PHILIP'S

STREET ATLAS

UNRIVALLED DETAIL FROM THE BEST-SELLING ATLAS RANGE

NAVIGATOR® DEVON

& PLYMOUTH

T0319298

www.philips-maps.co.uk
Philip's, a division of
Octopus Publishing Group Ltd
www.octopusbooks.co.uk
Carmelite House
50 Victoria Embankment
London EC4Y 0DZ
An Hachette UK Company
www.hachette.co.uk

First edition 2024
First impression 2024
DEVEA

ISBN 978-1-84907-646-3 (spiral)

© Philip's 2024

Ordnance Survey
Licensed Data

This product includes mapping data licensed from Ordnance Survey® with the permission of the Controller of His Majesty's Stationery Office. © Crown copyright 2024. All rights reserved. Licence number 100011710.

CONTENTS

III Key to map symbols

IV Key to map pages

VI Route planning

X Major administrative and Postcode boundaries

1 Street maps at 1¾ inches to 1 mile

150 Street maps at 3½ inches to 1 mile

261 Street maps of Exeter and Plymouth at 7 inches to 1 mile

264 Index of towns, villages, streets, hospitals, industrial estates, railway stations, schools, shopping centres, universities and places of interest

Key to map symbols

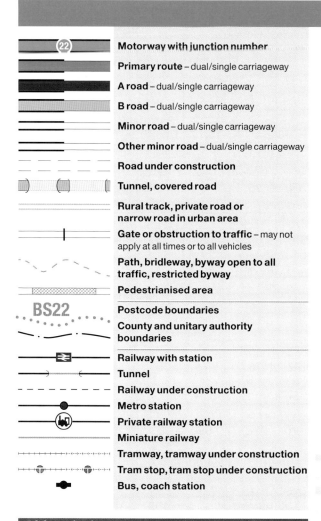

Motorway with junction number

Primary route – dual/single carriageway

A road – dual/single carriageway

B road – dual/single carriageway

Minor road – dual/single carriageway

Other minor road – dual/single carriageway

Road under construction

Tunnel, covered road

Rural track, private road or narrow road in urban area

Gate or obstruction to traffic – may not apply at all times or to all vehicles

Path, bridleway, byway open to all traffic, restricted byway

Pedestrianised area

BS22   Postcode boundaries

County and unitary authority boundaries

Railway with station

Tunnel

Railway under construction

Metro station

Private railway station

Miniature railway

Tramway, tramway under construction

Tram stop, tram stop under construction

Bus, coach station

Ambulance station

Coastguard station

Fire station

Police station

Accident and Emergency entrance to hospital

H   Hospital

+   Place of worship

Information centre – open all year

Shopping centre

P   Parking

P&R   Park and Ride

PO   Post Office

Camping site

Caravan site

Golf course

Picnic site

Church   Non-Roman antiquity

ROMAN FORT   Roman antiquity

Univ   Important buildings, schools, colleges, universities and hospitals

Built-up area

Woods

River Medway   Water name

River, weir

Stream

Canal, lock, tunnel

Water

Tidal water

263   Adjoining page indicators

58   87

The small numbers around the edges of the maps identify the 1-kilometre National Grid lines

The dark grey border on the inside edge of some pages indicates that the mapping does not continue onto the adjacent page

Enlarged maps only

Railway or bus station building

Place of interest

Parkland

Abbreviations

Acad	Academy	Meml	Memorial
Allot Gdns	Allotments	Mon	Monument
Cemy	Cemetery	Mus	Museum
C Ctr	Civic centre	Obsy	Observatory
CH	Club house	Pal	Royal palace
Coll	College	PH	Public house
Crem	Crematorium	Recn Gd	Recreation ground
Ent	Enterprise	Resr	Reservoir
Ex H	Exhibition hall	Ret Pk	Retail park
Ind Est	Industrial Estate	Sch	School
IRB Sta	Inshore rescue boat station	Sh Ctr	Shopping centre
Inst	Institute	TH	Town hall / house
Ct	Law court	Trad Est	Trading estate
L Ctr	Leisure centre	Univ	University
LC	Level crossing	W Twr	Water tower
Liby	Library	Wks	Works
Mkt	Market	YH	Youth hostel

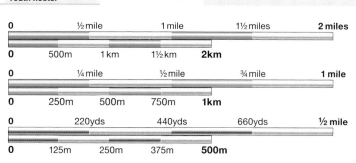

The map scale on the pages numbered in green is 1¾ inches to 1 mile
2.76 cm to 1 km • 1:36206

0	½ mile	1 mile	1½ miles	2 miles
0	500m	1 km	1½ km	2km

The map scale on the pages numbered in blue is 3½ inches to 1 mile
5.52 cm to 1 km • 1:18103

0	¼ mile	½ mile	¾ mile	1 mile
0	250m	500m	750m	1km

The map scale on the pages numbered in red is 7 inches to 1 mile
11.04 cm to 1 km • 1:9051

0	220yds	440yds	660yds	½ mile
0	125m	250m	375m	500m

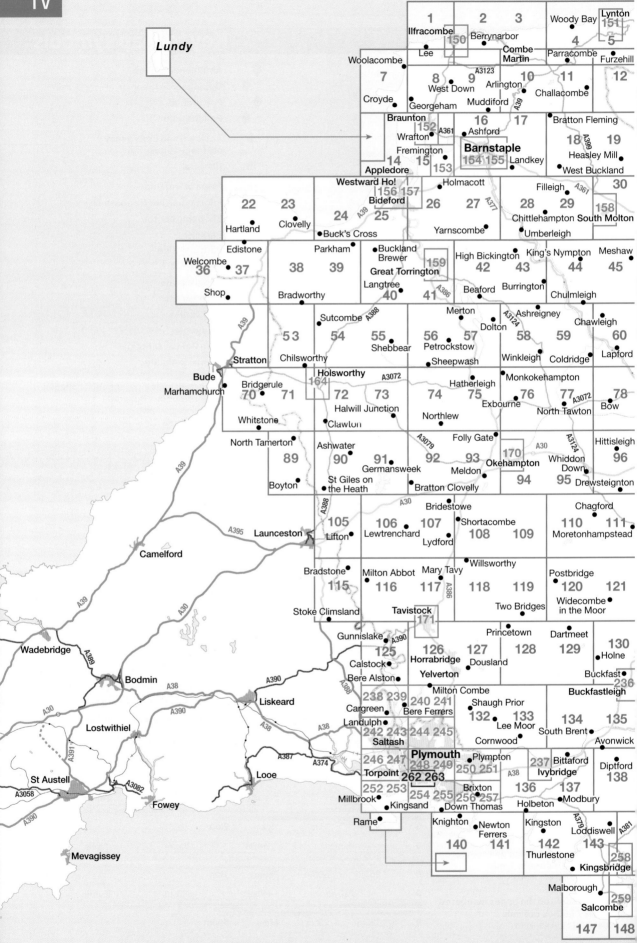

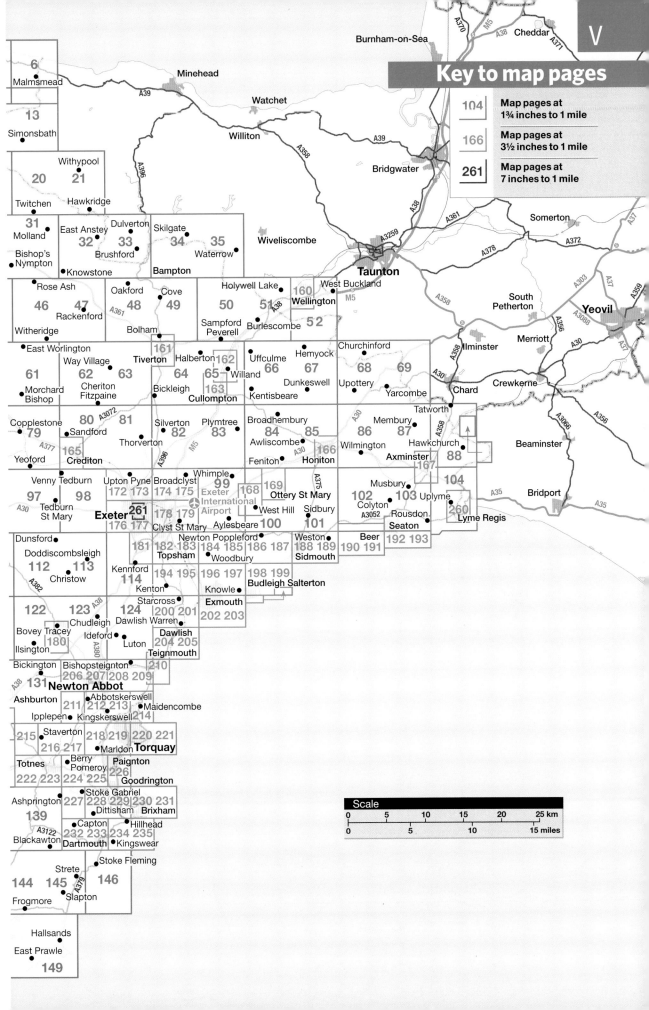

V

Key to map pages

104	Map pages at 1¾ inches to 1 mile
166	Map pages at 3½ inches to 1 mile
261	Map pages at 7 inches to 1 mile

Burnham-on-Sea
Cheddar
Minehead
Watchet
Malmsmead **6**
Williton
13
Simonsbath
Bridgwater
Somerton
Withypool
20 **21**
Twitchen
Hawkridge
Yeovil
31
Molland
East Anstey Dulverton Skilgate
32 **33** **34** **35**
Brushford Waterrow
Bishop's Nympton
Bampton
Wiveliscombe
Knowstone
Taunton
South Petherton
Rose Ash
Oakford Cove
Holywell Lake West Buckland
46 **47** **48** **49**
50 **51** **160**
Rackenford
Wellington
52
Witheridge
Bolham
Sampford Peverell
Burlescombe
Ilminster
Merriott
East Worlington
Churchinford
Crewkerne
Way Village
Halberton
Uffculme Hemyock
61 **62** **63**
161
162
66 **67** **68** **69**
Morchard Bishop
Cheriton Fitzpaine
Tiverton
64 **65**
Willand
Dunkeswell
Upottery
Chard
Bickleigh
Kentisbeare
Yarcombe
Beaminster
Copplestone
80 **81**
163
Cullompton
Tatworth
79
Sandford
Silverton Plymtree
Broadhembury
Membury
82 **83**
84 **85** **86** **87**
Yeoford
165
Thorverton
Awliscombe
Wilmington
Hawkchurch
88
Crediton
Feniton Honiton
Axminster
Bridport
Venny Tedburn
Upton Pyne Broadclyst
Whimple
166
167
Musbury
97 **98**
172 173 **174 175**
99
168 169
102 **103**
104
Tedburn St Mary
Exeter International Airport
Ottery St Mary
Colyton
Uplyme
Dunsford
178 179
West Hill Sidbury
Rousdon
260
Lyme Regis
Doddiscombsleigh
176 177
Clyst St Mary
100 **101**
Seaton
112 **113**
Aylesbeare
Weston Beer
192 193
Christow
181
114
Newton Poppleford
188 189
190 191
Kennford
182 183 **184 185** **186 187**
Sidmouth
122 **123**
Topsham
Woodbury
198 199
Bovey Tracey
Chudleigh
194 195 **196 197**
Budleigh Salterton
180
Kenton
Knowle
Ilsington
Starcross
124 **200 201**
Exmouth
Dawlish Warren
202 203
Ideford
Luton
Dawlish
Bickington
204 205
Bishopsteignton
Teignmouth
131
206 207 208 209
210
Newton Abbot
Ashburton
Abbotskerswell
211 212 213
Maidencombe
Ipplepen
Kingskerswell
214
Staverton
215
218 219 220 221
216 217
Marldon Torquay
Totnes
Berry Pomeroy
Paignton
222 223
224 225
226
Goodrington
Stoke Gabriel
Ashprington
227 228 229 230 231
Dittisham Brixham
139
Capton
Hillhead
232 233 234 235
Blackawton
Dartmouth Kingswear
Stoke Fleming
Strete
144 145 **146**
Frogmore
Slapton
Hallsands
East Prawle
149

Scale						
0	5	10	15	20	25 km
0		5		10		15 miles

Route planning

Scale

0		5		10km
0	1 2 3 4	5miles		

BRIDGWATER BAY

Foreland Pt.
Lynmouth Bay
Countisbury
Lynton
Lynmouth
Hurlstone Pt.
Porlock Bay
Selworthy Beacon 308
Minehead
Barbrook
East Ilkerton
Cheriton
Furzehill
Shallowford
Malmsmead
Brendon
Oare
Porlock Weir
Bossington
Allerford
Selworthy
Woodcombe
Periton
Alcombe
Marsh Street
Blue Anchor Bay
Watchet
Old Cleeve
East Quantoxhead
Kilton
Lilstock
Shurton
Burton
Stringston
Nether Stowey
EXMOOR
EXMOOR FOREST
Brendon Common
Pinkworthy Pond 487
Exe Plain
Challacombe
B3358
Holnicote Estate
DUNKERY BEACON 519
West Luccombe
Luccombe
Wootton Courtenay
Cowbridge
Timberscombe
Carhampton
Blue Anchor
Bilbrook
Rodhuish
Washford
Sampford Brett
Williton
Watchet
West Quantoxhead
Staple
Bicknoller
Holford
Kilve
Over Stowey
QUANTOCK FOREST
NATIONAL
Simonsbath
B3223
Edgcott
Exford
Luckwell Bridge
Wheddon Cross
Cutcombe
BRENDON FOREST
CROYDON HILL 365
Luxborough
Roadwater
Kingsbridge
Treborough
LYPE HILL 423
Monksilver
Yellow
Stogumber
Elworthy
Lower Vexford
Crowcombe
Flaxpool
West Bagborough
PARK
HORSEN HILL 443
Withypool Common
WINSFORD HILL 426
Withypool
Liscombe
Winsford
Exton
Bridgetown
Brompton Regis
BRENDON HILLS
Clatworthy Res.
Wimbleball Lake
Upton
Wiveliscombe
Willett
Tolland
Combe Florey
Bishops Lydeard
Cothelstone
North Radworthy
North Heasley
Heasley Mill
South Radworthy
Hawkridge
Molland Common
Twitchen
North Molton
Anstey Common
West Anstey
East Anstey
Molland
Dulverton
Battleton
Nightcott
Brushford
Oldways End
Exebridge
Bury
Morebath
Skilgate
Waterrow
HADDON HILL 355
Huish Champflower
HEYDON HILL 338
Chipstable
Maundown
Langley Marsh
Fitzhead
VALE OF TAUNTON
Halse
Norton Fitzwarren
DEANE
South Molton
Bish Mill
Newtown
Bishops Nympton
Ash Mill
Knowstone
Roachill
Oakfordbridge
Oakford
Shillingford
Petton
Clayhanger
Kittisford
Langford Budville
Appley
Thorne St. Margaret
Holywell Lake
Wellington
West Buckland
Milverton
Hillcommon
Oake
Hillfarrance
East Nynehead
Bradford-on-Tone
George Nympton
Alswear
Mariansleigh
Rose Ash
Romansleigh
Meshaw
Creacombe
Rackenford
STOODLEIGH BEACON 301
Stoodleigh
Cove
EXE VALLEY
East Mere
Whitnage
Hockworthy
Holcombe Rogus
Westleigh
Burlescombe
Sampford Arundel
Wrangway
Ford Street
Angersleigh
BLACKDOWN HILLS
Clayhidon
Cadbury Barton
Week
Lutworthy
West Worlington
East Worlington
Drayford
Witheridge
Templeton Bridge
Templeton
Loxbeare
Washfield
Calverleigh
Bolham
Chevithorne
Uplowman
Halberton
Appledore
Nicholashayne
Rosemary Lane
Stapley
Culmstock
Hemyock
Bolham Water
Smeatharpe
Chulmleigh
Cheldon
Thelbridge Barton
Washford Pyne
Nomansland
Pennymoor
Cruwys Morchard
Withleigh
Cotteylands
Cowleymoor
Tiverton
Ash Thomas
Sampford Peverell
Uffculme
Craddock
HACKPEN HILL 258
Ashill
Abbey
Chawleigh
Filleigh
Eastington
Black Dog
Way Village
Well Town
Wiland
Smithincott
Blackborough
Sheldon
Dunkeswell
Upottery
Nymet Rowland
Lapford
Morchard Bishop
Kennerleigh
Stockleigh English
Cheriton Fitzpaine
Upham
Cadeleigh
Butterleigh
Colebrook
Dulford
Kerswell
BLACK DOWN 283
Broadhembury
Luppitt
RAWRIDGE BEACON 261
Monkton
East Leigh
Ash Bullayne
Oldborough
East Village
Cadbury
Stockleigh Pomeroy
Bickleigh
Bradninch
Westcott
Mutterton
Norman's Green
Payhembury
Awliscombe
Buckerell
Combe Raleigh
Down St. Mary
Newbuildings
Copplestone
Sandford
Upton Hellions
Thorverton
Up Exe
Silverton
Hele
Langford
Clyst Hydon
Plymtree
Tale
Colestocks
Honiton
Offwell
Bow
Knowle
Shobrooke
Efford Shute
Nether Exe
Ellerhayes
Clyst St. Lawrence
Talaton
Fenny Bridges
Gittisham
Church Green
Farway
Nymet Tracey
Coleford
Crediton
Uton
Sweetham
Brampford Speke
Rewe
Stoke Canon
Budlake
Dog Village
Cranbrook
Rockbeare
Fairmile
Ottery St. Mary
Broad Down
Colebrooke
Hillerton
Yeoford
Venny Tedburn
Newton St. Cyres
Upton Pyne
Poltimore
Broadclyst
Jack in the Green
Clyst Honiton
Marsh Green
West Hill
Whimple
Wiggaton
Tipton St. John
Sidbury
Harcombe
Crockernwell
Tedburn St. Mary
Cowley
EXETER
Pinhoe
Whipton
EXETER INTERNATIONAL
Sowton
Aylesbeare
Farringdon
Venn Ottery
Harpford
Bowd
Sidford
Whitestone
Cheriton Bishop
Longdown
Wheatley
Ide
St. Thomas
Heavitree
Countess Wear
Alphington
Clyst St. Mary
Clyst St. George
Woodbury Salterton
Colaton Raleigh
Newton Poppleford
Salcombe Regis
Branscombe
Sidmouth
Drewsteignton
Sandypark
Easton
Dunsford
Shillingford St. George
Kennford
Exminster
Topsham
Ebford
Woodbury
Hawkerland
Yettington
Otterton
East Budleigh
Ladram Bay
Murchington
Chagford
Doccombe
Bridford
Bridfordmills
Doddiscombsleigh
Higher Ashton
Lower Ashton
Christow
Kenn
Powderham
Exton
Lympstone
Withycombe Raleigh
Knowle
Budleigh Salterton
Danger Pt.
Moretonhampstead
North Bovey
Manaton
Lustleigh
Water
Hennock
Bovey Tracey
Trusham
Ideford
Starcross
Cockwood
Exmouth
Littleham
Straight Pt.
HAMELDOWN TOR 529
Widecombe in the Moor
Bonehill
Haytor Vale
Brimley
Ilsington
Heathfield
Chudleigh
Chudleigh Knighton
Ashcombe
Luton
Little Haldon
Holcombe
Dawlish
Dawlish Warren
Liverton
Coldeast
Preston
RIPPON TOR 473

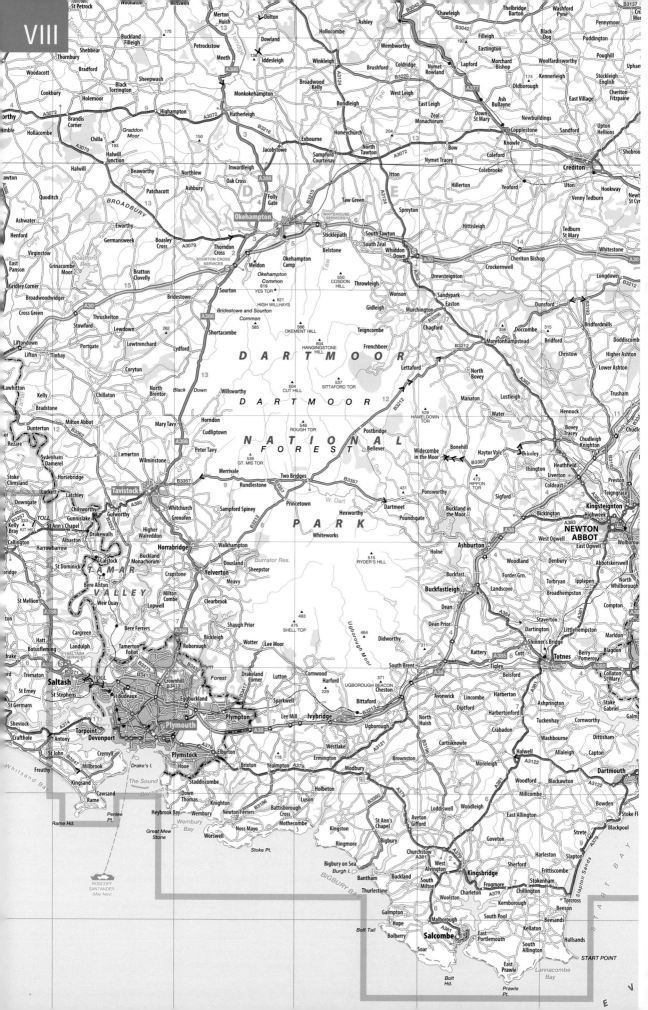

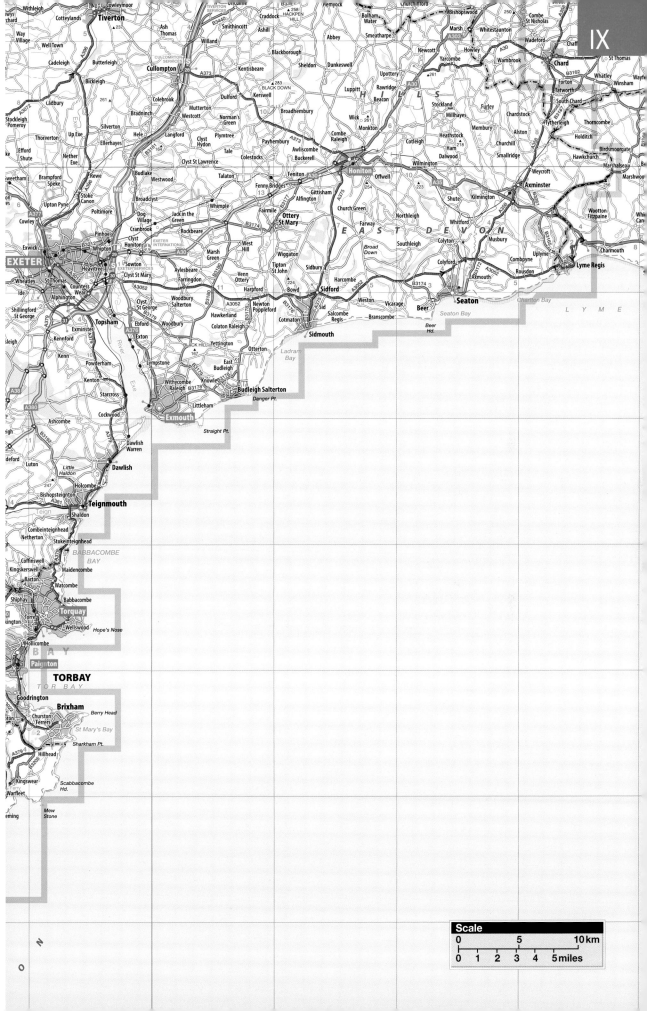

Scale

0   5   10km

0   1   2   3   4   5miles

Major administrative and Postcode boundaries

County and unitary authority boundaries

District boundaries

Postcode boundaries

Area covered by this atlas

Scale

0	5	10	15	20	25	30 km
0		5		10	15	20 miles

SS | ST

SX | SY

Somerset

Cornwall

Devon

North Devon

Mid Devon

East Devon

West Devon

Teignbridge

Torbay

South Hams

Torridge

City of Plymouth

Lynton
Ilfracombe
EX34
Woolacombe
Croyde
Braunton
EX33
EX31
EX35
Simonsbath
TA24
EX32
Barnstaple
Bideford
EX31
EX36
South Molton
Dulverton
TA22
TA4
Hartland
Clovelly
EX39
Umberleigh
EX37
Bampton
TA21
Wellington
Great Torrington
EX38
Chulmleigh
Witheridge
EX16
Tiverton
TA3
TA20
Dolton
EX18
FX15
Willand
Dunkeswell
EX19
Lapford
EX17
Silverton
EX14
TA20
Torridge
Black Torrington
EX22
Holsworthy
EX21
Hatherleigh
Bow
Crediton
Honiton
Axminster
Colyton
EX24
DT6
EX23
EX20
Okehampton
EX4
EX1
EX
11
Ottery St Mary
EX13
PL15
Exeter
EX5
EX2
EX10
EX12
Seaton
DT7
Lyme Regis
PL16
Lydford
West Devon
Chagford
EX6
Topsham
EX3
Sidmouth
Lifton
EX8
EX9
Budleigh Salterton
Milton Abbot
PL19
Bovey Tracey
Exmouth
PL17
Tavistock
EX7
Dawlish
PL18
PL20
Yelverton
Ashburton
Newton Abbot
TQ14
Teignmouth
Chagford
TQ13
TQ12
TQ2
Torquay
PL12
Buckfastleigh
TQ11
Totnes
TQ3
TQ1
City of Plymouth
PL5
PL6
TQ10
Paignton
Saltash
PL7
South Brent
TQ4
Brixham
PL11
PL21
Ivybridge
TQ9
TQ5
PL10
PL9
PL8
South Hams
Dartmouth
TQ6
PL1
PL2
PL3
PL4
Wembury
TQ7
Kingsbridge
Slapton
Salcombe
TQ8

SX | SY

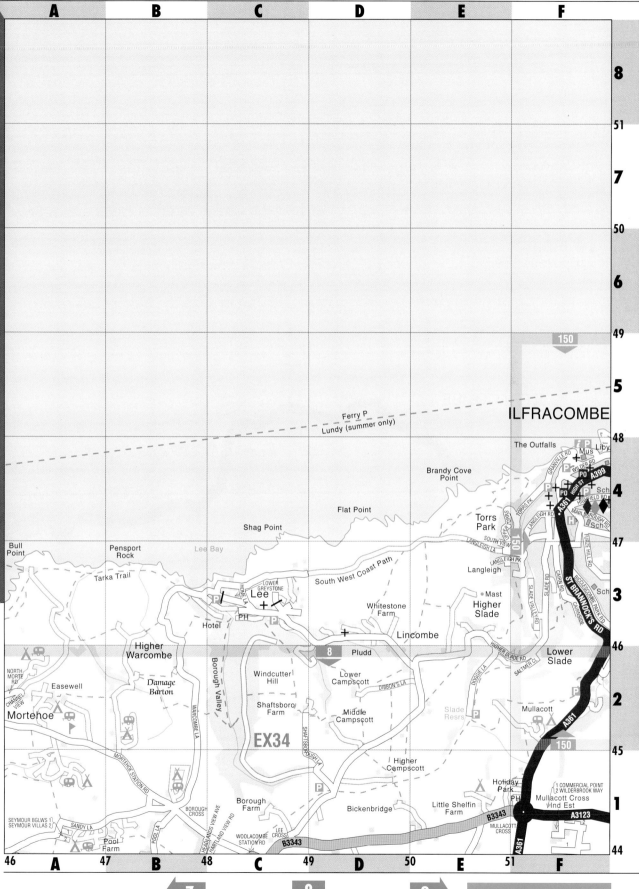

For full street detail of the highlighted area see page 150.

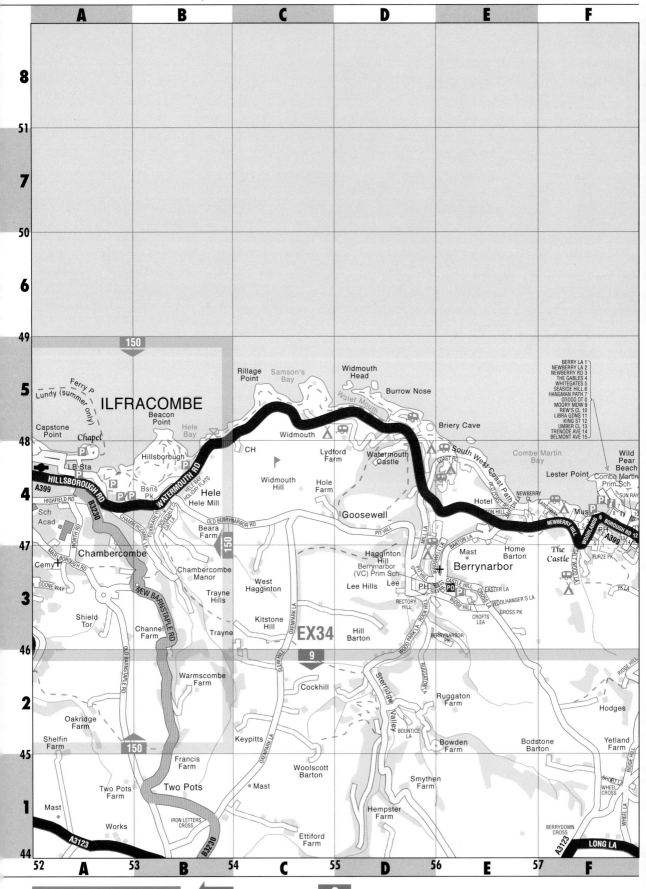

Scale: 1¾ inches to 1 mile

0 ¼ ½ mile
0 250m 500m 750m 1 km

A B C D E F

8

51

7

50

6

49

150

ILFRACOMBE

Ferry P
Lundy (summer only)

Rillage Point
Samson's Bay
Widmouth Head
Burrow Nose

Water Mouth

BERRY LA 1
NEWBERRY LA 2
NEWBERRY RD 3
THE GABLES 4
WHITEGATES 5
SEASIDE HILL 6
HANGMAN PATH 7
ONGGG GT 0
MOORY MDW 9
REW'S CL 10
LIBRA GDNS 11
KING ST 12
UMBER CL 13
TRENODE AVE 14
BELMONT AVE 15

5

Capstone Point
Chapel
Beacon Point
Hele Bay
Hillsborough
CH
Widmouth
Lydford Farm
Watermouth Castle
Briery Cave
South West Coast Path
Combe Martin Bay
Lester Point
Comba Martin Prim Sch
Wild Pear Beach

48

LB Sta
HILLSBOROUGH RD
A399
B3230
WATERMOUTH RD
Bsns Pk
HELE BAY HOLIDAY FLATS
Hele
Hele Mill
Widmouth Hill
Hole Farm
Goosewell
OLD COAST RD
Hotel
NEWBERRY HILL
COAST RD
SUN RAY
Mus
A399
BOROUGH RD 12
WOODLANDS

4

Highfield Rd
Sch Acad
CHAMBERCOMBE LA
DOUGDALE LA
CAT LA
OLD BERRYNARBOR RD
Beara Farm
150
PIT HILL
MILL LA
BARTON LA
Mast
Home Barton
The Castle
FURZE PK
NEWBERRY CL

47

Cemy
MARTINBOROUGH RD
WORTH RD
Chambercombe
Chambercombe Manor
Trayne Hills
West Hagginton
Hagginton Hill
Berrynarbor (VC) Prim Sch
Lee Hills
Lee
PH
SILVER
PO
P
Berrynarbor
CASTLE HILL
EASTER LA
WOOLHANGER'S LA
CROSS PK

3

DOONE WAY
Shield Tor
NEW BARNSTAPLE RD
Trayne Hills
Kitstone Hill
Trayne
OXENPARK LA
Hill Barton
WOOD PARK LA
ROCK HILL
RECTORY HILL
RIDGE HILL
Berrynarbor Pk
CROFTS LEA
CROSS LA

46

OLD BARNSTAPLE RD
Channel Farm
EX34
9
Sterridge Valley
Ruggaton Farm
RUGGATON LA
Hodges

2

Oakridge Farm
Warmscombe Farm
Cockhill
BOUNTICE LA
Bowden Farm
Bodstone Barton
Yetland Farm

45

Shelfin Farm
150
Francis Farm
Keypitts
Woolscott Barton
Smythen Farm
RIDGE HILL
SHORT WHEEL CROSS

1

Mast
Two Pots Farm
Two Pots
Mast
Hempster Farm
WHEEL LA
BERRYDOWN CROSS

Works
IRON LETTERS CROSS
Ettiford Farm
A3123
LONG LA

44

52 A 53 B 54 C 55 D 56 E 57 F

A3123
B3230

For full street detail of the highlighted area see page 150.

1

9

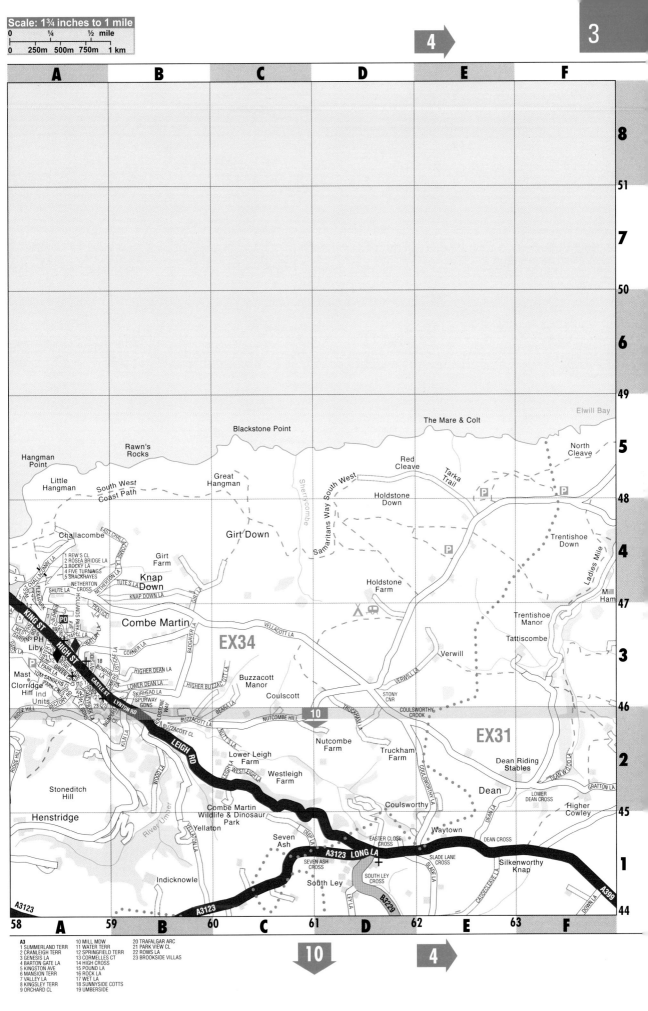

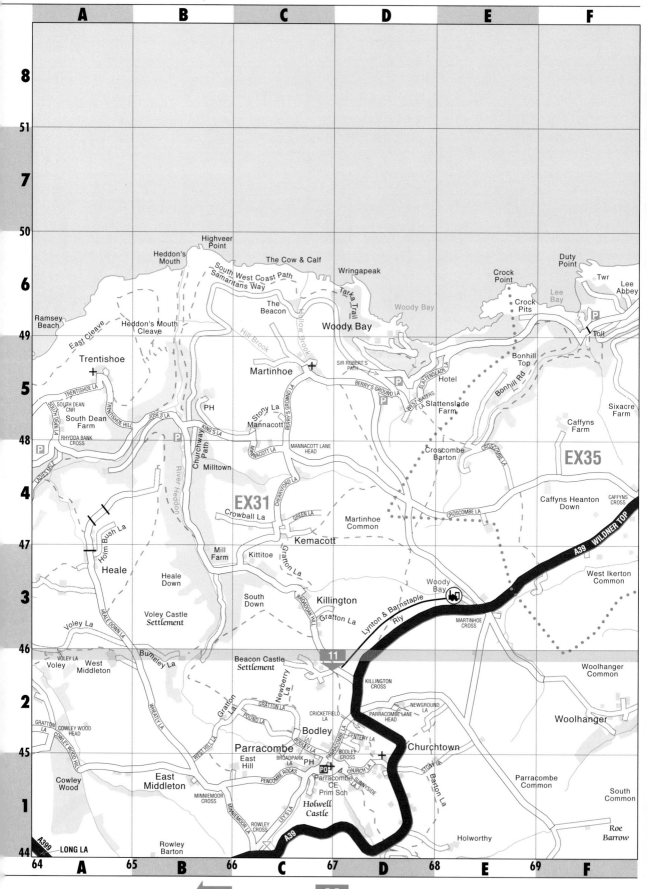

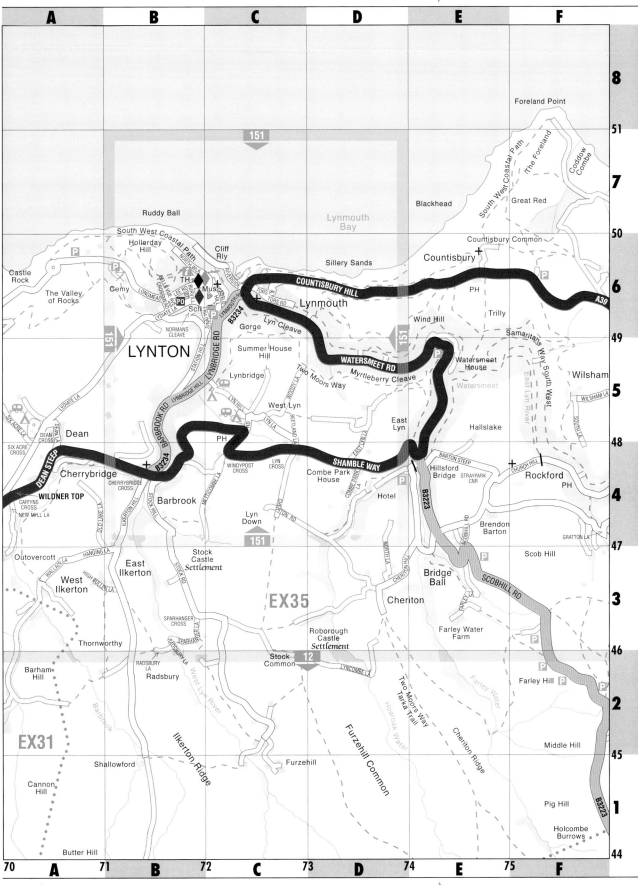

6

A   B   C   D   E   F

8

151

51

7

Foreland Point

Ruddy Ball

Lynmouth Bay

Blackhead

The Foreland

Coddow Combe

Great Red

South West Coastal Path

50

South West Coastal Path

Hollerday Hill

Cliff Rly

Countisbury Common

Countisbury

Sillery Sands

Castle Rock

The Valley of Rocks

Cemy

TH

Mus

PO

Sch

Countisbury Hill

Lynmouth

PH

A39

6

P

P

NORTH WLK
LEE RD
BEACH RD

Wind Hill

Trilly

LONGMEAD

LYDIATE LA

NORMANS CLEAVE

B3234

Gorge

Lyn Cleave

LYNTON

STATION HILL

Lynbridge Rd

Watersmeet Rd

151

Samaritans Way South West

Wilsham

49

Summer House Hill

Myrtleberry Cleave

Watersmeet House

Watersmeet

East Lyn River

WILSHAM LA

Lynbridge

Two Moors Way

West Lyn

East Lyn

Hallslake

SOUTH LA

5

48

LYNBRIDGE HILL

BARBROOK RD

LYN HILL

BEETLAND LA

PH

Dean

LYDIATE LA

Six Acre La

DEAN CROSS

SIX ACRE CROSS

B3234

Cherrybridge

CHERRYBRIDGE CROSS

Barbrook

WILDNER TOP

DEAN STEEP

CAFFYNS CROSS

NEW MILL LA

Windypost Cross

Lyn Cross

EAST LYN LA

COMBE PARK LA

Shamble Way

Combe Park House

Hotel

Hillsford Bridge

P

Barton Steep

STRAYPARK CNR

B3223

Church Hill

Rockford

PH

GRATTON LA

4

METICOMBE LA

STOCK HILL

CHERITON RD

Lyn Down

SCOBHILL RD

Brendon Barton

Outovercott

HANGING LA

WALLACE LA

HIGH BULLEN LA

East Ilkerton

Stock Castle Settlement

151

NORTH LA

CHERITON LN

Scob Hill

47

West Ilkerton

STOCK RD

Bridge Ball

FARLEY LN

P

SCOBHILL RD

Scobhill Rd

EX35

Cheriton

3

Thornworthy

SPARHANGER CROSS

SPARHAN

Roborough Castle Settlement

Farley Water Farm

P

46

Barham Hill

RADSBURY LA

Radsbury

Stock Common

12

LYNCOMBE LA

Two Moors Way Tarka Trail

Farley Water

Farley Hill

P

P

Middle Hill

2

RADSBURY LA

WEST LYN RIVER

Hoaroak Water

Cheriton Ridge

45

EX31

Shallowford

Furzehill

Furzehill Common

Ilkerton Ridge

Barbrook

Cannon Hill

Pig Hill

B3223

Holcombe Burrows

1

Butter Hill

44

70   A   71   B   72   C   73   D   74   E   75   F

12

6

For full street detail of the highlighted area see page 151.

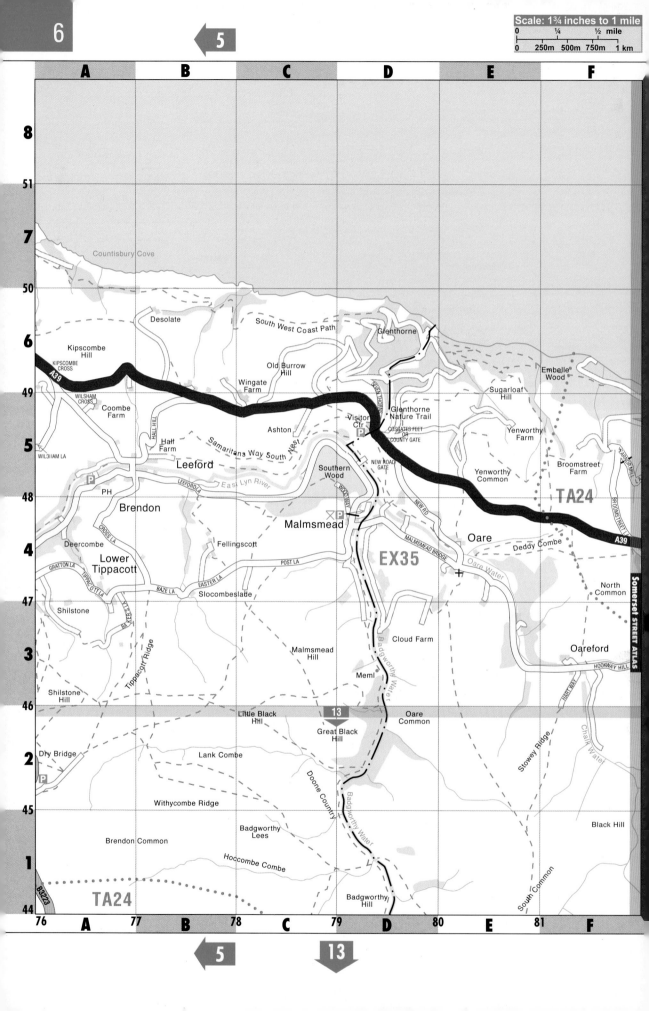

Scale: 1¾ inches to 1 mile

0   ¼   ½   mile
0   250m 500m 750m 1 km

A   B   C   D   E   F

8

51

7

50

6

Countisbury Cove

Desolate

South West Coast Path

Glenthorne

Kipscombe
Hill

KIPSCOMBE
CROSS

A39

Old Burrow
Hill

Wingate
Farm

Embelle
Wood

49

WILSHAM
CROSS

Coombe
Farm

Ashton

Nest

Glenthorne
Nature Trail

Sugarloaf
Hill

SEVEN THORNS

Yenworthy
Farm

5

WILSHAM LA

Hall
Farm

HALL HILL

Samaritans Way South

Southern
Wood

Visitor
Ctr
P

COSGATES FEET
OR
COUNTY GATE

NEW ROAD
GATE

Yenworthy
Common

Broomstreet
Farm

YENWORTHY LA

TA24

BROOMSTREET LA

Leeford

LEEFORD LA

East Lyn River

WOODWAY

48

P
PH

Brendon

CROSS LA

Malmsmead

NEW RD

Yenworthy
Common

MALMSMEAD BRIDGE

Oare

Deddy Combe

A39

4

GRATTON LA

TIPPACOTT LA

Deercombe

Lower
Tippacott

BAZE LA

EASTER LA

Fellingscott

POST LA

EX35

Oare Water

North
Common

BAKER'S LA

Slocombeslade

Oareford

47

Shilstone

Tippacott Ridge

Malmsmead
Hill

Cloud Farm

HOOKWAY HILL

HART WAY

3

Shilstone
Hill

Meml

Badgworthy Water

Stowey Ridge

Chalk Water

46

Little Black
Hill

13

Oare
Common

Great Black
Hill

2

Dry Bridge

P

Lank Combe

Doone Country

Badgworthy Water

Black Hill

45

Withycombe Ridge

1

B3223

TA24

Brendon Common

Badgworthy
Lees

Hoccombe Combe

Badgworthy
Hill

South Common

44

76   A   77   B   78   C   79   D   80   E   81   F

Somerset STREET ATLAS

Scale: 1¾ inches to 1 mile

Morte
Point

HEADLAND CT 1
KINEVOR CL 2
MORTEHOE STATION RD 3
ADA'S TERR 4

Mortehoe

PH

PO

Cemy

Mortehoe
& Her Ctr

Grunta
Beach

CASTLE
ROCK

Grunta
Pool

SHARP ROCK 5
UPPPER CLAYPARK 6

Hotel

Barricane
Beach

CROSSWAYS
CT

EX34

Woolacombe

Meml

ARLINGTON PL 1
THE GROVE 2
ARLINGTON RD 3
FROG ST 4
HUNTER LA 5
MILL LA 6
WEST RD 7
RAWNSLEY LA 8
FAIRHOLME RD 9
SPRINGFIELD RD 10
SANDY LANE CT 11
CLIFFSIDE 12

BEACH RD

PO

Hotel

Mill
Rock

CHALLACOMBE
HILL

Potter's
Hill

Dunes

Morte
Bay

Woolacombe
Sand

Woolacombe
Down

MARINE DR

Black
Rock

Putsborough
Sand

DOWN LA

Whiting
Hole

Long
Bar

Vention

Pickwell

South West Coast Path

VENTION RD

CLIFTON
CT

Croyde
Hoe

Ramson La

Manor
House

Putsborough

Baggy
Point

EX33

PUTSBOROUGH RD

Middlehill La

Middleborough
Hill

MOORBOROUGH LA

BROADWAY LA

New La

STENTAWAY LA

MEADOW LA

Hotel

Croyde
Bay

P

Tom's
Field

Ora Hill

MOOR
PARK CL

LANE HEAD CL

ORA CL

BEACH LA

PENNY
HILL

BROAD LA

Croyde

North
Hole

FROGS STREET HILL

Croyde Bay

CROYDE
SANDS
BGLWS

SANDY LA

PO

MILLERS BROOK

MARY'S RD

GEORGEHAM RD

Forda
Hill

Cross

Dunes

WEST CROYDE HILL

HOBB'S HILL

CLOUTMAN'S
LA

ORCHARD GR

MILKWAY LA

LITTLE CLEAVE RD

South
Hole
Farm

B3231

LANGSFIELD

WITHY

SOMERTHING LA

Chapel

1 ORA STONE PK
2 BONNICOTT LA
3 LEADENGATE FIELDS
4 LEADENGATE CL
5 SANDY WAY
6 ST HELEN'S CL
7 HOME FARM LA
8 WATERY LA
9 MYRTLE FARM VIEW
10 SEA BIRDS PK
11 BAY VIEW CL

LONG LA

CROYDE RD

Saunton
Down

B3231

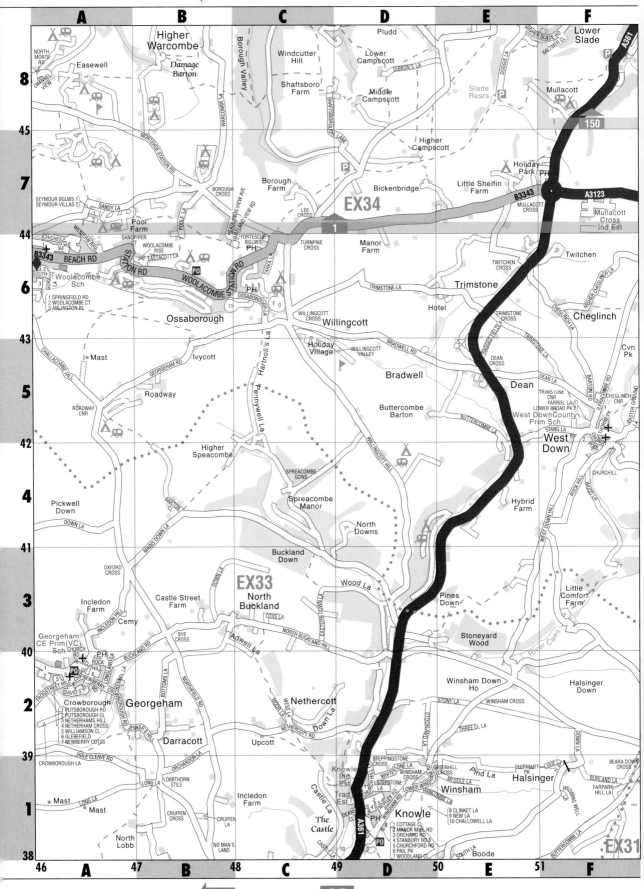

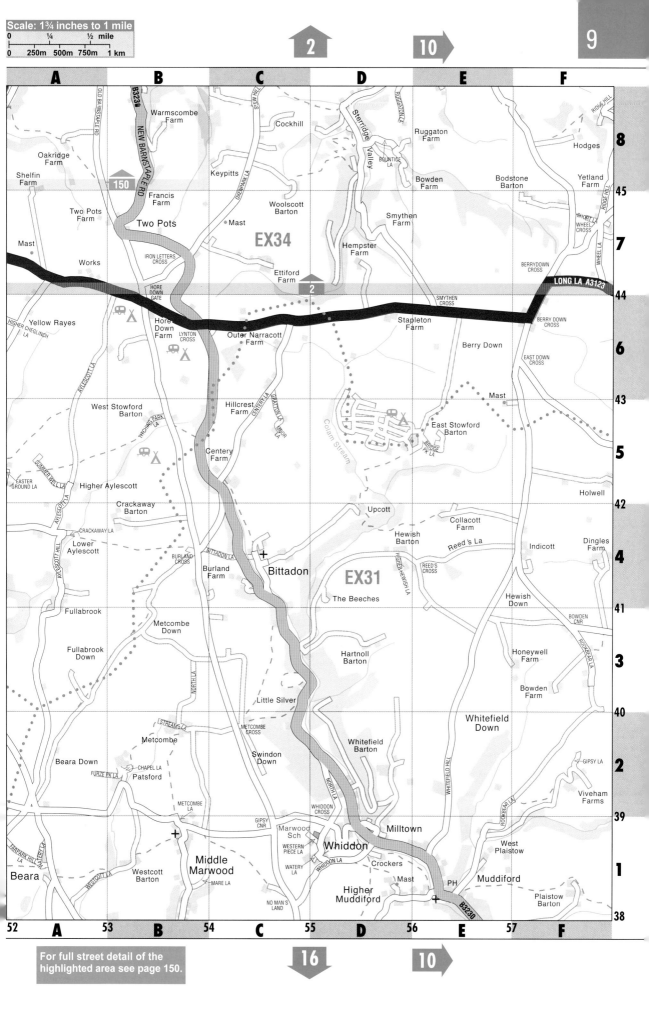

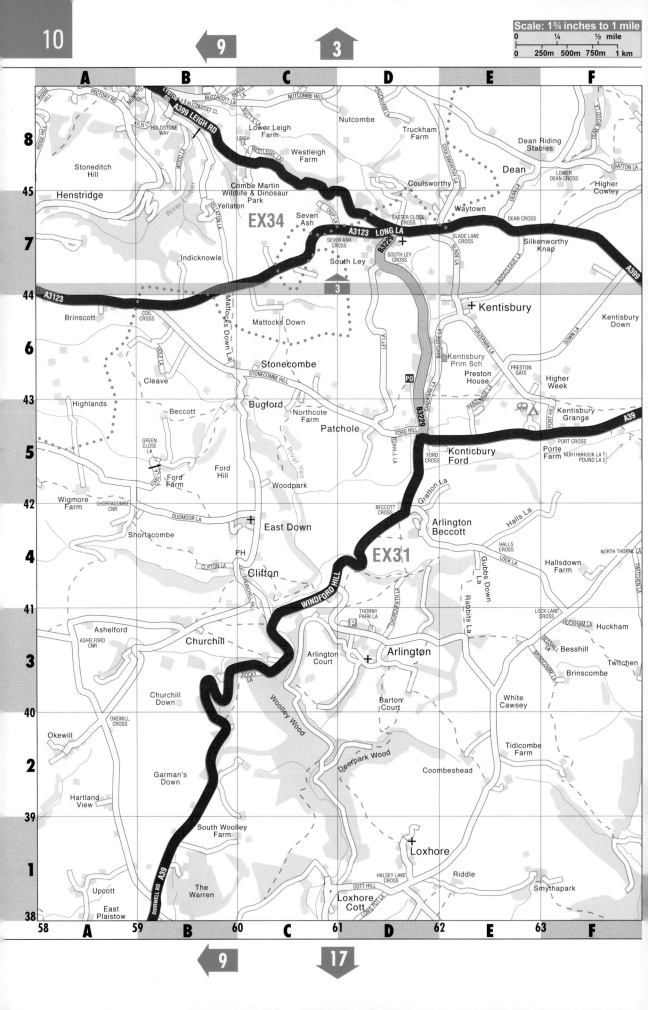

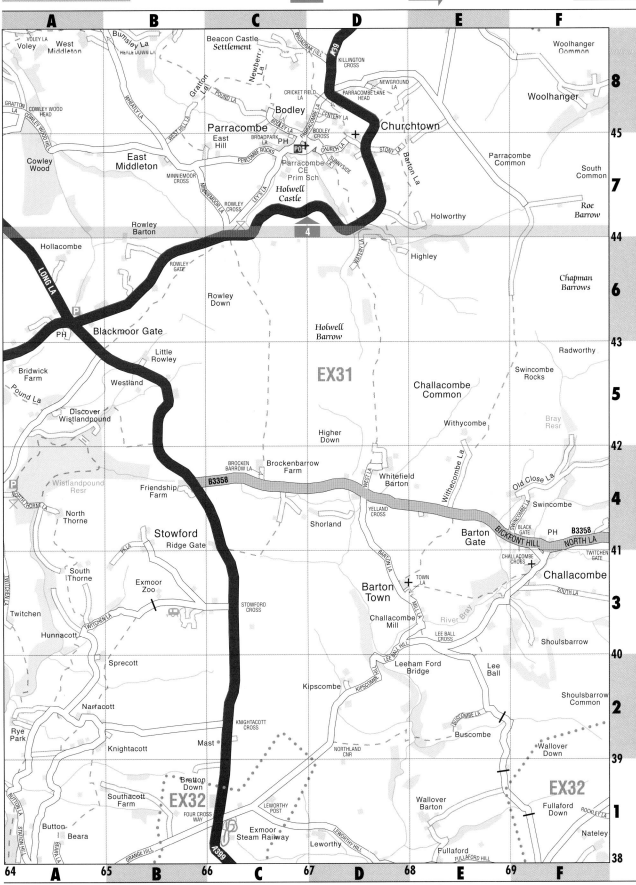

11

5

Scale: 1¾ inches to 1 mile

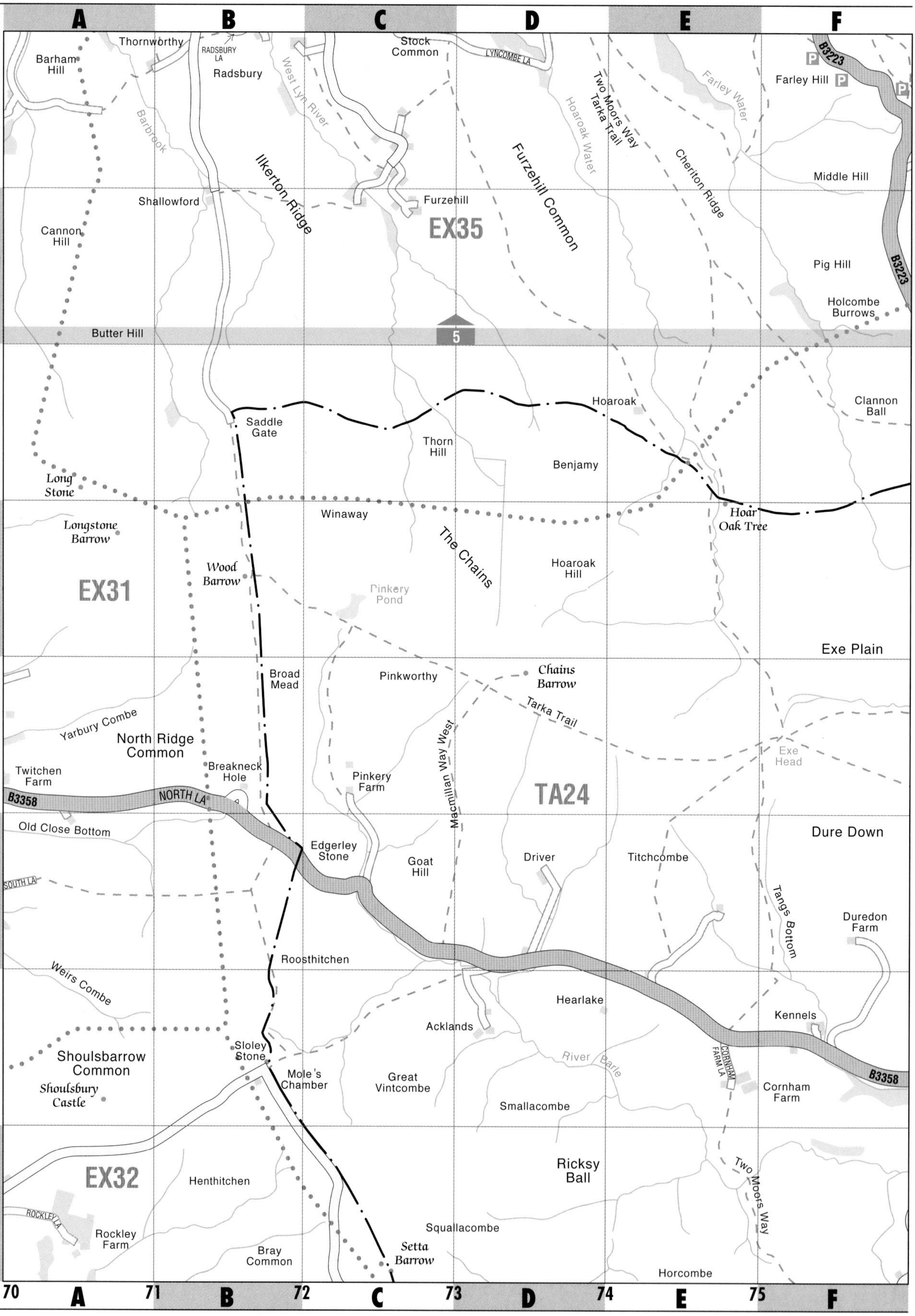

0 ¼ ½ mile

0 250m 500m 750m 1 km

A B C D E F

8

45

7

44

6

43

5

42

4

41

3

40

2

39

1

38

Barham Hill

Thornworthy

Radsbury

RADSBURY LA

Stock Common

LYNCOMBE LA

Farley Hill

B3223

P

P

West Lyn River

Barbrook

Ilkerton Ridge

Shallowford

Furzehill

EX35

Two Moors Way Tarka Trail

Hoaroak Water

Furzehill Common

Cheriton Ridge

Farley Water

Middle Hill

B3223

Cannon Hill

Pig Hill

Holcombe Burrows

Butter Hill

5

Saddle Gate

Hoaroak

Clannon Ball

Long Stone

Thorn Hill

Benjamy

Hoar Oak Tree

Longstone Barrow

Winaway

The Chains

Hoaroak Hill

EX31

Wood Barrow

Pinkery Pond

Exe Plain

Broad Mead

Pinkworthy

Chains Barrow

Tarka Trail

Yarbury Combe

North Ridge Common

Breakneck Hole

Pinkery Farm

Macmillan Way West

TA24

Exe Head

Twitchen Farm

B3358

NORTH LA

Old Close Bottom

Edgerley Stone

Goat Hill

Driver

Titchcombe

Dure Down

SOUTH LA

Roosthitchen

Tangs Bottom

Duredon Farm

Weirs Combe

Hearlake

Kennels

Shoulsbarrow Common

Sloley Stone

Mole's Chamber

Acklands

Great Vintcombe

River Barle

CORNHAM FARM LA

Cornham Farm

B3358

Shoulsbury Castle

Smallacombe

EX32

Henthitchen

Ricksy Ball

Two Moors Way

ROCKLEY LA

Rockley Farm

Bray Common

Setta Barrow

Squallacombe

Horcombe

70 A 71 B 72 C 73 D 74 E 75 F

11

19

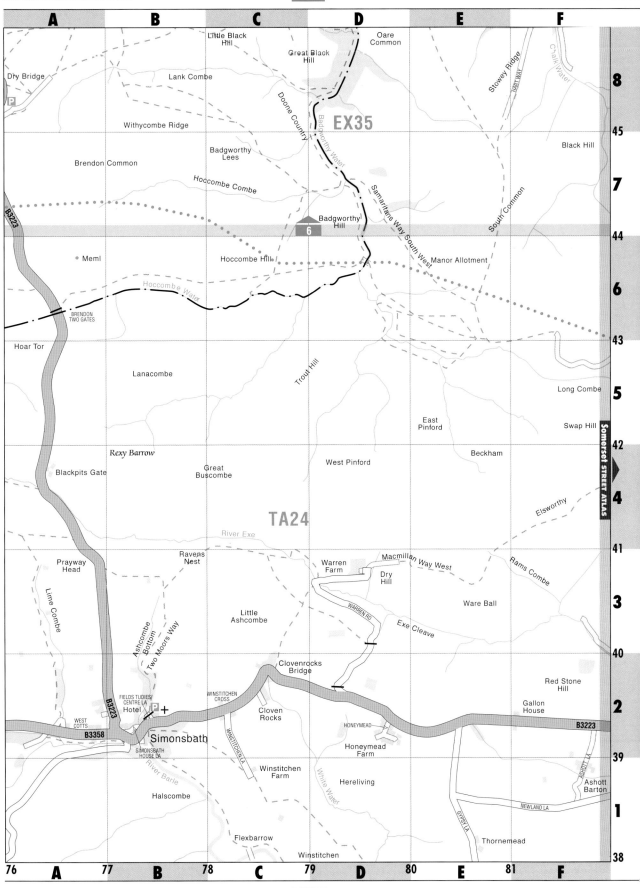

Dry Bridge

P

Little Black Hill

Great Black Hill

Oare Common

Lank Combe

Stowey Ridge

HART WAY

Chalk Water

EX35

Doone Country

Withycombe Ridge

Badgworthy Lees

Black Hill

Brendon Common

Hoccombe Combe

Badgworthy Water

Samaritans Way South West

South Common

B3223

Meml

Badgworthy Hill

6

Hoccombe Hill

Manor Allotment

Hoccombe Water

BRENDON TWO GATES

Hoar Tor

Lanacombe

Trout Hill

Long Combe

East Pinford

Swap Hill

Rexy Barrow

Great Buscombe

West Pinford

Beckham

Blackpits Gate

TA24

Elsworthy

River Exe

Prayway Head

Ravens Nest

Warren Farm

Macmillan Way West

Rams Combe

Dry Hill

Ware Ball

Lime Combe

Little Ashcombe

WARREN RD

Exe Cleave

Ashcombe Bottom

Two Moors Way

Clovenrocks Bridge

Red Stone Hill

FIELDS TUDIES/ CENTRE LA

Gallon House

B3223

WINSTITCHEN CROSS

Cloven Rocks

WEST COTTS

B3223

HONEYMEAD

B3358

Simonsbath

WINSTITCHEN LA

Honeymead Farm

SIMONSBATH HOUSE LA

River Barle

Winstitchen Farm

White Water

Hereliving

ASHOTT LA

Ashott Barton

Halscombe

GYPSY LA

NEWLAND LA

Thornemead

Flexbarrow

Winstitchen

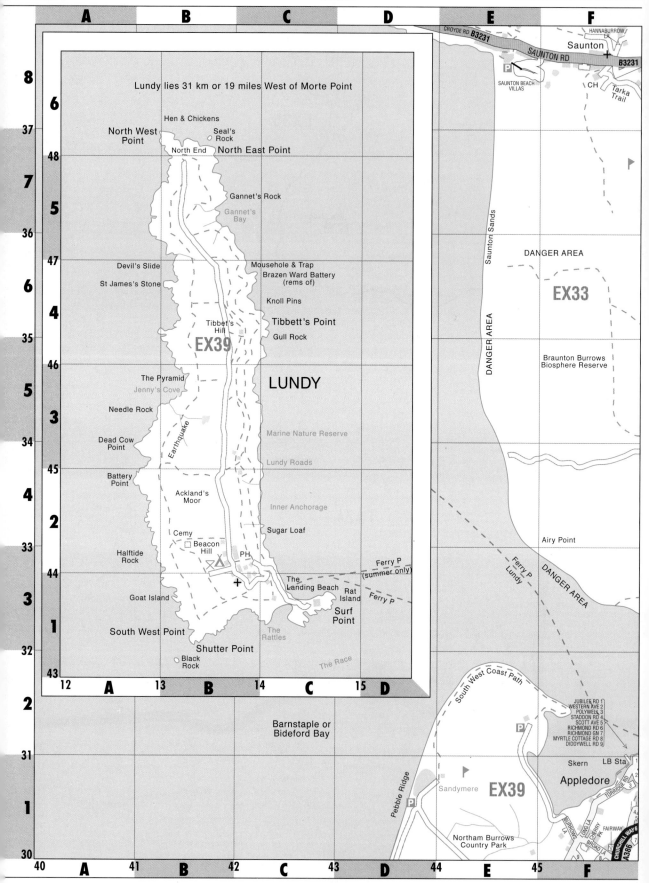

Scale: 1¾ inches to 1 mile

0   ¼   ½   mile
0 250m 500m 750m 1 km

A   **B**   **C**   **D**   **E**   **F**

CROYDE RD **B3231**

HANNABURROW LA

SAUNTON RD

Saunton

B3231

8

6

P

SAUNTON BEACH VILLAS

CH

Tarka Trail

Lundy lies 31 km or 19 miles West of Morte Point

Hen & Chickens

37

Seal's Rock

North West Point

48

North End   North East Point

7

5

Gannet's Rock

Gannet's Bay

36

Saunton Sands

DANGER AREA

47

Devil's Slide

Mousehole & Trap

EX33

Brazen Ward Battery (rems of)

St James's Stone

6

4

Knoll Pins

DANGER AREA

Tibbet's Hill

Tibbett's Point

35

Gull Rock

Braunton Burrows Biosphere Reserve

EX39

46

The Pyramid

LUNDY

5

Jenny's Cove

3

Needle Rock

34

Marine Nature Reserve

Dead Cow Point

Earthquake

Lundy Roads

45

Battery Point

4

Ackland's Moor

2

Inner Anchorage

Airy Point

33

Sugar Loaf

Cemy

44

Halftide Rock

Beacon Hill

PH

Ferry P (summer only)

DANGER AREA

Ferry P Lundy

3

1

Goat Island

The Landing Beach

Rat Island

Ferry P

South West Point

Surf Point

Shutter Point

The Rattles

32

Black Rock

The Race

43

12   **A**   **13**   **B**   **14**   **C**   **15**   **D**

South West Coast Path

2

JUBILEE RD 1
WESTERN AVE 2
POLYWELL 3
STADDON RD 4
SCOTT AVE 5
RICHMOND RD 6
RICHMOND GN 7
MYRTLE COTTAGE RD 8
DIDDYWELL RD 9

Barnstaple or Bideford Bay

P

31

Skern

LB Sta

Pebble Ridge

Appledore

Sandymere

1

P

EX39

Northam Burrows Country Park

FAIRWAY

30

40   **A**   **41**   **B**   **42**   **C**   **43**   **D**   **44**   **E**   **45**   **F**

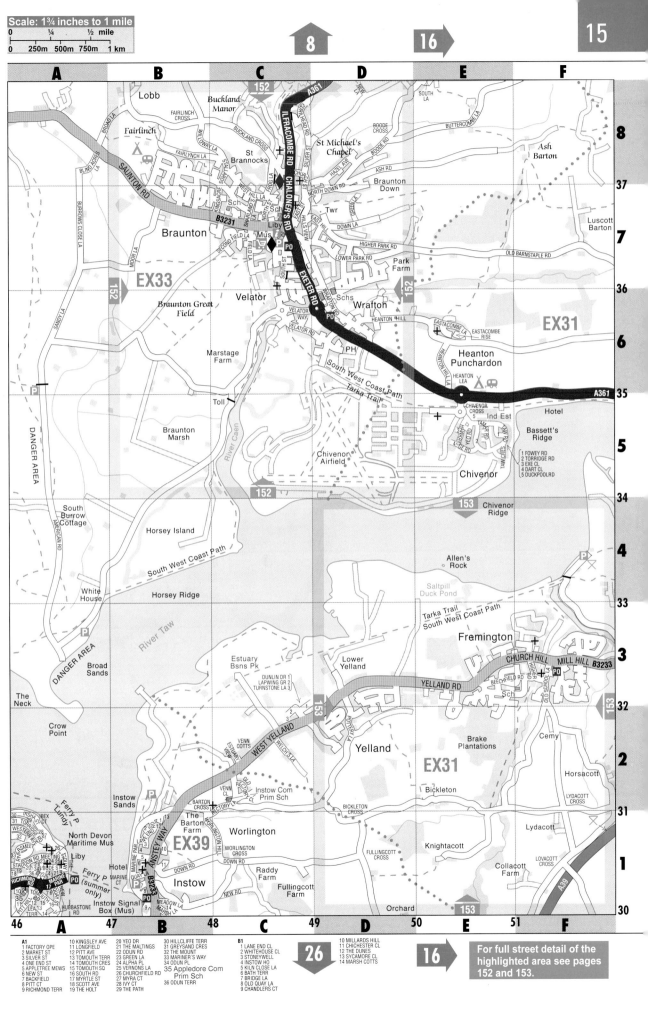

Scale: 1¾ inches to 1 mile

8

16

A1
1 FACTORY OPE
2 MARKET ST
3 SILVER ST
4 ONE END ST
5 APPLETREE MEWS
6 NEW ST
7 BACKFIELD
8 PITT CT
9 RICHMOND TERR
10 KINGSLEY AVE
11 LONGFIELD
12 PITT AVE
13 TOMOUTH TERR
14 TOMOUTH CRES
15 TOMOUTH SQ
16 SOUTH RD
17 MYRTLE ST
18 SCOTT AVE
19 THE HOLT
20 YEO DR
21 THE MALTINGS
22 ODUN RD
23 GREEN LA
24 ALPHA PL
25 VERNONS LA
26 CHURCHFIELD RD
27 MYRA CT
28 IVY CT
29 THE PATH
30 HILLCLIFFE TERR
31 GREYSAND CRES
32 THE MOUNT
33 MARINER'S WAY
34 ODUN PL
35 Appledore Com
Prim Sch
36 ODUN TERR

B1
1 LANE END CL
2 WHITEHOUSE CL
3 STONEYWELL
4 INSTOW HO
5 KILN CLOSE LA
6 BATH TERR
7 BRIDGE LA
8 OLD QUAY LA
9 CHANDLERS CT
10 MILLARDS HILL
11 CHICHESTER CL
12 THE DUNES
13 SYCAMORE CL
14 MARSH COTTS

26

16

For full street detail of the
highlighted area see pages
152 and 153.

A B C D E F

8

Marwood
WIGLEY CROSS
Whitehall
Pippacott
Lee House
Marwood Hill Gdns
Guineaford
Plaistow Mills
Kennacot Farm
Quarry
Sloley Barton
B3230

37

Prixford
SOUTH VIEW
MEREWOOD CL
PH
Kingsheanton
Broomhill Farm
Hotel
Broomhill Sculpture Gardens
North Hill

7

Waterlake
WATERLAKE LA
KNOWLE LA
Mainstone
OLD BARNSTAPLE RD
EX31
Varley Farm
PRIXFORD
South Hill

36

NORTH LA
Blakewell
Tutshill
Hartpiece Farm
Bradford Water

6

WINDY CROSS
West Ashford
Horridge
STRAND CL
ASHFIELD LA
LOOKOUT COTTS
Upcott
Ashford
GRATTAN LA
Shirwell Cross
B3230
SHIRWELL RD
Burridge
fort
A39
LIMEKILN LA
STRAND LA
HIGHER NEWCLOSE LA
Pilland
UPCOTT HILL
154
Roborough

35

A361
Strand House
Bradford House
HALL'S MILL
Westaway
ROBOROUGH RD
155
Raleigh House
SMOKY HOUSE LA
North Devon District
H
Pitt Farm
River Yeo

5

Sewage Works
South West Coast Path
Bradford
BRAUNTON RD
CHADDIFORD LA
WINDSOR RD
BELLAIRE
NORTHFIELD LA
LITTABOURNE
WESTAWAY PLAIN
NORTH RD
HIGHER RALEIGH RD
Raleigh

34

Pilton
UPCOTT AVE
RIVERSIDE RD
PILLAND WAY
B3149
PILTON CSWY
Coll
Schs
ABBEY RD
RALEIGH RD
ST GEORGE'S RD
BARNSTAPLE
Waytown

4

MEAD PARK CL 1
ELM COTTS 2
BICKINGTON LODGE 3
ELMFIELD RD 4
SEA KING CL 5
PENHILL VIEW 6
MUDDLEBRIDGE CL 7
Pottington
Bsns Pk
Ind Est
A39
ROLLE ST
C Ctr
Liby
Mkt
HIGH ST
ALEXANDRA RD
BEAR ST
Derby
Cemy
GORWELL
GOODLEIGH RD
WALTON WAY
Mast
Resr

33

Penhill
Clampitts
Muddlebridge
MEAD PK
Bickington
OAKLAND PK S
PARK AVE
LYNHURST AVE
WOODS LA
Sticklepath
OLD STICKLEPATH HILL
THE SQUARE
Mus
A3125
Ret Pk
Ltr Ctr
NEW RD
VICTORIA RD
FORCHES AVE
Sch
BARTON LA
154
Tarka Trail
Hollowcombe

3

MILL HILL
B3233
SHIELING RD
TEWS LA
LYDIACLEAVE
COMBREW LA
MIDDLE BROOK
BICKINGTON RD
B3233
ELLERSLIE RD
Sch
Ind Est
PO
STICKLEPATH HILL
Barnstaple
Ind Est
LADIES MILE
PARK LA
SOUTH ST
EASTERN AVE
B3138
Newport
Ind Acad
Superstore
Ind Est
A39
A361
WHIDDON DR

2

Combrew Farm
EX31
TEWS LA
CORVID CL
OLD BIDEFORD RD
FISHLEIGH RD
BRANNAM CRES
CEDAR DR
Ret Pk
A3125
Bsns Pk
PETROC
Ind Est
Crem
SANDRINGHAM GDN
WINDSOR GDNS
GRANGE AVE
ANDREW RD
PHILIP AVE
Herton
BIDEFORD RD
ELIZABETH DR
PETROC
Superstore Trad Est
Roundswell
Lake
Pill Farm
A361
Pill House
A39
A361
B3138
BISHOP'S TAWTON RD
CLIFTON RD
RUMSAM RD
ST JOHN'S LA
CHIRCOMBE AVE
LANDKEY RD
P&R
Whiddon
Rumsam
A377
VENN RD
WINDY ASH RD
VENN CROSS
155

31

A39
Rookabear
Brynsworthy
BRYNSWORTHY LA
Resr
ENTERPRISE RD
B3232
Upcott Farm
154
SOUTH VIEW
BISHOP'S TAWTON HILL
CHESTWOOD VILLAS
HAMMETTS LA
EX32
Chestwood
WINDY ASH CROSS

1

Factory
Hollamoor Clump
Tower
OLD EXETER RD
WHITEMOOR HILL
Whitemoor
Bishop's Tawton
Quarries
A377
NEW RD
SANCTUARY CL
SENTRY LA

30

52 A 53 B 54 C 55 D 56 E 57 F

E1
1 TAW VIEW
2 HIGHFIELD TERR
3 MOUNT PLEASANT
4 DEER WOOD VIEW
5 LAW MEMORIAL HO
6 CROSS FARM CT
7 SCHOOL LA
8 SANDERS LA
9 ROSE COTTS
10 VILLAGE ST
11 THE SQUARE
12 BISHOP'S TAWTON PRIM SCH

For full street detail of the highlighted area see pages 154 and 155.

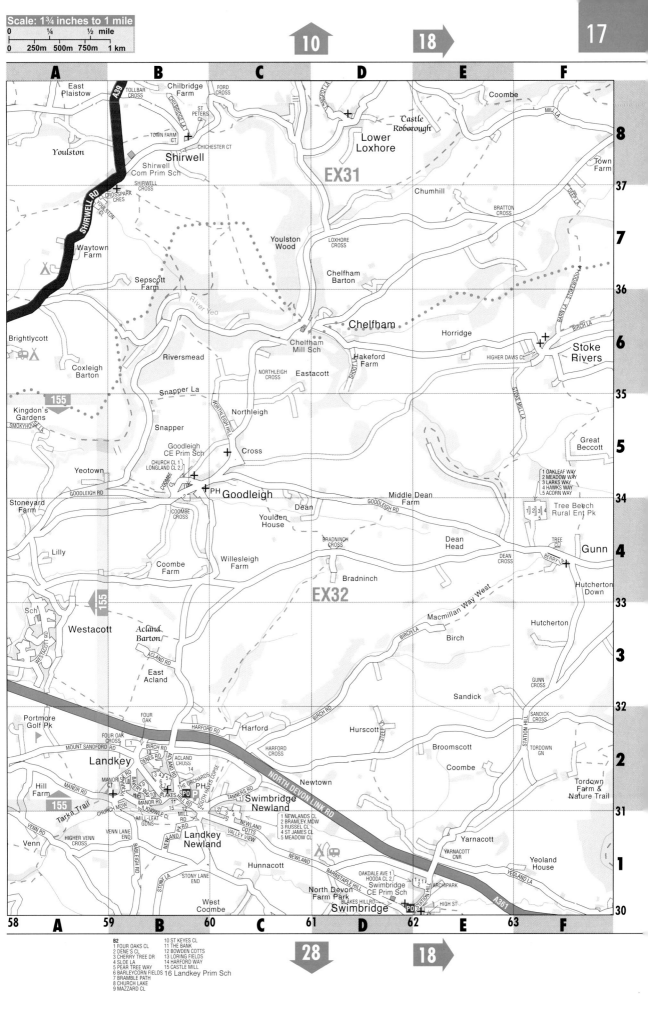

East Plaistow
Youlston
Chilbridge Farm
Ford Cross
TOLLBAR CROSS
CHILBRIDGE LA
ST PETERS CL
TOWN FARM CT
CHICHESTER CT
Shirwell
Shirwell Com Prim Sch
Coombe
MILL LA
Lower Loxhore
Castle Roborough
Town Farm
8
37

SHIRWELL RD
A39
CROSSPARK CRES
YOULSTON CL
SHIRWELL CROSS

EX31
Chumhill
DEER LA
BRATTON CROSS

Waytown Farm
Youlston Wood
Loxhore Cross
7
36

Sepscott Farm
River Yeo
Chelfham Barton
Chelfham
BARN LA
STOKEWOOD LA
BIRCH LA

Brightlycott
Riversmead
Chelfham Mill Sch
Horridge
Stoke Rivers
6
35

Coxleigh Barton
NORTHLEIGH CROSS
Eastacott
Hakeford Farm
HIGHER DAVIS CE
STOKE MILL LA

Snapper La
Kingdon's Gardens
155
SMOKYHOUSE LA
Snapper
Northleigh
NORTHLEIGH HILL
Cross
Great Beccott
5
34

Yeotown
Goodleigh CE Prim Sch
CHURCH CL 1
LONGLAND CL 2
COOMBE CL
PH
Goodleigh
Dean
Middle Dean Farm
GOODLEIGH RD
1 OAKLEAF WAY
2 MEADOW WAY
3 LARKS WAY
4 HAWKS WAY
5 ACORN WAY
Tree Beech Rural Ent Pk

Stoneyard Farm
GOODLEIGH RD
COOMBE CROSS
Youlden House
Dean
BRADNINCH CROSS
Dean Head
DEAN CROSS
TREE CL
BERRY LA
Gunn
4
33

Lilly
Coombe Farm
Willesleigh Farm
Bradninch
EX32
Hutcherton Down

155
Westacott
Acland Barton
ACLAND RD
Macmillan Way West
BIRCH LA
Birch
Hutcherton
3
32

Sch
East Acland
Hurscott
STEEP
Broomscott
Sandick
GUNN CROSS
SANDICK CROSS
STATION HILL
TORDOWN GN

Portmore Golf Pk
FOUR OAK CROSS
FOUR OAK CL
BIRCH RD
Harford
BIRCH RD
Coombe
Tordown Farm & Nature Trail
2
31

MOUNT SANDFORD RD
Landkey
HARFORD RD
HARFORD CROSS
Newtown
NORTH DEVON LINK RD
Yarnacott
YARNACOTT CNR
Yeoland House
YEOLAND LA
A361

MANOR RD
155
Tarka Trail
Swimbridge Newland
1 NEWLANDS CL
2 BRAMLEY MDW
3 RUSSEL CL
4 ST JAMES CL
5 MEADOW CL

Hill Farm
VENN RD
HIGHER VENN CROSS
Venn
VENN LANE END
MILL-LEAT GDNS
Landkey Newland
Hunnacott
STONY LA
STONY LANE END
VALLEY VIEW
BARNSTAPLE HILL
OAKDALE AVE 1
HOODA CL 2
Swimbridge CE Prim Sch
HIGH ST
Swimbridge
MARCHPARK
1
30

West Coombe
North Devon Farm Park
BLAKES HILL RD
PO

B2
1 FOUR OAKS CL
2 DENE S CL
3 CHERRY TREE DR
4 SLOE LA
5 PEAR TREE WAY
6 BARLEYCORN FIELDS
7 BRAMBLE PATH
8 CHURCH LAKE
9 MAZZARD CL
10 ST KEYES CL
11 THE BANK
12 BOWDEN COTTS
13 LORING FIELDS
14 HARFORD WAY
15 CASTLE MILL
16 Landkey Prim Sch

Scale: 1¾ inches to 1 mile

0   ¼   ½   mile
0   250m 500m 750m 1 km

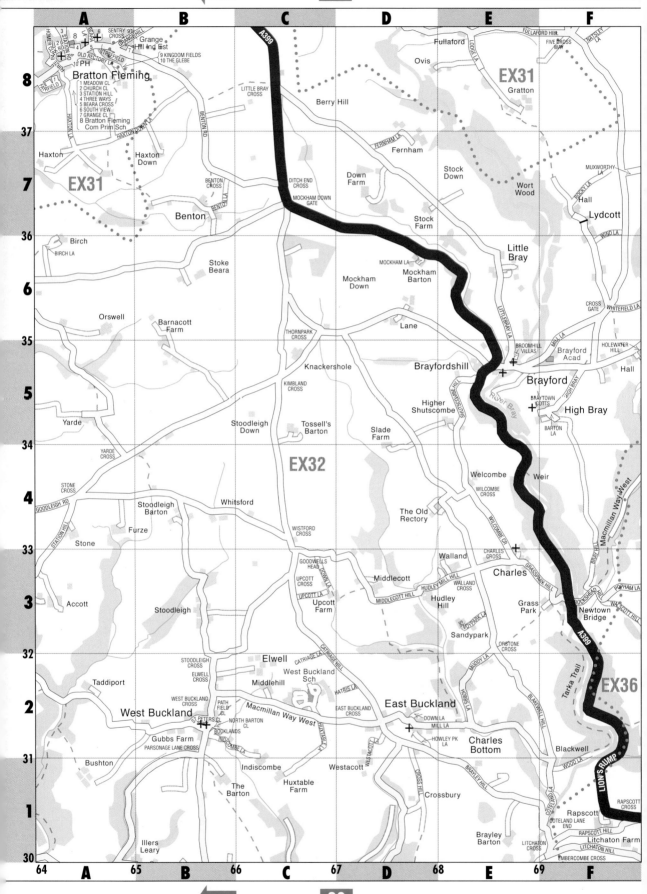

A   B   C   D   E   F

8

Station Rd
Grangehill
Sentry Cross
Old Rectory La
PH
Grange Hill Ind Est
9 Kingdom Fields
10 The Glebe
Grange
Bratton Fleming
1 MEADOW CL
2 CHURCH CL
3 STATION HILL
4 THREE WAYS
5 BEARA CROSS
6 SOUTH VIEW
7 GRANGE CL
8 Bratton Fleming
 Com Prim Sch

Little Bray Cross

Berry Hill

Fullaford
Ovis
Lodge La
Fullaford Hill
Five Cross Way
Hatsley La

EX31
Gratton

37

Haxton
Haxton Down

Fernham La
Fernham

Muxworthy La

7

EX31

Benton Cross
Benton La
Benton

Ditch End Cross

Mockham Down Gate

Down Farm

Stock Down

Wort Wood

Rocky La
Hall

Lydcott

Wind La

36

Birch
Birch La

Stoke Beara

Stock Farm

Mockham La

Little Bray

Cross Gate
Whitefield La
Holewater Hill

6

Orswell

Barnacott Farm

Thornpark Cross

Mockham Down

Mockham Barton

Lane

Little Bray La

Broomhill Villas

Mill La
Brayford Acad

Hall

35

Knackershole

Brayfordshill

River Bray

Brayton Cotts

Brayford

High Bray Hill

Hall

5

Yarde

Kimbland Cross

Stoodleigh Down

Tossell's Barton

Higher Shutscombe

Shutscombe Hill

River Bray

Weir

Barton La

High Bray

34

Yarde Cross

Slade Farm

EX32

Welcombe

Macmillan Way West

4

Stone Cross

Goodleigh Rd

Station Hill

Stoodleigh Barton

Whitsford

Furze

Wistford Cross

The Old Rectory

Wilcombe Cross

Wilcombe Cr

Bray Hill

33

Stone

Goodwells Head
Upcott Cross

Down La

Upcott La

Middlecott

Walland

Charles Cross

Charles

Grasspark Hill

Rockshead
Popham La
Rapscott Hill

3

Accott

Stoodleigh

Upcott Farm

Middlecott Hill

Hudley Mill Hill

Walland Cross

Hudley Hill

Sandypark La

Grass Park

Newtown Bridge

A399

32

Stoodleigh Cross

Elwell Cross

Elwell

Catriage Hill

West Buckland Sch

Catriage La

Middlehill

Sandypark

Orstone Cross

Muddy La

Blackwell Hill

Tarka Trail

EX36

2

Taddiport

West Buckland Cross

Path Field Cl

West Buckland

St Peters Cl

North Barton Cl

Middlehill

Harris La

Macmillan Way West

Huxtable La

East Buckland Cross

East Buckland

Down La
Mill La

Howley Pk La

Charles Bottom

Blackwell

1

Bushton

Gubbs Farm

Parsonage Lane Cross

Indiscombe La

Indiscombe

The Barton

Huxtable Farm

Westacott La

Westacott

Cross Hill

Crossbury

Brayley Hill

Wood La

Coteland Lane End

Lion's Rump

Coteland Lane End

Rapscott Cross

Rapscott

Litchaton Farm

30

Illers Leary

Brayley Barton

Litchaton Cross

Litchaton Hill

Embercombe Cross

A   B   C   D   E   F

64   65   66   67   68   69

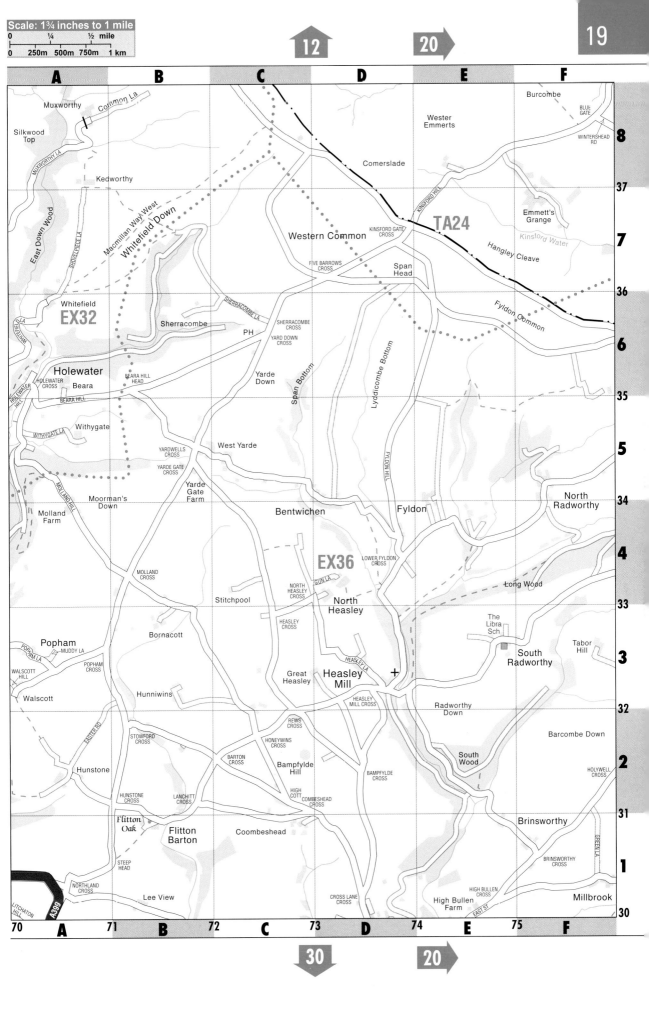

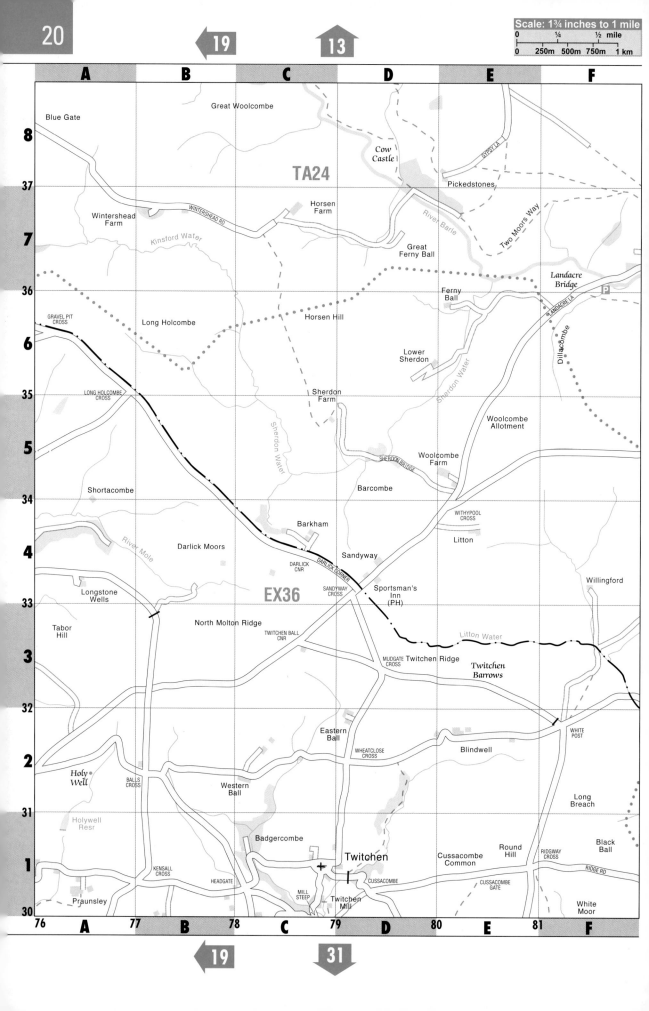

Scale: 1¾ inches to 1 mile

0   ¼   ½   mile

0   250m   500m   750m   1 km

A   **B**   **C**   **D**   **E**   **F**

Great Woolcombe

Blue Gate

8

Cow Castle

TA24

37

Pickedstones

GYPSY LA

Wintershead Farm

WINTERSHEAD RD

Horsen Farm

River Barle

Two Moors Way

7

Kinsford Water

Great Ferny Ball

Landacre Bridge

P

36

Ferny Ball

LANDACRE LA

Long Holcombe

Horsen Hill

GRAVEL PIT CROSS

Dillacombe

6

Lower Sherdon

35

LONG HOLCOMBE CROSS

Sherdon Farm

Sherdon Water

Woolcombe Allotment

5

Shortacombe

Sherdon Water

SHERDON BRIDGE

Woolcombe Farm

34

Barcombe

River Mole

Darlick Moors

Barkham

Sandyway

WITHYPOOL CROSS

4

DARLICK CNR

DARLICK BORNER

Litton

Willingford

33

Longstone Wells

EX36

North Molton Ridge

SANDYWAY CROSS

Sportsman's Inn (PH)

Tabor Hill

TWITCHEN BALL CNR

Litton Water

3

MUDGATE CROSS

Twitchen Ridge

Twitchen Barrows

32

WHITE POST

Eastern Ball

WHEATCLOSE CROSS

Blindwell

2

Holy Well

BALLS CROSS

Western Ball

Long Breach

31

Holywell Resr

Badgercombe

Cussacombe Common

Round Hill

RIDGWAY CROSS

Black Ball

1

KENSALL CROSS

HEADGATE

Twitchen

CUSSACOMBE

RIDGE RD

Praunsley

MILL STEEP

Twitchen Mill

CUSSACOMBE GATE

White Moor

30

76   **A**   **77**   **B**   **78**   **C**   **79**   **D**   **80**   **E**   **81**   **F**

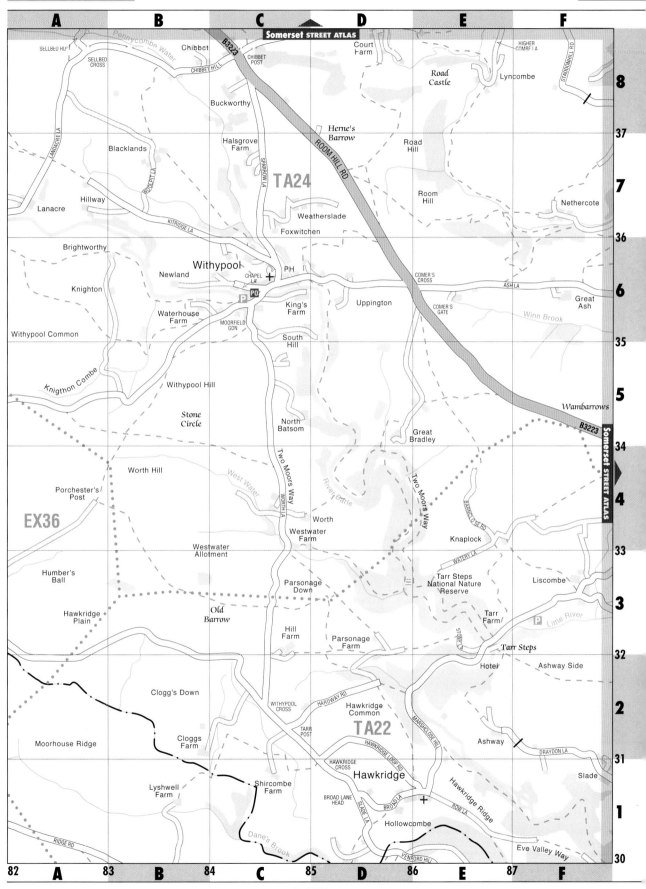

Scale: 1¾ inches to 1 mile
0   ¼   ½ mile
0   250m 500m 750m 1 km

SELLBED RD
SELLBED CROSS
Pennycombe Water
Chibbet
CHIBBET HILL
Chibbet Post
B3223
Court Farm
HIGHER COMBE LA
STADDONHILL RD

Road Castle
Lyncombe

Buckworthy
Herne's Barrow
Road Hill

Halsgrove Farm
Blacklands
SPARROW LA
TA24
Room Hill
Nethercote

Lanacre
Hillway
WOOLPIT LA
KITRIDGE LA
Weatherslade
Foxwitchen
ROOM HILL RD

Brightworthy
Withypool
Newland
CHAPEL LA
PH
Comer's Cross
ASH LA
Great Ash

Knighton
PO
P
King's Farm
Uppington
Comer's Gate
Winn Brook

Waterhouse Farm
MOORFIELD GDN
South Hill

Withypool Common
Knigthon Combe
Withypool Hill
Stone Circle
North Batsom
Great Bradley
Wambarrows
B3223

Somerset STREET ATLAS

Worth Hill
West Water
Two Moors Way
WORTH LA
River Barle
Two Moors Way
BARRICLOSE RD
WATERY LA
Knaplock
Liscombe

Porchester's Post
Worth
Westwater Farm
Tarr Steps National Nature Reserve
Little River
P

EX36
Westwater Allotment
Humber's Ball
Parsonage Down
Old Barrow
Tarr Farm
STORKS LA
Tarr Steps
Ashway Side

Hawkridge Plain
Hill Farm
Parsonage Farm
Hotel

Clogg's Down
Cloggs Farm
WITHYPOOL CROSS
HARDWAY RD
Hawkridge Common
TARR POST
TA22
MARSHCLOSE HILL
Ashway
DRAYDON LA

Moorhouse Ridge
HAWKRIDGE LOOP RD
HAWKRIDGE CROSS
Hawkridge
Hawkridge Ridge
Slade
ROW LA

Lyshwell Farm
Shircombe Farm
BROAD LANE HEAD
SLADE LA
BROAD LA
Hollowcombe
Eve Valley Way

RIDGE RD
Dane's Brook
VENFORD HILL

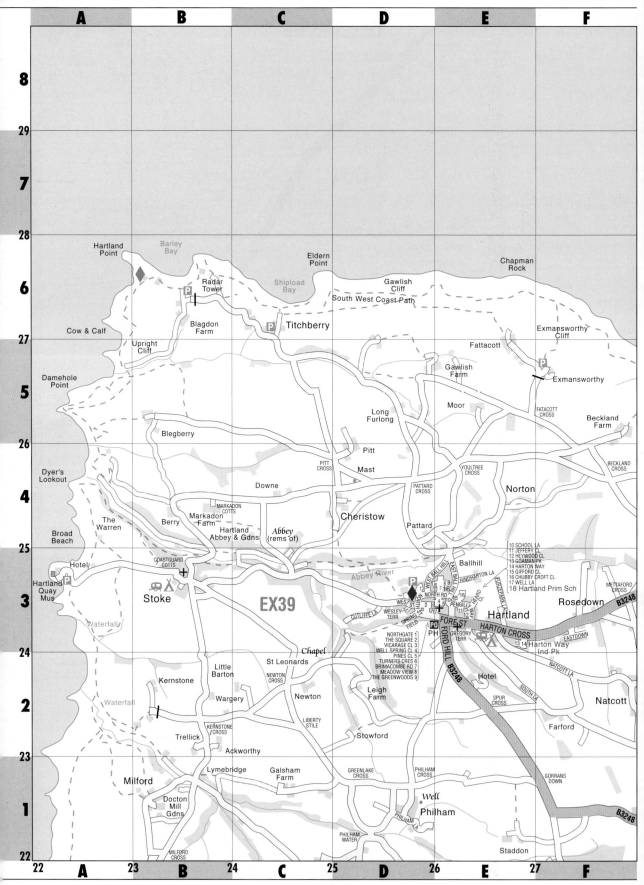

A   B   C   D   E   F

8

29

7

28

6

Hartland
Point
Barley
Bay
Eldern
Point
Chapman
Rock

Radar
Tower
Shipload
Bay
Gawlish
Cliff

Blagdon
Farm
South West Coast Path
Titchberry

Cow & Calf
Upright
Cliff
Exmansworthy
Cliff

27

Fattacott
Exmansworthy

Damehole
Point
Gawlish
Farm

5

Moor
FATACOTT
CROSS

Long
Furlong
Beckland
Farm

Blegberry
PITT
CROSS
Pitt
BECKLAND
CROSS

26

Downe
Mast
Norton

Dyer's
Lookout
PATTARD
CROSS

4

Markadon
Farm
MARKADON
COTTS
Cheristow
YOULTREE
CROSS

The
Warren
Berry
Hartland
Abbey & Gdns
Abbey
(rems of)
Pattard

Broad
Beach

Hartland
Quay Mus
COASTGUARD
COTTS
Ballhill
Rosedown

25

Abbey River
HINDHARTON LA
METTAFORD
CROSS
B3248

Hotel
10 SCHOOL LA
11 JEFFERY CL
12 HEYWOOD CL
13 GOAMAN PK
14 HARTON WAY
15 GIFFORD CL
16 CHUBBY CROFT CL
17 WELL LA
18 Hartland Prim Sch

Stoke
EX39
WEST BALL HIL
EAST BALL HIL
GAWLISH LA
PENGILLY
Hartland
EASTDOWN

3

NORTH RD
WESLEY
TERR
WESLEY
SPRING
FIELD
HARTON CROSS

Waterfall
CUTLIFFE LA
SPRING
FORD HILL
Harton Way
Ind Pk

24

Chapel
NORTHGATE 1
THE SQUARE 2
VICARAGE CL 3
WELL SPRING CL 4
PINES CL 5
TURNERS CRES 6
BRIMACOMBE RD 7
MEADOW VIEW 8
THE GREENWOODS 9
PO
PH
GREGORY
TERR
13 14
NATCOTT LA

St Leonards

Little
Barton
NEWTON
CROSS
Leigh
Farm
Hotel
SOUTH LA

Kernstone
Waterfall

2

Wargery
Newton
SPUR
CROSS
Natcott

KERNSTONE
CROSS
LIBERTY
STILE
Farford

Trellick
Ackworthy
Stowford

23

Lymebridge
Galsham
Farm
GREENLAKE
CROSS
PHILHAM
CROSS
GORRANS
DOWN

Milford
Well
Philham
B3248

Docton
Mill
Gdns
PHILHAM
LA

1

MILFORD
CROSS
PHILHAM
WATER
Staddon

22

A   22   B   23   24   C   25   D   26   E   27   F

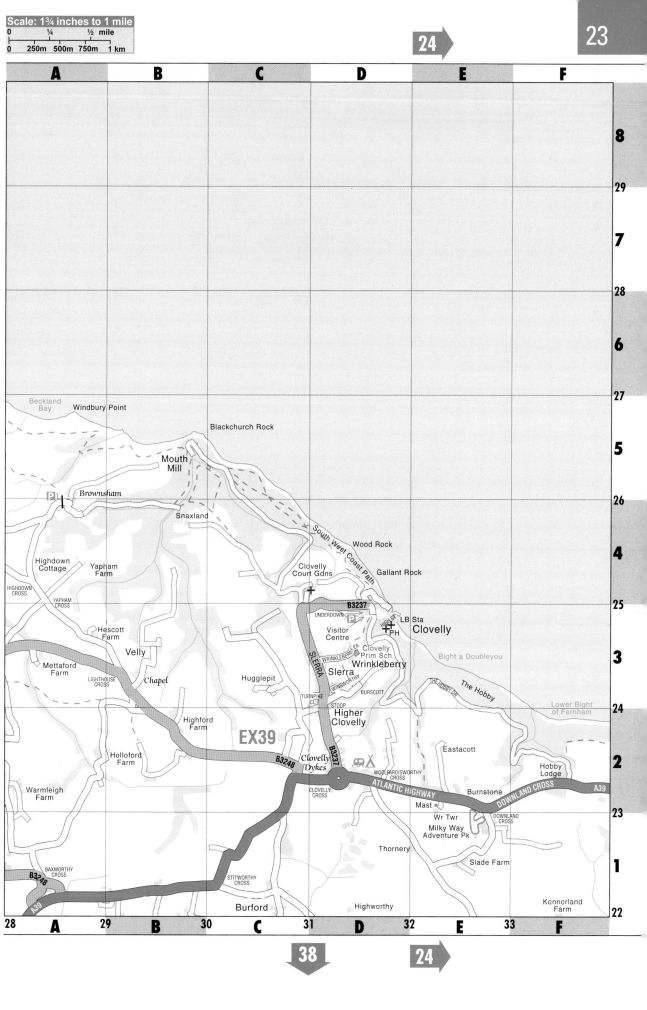

Scale: 1¾ inches to 1 mile

0   ¼   ½   mile
0   250m   500m   750m   1 km

A   B   C   D   E   F

8
29
7
28
6
27
5
26
4
25
3
24
2
23
1
22

Beckland Bay
Windbury Point
Blackchurch Rock
Mouth Mill
Brownsham
Snaxland
South West Coast Path
Wood Rock
Highdown Cottage
Yapham Farm
HIGHDOWN CROSS
YAPHAM CROSS
Clovelly Court Gdns
Gallant Rock
B3237
UNDERDOWN
LB Sta
Clovelly
Hescott Farm
Mettaford Farm
Velly
LIGHTHOUSE CROSS
Chapel
Hugglepit
Visitor Centre
WRINKLEBERY
Clovelly Prim Sch
Wrinkleberry
PH
SLERRA
Slerra
Bight a Doubleyou
The Hobby
THE HOBBY DR
WINSWORTHY
BURSCOTT
Burscott
Lower Bight of Fernham
TURNPIKE CL
STOOP
Higher Clovelly
Highford Farm
EX39
Holloford Farm
Warmleigh Farm
B3248
Clovelly Dykes
B3237
Eastacott
Hobby Lodge
WOOLFARDISWORTHY CROSS
A39
CLOVELLY CROSS
ATLANTIC HIGHWAY
DOWNLAND CROSS
Burnstone
Mast
Wr Twr
Milky Way Adventure Pk
DOWNLAND CROSS
BAXWORTHY CROSS
B3248
STITWORTHY CROSS
Thornery
Slade Farm
A39
Burford
Highworthy
Kennerland Farm

A   B   C   D   E   F
28   29   30   31   32   33

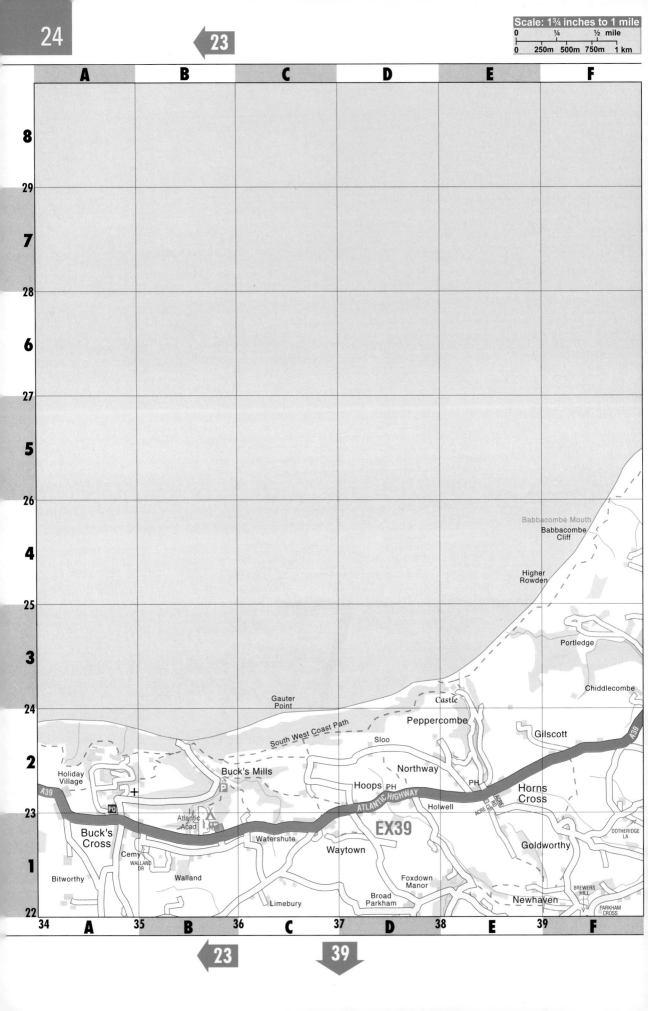

Babbacombe Mouth
Babbacombe Cliff
Higher Rowden
Portledge
Chiddlecombe
Gauter Point
Castle
Peppercombe
Gilscott
South West Coast Path
Sloo
Buck's Mills
Northway
Hoops PH
Horns Cross
P
PH
ATLANTIC HIGHWAY
Holwell
ACRE CL RD
A39
Holiday Village
A39
EX39
Goldworthy
DOTHERIDGE LA
PO
Atlantic Acad
Buck's Cross
Watershute
Waytown
Foxdown Manor
Newhaven
BREWERS HILL
Cemy
WALLAND DR
Bitworthy
Walland
Limebury
Broad Parkham
PARKHAM CROSS

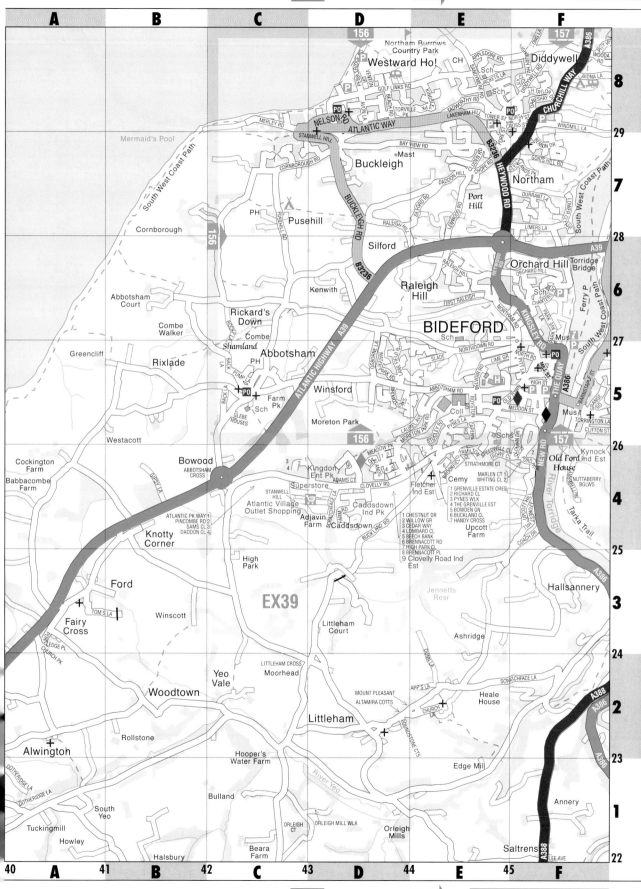

A   B   C   D   E   F

8
29
7
28
6
27
5
26
4
25
3
24
2
23
1
22

Mermaid's Pool

South West Coast Path

Cornborough

Abbotsham Court

Combe Walker

Greencliff

Rixlade

Westacott

Cockington Farm

Babbacombe Farm

Ford

Fairy Cross

TOM'S LA

Winscott

Woodtown

Rollstone

Alwington

DOTHERIDGE LA

Tuckingmill

Howley

South Yeo

Halsbury

Bulland

Beara Farm

Hooper's Water Farm

Yeo Vale

Moorhead

LITTLEHAM CROSS

Littleham

River Yeo

ORLEIGH CT

ORLEIGH MILL WLK

Orleigh Mills

Saltrens

LEE AVE

A388

Westward Ho!

Buckleigh

Pusehill

PH

Rickard's Down

Combe Shamland

Abbotsham

Winsford

Moreton Park

BUCKLEIGH RD B3236

Kenwith

ATLANTIC HIGHWAY A39

Bowood

ABBOTSHAM CROSS

Knotty Corner

Atlantic Village Outlet Shopping

Stanwell Hill

Adjavin Farm

Caddsdown

High Park

Littleham Court

EX39

Jennetts Resr

Kingdon Ent Pk

Superstore

Caddsdown Ind Pk

BUCKLAND RD

ATLANTIC PK WAY 1
PINCOMBE RD 2
SAMS CL 3
DADDON CL 4

Silford

Raleigh Hill

BIDEFORD

Port Hill

Northam

Diddywell

Orchard Hill

Torridge Bridge

CHURCHILL WAY

HEYWOOD RD B3236

KINGSLEY RD

NEW RD

A386

A39

THE QUAY

River Torridge

Tarka Trail

Hallsannery

Old Ford House

Kynock Ind Est

NUTTABERRY BGLWS

Ashridge

Heale House

MOUNT PLEASANT
ALTAMIRA COTTS

CHURCH LA

BOUNDSTONE CTS

APP'S LA

SCRATCHFACE LA

Edge Mill

Annery

A388 A386

Upcott Farm

1 GRENVILLE ESTATE CRES
2 RICHARD CL
3 PYNES WLK
4 THE GRENVILLE EST
5 BOWDEN GN
6 BUCKLAND CL
7 HANDY CROSS

1 CHESTNUT DR
2 WILLOW GR
3 CEDAR WAY
4 LOMBARD CL
5 BEECH BANK
6 BRENNACOTT RD
7 HIGH PARK CL
8 BRENNACOTT PL
9 Clovelly Road Ind Est

Fletcher Ind Est

Clovelly Rd

MARLEN CT 1
WHITING CL 2

STRATHMORE CT

Cemy

156

157

40   26

For full street detail of the highlighted area see pages 156 and 157.

40   A   41   B   42   C   43   D   44   E   45   F

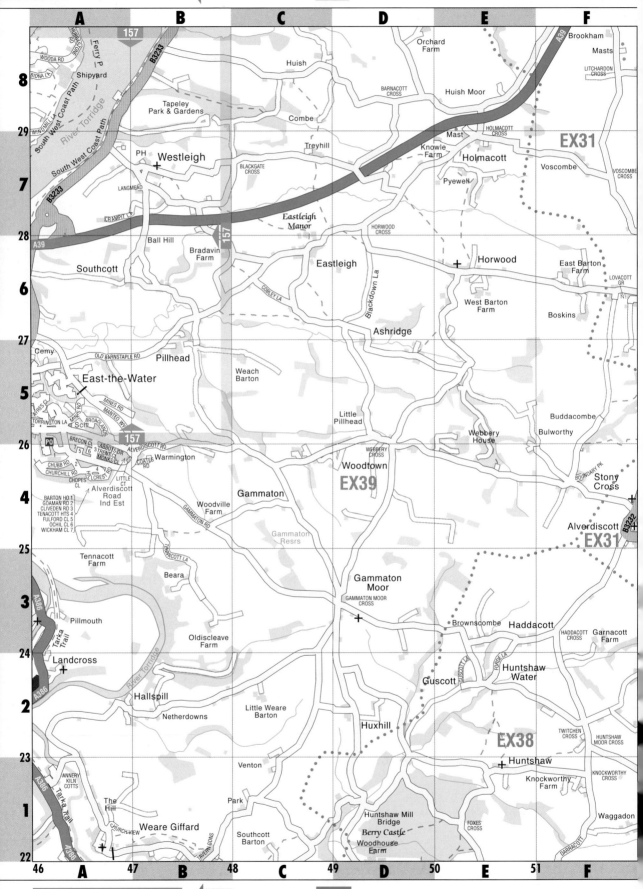

Scale: 1¾ inches to 1 mile

0   ¼   ½   mile
0   250m 500m 750m 1 km

A **B** **C** **D** **E** **F**

157

B3233

WOODA RD
BIDNA LA

WINDMILL LA
Shipyard

South West Coast Path

8

River Torridge

Tapeley
Park & Gardens

Orchard
Farm

Huish

Brookham

Masts

LITCHARDON
CROSS

29

Combe

Treyhill

BARNACOTT
CROSS

Huish Moor

Mast

HOLMACOTT
CROSS

EX31

PH   Westleigh

LANGMEAD

B3233

CRAMPIT

BLACKGATE
CROSS

Knowle
Farm

Mast

Holmacott

Voscombe

VOSCOMBE
CROSS

7

Eastleigh
Manor

HORWOOD
CROSS

Pyewell

28

157

A39

Ball Hill

Bradavin
Farm

Eastleigh

Horwood

East Barton
Farm

LOVACOTT
GR

Southcott

COBLEY LA

Blackdown La

West Barton
Farm

Boskins

6

27

Cemy

OLD BARNSTAPLE RD

Pillhead

Weach
Barton

Ashridge

East-the-Water

MINES RD
MANTEO RD
BROADLANDS

AYRES CL
TORRINGTON LA
MIN... RD
Sch

Little
Pillhead

Webbery
House

Buddacombe

Bulworthy

5

157

PO

BRECON CL
CHUBB RD
CHURCHILL RD
CHOPES
CL

ABBOTS DR
TRENT CL
MONKS CL
H... CRES

ALVERDISCOTT RD

COATES
RD

Warmington

WEBBERY
CROSS

Woodtown

BOUNDARY PK

Stony
Cross

26

BARTON HO 1
GOAMAN RD 2
CLIVEDEN RD 3
TENACOTT HTS 4
FULFORD CL 5
OCHIL CL 6
WICKHAM CL 7

LITTLE
CT

Alverdiscott
Road
Ind Est

Woodville
Farm

GAMMATON RD

Gammaton

EX39

Alverdiscott

B3232

EX31

4

Tennacott
Farm

TAPSCOTT LA

Beara

Gammaton
Resrs

25

A386

Pillmouth

Tarka Trail

Oldiscleave
Farm

Gammaton
Moor

GAMMATON MOOR
CROSS

Brownscombe

HADDACOTT
CROSS

Haddacott

Garnacott
Farm

3

Landcross

River Torridge

Hallspill

Netherdowns

Little Weare
Barton

Venton

Guscott

GUSCOTT LA

FORCE LA

Huxhill

Huntshaw
Water

EX38

TWITCHEN
CROSS

Huntshaw
Moor Cross

24

2

A386

Park

Southcott
Barton

Huntshaw Mill
Bridge
Berry Castle
Woodhouse
Farm

Huntshaw

FOXES
CROSS

Knockworthy
Farm

KNOCKWORTHY
CROSS

Waggadon

23

ANNERY
KILN
COTTS

The
Hill

CHURCH VIEW

Weare Giffard

TAVERN GDNS

DARRACOTT

1

A386

Tarka Trail

22

46   **A**   47   **B**   48   **C**   49   **D**   50   **E**   51   **F**

For full street detail of the
highlighted area see page 157.

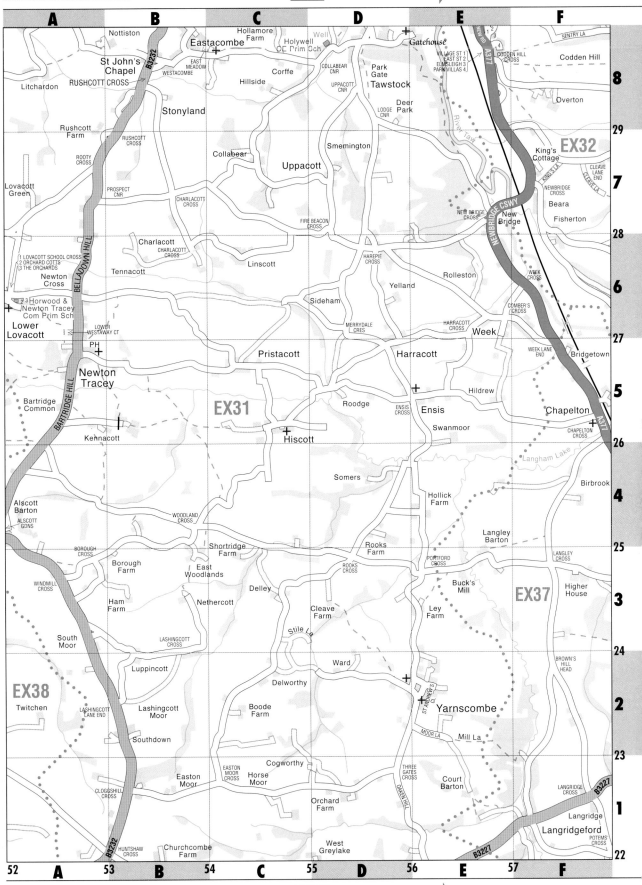

Scale: 1¾ inches to 1 mile

0   ¼   ½ mile

0   250m   500m   750m   1 km

A   B   C   D   E   F

16   28

8

Nottiston

St John's Chapel
RUSHCOTT CROSS
B3232

Eastacombe
Hollamore Farm
EAST MEADOW
WESTACOMBE

Holywell CE Prim Sch
Well
Gatehouse

VILLAGE ST 1
EAST ST 2
ELMSLEIGH 3
PARK VILLAS 4

CODDEN HILL CROSS

SENTRY LA

Codden Hill

A377
NEW RD

Litchardon

Corffe
Hillside

COLLABEAR CNR

Park Gate
Tawstock

Deer Park

UPPACOTT CNR

LODGE CNR

29

Stonyland

Collabear

Uppacott

Smemington

River Taw

EX32

King's Cottage
KING'S LA

Newbridge Cross

Overton

29

Rushcott Farm

RUSHCOTT CROSS

ROOTY CROSS

PROSPECT CNR

CHARLACOTT CROSS

BELLADOWN HILL

Fire Beacon Cross

New Bridge Cross

NEWBRIDGE CSWY

New Bridge

CLEAVE LANE END
CLEAVE LA

Beara

Fisherton

7

Lovacott Green

28

28

1 LOVACOTT SCHOOL CROSS
2 ORCHARD COTTS
3 THE ORCHARDS

Newton Cross

Charlacott
CHARLACOTT CROSS

Tennacott

Linscott

Harepie Cross

Yelland

Rolleston

Week Cross

6

Horwood & Newton Tracey Com Prim Sch

Lower Lovacott

LOWER WESTAWAY CT

PH

BARTRIDGE HILL

Newton Tracey

Sideham

MERRYDALE CRES

Pristacott

HARRACOTT CROSS

Harracott

COMBER'S CROSS

Week

WEEK LANE END

Bridgetown

27

Bartridge Common

EX31

Roodge

ENSIS CROSS

Ensis

Swanmoor

Hildrew

WEEK LANE END

A377

Chapelton

CHAPELTON CROSS

5

Kennacott

Hiscott

Somers

Hollick Farm

Langham Lake

Birbrook

26

Alscott Barton

ALSCOTT GDNS

WOODLAND CROSS

Langley Barton

LANGLEY CROSS

4

BOROUGH CROSS

Borough Farm

Shortridge Farm

Rooks Farm

ROOKS CROSS

PORTFORD CROSS

Buck's Mill

EX37

Higher House

25

WINDMILL CROSS

Ham Farm

East Woodlands

Nethercott

Delley

Cleave Farm

Stile La

Ley Farm

BROWN'S HILL HEAD

3

South Moor

LASHINGCOTT CROSS

Ward

24

EX38

Twitchen

Luppincott

LASHINGCOTT LANE END

Lashingcott Moor

Boode Farm

Delworthy

ST ANDREW'S CL

Yarnscombe

2

Southdown

Easton Moor

EASTON MOOR CROSS

Horse Moor

Cogworthy

MOOR LA

Mill La

23

CLOGGSHILL CROSS

Orchard Farm

THREE GATES CROSS

OAKEN HILL

Court Barton

LANGRIDGE CROSS
B3227

Langridge

1

B3232

HUNTSHAW CROSS

Churchcombe Farm

West Greylake

B3227

Langridgeford

POTEMS CROSS

22

52   A   53   B   54   C   55   D   56   E   57   F

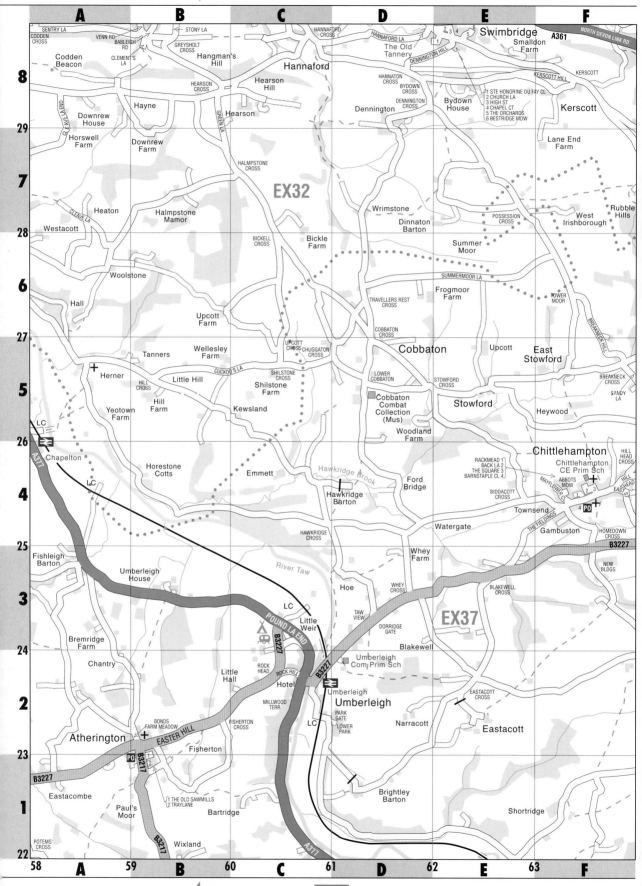

A   B   C   D   E   F

8

SENTRY LA
CODDEN
CROSS
STONY LA
VENN RD
BABLEIGH
RD
CLEMENT'S
LA
GREYSHOLT
CROSS
Hangman's
Hill
HANNAFORD
CROSS
HANNAFORD LA
The Old
Tannery
DENNINGTON HILL
Swimbridge
Smalldon
Farm
A361
NORTH DEVON LINK RD
Codden
Beacon
Hearson
Cross
Hearson
Hill
Hannaford
HANNATON
CROSS
BYDOWN
CROSS
Bydown
House
KERSCOTT HILL
KERSCOTT
Kerscott
Hayne
HEARSON
CROSS
Downrew
House
Hearson
Dennington
DENNINGTON
CROSS
1 STE HONORINE DU FAY CL
2 CHURCH LA
3 HIGH ST
4 CHAPEL CT
5 THE ORCHARDS
6 BESTRIDGE MDW

29

CLEAVE LA END
GREEN LA
Horswell
Farm
Downrew
Farm
HALMPSTONE
CROSS
Lane End
Farm

7

CLEAVE LA
Heaton
Halmpstone
Mamor
EX32
Wrimstone
POSSESSION
CROSS
West
Irishborough
Rubble
Hills

28

Westacott
BICKELL
CROSS
Bickle
Farm
Dinnaton
Barton
Summer
Moor
BREAKNECK HILL
TOWER
MOOR

Woolstone
SUMMERMOOR LA
Frogmoor
Farm

6

Hall
Upcott
Farm
TRAVELLERS REST
CROSS
COBBATON
CROSS
Cobbaton
Upcott
East
Stowford

27

Tanners
Wellesley
Farm
UPCOTT
CROSS
CHUGGATON
CROSS
LOWER
COBBATON
STOWFORD
CROSS
BREAKNECK
CROSS
SANDY
LA

Herner
CUCKOO'S LA
SHILSTONE
CROSS
Stowford
Heywood

5

HILL
CROSS
Little Hill
Shilstone
Farm
Cobbaton
Combat
Collection
(Mus)

LC
Yeotown
Farm
Hill
Farm
Kewsland
Chittlehampton
Chittlehampton
CE Prim Sch
HILL
HEAD
CROSS

26

Chapelton
A377
Horestone
Cotts
Emmett
Hawkridge Brook
Woodland
Farm
RACKMEAD 1
BACK LA 2
THE SQUARE 3
BARNSTAPLE CL 4
MAYFLOWER CL
ABBOTS
MDW
HILL
HEAD
EAST

4

LC
Hawkridge
Barton
Ford
Bridge
BIDDACOTT
CROSS
Townsend
PO
HOMEDOWN
CROSS

HAWKRIDGE
CROSS
Watergate
Gambuston
B3227

25

Fishleigh
Barton
River Taw
Whey
Farm
NEW
BLDGS

Umberleigh
House
Hoe
WHEY
CROSS
Blakewell
CROSS

3

LC
Little
Weir
TAW
VIEW
EX37
Blakewell

Bremridge
Farm
POUND LA END
B3227
DORRIDGE
GATE
EASTACOTT
CROSS

24

Chantry
Little
Hall
ROCK
HEAD
Umberleigh
Com Prim Sch
Blakewell

Fisherton
CROSS
Rock Hill
Hotel
B3227

2

Atherington
EASTER HILL
MILLWOOD
TERR
Umberleigh
Narracott
Eastacott

BONDS
FARM MEADOW
Fisherton
LC
PARK
GATE
LOWER
PARK

23

PO
B3217
Fisherton

B3227

1

Eastacombe
1 THE OLD SAWMILLS
2 TRAYLANE
Bartridge
Brightley
Barton
Shortridge

Paul's
Moor

22

POTEMS
CROSS
B3217
Wixland
A377

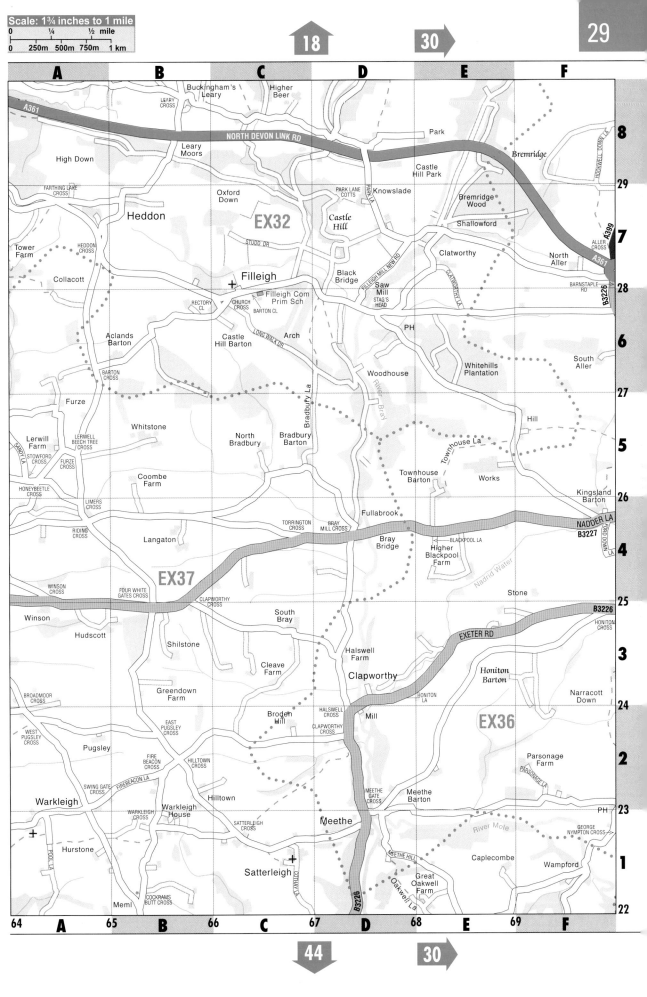

Scale: 1¾ inches to 1 mile
0 ¼ ½ mile
0 250m 500m 750m 1 km

A B C D E F

8

Litchaton Cross
A399
NADRID CROSS
Litchaton Cross
Nadrid Farm
Nadrid Farm
Hookwell Down La
Portgate Cross
Stonybridge Cross
Bridge Hill
Stony Bridge
West Park
Oakford Cross
Oakford Cl
Oakford Vills
Back La
Fore St
Higher East St
Broad Cl
East St
PO
PH
Bendle Lane Cross
Bendle La
Pitt La
Pitt
North Molton Prim Sch
Wheatlands Farm
North Lee Farm
Lee Cross
North Molton
1 THE SQUARE
2 JUBILEE GDNS
3 NORTH MOLTON CROSS
4 WINSOR MEADOW
5 ROBERTS FIELD

29

Coombe Farm
A399
North Cockerham
South Lee Cross
South Leigh
Holdridge La
Holdridge
Ley Cross
Upcott
Sannacott Farm
Higher Ley

7

Snurridge
A361
South Cockerham
Burcombe Farm
Burcombe Hill
Limeslake Farm
Burwell La
Burwell

28

West Ford
B3226
BARNSTAPLE RD
Ford La
Hacche La
Hacche Barton
158
Marsh La
East Marsh
River Mole
Bicknor Farm
Marsh La
Drewstone
Drewstone Cross
Walk La
Whitechapel Manor
Burwell

6

Hache Moor
Marsh Hall
Marsh La
Johnstone Moors
Rawstone Moors
Whitechapel La
Whitechapel Moors

27

Lime Way
Hacche La
Pathfields Bsns Pk
Park House
Piccavins La
Folly La
North Devon Link Rd
Rawstone

5

Mast
Honey Farm
Gunswell La
B322a
North Rd
Sch
Sch
Asab Dr
Kingsdons
Mole Bridge
Cuke Down La
Garliford Farm

26

158
B3227 NADDER LA
B3227
West St
Broad St
North St
East St
PO
Mus
Johnstone La
Johnstone
Garliford La
EX36
Bridge La
A361

4

Ford Down
South Molton United CE Prim Sch
Raleigh Pk
Livarot Wlk
Cooks Cross
B3137 NEW RD
Mill St
Poltimore Rd
Tucking Mill La
ALSWEAR NEW RD
Venford Villas
Gorton Hill
River Yeo
PH
B3227
Bishmill Gate
Silcombe Hill
Bish Mill
Waterhouse Farm
Aller Hill

25

B3226
Furzebray
George Nympton Rd
Alswear Old Rd
SOUTH MOLTON
South Molton Com Coll
Cemy
Great Hele Barton
Great Hele La
Grilstone
Silcombe Cross

3

Narracott La
Thorne Farm
Limer's Lane Cross
Limer's La
Blastridge Hill
Slough House
Slough La
Hall Park
SPIRE LAKE CL 1
JOEYS FIELD 2
PARSONAGE HILL 3
GLEBELAND VILLAS 4
MEADOW VIEW 5
ANGELHILL CROSS 6
SPIRELAKE 7

24

Narracott Farm
158
Cheyney Cross
Radley Cross
Crosse Farm
Barton
Little La
PO
Bishops Nympton Prim Sch
WEST ST

2

Hillside
Broomhouse La
Broomhouse Farm
Cheyney La
Ley
Great Frenchstone
1 GEORGE NYMPTON CROSS
2 THE ROW
FRENCHSTONE CROSS
Radley La
Radley
Westwood
Eastwood
Park
West Rock Rd

23

½
Culverhill Farm
George Nympton
Moorhouse La
Moorhouse
Polamarsh Hill

1

Mile Hill
Trayne Farm
Mill Farm
Garramarsh
Plcock La
B3137
Crooked Oaks
Bobby House La
Crooked Oak
Pitt Farm
Callards La
Moorhouse La
1 CHURCH GATE
2 MARIANSLEIGH CROSS
3 TOWNLIVING CROSS
Hilltown
Bishop's Nympton Cross

22

Woodhouse
Alswear
PH
Mariansleigh

70 A 71 B 72 C 73 D 74 E 75 F

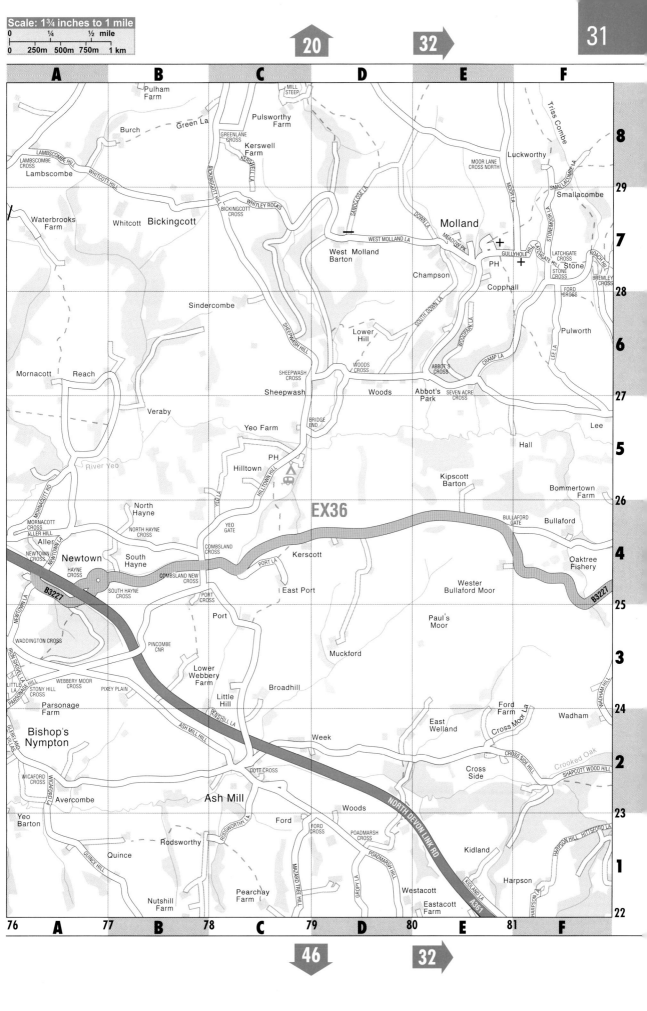

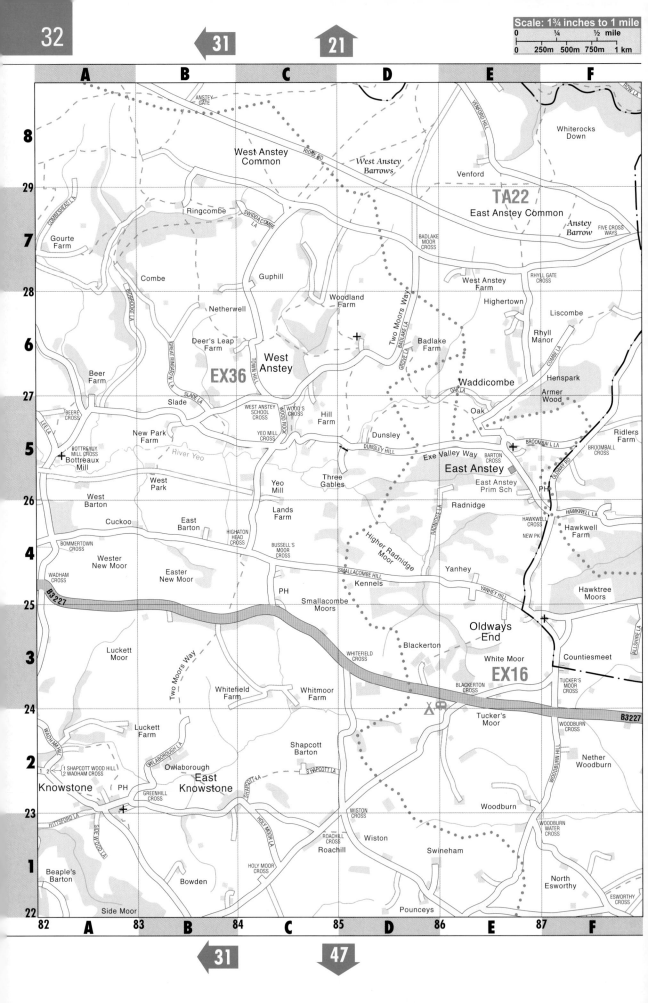

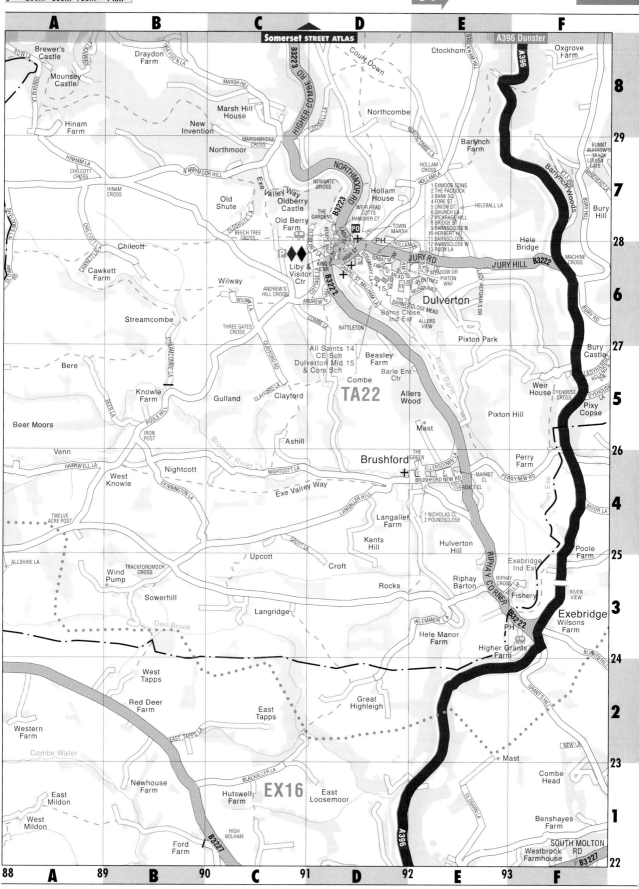

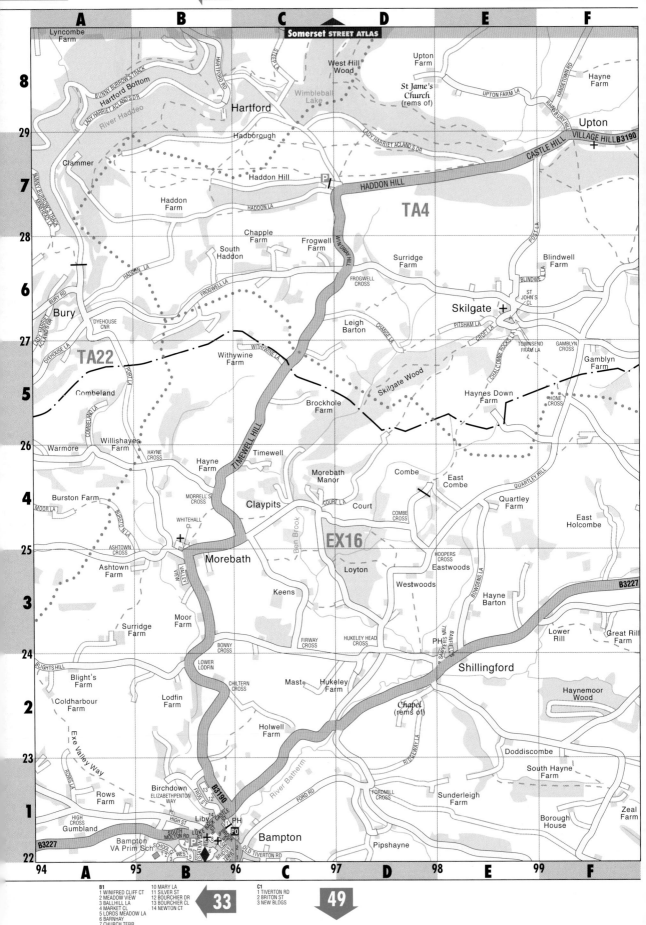

Somerset STREET ATLAS

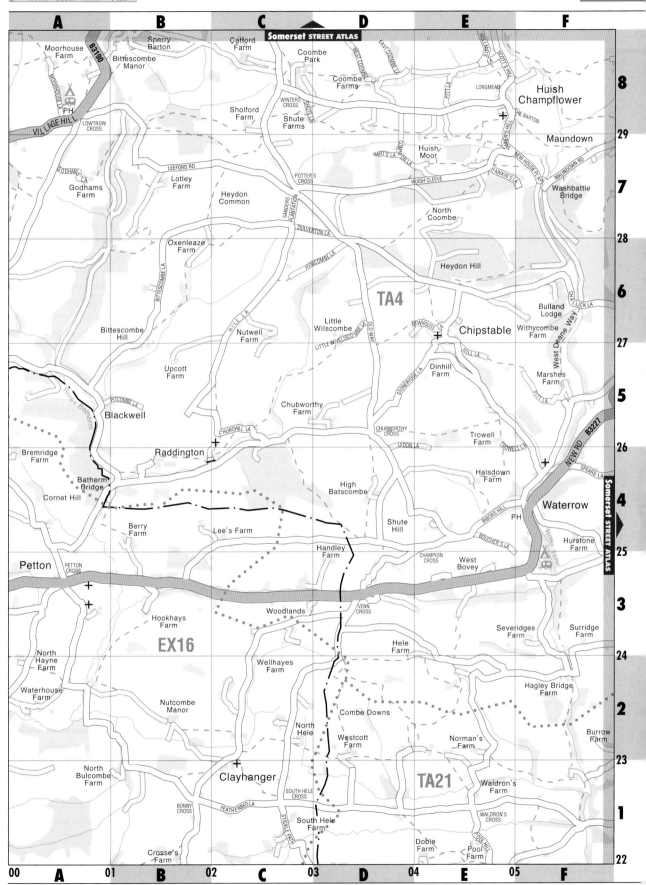

Scale: 1¾ inches to 1 mile

Somerset STREET ATLAS

Somerset STREET ATLAS

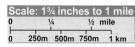

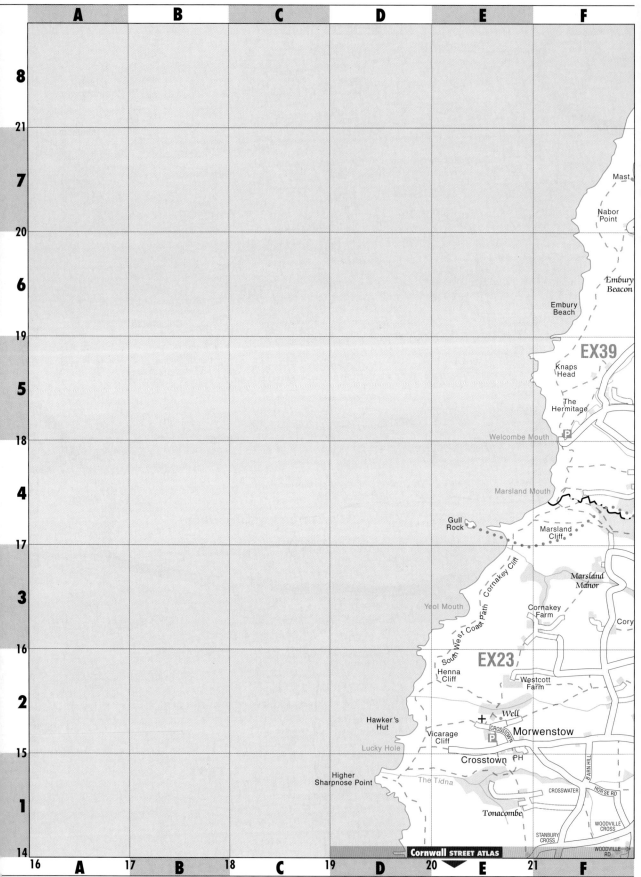

Mast

Nabor
Point

Embury
Beacon

Embury
Beach

EX39

Knaps
Head

The
Hermitage

Welcombe Mouth

Marsland Mouth

Gull
Rock

Marsland
Cliff

Marsland
Manor

Yeol Mouth

Cornakey Cliff

Cornakey
Farm

Cory

South West Coast Path

EX23

Henna
Cliff

Westcott
Farm

Hawker's
Hut

Well

Morwenstow

Vicarage
Cliff

CROSSTOWN

Lucky Hole

Crosstown

PH

BARN HILL

Higher
Sharpnose Point

The Tidna

CROSSWATER

HORSE RD

Tonacombe

WOODVILLE
CROSS

STANBURY
CROSS

WOODVILLE
RD

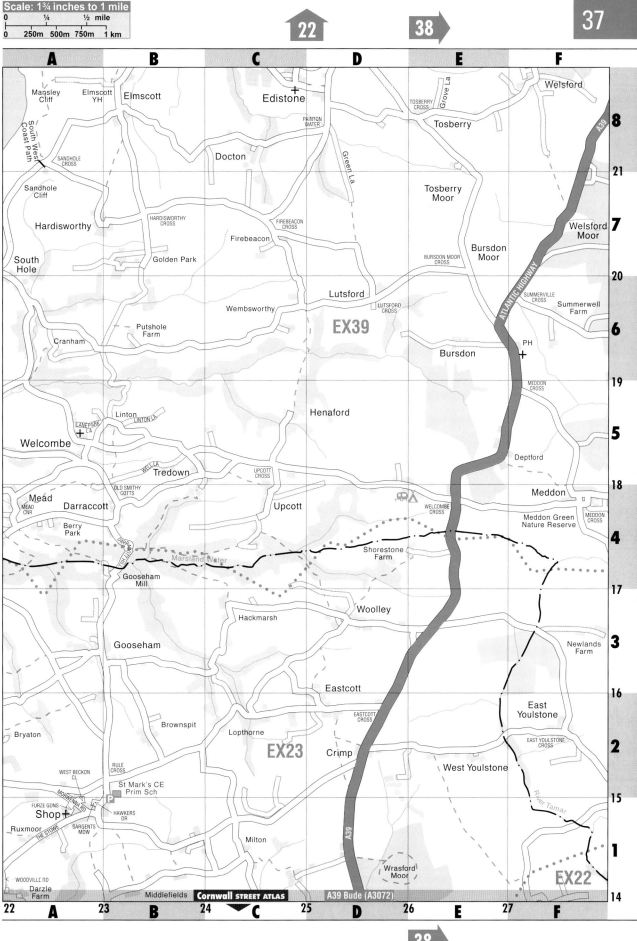

A   B   C   D   E   F

Mansley Cliff
Elmscott YH
Elmscott
Edistone
Tosberry Cross
Grove La
Welsford

8

South West Coast Path
Sandhole Cross
Docton
PAINTON WATER
Tosberry

21

Sandhole Cliff
Green La
Tosberry Moor

7

Hardisworthy
Hardisworthy Cross
Firebeacon Cross
Tosberry Moor
Welsford Moor

South Hole
Firebeacon
Bursdon Moor Cross
Bursdon Moor

20

Golden Park
Wembsworthy
Lutsford
Lutsford Cross
EX39
ATLANTIC HIGHWAY
Summerville Cross
Summerwell Farm

6

Putshole Farm
Bursdon
PH

Cranham

19

MEDDON CROSS

Linton
LINTON LA
Henaford
Deptford

5

LANE PARK LA
Welcombe
Meddon

WELL LA
Tredown
UPCOTT CROSS
MEDDON CROSS

18

OLD SMITHY COTTS
Upcott
WELCOMBE CROSS
Meddon Green Nature Reserve

Mead
MEAD CNR
Darraccott
DARRACOTT HILL
Shorestone Farm

4

Berry Park
Marsland Water
Gooseham Mill

17

Hackmarsh
Woolley
Newlands Farm

3

Gooseham
Eastcott
East Youlstone

16

Brownspit
Lopthorne
EASTCOTT CROSS
EAST YOULSTONE CROSS

2

Bryaton
EX23
Crimp
West Youlstone

RULE CROSS
WEST BECKON CL
River Tamar

15

MORWENNA RD
St Mark's CE Prim Sch
P
HAWKERS DR

FURZE GDNS
Shop
SARGENTS MDW

Ruxmoor
THE STOWE
Milton
A39
EX22

1

WOODVILLE RD
Darzle Farm
Wrasford Moor

14

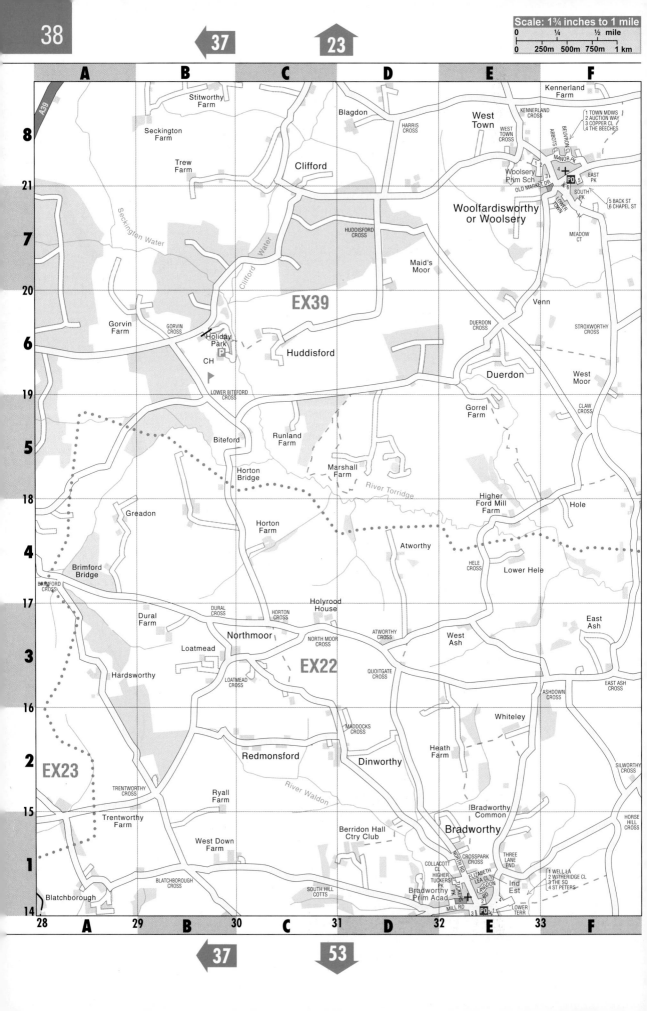

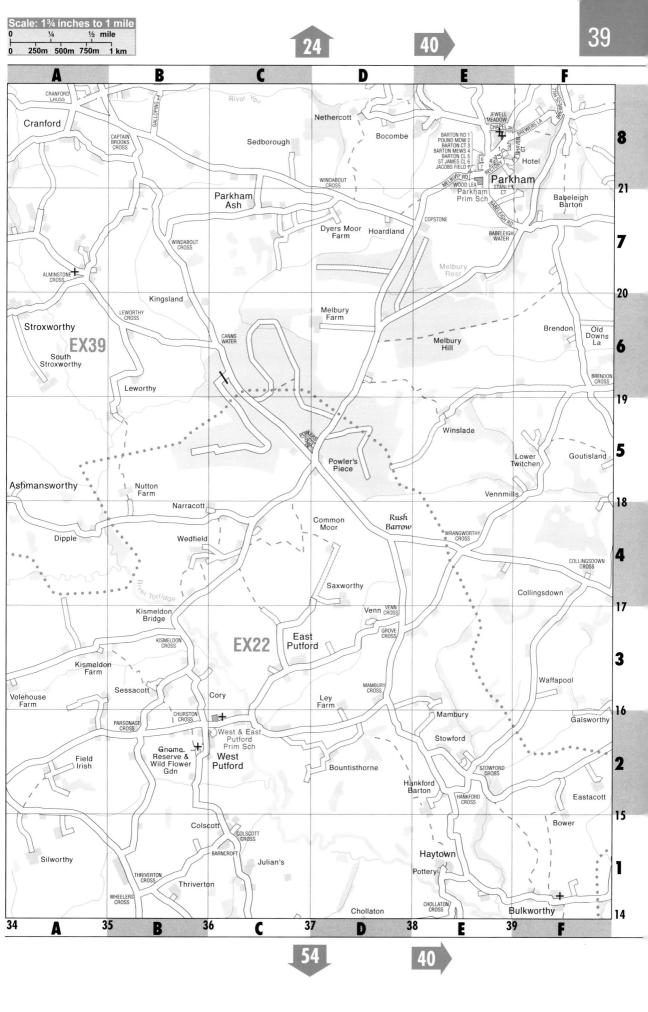

A   B   C   D   E   F

8
21
7
20
6
19
5
18
4
17
3
16
2
15
1
14

CRANFORD CROSS
Cranford
CAPTAIN BROOKS CROSS
GALLOPING 4
River You
Sedborough
Nethercott
Bocombe

JEWELL MEADOW
CHAPEL RD
BREWERS LA
THE SQUARE
BARTON RD 1
POUND MDW 2
BARTON CT 3
BARTON MEWS 4
BARTON CL 5
ST JAMES CL 6
JACOBS FIELD 7
RECTORY
MELBURY RD
WOOD LEA
Parkham Prim Sch
Parkham
STANLEY CT
Hotel
Babeleigh Barton
BABELEIGH RD

Parkham Ash
WINDABOUT CROSS
Dyers Moor Farm
Hoardland
Copstone
Babeleigh Water
Melbury Resr

ALMINSTONE CROSS
Kingsland
LEWORTHY CROSS
WINDABOUT CROSS
CANNS WATER
Melbury Farm
Melbury Hill
Brendon
Old Downs La
BRENDON CROSS

Stroxworthy
EX39
South Stroxworthy
Leworthy

POWLERS PIECE
Powler's Piece
Winslade
Lower Twitchen
Goutisland
Vennmills

Ashmansworthy
Nutton Farm
Narracott
Common Moor
Rush Barrow
WRANGWORTHY CROSS
COLLINGSDOWN CROSS

Dipple
Wedfield
Saxworthy
Collingsdown
River Tortridge

Kismeldon Bridge
KISMELDON CROSS
Venn
VENN CROSS
GROVE CROSS
Waffapool

EX22
East Putford
Kismeldon Farm
Sessacott
Cory
Ley Farm
MAMBURY CROSS
Mambury
Galsworthy

Volehouse Farm
PARSONAGE CROSS
CHURSTON CROSS
West & East Putford Prim Sch
Stowford
Field Irish
Gnome Reserve & Wild Flower Gdn
West Putford
Bountisthorne
Hankford Barton
HANKFORD CROSS
STOWFORD CROSS
Eastacott
Bower

Colscott
COLSCOTT CROSS
BARNCROFT
Julian's
Haytown
Pottery

Silworthy
THRIVERTON CROSS
Thriverton
Chollaton
CHOLLATON CROSS
Bulkworthy
WHEELERS CROSS

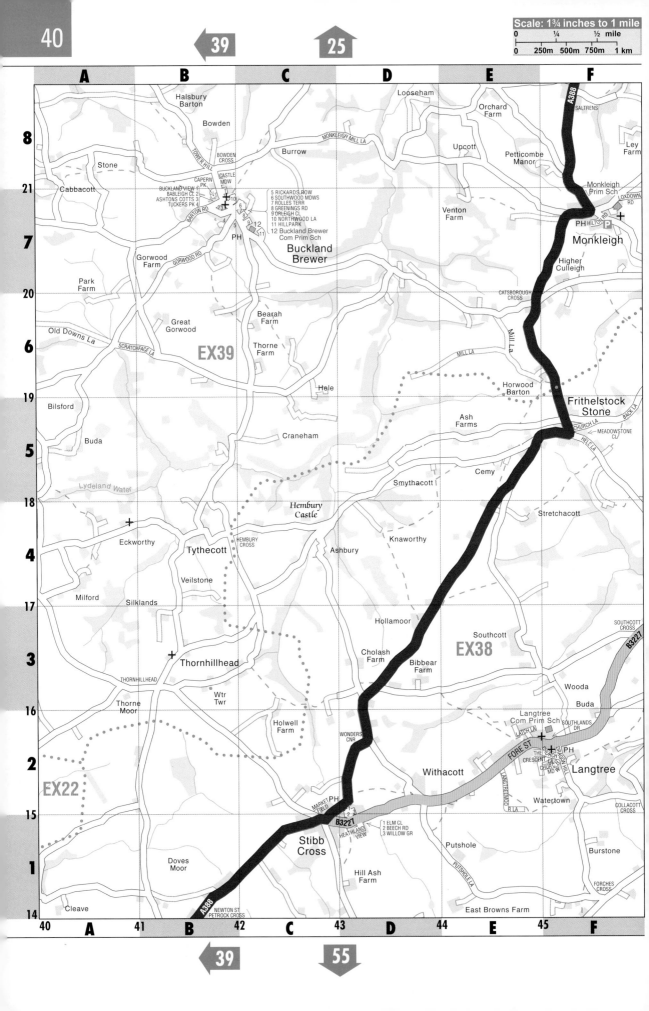

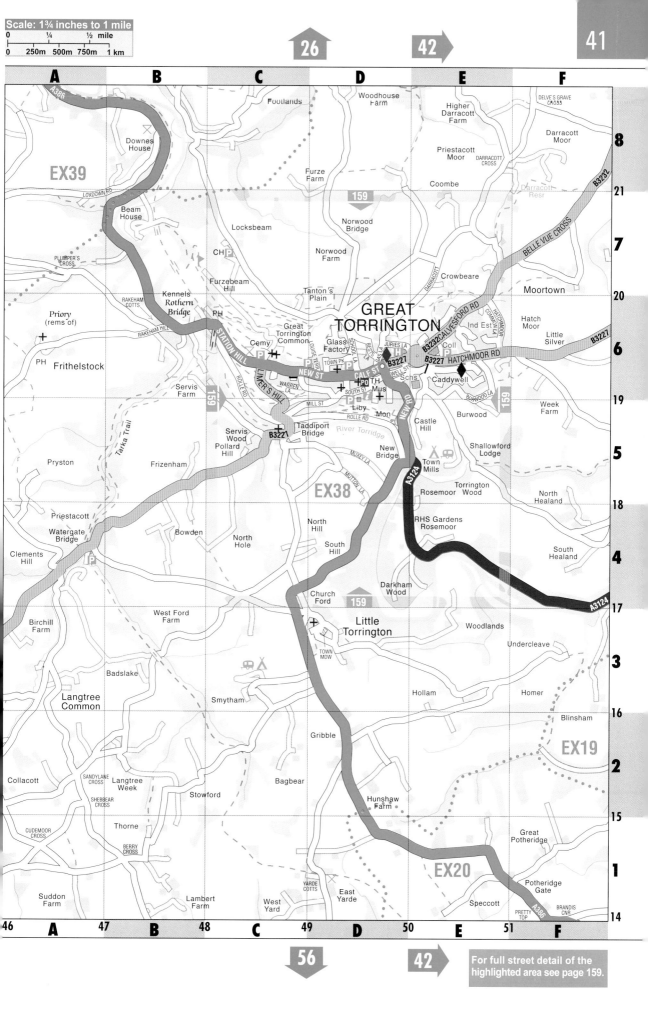

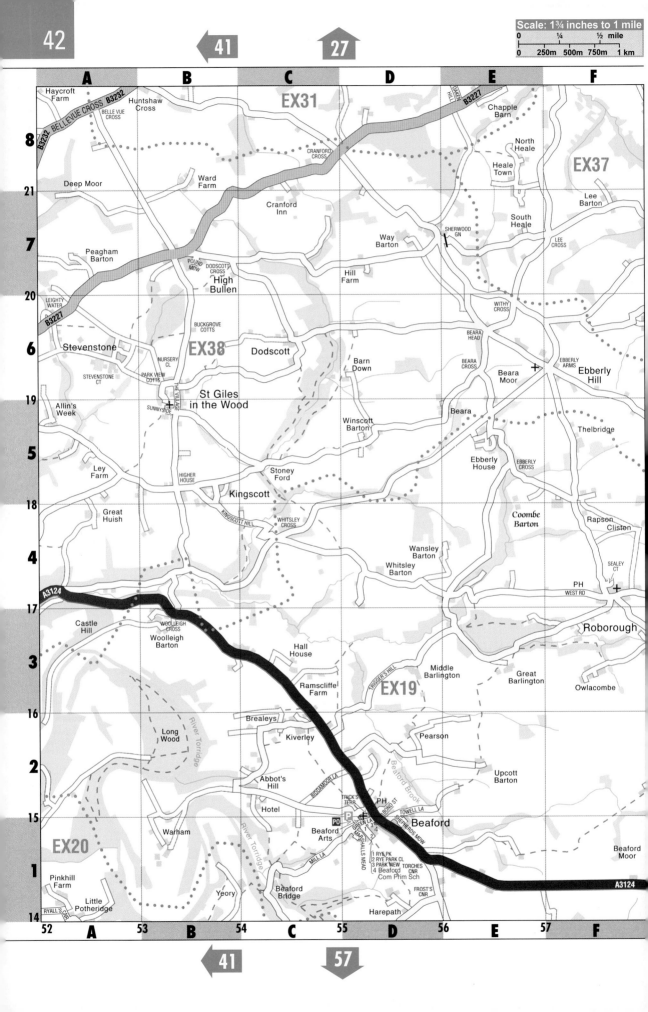

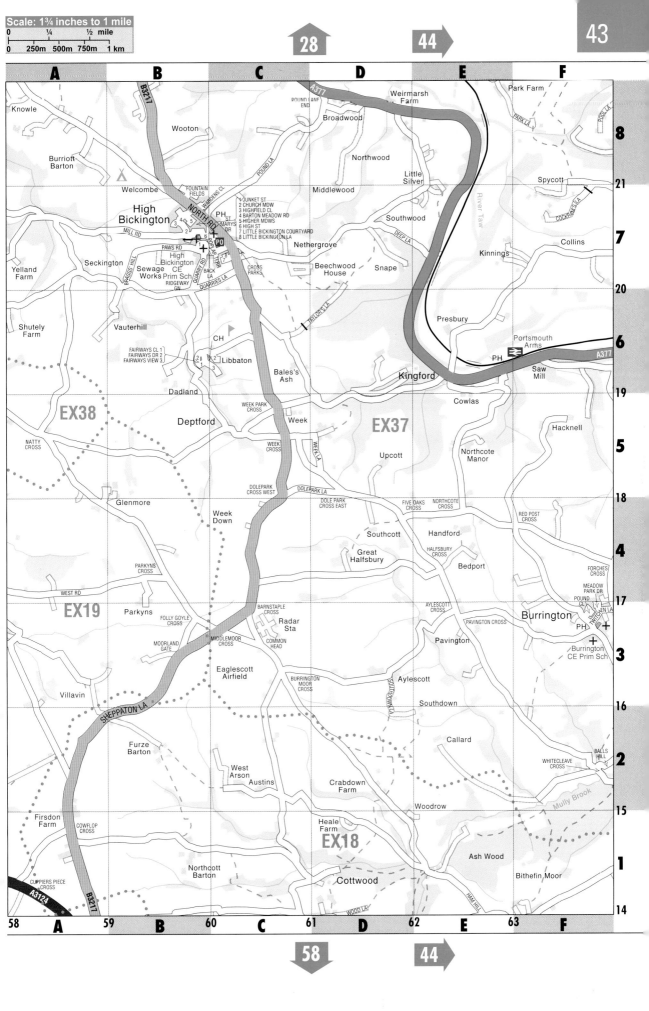

Scale: 1¾ inches to 1 mile

0   ¼   ½   mile
0   250m 500m 750m 1 km

A   B   C   D   E   F

8
21
7
20
6
19
5
18
4
17
3
16
2
15
1
14

Knowle
Burriott
Barton
Welcombe
High
Bickington
Mill Rd
Seckington
Sewage
Works
High
Bickington
CE
Prim Sch
Ridgeway
Gn
Yelland
Farm
Shutely
Farm
Vauterhill
FAIRWAYS CL 1
FAIRWAYS DR 2
FAIRWAYS VIEW 3
CH
Libbaton
Dadland
EX38
Deptford
NATTY
CROSS
Glenmore
Week
Down
PARKYNS
CROSS
WEST RD
EX19
Parkyns
FOLLY GOYLE
CROSS
MOORLAND
GATE
MIDDLEMOOR
CROSS
Villavin
SHEPPATON LA
Furze
Barton
West
Arson
Austins
Northcott
Barton
Firsdon
Farm
COWFLOP
CROSS
CUPPIERS PIECE
CROSS
A3124
B3217

Wooton
B3217
NORTH RD
POUND LA
WARDENS CL
FOUNTAIN
FIELDS
PH
ST
MARYS
DR
PO
PAWS RD
QUARRY RD
BACK
LA
QUARRIES LA
BRAGGS HILL
1 JUNKET ST
2 CHURCH MDW
3 HIGHFIELD CL
4 BARTON MEADOW RD
5 HIGHER MDWS
6 HIGH ST
7 LITTLE BICKINGTON COURTYARD
8 LITTLE BICKINGTON LA
CROSS
PARKS
Bales's
Ash
Week
WEEK PARK
CROSS
WEEK CROSS
WEEK LA
DOLEPARK
CROSS WEST
BARNSTAPLE
CROSS
Radar
Sta
COMMON
HEAD
Eaglescott
Airfield
BURRINGTON
MOOR
CROSS
West
Arson
Heale
Farm
EX18
Cottwood
WOOD LA

A377
ROUND LANE
END
Broadwood
Weirmarsh
Farm
Northwood
Middlewood
Little
Silver
Southwood
Nethergrove
TAYLOR'S LA
Beechwood
House
Snape
DEEP LA
Kingford
Cowlas
EX37
Upcott
DOLEPARK LA
DOLE PARK
CROSS EAST
FIVE OAKS
CROSS
Southcott
Great
Halfsbury
Southcott
Handford
HALFSBURY
CROSS
Bedport
AYLESCOTT
CROSS
Pavington
PAVINGTON CROSS
Aylescott
SOUTHDOWN LA
Southdown
Crabdown
Farm
Woodrow
Callard
Ash Wood
Bithefin Moor
HAM HILL

Park Farm
PARK LA
POOL LA
Spycott
COCKRILLS LA
Collins
River Taw
Kinnings
Presbury
Portsmouth
Arms
PH
Saw
Mill
A377
Hacknell
NORTHCOTE
CROSS
Northcote
Manor
RED POST
CROSS
FORCHES
CROSS
MEADOW
PARK DR
POUND
CL
Burrington
PH
WHITCHEN LA
Burrington
CE Prim Sch
WHITECLEAVE
CROSS
BALLS
HILL
Mully Brook

58
A   B   C   D   E   F
58   59   60   61   62   63

Map grid (A–F, 14–21)

Row 8 area: POOL LA, Haynetown, Edington, Newlands, HAYNE TOWN CROSS, NEWLAND CROSS, COTHAY LA, B3226, Watertown, Bias Wood, YEOTOWN CROSS, DANNELLA, SAMPSON CROSS, Sampson Barton, Stone, SLETCHCOTT CROSS, RED GATE, JOSE'S CROSS

Row 21: Chittlehamholt, PH, RUSSON LA, Arshaton Wood, River Mole, Hele, HELE CROSS, Sletchcott, Down Farm, Collacott Farm

Row 7: Highbullen, Hele Wood, Coley Lake, Huxford Farm, HUXFORD LA, ENTRANCE CROSS, WHITMORE LA

Row 20: Manor House, Whitmore, Lenton, LENTON LA, Smitha, Kingsnympton Park, PH, STEEPLE MDW

Row 6: Abbot's Marsh, A377, SNYDLAS LA, EX37, Snydles Farm, King's Nympton County Prim Sch, COOPERS CROSS, King's Nympton, BRANDY WELLS, NYMET VILLAS, KING'S CROSS, BEARA CROSS

Row 19: Braggamarsh, Bouchland Farm, Park Wood, Wooda, Beara, TONGUE LAKE LA, GREAT LIGHTLEIGH LA, SHORELAND CROSS

Row 5: BOLMSFORD LA, Weir, HILL HEAD CROSS, HEAD MILL, SPITTLE LA, Great Lightleigh, LIGHTLEIGH CROSS, WADDINGTON LA

Row 18: Hill, Head Wood, River Taw, Head Barton, Hill Head, JUNCTION POOL, BRIDGE CROSS, NEWNHAM LA, Spittle Farm, COOMBE, COMBE LA, Waddington

Row 4: Barnpool, POOL LA, NEWNHAM CROSS, B3226, Newnham Barton, SPITTLE CROSS, Cutland House, Cadbury Barton, Bunson

Row 17: FORCHES CROSS, TWO GATE CROSS, Catham, King's Hill, Fortescue Cross, Kings Nympton, HIGHER ELSTONE CROSS, ELSTONE CROSS, CUTLAND CROSS, PYNE MEADOW CROSS, TOLL BAR CROSS, DOBBSMOOR CROSS, ORANGE MOOR CROSS

Row 3: TWITCHEN LA, Hayne Barton, Twitchen, Churchland, Bircham, STATON RD, Elstone, Lakehead, Dobbs Moor Farm, Beacon

Row 16: BALLS CNR, CLEAVE LA, BALLS HILL, SOUTH MOLTON RD, GOLLAND LA, MILL MOOR CROSS, Colleton Mills, EX18, DOBBSMOOR CROSS, Thurle, Parsonage Farm, PARSONAGE CROSS

Row 2: Cleave, Golland, HANSFORD CROSS, Hansford Barton, FORD CROSS

Row 15: MILL LA, Mully Brook, Winswood, HANSFORD CROSS, BORNE CROSS, BONDS CROSS, Chulmleigh Com Coll, CHARNEYMORE CROSS, FOUR CROSSWAYS, Chulmleigh Prim Sch, LANGLEY LA

Row 1: Hook Farm, Borne, BAGGED LA, COLLETON GATE, Colleton Manor, NAP LA, Back Hill Ind Est, MALLINGBROOK CROSS, BACK HILL, Liby, LANGLEY, Chulmleigh, EAST ST, PO, CH

Row 14: A377, B3096, LEIGH RD, B3096, LEIGH VILLAS, DARTRIDGE MDWS, Ladywell La, LADYWELL MDWS, Cricket Cl, Park Mill La, Lodge La

E1
1 LAND PK
2 DARTMOOR VIEW
3 FOUR WAYS DR
4 THREE CROSSWAYS
5 BEACON RISE
6 LANGLEY GDNS
7 ROYAL CHARTER PK
8 WINDY CROSS
9 EGYPT LA
10 CHULMLEIGH HILL
11 FORE ST HILL
12 THE SQUARE
13 ROCK HILL
14 NEW ST
15 CHURCH CL

1 CRICKET CL
2 PARK MILL LA

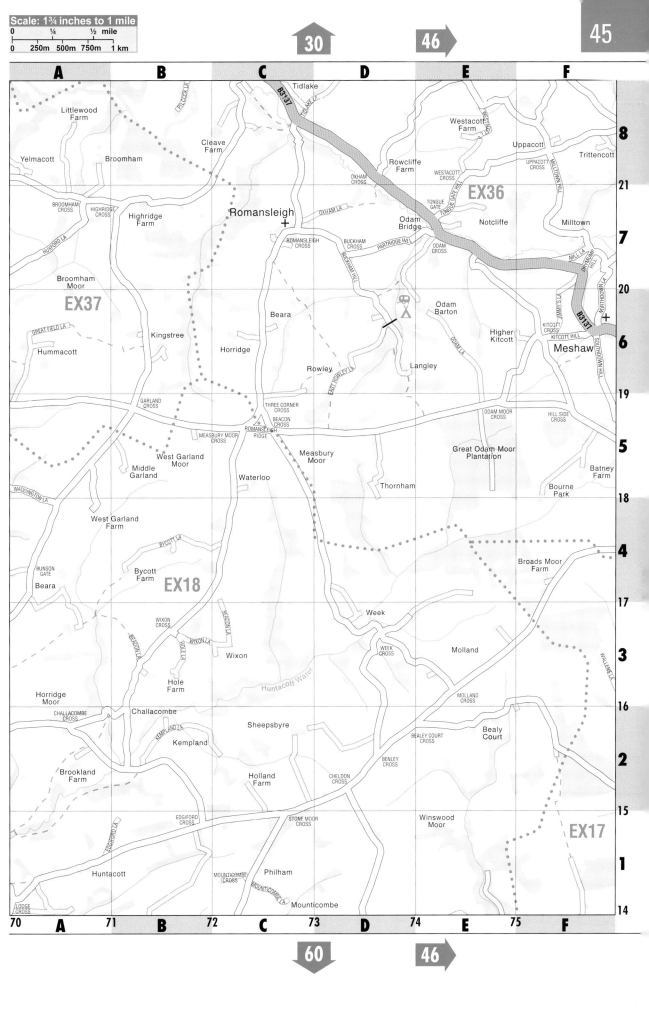

Scale: 1¾ inches to 1 mile

0   ¼   ½ mile
0   250m   500m   750m   1 km

A   B   C   D   E   F

8

TRITTENCOTT CROSS
Munson Farm
West Centry
QUINCE CROSS
RODSWORTHY LA
MAZARD TREE HILL
MOORLAND VIEW
GROPY LA
Rose Ash
BICKWILL CROSS
POADMARSH HILL
FIVE CROSSWAY
N DEVON LINK RD
A361
HARROW LA
Beaple's Moor

21

Cherridge
Whippenscott
WHIPPENSCOTT HILL
YARD LA
Overcott
Nethercott Manor Farm
Nutcombe Farm
Poole Farm
DISH'S HILL
BATSWORTHY CROSS

7

EX36
Bigbrook
Catkill
CATKILL CROSS
FANNY'S CROSS
Great Ash Moor
Batsworthy

20

Narracott
Burcombe
VENHAY CROSS
HARP'S CORNER CROSS
NEW ROAD CROSS
Ash Moor
DENSDON GATE
DITCHETT CROSS
BROADCLOSE HILL

6

CLEAVE HILL
B3137
Meshaw Barton
Blacklands
Middle Whitstone
Ditchett
DENSDON RD
NETTLEFORD HILL
CREACOMBE BARTON CROSS

19

SOUTHDOWN CROSS
MESHAW RECTORY CROSS
RECTORY LA
Great Whitstone
WHITSTONE LA
Heath Farm
Venhay
MAIRE RD
Maire
Crowdhole

5

MESHAW MOOR CROSS
GIDLEY ARMS CROSS
IRISHCOMBE GATE
Nettleford
CROWHOLE HILL
Surcombe River

18

BOURNE BRIDGE CROSS
MESHAW CROSS RDS
GIDLEY CROSS
IRISHCOMBE LA
Irishcombe Farm
GRENDON LA
CROWDHOLE CROSS

4

MOUSEBERRY CROSS
BURROW CROSS
Burrow
Wheadon Farm
WHEADON CROSS
The Grendons
Bradford Farm

17

Mouseberry
Blagrove
BLAGROVE HILL
West Yeo Moor
Broadridge Farm
Rowden Farm
Bradford Tracy

3

WEST YEO MOOR HILL
EX16

16

WALLENSLA
Lutworthy
RACKLEIGH LA
Long Stone
Stone Farm
Hellinghayes
HELLINGHAYES LA
Horseford Farm
Dart Raffe Moor
DART HILL
NEWHOUSE HILL
Newhouse
Essebeare
Betham Farm
BETHAM LA

2

COBLEY LA
Rackleigh
EX17
ADWORTHY LA
Adworthy
WEST YEO CROSS
Dart Raffe Farm
WITHERIDGE MILL CROSS
Two Moors Way
Hole Farm
PILLIVEN CROSS
HOLE HILL

15

AFFETON MOOR CROSS
Thornham
THORNHAM LA
THORNHAM CHAPEL CROSS
WILSON LA
West Yeo
NEWBRIDGE HILL
New Bridge
Little Dart River
CHURCH ST
TRACEY GN
RACKENFORD RD
BENDLEY HILL
FYFE ST
10 GREENSLADE RD
11 MELHUISH GL
12 BUTTS CL
13 EAST CL
14 LAKELANDS CL
15 CANNINGTON RD
South Coombe

1

Affeton Moor
Wilson
Town Moor
TOWN MOOR HILL
TOWN MOOR CROSS
COOMBE BALL HILL
THE SQUARE 1
PULLEN'S ROW 2
BROOMHOUSE PK 3
BENSON CL 4
JOAN SPRY CL 5
CHAPPLE RD 6
ANSTEYS CT 7
WIRIGA WAY 8
SHORTRIDGE CL 9
Old Market Field
Old Market Field Ind Est
BARTON LA
WEST ST
BROOKE RD
DRAYFORD RD
NORTH ST
PO
B3137
APPLE TREE
Witheridge
Witheridge CE Prim Sch

14

76   A   77   B   78   C   79   D   80   E   81   F

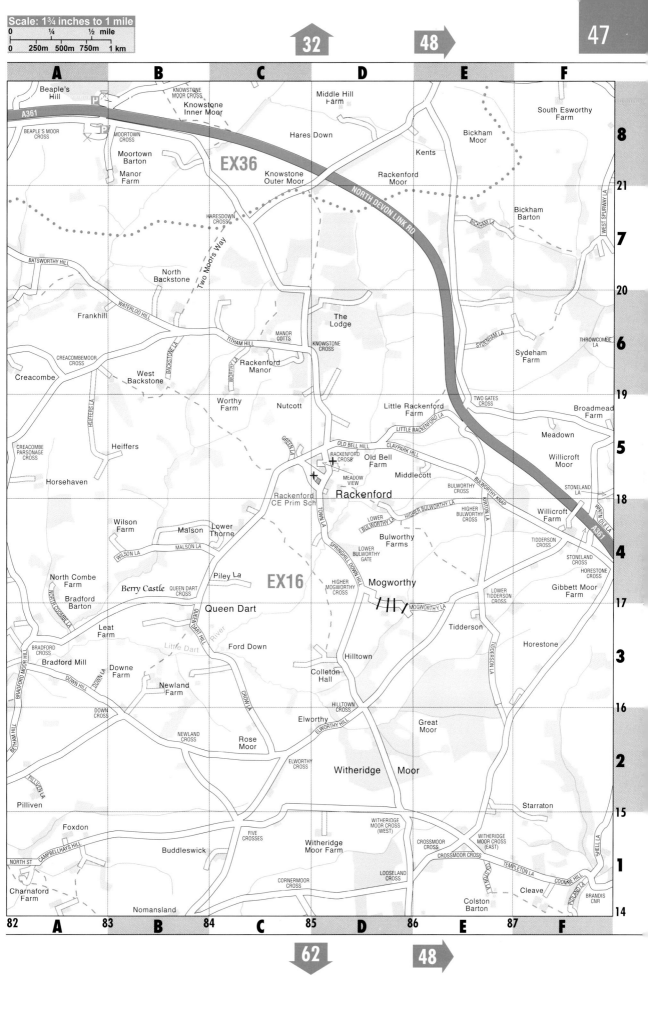

A   B   C   D   E   F

Gloyns Farm
Bowdens
FORDMOOR CROSS
Upcott Farm
B3227
HIGH WAY
Oakfordbridge
A396
Wonham House
ILTON RD
Black Cat
B3227
River Exe

West Spurway
WEST SPURWAY LA
SPURWAY HILL CROSS
Spurway Barton
PINKWORTHY CROSS
Holme Place
PH
NETHERCOTT CROSS
Oakford
ROOKERY HILL
Manor House
STUCKERIDGE CROSS
HAMSLADE HILL
Hamslade House
HAMSLADE CROSS
Stuckeridge House
Stuckeridge South
A396

21

Westcott La
SPURWAY HILL
Spurway Barton
PINKWORTHY HILL
Pinkworthy Farm
PINKWORTHY HILL
Nethercott Farm
PITCOTT HILL
NETHERCOTT HILL
HANGMAN'S HILL
Iron Mill Stream
Chample's Farm
Hangman's Hill Cross
HONEYMOOR LA
Down
Steart

7

Great Wood
SPURWAY HILL
West Mill
WARBRIGHTSLEIGH HILL
ALDRIDGE MILL HILL
WORKSWORTHY HILL
Stoodleigh Moor Cross
Stoodleighmoor
East Stoodleigh Barton

20

Throwcombe
THROWCOMBE LA
THROWCOMBE CROSS
Thorne Farm
Coleford Bottom
Wheatland
WHEATLAND LA
WHEATLAND CROSS
Ash
ASH CROSS
ASH HILL
Quoit-at-Cross
CARSCOMBE LA
Carscombe
Dryhill

6

Waspley Farm
Great Coleford
COLEFORD HILL
RULL HILL
Ash
ASH HILL CROSS
KISSING GATE CROSS
HILLCREST
Stoodleigh

19

Mast
WHITNOLE CROSS
Rull
RULL CROSS
FORD CROSS
WEST END LA
Rull
Ford Barton
Webland
Easterlands

5

BROADMEAD CROSS
West Whitnole
EX16
VIAL'S CNR
Slade Farm

18

Stoneland Farm
WHITNOLE LA
Blatchworthy Farm
Rifton
RIFTON LA
WEST END CROSS
PARKHOUSE LA

Rifton Moor
Diptford Farm
DIPTFORD LA
Hutswell
HAYDON CROSS
Pilemore Cross
SMITH'S LA
PARKHOUSE LA
Pylemoor

4

A361
STOODLEIGH CROSS
DIPTFORD GATE
Haydon
BUTTERMOOR CROSS
MORDON LA
Ennerleigh
PILEMORE LA
Hatherland

17

Source of the River Dart
HOLMEAD CROSS
Churchill Farm
CHURCHILL LA
NORTH DEVON LINK RD
Windbow
Moorhayes

3

NORTH COMBE CROSS
Loxbeare
Courtenay
STOODLEIGH CROSS
LONG LA
Stanterton
COURTENAY COTTS

16

North Coombe
Holmead Farm
Deepaller
STONEY LANE HILL
Pantacridge
Barton
Leigh Barton
LURLEY CROSS
Pitt
MOUSEBEARE LA
THE WEECHES
Washfield
WASHFIELD LA

2

South Coombe
BURCHES CROSS
Higher Way
Sidborough
Leigh
Fulford
Lurley
Beauchamp
BROOK LA

15

LITTLE ESWORTHY LA
Lower Way
CALVERLEIGH CROSS
Calverleigh
Harpridge

1

Templeton
TEMPLETON CROSS
West Bradley
TITCHEN'S LA
TOMBSTONE LA
Frogwell
Court
Palmers

14

WEST LA

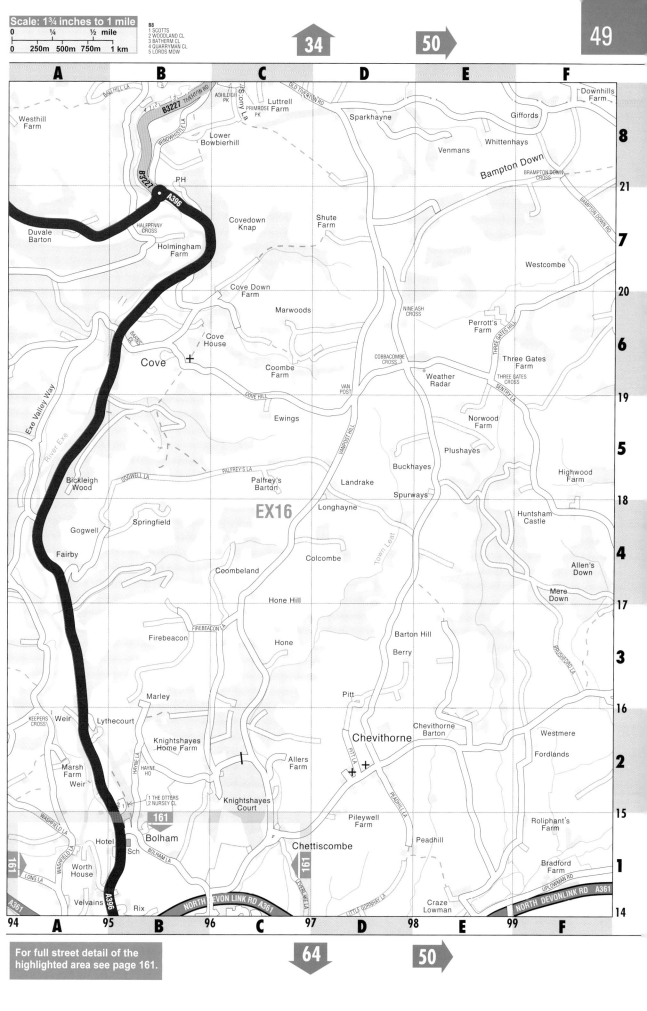

Scale: 1¾ inches to 1 mile

0   ¼   ½ mile
0   250m   500m   750m   1 km

B8
1 SCOTTS
2 WOODLAND CL
3 BATHERM CL
4 QUARRYMAN CL
5 LORDS MDW

Westhill Farm

Duvale Barton

BKW HILL LA

B3227 TIVERTON RD

WINDWHISTLE CLA

5

4 7 2 1 2

3

PRIMROSE PK

CHURCH PK

S ony La

Luttrell Farm

Lower Bowbierhill

OLD TIVERTON RD

Sparkhayne

Giffords

Whittenhays

Venmans

Downhills Farm

Bampton Down

Brampton Down Cross

Bampton Down Rd

PH

A396

HALFPENNY CROSS

Holmingham Farm

Covedown Knap

Shute Farm

Westcombe

Cove Down Farm

Marwoods

Nine Ash Cross

Perrott's Farm

Three Gates Hill

Cove

BARNS CLA

Cove House

Coombe Farm

Cobbacombe Cross

Weather Radar

Three Gates Farm

Three Gates Cross

Sentry La

Exe Valley Way

River Exe

Bickleigh Wood

GOGWELL LA

PALFREY'S LA

Palfrey's Barton

Cove Hill

Ewings

VAN POST

VANPOST HILL

Landrake

Buckhayes

Plushayes

Norwood Farm

Highwood Farm

EX16

Longhayne

Spurways

Huntsham Castle

Springfield

Gogwell

Fairby

Coombeland

Colcombe

Town Leat

Allen's Down

Mere Down

BRUSHFORD LA

Hone Hill

FIREBEACON LA

Firebeacon

Hone

Barton Hill

Berry

Keepers Cross

Weir

Lythecourt

Marley

Pitt

PITT LA

Chevithorne

Chevithorne Barton

Westmere

Fordlands

Knightshayes Home Farm

HAYNE LA

HAYNE HO

Allers Farm

Knightshayes Court

1 THE OTTERS
2 NURSEY CL

Marsh Farm Weir

161

Bolham

Sch

BOLHAM LA

Chettiscombe

161

EVERLAKE LA

Pileywell Farm

PEADHILL LA

Peadhill

Roliphant's Farm

Bradford Farm

WASHFIELD LA

Hotel

Worth House

161

LONG LA

WASHFIELD LA

Velvains

A396

Rix

A361

NORTH DEVON LINK RD A361

LITTLE GORNHAY LA

Craze Lowman

UPLOWMAN RD

NORTH DEVON LINK RD A361

For full street detail of the highlighted area see page 161.

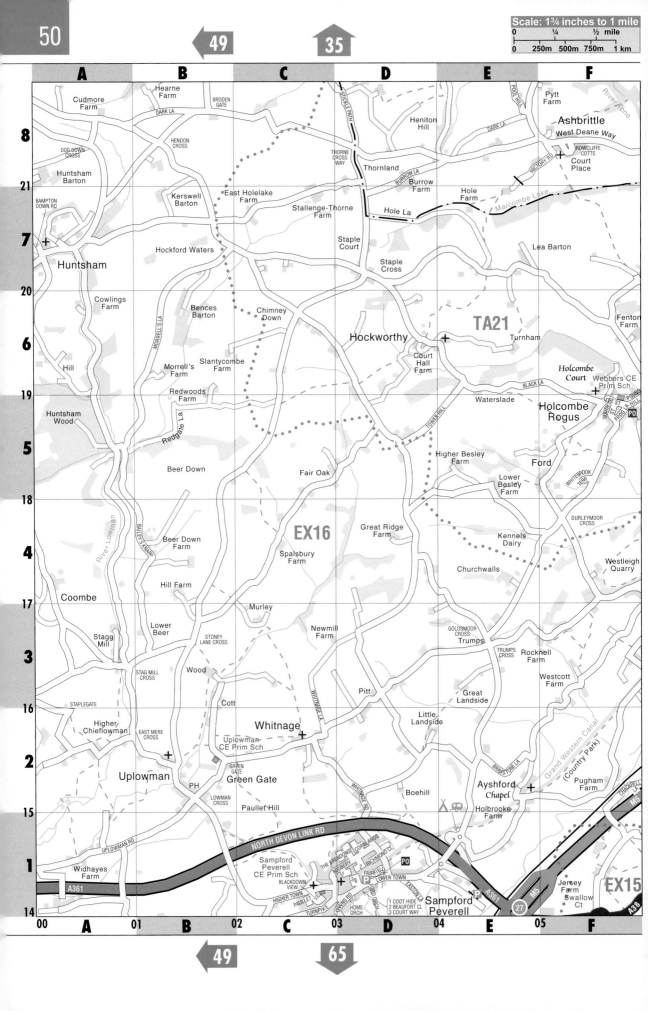

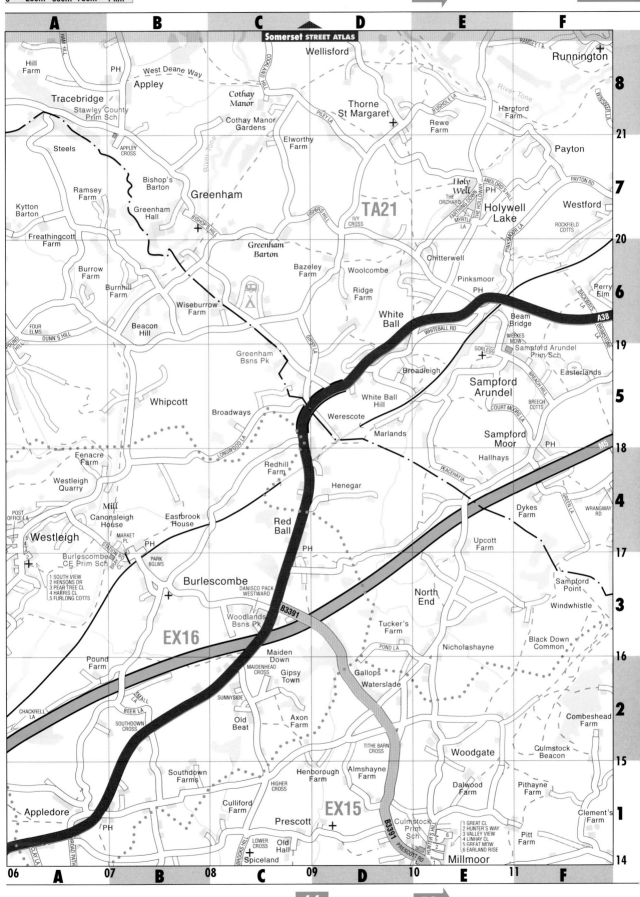

A   B   C   D   E   F

Somerset STREET ATLAS

Wellisford · Runnington

Hill Farm · HAM HILL · PH · West Deane Way · Appley · Cothay Manor · Thorne St Margaret · Rewe Farm · Harpford Farm · River Tone

8

Tracebridge · Stawley County Prim Sch · Cothay Manor Gardens · Holy Well · THE ORCHARD · Payton

21

Steels · APPLEY CROSS · Elworthy Farm · PILEY LA · PH · THE HOLLOWAY · MYRTLE LA · Holywell Lake · Westford · PAYTON RD

Ramsey Farm · Bishop's Barton · Greenham · FISHER'S HILL · TA21 · Chitterwell · ROCKFIELD COTTS

7

Kytton Barton · Greenham Hall · IVY CROSS · PINKSMOOR LA · Pinksmoor · PERRY ELM

20

Freathingcott Farm · BISHOP'S HILL · Greenham Barton · Bazeley Farm · Woolcombe · PH · BLACKWAYS LA

6

Burrow Farm · Wiseburrow Farm · Ridge Farm · White Ball · Beam Bridge · A38 · BRIMSTONE LA

Burnhill Farm · FOUR ELMS · DUNN'S HILL · Beacon Hill · GIPSY LA · WHITEBALL RD · GORLEGG · WEEKES MDW · Sampford Arundel Prim Sch · Easterlands

19

Greenham Bsns Pk · Broadleigh · Sampford Arundel · BREECH HILL

Whipcott · Broadways · White Ball Hill · BREECH COTTS

5

LONGWOOD LA · Werescote · Marlands · COURT MOORS LA · Sampford Moor · PH

Fenacre Farm · Redhill Farm · Henegar · Hallhays · M5

18

Westleigh Quarry · PEACEHAYIA · Dykes Farm · WRANGWAY RD

4

POST OFFICE LA · Mill · Canonsleigh House · Eastbrook House · Red Ball · Upcott Farm · GREEN LA · Sampford Point

Westleigh · MARKET PL · PH · PH · North End · Windwhistle

17

STATION RD · Burlescombe CE Prim Sch · PARK BGLWS · Burlescombe · DANISCO PACK WESTWARD

1 SOUTH VIEW
2 HENSONS DR
3 PEAR TREE CL
4 HARRIS CL
5 FURLONG COTTS

3

EX16 · B3391 · Woodlands Bsns Pk · Tucker's Farm · Nicholashayne · Black Down Common

CHACKRELL LA · Pound Farm · SMALL LA · Maiden Down · POND LA · Gallops · Waterslade

16

BEER LA · MAIDENHEAD CROSS · Gipsy Town · SOUTHDOWN CROSS · SUNNYSIDE · Axon Farm · Combeshead Farm

2

Appledore · Old Beat · TITHE BARN CROSS · Woodgate · Culmstock Beacon

Southdown Farms · HIGHER CROSS · Henborough Farm · Almshayne Farm · Dalwood Farm · Pithayne Farm

15

BROAD PATH · CLAY LA · PH · Culliford Farm · Prescott · EX15 · B3391 · Culmstock Prim Sch · Clement's Farm

1 GREAT CL
2 HUNTER'S WAY
3 VALLEY VIEW
4 LINHAY CL
5 GREAT MDW
6 EARLAND RISE

1

BROOKS HILL · LOWER CROSS · Old Hall · Spiceland · PRESCOTT RD · HUNTER'S HILL · Millmoor · Pitt Farm

14

A   B   C   D   E   F
06   07   08   09   10   11

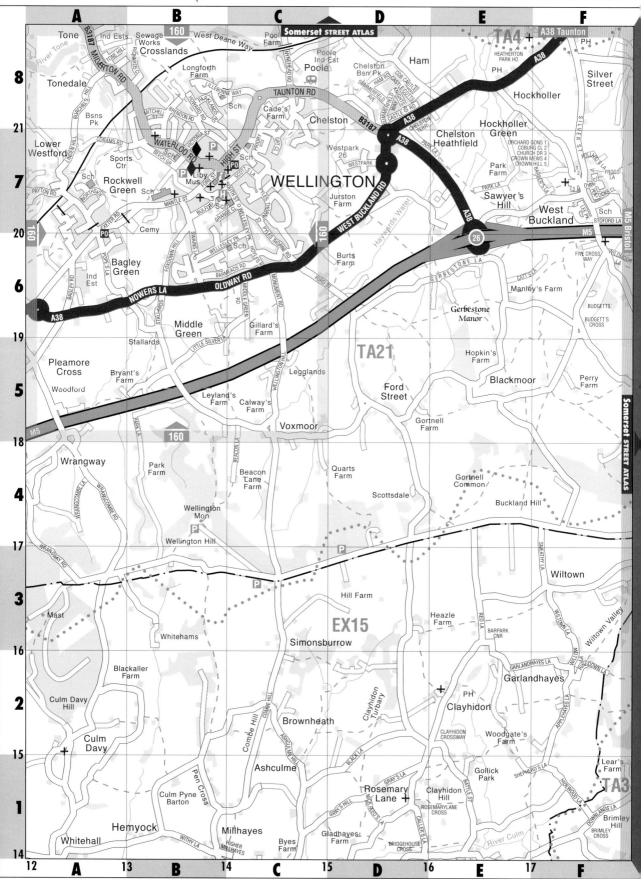

Scale: 1¾ inches to 1 mile

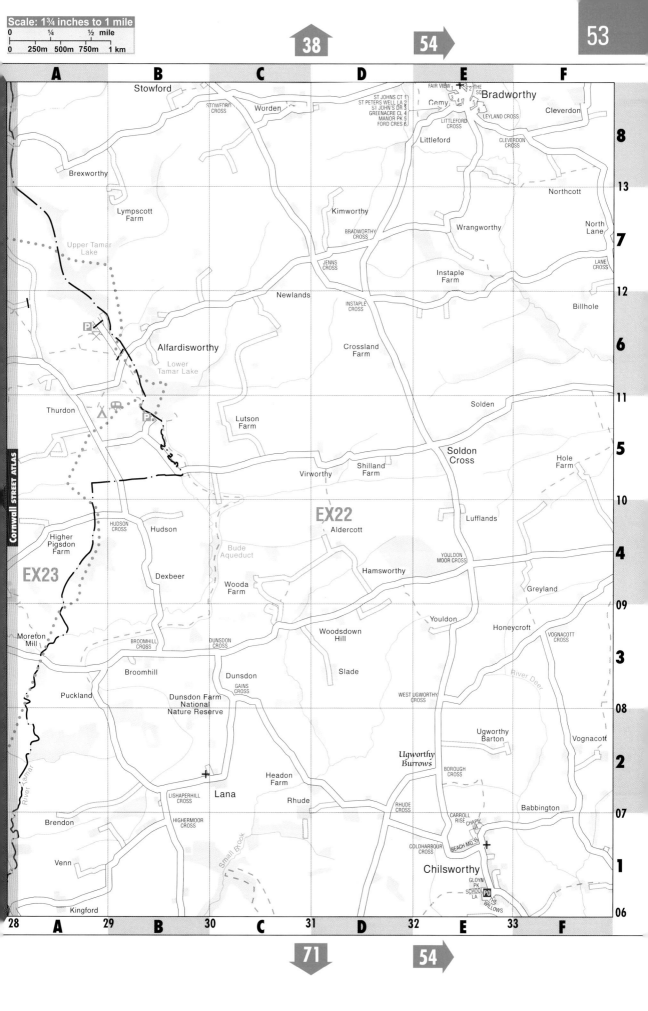

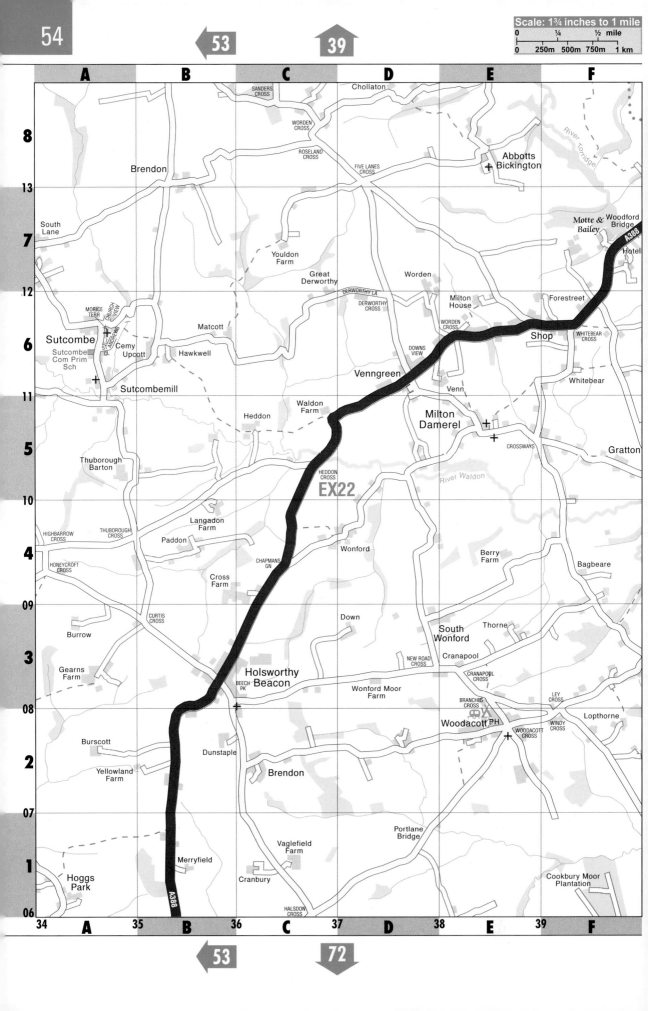

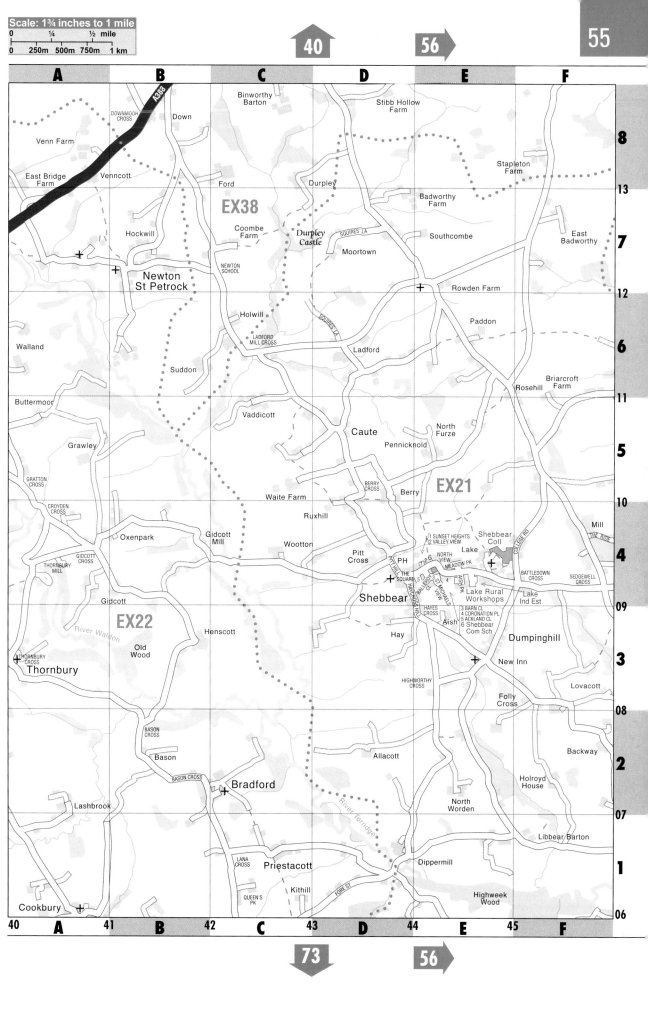

Scale: 1¾ inches to 1 mile

0 ¼ ½ mile
0 250m 500m 750m 1 km

A B C D E F

8

Venn Farm

East Bridge Farm

Venncott

Downmoor Cross

A388

Down

Binworthy Barton

Stibb Hollow Farm

Stapleton Farm

13

EX38

Hockwill

Ford

Coombe Farm

Durpley

Durpley Castle

Badworthy Farm

Southcombe

East Badworthy

7

Newton St Petrock

Newton School

Moortown

Squires La

Rowden Farm

12

Holwill

Squires La

Ladford Mill Cross

Ladford

Paddon

6

Walland

Suddon

Vaddicott

Caute

Pennicknold

North Furze

Rosehill

Briarcroft Farm

11

Buttermoor

Grawley

Berry Cross

Berry

EX21

5

Gratton Cross

Croyden Cross

Waite Farm

Ruxhill

Mill

THE RIDE

10

Oxenpark

Gidcott Mill

Wootton

Pitt Cross

PH

1 SUNSET HEIGHTS
2 VALLEY VIEW

North View

Lake

Shebbear Coll

COLLEGE RD

4

Thornbury Mill

Gidcott Cross

Gidcott

PITT HILL

THE SQUARE

BALLEROY CL

ST MICHAELS VIEW

MEADOW PK

AISH PK

Battledown Cross

Sedgewell Cross

Lake Ind Est

Lake Rural Workshops

EX22

River Waldon

Old Wood

Henscott

Shebbear

HACKNESS HILL

HAYES CROSS

3 BARN CL
4 CORONATION PL
5 ACKLAND CL
6 Shebbear Com Sch

Dumpinghill

09

Lovacott

Thornbury Cross

Thornbury

Hay

Aish

New Inn

3

HIGHWORTHY CROSS

Folly Cross

08

Bason Cross

Bason

BASON CROSS

Allacott

Backway

2

Lashbrook

Bradford

River Torridge

North Worden

Holroyd House

07

LANA CROSS

Priestacott

Kithill

FORE ST

Dippermill

1

QUEEN'S PK

Highweek Wood

Libbear Barton

Cookbury

06

A B C D E F

40 41 42 43 44 45

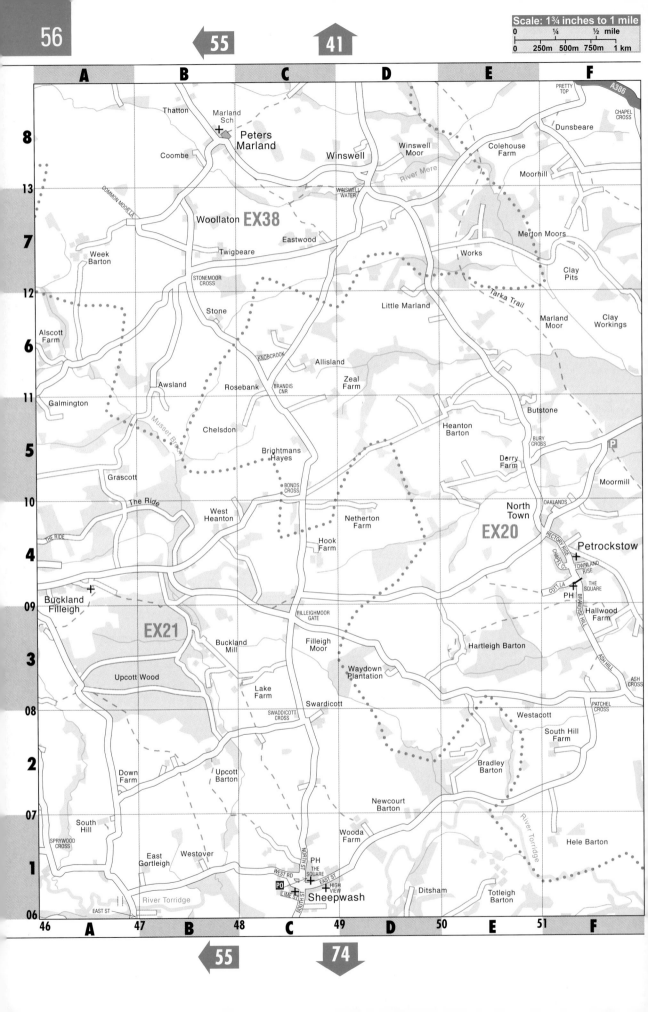

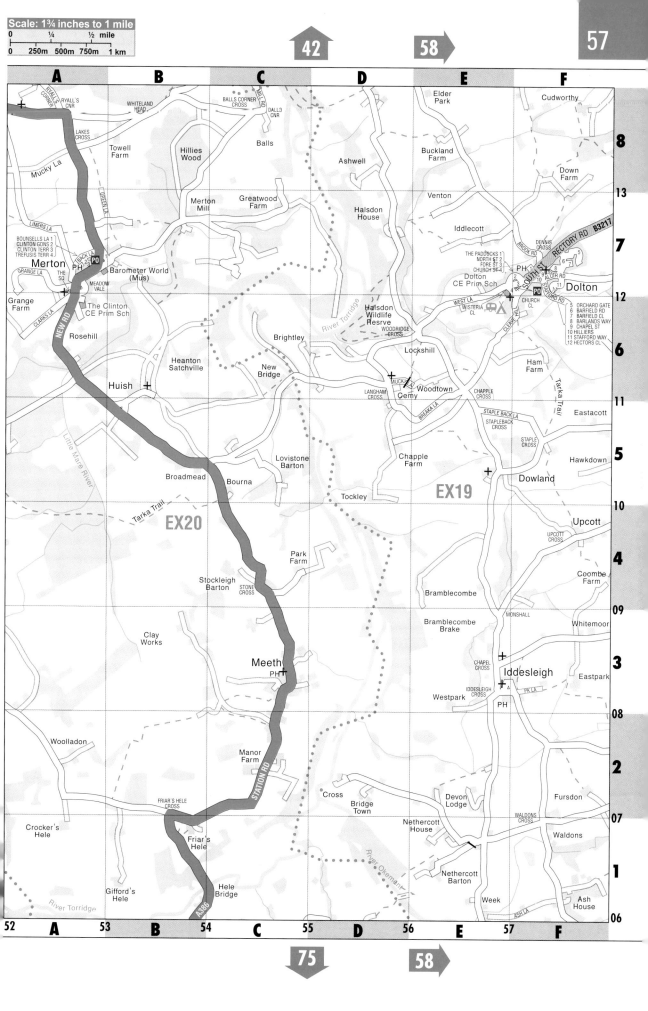

A   B   C   D   E   F

Cudworthy Moor
A3124
B3217
Dolton Beacon
Westacott Barton
East Westacott
Riddlecombe
Churchwater
THE SQUARE
CHURCH ST
GREEN HEDGES
PO
COLES CT
Ashreigney
BUSH CNR
BUSH CROSS
BEECH LEA
8

RECTORY RD
B3217
Hayes
LITTLE HAYES LA
HAYES LA
CHURCHWATER LA
VESTYARD LA
Westyard
HAM HILL
BURRIDGE CROSS
LEY CROSS
13

Wood Farm
MUDHOUSE CROSS
Coldharbour
HOLLOCOMBE MOOR HEAD
Eagle Down
Narracott
EX18
LAKE LA
REDLAND CROSS
Densham
7

Parsonage Farm
Cross Farm
Cherubeer
Hollocombe Moor
WINKLEIGH MOOR CROSS
HOLLOCOMBE MOOR GATE
HOLLOCOMBE CNR
NARRACOTT LA
SMITH'S LA
Redland
12

Aller Farm
Venton
Great Pitford
GREAT PITFORD LA
TWELVE OAKS CROSS
Hollocombe
FERRY MILL LA
6

Stafford Barton
Stafford Moor
Venton Moor
Durdon
Hollocombe Town
Woodterrill
SHUTE WOOD
STAFFORD RD
11

Stafford Moor Fishery
Furzepark Wood
WHITEHOUSE LA
Whitehouse
Woodroberts
Heath Farm
HEATH LA
5

FURZEPARK CROSS
Hawkdown
Dowland Moor
Riddiford
DOWN LA
BUTCHER'S MOOR LA
BERNER'S CROSS
Breechlea Ind Est
10

Pewson Barton
LOOSEDON CROSS
Heath Hill
SECKINGTON CROSS
SUMMER FIELD
FOUR SEASONS VILLAGE
Depot
10 CHURCH LA
11 CASTLE ST
12 SOUTH ST
13 COOPERS HILL
14 DIAL ST
15 QUEEN ST
16 CHURCH HILL
17 VINE ST
4

09

Henacroft
HENACROFT CROSS
Loosedon Barton
Gerrydon Farm
GERRYDOWN RD
West Chapple
SPRINGFIELD
AUTUMN FIELD
Cemy
TORRINGTON RD
HIGH LA
BARNSTAPLE
CARRIONPIT LA
Court Castle
EAST PARK LA
EGGESFORD RD
3

ASHPLANTS CL 1
KINGS MEADOW DR 2
KINGS FARM LA 3
SUNNY VIEW 4
OLD CHAPEL GDNS 5
CHULMLEIGH RD 6
COURT WLK 7
HIGH ST 8
FORE ST 9
LUTEHOUSE LA
EXETER RD
PO
08

Bryony Hill Farm
EX19
Barwick
BARWICK CROSS
Oakley House
THREE CROSS WAYS
HATHERLEIGH RD
Winkleigh
Winkleigh Com Prim Sch
TOWNSEND CROSS
B3220
CORSE LA
SHUTE
2

Pixton
PIXTON CROSS
Lower Ingley
FOUR CROSS WAYS
RED GATE
Stony Bridge
TOWNSEND HILL
1 FORGE END
2 LOWER TOWN
3 SOUTHERNHAY
4 FARMER FRANK'S LA
5 SHUTE LA
6 WESTCOTS DR
7 LENDON WAY
8 BULLOW VIEW
9 ELMS MDW
10 OLD BARN CL

BULLHEAD CROSS
Bullhead Farm
Inleigh Green
Upcott
VELLONDMOOR
Southcott
07

Hill Farm
Bude Farm
Hawksland
UPCOTT LA
BARNTOWN GATE
SUMMERS MOOR CROSS
1

Lake
Middlecott
Barntown
BARNTOWN LA
A3124
06

58   A   59   B   60   C   61   D   62   E   63   F

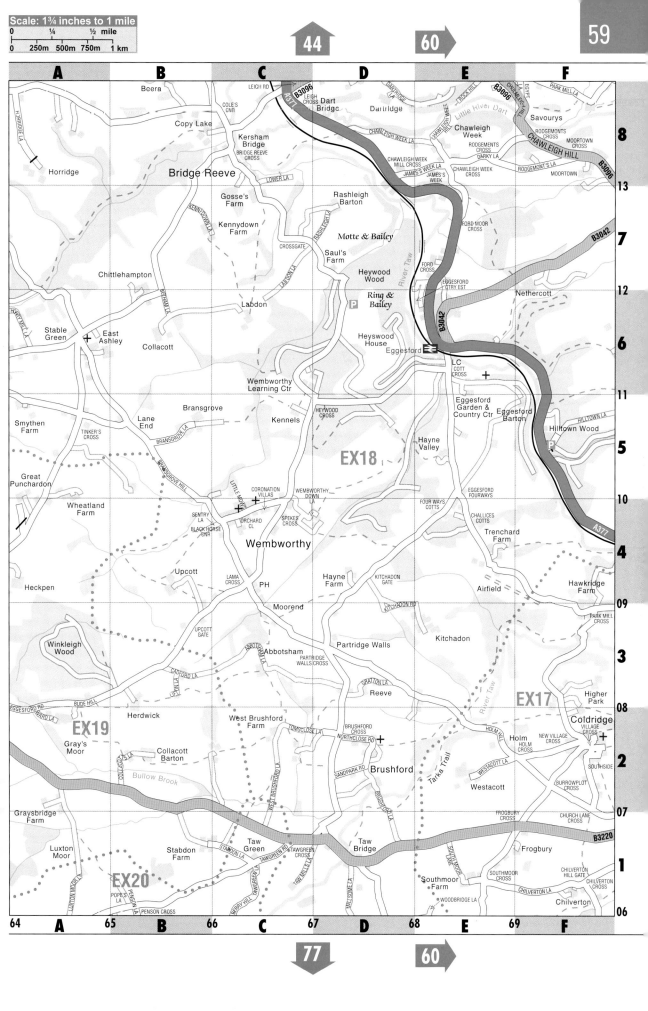

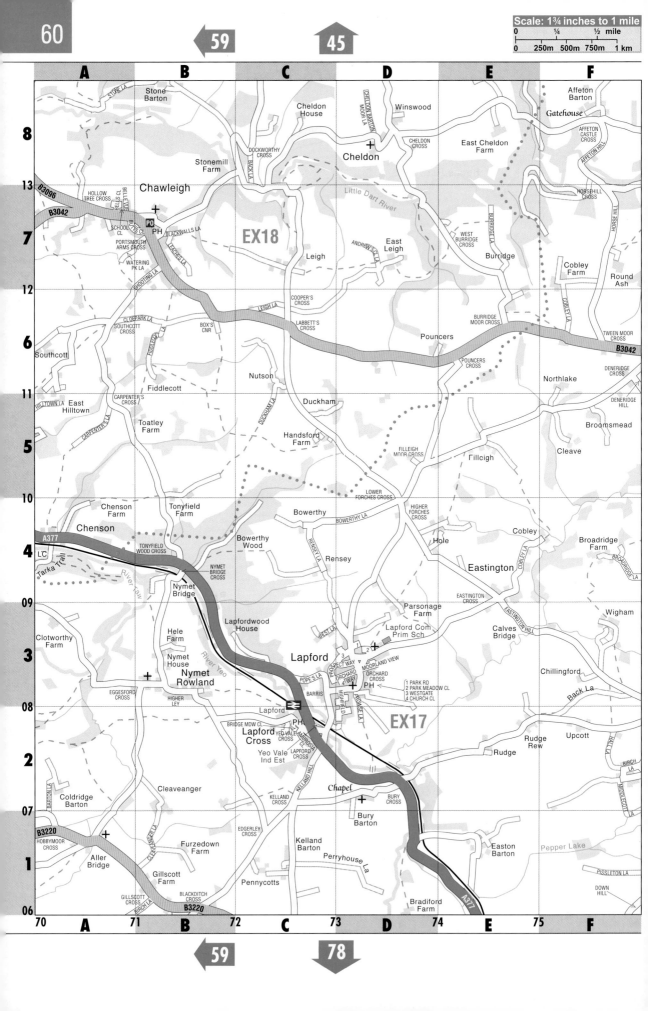

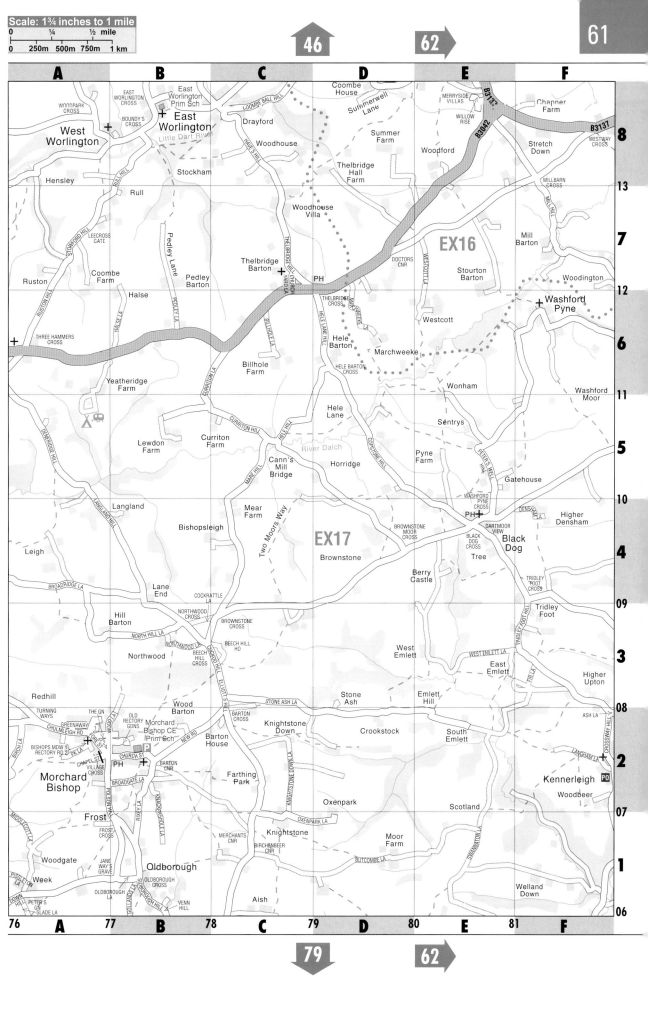

Scale: 1¾ inches to 1 mile
0   ¼   ½   mile
0   250m   500m   750m   1 km

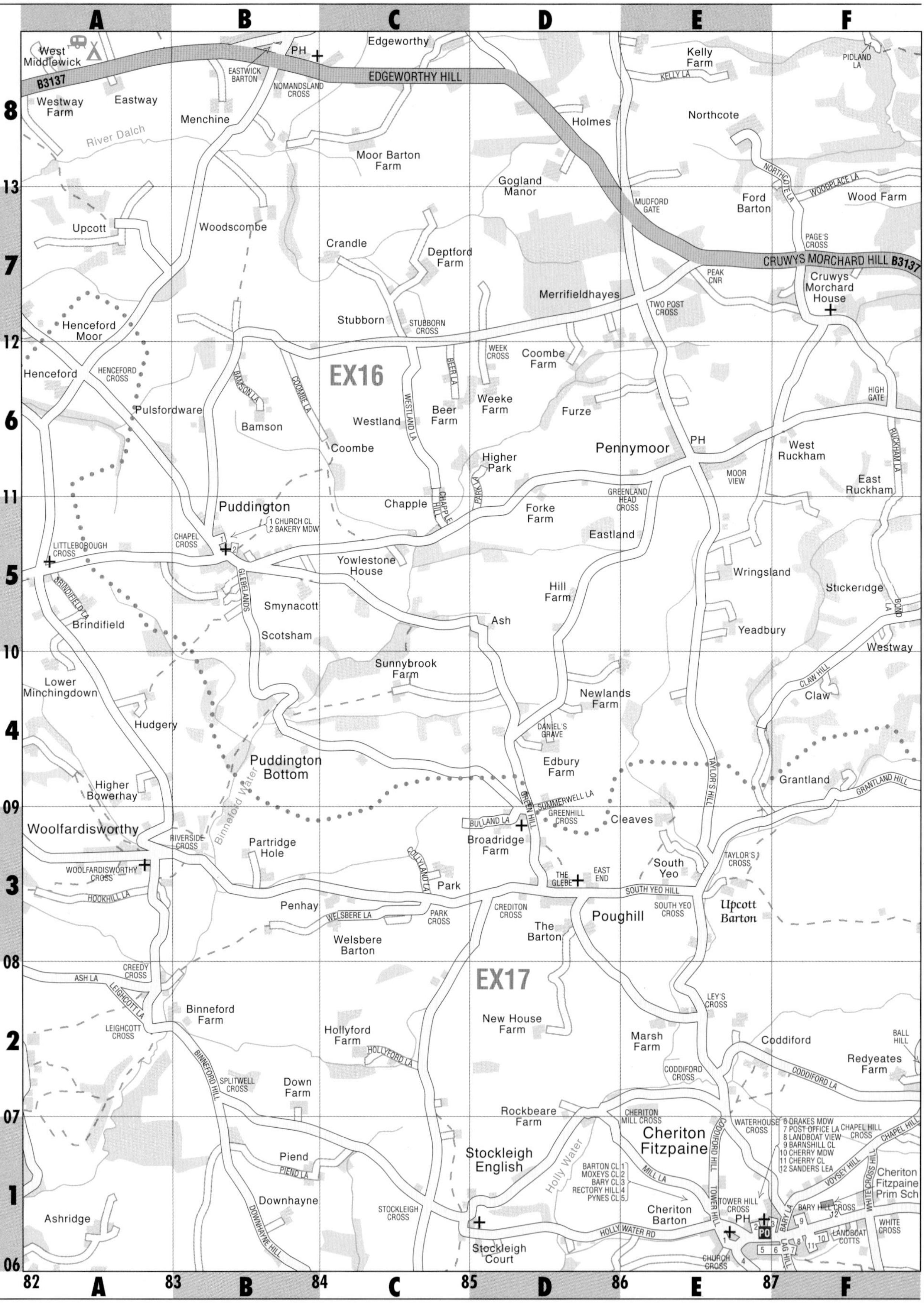

Grid columns: A B C D E F
Grid rows: 8 13 7 12 6 11 5 10 4 09 3 08 2 07 1 06

West Middlewick
B3137
Westway Farm
Eastway
River Dalch
Menchine
Eastwick Barton
Nomandsland Cross
PH
Edgeworthy
EDGEWORTHY HILL
Holmes
Kelly Farm
KELLY LA
Pidland La
Northcote
Upcott
Woodscombe
Moor Barton Farm
Gogland Manor
Mudford Gate
Northcote La
Woodblace La
Ford Barton
Wood Farm
Henceford Moor
Crandle
Deptford Farm
Page's Cross
CRUWYS MORCHARD HILL B3137
Peak Cnr
Henceford
Henceford Cross
Stubborn
Stubborn Cross
Merrifieldhayes
Two Post Cross
Cruwys Morchard House
Pulsfordware
EX16
Week Cross
Coombe Farm
Bamson La
Coombe La
Westland La
Beer La
Bamson
Westland
Beer Farm
Weeke Farm
Furze
Pennymoor
PH
West Ruckham
Ruckham La
High Gate
East Ruckham
Coombe
Higher Park
Chapple
Chapple Hill
Beer La
Forke Farm
Greenland Head Cross
Eastland
Moor View
Wringsland
Stickeridge
Bond La
Littleborough Cross
Puddington
Chapel Cross
1 Church Cl
2 Bakery Mdw
Yowlestone House
Ash
Hill Farm
Yeadbury
Claw Hill
Westway
Saundfield La
Glebelands
Brindifield
Smynacott
Scotsham
Sunnybrook Farm
Newlands Farm
Claw
Lower Minchingdown
Daniel's Grave
Hudgery
Edbury Farm
Grantland
Grantland Hill
Higher Bowerhay
Puddington Bottom
Binneford Water
Summerwell La
Green Hill
Greenhill Cross
Cleaves
Taylor's Hill
Woolfardisworthy
Riverside Cross
Partridge Hole
Bulland La
Broadridge Farm
South Yeo
Taylor's Cross
Upcott Barton
Woolfardisworthy Cross
Govanund La
Park
The Glebe
East End
South Yeo Hill
Poughill
Hookhill La
Penhay
Welsbere La
Park Cross
Crediton Cross
The Barton
South Yeo Cross
Ley's Cross
Ash La
Creedy Cross
Welsbere Barton
New House Farm
Marsh Farm
Coddiford
Ball Hill
Leighcott La
Binneford Farm
Hollyford Farm
Hollyford La
Coddiford Cross
Coddiford La
Redyeates Farm
Leighcott Cross
Splitwell Cross
Down Farm
Rockbeare Farm
Waterhouse Cross
Cheriton Mill Cross
Voysey Hill
Whitecross Hill
Cheriton Fitzpaine Prim Sch
Binneford Hill
Piend
Piend La
EX17
Stockleigh English
Holly Water
Cheriton Fitzpaine
Barton Cl 1
Moxeys Cl 2
Bary Cl 3
Rectory Hill 4
Pynes Cl 5
6 Drakes Mdw
7 Post Office La
8 Landboat View
9 Barnshill Cl
10 Cherry Mdw
11 Cherry Cl
12 Sanders Lea
Chapel Hill Cross
Chapel Hill
White Cross
Ashridge
Downhayne
Downhayne Hill
Stockleigh Cross
Cheriton Barton
Tower Hill Cross
Mill La
Comford Hill
Tower Hill
Bary Hill
PH
PO
Landboat Cotts
Stockleigh Court
Holly Water Rd
Church Cross

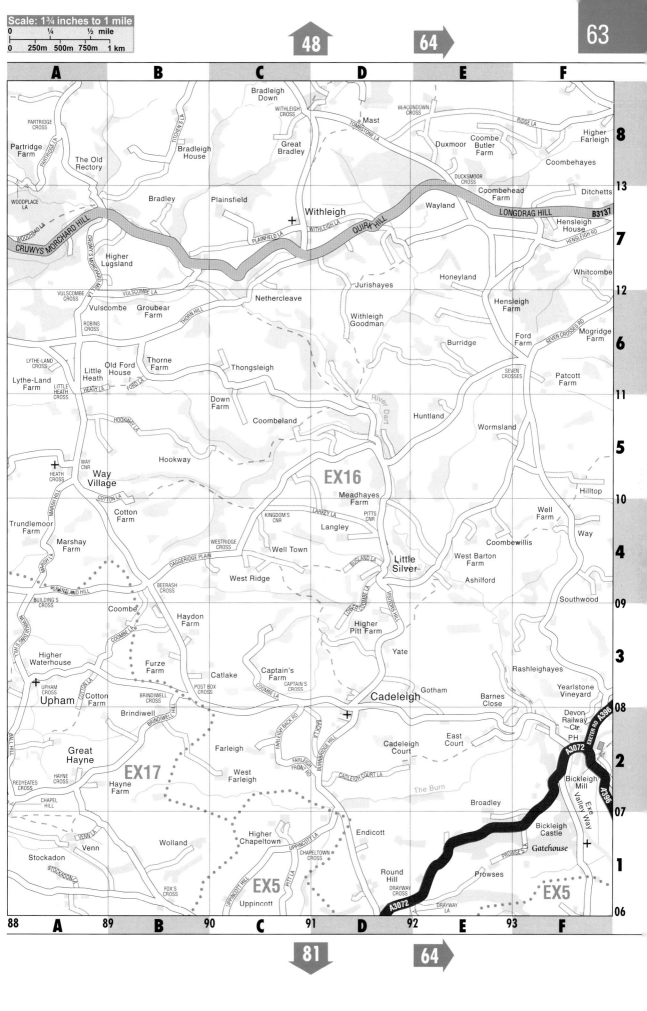

64

63

49

D7
1 LIME TREE MEAD
2 RENNIE RD
3 WESLEY CL
4 FRANCIS CRES
5 CHILCOTT CL
6 MARINA WAY
7 CHICHESTER PL
8 COLERIDGE RD
9 PUGSLEY RD
10 STARKEY CL
11 TIDCOMBE CL
12 ST LAWRENCE CL
13 RAYER RD
14 POLWHELE RD
15 WESTCOTT RD
16 RYDER CL
17 RIPPON CL
18 TIDCOMBE WLK

Column headers (top): A B C D E F

Row labels (left): 8 13 7 12 6 11 5 10 4 09 3 08 2 07 1 06

Weir
A361
PETROC
Moorhayes
LEA RD
Gornhay
Cross
Little Gornhay
River Lowman
NORTH DEVON LINK RD
A396
Loomend
WASHFIELD LA
RACKENFORD RD
GALE WAY
Sch
A3126
KENNEDY WAY
Cemy
PINNEX MOOR RD
BEECH RD
Sch
PO
Bsns Pk
GORNHAY CROSS
1 LITTLE GORNHAY LA
2 LOWER MOOR WAY
3 LOWMAN UNITS
4 CHINON CT
LOWMAN WAY
TIVERTON WAY
PUTSON CROSS
CHAMPION WAY
CH
HARTNOLL CROSS

LONGDRAG HILL
B3137
Cotteylands
BAKER'S HILL
Tiverton Castle
PARK HILL
PARK RD
BELMONT RD
COWLEY MOOR RD
ELMORE
CHAPEL'S RD
Cowleymoor
BLUNDELL'S RD
Sch
Blundell's Prep Sch
Blundell's Sch
Pool Anthony
WEST MANLEY LA
MANLEY RD
Hartnoll Farm
Grand Western Canal Country Park Nature Reserve

SEVEN CROSS RD
Sch
BROOK ST
CHURCH ST
WEST EXE
PETER ST
GOLD ST
A3126
GREAT WESTERN WAY
A396
TIVERTON
HOWDEN RD
BAMPTON ST
Shamel's End
Copplestone
161

HARTNOLL FARM
GLEBELANDS RD
LITELBURG RD
Tidcombe Prim Sch
Tidcombe Cross
East Manley
Curham
Manley

Cranmore Castle
HORN HILL
EXETER HILL
Collipriest
Newte's Hill
WARNICOMBE LA
Lower Warnicombe
LIMETREE CROSS
Thurlescombe
Rowridge
Crosssparks

Exe Valley Way
River Exe
161
EX16
Gogwell
NEWTE'S HILL
Warnicombe
THURLESCOMBE CROSS
Thornes Cross
Thornes Wood
Crosslands
Sock Hill

Ashley
ASHLEY BACK LA
HOLWELL LA
Holwell
Sewage Works
Saltars La
SECKERLEIGH CROSS
WHITE DOWN CROSS
Turley Down

CUSTOM LA
EXETER RD
West Pitt Farm
Rhode Farm
PITT LA
Seckerleigh
Chorland Farm
Cruwyshayes

Backswood Farm
Backs Wood
BACKSWOOD LA
BURROW CNR
BURROW CTYD
Oburnford
Way Mill

East Barton
Overleigh
Coombe Farm
Sunnyside Farm
East Butterleigh
EAST BUTTERLEIGH CROSS
Birchen Oak
Fulford Water
FORGES HILL

A396
Weir
Exeland
Henbere
Butterleigh
PH
FORGE LA
Fir La
Hayne Oak
CHESTNUT WLK
HOLLY WLK
Hillersdon House

Swallowhayes
Bickleigh-on-Exe CE Prim Sch
BELL MDW
MAJOR CROSS
Brithayes
Keens
HAYNE LA
Shutelake Farm
EX15
PONSFORD LA
HALSEWOOD GATE

Bickleigh
A396
Great Dorweeke
Fig Tree Farm
Billingsmoor Farm
Halsewood Farm
KNOWLE LA
Coombe Farm
BUNNEFORD CROSS

Burnhayes
EX5
Lower Dorweeke
Queenborough
Burn River
Hawk Aller

Column headers (bottom): A B C D E F

Grid numbers (bottom): 94 95 96 97 98 99

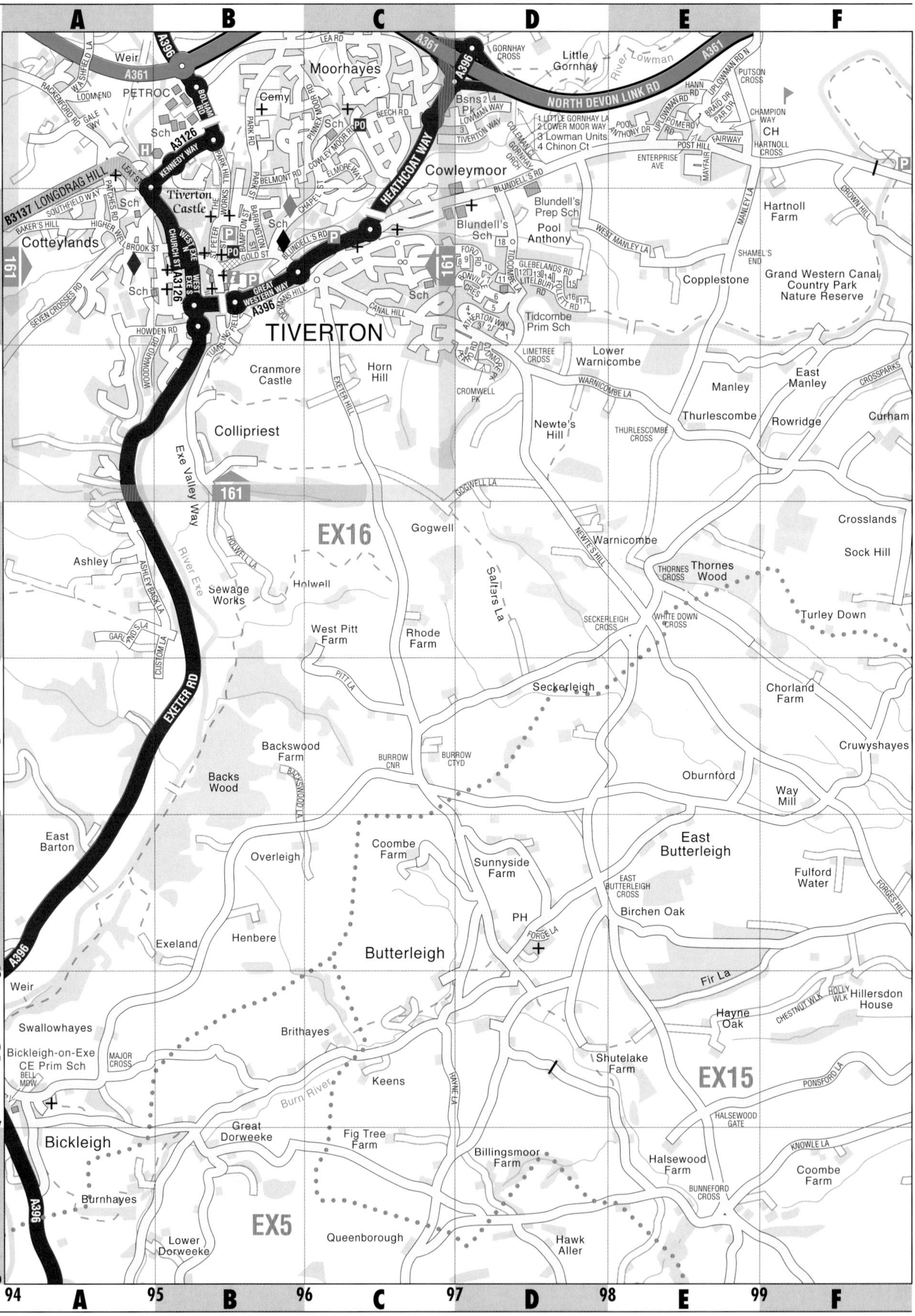

For full street detail of the highlighted area see page 161.

63

82

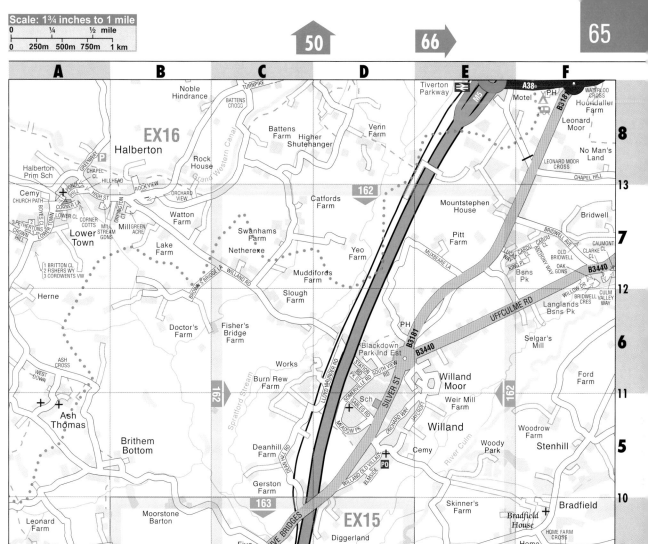

65
51

Scale: 1¾ inches to 1 mile

0 ¼ ½ mile
0 250m 500m 750m 1 km

A B C D E F

8

Gravel Pit
Broad Path
Uffculme
Clavia
Culm Haven 1
Coronation Cres 2
Prospect Cres 3
Russet Cl 4
Appletree Cl 5
Pippins Field 6
Caumont Cl 7
Culm Valley Way 8

9 ORCHARD WAY
10 TRAFALGAR CT
11 UFFCULME
12 ORCHARD CL
13 KITWELL ST
14 EAST ST
15 KENTS CL
16 AYSHFORD
17 MARKERS
18 GRANTLANDS

Five Fords
Brooks Hill
Ratsash La
River Culm

GREAT CL 1
LINHAY CL 2
MILLMOOR 3
Culmstock
The Cleeve
BLACKWATER RD
B3391
SILVER ST
FORE ST
UFFCULME RD
Hillmoor
HEMYOCK RD
B3391

Southey Barton
Northcott
Bowhayes Farm

13

Uffculme Sch
Libby
Chapel Hill
Highland Pk
The Spinney
Ashley Rd
Manor Cl
The Square
Bridge St
Limers Way
Uffculme Prim Sch
Pathfields
B3440
Uffculme Rd
Coll
Cemy
Well Mead Cl
Portway
Craddock
Lowmoor Farm
Craddock House
Park Farm
Hackpen Cross Way
Hackpen Hill

7

Coldharbour
Coldharbour Mill (Mus)
Smithincott
Gaddon
Twenty Acres
Reed's Cross
Hackpen Barton
Foxhill Farm
Leigh Cross

12

Ashill
Bramley Way
Mill La
Ashill Ctyd
Sanders Wy
PH
Batts Pk
Rull Green Farm
Heckpen View
Rull House
Leigh Court

6

Ashill Moor
Whitmoor
Nibbys Cross
Southill Barton
Allhallows Farm
Allercombe Farm
Leigh Hill Farm
Hayne Cross

11

EX15

Sowells Farm
Sandfield Farm
Blackborough House
Hayne Farm

5

Croyle Cross
Birchen Tree Cross
Yew Wood Cross
Halsbeer Farm
Mortimers Farm
Bodmiscombe

10

Jarmins Pit Cross
Croyle House
Pirzwell
Mortimers Cross
Blackborough
South Farm
Sheldon Hill
Landcroft La

4

Stockland Cross
France Farm
Ponchydown
Sheldon
Drift La
Church La Oakleigh
Slade
Shoots La

09

Kentisbeare
Kentisbeare CE Prim Sch
Wressing View
Fore St
Stoford Water
Hollis Green
Saint Hill
Drift Lane Cross
Westcott Cross
Westcott Farm
EX14

3

Parson's Cl
Silver St
Silver Pk
Bishops
Cut
Manor Cl
Kerswell Cl
PH
PO
Priest High St
Honest Heart Cross
Henland Farms
Downlands Cross
Golden Lane Cross
Sheldon Cross
Southcott Farm
Golden La

08

Yerris Rd
Moorhayne Cross
Kentisbeare House
Orway Ash Cross
Orway
Knowles Wood
Black Down
Forest Glade

2

Dulford House
Priory Wall Cross
Broad Rd
North Hill
Gliding Club
Hanger Farm

07

A373
Dulford Bshs Pk
Dulford Cross
Orway Cross
Long Cot

1

PH
Kerswell Priory
Wind Whistle Cross
Windwhistle Farm

06

Matthews Cross
Kerswell

06 A 07 B 08 C 09 D 10 E 11 F

65
84

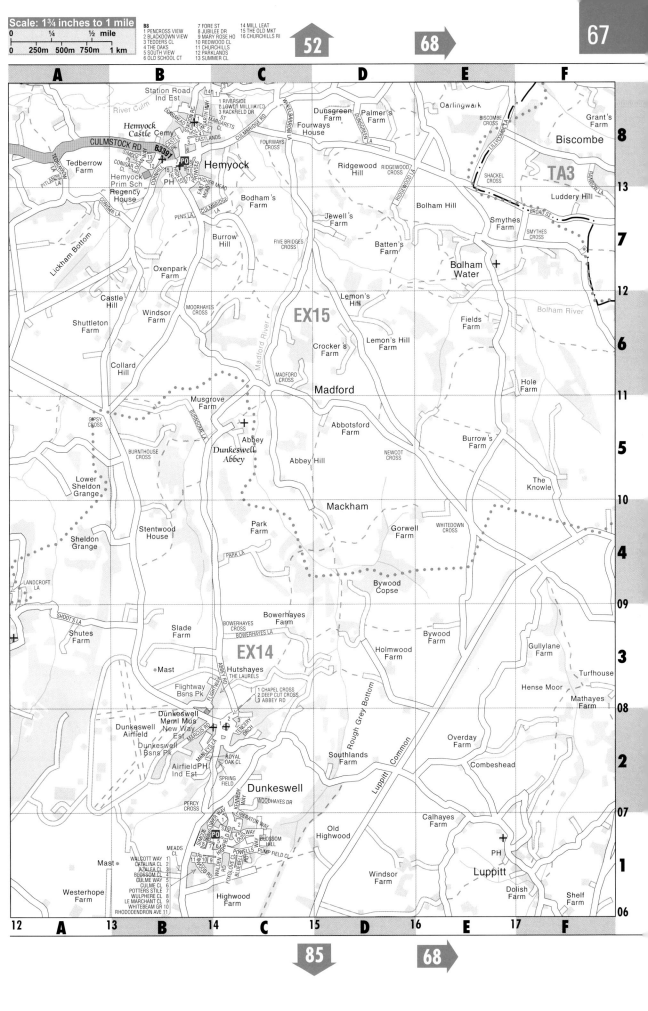

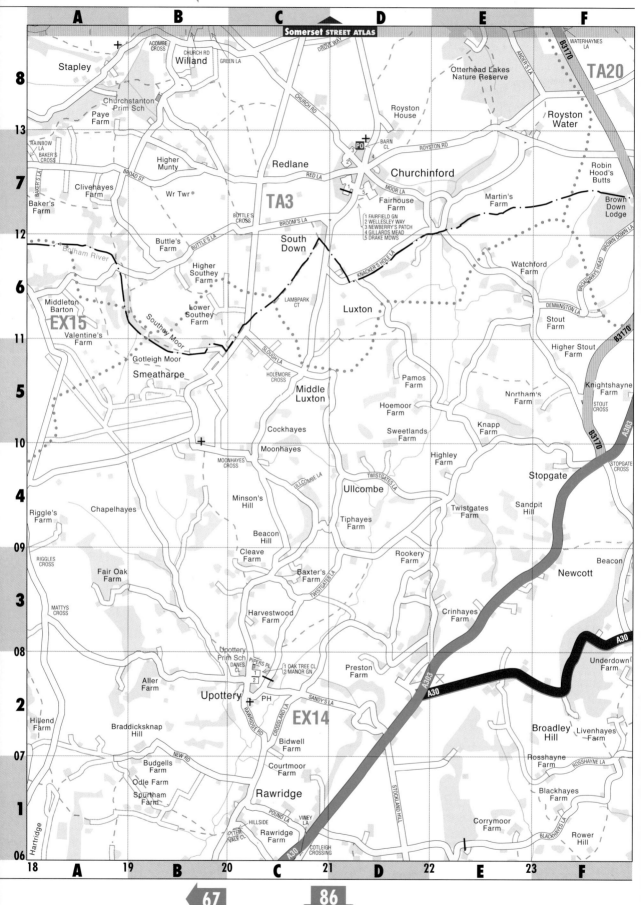

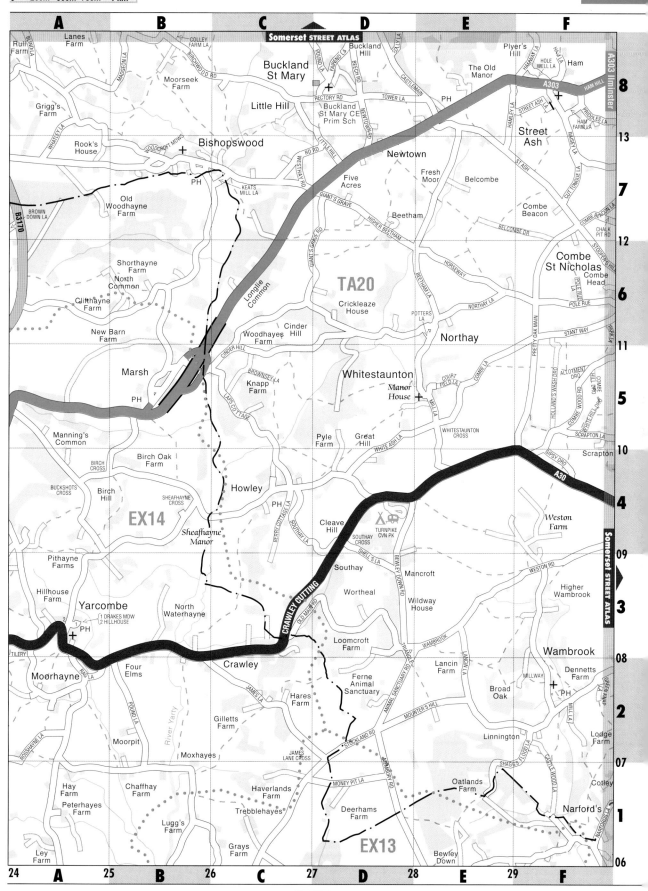

Somerset STREET ATLAS

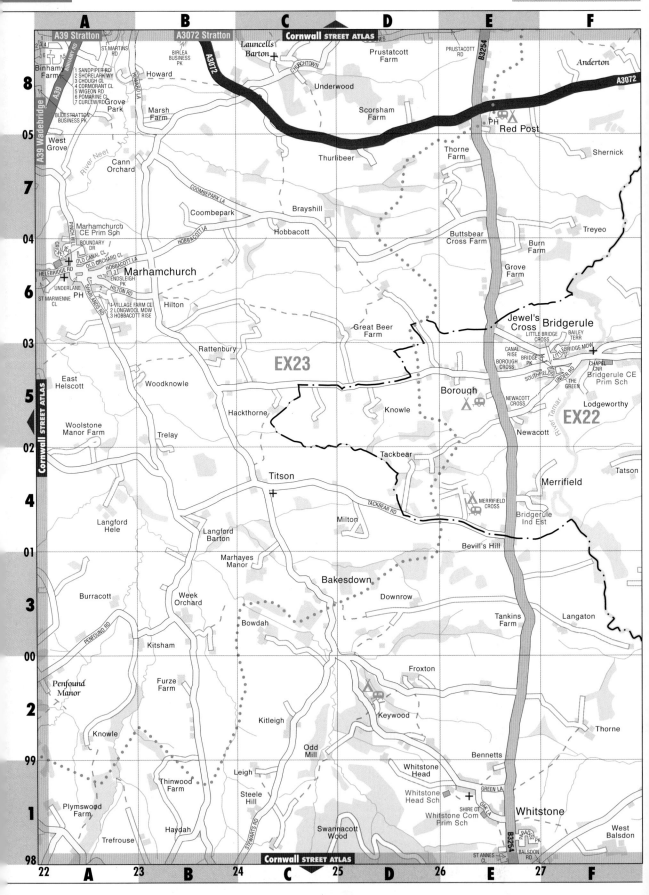

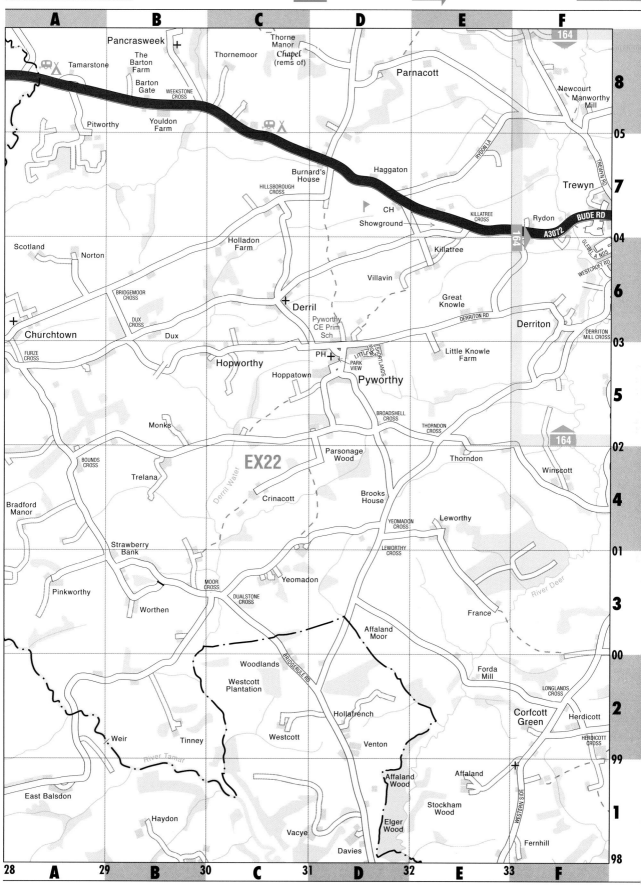

A   B   C   D   E   F

Pancrasweek
Tamarstone
The Barton Farm
Barton Gate
WEEKSTONE CROSS
Pitworthy
Youldon Farm
Thornemoor
Thorne Manor
Chapel (rems of)
Parnacott
Newcourt
Manworthy Mill

164

8

05

Scotland
Norton
Hillsborough Cross
Burnard's House
Haggaton
Killatree Cross
Trewyn
Rydon
BUDE RD
A3072
164

7

04

Holladon Farm
CH
Showground
Killatree
RYDON LA
TREWYN RD
GLEBE LANDS
WESTCROFT RD

Churchtown
Bridgemoor Cross
Dux Cross
Dux
Derril
Pyworthy CE Prim Sch
Villavin
Great Knowle
DERRITON RD
Derriton
Derriton Mill Cross

6

03

Furze Cross
Hopworthy
PH
Hoppatown
WESTLANDS MDW
PARK VIEW
LITTLE MDW
Pyworthy
Little Knowle Farm

5

Monks
Broadshell Cross
THORNDON CROSS

Bounds Cross
Trelana
EX22
Parsonage Wood
Thorndon
Winscott

164

02

Bradford Manor
Crinacott
Brooks House
Leworthy

4

01

Strawberry Bank
YEOMADON CROSS
LEWORTHY CROSS

Pinkworthy
Worthen
Moor Cross
Yeomadon
Dualstone Cross
Affaland Moor
France
River Deer

3

00

Weir
Tinney
Woodlands
Westcott Plantation
BRIDGERULE RD
Hollafrench
Forda Mill
Corfcott Green
Herdicott
LONGLANDS CROSS

2

99

East Balsdon
River Tamar
Haydon
Westcott
Venton
Affaland Wood
Affaland
Stockham Wood
WESTERN SIDE
HERDICOTT CROSS

Vacye
Elger Wood
Fernhill

1

Davies

98

For full street detail of the highlighted area see page 164.

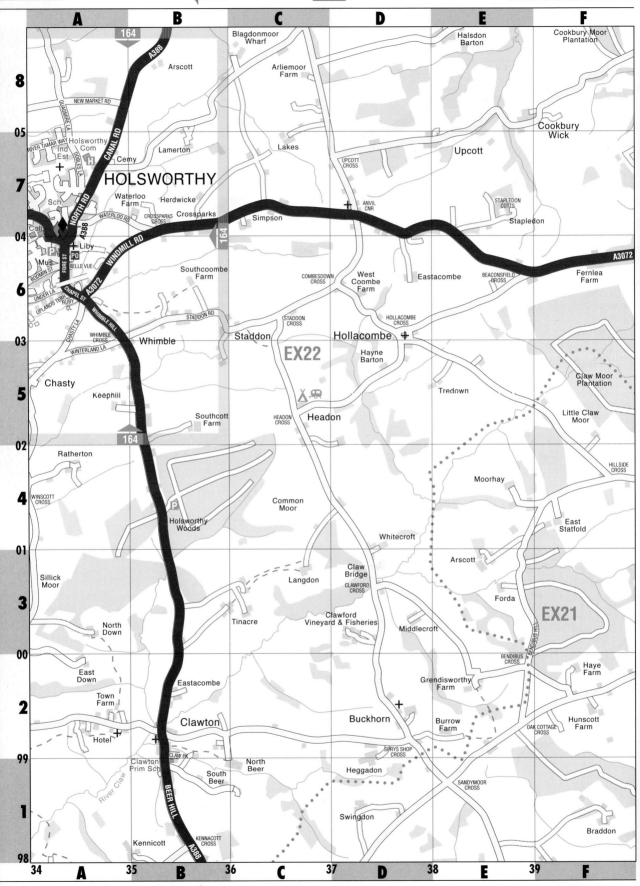

Scale: 1¾ inches to 1 mile

0 ¼ ½ mile
0 250m 500m 750m 1 km

A B C D E F

8

05

7

04

6

03

5

02

4

01

3

00

2

99

1

98

34 A 35 B 36 C 37 D 38 E 39 F

164
A388
Arscott
Blagdonmoor Wharf
Arliemoor Farm
Halsdon Barton
Cookbury Moor Plantation

Cookbury Wick

NEW MARKET RD
QUAGMIRE LA
River Tamar Way
Holsworthy Com
CANAL RD
Cemy
Lamerton
Lakes
Upcott
UPCOTT CROSS

Ind Est
H
HOLSWORTHY
NORTH RD
Waterloo Farm
Herdwicke
Crosssparks
CROSSSPARKS CROSS
Crossparks
Simpson
ANVIL CNR
Stapleton Cotts
Stapledon

Sch
A388
Liby
WINDMILL RD
WATERLOO RD
164
BEACONSFIELD CROSS
A3072
Fernlea Farm

P
PO
BELLE VUE
Mus
BODMIN ST
UNDER LA
CHAPEL ST
RUBY CL
UPLANDS TERR
A3072
Southcoombe Farm
COMBESDOWN CROSS
West Coombe Farm
Eastacombe

WHIMBLE HILL
STADDON RD
WHIMBLE CROSS
WINTERLAND LA
Whimble
Staddon
STADDON CROSS
HOLLACOMBE CROSS
Hollacombe
EX22

Chasty
Keephill
Southcott Farm
HEADON CROSS
Headon
Hayne Barton
Tredown
Claw Moor Plantation

Ratherton
Little Claw Moor
HILLSIDE CROSS

WINSCOTT CROSS
Common Moor
Whitecroft
Moorhay
East Statfold

Sillick Moor
Langdon
Claw Bridge
CLAWFORD CROSS
Arscott
Forda
EX21

North Down
Tinacre
Clawford Vineyard & Fisheries
Middlecroft
BENDIBUS HILL
BENDIBUS CROSS
Haye Farm

East Down
Town Farm
Eastacombe
Buckhorn
Grendisworthy Farm
Burrow Farm
OAK COTTAGE CROSS
Hunscott Farm

Hotel
CLAW PK
Clawton
North Beer
SPRYS SHOP CROSS
Heggadon
SANDYMOOR CROSS

Clawton Prim Sch
BEER HILL
South Beer
Swingdon
Braddon

River Claw
Kennicott
KENNACOTT CROSS
A388

For full street detail of the highlighted area see page 164.

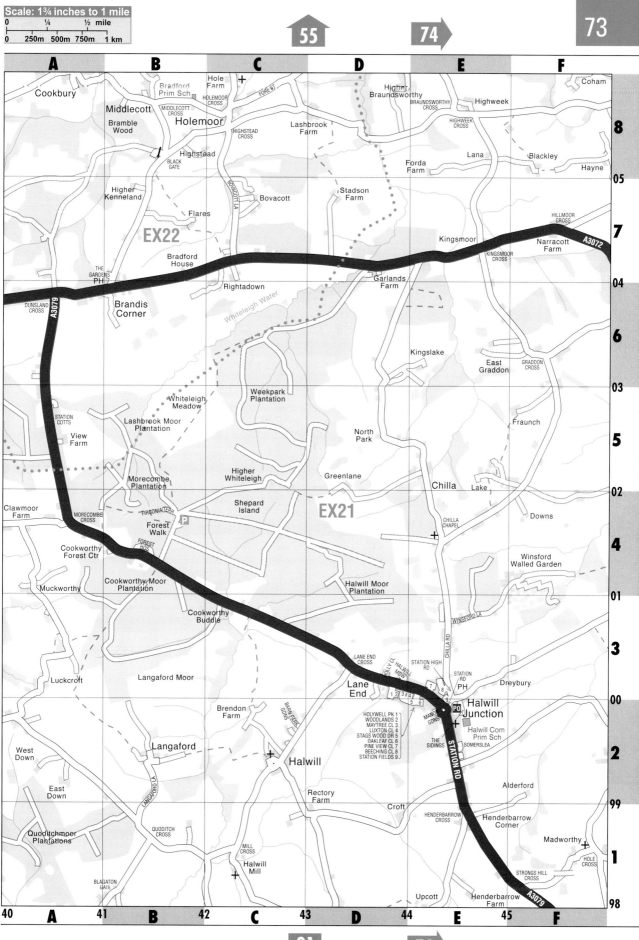

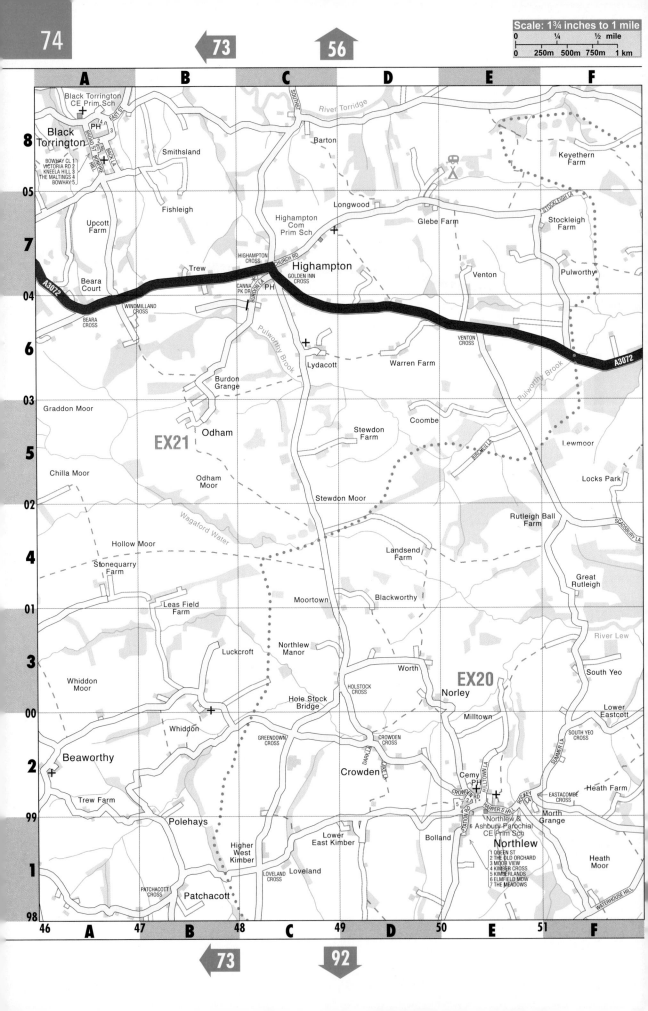
A   B   C   D   E   F

Black Torrington
CE Prim Sch
PH
Black
Torrington
BOWHAY CL 1
VICTORIA RD 2
KNEELA HILL 3
THE MALTINGS 4
BOWHAY 5

BROAD ST
BOWHAY HILL
BACK LA
EAST ST

Smithsland

8

05

Upcott
Farm
Fishleigh

River Torridge

Barton

Longwood   Glebe Farm

Keyethern
Farm

STOCKLEIGH LA

Stockleigh
Farm

7

04

A3072

Beara
Court
Beara
Cross

WINDMILLAND
CROSS

Trew

Highampton
Com Prim Sch

HIGHAMPTON
CROSS

CHURCH RD

CANNA
PK DR
BURDON LA

Highampton

GOLDEN INN
CROSS
PH

Venton

Pulworthy

Graddon Moor

Burdon
Grange

Pulworthy Brook

Lydacott

Warren Farm

VENTON
CROSS

A3072

Pulworthy Brook

6

03

EX21

Odham

Odham
Moor

Stewdon
Farm

Coombe

Lewmoor

5

02

Chilla Moor

Wagaford Water

Stewdon Moor

BIRCH LA

Locks Park

Rutleigh Ball
Farm

SCADSBURY LA

4

01

Hollow Moor

Stonequarry
Farm

Leas Field
Farm

Moortown

Landsend
Farm

Blackworthy

Great
Rutleigh

3

00

Whiddon
Moor

Luckcroft

Northlew
Manor

Hole Stock
Bridge

HOLSTOCK
CROSS

Worth

Norley

EX20

River Lew

South Yeo

Lower
Eastcott

2

99

Beaworthy

Trew Farm

Whiddon

GREENDOWN
CROSS

Polehays

Higher
West
Kimber

Lower
East Kimber

CROWDEN
CROSS

DARK LA
CREW LA

Crowden

STATION RD
CROWDEN
HILL

Milltown

HILLTOWN LA
Cemy
PH

Bolland

ROCKEY LA
SUMMER LA

Northlew &
Ashbury Parochial
CE Prim Sch

Northlew

1 QUEEN ST
2 THE OLD ORCHARD
3 MOOR VIEW
4 KIMBER CROSS
5 KIMBERLANDS
6 ELMFIELD MDW
7 THE MEADOWS

SOUTH YEO
CROSS

Heath Farm

EASTACOMBE
CROSS
Morth
Grange

Heath
Moor

WATERHOUSE HILL

1

98

46   A   47   B   48   C   49   D   50   E   51   F

LOVELAND
CROSS
Loveland

PATCHACOTT
CROSS
Patchacott

Scale: 1¾ inches to 1 mile

0 ¼ ½ mile
0 250m 500m 750m 1 km

| A | B | C | D | E | F |

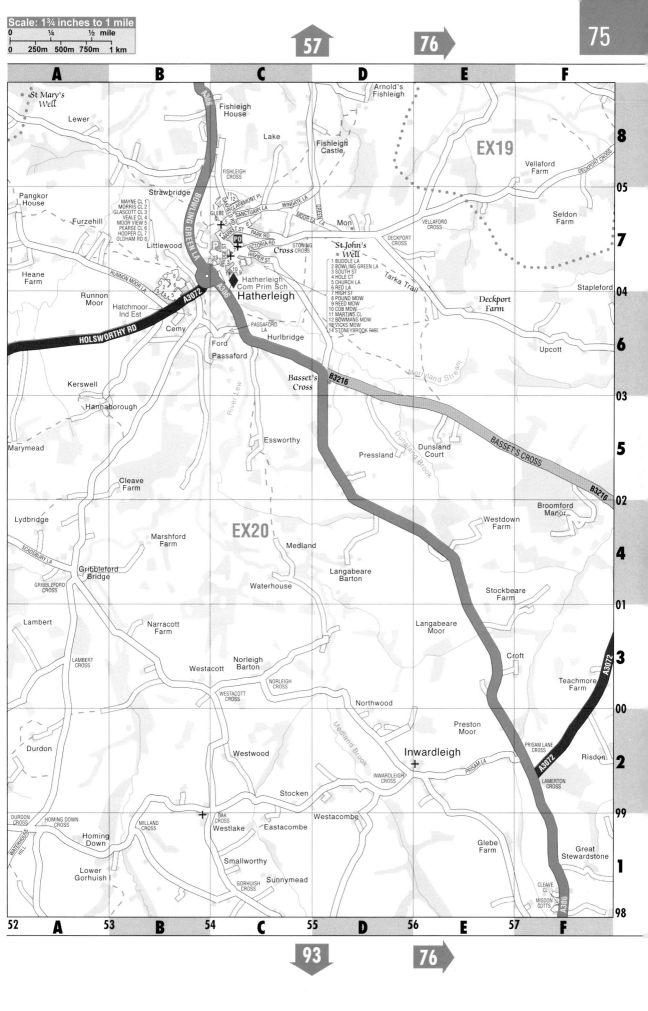

St Mary's Well
Lewer
Pangkor House
Furzehill
Heane Farm
Runnon Moor
Littlewood
Strawbridge
Fishleigh House
Lake
Fishleigh Castle
Arnold's Fishleigh
FISHLEIGH CROSS

EX19
Vellaford Farm
Seldon Farm
Stapleford

MAYNE CL 1
MORRIS CL 2
GLASCOTT CL 3
VEALE CL 4
MOOR VIEW 5
PEARSE CL 6
HOOPER CL 7
OLDHAM RD 8

RUNNON MOOR LA
A3072
HOLSWORTHY RD
Hatchmoor Ind Est
Cemy
Kerswell
Hannaborough
Marymead
Cleave Farm
Lydbridge
Gribbleford Bridge
GRIBBLEFORD CROSS
Lambert
LAMBERT CROSS
Durdon
DURDON CROSS
HOMING DOWN CROSS
WATERHOUSE HILL
Homing Down
Lower Gorhuish

BOWLING GREEN LA
A386
GLEBE
SANCTUARY LA
CLAREMONT PL
PARK RD
MARKET ST
VICTORIA RD
BRIDGE ST
DANIELL RD
PO
Cross
STONING CROSS
HIGHER ST
Hatherleigh
Hatherleigh Com Prim Sch
Ford
Passaford
PASSAFORD LA
Hurlbridge
River Lew
Basset's Cross
Essworthy
Medland
Waterhouse
Marshford Farm
Narracott Farm
Westacott
Norleigh Barton
NORLEIGH CROSS
WESTACOTT CROSS
Westwood
Westlake
OAK CROSS
MILLAND CROSS
Smallworthy
GORHUISH CROSS
Sunnymead
Eastacombe
Stocken
Westacombe

St John's Well
1 BUDDLE LA
2 BOWLING GREEN LA
3 SOUTH ST
4 HOLE CT
5 CHURCH LA
6 RED LA
7 HIGH ST
8 POUND MDW
9 REED MDW
10 COB MDW
11 MARTINS CL
12 BOWMANS MDW
13 VICKS MDW
14 STONEYBROOK RISE

Mon
MOOR LA
WINGATE LA
GREEN LA
DECKPORT CROSS
VELLAFORD CROSS
Tarka Trail
Deckport Farm
Upcott
Merryland Stream
B3216
Pressland
Dunsland Court
Dunsland Brook
BASSET'S CROSS
B3216
Broomford Manor
Westdown Farm
Stockbeare Farm
DECKPORT CROSS

EX20
Langabeare Barton
Langabeare Moor
Northwood
Croft
A3072
Teachmore Farm
Risdon
PRISAM LANE CROSS
PRISAM LA
A3072
LAMERTON CROSS
Preston Moor
Inwardleigh
INWARDLEIGH CROSS
Medland Brook
Glebe Farm
Great Stewardstone
CLEAVE CL
MISDON COTTS
A386

| A | B | C | D | E | F |

8
05
7
04
6
03
5
02
4
01
3
00
2
99
1
98

52 53 54 55 56 57

Scale: 1¾ inches to 1 mile
0 | ¼ | ½ mile
0 | 250m | 500m | 750m | 1 km

A | B | C | D | E | F

RATTENBURY CROSS
Wood Barton
Colehouse
Brixton Barton Farm
Broadwoodkelly
Clarkestown
SHORESGATE CROSS
A3124
Coulson
HUGHBALL CROSS
BURROW CROSS
COULSON CROSS
PH
P
Monkokehampton
MONKOKEHAMPTON CROSS
Stafford Beer Farm
Splatt
WOODCROFT LA
Woodcroft
Walson Barton
DECKPORT CROSS
Hole Brook
SPLATTS CROSS
Redhays
WALSON LA
CADDITON CROSS
05
EX19
SOUTH DOWN CROSS
CORSTONE CROSS
Taylor's Down
Moorend Farm
Beer
Holme Down
Southdown Farm
WOODCROFT CROSS
Corstone
Lewersland Farm
7
Corstone Moor
BUDE MOOR CROSS
04
Easterbrook
Fursdon
BONDLEIGH MOOR CROSS
Honeychurch Moor
Stapleford
Waterhouse
Bude Farm
POST BOX CROSS
6
Woodhall Bridge
Coxwell Farm
Tor Down Farm
Westacott
FISHINGCLOSE CROSS
HONEYCHURCH MOOR CROSS
TERRIS CROSS
Woodhall
Narracott
Chattafin
REDPOST CROSS
03
Cadham
FARTHINGLAND CROSS
EX20
Honeychurch
ROWTRY CROSS
Frankland
Beerhill
5
Brooklyns
THE BELLANDS
THE TUMBELS
TOWN LIVING DRO
MAYFIELD RD
FORE ST
HIGHER LA
BEERHILL LA
A3124
Langmead Farm
1 THE SHRUBBERY
2 DUCK LA
3 MANOR GDNS
4 BLENHEIM LA
PO
Solland
HONEYCHURCH LA
REDPOST CROSS
02
Jacobstowe
B3276
Exbourne CE Prim Sch
STOWFORD LA
HIGH ST
CLISTON VIEW
HOLEBROOK CROSS
PH
Cliston
HUCKLAND CROSS
LONGMEAD LA
Combe
BARTON HEAD CROSS
EXBOURNE CROSS
HOLE HILL
SOLLAND LA
CLISTON LA
CLISTON LA
PEACEGATE CROSS
WEST BARTON LA
Bulland CROSS
4
Buskin Farm
Exbourne
SOLLAND CROSS
THORNBURY CROSS
CHAPPLE LA
BULLAND CROSS
HARVEYS CL
Sampford Courtenay
A3072
RECTORY HILL
PH
TRECOTT CROSS
01
Shilstone
Swanstone
LANDERDOWN LA
Underdown Farm
Paize Farm
Sampford Chapple
SAMPFORD CROSS
BROOKE CL
GREEN HILL
Trecott
WALSPRINGS LA
RAMSEY LA
3
Hayes Barton
Tarka Trail
River Okement
Swanstone Moor
Brookfield
Chapple Moor
Southey
SOUTHEY LA
00
South Dornaford
Dornaford Park
Common Moor
2
Risdon
Dornaford Cross
Hatherton Sampford Moors
PH
B3215
Goldburn
Berrydown Plantation
Ventown
THE BEACHES
Black Moor
1
GOLDBURN CROSS
Hill Farm
Sewage Works
Wood Farm
Dartmoor Rly
BELSTONE CNR CROSS
Witheybrook
98
B3215
Incott

58 | A | 59 | B | 60 | C | 61 | D | 62 | E | 63 | F

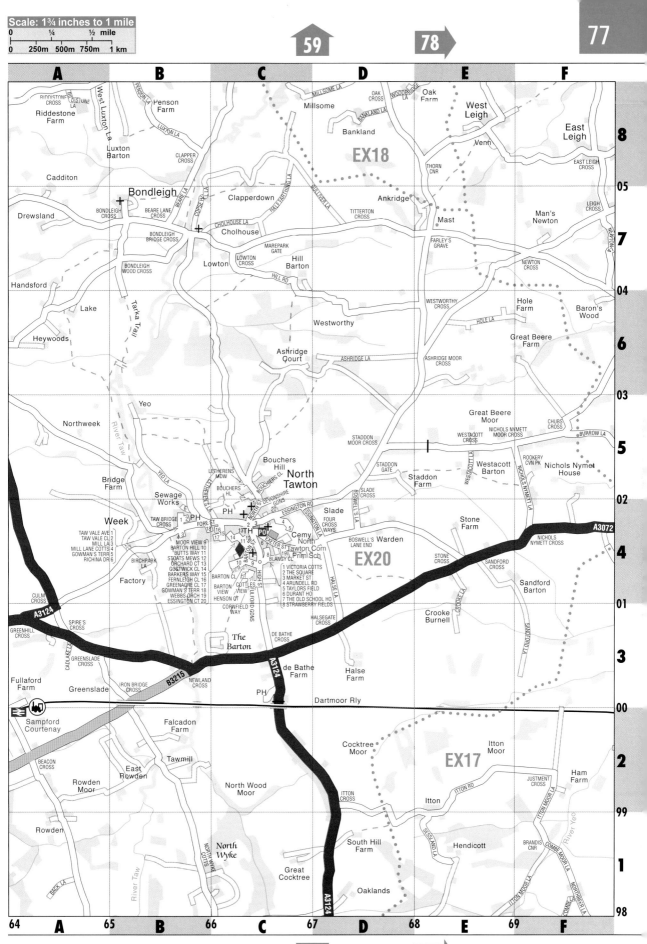

Scale: 1¾ inches to 1 mile
0 ¼ ½ mile
0 250m 500m 750m 1 km

A B C D E F

8
05
7
04
6
03
5
02
4
01
3
00
2
99
1
98

Birch Farm
BIRCH LA
Trinity Leigh
BLACKDITCH LA
LOOSE AREA LA
Birch Cross
MOOR LA
Loosebeare Cross
Loosebeare
B3220
Loosebeare Cross
STOPGATE CROSS
Nymphayes
NYMPHAYES LA
WEEK CROSS LA
Higher Week
Middle Yeo Farm
YEO RD
Ellicombe
A377
Sharland Farm
SHARLAND LA
DOWN HILL
Morchard Road
B3220
PH
Morchard Road
SHOBROOKE LA
Foldhay
Gissage Lake
CHURCHILL GDNS
GISSAGE HILL GDNS
Rowans
WESTERN RD
EASTERN RD
BEER LA
WAIE COTTS
Waie PH
Zeal Monachorum
River Yeo
Thorne Farm
Down St Mary
1 THE GREEN
2 BEECH DR
3 GLEBELAND
4 STURT COTTS
UNION HILL
BARN HILL
Wolfin Farm
Barn Shelley
Shobrooke Farm
WATER BRIDGE CROSS
CH
Foldhay Cross
FOLDHAY LA
Gillhouse Farm
Cvn Pk
WAIE CROSS
Oak Tree Farm
Bartonbury
Bartonbury Cross
Two Moors Way
LAMMACOTT LA
QUARRY LA
CHAFFCOMBE LA
Eppletons Farm
THREE CROSSWAYS
Hayne
HAYNE CROSS
Tuckingmill
FURZEPARK LA
Thorne
Lammacott Farm
LAMMACOTT CROSS
Chaffcombe Cross
Wr Twr
Reeve Castle
CLAPPER CROSS
Sutton Farm
SERSTONE CROSS
ALLER GATE
Clannaborough Cross
A3072
BEERS HILL
Beers
Burrow
BURROW LA
LOWER BURSTON
PITT LA
PAUSEY LA
JESSEY'S LA
Serstone Farm
1 MILL LEAT COTTS
2 HOBBS WAY
3 GREGORY CL
4 COLLATONS WLK
5 NYMET AVE
6 GRATTANS WAY
7 ITER CT
8 CHURCHLANDS
9 JUNCTION RD
EX17
Clannaborough Barton
Burston
MARSH LA
BURSTON CROSS
WATER LA
ITER CNR
Bow
ITER CROSS
Grattans
Blackpool Cross
Sweetfield
A3072
HAMPSON CROSS
Hampson
PH
MILL LA
GODFREYS GDNS
BOW MILL LA
NATSON MILL LA
2 LILIAN CL
GOSS MDW
WHEATLY COTTS
Bow Com Prim Sch
ST MARTIN'S
ITER PK
Works West Halse
Collatons
BLACKPOOL RD
Appledore Farm
Paschoe
FORD HILL
Ford Farm
HAMPSON LA
BOWPOUND CROSS
Langford
LANGFORD CROSS
Natson
STATION RD
Glebe House
WALSON RD
Walson Cross
Whelmstone Barton
WHELMSTONE CROSS
LANDSEND LA
WEBBER LA
Broadnymett Chapel
Little Langford
Nymet Tracey
MUDGE LA
THORNE LA
Thorne Farm
Landsend Barton
Butterlands Park
Broadnymett Moor
BOW STATION CROSS
Common Moor
HILLDOWN RD
Newcott Farm
Coxmoor
Brownsland
Hilldown
HILLDOWN CROSS
THORNEMOOR LA
Prestons
COXMOOR LA
West Begbeer
HILLDOWN LA
Downhayes
COXMOOR CROSS
Treedown Farm
SPESTOS LA
Spestos
West Wotton
Great Wotton
Great Begbeer Farm
Bowbeer
BOWBEER LA
HILLERTON CROSS
Hillerton
Grange Place
Blue Violet
THORNE LA
Birchman's Cross
Wood Farm
BOW BEER CROSS

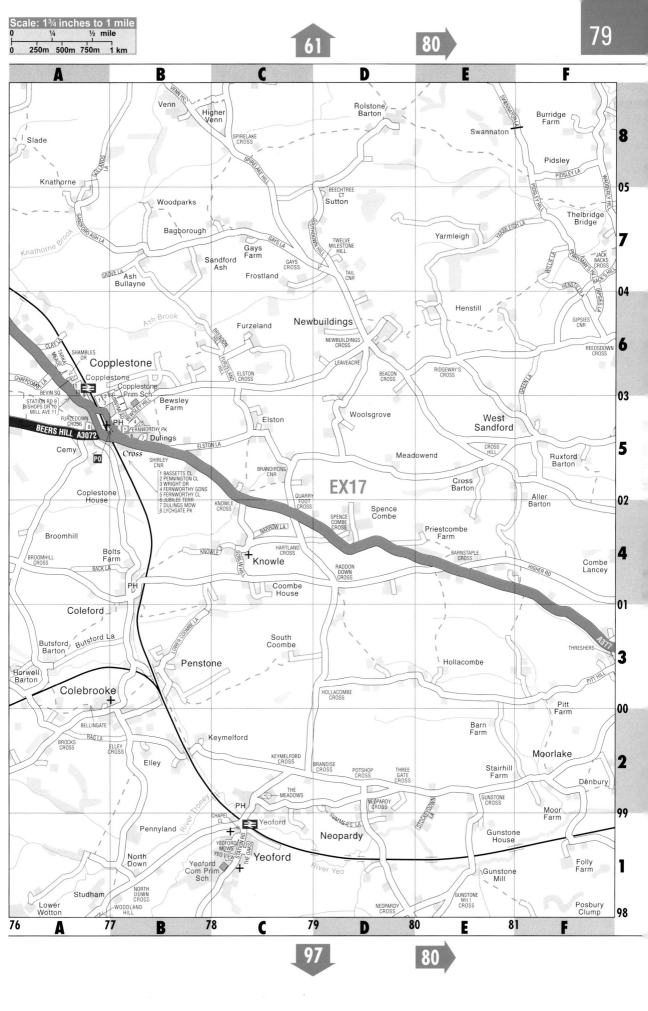

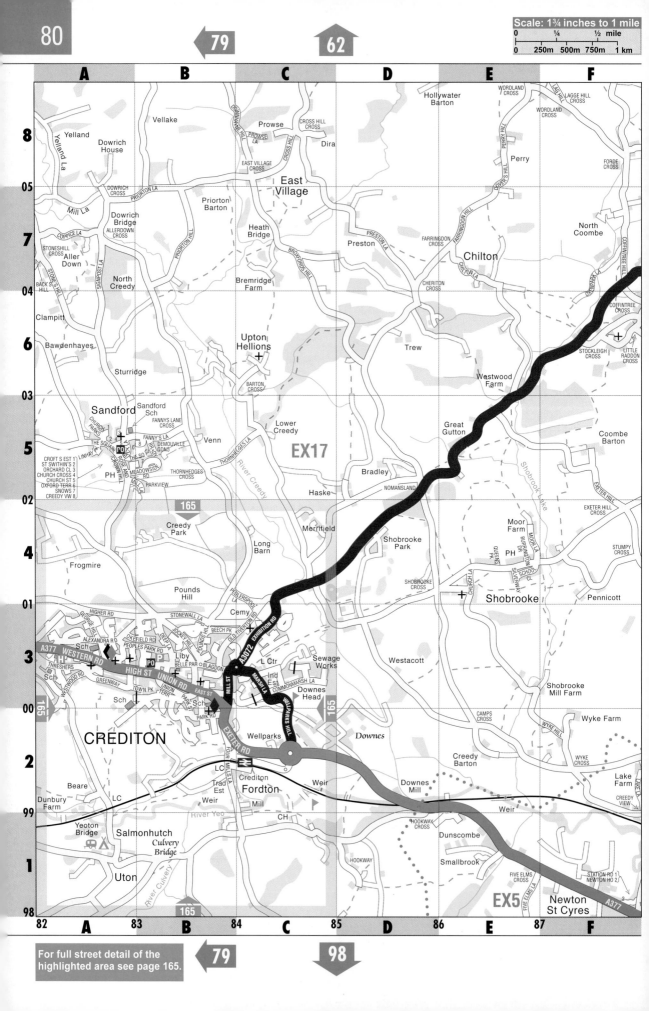

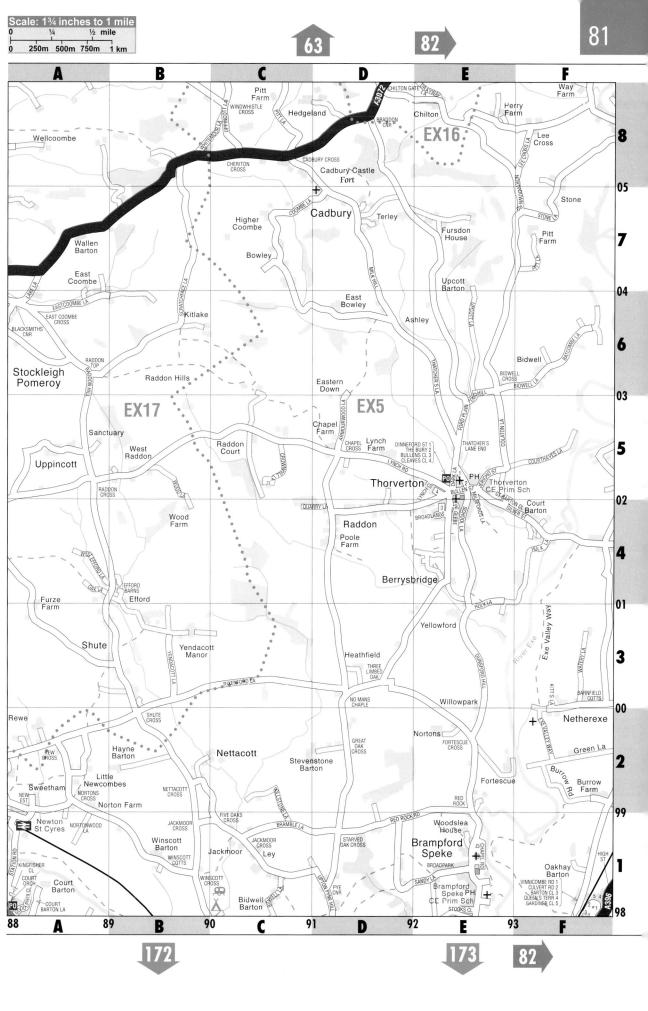

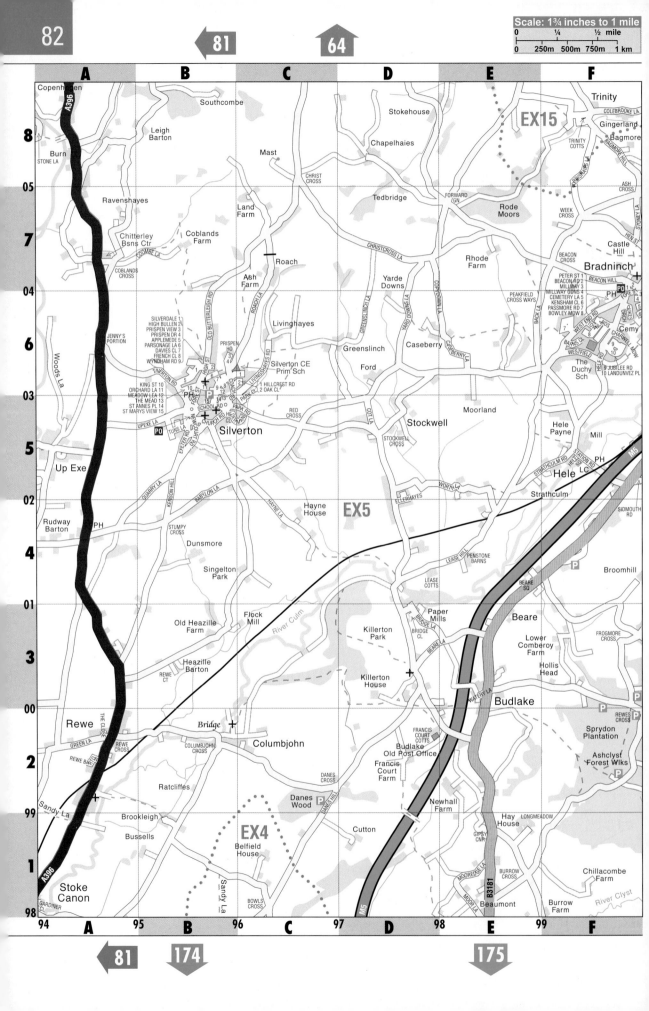

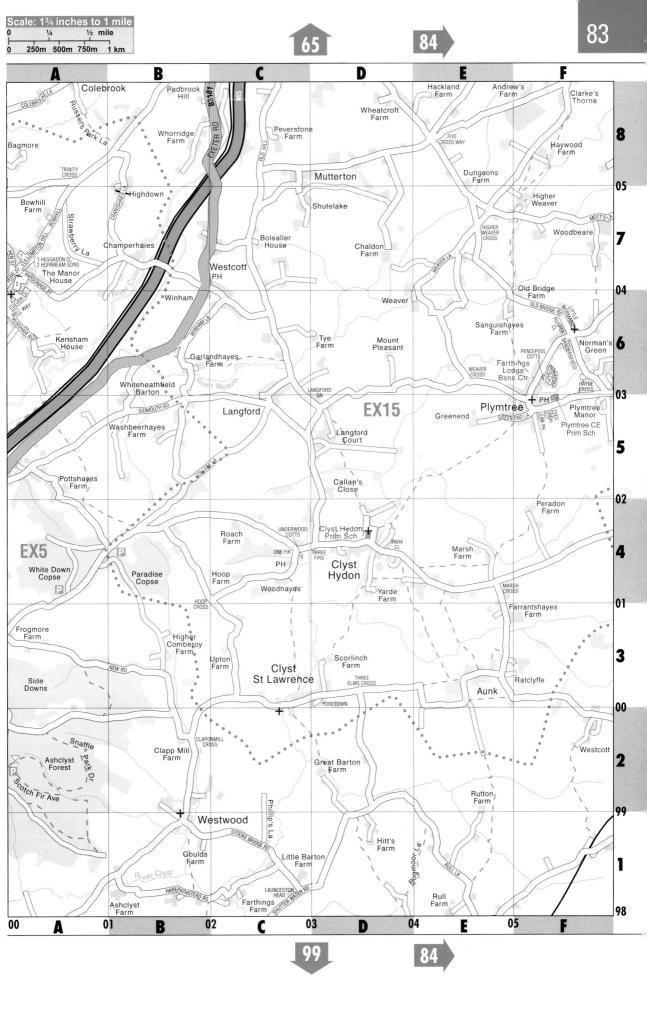

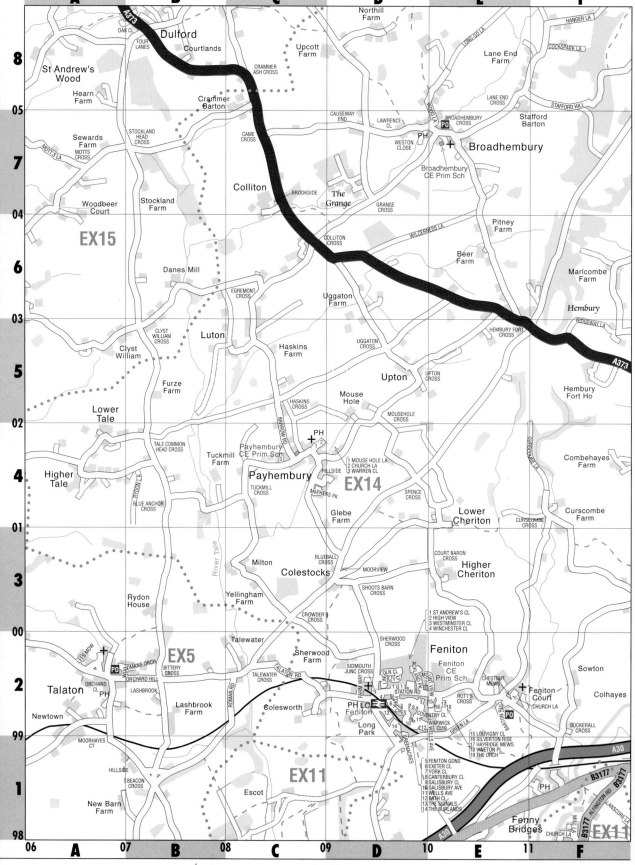

Scale: 1¾ inches to 1 mile

0 ¼ ½ mile
0 250m 500m 750m 1 km

A **B** **C** **D** **E** **F**

A373
Oak Cl
Dulford
Four Lanes
Courtlands
St Andrew's Wood
Hearn Farm
Crammer Ash Cross
Upcott Farm
Northill Farm
Longbd La
Lane End Farm
Worth La
Cockspark La
Hanger La

8

Sewards Farm
Stockland Head Cross
Crammer Barton
Came Cross
Causeway End
Lawrence Cl
Weston Close
PO
Broadhembury Cross
Lane End Cross
Stafford Barton
Stafford Hill

05

Motts La
Motts Cross
Stockland Farm
PH
Broadhembury
Broadhembury CE Prim Sch

7

Woodbeer Court
Colliton
Brookside
The Grange
Grange Cross
Pitney Farm

04

EX15
Danes Mill
Egremont Cross
Colliton Cross
Wilderness La
Beer Farm
Marlcombe Farm

6

Clyst William Cross
Luton
Haskins Farm
Uggaton Farm
Uggaton Cross
Hembury Fort Cross
Hembury
Ridgeway La
A373

03

Clyst William
Furze Farm
Upton
Upton Cross
Hembury Fort Ho

5

Lower Tale
Haskins Cross
Mouse Hole
Mousehole Cross
Curscombe La
Combehayes Farm

02

Tale Common Head Cross
Tuckmill Farm
Payhembury CE Prim Sch
PH
Hillside
1 MOUSE HOLE LA
2 CHURCH LA
3 WARREN CL
Spence Cross
Curscombe Cross
Curscombe Farm

4

Higher Tale
Barrow Rd
Payhembury
Tuckmill Cross
Markers Pk
EX14
Lower Cheriton

Blue Anchor Cross
Glebe Farm
Court Baron Cross

01

River Tale
Milton
Blueball Cross
Colestocks
Moorview
Shoots Barn Cross
Higher Cheriton

3

Rydon House
Yellingham Farm
Crowder's Cross
1 ST ANDREW'S CL
2 HIGH VIEW
3 WESTMINSTER CL
4 WINCHESTER CL

00

Lees Mdw
Talewater
Sherwood Farm
Sherwood Cross
Feniton
Feniton CE Prim Sch
Sowton

Sidmans Orch
EX5
Bittery Cross
Talaton Rd
Sidmouth Junc Cross
Fairway
Qln Cl
Linc Pk
Station Rd
Chestnut Mews
Feniton Court
Church La
Colhayes

2

Talaton
PO
Orchard Hill
Lashbrook
Talewater Cross
Roman Rd
Colesworth
PH LC
Feniton
Warwick Cl
Country Cl
Rutt's Cross
PO
Buckerall Cross

Newtown
Lashbrook Farm
Long Park
Greenacres Cl
Wells Ave
Green La

99

Moorhayes Ct
Beacon Cross
Hillside
Escot
EX11
15 LOUVIGNY CL
16 SILVERTON RISE
17 HAYRIDGE MEWS
18 VMIETON PL
19 THE ORCH
A30
B3177

1

New Barn Farm
5 FENITON GDNS
6 EXETER CL
7 YORK CL
8 CANTERBURY CL
9 SALISBURY CL
10 SALISBURY AVE
11 WELLS AVE
12 BATH CL
13 THE SIGNALS
14 THE BURLANDS
PH
Fenny Bridges
Mill La
Alfington Rd
Lanscore La
B3177
Church La
EX11

98

06 **A** **07** **B** **08** **C** **09** **D** **10** **E** **11** **F**

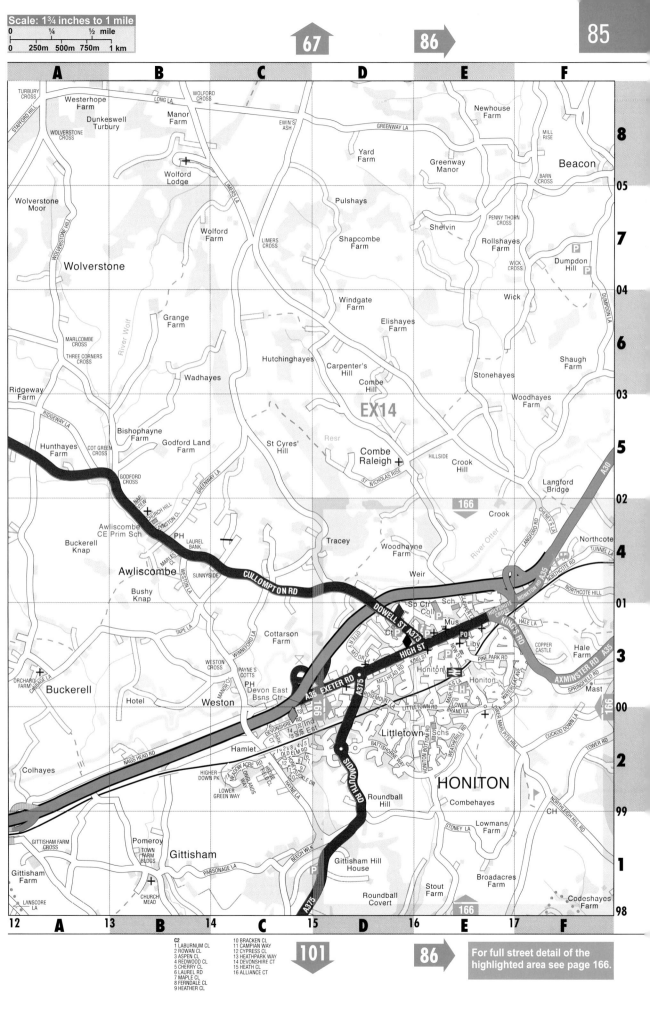

A B C D E F

8

05

7

04

6

03

5

02

4

01

3

00

2

99

1

98

TURBURY CROSS
STAFFORD HILL
Westerhope Farm
Dunkeswell Turbury
WOLVERSTONE CROSS
LONG LA
WOLFORD CROSS
Manor Farm
EWIN'S ASH
GREENWAY LA
Newhouse Farm
MILL RISE
Wolford Lodge
Yard Farm
Greenway Manor
Beacon
BARN CROSS
Wolverstone Moor
Pulshays
Shelvin
PENNY THORN CROSS
Rollshayes Farm
WOLVERSTONE HILL
Wolford Farm
LIMERS CROSS
Shapcombe Farm
WICK CROSS
Dumpdon Hill
DUMPDON LA
Wolverstone
LIMERS LA
Windgate Farm
Wick
MARLCOMBE CROSS
Grange Farm
Elishayes Farm
Shaugh Farm
RIVER WOLF
THREE CORNERS CROSS
Wadhayes
Hutchinghayes
Carpenter's Hill
Stonehayes
Woodhayes Farm
Ridgeway Farm
Combe Hill
RIDGEWAY LA
Bishophayne Farm
Godford Land Farm
St Cyres' Hill
Resr
EX14
HILLSIDE
Crook Hill
Langford Bridge
A30
Hunthayes Farm
COT GREEN CROSS
Combe Raleigh
ST NICHOLAS RISE
166
Crook
CHERRY LA
LANGFORD RD
NORTHCOTE
NAP VIEW
GODFORD CROSS
CHURCH HILL
AXINGTON CL
Awliscombe CE Prim Sch
GREENWAY LA
PH
LAUREL BANK
Tracey
Woodhayne Farm
RIVER OTTER
TUNNEL LA
Buckerell Knap
Awliscombe
MARLES LA
WESTON LA
CULLOMPTON RD
Weir
MONKTON RD
NORTHCOTE RD
A35
NORTHCOTE HILL
Bushy Knap
SUNNYSIDE
DOWELL ST A373
Sp Ctr Coll
Sch
HOLYBRUTE CROSS
HALE LA
TAPE LA
WINNEFORD LA
Cottarson Farm
HIGH ST
Mus
PO
KING'S RD
COPPER CASTLE
Hale Farm
A35
Buckerell
ORCHARD FARM LA
CABBAGE LA
WESTON CROSS
PAYNE'S COTTS
PH
Devon East Bsns Ctr
A35 EXETER RD
A373
MOOR
OTTER
Liby
PINE PARK RD
Honiton
WATERLEAT AVE
SPRINGFIELD RD
Mast
MANOR CL
ROSEMOUNT LA
MILLHEAD RD
KING RD
LOWER BRAND LA
AXMINSTER RD A35
166
Hotel
166
Weston
13
DEVONSHIRE LA
Ind Est
Littletown RD
Schs
RIVER MARI PITS HILL
00
Hamlet
14
PINE ES
OLD ELM RD
BATTISHORNE WAY
HONITON BOTTOM RD
WEATHERILL RD
CUCKOO DOWN LA
TOWER RD
Colhayes
NAGS HEAD RD
HIGHER DOWN PK
MEADOW ACRE RD
HONEYSUCKLE DR
LONGLANDS WAY
HERNE RISE
Littletown
Schs
HONITON
NORTHLEIGH HILL RD
LOWER GREEN WAY
HAYNE LA
SIDMOUTH RD
Roundball Hill
Combehayes
CH
Pomeroy
TOWN FARM BLDGS
PARSONAGE LA
BEECH WLK
Roundball Covert
STONEY LA
Lowmans Farm
Broadacres Farm
Gittisham
Gittisham Hill House
Stout Farm
Codeshayes Farm
GITTISHAM FARM CROSS
CHURCH MEAD
A375
166
Gittisham Farm
LANSCORE LA

12 A 13 B 14 C 15 D 16 E 17 F

C2
1 LABURNUM CL
2 ROWAN CL
3 ASPEN CL
4 REDWOOD CL
5 CHERRY CL
6 LAUREL RD
7 MAPLE CL
8 FERNDALE CL
9 HEATHER CL
10 BRACKEN CL
11 CAMPIAN WAY
12 CYPRESS CL
13 HEATHPARK WAY
14 DEVONSHIRE CT
15 HEATH CL
16 ALLIANCE CT

Scale: 1¾ inches to 1 mile
0 ¼ ½ mile
0 250m 500m 750m 1 km

A B C D E F

8

Pound Farm
Mohun's Ottery
Underdown Farm
Hugginshayes Farm
Hill Grounds
Witch La
North Hill Farm
North Hill La

05

Halsdon House
Hayne Farm
Mast
Bowood Farm
Post La
Leywood
Barn Park Farm
Brimpit Farm
Lake Farm
White's La
Hornshayes Bridge
Hornshayes Knap Cross

7

Whitehall Farm
River Otter
Aplins Farm
Yard Cross
Viney La
Westwood Farm
South Wood Farm
Snodwell Farm
Short Moor
Groundhead Rd
Stockland Hill

04

Butler Way
Dumpdon View
Monkton Barton
Viney Cross
Wood La
Bull Farm
Wood Cross
Royal Oak Cross
Shortmoor Cross
Golden Square
Stockland Little Castle
Millhayes Cross
Millhayes
Millhayes Rd

6

PH
Old Chard Rd
Three Mariners Cross
Cotleigh Bridge
Feath Fibed La
Shrubbery La
Hussey's Cross
Hussey's La
Cawley's La

03

Ford Bridge
Monkton Rd
Monkton
Ford Cross
Hedgend Rd
Stadbury La
Stadbury Cross
Holmsleigh Cross
Holmsleigh Green
Wellhayes Farm
Stockland Great Castle
Ewecroft La
Shore Bottom
Shore Head
Broadhayes House
Ruft Farm

Luppitt Rd

5

Holmsleigh Rd
Holmsleigh Farm
Viney Lane Cross
Cotleigh
Cotleigh Cross
Rye Pk
Hill's La
Gully La
Broadhayes Cross
Goren Farm

02

Cotleigh Court
Umborne Brook
Court Place Farm
Lower Ridge

4

A35
Cleverhayes La
Southcote La
Cleverhayes Farm
Four Cross
Whitehorn Farm
Southcote La
Southcote Farm
Wylmington Hayes
Ridge Cross
Mast
Ridge Court Farm
Ham Cross
Ham
Yonder Ridge
Ham Rd

Tunnel La
Northcote Hill

EX14

01

Tower Cross
Spilcombe Copse
Cleave Cross
Cleave La
Hayne La
Mansfield Farm
Coombes Head Farm
Combehead Droveway
Combehead La
Hawley Bottom

00

Axminster Rd
Hutgate Rd
Northgate La
Mount Pleasant
Cleave
Ridgeway Farm
Ridge La
Wilmington
Whitefield PH
Ford Farm
Larkshayes Knap
Larkshayes Cross
Larkshayes Groveway
Hawley Cross

EX13

3

Springfield Rd
Tower Rd
Twr
Ramsden La
Woodlands Cl
Four Acres Cl
Featherbed La
Offwell CE Prim Sch
East Devon Bsns Pk
Orchard Cl
Whitehayes Cl
The Firs
Moorcox
Walmington La
Moorcox Cross
Burrow Knap

2

Tower Rd
Offwell House
Offwell
Colyton Cross
North Coombe Rd
Widworthy Ct
Castle Hill
Barton
New Rd
Widworthy
Dalwood Hill
Worham's La
Burrow Knap Way

99

West Colwell
Offwell Brook
Suttons Cross
New Road Cross
Worham's Farm
Burrow Cnr
Old Taunton Rd

1

Broaddown Cross
Northleigh Hill Rd
Glanville Rd
Colwell Barton
Mill La
Village La
Rock La
Hotel
Stoneyhouse La
Sutton Barton
Widworthy Hill
Halshayne
Colhayne La
A35
Colhayne Farm
Colcombe La

98

18 A 19 B 20 C 21 D 22 E 23 F

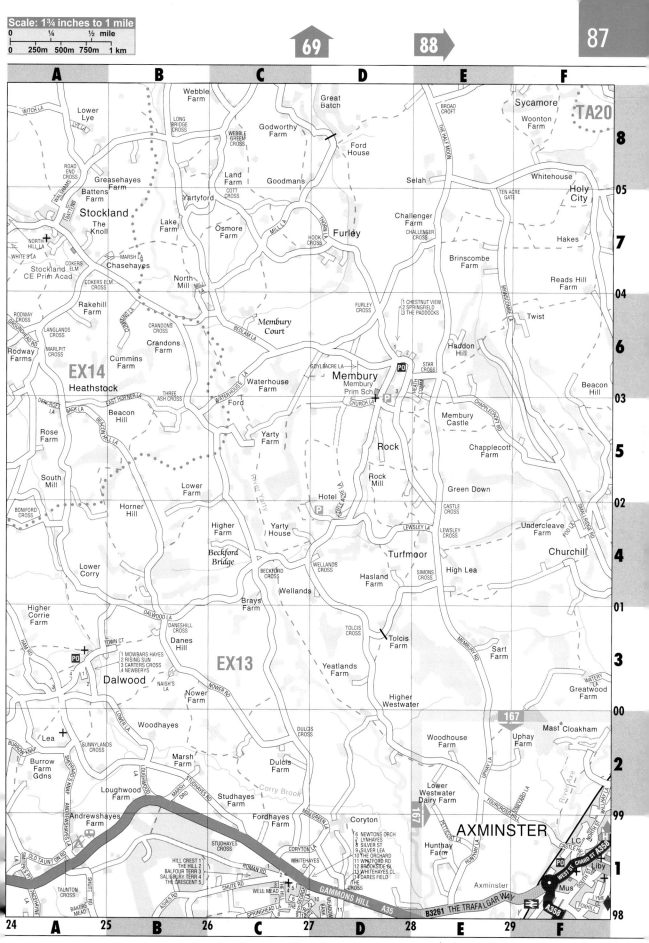

Scale: 1¾ inches to 1 mile

0   ¼   ½   mile
0 250m 500m 750m 1 km

A **B** **C** **D** **E** **F**

TA20

Sycamore
Woonton Farm

Lower Lye
Witch La
Lye La

Webble Farm

Great Batch

Broad Croft

The Half Moon

Whitehouse

Holy City

Road End Cross
Walshams
Battens

Greasehayes Farm

Long Bridge Cross

Godworthy Farm

Ford House

Selah

Ten Acre Gate

Hakes

Battens Farm
Stockland

Yartyford

Land Farm

Goodmans

Challenger Farm

Reads Hill Farm

The Knoll

Lake Farm

Webble Green Cross

Cott Cross

Hook La

Furley

Challenger Cross

Brinscombe Farm

Brinscombe La

White S La

Marsh La
Chasehayes

North Mill

Mill La

Thorn La

Hook Cross

Furley Cross

1 Chestnut View
2 Springfield
3 The Paddocks

Twist

Stockland CE Prim Acad

Cokers Elm

Cokers Elm Cross

Rakehill Farm

Crandons Cross

Bedlam La

Membury Court

Haddon Hill

Star Cross

Beacon Hill

Rodway Cross

Langlands Cross

Cummins La

Crandons Farm

PO
Membury
Membury Prim Sch

Chapplecroft Rd

Groundhead Rd

Marlpit Cross

Cummins Farm

Waterhouse La

Goylbacre La

Heath Comm

Membury Castle

Rodway Farms

EX14
Heathstock

Three Ash Cross

Waterhouse Farm

Church La

Rock

Chapplecott Farm

Dencroft La
Back La
Beacon Hill La

East Horner La

Ford

Yarty Farm

Green Down

Rose Farm
Beacon Hill

Lower Farm

River Yarty

Rock Mill

Castle Cross

Undercleave Farm

Pol La

Smallridge Rd

Churchill

South Mill

Horner Hill

Hotel
P

Coly Ridge La

Lewsley La

Lewsley Cross

Boniford Cross

Higher Farm

Yarty House

Turfmoor

Membury Rd

Lower Corry

Beckford Bridge

Beckford Cross

Wellands Cross

Hasland Farm

Simons Cross

High Lea

Higher Corrie Farm

Dalwood La

Daneshill Cross

Brays Farm

Wellands

Sart Farm

Ham Rd

Town Ct

Danes Hill

1 Mowbars Hayes
2 Rising Sun
3 Carters Cross
4 Newberys

EX13

Tolcis Cross

Tolcis Farm

Watery La
Greatwood Farm

PO
Dalwood

Naish's La

Nower Rd

Yeatlands Farm

167

Lower La

Nower Farm

Higher Westwater

Mast Cloakham

Lea

Woodhayes

Dulcis Cross

Woodhouse Farm

Uphay Farm

Sunnylands Cross

Marsh Farm

Dulcis Farm

Uphay La

River Axe

Burrow Knap

Burrow Farm Gdns

Sheppard's Knap

Loughwood

Loughwood Farm

Studhayes Rd

Marsh Dro

Studhayes Farm

Corry Brook

Lower Westwater Dairy Farm

Tourcross Hill

Pettman La

Linecard La

AXMINSTER

Mury La

LC

Andrewshayes Farm

Andrewshayes La

Fordhayes Farm

Millgreen La

Coryton

Hunthay Farm

Castle Hc

PO

West St

Chard St A358

North St

Liby

Smiths Ft
Old Taunton Rd
Shute La

Studhayes Cross

Coryton La

Whitehayes Cl

The Cross

6 Newtons Orch
7 Lynhayes
8 Silver St
9 Silver Lea
10 The Orchard
11 Whitford Rd
12 Brookside Cl
13 Whitehayes Cl
14 Dares Field

Hunthay La

George St
The Hill
Mus

Lyme Cl

Taunton Cross

Bakers La Mead

Hill Crest 1
The Hill 2
Balfour Terr 3
Salisbury Terr 4
The Crescent 5

Roman Rd

Ashes Rd

Shute Rd

Well Mead

Springhead La

Meadow Bank

Gammons Hill
A35

Coryton

Axminster

B3261 THE TRAFALGAR WAY

A358

Foxhill

Packhayne La

8
05
7
04
6
5
02
4
01
3
00
2
99
1
98

24 A **25** B **26** C **27** D **28** E **29** F

For full street detail of the highlighted area see page 167.

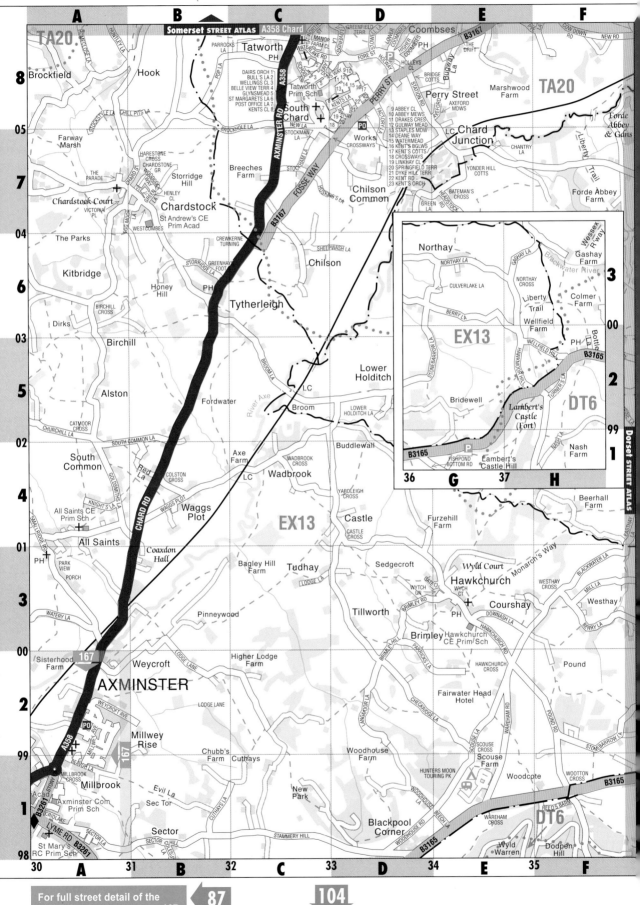

Somerset STREET ATLAS   A358 Chard

TA20

Brockfield
Hook
Tatworth
PH

DAIRS ORCH 1
BULL'S LA 2
BELLE VIEW TERR 4
GLYNSMEAD 5
ST MARGARETS LA 6
POST OFFICE LA 7
KENTS CL 8

Coombses
Perry Street
Marshwood Farm
TA20

Forde Abbey & Gdns

South Chard
Chilson Common

9 ABBEY CL
10 ABBEY MEWS
11 DRAKES CRES
12 GULWAY MEAD
13 STAPLES MDW
14 DEANE WAY
15 WATERMEAD
16 KENT'S BGLWS
17 KENT'S COTTS
18 CROSSWAYS
19 LINKHAY CL
20 SPRINGFIELD TERR
21 DYKE HILL TERR
22 KENT RD
23 KENT'S ORCH

Lc Chard Junction

Farway Marsh

Harestone Cross
Chardstock Court
Chardstock
St Andrew's CE Prim Acad
Storridge Hill
Breeches Farm

Forde Abbey Farm

The Parks
Kitbridge
Honey Hill
Tytherleigh
Chilson

Dirks
Birchill Cross
Birchill
Alston

Northay
Northay Cross
Gashay Farm
Colmer Farm
Liberty Trail
Wellfield Farm
EX13
Bridewell
Wellfield Hill
PH
B3165
DT6
Lambert's Castle (Fort)
Lambert's Castle Hill
B3165
Fishpond Bottom Rd
Nash Farm

Fordwater
Broom
Lower Holditch
Lower Holditch La

Catmoor Cross
Churchill La
South Common La
South Common
Red La
Colston Cross
Axe Farm
LC
Wadbrook
Buddlewall
Beerhall Farm

Knight's La
All Saints CE Prim Sch
Waggs Plot
EX13
Castle
Castle Cross
Furzehill Farm
Yardleigh Cross

PH
Park View
Porch
All Saints
Coaxdon Hall
Bagley Hill Farm
Tudhay
Sedgecroft
Wyld Court
Hawkchurch
Courshay
Westhay Cross
Westhay

Watery La
Pinneywood
Tillworth
Brimley
Hawkchurch CE Prim Sch
Pound

Sisterhood Farm
167
Weycroft
Higher Lodge Farm
Lodge Lane
Hawkchurch Cross
Fairwater Head Hotel

AXMINSTER
Lodge Lane
Woodhouse Farm
Scouse Cross
Scouse Farm
Woodcote
Wootton Cross

Weycroft Ave
Millwey Rise
Chubb's Farm
Cuthays
New Park
Hunters Moon Touring Pk
B3165

Axminster Com Prim Sch
Millbrook
Evil La
Sec Tor
Blackpool Corner
Wareham Cross
DT6

St Mary's RC Prim Sch
B3261
Sector
Cuthays La
Stammery Hill
Wyld Warren
Dodpen Hill

TA20

DT6

Dorset STREET ATLAS

87

104

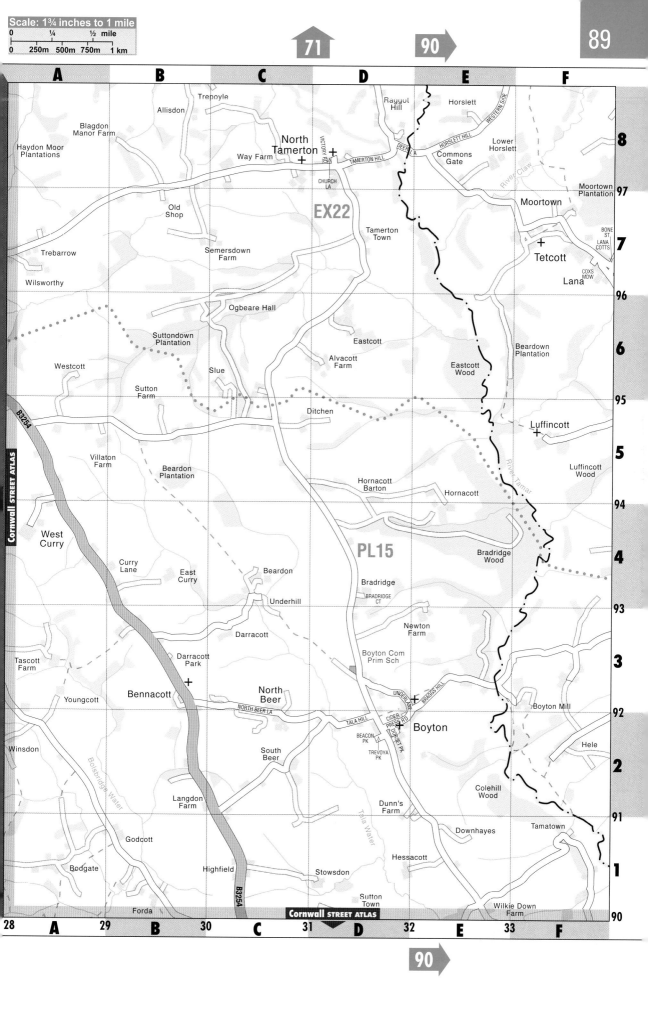

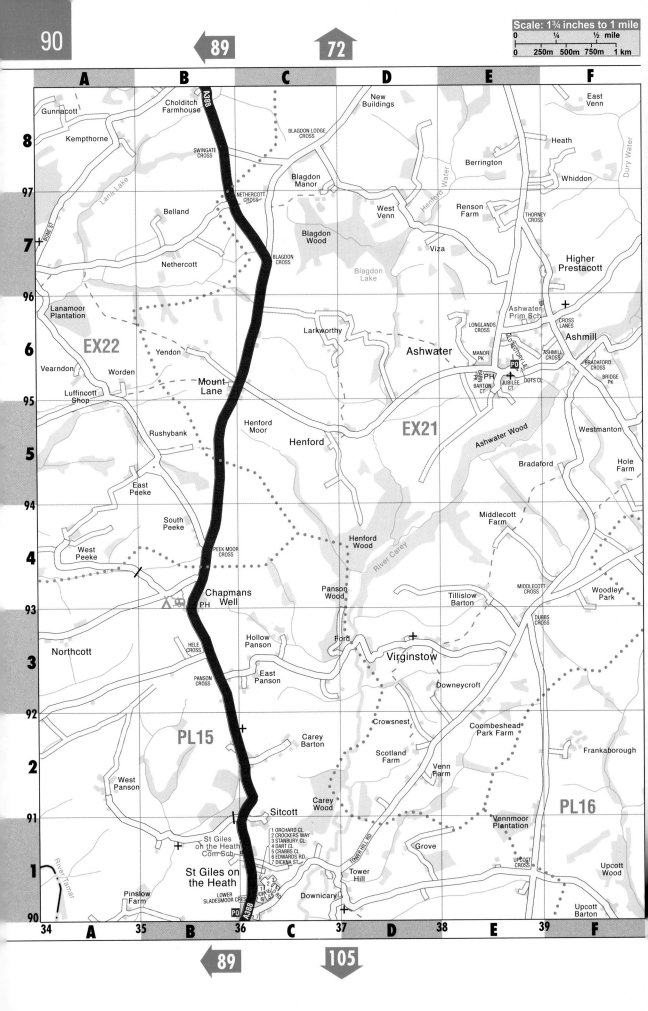

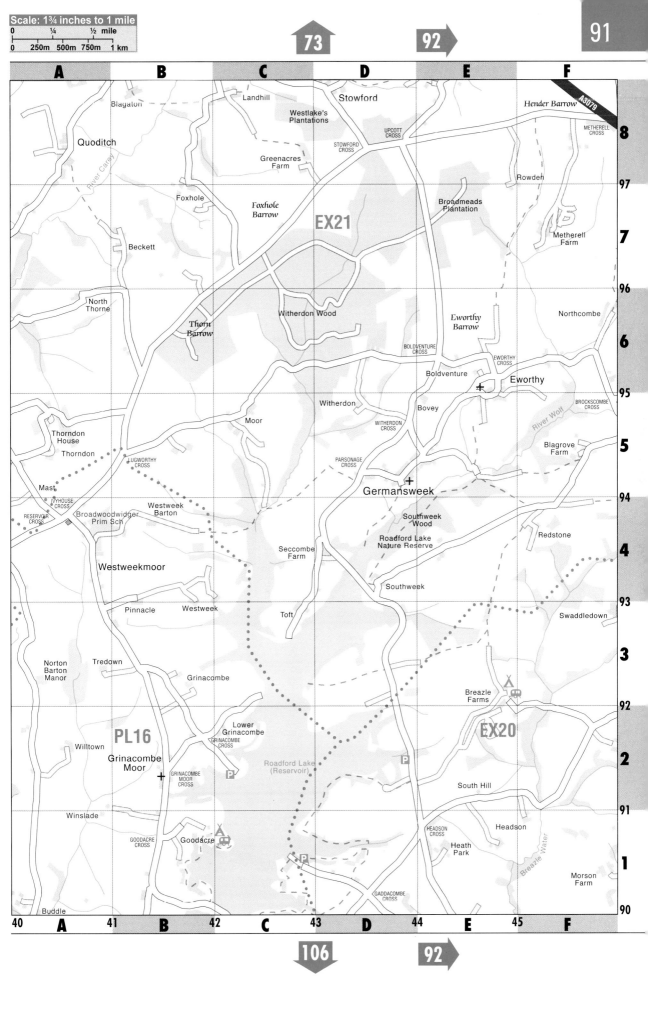

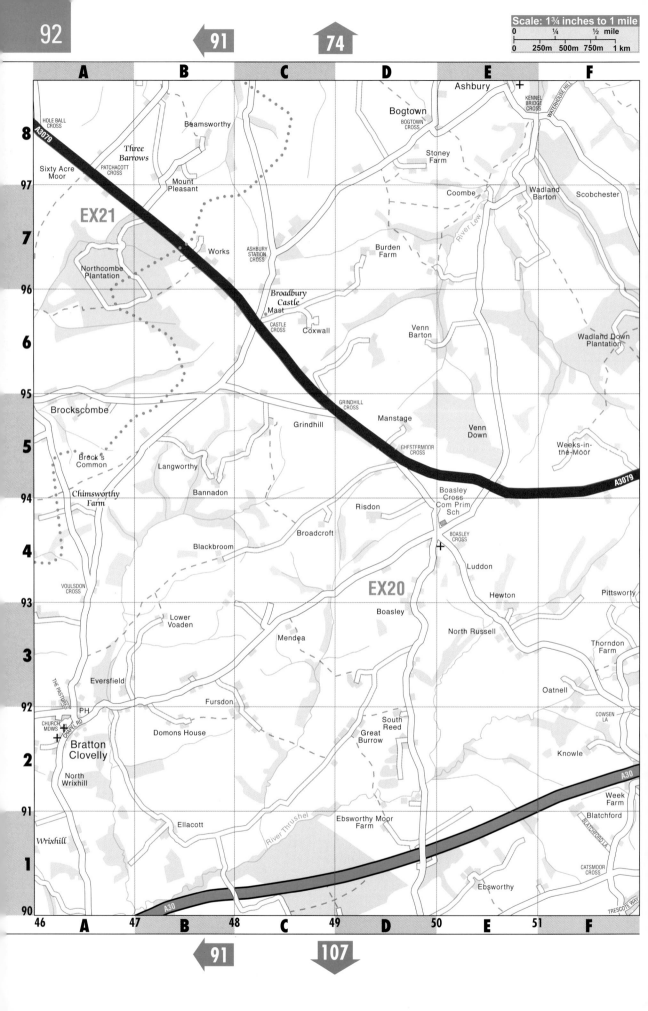

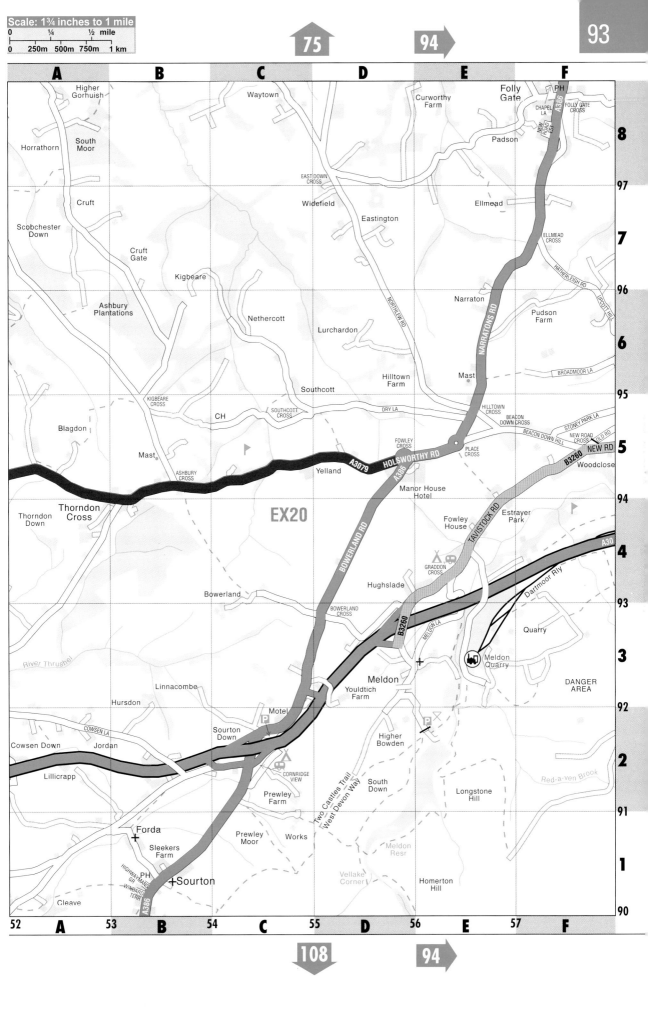

A   B   C   D   E   F

8

Abbeyford Woods Forest Wlks   Brightley   Agistment Farm   Appledore Farm   West Hill   Lydcott   Trehill Farm   Aller La   SHOALGATE CROSS

BRIGHTLEY CROSS

97   Mast   170   Knowle Farm   Webber Hill Farm   Glendon Cross   Glendon   Church Hill Cross   Restland   Restland La

OKEHAMPTON   Chichacott   Chichacott Rd   North Alfordon   Corscombe   Beer

7   Hook   Knowle Bridge   Barton Farm   Chichacott Cross   Ind Est   Beer Cross   Reddaway

Higher Upcott   Tarka Trail   Fern Mdw   Ind Est   Stockley   Ball Hill Farm   Corscombe La

96   Oaklands   Sch   Crediton Rd   Stockley Hamlet   Corscombe Down

Upcott Hill   Okehampton Com   Baldwin Dr   Cranmere Rd   Fatherford Farm   Crossway Cross   A30

Sch   Glendale Rd   Exeter Rd   Hameldown Rd   B3260

6   Lodge   Liby   TH   H   B3215   Motel   Coombe Head   Bude

Eore St   East St   Giblands Cross   Great West Tor Rd   Tongue End Cross   Greenhill Farm

95   PO   The Beacon   Fatherford Rd   Westlake   Eastlake   Crossway Cross

West St   New Rd   Ball Hill   Coll   Tor Down   Priestacott   EX20

Castle La   Dartmoor Way   Westlake   Skaigh   Grove Mdw

5   B3260   Okehampton   Tarka Trail   Tor Down   Belstone Cross   Belstone Cleave   Skaigh Warren

West Devon Way   Parklands   YH   West Cleave

Castle   Two Castles Trail   Camp Rd   Cleave House   Belstone Cross

94   CH   A30   Well & Cross   YH   East Hill   Old Rectory Farm   Belstone   PH

Okehampton Park   Camp Rd   Lower Halstock   Belstone   Birchy Lake

Moor Brook   Halstock Wood   Tarka Trail

93   Camp   170   Moorgate Farm   East Bowden   East Bowden Wood   Watchet Hill

East Hill   Higher Halstock   Nine Stones

3   Black Down   Danger Area   Black-a-ven Brook   Scarey Tor   Belstone Common   River Taw   Foxes' Holt

Cullever Steps   Belstone Tor   Irishman's Wall

92

2   Cosdon Hill

East Okemont Farm   South Tawton Common

91   West Mill Tor   White Hill   Small Brook

1   Danger Area   Taw Marsh

Yes Tor   New Bridge   East Mill Tor   Oke Tor   Raybarrow Pool

90

58   A   59   B   60   C   61   D   62   E   63   F

For full street detail of the highlighted area see page 170.

93   109

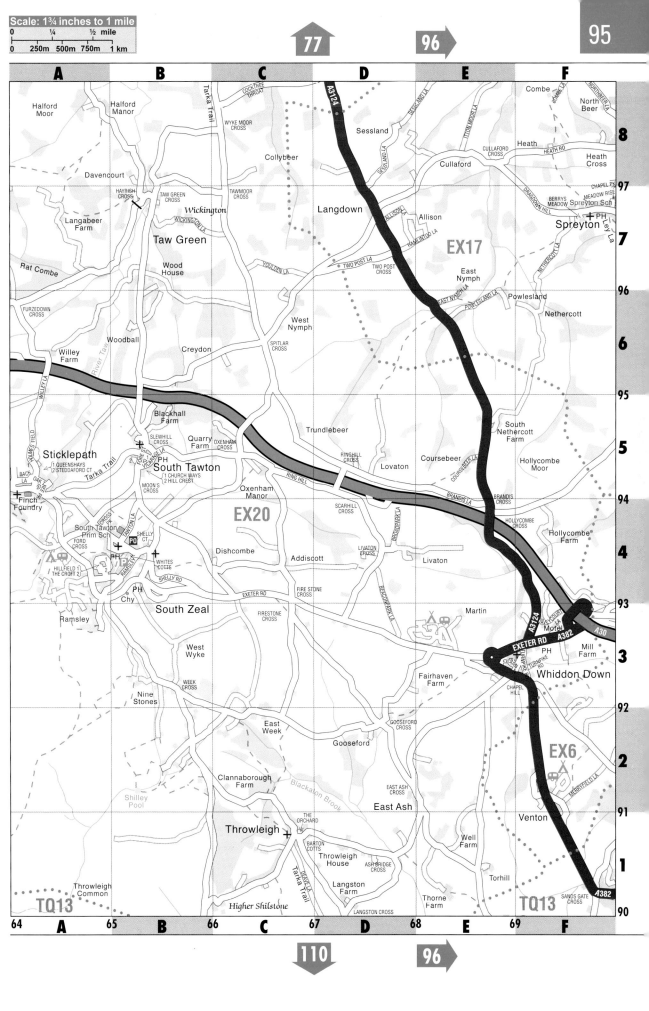

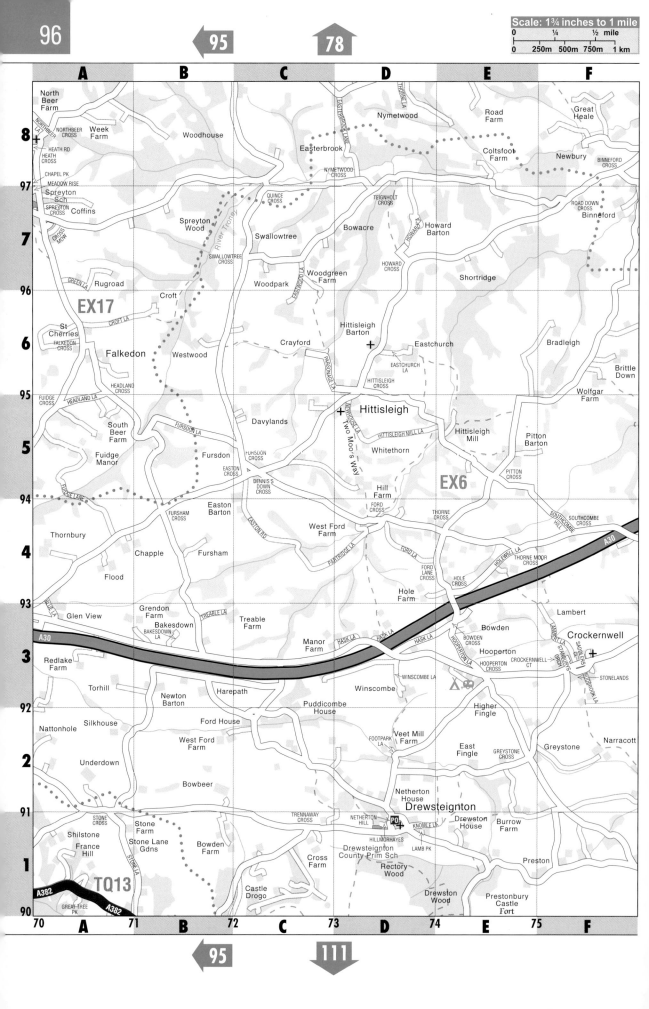

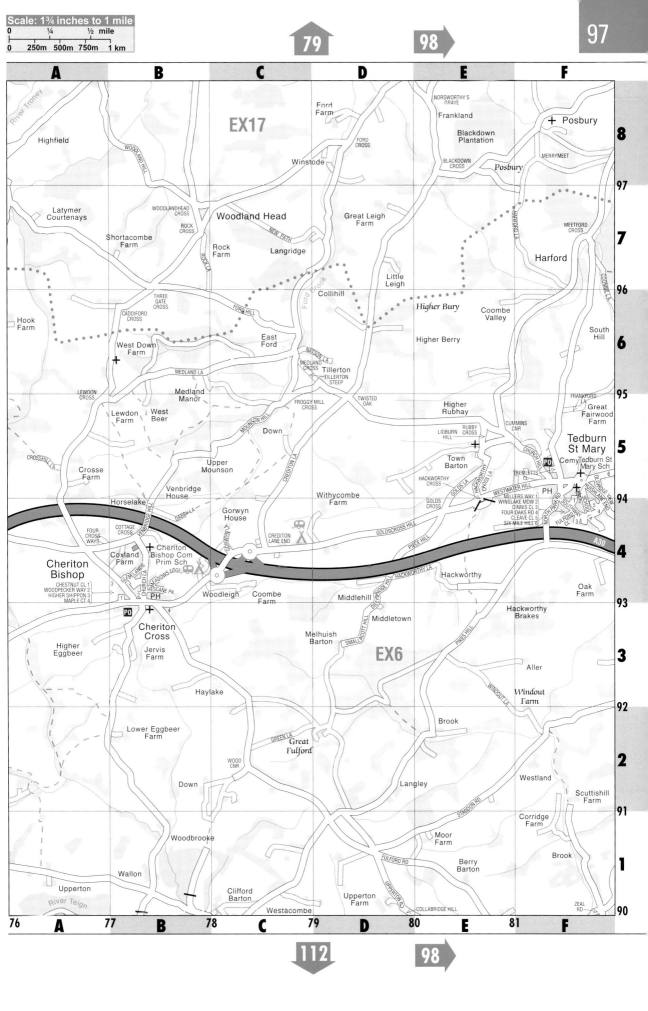

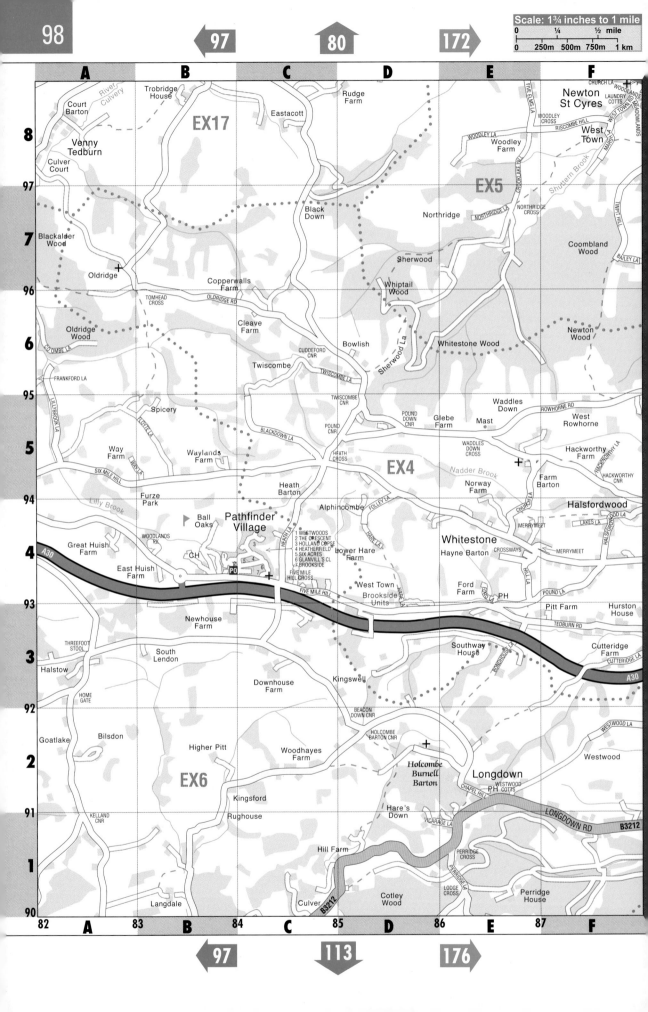

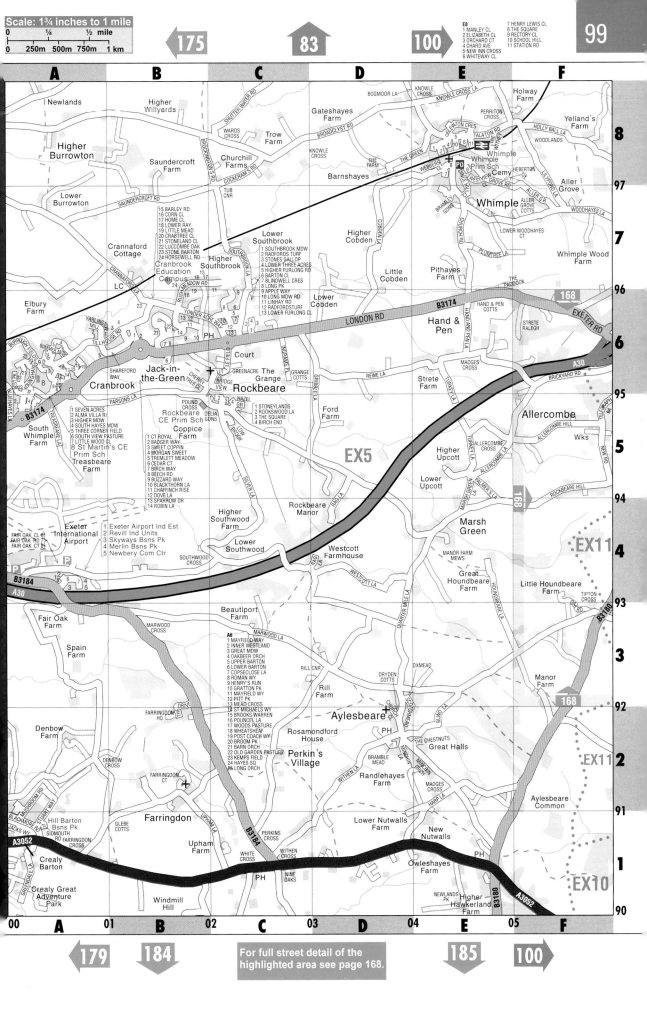

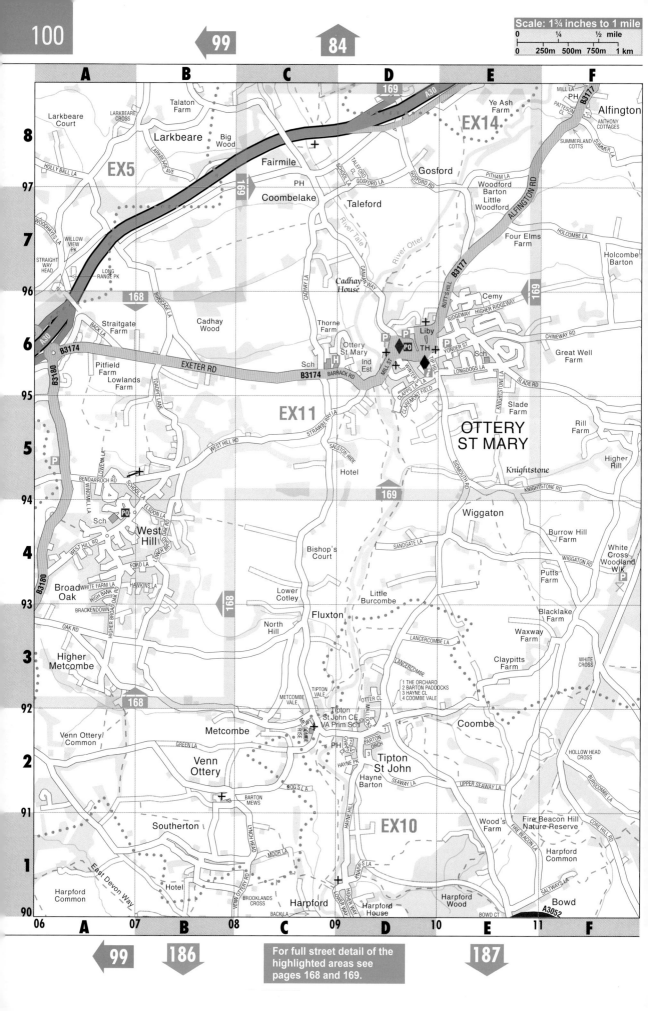

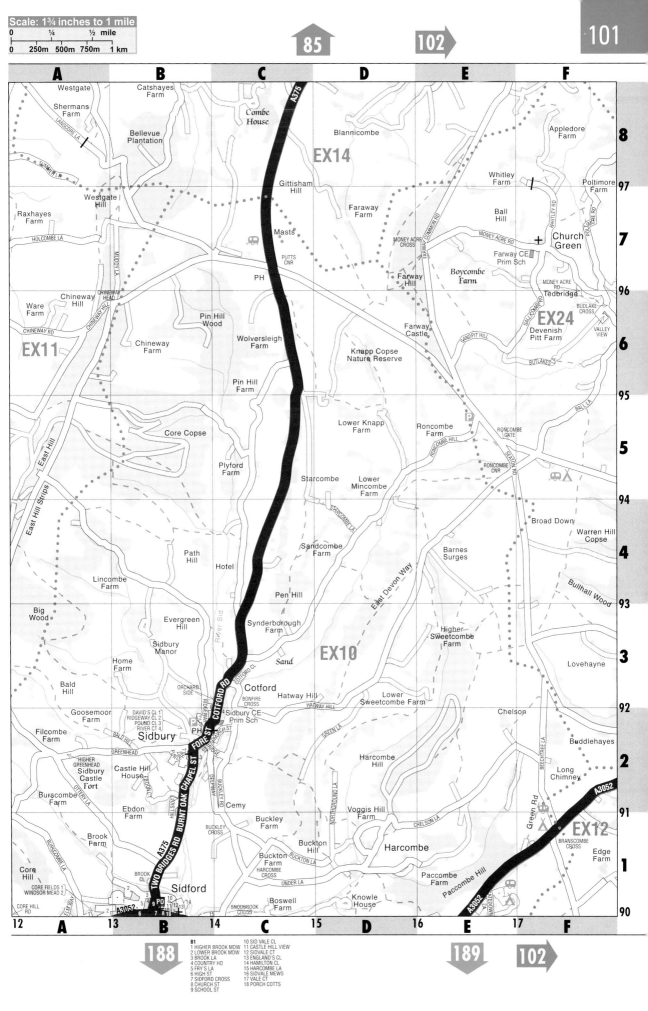

101
86

Scale: 1¾ inches to 1 mile

0 ¼ ½ mile
0 250m 500m 750m 1 km

A B C D E F

8

Glanville Farm
EX14
Townshayne Common
Slade
Home Bush
EX14
Watchcombe
COLCOMBE LA
CHURCH PATH
Bucknole Cross
Summerdown
OFFWELL TURN
Smallicombe Farm
Cookshayes Farm
EX13
Umborne

97

Offwell Brook
Northleigh Cross
Blamphayne Farm
Stockers Farm
Sutton Thorn
Blamphayne Cross
PAINTER'S CROSS
BLIND LA
EASY BRIDGE CROSS

7

Bucknole Farm
COMBE LA
Tricombe
Rockerhayne Cross
Parehayne Hill
Parehayne Farm
Logshayne Farm
LILYLAKE CROSS
COOKLEY LA
CHAPEL KNAP

WARREN LA
BUCKNOLL HILL RD
Chilcombe
CHILCOMBE CROSS
Northleigh
Rockerhayne

96

Netherton Barton
HILLSIDE
BUCKHOUSE
Ball Hill
Road Pitt Farm
Hamberhayne Farm
Carswells Moor
Downhayne Farm
Tritchayne
THREE SYCAMORES CROSS
Yardbury Farm

BALL LA
CHILCOMBE LA
Farway
COLYTON RD
FARWOOD CROSS
HAMBERHAYNE CROSS
Barritshayes
GATE CROSS
WATERY LA
TOM'S CLOSE HILL

6

WOODBRIDGE LA
Farwood Barton
PURLBRIDGE CROSS
COLEMAN'S CROSS
NORTHLEIGH RD
East Devon Way
Streathayne House
Hooperhayne
RED CROSS
Gittshayne Farm
GITTSHAYNE LA

Goldacre Farm
SUDDON'S CROSS
Woodbridge
SUDDON'S LA
BLACKACRE RD
DOWNHAYNE RD
HOOPERHAYNE RD

95

Widcombe Barton Farm
Holnest Farm
HORNSHAYNE RD
Knowle Hill
Bonehayne
River Coly
RATSHOLE GATE
WILLHAYNE LA

Widcombe Wood
Hornshayne Farm
STUBBING CROSS
Moorplash Farm
BONEHAYNE AND PURLBRIDGE RD
Heathayne
HEATHAYNE CROSS
SIDMOUTH RD

5

EX24
Great Pen
Wadden
QITTSHAYNE LA
SOUTHLEIGH RD
GUERNSEY CNR
SOUTH LA

Whitmoor
Blackley Down
Scruel Barton
Ox Hill
OX HILL LA
RIDGWAY LA
CLAYLA

94

Glebe House
Southleigh
WADDENS CROSS
Ridgeway
NEW SIDMOUTH RD
OLD SIDMOUTH RD

Higher Wiscombe
Eppitts
HILLSIDE
Morganhayes
MORGANHAYES CROSS
JOBBLE'S LA
SAND PIT HILL
Bolshayne Farm

93

Wiscombe Park
Southleigh Hills
Colyton Hill
WHITE GATE
Whitwell Farm
WHITWELL LA
SALTER'S LA

Blackbury Castle Settlement
Weekhayne
Morganhayes Covert
Holyford
HOLYFORD LA

3

SOUTHLEIGH HILL CROSS
P
Stockham
GREEN LA
Pratt's Hill
Holyford Woods Nature Reserve

Little Farm
BURNBREACH CNR
Ashdown Farm
Seaton Down

92

Radish Plantation
SEATON RD
TRAVISTALA
PH
Borcombe Farm
Bovey Down
EX12
HAREPATH HILL
A3052
BARNARDS LA

2

A3052
Meml
STAFFORD CROSS
GATCOMBE ASH
Hotel
Gatcombe Farm
B3172
AXEVIEW RD
WYCHALL PK

91

190
Hangman's Stone
B3174
191
Seaton Down Hill
SEATON DOWN HILL

Elverway Farm
LOCKSEY'S LA
HOLLYHEAD RD
Couchill Farm
CHURSTON RISE
MARGPITLA

1

190
Rockenhayne
Bovey House
B3174
HOLYHEAD CROSS
STOVARLONG LA
BURNS LA
DUFFIELD RD

90

WOODHEAD CROSS
BOVEY LA
Woodhead
B3174
SELLER'S WOOD HILL

18 A 19 B 20 C 21 D 22 E 23 F

101
190
191

For full street detail of the highlighted area see pages 190 and 191.

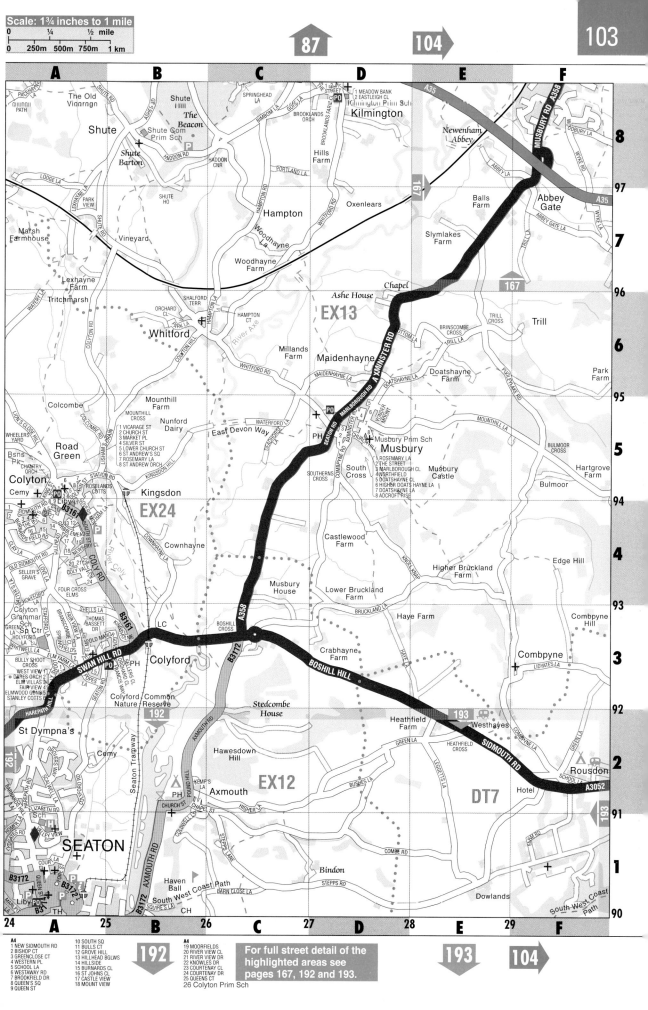

Scale: 1¾ inches to 1 mile

0 ¼ ½ mile
0 250m 500m 750m 1 km

A B C D E F

8

Old Park Farm
Lower Beavor
Beavor Grange
Coles's Farm
Coles's La
Woodside Cl
Higher Pound Farm
Wyld Warren
Dodpen Hill Ridge Farm
B3261 LYME RD
Furzeleigh House
Bever Batch
Lower Pound Farm
Champernhayes Marsh
Woodbury La
Old Park
Furzeleigh Farm
Axe Valley Cl
Marsh Farm
Wootton Hill

97

Chattan
A35
B3261
Cooks La
Monkton Wyld Cross
Pound La
DT6
Champernhayes La

7

Wyke Green
167
Burrowshot Cross
Pidgeon's La
Coppice Cl
PH
Crewkerne Rd
Green La
Scott's La B3165
Monkton Wyld
Eggon La
Higher Wyld Farm
Monkton Wyld La
Champernhayes Farmhouse
Spence Farm
Spence La

EX13
Raymond's Hill
PO
Charmouth Rd
B3165
Red Cross
Monkton Wyld
Meerhay La

96

Trinity Hill Nature Reserve
Rocombe Cross
Harcombe Cross
Redlane Cross
Harcombe Rd
Penn
Thistle Hill
Westover Hill
Hogchester Farm
Mill La

P
St Marys
Yawl Cross
Yawl Hill
Yawl Hill La
Harcombe Bottom
Haddon's La
Rookery
260
Hole Common
Cemy
Dorset Street Atlas A35 Bridport

6

Woodhouse Hill
Yawl Bottom
Knoll Hill
Rocombe Bottom
Carswell Farm
The Coach Rd
Whitty Hill
Rhode Hill
Sleech Wood
Hole Common
Fern Hill
Hotel FERNHILL HTS
A3052
A35
Lily Farmhouse
Axminster Rd

5

Five Barrow La
Trinity Hill Rd
St Mary's La
Yawl Cres
Lyme Rd
Cathole La
Yawl
Uplyme
Sch
Spring Head Rd
Liberty Trail
Rhode La
Rhode Barton
Rhode Hill
Dragon's Hill
Charmouth Bypass
CH
P&R
Timber Hill
Charmouth
Charberry Rise 1
Westcliff Rd 2
Greenhayes 3
Downside Cl 4
Old Lyme Hill
Old Lyme Rd

94

West Hill Farm
East Devon Way
Woodhouse La
Woodhouse
Hotel
PO
Pound La
Mill La
Croggs La
Kippers La
DT7
Wessex Ridgeway
River Lim
Talbot Rd
Timber Hill
Black Ven

4

Shapwick Hill
Holcombe La
Holcombe
Hook Farm
260
Whalley La
Barbers La
Gore La
Sch
Up Lyme Rd
Haye La
Woodmead
South Ave
Queens Wk
Cemy
Sch
Kingsway
Anning Rd
Charmouth Rd
260
The Spittles

3

Combpyne Hill
Cannington Farm
Canning Dn La
Horseman's Hill
Shire La
Somers Rd
Up Lyme Rd
Silver St
B3165
PO
Mill
Broad St
Church St
Lyme Bay

2

Lidyates La
Shapwick Grange Farm
P&R
Sidmouth Rd
Pound St
Pine Ave
Cobb Rd
Marine Par
TH
Mus
LYME REGIS
Pinhay Hollow
Ware La
Ware Farm
Underhill Farm
Cobb
P
Aquarium
The Cobb
Poker's Pool

A3052
Charton Cross
Pinhay
South West Coast Path
Seven Rock Point
260

1

Whitlands House
Pinhay Bay

90

Charton
Humble Point

30 A 31 B 32 C 33 D 34 E 35 F

For full street detail of the highlighted areas see pages 167 and 260.

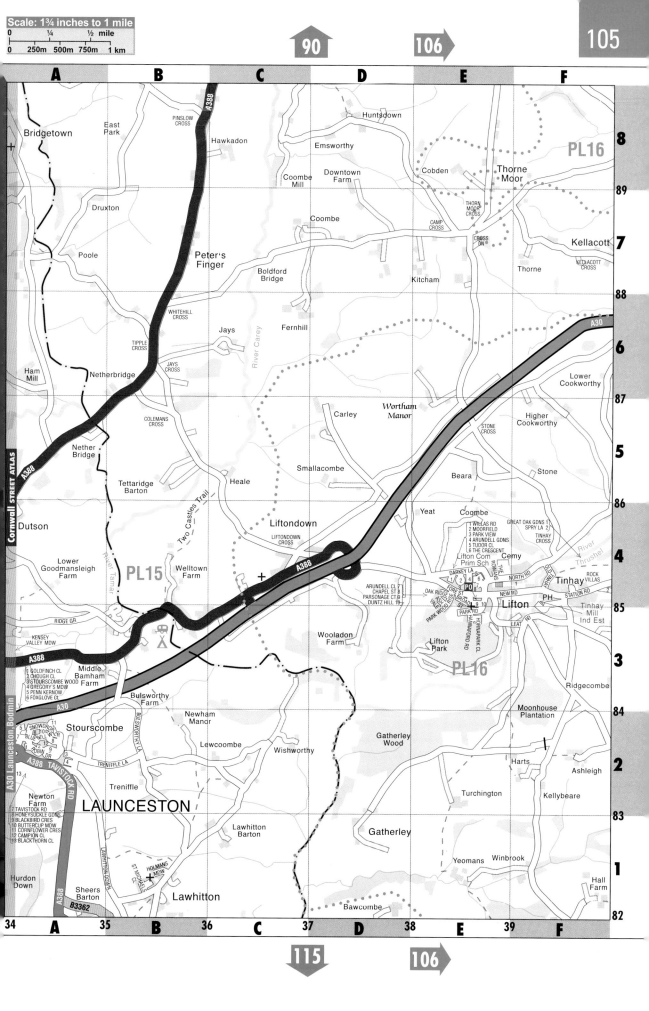

Scale: 1¾ inches to 1 mile

Cornwall STREET ATLAS

A30 Launceston, Bodmin

PL16

PL15

PL16

Bridgetown
East Park
Pinslow Cross
Hawkadon
Huntsdown
Cobden
Thorne Moor
Druxton
Emsworthy
Coombe Mill
Downtown Farm
Coombe
THORN MOOR CROSS
CAMP CROSS
CROSS GN
Kellacott
Poole
Peter's Finger
Boldford Bridge
Kitcham
Thorne
KELLACOTT CROSS
WHITEHILL CROSS
TIPPLE CROSS
Jays
River Carey
Fernhill
A30
Ham Mill
Netherbridge
JAYS CROSS
Lower Cookworthy
Nether Bridge
COLEMANS CROSS
Carley
Wortham Manor
STONE CROSS
Higher Cookworthy
A388
River Tamar
Tettaridge Barton
Heale
Smallacombe
Beara
Stone
Dutson
Two Castles Trail
Liftondown
LIFTONDOWN CROSS
Yeat
Coombe
1 WILLAS RD
2 MOORFIELD
3 PARK VIEW
4 ARUNDELL GDNS
5 TUDOR CL
6 THE CRESCENT
GREAT OAK GDNS 1
SPRY LA 2
TINHAY CROSS
River Thrushel
Lower Goodmansleigh Farm
Welltown Farm
A388
Lifton Com Prim Sch
DARKEY LA
THE ROWANS
NORTH RD
OLD HWYN
ROCK VILLAS
Tinhay
ARUNDELL CL 7
CHAPEL ST 8
PARSONAGE CT 9
DUNTZ HILL 10
OAK RIDGE
FORE ST
BROAD ST
PO
NEW RD
Lifton
STATION RD
PH
Tinhay Mill Ind Est
RIDGE GR
KENSEY VALLEY MDW
A388
A30
1 GOLDFINCH CL
2 CHOUGH CL
3 STOURSCOMBE WOOD
4 GREGORY'S MDW
5 PENN KERNOW
6 FOXGLOVE CL
Middle Bamham Farm
Wooladon Farm
PARK WOOD
HORNAPARK CL
HARNAFORD RD
PARK RD
LEAT RD
Lifton Park
Ridgecombe
Bulsworthy Farm
Moonhouse Plantation
Stourscombe
BULSWORTHY LA
Newham Manor
Lewcoombe
Wishworthy
Gatherley Wood
Harts
Ashleigh
SNOWDROP
BLUEBELL
ROBIN
TRENIFFLE LA
Treniffle
Turchington
Kellybeare
Newton Farm
7 TAVISTOCK RD
8 HONEYSUCKLE GDNS
9 BLACKBIRD CRES
10 BUTTERCUP MDW
11 CORNFLOWER CRES
12 CAMPION CL
13 BLACKTHORN CL
LAUNCESTON
A388 TAVISTOCK RD
LAWHITTON DOWN
Lawhitton Barton
Gatherley
Yeomans
Winbrook
Hurdon Down
Sheers Barton
B3362
ST MICHAELS CL
HOLMANS MDW
Lawhitton
Bawcombe
Hall Farm

90
106
115
106

105
91

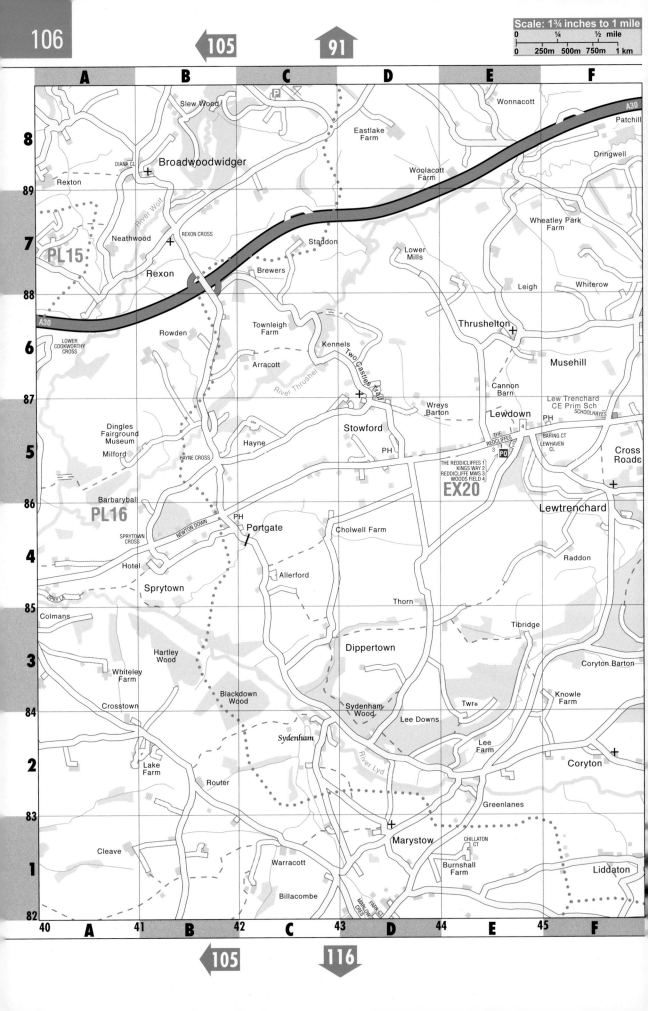

A30
Patchill
Wonnacott
Dringwell
Eastlake Farm
Slew Wood
Woolacott Farm
Wheatley Park Farm
Broadwoodwidger
DIANA CL
Rexton
Whiterow
Leigh
Lower Mills
Staddon
River Wolf
PL15
Neathwood
REXON CROSS
Rexon
Brewers
Thrushelton
Rowden
Townleigh Farm
Kennels
Musehill
LOWER COOKWORTHY CROSS
Arracott
River Thrushel
Two Castles Trail
Cannon Barn
Lew Trenchard CE Prim Sch
SCHOOLHAYES
Wreys Barton
Lewdown
PH
Dingles Fairground Museum
Hayne
Stowford
THE REDDICLIFFES
PH
BARING CT
LEWHAVEN CL
Milford
HAYNE CROSS
4
Cross Roads
PO
THE REDDICLIFFES 1
KINGS WAY 2
REDDICLIFFE MWS 3
WOODS FIELD 4
Barbaryball
EX20
PL16
Lewtrenchard
PH
Portgate
Cholwell Farm
NEWTON DOWN
SPRYTOWN CROSS
Raddon
Hotel
Allerford
Coryton Barton
Sprytown
Thorn
Colmans
Knowle Farm
Hartley Wood
Dippertown
Tibridge
Whiteley Farm
Twr
Sydenham Wood
Lee Downs
Crosstown
Blackdown Wood
Lee Farm
Coryton
Sydenham
River Lyd
Lake Farm
Router
Greenlanes
Cleave
Marystow
CHILLATON CT
Liddaton
Warracott
Burnshall Farm
Billacombe
PARK CT
MARLOW CROSS

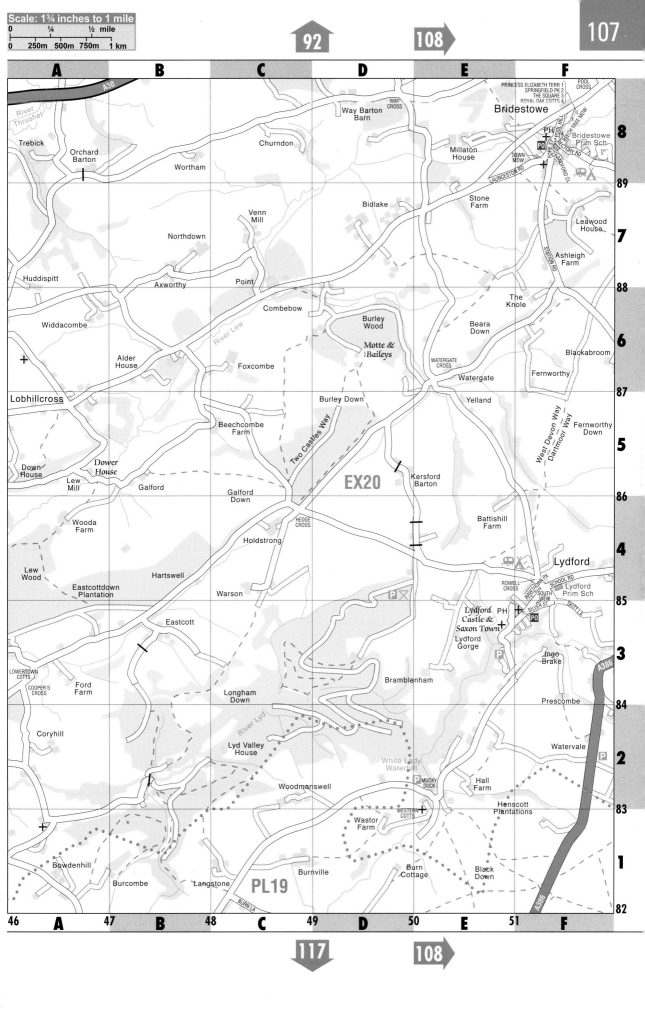

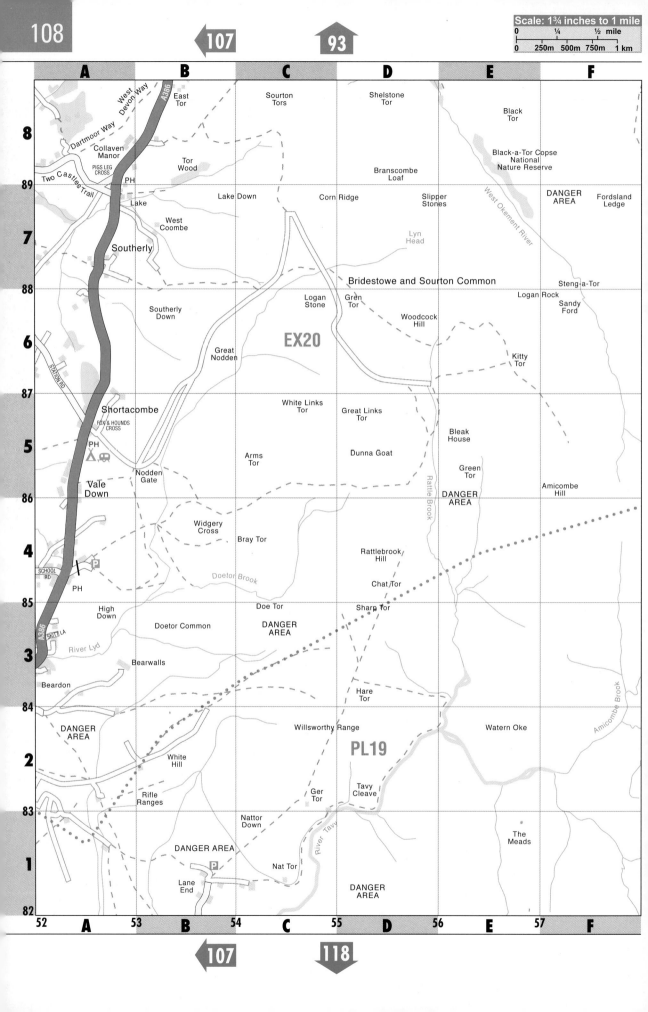

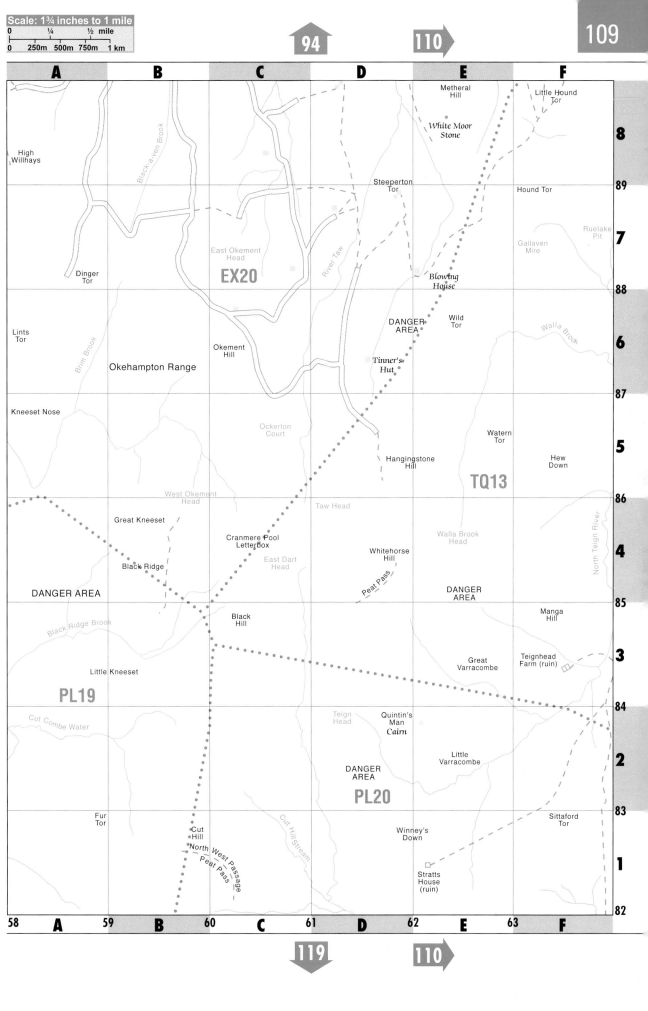

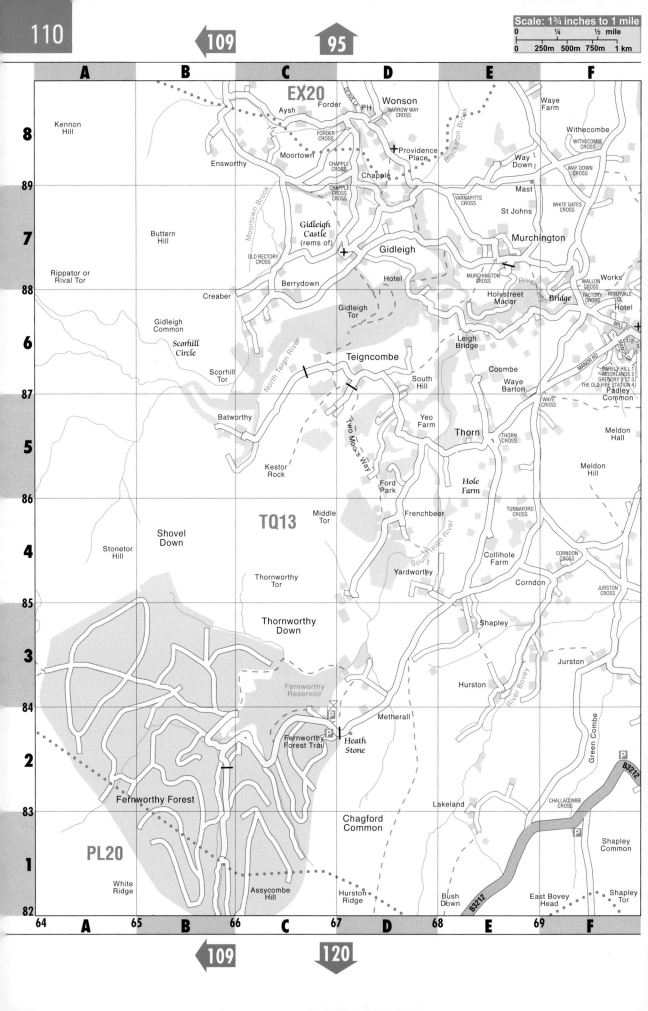

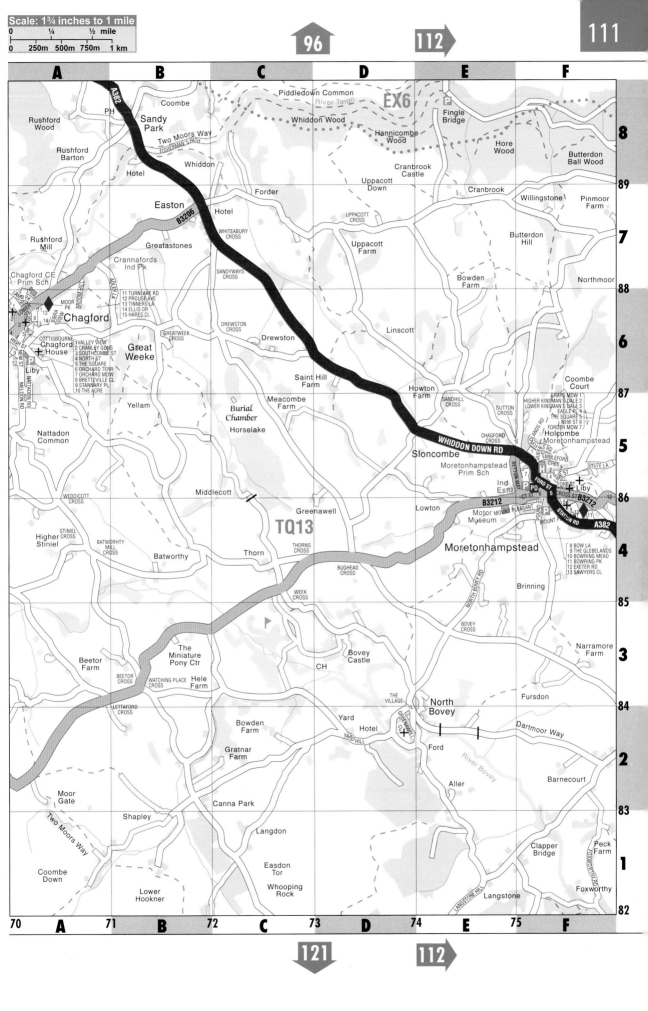

Scale: 1¾ inches to 1 mile

0   ¼   ½   mile
0   250m   500m   750m   1 km

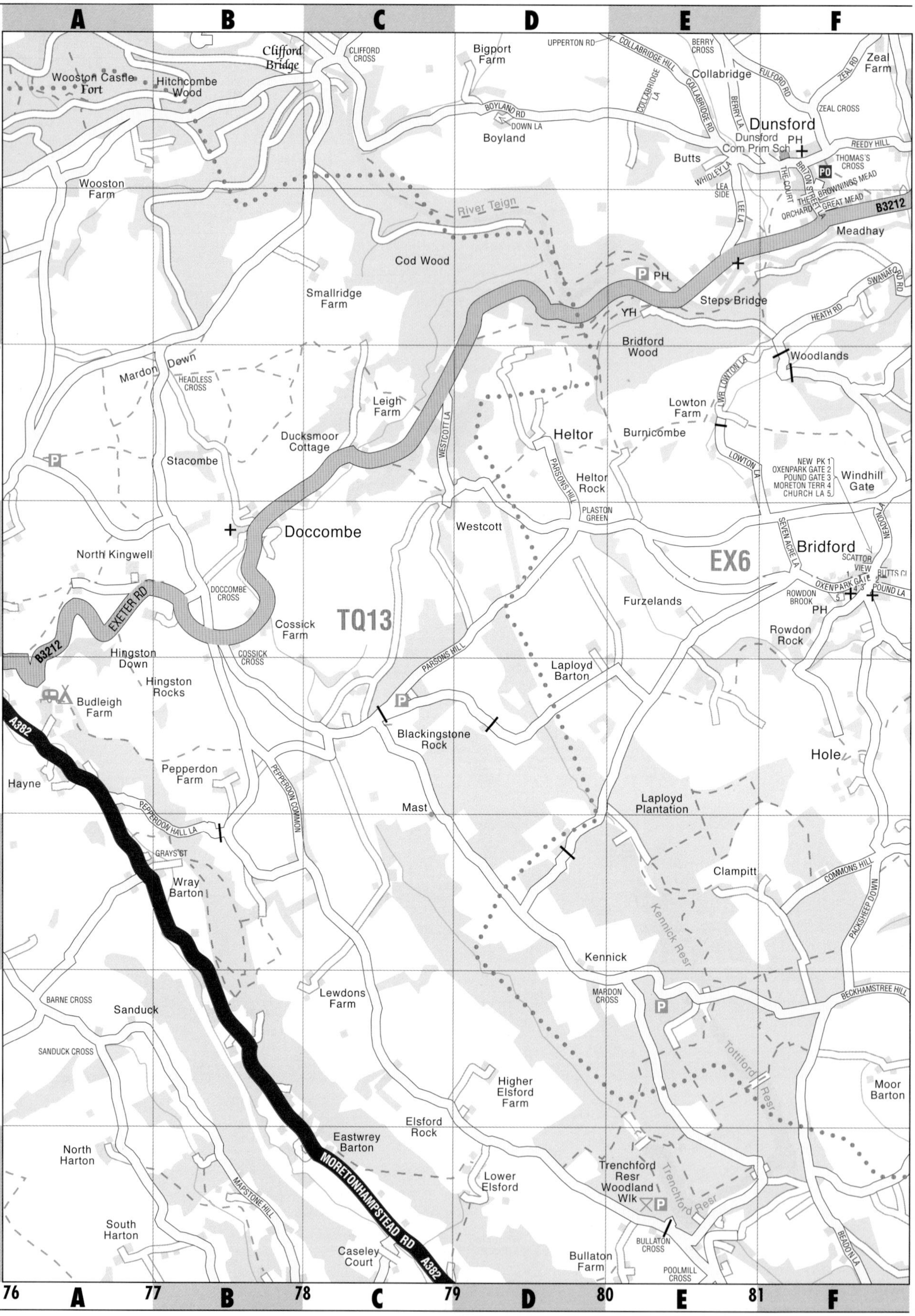

A B C D E F

8 89 7 88 6 87 5 86 4 85 3 84 2 83 1 82

Wooston Castle Fort
Hitchcombe Wood
Clifford Bridge
Clifford Cross
Bigport Farm
UPPERTON RD
COLLABRIDGE HILL
BERRY CROSS
Collabridge
FULFORD RD
ZEAL FARM
ZEAL CROSS
COLLABRIDGE LA
COLLABRIDGE RD
BERRY LA
Dunsford
Dunsford Com Prim Sch
PH
REEDY HILL
Butts
WHIDLEY LA
LEA SIDE
LEE LA
THOMAS'S CROSS
PO
BRITON STREET
THE COURT
ORCHARD
GREAT MEAD
BROWNING'S MEAD
B3212
Meadhay
Wooston Farm
BOYLAND RD
DOWN LA
Boyland
River Teign
Cod Wood
SWANAFORD RD
P PH
Steps Bridge
HEATH RD
Smallridge Farm
YH
Bridford Wood
Woodlands
LWR LOWTON LA
Mardon Down
HEADLESS CROSS
Leigh Farm
Lowton Farm
Burnicombe
LOWTON LA
Ducksmoor Cottage
WESTCOTT LA
Heltor
NEW PK 1 OXENPARK GATE 2 POUND GATE 3 MORETON TERR 4 CHURCH LA 5
Windhill Gate
Stacombe
Heltor Rock
PLASTON GREEN
P
North Kingwell
Doccombe
Westcott
PARSONS HILL
SEVEN ACRE LA
Bridford
SCATTOR VIEW
EX6
BUTTS CI
MALDON LA
OXENPARK GATE
POUND LA
PH
Doccombe Cross
Cossick Farm
TQ13
Furzelands
Rowdon Brook
Rowdon Rock
B3212
EXETER RD
Cossick Cross
Hingston Down
Hingston Rocks
PARSONS MILL
Laployd Barton
Hole
B3212
Budleigh Farm
A382
Pepperdon Farm
Blackingstone Rock
Hayne
PEPPERDON HALL LA
PEPPERDON COMMON
Mast
Laployd Plantation
Clampitt
COMMONS HILL
GRAYS GT
Wray Barton
Kennick
Kennick Resr
PACKSHEEP DOWN
BECKHAMSTREE HILL
Barne Cross
Sanduck
Lewdons Farm
MARDON CROSS
P
TOTTIFORD RESR
Moor Barton
Sanduck Cross
Higher Elsford Farm
Elsford Rock
North Harton
MAPSTONE HILL
MORETONHAMPSTEAD RD
Eastwrey Barton
Lower Elsford
Trenchford Resr Woodland Wlk
P
TRENCHFORD RESR
BEADON LA
South Harton
Caseley Court
A382
Bullaton Farm
BULLATON CROSS
POOLMILL CROSS

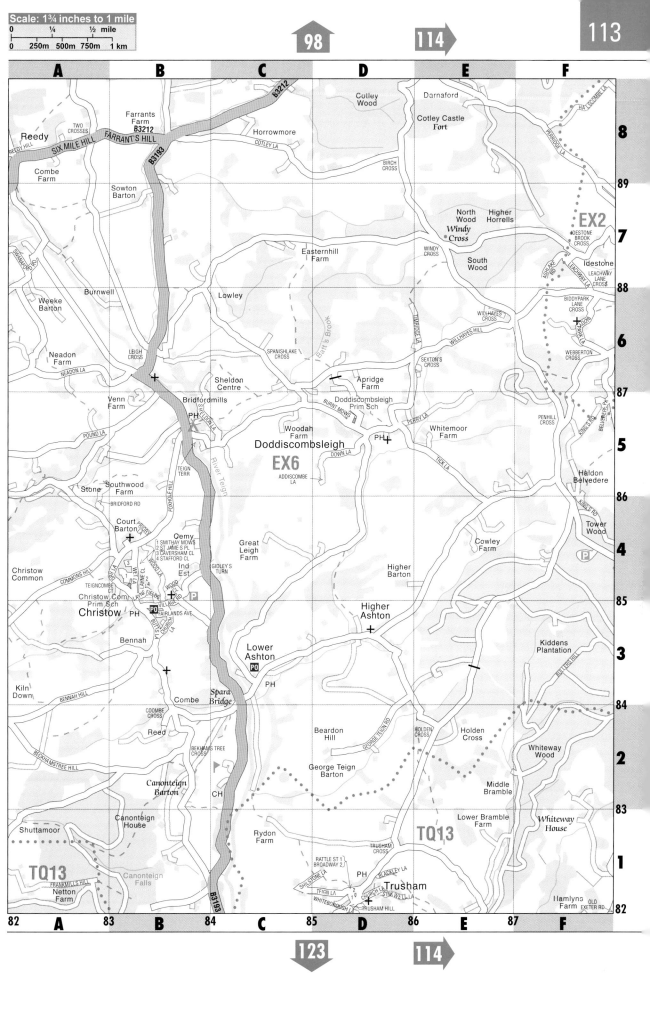

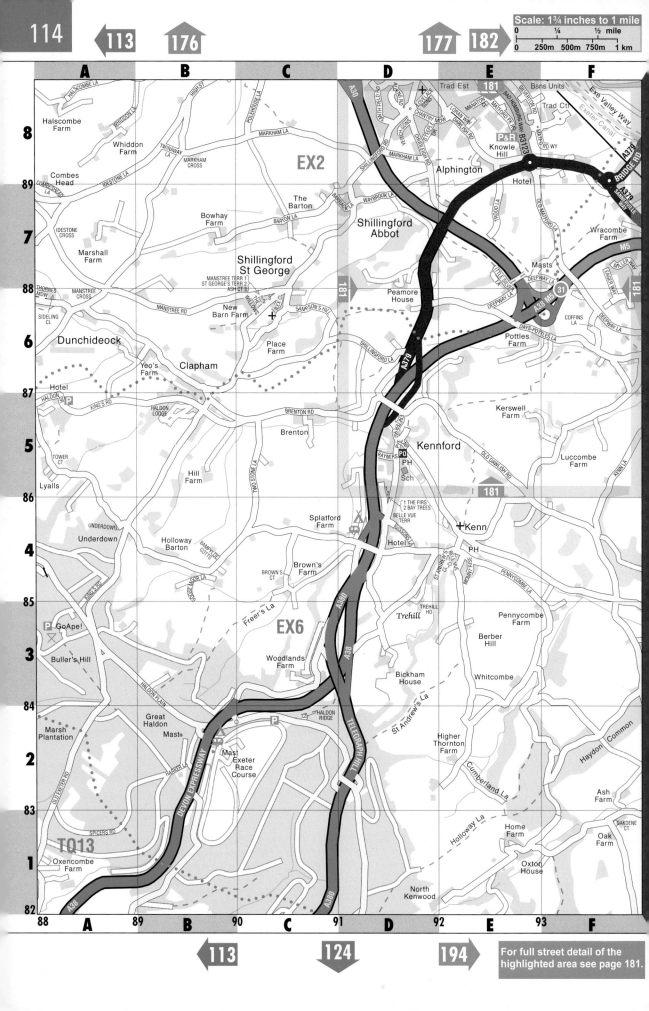

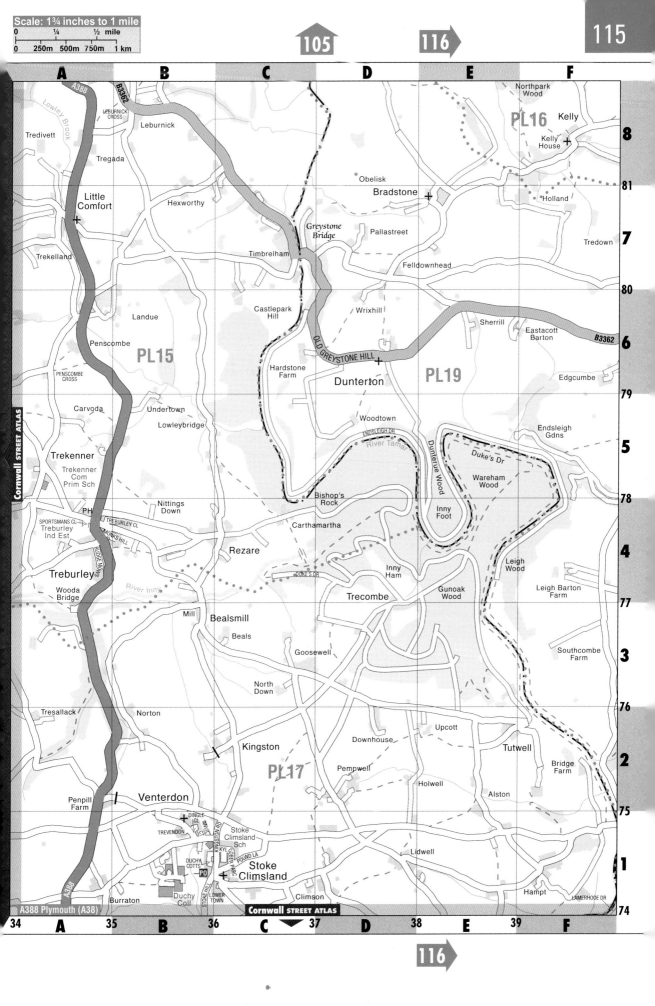

115
106

A **B** **C** **D** **E** **F**

Meadwell

Borough

Higher
Chillaton

PL16

Chillaton

PH
RIVERSIDE

Shute

Quither

Week

81

Downhouse

Narracott

Uppaton

Metherell

7

White Tor

Willesley

Quither Common

80

Beechwood

Cardwell

Higher
Edgecumbe

EDGCUMBE RD

1 LUTYENS FOLD
2 TAMAR VIEW
3 EDGCUMBE TERR

Milton
Abbot

PH THE VILLAGE

LONGCROSS COTTS

Mast

Heathfield

6

B3362

FORE ST OLD GREYSTONE HL

Longbrook
Farm

Longcross

THE PARADE

VICARAGE GDN

VENN
HILL

Milton Abbot Sch

79

Milton
Green

Short Burn
Farm

Foghanger

Higher
Haye

Tamar Valley Discovery Trail

5

Pittescombe

Coombe
Farm

Tuelldown

Willestrew

Great Haye
Farm

78

PL19

Hurlditch
Court

4

Hardicott
Farm

Tuell

Collacombe
Down

Chestnut Cl 1
Chestnut Terr 2

Court Barton Mews

Ford
Farm

Wonwood

Collacombe
Cross

CHERRY
CT

ORCHARD CT

CHURCH

Lamerton CE (VC)
Prim Sch

77

Youngcott

Derriton
Farm

Culverhill

Collacombe
Manor

Belgrove
House

TRENANCE
DR

GREEN HILL

SMITHWAYES

Beckadon

3

Beera
Farm

Portington

PH OUTER
DOWN

Lamerton

THE FARRIERS

76

Sydenham
Damerel

SUMMER GREEN 1
FORTESSQUE CT 2

Rushford

Venn
House

ORCHARD
COTTS

SYDENHAM
CROSS

LANE END
CROSS

Hartwell

Cholwell

Ottery Park
Ind Est

2

River Lumburn

Woodley

Ottery

OTTERY
COTTS

75

PH

PH

Townlake

Combe

Ogbeare

Three Oaks

Mill Hill

Millhill

1

1 TAMAR COTTS
2 TAMAR TERR

LAMERHOOE DR

Horsebridge

Grenoven
Wood

Hele
Farm

Woodovis
House

B3362

Rubbytown
Farm

Artiscombe

MILL HILL
COTTS

MILL HILL LA

CREASE LA

LAMERHOOE
CROSS

LAMERHOOE DR

WHEAL MARIA
COTTS

WHEAL MARIA

BLANCHDOWN DR

74

40 **41** **42** **43** **44** **45**

A **B** **C** **D** **E** **F**

115
125

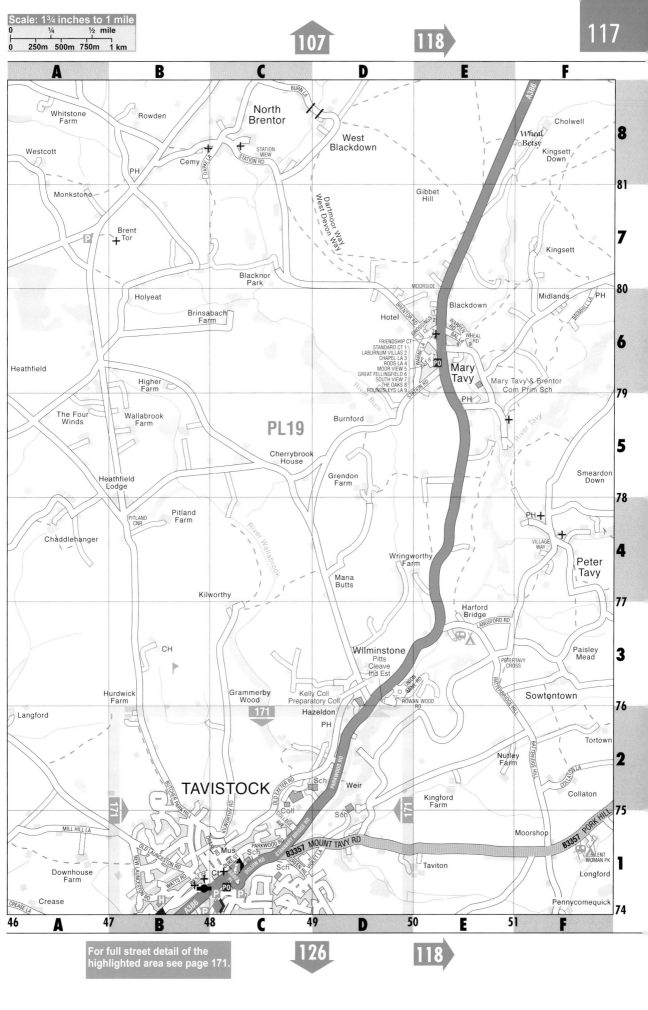

Scale: 1¾ inches to 1 mile

0   ¼   ½ mile
0 250m 500m 750m 1 km

107

118

117

A   B   C   D   E   F

8
81
7
80
6
79
5
78
4
77
3
76
2
75
1
74

Whitstone Farm
Rowden
North Brentor
West Blackdown
Cholwell
Wheal Betsy
Kingsett Down

Westcott
STATION VIEW
BURN LA
Gibbet Hill
Kingsett

Monkstone
PH
Cemy
DARKE LA
STATION RD
Dartmoor Way
West Devon Way
MOORSIDE
Blackdown
Midlands
PH
BRIMHILL LA

Brent Tor
P
Blacknor Park
BRENTOR RD
CROSSINGS
WARNE LA
WARREN
HOL LA
BAL LA
WHEAL RD
Mary Tavy
Mary Tavy & Brentor Com Prim Sch

Holyeat
Brinsabach Farm
Hotel
FRIENDSHIP CT
STANDARD CT 1
LABURNUM VILLAS 2
CHAPEL LA 3
RODS LA 4
MOOR VIEW 5
GREAT FELLINGFIELD 6
SOUTH VIEW 7
THE OAKS 8
ROUNDSLEYS LA 9
PO
PH

Heathfield
Higher Farm
River Burn
PL19
Burnford
STATION RD
River Tavy

The Four Winds
Wallabrook Farm
Cherrybrook House

Heathfield Lodge
PITLAND CNR
Pitland Farm
Grendon Farm
Smeardon Down

Chaddlehanger
River Wallabrook
PH
VILLAGE WAY
Peter Tavy

Kilworthy
Mana Butts
Wringworthy Farm

CH
Harford Bridge
LANGSFORD RD
Paisley Mead

Hurdwick Farm
Grammerby Wood
Wilminstone
Pitts Cleave Ind Est
UNION MINE RD
ROWAN WOOD RD
PETERTAVY CROSS
BATTERIDGE HILL
Sowtontown

Langford
171
Kelly Coll Preparatory Coll
Hazeldon
PH
Tortown

MILL HILL LA
BUTCHER PARK HILL
171
KILWORTHY HILL
OLD EXETER RD
PARKWOOD RD
Sch
Weir
171
Kingford Farm
Nutley Farm
COLLATON LA
Collaton

TAVISTOCK
DRAKE RD
Coll
COLLEGE AVE
PARKWOOD RD
STANNARY BRIDGE RD
Sch
Moorshop
B3357 PORK HILL
SILENT WOMAN PK

NEW LAUNCESTON RD
OLD LAUNCESTON RD
WATTS RD
DUKE ST
DOLVIN RD
Ct
Mus
GREEN HILL
DUKE LA
Sch
B3357 MOUNT TAVY RD
Taviton
Longford

CREASE LA
Crease
Downhouse Farm
H
A386
PO
P
P
P
Pennycomequick

46 A 47 B 48 C 49 D 50 E 51 F

126

118

For full street detail of the highlighted area see page 171.

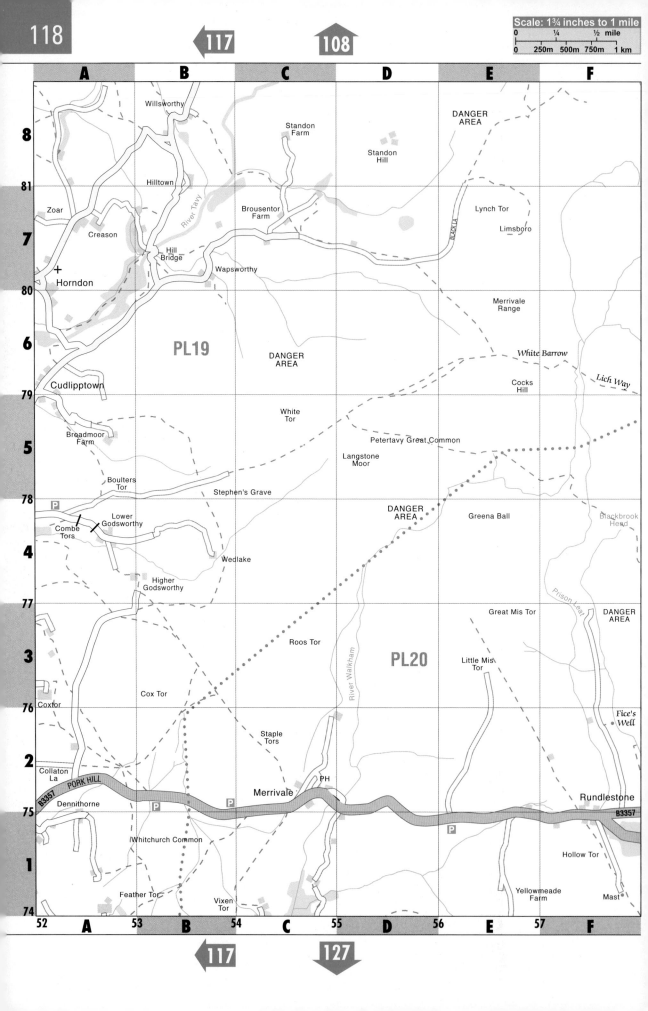

Scale: 1¾ inches to 1 mile
0   ¼   ½ mile
0 250m 500m 750m 1 km

A   B   C   D   E   F

8

Willsworthy

DANGER AREA

Standon Farm

Standon Hill

81

Hilltown

River Tavy

Brousentor Farm

Lynch Tor

BLACKLA

Limsboro

7

Zoar

Creason

Hill Bridge

Wapsworthy

+ Horndon

80

Merrivale Range

6

PL19

DANGER AREA

White Barrow

Lich Way

Cocks Hill

Cudlipptown

79

White Tor

Petertavy Great Common

5

Broadmoor Farm

Langstone Moor

Boulters Tor

Stephen's Grave

DANGER AREA

Greena Ball

Blackbrook Head

78

Combe Tors

Lower Godsworthy

4

Higher Godsworthy

Wedlake

Prison Leat

DANGER AREA

77

Great Mis Tor

Roos Tor

PL20

3

Cox Tor

River Walkham

Little Mis Tor

76

Coxtor

Staple Tors

Fice's Well

2

Collaton La

PORK HILL

PH

Merrivale

Rundlestone

B3357

Dennithorne

P   P

B3357

75

Whitchurch Common

Hollow Tor

1

Feather Tor

Vixen Tor

Yellowmeade Farm

Mast

74

52   A   53   B   54   C   55   D   56   E   57   F

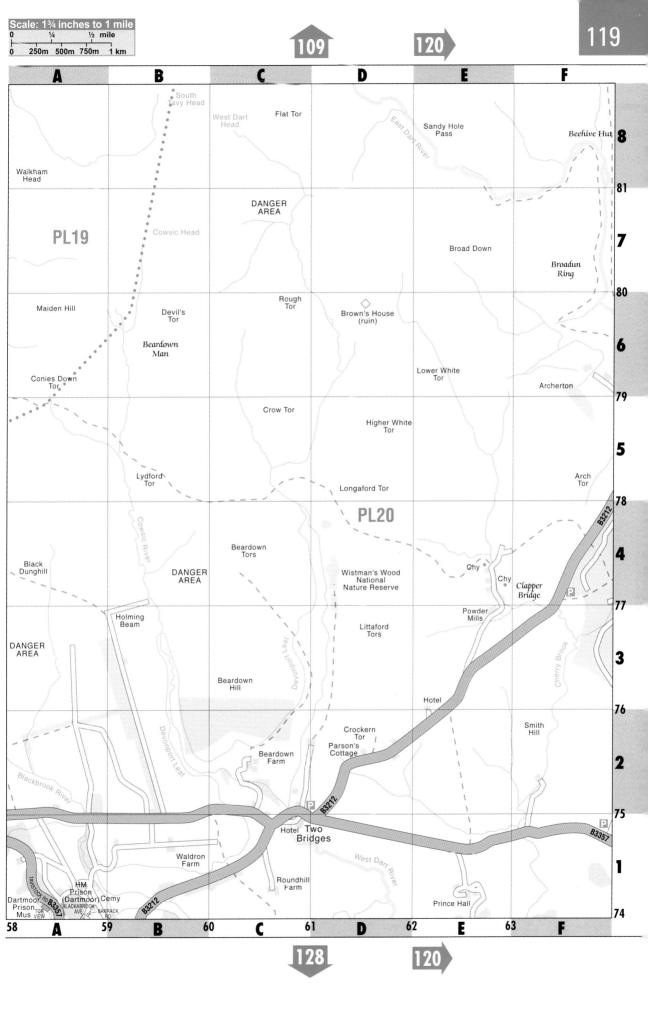

Scale: 1¾ inches to 1 mile

0   ¼   ½   mile
0   250m   500m   750m   1 km

109

120

119

A   B   C   D   E   F

8

81

7

80

6

79

5

78

4

77

3

76

2

75

1

74

Walkham
Head

PL19

South
Tavy Head

West Dart
Head

Flat Tor

East Dart River

Sandy Hole
Pass

Beehive Hut

Cowsic Head

DANGER
AREA

Broad Down

Broadun
Ring

Maiden Hill

Devil's
Tor

Beardown
Man

Rough
Tor

Brown's House
(ruin)

Lower White
Tor

Archerton

Conies Down
Tor

Crow Tor

Higher White
Tor

Lydford
Tor

Longaford Tor

PL20

Arch
Tor

B3212

Black
Dunghill

Cowsic River

DANGER
AREA

Beardown
Tors

Wistman's Wood
National
Nature Reserve

Chy

Chy

Clapper
Bridge

P

Holming
Beam

Devonport Leat

Powder
Mills

Cherry Brook

DANGER
AREA

Beardown
Hill

Littaford
Tors

Hotel

Smith
Hill

Blackbrook River

Devonport Leat

Beardown
Farm

Crockern
Tor

Parson's
Cottage

B3212

P

Beardown
Farm

B3212

P

B3357

TAVISTOCK RD

Waldron
Farm

Hotel

Two
Bridges

West Dart River

Dartmoor
Prison
Mus

HM
Prison
(Dartmoor)

Cemy

BLACKABROOK
AVE

BARRACK
RD

B3212

Roundhill
Farm

Prince Hall

B3357

TOR
VIEW

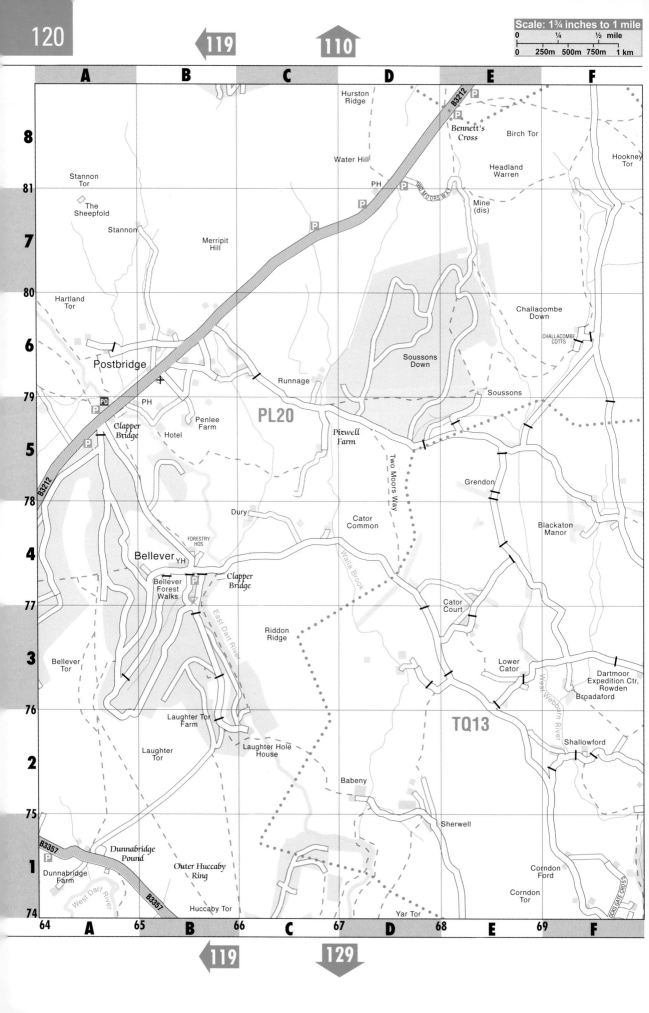

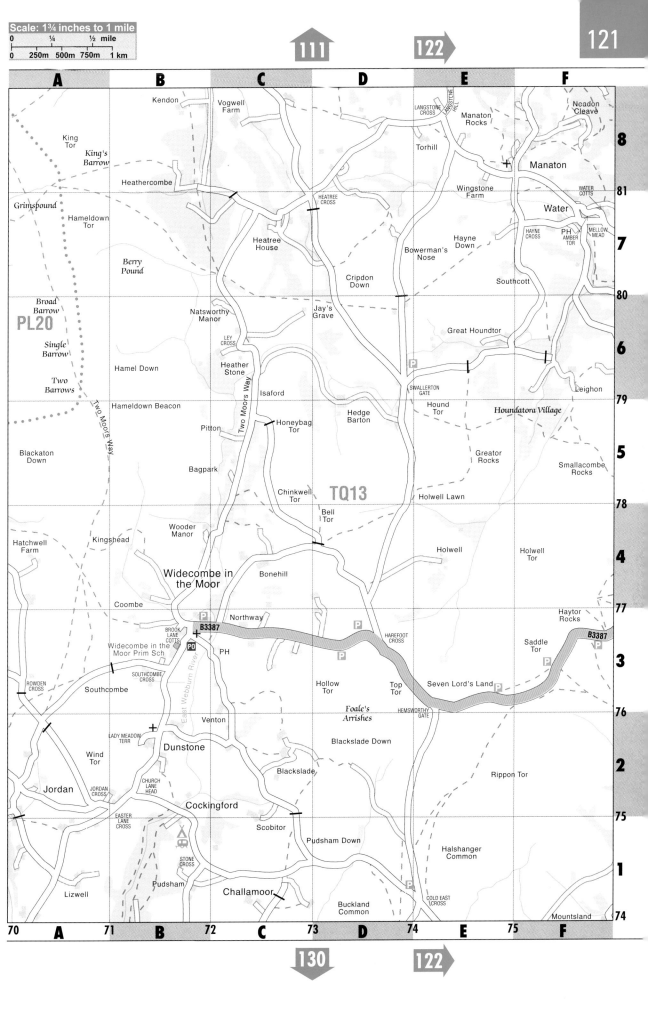

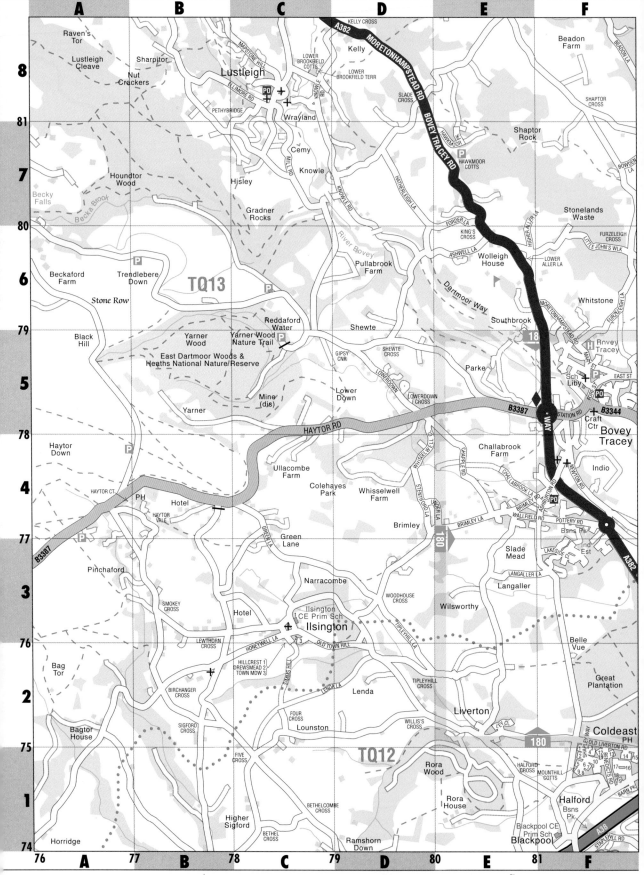

Scale: 1¾ inches to 1 mile
0   ¼   ½   mile
0   250m   500m   750m   1 km

8

Raven's Tor
Lustleigh Cleave
Sharpitor
Nut Crackers
MADSTONE HILL
Lustleigh
KELLY CROSS
Kelly
Lower Brookfield Cotts
Lower Brookfield Terr
A382
MORETONHAMPSTEAD RD
BOVEY TRACEY RD
Beadon Farm
BEADON LA
BOWDEN LA

ELLIMORE RD
PO
Wrayland
PETHYBRIDGE
KNOWLE RD
SLADE CROSS
Slade Cross
SHAPTOR CROSS

81

7

Houndtor Wood
Hisley
MILL RD
Knowle
KNOWLE RD
HATHERLEIGH LA
HAWKMOOR
P
Hawkmoor Cotts
Shaptor Rock
FURZELEIGH CROSS
LITTLE JOHN'S WLK

Becky Falls
Becka Brook

80

Beckaford Farm
Stone Row
Trendlebere Down
P
TQ13
Gradner Rocks
River Bovey
Pullabrook Farm
FORDER LA
King's Cross
ASHWELL LA
HIGHER ALLER LA
Wolleigh House
LOWER ALLER LA
Stonelands Waste
Whitstone

6

Black Hill
Reddaford Water
Yarner Wood
Yarner Wood Nature Trail
P
P
Shewte
Dartmoor Way
Southbrook
MORETONHAMPSTEAD RD
FURZELEIGH LA
Bovey Tracey
18
H

79

East Dartmoor Woods & Heaths National Nature Reserve
SHEWTE CROSS
GIPSY CNR
Parke
Sch Liby
PO
EAST ST
Craft Ctr
B3387
B3344

5

Yarner
Mine (dis)
Lower Down
LOWERDOWN
LOWERDOWN CROSS
B3387
WAY
STATION RD
Bovey Tracey

78

Haytor Down
P
HAYTOR RD
Ullacombe Farm
Colehayes Park
Whisselwell Farm
WHISSELWELL LA
STENTIFORD LA
Challabrook Farm
CHALLABROOK LA
Indio
NEWTON RD
POT LA

4

HAYTOR CT
PH
Hotel
HAYTOR VALE
Green Lane
GREEN LA
Whisselwell Farm
Brimley
CHAPPLE RD
BRIMLEY LA
180
Slade Mead
BRIMLEY RD
EMBLEFORD
PO
WALLFIELD RD
POTTERY RD
Bsns Pk
LANGALLER LA
Ind Est
LAKESIDE CL

77

B3387
P
Pinchaford
Smokey Cross
Hotel
SIMMS HILL
Narracombe
Woodhouse Cross
Wilsworthy
Langaller
Belle Vue
A382

3

Bag Tor
Birchanger Cross
LEWTHORN CROSS
HONEYWELL LA
Ilsington CE Prim Sch
Ilsington
OLD TOWN HILL
TIPLEYHILL LA
Great Plantation

2

Bagtor House
Sigford Cross
FIVE CROSS
FOUR CROSS
Lounston
Lenda
LENDA LA
TIPLEYHILL CROSS
WILLIS'S CROSS
Liverton
SHAPLEY WAY
Coldeast PH
OLD LIVERTON RD
BENEDICTS RD
BARN PK

HILLCREST 1
DREWSMEAD 2
TOWN MDW 3
1
2 3
180
HALFORD CROSS
MOUNTHILL COTTS
STAPLEHILL RD

75

1

Horridge
Higher Sigford
BETHEL CROSS
BETHELCOMBE CROSS
Ramshorn Down
Rora Wood
Rora House
Blackpool CE Prim Sch
Blackpool
Halford
Bsns Pk
A38

74

TQ12

76   **A**   77   **B**   78   **C**   79   **D**   80   **E**   81   **F**

121   131   For full street detail of the highlighted area see page 180.

F1
1 LASKEYS HEATH
2 TAYLORS NEWTAKE
3 LEAT MDW
4 ROWELLS MEAD
5 BEAUMONT CL
6 DIVETT DR
7 MUNRO MEAD
8 POMEROY PL
9 FLOWERS MDW
10 KITTERSLEY DR
11 CHAPEL LA
12 BEANHAY CL
13 BENLEARS ACRE
14 BICKFORDS GN
15 SUMMERLANDS CT
16 SUMMERHILL RD
17 SUMMERHILL CRES
18 SUMMERHILL CL
19 BENEDICTS CL

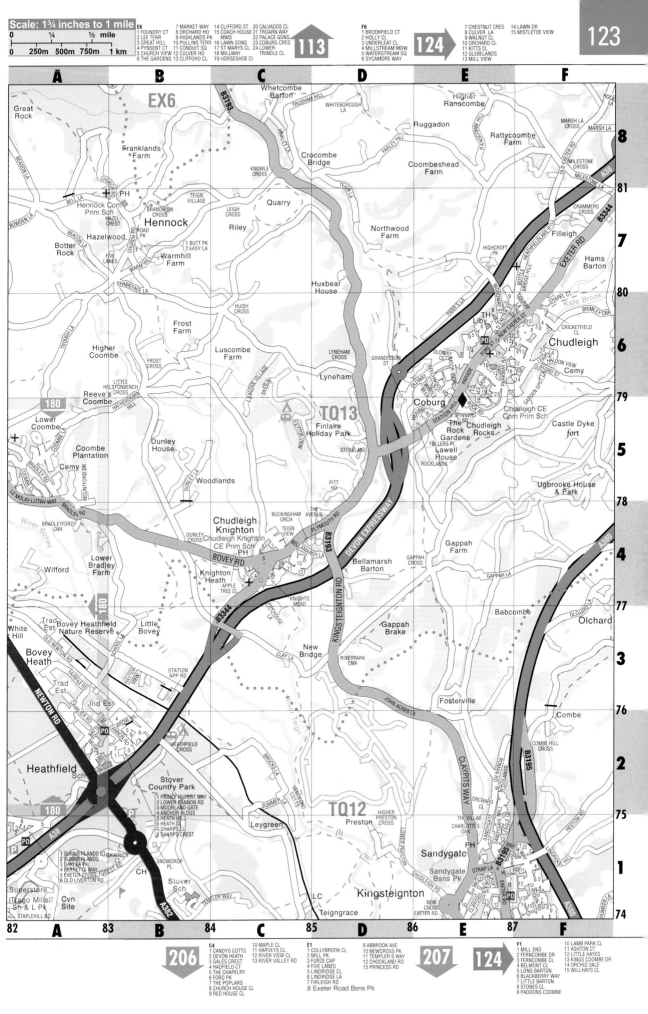

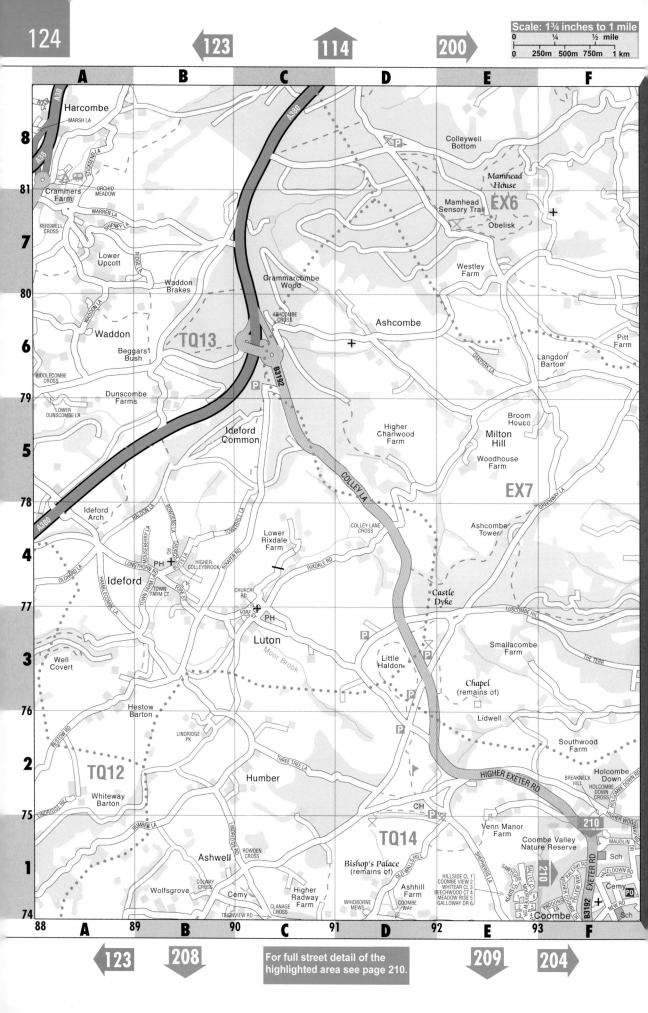

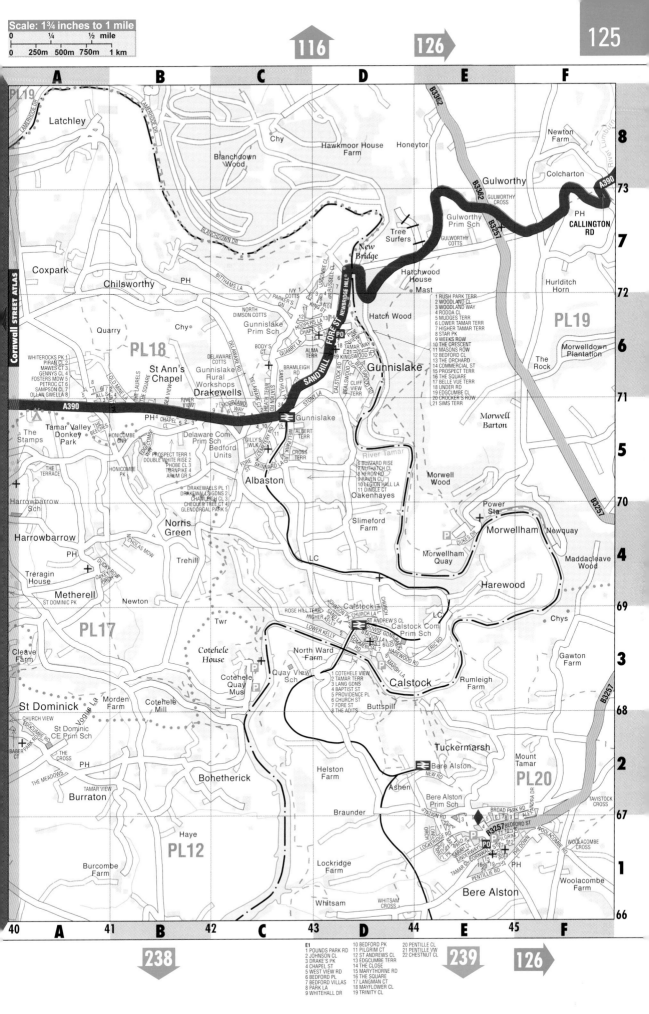

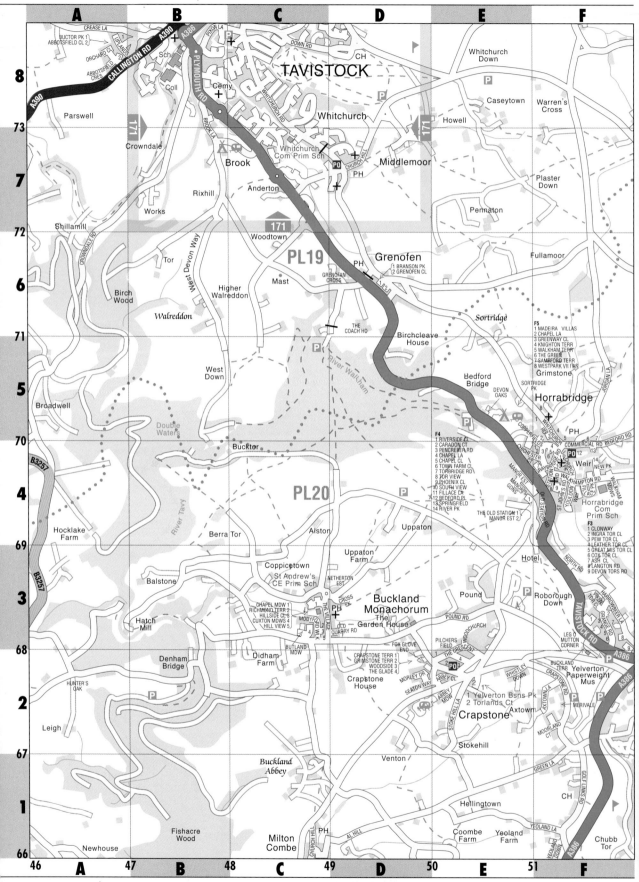

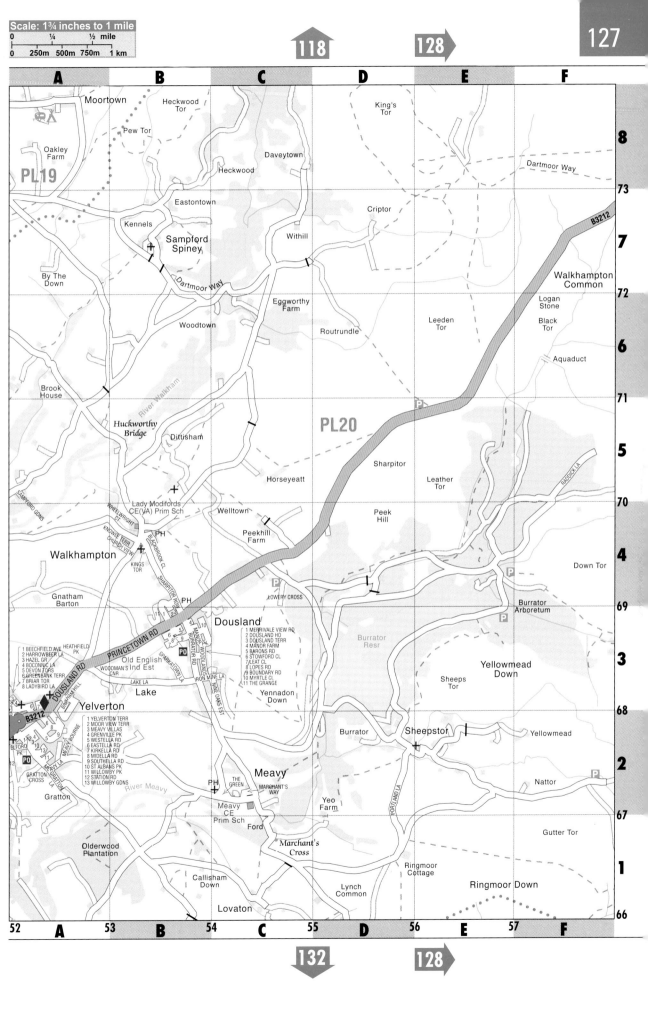

Scale: 1¾ inches to 1 mile

0   ¼   ½ mile
0   250m 500m 750m 1 km

118
128
132
128

PL19

Moortown
Heckwood Tor
Pew Tor
Oakley Farm
Heckwood
Daveytown
King's Tor
Dartmoor Way
Eastontown
Criptor
Kennels
Withill
Sampford Spiney
B3212
Walkhampton Common
Dartmoor Way
Logan Stone
Eggworthy Farm
Woodtown
Routrundle
Leeden Tor
Black Tor
Aquaduct
By The Down
Brook House
PL20
Huckworthy Bridge
Dittisham
Sharpitor
Leather Tor
Raddick La
Sampford Gdns
Horseyeatt
Peek Hill
Down Tor
Lady Modifords CE(VA) Prim Sch
Welltown
Wheelwright Ct
Peekhill Farm
Knowle Terr
Church View
PH
Walkhampton
Kings Tor
Gnatham Barton
Lowery Cross
Burrator Arboretum
Blackabrook Cl
Sharpiton Row
PH
Dousland

1 Merrivale View Rd
2 Dousland Ho
3 Dousland Terr
4 Manor Farm
5 Barons Rd
6 Stowford Cl
7 Leat Cl
8 Lopes Rd
9 Boundary Rd
10 Myrtle Cl
11 The Grange

Burrator Resr
Yellowmead Down
Sheeps Tor
Princetown Rd
Dousland Rd
Heathfield Pk
1 Beechfield Ave
2 Harrowbeer La
3 Hazel Gr.
4 Boconnic La
5 Devon Tors
6 Greenbank Terr
7 Briar Tor
8 Ladybird La
Old English Ind Est
Woodman's Cnr
Lake La
Manor
Woodland
Burrator Rd
Iron Mine La
Sparkatownla
PO
Lake
Nine Oaks Est
Yennadon Down
Sheepstor
Yellowmead
Yelverton
1 Yelverton Terr
2 Moor View Terr
3 Meavy Villas
4 Grenville Pk
5 Westella Rd
6 Eastella Rd
7 Kirkella Rd
8 Midella Rd
9 Southella Rd
10 St Albans Pk
11 Willowby Pk
12 Station Rd
13 Willowby Gdns
B3212
Dinkham Hill
Meavy Bourne
Elford Pk
Burrator
Nattor
PO
Gratton Cross
Gratton
River Meavy
Pinkham Hill
Meavy La
Gratton La
PH
The Green
Marchant's Way
Meavy
Yeo Farm
Portland La
Olderwood Plantation
Meavy CE Prim Sch
Ford
Marchant's Cross
Gutter Tor
Callisham Down
Lynch Common
Ringmoor Cottage
Ringmoor Down
Lovaton

Scale: 1¾ inches to 1 mile

0   ¼   ½ mile
0   250m   500m   750m   1 km

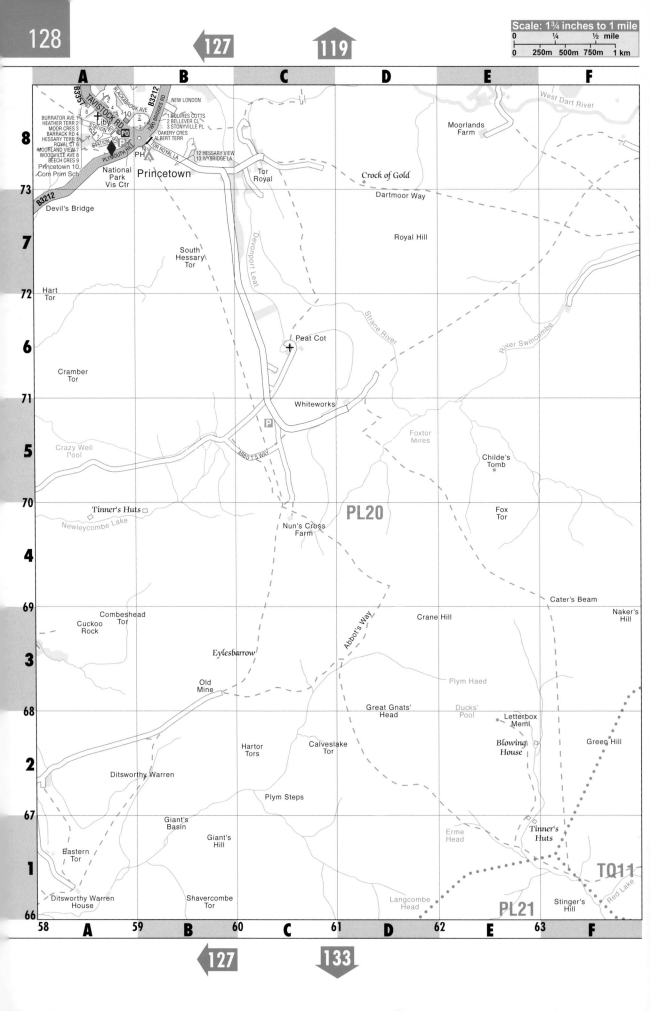

A   **B**   **C**   **D**   **E**   **F**

West Dart River

B3357   TAVISTOCK RD   BLACKABROOK AVE   B3212   TWO BRIDGES RD

NEW LONDON

1 SQUIRES COTTS
2 BELLEVER CL
3 STONYVILLE PL

Moorlands Farm

Liby

BURRATOR AVE 1
HEATHER TERR 2
MOOR CRES 3
BARRACK RD 4
HESSARY TERR 5
MOORLAND VIEW 7
WOODVILLE AVE 8
BEECH CRES 9
Princetown 10.
Com Prim Sch

STATION RD
PO
P
PLYMOUTH HILL
PH

OAKERY CRES
ALBERT TERR
TOR ROYAL LA
12 HESSARY VIEW
13 IVYBRIDGE LA

8

Crock of Gold

National Park Vis Ctr

Princetown

Tor Royal

73

Devil's Bridge

B3212

Dartmoor Way

7

South Hessary Tor

Royal Hill

Devonport Leat

72

Hart Tor

Strane River

River Swincombe

6

Peat Cot

Cramber Tor

Whiteworks

71

Foxtor Mires

5

Crazy Well Pool

P

ABBOT S WAY

Childe's Tomb

70

Tinner's Huts

Fox Tor

Newleycombe Lake

Nun's Cross Farm

PL20

4

Combeshead Tor

Cater's Beam

69

Cuckoo Rock

Crane Hill

Naker's Hill

3

Eylesbarrow

Abbot's Way

Plym Haed

68

Old Mine

Great Gnats' Head

Ducks' Pool

Letterbox Meml

Green Hill

Hartor Tors

Calveslake Tor

Blowing House

2

Ditsworthy Warren

Plym Steps

Tinner's Huts

67

Giant's Basin

Giant's Hill

Erme Head

P

TQ11

1

Eastern Tor

Langcombe Head

Stinger's Hill

Red Lake

Ditsworthy Warren House

Shavercombe Tor

PL21

66

58   **A**   59   **B**   60   **C**   61   **D**   62   **E**   63   **F**

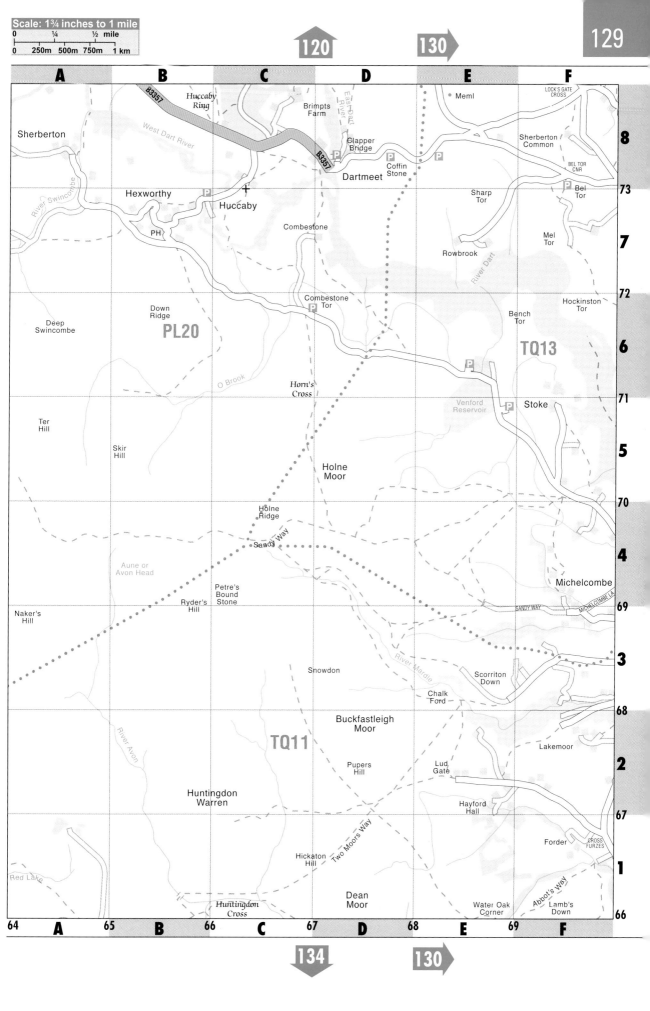

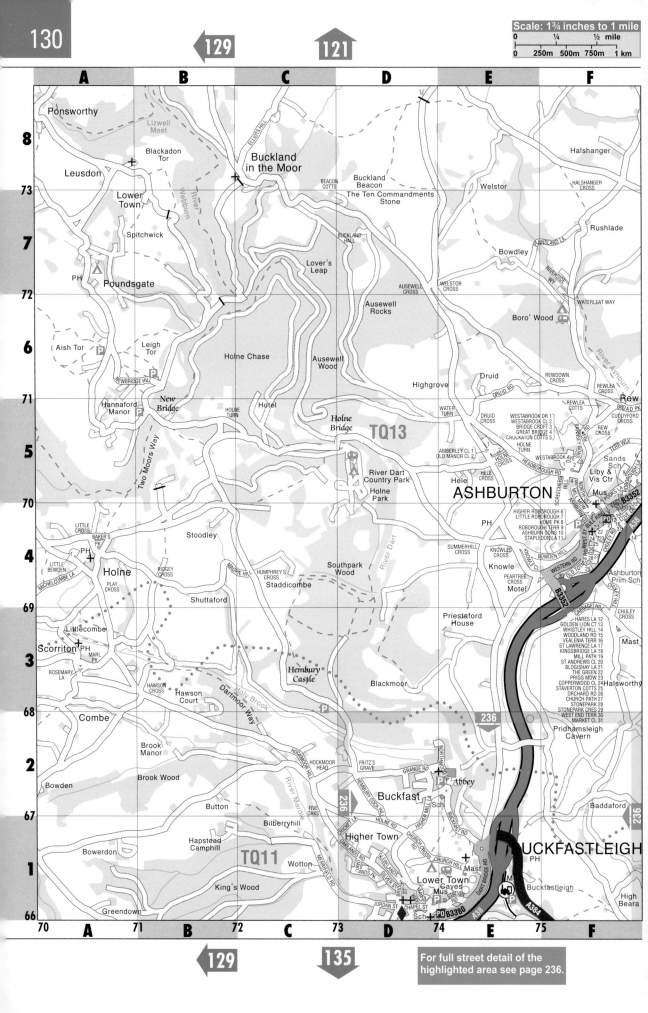

129
121

Scale: 1¾ inches to 1 mile

0   ¼   ½   mile
0 250m 500m 750m 1 km

A B C D E F

Ponsworthy

Lizwell Meet

Leusdon

Blackadon Tor

Lower Town

Spitchwick

Buckland in the Moor

Beacon Cotts

Buckland Hall

The Ten Commandments Stone

Welstor

Halshanger

Halshanger Cross

Rushlade

Bowdley

Lover's Leap

Ausewell Cross

Welstor Cross

River Webburn

PH

Poundsgate

Aish Tor

Leigh Tor

Ausewell Rocks

Ausewell Wood

Druid

Rewdown Cross

Boro' Wood

Waterleat Way

Riverside Wy

River Ashburn

Holne Chase

Highgrove

Rewlea Cross

Rew

Hannaford Manor

New Bridge

Holne Turn

Hotel

Holne Bridge

TQ13

Water Turn

Druid Cross

Westabrook Dr 1
Westabrook Ct 2
Bridge Croft 3
Great Bridge 4
Chuckaton Cotts 5

Rewlea Cotts

Rew Cross

Cuddyford Cross

Two Moors Way

Holne Turn

Amberley Cl 1
Old Manor Cl 2

Holne Turn

Westabrook Ave

Hele

Sands Sch

Liby & Vis Ctr

ASHBURTON

Mus

B3352

Little Cross

BAKER'S PK

Stoodley

River Dart Country Park

Holne Park

Higher Roborough 6
Little Roborough 7
Home Pk 8
Roborough Terr 9
Ashburn Dons 10
Stapledon La 11

PO

PH

Little Bewden

PH

Holne

RIDGEY CROSS

MAGPIE HILL

HUMPHREY'S CROSS

Staddicombe

Southpark Wood

River Dart

Summerhill Cross

Knowles Cross

Knowle

Bowden Hill

Ashburton Prim Sch

Chuley Cross

Littlecombe

Scorriton

PH

MARL PK

Shuttaford

Priestaford House

Peartree Cross

Motel

Mast

B3352

HARES LA 12
GOLDEN LION CT 13
WHISTLEY HILL 14
WOODLAND RD 15
VEALENIA TERR 16
ST LAWRENCE LA 17
KINGSBRIDGE LA 18
MILL PATH 19
ST ANDREWS CL 20
BLOGISHAY LA 21
THE GREEN 22
PRIGG MDW 23
COPPERWOOD CL 24
STAVERTON COTTS 25
ORCHARD RD 26
CHURCH PATH 27
STONEPARK 28
STONEPARK CRES 29
WEST END TERR 30
MARKET CL 31

ROSEMARY LA

Hembury Castle

Blackmoor

Halsworthy

Combe

HAWSON CROSS

Hawson Court

Holy Brook

Dartmoor Way

P

236

Pridhamsleigh Cavern

Bowden

Brook Manor

Brook Wood

HOCKMOOR HILL

Hockmoor Head

Fritz's Grave

Grange Rd

Abbey

Sch

236

236

Button

FIVE OAKS

River Mardle

236

Buckfast

Holne Rd

Higher Mill

Buckfast Rd

Baddaford

Bilberryhill

CRICKET LA

HEMBURY COCK HILL

CHURCH CROSS

Bowerdon

Hapstead Camphill

TQ11

Wotton

MERRIFIELD RD

OAKLANDS RD

Higher Town

Church Hill

Mast

BUCKFASTLEIGH

PH

King's Wood

SILVER STREET

Lower Town

Caves Mus

DART BRIDGE RD

P

Buckfastleigh

High Beara

Greendown

JORDAN ST

CHAPEL ST

Sch

PO

B3380

A38

A384

129
135

For full street detail of the highlighted area see page 236.

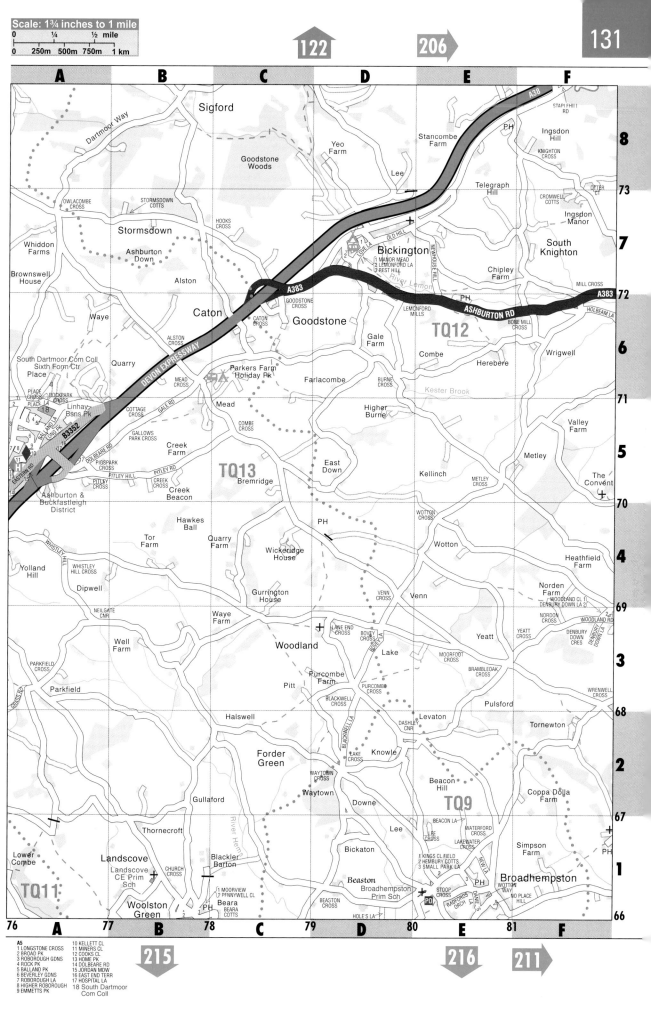

241
127

Scale: 1¾ inches to 1 mile

0   ¼   ½ mile
0 250m 500m 750m 1 km

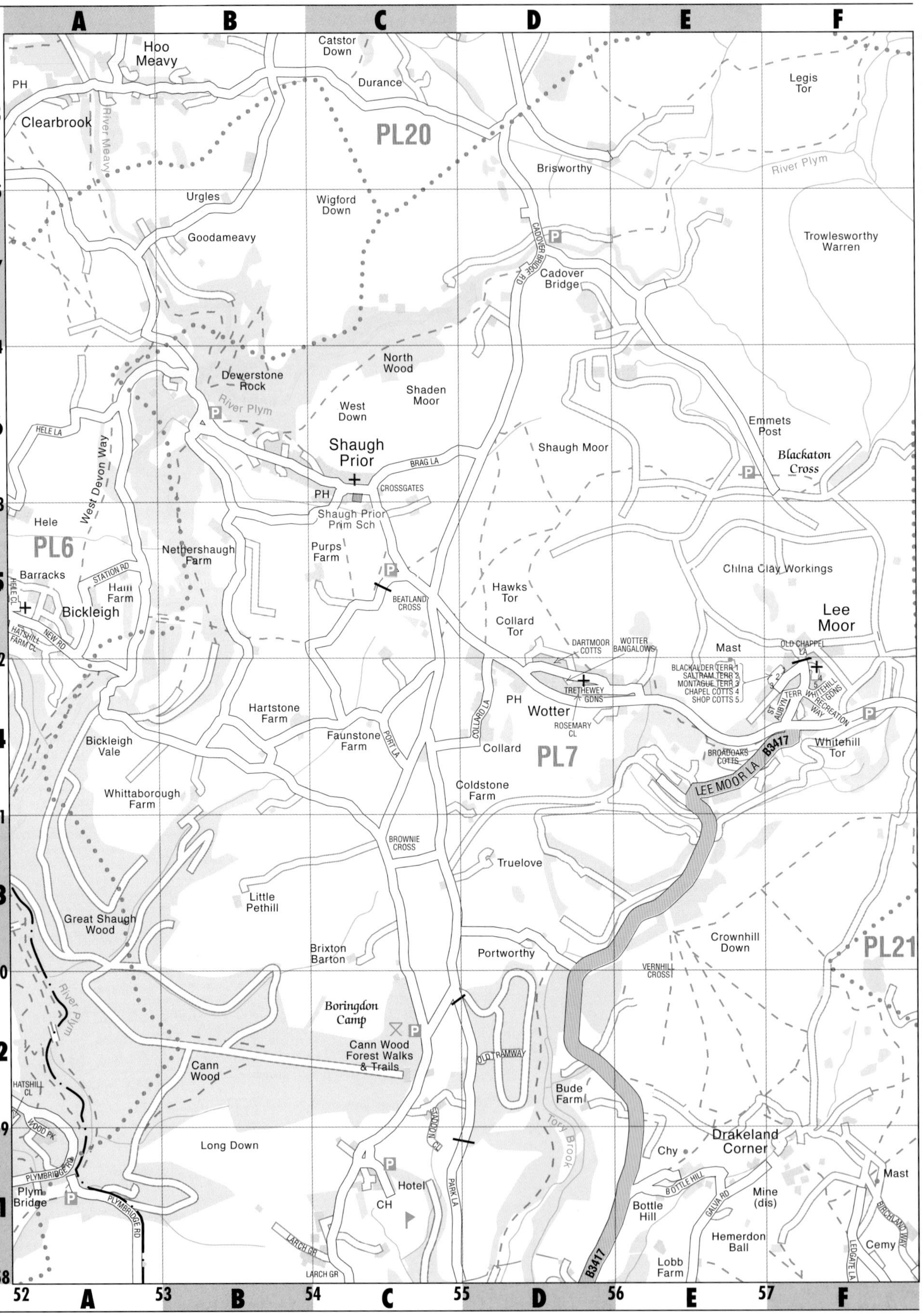

A **B** **C** **D** **E** **F**

Hoo Meavy

PH

Clearbrook

Catstor Down

Durance

PL20

Legis Tor

River Plym

River Meavy

Urgles

Goodameavy

Wigford Down

Brisworthy

Trowlesworthy Warren

CADOVER BRIDGE RD

P

Cadover Bridge

Dewerstone Rock

North Wood

P

River Plym

West Down

Shaden Moor

Shaugh Moor

Emmets Post

P

Blackaton Cross

HELE LA

West Devon Way

Shaugh Prior

BRAG LA

PH

CROSSGATES

Shaugh Prior Prim Sch

China Clay Workings

Hele

PL6

Nethershaugh Farm

Purps Farm

P

BEATLAND CROSS

Hawks Tor

Collard Tor

Mast

OLD CHAPPEL LA

Lee Moor

Barracks

STATION RD

Ham Farm

HELE CL

Bickleigh

NEW RD

HATSHILL FARM CL

DARTMOOR COTTS

WOTTER BANGALOWS

BLACKALDER TERR 1
SALTRAM TERR 2
MONTAGUE TERR 3
CHAPEL COTTS 4
SHOP COTTS 5

ALBITHA TERR
WHITEHILL GDNS
RECREATION WAY

P

Hartstone Farm

PORT LA

Faunstone Farm

COLLARD LA

PH

TRETHEWEY
GDNS

Wotter

ROSEMARY CL

PL7

BROADOAKS COTTS

B3417

LEE MOOR LA

Whitehill Tor

Bickleigh Vale

Collard

Whittaborough Farm

Coldstone Farm

BROWNIE CROSS

Truelove

Crownhill Down

PL21

River Plym

Great Shaugh Wood

Little Pethill

Portworthy

VERNHILL CROSS

HATSHILL CL

Brixton Barton

Boringdon Camp

P

Cann Wood Forest Walks & Trails

OLD TRAMWAY

Bude Farm

Tory Brook

Drakeland Corner

Mast

WOOD PK

Cann Wood

Long Down

P

SANDON LA

PARK LA

Chy

BOTTLE HILL

Mine (dis)

PLYMBRIDGE RD

Plym Bridge

P

PLYMBRIDGE RD

Hotel

CH

B3417

Bottle Hill

GALVA RD

Hemerdon Ball

Lobb Farm

BUCKLAND WAY

LEGIS LA

Cemy

LARCH GR

LARCH GR

A **B** **C** **D** **E** **F**

245
250
251

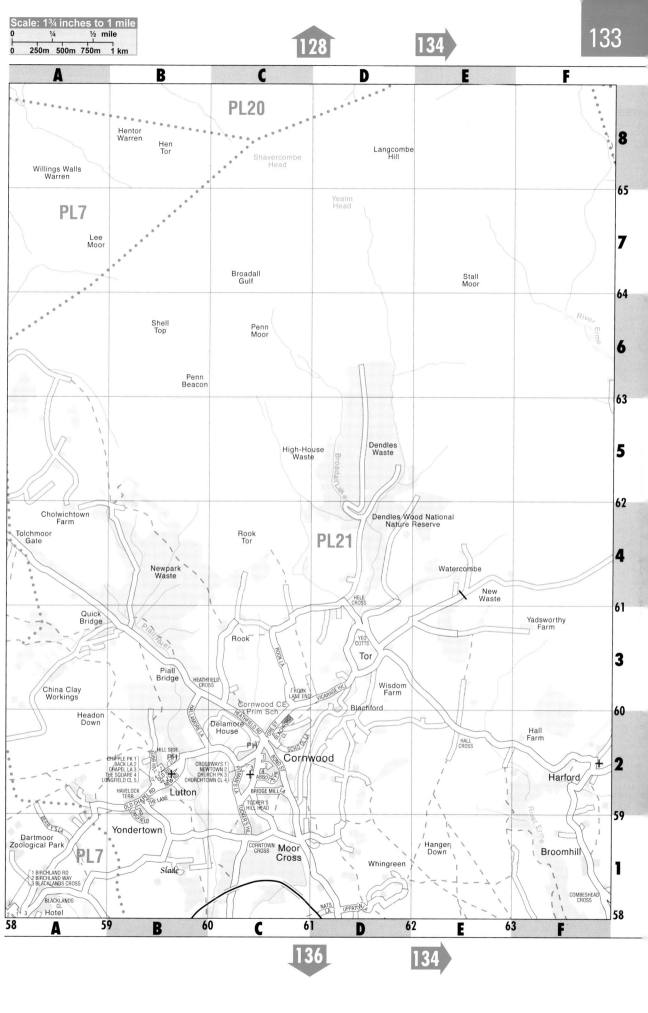

Scale: 1¾ inches to 1 mile

0   ¼   ½   mile
0   250m 500m 750m 1 km

128

134

133

A   B   C   D   E   F

PL20

Hentor Warren

Hen Tor

Shavercombe Head

Langcombe Hill

Willings Walls Warren

8

65

PL7

Yealm Head

Lee Moor

7

64

Broadall Gulf

Stall Moor

Shell Top

Penn Moor

6

63

Penn Beacon

High-House Waste

Dendles Waste

5

Broadall Lake

62

Cholwichtown Farm

Dendles Wood National Nature Reserve

Tolchmoor Gate

Rook Tor

PL21

4

Watercombe

Newpark Waste

New Waste

61

Hele Cross

Yadsworthy Farm

Quick Bridge

Piall River

Rook

Yeo Cotts

3

China Clay Workings

Piall Bridge

Heathfield Cross

Rook La

Tor

Wisdom Farm

Hall Cross

Rook Lane End

Vicarage Hill

Blachford

Headon Down

Cornwood CE Prim Sch

60

Delamore House

Heathfield Rd

Forest St

Blacklands Cl

Scho Cul La

Hall Farm

Hill Side

PH

PH

Bond St

Cornwood

Hall Cross

2

CHIPPLE PK 1
BACK LA 2
CHAPEL LA 3
THE SQUARE 4
LONGFIELD CL 5

CROSSWAYS 1
NEWTOWN 2
CHURCH PK 3
CHURCHTOWN CL 4

Abbot's

Harford

Gibb Hill La

Hillamore La

Pytman's La

Havelock Terr

Old Chapel Rd

The Lane

Bridge Mill La

Lutton

Tucker's Hill Head

Longfield

59

Berry's La

Yondertown

Tucker's Hill

Dartmoor Zoological Park

PL7

Corntown Cross

Moor Cross

Hanger Down

Broomhill

Whingreen

River Erme

1

1 BIRCHLAND RD
2 BIRCHLAND WAY
3 BLACKLANDS CROSS

Slade

Combeshead Cross

1
2
3

BLACKLANDS CL

Hotel

Nats La

Uppaton La

58

58   A   59   B   60   C   61   D   62   E   63   F   58

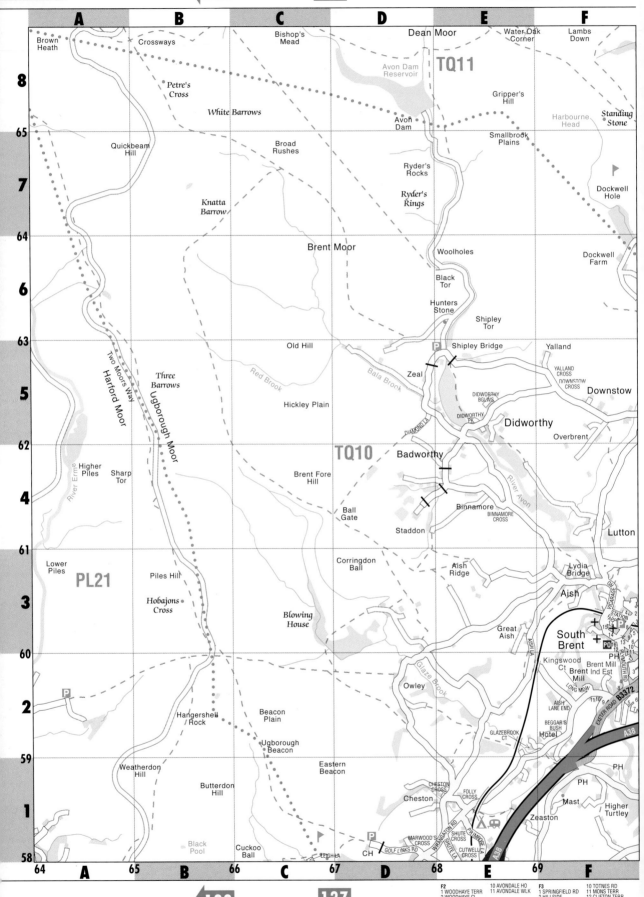

Scale: 1¾ inches to 1 mile

0   ¼   ½ mile
0   250m 500m 750m 1 km

A   B   C   D   E   F

Brown Heath
Crossways
Bishop's Mead
Dean Moor
Water Oak Corner
Lambs Down
TQ11
Avon Dam Reservoir
Petre's Cross
White Barrows
Gripper's Hill
Harbourne Head
Standing Stone
Avon Dam
Smallbrook Plains
Quickbeam Hill
Broad Rushes
Ryder's Rocks
Dockwell Hole
Knatta Barrow
Ryder's Rings
Brent Moor
Woolholes
Dockwell Farm
Black Tor
Hunters Stone
Shipley Tor
Old Hill
Shipley Bridge
Yalland
Two Moors Way
Red Brook
Bala Brook
Zeal
YALLAND CROSS
DOWNSTOW CROSS
Three Barrows
Harford Moor
Ugborough Moor
Hickley Plain
DIDWORTHY BGLWS
DIDWORTHY PK
Downstow
Didworthy
River Avon
DIAMOND LA
Badworthy
Overbrent
TQ10
River Erme
Higher Piles
Sharp Tor
Brent Fore Hill
Binnamore
BINNAMORE CROSS
Lutton
Staddon
Lower Piles
Ball Gate
PL21
Piles Hill
Corringdon Ball
Aish Ridge
Lydia Bridge
Aish
Hobajons Cross
Blowing House
Great Aish
South Brent
Owley
Kingswood Ct
Brent Ind Est
Brent Mill
Mill
Glaze Brook
LONG MDW
AISH LA
EXETER ROAD
B3372
Hangershell Rock
Beacon Plain
AISH LANE END
GLAZEBROOK CT
BEGGAR'S BUSH
Hotel
A38
Weatherdon Hill
Ugborough Beacon
Eastern Beacon
PH
Butterdon Hill
Cheston
CHESTON CROSS
FOLLY CROSS
Zeaston
Mast
Higher Turtley
Black Pool
Cuckoo Ball
MARWOOD'S CROSS
SHUTE CROSS
CUTWELL CROSS
CH
GOLF LINKS RD
WRANGATON RD
SHUTE LA
PRIMROSE LA
LEIGH LA

64 65 66 67 68 69

A   B   C   D   E   F

F2
1 WOODHAYE TERR
2 WOODHAYE CL
3 CLOBELLS
4 BEACON TERR
5 ST MICHAELS TERR
6 CORN PK
7 GREENFIELD DR
8 BEACON VIEW
9 NEW ORCHARD

10 AVONDALE HO
11 AVONDALE WLK

F3
1 SPRINGFIELD RD
2 HILLSIDE
3 BISHOPS MEAD
4 BROOKWOOD CL
5 ASHWOOD
6 CHAPEL FIELDS
7 BALMORAL LA
8 STATION RD
9 MANOR CT

10 TOTNES RD
11 MONS TERR
12 CLIFTON TERR
13 FORE ST
14 CHURCH ST
15 WELLINGTON SQ
16 STOCKBRIDGE LA
17 OLD STATION YARD

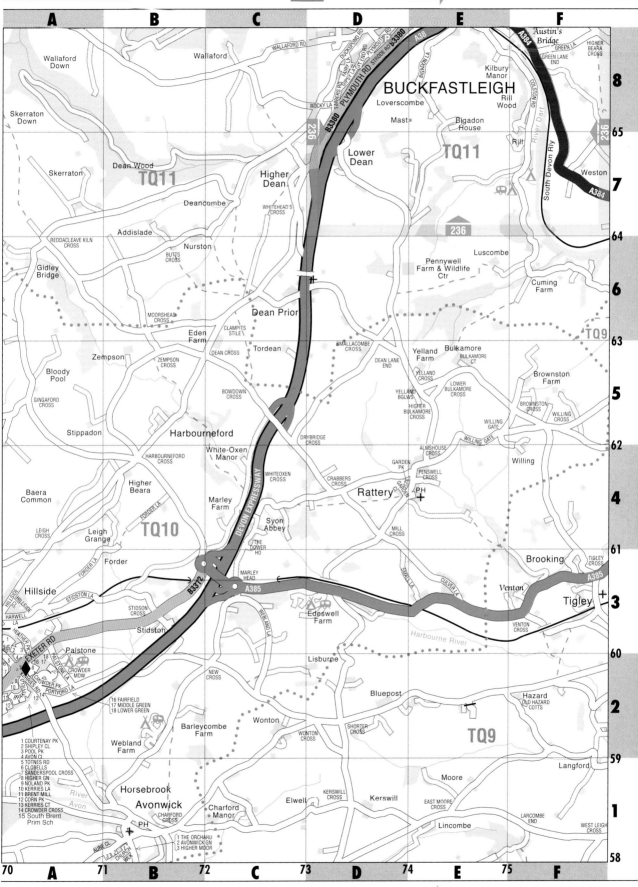

Scale: 1¾ inches to 1 mile

0   ¼   ½   mile
0   250m   500m   750m   1 km

130

215

135

A   B   C   D   E   F

8

Wallaford
Down

Wallaford

WALLAFORD RD

Austin's
Bridge

GREEN LA

HIGHER
BEARA
CROSS

GREEN LANE
END

A384

DUCKSPOND RD

TIMBERS RD

RIPS LANE END

FIAY LA

PLYMOUTH RD   STRODE RD   PLYMOUTH RD

B3380

ROCKY LA

A38

BIGADON LA

BUCKFASTLEIGH

Kilbury
Manor

Rill
Wood

65

Skerraton
Down

B3380

236

Loverscombe

Mast

Bigadon
House

Rill

Weston

A384

7

Skerraton

Dean Wood

TQ11

Higher
Dean

Lower
Dean

TQ11

South Devon Rly

River Dart

236

Deancombe

WHITEHEAD'S
CROSS

64

Addislade

Nurston

BUTTS
CROSS

Luscombe

Cuming
Farm

6

REDDACLEAVE KILN
CROSS

Gidley
Bridge

Pennywell
Farm & Wildlife
Ctr

TQ9

63

MOORSHEAD
CROSS

Eden
Farm

CLAMPITS
STILE

Dean Prior

SMALLACOMBE
CROSS

Yelland
Farm

Bulkamore

BULKAMORE
CT

Brownston
Farm

Zempson

ZEMPSON
CROSS

DEAN CROSS

Tordean

DEAN LANE
END

YELLAND
CROSS

LOWER
BULKAMORE
CROSS

BROWNSTON
CROSS

WILLING
CROSS

5

Bloody
Pool

GINGAFORD
CROSS

BOWDOWN
CROSS

YELLAND
BGLWS

HIGHER
BULKAMORE
CROSS

WILLING
GATE

WILLING GATE

62

Stippadon

Harbourneford

DRYBRIDGE
CROSS

ALMSHOUSE
CROSS

Willing

HARBOURNEFORD
CROSS

White-Oxen
Manor

CRABBERS
CROSS

GARDEN
PK

PENSWELL
CROSS

Baera
Common

Higher
Beara

FORDER LA

TQ10

WHITEOXEN
CROSS

Marley
Farm

Rattery

GARDEN

GARDEN

PH

4

LEIGH
CROSS

Leigh
Grange

Syon
Abbey

MILL
CROSS

Brooking

TIGLEY
CROSS

61

Forder

FORDER LA

THE
DOWER
HO

DEVON EXPRESSWAY

Venton

A385

Tigley

Hillside

HILLSIDE

HILL SIDE

STIDSON LA

B3372

MARLEY
HEAD

A385

SMALL LA

CULVER LA

VENTON
CROSS

3

HARWELL

HEATHER PK

PALSTONE LA

STIDSON
CROSS

Stidston

WEBLAND LA

Edeswell
Farm

Harbourne River

60

EXETER RD

Palstone

CROWDER
MDW

NEW
CROSS

Lisburne

Bluepost

Hazard

OLD HAZARD
COTTS

2

1 COURTENAY PK
2 SHIPLEY CL
3 POOL PK
4 AVON CL
5 TOTNES RD
6 CLOBELLS
7 SANDERSPOOL CROSS
8 HIGHER GN
9 NOLAND PK
10 KERRIES LA
11 BRENT MILL
12 CORN PK
13 KERRIES CT
14 CROWDER CROSS
15 South Brent
Prim Sch

16 FAIRFIELD
17 MIDDLE GREEN
18 LOWER GREEN

CROWDER PK

PORTFORD LA

Webland
Farm

Barleycombe
Farm

Wonton

WONTON
CROSS

SHORTER
CROSS

TQ9

Langford

59

River Avon

Horsebrook

Avonwick

CHARFORD
CROSS

Charford
Manor

PH

Elwell

KERSWILL
CROSS

Kerswill

EAST MOORE
CROSS

Moore

Lincombe

LARCOMBE
END

WEST LEIGH
CROSS

1

AUNE CL

CHURCH
WLK

1 THE ORCHARD
2 AVONWICK GN
3 HIGHER MOOR

58

70   A   71   B   72   C   73   D   74   E   75   F

138

222

For full street detail of the
highlighted area see page 236.

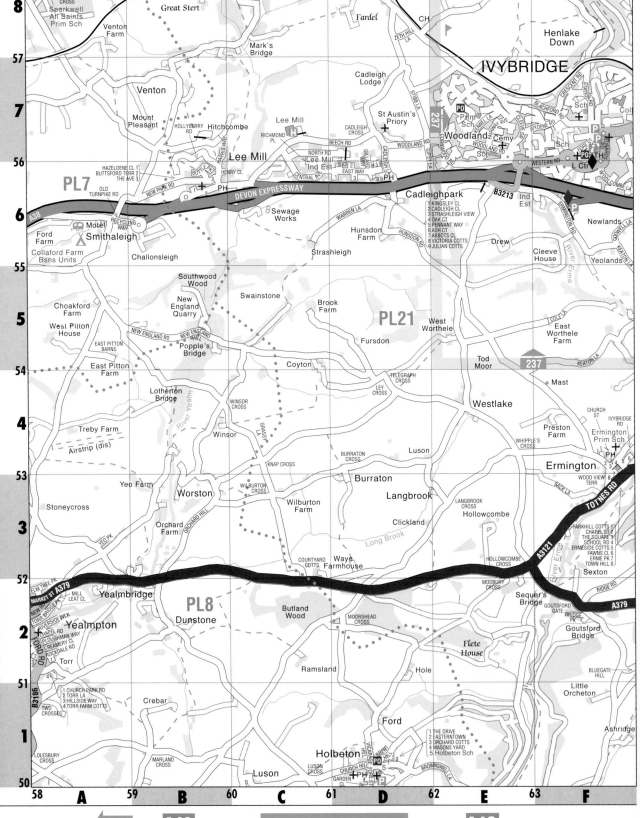

257   141   142

For full street detail of the highlighted area see page 237.

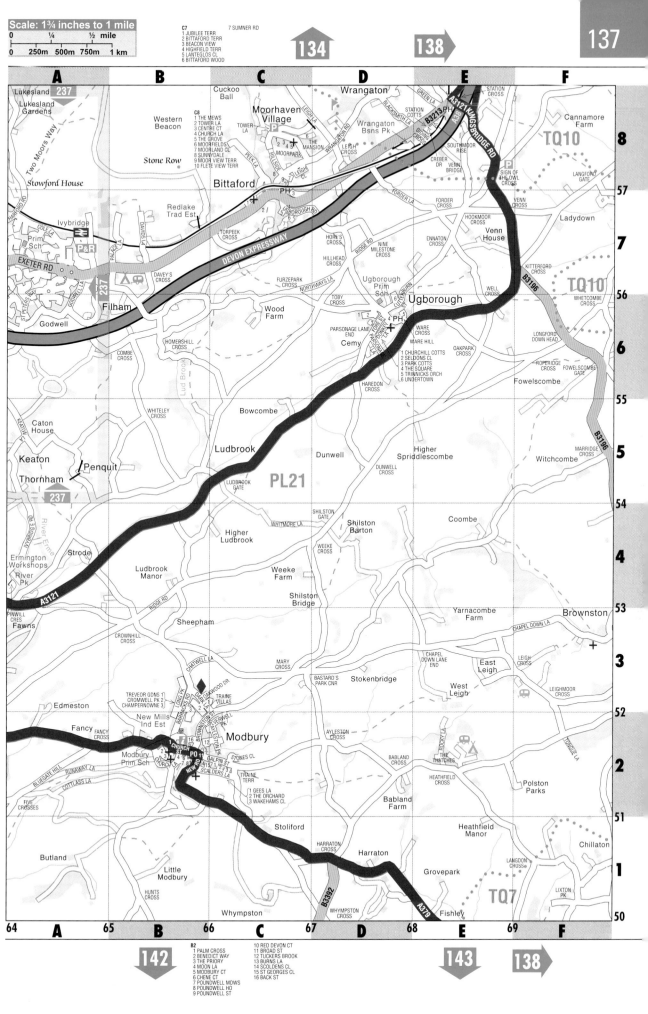

137
135

Scale: 1¾ inches to 1 mile

0   ¼   ½ mile
0 250m 500m 750m 1 km

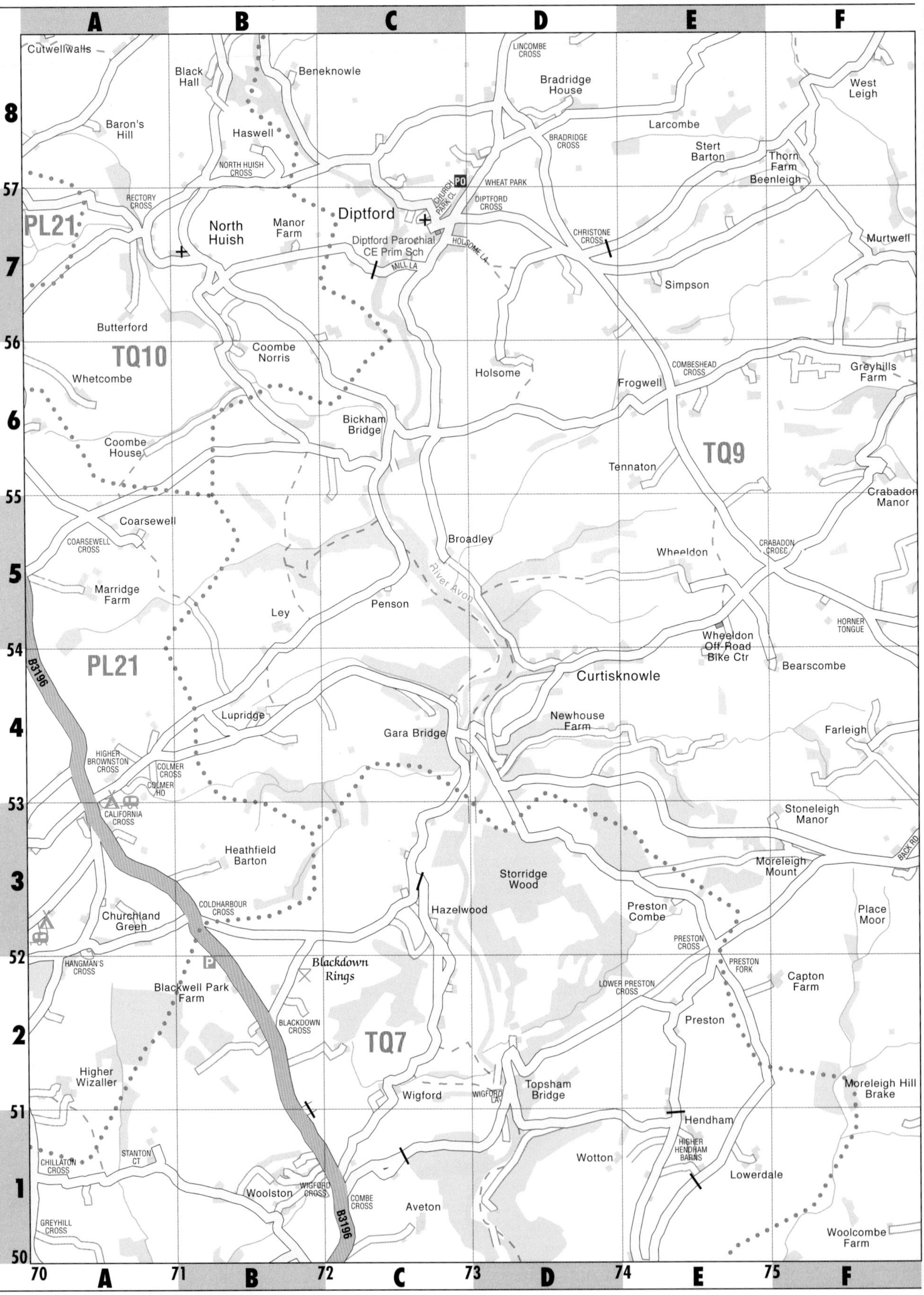

A B C D E F

8
Cutwellwalls
Baron's Hill
Black Hall
Beneknowle
Haswell
LINCOMBE CROSS
Bradridge House
West Leigh
Larcombe

57
NORTH HUISH CROSS
PO
WHEAT PARK
Stert Barton
Thorn Farm
Beenleigh
RECTORY CROSS
CHURCH PARK CL
BRADRIDGE CROSS
DIPTFORD CROSS

7
PL21
North Huish
Manor Farm
Diptford
Diptford Parochial CE Prim Sch
HOLSOME LA
CHRISTONE CROSS
Murtwell
MILL LA
Simpson

Butterford
Coombe Norris
Holsome
Frogwell
COMBESHEAD CROSS
Greyhills Farm

56
TQ10
Whetcombe

6
Coombe House
Bickham Bridge
Tennaton
TQ9

55
Coarsewell
Broadley
Wheeldon
CRABADON CROSS
Crabadon Manor

5
COARSEWELL CROSS
Marridge Farm
Ley
Penson
River Avon
HORNER TONGUE

54
PL21
Wheeldon Off-Road Bike Ctr
Bearscombe

4
Lupridge
Gara Bridge
Newhouse Farm
Curtisknowle
Farleigh
HIGHER BROWNSTON CROSS
COLMER CROSS
COLMER HO

53
CALIFORNIA CROSS
Heathfield Barton
Storridge Wood
Preston Combe
Stoneleigh Manor
Moreleigh Mount
BACK RD

3
Churchland Green
COLDHARBOUR CROSS
Hazelwood
PRESTON CROSS
Place Moor

52
HANGMAN'S CROSS
P
Blackdown Rings
Lower Preston Cross
PRESTON FORK
Capton Farm
Blackwell Park Farm
BLACKDOWN CROSS

2
Higher Wizaller
TQ7
Wigford
WIGFORD LA
Topsham Bridge
Preston
Moreleigh Hill Brake

51
STANTON CT
Wigford
Hendham
HIGHER HENDHAM BARNS

1
CHILLATON CROSS
Woolston
WIGFORD CROSS
Wotton
Lowerdale
GREYHILL CROSS
COMBE CROSS
Aveton
Woolcombe Farm
B3196

50
70 A 71 B 72 C 73 D 74 E 75 F

137
143
144

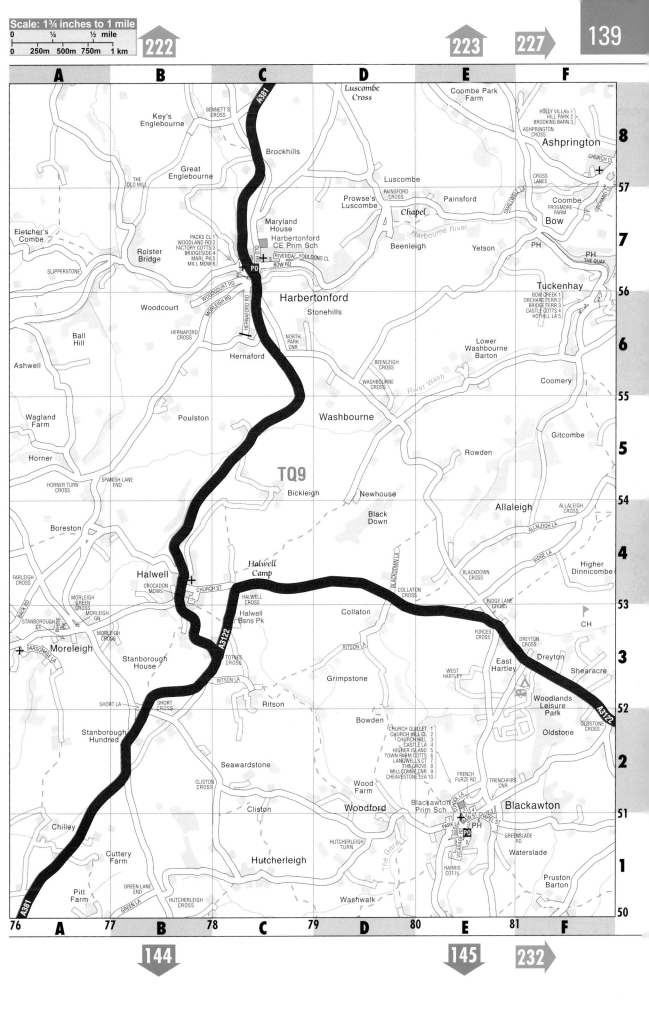

A   B   C   D   E   F

8

Key's
Englebourne

Bennett's
Cross

Luscombe
Cross

Coombe Park
Farm

HOLLY VILLAS 1
HILL PARK 2
BROOKING BARN 3
ASHPRINGTON
CROSS

Ashprington

Brockhills

Great
Englebourne

Luscombe

CROSS
LANES

CHURCH CL

57

Fletcher's
Combe

THE
OLD MILL

Maryland
House

Harbertonford
CE Prim Sch

PACKS CL 1
WOODLAND RD 2
FACTORY COTTS 3
BRIDGESIDE 4
MARL PK 5
MILL MDW 6

Rolster
Bridge

Prowse's
Luscombe

PAINSFORD
CROSS

Chapel

Painsford

Harbourne River

Beenleigh

Yetson

PH

Coombe
FROGMORE
FARM

Bow

PH
THE QUAY

7

SLIPPERSTONE

Woodcourt

RIVERDA
BOW RD
YOULDONS CL

PO

Harbertonford

Stonehills

BOW CREEK 1
ORCHARD TERR 2
BRIDGE TERR 3
CASTLE COTTS 4
HOTHILL LA 5

Tuckenhay

56

Ball
Hill

WOODCOURT RD

MORLEIGH RD

HERNAFORD RD

HERNAFORD
CROSS

Hernaford

NORTH
PARK CNR

BEENLEIGH
CROSS

Lower
Washbourne
Barton

6

Ashwell

WASHBOURNE
CROSS

River Wash

Coomery

55

Wagland
Farm

Poulston

Washbourne

Gitcombe

5

Horner

TQ9

Bickleigh

Rowden

Allaleigh

ALLALEIGH
CROSS

54

HORNER TURN
CROSS

SPANISH LANE
END

Newhouse

Black
Down

ALLALEIGH LA

RIDGE LA

Higher
Dinnicombe

4

Boreston

Halwell
Camp

Blackdown
Cross

BLACKDOWN LA

BLACKDOWN
CROSS

FARLEIGH
CROSS

Halwell

CROCADON
MDWS

CHURCH ST

HALWELL
CROSS

COLLATON
CROSS

RIDGE LANE
CROSS

CH

53

MORLEIGH
GREEN
CROSS

Halwell
Bsns Pk

Collaton

FORCES
CROSS

DREYTON
CROSS

Dreyton

BACK
RD

WHITE
LA

MORLEIGH
GN

MORLEIGH
CROSS

TOTNES
CROSS

RITSON LA

East
Hartley

Shearacre

3

PARSONAGE LA

Moreleigh

Stanborough
House

RITSON LA

Ritson

Grimpstone

WEST
HARTLEY

Woodlands
Leisure
Park

A3122

OLDSTONE
CROSS

52

SHORT LA

SHORT
CROSS

Stanborough
Hundred

Bowden

CHURCH QUILLET 1
CHURCH HILL CL 2
CHURCH HILL 3
CASTLE LA 4
HIGHER ISLAND 5
TOWN FARM COTTS 6
LANGWELLS CT 7
THE GROVE 8
MILLCOMBE CNR 9
CHEAVESTONE LEA 10

Oldstone

2

CLISTON
CROSS

Seawardstone

Wood
Farm

FRENCH
FURZE RD

TRENCHFIRS
CNR

Chilley

Cliston

Woodford

Blackawton
Prim Sch

PO   PH

Blackawton

51

Cuttery
Farm

GREEN LANE
END

HUTCHERLEIGH
TURN

The Gara

PARK LA

VICARAGE RD

GREENSLADE
RD

Waterslade

1

Pitt
Farm

A381

GREEN LA

HUTCHERLEIGH
CROSS

Hutcherleigh

Washwalk

HARRIS
COTTS

Pruston
Barton

50

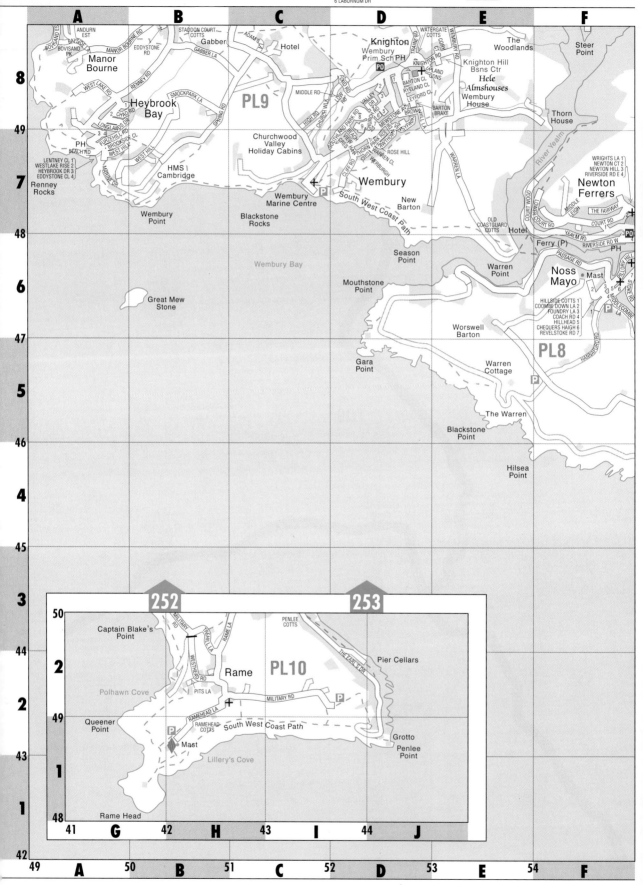

D8
1 WEMBURY MDW
2 HIGHFIELD DR
3 CROSS PARK RD
4 CROSSWAYS
5 COLLIERS CL
6 LABURNUM DR

7 SEA VIEW DR
8 SOUTHLAND PARK CRES
9 HILLCREST CL

Scale: 1¾ inches to 1 mile

0   ¼   ½ mile
0 250m 500m 750m 1 km

Map labels

Manor Bourne

ANDURN EST

BOVISAND ES
BOVISAND PK
BAYSIDE

MANOR BOURNE RD
EDDYSTONE RD

STADDON COURT COTTS

Gabber

GABBER LA

Hotel

ADAM'S LA

Knighton

Wembury Prim Sch PH
PO

WATERGATE COTTS

The Woodlands

Steer Point

WEST CAKE RD

RENNEY RD

SMOCKPARK LA

SPRING RD

PL9

MIDDLE RD

Wembury House

Knighton Hill Bsns Ctr
Hele Almshouses

BARTON BRAKE

Thorn House

Heybrook Bay

LONGLANDS DR
CYAD RD
FURZEHILL RD
BROOKSIDE CL

3 4

PH
BEACH RD

LENTNEY CL 1
WESTLAKE RISE 2
HEYBROOK DR 3
EDDYSTONE CL 4

WEST HILL

WEST HILL

MARINE DR

HMS Cambridge

HIGH RD
CHURCH WLK

Churchwood Valley Holiday Cabins

CLIFF RD

ROSE HILL

Wembury

River Yealm

WRIGHTS LA 1
NEWTON CT 2
NEWTON HILL 3
RIVERSIDE RD E 4

Newton Ferrers

Renney Rocks

Wembury Point

Blackstone Rocks

Wembury Marine Centre

South West Coast Path

New Barton

WARREN LA

Old COASTGUARD COTTS

Hotel

COURT WOOD RD
LOWER COURT RD

MIDDLE LEIGH

THE FAIRWAY

COURT RD

Ferry (P)

PASSAGE RD

YEALM RD

Riverside RD W
PO
PH

PILLORY HILL

Wembury Bay

Season Point

Mouthstone Point

Warren Point

Noss Mayo
Mast

HILLSIDE COTTS 1
COOMBE DOWN LA 2
FOUNDRY LA 3
COACH RD 4
HILLHEAD 5
CHEQUERS HAIGH 6
REVELSTOKE RD 7

MIDDLECOMBE LA

Great Mew Stone

Worswell Barton

Gara Point

Warren Cottage

PL8

HANNAFORD RD

The Warren

Blackstone Point

Hilsea Point

Captain Blake's Point

MILITARY RD
REPHIL LA
RAME LA

PENLEE COTTS

Pier Cellars

THE EARL'S DR

Rame
PL10

WESTHERD RD
PITS LA

Polhawn Cove

Queener Point

RAMEHEAD LA

MILITARY RD

P

Grotto

RAMEHEAD COTTS

South West Coast Path

Penlee Point

Mast

Lillery's Cove

Rame Head

41   42   43   44

G   H   I   J

49 A 50 B 51 C 52 D 53 E 54 F

50
44
2
49
43
1
48
42

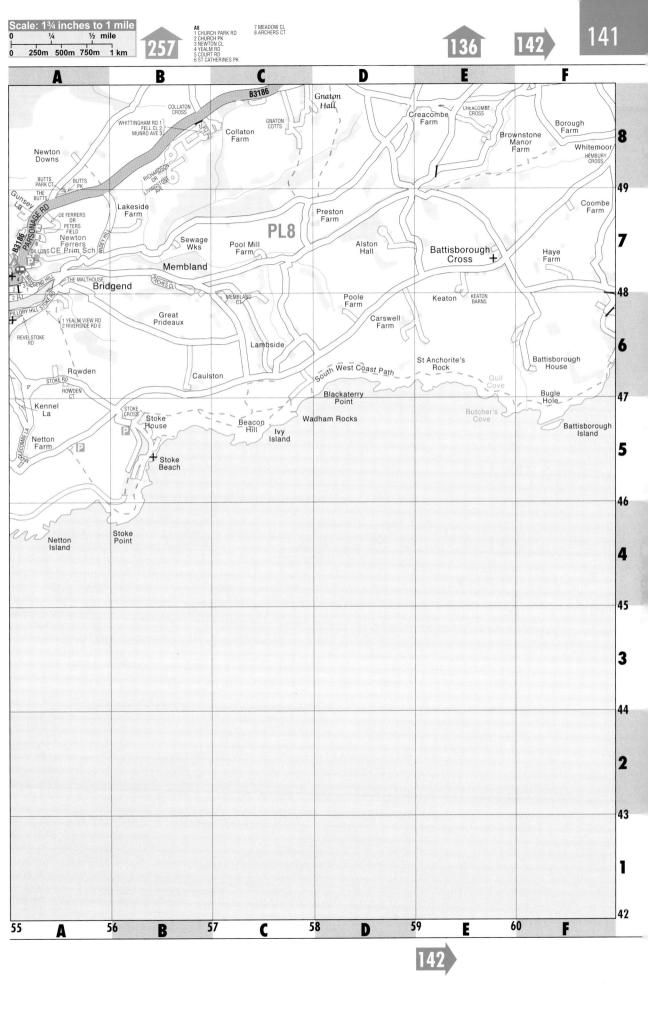

A B C D E F

8

49

7

48

6

47

5

46

4

45

3

44

2

43

1

42

GARDEN CL
FORE ST
WHITEMOOR CROSS
Efford House

BROWNSWELL LA

Great Orcheton Farm

PL21

B3392

PL8

Clyng Mill
Oldaport
Tor Rock

Wastor

Shearlangstone

SEVEN STONES CROSS

Highlands

Cumery

Pamflete House

River Erme

PIPERS CROSS
WASTOR CROSS

Langston

OLDHOUSE LA

Tuffland

Torr Down

COCKS PK
WASTOR PK

LANGSTON CROSS
South Langston

Owen's Hill

Wonwell Court

BLACKPOST CROSS
FOUR CROSS

Great Torr

RENTON LA

St Ann's Chapel

Holy Well

Mothecombe

P

Kingston

+ PH

1 CHURCH PK
2 ROCK COTTS
3 PARK VIEW TERR
4 HOME FARM CL
5 YELLANDS PK
6 ARNOLD'S CL
7 CHAPEL ROW
8 WESTENTOWN
9 OVERLANGS

MARWELL CROSS

Renton La

BLACKBERRY LA

PH

HILLTOP
P
PO

BULLHORN CROSS

PARK COTTS

BOWLS CROSS

BIGBURY CT

Erme Mouth

Wonwell Beach

Malthouse Point

Okenbury

Marwell

Houghton

Bigbury

PH

Scobbiscombe

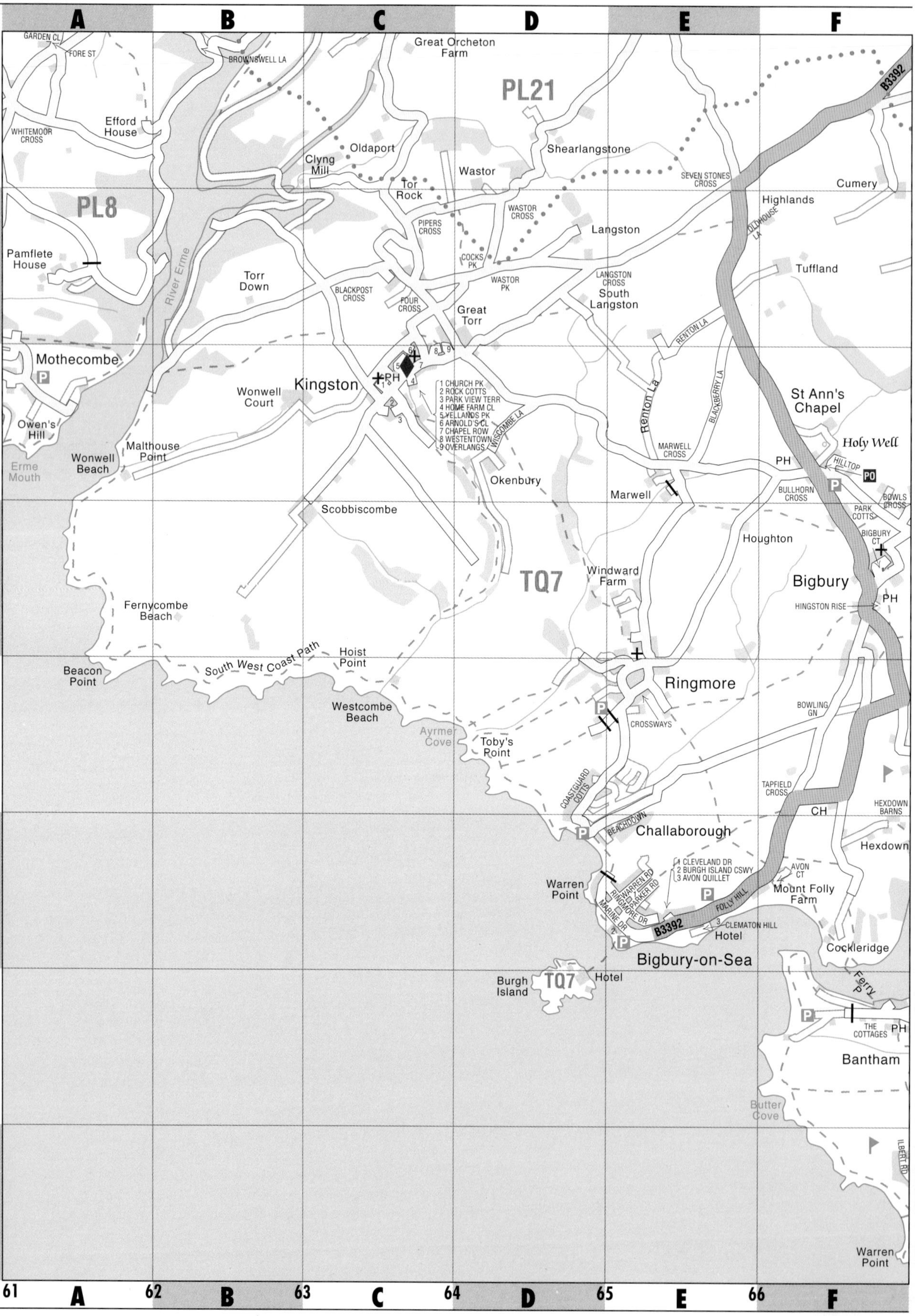

Windward Farm

TQ7

HINGSTON RISE

Fernycombe Beach

South West Coast Path

Hoist Point

Ringmore

BOWLING GN

Beacon Point

Westcombe Beach

Ayrmer Cove

Toby's Point

P
CROSSWAYS

TAPFIELD CROSS

CH

HEXDOWN BARNS

Challaborough

Hexdown

COASTGUARD COTTS

P
BEACHDOWN

AVON CT

Mount Folly Farm

Warren Point

1 CLEVELAND DR
2 BURGH ISLAND CSWY
3 AVON QUILLET

P
FOLLY HILL

Cockleridge

HOWARREN RD
PARKER RD
MARINE DR

B3392
Hotel

CLEMATON HILL

Ferry P

P

Burgh Island

TQ7

Hotel

Bigbury-on-Sea

P
THE COTTAGES
PH

Bantham

Butter Cove

ILBERT RD

Warren Point

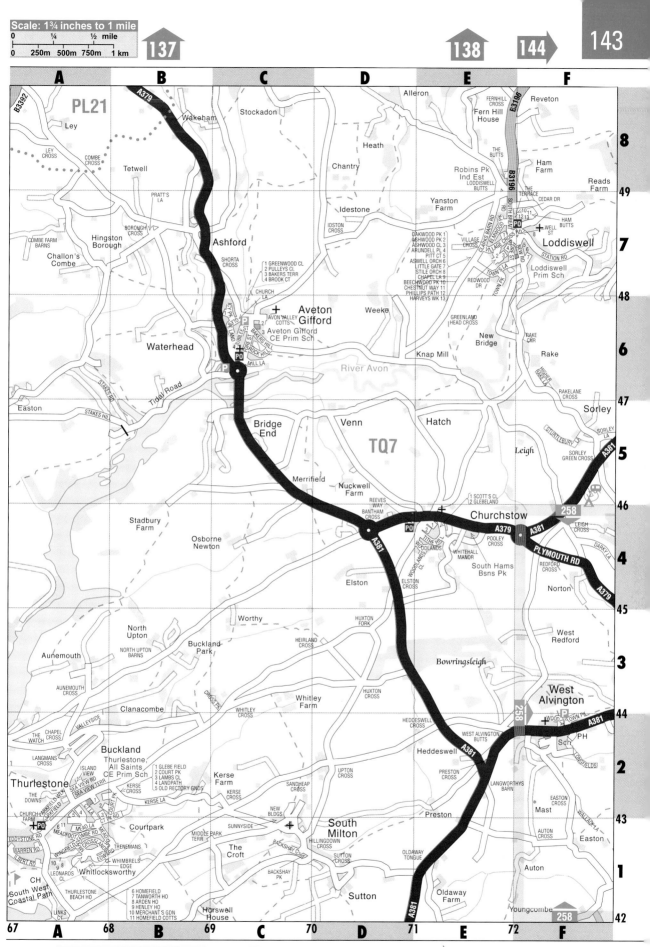

PL21

Ley
LEY CROSS
COMBE CROSS
Tetwell
Wakeham
Stockadon
Alleron
Fern Hill House
FERNHILL CROSS
Reveton

THE BUTTS
Ham Farm
Reads Farm

Robins Pk Ind Est
LODDISWELL BUTTS
Yanston Farm
CEDAR DR
THE TERRACE
HAM BUTTS

Challon's Combe
COMBE FARM BARNS
Hingston Borough
BOROUGH CROSS
PRATT'S LA
Ashford
SHORTA CROSS
CHURCH LA
Idestone
IDSTON CROSS
CLARKS BARN RD
WELL ST
ELAND RD
Village Cross
TOWN'S LA
Loddiswell

OAKWOOD PK 1
ASHWOOD PK 2
ASHWOOD PK 3
ARUNDELL 4
PITT CT 5
ASWELL ORCH 6
LITTLE GATE 7
STILE ORCH 8
CHAPEL LA 9
BEECHWOOD PK 10
CHESTNUT WAY 11
PHILLIPS PATH 12
HARVEYS WK 13

1 GREENWOOD CL
2 PULLEYS CL
3 BAKERS TERR
4 BROOK CT

Loddiswell Prim Sch
Station Rd
STATION RD

Aveton Gifford
AVON VALLEY COTTS
Aveton Gifford CE Prim Sch
Weeke
Waterhead
REDWOOD DR
GREENLAND HEAD CROSS

MILL LA
River Avon
Knap Mill
New Bridge
Rake
RAKE CNR
HIGHER RAKE LA
RAKELANE CROSS

Easton
STAKES HILL
Tidal Road

Bridge End
Venn
Hatch
TQ7
Leigh
Sorley
STURTLEBURY
SORLEY LA
SORLEY CROSS
A381

Merrifield
Nuckwell Farm
REEVES WAY
BANTHAM CROSS
1 SCOTT S CL
2 GLEBELAND
Churchstow
258
A381

Stadbury Farm
Osborne Newton
TITHE HILL
WOODLANDS
DOLANDS
A379
Pooley Cross
A381
LEIGH CROSS
DARKY LA
PLYMOUTH RD

Whitehall Manor
South Hams Bsns Pk
Redford Cross
REDFORD CROSS
Norton
A379

Elston
ELSTON CROSS

North Upton
NORTH UPTON BARNS
Buckland Park
Worthy
HEIRLAND CROSS
HUXTON FORK
West Redford

Aunemouth
AUNEMOUTH CROSS
Clanacombe
CROSS PK
Whitley Farm
HUXTON CROSS
Bowringsleigh
West Alvington

THE WATCH
CHAPEL CROSS
VALLEYSIDE
LANGMANS CROSS
WHITLEY CROSS
HEDDESWELL CROSS
WEST ALVINGTON BUTTS
WOOD ST
TOWN PK
A381
Sch
PH

Buckland
Thurlestone, All Saints CE Prim Sch
ISLAND VIEW
SEA VIEW RD
SEA VIEW TERR
KERSE CROSS
Kerse Farm
KERSE LA
UPTON CROSS
Heddeswell
Preston
PRESTON CROSS
Langworthys Barn
LONGFIELDS
Easton CROSS
Mast

Thurlestone
THE DOWNS
CHURCH FARM
MEADFOOT
COMBE RD
Courtpark
MIDDLE PARK
TERR
Sunnyside
HILLINGDOWN CROSS
South Milton
SUTTON CROSS
Auton
AUTON CROSS
WALLACE LA
Easton

1 GLEBE FIELD
2 COURT PK
3 LAMBS CL
4 LANDPATH
5 OLD RECTORY GNDS

EDDYSTONE RD
WARREN RD
ALBERT RD
WHIMBRELS EDGE
Whitlocksworthy
LEONARDS CL
Trenemans
The Croft
BACKSHAY CV
BACKSHAY PK
NEW BLDGS
Sutton
Oldaway Tongue
Oldaway Farm
A381
Youngcombe
258

CH
South West Coastal Path
LINKS CL
THURLESTONE BEACH HO
6 HOMEFIELD
7 TANWORTH HO
8 ARDEN HO
9 HENLEY HO
10 MERCHANT'S GDN
11 HOMEFIELD COTTS
Horswell House

For full street detail of the highlighted area see page 258.

147   144   148

Scale: 1¾ inches to 1 mile
0   ¼   ½ mile
0   250m   500m   750m   1 km

A   B   C   D   E   F

8

Wood Barton
SILVERIDGE LA
LOWERDALE TURN
Torr Brook
Grimpstonleigh
Morecombe Farm
A381
Yetsonais Farm
GREEN LA
HINGSTON POST
Higher Poole Farm
Pasture Farm

49

Woodleigh
The Mounts
Yetsonais Cross
FALLAPIT TURN
Fallapit House
TOWNSEND TERR
Barnston Farm
Kellaton Cross
DARTMOUTH RD
Lower Combe Farm
Pasture Cross

7

TORR LA
FIRS CROSS
Nutcombe Farm
ADDLEHOLE
GREENHILL
BUNKERS FARM
LISTER WAY
East Allington
Kellaton Farm
Higher Combe Farm
TOR LANE END
GREENHILL TERR 1
VINEYARD TERR 2
BARNFIELD 3
LABURNUM WAY 4
East Allington Prim Sch

48

Torr Quarry Ind Est
SANDY LANE END
TQ9

6

LOWER WARCOMBE CROSS
Field Study Centre
BOROUGH LA
Borough
STUMPYPOST CROSS
Higher Norton Farm

Warcombe
SLADE CROSS
LEDSTONE CROSS
Knighton
Cross
Colehanger

47

SORLEY LA
A381
HIGHER WARCOMBE CROSS
Slade
HILL LA
SANDY LA
RYE LA
Ledstone
Goveton
Flear Farm
COLE'S CROSS
VENN CROSS
VENTON CT

5

Coombe Farm
Sigdon
HILL CROSS
Buckland-Tout-Saints
Hotel
Rimpston Farm
Netherton
KINGSBRIDGEFORK CROSS
PINHEY'S CROSS
Valley Springs

46

258
Croft
Centry
Malston Mill
SELCOMBE CROSS
Fursdon
FURSDON CROSS

4

KINGSBRIDGE
TQ7
NARROWMOOR CROSS
MALSTON CROSS
Malston Barton
HARLESTON CROSS

45

DARK LA
PLYMOUTH RD
WALLINGFORD RD
STENTIFORD HILL
South Hams
BELLE HILL
BELLE CROSS RD
Bearscombe
Ranscombe
MAREPARK CROSS
STANCOMBE CROSS

3

COOKWORTHY RD
Mus
TH
A379
Coll
CHURCH ST
WOODBURY RD
Sch
Dodbrooke
STOGGY LA
Bowcombe
SHERFORD DOWN CROSS
FURZE CROSS
Sherford Down
SHERFORD DOWN RD
ROSE COTTS
Sherford
FORE ST
PO

44

Ind Est
A381
Liby
Coll
DERBY RD
Ind Est
EBRINGTON ST
BOWCOMBE RD
258
BOWDEN CROSS
Bowden
PEASPARK CROSS
Homefield

PROMENADE
A379
BIDGE HOUSE LA
DUNCOMBE CROSS

2

Southville
EMBANKMENT RD
ROPEWALK
The Grange
1 HERONS REACH
2 WEST CHARLETON CT
3 SAUNDERS WAY
4 CHARLETON COURT BARNS
Keynedon Barton
Frogmore
PH
OLD FROGMORE RD
Coombe Park
PORT LANE CL
PRIMROSE CL

43

Park Farm
Cemy
Ferry P (Summer only)
CHURCH LA
CHARLETON WAY
COMPTON RD
East Charleton
EAST FARM
DANIELS LA
APPLE TREE CL
Hotel
A379
Mill Farm
COOMBE MDWS
COPPERFIELD

1

Kingsbridge Estuary
CURLEW DR
SICKLEMANS CL
TYE LA
MARSH LA
Charleton CE Prim Sch
Frogmore Creek
CREEK CL
WILLOWS CL
ORCHARD CL
LOO CROSS
Sewage Works
West Charleton
ORCHARD VIEW 1
WINSLADE CL 2
Winslade Manor
WINSLADE CT
GERSTON LA
258

42

73   A   74   B   75   C   76   D   77   E   78   F

River Avon
TORR LA

For full street detail of the highlighted area see page 258.

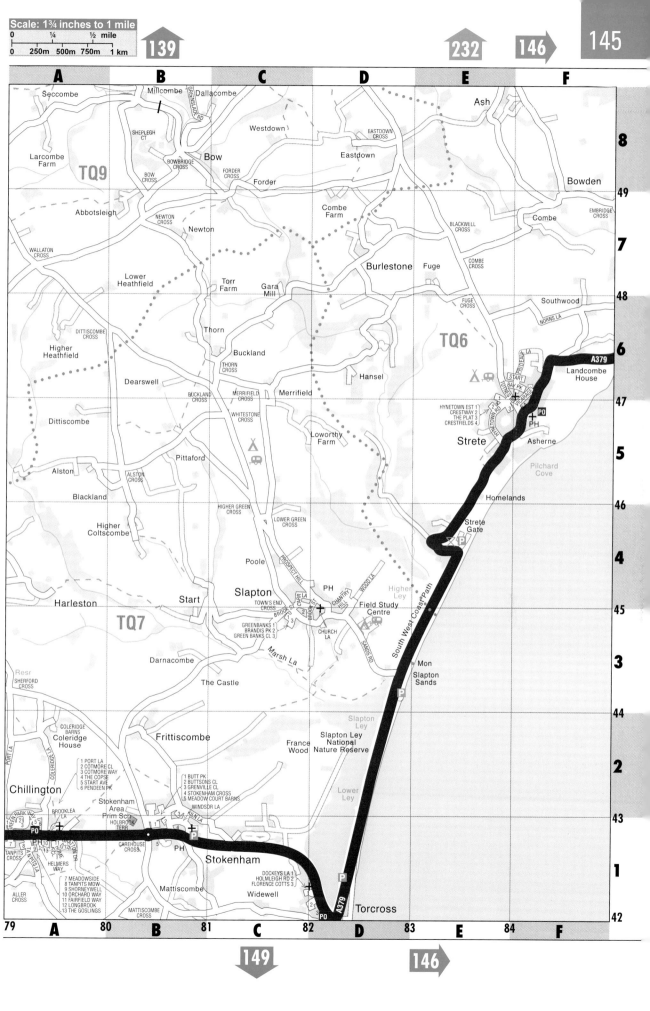

145
233
234

Scale: 1¾ inches to 1 mile
0   ¼   ½ mile
0 250m 500m 750m 1 km

Worden
Venn
Thorn

TQ6

Newfoundland
Cove

TQ6

SW Coast Path

Lookout
Sta
Inner Froward
Point

Blackstone
Point

Lower
Week

B3205

WEEKE HILL

VENN
CROSS

VENN LA

A379

DARTMOUTH RD

B3205

REDLAP
CROSS

COMPASS COVE
COTTS

CASTLE RD

Compass Cove

POUNDHOUSE
CROSS

DEER PARK

Poundhouse

REDLAP RD

8

VENN PK 1
VENN WAY 2
GRATTON CL 3
VENN CL 4
BAY VIEW CL 5
BAY VIEW EST 6
HAREFIELD DR 7
GLEBE PK 8
RAVENSBOURNE LA 9

EMBRIDGE HILL

49

SCHOOL RD

Liby

Redcroft
Heights

REDLAP LA

PH

Little
Dartmouth

Redlap
House

Combe
Point

Stoke
Fleming

BLACKPOOL VALLEY RD

Stoke Fleming
Com Prim Sch

MANOR CT 10
RECTORY LA 11
BAILEYS MDW 12
MILL LA

HOCKEY
FIELDS

7

WGN PARK

CHURCH RD

SHADY LA

Redlap
Cove

Dancing
Beggars

13 CHAPEL LA
14 STOKE HOUSE GDNS
15 WHITE LADIES
16 PENHILL CHALETS
17 BIDDERS WLK

Sanders

OLD RD

NEW RD

Leonard's
Cove

48

Blackpool
Gardens

NORNS
LA

BLACKPOOL HILL

Blackpool

A379

6

Matthew's
Point

47

Forest
Cove

5

46

4

45

3

44

2

43

1

42

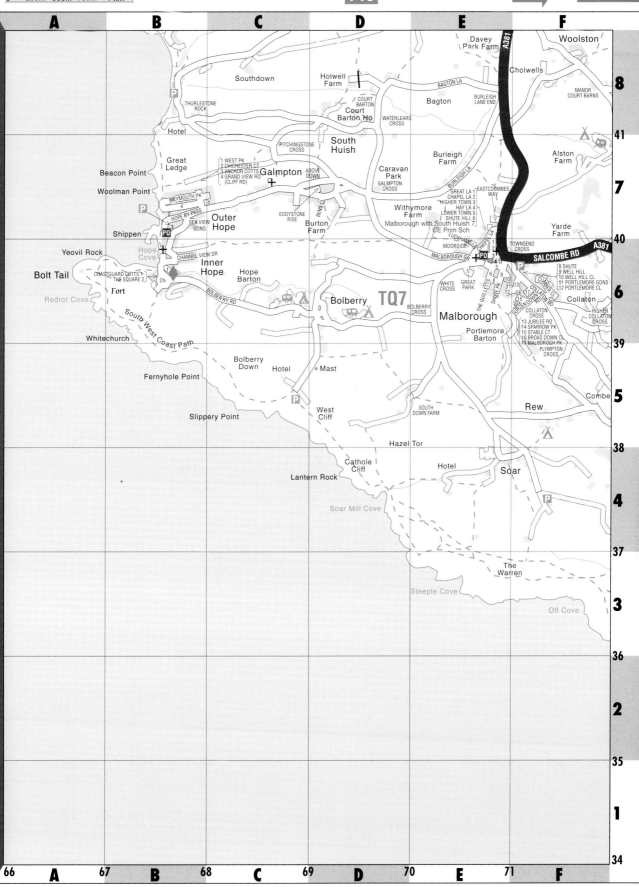

A | B | C | D | E | F

8
41
7
40
6
39
5
38
4
37
3
36
2
35
1
34

Davey Park Farm
A381
Woolston
Cholwells
Southdown
Holwell Farm
Court Barton Ho
COURT BARTON
South Huish
Bagton
BAGTON LA
BURLEIGH LANE END
MANOR COURT BARNS
THURLESTONE ROCK
Hotel
Great Ledge
PITCHINGSTONE CROSS
WATERLEARS CROSS
Burleigh Farm
Alston Farm
Beacon Point
Galmpton
1 WEST PK
2 CHICHESTER CT
3 ANCHOR COTTS
4 GRAND VIEW RD (CLIFF RD)
ABOVE DOWN
Caravan Park
GALMPTON CROSS
BURLEIGH LA
EASTCOOMBES WAY
GREAT LA 1
CHAPEL LA 2
HIGHER TOWN 3
HAY LA 4
LOWER TOWN 5
SHUTE HILL 6
Woolman Point
WEYMOUTH PK
HOPE BY-PASS
Withymore Farm
Malborough with South Huish 7
CE Prim Sch
Yarde Farm
Shippen
SEA VIEW GDNS
EDDYSTONE RISE
BEVS CL
Burton Farm
LUCKHAMS
MOORSIDE
TOWNSEND CROSS
SALCOMBE RD
A381
Yeovil Rock
Hope Cove
CHANNEL VIEW DR
Inner Hope
Hope Barton
White Cross
Great Park
8 SHUTE
9 WELL HILL
10 WELL HILL CL
11 PORTLEMORE GDNS
12 PORTLEMORE CL
Bolt Tail
COASTGUARD COTTS 1
THE SQUARE 2
Outer Hope
BOLBERRY RY RD
Bolberry
TQ7
Bolberry Cross
Collaton
Fort
Malborough
CUMBER CL
COLLATON RD
13 JUBILEE RD
14 SPARROW PK
15 STABLE CT
16 BROAD DOWN CL
17 MALBOROUGH PK
HIGHER COLLATON CROSS
Redrot Cove
Portlemore Barton
COLLATON CROSS
PLYMPTON CROSS
Whitechurch
South West Coast Path
Bolberry Down
Hotel
Mast
Bolberry Cross
Fernyhole Point
West Cliff
SOUTH DOWN FARM
Rew
Combe
Slippery Point
Hazel Tor
Soar
Cathole Cliff
Hotel
Lantern Rock
Soar Mill Cove
The Warren
Steeple Cove
Off Cove

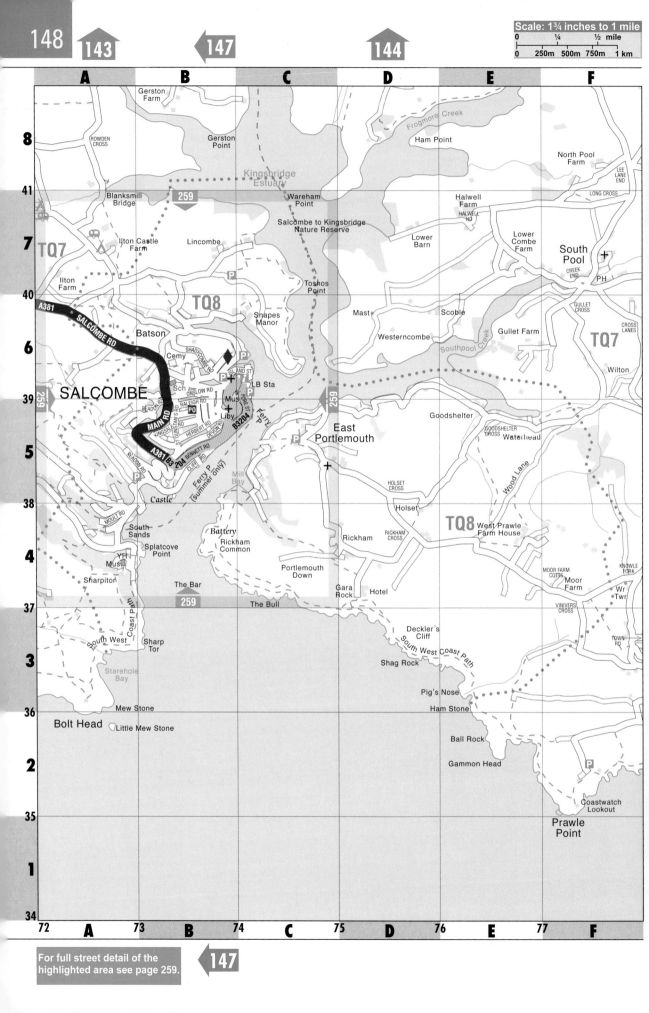

148

143

147

144

Scale: 1¾ inches to 1 mile

0 ¼ ½ mile
0 250m 500m 750m 1 km

A B C D E F

Gerston Farm

Gerston Point

Ham Point

North Pool Farm

LEE LANE END

LONG CROSS

8

Frogmore Creek

Kingsbridge Estuary

Blanksmill Bridge

259

Wareham Point

Halwell Farm

HALWELL HO

41

TQ7

Ilton Castle Farm

Lincombe

Salcombe to Kingsbridge Nature Reserve

Lower Barn

Lower Combe Farm

South Pool

CREEK END

PH

7

Ilton Farm

Toshos Point

40

A381

SALCOMBE RD

TQ8

Snapes Manor

Mast

Westerncombe

Scoble

GULLET CROSS

TQ7

CROSS LANES

Batson

Cemy

SHADYCOMBE RD

Southpool Creek

Wilton

6

259

Sch

ISLAND ST

LB Sta

Goodshelter

GOODSHELTER CROSS

Waterhead

GULLET FARM

SALCOMBE

MAIN RD

ONSLOW RD

RALEIGH RD

Mus

Liby

B3204

East Portlemouth

39

BEADON RD

KINGSALE RD

ST DUNSTAN'S RD

PO

HERBERT RD

DEVON RD

Ferry

Ferry

Wood Lane

5

A381 B3 204

BENNETT RD

CLIFF RD

Ferry P (summer only)

Mill Bay

HOLSET CROSS

West Prawle Farm House

TQ8

38

MOULT RD

Castle

Battery

Rickham Common

Holset

RICKHAM CROSS

Rickham

South Sands

Splatcove Point

Portlemouth Down

MOOR FARM COTTS

Moor Farm

KNOWLE FORK

Wr Twr

4

YH

Mus

Sharpiton

Gara Rock

Hotel

VINIVERS CROSS

37

The Bar

259

The Bull

Deckler's Cliff

TOWN RD

3

South West Coast Path

Sharp Tor

South West Coast Path

Shag Rock

Starehole Bay

Pig's Nose

36

Mew Stone

Ham Stone

Bolt Head

Little Mew Stone

Ball Rock

2

Gammon Head

P

35

Coastwatch Lookout

Prawle Point

1

34

72 A 73 B 74 C 75 D 76 E 77 F

For full street detail of the highlighted area see page 259.

147

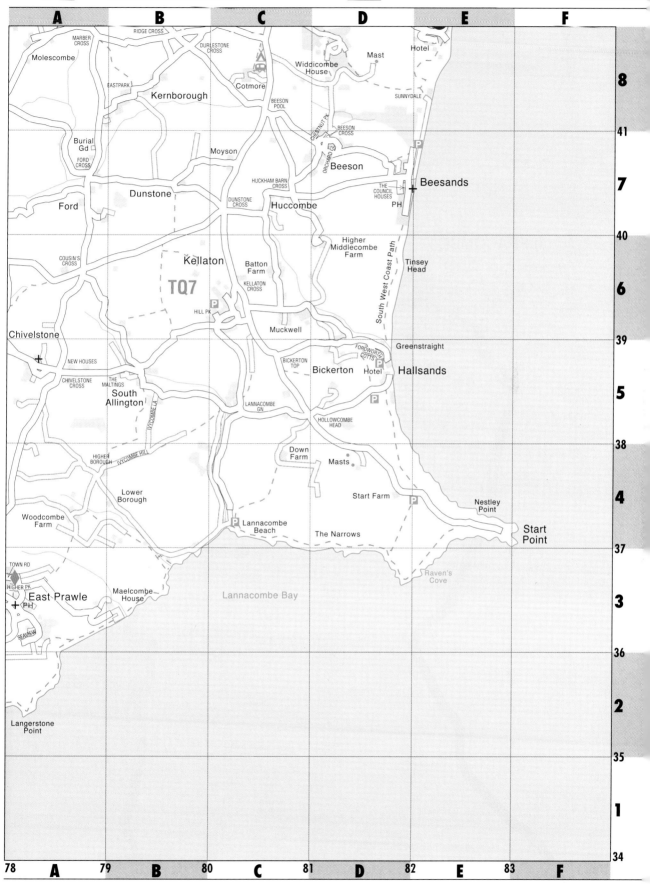

ILFRACOMBE

EX34

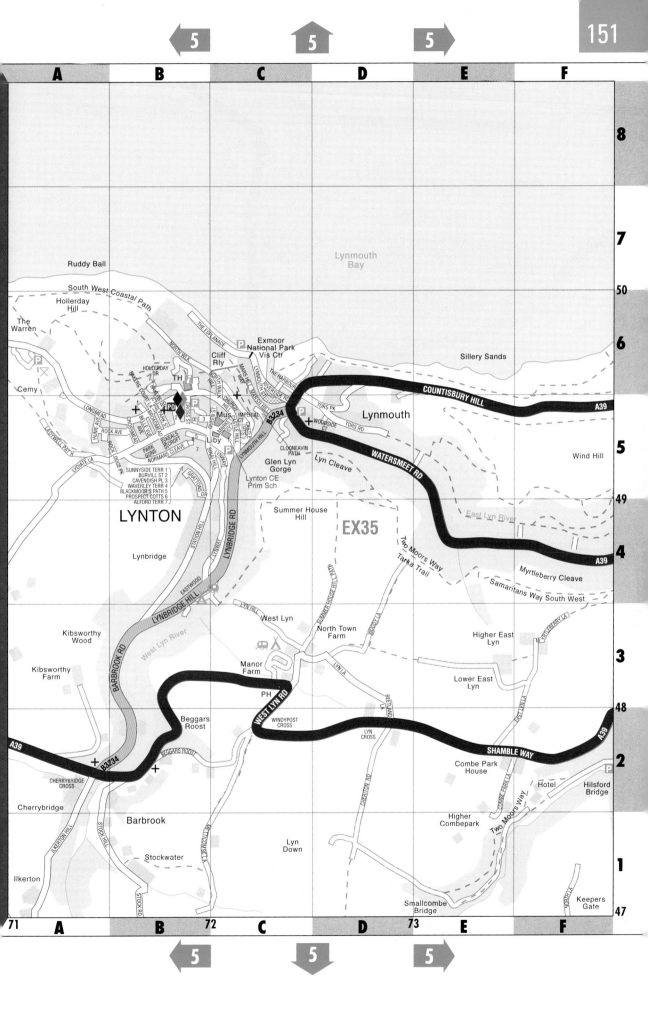

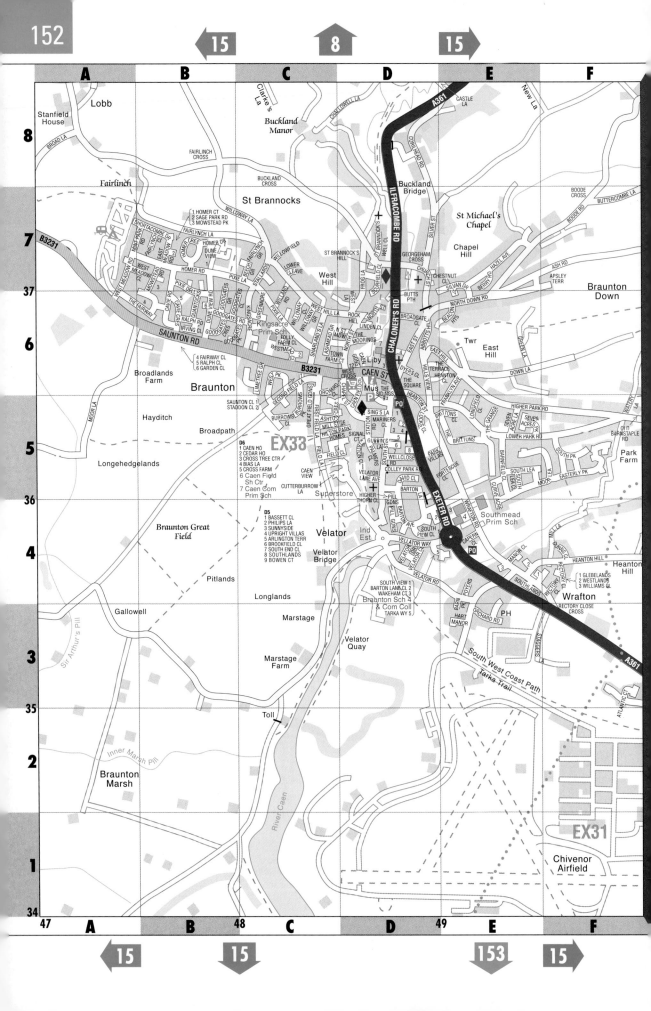

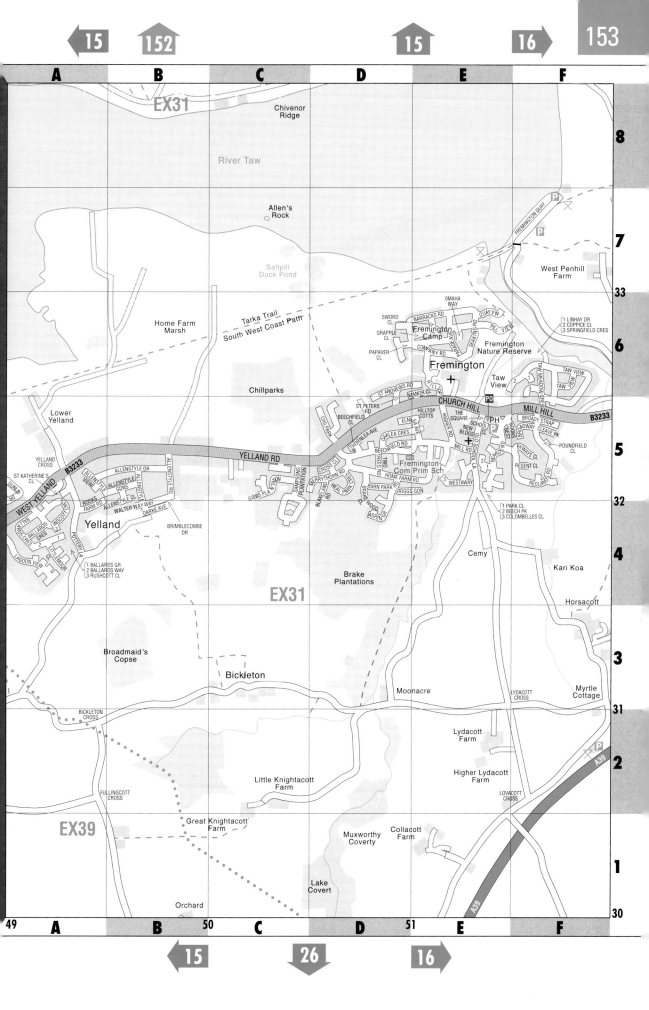

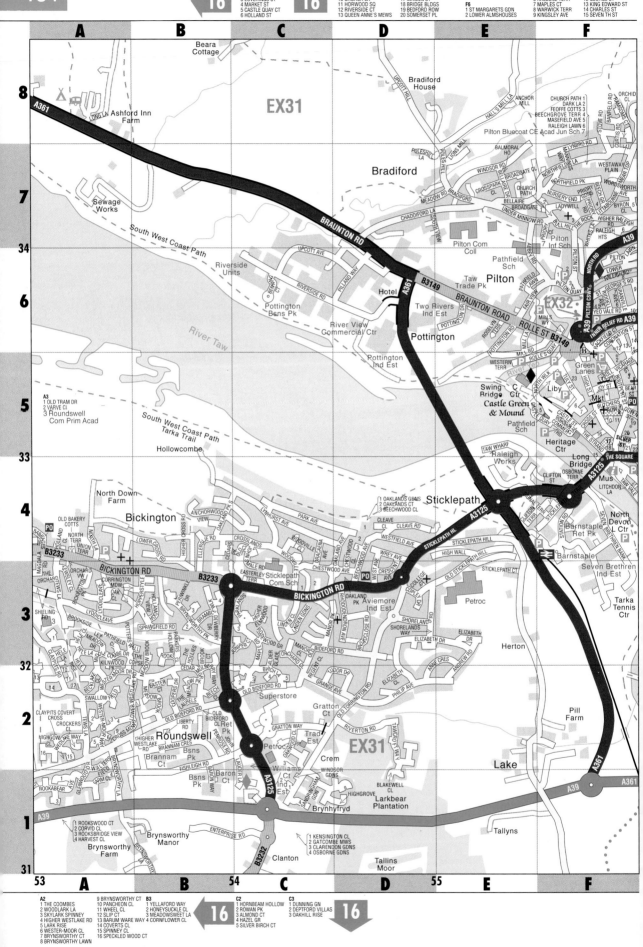

F5
1 GREEN LA
2 NORAH BELLOT CT
3 LOVERINGS CT
4 MARKET ST
5 CASTLE QUAY CT
6 HOLLAND ST

7 PAIGES LA
8 PATERNOSTER ROW
9 ST PETER'S TERR
10 CHURCH LA
11 HORWOOD SQ
12 RIVERSIDE CT
13 QUEEN ANNE'S MEWS

14 QUEEN ANNE'S CT
15 BRIDGE CHAMBERS
16 THEATRE LA
17 MAIDEN ST
18 BRIDGE BLDGS
19 BEDFORD ROW
20 SOMERSET PL

21 DIAMOND ST
22 BELLE MEADOW CT
23 GAMMON WLK

F6
1 ST MARGARETS GDN
2 LOWER ALMSHOUSES

3 REFORM ST
4 CRANLEIGH
5 YEO VALE HO
6 HALDENE TERR
7 MAPLES CT
8 WARWICK TERR
9 KINGSLEY AVE

10 MARGROVE TERR
11 ROWAN ST
(MERMAID WLK)
12 GEORGE ST
13 KING EDWARD ST
14 CHARLES ST
15 SEVEN TH ST

A2
1 THE COOMBES
2 WOODLARK LA
3 SKYLARK SPINNEY
4 HIGHER WESTLAKE RD
5 LARK RISE
6 WESTER-MOOR CL
7 BRYNSWORTHY CT
8 BRYNSWORTHY LAWN

9 BRYNSWORTHY CT
10 PANCHEON CL
11 WHEEL CL
12 SLIP CT
13 BARUM WARE WAY
14 COVERTS CL
15 SPINNEY CL
16 SPECKLED WOOD CT

B3
1 YELLAFORD WAY
2 HONEYSUCKLE CL
3 MEADOWSWEET LA
4 CORNFLOWER CL

C2
1 HORNBEAM HOLLOW
2 ROWAN PK
3 ALMOND CT
4 HAZEL GR
5 SILVER BIRCH CT

C3
1 DUNNING GN
2 DEPTFORD VILLAS
3 OAKHILL RISE

A6
1 ST GEORGE'S TERR
2 LANSDOWN TERR
3 VERONA CT
4 GRANGE CT
5 CARRINGTON TERR
6 PORTLAND BLDGS

7 HIGHER MAUDLIN ST
8 NEW BLDGS
9 MAGDALENE LAWN
10 RICHMOND WLK

A7
1 CLAUDE DIX CL
2 CHARLES HUDSON LA
3 RALEIGH COTTS
4 OSWALD BROWNING WAY
5 MASEFIELD AVE
6 WORDSWORTH AVE

7 PILTON LAWN

B5
1 SABRE WLK
2 METEOR WLK
3 NORTH GARRON
4 THE FIRS
5 RAVELEIGH GDNS
6 GOODLEIGH RD

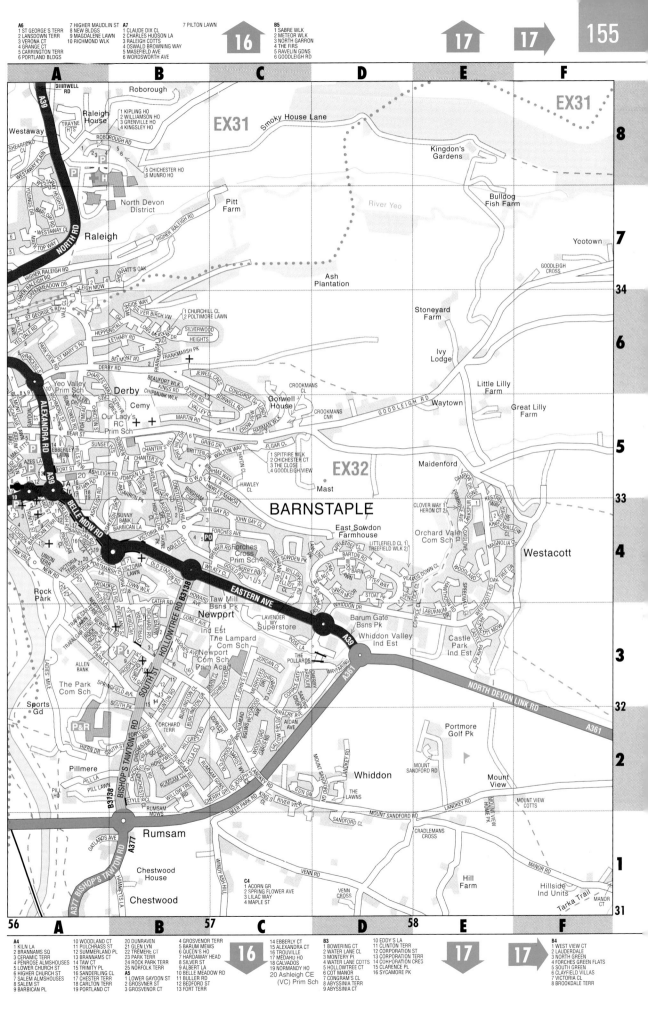

A4
1 KILN LA
2 BRANNAMS SQ
3 CERAMIC TERR
4 PENROSE ALMSHOUSES
5 LOWER CHURCH ST
6 HIGHER CHURCH ST
7 SALEM ALMSHOUSES
8 SALEM ST
9 BARBICAN PL

10 WOODLAND CT
11 PULCHRASS ST
12 SUMMERLAND PL
13 BRANNAMS CT
14 TAW CT
15 TRINITY PL
16 SANDERLING CL
17 CHESTER TERR
18 CARLTON TERR
19 PORTLAND CT

20 DUNRAVEN
21 GLEN LYN
22 TREMEER CT
23 PARK TERR
24 ROCK PARK TERR
25 NORFOLK TERR

A5
1 LOWER GAYDON ST
2 GROSVNER ST
3 GROSVENOR CT

4 GROSVENOR TERR
5 BARUM MEWS
6 QUEEN'S HO
7 HARDAWAY HEAD
8 SILVER ST
9 ALBERT LA
10 BELLE MEADOW RD
11 BULLER RD
12 BEDFORD ST
13 FORT TERR

14 EBBERLY CT
15 ALEXANDRA CT
16 TROUVILLE
17 MEDAHU HO
18 CALVADOS
19 NORMANDY HO
20 Ashleigh CE (VC) Prim Sch

C4
1 ACORN GR
2 SPRING FLOWER AVE
3 LILAC WAY
4 MAPLE ST

B3
1 BOWERING CT
2 WATER LANE CL
3 MONTERY PL
4 WATER LANE COTTS
5 HOLLOWTREE CT
6 COT MANOR
7 CONGRAM'S CL
8 ABYSSINIA TERR
9 ABYSSINIA CT

10 EDDY'S LA
11 CLINTON TERR
12 CORPORATION ST
13 CORPORATION TERR
14 CORPORATION CRES
15 CLARENCE PL
16 SYCAMORE PK

B4
1 WEST VIEW CT
2 LAUDERDALE
3 NORTH GREEN
4 FORCHES GREEN FLATS
5 SOUTH GREEN
6 CLAYFIELD VILLAS
7 VICTORIA CL
8 BROOKDALE TERR

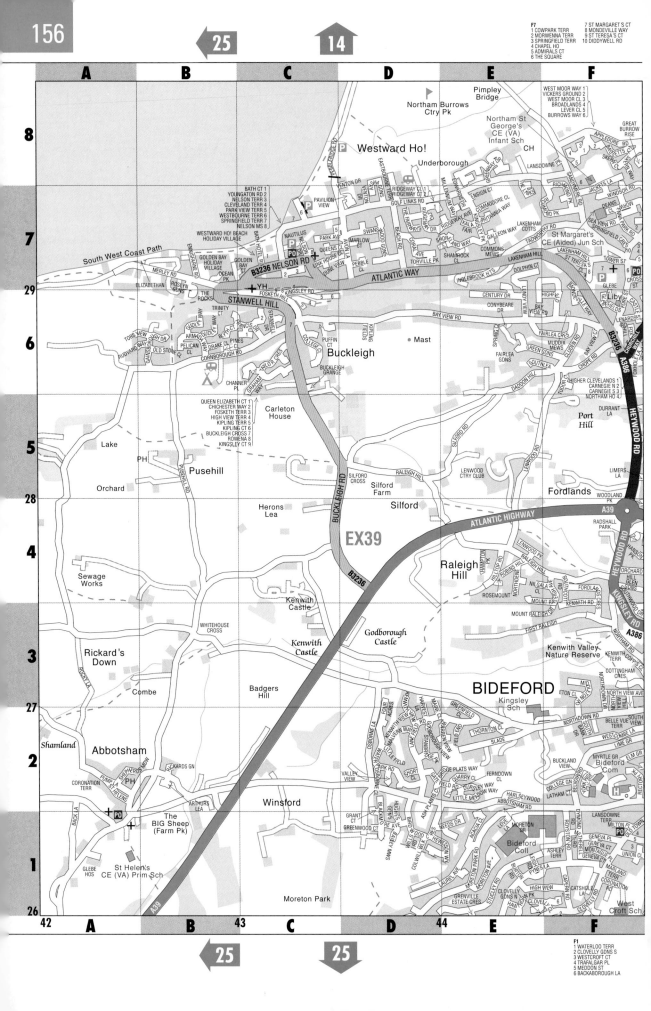

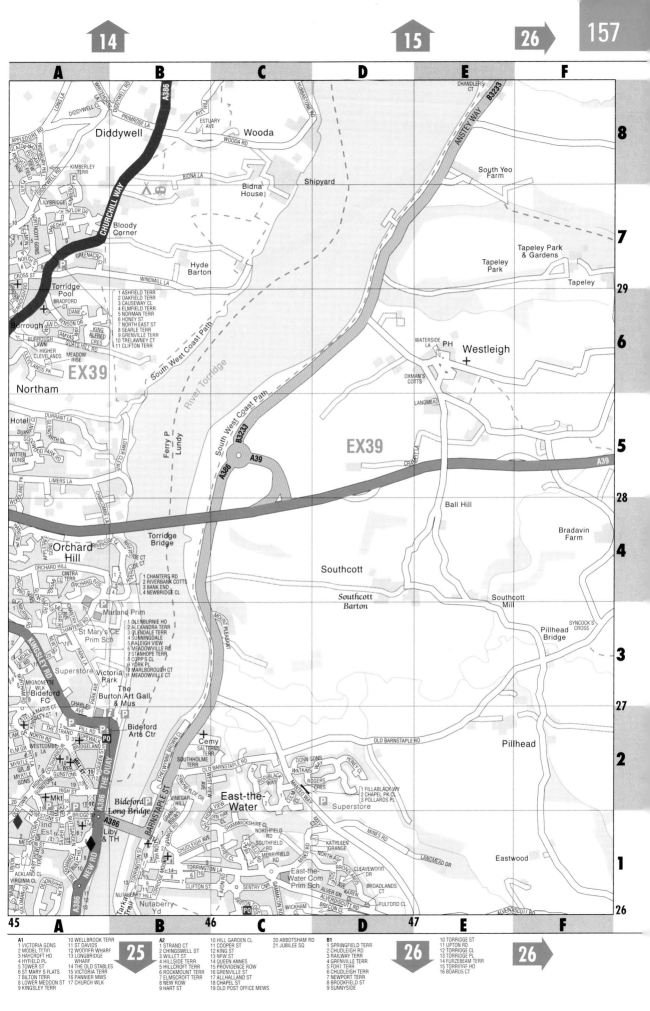

A386
Diddywell
Wooda
CHANDLERS CT
B3233
ANSTEY WAY
WHITEHOUSE RD
DIDDYWELL RD
DIDDYWELL CL
PRIMROSE LA
PITT LA
ESTUARY AVE
WOODA RD
BIDNA LA
Shipyard
South Yeo Farm
APPLEDORE RD
LONG LA
GLAZE
HIGHBURY HILL
DIDDYWELL
KIMBERLEY TERR
Bidna House
Tapeley Park & Gardens
LILYBRIDGE
HT TAYLOR DR
CHURCHILL WAY
Bloody Corner
Hyde Barton
Tapeley Park
LANESHAY
NORTH LA
Tapeley

8

7

29

1 ASHFIELD TERR
2 OAKFIELD TERR
3 CAUSEWAY CL
4 ELMFIELD TERR
5 NORMAN TERR
6 HONEY ST
7 NORTH EAST ST
8 SEARLE TERR
9 GRENVILLE TERR
10 TRELAWNEY CT
11 CLIFTON TERR

GREENACRE CL
Torridge Pool
BRADFORD
DANE CL
BENSON DR
KING ALFRED CRES
WINDMILL LA
Burrough
BURROUGH RD
CROSS ST
NORTH LA
AMYAS
GOATS HILL RD
HIGHER CLEVELANDS
MEADOW RISE
BURROUGH LAWN
CLEVELANDS PK
EX39
Northam

Waterside La PH
Westleigh
OXMAN'S COTTS
LANGMEAD

6

Hotel
Hotel Cl
DURRANT LA
GOODPARK RD
DURRANT CL
NORTH CL
WITTEN GDNS
LOWER CL EAVE
LIMERS LA
WOODLAND PK
CHROME LA
River Torridge
South West Coast Path
Ferry P Lundy
B3233
A386
A39
EX39
South West Coast Path
CRANFORD
A39

5

28

Orchard Hill
APPLETREE CL
ORCHARD HILL
CINTRA TERR
ORCHARD RISE
RIVERSIDE CT
RIVERS
Torridge Bridge

1 CHANTERS RD
2 RIVERBANK COTTS
3 BANK END
4 NEWBRIDGE CL

Southcott
Ball Hill
Bradavin Farm

4

KINGSLEY RD
NEW RD
St Mary's CE Prim Sch
Marland Prim
Superstore
Victoria Park
PARK LA
PARK AVE

1 GLENBURNIE HO
2 ALEXANDRA TERR
3 GLENDALE TERR
4 SUNNINGDALE
5 RALEIGH VIEW
6 MEADOWVILLE RD
7 STANHOPE TERR
8 COPP'S CL
9 YORK PL
10 MARLBOROUGH CT
11 MEADOWVILLE CT

MOUNT PLEASANT
Southcott Barton
Southcott Mill
Pillhead Bridge
SYNCOCK'S CROSS

3

27

Bideford FC
MIGNONETTE WLK
STELLA MARIS CT
KINGSLEY ST
THE STRAND
NORTH RD
WESTCOMBE LA
The Burton Art Gall & Mus
CHARLES AVE
PILL RD
ROPEWALK
BRIDGELAND ST
Bideford Arts Ctr
Cemy
SALTERNS TERR
SOUTHHOLME TERR
ETHELWYNNE BROWN CL
OLD BARNSTAPLE RD
Old Barnstaple Rd
Pillhead

DONN GDNS
WATKINS
HONEY ST
ROGERS CRES
1 FILLABLACK WY
2 CHAPEL PK CL
3 POLLARDS PL
Superstore

2

THE QUAY
BARNSTAPLE ST
Bideford Long Bridge
BRIDGE ST
A386
Liby & TH
Mkt
HIGH ST
QUEEN ST
LOWER GUNSTONE
MYRTLE GR
LIME GR
ELM GR
A386
Ind Est
MEDDON ST
NEW RD
VINEGAR HILL
WEST VIEW
WEST VIEW AVE
East-the-Water
BIDIBLACK WAY
MANTEO WAY
MAY ST

1

DEVONSHIRE PK
VIRGINIA CL
ACKLAND CL
SOLOMAN
A386
NEW RD
Bideford
CHUDLEIGH AVE
AYRES VIEW
FORDE VIEW
TORRINGTON LA
CLIFTON ST
SENTRY CNR
Nutaberry Yd
Tarka Trail
East-the-Water Com Prim Sch
WICKHAM LA
GAMMACON RD
BRECON CL
FULFORD CL
ALVERDISCOTT RD
BROADLANDS CT
KATHLEEN GRANGE
CLEAVEWOOD DR
Eastwood
MINES RD
LANGMEAD DR
ALVERDISCOTT RD

26

A1
1 VICTORIA GDNS
2 MODEL TERR
3 HAYCROFT HO
4 HYFIELD PL
5 TOWER ST
6 ST MARY S FLATS
7 BILTON TERR
8 LOWER MEDDON ST
9 KINGSLEY TERR
10 WELLBROOK TERR
11 ST DAVIDS
12 WOODFR WHARF
13 LONGBRIDGE WHARF
14 THE OLD STABLES
15 VICTORIA TERR
16 PANNIER MWS
17 CHURCH WLK

A2
1 STRAND CT
2 CHINGSWELL ST
3 WILLET ST
4 HILLSIDE TERR
5 HILLCROFT TERR
6 ROCKMOUNT TERR
7 ELMSCROFT TERR
8 NEW ROW
9 HART ST
10 HILL GARDEN CL
11 COOPER ST
12 KING ST
13 NEW ST
14 QUEEN ANNES
15 PROVIDENCE ROW
16 GRENVILLE ST
17 ALLHALLAND ST
18 CHAPEL ST
19 OLD POST OFFICE MEWS
20 ABBOTSHAM RD
21 JUBILEE SQ

B1
1 SPRINGFIELD TERR
2 CHUDLEIGH RD
3 RAILWAY TERR
4 GRENVILLE TERR
5 FORT TERR
6 CHUDLEIGH TERR
7 NEWPORT TERR
8 BROOKFIELD ST
9 SUNNYSIDE
10 TORRIDGE ST
11 UPTON RD
12 TORRIDGE CL
13 TORRIDGE PL
14 FURZEBEAM TERR
15 TORRIDGE HO
16 BOARDS CT

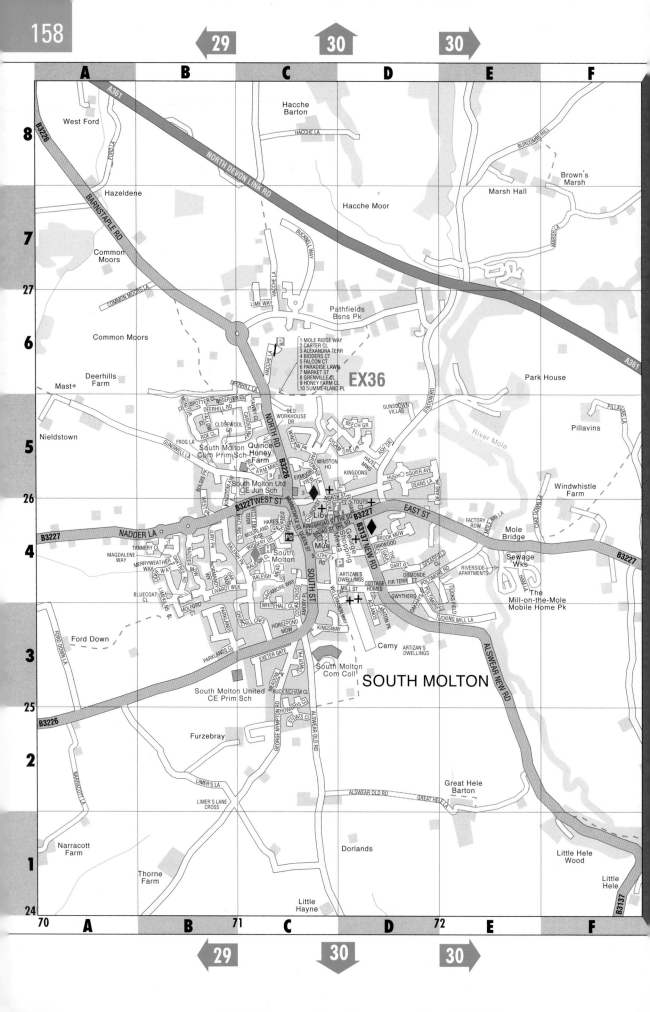

EX36

1 MOLE RIDGE WAY
2 CARTER CL
3 ALEXANDRA TERR
4 BIDDERS CT
5 FALCON CT
6 PARADISE LAWN
7 MARKET ST
8 GRENVILLE CL
9 HONEY FARM CL
10 SUMMERLAND PL

SOUTH MOLTON

South Molton Com Coll

South Molton United
CE Prim Sch

South Molton Utd
CE Jun Sch

South Molton
Cum Prim Sch

Quince
Honey
Farm

West Ford
Hazeldene
Common Moors
Common Moors
Deerhills Farm
Mast
Nieldstown
Ford Down
Narracott Farm
Thorne Farm
Furzebray
Limer's Lane Cross
Dorlands
Little Hayne
Little Hele Wood
Little Hele
Great Hele Barton
Hacche Barton
Hacche Moor
Marsh Hall
Brown's Marsh
Park House
Pillavins
Windwhistle Farm
Mole Bridge
The Mill-on-the-Mole Mobile Home Pk
Sewage Wks
Pathfields Bsns Pk
Gunsdown Villas
Ford Down

North Devon Link Rd
Barnstaple Rd
A361
B3226
B3227
Nadder La
B3227
West St
East St
South St
New Rd
Alswear New Rd
B313
B3227
B3137
Alswear Old Rd
B3226
Great Hele La

River Mole

Cemy

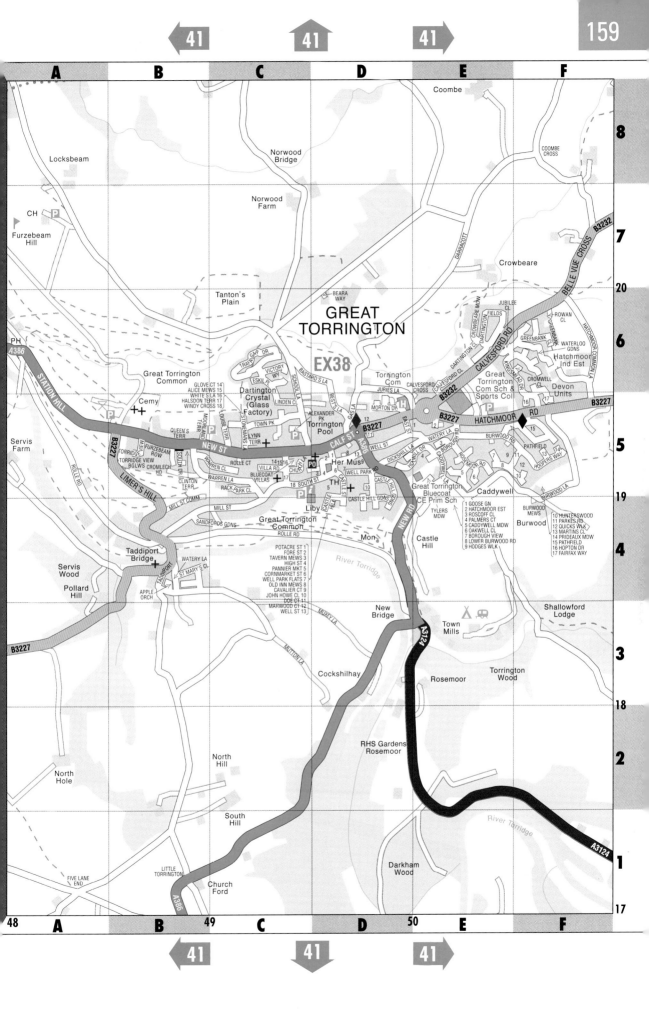

A B C D E F

8

7

20

6

5

19

4

3

18

2

1

17

Coombe

COOMBE CROSS

Locksbeam

CH P

Furzebeam Hill

PH

A386

STATION HILL

Servis Farm

B3227

Cemy

Great Torrington Common

Norwood Bridge

Norwood Farm

Tanton's Plain

BEARA WAY

GREAT TORRINGTON

EX38

Crowbeare

B3232

BELLE VUE CROSS

CROWBEARE MDW

DARRACOTT

JUBILEE FIELDS

DARTINGTON CL

ROWAN CL

GREENBANK

GREENBANK CL

WATERLOO GDNS

HATCHMOOR COMMON LA

Hatchmoor Ind Est

CALVESFORD RD

Torrington Com

CALVESFORD CROSS

DARTINGTON RD

B3232

Great Torrington Com Sch & Sports Coll

KINGSMEAD DR

CROMWELL

Devon Units

B3227

GLOVE CT 14
ALICE MEWS 15
WHITE S LA 16
HALSDON TERR 17
WINDY CROSS 18

TRAPP GAP DR
ESKIL WY
VICTORY WY

Dartington Crystal (Glass Factory)

SCHOOL LA

LINDEN CL

BEST'S LA
BASTARD'S LA

Alexander Pk Torrington Pool

GAS LA

JURIES LA

MORTON DR

H

CALVESFORD CL

EAST ST

B3227

HATCHMOOR RD

BURWOOD RD

Pathfield

16

15

HOPPERS WY

TORRIDGE VIEW
BGLWS
TORRIDGE
VIEW
Servis Farm

QUEEN'S TERR

MORLAND TERR

LOUISE TERR

TOWN PK

STONEMA'S LA

NEW ST

P

P

P

LYNN TERR

VILLA RD

ROLLE CT

WARREN LA

141516

CHU ST

CALF ST

A386

WELL ST

DICKSHILL LA

HOWELL RD

BOROUGH RD

CADDYWELL RD

ROSEMOOR RD

BURWOOD LA

BURWOOD MEWS

Caddywell

1 GOOSE GN
2 HATCHMOOR EST
3 ROSCOFF CL
4 PALMERS CT
5 CADDYWELL MDW
6 OAKWELL CT
7 BOROUGH VIEW
8 LOWER BURWOOD RD
9 HODGES WLK

10 HUNTERSWOOD
11 PARKES RD
12 QUICKS WLK
13 MARTINS CL
14 PRIDEAUX MDW
15 PATHFIELD
16 HOPTON DR
17 FAIRFAX WY

Burwood

Great Torrington Bluecoat CE Prim Sch

TYLERS MDW

LIMER'S HILL

ROLLE RD

SOUTH DR

CLINTON TERR

CROMLECH HO

RACK PARK CL

SANDFORDS GDNS

MILL ST

MILL ST COMM

Bluecoat Villas

18 SOUTH ST

P

Castle Hill

Liby

TH

CASTLE HILL

CASTLE HILL GDNS

NEW RD

Great Torrington Common

Taddiport Bridge

TADDIPORT

ST MARY'S CL

WATERY LA

POTACRE ST 1
FORE ST 2
TAVERN MEWS 3
HIGH ST 4
PANNIER MKT 5
CORNMARKET ST 6
WELL PARK FLATS 7
OLD INN MEWS 8
CAVALIER CT 9
JOHN HOWE CL 10
DOE CT 11
MARWOOD CT 12
WELL ST 13

Mon

Servis Wood

Pollard Hill

APPLE ORCH

River Torridge

MUXEY LA

New Bridge

A3124

Town Mills

Shallowford Lodge

B3227

MUTTON LA

Cockshilhay

Rosemoor

Torrington Wood

North Hole

North Hill

South Hill

RHS Gardens Rosemoor

Darkham Wood

River Torridge

A3124

FIVE LANE END

LITTLE TORRINGTON

A386

Church Ford

Somerset STREET ATLAS

| A | B | C | D | E | F |

WELLINGTON

Tone
B3187
Lowmoor Ind Est
West Deane Way
Sewage Works
Blackham Copse
Poole Farm
Long Copse

JOHN COLE CL 1
FOLLETT CL 2
PROCTOR RD 3
TREDWIN CL 4
MAURICE JENNINGS DR 5

Crosslands
Tonedale Ind Est
Thomas Fox Rd
Wharf Cotts
Five Hos
Longmead Cotts
Tonedale
Garden Terr
Stoneleigh
Canal Cl
Richards Cl
Milverton Rd

Poole Ind Est
Poole
Nynehead Rd
Cadeside Cvn Site
Cades Gdns
Taunton Rd
B3187

Longforth Farm
Palmers Mead
Luke's Dr
Gala Dr
Gregory's Dre
Rices
Lillebonne Way
Factory
Works

Tonedale Bsns Pk
Burchill's Hill
Weaver's Reach
Station Rd
High Path
Springfield Rd
Riverside
Riverside

Holyoake St
Mitchell St
Owen St
Seymour St
Bonet St
Ivy Ho
Quantock Rd
Brendon Rd
George St
Popham Flats
Mancer Cl
Victoria St
Penny Dr
Howard Rd
Parklands Rd
Thomas St
Stedham's Cl
Isambard Kingdom Brunel Prim Sch
Drake's Place
Priory Ct
Drake's St
Churchfields
Baynes Cl
Kelway Rd
Priory
Numbers Rd
Lillebonne Way
Cades Mead
Torres Vedras
Bramley Cl
Aspin Rd
Aspin Cl
Popham Rd
Damson Pl
Rd
Nash Dr
Blackdown Mdw

Tonedale Farm
Winsbere La
Linden Hill
Linden Hill
Lower Westford
Corams La
Riverside
Sports Ctr
Beech Gr
Ye Gables
Beech Grove Prim Sch
Court Fields Com Sch
Court Dr
Waterloo Rd
North St
Burcage
White Hart La
Lancer Cl
Mus
Liby
Bsns Pk
Acre Cl
St John's CE Prim Sch
The Old Vicarage
Buckwell
Baker's La
St Johns
Gladstone Terr
Parker Cl
Jurston La
Mitchell's Pool
1 Pear Tree Way
2 Damson Cres
Jurston Farm

Lower Westford
Water Path
Orchard Cl
Allendale
Brook La
Northside
Owen Ground
The Well
Rockwell Green CE Prim Sch
Rockwell Green
Hyacinth Terr
Mantle St
Taylor Pl
Court Dr
Griggs Dri
Clifford Mews
Wellington Jun Sch
Wellington Sch
Laburnum Rd
Chestnut Dr
Hawthorne Rd
Sanford Mws
Jurston Fields
Kenyon Rd
Sanford Hse
Jeffries Rd
Wellington Relief Rd

Westford Ct
Payton Rd
Westford Dr
Rockwell Dr
Dobree Rd
Greenway Rd
Northside Gw
Rockwell Gate
Hilly Head
Exeter Rd
Trinity Cl
Champford La
Martins Cl
Bullens Cl
Rookery Terr 1
Court Terr 2
Trinity Row 3
Walkers Gate
Eight Acre La
Mornington Pk
Wesley Pk
Pyles Thorne Cl
Oldway Ho
Blackmoor Rd
Oldway Hse
Jurston Rise

Frank Webber Rd
Warre Cl
Dobree Rd
Exeter Rd
Gillards Cl
Cemy
Foxdown Ho
Foxdown Hill
Swains La
Swains Rd
Corner Cl
Ardwyn
Elworthy Dr
Wellesley Pk
Hoyles Cl
Webbers Cl
Damson Cres
Oakfield
Pyles Thorne
West Buckland Rd
A38
Burts Farm

TA21
Farthing's Pitts
Cox Rd
Immenstadt Dr
The Brambles
Blackberry La
John Grove
Lyddon Cl
Carters Way
Post Rd
Barn Meads Rd
Wellesley Park Prim Sch
Monument Rd
Ford St
Ford Farm
Woodlands

Pitt Farm
Barrington Way
Pope's La
Blackdown Rd
Andrew Allan Rd
Wellington Relief Rd
Burroughway
Rope Wlk
Oldway Rd
Middle Green Rd
Robin's Close
Gillard's Farm
M5

Exeter Road Cvn Pk
Dott's Cl
Elizabeth Cl
Ross Cl
Morris Cl
Bagley Rd
Ryelands Farm Ind Est
Blackboy Farm
Standle
Stallards
Middle Green Farm
Middle Green

Brunstone Rd
A38
Bagley Green
Bagley Farm
Standle
Standle
Middle Green
Standand

Pleamore Cross
Greenacres
Legglands

Wrangcombe Rd
Bryant's Farm
Long Wood
Park La
Leyland's Farm
Calway's Farm
Briscoe House

Woodford
Higher Woodford
Little Silver La
Wellington Hill
Voxmoor
M5

| A | B | C | D | E | F |

D5
1 THE GARDENS
2 CHAMPFORD MEWS
3 POUND TERR
4 MARTINS BLDGS
5 IMPROVEMENT PL
6 WILLCOCKS CL
7 LABURNUM COTTS
8 JUBILEE CT

D6
1 THE LAWN
2 BEECH CT
3 BELVEDERE CT
4 OLD CT MWS
5 CORNHILL

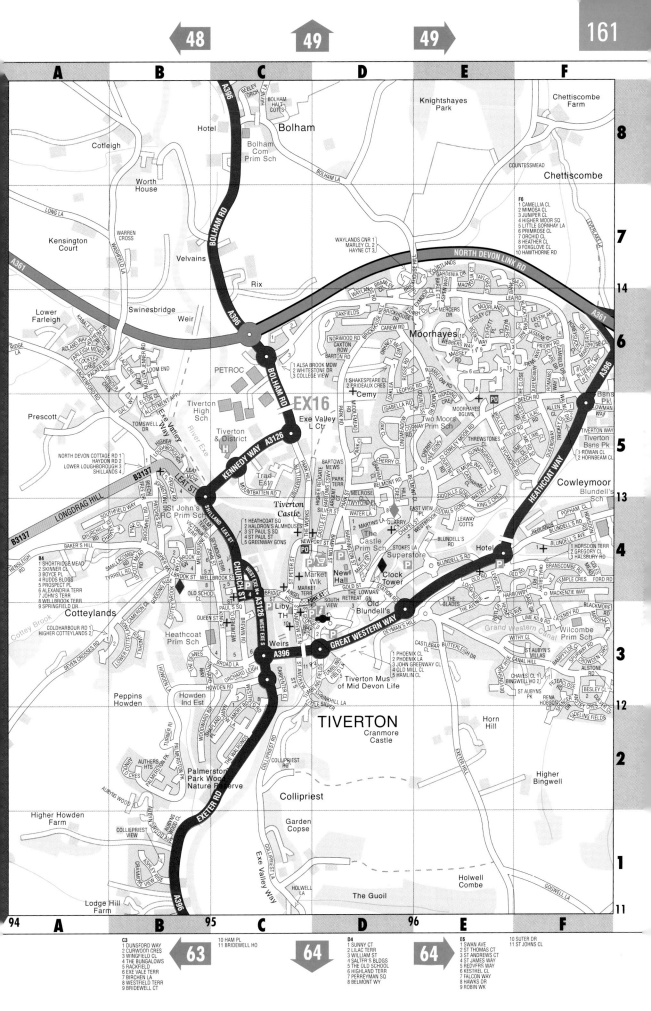

C3
1 DUNSFORD WAY
2 CURWOOD CRES
3 WINGFIELD CL
4 THE BUNGALOWS
5 RACKFIELD
6 EXE VALE TERR
7 BIRCHEN LA
8 WESTFIELD TERR
9 BRIDEWELL CT

10 HAM PL
11 BRIDEWELL HO

D4
1 SUNNY CT
2 LILAC TERR
3 WILLIAM ST
4 SALTFR'S BLDGS
5 THE OLD SCHOOL
6 HIGHLAND TERR
7 PERREYMAN SQ
8 BELMONT WY

E6
1 SWAN AVE
2 ST THOMAS CT
3 ST ANDREWS CT
4 ST JAMES WAY
5 REDVERS WAY
6 KESTREL CL
7 FALCON WAY
8 HAWKS DR
9 ROBIN WK

10 SUTER DR
11 ST JOHNS CL

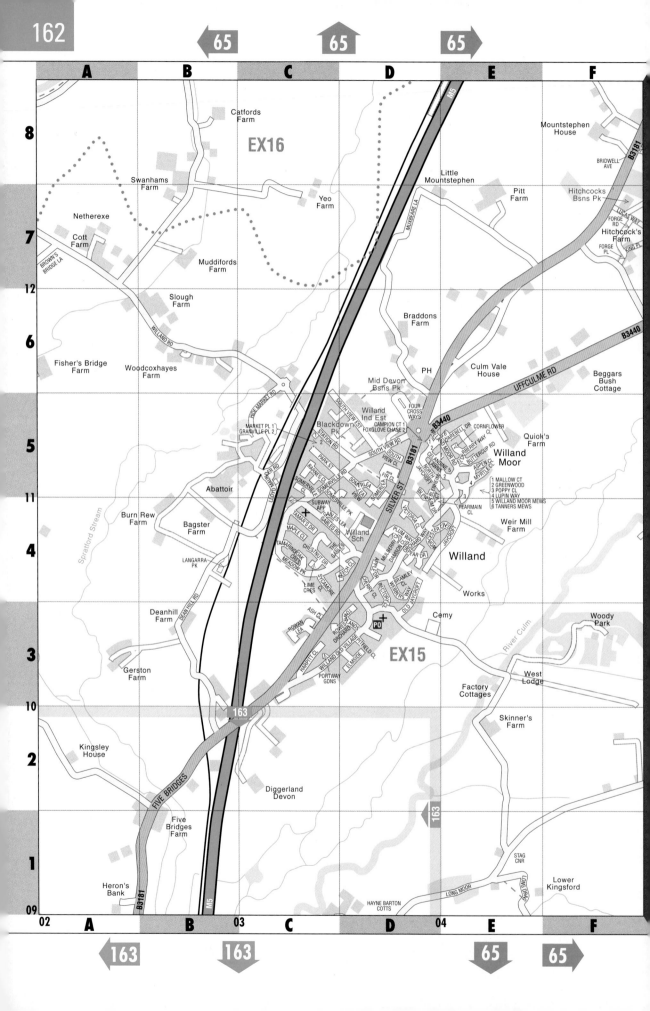

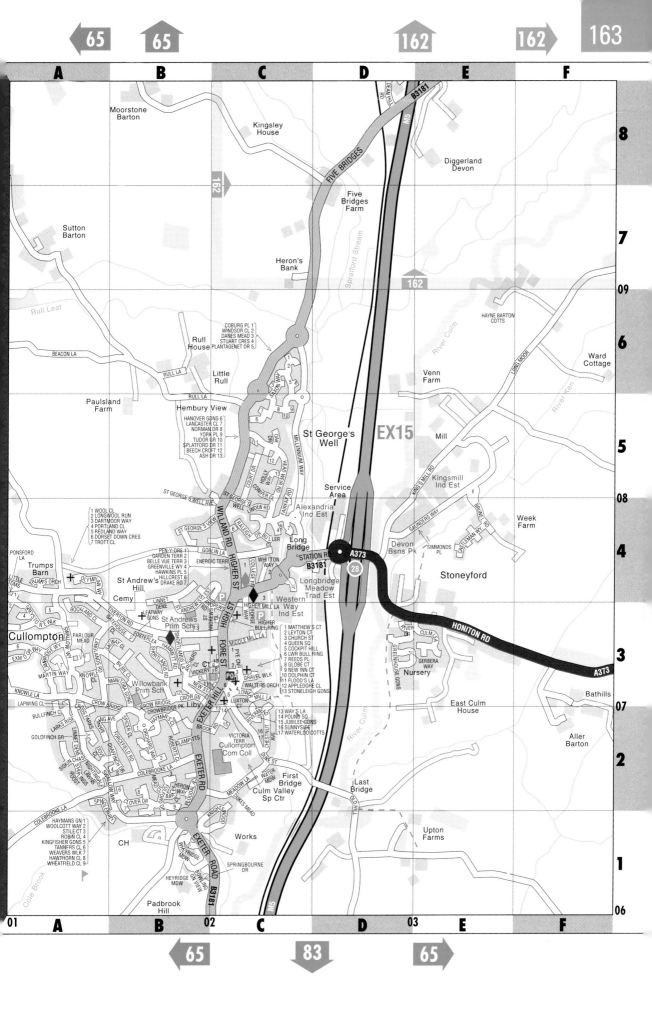

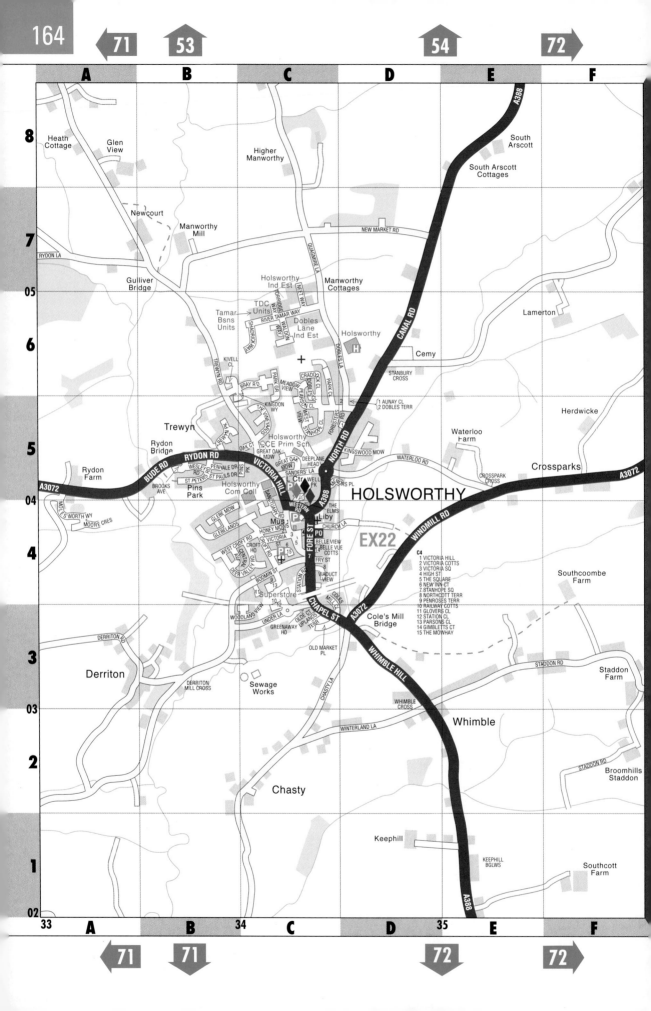

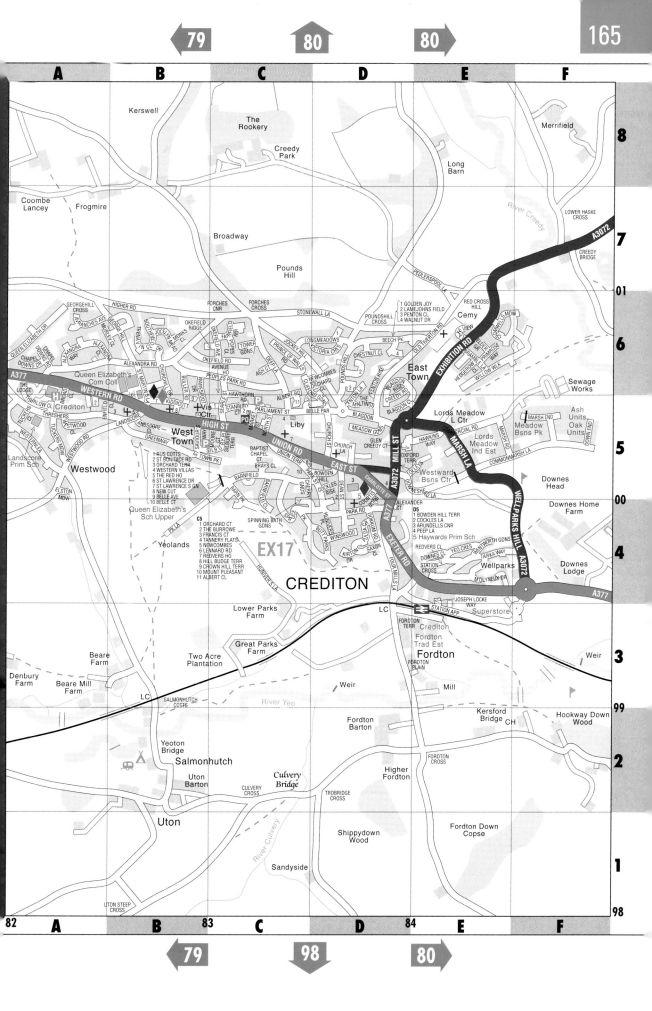

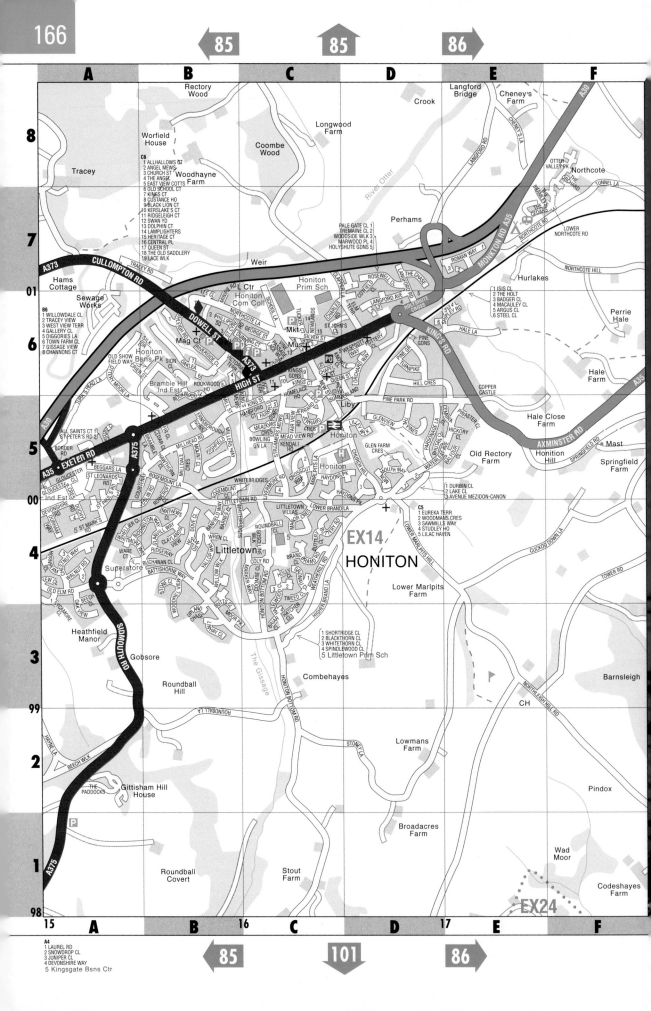

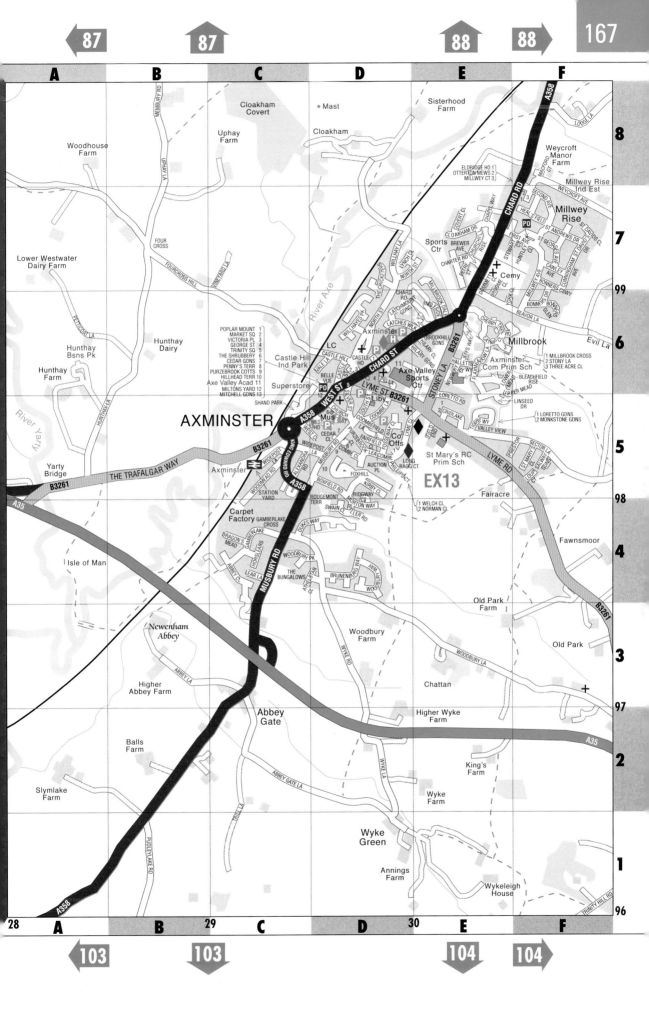

A   B   C   D   E   F

8
7
99
6
5
98
4
3
97
2
1
96

Woodhouse Farm

Cloakham Covert

Uphay Farm

• Mast

Cloakham

Sisterhood Farm

Weycroft Manor Farm

Lower Westwater Dairy Farm

FOUR CROSS

River Axe

ELDRIDGE HO 1
OTTERTON MEWS 2
MILLWEY CT 3

Millwey Rise Ind Est

Millwey Rise

Sports Ctr

Cemy

PO

Hunthay Bsns Pk

Hunthay Dairy

POPLAR MOUNT 1
MARKET SQ 2
VICTORIA PL 3
GEORGE ST 4
TRINITY SQ 5
THE SHRUBBERY 6
CEDAR GDNS 7
PENNY'S TERR 8
PURZEBROOK COTTS 9
HILLHEAD TERR 10
Axe Valley Acad 11
MILTONS YARD 12
MITCHELL GDNS 13

Axminster

LC

Castle Hill Ind Park

Superstore

Millbrook

1 MILLBROOK CROSS
2 STONY LA
3 THREE ACRE CL

Axminster Com Prim Sch

Bleachfield Rise

LINSEED DR

1 LORETTO GDNS
2 MONKSTONE GDNS

Hunthay Farm

Axe Valley Sports Ctr

Castle Hill

WEST ST

Mus

P

Liby

B3261

P

Co Offs

St Mary's RC Prim Sch

EX13

Fairacre

River Yarty

AXMINSTER

THE TRAFALGAR WAY

B3261

Axminster

Station Yard

A358

Widepost

AUCTION

10

FOXHILL

Long Ragg Ct

Fawnsmoor

Yarty Bridge

A35

1 WELCH CL
2 NORMAN CL

Old Park Farm

Old Park

Carpet Factory

Gamberlake Cross

Dragon's Mead

THE BUNGALOWS

Woodbury Pk

Woodbury Farm

Isle of Man

MUSBURY RD

Lear La

Chattan

Higher Wyke Farm

Newenham Abbey

ABBEY LA

Higher Abbey Farm

Abbey Gate

WYKE RD

Woodbury Farm

A35

Balls Farm

ABBEY GATE LA

King's Farm

Wyke Farm

Slymlake Farm

PUDLEY LAKE RD

Wyke Green

Annings Farm

Wykeleigh House

TRINITY HILL RD

A358

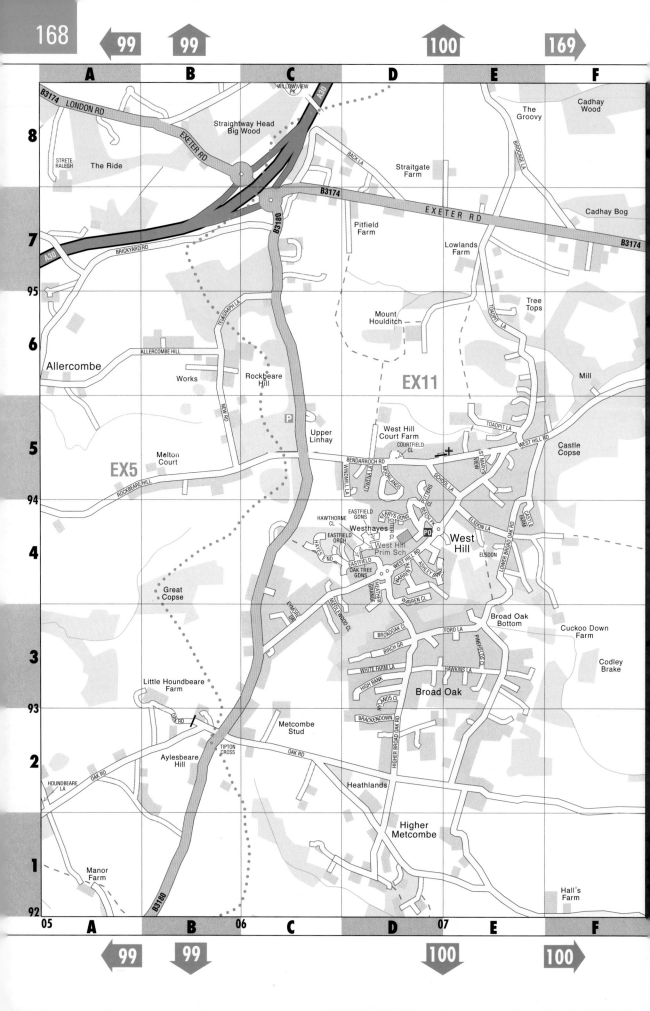

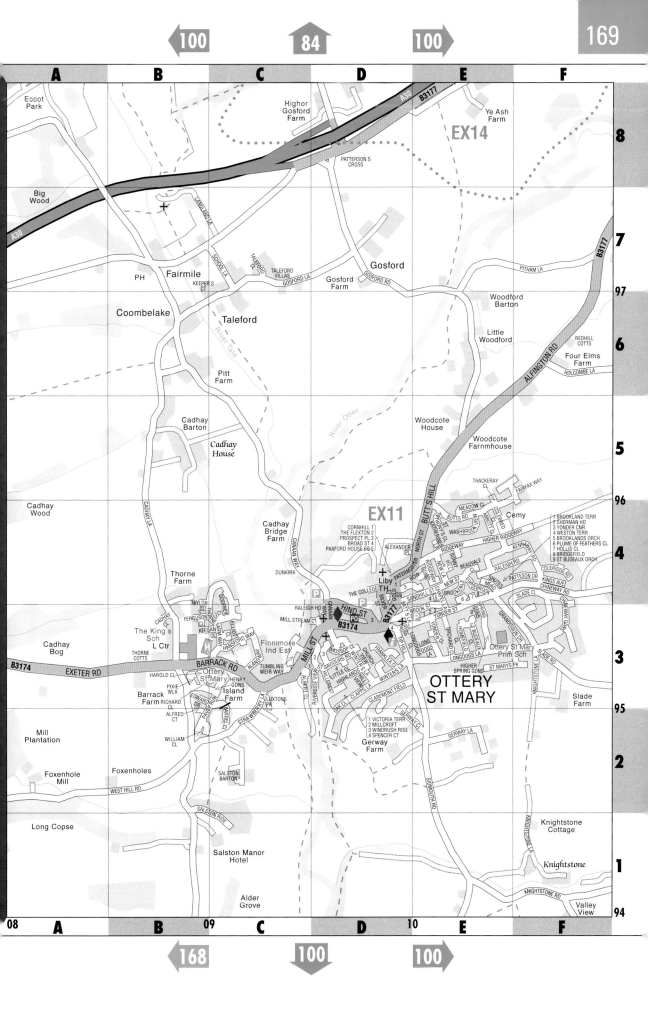

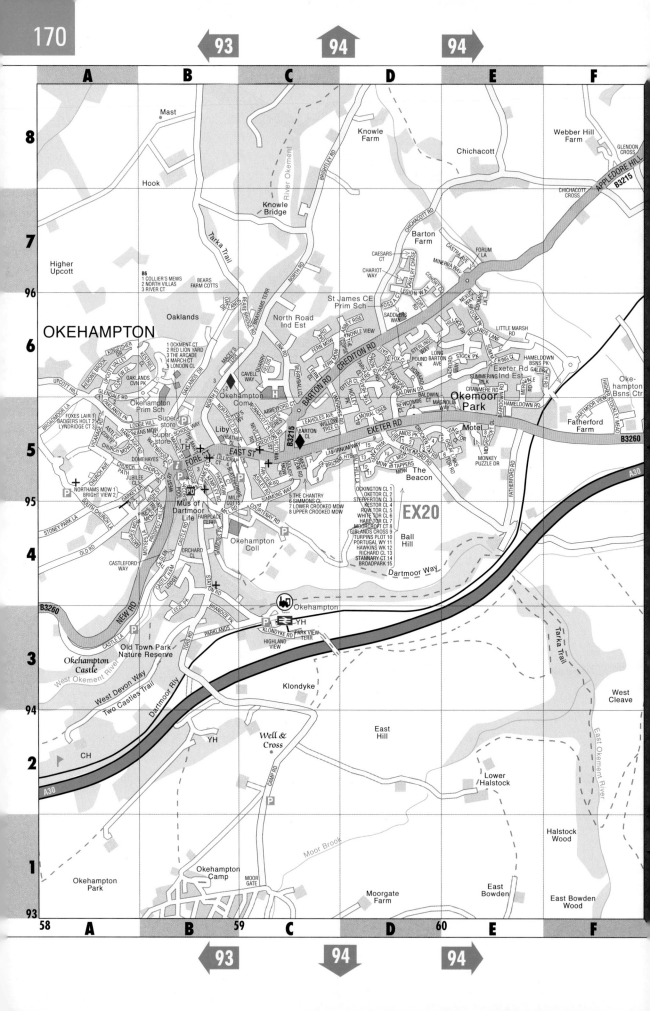

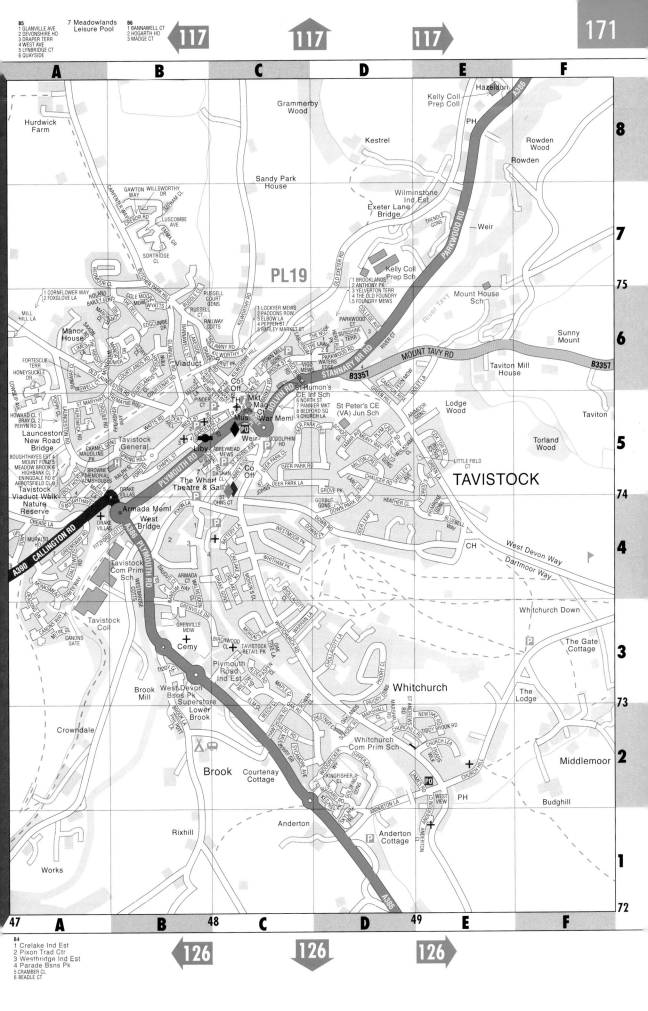

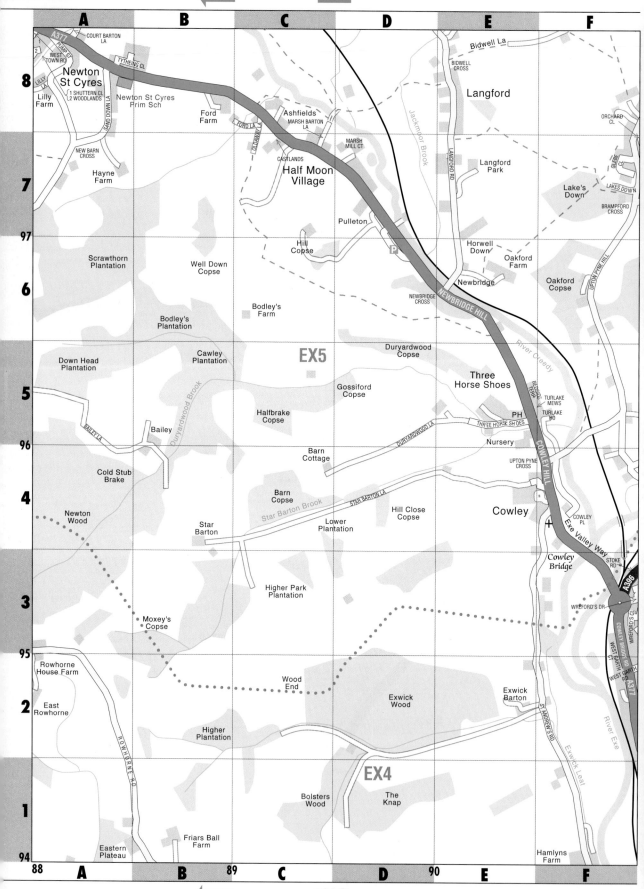

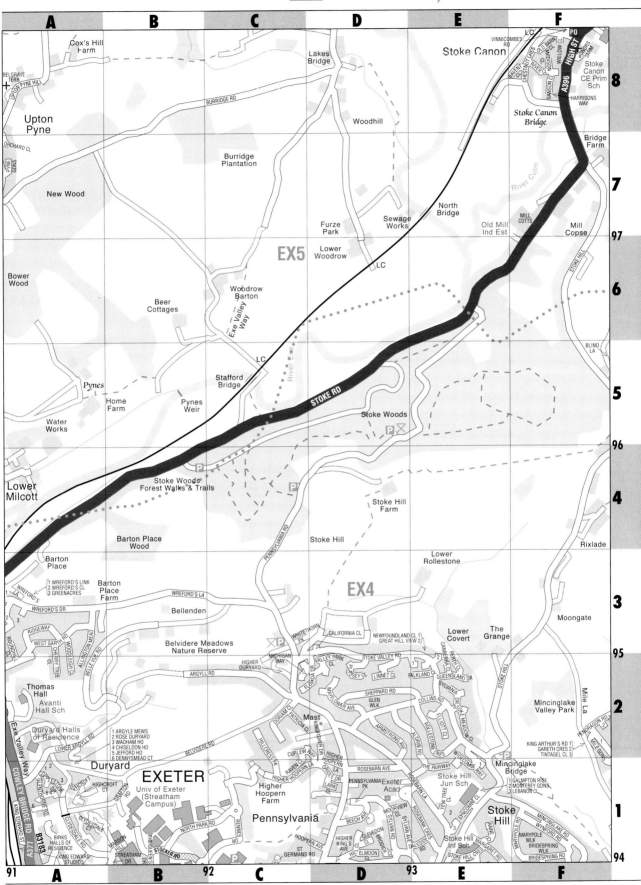

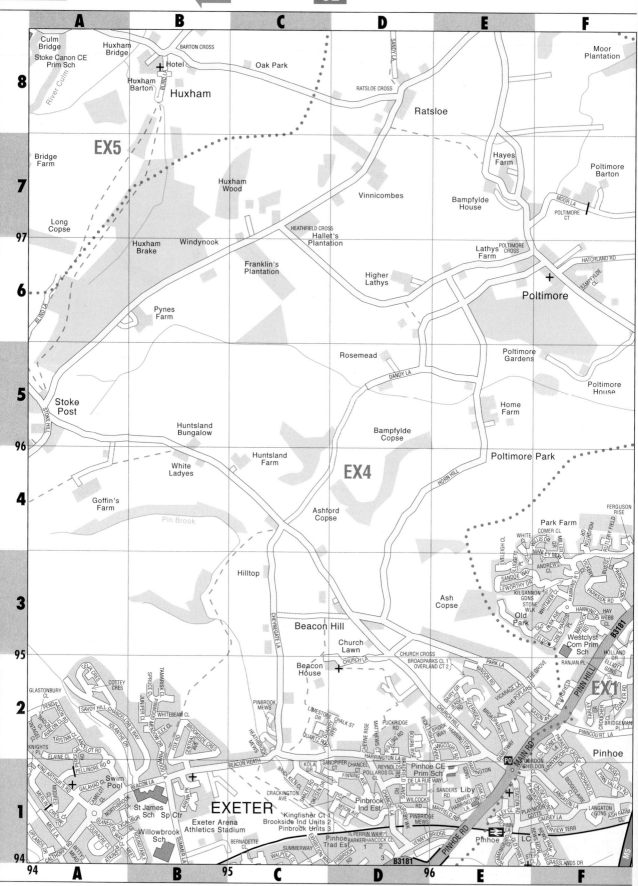

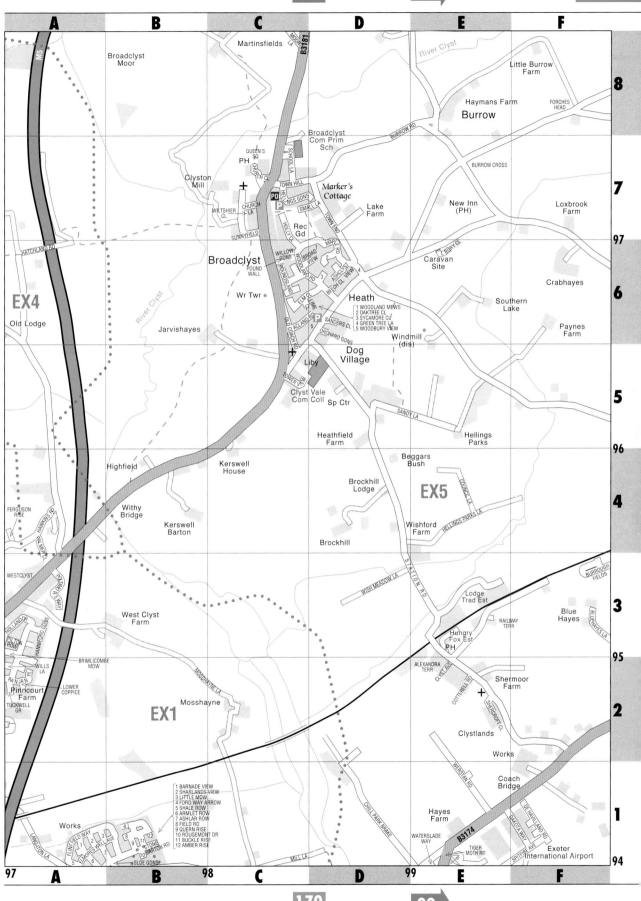

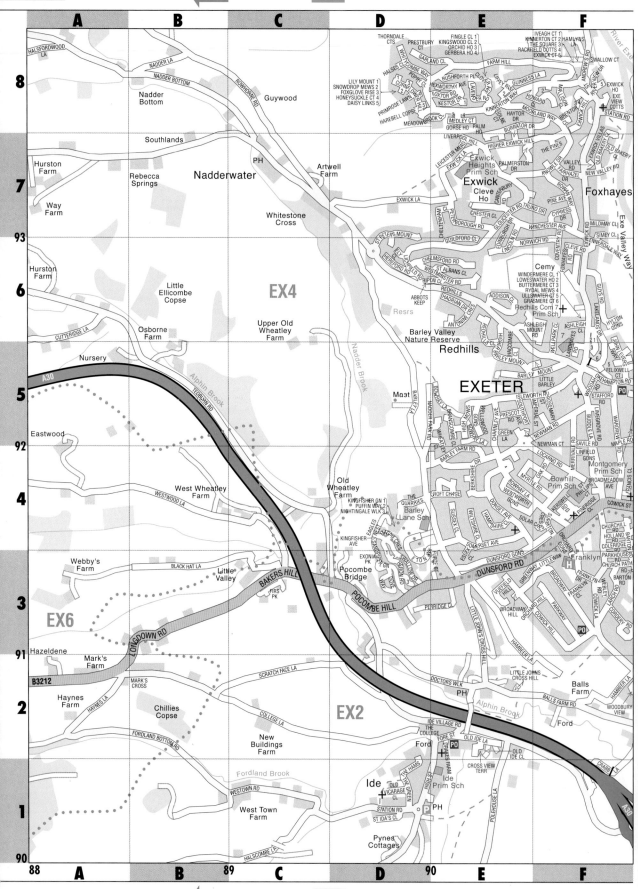

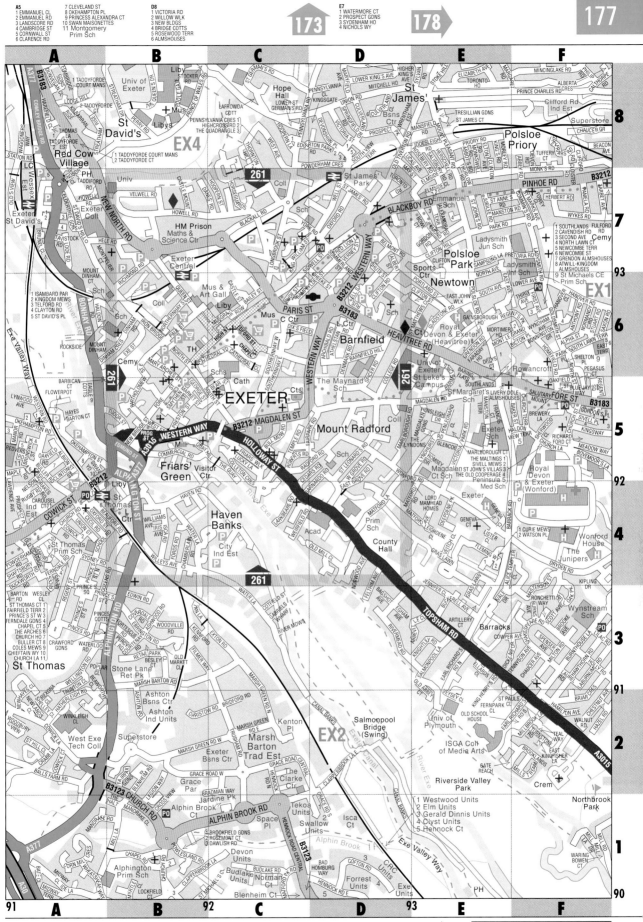

A5
1 EMMANUEL CL
2 EMMANUEL RD
3 LANDSCORE RD
4 CAMBRIDGE ST
5 CORNWALL ST
6 CLARENCE RD

7 CLEVELAND ST
8 OKEHAMPTON PL
9 PRINCESS ALEXANDRA CT
10 SWAN MAISONETTES
11 Montgomery
   Prim Sch

D8
1 VICTORIA RD
2 WILLOW WLK
3 NEW BLDGS
4 BRIDGE COTTS
5 ROSEWOOD TERR
6 ALMSHOUSES

E7
1 WATERMORE CT
2 PROSPECT GDNS
3 SYDENHAM HO
4 NICHOLS WY

For full street detail of the highlighted area see page 261.

177
174

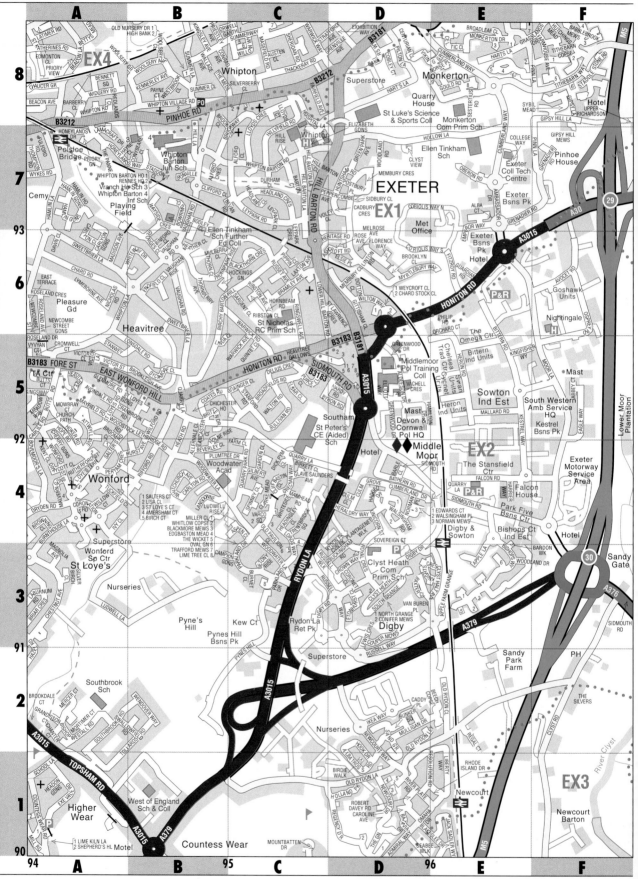

177
182

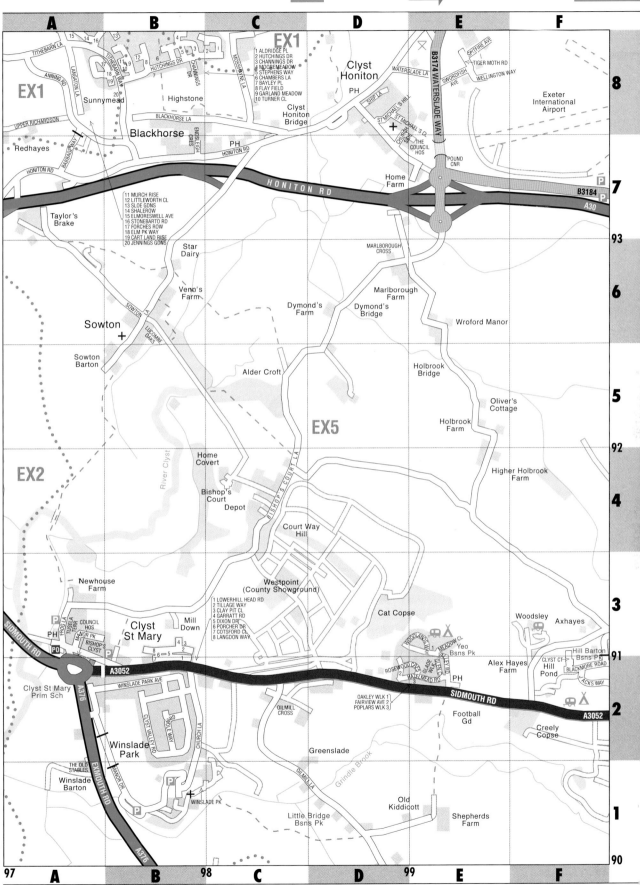

EX1

EX1
1 ALDRIDGE PL
2 HUTCHINGS DR
3 CHANNINGS DR
4 MOORE MEADOW
5 STEPHENS WAY
6 CHAMBERS LA
7 BAYLEY PL
8 FLAY FIELD
9 GARLAND MEADOW
10 TURNER CL

Clyst
Honiton

Sunnymead

Highstone

Clyst
Honiton
Bridge

Blackhorse

PH

Redhayes

Taylor's
Brake

11 MURCH RISE
12 LITTLEWORTH CL
13 SLOE GDNS
14 SHALEROW
15 ELMORESWELL AVE
16 STONEBARTO RD
17 FORCHES ROW
18 ELM PK WAY
19 CART LAND RISE
20 JENNINGS GDNS

HONITON RD

Home
Farm

B3184
A30

MARLBOROUGH
CROSS

Star
Dairy

Venn's
Farm

Marlborough
Farm

Dymond's
Farm

Dymond's
Bridge

Wroford Manor

EX1

Sowton

Sowton
Barton

Alder Croft

Holbrook
Bridge

Oliver's
Cottage

EX5

Holbrook
Farm

Home
Covert

Bishop's
Court
Depot

Higher Holbrook
Farm

EX2

Court Way
Hill

Newhouse
Farm

Westpoint
(County Showground)

1 LOWERHILL HEAD RD
2 TILLAGE WAY
3 CLAY PIT CL
4 GARRATT RD
5 DIXON DR
6 PORCHER DR
7 COTSFORD CL
8 LANGDON WAY

Cat Copse

Woodsley

Axhayes

Clyst
St Mary

Mill
Down

Yeo
Bsns Pk

Hill Barton
Bsns Pk

CLYST CT

Alex Hayes
Farm

Hill
Pond

BLACKMORE ROAD

JACK'S WAY

A3052

Clyst St Mary
Prim Sch

WINSLADE PARK AVE

OILMILL
CROSS

OAKLEY WLK 1
FAIRVIEW AVE 2
POPLARS WLK 3

SIDMOUTH RD
A3052

Football
Gd

Creely
Copse

SIDMOUTH RD

Winslade
Park

THE OLD
STABLES

Winslade
Barton

WINSLADE PK

Greenslade

OILMILL LA

Grindle Brook

Little Bridge
Bsns Pk

Old
Kiddicott

Shepherds
Farm

EXMOUTH RD
A376

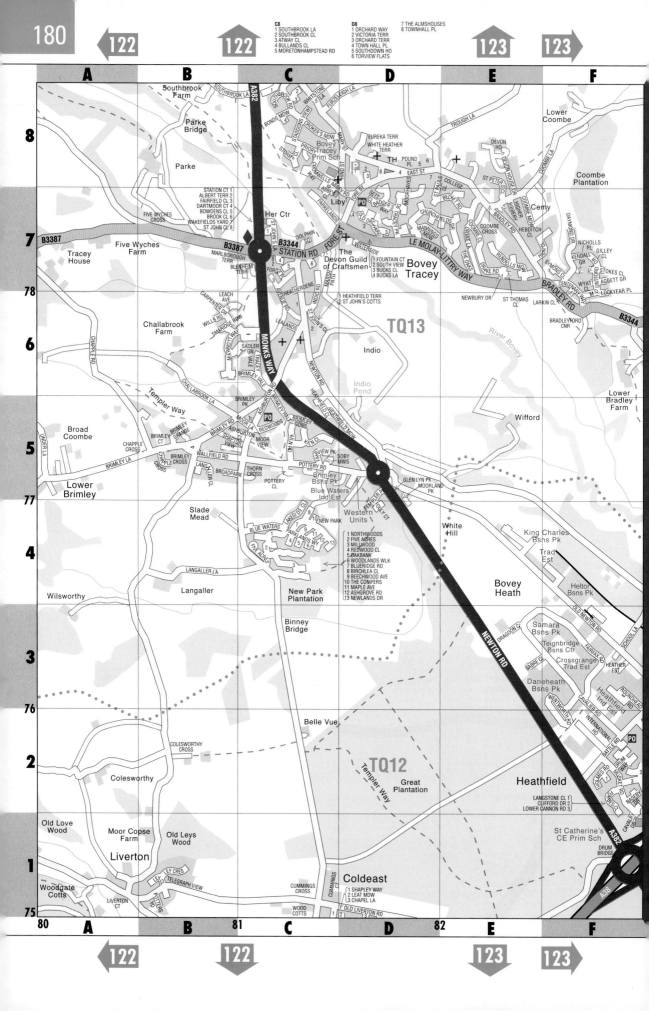

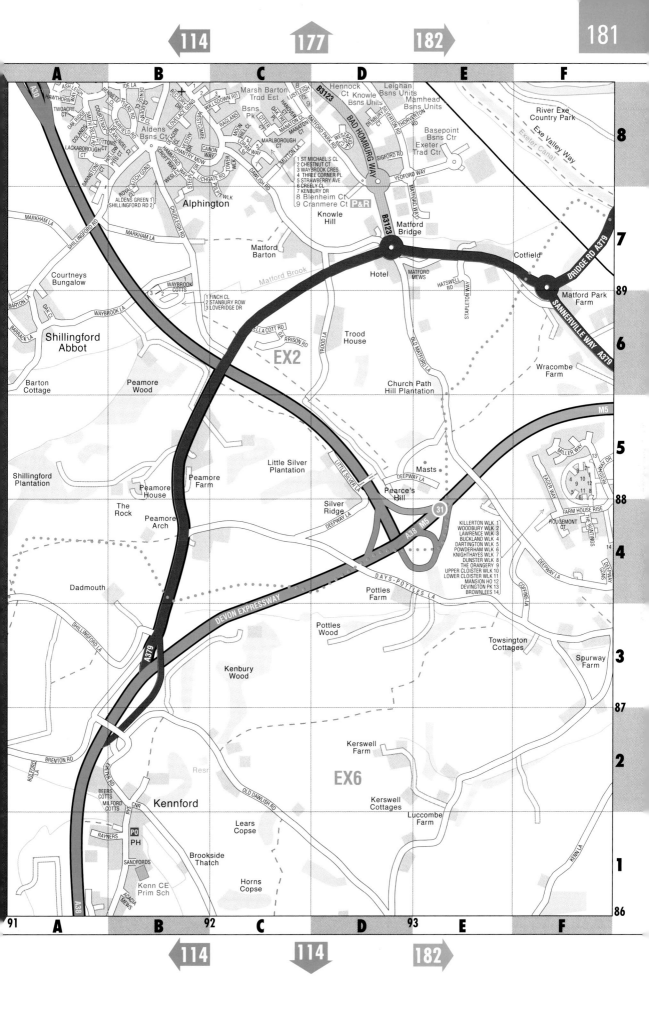

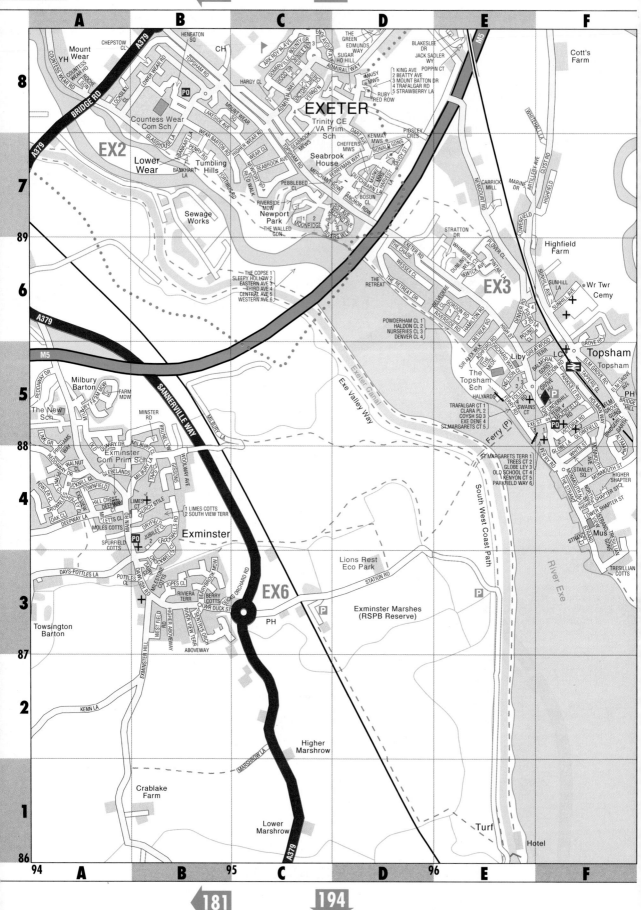

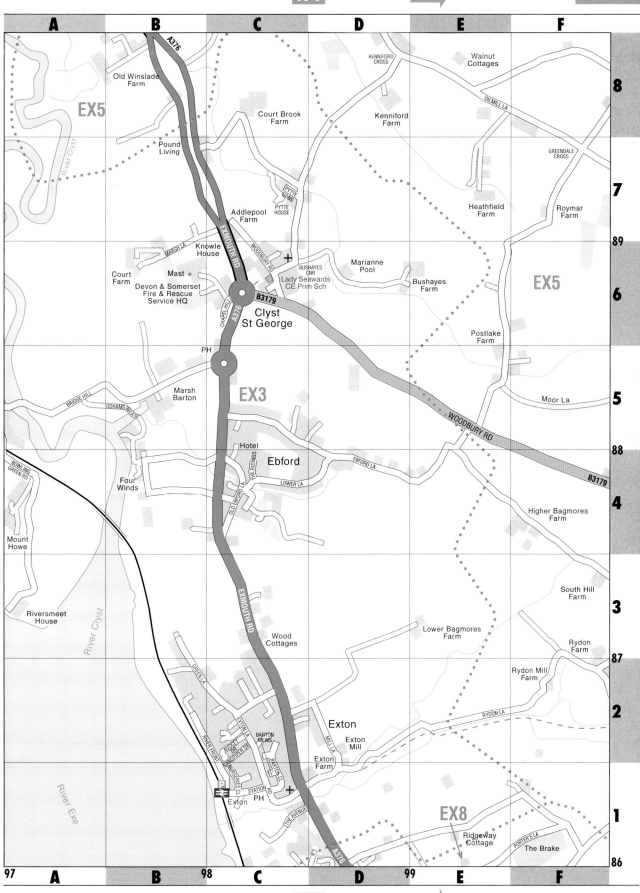

A376

Old Winslade Farm

EX5

River Clyst

Court Brook Farm

KENNIFORD CROSS

Walnut Cottages

Kenniford Farm

OILMILL LA

8

Pound Living

GREENDALE CROSS

7

Addlepool Farm

PYTTE CGNS

PYTTE HOUSE

Heathfield Farm

Roymar Farm

Marsh La

Knowle House

WOODBURY RD

Marianne Pool

89

EXMOUTH RD

BUSHAYES CNR

Lady Seawards CE Prim Sch

Bushayes Farm

EX5

Court Farm

Mast

Devon & Somerset Fire & Rescue Service HQ

B3179

Clyst St George

CHAPEL HILL

A376

6

Postlake Farm

PH

BRIDGE HILL

ODHAMS WEARE

Marsh Barton

EX3

WOODBURY RD

Moor La

5

Hotel

Ebford

THE RIDINGS

EBFORD LA

88

B3179

Four Winds

OLD EBFORD LA

LOWER LA

Higher Bagmores Farm

Mount Howe

4

Riversmeet House

River Clyst

EXMOUTH RD

South Hill Farm

3

Wood Cottages

Lower Bagmores Farm

Rydon Farm

GREEN LA

87

Rydon Mill Farm

RYDON LA

2

RIVER FRONT

SANDPIPERS DR

AVOCET DR

EXTON LA

BARTON MEWS

Exton

MILL LA

BARTON RD

Exton Mill

Exton Farm

P

STATION RD

Exton

PH

THE AVENUE

EX8

A376

Ridgeway Cottage

PORTER'S LA

The Brake

1

86

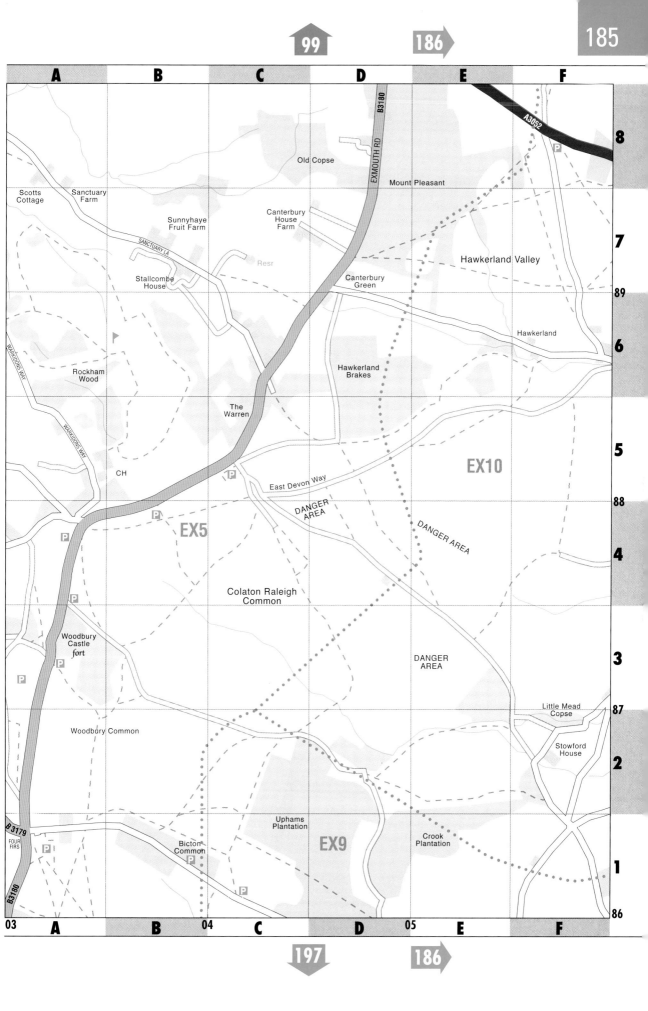

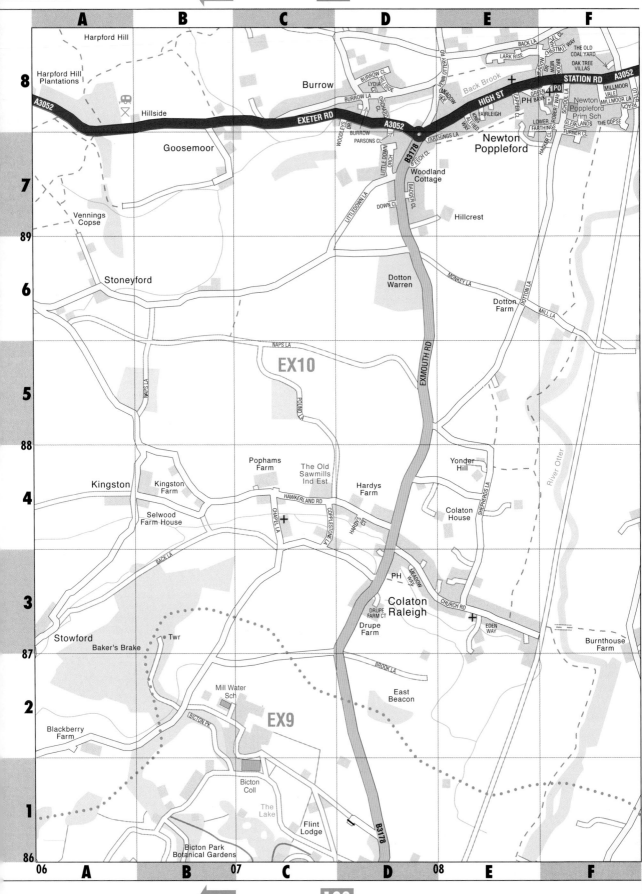

185
100

A   B   C   D   E   F

8

7

89

6

5

88

4

3

87

2

1

86

Harpford Hill

Harpford Hill Plantations

Hillside

Goosemoor

Vennings Copse

Stoneyford

A3052

EXETER RD

A3052

Burrow

BURROW CL
LYDIA CL
HILLSIDE
BURROW LA
ORCHARD CL

WOODLEYS DR
BURROW PARSONS CL

LITTLE DOWN ORCH

LITTLEDOWN LA

DOWN CL

B3178

BEECH CL

FARTHINGS LA

Woodland Cottage

BADGER CL

Hillcrest

MONKEY LA

Dotton Warren

Dotton Farm

DOTTON LA

MILL LA

VENN OTTERY RD

MEADOW DR

BACK LA

LARK RISE

MICHAEL CL
CHESTNUT WAY

BROOK

HIGH ST

Back Brook

STATION RD   A3052

THE OLD COAL YARD

OAK TREE VILLAS

MILLMOOR VALE
MILLMOOR LA

FAIRLEIGH
KING ALFRED WAY

GREEN CL
BANK
PH

P
PO

LOWER FARTHINGS

HAMER CL
ROBERT WAY

SCHOOL LA

GLEBELANDS

TURNER CL

Newton Poppleford Prim Sch

THE COPSE

OTTER REACH

Newton Poppleford

EX10

NAPS LA

NAPS LA

LONDON DR

EXMOUTH RD

Pophams Farm

The Old Sawmills Ind Est

Hardys Farm

HAWKERLAND RD

CHAPEL LA

COPPLESTONE LA

HARDYS CT

Yonder Hill

Colaton House

SHEPHERDS LA

River Otter

Kingston

Kingston Farm

Selwood Farm House

BACK LA

PH

MEADOW WAY

Colaton Raleigh

CHURCH RD

EDEN WAY

Stowford

Baker's Brake

Twr

DRUPE FARM CT

Drupe Farm

BROOK LA

East Beacon

Burnthouse Farm

Blackberry Farm

BICTON PK

Mill Water Sch

EX9

Bicton Coll

The Lake

Flint Lodge

B3178

Bicton Park Botanical Gardens

06   A   B   07   C   D   08   E   F

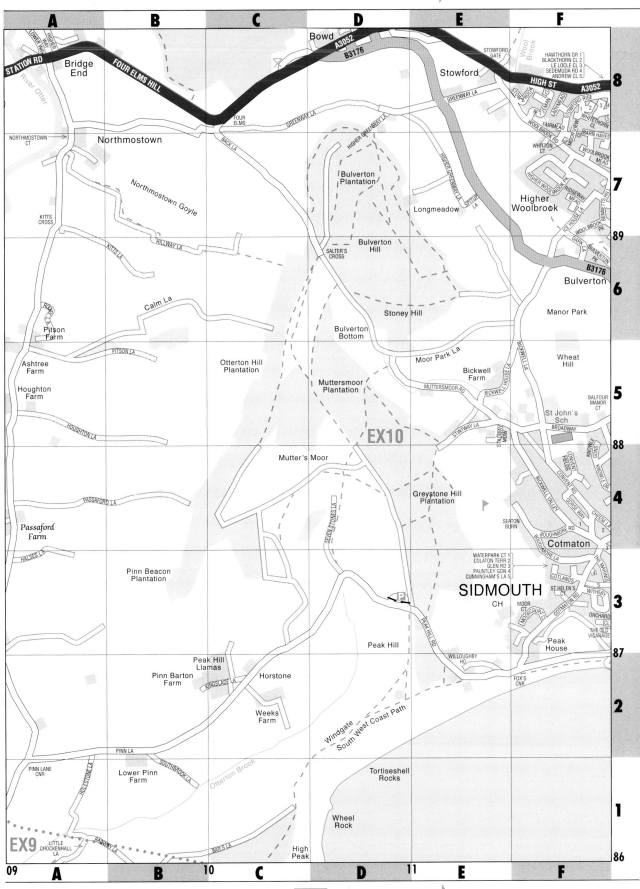

A B C D E F

8
7
89
6
5
88
4
88
3
87
2
1
86

STATION RD
Bridge End
River Otter
FOUR ELMS HILL
Northmostown
NORTHMOSTOWN CT
Northmostown Goyle
KITTS CROSS
KITTS LA
HILLWAY LA
BACK LA
Calm La
PITSON LA
Pitson Farm
FOX LA
Ashtree Farm
Houghton Farm
HOUGHTON LA
PASSAFORD LA
Passaford Farm
HALSES LA
Pinn Beacon Plantation
Otterton Hill Plantation
Muttersmoor Plantation
Mutter's Moor
SEVEN STONES LA
Peak Hill Llamas
Pinn Barton Farm
KINGSSLADE LA
Horstone
Weeks Farm
PINN LA
SOUTHBROOK LA
HOLESTONE LA
PINN LANE CNR
Lower Pinn Farm
Otterton Brook
BARTS LA
RADWAY LA
LITTLE CHOCKENHALL LA
EX9
High Peak
Wheel Rock
Windgate
South West Coast Path
Tortiseshell Rocks
Peak Hill
Peak Hill Rd
WILLOUGHBY HO
FOX'S CNR
Peak House
SIDMOUTH
CH
MOOR CT
MOORCOURT
COTMATON RD
ORCHARD CL
THE OLD VICARAGE
ST HELEN'S CT
COTLANDS
WITHEBY
THE MARINO
Cotmaton
BOUGHMORE LA
BOUGHMORE RD
SEATON BURN
WATERPARK CT 1
COLATON TERR 2
GLEN RD 3
PAUNTLEY GDN 4
CUNNINGHAM S LA 5
CHEESE LA
2
GORSE WAY
BICKWELL VALLEY
CONVENT RD
CONVENT FIELDS
KNOWLE DR
KNOWLE GDNS
KNOWLE CR
Greystone Hill Plantation
STINTWAY LA
STACKWAY MDW
Bickwell Farm
MUTTERSMOOR RD
BICKWELL LA
BICKWELL HOUSE LA
Moor Park La
Bulverton Bottom
Stoney Hill
Bickwell
Broadway
St John's Sch
BALFOUR MANOR CT
Wheat Hill
Manor Park
P
EX10
Bulverton Hill
SALTER'S CROSS
Bulverton Plantation
Longmeadow
HIGHER GREENWAY LA
SPITUR LA
HIGHER GREENWAY LA
Greenway La
Stowford
Bowd
A3052
B3176
Greenway La
STOWFORD GATE
HIGH ST
A3052
Wool Brook
HAWTHORN DR 1
BLACKTHORN CL 2
LE LOCLE CL 3
SEDEMUDA RD 4
ANDREW CL 5
STOWFORD RISE
WHITTON CT
WOOLBROOK RD
FAIRMEAD
LARKMEAD
MOORVIEW
WHITETHORN CL
BARN HAYES
WOOLBROOK MEAD
HIGHER WOOLBROOK PK
RIDGEWAY
WOOLBROOK MEAD
ICE HOUSE LA
BENNETT'S HILL
WOOLBROOK PK
DARK LA
BULVERTON PK
Higher Woolbrook
Bulverton
B3176
FOUR ELMS

188

A7
1 St Nicholas CE Prim Sch

B7
1 RALEIGH HO
2 OLD FARM BGLWS
3 Manstone Workshops

← 187   ↑ 101

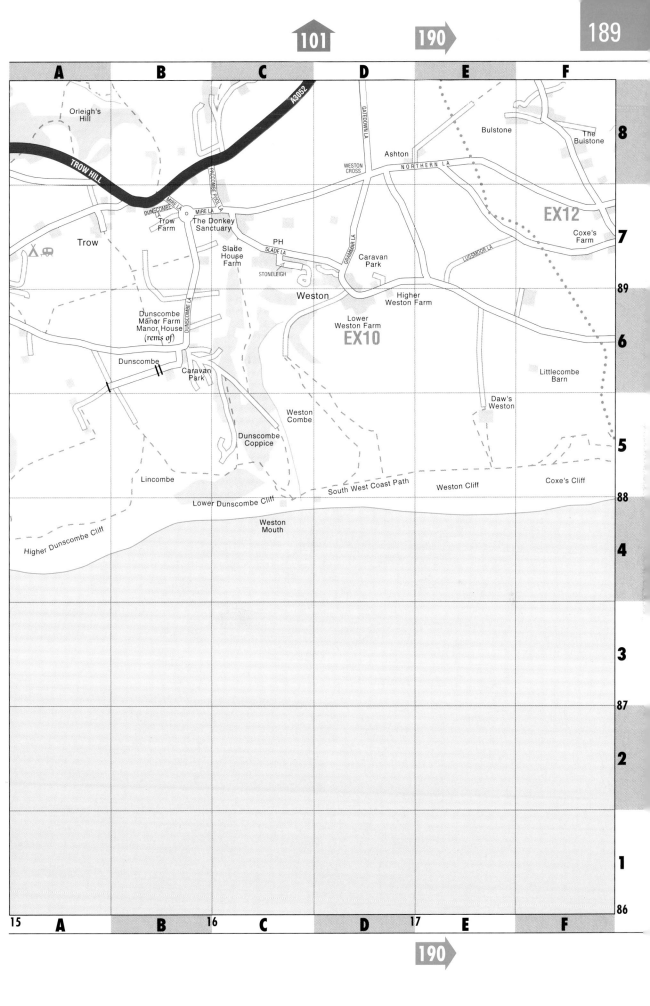

A   B   C   D   E   F

Orleigh's
Hill

A3052

8

Bulstone

The
Bulstone

Ashton

Weston
Cross

GATEDOWN LA

NORTHERN LA

EX12

7

Coxe's
Farm

TROW HILL

Dunscombe LA

MIRE LA

Trow
Farm

The Donkey
Sanctuary

PH

SLADE LA

Slade La

Trow

Slade
House
Farm

STONELEIGH

GRAMMAR LA

Caravan
Park

LUGSMOOR LA

89

Weston

Higher
Weston Farm

Dunscombe LA

Dunscombe
Manor Farm
Manor House
(rems of)

Lower
Weston Farm

EX10

6

Littlecombe
Barn

Dunscombe

Caravan
Park

Daw's
Weston

5

Weston
Combe

Dunscombe
Coppice

Lincombe

South West Coast Path

Weston Cliff

Coxe's Cliff

88

Lower Dunscombe Cliff

Weston
Mouth

Higher Dunscombe Cliff

4

3

87

2

1

86

101
102

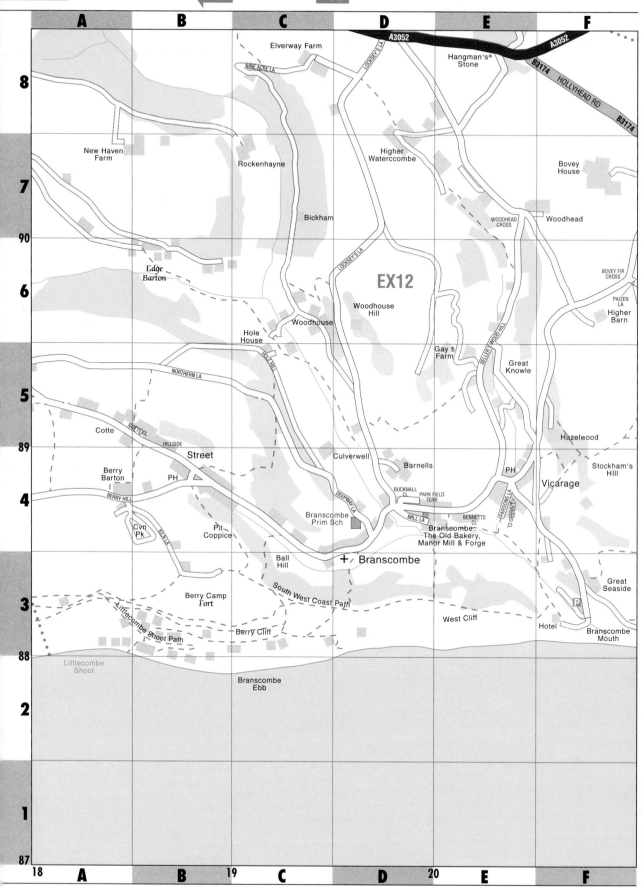

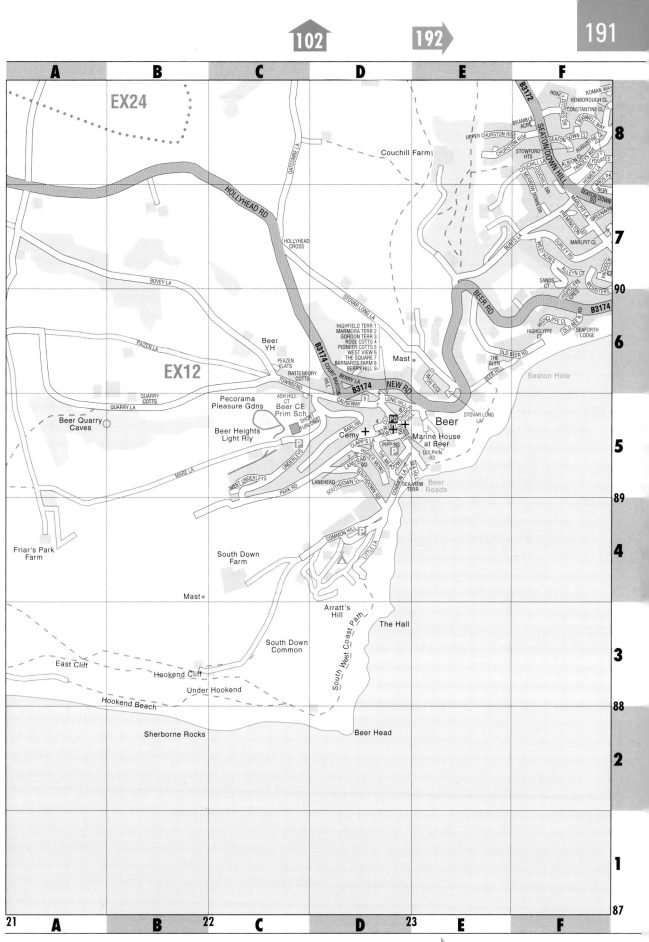

EX24

HOLLYHEAD RD

GATCOMBE LA

Couchill Farm

HOLLYHEAD CROSS

BOVEY LA

ROMAN WAY

HONEY DITCHES DR   VENBOROUGH CL

CONSTANTINE CL

BRAMBLE ACRE

BOSWELL WAY

Upper Churston Rise

CHURSTON RISE

STOWFORD HTS

ALBION CL

SEATON DOWN CL

TRACEYS AVE

AUGUSTINE CL

LYDGATES RD

NEW NIDS PK

HOMER RD

SEATON DOWN RD

GREENWAY

MARLPIT LA

FLEMMINGTON RD

COLCHILL LA

MERKINS DOWN DR

COLCHILL DR

SEATON DOWN HILL

B3172

STOVAR LONG LA

BEER RD

BURNTS LA

MARLPIT CL

DURLEY RD

WEST ACRES

ALLEYN CT

PADDOCK

WESSITERS

SANDS CT

HIGHCLIFFE CRES

HIGHCLIFFE CL

HIGHCLYFFE CT

OLD BEER RD

B3174

SEAFORTH LODGE

90

Beer YH

EX12

PAIZEN LA

PEAZEN FLATS

RATTENBURY COTTS

TOWNSEND

QUARRY COTTS

QUARRY LA

Beer Quarry Caves

MARE LA

WEST UNDERLEYS

UNDERLEYS

PARK RD

Pecorama Pleasure Gdns

Beer CE Prim Sch

ASH HILL CT

SHORT FURLONG

Beer Heights Light Rly

HIGHFIELD TERR 1
MARMORA TERR 2
GORDON TERR 3
ROSE COTTS 4
PIONEER COTTS 5
WEST VIEW 6
THE SQUARE 7
BARNARDS FARM 8
BERRY HILL 9

B3174 COURT BARTON HILL

BERRY LA

CAUSEWAY

B3174

NEW RD

LONG HILL

Mast

HILL

THE GLEN

OLD BEER RD

BEER HILL

Seaton Hole

Beer

Marine House at Beer

STOVAR LONG LA

DOLPHIN RD

Cemy

BARLINE

CLAPP'S LA

LANEHEAD RD

LANEHEAD

HIGHER MEWS

SOUTHDOWN RD

SOUTHDOWN CL

PO

PIPPINS

THE MEADOWS

COMMON LA

SEA VIEW TERR

Beer Roads

Friar's Park Farm

South Down Farm

Mast

Common Hill

South Down Common

Arratt's Hill

South West Coast Path

The Hall

East Cliff

Hookend Cliff

Under Hookend

Hookend Beach

Sherborne Rocks

Beer Head

LITTLE LA

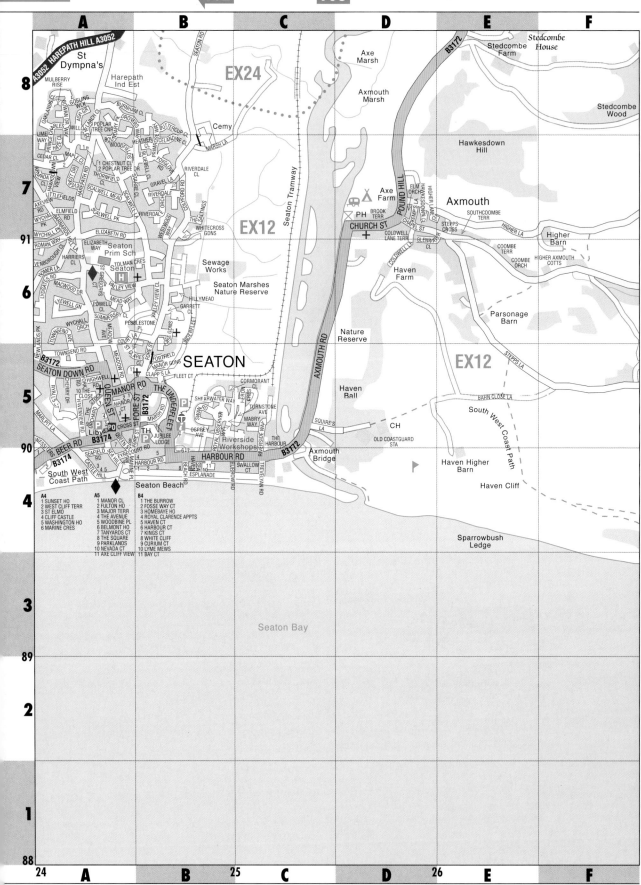

A4
1 SUNSET HO
2 WEST CLIFF TERR
3 ST ELMO
4 CLIFF CASTLE
5 WASHINGTON HO
6 MARINE CRES

A5
1 MANOR CL
2 FULTON HO
3 MAJOR TERR
4 THE AVENUE
5 WOODBINE PL
6 BELMONT HO
7 TANYARDS CT
8 THE SQUARE
9 PARKLANDS
10 NEVADA CT
11 AXE CLIFF VIEW

B4
1 THE BURROW
2 FOSSE WAY CT
3 HOMEBAYE HO
4 ROYAL CLARENCE APPTS
5 HAVEN CT
6 HARBOUR CT
7 KINGS CT
8 WHITE CLIFF
9 CURIUM CT
10 LYME MEWS
11 BAY CT

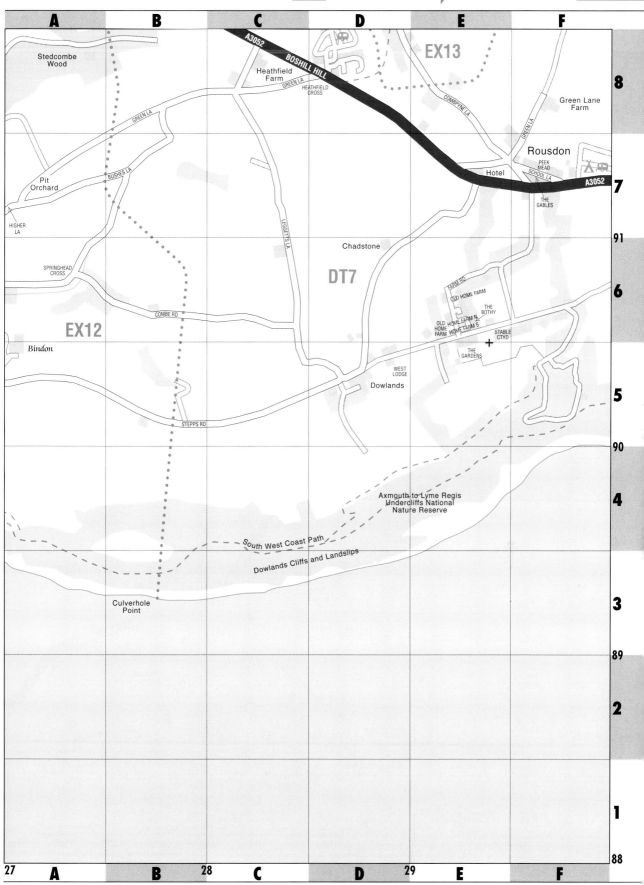

A   B   C   D   E   F

8
7
91
6
5
90
4
3
89
2
1
88

Stedcombe Wood

A3052

BOSHILL HILL

Heathfield Farm

GREEN LA

Heathfield Cross

EX13

COMBPYNE LA

Green Lane Farm

GREEN LA

Rousdon

Hotel

PEEK MEAD

SCHOOL LA

A3052

THE GABLES

Pit Orchard

BUSHES LA

GREEN LA

HIGHER LA

LEGGETTS LA

Chadstone

DT7

FARM RD

OLD HOME FARM

THE BOTHY

OLD HOME FARM

HOME FARM N

HOME FARM S

STABLE CTYD

SPRINGHEAD CROSS

COMBE RD

EX12

Bindon

WEST LODGE

THE GARDENS

Dowlands

STEPPS RD

Axmouth to Lyme Regis Undercliffs National Nature Reserve

South West Coast Path

Dowlands Cliffs and Landslips

Culverhole Point

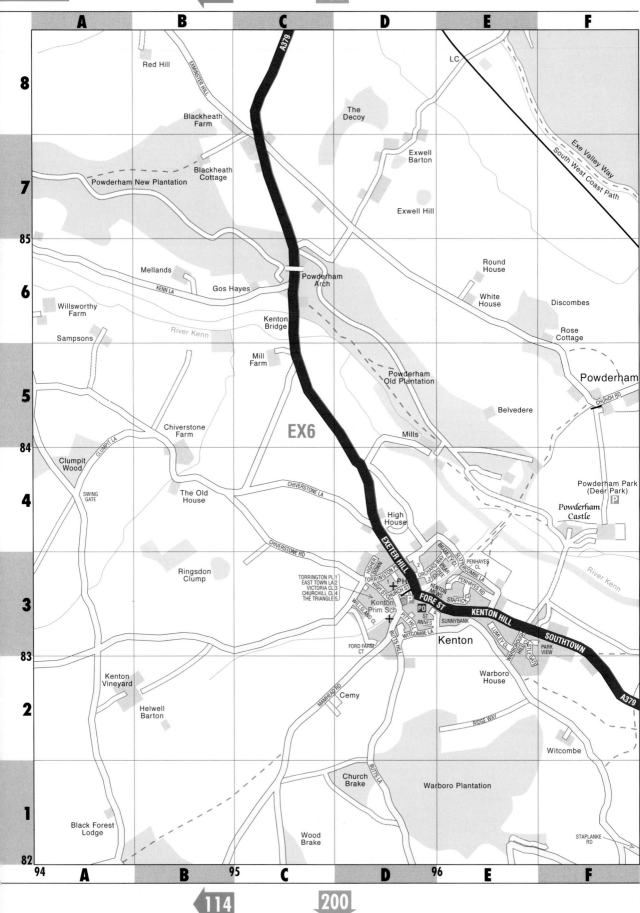

A B C D E F

8

7

85

6

5

84

4

3

83

2

1

82

94 A 95 B C 96 D E F

Red Hill

EMINSTER HILL

Blackheath
Farm

Powderham New Plantation

Blackheath
Cottage

The Decoy

LC

Exwell
Barton

Exe Valley Way

South West Coast Path

Exwell Hill

Round
House

Mellands

KENN LA

Gos Hayes

Powderham
Arch

White
House

Discombes

6

Willsworthy
Farm

River Kenn

Kenton
Bridge

Rose
Cottage

Powderham

Sampsons

Mill
Farm

Powderham
Old Plantation

CHURCH RD

Belvedere

P

Chiverstone
Farm

EX6

Mills

Powderham Park
(Deer Park)

Clumpit
Wood

CLUMPIT LA

SWING
GATE

The Old
House

CHIVERSTONE LA

High
House

Powderham
Castle

P

Ringsdon
Clump

CHIVERSTONE RD

HIGHER TOWN

TORRINGTON PL 1
EAST TOWN LA 2
VICTORIA CL 3
CHURCHILL CL 4
THE TRIANGLE 5

TORRINGTON PL

HIGH ST

EXETER HILL

CHURCH ST

PH

P

2

ORCHARD WAY

KENTON
MEWS

BRAMLEY CL

SUTHCOMBE LA

PENHAYES
CL

PENHAYES RD

River Kenn

Kenton
Prim Sch

WILLSLAND CL

BUTTS HILL

PITT HILL

PO

ST
ANNES

4

WITCOMBE LA

STAFFICK

FORE ST

KENTON HILL

SOUTHTOWN

SUNNYBANK

A379

FORD FARM
CT

Kenton

Warboro
House

WARBOROUGH

HIGH CASTLE GATE

LUMLEY CL

Park
View

Kenton
Vineyard

MANHEAD RD

Cemy

RIDGE WAY

Witcombe

Helwell
Barton

Church
Brake

BUTTS LA

Warboro Plantation

STAPLANKE
RD

Black Forest
Lodge

Wood
Brake

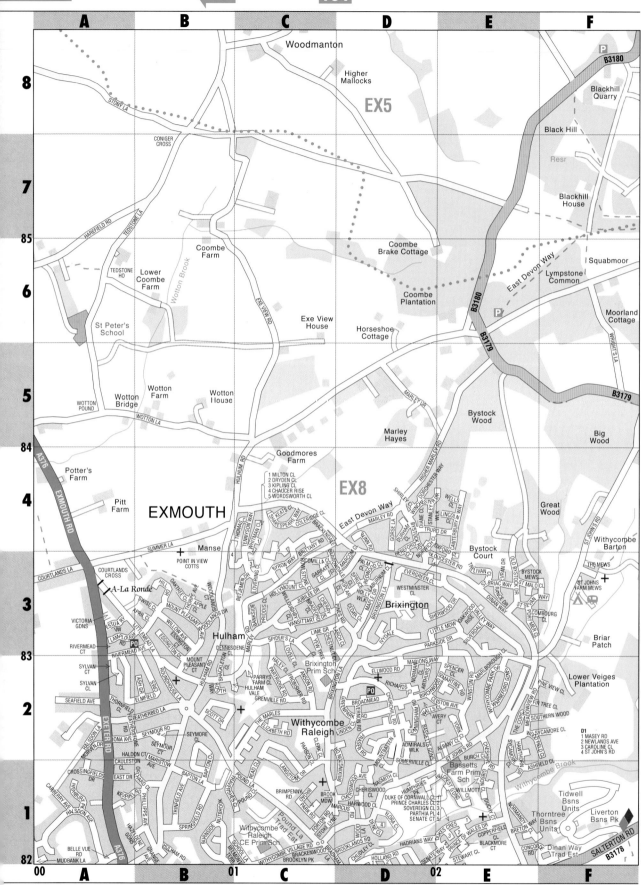

195
184

A B C D E F

8

7

85

6

5

84

4

3

83

2

1

82

Woodmanton

Higher
Mallocks

EX5

Blackhill
Quarry

Black Hill

Resr

Blackhill
House

Squabmoor

STONY LA

CONIGER
CROSS

HAREFIELD RD

TEDSTONE LA

Coombe
Farm

Wotton Brook

Coombe
Brake Cottage

East Devon Way

Lympstone
Common

B3180

P

TEDSTONE
HO

Lower
Coombe
Farm

EXE VIEW RD

Coombe
Plantation

Horseshoe
Cottage

Coombe
Brake Cottage

B3180

P

B3179

Moorland
Cottage

WRIGHT'S LA

St Peter's
School

Exe View
House

B3179

Bystock
Wood

Big
Wood

WOTTON POUND

Wotton
Farm

Wotton
Farm

Wotton
House

WOTTON LA

Marley
Hayes

MARLEY DR

A376

Potter's
Farm

Pitt
Farm

SUMMER LA

Goodmores
Farm

1 MILTON CL
2 DRYDEN CL
3 KIPLING CL
4 CHAUCER RISE
5 WORDSWORTH CL

EX8

East Devon Way

MARLEY RD

HIGHER MARLEY RD

Great
Wood

Withycombe
Barton

EXMOUTH

EXMOUTH RD

Manse

Point in View
Cotts

COURTLANDS LA

Courtlands
Cross

A-La Ronde

Hulham

Brixington

HULHAM RD

Bystock
Court

Bystock
Mews

St Johns
Farm Mews

St Johns
Farm Mews

THE MEWS

Briar
Patch

VICTORIA
GDNS

RIVERMEAD
CT

PO

Brixington
Prim Sch

Lower Veiges
Plantation

SYLVAN
CT

SYLVAN
CL

SEAFIELD AVE

Withycombe Brook

PINE VIEW LA

FIR TREE LA

Mount
Pleasant
Ct

PO

Withycombe
Raleigh

Bassetts
Farm Prim
Sch

D1
1 MASEY RD
2 NEWLANDS AVE
3 CAROLINE CL
4 ST JOHN'S RD

Tidwell
Bsns
Units

Thorntree
Bsns
Units

Liverton
Bsns Pk

Withycombe
Raleigh
CE Prim Sch

Withycombe
Village Rd

BRACKENWOOD

Brooklyn Pk

Dinan Way
Trad Est

SALTERTON RD

B3178

BELLE VUE
RD

MUDBANK LA

00 01 02

A B C D E F

195
202

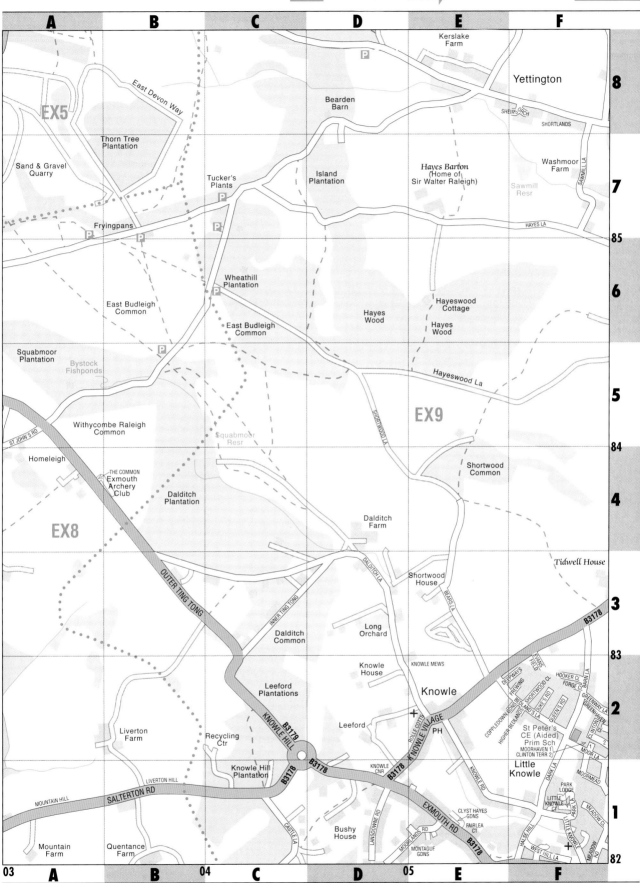

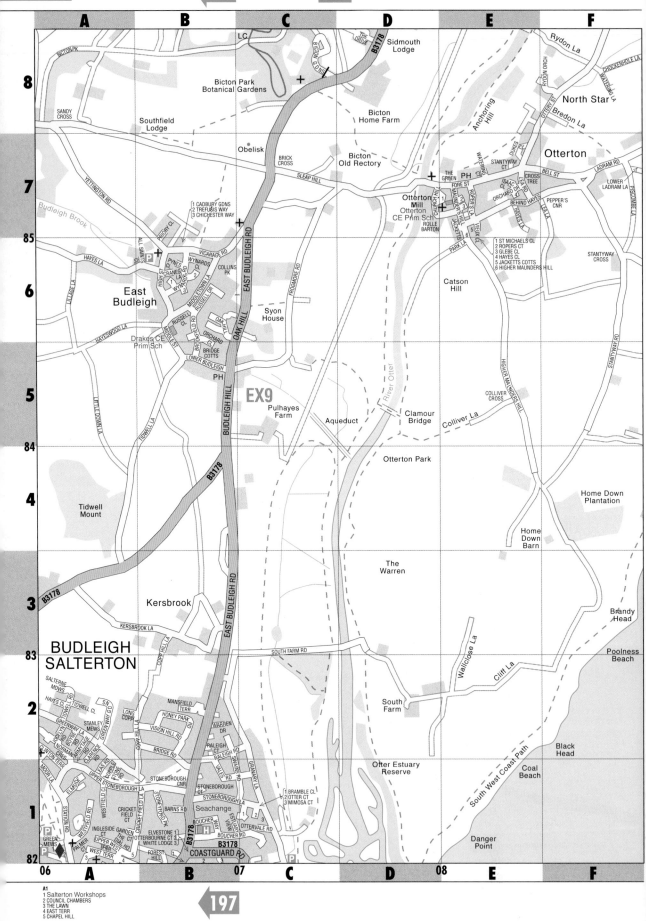

A1
1 Salterton Workshops
2 COUNCIL CHAMBERS
3 THE LAWN
4 EAST TERR
5 CHAPEL HILL

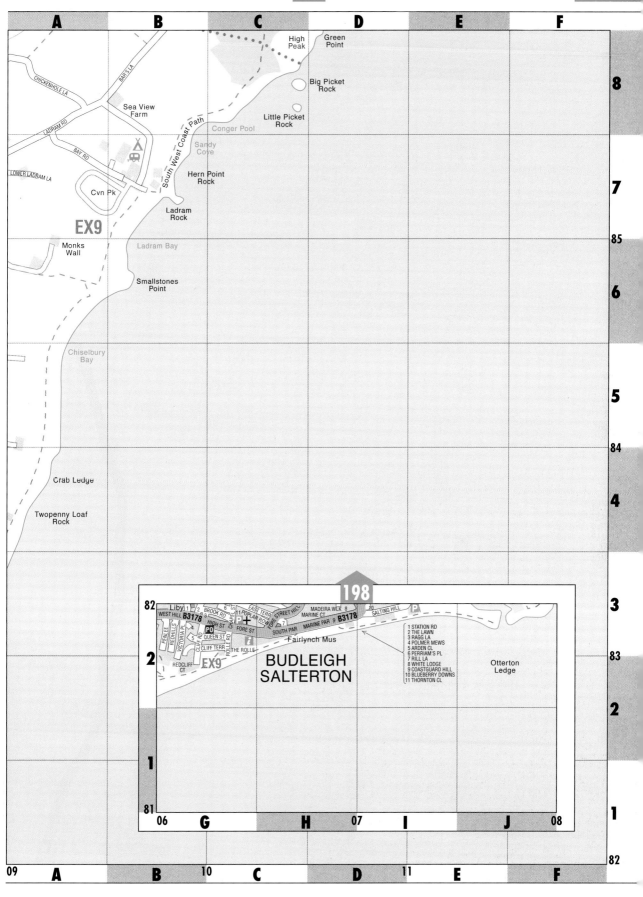

CHICKENHOLE LA

BARS LA

LADRAM RD

Sea View Farm

BAY RD

LOWER LADRAM LA

Cvn Pk

EX9

Monks Wall

South West Coast Path

High Peak

Green Point

Big Picket Rock

Little Picket Rock

Conger Pool

Sandy Cove

Hern Point Rock

Ladram Rock

Ladram Bay

Smallstones Point

Chiselbury Bay

Crab Ledge

Twopenny Loaf Rock

8

85

7

6

5

84

4

198

Liby 1
WEST HILL **B3178**
PENLEE
REDHILLS
VICTORIA PL
CLIFF RD
REDCLIFF CT
EX9
CLIFF TERR
QUEEN ST
PO
HIGH ST
BROOK RD
CHAPEL ST
ROLLE RD
THE ROLLE
EAST TERR
POPLAR ROW
FORE ST
FORD STREET HILL
SOUTH PAR
MADEIRA WLK 8
MARINE CT
MARINE PAR 9 **B3178**
SALTING HILL
P
Fairlynch Mus

BUDLEIGH SALTERTON

1 STATION RD
2 THE LAWN
3 RAGG LA
4 POLMER MEWS
5 ARDEN CL
6 PERRIAM'S PL
7 RILL LA
8 WHITE LODGE
9 COASTGUARD HILL
10 BLUEBERRY DOWNS
11 THORNTON CL

Otterton Ledge

82

3

83

2

2

1

81

2

1

09 A | B 10 | C | D 11 | E | F

06 G | H 07 | I | J 08

82

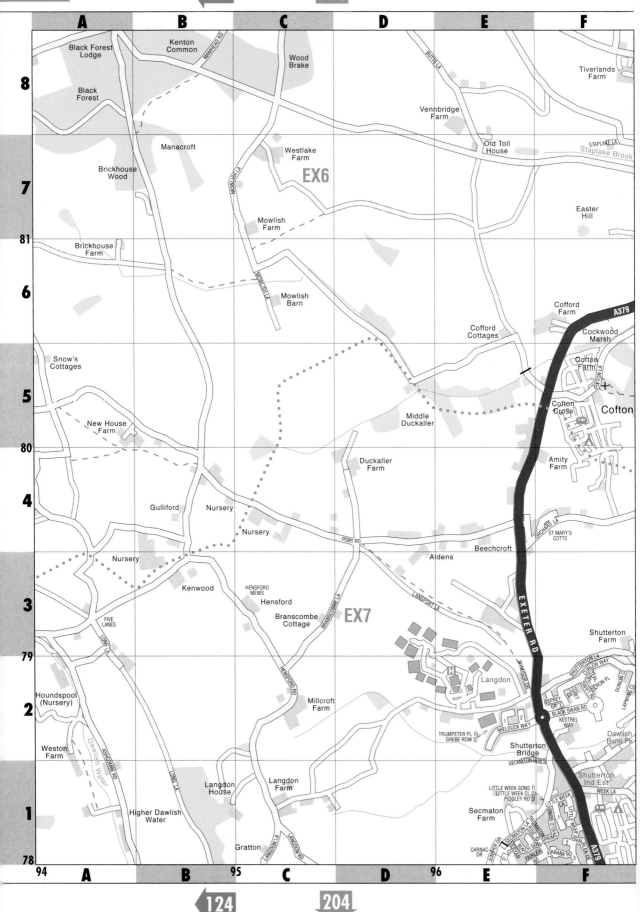

A B C D E F

8

Black Forest
Lodge

Kenton
Common

Wood
Brake

Tiverlands
Farm

Black
Forest

MAMHEAD RD

Vennbridge
Farm

Old Toll
House

STAPLAKE LA

Staplake Brook

Manacroft

Westlake
Farm

EX6

7

Brickhouse
Wood

MOWLISH LA

Easter
Hill

81

Brickhouse
Farm

Mowlish
Farm

Mowlish
Barn

MOWLISH LA

6

Cofford
Farm

A379

Cofford
Cottages

Cockwood
Marsh

Snow's
Cottages

Cofton
Farm

CARTON LA

Cofton
Cross

Cofton

5

Middle
Duckaller

New House
Farm

80

Amity
Farm

Duckaller
Farm

4

Gulliford

Nursery

PORT RD

Beechcroft

ORCHARD LA

ST MARY'S
COTTS

Nursery

Aldens

Nursery

LANGPORT LA

EXETER RD

Kenwood

HENSFORD MEWS

Hensford

BRANSCOMBE LA

EX7

Shutterton
Farm

3

Branscombe
Cottage

79

FIVE
LANES

LONG LA

HENSFORD RD

WINDSOR DR

SHUTTERTON LA

CURLEW WAY

DUNLIN CL

Houndspool
(Nursery)

H

Langdon

OSPREY
GR

EGRET
RD

SWIFT RD

HERON PL

LAPWING CL

2

Millcroft
Farm

Black Swan Rd

KESTREL
WAY

Dawlish
Bsns Pk

Weston
Farm

Dawlish Water

ASHCOMBE RD

TRUMPETER PL 1
GREBE ROW 2

SHELDUCK WAY

Shutterton
Bridge

SECMATON GDNS

Shutterton
Ind Est

WEEK LA

LONG LA

LANGDON LA

Langdon
House

Langdon
Farm

LITTLE WEEK GDNS 1
LITTLE WEEK CL 2
PIDGLEY RD 3

LITTLE WEEK LA

1

Secmaton
Farm

Higher Dawlish
Water

LANGDON RD

Gratton

CARNAC
DR

JUNIPER DR

FIRBANK RD

A379

78

94 A 95 B C 96 D E F

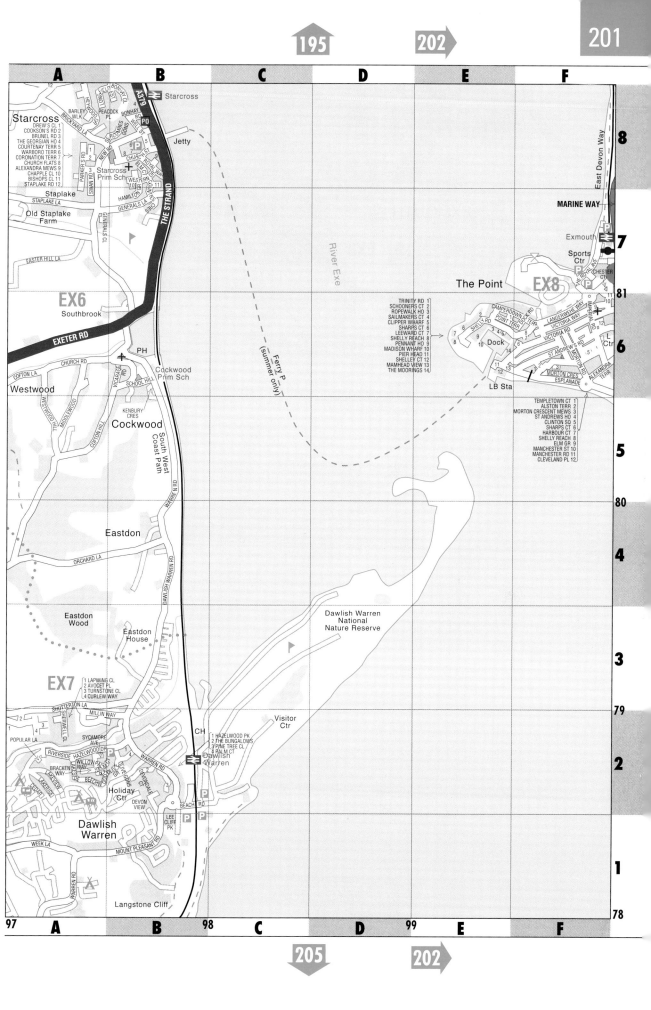

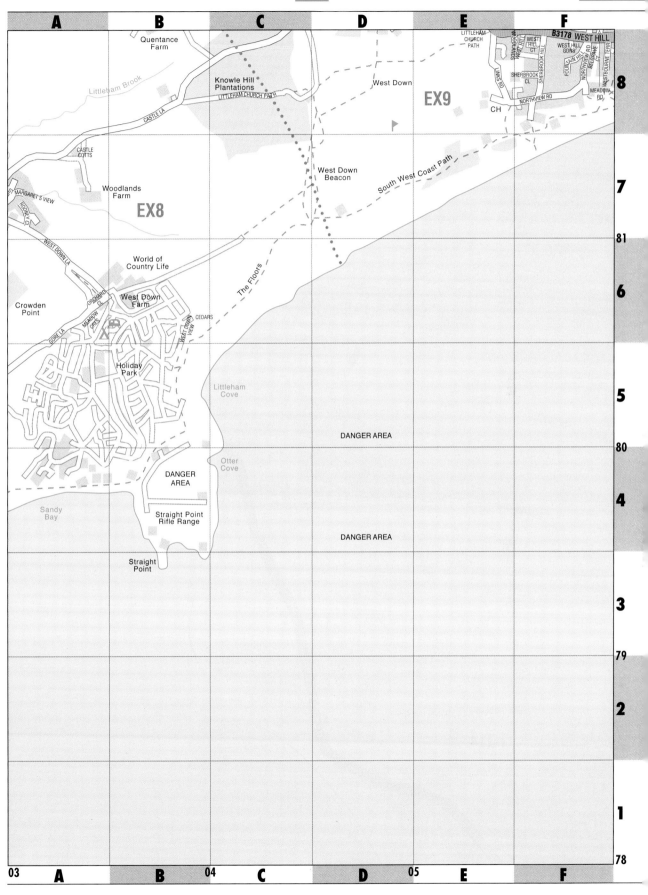

Quentance Farm

Knowle Hill Plantations

Littleham Brook

CASTLE LA

LITTLEHAM CHURCH PATH

West Down

EX9

West Down Beacon

South West Coast Path

LITTLEHAM CHURCH PATH

B3178 WEST HILL

WEST HILL

WEST HILL CT

SHERBROOK CL

WEST HILL GDNS

FOUNTAIN HILL

NORTHVIEW RD

BELGRAVE CT

WESTBOURNE TERR

MEADOW RD

LINKS RD

SHERBROOK HILL

NORTHVIEW RD

CH

CASTLE COTTS

ST MARGARET'S VIEW

RODNEY CL

Woodlands Farm

EX8

WEST DOWN LA

World of Country Life

Crowden Point

GORE LA

ORCHARD CL

MEADOW CRES

West Down Farm

WEST DOWN VIEW

CEDARS

The Floors

Holiday Park

Littleham Cove

DANGER AREA

Sandy Bay

Otter Cove

DANGER AREA

DANGER AREA

Straight Point Rifle Range

Straight Point

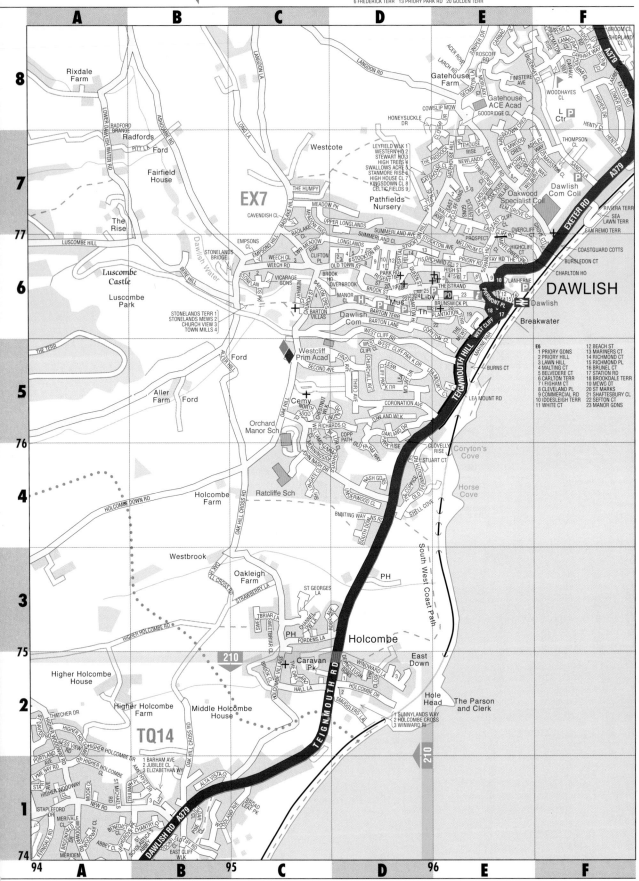

D6
1 PENFIELD GDNS
2 RED LION PL
3 SIDNEY CT
4 HOOPERN TERR
5 MANOR CT
6 FREDERICK TERR
7 SCHOOL HILL
8 QUEEN LA
9 STOCKTON LA
10 HATCHER ST
11 BLACKSWAN PL
12 LUSCOMBE TERR
13 PRIORY PARK RD
14 HALDON TERR
15 ORCHARD GDNS
16 PRINCES ST
17 KING ST
18 ALBERT ST
19 TOWN TREE HILL
20 GOLDEN TERR
21 OLD MANOR CT
22 WEDLAKE MEWS
23 ALEXANDER RD
24 BROOKLANDS
25 LAWN TERR

E6
1 PRIORY GDNS
2 PRIORY HILL
3 LAWN HILL
4 MALTING CT
5 BELVEDERE CT
6 CARLTON TERR
7 FIGHAM CT
8 CLEVELAND PL
9 COMMERCIAL RD
10 IDDESLEIGH TERR
11 WHITE CT
12 BEACH ST
13 MARINERS CT
14 RICHMOND CT
15 RICHMOND PL
16 BRUNEL CT
17 STATION RD
18 BROOKDALE TERR
19 MCWC OT
20 ST MARKS
21 SHAFTESBURY CL
22 SEFTON CT
23 MANOR GDNS

Stonelands Terr 1
Stonelands Mews 2
Church View 3
Town Mills 4

| A | B | C | D | E | F |

8

EX7

WARREN RD

South West Coast Path

Langstone Rock

A379

PINEWOOD CL

PO

THE ROCKSTONE

7

77

6

5

76

4

3

75

2

1

74

97 **A** **B** 98 **C** **D** 99 **E** **F**

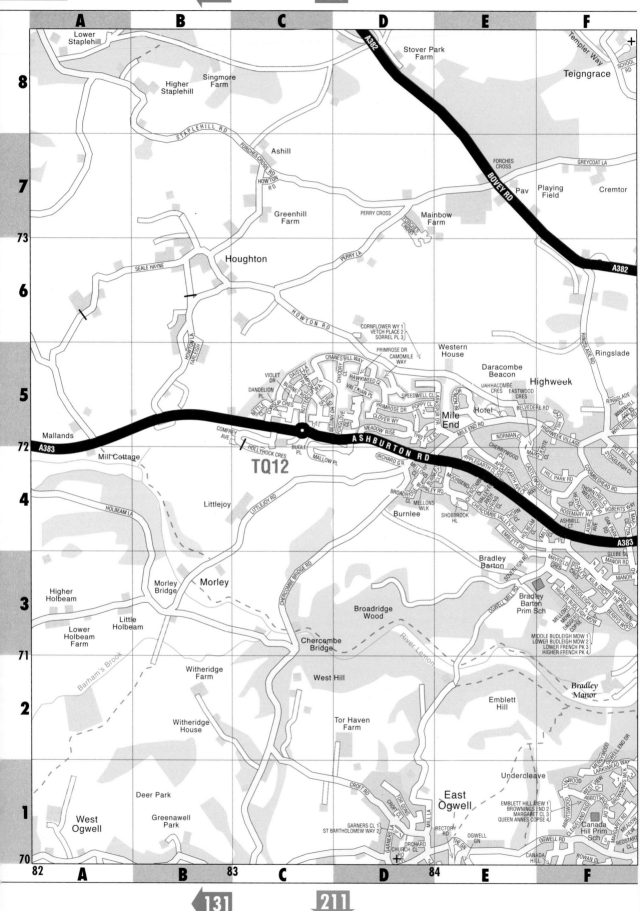

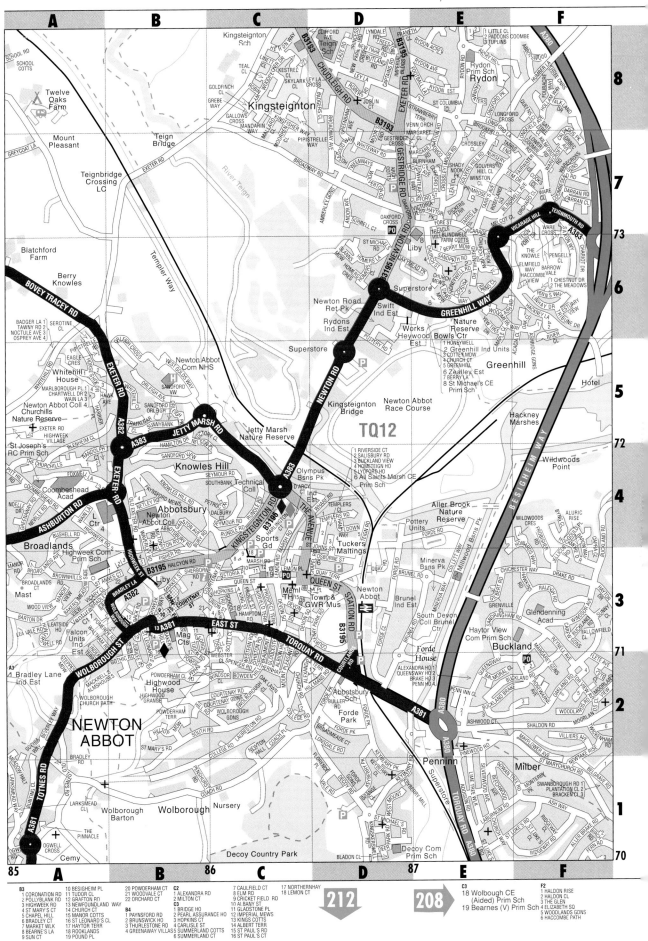

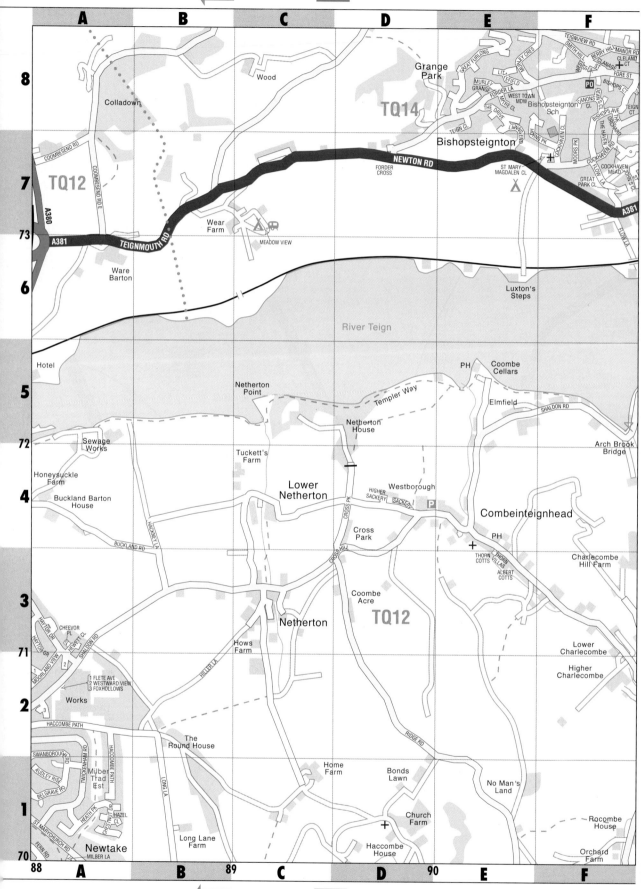

214

F7		
1 UPPER HERMOSA RD	7 QUINNEL HO	14 DOUGLAS HO
2 ROPE WLK	8 CHELSEA PL	15 ST JAMES'S PREC
3 ELMHURST CT	9 GLOUCESTER RD	16 ST JAMES HO
4 MINDEN RD	10 BOSCAWEN PL	17 SPERANZA GR
5 HERMOSA GDNS	11 GROVE TERR	18 FORE ST
6 GROVE CRES	12 GROVE AVE	19 SAXE ST
	13 BITTON PARK RD	

210

209

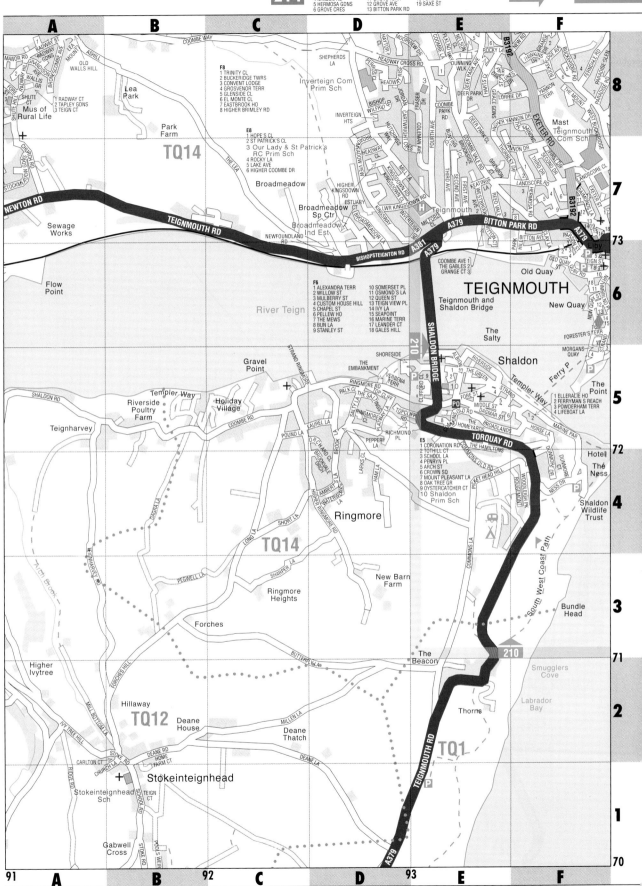

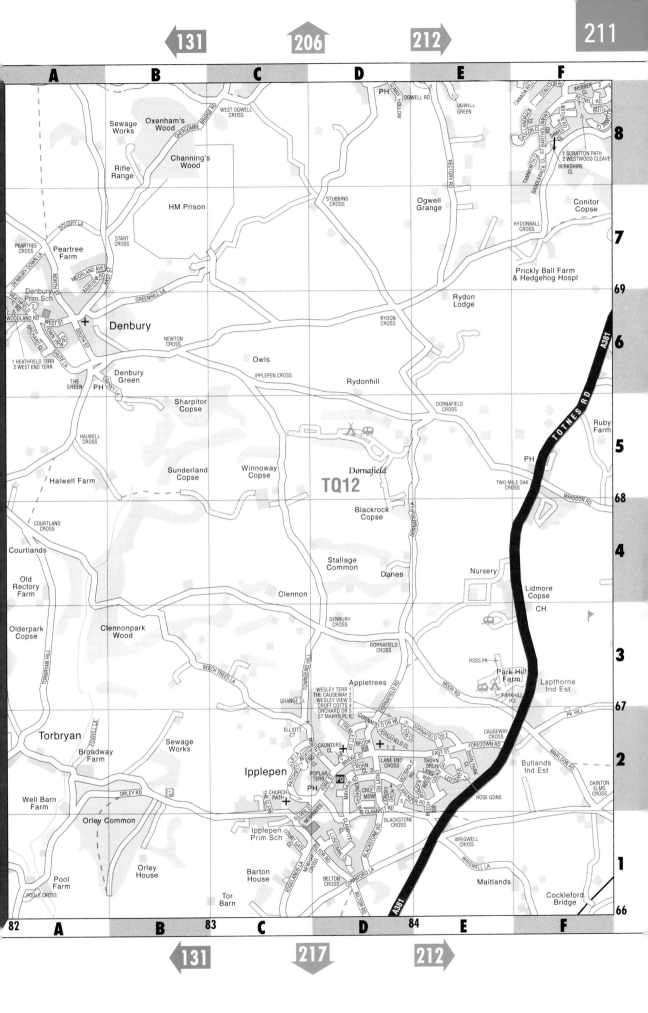

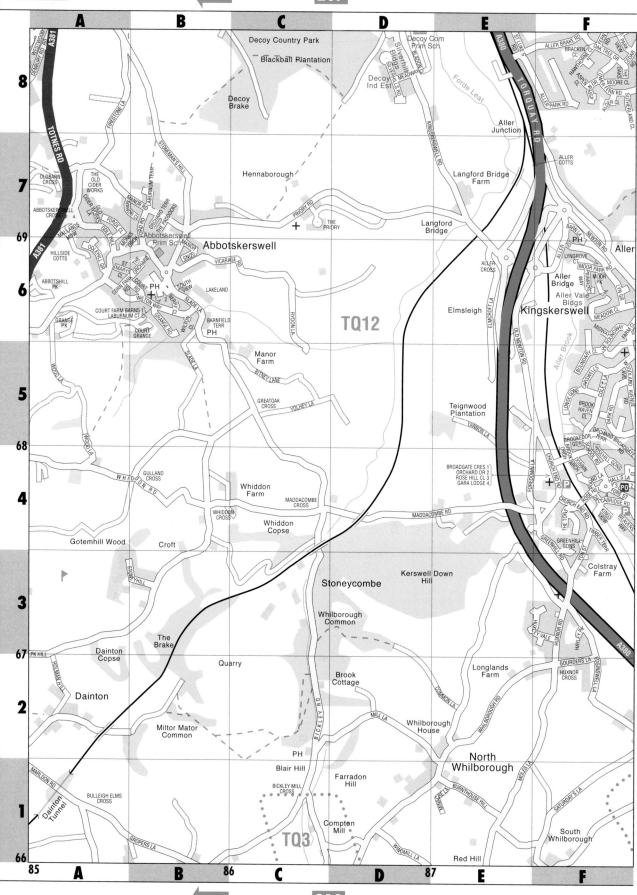

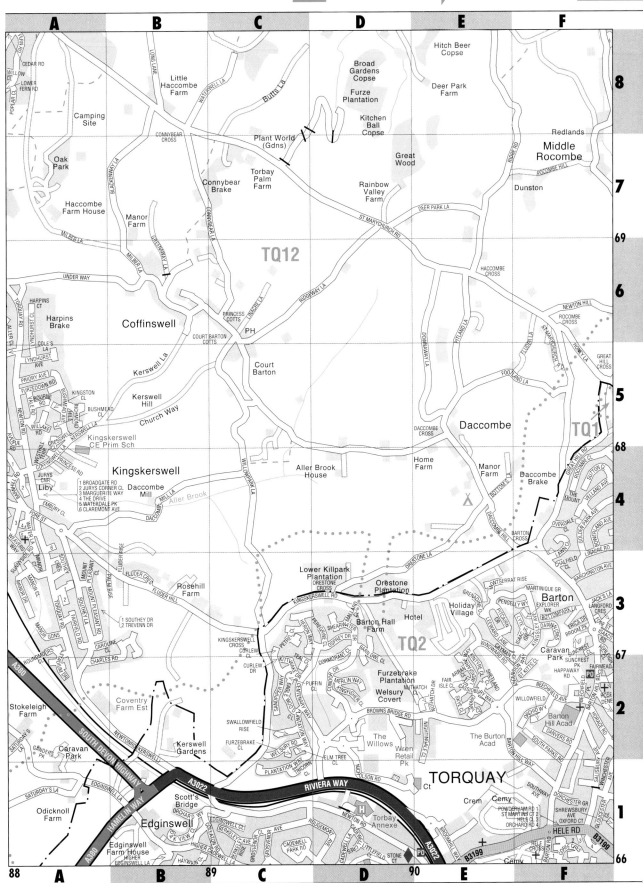

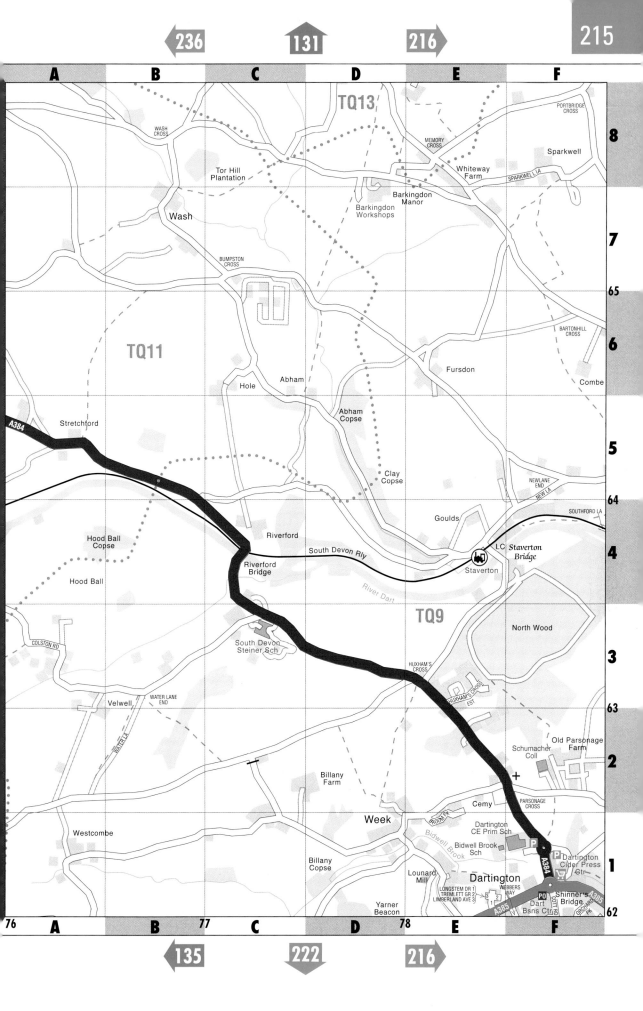

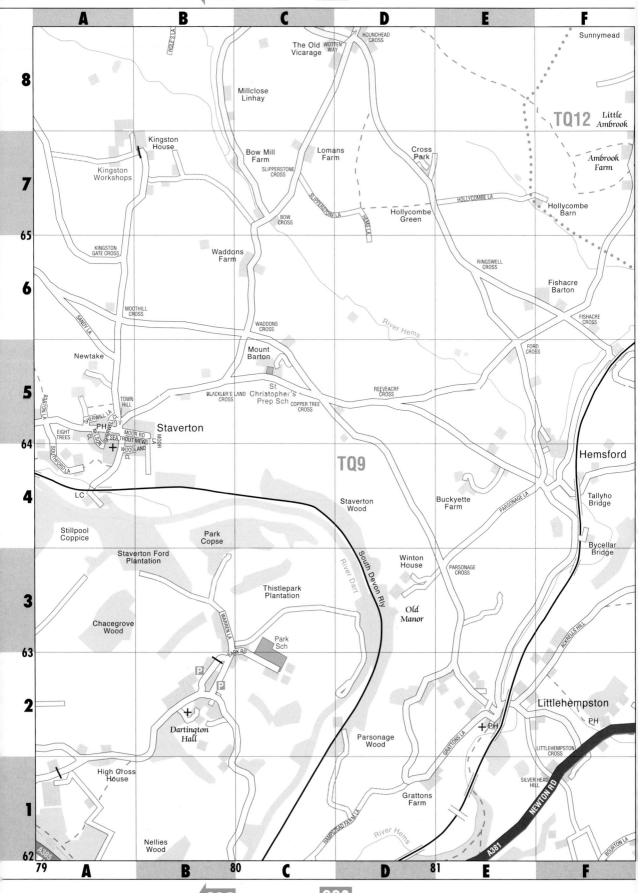

A B C D E F

8

7

65

6

5

64

4

3

63

2

1

62

Map labels:

Sunnymead

TQ12 Little Ambrook

Ambrook Farm

Houndhead Cross

The Old Vicarage

Wotten Way

Kingston House

Millclose Linhay

Bow Mill Farm

Lomans Farm

Slipperstone Cross

Cross Park

Hollycombe La

Hollycombe Barn

Kingston Workshops

Bow Cross

Slipperstone La

Hems La

Hollycombe Green

Fishacre Barton

Kingston Gate Cross

Waddons Farm

Ringswell Cross

Fishacre Cross

Moothill Cross

Waddons Cross

River Hems

Ford Cross

Sandy La

Newtake

Mount Barton

St Christopher's Prep Sch

Blackler's Land Cross

Copper Tree Cross

Reeveacre Cross

Town Hill

Staverton

PH

Eight Trees

Moor Rd

Trout Mews

Woodland Cl

Moor

Hemsford

Tallyho Bridge

Barton La

Southford La

Cherwill La

Nelson Cl

Sea Cl

TQ9

Staverton Wood

Buckyette Farm

Parsonage La

Bycellar Bridge

LC

Stillpool Coppice

Park Copse

Staverton Ford Plantation

Thistlepark Plantation

River Dart

South Devon Rly

Winton House

Parsonage Cross

Chacegrove Wood

Warren La

Park Rd

Park Sch

Old Manor

Ackrells Hill

P

P

Littlehempston

PH

Dartington Hall

Parsonage Wood

Grattons La

PH

Littlehempston Cross

High Cross House

Silver Head Hill

Newton Rd

Nellies Wood

Hampstead Farm La

River Hems

Grattons Farm

A381

Bourton La

A385

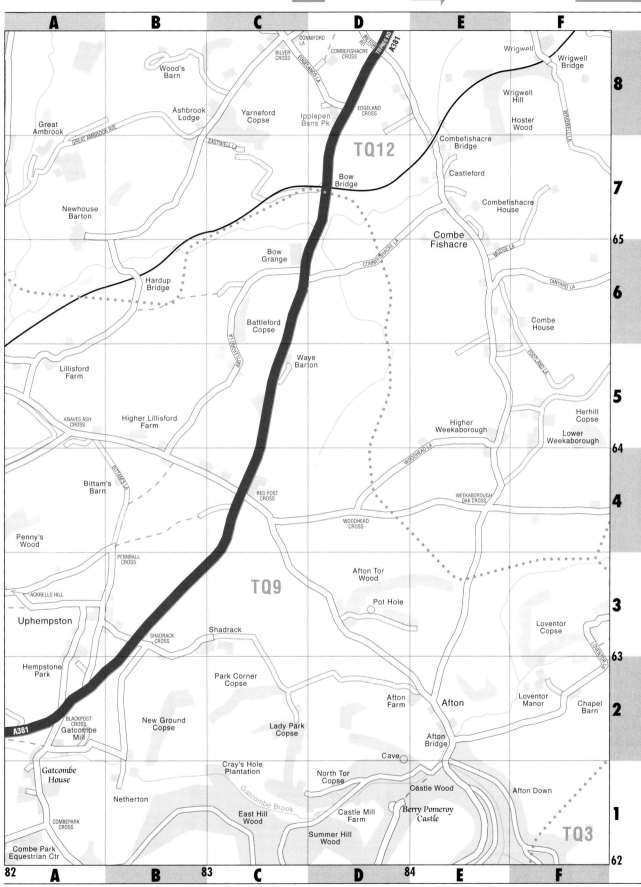

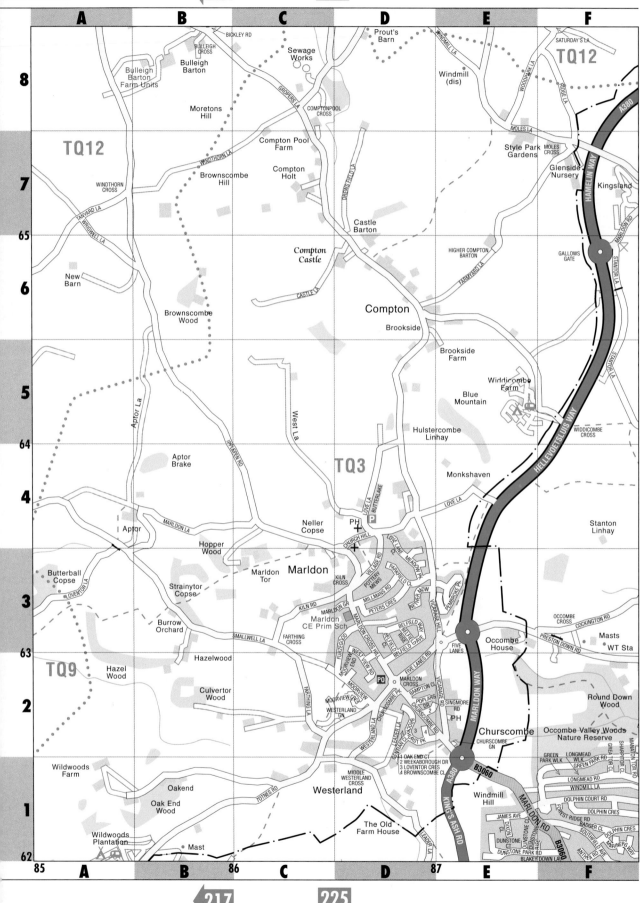

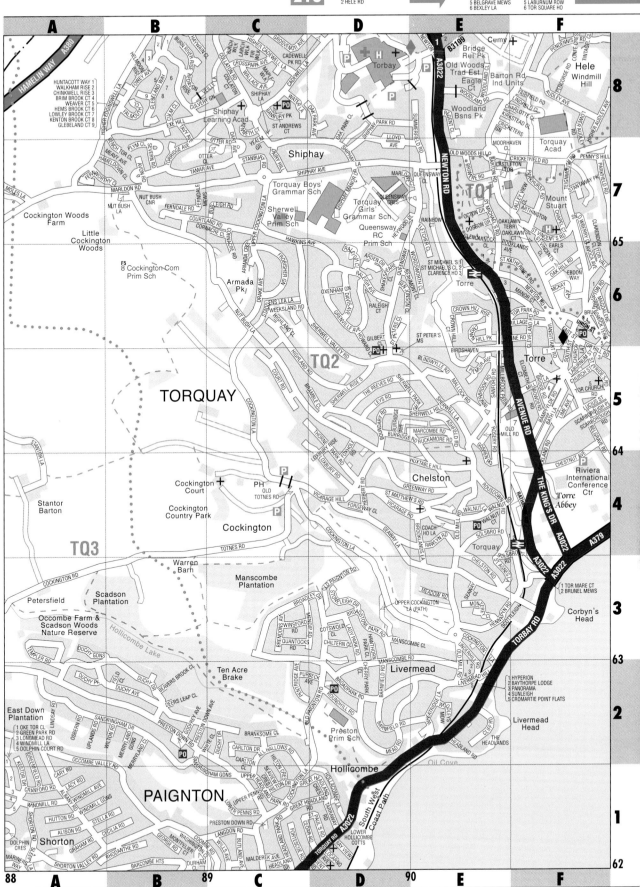

A6
1 KIERAN CT
2 UPTON CT
3 TOR DALE
4 SUNBURY TERR
5 ST IVES CT
6 WILNCOTE LODGE

A7
1 WILLIS CT
2 EMPIRE CT
3 ORCHARD PL
4 MYRTLE ROW
5 UPTON ST JAMES CE PRIM SCH

← **219**

B5
1 BETHEL TERR
2 ST MICHAEL'S TERR
3 ALBERT CT
4 MYRTLE ROW
5 EDGEMOUNT HO
6 LOWER WARBERRY RD

B6
1 WELLINGTON PL
2 MOUNT PLEASANT RD
3 WARBERRY VALE
4 ORCHARD CT
5 SIMON CT
6 PRINCES CT

214

7 ELLACOMBE ACAD

B8
1 WARBRO CT
2 EXCELSIOR MEWS
3 PLAINMOOR RD

B7
4 BLYTHWOODS CRES

1 HOMELANDS PRIM SCH
2 ST MARGARET'S ACAD
3 PRIORY RC PRIM SCH
4 FORE ST

D5
1 MANORGLADE CT
2 ST RONANS
3 WELLSWOOD MANOR
4 MAXSTOKE CT
5 UNDERHEATH
6 HAZELWOOD

TQ2 · TQ1 · TORQUAY
Plainmoor · Babbacombe · Ellacombe · Upton · Wellswood · Kents Cavern
Oddicombe Beach · Babbacombe Cliff Rly · Long Quarry Point · Anstey's Cove · Devil's Point
The Market Forum · Princes Theatre · Torquay Marina · Clock Tower · New Harbour · Town Dock · Living Coasts · Meadfoot Beach

← **219**

A B C D E F

8

7

65

6

Bishop's Wlk

Black
Head

5

Brandy
Cove

64

RICHMOND CT

Hope Cove

BISHOPS
CL

BISHOPS RISE

TQ1

ILSHAM MARINE DR

4

WHIDBORNE AVE

Hope's
Nose

THATCHER AVE

Lead Stone
or Flat Rock

MARINE
MOUNT

South West Coast Path

Thatcher
House

COMPASS
SOUTH

3

Thatcher
Point

63

Ore Stone

Thatcher
Rock

2

1

62

94 A 95 B C 96 D E F

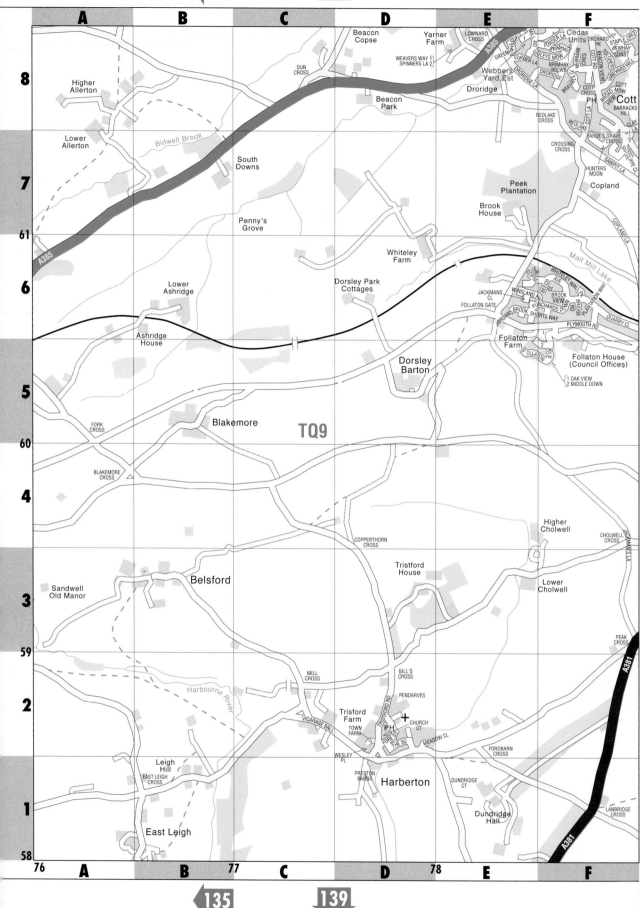

A **B** **C** **D** **E** **F**

8

Higher Allerton

Beacon Copse

Yarner Farm

Lownard Cross

Cedar Units

7

Lower Allerton

Bidwell Brook

South Downs

Dun Cross

Beacon Park

Weavers Way
Spinners La 1
Spinners La 2

Webbers Yard Est

Droridge

Redlake Cross

Crossing Cross

Cott

Barracks Hill

Peek Plantation

Copland

61

Penny's Grove

Whiteley Farm

Brook House

Hunters Moon

6

Lower Ashridge

Dorsley Park Cottages

Jackmans Cl

Follaton Gate

The Copse

Winsland Av

Brook View

Shorts Way

Plymouth Rd

Quarry Cl

Ashridge House

Follaton Farm

Follaton House (Council Offices)

Dorsley Barton

1 Oak View
2 Middle Down

5

Blakemore

TQ9

Fork Cross

60

Blakemore Cross

Higher Cholwell

Cholwell Cross

Jackman's La

4

Copperthorn Cross

Tristford House

Lower Cholwell

Sandwell Old Manor

Belsford

3

Peak Cross

59

Harbourne River

Mill Cross

Gill's Cross

Pendarves

A381

2

Vicarage Ball

Trisford Farm

Tristford Rd

Town Farm

PH

Fore St

The Sq

Church Ct

Meadow Cl

Fordbarn Cross

Leigh Hill

East Leigh Cross

Wesley Pl

Preston Barns

Harberton

Dundridge Ct

Lanbridge Cross

1

East Leigh

Dundridge Hall

A381

58

A 76 **B** 77 **C** **D** 78 **E** **F**

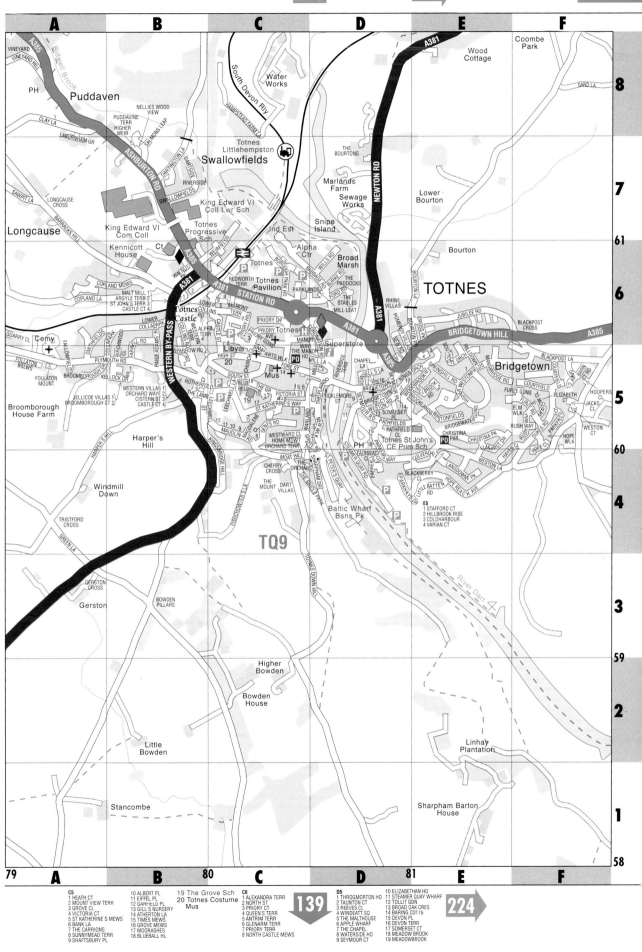

C5
1 HEATH CT
2 MOUNT VIEW TERR
3 GROVE CL
4 VICTORIA CT
5 ST KATHERINE S MEWS
6 BANK LA
7 THE CARRIONS
8 SUNNYMEAD TERR
9 SHAFTSBURY PL

10 ALBERT PL
11 EIFFEL PL
12 GARFIELD PL
13 GILL'S NURSERY
14 ATHERTON LA
15 TIMES MEWS
16 GROVE MEWS
17 MOORASHES
18 BLUEBALL HL

19 The Grove Sch
20 Totnes Costume Mus

C6
1 ALEXANDRA TERR
2 NORTH ST
3 PRIORY CT
4 QUEEN'S TERR
5 ANTRIM TERR
6 GLENARM TERR
7 PRIORY TERR
8 NORTH CASTLE MEWS

D5
1 THROGMORTON HO
2 TAUNTON CT
3 REEVES CL
4 WINDEATT SQ
5 THE MALTHOUSE
6 APPLE WHARF
7 THE CHAPEL
8 WATERSIDE HO
9 SEYMOUR CT

10 ELIZABETHAN HO
11 STEAMER QUAY WHARF
12 TOLLIT GDN
13 BROAD OAK CRES
14 BARING COTTS
15 DEVON PL
16 DEVON TERR
17 SOMERSET CT
18 MEADOW BROOK
19 MEADOWBROOK

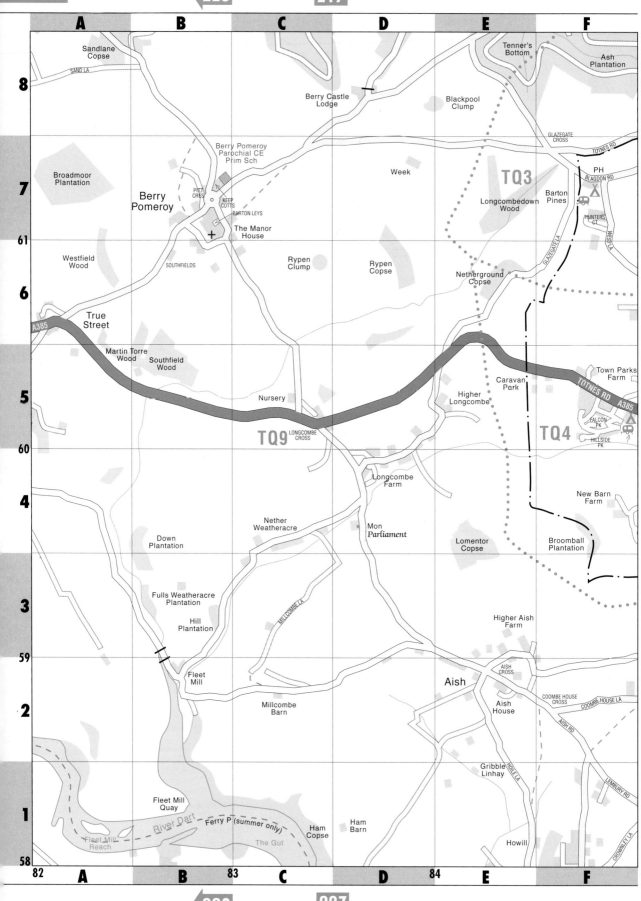

Sandlane Copse

SAND LA

Broadmoor Plantation

Berry Pomeroy Parochial CE Prim Sch

Berry Castle Lodge

Blackpool Clump

Tenner's Bottom

Ash Plantation

GLAZEGATE CROSS

TOTNES RD

TQ3

Week

BLAGDON RD

PH

Berry Pomeroy

PITT CRES

KEEP COTTS

BARTON LEYS

Longcombedown Wood

Barton Pines

HUNTERS CT

The Manor House

Westfield Wood

SOUTHFIELDS

Rypen Clump

Rypen Copse

Netherground Copse

WEST LA

GLAZEGATE LA

True Street

A385

Martin Torre Wood

Southfield Wood

Nursery

Higher Longcombe

Caravan Park

TOTNES RD

Town Parks Farm

TQ9

LONGCOMBE CROSS

A385

FALCON PK

TQ4

HILLSIDE PK

Longcombe Farm

Down Plantation

Nether Weatheracre

Mon Parliament

Lomentor Copse

New Barn Farm

Broomball Plantation

Fulls Weatheracre Plantation

MILLCOMBE LA

Higher Aish Farm

Hill Plantation

Fleet Mill

AISH CROSS

Aish

COOMBE HOUSE CROSS

COOMBE HOUSE LA

Millcombe Barn

Aish House

AISH RD

Gribble Linhay

HOLE LA

LEMBURY RD

Fleet Mill Quay

River Dart

Ferry P (summer only)

Ham Copse

Ham Barn

Fleet Mill Reach

The Gut

Howill

CROWLEY LA

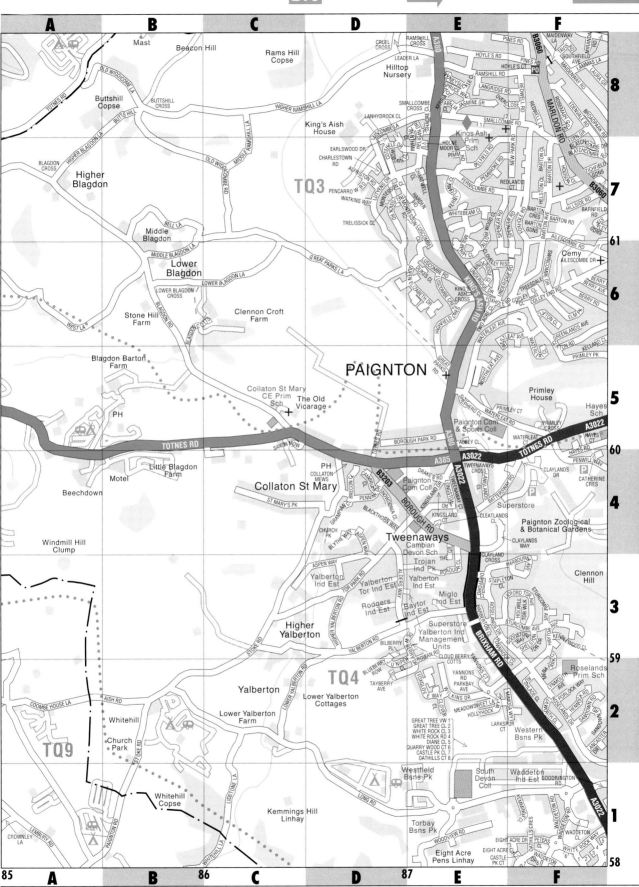

A   B   C   D   E   F

8
7
61
6
5
60
4
3
59
2
1
58

Mast
Beacon Hill
Rams Hill Copse
CRUEL CROSS
RAMSHILL CROSS
LEADER LA
Hilltop Nursery
PINES RD
HOYLE'S RD
HOYLE'S CT
B3060
PO
MAIDENWAY
SOUTHFIELD AVE
LAMMAS LA
MAIDENWAY RD
LAURA CT

Buttshill Copse
OLD WIDDICOMBE LA
Buttshill Cross
BUTT'S HILL
WGHER RAMSHILL LA
King's Aish House
SMALLCOMBE CL
LANHYDROCK CL
HONEYSUCKLE CL
SPRUCE AV
ABBE LA
JASMINE GR
RAMSHILL RD
LANGRIDGE RD
OVER CLOSE
REDWELL RD
REDWELL LA
A380
B3060
MARLDON RD
ROSEMARY GDNS
EDENVALE RD
BROADPARK RD

TOTNES RD
Higher Blagdon
BLAGDON CROSS
HIGHER BLAGDON LA
OLD WIDDICOMBE RD
MIDDLE RAMSHILL LA
EARLSWOOD DR
CHARLESTOWN RD
PENCARRO W
LUTTON TER
MONTESSON CL
WATKINS WAY
TRELISSICK CL
TQ3
Kings Ash Prim Sch
HOLNE MOOR CL
PIMM
NEW PARK RD
REDLANDS CT
FERNICOMBE RD
PENROHE RD
SPENCER RD
BARTON CRES
BARTON GDNS
BARTON AVE
BARTON DR
BARTON RD
HELSTON CL
MILLSIDE RD
AILESCOMBE RD
BLACKCOMBE RD
BLACKCOMBE RD
TICHFIELD GDNS
BARNFIELD RD
SELE CL

Middle Blagdon
BELL LA
Lower Blagdon
LOWER BLAGDON LA
GREAT PARKS LA
WHITEBEAM CL
FERN CL
LISCOMBE WAY
LISCOMBE CL
QUEEN ELIZABETH DR
KING'S AISH CROSS
FOXHOLE RD
COPLEY CL
COLLEY END RD
CLAYTON CL
Cemy
AILESCOMBE DR
BERRY CL
BERRY RD
BERRY PK

Lower Blagdon
LOWER BLAGDON CROSS
Stone Hill Farm
Clennon Croft Farm
BLAGDON RD
BLAGDON COTTS
KINGS AISH RD
HIGHFIELD CL
OTELY RISE
WATERLEAT AVE
WATRI CL
GREENLANDS AVE
ELM PK
KELLAND CL
TON RD
Primley Pk

Blagdon Barton Farm
WEST LA
Collaton St Mary CE Prim Sch
The Old Vicarage
PAIGNTON
GREAT PARKS RD
SHEPHERD CL
NORTHFIELD AVE
WATERLEAT RD
Primley House
Primley Ct
Hayes Sch
Primley Pk

PH
TOTNES RD
SAXON MOW
LYDWELL RD
Borough Park Rd
A380
A3022
A3022
Paignton Com & Sports Coll
WATERLEAT CT
Hayes CT
PENWILL WAY
A3022
Hayes
TOTNES RD
60

Beechdown
Motel
Little Blagdon Farm
COLLATON MEWS
Collaton St Mary
ST MARY'S PK
GRAMPIAN CL
BRECON CL
SNOWDON CL
CAMBRIAN CL
PENNY
BLACKTHORN WAY
B3203
BOROUGH RD
Paignton Com Coll
DRAKES RD
KINGSLAND RD
KINGSLAND CT
TWEENAWAYS CROSS
LANGLANDS RD
BATTERSWAY RD
Superstore
CLAYLANDS DR
A3022
CLEATLANDS CL
Superstore
CATHERINE CRES
P
Windmill Hill Clump
CHURCH PK
BLYTHE WAY
ASPEN WAY
Tweenaways
Cambian Devon Sch
Trojan Ind Pk
CLAYLAND CROSS
CLAYLANDS WAY
Paignton Zoological & Botanical Gardens
Clennon Hill
ASPEN WAY
TOR PARK RD
ALDERS WAY
Yalberton Ind Est
Yalberton Tor Ind Est
Yalberton Ind Est
Rodgers Ind Est
Baytor Ind Est
Miglo Ind Est
THE BOROUGH
STAPLETON CL
HARBOURN
LIDFORD TOR AVE
STURCOMBE AVE
HOLWILL TOR WLK
KENALWOOD CL
3
Higher Yalberton
STOKE RD
HIGHER YALBERTON RD
VALBERTON RD
BILBERRY PL
BLUEBERRY ROW
JUNIPER
ROWAN RD
Superstore
Yalberton Ind Management Units
Cloud Berry Cotts
YANNONS RD
PARKBAY AVE
WOODSTONE
CASTLE PK CL
TOR HILL
BRIXHAM RD
MARWOOD
LYNMOUTH
PORLOCK WAY
HENACRE RD
Roselands Prim Sch
59
COOMBE HOUSE LA
AISH RD
LOWER YALBERTON RD
Yalberton
TQ4
Lower Yalberton Cottages
TAYBERRY AVE
E WAY
KINS DR
MEADOWSWEET LA
HOLLYHOCK
ROSELANDS DR
SANDOWN RD
LANCASTER DRI
2
TQ9
Whitehill
Church Park
Lower Yalberton Farm
GREAT TREE VW 1
GREAT TREE CL 2
WHITE ROCK CL 3
WHITE ROCK RD 4
DIANE CL 5
QUARRY WOOD CT 6
CASTLE PK CL 7
OATHILLS CT 8
LARKSUR
Western Bsns Pk
CROWNLEY LA
LEMBURY RD
PAIGNTON RD
LIBSTONE LA
WHITEHILL LA
Whitehill Copse
Kemmings Hill Linhay
LONG RD
WOODVIEW RD
Westfield Bsns Pk
South Devon Coll
Waddeton Ind Est
GOODRINGTON RD
WADDETON RD
EIGHT ACRE DR
OATHILLS CRES
PETERS
WHITE ROCK WAY
WADDETON CL
1
Torbay Bsns Pk
Eight Acre Pens Linhay
EIGHT ACRE CL
CASTLE PK CT
A3022
58

85   A   86   B   C   87   D   E   F

A5
1 HIGHER MANOR TERR
2 CONWAY CRES
3 ELMBANK GDNS
4 CONWAY HO
5 MERRITT FLATS
6 FLEMONS CT

A6
1 PLEASANT TERR
2 HILLSIDE TERR
3 LAURA PL
4 BANNER CT
5 CLIFTON BANK

A7
1 KIRKHAM CT
2 LOWER PK

225

B5
1 TOR SANDS
2 WHITESTONE ORCH
3 THE OLD CIDER PRESS
4 Curledge Street Acad

219

A
B
C
D
E
F
8
7
61
6
5
60
4
3
59
2
1
58
88
89
90
Preston
TQ3
Oldway
Oldway Mansion
Oldway Prim Sch
Torbay Sch
Liby
Crossways
Victoria
PAIGNTON
Promenade Pier
South West Coast Path
Pirates Bay Adventure Golf
Paignton
Paignton Harbour
Roundham Head
St Michaels
Meml
TA Ctr
Seashore Ctr
Goodrington Sands
Spashdown @ Quaywest
Paignton Zoo & Botanical Gdns
Torbay L Ctr
TQ4
Clennon Hill
Holiday Centre
Goodrington
Sugar Loaf Hill & Saltern Cove Nature Reserve
Saltern Cove
Shell Cove
Dartmouth Steam Rly
Tor Bay
DARTMOUTH RD
TORQUAY RD
TOTNES RD
HYDE RD
TORBAY RD
SANDS RD
ESPLANADE RD
MARINE DR
EUGENE RD
A3022
A379
B3201
B3060
1 ROSEMARY CT
2 DOWER CT
3 BISHOPSTONE GDNS
4 THE CLARIDGE
5 SEAWAY GDNS
6 SEAWAY CRES
7 BROOKFIELD HO
8 PRESTON DOWN RD
B7
1 WOODLAND MEWS
2 HADDON CT
3 KILLERTON CL
4 MILL LA
5 KIRKHAM ST
6 FARNHAM TERR
7 Sacred Heart RC Sch
8 The Polsham Ctr
1 KINGSMEAD HO
2 MEADCOURT
3 LOGAN RD
4 WILBARN RD
B6
1 BRENT RD
2 MILLBROOK RD
3 ST JOHN'S CT
4 CHURCH ST MEWS
5 CROWN AND ANCHOR WAY
6 CHURCH PATH
7 LACEY HO
8 GERSTON PL
9 CROSSWAYS
10 JACK BEARS HO
11 RADFORD HO
12 GREAT WESTERN RD
13 Kirkham Ho
14 St Hilary Sch of English
15 Paignton Com Coll
16 Paignton Health & Wellbeing Centre
1 PARKSIDE RD
2 BERRY SQ
3 PAGE HO
1 ADELPHI MANS
2 KINGSWOOD CT
3 CLEVELAND CT
4 BARRINGTON CL
5 PINEWOOD CT
6 HOMEBOURNE HO
7 SUMMERFIELD CT
8 THE MOORINGS
9 THE ANCHORAGE
10 LANCASTER HO
11 ROUNDHAM HO
12 OSMOND LODGE
13 ROSEMOUNT
1 YOUNG'S PARK LA
2 BRAESIDE MEWS
3 BOSUNS POINT
4 SEABOURNE CT
BLACKBROOK WLK 1
BIDWELL WLK 2
CHERRY BROOK WLK 3
MONTEREY 4
CRYSTAL CL 1
HOOKHILLS RD 2

225
229

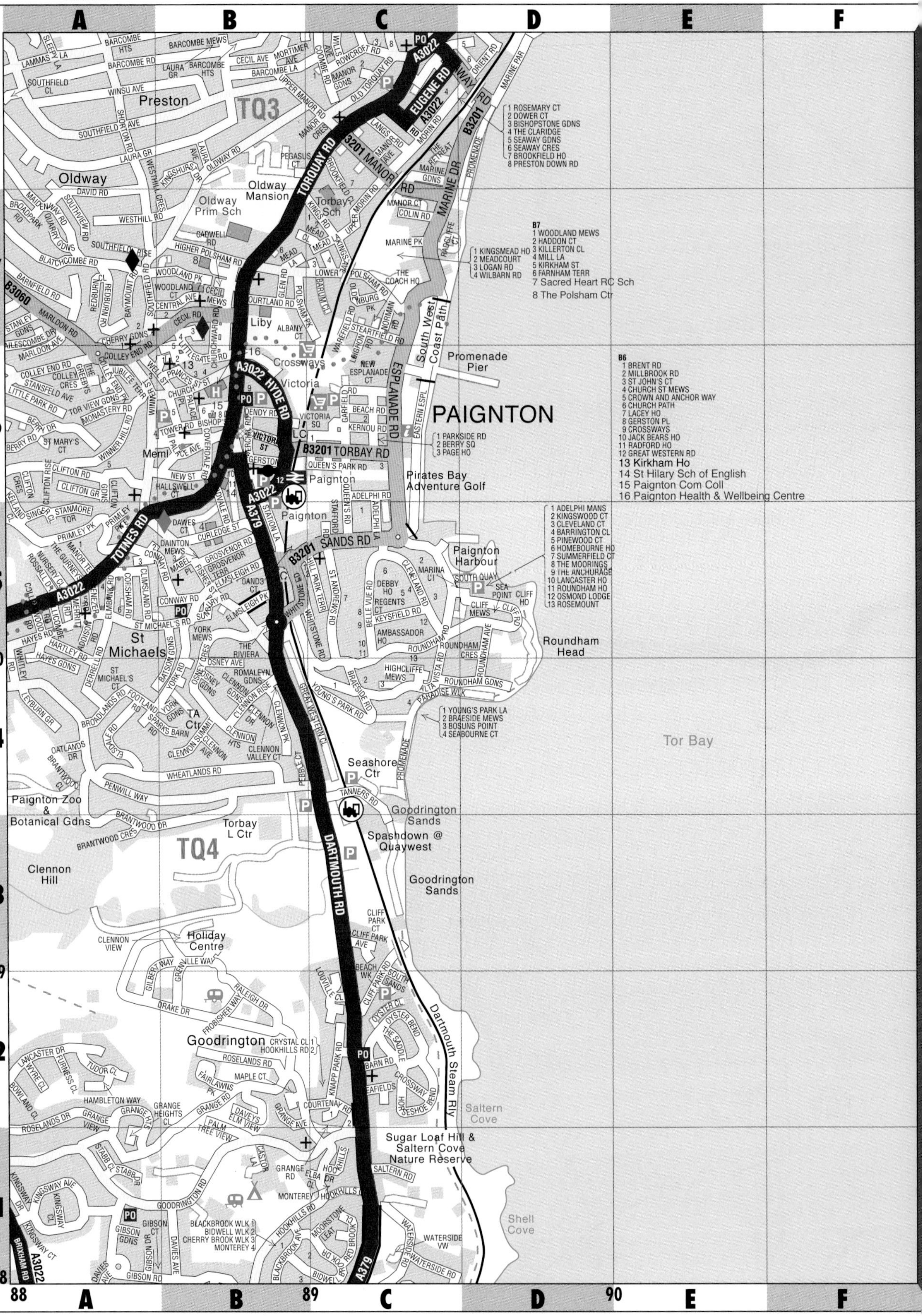

A B C D E F

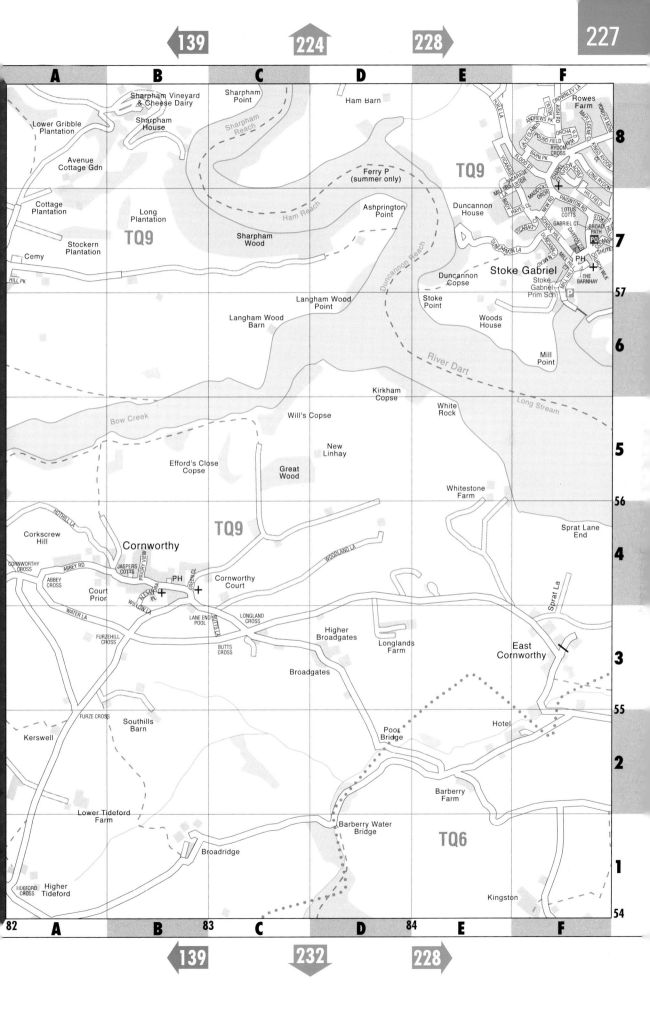

8

Lower Gribble
Plantation

Sharpham Vineyard
& Cheese Dairy

Sharpham
House

Sharpham
Point

Ham Barn

Rowes
Farm

Avenue
Cottage Gdn

Sharpham Reach

Ferry P
(summer only)

TQ9

Duncannon
House

8

Cottage
Plantation

Long
Plantation

Sharpham
Wood

Ham Reach

Ashprington
Point

Stoke Gabriel

7

Stockern
Plantation

TQ9

Duncannon Reach

Duncannon La

PH

57

Cemy

HILL PK

Langham Wood
Point

Langham Wood
Barn

Duncannon
Copse

Stoke
Point

Woods
House

Stoke
Gabriel
Prim Sch

6

River Dart

Mill
Point

Bow Creek

Kirkham
Copse

White
Rock

Long Stream

5

Will's Copse

New
Linhay

Whitestone
Farm

56

Efford's Close
Copse

Great
Wood

Corkscrew
Hill

TQ9

Sprat Lane
End

4

Cornworthy

WOODLAND LA

Sprat La

Cornworthy
Cross

JASPERS
COTTS

PH

Cornworthy
Court

Abbey
Cross

Court
Prior

Green Cl

East
Cornworthy

3

Water La

Lane End
Pool

Longland
Cross

Higher
Broadgates

Longlands
Farm

55

Furzehill
Cross

Butts
Cross

Broadgates

Hotel

Kerswell

Furze Cross

Southills
Barn

Pool
Bridge

2

Lower Tideford
Farm

Barberry
Farm

Broadridge

Barberry Water
Bridge

TQ6

1

Tideford
Cross

Higher
Tideford

Kingston

54

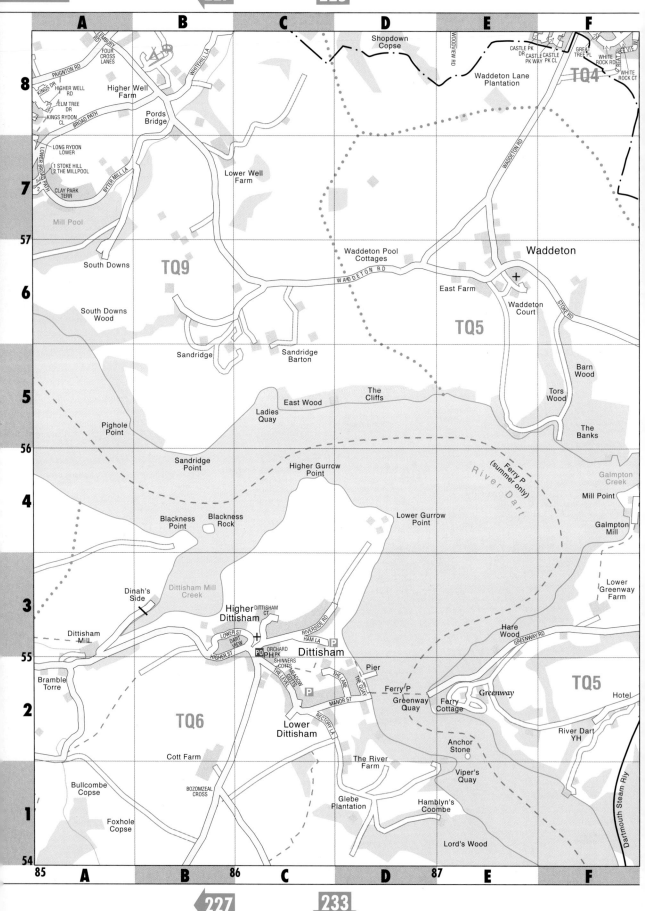

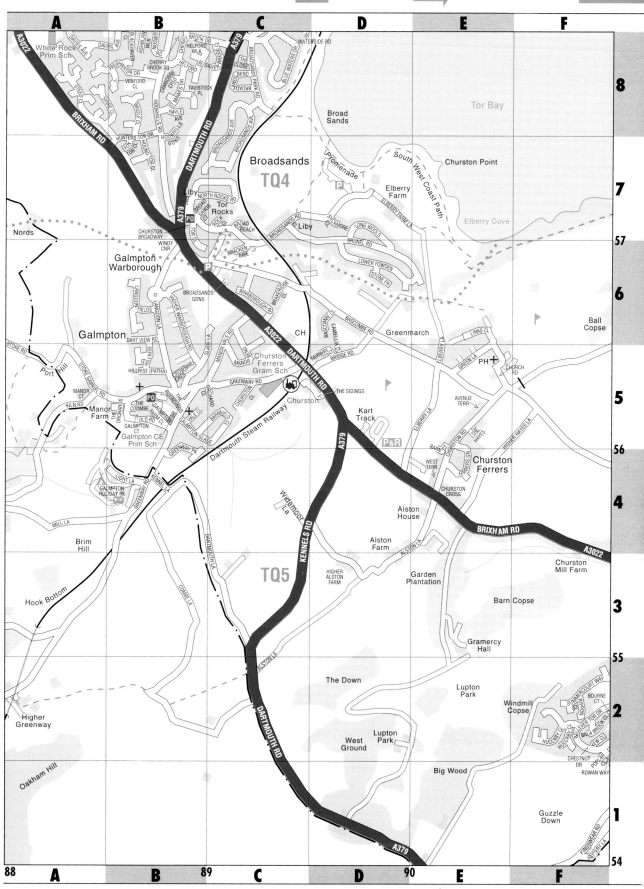

C3
1 GARROW CL
2 EVELEIGH CL
3 DOCTORS RD
4 GREENSWOOD RD
5 CLENNON CT
6 MAYFLOWER DR
7 HANOVER CL
8 ORCHARD CL
9 GREENSWOOD CL
10 CASTOR MWS

C4
1 PRINCE WILLIAM CT
2 SAXON HTS
3 CAVERN RD
4 TINKERS WOOD CT
5 WATERMILL CT
6 PARKHAM TWRS
7 CHURCHILL CT
8 BOLTON CT
9 WINDMILL CT
10 WREN CT
11 GREAT GATE FLATS
12 PARKHAM TERR

C5
1 HARBOUR VIEW CL
2 LINDEN CT
3 PROSPECT RD
4 CHURCH ST
5 CHURCH HILL W
6 CHURCH HILL E
7 APTERS HILL
8 MARKET ST
9 UNION LA
10 SOMERSET CT
11 BANK LA
12 BREWERY LA
13 PRINGS CT

D5
1 PARADISE PL
2 FURZE LA
3 THE STRAND
4 PUMP ST
5 ST PETER'S HILL
6 TEMPERANCE PL
7 MARINERS CT
8 HEADLAND CT
9 RANSCOMBE CT

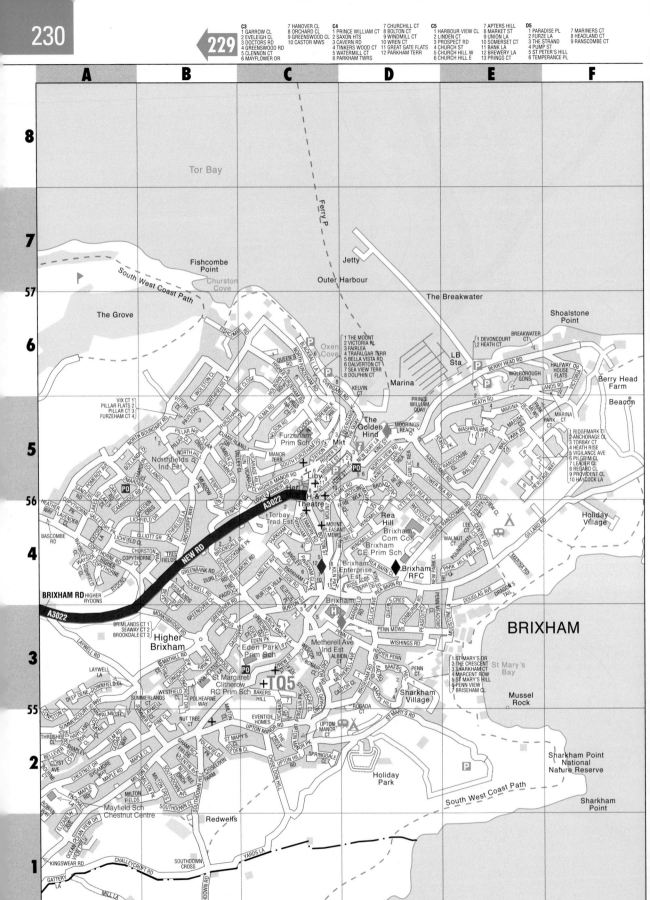

A B C D E F

8

7

57

6

Quay

Berry Head

Berry Head
National
Nature Reserve

TQ5

Berry Head
Fort

Berry Head
Common

Berry Head
Country Park

P

GILLARD
RD

5

56

Mew
Stone

Cod
Rock

Durl Head
Durl
Rock

4

3

55

2

1

54

94 A B 95 C D 96 E F

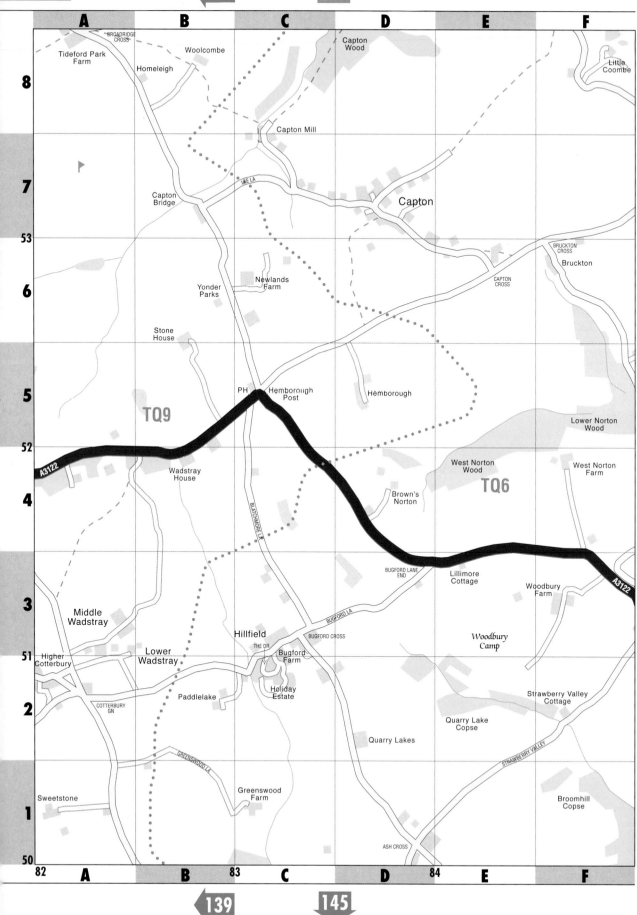

A B C D E F

8
7
53
6
5
52
4
3
51
2
1
50

82 A 83 B C 84 D E F

Broadridge Cross
Tideford Park Farm
Woolcombe
Homeleigh
Capton Wood
Little Coombe
Capton Mill
Capton Bridge
ICE LA
Capton
Bruckton Cross
Bruckton
Yonder Parks
Newlands Farm
Capton Cross
Stone House
Hemborough Post
PH
Hemborough
Lower Norton Wood
TQ9
West Norton Wood
West Norton Farm
A3122
Wadstray House
Brown's Norton
TQ6
BLATCHMORE LA
Bugford Lane End
Lillimore Cottage
Woodbury Farm
A3122
Middle Wadstray
Bugford La
Woodbury Camp
Higher Cotterbury
Lower Wadstray
Hillfield
THE DR
Bugford Farm
Bugford Cross
Strawberry Valley Cottage
Cotterbury Gn
Paddlelake
Holiday Estate
Quarry Lake Copse
Strawberry Valley
Greenswood La
Quarry Lakes
Sweetstone
Greenswood Farm
Broomhill Copse
Ash Cross

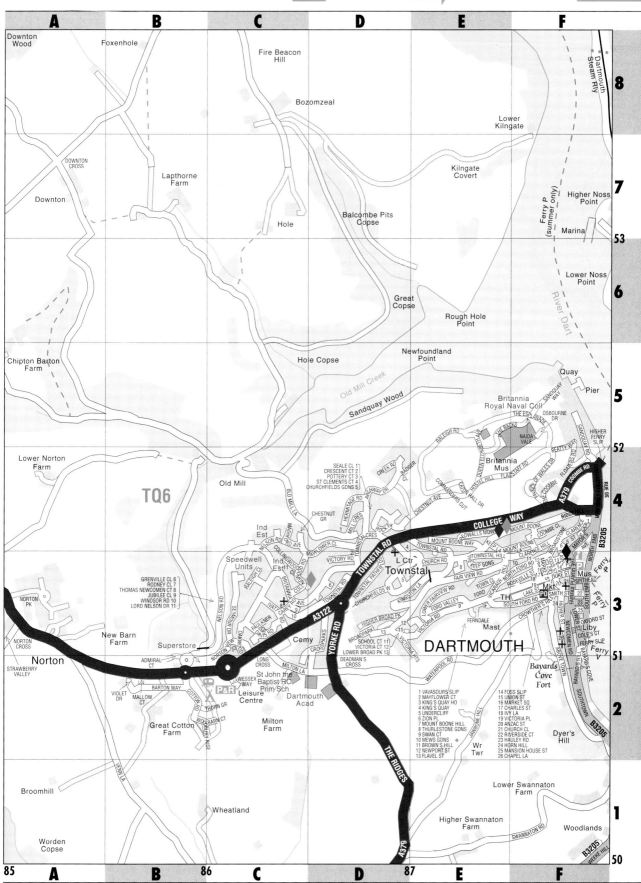

8

Dartmouth Steam Rly

Downton Wood

Foxenhole

Fire Beacon Hill

Bozomzeal

Lower Kilngate

7

Lapthorne Farm

Kilngate Covert

Higher Noss Point

Hole

Ferry P (summer only)

Marina

53

Downton

Balcombe Pits Copse

Lower Noss Point

6

Chipton Barton Farm

Great Copse

River Dart

Rough Hole Point

Hole Copse

Newfoundland Point

Quay

Pier

5

Lower Norton Farm

Sandquay Wood

Britannia Royal Naval Coll

THE ESPLANADE

NAIDA VALE

Higher Ferry Slip

52

TQ6

Old Mill

Britannia Mus

4

SEALE CL 1
CRESCENT CT 2
POTTERY CT 3
ST CLEMENTS CT 4
CHURCHFIELDS GDNS 5

COLLEGE WAY

A379 COOMBE RD

RUE DE

B3205

Ind Est

Ind Est

TOWNSTAL RD

L Ctr
Townstal

3

GRENVILLE CL 6
RODNEY CL 7
THOMAS NEWCOMEN CT 8
JUBILEE CL 9
WINDSOR RD 10
LORD NELSON DR 11

Speedwell Units

A3122

YORKE RD

DARTMOUTH

Cemy

Ferry

51

NORTON PK

New Barn Farm

Superstore

Cemy

FERNDALE Mast

Bayards Cove Fort

NORTON CROSS

Norton

ADMIRAL CT

St John the Baptist RC Prim Sch

SCHOOL CT 11
VICTORIA CT 12
LOWER BROAD PK 13

DEADMAN'S CROSS

1 VAVASOURS SLIP
2 MAYFLOWER CT
3 KING'S QUAY HO
4 KING'S QUAY
5 UNDERCLIFF
6 ZION PL
7 MOUNT BOONE HILL
8 THURLESTONE GDNS
9 SWAN CT
10 MEWS GDNS
11 BROWN'S HILL
12 NEWPORT ST
13 FLAVEL ST

14 FOSS SLIP
15 UNION ST
16 MARKET SQ
17 CHARLES ST
18 IVY LA
19 VICTORIA PL
20 ANZAC ST
21 CHURCH CL
22 RIVERSIDE CT
23 HAULEY RD
24 HORN HILL
25 MANSION HOUSE ST
26 CHAPEL LA

STRAWBERRY VALLEY

VIOLET DR

MALLOW CT

P&R

Leisure Centre

Dartmouth Acad

Dyer's Hill

B3205

2

Great Cotton Farm

Milton Farm

Wr Twr

THE RIDGES

Lower Swannaton Farm

1

Broomhill

Wheatland

A379

Higher Swannaton Farm

SWANNATON RD

Woodlands

B3205

WEEKE HILL

50

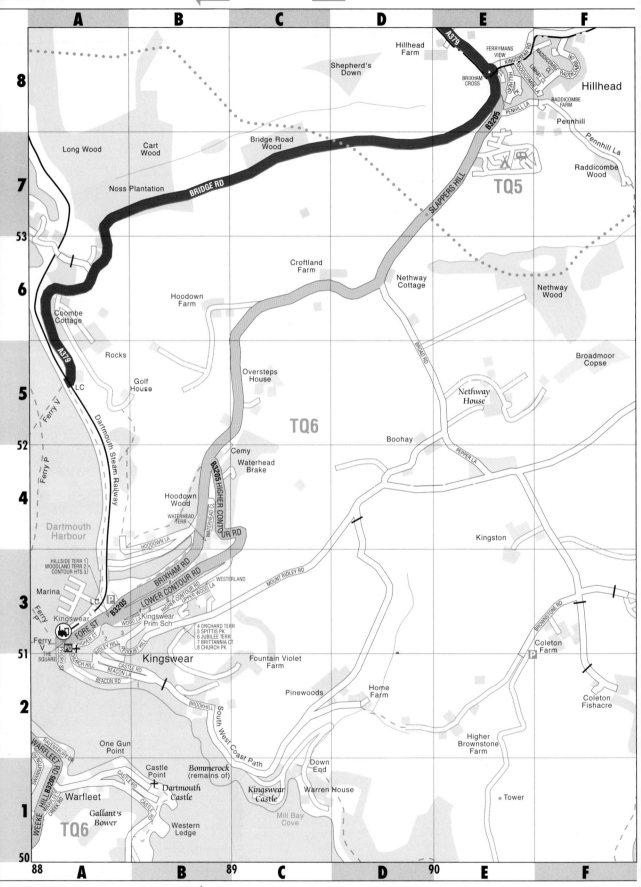

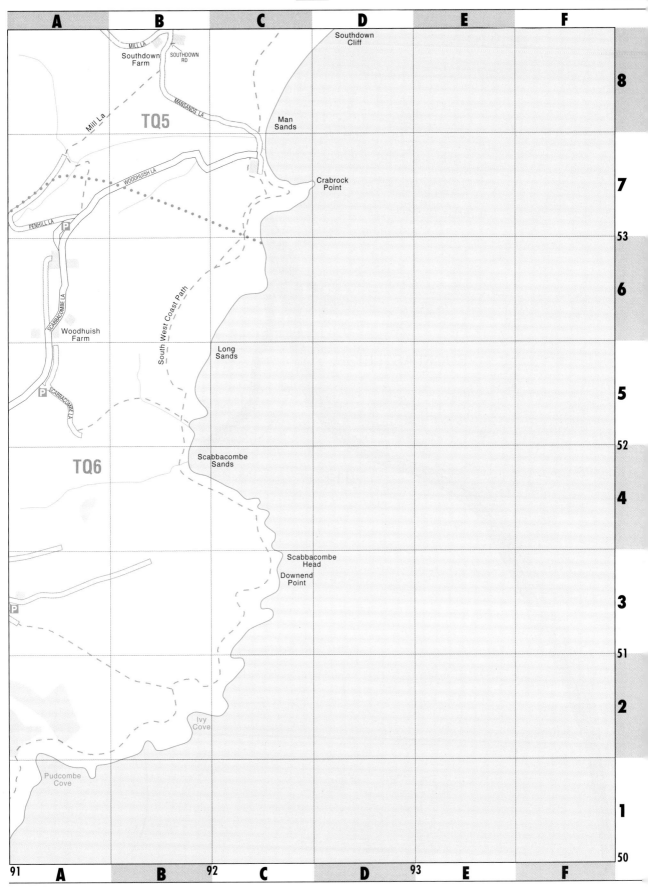

MILL LA

Southdown
Farm

SOUTHDOWN
RD

Southdown
Cliff

Mill La

MANSANDS LA

TQ5

Man
Sands

WOODHUISH LA

Crabrock
Point

PENHILL LA

P

SCABBACOMBE LA

Woodhuish
Farm

South West Coast Path

Long
Sands

P SCABBACOMBE LA

TQ6

Scabbacombe
Sands

Scabbacombe
Head

Downend
Point

P

Ivy
Cove

Pudcombe
Cove

130 130 131

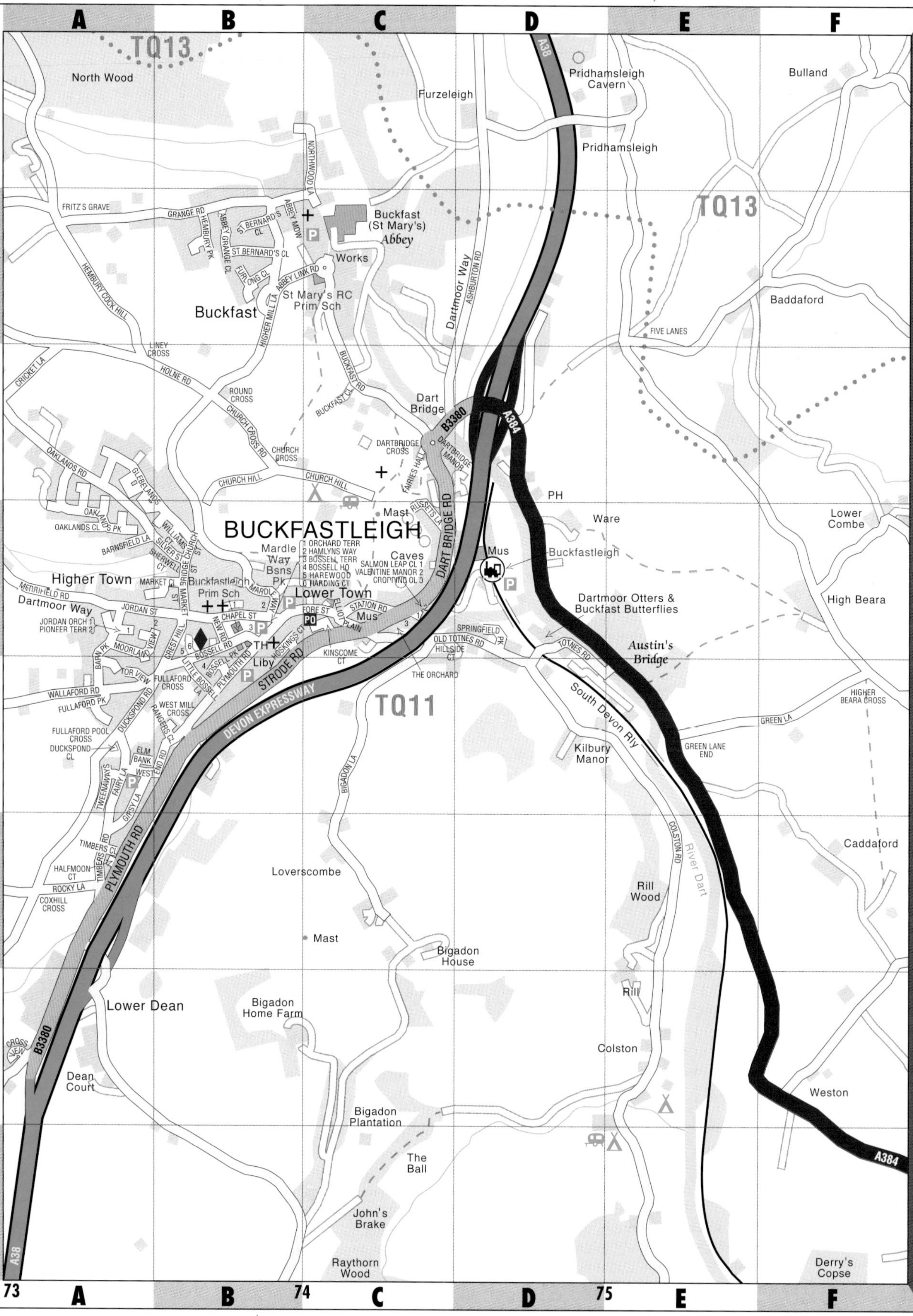

A B C D E F
8
7
67
6
5
66
4
3
65
2
1
64
73
74
75
TQ13
TQ11
North Wood
Furzeleigh
Pridhamsleigh Cavern
Pridhamsleigh
Bulland
FRITZ'S GRAVE
GRANGE RD
HEMBURY PK
ABBEY GRANGE CL
ST BERNARD'S CL
NORTHWOOD LA
ABBEY MDW
Buckfast (St Mary's) Abbey
Works
ST BERNARD'S CL
FURLONG CL
ABBEY LINK RD
St Mary's RC Prim Sch
HIGHER MILL LA
HEMBURY COCK HILL
Buckfast
Dartmoor Way
ASHBURTON RD
Baddaford
FIVE LANES
A38
LINEY CROSS
CRICKET LA
HOLNE RD
ROUND CROSS
CHURCH CROSS RD
BUCKFAST RD
BUCKFAST CL
Dart Bridge
B3380
A384
DARTBRIDGE CROSS
DARTBRIDGE MANOR
CHURCH CROSS
OAKLANDS RD
GLEBELANDS
CHURCH HILL
CHURCH HILL
FAIRIES HALL
OAKLANDS PK
OAKLANDS CL
BARNSFIELD LA
WILLIAMS CT
SILVER ST
SHERWELL CT
BRIDGE ST
CHURCH ST
Mast
RUSSETS LA
DART BRIDGE RD
PH
Ware
Lower Combe
BUCKFASTLEIGH
Mardle Way Bsns Pk
1 ORCHARD TERR
2 HAMLYNS WAY
3 BOSSELL TERR
4 BOSSELL HO
5 HAREWOOD
6 HARDING CT
Caves
SALMON LEAP CL 1
VALENTINE MANOR 2
CROPPING CL 3
Mus
Buckfastleigh
Higher Town
MARKET CL
Buckfastleigh Prim Sch
MARKET ST
MARDLE WAY
Lower Town
MERRIFIELD RD
Dartmoor Way
JORDAN ST
CHAPEL ST
FORE ST
STATION RD
Mus
ELLIOT PLAIN
PO
JORDAN ORCH 1
PIONEER TERR 2
CREST HILL
VIEW
MOORLAND
NEW RD
BOSSELL RD
TH
HOSKINGS CT
SPRINGFIELD PK
OLD TOTNES RD
HILLSIDE CT
KINSCOME CT
TOTNES RD
Dartmoor Otters & Buckfast Butterflies
High Beara
Austin's Bridge
BARN PK
TOR VIEW
BOSSELL PK
LITTLE BOSSELL
PLYMOUTH RD
Liby
STRODE RD
THE ORCHARD
WALLAFORD RD
FULLAFORD PK
FULLAFORD CROSS
DUCKSPOND RD
WEST MILL CROSS
RANGERS CL
DEVON EXPRESSWAY
South Devon Rly
HIGHER BEARA CROSS
GREEN LA
FULLAFORD POOL CROSS
DUCKSPOND CL
ELM BANK
WEST END RD
Kilbury Manor
GREEN LANE END
TWEENAWAYS
FAIRY LA
GIPSY LA
BIGADON LA
COLSTON RD
River Dart
TIMBERS RD
TIMBERS CL
HALFMOON CT
ROCKY LA
COXHILL CROSS
PLYMOUTH RD
Loverscombe
Caddaford
Rill Wood
Mast
Bigadon House
Lower Dean
Rill
Bigadon Home Farm
CROSS VIEW
B3380
Colston
Dean Court
Weston
Bigadon Plantation
The Ball
A384
John's Brake
Raythorn Wood
Derry's Copse
A38

135 135 215

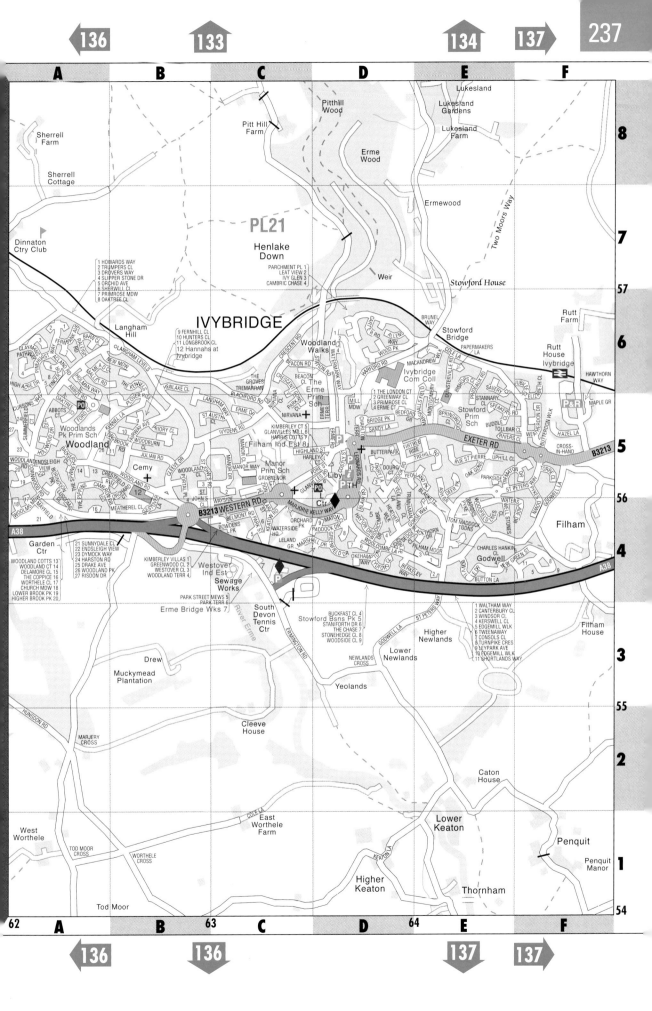

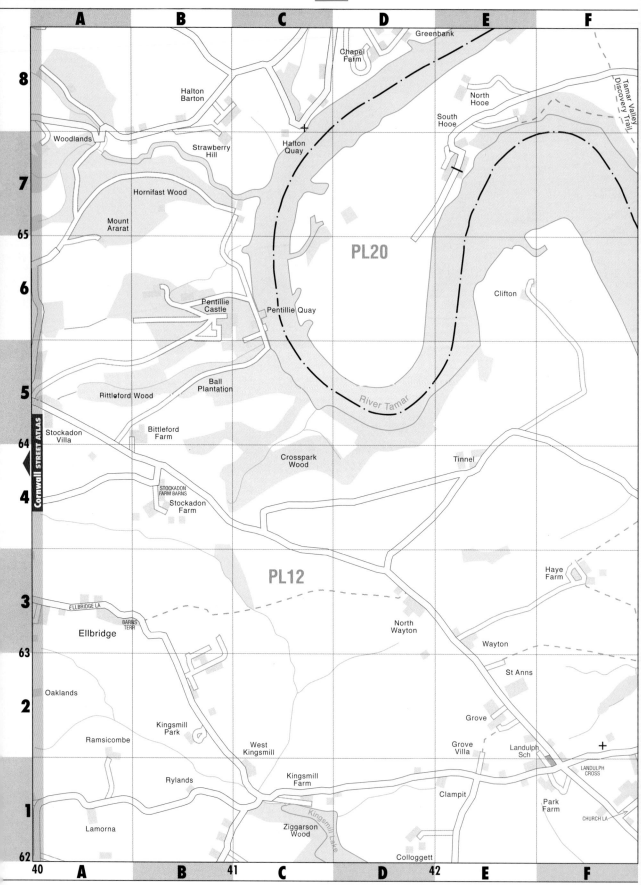

Greenbank

Chapel
Farm

Halton
Barton

North
Hooe

Woodlands

Strawberry
Hill

South
Hooe

Tamar Valley
Discovery Trail

Halton Quay

Hornifast Wood

PL20

Mount
Ararat

Clifton

Pentillie
Castle

Pentillie Quay

Ball
Plantation

Rittleford Wood

River Tamar

Stockadon
Villa

Bittleford
Farm

Crosspark
Wood

Tinnel

Cornwall STREET ATLAS

STOCKADON
FARM BARNS

Stockadon
Farm

PL12

Haye
Farm

ELLBRIDGE LA

North
Wayton

Wayton

BARNS
TERR

Ellbridge

St Anns

Oaklands

Grove

Ramsicombe

Kingsmill
Park

Grove
Villa

Landulph
Sch

LANDULPH
CROSS

West
Kingsmill

Rylands

Kingsmill
Farm

Clampit

Park
Farm

CHURCH LA

Lamorna

Ziggarson
Wood

Kingsmill Lake

Colloggett

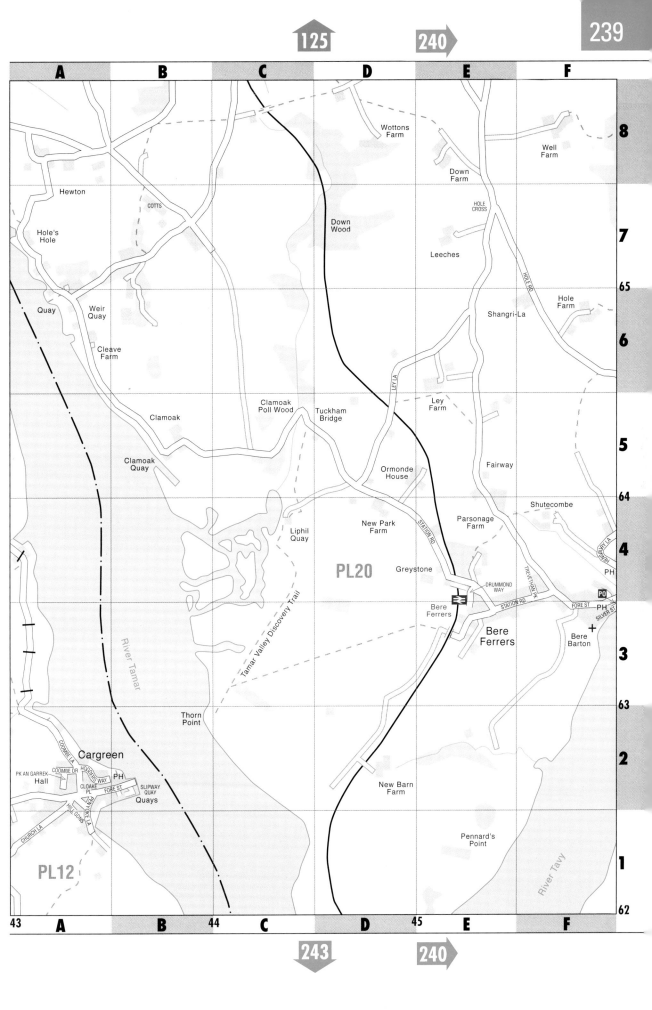

239
126

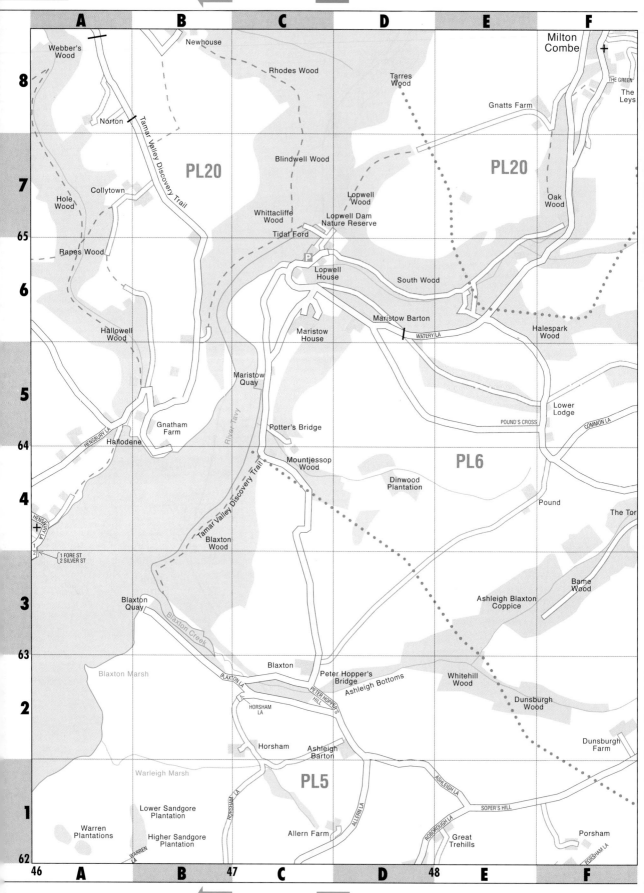

A B C D E F

239
244

Webber's Wood

Newhouse

Rhodes Wood

Tarres Wood

Milton Combe

THE GREEN

The Leys

Norton

Tamar Valley Discovery Trail

PL20

Blindwell Wood

Gnatts Farm

PL20

8

Hole Wood

Collytown

Lopwell Wood

Oak Wood

7

Whittacliffe Wood

Lopwell Dam Nature Reserve

65

Rapes Wood

Tidal Ford

P

Lopwell House

South Wood

Maristow Barton

Halespark Wood

WATERY LA

Hallowell Wood

Maristow House

6

River Tavy

Maristow Quay

Lower Lodge

POUND'S CROSS

COMMON LA

5

HENSBURY LA

Hallodene

Gnatham Farm

Potter's Bridge

64

Mountjessop Wood

PL6

Dinwood Plantation

Pound

The Tor

HENSBURY LA

1 FORE ST
2 SILVER ST

Tamar Valley Discovery Trail

Blaxton Wood

Bame Wood

4

Blaxton Quay

Ashleigh Blaxton Coppice

3

Blaxton Creek

63

Blaxton Marsh

BLAXTON LA

Blaxton

Peter Hopper's Bridge

Ashleigh Bottoms

Whitehill Wood

Dunsburgh Wood

PETER HOPPER'S HILL

HORSHAM LA

Horsham

Ashleigh Barton

Dunsburgh Farm

2

Warleigh Marsh

PL5

ASHLEIGH LA

SOPER'S HILL

1

HORSHAM LA

Lower Sandgore Plantation

ALLERN LA

ROBOROUGH LA

Great Trehills

Porsham

Warren Plantations

Higher Sandgore Plantation

Allern Farm

PORSHAM LA

WARREN LA

62

46 A B 47 C D 48 E F

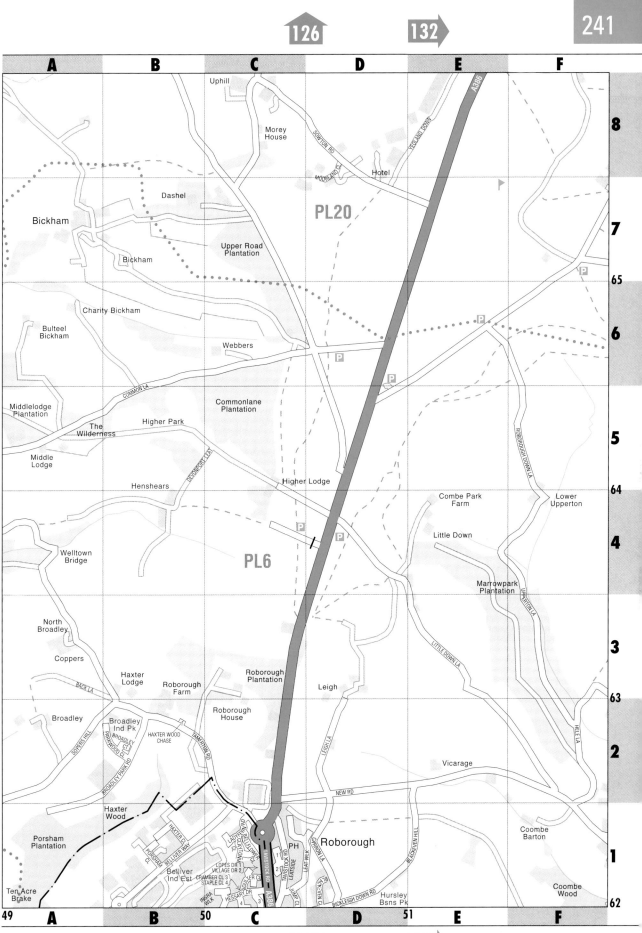

Uphill

Morey House

Hotel

PL20

Bickham

Dashel

Bickham

Upper Road Plantation

Charity Bickham

Bulteel Bickham

Webbers

Middlelodge Plantation

Commonlane Plantation

COMMON LA

Higher Park

The Wilderness

Middle Lodge

Henshears

Higher Lodge

Combe Park Farm

Lower Upperton

Little Down

ROBOROUGH DOWN LA

DEVONPORT LEAT

PL6

Welltown Bridge

Marrowpark Plantation

UPPERTON LA

North Broadley

Coppers

Roborough Plantation

Leigh

LITTLE DOWN LA

Haxter Lodge

Roborough Farm

BACK LA

Broadley

Broadley Ind Pk

HAXTER WOOD CHASE

Roborough House

SOPERS HILL

BROADLEY PARK RD

PARKWOOD RD

BROADLEY CT

TAMERTON RD

LEIGH LA

Vicarage

HELE LA

Haxter Wood

HAXTER CL

PORSHAM CL

BELLIVER WAY

NEW RD

Coombe Barton

Porsham Plantation

Belliver Ind Est

LADYSMITH

CLAYTON CL

LADY BELLFLOWER

BAXTER CL

PH

Roborough

CAPTON LA

BLACKEVEN HILL

Coombe Wood

Ten Acre Brake

INGRA WLK

LOPES DR 1
VILLAGE DR 2
CRAMBER CL 3
STAPLE CL 4

HESSARY DR

CROWTHER CL

STAPLE CL

TAVISTOCK RD

LEATSIDE

JUMP CL

PICKAVEN HILL

BICKLEIGH DOWN RD

Hursley Bsns Pk

A386

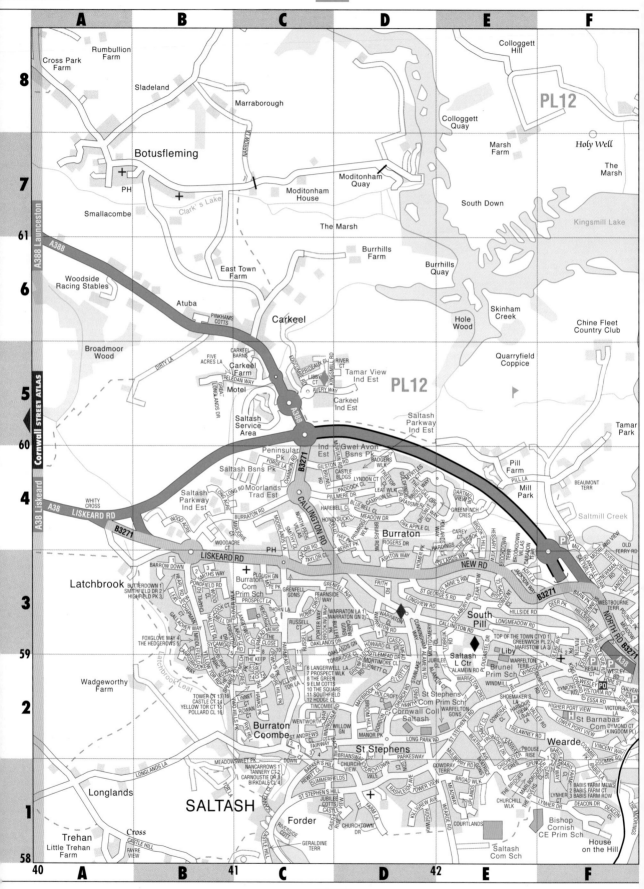

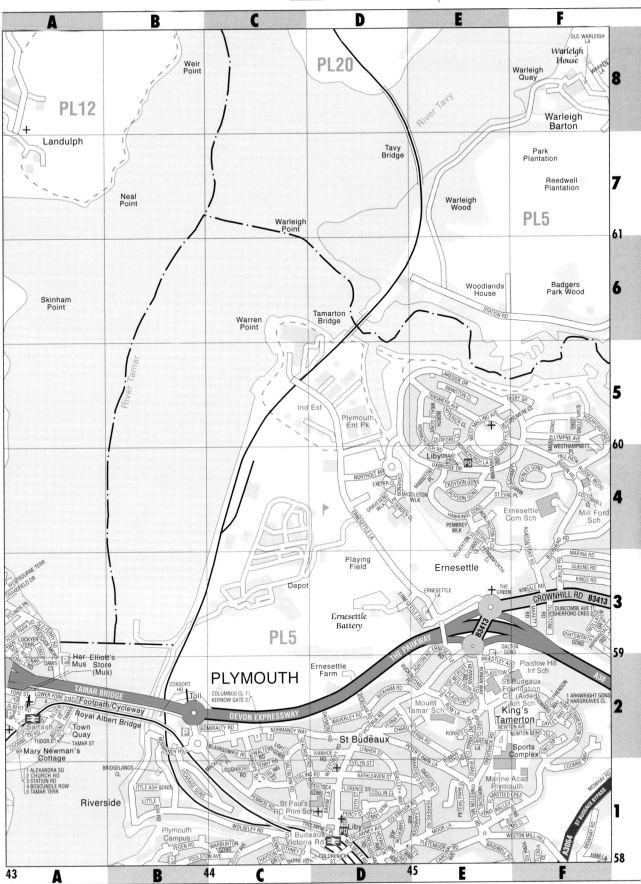

D1
1 Victoria Road
Prim Sch

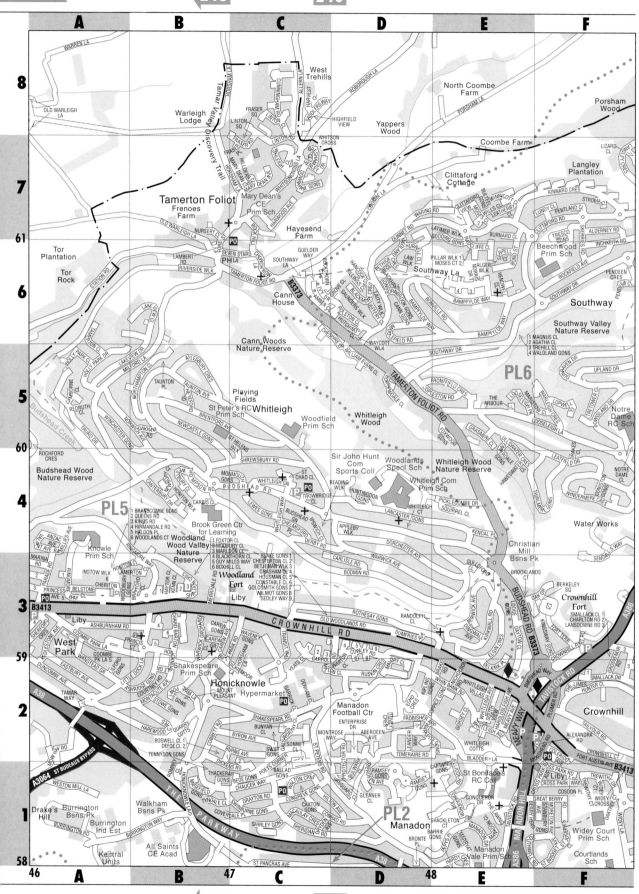

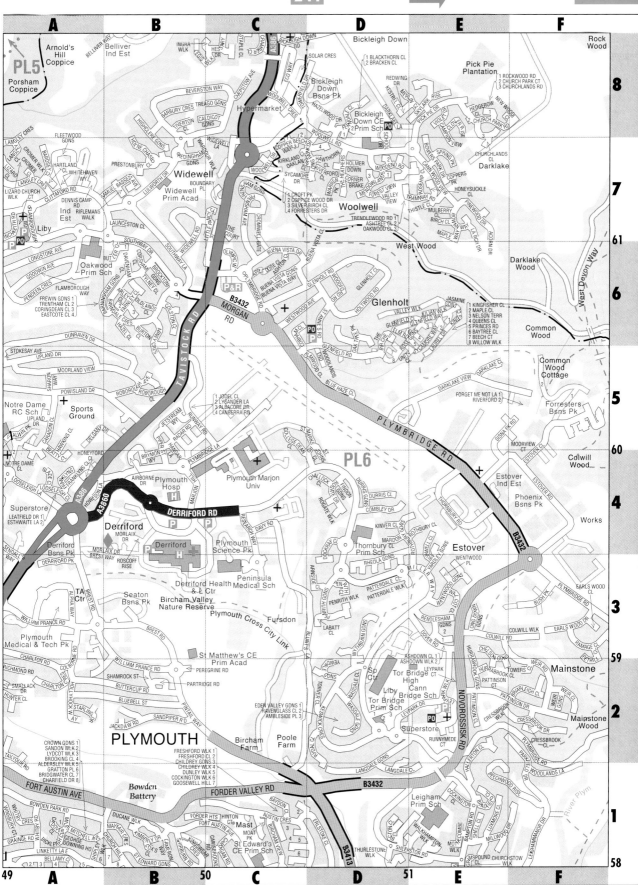

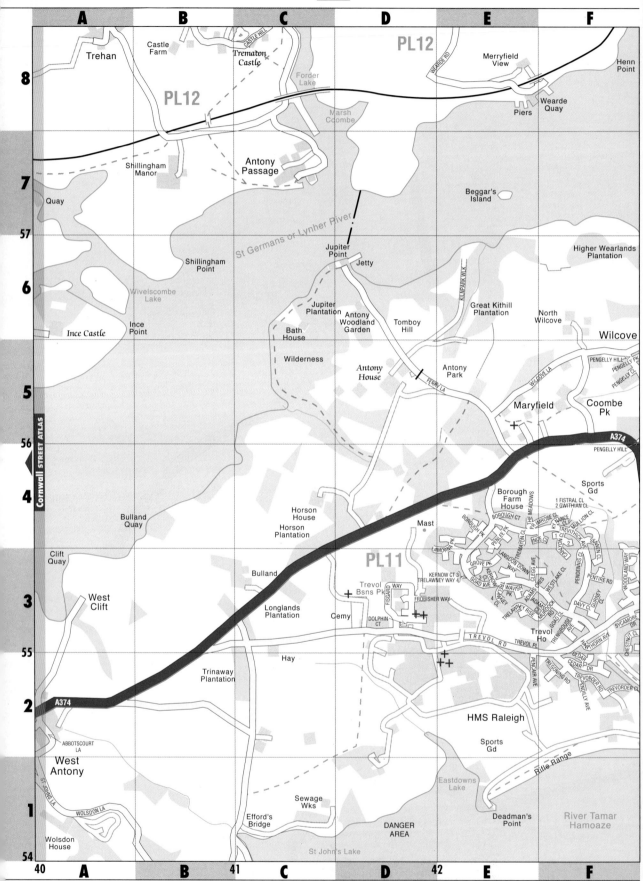

247   244
247   254

For full street detail of the highlighted area see pages 262 and 263.

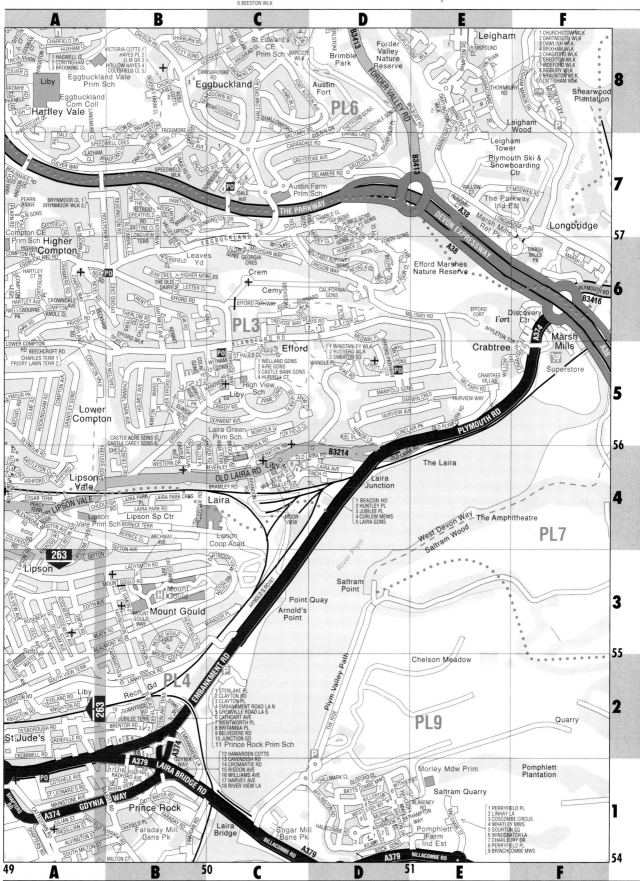

245
250

C7
1 BRAMBLE WLK
2 BOWHAYS WLK
3 BRISMAR WLK
4 MOORFIELD AVE
5 BEAUDYN WLK
6 BEESTON WLK

For full street detail of the highlighted area see page 263.

E7
1 PERSEVERANCE COTTS
2 BLANCHARD PL
3 MAYHEW GDNS

A **B** **C** **D** **E** **F**

8

China Clay
Works

Triumphal
Arch

Hilltops

Boringdon Hall

Brockhole
Wood

Elfordleigh
Wood

Binicliff
Wood

CH

The Croft

Boringdon
Cottages

7

Prym Valley Rlwy

Triumphal
Cres

Ashcombe Cl

Plymtree Dr

Plymbridge Cl

South View

South View

Devonia Cl

Rhodes Cl

Elford Cres

Brett Wlk

Delacombe Cl

NEWNHAM RD

B3417

Cundy Cl

Tithe Rd

Wheatridge

Church Cl

Longacre

Higher Cl

Woodford Cl

Plymbridge Rd

Buckland Cl

Meadow Way

Long Mow

Deeble Cl

Waddon Cl

Rashleigh Ave

Avent Wlk

Joshua Pk

Kay Cl

Wallpark Cl

57

Marsh
Mills

St Margarets Rd

Oakapple Cl

Park Cl

Woodford
Prim Sch

Litchaton

Larkham La

Woodford

Crossway

The Mead

Jessops

Courtland Cres

Boringdon
Prim Sch

Perryman Cl

Fairfield

Clifton Cl

Colebrook La

Farriers
Cotts

Colebrook

Newnham
Ind Est

Lister Cl

Boringdon Mill
Bsns Ctr

P&R
LC

Marsh
Mills

The Knoll

Lynwood Ave

Coppard
Mdws

Unicorn

Reynolds Rd

St Marys Rd

Sherwood Gdns

Seymour Rd

Molesworth Rd

Hele's
Sch

Stonebarton Cl

Acorn
Gdns

Stonebarton Rd

Alston
Pk

Treverbyn Rd

Revell Park Rd

The Lane

Boringdon
Village

Hemerdon Way

Raymond Way

Linkadell

Colebrook Rd

1 Tory Brook Ave
2 Tory Brook Ct
3 Whitewater Ct

Glenside
Rd

GLEN RD

B3417 STRODE RD

Pinewood Cl

Stoggy La

Torridge Rd

Westfield

B3416

6

B3416
LC

Cot Hill Cl

Cot Hill
Trad Est

Trad Est

PLYMOUTH RD

Dingle Rd

Oakfield Rd

Morley
Rd

Meadow View

St Marys Ct

Woodland Rd

Borringdon
Terr

Chamberlayne
Dr

Earls Mill Rd

Moorland Dr

George Ave

Moorland
Vws

Grebe
Cl

Aylwin Cl

Plympton

Ridgeway
Sch

Ridge Park Rd

Chaddlewood

Mallard Cl

5

Sewage
Works

Marsh Rd

Chantry
Ct

Cot Hill

Merafield Rd

Valley Rd

Ind & Trad Est

Underwood

Dudley Rd

Underlane

Plympton St Mary
Inf & Old Priory
Jun Acad

Brookingfield Cl

Potters Way

Lavinia

Hawkmoor
Dr

Sovereign

Ridgeway

Old Priory

Priory Mill

Longbrook Barton

Osmand
Gdns

Priory Rd

St Stephen

Ridgeway
Sp Ctr

Highbridge
Ct

Stannary

George
Cross

George La

Manor Park Cl

Manor
Park

56

Morley Cl

Robert Adams Cl

Merafield
Park

Maple Gr

Elaine Cl

Woodland Dr

Amados Cl

Merafield Rise

Merafield Rd

Kennel Hill Cl

Kennel
La

Rock
Terr

Copse Cl

Copse Rd

Hill Cl

Willow
Cotts

Underwood Rd

Sydney Cl

Redvers

Plympton
St Maurice

Longcause Com
Spcl Sch

Grange Rd

4

Saltram
House

Saltram
Park

P

Merafield
Farm Cotts

Grantham
Cl

Amados Rise

Amados Dr

Amados Hill

Hardwick Wood
Mast

PL7

1 WARELWAST CL
2 GATEHOUSE LA

Drunken Bridge Hill

Dorsmouth
Rock

Woodside

COTTAGE MEWS 1
ILBERT COTTS 2
CASTLEHAYES GDNS 3
WOODBINE COTTS 4
DORSMOUTH TERR 5
ST MAURICE MEWS 6

Castle
Barbican

Barbican Rd

School
La

Maurice
Mws

Castle La

Back La

St Peter

Cotton Cl

Hele Gdns

Woolcombe Ave

3

Stable
House

P

Television
Relay Sta

Telegraph
Cottage

The Gables

PLYMOUTH

Ridge Rd

Six O Clock
La

Allotment
La

New Barn Hill

St Elizabeth
Cl

Longbrook St

Wolverwood La

St Stephens

St Thomas
Cl

Magdalen
Gdns

Eagle Gdns

Plympton
St Maurice
Prim Sch

55

The Belt

DEVON EXPRESSWAY

Heather
Grange

Vinery La

A38

2

Sellar
Acres

Merafield Rd

P

Cemy

Wixenford
Brake

New Barne
Farm

Vealeholme

1

Wixenford
Farm

Colesdown Hill

Haye
Farm

Haye Rd

Hatch Rd

PL9

Moorcroft
Quarry

Haye Road
Nurseries

Priors Park
Nursery

Vinery La

Furze
Park

Hercules Rd

Higher
Sherford

54

THIRD AVE
SECOND AVE

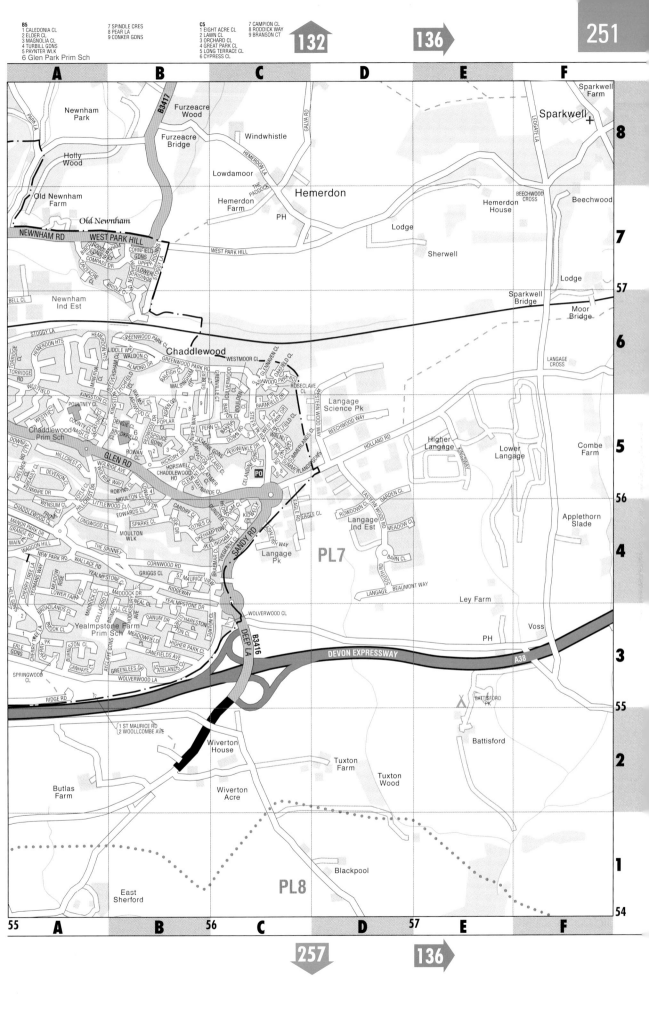

246

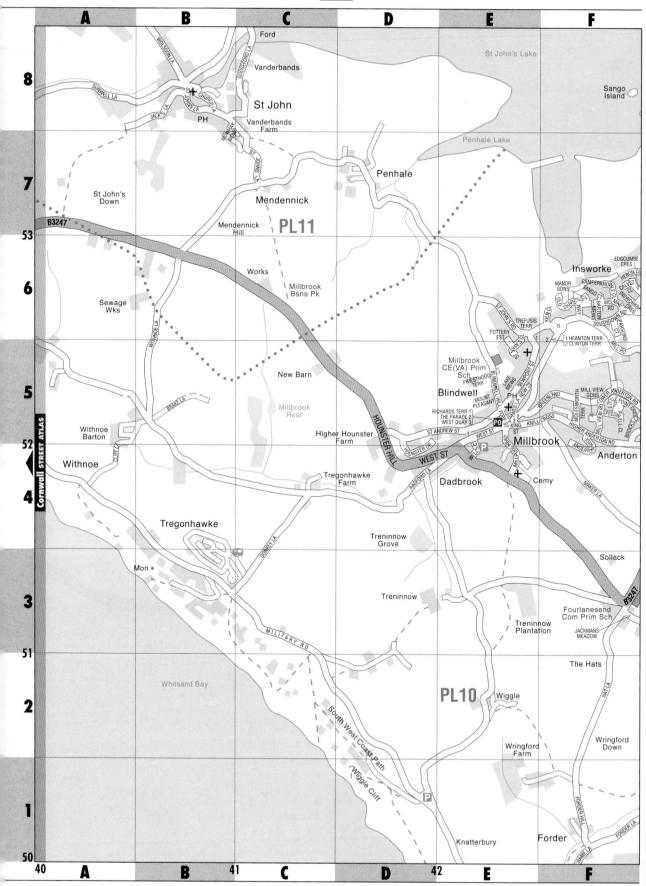

140

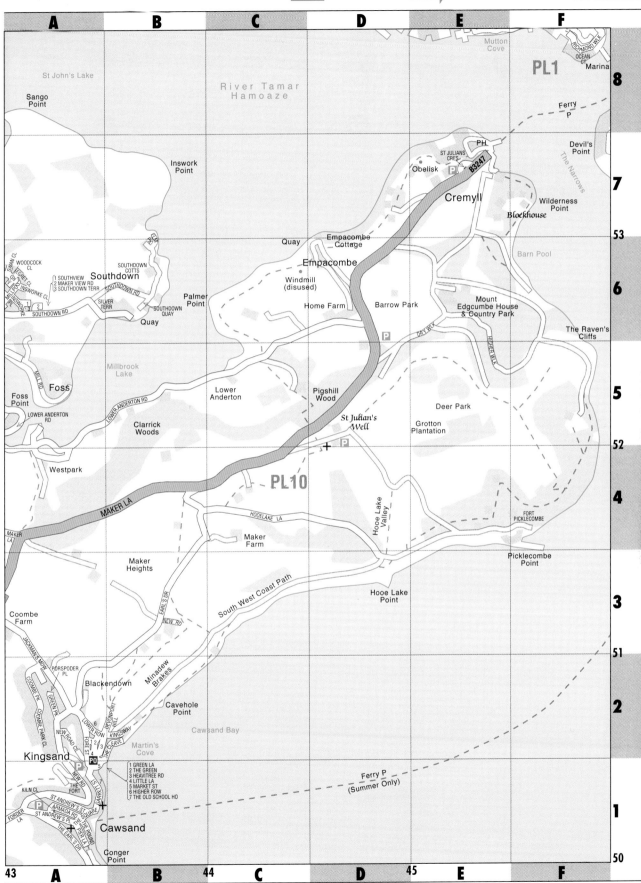

PL1

St John's Lake

River Tamar
Hamoaze

Sango
Point

Mutton
Cove

Marina

RICHMOND WLK

OCEAN CT

Ferry
P

Devil's
Point

Inswork
Point

Obelisk

ST JULIANS
CRES

PH

B3247

The Narrows

Cremyll

Wilderness
Point

Blockhouse

Barn Pool

Quay

Empacombe
Cottage

Empacombe

WOODCOCK
CL

1 SOUTHVIEW
2 MAKER VIEW RD
3 SOUTHDOWN TERR

SWAN CL

EGRET CL

SILVERET CL

INSWORKE CL

MILLBROOK

Southdown

SOUTHDOWN
COTTS

SOUTHDOWN RD

SILVER
TERR

SOUTHDOWN RD

SOUTHDOWN QUAY

Palmer
Point

Quay

Windmill
(disused)

Home Farm

Barrow Park

Mount
Edgcumbe House
& Country Park

The Raven's
Cliffs

DRY WLK

HIGHER WLK

Millbrook
Lake

Foss

Foss
Point

LOWER ANDERTON
RD

MILL RD

LOWER ANDERTON RD

Clarrick
Woods

Lower
Anderton

Pigshill
Wood

St Julian's
Well

Deer Park

Grotton
Plantation

Westpark

PL10

MAKER LA

MAKER
LA

HOOELAKE LA

Maker
Farm

Hooe Lake
Valley

FORT
PICKLECOMBE

Picklecombe
Point

Maker
Heights

EARL'S DR

NEW RD

South West Coast Path

Hooe Lake
Point

Coombe
Farm

JACKMAN'S MDW

PORSPODER
PL

Blackendown

Minadew
Brakes

Cavehole
Point

COOMBE PK

GREEN PK

DEVONPORT
HILL

COOMBE PARK CL

LOWER ROW

KINGSWAY

THE CLEAVE

Cawsand Bay

Martin's
Cove

Kingsand

NEW RD

FORE ST

THE BOUND

1 2 3
4 5

PO

1 GREEN LA
2 THE GREEN
3 HEAVITREE RD
4 LITTLE LA
5 MARKET ST
6 HIGHER ROW
7 THE OLD SCHOOL HO

Ferry P
(Summer Only)

KILN CL

FORDER
LA

ST ANDREW'S ST

ARMADA RD

ST ANDREW'S PL

THE EARL'S DR

PEEL LA

THE SQUARE

THE POUND

Cawsand

The Fort

Conger
Point

253
248

For full street detail of the highlighted area see pages 262 and 263.

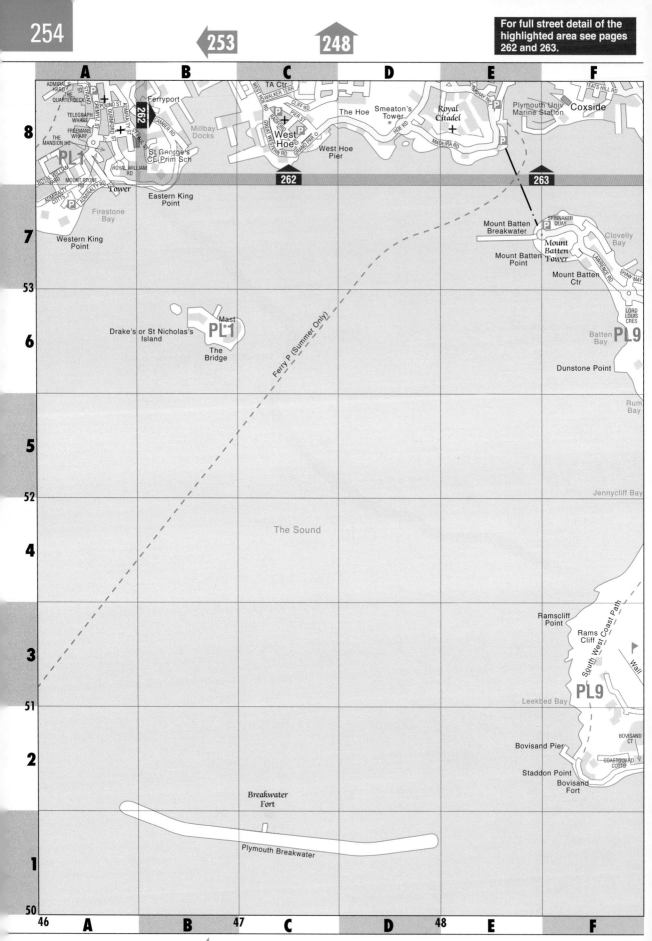

A B C D E F

8

ADMIRAL'S HARD
THE QUARTERDECK
TELEGRAPH WHARF
FREEMANS WHARF
THE MANSION HO
PL1
ROYAL WILLIAM YARD
MOUNT STONE RD
ADMIRALTY COTTS
Tower
Western King Point
Firestone Bay

Ferryport
262
CAMBER RD
Millbay Docks
St George's CE Prim Sch
Eastern King Point

TA Ctr
WEST HOE RD
WALKER TERR
CLIFF RD
PIER ST
West Hoe
GREAT WESTERN RD
GRAND PAR
West Hoe Pier
262

The Hoe
HOE RD
Smeaton's Tower

MARHAY HILL
Royal Citadel
MADEIRA RD

Plymouth Univ Marine Station
P
Coxside
TEATS HILL RD
263

SPINNAKER QUAY
Mount Batten Breakwater
P
Mount Batten Point
Mount Batten Tower
LAWRENCE RD
SHAW WAY
Clovelly Bay
Mount Batten Ctr
LORD LOUIS CRES
PL9

53

7

Drake's or St Nicholas's Island
Mast
PL1
The Bridge

Ferry P (Summer Only)

Batten Bay
Dunstone Point

Rum Bay

6

53

52

5

Jennycliff Bay

4

The Sound

Ramscliff Point
Rams Cliff
South West Coast Path
Wall

3

51

Leekbed Bay
PL9

Bovisand Pier
Staddon Point
Bovisand Fort
BOVISAND CT
COASTGUARD COTTS

2

Breakwater Fort

Plymouth Breakwater

1

50

46 A B 47 C D 48 E F

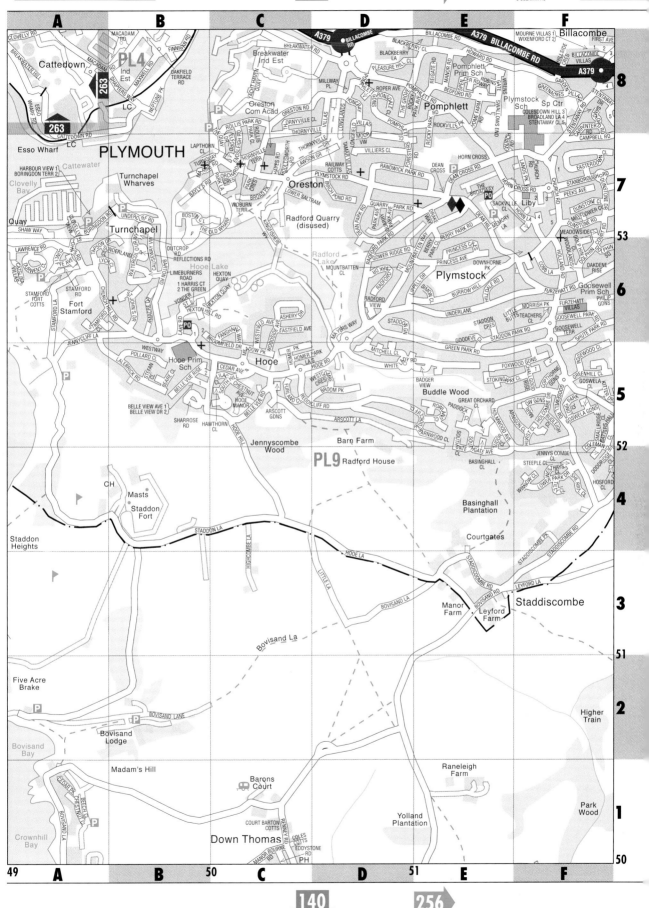

249

256

F5
1 CHALLGOOD CL
2 ORCHARDTON TERR

F7
1 THE DUKES RYDE
2 MAPLE CT
3 MAGNOLIA CT
4 HORN LANE FLATS
5 SELKIRK HO

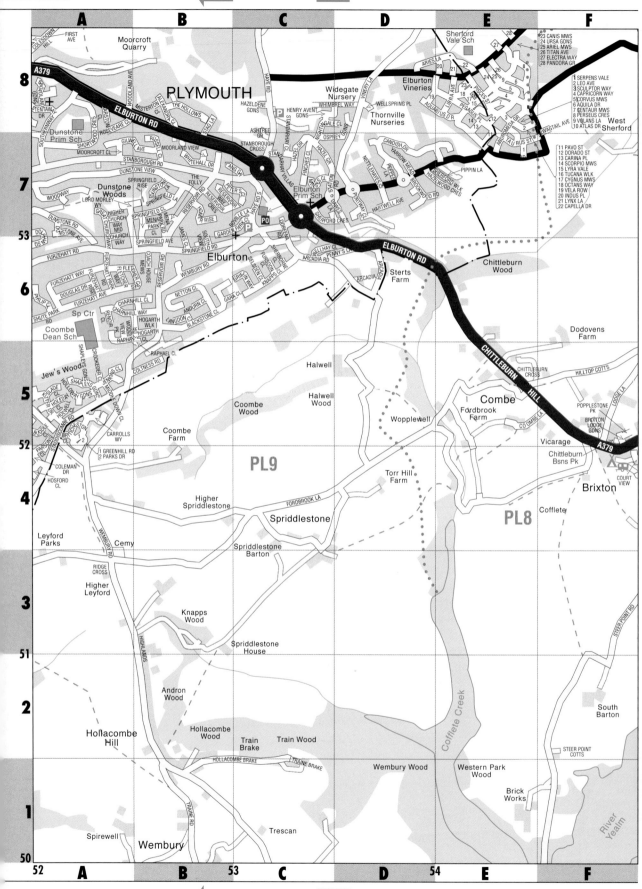

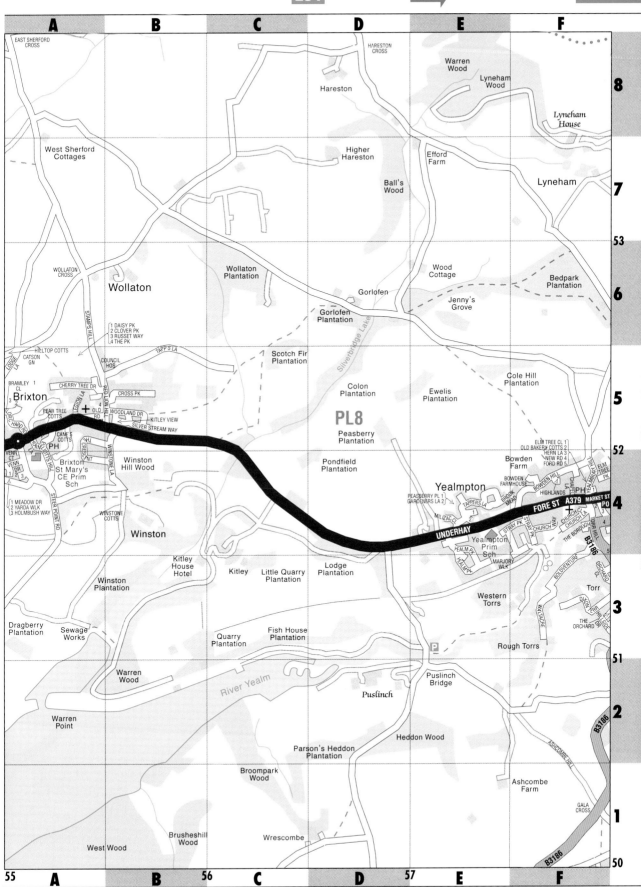

A B C D E F

8
7
53
6
5
52
4
3
51
2
1
50

EAST SHERFORD CROSS

West Sherford Cottages

HARESTON CROSS

Hareston

Warren Wood

Lyneham Wood

Lyneham House

Higher Hareston

Efford Farm

Lyneham

Ball's Wood

WOLLATON CROSS

Wollaton

Wollaton Plantation

Gorlofen

Wood Cottage

Bedpark Plantation

Jenny's Grove

HILLTOP COTTS
CATSON GN

1 DAISY PK
2 CLOVER PK
3 RUSSET WAY
4 THE PK

Gorlofen Plantation

Silverbridge Lake

Scotch Fir Plantation

Cole Hill Plantation

BRAMLEY CL
CHERRY TREE DR
CROSS PK

Colon Plantation

Ewelis Plantation

Brixton

PL8

PEAR TREE COTTS
WOODLAND DR
KITLEY VIEW
SILVER STREAM WAY

Peasberry Plantation

ELM TREE CL 1
OLD BAKERY COTTS 2
HERN LA 3
NEW RD 4
FORD RD 5

Bowden Farm

Winston Hill Wood

Pondfield Plantation

Yealmpton

Bowden Farmhouse

BOWDEN HILL

HIGHLANDS

Brixton St Mary's CE Prim Sch

PEASBERRY PL 1
GARDENERS LA 2

TAPPERS LA

BROOK MEAD

FORE ST A379

MARKET ST
PO

1 MEADOW DR
2 YARDA WLK
3 HOLMBUSH WAY

Winston Cotts

MILIZAC CL

UNDERHAY

Yealmpton Prim Sch

THE BOROUGH

B3186

Winston

Kitley House Hotel

Kitley

Little Quarry Plantation

Lodge Plantation

PALM PK

MARJORY WLK

Western Torrs

Torr

THE ORCHARD

BOLDVENTURE

Winston Plantation

Dragberry Plantation

Sewage Works

Quarry Plantation

Fish House Plantation

Rough Torrs

WALTACRE

Warren Wood

River Yealm

Puslinch Bridge

ASHCOMBE HILL

B3186

Warren Point

Puslinch

Heddon Wood

West Wood

Brusheshill Wood

Wrescombe

Parson's Heddon Plantation

Broompark Wood

Ashcombe Farm

GALA CROSS

B3186

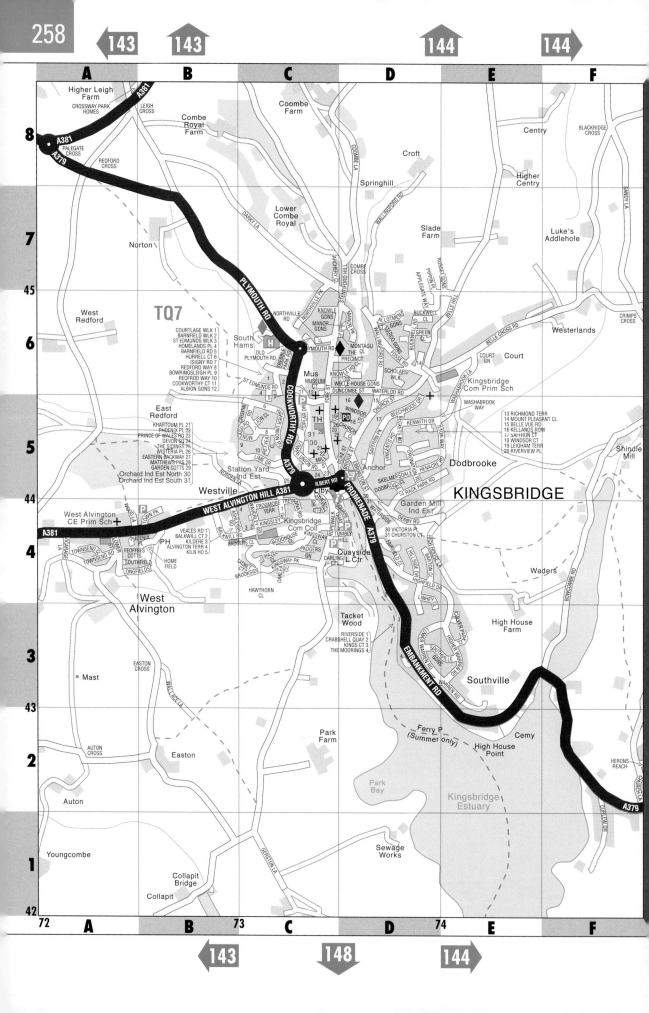

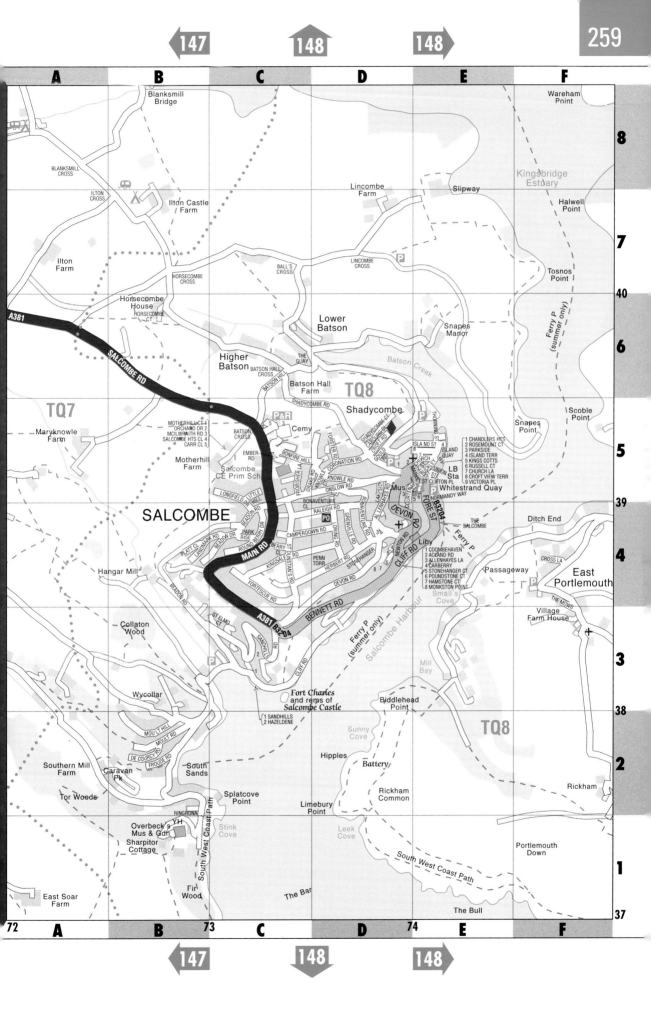

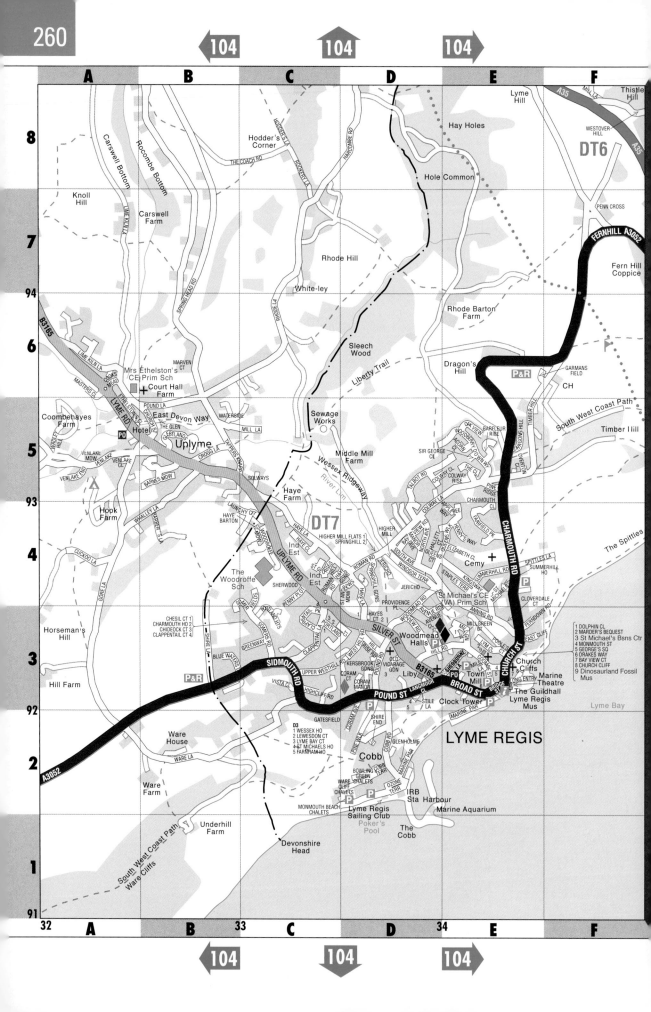

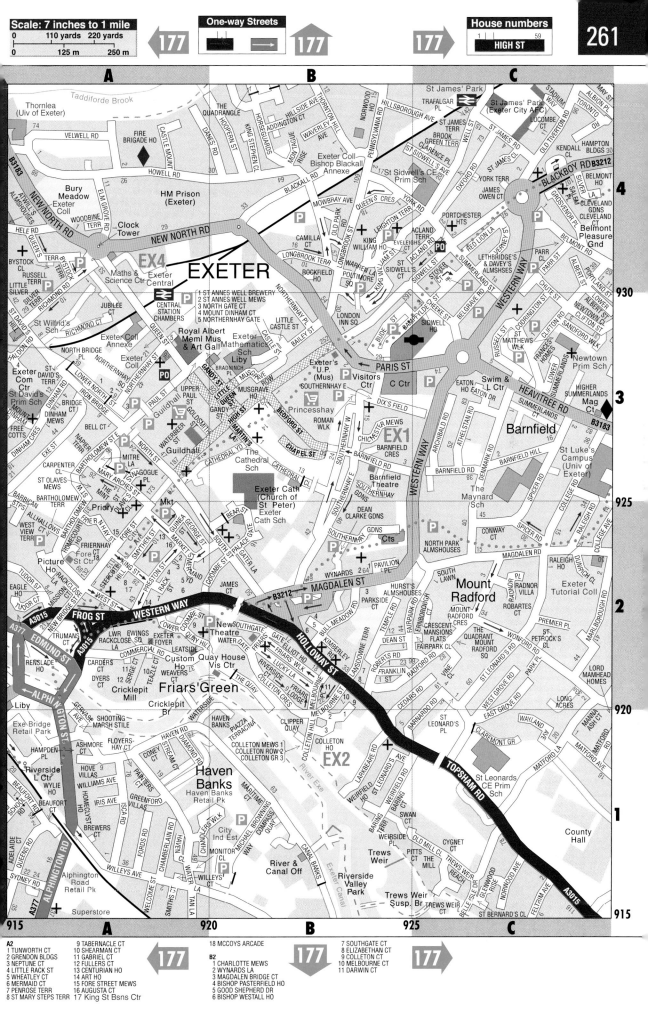

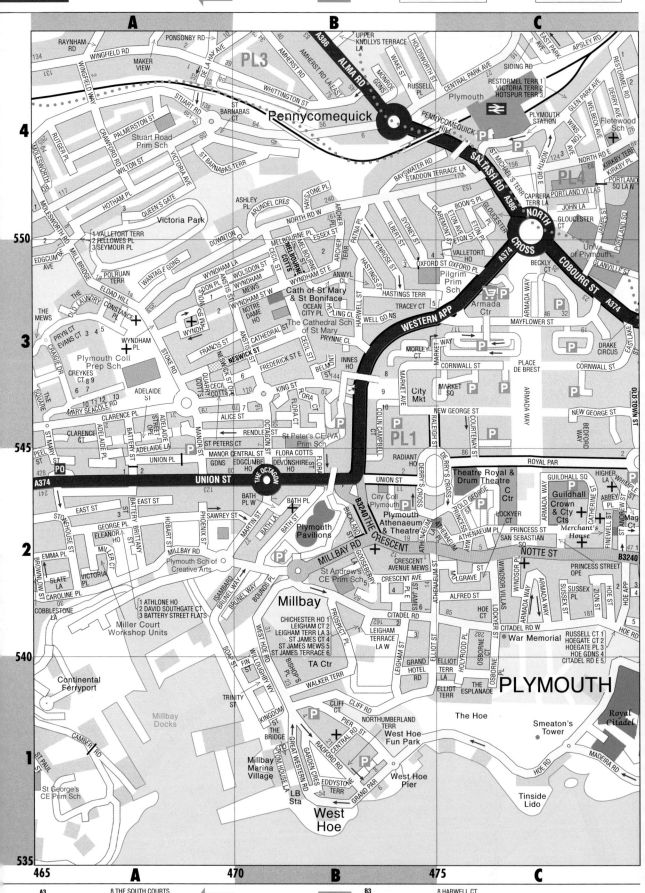

A3		B3
1 WYNDHAM MEWS	8 THE SOUTH COURTS	1 ANSON HO
2 HOLLYWOOD TERR	9 LYSTER CT	2 MELBOURNE GN
3 NORBURY CT	10 HOWESON CT	3 ETON TERR
4 THE NORTH COURTS	11 Millfields Trust Bus Units	4 OXFORD TERR
5 THE EAST COURTS	12 McDONALD CT	5 CAMBRIDGE LA W
6 GORDON CT	13 STONLEY CT	6 FREDERICK ST W
7 FELLOWES CT		7 ALICE LA

8 HARWELL CT	
9 FRANKFORT GATE	
10 COLIN CAMPBELL CT	

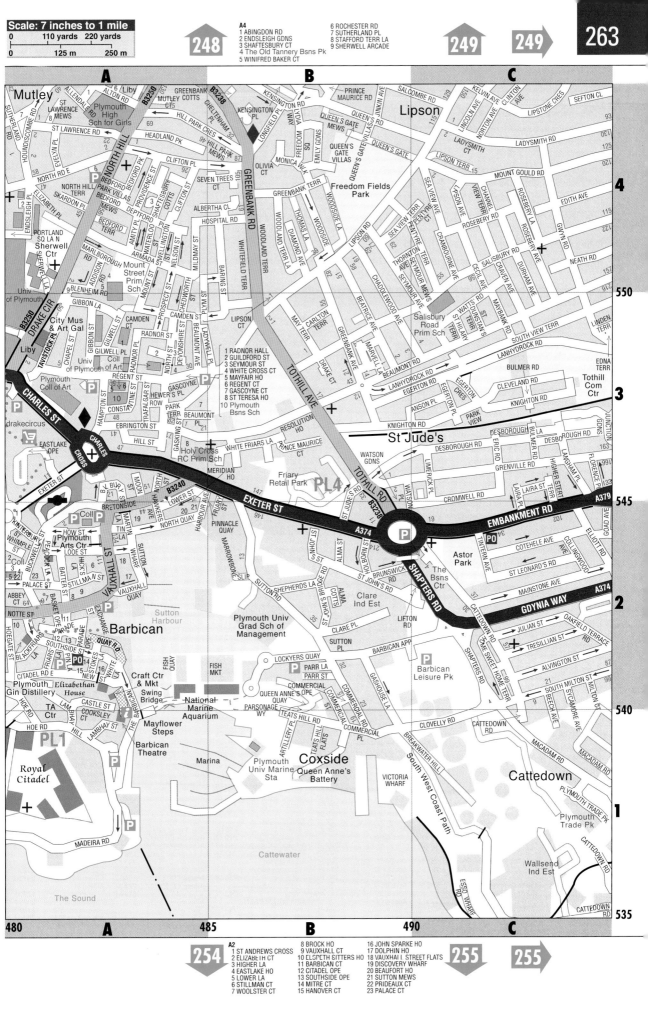

Index

Place name May be abbreviated on the map

Location number Present when a number indicates the place's position in a crowded area of mapping

Locality, town or village Shown when more than one place has the same name

Postcode district District for the indexed place

Page and grid square Page number and grid reference for the standard mapping

Church Rd **6** **Beckenham BR2..........53** C6

Cities, towns and villages are listed in CAPITAL LETTERS

Public and commercial buildings are highlighted in **magenta**   **Places of interest** are highlighted in blue

Abbreviations used in the index

Acad	**Academy**	Comm	**Common**	Gd	**Ground**	L	**Leisure**
App	**Approach**	Cott	**Cottage**	Gdn	**Garden**	La	**Lane**
Arc	**Arcade**	Cres	**Crescent**	Gn	**Green**	Liby	**Library**
Ave	**Avenue**	Cswy	**Causeway**	Gr	**Grove**	Mdw	**Meadow**
Bglw	**Bungalow**	Ct	**Court**	H	**Hall**	Meml	**Memorial**
Bldg	**Building**	Ctr	**Centre**	Ho	**House**	Mkt	**Market**
Bsns, Bus	**Business**	Ctry	**Country**	Hospl	**Hospital**	Mus	**Museum**
Bvd	**Boulevard**	Cty	**County**	HQ	**Headquarters**	Orch	**Orchard**
Cath	**Cathedral**	Dr	**Drive**	Hts	**Heights**	Pal	**Palace**
Cir	**Circus**	Dro	**Drove**	Ind	**Industrial**	Par	**Parade**
Cl	**Close**	Ed	**Education**	Inst	**Institute**	Pas	**Passage**
Cnr	**Corner**	Emb	**Embankment**	Int	**International**	Pk	**Park**
Coll	**College**	Est	**Estate**	Intc	**Interchange**	Pl	**Place**
Com	**Community**	Ex	**Exhibition**	Junc	**Junction**	Prec	**Precinct**

Prom	**Promenade**
Rd	**Road**
Recn	**Recreation**
Ret	**Retail**
Sh	**Shopping**
Sq	**Square**
St	**Street**
Sta	**Station**
Terr	**Terrace**
TH	**Town Hall**
Univ	**University**
Wk, Wlk	**Walk**
Wr	**Water**
Yd	**Yard**

Index of towns, villages, streets, hospitals, industrial estates, railway stations, schools, shopping centres, universities and places of interest

3rd–Ald

3rd Ave **8** EX2.......178 D5

A

Abbeville Cl EX2 .....177 E3
Abbey Cl
　Axminster EX13 .....167 C4
　Bovey Tracey TQ13 ...180 C7
　Crapstone PL20 .....126 E2
　Paignton TQ3 ......225 E5
　Tatworth TA20.......88 D8
　Teignmouth TQ14 ...210 C7
Abbey Cross TQ9....227 A4
Abbey Ct
　Exeter EX2 ....178 F5
　Plymouth PL1 .....263 A2
Abbeydale EX10 .....188 A3
Abbeyfield Ho **7**
　TQ14............210 C5
Abbeyford Ct EX20 ...170 C5
ABBEY GATE 167 C2
Abbey Gate La EX13..167 C2
Abbey Grange Cl
　TQ11............236 B7
Abbey La EX13.....167 B3
Abbey Link Rd TQ11..236 B7
Abbey Mdw
　Buckfast TQ11.......236 B7
　Yelverton PL20 ......126 E2
Abbeymead Mews
　PL19............171 C5
Abbey Mews
　Tatworth TA20........88 D8
　Torquay TQ1 ....220 B8
Abbey Pl
　Plymouth PL1 .....262 C2
　Tavistock PL19 .....171 C5
Abbey Rd
　Barnstaple EX31.....154 E6
　Bovey Tracey TQ13 ...180 D7
　Cornworthy TQ9 .....227 A4
　Dunkeswell EX14 .....67 C2
　Dunkeswell EX15 .....67 C3
　Exeter EX4 ....177 F7
　Torquay TQ2 ......220 A5
Abbey Rise
　Okehampton EX20 ...170 D6
　Tavistock PL19 .....171 C5
Abbey Sch The TQ1..220 C8

Abbot Rd PL21.......237 A6
ABBOTSBURY 207 B4
Abbotsbury Rd TQ12 .207 B4
Abbotsbury Sch
　TQ12.............207 D2
Abbotsbury Way PL2 247 F8
Abbots Cl
　Lee Mill PL21 ......136 D6
　Woolfardisworthy EX39 . 38 F8
Abbotscourt La PL11.246 A2
Abbots Ct PL21.....237 A5
Abbots Dr EX39.......26 A4
Abbotsfield Cl PL19 ..126 A8
Abbotsfield Cres
　PL19............126 A8
ABBOTSHAM........156 A2
Abbotsham Cross
　EX39............25 C4
Abbotsham La EX19...59 C3
Abbotsham Rd
　Bideford EX39.......156 E2
　20 Bideford EX39.....157 A2
Abbotshill Pk TQ12...212 A6
Abbots Keep EX4 ....176 D6
ABBOTSKERSWELL.212 B6
Abbotskerswell Cross
　TQ12............212 A7
Abbotskerswell Prim Sch
　TQ12............212 B6
Abbots Mdw EX37.....28 F4
Abbot's Rd EX4 .....177 E8
Abbotsridge Dr TQ12 206 F1
Abbot's Way PL20...128 C5
Abbotswood
　East Ogwell TQ12 ...206 F1
　Kingsteignton TQ12 ...207 F8
ABBOTTS
　BICKINGTON......54 E8
Abbotts Hill EX33 ....152 D6
Abbotts Pk PL21.....133 C2
Abbotts Rd PL3 .....248 E6
Abbrook Ave **9**
　TQ12............123 E1
Abelia Cl TQ3 ......225 E8
Aberdeen Ave
　Plymouth PL5 .....244 D1
　Plymouth TQ12 .....244 D2
Aberfeldy **9** TQ1 ...220 C5
Abingdon Rd **1** PL4..263 A4
Abney Cres PL6......245 B6
Above Down TQ7 ...147 D7

Above Town TQ6....233 F2
Aboveway EX3......182 B3
Abscott La PL9.......255 C5
Abyssinia Ct **9** EX32 .155 B3
Abyssinia Terr **8**
　EX32.............155 B3
Acacia Cl
　Bideford EX39.......156 E1
　Kingsteignton TQ12 ...207 F6
Acacia Mews EX6....181 B1
Acadia Rd TQ1.....220 E4
Acer Row EX7 ......204 E8
Ackland Cl
　Bideford EX39.......157 A1
　Shebbear EX21.......55 E4
Ackland Terr EX4 ....261 C4
Acklington Pl PL5....243 E4
Ackrells Hill
　Littlehempston TQ9 ...216 F3
　Uphempston TQ9 ....217 A3
Acland Cross EX32 ...17 B2
Acland Rd
　Broadclyst EX5.......175 C6
　Exeter EX4 ....261 C4
　Ivybridge PL21.......237 A6
　Landkey EX32 ....17 B2
　Salcombe TQ8.......259 D4
Aclands EX36......158 D3
Acland Terr EX4 ....261 C4
Acland Way EX16 ....161 A6
Acombe Cross TA3....68 B8
Acorn Dr PL6.......245 E7
Acorn Gdns PL7......250 D6
Acorn Gr **1** EX32 ...155 C4
Acorn Way EX32 .....17 F4
Acre Cl EX39.........24 E2
Acre Cotts
　Plymouth PL1 ......247 F3
　Plymouth PL5 ......247 F3
　Wellington TA21 ....160 E6
Acre La TQ1 ......220 E6
Acre Pl PL1.......247 F3
Acre Rd EX39 ......24 E2
Acre The TQ13......111 A6
Adams Cl
　Plymouth PL5 .....243 F1
　Torpoint PL11.......246 F3
Adams Cres PL11 ...246 E3
Adams Ct EX39.......25 D4
Adam's La PL9......140 C8
Ada's Terr EX34.......7 F8
Adcroft Rise EX13....103 D5
Adder Rd EX31.......16 B6

Addington Ct EX4....261 B4
Addiscombe La EX6..113 D5
Addison Cl EX4 .....176 E6
Addison Rd
　Newton Abbot TQ12 ...207 E1
　Paignton TQ4 ......226 A5
　Plymouth PL4 ......263 A4
Addlehole TQ9.......144 D7
Adelaide Ct
　Exeter EX2 ....261 A1
　Exmouth EX8.......202 A5
Adelaide La PL1 .....262 A2
Adelaide Pl PL1......262 A3
Adelaide St
　Plymouth PL1 ......262 A3
　2 Plymouth, Ford PL2 247 F5
Adelaide Street Ope
　PL1............262 A3
Adelaide Terr **6**
　EX34............150 B6
Adela Rd PL11......247 A3
Adelphi La TQ4 .....226 C5
Adelphi Mans TQ4 ...226 C5
Adelphi Rd TQ4.....226 C6
Adit La PL12........242 E3
Adits The PL18.......125 D3
Adley La TQ13 ......111 B7
Admiral Ct TQ6 ....233 B2
Admirals Ct
　22 Exmouth EX8......202 A6
　5 Northam EX39.....156 F7
Admiral's Hard PL1 ...254 A8
Admiral Swimming Ctr
　TQ5.............230 D4
Admirals Wlk
　Exmouth EX8.......196 D2
　Teignmouth TQ14 ...210 A8
Admiralty Cotts PL1..254 A7
Admiralty Ope S PL5 .247 E6
Admiralty Rd
　Plymouth, Millbay
　　PL1............254 A8
　Plymouth, St Budeaux
　　PL5............243 C2
Admiralty St Ope N
　PL5.............247 E6
Admiralty St
　Plymouth, Keyham
　　PL2............247 E6
　Plymouth, Millbay PL1 .254 A8
Admiral Way
　Exeter EX1 ....178 D1
　Exeter EX3 ....182 D8

Admiral Wy EX2 .....182 C8
Adrian Cl EX39.......157 A4
Adworthy La EX17....46 B2
Affeton Castle Cross
　EX17............60 F8
Affeton Hill EX17.....60 F8
Affeton Moor Cross
　EX17.............46 A2
Afflington Rd PL3....249 D1
AFTON...........217 E2
Agatha Cl **2** TQ12...244 E6
Agaton Fort Rd PL5 ..243 F4
Agaton Rd PL5......243 E3
Aggett Gr TQ13 .....180 F7
Aidan Ave EX32 ....155 C2
Ailescombe Dr TQ3 ..225 F6
Ailescombe Rd TQ3 ..225 F6
Ainslie Terr PL2......247 E7
Airborne Dr PL6 ....245 B4
Aire Gdns PL3 ......249 B5
Airfield Ind Est EX14 ..67 B2
AISH
　Paignton............224 F2
　South Brent 134 F3
Aish Cross TQ9 .....224 E2
Aish La TQ10.......134 E2
Aish Lane End TQ10 ..134 F2
Aish Pk EX21 ....55 E4
Aish Rd
　Paignton TQ4 ......225 B2
　Stoke Gabriel TQ9 ....224 F2
Alamein Ct PL12 ....242 E2
Alanmere Rd
　Saltash PL12.......242 D2
　Saltash PL12.......242 E2
Alandale Cl TQ14.....210 C6
Alandale Rd TQ14....210 C6
Alansway EX11 ....169 C3
A-La Ronde ★ EX8...196 A3
Albacore Dr PL6 ....245 B5
Alba Ct EX1........178 E7
Albany Cl EX8......196 E2
Albany Ct TQ3 ......226 B7
Albany Rd TQ3.....219 A1
Albany St
　10 Newton Abbot
　　TQ12............207 C3
　Plymouth PL1 ......247 E2
Albany St

Albert Cl
　11 Crediton EX17 .....165 C5
　Ottery St Mary EX11 ...169 C3
Albert Cotts TQ12 ...208 E3
Albert Ct
　7 Ilfracombe EX34 ....150 C6
　3 Torquay TQ1.......220 B5
Albertha Cl PL4 .....263 B4
Albert La **9** EX32 ...155 A5
Albert Pl
　Exmouth EX8.......202 A6
　10 Totnes TQ9.......223 C5
Albert Rd
　Crediton EX17 .....165 C5
　Plymouth PL2 .....247 F3
　Saltash PL12.......243 A2
　Torquay TQ1 ......220 B5
Albert St
　18 Dawlish EX7 .....204 D6
　Exeter EX1 ....261 C4
　Exeter EX2 ....177 D7
Albert Terr
　Bovey Tracey TQ13 ...180 C7
　Gunnislake PL18.....125 C5
　14 Newton Abbot
　　TQ12............207 C3
　Princetown PL20 ....128 B8
Albert Villas PL2 ....247 E4
Albion Cl EX12......191 F8
Albion Ct
　Brixham TQ5........230 C3
　6 Exmouth EX8......202 A7
　Torpoint PL11.......247 B3
Albion Dr PL2.......248 B7
Albion Gdns TQ7....258 C6
Albion Hill
　Exmouth EX8.......202 B7
　Newton Abbot TQ12 ...207 C2
Albion Pl
　Exeter EX4 ....261 C4
　Exmouth EX8.......202 A7
Albion Rd PL11 .....247 B3
Albion St
　Exeter EX4 ....177 A5
　Exmouth EX8.......202 A7
　Teignmouth TQ14 ...210 A3
Albion Terr **9** EX8 ...202 A7
Alcester Cl PL2 .....247 E4
Alcester St PL2 .....247 F4
Aldborough Ct EX8...202 B7
Aldens Bsns Ct EX2..181 B8
Aldens Green EX2....181 B8
Aldens Rd EX2 ....181 B8

Alden Wlk PL6 . . . . . . 249 B7
Alder Cl
 Newton Abbot TQ12 . . . 212 F8
 Teignmouth TQ14 . . . . 210 B7
Alder Glade EX31 . . . . 154 C3
Alderney Rd PL6 . . . . . 244 F7
Alder Rd PL19 . . . . . . 171 C3
Aldersley Wlk PL6 . . . . 245 A1
Alderson Dr EX2 . . . . . 178 D5
Alders Way TQ4 . . . . . 225 D3
Aldridge Mill Hill
 EX16 . . . . 48 C6
Aldridge Pl EX1 . . . . . 179 C8
Aldrin Rd EX4 . . . . . . 173 D2
Alexander Ct EX17 . . . 165 D4
Alexander Pk EX38 . . . 159 C5
Alexander Pl EX1 . . . . 169 D4
Alexander Wlk **23** EX7 .204 D4
Alexander Wlk **4**
 EX2 . . . . 178 D5
Alexandra Cl
 Crediton EX17 . . . . . . 165 A6
 Plymouth PL9 . . . . . . 256 B8
Alexandra Ct **15**
 EX32 . . . . 155 A5
Alexandra Dr PL20 . . . 125 F1
Alexandra Ho TQ12. . . 207 C2
Alexandra La TQ1 . . . . 220 B6
Alexandra Mews EX6 201 B8
Alexandra Pl
 Cornworthy TQ9 . . . . . 227 B4
 5 Plymouth PL4. . . . 248 E4
Alexandra Rd
 Axminster EX13 . . . . . 167 C5
 Barnstaple EX32. . . . . 155 A5
 Crediton EX17. . . . . . 165 B6
 1 Newton Abbot
 TQ12. . . . . 207 C2
 Plymouth PL3 . . . . . . 249 A4
 Plymouth, Crownhill
 PL6. . . . . 244 F2
 Plymouth, Ford PL2. . . 247 F5
 Plymouth, Mutley PL4. . 248 F4
 Torquay TQ1 . . . . 220 B6
 Wellington TA21 . . . . . 160 D6
Alexandra Sq PL12 . . . 243 A4
Alexandra Terr
 Bideford EX39. . . . . . 157 A3
 Clyst Honiton EX5 . . . . 175 E2
 Exeter EX4 . . . . 177 E7
 Exmouth EX8. . . . . . . 201 F6
 Newton Abbot TQ12 . . 207 C2
 Plymouth PL2 . . . . . . 247 F5
 South Molton EX36 . . . 158 C5
 1 Teignmouth TQ14 . 210 B4
 Torpoint PL5 . . . . 247 B2
 1 Totnes TQ9 . . . . . 223 C6
Alexandra Way EX17 . 165 A6
Alexandria Ind Est
 EX15 . . . . 163 D4
Alexandria Rd EX10 . . 188 A6
Alexandria Terr **6**
 EX16 . . . . 161 B4
Alexandria Trad Est
 EX10 . . . . 188 A6
ALFARDISWORTHY . . 53 B6
ALFINGTON 100 F8
Alfington Rd
 Alfington EX11 . . . . . . 84 F1
 Ottery St Mary EX11 . . 169 F6
Alford Cl EX1 . . . . 178 C7
Alford Cres EX1. . . . . . 178 B7
Alford Terr EX35 . . . . . 151 B5
Alfred Ct EX11 . . . . . . 169 B2
Alfred Pl PL2 . . . . 247 F5
Alfred Rd PL2 . . . . 247 F5
Alfred St PL1 . . . . 262 C2
Alfriston Rd TQ3 . . . . . 225 D7
Alger Wlk PL6 . . . . . . 244 E6
Al Hill PL20 . . . . 126 D1
Alice La **7** PL1. . . . . . 262 B3
Alice Mews EX38. . . . . 159 C5
Alice St PL1 . . . . 262 A3
Alison Rd TQ3 . . . . . . 219 A1
ALLALEIGH 139 E4
Allaleigh Cross TQ9 . . 139 E4
Allaleigh La TQ9 . . . . . 139 F4
Allaway EX10 . . . . 188 B6
Allen Bank EX32 . . . . . 155 A3
Allenby Rd PL2 . . . . . . 248 A6
Allen Cl EX16 . . . . 161 F5
Allendale Cl TA21. . . . 160 A5
Allendale Rd PL4. . . . . 263 A4
Allenhayes La TQ8 . . . 259 D4
Allenhayes Rd TQ8 . . . 259 D4
Allens Rd PL21. . . . . . 237 D6
Allenstyle Cl EX31 . . . 153 B5
Allenstyle Dr EX31 . . . 153 B5
Allenstyle Gdns EX31 153 B5
Allenstyle Rd EX31 . . . 153 B5
Allenstyle View EX31 . 153 A5
Allenstyle Way EX31 . 153 B5
Aller Brake Rd TQ12 . . 212 F8
Aller Brook Nature
 Reserve★ TQ12. . . . . 207 E4
Aller Cl TQ12 . . . . 213 A6
ALLERCOMBE 168 A6
Allercombe Cross EX5 99 E5
Allercombe Hill EX5. . 168 A6
Allercombe La EX5. . . . 99 E5
Aller Cotts TQ12 . . . . . 212 F7
Aller Cross
 Chillington TQ7 . . . . . 145 A1
 Kentisbeare EX15. . . . . 65 F1
 Kingskerswell TQ12 . . . 212 F7
 South Molton EX36. . . . 29 F7
Allerdown Cross EX17 80 A7
Aller Gate EX17 . . . . . 78 D5

Aller Gr EX5 . . . . 99 F7
Aller Grove Cotts EX5 . 99 F7
Aller Hill
 Bishop's Nympton
 EX36. . . . . 30 F4
 Bishops Nympton EX36. . 31 A4
 Dawlish EX7. . . . . . . 204 B5
Aller La EX20 . . . . 94 F8
Aller Park Rd TQ12 . . . 212 F8
Aller Rd
 Dolton EX19 . . . . 57 F7
 Kingskerswell TQ12 . . . 212 F6
Allers View TA22 . . . . . 33 C6
Allerton Wlk PL6 . . . . 249 B7
Aller Vale Bldgs
 TQ12. . . . . 212 F6
Allervale Cl EX2. . . . . 178 B4
Alleyn Ct EX12 . . . . . . 191 F7
Alleyn Gdns PL3 . . . . . 248 E8
Allhalland St **17**
 EX39. . . . . 157 A2
Allhallows Ct
 Exeter EX4 . . . . 261 A2
 1 Honiton EX14. . . . 166 C6
 Allhallows Mus★
 EX14. . . . . 166 C6
All Hallows Rd TQ3 . . 219 C3
Alliance Ct **16** EX14. . 85 C2
Allington Mead EX4 . . 173 A3
Allington Terr EX17 . . . 78 F7
Allison La EX17 . . . . . . 95 D7
Allotment Dro TA20 . . . 69 F5
Allotment Gdns TQ7. . 258 D6
ALL SAINTS 88 A4
All Saints Babbacombe
 CE Prim Sch TQ1. . . . 220 D6
All Saints CE Acad
 PL5. . . . . 244 B1
All Saints CE Prim Sch
 EX13. . . . . 88 A4
All Saints CE Sch
 TA22. . . . . 33 D6
All Saints Cl EX9 . . . . 198 B6
All Saints Cl EX14 . . . 166 A5
All Saints Marsh CE Prim
 Sch TQ12. . . . . 207 D3
All Saints Mews **11**
 EX8. . . . . 202 A7
All Saint's Rd PL18 . . 125 B5
All Saint's Rd EX14 . . . 188 A4
All Saints' Rd TQ1. . . . 220 C7
Allshire La EX16 . . . . . 32 F3
Alma Cotts PL4 . . . . . 263 B2
Alma La EX10 . . . . . . 188 C4
Alma Rd
 Brixham TQ5 . . . . 230 C5
 Plymouth PL3 . . . . . . 248 C4
Alma St PL4 . . . . 263 B2
Alma Terr PL18 . . . . . 125 D6
Alma Villa Rise EX5 . . . 99 A5
Almeria Ct PL7. . . . . . 250 D4
Alminstone Cross
 EX39. . . . . 39 A7
Almond Ct **3** EX31. . 154 C2
Almond Dr PL7 . . . . . 251 B6
Almshouse Cross
 TQ10. . . . . 135 E4
Almshouses **4** EX4 . 177 D8
Almshouses The **7**
 TQ13. . . . . 180 D8
Alpha Ctr TQ9 . . . . . . 223 C6
Alpha Pl **24** EX39 . . . 15 A1
Alpha St EX1. . . . . . . 177 F6
Alpha Terr TQ9 . . . . . 223 B6
Alpha Way PL6. . . . . . 249 C7
Alphin Brook Ct EX2 177 C1
Alphin Brook Rd EX2 177 C1
ALPHINGTON 181 B7
Alphington Prim Sch
 EX2. . . . . 177 B1
Alphington Rd EX2. . . 177 B3
Alphington Road Ret Pk
 EX1. . . . . 261 A1
Alphington St EX2 . . . 261 A1
Alpine Rd TQ1 . . . . . . 220 B5
Alsa Brook Mdw
 EX16. . . . . 161 C6
Alscott Gdns EX31. . . . 27 A4
ALSTON 88 A5
Alston Cross
 Ashburton TQ13. . . . . 131 B6
 Slapton TQ7 . . . . 145 B5
Alstone Rd EX16 . . . . 161 F3
Alston La TQ5 . . . . . . 229 D4
Alston Pk PL7. . . . . . . 250 D6
Alston Terr EX8. . . . . . 201 F6
ALSWEAR 30 C1
Alswear New Rd
 Alswear EX36 . . . . 30 C1
 South Molton EX36. . . 158 E3
Alswear Old Rd
 South Molton EX36. . . 158 C2
 South Molton EX36. . . 158 D2
Altamira EX3 . . . . 182 F5
Altamira Cotts EX39. . . 25 D2
Alta Vista Cl TQ14. . . . 210 D7
Alta Vista Rd TQ4 . . . . 226 C4
Alton Pl EX14 . . . . 248 E4
Alton Rd PL4. . . . . . . 263 A4
Aluric Rise TQ12 . . . . 207 F4
ALVERDISCOTT 26 F4
Alverdiscott Rd EX39 . . 26 B4
Alverdiscott Road Ind Est
 EX39. . . . . 26 A4
Alver Gn EX39. . . . . . 157 D1
Alvington St PL4 . . . . 263 C2
Alvington Terr TQ7. . . 258 C4

ALWINGTON 25 A2
Alwin Pk PL6 . . . . 245 A5
Alwyns Cl **3** TQ14. . . 210 C5
Alwyns Ct **5** TQ14 . . 210 C5
Amacre Dr PL9 . . . . . 255 B6
Amados Cl PL7. . . . . . 250 B4
Amados Dr PL7 . . . . . 250 C4
Amados Rise PL7 . . . . 250 C4
Ambassador Dr EX1. . 178 E7
Ambassador Ho EX8 226 C5
Amber Cl TQ12. . . . . . 244 C6
Amberley Cl TQ13. . . . 130 E5
Amberley Gdns
 TQ12. . . . . 207 D7
Amber Rise EX1. . . . . 175 B1
Amber Tor TQ13 . . . . 121 F7
Ambleside Pl PL6. . . . 245 D2
Ambrosia Cl EX17. . . . 60 C2
American Rd EX33 . . . . 15 A4
Amersham Ct EX2. . . 178 A4
Amethyst Dr TQ14. . . 204 B1
Amherst Rd PL3 . . . . 262 B4
Amherst Rd La East
 PL3 . . . . 262 B4
Amity Pl PL4 . . . . 263 A4
Amory Pl EX36 . . . . . 158 C4
Amory Rd
 Dulverton TA22 . . . . . . 33 D6
 Tiverton EX16 . . . . . . 161 C2
Amyas Way EX39. . . . 157 A6
Amyatt's Terr EX11. . . 188 B3
Anchorage Cl TQ5 . . . 230 E5
Anchorage The TQ4. . 226 C5
Anchor Bldgs TQ12. . . 123 B2
Anchor Cotts TQ7. . . 147 B7
Anchor Mill EX31 . . . 154 E8
Anchor Row EX3. . . . 182 D7
Anchor Sh Ctr TQ7 . . 258 D5
Anchorwood View
 EX31. . . . . 154 B4
Ander's La TA3 . . . . . . 68 E8
ANDERTON 252 F4
Anderton Cl PL19 . . . 171 L1
Anderton Ct PL19. . . . 171 C2
Anderton La PL19 . . . 171 D2
Anderton Rise PL10 . . 252 F4
Andor Ave TQ12. . . . . 207 D7
Andrew Allan Rd
 TA21. . . . . 160 B4
Andrew Cl EX10. . . . . 187 F8
Andrew Rd EX31 . . . . 154 E3
Andrews Cl EX1. . . . . 154 E3
Andrew's Cl La EX17 . . 60 C7
Andrewshayes La
 EX13. . . . . 87 A1
Andrew's Hill TA22. . . . 33 D6
Andrew's Hill Cross
 TA22. . . . . 33 C6
Andrews Pk TQ9 . . . . 227 F8
Andromeda Gr PL9. . . 256 E7
Andurn Cl PL9 . . . . . . 256 B6
Andurn Est PL9 . . . . . 140 A8
Angel Hill EX16 . . . . . 161 C4
Angelhill Cross EX36. . 36 F2
Angel Mews **2** EX14 166 C6
Angel The **4** EX14. . 166 C6
Animal Sanctuary Rd
 TA20. . . . . 69 D2
Anne Cl EX4. . . . . . . 173 E1
Anne Cres EX31. . . . . 154 E3
Annery Kiln Cotts
 EX39. . . . . 26 A1
Anning Rd
 Blackhorse EX1. . . . . 179 A8
 Lyme Regis DT7 . . . . . 260 E4
Ann's Pl PL3. . . . . . . 248 A4
Anson Ho **1** PL1. . . 262 B3
Anson Pl
 Plymouth, Devonport
 PL2. . . . . 247 F4
 Plymouth, St Jude's
 PL4. . . . . 263 C3
Anson Rd EX36 . . . . . 196 C2
Anstey Cres EX16. . . 161 F3
Anstey Gate TA22. . . . 32 B8
Ansteys Cl TQ1. . . . . 220 E5
Ansteys Cove Rd
 TQ1. . . . . 220 E6
Ansteys Ct EX16. . . . . 46 E1
Anstey Way
 Instow EX39. . . . . 15 B1
 Instow EX39. . . . . . . 157 E8
Anstis Ct EX10 . . . . . 188 A4
Anstis St PL1 . . . . . . 262 A3
Anthea Rd TQ3. . . . . 218 F1
Anthony Cottages
 EX10. . . . . 100 F8
Anthony Rd EX1. . . . . 177 D6
Anthony Way PL15. . . 65 F7
Antonine Cres EX4 . . 176 E6
Antony Ho PL2. . . . . . 248 C8
 Antony House★
 PL11. . . . . 246 D5
 Antony Woodland Gdn★
 PL11. . . . . 246 D6
Antrim Terr **5** TQ9. . 223 B6
Anvil Cnr EX22. . . . . . 72 D7
Anvil Ct PL17. . . . . . . 115 B1
Anwyl Cl PL1 . . . . . . 262 B3
Anzac Ave PL5. . . . . . 244 A4
Anzac St TQ6. . . . . . . 233 F3
Applebee Way TQ7. . . 260 E4
Applebee Wlk PL5. . . 244 D4
Apple Cl PL15. . . . . . . 196 B3
APPLEDORE
 Bideford 14 F1
 Uffculme 51 A1

Appledore Cl
 Cullompton EX15 . . . . 163 B3
 Plymouth PL6 . . . . . . 245 C6
Appledore Com Prim Sch
 35 EX39 . . . . 15 A1
Appledore Hill EX20. . 170 F8
Appledore Rd
 Bideford EX39. . . . . . 156 F8
 Northam EX39 . . . . . . 157 A8
Apple Dr EX15 . . . . . . 162 D4
Apple Farm Grange
 EX2. . . . . 178 E3
Applegarth Ave TQ12 206 E1
Applegarth Cl TQ12 . . 206 E4
Applegate Way TQ7 . . 258 D7
Applehayes EX8 . . . . . 202 C5
Applehayes La EX15. . 52 F2
Apple La EX2 . . . . 178 E4
Apple Orch EX38 . . . . 159 C5
Appleton Tor Cl PL3. . 249 F5
Appletree Cl
 Barnstaple EX32. . . . . 155 D4
 Uffculme EX15 . . . . . . 66 A7
Apple Tree Cl
 Chudleigh Knighton
 TQ12. . . . . 123 C4
 Frogmore TQ7 . . . . . . 144 E1
 Witheridge EX16. . . . . 46 E1
Appletree Gdns EX39 157 A4
Appletree Mews **5**
 EX39. . . . . 15 A1
Apple Way EX5 . . . . . . 99 C6
Apple Wharf **6** TQ9 223 D5
APPLEY 51 B8
Appley Cross TA21. . . 51 B7
App's La EX39 . . . . 25 E2
April Cl EX8 . . . . 196 B3
Apsley Ho TQ1. . . . . . 220 C3
Apsley Rd PL4. . . . . . 248 D4
Apsley Terr
 Braunton EX33 . . . . . . 152 F7
 1 Ilfracombe EX34 150 C5
Apsley Villas **4** EX34 150 C5
Apters Hill **7** TQ5. . . 230 C5
Aquarius Dr PL9 . . . . 256 D8
Aquila Dr PL9. . . . . . . 256 E8
Arbour Cl EX34 . . . . . 150 B3
Arbour The PL6. . . . . 244 E5
Arcade Rd EX34. . . . . 150 B6
Arcade The EX20. . . . 170 B5
Arcadia PL9 . . . . 256 D6
Arcadia Rd PL9 . . . . . 256 D6
Arch Cotts TQ12 . . . . 207 D7
Archer Pl PL1. . . . . . . 262 B4
Archers Cl EX15. . . . . 163 B3
Archers Ct **8** PL8. . . 141 A7
Archer Terr PL1. . . . . 262 B3
Archery Ct TQ7 . . . . . 258 C7
Arches The EX2. . . . . 177 A4
Archibald Rd EX1. . . . 261 C3
Archipark EX32 . . . . . . 17 E1
Architect Way PL5 . . . 247 B8
Arch St **5** TQ14. . . . 210 A3
Arch The EX5. . . . . . . 184 B3
Archway Ave PL4 . . . . 249 B3
Archway Dr TQ6 . . . . 233 D4
Arcot Gdns EX10. . . . 188 B6
Arcot Pk EX10 . . . . . . 188 B6
Arcot Rd EX10 . . . . . . 188 B6
Arden Cl EX9 . . . . . . 199 G2
Arden Dr TQ2 . . . . . . 219 D6
Arden Gr PL2 . . . . . . 248 C8
Arden Ho TQ7 . . . . . . 143 A1
Ardenney Ct EX8. . . . 202 C5
Ardwyn TA21 . . . . . . 160 D4
Arena Pk EX4 . . . . . . 174 B1
Argent Cl EX14 . . . . . 161 D4
Argus Cl EX14. . . . . . 166 C6
Argyle Mews EX4 . . . 173 A1
Argyle Terr TQ9. . . . . 223 B6
Argyll Rd EX4 . . . . . . 173 B2
Ariel Mws PL9 . . . . . 256 E8
Aries La PL9 . . . . 256 D8
Arimoor Gdns PL19. . 171 C5
Ark Royal Ave EX2 . . . 182 C8
Ark Royal Cl PL5. . . . 247 B8
Arkwright Gdns PL5. . 243 F2
Arley Cl PL6 . . . . 245 B6
ARLINGTON
 BECCOTT 10 D4
ARLINGTON. 10 D3
 Arlington Court★
 EX31. . . . . 10 D3
Arlington Pl EX34. . . . 8 A6
Arlington Rd
 Plymouth PL4 . . . . . . 248 F4
 Woolacombe EX34 . . . . 7 F6
Arlington Terr **5**
 EX33. . . . . 152 D5
Armada Cl EX12. . . . . 192 A7
Armada Cres
 Paignton TQ3 . . . . . . 219 B2
 Torquay TQ2 . . . . 219 C6
Armada Ct PL19. . . . . 171 B4
Armada Dr TQ14 . . . . 210 A8
Armada Rd PL10 . . . . 253 A1
Armada (Sh) Ctr PL1 262 C3
Armada St PL4. . . . . . 263 A4
Armada Way
 Plymouth PL1 . . . . . . 262 C2
 Plymouth PL3 . . . . . . 262 C4
 Westward Ho! EX39 . . 156 B6
Armlet Row EX1 . . . . 175 B1
Armourwood La EX5 . . 81 D5
Armstrong Ave EX4 . . 173 D2
Armytage Rd EX9 . . . 198 A3
Arnison Cl PL9. . . . . . 255 F5

Arnold Cres EX16. . . . 161 B2
Arnold's Cl TQ7. . . . . 142 C6
Arnold's Point PL4. . . 249 C3
Arnside EX16 . . . . . . 245 D3
Arran Cl TQ2. . . . . . . 213 E2
Arscott Gdns Pl 9 . . . 255 C5
Arscott La PL9 . . . . . 255 D5
Arthington TQ1 . . . . . 219 F7
Art Ho **14** EX1 . . . . . 261 A2
Arthurs Cl EX8 . . . . . 196 D2
Arthurs Lea EX39 . . . 156 F5
Arthur Terr PL11 . . . . 247 B2
Artillery Ave EX2 . . . . 182 E7
Artillery Ct EX2 . . . . . 177 E3
Artillery Pl PL4 . . . . . 263 B1
Artizan's Dwellings
 EX36. . . . . 158 D4
Arum Gr PL18 . . . . . . 125 B5
Arun Cl PL3. . . . . 249 C5
Arundel Cl EX2 . . . . . 181 B8
Arundel Cres PL1. . . . 262 B4
Arundell Cl PL16 . . . . 105 E4
Arundell Gdns PL16 . . 105 E4
Arundell Pl TQ7 . . . . . 143 E7
Arundell Rd EX20 . . . 77 C4
Arundells Cnr **3**
 EX17. . . . . 165 D5
Arundel Terr PL2 . . . . 247 F4
Ascension Way TQ2 . . 213 F2
Ascerton Cl EX10 . . . 188 B5
Ascerton Rd EX10 . . . 188 B5
ASH. 145 E8
Ashacre Cross TQ1. . . 214 B6
Ash Bridge Cross
 EX20. . . . . 95 D1
ASHBRITTLE 50 F8
Ashbrook St PL9 . . . . 249 D1
Ashburgh Parc PL12 . 242 B3
Ashburn Cl TQ13 . . . . 130 C4
Ashburn Gdns TQ13 . 130 F5
Ashburnham Rd PL5 . 244 A3
Ashburn Wlk TQ4 . . . 229 B8
ASHBURTON 130 E5
Ashburton &
 Buckfastleigh District
 Hosp TQ13. . . . . . . 131 A5
 Ashburton Mus★
 TQ13. . . . . 130 F4
Ashburton Cl TQ13 . . 180 C5
Ashburton Prim Sch
 TQ13. . . . . 130 F4
Ashburton Rd
 Bovey Tracey TQ13 . . 180 C5
 Buckfast TQ11. . . . . . 236 D7
 Newton Abbot TQ12 . . 206 D4
 Totnes TQ9. . . . . 223 B7
ASHBURY. 92 E8
Ashbury Cross 93 B5
Ashbury Station Cross
 EX20. . . . . 92 C7
Ash Cl
 Willand EX15 . . . . . . 162 C3
 7 Yelverton PL20. . 126 F3
Ashclyst View EX5 . . . 175 D6
ASHCOMBE. 124 D6
Ashcombe Cl PL7 . . . 250 C7
Ashcombe Cross
 EX7. . . . . 124 C6
Ashcombe Hill PL8. . . 257 F2
Ashcombe Rd EX7 . . . 204 B8
Ashcroft Rd EX1 . . . . 178 D6
Ash Cross
 Bradninch EX5 . . . . . . 82 F7
 Dartmouth TQ6. . . . . 232 D1
 Halberton EX16 . . . . . 65 A6
 Oakford EX16. . . . . . . 48 D6
 Petrockstow EX20 . . . . 56 F3
Ash Ct
 Crediton EX17. . . . . . 165 C6
 Lee Mill PL21. . . . . . 136 D6
 Shillingford St George
 EX2. . . . . 114 C6
ASHCULME 52 C1
Ashdown Cl PL6 . . . . 245 E8
Ashdown Cross EX22. . 38 F3
Ashdown Wlk PL6. . . 245 E8
Ash Dr
 Cullompton EX15 . . . . 163 C3
 South Molton EX36. . . 158 C5
Asheldon Ho TQ1 . . . 220 E5
Asheldon Manor
 TQ1. . . . . 220 E5
Asheldon Rd TQ1 . . . 220 E5
Ashelford Cnr EX31 . . 10 A3
Ashery Dr PL9 . . . . . . 255 C6
Ashes Rd
 Dalwood EX13 . . . . . . 87 B1
 Shute EX13. . . . . 103 B8
Ash Farm Cl EX1 . . . . 174 F1
Ashfield Cl
 Ashford EX31 . . . . 16 B6
 Exmouth EX8. . . . . . . 196 E1
Ashfield La EX31. . . . . 16 B6
Ashfield Rd TQ2 . . . . 219 E5
Ashfield Terr EX39 . . . 157 A7
ASHFORD
 Aveton Gifford 143 C7
 Barnstaple. 16 B6
Ashford Cl PL3. . . . . . 249 A4
Ashford Cres PL3 . . . 249 A4
Ashford Hill PL4 . . . . 249 A4
Ashford Rd
 Plymouth PL4 . . . . . . 248 F4
 Topsham EX3 . . . . . . 182 E5
 Wellington TA21 . . . . . 160 D4
Ash Gr
 Exmouth EX8. . . . . . . 196 B2

Ash Gr continued
 Ivybridge PL21. . . . . . 237 E5
 Plymouth PL2 . . . . . . 247 F7
 Seaton EX12. . . . . . . 192 A8
Ashgrove Rd TQ13 . . . 180 C4
Ash Hill
 Oakford EX16. . . . . . . 48 D6
 Petrockstow EX20 . . . . 56 F3
Ash Hill Cross EX16 . . 48 D6
Ash Hill Ct EX12. . . . 191 C5
Ash Hill Rd TQ1 . . . . 220 A6
ASHILL 66 D6
Ashill TQ14 . . . . 209 A8
Ashill Ctyd EX15 . . . . 66 C6
Ash La
 Iddesleigh EX19 . . . . . . 57 F1
 Withypool TA24. . . . . . 21 F6
 Woolfardisworthy EX17 . 62 A2
Ashlake Rd EX6 . . . . 113 F7
Ashlar Row EX1. . . . . 175 B1
Ash Leigh EX2 . . . . . 181 A8
Ashleigh CE (VC) Prim
 Sch **20** EX32 . . . . . 155 A5
Ashleigh Cl
 Exeter EX4 . . . . 176 F6
 Plymouth PL5 . . . . . . 244 C7
 Teignmouth TQ14 . . . . 210 B7
 Torquay TQ2 . . . . 213 F3
Ashleigh Cres EX32 . . 155 A5
Ashleigh Ct TQ1 . . . . 220 D3
Ashleigh Dr TQ14 . . . 210 B7
Ashleigh La PL5. . . . . 240 D1
Ashleigh Mount
 TQ14. . . . . 210 B7
Ashleigh Mount Rd
 EX4. . . . . 176 F6
Ashleigh Pk
 Bampton EX16 . . . . . . 49 C8
 Teignmouth TQ14 . . . . 210 B7
Ashleigh Rd
 Barnstaple EX32. . . . . 155 A5
 Exmouth EX8. . . . . . . 202 C7
 Honiton EX14. . . . . . 166 B6
 Kingsbridge TQ7 . . . . 258 B4
Ashleigh Rise TQ14 . . 210 B7
Ashleigh Way
 Plymouth PL7 . . . . . . 251 C4
 Teignmouth TQ14 . . . . 210 B7
Ashley Back La EX16 . . 64 A5
Ashley Brake EX11. . . 168 D4
Ashley Cl EX15. . . . . . 66 B8
Ashley Cres EX10 . . . 188 A7
Ashley Ho **2** EX8 . . 202 B6
Ashley Pl PL1. . . . . . 262 B4
Ashley Priors La TQ1 214 C4
Ashley Rd
 Okehampton EX20 . . . 170 C5
 Uffculme EX15 . . . . . . 66 A7
Ashley Rise EX16. . . . 161 B1
Ashley Terr
 Bideford EX39. . . . . . 156 F1
 13 Ilfracombe EX34 150 B5
Ashley Way EX7 . . . . . 204 F7
ASHMANSWORTHY . . 39 A5
Ashmead Gr EX33. . . 152 C6
ASHMILL 90 F6
ASH MILL 31 C2
Ashmill Cross EX21. . . 90 F6
Ashmill Ct TQ12. . . . 206 F4
Ash Mill Hill EX36 . . . 31 B2
Ashmore Ct EX2 . . . . 261 A1
Ashott La TA24. . . . . . 13 F1
Ashplants Cl EX36 . . . 58 F3
Ash Plants Cl EX39. . 156 D2
ASHPRINGTON 139 F8
Ashprington Cross
 TQ9. . . . . 139 F8
Ash Rd
 Braunton EX33 . . . . . . 152 F7
 Kingsteignton TQ12 . . 207 E6
ASHREIGNEY 58 F8
ASHRIDGE 26 D6
Ashridge Gdns
 Kingsteignton TQ12 . . 207 F6
 Plymouth PL5 . . . . . . 244 B2
Ashridge La EX20 . . . 77 D6
Ashridge Moor Cross
 EX20. . . . . 77 E6
ASH THOMAS 65 A3
Ashton Bsns Ctr EX2 . 177 B2
Ashton Cl PL6. . . . . . 245 C6
Ashton Cres EX33 . . . 152 C5
Ashton Ct **11** TQ12. . 123 F1
Ashton Ind Units EX2 177 B2
Ashton Rd EX2 . . . . . 177 B2
Ashtons Cotts EX39 . . 40 B7
Ashton Terr TQ1 . . . . 220 B5
Ashton Way TQ12 . . . 242 D3
Ashtown Cross EX16. . 34 A3
Ashtree Cl PL6. . . . . . 245 D7
Ashtree Gr PL9 . . . . . 256 C8
Ash Units EX17 . . . . . 165 F5
Ash Vale PL16 . . . . . . 105 E4
ASHWATER 90 D6
Ashwater Prim Sch
 EX21. . . . . 90 F6
Ash Way TQ12 . . . . . 207 F1
ASHWELL. 124 B1
Ashwell La TQ13. . . . 122 E6
Ashwickla TA24. . . . . . 33 A8
Ashwood **5** TQ10. . 134 F3
Ash Way
 Loddiswell TQ7 . . . . . 143 E7
 Plymouth PL7 . . . . . . 251 B5
Ashwood Ct TQ12. . . 207 E2

Ashwood Park Rd PL7 ... 251 C6
Ashwood Pk TQ7 ... 143 F7
Ashwood Rd EX2 ... 177 B3
Aspen Cl
Exeter EX2 ... 178 C4
3 Honiton EX14 ... 85 C2
Newton Abbot TQ12 ... 212 F8
Tavistock PL19 ... 171 C3
Willand EX15 ... 162 E5
Aspen Dr TQ12 ... 212 F8
Aspen Gdns PL7 ... 251 B5
Aspen Gr EX31 ... 153 D4
Aspen Way
Paignton TQ4 ... 225 D3
Tiverton EX16 ... 161 E7
Aspin Cl TA21 ... 160 F6
Aspin Rd TA21 ... 160 F6
Astley Corte EX20 ... 170 A5
Astor Dr PL4 ... 249 C3
Aswell Orch TQ7 ... 143 F7
Athelstan Cl EX13 ... 167 D4
Athelstan Rd EX1 ... 261 C3
Athenaeum La PL1 ... 262 B2
Athenaeum Pl PL1 ... 262 C2
Athenaeum St PL1 ... 262 B2
ATHERINGTON ... 28 A2
Atherton La 14 TQ9 ... 223 C5
Atherton Pl PL2 ... 247 E4
Atherton Way EX16 ... 64 D7
Athlone Ho PL1 ... 262 A2
Atkinson Cl EX4 ... 174 A1
Atlantic Acad EX39 ... 24 B1
Atlantic Ct EX33 ... 152 F3
Atlantic Highway EX39 ... 156 E4
Atlantic Park Way EX39 ... 25 C4
Atlantic Village Outlet Shopping EX39 ... 25 D4
Atlantic Way EX39 ... 156 D7
Atlas Dr PL9 ... 256 E8
Attwyll Ave EX2 ... 178 A5
Atway Cl 3 TQ13 ... 180 C8
Atwill-Kingdom Almshouses EX1 ... 177 E6
Atwill's Almshouses EX4 ... 261 A4
Atworthy Cross EX22 ... 38 D3
Aubyns Wood Ave EX16 ... 161 B1
Aubyns Wood Cl EX16 ... 161 B1
Aubyns Wood Rise EX16 ... 161 B1
Auckland Rd 3 PL2 ... 248 A5
Auctioneers Cl PL7 ... 250 D5
Auction Pl EX13 ... 167 D5
Auction Way EX39 ... 38 F8
Audley 2 EX10 ... 188 A4
Audley Ave TQ2 ... 219 F8
Audley Rise TQ12 ... 208 A1
Augusta Ct 16 EX1 ... 261 A2
Augustine Cl EX12 ... 191 F8
Aunay Cl EX22 ... 164 D5
Aune Cl TQ10 ... 135 B1
Aunemouth Cross TQ7 ... 143 A3
AUNK ... 83 E3
Ausewell Cross TQ13 130 D7
Austen Cl EX4 ... 178 C8
Austin Ave PL2 ... 248 A6
Austin Cres PL6 ... 245 C1
Austin Farm Prim Sch PL6 ... 249 C7
Authers Hts EX16 ... 161 B2
Auton Cross TQ7 ... 258 A2
Autumn Field EX19 ... 58 E3
Avalon Cl EX4 ... 174 A2
Avanti Hall Sch EX4 ... 173 A2
Aveland Rd TQ1 ... 220 C7
Avent Wlk PL7 ... 250 F7
Avenue Cl DT7 ... 260 D3
Avenue Cottage Gdn★ TQ9 ... 227 A8
Avenue Ho EX17 ... 165 C6
Avenue Mezidon-Canon EX14 ... 166 D5
Avenue Rd
Bovey Tracey TQ13 ... 180 C6
Ilfracombe EX34 ... 150 B6
Kingskerswell TQ12 ... 213 A5
Lyme Regis DT7 ... 260 D3
Torquay TQ2 ... 219 F5
Avenue Terr TQ5 ... 229 E5
Avenue The
Chudleigh Knighton TQ13 ... 123 D4
Exton EX3 ... 183 C1
Newton Abbot TQ12 ... 207 D4
4 Seaton EX12 ... 192 A5
Tiverton EX16 ... 161 E3
Avery Ct EX8 ... 196 D2
Avery Hill TQ12 ... 207 E8
Avery Way PL12 ... 242 C5
Ave The 3 PL7 ... 136 B6
AVETON GIFFORD ... 143 C6
Aveton Gifford CE Prim Sch TQ7 ... 143 C6
Aviemore Ind Est EX31 ... 154 D3
Avoca Ave TQ1 ... 219 F6
Avocet Dr EX3 ... 183 C2
Avocet Pl EX7 ... 201 A2
Avocet Rd EX2 ... 178 F6
Avon Cl
Plymouth PL3 ... 249 D6
South Brent TQ10 ... 135 A2
Avon Ct TQ7 ... 142 F3
Avondale Ho 10 TQ10 134 F2
Avondale Rd
Exeter EX2 ... 178 A5
Exmouth EX8 ... 202 D8
Avondale Wlk 11 TQ10 ... 134 F2
Avon Dam★ TQ11 ... 134 D8
Avon La EX39 ... 156 D7
Avon Quillet TQ7 ... 142 E3
Avon Rd
Bideford EX39 ... 157 C1
Torquay TQ2 ... 219 B7
Avon Valley Cotts TQ7 ... 143 C6
AVONWICK ... 135 B1
Avonwick TQ1 ... 220 C7
Avonwick Gn TQ10 ... 135 B1
Avranches Ave EX17 ... 165 A6
AWLISCOMBE ... 85 B4
Awliscombe CE Prim Sch EX14 ... 85 B4
Axe Cl PL3 ... 249 D6
Axe Cliff View 11 EX12 ... 192 A5
Axeford TA20 ... 88 E8
Axeford Mdws TA20 ... 88 E8
Axe Valley Cl EX13 ... 104 C7
Axe Valley Sports Ctr EX13 ... 167 E6
Axeview Rd EX12 ... 192 A7
AXMINSTER ... 167 C6
Axminster Community Prim Acad EX13 ... 167 D6
Axminster Com Prim Sch EX13 ... 167 E6
Axminster Hospl EX13 ... 167 D6
Axminster Mus★ EX13 ... 167 D5
Axminster Rd
Charmouth DT6 ... 104 F4
Honiton EX14 ... 166 F5
Maidenhayne EX24 ... 103 D6
Musbury EX13 ... 103 D5
Offwell EX14 ... 86 A3
Tatworth TA20 ... 88 C7
Axminster Sta EX13 ... 167 C5
AXMOUTH ... 192 F7
Axmouth Rd
Axmouth EX24 ... 103 B2
Seaton EX12 ... 192 C5
Axmouth to Lyme Regis National Nature Reserve★ DT7 ... 193 D4
Axtown La PL20 ... 126 F2
Aycliffe Gdns PL7 ... 251 A3
AYLESBEARE ... 99 D2
Aylesbury Cres PL5 ... 244 B5
Aylescott Cross EX37 ... 43 E3
Aylescott Hill EX34 ... 9 A4
Aylescott La EX34 ... 9 A4
Ayleston Cross PL21 137 D2
Ayleston Pk PL21 ... 137 C2
Aylwin Cl PL7 ... 250 E6
Ayres Cl EX39 ... 157 C1
Ayreville Rd PL2 ... 248 B7
Aysha Gdns EX39 ... 156 D8
AYSHFORD ... 50 E2
Ayshford EX15 ... 66 A7
Azalea Cl EX14 ... 67 C1
Azes La EX32 ... 155 A5

B

BABBACOMBE ... 220 D7
Babbacombe Bsns Pk TQ1 ... 220 E7
Babbacombe Cl PL6 ... 249 E8
Babbacombe Cliff TQ1 ... 220 D7
Babbacombe Cliff Rly★ TQ1 ... 220 D8
Babbacombe Downs Rd TQ1 ... 220 D8
Babbacombe Model Village★ TQ1 ... 220 C8
Babbacombe Rd TQ1 220 E6
Babbage Rd TQ9 ... 223 D6
Babbages EX31 ... 154 A4
Babbage Wy EX5 ... 179 A7
Babblebrook Mews EX1 ... 178 F8
Babeleigh Rd EX39 ... 39 E7
Babeleigh Water EX39 39 E7
Baber Ct PL12 ... 125 A2
Babis Farm Cl PL12 ... 242 F1
Babis Farm Ct PL12 ... 242 F1
Babis Farm Mews PL12 ... 242 F2
Babis Farm Row PL12 ... 242 F1
Babis Farm Way PL12 ... 242 F2
Babis La PL12 ... 242 F1
Babland Cross PL21 ... 137 D2
Bableigh Cl EX39 ... 40 B7
Bableigh Rd
Landkey EX32 ... 17 B1
Swimbridge EX32 ... 28 B8
Baby La TA22 ... 33 E7
Babylon La EX5 ... 82 B5
Backaborough La 6 EX39 ... 156 F1
Backfield 7 EX39 ... 15 A1
Back Hill PL12 ... 242 D2
Back Hill Ind Est EX18 . 44 E1
Back La
Abbotsham EX39 ... 156 A1
Bickleigh EX16 ... 63 D2
Black Torrington EX21 ... 74 A8
Bradninch EX5 ... 82 E6
Chawleigh EX18 ... 60 C8
Chittlehampton EX37 ... 28 F4
Chulmleigh EX18 ... 44 E1
Colaton Raleigh EX10 ... 186 B3
Copplestone EX17 ... 79 A4
Ermington PL21 ... 136 F3
Frithelstock Stone EX38 . 40 F5
High Bickington EX38 ... 43 C7
Lutton PL21 ... 133 B2
Merton EX20 ... 57 A7
Newton Poppleford EX10 ... 186 E8
North Molton EX36 ... 30 D8
Okehampton/North Tawton EX20 ... 77 A1
Ottery St Mary EX10 ... 100 A6
Ottery St Mary EX10 ... 168 D8
Plymouth PL7 ... 250 E4
Roborough PL6 ... 241 A3
Sandford EX17 ... 80 A5
Sidmouth EX10 ... 187 C7
Sticklepath EX20 ... 95 A5
Stockland EX14 ... 87 A5
Whimple EX11 ... 168 D8
Back Rd
Calstock PL18 ... 125 D3
Moreleigh TQ9 ... 139 A3
Newton Abbot TQ12 ... 207 B3
Backshay Cl TQ7 ... 143 C1
Backshay Pk TQ7 ... 143 C1
Back's Hill
Crediton EX17 ... 79 F7
Sandford EX17 ... 80 A7
Back St
Bampton EX16 ... 34 B1
16 Modbury PL21 ... 137 B2
Woolfardisworthy EX39 . 38 F8
Backs The TQ6 ... 233 E5
Backstone La EX16 ... 47 B6
Backswood La EX16 ... 64 B4
Backways La TA21 ... 51 F6
Backwells Mead EX24 ... 102 B6
Badgaver La EX34 ... 3 B3
Badger Cl
Dartmouth TQ6 ... 233 D4
10 Exeter EX2 ... 178 D5
Honiton EX14 ... 166 E7
Newton Poppleford EX10 ... 186 D7
Paignton TQ3 ... 218 F1
Badger La 1 TQ12 ... 207 A5
Badgers Cl
Ivybridge PL21 ... 237 A5
Kingsbridge TQ7 ... 258 C4
Kingsteignton TQ12 ... 207 D8
Badgers Gn TQ7 ... 258 C4
Badgers Holt EX20 ... 170 A5
Badger's Way TQ13 ... 180 D7
Badgers Wlk PL12 ... 242 D4
Badger View PL9 ... 255 E5
Badger Way EX5 ... 99 B6
Bad Homburg Way EX2 ... 181 D8
Badlake Cl EX7 ... 204 C7
Badlake Hill EX7 ... 204 C7
Badlake La EX36 ... 32 D6
Badlake Moor Cross TA22 ... 32 D7
Badon Cl EX4 ... 174 A2
BADWORTHY ... 134 D4
BAGLEY GREEN ... 160 A3
Bagley Rd TA21 ... 160 A3
Bagmore Hill EX5 ... 82 F8
Bagshot Ave EX2 ... 177 D3
Bagton La TQ7 ... 147 E8
Bailey La EX5 ... 98 F7
Bailey Mws EX39 ... 156 D1
Bailey's Knapp EX16 ... 50 B4
Baileys Mdw TQ6 ... 146 B7
Bailey St EX4 ... 261 B3
Bailey Terr EX22 ... 70 F5
Bainbridge Ave PL3 ... 248 F7
Bainbridge Ct PL7 ... 250 E7
Baker Cl EX10 ... 188 A8
Bakers Cl PL7 ... 251 C5
Bakers Cotts EX8 ... 195 F5
Bakers Court La EX35 ... 151 B5
Baker's Cross TA3 ... 68 A7
Bakers Ct EX35 ... 151 B5
Bakers Hill
Aveton Gifford TQ7 ... 143 C6
Brixham TQ5 ... 230 C3
Exeter EX2 ... 176 C3
Baker's Hill
Newton Abbot TQ12 ... 207 B3
Tiverton EX16 ... 161 A4
Baker's La
Churchinford TA3 ... 68 A7
Lower Tippacott EX35 ... 6 A3
Wellington TA21 ... 160 E6
Bakers Mead EX13 ... 87 A1
Baker's Pk TQ13 ... 130 A4
Bakers Pl PL1 ... 247 F1
Baker St EX2 ... 177 F5
Bakers Terr TQ7 ... 143 C6
Bakers View TQ12 ... 207 A3
Bakers Wy EX4 ... 178 D8
Bakery La EX8 ... 202 A7
Bakery Mdw EX16 ... 62 B5
Bakery Way EX32 ... 17 B2
BAKESDOWN ... 70 C3
Bakesdown La EX6 ... 96 B3
Bala Brook Cl TQ5 ... 229 F2
Bald Hill EX10 ... 101 B2
Baldwin Ct EX20 ... 170 D6
Balfour Cl EX14 ... 166 E5
Balfour Gdns EX10 ... 188 A6
Balfour Manor EX10 ... 188 A5
Balfour Manor Ct EX10 ... 187 F5
Balfour Mews EX10 ... 188 A5
Balfours EX10 ... 188 A6
Balfour Terr
Kilmington EX13 ... 87 C1
Plymouth PL2 ... 247 E4
Balkwill Ct TQ7 ... 258 C4
Balkwill Rd TQ7 ... 258 B4
Bal La PL19 ... 117 E6
Balland La TQ13 ... 131 A5
Balland Pk 5 TQ13 ... 131 A5
Ballards Cres EX31 ... 153 A4
Ballards Gr EX31 ... 153 A4
Ballards Way EX31 ... 153 A4
Balleroy Cl EX21 ... 55 E4
Ball Hill
Cheriton Fitzpaine EX17 ... 62 F2
Cheriton Fitzpaine EX17 . 63 A2
Ballhill La EX16 ... 49 B8
Ball Hill La EX20 ... 170 D5
Ball La EX24 ... 101 F5
Ball Mdw EX20 ... 170 D5
Balls Cnr EX37 ... 44 A3
Balls Corner EX20 ... 57 C8
Balls Corner Cross EX20 ... 57 C8
Balls Cross EX36 ... 20 B2
Ball's Cross TQ8 ... 259 C7
Balls Farm Rd EX2 ... 176 F2
Balls Hill EX37 ... 44 A2
Balmoral Ave PL2 ... 247 F5
Balmoral Cl TQ12 ... 207 E2
Balmoral Cres EX20 ... 170 D5
Balmoral Gdns EX3 ... 182 F5
Balmoral Ho EX31 ... 154 E7
Balmoral La 7 TQ10 ... 134 F3
Balmoral Terr 12 EX34 ... 150 B5
Balsdon Rd EX22 ... 70 E1
Baltic Wharf Bsns Pk TQ9 ... 223 D4
Bamfylde Cotts EX6 ... 114 B4
Bampflyde Way PL6 ... 244 D6
Bampfylde Cl
Poltimore EX4 ... 174 F6
Tiverton EX16 ... 161 F3
Bampfylde Cross EX36 ... 19 D2
Bampfylde Rd TQ2 ... 219 F5
Bampfylde St EX1, EX4 ... 261 C3
BAMPTON ... 34 C1
Bampton Cl TQ3 ... 218 D2
Bampton Down Rd EX16 ... 49 F7
Bampton Rd PL6 ... 245 E1
Bampton St EX16 ... 161 D4
Bampton VA Prim Sch EX16 ... 34 B1
Bamson La EX16 ... 62 B6
Banbury Pk TQ2 ... 219 C8
Banfield Rd EX31 ... 154 F8
Banfield Way EX14 ... 166 B4
Bankart La EX3 ... 182 B7
Bank End EX39 ... 157 B4
Bankhart La EX3 ... 182 B7
Bank La
11 Brixham TQ5 ... 230 C5
6 Totnes TQ9 ... 223 C5
Bankland La EX20 ... 77 D8
Banks Cl EX16 ... 49 C1
Banksia Cl EX16 ... 161 E7
Bankside EX8 ... 196 C3
Bank Sq TA22 ... 33 D6
Bank St
Newton Abbot TQ12 ... 207 B3
12 Teignmouth TQ14 ... 210 C4
Bank The 11 EX32 ... 17 B2
Bannawell Ct 1 PL19 ... 171 B6
Bannawell St PL19 ... 171 B6
Banner Ct 4 TQ3 ... 226 A6
BANTHAM ... 142 F2
Bantham Cross TQ7 ... 143 D4
Baptist Chapel Ct EX17 ... 165 C5
Baptist St PL17 ... 125 D3
Bapton Cl EX8 ... 196 B2
Bapton La EX8 ... 196 B1
Barberry Cl EX4 ... 178 A8
Barbers La EX13 ... 104 C3
Barber's La
Uplyme DT7 ... 260 B4
West Buckland TA21 ... 52 F7
BARBICAN ... 263 A2
Barbican App PL4 ... 263 B2
Barbican Cl EX32 ... 155 A4
Barbican Ct
Exeter EX4 ... 177 A5
11 Plymouth PL4 ... 263 A2
Barbican La EX32 ... 155 B4
Barbican L Pk PL4 ... 263 C2
Barbican Pl 9 EX32 ... 155 A4
Barbican Rd
Barnstaple EX32 ... 155 A4
Plymouth PL7 ... 250 E4
Barbican Stps EX4 ... 261 A2
Barbican Terr EX32 ... 155 A4
Barbican The PL1 ... 263 A2
Barbican Theatre★ PL1 ... 263 A1
BARBROOK ... 151 B1
Barbrook Rd EX35 ... 151 B3
Barbury Cres PL6 ... 245 B8
Barchington Ave TQ2 213 F3
Barcombe Hts TQ3 ... 226 B8
Barcombe La TQ3 ... 226 B8
Barcombe Mews TQ3 ... 226 B8
Barcombe Rd TQ3 ... 226 A8
Barcote Wlk PL6 ... 249 C8
Bardon Walk EX2 ... 178 E3
Bardsey Cl PL6 ... 245 A7
Barewell Cl TQ1 ... 220 B8
Barewell Rd TQ1 ... 220 B8
Barfield Cl EX19 ... 57 F7
Barfield Rd EX19 ... 57 F7
Barfleur Rise DT7 ... 260 E5
Barham Ave TQ14 ... 204 B1
Baring Cotts 14 TQ9 ... 223 D5
Baring Cres EX1 ... 177 E6
Baring Ct
Exeter EX2 ... 261 B1
Lewtrenchard EX20 ... 106 F5
Baring Flats EX1 ... 177 E6
Baring St PL4 ... 263 B4
Baring Terr EX1 ... 261 B1
Barkerhancock Cl EX4 ... 174 D1
Barker's Hill PL12 ... 242 C1
Barkers Way EX20 ... 77 C4
Barkingdon Workshops TQ9 ... 215 D7
Barlands Way EX19 ... 57 F7
Barle Cl EX2 ... 178 D4
Barle Ct EX16 ... 161 E7
Barle Ent Ctr TA22 ... 33 D5
Barley Cl EX15 ... 163 B2
Barleycorn Fields 6 EX32 ... 17 B2
Barley Farm Rd EX4 ... 176 E4
Barley La EX4 ... 176 D5
Barley Lane Sch EX4 176 D4
Barley Market St PL19 ... 171 C6
Barley Mount EX4 ... 176 F5
Barley Rd EX5 ... 99 B6
Barley Valley Nature Reserve★ EX4 ... 176 D6
Barley Wlk EX6 ... 201 A8
Barline EX12 ... 191 D5
Barlow Gdns PL2 ... 248 B7
Barlow Rd EX31 ... 155 A7
Barnacott Cross EX39 . 26 D8
Barnade View EX1 ... 175 B1
Barnardo Rd EX2 ... 261 C1
Barnards Farm EX12 . 191 D5
Barnards Hill La EX12 ... 192 A7
Barn Cl
Barnstaple EX32 ... 155 C3
Churchinford TA3 ... 68 D7
Ivybridge PL21 ... 237 A6
Plymouth PL7 ... 251 D4
Shebbear EX21 ... 55 E4
Whiddon Down EX20 ... 95 F3
Barn Close La EX12 ... 192 E5
Barnclose Rd TA22 ... 21 E4
Barncroft EX22 ... 39 C1
Barn Cross EX14 ... 85 F8
Barn Ct
Churston Ferrers TQ5 ... 229 E4
Dartmouth TQ6 ... 233 C2
Barn Ct Rd TQ9 ... 223 F5
Barndale Cres PL6 ... 245 B6
BARNE BARTON ... 247 C8
Barne Cl PL5 ... 247 C8
Barne Cross TQ13 ... 112 A2
Barne La PL5 ... 243 D1
Barne Rd PL5 ... 247 C8
Barnes Cl
Honiton EX14 ... 166 B4
Willand EX15 ... 162 C5
Barnes Close Mead TA22 ... 33 D6
Barnes Mdw DT7 ... 260 B5
BARNFIELD ... 261 C3
Barnfield
Crediton EX17 ... 165 C5
East Allington TQ9 ... 144 D7
Barnfield Ave EX8 ... 202 D7
Barnfield Cl
Braunton EX33 ... 152 E5
Crediton EX17 ... 165 C5
Galmpton TQ5 ... 229 C5
Barnfield Cotts EX5 ... 81 F3
Barnfield Cres EX1 ... 261 B3
Barnfield Dr PL7 ... 251 C5
Barnfield Hill EX1 ... 261 C3
Barnfield Rd
Brixham TQ5 ... 230 D3
Exeter EX1 ... 261 B3
Kingsbridge TQ7 ... 258 C6
Paignton TQ3 ... 225 F7
Paignton TQ3 ... 226 A7
Torquay TQ2 ... 219 D2
Barnfield Terr TQ12 ... 212 B6
Barnfield Theatre★ EX1 ... 261 B3
Barnfield Wlk TQ7 ... 258 C6
Barnhay 6 EX16 ... 34 B1
Barn Hayes EX10 ... 187 F7
Barnhay The TQ9 ... 227 F7
Barn Hill
Down St Mary EX17 ... 78 F7
Morwenstow EX23 ... 36 F1
Barnhill Rd TQ12 ... 213 A4
Barningham Gdns PL6 ... 245 B6
Barn La
Budleigh Salterton EX9 ... 197 F2
Kingskerswell TQ12 ... 212 F7
Stoke Rivers EX32 ... 17 F6
Barn Meads Rd TA21 . 160 E4
Barn Orchard 21 EX5 .. 99 A6
Barn Owl Cl TQ2 ... 213 D3
Barnpark Cl TQ14 ... 210 C6
Barn Park Cl TQ12 ... 211 E2
Barn Park Gdns EX21 .. 73 C2
Barnpark Rd TQ14 ... 210 C5
Barn Park Rd
Fremington EX31 ... 153 D5
Plymouth PL3 ... 248 D6
Barnpark Terr TQ14 .. 210 C6
Barn Pk
Ashwater EX21 ... 90 E6
Buckfastleigh TQ11 ... 236 A5
Coldeast TQ12 ... 122 F1
Crediton EX17 ... 165 C5
Saltash PL12 ... 242 F3
Stoke Gabriel TQ9 ... 227 F8
Wrafton EX33 ... 152 E3
Barn Rd TQ4 ... 226 C2
Barns Cl
Bradninch EX5 ... 82 F6
Cove EX16 ... 49 B6
Kingsteignton TQ12 ... 207 E6
Barnsclose TA22 ... 33 D6
Barns Close Ind Est TA22 ... 33 D6
Barnsclose N TA22 ... 33 D6
Barnsclose W TA22 ... 33 D6
Barnsey Gdns TQ13 ... 130 F5
Barnsfield La TQ11 ... 236 A5
Barnshill Cl EX17 ... 62 F1
Barnsley Cl 1 TQ14 ... 210 C5
Barnsley Dr TQ14 ... 210 C6
Barns Rd EX9 ... 198 B1
BARNSTAPLE ... 155 C4
Barnstaple Cl
Chittlehampton EX37 ... 28 F4
Plymouth PL6 ... 249 E7
Barnstaple Cross
Burrington EX37 ... 43 C3
Crediton EX17 ... 79 E4
Barnstaple Heritage Ctr★ EX31 ... 154 F5
Barnstaple Hill EX32 .. 17 D1
Barnstaple Rd
Filleigh EX32 ... 29 F7
South Molton EX36 ... 30 A6
South Molton EX36 ... 158 A7
Barnstaple Ret Pk EX31 ... 154 F4
Barnstaple St
Bideford EX39 ... 157 B2
South Molton EX36 ... 158 C4
Winkleigh EX19 ... 58 F3
Barnstaple Sta EX31 . 154 F4
Barns Terr PL12 ... 238 A3
Barnstone Ct EX2 ... 181 A8
Barntown Gate EX19 .. 58 E1
Barntown La EX19 ... 58 D1
Barnwood Cl PL9 ... 255 E5
Barometer World (Mus)★ EX20 ... 57 A7
Baron Ct EX31 ... 154 B1
Barons Pyke PL21 ... 237 E4
Barons Rd PL20 ... 127 B3
Baron Way
Barnstaple EX31 ... 154 B1
Newton Abbot TQ12 ... 207 F4
Barossa Pl 10 PL5 ... 247 B3
Barossa Rd PL11 ... 247 B3
Barpark Cnr EX15 ... 52 E3
Barrack La EX2 ... 181 A6
Barrack Pl PL1 ... 248 A1
Barrack Rd
Exeter EX2 ... 177 E4
Ottery St Mary EX11 ... 169 C3
Princetown PL20 ... 128 B8
Yelverton PL20 ... 119 A1
Barracks Hill TQ9 ... 223 A7
Barracks Rd
Fremington EX31 ... 153 E6
Modbury PL21 ... 137 B3
Barrack St PL1 ... 247 E2
Barradon Cl TQ2 ... 214 A4
Barrel Cl EX11 ... 169 C3
Barrington Ct TQ4 ... 226 C5
Barrington Ho TQ1 ... 220 E5
Barrington Mead EX10 ... 188 B4
Barrington Rd TQ1 ... 220 E5
Barrington St EX16 ... 161 D4
Barrington Wy TA21 ... 160 B4
Barris EX17 ... 60 C3
Barrowdale Cl EX8 ... 196 C3
Barrow Down PL12 ... 242 B3
Barrow Rd EX14 ... 84 C4
Barrow Way Cross EX20 ... 110 D8
Bar's La EX9, EX10 ... 199 B8
Bartholomew Rd PL2 248 B5
Bartholomew Street E EX4 ... 261 A3
Bartholomew Street W EX4 ... 261 A2
Bartholomew Terr EX4 ... 261 A2

BARTON 213 F3
Barton Ave
  Braunton EX33 . . . .152 D4
  Paignton TQ3 . . . . .225 F7
  Plymouth PL2 . . . . .247 E5
Barton Brake PL9 . . .140 D8
Bartonbury Cross
  EX17 . . . . .78 E6
Barton Cl
  Cheriton Fitzpaine
    EX17 . . . . .62 E1
  Cranbrook EX5 . . . . .99 C6
  Exton EX3 . . . . . . .183 C1
  Filleigh EX32 . . . . . .29 C6
  Georgeham EX33 . . . . .8 B4
  Kingsbridge TQ7 . . . .258 D4
  North Tawton EX20 . . . .77 C4
  Okehampton EX20 . . .170 C5
  Paignton TQ3 . . . . .225 F7
  Parkham EX39 . . . . . .39 E8
  Plymouth PL7 . . . . .251 C5
  Stoke Canon EX5 . . . .81 F1
  Wembury PL9 . . . . .140 D8
Barton Cnr EX17 . . . .61 B2
Barton Cotts EX20 . . .95 C1
Barton Cres
  Dawlish EX7 . . . . . .204 C6
  Paignton TQ3 . . . . .225 F7
Barton Cross
  East Anstey EX16 . . . .32 E5
  Filleigh EX32 . . . . . .29 A6
  Heasley Mill EX36 . . . .19 C2
  Instow EX39 . . . . . . .15 B2
  Morchard Bishop EX17 . .61 C2
  Poltimore EX5 . . . . .174 B8
  Sandford EX17 . . . . . .80 C6
  Torquay TQ2 . . . . . .213 F4
Barton Ct
  Ashwater EX21 . . . . . .90 E6
  Exeter EX1 . . . . . . .178 C7
  Parkham EX39 . . . . . .39 E8
  Sidmouth EX10 . . . . .188 A3
Barton Dr
  Newton Abbot TQ12 . .206 F3
  Paignton TQ3 . . . . .225 F7
BARTON GATE 11 E4
Barton Gate La EX34 . . .3 A3
Barton Gdns TQ3 . . . .225 F7
Barton Head Cross
  EX20 . . . . .76 C4
Barton Hill
  Berrynarbor EX34 . . . . .2 E4
  Daccombe TQ1, TQ12 . .214 A6
  Dawlish EX7 . . . . . .204 D6
  North Tawton EX20 . . . .77 C4
Barton Hill Acad TQ2 .213 F2
Bartonhill Cross TQ9 .215 F6
Barton Hill Rd TQ2 . .213 F2
Barton Hill Way TQ2. .213 F2
Barton Ho EX39 . . . . . .26 A4
Barton La
  Barton Town EX31 . . . .11 D3
  Berrynarbor EX34 . . . . .2 E4
  Braunton EX32 . . . . .152 D5
  Brayford EX32 . . . . . .18 F4
  Dawlish EX7 . . . . . .204 D6
  Lapford EX17 . . . . . .60 A2
  Shillingford Abbot EX2 .114 C7
  Staverton TQ9 . . . . .216 A3
  Witheridge EX16 . . . . .46 E1
Barton Lane Cl EX33 .152 D4
Barton Leys TQ9 . . . .224 B7
Barton Meadow Rd
  EX37 . . . . .43 B7
Barton Mews
  Exton EX3 . . . . . . .183 C1
  Millbrook PL10 . . . . .252 F6
  Parkham EX39 . . . . . .39 E8
  Venn Ottery EX11 . . . .100 B2
Barton Orch EX10 . . . .100 D2
Barton Paddocks
  EX10 . . . . .100 D2
Barton Rd
  Barnstaple EX32 . . . .155 D4
  Buckland Brewer EX39 . .40 B7
  Exeter EX2 . . . . . . .176 F4
  Okehampton EX20 . . .170 C5
  Paignton TQ3 . . . . .225 F7
  Parkham EX39 . . . . . .39 E8
  Plymouth PL9 . . . . .255 B6
  Tiverton EX16 . . . . .161 D6
  Torquay TQ1, TQ2 . . .219 E7
  West Down EX34 . . . . . .8 F5
  Woolacombe EX34 . . . . .7 F6
Barton Rise EX14 . . . . .84 E2
Barton Road Ind Units
  TQ2 . . . . .219 E8
Barton St EX20 . . . . . .77 C4
Barton Steep EX35 . . . . .5 E4
Barton Terr EX7 . . . .204 D6
Barton The TA4 . . . . . .35 E8
Barton Tors EX39 . . . .157 C1
BARTON TOWN 11 D3
Barton View EX20 . . . . .77 C4
Barton Villas EX7 . . .204 C6
Barton Way TQ6 . . . .233 B2
Bartows Cswy EX16 . .161 D5
Bartows Mews EX16 . .161 D5
Bartridge Hill EX31 . . .27 A5
Barum Arc EX32 . . . .155 A5
Barum Ct TQ3 . . . . .226 C7
Barum Gate Bsns Pk
  EX32 . . . . .155 D3
Barum Mews 5
  EX32 . . . . .155 A5
Barum Ware Way 13
  EX31 . . . . .154 A2
Barwick Cross EX19 . . .58 B2

Bary Cl EX17 . . . . .62 F1
Bary Hill Cross EX17. . .62 F1
Bary La EX17 . . . . .62 F1
Bascombe Cl TQ5 . . . .229 D6
Bascombe Rd
  Brixham TQ5 . . . . . .230 A4
  Churston Ferrers TQ5. .229 D6
Basepoint Bsns Ctr
  EX2 . . . . .181 E8
Basinghall Rd PL9 . . .255 E5
Basket Ope PL4 . . . . .263 A2
Bason Cross
  Bradford EX22 . . . . . .55 B2
  Shebbear EX22 . . . . . .55 B2
Basset's Cross EX20. . .75 E5
Bassett Cl 1 EX33 . . .152 D5
Bassetts Cl
  Copplestone EX17 . . . .79 A5
  Northam EX39 . . . . .156 F8
Bassetts Farm Prim Sch
  EX8 . . . . .196 E1
Bassetts Gdns EX8 . . .196 E2
Bastard's La EX38 . . .159 D6
Bastard's Park Cnr
  PL21 . . . . .137 D3
Batavia Dr EX2 . . . . .178 D1
Batcombe La EX5 . . . . .81 F6
Bate Cl EX2 . . . . . . .177 A1
Bateman's Cross EX13. .88 E7
Bath Cl EX14 . . . . .84 D2
Bath Ct EX39 . . . . . . .156 C7
Batherm Cl 3 EX16 . . .49 B8
Bathern Rd EX2 . . . . .178 D1
Bath Hotel Rd EX39 . .156 C7
Bath La
  Plymouth PL1 . . . . . .262 B2
  Torquay TQ2 . . . . . .219 F5
Bath Meadow Dr TA22. 33 E6
Bath Pl
  Ilfracombe EX34 . . . .150 B6
  Plymouth PL1 . . . . . .262 B2
Bath Place W PL1 . . . .262 B2
Bath Rd EX8 . . . . . . .202 A6
Bath St PL1 . . . . .262 B2
Bath Terr
  6 Instow EX39 . . . . .15 B1
  11 Teignmouth TQ14 . .210 C4
Batson Cross TQ8 . . . .259 C5
Batson Gdns TQ4 . . . .226 B4
Batson Hall Cross
  TQ8 . . . . .259 C6
Batson Hill TQ8 . . . . .259 C5
BATSWORTHY 46 F6
Batsworthy Cross
  EX16 . . . . .46 F7
Batsworthy Hill EX16. .47 A7
Battens EX14 . . . . .87 A7
Battens Cross EX16 . . .65 C8
Batterbridge Hill
  PL19 . . . . .117 E3
Batteridge Hill PL19. .117 F2
Battershall Cl PL9. . . .255 F5
Batter St PL4 . . . . . . .263 A2
Battersway Rd TQ4. . .225 E4
Battery La PL19 . . . . .171 C4
Battery St PL1 . . . . . .262 A2
Battery Street Flats
  PL1 . . . . .262 A2
BATTISBOROUGH
  CROSS 141 E7
Battisford Pk PL7 . . . .251 E3
Battishorne Way
  EX14 . . . . .166 B4
Battle Abbey Way 2
  EX1 . . . . .178 F8
Battledown Cross
  EX21 . . . . .55 F4
Battleford La TQ9 . . . .217 C5
Battle Rd TQ12 . . . . . .180 F2
Battle St EX15 . . . . . .52 E1
Battleton TA22 . . . . . . .33 D6
Batts Combe Mws
  PL3 . . . . .249 D1
Batt's La EX11 . . . . . .169 D3
Batts Pk EX15 . . . . . . .66 C6
Batworthy Mill Cross
  TQ13 . . . . .111 A4
Bavent Cl EX5. . . . . . .173 F8
Baxter Cl EX2 . . . . . .178 D3
Baxworthy Cross EX39 23 A1
Bayard's Cove TQ6. . .233 F3
Bayard's Cove Fort ★
  TQ6. . . . . .233 F2
Bayard's Hill TQ6 . . . .233 F3
Bayclose La EX31 . . . . .10 E6
Bay Ct 11 EX12 . . . . . .192 B4
Baydon Cl PL6 . . . . . .245 C1
Bay Fort Mans TQ1. . .220 A4
Bayley Pl EX1 . . . . . . .179 B8
Bayly's Rd PL9 . . . . . .255 B7
Baymount Rd TQ3. . . .226 A7
Baynes Cl TA21 . . . . . .160 E7
Bay Rd EX9 . . . . .199 A7
Bayside La PL9. . . . . . .140 A8
Bayswater Rd PL1. . . .262 B4
Baythorpe Lodge
  TQ2 . . . . .219 E2
Baytor Ind Est TQ4 . . .225 E3
Baytree Cl PL6 . . . . . .245 D6
Baytree Gdns PL2 . . . .248 A7
Bay Trees EX6 . . . . . .114 D4
Bay View TQ3 . . . . . .219 D1
Bay View Cl
  Croyde EX33 . . . . .7 E1
  Stoke Fleming TQ6 . . .146 B7
Bay View Ct
  Lyme Regis DT7 . . . . .260 E3
  Northam EX39 . . . . .156 F6

Bay View Dr TQ14 . . . .210 C6
Bay View Est TQ6 . . . .146 B7
Bay View Rd
  Lyme Regis DT7 . . . . .260 D4
  Northam EX39 . . . . .156 E6
  Woolacombe EX34 . . . . .7 F6
Baze La EX35 . . . . .6 B4
Bazley Sq 3 EX1 . . . .178 E8
Beachdown TQ7 . . . . .142 E3
Beach Mdw EX22 . . . . .53 E1
Beach Rd
  Croyde EX33 . . . . .7 D2
  Dawlish Warren EX7. . .201 B2
  Heybrook Bay PL9. . . .140 A7
  Ilfracombe EX34. . . . .150 F6
  Seaton EX12 . . . . . . .192 B4
  Torquay TQ1 . . . . . . .220 D7
  Westward Ho! EX39 . .156 D7
  Woolacombe EX34 . . . . .8 A6
Beach St 12 EX7. . . . .204 E6
Beach View Cres
  PL9 . . . . .140 D7
Beach Wlk TQ4 . . . . . .226 C2
BEACON 85 F8
Beacon Ave EX4 . . . . .178 A8
Beacon Castle EX34 . . .150 A6
Beacon CE VA Prim Sch
  The 24 EX18 . . . . . .202 A6
Beacon Cl PL21 . . . . . .237 C6
Beacon Cotts TQ13 . . .130 C8
Beacon Cross
  Bradninch EX5 . . . . . .82 F7
  Copplestone EX17 . . . .79 D6
  North Tawton EX20 . . . .77 A2
  Romansleigh EX36 . . . .45 C5
  Talaton EX5. . . . . . . .84 B1
Beacon Down Ave
  PL2 . . . . .248 B7
Beacon Down Cnr
  EX6. . . . . .98 D2
Beacondown Cross
  EX16. . . . . .63 E8
Beacon Down Cross
  EX20. . . . . .93 E5
Beacon Down Hill
  EX20. . . . . .93 F5
Beacon Dr TQ12 . . . . .206 E5
Beaconfield Rd PL2 . . .248 B7
Beacon Heath EX4 . . .174 C1
BEACON HILL 174 C3
Beacon Hill
  Bradninch EX5 . . . . . .82 F7
  16 Exmouth EX8 . . . . .202 A6
  Torquay TQ1 . . . . . . .220 B3
Beacon Hill La EX14 . . .87 A5
Beacon Ho PL3 . . . . . .249 D4
Beacon Hts EX33 . . . .152 E6
Beacon La
  Broadhempston TQ9. . .131 E4
  Chulmleigh EX18. . . . . .45 C3
  Cullompton EX15 . . . . .65 A3
  Exeter EX4 . . . . . . .178 A8
  Hennock TQ13. . . . . .123 A7
  Kingswear TQ6 . . . . .234 A2
  Wellington TA21 . . . . . .52 C4
Beaconpark La EX20 . . .95 D3
Beacon Park Rd PL2. . .248 B7
Beacon Pk PL15. . . . . . .89 D7
Beacon Pl EX8 . . . . . .202 A6
Beacon Quay TQ1 . . . .220 B3
Beacon Rd
  Bradninch EX5 . . . . . .82 F7
  Ivybridge PL21 . . . . .237 C6
  Kingswear TQ6 . . . . .234 A2
Beacon Rise 5 EX18 . . .44 E1
Beaconsfield Cross
  EX22. . . . . .72 E6
Beacon Terr
  4 South Brent TQ10. . .134 F2
  Torquay TQ1 . . . . . . .220 B3
Beacon The EX8 . . . . .202 A6
Beacon View
  3 Bittaford PL21 . . . .137 C7
  Dartington TQ9 . . . . .222 F8
  8 South Brent TQ10. . .134 F2
Beadle St 6 PL19. . . . .171 B4
Beadon Dr TQ8 . . . . . .259 C4
Beadon La
  Bovey Tracey TQ13 . . .123 A8
  Chulmleigh EX18. . . . . .45 B3
  Hennock TQ13. . . . . .112 F1
Beadon Rd TQ8 . . . . . .259 B4
BEAFORD 42 D1
Beaford Arts ★ EX19. . .42 D1
Beaford Com Prim Sch
  EX19. . . . . .42 D1
Beagle Rd PL9 . . . . . .247 F1
Bealey Court Cross
  EX18. . . . . .45 E2
BEALSMILL 115 C3
Bealswood Cl PL18. . . .125 D6
Bealswood Rd PL18 . . .125 D6
Beanhay Cl 12 TQ12 . .122 F1
Beans Mdw EX20. . . . .170 A5
Beaple's Moor Cross
  EX36. . . . . .47 A8
BEARA 9 A1
Beara Cotts TQ13 . . . .131 C1
Beara Cross
  Bratton Fleming EX31. . .18 A8
  Highampton EX21. . . . .74 A6
  King's Nympton EX37 . . .44 F6
  Roborough EX38. . . . . .42 E6
Beara Down Cross
  EX31. . . . . .8 F1
Beara Head EX38 . . . . .42 E6
Beara Hill EX32 . . . . . .19 A5

Beara Hill Head EX36. . .19 B6
Beara La
  Bratton Fleming EX31. . .18 A8
  Combe Martin EX34 . . . .3 C3
Beara Way EX38 . . . . .159 D6
Beardown Rd EX20. . . .170 E5
Beards Rd EX31 . . . . .153 E5
BEARE 82 E3
Beare Bridge Rd
  EX20. . . . . .170 C6
Beare Cl PL9. . . . . . . .255 B5
Beare Copse La EX19. .58 F2
Beare La
  Beare EX5. . . . . .82 E3
  Bondleigh EX20 . . . . . .77 B7
Beare Lane Cross
  EX20. . . . . .77 B7
Beare Sq EX5 . . . . . . .82 A7
Bearne's (V) Prim Sch 19
  TQ12. . . . . .207 C3
Bearsdown Cl PL6 . . . .249 C8
Bearsdown Rd PL6 . . . .249 C8
Bears Farm Cotts
  EX20. . . . . .170 B7
Bears La EX9 . . . . . . .197 E3
Bear St
  Barnstaple EX32. . . . .155 A5
  Exeter EX1 . . . . .261 B2
BEASTON 131 D1
Beaston Cross TQ9. . . .131 D1
Beatland Cross PL7 . . .132 C5
Beatlands Rd EX10 . . .188 B4
Beatrice Ave
  Plymouth, Keyham
    PL2. . . . . .247 E5
  Plymouth, St Jude's
    PL4. . . . . .263 B3
  Saltash PL12. . . . . . .242 E2
Beatrice Gdns PL12 . . .242 E1
Beattie Rd PL5. . . . . . .247 B8
Beatty Ave EX2 . . . . . .182 C8
Beatty Cl PL6 . . . . . . .245 A4
Beatty Way TQ6 . . . . .233 F4
Beauchamp Cres
  PL2. . . . . .248 C7
Beauchamp Rd 2 . . . .248 C7
Beaudyn Wlk 5 PL6. . .249 C7
Beaufort Cl
  Plymouth PL5 . . . . . .247 C6
  Sampford Peverell EX16 50 D1
Beaufort Ct EX2 . . . . .261 A1
Beaufort Ho 20 PL4 . . .263 A2
Beaufort Rd EX2 . . . . .261 A1
Beaufort Wlk EX32 . . .155 B6
Beauly Cl PL7. . . . . . . .251 A5
Beaumaris Gdns
  PL3. . . . . .248 F8
Beaumaris Rd PL3 . . . .248 F7
Beaumont Ave PL4. . . .263 A4
Beaumont Cl
  5 Coldeast TQ12 . . . .122 F1
  Torquay TQ2 . . . . . . .219 D6
Beaumont Pl PL4 . . . . .263 A3
Beaumont Rd
  Newton Abbot TQ12 . .207 C3
  Plymouth PL4 . . . . . .263 B3
  Totnes TQ9 . . . . .223 C5
Beaumont St PL2 . . . . .248 A5
Beaumont Terr PL12 . .242 F4
Beaumont Way PL7 . . .251 D4
Beauvale Cl EX11 . . . . .169 E4
Beavers Brook Cl
  TQ3. . . . . .219 B2
Beavor La EX13 . . . . . .167 F6
BEAWORTHY 74 A2
Beaworthy Cl EX2. . . . .177 A3
Beccott Cross EX31 . . . .10 D4
Becket Rd TQ13. . . . . .180 E7
Beckets Rd TQ7 . . . . .258 D5
Beckford Cl PL7 . . . . . .251 A5
Beckford Cross EX13 . . .87 C4
Beckham Pl PL3 . . . . . .249 A6
Beckhamstree Hill
  EX6. . . . . .112 F2
Becklake Cl EX31 . . . . .154 A2
Beckland Cross EX39 . . .22 F4
Beckly Ct PL1. . . . . . . .262 C3
Becky Falls ★ TQ13 . . .122 A7
Bede Gdns PL5 . . . . . .244 C1
Bedford Cl PL18 . . . . .125 C6
Bedford Ct EX10 . . . . .188 B3
Bedford Flats EX10 . . .188 A3
Bedford Gr PL21 . . . . .237 D5
Bedford Mews PL4 . . . .263 A4
Bedford Park Villas
  PL4. . . . . .263 A4
Bedford Pk
  10 Bere Alston PL20. . .125 E1
  Plymouth PL4 . . . . . .263 A4
Bedford Pl
  6 Bere Alston PL20. . .125 E1
  12 Horrabridge PL20 . .126 F4
Bedford Rd
  Horrabridge PL20. . . .126 F4
  Plymouth PL9 . . . . . .255 E8
  Torquay TQ1 . . . . . . .220 D8
Bedford Row 19
  EX31 . . . . .154 F5
Bedford Sq
  Sidmouth EX10 . . . . .188 B3
  Tavistock PL19 . . . . .171 C5
Bedford St
  12 Barnstaple EX32 . . .155 A5
  Bere Alston PL20 . . . .125 E1
  Exeter EX4 . . . . .261 B3
  Plymouth PL2 . . . . . .247 F5
Bedford Terr PL4 . . . . .263 A4
Bedford Units PL18 . . .125 C5

Bedford Villas 7
  PL20. . . . . .125 E1
Bedford Way PL1 . . . . .262 C3
Bedlam La EX13. . . . . . .87 C6
Bedland's La EX9 . . . . .197 F2
Beech Ave
  Exeter EX4 . . . . .173 D1
  Plymouth PL4 . . . . . .263 C2
Beech Bank EX39 . . . . .25 D4
Beech Cl
  Barnstaple EX31 . . . . .154 B2
  Broadclyst EX5 . . . . .175 D6
  Honiton EX14 . . . . . .166 A4
  Tavistock PL19 . . . . .171 C2
  Torpoint PL11 . . . . . .247 A3
  Totnes TQ9 . . . . .222 F6
  Wembury PL9 . . . . . .255 A1
  Willand EX15 . . . . . .162 D4
Beech Copse EX1 . . . . .178 E2
Beech Cres PL20. . . . . .128 A8
Beech Croft EX15 . . . . .163 C5
Beechcroft Rd
  Plymouth, Lower Compton
    PL3. . . . . .249 A6
  Plymouth, North Prospect
    PL2. . . . . .248 B7
Beech Ct
  Plymouth PL6 . . . . . .245 D5
  2 Wellington TA21. . . .160 C6
Beech Dr
  Down St Mary EX17 . . . .78 E7
  Ipplepen TQ12 . . . . . .211 E2
Beeches Cl EX5 . . . . . .184 B2
Beeches The
  Okehampton EX20 . . . .76 E1
  St Ann's Chapel PL18 . .125 A5
  Woolfardisworthy EX39 . 38 F8
Beechfield Ave
  Torquay TQ2 . . . . . . .213 F2
  Yelverton PL20 . . . . . .127 A3
Beechfield Cl EX31 . . . .153 D5
Beechfield Gr PL3. . . . .248 E6
Beechfield Pl TQ2. . . . .213 F2
Beechfield Rd EX31 . . .153 D5
Beech Gr
  Barnstaple EX31. . . . .154 F7
  Braunton EX33 . . . . .152 C7
  South Molton EX36 . . .158 D5
  Wellington TA21 . . . .160 C6
Beech Grove Prim Sch
  TA21. . . . . .160 C6
Beechgrove Terr
  TA21. . . . . .154 F7
Beech Hill TA21 . . . . . .160 F5
Beech Hill Cross EX17. .61 B3
Beech Hill Ho EX17. . . .61 C3
Beeching Cl EX21 . . . . .73 E3
Beech La EX13 . . . . . . .88 E1
Beech Lea EX18. . . . . . .58 F8
Beechlea Ind Est EX19. 58 F4
Beech Pk
  Buckland St Mary
    TA20. . . . . .69 D8
  Cranbrook EX5 . . . . . .99 B6
  Lee Mill PL21 . . . . . .136 C7
  Stibb Cross EX38 . . . . .40 D1
  Tiverton EX16 . . . . . .64 C8
  Tiverton EX16 . . . . . .161 F5
Beech Tree Cross
  TA22. . . . . .33 C7
Beechtree Ct EX17 . . . .79 D7
Beech Tree Dr EX16 . . .161 B6
Beechtree La EX10,
  E12. . . . . .101 F2
Beech Tree Mdw
  EX20. . . . . .107 D8
Beech Trees La
  TQ12. . . . . .211 C3
Beech Wlk EX14 . . . . . .85 C5
Beechwood Ave
  Bovey Tracey TQ13 . . .180 C4
  Newton Abbot TQ12 . .207 E1
  Plymouth PL4 . . . . . .248 B8
Beechwood Cl EX31 . . .154 D4
Beechwood Cres
  EX7. . . . . .201 A2
Beechwood Cross
  PL7. . . . . .251 F7
Beechwood Dr TQ7 . . .258 D5
Beechwood Pk 10
  TQ7. . . . . .143 E7
Beechwood Prim Sch
  PL6. . . . . .244 F6
Beechwood Rd TQ13 . .123 C6
Beechwood Rise PL6 . .245 C1
Beechwood Terr PL4 . .248 B8
Beechwood Way PL7 . .251 D5
Bee Farm Mws EX36. . .158 C5
Beeley Orch EX16 . . . .161 C8
Beenleigh Cross TQ9 . .139 D6
BEER 191 E5
Beerash Cross EX16 . . .63 B4
Beer CE Prim Sch
  EX12. . . . . .191 C5
Beer Cross EX20 . . . . . .94 C6
Beere Cross EX36 . . . . .32 C5
Beer Heights Light Rly ★

Beer Hill
  Clawton EX22 . . . . . . .72 B1
  Seaton EX12 . . . . . . .191 E6
Beerhill La EX20 . . . . . .76 F5
Beer La
  Burlescombe EX16 . . . .51 B2
  Dulverton TA22 . . . . . .33 B5
  Puddington EX16 . . . . .62 C6
  Zeal Monachorum EX17 . 78 C7
Beer Quarry Caves ★
  EX12. . . . . .191 A5
Beer Rd EX12 . . . . . . .191 E6
Beers Cotts EX6 . . . . .181 B2
Beers Hill EX17 . . . . . .79 A5
BEESANDS 149 E7
Beesands TQ7 . . . . . . .149 E7
BEESON 149 D7
Beeson Cross TQ7 . . . .149 D7
Beeson Pool TQ7 . . . . .149 C8
Beeson Wlk 6 PL6 . . . .249 C7
Beetham La EX35 . . . . .69 E6
Beetland La EX35 . . . . .151 D2
Beetor Cross TQ13 . . . .111 B3
Beggar's Bush TQ10. . .134 F2
Beggars La EX14 . . . . .166 A5
Beggars Roost EX35. . .151 E6
Behind Hayes EX9. . . . .198 E7
Bekhams Tree Cross
  EX6. . . . . .113 B2
Belair Rd PL2 . . . . . . .248 C7
Belaire Dr EX31. . . . . .154 E7
Bellaire EX31. . . . . . . .154 E7
Bellamarsh La TQ13 . .123 C4
Bellamy Cl PL6. . . . . . .245 A1
Bellamys The EX20. . . . .76 C5
Bella Vista Rd TQ5 . . .230 C6
Bell Cl PL7. . . . . .250 F6
Bell Ct EX4 . . . . .261 A3
Belle Acre Cl PL3 . . . . .248 F6
Belle Ave EX17 . . . . . .165 B5
Belle Cross Rd TQ7. . . .258 E6
Belle Ct EX17 . . . . . . .165 B5
Belle Hill TQ7 . . . . . . .258 E6
Belle Isle Dr EX2 . . . . .261 C1
Belle Meadow Ct 22
  EX32. . . . . .154 F5
Belle Meadow Rd 10
  EX32. . . . . .155 A5
Belle Parade EX17 . . . .165 D5
BELLEVER 120 B4
Bellever Cl 2 PL20. . . .128 B8
Bellever Tor 5 TQ5 . . .229 F2
Belle View EX22 . . . . .164 C4
Belle View Terr TA20. . .88 C8
Belle Vue
  Axminster EX13 . . . . .167 D6
  Chawleigh EX18 . . . . .60 A7
  Holsworthy TA20. . . . . .72 A6
  Holsworthy TA20. . . . .164 C4
Belle Vue Ave
  Lynton EX35 . . . . . . .151 B5
  Plymouth PL9 . . . . . .255 B5
Belle Vue Cl PL21 . . . . .136 D2
Belle Vue Cotts EX22 .164 C4
Belle Vue Cross
  Great Torrington EX38 . .41 F7
  Great Torrington EX38 . .42 A8
  Great Torrington EX38 .159 F7
Belle Vue Dr PL9 . . . . .255 B5
Belle Vue Rd
  Exeter EX4 . . . . .173 A2
  Exmouth EX8. . . . . . .202 A8
  Kingsbridge TQ7 . . . . .258 D5
  Paignton TQ4 . . . . . .226 C5
  Plymouth PL9 . . . . . .255 C5
  Saltash PL12 . . . . . . .242 F2
Belle Vue Rise
  Plymouth PL9 . . . . . .255 B5
Bellevue Sq PL11 . . . . .247 B2
Belle Vue Terr
  Bideford EX39. . . . . .156 F2
  Cullompton EX15 . . . .163 C4
  Gunnislake PL18. . . . .125 D6
  Kenford EX6 . . . . . . .114 D4
Bellflower Cl PL6 . . . . .241 C1
Bellgate EX17 . . . . .79 A2
Bellingham Cres PL7 . .251 C4
Belliver Ind Est PL6 . . .241 B1
Belliver Way PL6. . . . . .241 B1
Bell La
  Hennock TQ13. . . . . .123 A7
  Paignton TQ3 . . . . . .225 B7
Bell Mdw EX16. . . . . . .64 A2

Bellrock Cl TQ2 . . . . . . 214 B3
Bells Cl EX18 . . . . 60 A7
Bell St EX9 . . . . 198 F7
Belmont EX32 . . . . 155 A5
Belmont Ave
  Combe Martin EX34 . . . . . 2 F4
  Ilfracombe EX34 . . . . . . 150 A5
Belmont Cl
  ⁴ Kingsteignton
  TQ12 . . . . 123 F1
  Tiverton EX16 . . . . 161 D5
Belmont Ct ⁸ PL3 . . . . . 248 A4
Belmont Ho
  Exeter EX4 . . . . 261 C4
  ⁶ Seaton EX12 . . . . 192 A5
Belmont Pl PL3 . . . . 248 A4
Belmont Rd
  Barnstaple EX32 . . . . . . 155 B6
  Brixham TQ5 . . . . 230 C4
  Exeter EX1 . . . . 261 C4
  Ilfracombe EX34 . . . . . . 150 A5
  Ivybridge PL21 . . . . 237 C4
  Tiverton EX16 . . . . 161 D5
  Torquay TQ1 . . . . 220 C6
Belmont St PL1 . . . . 262 B3
Belmont Terr
  Exmouth EX8 . . . . 196 C1
  Totnes TQ9 . . . . 223 C6
Belmont Villas ⁸
PL2 . . . . 248 A3
Belmont Wy ⁸ EX16 . 161 D4
BELSFORD 222 B3
BELSTONE 94 D4
Belstone Cl PL5 . . . . . . 244 A3
Belstone Cnr Cross
EX20 . . . . 76 E1
Belstone Cross EX20 . . . 94 E4
Bel Tor Cnr TQ13 . . . . . 129 F8
Beltor Cross TQ12 . . . . . 211 D1
Belvedere Cl EX3 . . . . . 182 E6
Belvedere Ct
  ⁵ Dawlish EX7 . . . . 204 E6
  ³ Wellington TA21 . . . . 160 D6
Belvedere Pk EX2 . . . . . 113 F5
Belvedere Rd
  Exmouth EX8 . . . . 202 A7
  Ilfracombe EX34 . . . . . . 150 B6
  Newton Abbot TQ12 . . . 206 E5
  Plymouth PL4 . . . . 249 B2
Belvidere Meadows
  Nature Reserve ★
  EX4 . . . . 173 A3
Belvidere Rd EX4 . . . . . 173 B2
Belvoir Rd EX39 . . . . . . 156 F2
Benbow St PL2 . . . . 247 F4
Bench Tor Cl TQ2 . . . . . 219 B7
Bendarroch Rd EX11 . . 168 D5
Bendibus Cross EX22 . . . 72 E2
Bendibus Hill EX21 . . . . . 72 E3
Bendle La EX36 . . . . 30 E8
Bendle Lane Cross
EX36 . . . . 30 E8
Bendley Hill EX16 . . . . . . 46 E1
Benedict Cl TQ14 . . . . . 210 C2
Benedicts Ct TQ12 . . . . 122 F1
Benedicts Rd TQ12 . . . . 122 F1
Benedict Way ²
PL21 . . . . 137 E2
Ben Jonson Cl TQ2 . . . 219 D6
Benlears Acre ¹³
TQ12 . . . . 122 F1
Benley Cross EX18 . . . . . 45 D2
BENNACOTT 89 B3
Bennah Hill EX6 . . . . . . 113 A3
Bennets La PL12 . . . . . . 242 F3
Bennett Cl EX2 . . . . 181 B8
Bennett Rd TQ8 . . . . . . 259 D3
Bennetts Cl EX12 . . . . . 190 E4
Bennett's Cross TQ9 . . 139 C8
Bennetts Hill EX10 . . . . 187 F7
Bennett Sq EX4 . . . . . . 178 A8
Bennett St PL1 . . . . 247 E1
Benning Ct EX31 . . . . . . 154 C6
Bens Cl TQ7 . . . . 147 D7
Benson Cl EX16 . . . . 46 E1
Benson Dr EX39 . . . . . . 157 A6
BENTON 18 B7
Benton Cross EX32 . . . . . 18 B7
Benton La EX31 . . . . 18 B7
Benton Rd EX32 . . . . 18 B8
BENTWICHEN 19 C4
Ben Venue Cl TQ1 . . . . 220 C5
Berachah Rd TQ1 . . . . . 220 B6
BERE ALSTON 125 E1
Bere Alston Prim Sch
PL20 . . . . 125 D1
Bere Alston Sta PL20 . 125 E2
Berea Rd TQ1 . . . . 220 C6
BERE FERRERS 239 E3
Bere Ferrers Sta
PL20 . . . . 239 E3
Bere Hill EX7 . . . . 204 B6
Beresford St PL2 . . . . . 248 A4
Berkeley Ave TQ2 . . . . 213 C1
Berkeley Pl ⁶ EX34 . . 150 B5
Berkeley Rise TQ2 . . . . 213 C1
Berkeley Sq TQ2 . . . . . 244 F3
Berkeley Way PL21 . . . 237 C4
Berkshire Cl TQ12 . . . . 211 F8
Berkshire Dr
  Exeter EX4 . . . . 176 E4
  Plymouth PL2 . . . . 247 F5
Bernadette Cl EX4 . . . . 174 C1
Berner's Cross EX19 . . . 58 F4
Bernice Cl PL4 . . . . 249 B4

Bernice Terr PL4 . . . . . 249 B4
Berretts Way TQ12 . . . 123 A1
Berrow Park Rd PL3 . . 248 E6
Berryball Cl EX20 . . . . . 170 C6
Berrybrook Mdw
EX6 . . . . 182 B3
Berry Cl
  Abbotskerswell TQ12 . . 212 B6
  Exmouth EX8 . . . . 202 E8
  Salcombe TQ8 . . . . 259 C4
Berry Cottage La TA20 . 69 A2
Berry Cotts EX6 . . . . . . 182 B3
Berry Cross
  Dunsford EX6 . . . . 112 C8
  Langtree EX38 . . . . 41 B1
  Shebbear EX21 . . . . 55 D5
Berrydown Cross EX34 . . 2 F1
Berry Down Cross EX34 . 9 F6
Berry Dr TQ3 . . . . 226 A6
Berry Head Country Pk ★
TQ5 . . . . 231 A5
Berry Head Gdns
PL6 . . . . 244 E1
Berry Head National
  Nature Reserve ★
  TQ5 . . . . 231 A6
Berry Head Rd TQ5 . . 230 E6
Berry Hill
  Beer EX12 . . . . 191 D5
  Bishopsteignton TQ14 . 208 F8
  Branscombe EX12 . . . . . 190 A4
  North Tawton EX20 . . . . 59 C1
Berry La
  Axminster EX13 . . . . 88 F3
  Beer EX12 . . . . 191 D6
  Combe Martin EX34 . . . . 2 F4
  Dunsford EX6 . . . . 112 C8
  Gunn EX32 . . . . 17 F4
  Kingsteignton TQ12 . . . 207 E6
Berry Mdw TQ12 . . . . . 207 E6
BERRYNARBOR 2 E3
Berrynarbor Pk EX34 . . 2 E3
Berrynarbor (VC) Prim
  Sch EX34 . . . . 2 E3
Berry Park Cl PL9 . . . . 255 E6
Berry Park Rd PL9 . . . 255 E7
Berry Pk PL12 . . . . 242 D4
BERRY POMEROY 217 D1
Berry Pomeroy Castle ★
TQ9 . . . . 217 D1
Berry Pomeroy Parochial
  CE Prim Sch TQ9 . . . . 224 D7
Berry Rd
  Barnstaple EX32 . . . . . 155 C4
  Braunton EX33 . . . . 152 E7
  Paignton TQ3 . . . . 225 F6
BERRYSBRIDGE 81 E4
Berry's Ground La EX31 4 C5
Berrys Meadow EX17 . . 95 F7
Berry Sq TQ4 . . . . 226 C6
Berrys Wood TQ12 . . . . 206 F3
Berthon Rd PL5 . . . . . . 247 C8
Berwick Ave PL5 . . . . . 244 E3
Besigheim Pl ¹⁰
TQ12 . . . . 207 B3
Besigheim Way TQ12 207 F4
Besley Cl EX16 . . . . 161 F3
Besley Ct EX2 . . . . 177 B3
Besshill La EX31 . . . . 10 F3
Best Pk EX5 . . . . 99 A6
Bestridge Mdw EX32 . . 18 A8
Bests La
  Great Torrington EX38 . . 41 D6
  Great Torrington EX38 . 159 D5
Best's La EX38 . . . . 159 D5
Betham Hill EX16 . . . . . . 46 F2
Bethany Gdns PL2 . . . . 248 A5
Bethel Cross TQ12 . . . . 122 C1
Bethel Terr ¹ TQ1 . . . 220 B5
Betjeman Cl EX10 . . . . 187 F8
Betjeman Wlk PL5 . . . . 244 C3
Betjemen Dr EX8 . . . . . 196 C3
Betony Dr TQ12 . . . . . . 206 C5
Betony Rise EX2 . . . . . . 178 C3
Betton Way TQ13 . . . . . 111 F5
Betton Way Ind Est
TQ13 . . . . 111 E5
Bettys Mead
  Exeter EX4 . . . . 174 A1
  Exeter EX4 . . . . 178 A8
Beuvron Cl EX39 . . . . . . 38 F8
Bevan Rd
  Barnstaple EX32 . . . . . 155 A5
  Exeter EX1 . . . . 178 C7
Beverley Cl EX2 . . . . . . 178 B4
Beverley Gdns ⁶
TQ13 . . . . 131 A5
Beverley Rd PL3 . . . . . . 249 C4
Beverley Rise TQ5 . . . . 230 B4
Beverley Way TQ12 . . . 207 A2
Beverston Way PL6 . . . 245 B8
Bevil Cl EX39 . . . . 157 A1
Bevin Sq EX17 . . . . 79 A6
Beweys Pk PL12 . . . . . 242 C2
Bewhay Gdns TQ9 . . . . 222 F8
Bewick Ave EX3 . . . . . . 182 E6
Bewley Down Rd
TA20 . . . . 69 D3
Bewsley Hill EX17 . . . . . 79 B5
Bexley La ⁵ TQ2 . . . . . 219 F5
Beyrout Pl ⁶ PL1 . . . . 247 F3
Bhutan Cl EX14 . . . . . . 166 D5
Bias La ⁴ EX33 . . . . . . 152 D6

Bibors Hill TA4 . . . . 35 E4
Bicclescombe Ct
EX34 . . . . 150 B4
Bicclescombe Gdns
EX34 . . . . 150 B4
Bicclescombe Park Rd
EX34 . . . . 150 B4
Bickell Cross EX32 . . . . . 28 C6
Bickern Rd PL11 . . . . . . 247 B3
BICKERTON 149 D5
Bickerton Top TQ7 . . . 149 C5
Bickfont Hill EX11 . . . . . 11 F4
Bickford La ² TQ14 . 210 C3
Bickfords Gn ¹⁴
TQ12 . . . . 122 F1
BICKHAM 241 A7
Bickham La EX16 . . . . . . 47 E7
Bickham Park Rd
PL3 . . . . 248 D7
Bickham Rd PL5 . . . . . . 243 D7
BICKINGCOTT 31 B7
Bickingcott Cross
EX36 . . . . 31 C7
Bickingcott Hill EX36 . 31 C8
BICKINGTON
  Ashburton 131 D7
  Barnstable 154 B4
Bickington Lodge
EX31 . . . . 16 A3
Bickington Pk EX31 . . . 154 A3
Bickington Rd EX31 . . . 154 C3
BICKLEIGH
  Plymouth 132 A5
  Tiverton 64 A1
Bickleigh Castle ★
EX16 . . . . 63 F1
Bickleigh Cl
  Exeter EX4 . . . . 174 D2
  Plymouth PL6 . . . . 245 A1
Bickleigh Down Bsns Pk
PL6 . . . . 245 D8
Bickleigh Down CE Prim
  Sch PL6 . . . . 245 D7
Bickleigh Down Rd
PL6 . . . . 241 D1
Bickleigh Mill ★ EX16 . 63 F2
Bickleigh-on-Exe CE
  Prim Sch EX16 . . . . 64 A2
BICKLETON 153 C3
Bickleton Cross
EX31 . . . . 153 A2
Bickley Mill Cross
TQ12 . . . . 212 C1
Bickley Rd TQ12 . . . . . 212 C2
Bickwell House La
EX10 . . . . 187 E5
Bickwell La EX10 . . . . . 187 F5
Bickwell Valley EX10 187 F4
Bickwell Cross EX36 . . . 46 D8
Bicton Cl PL6 . . . . 245 D1
Bicton Coll EX9 . . . . . . 186 C1
Bicton Gdns EX9 . . . . . 198 C8
Bicton Park Botanical
  Gdns ★ EX9 . . . . 198 C8
Bicton Pk
  Bicton EX9 . . . . 186 B2
  Bicton EX9 . . . . 198 A8
Bicton Pl
  Exeter EX1 . . . . 177 F6
  Exmouth EX8 . . . . 202 A6
Bicton St
  Barnstaple EX32 . . . . . 155 A5
  Exmouth EX8 . . . . 202 A6
Bicton Villas EX8 . . . . . 202 B6
Bidbrooke La EX36 . . . . 32 A6
Biddacott Cross EX37 . 28 C4
Biddamoor La EX19 . . . 42 C2
Bidders Cl TQ6 . . . . 146 B7
Bidders Ct EX36 . . . . . . 158 C4
Bidders Wlk TQ6 . . . . . 146 B7
Biddiblack Way
TQ6 . . . . 157 C2
Biddick Dr PL2 . . . . 247 F6
Biddington Way
EX14 . . . . 166 A4
Biddlecombe Cross
TQ13 . . . . 124 A6
Biddypark La EX2 . . . . 113 F6
Biddypark Lane Cross
EX2 . . . . 113 F6
BIDEFORD 156 E3
Bideford Arts Ctr ★
EX39 . . . . 157 A2
Bideford Coll EX39 . . . 156 E1
Bideford Com Hospl
EX39 . . . . 156 F2
Bideford Wlk PL6 . . . . 249 E8
Bidmead Cl EX8 . . . . . . 202 E7
Bidna La EX39 . . . . 157 B8
Bidwell Brook Dr
TQ4 . . . . 226 C1
Bidwell Brook Sch
TQ9 . . . . 215 F1
Bidwell Cross
  Langford EX5 . . . . 172 E8
  Thorverton EX5 . . . . 81 E6
Bidwell La
  Brampford Speke EX5 . . 81 C1
  Thorverton EX5 . . . . 81 F6
Bidwell Wlk TQ4 . . . . . 226 B1
Biera View TQ13 . . . . . 111 A6
Bigadon La TQ11 . . . . 236 C4
BIGBURY 142 F5
Bigbury Ct TQ7 . . . . . . 142 F5
BIGBURY-ON-SEA 142 F4
Bigbury Way TQ2 . . . . 214 B2
Bigbury Wlk PL6 . . . . . 249 E8
Biggin Hill PL5 . . . . 243 F4

BIG Sheep (Farm Pk)
  The ★ EX39 . . . . 156 B1
Bilberry Pl TQ3 . . . . . . 225 D2
Bilbie Cl EX15 . . . . 163 B3
Bilbury St PL4 . . . . 263 A3
BILLACOMBE 255 F8
Billacombe Rd PL9 . . . 249 E1
Billacombe Villas
PL9 . . . . 255 F8
Bill Douglas Centre for
  the History of Cinema &
  Popular Culture (Mus) ★
  EX4 . . . . 177 B8
Billhole La EX17 . . . . 61 C6
Billings Cl PL6 . . . . 244 D6
Billington Cl PL6 . . . . . 249 B7
Bilton Terr ⁷ EX39 . . 156 F1
Biltor Rd TQ12 . . . . 211 D1
Bilver Cross TQ12 . . . . 217 C8
Bimbom La EX13 . . . . . 103 C8
Bindon Rd EX4 . . . . 174 E2
Binford St EX1 . . . . 178 B6
Bingfield Cl TQ1 . . . . . 220 C5
Bingham Cres EX32 . . . 155 B4
Bingwell Ho EX16 . . . . 161 F3
Binhamy Rd EX23 . . . . . 70 A8
Binkham Hill PL20 . . . . 127 A3
Binnamore Cross
TQ10 . . . . 134 E4
Binneford Cross EX17 . 96 F8
Binneford Hill EX17 . . . 62 B2
Bircham Valley Nature
  Reserve PL6 . . . . 245 B3
Bircham View PL6 . . . . 245 C1
Birchanger Cross
EX36 . . . . 31 C7
Birch Cl PL6 . . . . 245 E7
Birch Cross
  Doddiscombsleigh
  EX6 . . . . 113 D8
  Yarcombe EX14 . . . . 69 A4
  Zeal Monachorum EX17 . 78 B8
Birch Ct EX2 . . . . 178 A4
Birch End EX5 . . . . 99 C5
Birchenbeer Cnr EX17 61 C1
Birchen La
  Highampton EX20,
  EX21 . . . . 74 E5
  ⁷ Tiverton EX16 . . . . . 161 C3
Birchen Tree Cross
EX15 . . . . 66 C4
Birches The PL6 . . . . . . 245 D6
Birchfield Ave PL2 . . . . 248 B6
Birch Gr EX11 . . . . 168 D3
BIRCHILL 88 A5
Birchill Cross EX13 . . . . 88 A6
Birch La
  Barnstaple EX31 . . . . . 154 C2
  Landkey EX32 . . . . 17 D3
  Morchard Bishop EX17 . 61 A2
  Stoke Rivers EX32 . . . . . 17 F6
  Stoke Rivers EX32 . . . . . 18 A6
  Zeal Monachorum EX17 . 78 A8
Birchland Rd PL7 . . . . . 133 A4
Birchland Way PL7 . . . 136 A8
Birchlea TQ13 . . . . 180 C4
Birchman's Cross
EX17 . . . . 78 E1
Birchpark La EX20 . . . . 77 B4
Birch Pond Rd PL9 . . . 255 D7
Birch Rd
  Landkey EX32 . . . . 17 B2
  Lympstone EX8 . . . . . . 195 F5
  Newton Abbot TQ12 . . . 207 F1
  Wellington TA21 . . . . . 160 E5
Birch Way EX5 . . . . 99 B6
Birch Wlk TQ2 . . . . 219 C8
Birchwood Cl
  Tavistock PL19 . . . . . . 171 C3
  Totnes TQ9 . . . . 223 E4
Birchwood Gdns PL7 251 A7
Birchwood Rd
  Buckland St Mary
  TA20 . . . . 69 B8
  Exmouth EX8 . . . . 196 D2
Birchy Barton Hill
EX1 . . . . 178 B6
Birdcage La EX11 . . . . . 168 E8
Birdie Walk EX2 . . . . . . 178 C1
Birdshaven TQ2 . . . . . . 219 E5
Birdswell La EX24 . . . . . . 2 D3
Birdwood Cres EX39 . . 156 F1
Birkbeck Cl PL7 . . . . . . 250 E7
Birkdale Cl PL12 . . . . . 242 C2
Birkett Cl EX2 . . . . 178 C4
Birks Halls of Residence
EX4 . . . . 173 A1
Birlea Business Pk
EX23 . . . . 70 B8
BISCOMBE 67 F8
Biscombe Cross TA3 . . 67 E8
Biscombe Gdns PL12 243 A2
BISH MILL 30 E4
Bishmill Gate EX36 . . . . 30 E4
Bishop Cornish CE Prim
  Sch PL12 . . . . 242 F1
Bishop Ct ² EX24 . . . 103 A4
Bishop Pasterfield Ho ⁴
EX2 . . . . 261 B2
Bishops Ave TQ14 . . . . 208 F8
Bishops Cl
  Ivybridge PL21 . . . . . . 237 E6
  Saltash PL12 . . . . 242 E3
  Starcross EX6 . . . . 201 B8
Bishop's Clyst EX5 . . . 179 A3
Bishops Court Ind Est
EX2 . . . . 178 E4

Bishop's Court La
EX5 . . . . 179 C4
Bishops Ct TQ14 . . . . . 208 F8
Bishops Dr EX17 . . . . . . 79 A6
Bishop's Hill TA21 . . . . . 51 B7
Bishops Mdw EX17 . . . . 61 A2
Bishops Mead ⁸
TQ10 . . . . 134 F3
BISHOPS NYMPTON . . 31 A2
Bishops Nympton
EX36 . . . . 31 C1
Bishop's Nympton Cross
EX36 . . . . 30 F1
Bishops Nympton Prim
  Sch EX36 . . . . 30 F2
Bishop's Pl
  Paignton TQ3 . . . . 226 B6
  Plymouth PL1 . . . . 262 B1
Bishops Rise
  Kentisbeare EX15 . . . . . 66 A3
  Torquay TQ1 . . . . 221 A4
BISHOP'S TAWTON . . 16 F1
Bishop's Tawton Prim Sch
  ¹² EX32 . . . . 16 E1
Bishop's Tawton Rd
  Barnstaple EX32 . . . . . 155 B2
  Bishop's Tawton EX32 . . 16 E1
BISHOPSTEIGNTON . 208 E7
Bishopsteignton Mus of
  Rural Life ★ TQ14 . . . 209 A8
Bishopsteignton Rd
TQ14 . . . . 209 D6
Bishopsteignton Sch
TQ14 . . . . 208 F8
Bishopstone Gdns
TQ3 . . . . 226 C8
Bishops Way ⁸ EX1 . 178 E3
BISHOPSWOOD 69 C7
Bishops Wy EX2 . . . . . 178 E3
Bishop Westall Ho ⁶
EX2 . . . . 261 B2
Bishop Westall Rd
EX2 . . . . 178 A2
Bishop Wilfrid Rd
TQ14 . . . . 209 D8
Bitney La TQ12 . . . . . . 212 C5
BITTADON 9 C4
Bittadon La EX31 . . . . . . 9 C4
BITTAFORD 137 C8
Bittaford Terr ²
PL21 . . . . 137 C7
Bittaford Wood ⁶
PL21 . . . . 137 C7
Bittam's La TQ9 . . . . . . 217 B4
Bittern Ind Units EX2 178 E5
Bittern Rd EX1 . . . . 178 E6
Bittery Cross EX5 . . . . . 84 B2
Bittescombe La TA4 . . . 35 B6
Bitthams La PL18 . . . . . 125 C2
Bitton Ave TQ14 . . . . . 210 B5
Bitton Ct TQ14 . . . . . . 210 A5
Bitton Park Rd ¹³
TQ14 . . . . 210 B5
Blachford Cl PL21 . . . . 133 C2
Blachford Rd PL21 . . . 237 C5
Blackabrook Ave
  Princetown PL20 . . . . . 119 A1
  Princetown PL20 . . . . . 128 A8
Blackacre Rd EX24 . . . 102 C6
Blackalder Terr PL7 . . . 132 F4
Blackaller La EX16 . . . . 33 C1
Blackall Rd EX4 . . . . . . 261 B4
Black-a-Tor Copse
  National Nature
  Reserve ★ EX20 . . . . . 108 E8
BLACKAWTON 139 F2
Blackawton Prim Sch
TQ9 . . . . 139 E2
Blackball La TQ5 . . . . . 230 C6
Blackberry Cl
  Plymouth PL9 . . . . 255 E8
  Totnes TQ9 . . . . 223 E4
Blackberry Ct TA21 . . . 160 D4
Blackberry La
  Bigbury TQ7 . . . . 142 E6
  Plymouth PL9 . . . . 255 E8
Blackberry Way ⁶
TQ12 . . . . 123 F1
Blackbird Cres PL15 . . 105 A2
BLACKBOROUGH 66 D4
Blackboy Rd EX1 . . . . . 177 E7
Blackbrook Ave TQ4 . . 226 B1
Blackbrook Cl PL20 . . . 127 B4
Blackbrook Wlk TQ4 . 226 B1
Blackditch Cross EX17 60 B1
Blackditch La EX17 . . . 78 B8
BLACK DOG 61 E4
Black Dog Cross EX17 . 61 E4
Blackdown Bsns Pk
TA21 . . . . 160 E6
Blackdown Cross
  Cornworthy TQ9 . . . . . 139 E4
  Loddiswell TQ7 . . . . . . 138 B2
  Tedburn St Mary EX17 . 97 E8
Blackdown La
  Halwill TQ9 . . . . 139 D4
  Tedburn St Mary EX4 . . 98 C5
Blackdown Mdw
TA21 . . . . 160 F7
Blackdown Pk EX15 . . 162 C5
Blackdown Rd TA21 . . 160 B4
Blackdown View
  ² Hemyock EX15 . . . . . 67 B8
  Sampford Peverell EX16 50 C1
Blackenway La TQ12 . 213 B7
Blackerton Cross
EX16 . . . . 32 E3
Blackett Cl PL21 . . . . . 237 E4

Blackeven Cl PL6 . . . . . 241 D1
Blackeven Hill PL6 . . . . 241 E1
Blackfriars La PL1 . . . . 263 A2
Black Gate
  Challacombe EX31 . . . . . 11 F4
  Holemoor EX22 . . . . 73 B8
Blackgate Cross EX39 . 26 C7
Blackhall Gdns PL6 . . . 244 D6
Black Hat La EX6 . . . . . 176 B3
Blackhaven Cl TQ4 . . . 229 B8
Blackhayes La EX14 . . . 68 F1
BLACKHORSE 179 B7
Black Horse Cnr EX18 . 59 C4
Blackhorse La EX5 . . . 179 B8
Black La
  Hemyock EX15 . . . . 52 D2
  Holcombe Rogus TA21 . . 50 E6
  Peter Tavy PL19 . . . . . 118 E7
Blacklands PL7 . . . . 133 A1
Blackler's Land Cross
TQ9 . . . . 216 B5
Blackley La TQ13 . . . . . 113 D1
Black Lion Ct ⁹
EX14 . . . . 166 C6
BLACKMOOR 52 E5
BLACKMOOR GATE . . . 11 A6
Blackmoor Rd TA21 . . 160 F4
Blackmoor's Path
EX35 . . . . 151 B5
Blackmore Ave EX39 . 156 D1
Blackmore Cres PL6 . 244 D6
Blackmore Ct EX8 . . . . 196 C1
Blackmore Dr EX10 . . . 188 B4
Blackmore Mews
EX2 . . . . 178 C4
Blackmore Rd
  Exeter EX5 . . . . 99 A1
  Tiverton EX16 . . . . 161 F3
Blackmore Theatre ★
EX8 . . . . 202 A6
BLACKPOOL 122 F1
Blackpool CE Prim Sch
TQ12 . . . . 122 F1
BLACKPOOL CORNER 88 D1
Blackpool Cross EX17 . 78 D4
Blackpool Gdns ★
TQ6 . . . . 146 A7
Blackpool Hill TQ6 . . . 146 A6
Blackpool La EX36 . . . . 29 C4
Blackpool Rd EX17 . . . . 78 D4
Blackpool Valley Rd
TQ6 . . . . 146 A7
Blackpost Cross
  Kingston TQ7 . . . . 142 C7
  Totnes TQ9 . . . . 223 F6
  Totnes, Littlehempston
  TQ9 . . . . 217 A2
Blackpost La TQ9 . . . . 223 F5
Blackridge Cross
TQ7 . . . . 258 F8
Blacksmith La TQ13 . . 131 D1
Blacksmiths Cnr EX17 81 A6
Blackstone Cl PL9 . . . . 256 E5
Blackstone Cross
TQ12 . . . . 211 D1
Blackstone Rd TQ12 . . 211 D1
Blackswan Pl ¹¹ EX7 . 204 D6
Black Swan Rd EX7 . . . 200 F2
Blackthorn Ave EX16 . 161 F6
Blackthorn Cl
  Honiton EX14 . . . . 166 C4
  Launceston PL15 . . . . . 105 A3
  Plymouth, Honicknowle
  PL5 . . . . 244 B3
  Plymouth, Woolwell
  PL6 . . . . 245 D6
  Sidmouth EX10 . . . . . . 187 F5
Blackthorn Cres EX1 . 178 C6
Blackthorn Dr PL21 . . 237 E4
Blackthorn La EX5 . . . . 99 B6
Blackthorn Way TQ4 . 225 D4
BLACK TORRINGTON . 74 A8
Black Torrington CE Prim
  Sch EX21 . . . . 74 A8
Blackwalls La EX18 . . . 60 B7
Blackwater La EX13 . . . 88 F3
Blackwater Rd EX15 . . . 66 E8
BLACKWELL 35 B5
Blackwell Cross
  Broadhempston
  TQ13 . . . . 131 D3
  Strete TQ6 . . . . 145 E7
Blackwell La TQ13 . . . 131 D3
Bladder La PL5 . . . . . . 244 E2
Bladon Cl
  Newton Abbot TQ12 . . . 207 D1
  Newton Abbot TQ12 . . . 212 D8
Blagaton Gate EX21 . . 73 B1
Blagdon Cl EX17 . . . . . 165 D5
Blagdon Cl EX17 . . . . . 165 D5
Blagdon Cotts TQ3 . . . 225 B6
Blagdon Cross
  Ashwater EX21 . . . . 90 C7
  Paignton TQ3 . . . . 225 B6
Blagdon Lodge Cross
EX21 . . . . 90 C4
Blagdon Rd TQ3 . . . . . 225 B6
Blagdon Rise EX17 . . . 165 D6
Blagrove Hill EX17 . . . . 46 C3
Blairgowrie Rd PL5 . . . 243 C2
Blair Rd PL21 . . . . 237 D5
Blake Cl TQ1 . . . . 220 B8
Blake Gdns PL5 . . . . . . 244 C3
Blakeland Rd EX31 . . . 153 D5
BLAKEMORE 222 B5
Blakemore Cross
TQ9 . . . . 222 A4
Blakeney Rd PL3 . . . . . 249 D1

Blakes Hill Rd
Landkey EX32 . . . . 17 B2
Swimbridge EX32 . . . . . . 17 D1
Blakeslee Dr
Exeter EX1 . . . . 178 E1
Exeter EX3 . . . . 182 E8
Blakewell Cl EX31 . . . . 154 D1
Blakewell Cross EX37 . 28 E3
Blakewell Hill EX32 . . . 18 E2
Blakey Down La TQ3 . 218 F1
Blamphayne Cross
EX24 . . . . 102 D7
Blanchard Pl 2 PL7 . . 250 E7
Blanchdown Dr PL18 125 C7
Blandford Rd PL3 . . . . 249 C6
Blangy Cl EX20 . . . . 77 C4
Blanksmill Cross
TQ7 . . . . 259 A8
Blatchborough Cross
EX22 . . . . 38 B1
Blatchcombe Dr TQ3 225 F7
Blatchcombe Rd
TQ3 . . . . 226 A7
Blatchford La EX20 . . . . 92 F2
Blatchfords Ct EX20 . . 170 B5
Blatchmore La TQ6 . . 232 C4
Blaxton La PL5 . . . . 240 C2
Bleachfield Rise
EX13 . . . . 167 E6
Blenheim Cl
Newton Abbot TQ12 . . . 207 A5
Torquay TQ1 . . . . 220 E4
Willand EX15 . . . . 162 D5
Blenheim Ct EX2 . . . . . 177 C1
Blenheim Ct EX15 . . . . 162 D5
Blenheim Dr EX15 . . . . 162 D4
Blenheim La EX20 . . . . . 76 C4
Blenheim Rd
Exeter EX2 . . . . 177 B2
Plymouth PL4 . . . . 263 A4
Blenheim Terr TQ13 . . 180 C7
Bligh Cl TQ14 . . . . 210 A8
Blights Hill EX16, TA22 . 33 F3
Blind Acres La EX33 . . . 15 A8
Blind La
Aylesbeare EX5 . . . . 99 E2
Buckland St Mary TA20 . . 69 A8
Exeter EX4 . . . . 173 F5
Huxham EX5 . . . . 174 B8
Stoke Canon EX4 . . . . . . 174 A6
Umborne EX13 . . . . 102 F8
BLINDWELL 252 E5
Blindwell Ave TQ12 . . 207 F7
Blindwell Cres EX5 . . . . 99 C6
Blindwell Farm Cotts
TQ12 . . . . 207 E7
Blindwell Hill PL10 . . . 252 E5
Blindwell La TA4 . . . . . . 34 E6
Blindwylle Rd TQ2 . . . 219 E5
Blogishay La TQ13 . . . 130 F4
Bloomball Cl PL3 . . . . 249 B6
Blossom Cl EX14 . . . . . . 67 C1
Blossom Hill EX14 . . . . . 67 C1
Blue Anchor Cross
EX14 . . . . 84 B4
Blueball Cross EX14 . . . 84 D3
Blueball Hill 18 TQ9 . . 223 C5
Blue Bell TQ9 . . . . 223 C5
Bluebell Ave EX16 . . . . 161 F6
Bluebell Cl
Saltash PL12 . . . . 242 D4
Seaton EX12 . . . . 192 B7
Bluebell Rd EX14 . . . . . . 67 C1
Bluebell St PL6 . . . . . . 245 B2
Bluebell Way
Launceston PL15 . . . . . 105 A2
Tavistock PL19 . . . . 171 E4
Blueberry Downs
EX9 . . . . 199 I2
Blueberry Row TQ3 . . 225 D2
Blue Cedar Ct EX8 . . . 202 B6
Bluecoat Cl EX36 . . . . . 158 B4
Bluecoat Villas EX38 . 159 C5
Blue Gate TA24 . . . . 19 F8
Bluegate Hill PL21 . . . 137 A2
Bluehayes La
Clyst Honiton EX5 . . . . . 175 F3
Rockbeare EX5 . . . . 99 A5
Blue Haze Cl PL6 . . . . . 245 D5
Blue Jay Way EX2 . . . . 177 F6
Blue La EX17 . . . . 96 A3
Blueridge Rd TQ13 . . . 180 C4
Bluett Rd TA21 . . . . 160 D4
Blue Waters TQ13 . . . . 180 C4
Blue Waters Dr
Lyme Regis DT7 . . . . . . 260 B3
Paignton TQ4 . . . . 229 C8
Blue Waters Ind Est
TQ13 . . . . 180 C5
Blundell's Ave EX16 . . 161 F4
Blundells Prep Sch
EX16 . . . . 64 D8
Blundell's Rd
Tiverton EX16 . . . . 161 E4
Tiverton, Cowleymoor
EX15 . . . . 64 D8
Blundell's Sch EX16 . . . 64 D7
Blunt's La PL6 . . . . 245 C3
Blyth Ct EX39 . . . . 156 B6
Blythe Way TQ3 . . . . . 225 D4
Blythwoods Cres 4
TQ1 . . . . 220 B7
Boarden Barn EX8 . . . 202 B6
Boards Ct 16 EX39 . . . . 157 B1
Boasley Cross EX20 . . . 92 E4
Boasley Cross Com Prim
Sch EX20 . . . . 92 E4
Bockland Cl EX15 . . . . 163 A3
Boconnic La PL20 . . . . 127 A3
BODLEY 4 C2
Bodley Cl EX1 . . . . 178 B7
Bodley Cross EX31 . . . . . 4 D1
Bodley La EX31 . . . . 4 C2
Bodmin Rd PL5 . . . . . . 244 D3
Bodmin St EX22 . . . . . . 164 C4
Body Hayes Cl TQ9 . . . 227 F7
Body's Ct PL18 . . . . 125 C6
Bogmoor La EX5 . . . . . . 99 D8
BOGTOWN 92 D8
Bogtown Cross EX20 . . 92 D8
BOHETHERICK 125 B2
BOLBERRY 147 D6
Bolberry Cross TQ7 . . 147 E6
Bolberry Rd TQ7 . . . . . 147 C6
Boldventure PL8 . . . . . 257 F3
Boldventure Cross
EX21 . . . . 91 E6
BOLHAM 161 C8
Bolham Halt Cotts
EX16 . . . . 161 C8
Bolham La EX16 . . . . . 161 D8
Bolham Prim Com Sch
EX16 . . . . 161 C8
Bolham Rd EX16 . . . . . 161 C7
BOLHAM WATER 67 E7
Bolt House Cl PL19 . . . 171 A5
Bolton Ct 8 TQ5 . . . . . 230 C4
Bolton St TQ5 . . . . 230 C4
Bommertown Cross
EX36 . . . . 32 A4
Bonair Cl TQ5 . . . . 230 C3
Bonaventure Cl TQ8 . . 259 D5
Bonaventure Rd TQ8 259 D5
Bondhouse La EX6 . . . . 98 E3
Bond La EX16 . . . . 62 F5
BONDLEIGH 77 B7
Bondleigh Bridge Cross
EX20 . . . . 77 B7
Bondleigh Cross EX20 . 77 B7
Bondleigh Moor Cross
EX20 . . . . 76 F6
Bondleigh Wood Cross
EX20 . . . . 77 B7
Bonds Cross
Chulmleigh EX18 . . . . . . 44 E1
Petrockstow EX20 . . . . . 56 C5
Bonds Farm Meadow
EX37 . . . . 28 B2
Bond's La EX5 . . . . 184 B5
Bonds Mdw TQ13 . . . . 180 C8
Bond St
Beaford EX19 . . . . 42 D2
Cornwood PL21 . . . . . . 133 C2
Plymouth PL6 . . . . 244 E6
Bonehayne and
Purlbridge Rd EX24 102 E5
Bone Mill Cross
TQ12 . . . . 131 F6
Bone St
Tetcott EX22 . . . . 89 F7
Tetcott EX22 . . . . 90 A7
Bonfire Cross EX10 . . . 101 C3
Bonfire Hill
Black Torrington EX21 . . . 74 A8
Salcombe TQ8 . . . . 259 C5
Bonfire La EX5 . . . . 184 C3
Bonhay Cl EX6 . . . . 201 B8
Bonhay Rd
Exeter EX4 . . . . 177 A6
Starcross EX6 . . . . 201 B8
Boniford Cross EX14 . . 87 A4
Bonners Cswy EX13 . . 167 F7
Bonners Dr EX13 . . . . . 167 F6
Bonners Glen EX13 . . . 167 F6
Bonnicott La EX33 . . . . . 7 D1
Bonnington Gr EX1 . . 177 F6
Bonny Cross
Clayhanger EX16 . . . . . . 35 B1
Morebath EX16 . . . . 34 B3
Bonville Cl EX1 . . . . . . 178 B7
Bonville Cres EX16 . . . . 64 D7
Bonville Dr PL21 . . . . . 237 E4
Bonville Rd PL6 . . . . . . 244 E6
Boobery EX16 . . . . 50 D1
Boode Cross EX33 . . . . 152 F7
Boode Rd EX33 . . . . . . 152 F7
Booklands EX32 . . . . . . 18 B2
Boon's Pl PL1 . . . . 262 C4
Booth Way EX8 . . . . . . 196 B2
Borden Gate EX16 . . . . . 50 B8
Border Rd EX14 . . . . . . 166 A5
Boringdon Ave PL5 . . 247 D8
Boringdon Cl PL7 . . . . 250 D7
Boringdon Hill PL7 . . . 250 E7
Boringdon Mill Bsns Ctr
PL7 . . . . 250 F6
Boringdon Pk PL21 . . . 237 A5
Boringdon Prim Sch
PL7 . . . . 250 D7
Boringdon Rd
Plymouth, Plympton
PL7 . . . . 250 D6
Plymouth, Turnchapel
PL9 . . . . 255 A7
Boringdon Terr
Plymouth, Plympton
PL7 . . . . 250 D6
Plymouth, Turnchapel
PL9 . . . . 255 A7
Boringdon Villas PL7 250 D6
BORNE 44 B1
Borne Cross EX37 . . . . . 44 B2
BOROUGH 70 E5
Borough Cl TQ4 . . . . . 225 E3
Borough Cross
Aveton Gifford TQ7 . . . . 143 B7
Borough Cross *continued*
Bridgerule EX22 . . . . 70 E5
Chilsworthy EX22 . . . . . . 53 E2
Newton Tracey EX31 . . . . 27 A3
Woolacombe EX34 . . . . . . 1 B1
Borough Ct PL11 . . . . . 246 E4
Borough La TQ9 . . . . . 144 B6
Borough Park Rd
Paignton TQ3 . . . . 225 E5
Totnes TQ9 . . . . 223 C6
Borough Pk PL11 . . . . 246 E4
Borough Rd
Combe Martin EX34 . . . . . 2 F4
Great Torrington EX38 . 159 E5
Paignton TQ4 . . . . 225 E4
Torquay TQ1 . . . . 214 B1
Borough The PL8 . . . . 257 F4
Borough View EX38 . . 159 E5
Borrowdale Cl PL6 . . . 244 D5
Boscastle Gdns PL2 . . 248 C8
Boscawen Pl
Plymouth PL2 . . . . 247 E4
10 Teignmouth TQ14 . . . 210 B5
Boscundle Row PL12 243 A2
Boshill Hill
Axmouth DT7 . . . . 193 C8
Colyford DT7, EX12 . . . . 103 D3
Bossell Ho TQ11 . . . . . 236 B4
Bossell Pk TQ11 . . . . . 236 B4
Bossell Rd TQ11 . . . . . 236 B5
Bossell Terr TQ11 . . . . 236 B5
Boston Cl PL4 . . . . 255 B7
Bosun Cl EX3 . . . . 182 D7
Bosuns Point TQ4 . . . 226 C4
Boswell Cl PL5 . . . . . . 244 B2
Boswell's La EX20 . . . . 77 D4
Boswell's Lane End
EX20 . . . . 77 D4
Boswell Way EX12 . . . 191 F8
Bothy The DT7 . . . . . . 193 E6
Bottle Bridge Hill
TQ13 . . . . 123 F7
Bottle Hill PL21 . . . . . . 132 E1
Bottle Pk PL21 . . . . 136 B6
Bottom La EX13 . . . . . . 103 D6
Bottompark La TQ2 . . 213 F3
Bottoms La EX33 . . . . . . 8 B2
Bottom's La TQ12 . . . . 213 E4
Bottreaux Mill Cross
EX36 . . . . 32 A5
BOTUSFLEMING 242 B7
Boucher Rd EX9 . . . . . 198 B1
Bouchers Hill EX20 . . . . 77 C5
Boucher's La TA4 . . . . . 35 E4
Boucher Way EX9 . . . . 198 B1
Bouchiers Cl EX20 . . . . 77 C5
Boughmore La EX10 . . 187 F3
Boughmore Rd EX10 . 187 F4
Boughthayes Est
PL19 . . . . 171 A5
Boulden Cl PL7 . . . . . . 251 C5
Boulter Cl PL6 . . . . 241 C1
Boundary Cl TQ12 . . . . 212 F5
Boundary Dr EX23 . . . . . 70 A6
Boundary Pk
Bideford EX39 . . . . 26 F4
Seaton EX12 . . . . 192 A8
Boundary Pl PL6 . . . . . 245 C7
Boundary Rd
Dousland PL20 . . . . 127 B3
Torquay TQ2 . . . . 219 D5
Bounds Cross EX22 . . . . 71 A4
Bounds Pl PL1 . . . . 262 B2
Boundstone Cotts
EX39 . . . . 25 D2
Bound The PL10 . . . . . 253 A1
Boundy's Cross EX17 . . 61 B8
Bounsells La EX20 . . . . 57 A7
Bountice La
Berrynarbor EX34 . . . . . . 2 D2
Berrynarbor EX34 . . . . . . 9 D8
Bourchier Cl 13 EX16 . . 34 B1
Bourchier Dr 12 EX16 . 34 B1
Bourne Bridge Cross
EX36 . . . . 46 A5
Bourne Cl PL3 . . . . 249 D6
Bourne Ct TQ5 . . . . 229 F2
Bourne Rd TQ12 . . . . . 213 A5
Bourn Rise EX4 . . . . . . 174 D2
Bourton La
Littlehempston TQ9 . . . . 216 F1
Totnes TQ9 . . . . 223 E6
Bourton Rd TQ9 . . . . . 223 E6
Bourtons The TQ9 . . . 223 D7
Boutport St (Mermaid
Wlk) 11 EX31 . . . . 154 F6
Boutport St EX31 . . . . 154 F5
Bovacott La EX22 . . . . . 73 C7
Bovemoor's La EX2 . . 178 A4
Bove Park Rd TQ2 . . . . 214 A4
Bovet St TA21 . . . . 160 C6
Bovey Cross
Broadhempston
TQ13 . . . . 131 D3
Moretonhampstead
TQ13 . . . . 111 E3
Bovey Fir Cross EX12 190 F6
BOVEY HEATH 180 E4
Bovey Heathfield Nature
Reserve ★ TQ12 . . . . . 123 A3
Bovey La
Beer EX12 . . . . 191 B7
Broadhempston TQ12,
TQ13 . . . . 131 D3
Bovey Rd TQ13 . . . . . . 123 C4
BOVEY TRACEY 180 D7
Bovey Tracey Heritage
Ctr ★ TQ13 . . . . 180 C7
Bovey Tracey Prim Sch
TQ13 . . . . 180 C8
Bovey Tracey Rd
TQ13 . . . . 122 E7
Boville La PL9 . . . . 256 C7
Bovisand Ct PL9 . . . . . 254 F2
Bovisand Est PL9 . . . . 140 A8
Bovisand La
Down Thomas PL9 . . . . . 255 D2
Staddiscombe PL9 . . . . 255 D3
Bovisand Pk
Down Thomas PL9 . . . . . 255 A1
Heybrook Bay PL9 . . . . . 140 A8
Bovisand Rd PL9 . . . . . 255 E3
BOW
Ashprington 139 F7
Blackawton 145 B8
Copplestone 78 C4
Bow Beer Cross EX17 . . 78 A1
Bowbeer La EX17 . . . . . 78 B1
Bowbridge Cross
TQ9 . . . . 145 B8
Bowcombe Rd
Kingsbridge TQ7 . . . . . . 144 B2
Kingsbridge TQ7 . . . . . . 258 F4
Bow Com Prim Sch
EX17 . . . . 78 C4
Bow Creek TQ9 . . . . . . 139 F6
Bow Cross
Blackawton TQ9 . . . . . . 145 B8
Staverton TQ9 . . . . 216 C7
BOWD 100 F1
Bowd Ct EX10 . . . . 100 E1
BOWDEN 145 F8
Bowden Cnr EX31 . . . . . . 9 F3
Bowden Cotts 12 EX32 . 17 B2
Bowden Cross
Buckland Brewer EX39 . . 40 B8
Drewsteignton EX6 . . . . . 96 E3
Kingsbridge TQ7 . . . . . . 144 C3
Bowden Farmhouse
PL8 . . . . 257 F4
Bowden Gn EX39 . . . . . . 25 E4
Bowden Hill
Ashburton TQ13 . . . . . . 130 F4
Crediton EX17 . . . . 165 D5
Newton Abbot TQ12 . . . 207 C2
Yealmpton PL8 . . . . 257 F4
Bowden Hill Terr 1
EX17 . . . . 165 D5
Bowden La TQ13 . . . . . 123 A7
Bowden Park Rd PL6 245 A1
Bowden Pillars TQ9 . . 223 B3
Bowden Rd TQ12 . . . . . 211 E2
Bowdens Cl TQ13 . . . . 180 C7
Bowdens La
Ideford TQ13 . . . . 124 B4
Shillingford EX16 . . . . . . 34 E3
Bowdens Pk PL21 . . . . 237 C4
Bowdown Cross
TQ10 . . . . 135 C5
Bowe Ct EX1 . . . . 177 E7
Bowen Ct 9 EX33 . . . . 152 D5
Bowerhayes Cross
EX14 . . . . 67 C3
Bowerhayes La EX14 . . 67 C3
Bowering Ct 1 EX32 . 155 B3
Bowerland Ave
Torquay TQ2 . . . . 213 F4
Torquay TQ3 . . . . 214 A4
Bowerland Cross
EX20 . . . . 93 D3
Bowerland Rd EX20 . . . 93 D4
Bowers Park Dr PL6 . . 245 E7
Bowers Rd PL2 . . . . . . 248 B5
Bowerthy La EX17 . . . . 60 D4
Bowhay EX21 . . . . 74 A8
Bowhay Cl EX21 . . . . . . 74 A8
Bowhay La
Combe Martin EX34 . . . . . 3 A3
Exeter EX4 . . . . 176 E4
Bowhays Wlk 2 PL6 . 249 C7
Bowhill EX5 . . . . 83 A7
Bowhill Prim Sch
EX4 . . . . 176 F4
Bow La TQ13 . . . . 111 F4
Bowland Cl TQ4 . . . . . . 226 A2
Bowley Mdw EX5 . . . . . 82 F6
Bowling Gn TQ7 . . . . . 142 F4
Bowling Gn La EX14 . 166 C5
Bowling Gn View
EX15 . . . . 163 B1
Bowling Green Chalets
DT7 . . . . 260 D2
Bowling Green La
Combe Martin EX34 . . . . . 3 A3
Hatherleigh EX20 . . . . . . 75 B7
Bowling Green Rd
EX3 . . . . 183 A4
Bowls Cross
Bigbury TQ7 . . . . 142 F5
Stoke Canon EX4 . . . . 82 C1
Bowmans Mdw EX20 . . 75 C7
Bow Mill La EX17 . . . . . 78 B4
BOWOOD 25 B4
Bowpound Cross EX17 78 B7
Bow Rd TQ9 . . . . 139 C7
Bowring Cl EX1 . . . . . . 178 B7
Bowring Mead TQ13 . 111 F4
Bowring Pk TQ13 . . . . 111 F4
Bowringsleigh Pl
TQ7 . . . . 258 C5
Bow Station Cross
EX17 . . . . 78 C2
Boxfield Rd EX13 . . . . 167 D5
Boxhill Cl PL5 . . . . 244 B3
Boxhill Gdns PL2 . . . . 248 C8
Box's Cnr EX18 . . . . 60 B6
Boyce Pl 3 EX16 . . . . . 161 B4
Boyds Dr TQ14 . . . . . . 210 C5
Boyes Cl EX16 . . . . 65 A7
Boyland Rd EX6 . . . . . 112 D8
Boyne Rd EX9 . . . . 198 A2
BOYTON 89 E2
Boyton Com Prim Sch
PL15 . . . . 89 D3
Bozomzeal Cross
TQ6 . . . . 228 B1
Bracken Cl
10 Honiton EX14 . . . . 85 C2
Newton Abbot TQ12 . . . 212 F8
Plymouth PL6 . . . . 245 D8
Brackendale EX8 . . . . 196 C4
Brackendown EX11 . . 168 D2
Bracken Rise TQ4 . . . . 229 C6
Bracken Way EX7 . . . . 201 A2
Brackenwood EX8 . . . 196 C1
Bradaford Cross EX21 . 90 F6
Bradbury La EX32 . . . . . 29 D6
Bradden Cres TQ5 . . . 230 B4
Braddon Cnr EX16 . . . . 81 D8
Braddons Cliffe TQ1 . 220 B4
Braddons Hill PL7 . . . . 250 B7
Braddons Hill Road E
TQ1 . . . . 220 B4
Braddons Hill Road W
TQ1 . . . . 220 B4
Braddons St TQ1 . . . . 220 B4
BRADFIELD 65 F4
Bradfield Cl PL6 . . . . . 245 E1
Bradfield Rd EX4 . . . . 174 D1
BRADFORD 55 C2
Bradford Cl
Exmouth EX8 . . . . 196 C3
Plymouth PL6 . . . . 249 B7
Bradford Cross EX16 . . 47 A3
Bradford Ct EX39 . . . . 157 A6
Bradford Moor Hill
EX16 . . . . 47 A3
Bradford Prim Sch
EX22 . . . . 73 B8
Bradham Ct EX8 . . . . . 202 D8
Bradham La EX8 . . . . . 202 D8
BRADIFORD 154 D7
Bradiford EX31 . . . . . . 154 E7
Bradley Barton Prim Sch
TQ12 . . . . 206 E3
Bradley Ct 6 TQ12 . . . 207 B3
Bradleyford Cnr
TQ13 . . . . 180 F6
Bradley La TQ12 . . . . . 207 A3
Bradley Lane Ind Est 1
TQ12 . . . . 207 A3
Bradley Manor ★
TQ12 . . . . 206 F2
Bradley Park Rd TQ1 . 214 B1
Bradley Rd
Bovey Tracey TQ13 . . . . 180 E7
Newton Abbot TQ12 . . . 207 A1
Plymouth PL4 . . . . 248 F4
Bradman Way EX2 . . . 177 C2
BRADNINCH 82 F7
Bradninch Cross EX32 17 D4
Bradninch Pl EX4 . . . . 261 B3
Bradridge Cross TQ9 138 D8
Bradridge Ct PL15 . . . . . 89 D4
BRADSTONE 115 D7
BRADWELL 8 D5
Bradwell EX34 . . . . 150 A5
Bradwell Rd EX34 . . . . . . 8 D5
BRADWORTHY 38 E1
Bradworthy Cross
EX22 . . . . 53 D7
Bradworthy Prim Acad
EX22 . . . . 38 E1
Brady Cl EX17 . . . . 80 B5
Braemar Cl PL7 . . . . . . 251 C4
Braeside Mews TQ4 . . 226 C4
Braeside Rd
Paignton TQ4 . . . . 226 C4
Torquay TQ2 . . . . 214 A4
Braggs Hill PL15 . . . . . . 89 E3
Braggs' Hill EX37 . . . . . 43 B7
Brag La PL7 . . . . 132 C6
Brahms Way EX32 . . . . 155 C5
Braid Dr EX16 . . . . 64 E8
Brakefield TQ10 . . . . . 135 A2
Brake Ho TQ12 . . . . . . 207 E2
Brake La PL10 . . . . 252 B5
Brake Rd PL5 . . . . 244 E2
Brakeridge Cl TQ5 . . . 229 C6
Brake Wood Cl EX31 . 153 D5
Bramble Acre EX2 . . . . 191 F8
Bramble Cl
Budleigh Salterton
EX9 . . . . 198 C1
Dartington TQ9 . . . . 222 F8
Plymouth PL3 . . . . 249 B7
Sidmouth EX10 . . . . 188 B8
Torquay TQ2 . . . . 219 D5
Bramble Hill Ind Est
EX14 . . . . 166 B6
Bramble La
Brampford Speke EX5 . . . 81 C1
Crediton EX17 . . . . 165 E6
Honiton EX14 . . . . 166 B5
Bramble Mead EX5 . . . . 99 D2
Brambleoak Cross
TQ12 . . . . 131 E3
Bramble Path 7 EX32 . 17 B2
Brambles The TA21 . . 160 D4
Bramble Wlk
Barnstaple EX31 . . . . . . 154 B3
1 Plymouth PL6 . . . . . . 249 C7
Bramfield Pl PL6 . . . . . 249 D7
Bramleigh Rd PL18 . . . 125 C6
Bramley Ave EX1 . . . . . 178 C6
Bramley Cl
Brixton PL8 . . . . 257 A5
Kenton EX6 . . . . 194 E3
Tiverton EX16 . . . . 161 D7
Wellington TA21 . . . . . . 160 F7
Willand EX15 . . . . 162 D4
Bramley Gdns EX5 . . . . 99 E7
Bramley Mdw EX32 . . . 17 C2
Bramley Rd PL3 . . . . . . 249 C4
Bramleys The EX14 . . 166 E7
Bramley Way EX15 . . . . 66 C6
Brampford Cross
EX5 . . . . 172 F7
BRAMPFORD SPEKE . . 81 E1
Brampford Speke CE
Prim Sch EX5 . . . . 81 E1
Brampton Down Cross
EX16 . . . . 49 F8
Branches Cross EX22 . . 54 E3
Brancker Rd PL2 . . . . . 248 C6
Brand Cl EX14 . . . . 166 C4
Brandiron Cross EX6 123 B7
Brandirons Cnr EX17 . . 79 C5
Brandis Cnr
Little Torrington EX20 . . . 41 F1
North Tawton EX17 . . . . . 77 F1
Petrockstow EX20 . . . . . 56 C6
Rackenford EX16 . . . . . . 47 F1
BRANDIS CORNER 73 B6
Brandis Cross EX20 . . . 95 E4
Brandise Cross EX17 . . 79 C2
Brandise Hill EX20 . . . . 56 F3
Brandis La EX20 . . . . . . 95 E4
Brandis Pk TQ7 . . . . . . 145 C3
Brandize Pk EX20 . . . . 170 B3
Brandon Rd PL3 . . . . . 249 C4
Brand Rd EX14 . . . . 166 C4
Brandreth Rd 3 PL3 . 248 F6
Brandy Wells EX37 . . . . 44 E6
Branksome Cl TQ3 . . . 219 C2
Brannam Cres EX31 . . 154 B2
Brannam Ct EX31 . . . . 154 B2
Brannams Ct 13
EX32 . . . . 155 A4
Brannams Sq 2
EX32 . . . . 155 A4
BRANSCOMBE 190 D3
Branscombe Cl
Colyford EX24 . . . . 103 A3
Exeter EX4 . . . . 176 E5
Torquay TQ1 . . . . 220 D6
Branscombe Cross
EX10 . . . . 101 F1
Branscombe Gdns
PL5 . . . . 244 A3
Branscombe La EX7 . . 200 C3
Branscombe Prim Sch
EX12 . . . . 190 D4
Branscombe Rd EX16 161 F4
Branscombe: The Old
Bakery, Manor Mill &
Forge ★ EX12 . . . . 190 D4
Bransgrove Hill EX18 . . 59 B5
Bransgrove La EX18 . . . 59 B5
Branson Ct 9 PL7 . . . 251 C5
Branson Pk PL19 . . . . . 126 D6
Brantwood Cl TQ4 . . . 226 A4
Brantwood Cres TQ4 226 A3
Brantwood Dr TQ4 . . . 226 A3
BRATTON CLOVELLY . . 92 A2
Bratton Cross EX31 . . . 17 E7
BRATTON FLEMING . . . 18 A8
Bratton Fleming Com
Prim Sch EX31 . . . . 18 A8
Braundsworthy Cross
EX21 . . . . 73 E8
BRAUNTON 152 B6
Braunton Burrows
Biosphere Reserve ★
EX33 . . . . 15 F5
Braunton & District Mus ★
EX33 . . . . 152 D6
Braunton Rd EX31 . . . 154 D7
Braunton Sch & Com Coll
EX33 . . . . 152 E4
Braunton Wlk PL6 . . . 249 E8
Bray Cl
Burlescombe EX16 . . . . . 51 B3
Tavistock PL19 . . . . 171 A5
BRAYFORD 18 F5
Brayford Acad EX32 . . . 18 F5
Brayford Ct PL5 . . . . . . 244 B3
BRAYFORDSHILL 18 E5
Brayhams Terr EX20 . 170 C6
Bray Hill EX32 . . . . 18 F3
Brayley Hill EX32 . . . . . 18 E1
Bray Mill Cross EX37 . . 29 D4
Bray Rd EX22 . . . . 164 C6
Brays Cl EX17 . . . . 165 C5
Braytown Cotts EX32 . . 18 F5
Breach Hill TA21 . . . . . . 51 F5
Breaka La EX19 . . . . 57 E5
Breakneck Cross EX37 28 F5
Breakneck Hill
Chittlehampton EX37 . . . 28 F5
Teignmouth TQ14 . . . . . 124 F2
Breakwater Ct TQ5 . . . 230 E6
Breakwater Hill
Plymouth PL4 . . . . 263 C1
Plymouth PL9 . . . . 255 A8
Breakwater Ind Est
PL9 . . . . 255 C8
Breakwater Rd PL9 . . 255 C8
Brean Down Cl PL3 . . 248 E6

Brean Down Rd PL3 248 E7
Brecon Cl
Bideford EX39 157 D1
East-the-Water EX39 26 A5
Paignton TQ4 225 D4
Plymouth PL3 249 A7
Breech Cotts TA21 51 F5
Bremley Cross EX36 31 F7
BRENDON
Bradworthy 54 B8
Holsworthy Beacon 54 C2
Lynton 6 A5
Brendon Cross EX39 39 F6
Brendon Hill EX17 79 C6
Brendon Rd TA21 160 D7
Brendons Ave TQ2 219 C3
Brendons The EX16 50 D1
Brendon Two Gates
TA24 13 A6
Brennacott Pl EX39 25 D4
Brennacott Rd EX39 25 D4
Brent Cl EX5 184 C3
Brentford Ave PL5 244 B5
Brent Hill PL8 136 D1
Brent Knoll Rd 1
PL3 248 E6
Brent Mill TQ10 135 A2
Brent Mill Ind Est
TQ10 134 F2
Brenton Rd EX6 114 C5
Brentor Cl EX4 176 F8
Brentor Rd
Mary Tavy PL19 117 D6
Plymouth PL4 249 B2
Brent Rd 1 TQ3 226 B6
Brent Tor★ PL19 117 B7
Brest Rd PL6 245 A3
Brest Way PL6 245 A3
Bretonside PL4 263 A2
Breton Way EX8 196 E1
Bretteville Cl
Chagford TQ13 111 A6
Woodbury EX5 184 C3
Brett Wlk PL7 250 F7
Brewer Ave EX13 167 E7
Brewer Rd EX32 155 C4
Brewers Ct EX1 261 A1
Brewers Hill EX39 39 F8
Brewers La EX39 39 F8
Brewery La
12 Brixham TQ5 230 C5
Exeter EX2 177 F5
Sidmouth EX10 188 B5
Brewin Rd EX16 161 C3
Briansway PL12 242 D2
Briar Cl
Exmouth EX8 202 D8
Honiton EX14 166 C3
Briar Cres EX2 177 F2
Briardale Rd PL2 247 F6
Briarleigh Cl PL6 245 F2
Briar Rd PL3 248 F7
Briars Row PL12 242 D4
Briar Tor PL20 127 A3
Briary La TQ1 220 B5
Briary Mews 13 TQ1 220 D4
Brick Cross EX9 198 C7
Brickfields Sp Ctr
PL1 247 F2
Brickhouse Dr EX16 161 D6
Brickhouse Hill
Bolham EX16 49 C1
Tiverton EX16 161 D6
Brick Kiln Cl EX4 174 C1
Brickyard La EX6 201 A8
Brickyard Rd EX5 168 A7
Bridespring Rd EX4 173 F1
Bridespring Wlk EX4 173 F1
BRIDESTOWE 107 F8
Bridestowe Prim Sch
EX20 107 F8
Bridewell Ct 9 EX16 161 C3
Bridewell Ho 11
EX16 161 C3
BRIDFORD 112 F5
Bridford Rd
Christow EX6 113 A4
Exeter EX2 177 C2
BRIDGE BALL 5 E3
Bridge Bldgs 18
EX31 154 F5
Bridge Chambers 15
EX31 154 F5
Bridge Cl EX5 82 D3
Bridge Cotts
Chard Junction TA20 88 D8
East Budleigh EX9 198 B5
4 Exeter EX4 177 D8
Lympstone EX8 195 D5
Bridge Croft TQ13 130 F5
Bridge Cross
Bishops Nympton
EX36 30 F4
Fortescue Cross EX37 44 B4
Bridge Ct EX4 261 A3
BRIDGE END
Aveton Gifford 143 C5
Newton Poppleford 187 A8
Bridge End EX36 31 C5
Bridgefield EX11 169 E4
Bridge Hill
Topsham EX3 182 F5
Topsham EX3 183 A5
Bridgehill Garth EX3 182 F5
Bridge Ho 1 TQ12 207 C4
Bridgehouse Cross
EX15 52 D1
Bridge La
Budlake EX5 82 D3
7 Instow EX39 15 B1
Bridgelands Cl PL5 243 B1
Bridgeland St EX39 157 A2
Bridgeman Pl EX1 174 F2
Bridge Meadow Cl
EX17 60 C2
Bridge Mill La PL21 133 C2
Bridgemoor Cross
EX22 71 B6
BRIDGEND 141 A7
Bridgend Hill PL8 141 A7
Bridge Park La EX31 9 E5
Bridge Pk
Ashwater EX21 90 F6
Bridgerule EX22 70 F5
Ermington PL21 136 F2
Ivybridge PL21 237 D5
Bridge Plats Way
EX39 156 E2
Bridge Rd
Budleigh Salterton
EX9 198 B2
Churston Ferrers TQ5 229 D5
Exeter EX2, EX6 182 A8
Exmouth EX8 202 A8
Kingswear TQ5, TQ6 234 B7
Teignmouth TQ14 210 A3
Torquay TQ2 219 F5
Totnes TQ9 222 F6
BRIDGE-REEVE 59 B8
Bridge Reeve Cross
EX18 59 C8
Bridge Ret Pk TQ2 219 E8
BRIDGERULE 70 F6
Bridgerule CE Prim Sch
EX22 70 F5
Bridgerule Ind Est
EX22 70 E4
Bridgerule Rd TA20 71 C2
Bridgeside TQ9 139 C7
Bridge St
Bideford EX39 157 A1
Buckfastleigh TQ11 236 B5
Dulverton TA22 33 D6
Hatherleigh EX20 75 C7
Ipplepen TQ12 211 D2
Kingsbridge TQ7 258 D5
Lyme Regis DT7 260 E3
Sidbury EX10 101 B2
Tiverton EX16 161 C4
Uffculme EX15 66 A7
Bridges The PL12 242 E1
Bridge Terr
Ashprington TQ9 139 F6
Bampton EX16 34 B1
Bridge The PL1 262 B1
BRIDGETOWN
Launceston 105 A8
Totnes 223 F5
Bridgetown TQ9 223 D5
Bridgetown Ct TQ9 223 D5
Bridgetown Hill TQ9 223 E6
Bridge View EX5 99 C6
Bridge View Cl 2
EX1 178 E3
Bridge Vw PL5 247 D8
Bridgewater Gdns
TQ9 223 E5
Bridgwater Cl PL6 245 B1
Bridle Cl
Paignton TQ4 229 B8
Plymouth PL7 251 B7
Bridle Path The TQ9 223 C4
Bridle Way PL12 242 D4
Bridwell Ave
Uffculme EX15 65 F7
Uffculme EX15 162 F8
Bridwell Cl PL5 247 E8
Bridwell Cres EX15 65 F7
Bridwell Lane N PL5 247 E8
Bridwell Rd PL5 247 E8
BRIGHTLEY 94 B8
Brightley Cross EX20 94 B8
Brightley Rd EX20 170 C8
Bright View EX20 170 A4
Brimacombe Rd
EX39 22 E3
Brim Brook Ct TQ2 219 B8
Brimford Cross EX39 38 A4
Brimhay TQ9 222 F8
Brimhay Bglws TQ9 222 F8
Brim Hill TQ1 214 C5
Brimhill Cl PL7 251 B3
Brimhill La PL19 117 F6
Brimlands TQ5 230 B4
Brimlands Ct TQ5 230 B4
BRIMLEY 88 D3
Brimley Bsns Pk
TQ13 180 C5
Brimley Cnr TQ13 123 F6
Brimley Cross
Bovey Tracey TQ13 180 B5
Hemyock TA3 52 F1
Brimley Ct
Bovey Tracey TQ13 180 B5
Teignmouth TQ14 210 C6
Brimley Dr TQ14 210 C5
Brimley Gdns TQ13 180 C5
Brimley Grange
TQ13 180 B5
Brimley Halt TQ13 180 C5
Brimley Hill EX13 88 D2
Brimley La TQ13 180 A5
Brimley Pk TQ13 180 C5
Brimley Rd
Axminster EX13 88 D3
Bovey Tracey TQ13 180 B5
Brimley Vale TQ13 180 C6
Brimlicombe Mdw
EX1 175 A3
Brimpenny Rd EX8 196 C1
Brimstone La
Rockwell Green
TA21 160 A2
Sampford Arundel TA21 51 F6
Sampford Peverell EX16 50 E2
Brinchcombe Mws 9
PL3 249 D1
Brindifield La EX17 62 A5
Brindiwell Cross EX17 63 B3
Brindiwell Hill EX17 63 B2
Brinkburn Ct EX10 188 A3
Brinscombe Cross
EX13 103 E6
Brinscombe La
Arlington EX31 10 F3
Membury EX13 87 E6
BRINSWORTHY 19 F1
Brinsworthy Cross
EX36 19 F1
Briseham Cl TQ5 230 D3
Briseham Rd TQ5 230 D3
Brismar Wlk 3 PL6 249 C7
Britannia Ave TQ6 233 C3
Britannia Mus★ TQ6 233 E4
Britannia Pl PL4 249 B2
Britannia Row 5
EX34 150 C6
Britannia Royal Naval Coll
TQ6 233 F5
Britannia Way EX39 156 E7
BRITHEM BOTTOM 65 B5
Briticheston Cl PL9 256 A5
Briton St 2 EX16 34 C1
Briton Streetlane
EX6 112 F7
Brittannia Ct TQ6 234 B3
Brittany Rd EX8 196 C4
Britten Dr
Barnstaple EX32 155 B5
Exeter EX2 178 B5
Britton Cl EX16 65 A7
Brittons Cl EX33 152 E5
Brittons The EX33 152 E5
Briwere Rd TQ1 219 E7
BRIXHAM 230 C3
Brixham CE Prim Sch
TQ5 230 D4
Brixham Com Coll
TQ5 230 D4
Brixham Cross TQ5 234 E8
Brixham Enterprise Est
TQ5 230 D4
Brixham Heritage Mus★
TQ5 230 C5
Brixham Hospl TQ5 230 C3
Brixham Rd
Brixham TQ5 230 A3
Churston Ferrers TQ5 229 E4
Kingswear TQ6 234 B3
Paignton TQ4 225 E3
Brixham Theatre★
TQ5 230 C5
Brixham Wlk PL6 249 E8
BRIXINGTON 196 D3
Brixington Dr EX8 196 D1
Brixington La EX8 196 C2
Brixington Prim Sch
EX8 196 C2
BRIXTON
South Hams PL8 256 F4
South Hams PL8 257 A5
Brixton Lodge Gdns
PL8 256 F5
Brixton St Mary's CE Prim
Sch PL8 257 A4
Broadacre Dr TQ5 230 D5
Broad Cl
Crediton EX17 165 A6
North Molton EX36 30 E8
Broadclose Hill EX16 46 F6
Broadclose Rd EX31 154 D3
BROADCLYST 175 C6
Broadclyst Com Prim Sch
EX5 175 C7
Broadclyst Rd EX5 99 D8
Broadclyst Sports Ctr
EX5 175 D5
Broad Croft EX13 87 E8
Broad Down Cl TQ7 147 F6
Broaddown Cross
EX14 86 A1
Broadfield Rd EX32 155 B4
Broadfields Rd EX2 178 C5
Broadgate
Barnstaple EX31 154 E7
Exeter EX1 261 A3
Broadgate Cl
Barnstaple EX31 154 E7
Braunton EX33 152 D6
Broadgate Cres
TQ12 212 F4
Broadgate La EX17 61 B2
Broadgate Rd TQ12 213 A4
Broadhayes Cross
EX14 86 E5
BROADHEMBURY 84 E7
Broadhembury CE Prim
Sch EX14 84 E7
Broadhembury Cross
EX14 84 E7
BROADHEMPSTON 131 F1
Broadhempston Prim Sch
TQ9 131 E1
Broad La
Appledore EX39 14 F1
Braunton EX33 152 A8
Hawkridge TA22 21 D1
Tiverton EX16 161 C3
Broadland Gdns PL9 256 A8
Broadland La PL9 255 F8
BROADLANDS 207 A4
Broadlands
Bideford EX39 157 D1
Northam EX39 156 F8
Teignmouth TQ14 210 A3
Thorverton EX5 81 E4
Broadlands Ave
TQ12 207 A3
Broadlands Cl PL7 251 A3
Broadlands Ct
Bideford EX39 157 D1
Newton Abbot TQ12 207 A3
Broadlands Rd TQ4 226 A4
Broad Lane Head
TA22 21 D1
Broadleaf Cl EX1 178 E8
Broad Leaf Pk
Dawlish TQ14 210 E7
Teignmouth EX7 204 C1
Broadley Ct PL6 241 B2
Broadley Dr TQ2 219 C3
BROADLEY HILL 68 F2
Broadley Ind Pk PL6 241 B2
Broadley Park Rd
PL6 241 B2
Broadmead
Exmouth EX8 196 D2
Woodbury EX5 184 B3
Broadmead Bglws
EX32 155 C2
Broadmead Cross
EX16 48 A5
Broadmeade Ct
TQ12 207 D2
Broadmead Gdns
EX35 151 B5
Broadmeadow Ave
EX4 176 F4
Broadmeadow Ind Est
TQ14 209 D7
Broadmeadow La
TQ14 209 D7
Broadmeadow Sports Ctr
TQ14 209 D7
Broadmeadow View
TQ14 209 D7
Broadmoor Cross
EX37 29 A2
Broadmoor La EX20 170 A5
BROAD OAK 168 D3
Broadoak Cl EX11 168 D3
Broad Oak Cres 13
TQ9 223 D5
Broadoak Hill EX31 4 C3
Broadoaks Cotts PL7 132 E4
Broadpark
Bovey Tracey TQ13 180 B5
Brampford Speke EX5 81 E1
Dartmouth TQ6 233 D3
Okehampton EX20 170 D5
Broad Park Ave EX34 150 A5
Broad Park Cl EX33 7 E2
Broad Park Cres
EX34 150 A4
Broadpark La
Parracombe EX31 4 C2
Parracombe EX31 11 C8
Whiddon Down EX20 95 D4
Broadpark Rd
Paignton TQ3 226 A7
Torquay TQ2 219 D2
Broad Park Rd
Bere Alston PL20 125 E2
Exmouth EX8 196 C1
Plymouth PL3 248 D6
Broadparks Ave EX4 174 E2
Broadparks Cl EX4 174 E2
Broad Path
Stoke Gabriel TQ9 228 A8
Uffculme EX15 66 A8
Broad Pk
Ashburton TQ13 130 F5
Plymouth PL9 255 C7
Broad Rd
Kerswell EX15 66 C1
Kingswear TQ6 234 D5
Broad Reach TQ4 229 C7
Broadridge Cl TQ12 206 D4
Broadridge Cross
TQ9 232 A8
Broadridge La EX17 61 A4
BROADSANDS 229 C7
Broadsands Ave TQ4 229 C7
Broadsands Bend
TQ4 229 C8
Broadsands Ct TQ4 229 B7
Broadsands Gdns
TQ5 229 C6
Broadsands Park Rd
TQ4 229 C8
Broadsands Rd TQ4 229 C7
Broadshell Cross
EX22 71 D5
Broad St
Black Torrington EX21 74 A8
Churchinford TA3 68 A7
Ilfracombe EX34 150 C6
Lifton PL16 105 E4
Lyme Regis DT7 260 E3
Broad St *continued*
11 Modbury PL21 137 B2
Ottery St Mary EX11 169 D3
South Molton EX36 158 C4
Broadstone TQ6 233 F4
Broadstone Park Rd
TQ2 219 D3
Broad View
Broadclyst EX5 175 C6
Dartington TQ9 222 F8
Broadway
Exeter EX2 176 F3
Fremington EX31 153 F5
Sidmouth EX10 187 F5
Trusham TQ13 113 D1
Woodbury EX5 184 C2
Broadway Ave TQ12 207 D7
Broadway Hill EX2 176 E3
Broadway La EX33 7 D3
Broadway Rd TQ12 207 C7
Broadways Head EX14,
TA20 68 F6
Broadway The
Exmouth EX8 202 E8
Plymouth PL9 255 E7
Broad Wlk PL12 242 E1
BROADWOODKELLY 76 D8
BROADWOODWIDGER
106 B8
Broadwoodwidger Prim
Sch PL16 91 A4
Broady Strap EX31 153 F5
Brockenbarrow La
EX31 11 C4
BROCKFIELD 88 A8
Brock Ho 8 PL4 263 A2
Brockhole La
Plymouth PL7 250 E8
Tatworth EX13, TA20 88 B7
Brockhurst Pk TQ3 218 D2
Brockington's Rd EX5 99 C8
Brockley Rd PL3 249 C4
BROCKSCOMBE 92 A5
Brockscombe Cross
EX21 91 F5
Brocks Cross EX17 79 A2
Brocks La
Heathfield TQ12 123 C2
Millbrook PL10 252 F5
Brockton Gdns PL6 245 B6
Brodick Cl EX4 173 D1
Bromhead Ct PL6 249 A8
Bromley Ho 6 PL2 248 A4
Bromley Pl 5 PL2 248 A4
Bronescombe Ave
TQ14 209 A8
Bronshill Ho TQ1 220 B6
Bronshill Mews TQ1 220 B6
Bronshill Rd TQ1 220 B6
Bronte Pl PL5 244 D1
BROOK 171 B2
Brook Cl
Bovey Tracey TQ13 180 C7
Exeter EX1 178 B8
Holcombe EX7 210 E8
Plymouth PL7 251 A3
Sidford EX10 101 B1
Brook Ct
Aveton Gifford TQ7 143 C6
Barnstaple EX31 154 B3
Brookdale EX11 169 E4
Brookdale Ave EX34 150 A5
Brookdale Cl TQ5 230 B4
Brookdale Ct
Brixham TQ5 230 B4
Exeter EX2 178 A2
Brookdale Pk TQ5 230 B4
Brookdale Terr
8 Barnstaple EX32 155 B4
18 Dawlish EX7 204 E6
Brookdown Terr
PL12 242 E3
Brookdown Villas
PL12 242 E3
Brooke Ave EX2 177 F3
Brooke Cl
Saltash PL12 243 A2
Sampford Courtenay
EX20 76 F3
Brookedor TQ12 212 F5
Brookedor Gdns
TQ12 212 F5
Brooke Rd EX16 46 E1
Brookesby Hall TQ1 220 D3
Brookfield EX39 25 E4
Brookfield Cl
6 Braunton EX33 152 D5
Kingsteignton TQ12 207 E7
Paignton TQ3 226 C8
Plymouth PL7 251 B5
Brookfield Cotts EX8 195 D5
Brookfield Ct 1
TQ13 123 F6
Brookfield Dr
7 Colyton EX24 103 A4
Teignmouth TQ14 210 C7
Brookfield Gdns EX2 177 B1
Brookfield Ho TQ3 226 C8
Brookfield Pl EX34 150 B5
Brookfield Rd EX9 198 B6
Brookfields Cl PL1 247 F1
Brookfield St 8
EX39 157 B1
Brook Green Ctr for
Learning PL5 244 B4
Brook Green Terr
EX4 261 C4
Brook Haven Cl TQ12 212 F5
Brookhayes Cl EX8 202 B8
Brookhill TQ6 234 B2
Brookhill Gdns EX13 167 E6
Brook Ho EX7 204 C6
BROOKING 135 F3
Brooking Barn TQ9 139 F8
Brooking Cl PL6 249 A8
Brookingfield Cl PL7 250 C5
Brooking Way PL12 242 C3
Brook La
Calverleigh EX16 48 F2
Colaton Raleigh EX9 186 D2
Shaldon TQ14 209 D5
3 Sidford EX10 101 B1
Tavistock PL19 171 B2
Washfield EX16 48 F1
Brooklands
24 Dawlish EX7 204 D6
Exeter EX2 177 F2
Tavistock PL19 171 D6
Totnes TQ9 223 D5
Brooklands Cross
EX10 100 C1
Brooklands Ct PL6 244 E3
Brooklands Farm Cl
EX13 103 D8
Brooklands La TQ2 219 E4
Brooklands Orch
Kilmington EX13 103 D8
Ottery St Mary EX11 169 E4
Brooklands Rd
Exmouth EX8 196 D1
Rockwell Green TA21 160 B5
Brookland Terr EX11 169 E3
Brook Lane Cotts
TQ13 121 B3
Brooklea La TQ7 145 A1
Brookleigh Ave EX1 178 B5
Brooklyn Cl EX1 178 D6
Brooklyn Pk EX8 196 C1
Brookman Ct 1 TQ3 225 E8
Brook Mdw
Exmouth EX8 196 C1
Newton Poppleford
EX10 186 F8
South Molton EX36 158 D4
Brook Mead PL8 257 E4
Brook Orch TQ12 212 F4
Brook Rd
Budleigh Salterton
EX9 199 G2
Cullompton EX15 163 B2
Dolton EX19 57 F7
Ipplepen TQ12 211 D2
Ivybridge PL21 237 D5
Brooks Ave EX22 164 B5
Brooks Hill EX15 66 C8
Brookside
Barnstaple EX31 154 A3
Broadhembury EX14 84 C7
Kingsbridge TQ7 258 C4
Pathfinder Village EX6 98 C4
Sidmouth EX10 188 A7
Brookside Cl
Heybrook Bay PL9 140 A7
Kilmington EX13 87 C1
Teignmouth TQ14 210 A5
Brookside Cres EX4 174 B2
Brookside Ind Units
EX4 174 D1
Brookside Units EX4 98 D4
Brookside Villas 23
EX34 3 A3
Brooks Pl TA21 160 E6
Brook St
Bampton EX16 34 B1
Dawlish EX7 204 D6
Ottery St Mary EX11 169 E3
Slapton TQ7 145 C3
Tavistock PL19 171 C6
16 Teignmouth TQ14 210 C5
Brooks Warren 15
EX5 99 A6
Brook Terr EX12 192 D7
Brook The PL12 242 E4
Brookvale Orch
TQ14 209 D4
Brook View TQ9 222 F6
Brookway EX1 178 C7
Brook Way
Exeter EX4 174 E2
Kingsteignton TQ12 123 F1
Brookwood Cl 4
TQ10 134 F3
Brookwood Rd PL9 256 D7
Broomball Cross TA22 32 F5
Broomball La EX16 32 E5
Broomborough Ct
TQ9 223 B5
Broomborough Dr
TQ9 223 A5
Broom Cl
Dawlish EX7 204 F8
Exeter EX2 178 A5
Broome Cl EX13 167 E6
Broomfield Dr PL9 255 C5
Broomham Cross
EX37 45 A7
BROOMHILL 133 F1
Broom Hill
Chagford TQ13 111 A6
Saltash PL12 242 D2
Broomhill Cross
Chilsworthy EX22 53 B3
Copplestone EX17 79 A4
Broomhill Rd EX16 161 B4
Broomhill Sculpture
Gdns★ EX31 16 E7

Broomhill Villas EX32 . . . 18 E5
Broomhill Way TQ2 . . . 213 E1
Broomhouse La EX36 . . . 30 A2
Broomhouse Pk EX16 . . . 46 E1
Broom La EX13 . . . 88 C5
Broom Pk
Dartington TQ9 . . . 215 E1
Okehampton EX20 . . . 170 E6
Plymouth PL9 . . . 255 D5
20 Rockbeare EX5 . . . 99 A6
Torquay TQ2 . . . 213 F3
Broom's La TA3 . . . 68 C7
Broomstreet La TA24 . . . 6 F4
Broughton Cl PL3 . . . 248 F7
Brow Hill TQ12 . . . 123 B2
Brown Down La
Churchinford TA20 . . . 68 F7
Churchinford TA20 . . . 69 A7
Browne Memorial Almshouses PL19 . . . 171 A5
BROWNHEATH . . . 52 C2
Brownhill La PL9 . . . 140 D8
Brownhills Rd TQ12 . . . 207 A3
Brownie Cross PL7 . . . 132 C3
Browning Cl EX2 . . . 178 A4
Browning Rd PL2 . . . 248 A5
Brownings End TQ12 . . . 206 F1
Brownings Mead EX6 . . . 112 F7
Brownings Wlk TQ12 . . . 206 F1
Brownlands Cl EX10 . . . 188 C5
Brownlands Rd EX10 . . . 188 C5
Brownlees EX6 . . . 182 A4
Brownlow St PL1 . . . 262 A2
Brown's Bridge La EX15 . . . 65 B7
Browns Bridge Rd TQ2 . . . 213 D2
Brownscombe Cl TQ3 . . . 218 D2
Brown's Ct EX6 . . . 114 C4
Brownsey La TA20 . . . 69 C5
Brown's Hill TQ6 . . . 233 F3
Brown's Hill Head EX37 . . . 27 F2
BROWNSTON . . . 137 F3
Brownston Cross TQ10 . . . 135 F5
Brownstone Cross EX17 . . . 61 C3
Brownstone Moor Cross EX17 . . . 61 D4
Brownstone Rd TQ6 . . . 234 E3
Brownston St PL21 . . . 137 B2
Brownswell La
Holbeton PL7 . . . 136 E1
Holbeton PL8 . . . 142 B8
Broxfords Hill EX17 . . . 80 C7
Broxton Dr PL9 . . . 249 E1
Bruckland La EX12, EX13 . . . 103 D3
Bruckton Cross TQ6 . . . 232 F6
Brunel Ave
Plymouth PL2 . . . 247 F5
Torquay TQ2 . . . 214 B4
Brunel Cl
Exeter EX4 . . . 177 A7
Teignmouth TQ14 . . . 210 C6
Brunel Ct 16 EX7 . . . 204 E6
Brunel Ind Est TQ12 . . . 207 D3
Brunel Mews TQ2 . . . 219 F4
Brunel Prim Sch PL12 . . . 242 E2
Brunel Rd
Cullompton EX15 . . . 163 E4
Newton Abbot TQ12 . . . 207 D3
Paignton TQ4 . . . 229 D6
Saltash PL12 . . . 242 C4
Starcross EX6 . . . 201 A8
Brunel Terr 3 PL2 . . . 247 F5
Brunel Vw EX6 . . . 182 B5
Brunel Way
Ivybridge PL21 . . . 237 E6
Plymouth PL1 . . . 262 A2
Brunenburg Way EX13 . . . 167 D4
Brunswick Ho 2 TQ12 . . . 207 B4
Brunswick Pl
Dawlish EX7 . . . 204 E6
10 Plymouth PL2 . . . 247 F4
Brunswick Rd PL4 . . . 263 B2
Brunswick Sq 4 TQ1 . . . 219 F6
Brunswick St
Exeter EX4 . . . 177 A5
Teignmouth TQ14 . . . 210 C4
Brunswick Terr TQ1 . . . 219 F6
BRUSHFORD
Bondleigh . . . 59 D2
Dulverton . . . 33 D4
Brushford La
Chevithorne EX16 . . . 49 F3
Chulmleigh EX18 . . . 59 D2
Brushford New Rd TA22 . . . 33 E4
Brymon Wy PL6 . . . 245 B4
Brynmoor Cl PL3 . . . 249 A7
Brynmoor Pk PL3 . . . 249 A6
Brynmoor Wlk PL3 . . . 249 A6
Brynsworthy Ct 7 EX31 . . . 154 A2
Brynsworthy La EX31 . . . 154 A1
Brynsworthy Lawn 8 EX31 . . . 154 A2
Brynsworthy Pk EX31 . . . 154 B3
Bsns Ctr The PL4 . . . 263 C2
Buchanan Cl EX14 . . . 166 B4
Buckerall Cross EX14 . . . 84 F2
BUCKERELL . . . 85 A3
Buckerell Ave EX2 . . . 177 E3
Buckeridge Ave TQ14 . . . 210 B6
Buckeridge Rd
Exmouth EX8 . . . 202 E7
Teignmouth TQ14 . . . 210 B6
Buckeridge Twrs 2 TQ14 . . . 210 B6
BUCKFAST . . . 236 B7
Buckfast Cl
Buckfast TQ11 . . . 236 C6
Ivybridge PL21 . . . 237 D4
Plymouth PL2 . . . 248 A8
BUCKFASTLEIGH . . . 236 C5
Buckfastleigh Prim Sch TQ11 . . . 236 B5
Buckfastleigh Sta* TQ11 . . . 236 D5
Buckfast Rd TQ11 . . . 236 C6
Buckfast (St Mary's) Abbey* TQ11 . . . 236 C7
Buckgrove Cotts EX38 . . . 42 B6
Buckham Cross EX36 . . . 45 D7
Buckham Hill EX36 . . . 45 D7
BUCKHORN . . . 72 D2
Buckhouse La EX24 . . . 102 C7
Buckingham Cl
Exmouth EX8 . . . 202 E7
South Molton EX36 . . . 158 C3
Buckingham Orch TQ13 . . . 123 C4
Buckingham Pl PL5 . . . 243 E2
Buckingham Rd EX2 . . . 178 D3
BUCKLAND
Newton Abbot . . . 207 E3
Thurlestone . . . 143 B2
Buckland Abbey* PL20 . . . 126 C1
Buckland Brake TQ12 . . . 207 E2
BUCKLAND BREWER . . . 40 C7
Buckland Brewer Com Prim Sch EX39 . . . 40 C7
Buckland Cl
Bideford EX39 . . . 25 E4
Plymouth PL7 . . . 250 D7
Buckland Cross
Braunton EX33 . . . 152 C8
Slapton TQ7 . . . 145 C6
BUCKLAND FILLEIGH . . . 56 A4
Buckland Hall TQ13 . . . 130 D7
BUCKLAND IN THE MOOR . . . 130 C8
BUCKLAND MONACHORUM . . . 126 D3
Buckland Rd
Caddsdown EX39 . . . 25 D4
Georgeham EX33 . . . 8 B3
Netherton TQ12 . . . 208 A4
Newton Abbot TQ12 . . . 207 F4
BUCKLAND ST MARY . . . 69 C8
Buckland St Mary CE Prim Sch TA20 . . . 69 D8
Buckland St PL1 . . . 262 B2
Buckland Terr PL20 . . . 126 F2
BUCKLAND-TOUT-SAINTS . . . 144 C4
Buckland View
Bideford EX39 . . . 156 F2
Buckland Brewer EX39 . . . 40 B7
Newton Abbot TQ12 . . . 207 D4
Buckland Wlk EX6 . . . 181 F5
BUCKLEIGH . . . 156 D6
Buckleigh Cross EX39 . . . 156 C6
Buckleigh Grange EX39 . . . 156 C6
Buckleigh Rd EX39 . . . 156 C5
Buckle Rise EX1 . . . 175 B1
Buckley Cross EX10 . . . 101 C1
Buckley Rd EX10 . . . 101 C2
Buckley St TQ8 . . . 259 E5
Bucknall Cl EX12 . . . 190 D4
Bucknell Way EX36 . . . 158 C7
Bucknill Cl EX6 . . . 182 A4
Bucknole Cross EX14 . . . 102 A8
Bucknole Hill Rd EX24 . . . 102 A7
Bucks Cl TQ13 . . . 180 D7
BUCK'S CROSS . . . 24 A1
Buckshots Cross EX14 . . . 69 A4
Bucks La 4 TQ13 . . . 180 D7
BUCK'S MILLS . . . 24 B2
Buckthorn Ct TQ12 . . . 244 C6
Buckton La EX10 . . . 101 C1
Buckwell TA21 . . . 160 E6
Buckwell Cl TQ7 . . . 258 D6
Buckwell Rd TQ7 . . . 258 D6
Buckwell St PL1, PL4 . . . 263 A2
Buctor Pk PL19 . . . 126 A8
Budbrook La EX6 . . . 96 F3
Buddle Cl
Ivybridge PL21 . . . 237 E5
Plymouth PL9 . . . 256 A5
Tavistock PL19 . . . 171 B6
Buddle La
Exeter EX4 . . . 176 F5
Hatherleigh EX20 . . . 75 C7
Bude Hill EX19 . . . 59 A3
Bude Moor Cross EX19 . . . 76 D7
Bude Rd EX22 . . . 164 B5
Bude St
Appledore EX39 . . . 15 A1
Exeter EX4 . . . 261 B3
Bude-Stratton Business Pk EX23 . . . 70 A8
Budge Mdws PL15 . . . 115 A4
Budgetts TA21 . . . 52 F6
Budgett's Cross TA21 . . . 52 F6
BUDLAKE . . . 82 E3
Budlake Cross EX24 . . . 101 F6
Budlake Old Post Office* EX5 . . . 82 D2
Budlake Rd EX2 . . . 177 C1
Budlake Units EX2 . . . 177 C1
Budleigh Cl
Plymouth PL9 . . . 255 F5
Torquay TQ1 . . . 220 D6
Budleigh Hill EX9 . . . 198 B5
BUDLEIGH SALTERTON . . . 198 A2
Budshead Gn PL5 . . . 244 C4
Budshead Rd PL5 . . . 244 C4
Budshead Way PL5 . . . 244 E2
Budshead Wood Nature Reserve* PL5 . . . 244 A4
Buena Vista Cl PL6 . . . 245 D6
Buena Vista Dr PL6 . . . 245 C6
Buena Vista Gdns PL6 . . . 245 C6
Buena Vista Way PL6 . . . 245 C6
BUGFORD . . . 10 C5
Bugford Cross TQ6 . . . 232 C3
Bugford La TQ6 . . . 232 D3
Bugford Lane End TQ6 . . . 232 D3
Bughead Cross TQ13 . . . 111 D4
Bughole La TA21 . . . 51 E8
Bugle Pl TQ12 . . . 206 C5
Building's Cross EX17 . . . 63 A4
Bulford TA21 . . . 160 D5
Bulford La
Kennford EX6 . . . 181 A2
Wellington TA21 . . . 160 D5
Bulgis Pk EX36 . . . 158 B5
Bulkamore Ct TQ10 . . . 135 E5
BULKWORTHY . . . 39 F1
Bullaford Gate EX36 . . . 31 E4
Bulland Cross EX20 . . . 76 E4
Bulland La
Poughill EX17 . . . 62 D3
Sampford Courtenay EX20 . . . 76 F4
Bullands Cl 4 TQ13 . . . 180 C8
Bullaton Cross TQ13 . . . 112 E1
Bull Ct EX31 . . . 154 F5
Bulleid Cl PL2 . . . 247 F7
Bulleigh Barton Farm Units TQ12 . . . 218 B8
Bulleigh Cross TQ12 . . . 218 B8
Bulleigh Elms Cross TQ12 . . . 212 A1
Bullens Cl EX5 . . . 81 E4
Bullen St EX5 . . . 81 E5
Buller Cl
Cullompton EX15 . . . 163 C4
Plymouth PL7 . . . 250 F4
Torpoint PL11 . . . 247 A3
Buller Ct EX2 . . . 177 A4
Buller Pk PL12 . . . 242 D3
Buller Rd
11 Barnstaple EX32 . . . 155 A5
Crediton EX17 . . . 165 B6
Exeter EX4 . . . 177 A5
Newton Abbot TQ12 . . . 207 D2
Torpoint PL11 . . . 247 B3
Bullers Hill EX6 . . . 113 F3
Bullfinch Cl EX15 . . . 163 A2
Bullhead Cross EX19 . . . 58 B2
Bull Hill
Barnstaple EX31 . . . 154 F7
Bideford EX39 . . . 157 A1
Bullhorn Cross TQ7 . . . 142 F6
Bull Meadow Rd EX2 . . . 261 B2
Bullow View EX19 . . . 58 F2
Bull Ring TQ13 . . . 130 F4
Bulls Ct 11 EX24 . . . 103 A4
Bull's La TA20 . . . 88 C8
Bully Shoot Cross EX24 . . . 103 A3
Bulmer Rd PL4 . . . 263 C3
Bulmoor Cross EX13 . . . 103 F5
Bulsworthy La PL15 . . . 105 B2
Bulteel Gdns PL6 . . . 244 E7
BULVERTON . . . 187 F6
Bulverton Pk EX10 . . . 187 F6
Bulwark Cl TQ12 . . . 244 D2
Bulworthy Cross EX16 . . . 47 E5
Bulworthy Knap EX16 . . . 47 E5
Bumpston Cross TQ11 . . . 215 C7
Bungalows The
Axminster EX13 . . . 167 C4
Dawlish Warren EX7 . . . 201 B2
4 Tiverton EX16 . . . 161 C3
Bunkers Farm TQ9 . . . 144 E7
Bunker Square EX2 . . . 178 D2
Bun La 8 TQ14 . . . 210 B4
Bunneford Cross EX15 . . . 64 E1
Bunn Rd EX8 . . . 196 D4
Bunny Burrow's Track
Bury TA22 . . . 33 F7
Bury TA22 . . . 34 A7
Hartford TA4 . . . 34 A8
Bunson Gate EX18 . . . 45 A4
Bunting Cl
Newton Abbot TQ12 . . . 207 A1
Teignmouth TQ14 . . . 210 A5
Buntings The EX6 . . . 181 F4
Bunts La EX12 . . . 191 F7
Bunyan Cl PL5 . . . 244 C2
Burch Cl EX8 . . . 196 E2
Burches Cross EX16 . . . 48 A1
Burch Gdns EX7 . . . 200 E1
Burchills Cl TA21 . . . 160 A6
Burchill's Hill TA21 . . . 160 B7
Burcombe Hill EX36 . . . 158 E8
Burdon La EX21 . . . 74 C7
BURFORD . . . 23 C1
Burgage TA21 . . . 160 D6
Burgh Island Cswy TQ7 . . . 142 E3
Burgmanns Hill EX8 . . . 195 D3
Burke Rd TQ9 . . . 223 D6
Burland Cross EX31 . . . 9 B4
Burland La EX33 . . . 8 F1
Burlands The EX14 . . . 84 D2
Burleigh La
Malborough TQ7 . . . 147 E7
Plymouth PL3 . . . 248 D7
Burleigh Lane End TQ7 . . . 147 E8
Burleigh Manor PL3 . . . 248 D7
Burleigh Park Rd PL3 . . . 248 D6
Burleigh Rd TQ2 . . . 219 C7
BURLESCOMBE . . . 51 B3
Burlescombe CE Prim Sch EX16 . . . 51 B3
BURLESTONE . . . 145 D7
Burlington Cl EX32 . . . 155 B3
Burlington Gr EX32 . . . 155 B2
Burnard Cl PL6 . . . 244 E7
Burnards Cl 15 EX24 . . . 103 A4
Burnards Field Rd EX24 . . . 103 A4
Burnbreach Cnr EX24 . . . 102 B2
Burnbridge Hill EX16 . . . 63 D2
Burne Cross TQ12 . . . 131 D6
Burnet Cl EX2 . . . 178 C3
Burnet Rd TQ12 . . . 206 C5
Burnett Cl PL12 . . . 242 D2
Burnett Rd PL6 . . . 248 F8
Burnham Cl EX12 . . . 192 A8
Burnham Ct TQ12 . . . 207 E7
Burnham Park Rd PL3 . . . 248 D6
Burniston Cl PL7 . . . 251 A3
Burnistone Cl PL7 . . . 251 A3
Burn La
Lydford PL19 . . . 107 C1
North Brentor PL19 . . . 117 C8
Burnley Cl TQ12 . . . 206 D4
Burnley Rd TQ12 . . . 206 D4
Burn River Rise TQ2 . . . 219 B8
Burns Ave
Exeter EX2 . . . 177 F3
Plymouth PL5 . . . 244 C2
Burns Ct EX7 . . . 204 E5
Burnside EX8 . . . 196 B1
Burnside Rd EX34 . . . 150 A3
Burns La 13 PL21 . . . 137 B2
Burnsome La EX14, EX15 . . . 67 B5
Burnthouse Cross EX14 . . . 67 B5
Burnthouse Hill TQ12 . . . 212 E1
Burnthouse La EX2 . . . 177 F3
Burnt Mdws EX6 . . . 113 D5
Burnt Oak EX10 . . . 101 B1
BURRATON
Ermington . . . 136 D3
St Dominick . . . 125 A2
Saltash . . . 242 D4
Burraton Com Prim Sch PL12 . . . 242 C3
BURRATON COOMBE . . . 242 C2
Burraton Cross PL21 . . . 136 D4
Burraton Rd PL12 . . . 242 C4
Burrator Arboretum* PL20 . . . 127 E3
Burrator Ave PL20 . . . 128 A8
Burrator Dr EX4 . . . 176 E8
Burrator Rd PL20 . . . 127 B3
BURRIDGE . . . 16 E6
Burridge Ave TQ2 . . . 219 D5
Burridge Cross EX18 . . . 58 F8
Burridge La
Chawleigh EX17 . . . 60 E7
Torquay TQ2 . . . 220 A5
Burridge Moor Cross EX18 . . . 60 E6
Burridge Rd
Torquay TQ2 . . . 219 D5
Upton Pyne EX5 . . . 173 B8
BURRINGTON . . . 43 F3
Burrington Bsns Pk PL2 . . . 244 A1
Burrington CE Prim Sch EX37 . . . 43 F3
Burrington Dr EX17 . . . 80 E4
Burrington Ind Est PL5 . . . 244 A1
Burrington Moor Cross EX37 . . . 43 C3
Burrington Rd PL5 . . . 244 A1
Burrington Way PL5 . . . 244 B1
Burrough Fields EX5 . . . 99 A6
Burrough Lawn EX39 . . . 157 A6
Burrough Rd EX39 . . . 157 A6
Burrough Way TA21 . . . 160 D4
BURROW
Broadclyst . . . 175 E8
Newton Poppleford . . . 186 C8
Burrow EX10 . . . 186 D8
Burrow Cl EX10 . . . 186 D8
Burrow Cnr
Butterleigh EX16 . . . 64 C4
Dalwood EX13 . . . 86 F2
Burrow Cross
Budlake EX5 . . . 82 E1
Burrow EX5 . . . 175 E7
Meshaw EX17 . . . 46 A4
Monkokehampton EX19 . . . 76 A8
Burrow Ctyd EX16 . . . 64 C4
Burrowe The 2 EX17 . . . 165 C5
Burrow Farm Gdns* EX13 . . . 87 A2
Burrow Hill PL9 . . . 255 E6
Burrow Knap EX13 . . . 87 A2
Burrow Knap Way EX13 . . . 86 F2
Burrow La
Ashbrittle TA21 . . . 50 D8
Bow EX17 . . . 78 A5
Newton Poppleford EX10 . . . 186 D8
Burrowplot Cross EX17 . . . 59 F2
Burrow Rd
Burrow EX5 . . . 175 E8
10 Ilfracombe EX34 . . . 150 B5
Seaton EX12 . . . 192 B4
Burrows Cl EX33 . . . 152 C5
Burrows Close La EX33 . . . 15 A7
Burrowshot Cross EX13 . . . 104 B7
Burrows La EX39 . . . 14 F1
Burrows Pk EX33 . . . 152 C5
Burrows Way EX39 . . . 156 F8
Burrow The 1 EX12 . . . 192 B4
Burscombe La EX10 . . . 101 A1
Burscott EX39 . . . 23 D3
Bursdon Moor Cross EX39 . . . 37 E7
Bursledon Ct EX7 . . . 204 F6
BURSTON . . . 78 B5
Burston Cross EX17 . . . 78 B4
Burston La EX16 . . . 34 A4
Burton Acad The TQ2 . . . 213 E2
Burton Art Gallery & Mus The* EX39 . . . 157 A3
Burton Cl PL6 . . . 245 B6
Burton Pl TQ5 . . . 230 C4
Burton Rd EX39 . . . 156 E1
Burton St TQ5 . . . 230 C3
Burton Villa Cl TQ5 . . . 230 C4
Burvill St EX35 . . . 151 B5
Burwell Cl PL6 . . . 245 E4
Burwell La EX36 . . . 30 F7
Burwood La EX38 . . . 159 F5
Burwood Mews EX38 . . . 159 F4
Burwood Rd EX38 . . . 159 E5
BURY . . . 34 A6
Bury Cross
Lapford EX17 . . . 60 D2
Petrockstow EX20 . . . 56 F5
Bury Hill TA22 . . . 33 F7
Bury Rd
Bury TA22 . . . 34 A6
Dulverton TA22 . . . 33 F6
Newton Abbot TQ12 . . . 207 B4
Bury The EX5 . . . 81 E5
Buscombe La EX31 . . . 11 E2
Bushayes Cnr EX3 . . . 183 C6
Bush Cnr EX18 . . . 58 F8
Bush Cross EX18 . . . 58 F8
Bushell Rd TQ12 . . . 207 A4
Bushes La EX12, DT7 . . . 193 B7
Bushmead Ave TQ12 . . . 213 A5
Bushmead Cl TQ2 . . . 213 A5
Bush Pk PL6 . . . 245 F3
Busland La EX16 . . . 63 D4
Bussel Cl EX4 . . . 174 F3
Bussell's Moor Cross EX36 . . . 32 C4
Butcher Park Hill PL19 . . . 171 B7
Butcher's Moor La EX19 . . . 58 E4
Butchers Row EX31 . . . 154 F5
Butcombe La EX17 . . . 61 D1
Bute Rd PL4 . . . 249 A4
Butlakes La EX24 . . . 101 F6
Butland Ave TQ3 . . . 219 C1
Butland Mdw PL19 . . . 126 C3
Butland Rd TQ12 . . . 207 D8
Butlands Ind Est TQ12 . . . 211 F2
Butler Cl
Plymouth PL6 . . . 245 B6
Tiverton EX16 . . . 161 E3
Butler Way EX14 . . . 86 A6
Buttercombe Cl TQ12 . . . 211 F8
Buttercombe La
Braunton EX33 . . . 15 E8
Knowle EX31, EX34 . . . 8 F1
West Down EX34 . . . 8 E5
Buttercup Cl EX12 . . . 192 B8
Buttercup Mdw PL15 . . . 105 A2
Buttercup Rd
Plymouth PL6 . . . 245 B2
Willand EX15 . . . 162 E5
Buttercup Way TQ12 . . . 206 C5
Butterdon Wlk PL21 . . . 237 F5
Butterdown PL12 . . . 242 B3
Butterfly La TQ12 . . . 209 C2
Butterlake TQ3 . . . 218 D3
BUTTERLEIGH . . . 64 C3
Butterleigh Dr EX16 . . . 161 E3
Buttermere Ct EX4 . . . 176 F5
Buttermoor Cross EX16 . . . 48 D3
Butterpark PL21 . . . 237 D5
Buttery Cl EX14 . . . 166 C4
Buttery Rd EX14 . . . 166 C4
Buttgarden St EX39 . . . 157 A1
Buttle's Cross TA3 . . . 68 C7
Buttle's La TA3 . . . 68 B6
Button La
Bratton Fleming EX31 . . . 11 A1
Ivybridge PL21 . . . 237 E4
Butt Park Rd PL5 . . . 244 B3
Butt Parks EX17 . . . 165 D4
Butt Pk
Hennock TQ13 . . . 123 B7
Stokenham TQ7 . . . 145 B1
Butts Cl
Bridford EX6 . . . 112 F5
Chawleigh EX18 . . . 60 B7
Honiton EX14 . . . 166 B4
Witheridge EX16 . . . 46 E1
Butts Cross
Buckfastleigh TQ11 . . . 135 B6
Cornworthy TQ9 . . . 227 C3
Butts Ct EX2 . . . 178 A5
Buttsford Terr PL21 . . . 136 B6
Butts Hill
Kenton EX6 . . . 194 D3
Paignton TQ3 . . . 225 B8
Butt's Hill EX11 . . . 169 E4
Buttshill Cross TQ3 . . . 225 B8
Butts La
Christow EX6 . . . 113 B3
Ideford TQ13 . . . 124 B4
Kenton EX6 . . . 194 D1
Starcross EX6 . . . 200 D8
Buttsons Cl TQ7 . . . 145 B1
Butts Park Ct PL8 . . . 141 A7
Butts Path EX33 . . . 152 D6
Butts Pk PL8 . . . 141 A7
Butts Rd
Exeter EX2 . . . 178 A5
Ottery St Mary EX11 . . . 169 E4
Butts The
Colyton EX24 . . . 103 A4
Loddiswell TQ7 . . . 143 E8
Newton Ferrers PL8 . . . 141 A7
Butts Way EX20 . . . 77 C4
Buzzacott Cl EX34 . . . 3 B2
Buzzacott La EX34 . . . 3 B2
Buzzard Rd PL19 . . . 171 D2
Buzzard Rise PL18 . . . 125 C5
Buzzard Way EX5 . . . 99 B6
Byard Cl PL5 . . . 243 E1
Bycott La EX18 . . . 45 B4
Bydown Cross EX32 . . . 28 D8
Bye Cross EX33 . . . 8 B3
Byes Cl EX10 . . . 188 C8
Byeside Rd EX10 . . . 188 C8
Byes La EX10 . . . 188 D8
Bygones (Mus)* TQ1 . . . 220 C8
Byland Rd PL3 . . . 249 A6
Byng Cl TQ12 . . . 207 F4
Byron Ave PL5 . . . 244 C2
Byron Cl EX31 . . . 154 F7
Byron Rd
Exeter EX2 . . . 178 C5
Torquay TQ1 . . . 220 A8
Byron Way EX8 . . . 196 C3
Bystock Cl EX4 . . . 261 A4
Bystock Mews EX8 . . . 196 E3
Bystock Rd EX8 . . . 196 D4
Bystock Terr EX4 . . . 261 A4
Byter Mill La TQ9 . . . 228 A7
Byways Cl EX31 . . . 153 F5

C

Cabbage Hill TQ13 . . . 130 F4
Cabbage La EX14 . . . 85 A3
Cabot Cl PL12 . . . 242 E2
Cabourg Cl TQ8 . . . 259 D5
CADBURY . . . 81 D7
Cadbury Cres EX1 . . . 178 D7
Cadbury Cross EX17 . . . 81 C8
Cadbury Gdns EX9 . . . 198 B6
Caddecleave La
Kentisbury EX31 . . . 3 E1
Kentisbury EX31 . . . 10 E6
Caddiford Cross EX17 . . . 97 B6
Cadditon Cross EX20 . . . 76 F7
Caddsdown Ind Pk EX39 . . . 25 D4
Caddy Pl EX2 . . . 178 D2
Caddywell La EX38 . . . 159 E5
Caddywell Mdw EX38 . . . 159 E5
CADELEIGH . . . 63 D3
Cades Gdns TA21 . . . 160 E7
Cades Mead TA21 . . . 160 F7
Cadewell Cres TQ2 . . . 213 D1
Cadewell La TQ2 . . . 219 C8
Cadewell Park Rd TQ2 . . . 213 C1
Cadewell Pk Rd TQ2 . . . 213 C1
Cadford La EX19 . . . 59 B3
Cadhay Cl EX11 . . . 169 B3
Cadhay House* EX11 . . . 169 B5
Cadhay La EX11 . . . 169 B4
Cadlake La EX20 . . . 77 A3
Cadleigh Cl PL21 . . . 136 D6

Cadleigh Court La
EX16 . . . . .63 D2
Cadleigh Cross PL21 .136 D7
Cadleigh La PL21 . . . .136 D6
CADLEIGHPARK 136 D6
Cadover Bridge Rd
PL20 . . . . .132 D7
Cadover Cl PL6 . . . . .245 A1
Cadway Cl EX1 . . . . . .169 B3
Cadwell Rd TQ3. . . . . .226 B7
Caen Com Prim Sch ☑
EX33 . . . . .152 D6
Caen Field EX33 . . . . .152 D6
Caen Field Sh Ctr ☑
EX33. . . . . .152 D6
Caen Gdns EX33 . . . . .152 D6
Caen Ho ☑ EX33. . . . . .152 D6
Caen St EX33 . . . . .152 D6
Caen View EX33. . . . . .152 C5
Caernarvon Gdns
PL2 . . . . .248 B7
Caesars Ct EX20 . . . . .170 D7
Caffyns Cross EX35. . . . .5 A4
Cairn Rd EX34 . . . . . . .150 B4
Cairnside EX34 . . . . .1 F3
Cairn Side EX34. . . . . .150 B3
Cake Down La EX36 . .158 E4
Calder Cl PL3 . . . . .249 B6
Caldicot Gdns PL6 . . .245 C8
Caledonia EX34 . . . . .1 F3
California Cl EX4. . . . .173 D3
California Cross
PL21 . . . . .138 A3
California Gdns PL3 .249 D6
Callard's La EX36 . . . . .30 E1
Caller's La EX15. . . . . . .52 D1
Callington Rd
Gulworthy PL19 . . . . . .125 F7
Saltash PL12. . . . . .242 E3
Tavistock PL19 . . . . . . .171 A4
CALSTOCK 125 D3
Calstock Cl PL2 . . . . . .248 C8
Calstock Com Prim Sch
PL12 . . . . .125 D3
Calstock Rd PL18 . . . .125 D6
Calstock Sta PL18. . . .125 D3
Calthorpe Rd EX4 . . . .177 F8
Calvados ☑ EX32 . . . .155 A5
Calvados Cl ☑ TQ13. .123 E6
Calvados Pk TQ12. . . .207 F7
CALVERLEIGH 48 E1
Calverleigh Cross
EX16. . . . . .48 C1
Calvesford Cl EX38. . .159 E6
Calvesford Cross
EX38 . . . . .159 E5
Calvesford Rd EX38 . .159 E6
Calvez Cl PL10 . . . . . . .252 F6
Cambercombe Terr ☑
EX34 . . . . .150 D5
Camber Rd PL1 . . . . . . .262 A1
Cambian Devon Sch
TQ3. . . . . .225 E4
Camborne Cl PL5 . . . .244 A5
Camborne Cres TQ4. .229 B8
Cambrian Cl TQ4. . . . .225 D4
Cambric Chase PL21 .237 D6
Cambridge Gr ☑
EX34 . . . . .150 C5
Cambridge Lane W ☑
PL1. . . . . .262 B3
Cambridge Rd
Brixham TQ5 . . . . .230 A4
Plymouth PL2. . . . . . . .247 F5
Torquay TQ1 . . . . .214 B1
Cambridge St ☑ EX4 .177 A5
Cambridge Terr
EX10 . . . . .188 B4
Cambridge Wy EX15 .163 A4
Camden Ct PL4 . . . . . . .263 A3
Camden Rd TQ1 . . . . . .220 B5
Camden St PL4 . . . . . . .263 A3
Came Cross EX14 . . . . .84 C7
Camellia Cl
Churston Ferrers
TQ5. . . . . .229 D5
☑ Tiverton EX16 . . . . .161 F6
Camelot Cl EX4 . . . . . .174 A1
CAMELS HEAD 247 E7
Cameron Cl EX16 . . . .161 B3
Cameron Dr PL21 . . . .237 A5
Cameron Way PL6 . . . .245 B1
Camfield Dr EX16 . . . .161 F6
Camilla Ct EX4. . . . . . .261 B4
Camilla Terr PL2. . . . .248 D7
Camomile Way TQ12 .206 D5
Campbellhays Hill
EX16. . . . . .47 A1
Campbell Rd PL9 . . . . .255 F7
Camp Cross PL15 . . . .105 E7
Camperdown Rd
TQ8. . . . . .259 C4
Camperdown St PL2 .247 F4
Camperdown Terr
EX8. . . . . .201 F6
Camperknowle Cl
PL10 . . . . .252 F6
Campian Way ☑ EX14 .85 C2
Campion Cl
Launceston PL15 . . . . .105 A4
☑ Plymouth PL7. . . . . .251 C5
Saltash PL12. . . . . .242 D4
Campion Ct
Torquay TQ1 . . . . .214 B1

Campion Ct continued
Willand EX15 . . . . .162 D5
Campion Dr EX32 . . . .155 E5
Campion Gdns EX2. . .178 C3
Campion Pl TQ12 . . . .206 C5
Campion Rise PL19 . .171 D6
Campion View PL6. . . .245 B8
Camp Rd EX20 . . . . . . .170 C2
Camps Cross EX17 . . . .80 E2
Canada Hill
East Ogwell TQ12 . . . .206 F1
Ogwell TQ12 . . . . .211 F8
Canada Hill Prim Sch
TQ12. . . . . .206 F1
Canal Banks EX2. . . . .177 D2
Canal Cl TA21. . . . . . . .160 B8
Canal Hill EX16 . . . . . .161 F3
Canal Rd
Holsworthy EX22 . . . . .164 D6
Tavistock PL19 . . . . . . .171 B5
Canal Rise 70 F5
Canberra Cl EX4 . . . . .173 E2
Canberra Rd PL6. . . . .245 B5
Candar The EX34. . . . .150 B6
Candish Dr PL9 . . . . . .256 D7
Candys Cotts ☑
TQ13. . . . . .123 C4
Canefields Ave PL7 . .251 B3
Cane's Cotts PL8. . . . .257 A5
Canhaye Cl PL7 . . . . . .251 A3
Canis Mws PL9 . . . . . .256 E8
Canna Pk Dr EX21 . . . . .74 C7
Cann Bridge Sch PL6 245 E2
Cann Gdns PL6 . . . . . . .244 D6
Cannington La DT7. . .104 B3
Cannington Rd EX16 . . .46 E1
Cannon Rd TQ12 . . . . .123 B2
Cannon St PL1. . . . . . . .247 D2
Canns Water EX39 . . . .39 C6
Cann Woods Nature
Reserve★ PL6 . . . . . .244 C5
Cann Wood View
PL6. . . . . .245 E7
Canons Cl TQ14. . . . . .208 F8
Canons Gate PL19. . . .171 A3
Canons Way PL19 . . . .171 A3
Canonteign Falls★
EX6. . . . . .113 B1
Canon Way EX2. . . . . .181 B8
Canterbury Cl
Feniton EX14 . . . . .84 D2
Ivybridge PL21 . . . . . . .237 E4
Canterbury Dr PL5 . . .244 B4
Canterbury Rd EX4. . .176 E7
Canterbury Way EX8 .196 E4
Capel La EX8 . . . . .202 F8
Capella Dr PL9. . . . . . .256 E8
Capern Cl EX33 . . . . . .152 E4
Capern Pk EX39. . . . . . .40 B7
Capern Rd EX39. . . . . .156 F1
Capper Cl EX10 . . . . . .186 E8
Capra Cl TQ12 . . . . . . .207 F4
Caprera Terr La PL3. .262 C4
Capricorn Way PL9 . .256 E8
Capstone Cres EX34. .150 C6
Capstone Pde EX34 . .150 D5
Capstone Pl ☑ EX34 .150 C6
Capstone Rd EX34 . . .150 C6
Captain Brooks Cross
EX39. . . . . .39 B8
Captain's Cross EX16. .63 C3
Captains Gdns PL5. . .244 A5
Captains Rd TQ12 . . . .207 D8
CAPTON 232 D7
Capton Cross TQ6. . . .232 E6
Caradon Cl PL6 . . . . . .245 A5
Caradon Ct ☑ PL20 . . .126 F4
Caradon Terr PL12 . . .242 E3
Carbeile Jun Sch
PL11. . . . . .247 A3
Carbeile Rd PL11. . . . .247 A2
Carberry TQ8. . . . . .259 D4
Carberry Ave EX8 . . . .196 A1
Carbis Cl TQ12. . . . . . .244 B4
Carders Ct EX2 . . . . . .261 A2
Carder Way EX36 . . . .158 C5
Cardiff Cl PL7. . . . . . . .251 B4
Cardigan Rd PL6. . . . .245 C1
Cardinal Ave PL5. . . . .247 D8
Cardu Cl EX15 . . . . .65 F7
Carehouse Cross
TQ7. . . . . .145 B1
Careswell Ave PL2 . . .247 F8
Carew Ave PL5. . . . . . .244 B3
Carew Gdns
Newton Abbot TQ12 . .207 F3
Plymouth PL5 . . . . .244 B3
Saltash PL12. . . . . .242 D3
Carew Gr PL5. . . . . .244 B3
Carew Rd EX16 . . . . . . .161 D6
Carew Terr PL11. . . . . .247 B2
Carew Wharf PL11 . . .247 C2
Carew Wharf Bsns Ctr
PL11. . . . . .247 C2
Carey Ct PL12. . . . . . . .242 E3
Carey Rd TQ6. . . . . .233 C3
CARGREEN 239 A2
Carhaix Way EX7. . . . .204 F8
Carina Pl TQ3 . . . . .256 E8
Carisbrooke Rd PL6. .245 C1
CARKEEL 242 C6
Carlile Rd
Brixham TQ5 . . . . .230 A5
Exeter EX2 . . . . .178 A5

Carling Ct TQ7. . . . . . .258 C4
Carlisle Rd PL5 . . . . . .244 D3
Carlton St ☑ TQ12. . . .207 C3
Carlton Cl
Paignton TQ3 . . . . .219 C2
Plymouth PL3 . . . . .249 B5
Carlton Ct TQ12. . . . . .209 B2
Carlton Dr TQ3 . . . . . . .219 C2
Carlton Hill EX8. . . . . .202 A5
Carlton Mews TQ1 . . .220 C6
Carlton Pl ☑ TQ14 . . . .210 C4
Carlton Rd
Exeter EX2 . . . . .178 B4
Torquay TQ1 . . . . .220 C6
Carlton Terr
☑ Barnstaple EX32 . . .155 A4
☑ Dawlish EX7. . . . . . .204 E6
Plymouth, Lipson PL4. .263 B3
Plymouth, Weston Mill
PL5. . . . . .247 E8
Carlyle Ave EX32. . . . .155 A6
Carlyon Cl
Exeter EX1 . . . . .178 A6
Torpoint PL11. . . . . . . .246 F4
Carlyon Gdns EX1. . . .178 A6
Carmarthen Rd PL4 . .249 B2
Carmel Gdns PL19 . . .171 A5
Carnac Dr
Dawlish EX7. . . . . .200 E1
Dawlish EX7. . . . . .204 E8
Carnegie N EX39 . . . . .156 F6
Carnegie S EX39 . . . . .156 F6
Carnock Rd PL2. . . . . .248 D3
Carnoustie Dr PL12 . .242 C2
Carolina Gdns PL2 . . .247 F7
Caroline Ave EX2 . . . .178 D1
Caroline Cl
Exmouth EX8. . . . . .196 D1
Kingskerswell TQ12 . . .213 A3
Carousel Ct EX4 . . . . . .177 A4
Carpenter Cl
Exeter EX4 . . . . .261 A3
Tiverton EX16 . . . . .161 C3
Carpenter Dr TQ13 . . .180 B6
Carpenter Rd PL9 . . . .255 F8
Carpenter's Cross
EX18. . . . . .60 A5
Carpenter's La EX18. . .60 A5
Carpenter Way PL19 .171 B7
Carradale Rd PL6 . . . .249 C7
Carr Cl TQ8. . . . . .259 C5
Carrick Mill EX3 . . . . .182 E7
Carrington Terr ☑
EX32. . . . . .155 A6
Carrionpit La EX19 . . .58 F3
Carrions The ☑ TQ9 .223 C5
Carrisbrooke Way
PL12 . . . . .242 B2
Carroll Rd PL5 . . . . . . .244 C2
Carroll Rise EX7. . . . . .204 E6
Carrolls Way PL9 . . . .256 A5
Carron La PL6 . . . . .241 D1
Carscombe La EX16 . . .48 E6
Carslake Cl EX10. . . . .188 C7
Carswells TQ12 . . . . . .212 F5
Carter Ave EX8 . . . . . .202 A8
Carter Cl EX36 . . . . . . .158 C5
Carter Rd PL21. . . . . . .237 D6
Carters Cross EX13. . . .87 A3
Cart Land Rise EX1. . .179 B8
Cartwright Cres
TQ14. . . . . .209 D8
Cary Ave TQ1 . . . . .220 C7
Cary Castle TQ1. . . . . .220 B8
Cary Parade TQ2 . . . .220 B4
Cary Park Rd TQ1 . . . .220 C7
Cary Pk TQ1 . . . . .220 C7
Cary Rd
Paignton TQ3 . . . . .219 A1
Torquay TQ2 . . . . .220 A4
Caseberry La EX5 . . . . .82 E6
Case Gdns EX12. . . . . .192 B6
Cassiobury Way TQ2 .213 E2
Castlands EX5 . . . . .172 C4
CASTLE 88 C4
Castle Acre Gdns
PL3 . . . . .249 B5
Castle Bank Gdns
PL3. . . . . .249 B5
Castle Barbican PL7. .250 E4
Castlebar Cl EX16. . . .161 E5
Castle Bldgs PL12. . . .242 D4
Castle Carey Gdns
PL3. . . . . .249 B5
Castle Cir TQ1 . . . . .220 A5
Castle Circus Ct
TQ1. . . . . .220 A5
Castle Cotts
Exmouth EX8. . . . . .203 A7
Tuckenhay TQ9 . . . . . .139 F6
Wellington TA21 . . . . . .52 D8
Woodbury EX5 . . . . . . .184 C3
Castle Cross
Axminster EX13 . . . . . . .88 D4
Bratton Clovelly EX20. . .92 C6
Membury EX13 . . . . . . .87 E4
Castle Ct
Saltash PL12. . . . . .242 C2
Torquay TQ1 . . . . .220 C7
☑ Totnes TQ9 . . . . . . .223 B4
Totnes TQ9 . . . . .223 B6
Castle Drogo★ EX6 . . . .96 C1
Castle Farm EX11 . . . .168 E4
Castleford Way EX20 .170 B4
Castle Gate EX6. . . . . .194 C3
Castle Ham Lodge
EX20. . . . . .170 B4

Castlehayes Gdns
PL7. . . . . .250 E4
Castle Hill
Axminster EX13 . . . . . .167 D6
Berrynarbor EX34. . . . . .2 E3
Great Torrington EX38 .159 D4
Ilfracombe EX34. . . . . .150 C6
Lynton EX35 . . . . .151 C5
Saltash PL12. . . . . .242 B1
Seaton EX12. . . . . .192 A4
Upton TA4 . . . . .34 E7
Castle Hill Ave EX34. .150 C6
Castle Hill Gdns
EX38. . . . . .159 D5
Castle Hill Ind Pk
EX13. . . . . .167 C6
Castle Hill View ☑
EX10. . . . . .101 B1
Castle Hill Villas ☑
EX34. . . . . .150 C6
Castle Ho EX13 . . . . . . .167 D6
Castle Hts EX35. . . . . .151 C5
Castle La
Blackawton TQ9. . . . . .139 E2
Budleigh Salterton
EX9. . . . . .197 C1
Exmouth EX8, EX9. . . .203 B8
Okehampton EX20 . . . .92 F1
Paignton TQ3 . . . . .218 C6
Plymouth PL7 . . . . .250 E4
Torquay TQ1 . . . . .220 B5
Woodbury EX5 . . . . . . .184 D3
Castlemain TA20. . . . . .69 D8
Castleman Wy EX15 .163 E4
Castle Mdw EX30. . . . .40 D8
Castlemead Cl PL12. .242 D4
Castlemead Dr PL12. .242 D3
Castle Mill ☑ EX32. . .17 B2
Castle Mount
Exeter EX2 . . . . .177 B7
Exeter EX4 . . . . .261 A4
Castle Park Ind Est
EX32. . . . . .155 E3
Castle Park Rd EX32. .155 E3
Castle Pk EX15. . . . . . . .67 B8
Castle Pk Cl
☑ Paignton TQ3 . . . . .225 F1
Paignton TQ4 . . . . .228 F8
Castle Pk Ct TQ3 . . . . .225 F1
Castle Pk Dr TQ4. . . . .228 F8
Castle Pk Way TQ4 . .228 F8
Castle Prim Sch The
EX16. . . . . .161 D4
Castle Quay EX31 . . . .154 F5
Castle Quay Ct ☑
EX31. . . . . .154 F5
Castle Rd
Dartmouth TQ6 . . . . . .234 B1
Kingswear TQ6 . . . . . . .234 A2
Okehampton EX20 . . . .170 B4
Torquay TQ1 . . . . .220 B5
Wellington TA21 . . . . . .52 D8
Castle Rise
Plymouth PL3 . . . . .249 B4
Saltash PL12. . . . . .242 D1
Castle Rock EX34 . . . . .7 F7
Castle St
Axminster EX13 . . . . . .167 D6
Bampton EX16 . . . . .34 B1
Barnstaple EX31. . . . . .154 F5
Combe Martin EX34 . . . .3 A3
Exeter EX2 . . . . .177 C6
Exeter EX4 . . . . .261 B3
Great Torrington EX38 .159 D5
Northam EX39 . . . . . . .156 F6
Plymouth PL1. . . . . . . .263 A2
Tiverton EX16. . . . . . . .161 D4
Totnes TQ9 . . . . .223 C6
Winkleigh EX19. . . . . . .58 F3
Castle Terr ☑ EX34 . . .150 C6
Castleton Cl PL3 . . . . .249 B4
Castleton Tor TQ1 . . . .219 F7
Castle View
☑ Colyton EX24. . . . . .103 A4
Saltash PL12. . . . . .242 D1
Castle Way TQ12 . . . . .206 E4
Castlewood Ave
TQ12. . . . . .206 F4
Castle Wood La TA20. .69 F1
Castor Cl TQ5. . . . . .230 D3
Castor La TQ4 . . . . .226 B1
Castor Mws ☑ TQ5. . .230 A3
Castor Rd TQ5 . . . . . . .230 C3
Castra Ave EX20 . . . . .170 E7
Catalina Cl EX14 . . . . . .67 C1
Catalina Villas PL9 . .255 A6
Cater Rd EX32 . . . . .155 B4
Cat & Fiddle Pk EX5 . .179 E3
Catharine Cl EX16 . . .161 E5
Cathcart Ave PL4 . . . .249 B2
Cathedral Cl EX1. . . . .261 B3
Cathedral of St Mary's &
St Boniface★ PL1. . . .262 B3
Cathedral School of St
Mary The PL1. . . . . . .262 B3
Cathedral St PL1. . . . .262 B3
Catherine Cres TQ4 . .225 F1
Catherine St
Exeter EX1 . . . . .261 B3
Plymouth PL1. . . . . . . .262 C2
Cathole La DT7 . . . . . . .104 B5
Catkill Cross EX36 . . . .46 C7
Cat La EX34. . . . . .150 B5
Catmoor Cross EX13. . .88 A5
Catnip Cl EX13. . . . . . . .167 E6
CATON 131 C6

Caton Cross TQ12. . . .131 C6
Cator TQ9 . . . . .227 F8
Catriage Hill EX32. . . . .18 C2
Catriage La EX32. . . . . .18 C2
Catsborough Cross
EX39. . . . . .40 E6
Catshole La EX39 . . . .156 F1
Catsmoor Cross EX20 .92 F1
Catson Gn PL8. . . . . . . .257 A5
CATTEDOWN. 263 C1
Cattedown Rd PL3 . . .263 C1
Catterick Cl PL5 . . . . .243 E5
Cattewater Rd PL4 . . .249 B1
Cattewater Rd PL4 . . .249 B1
Cattledown Ind Est
PL9 . . . . .255 B8
Catt's La TA21 . . . . .52 E6
Caulston Ct EX8. . . . . .196 A2
Caulfield Ct ☑ TQ12. .207 C3
Caumont Cl EX15 . . . . .65 F7
Caunters Cl TQ12 . . . .211 D2
Causeway EX12 . . . . . .191 D5
Causeway EX39. . . . . . .157 A7
Causeway Cross
TQ12. . . . . .211 E2
Causeway End EX14. . .84 D7
Causeway The TQ12 . .211 D2
CauseWy View PL4. . .255 B6
Causey Gdns EX1 . . . .174 F1
Causey La EX1 . . . . . . .174 F1
CAUTE. 55 D5
Cavalier Ct EX38 . . . . .159 D5
Cavalier Rd TQ12 . . . .180 F3
Cavalry Chase EX20 . .170 D7
Cavalry Dr TQ12 . . . . .180 F1
Cavell Way EX20 . . . . .170 C6
Cavendish Cl EX7 . . . .204 C7
Cavendish Pl EX35 . . .151 B5
Cavendish Rd
Exeter EX1 . . . . .177 F6
Plymouth PL4 . . . . .249 B1
Cavern Rd
☑ Brixham TQ5. . . . . .230 C4
Torquay TQ1 . . . . .220 B5
Caversham Cl EX6 . . . .113 B4
Cavie Cres EX33 . . . . .152 B6
Cavie Rd EX33 . . . . . . .152 B6
Cawkett La TA22 . . . . . .33 A6
Cawley Ave EX13 . . . . .167 F7
Cawley's La EX14 . . . . .86 F6
CAWSAND 253 B1
Caxton Gdns PL5. . . . .244 C1
Caxton Row EX16 . . . .161 D6
Cayley Way PL5 . . . . . .243 F2
Cayman Cl TQ2 . . . . . .213 E3
Cecil Ave
Paignton TQ3 . . . . .226 B8
Plymouth PL4 . . . . .263 C4
Cecil Cotts PL1 . . . . . . .262 A3
Cecilia Rd TQ3. . . . . . . .219 B1
Cecil Mews TQ3 . . . . . .226 B7
Cecil Rd
Exeter EX2 . . . . .177 A4
Paignton TQ3 . . . . .226 B7
Cecil St PL1 . . . . .262 B3
Cedar Ave
Plymouth PL3 . . . . .249 B4
Saltash PL12. . . . . .242 F2
Cedar Ave PL9 . . . . .255 C5
Cedar Cl
Axminster EX13 . . . . . .167 D5
Exmouth EX8. . . . . .196 D3
Honiton EX14 . . . . .166 B5
Seaton EX12. . . . . .192 A7
Teignmouth TQ14 . . . .210 D7
Torpoint PL11. . . . . . . .246 F2
Cedar Court Rd TQ1. . .220 B7
Cedarcroft Rd PL2 . . .248 B7
Cedar Ct
Rockbeare EX5. . . . . . . .99 B6
Saltash PL12. . . . . .242 F2
Wellington TA21 . . . . . .160 E5
Cedar Dr
Loddiswell TQ7. . . . . . .143 F7
Torpoint PL11. . . . . . . .246 F2
Cedar Gdns EX13. . . . .167 D5
Cedar Gr EX31 . . . . .154 B2
Cedar Ho ☑ EX33 . . . . .152 D6
Cedar Pk PL9 . . . . .255 A1
Cedar Rd
Newton Abbot TQ12 . .212 F8
Paignton TQ3 . . . . .219 C1
Tiverton EX16. . . . . . . .161 F5
Cedars The EX14. . . . .166 E7
Cedar Units TQ9 . . . . .222 F8
Cedar Way
Bideford EX39. . . . . .25 D4
Brixham TQ5 . . . . .230 A2
Celandine Cl EX12 . . .192 B7
Celandine Gdns PL7. .251 C5
Celandine Lawns
EX15. . . . . .162 D5
Celia Cres EX4 . . . . . . .174 A2
Celtic Cl EX1 . . . . .178 E8
Celtic Fields EX7. . . . .204 E7
Cembra Cl EX14. . . . . .166 E5
Cemetery La EX5. . . . . .82 F6
Cemetery Rd PL18 . . .125 C5
Centaur Mws PL9 . . . .256 E8
Centenary Rd ☑ PL5 .247 E2
Centenary Way
Bovey Tracey TQ13 . . .180 F7
Torquay TQ2 . . . . .213 C2
Centry La
Bittadon EX31. . . . . .9 C5
Parracombe EX31. . . . . .4 D2

Central Ave
Exeter, Countess Wear
EX2. . . . . .182 D7
Exeter, Whipton EX4 . .174 B2
Holsworthy EX22 . . . . .164 B4
Lee Mill EX22 . . . . .136 C6
Paignton TQ3 . . . . .226 B8
Central Park Ave
PL4. . . . . .262 C4
Central Pl ☑ EX14 . . .166 C6
Central Rd PL1 . . . . . . .262 B1
Central St PL3 . . . . . . .262 B3
Central Station Chambers
EX4. . . . . .261 A3
Centre ☑ PL21 . . . . . . .137 C8
Centry Ct TQ5. . . . . . . .230 E4
Centry Rd TQ5 . . . . . . .230 E4
Centurion Cl EX1. . . . .178 D8
Centurian Ho ☑ EX1 .261 A3
Century Dr EX39 . . . . .156 E6
Ceramic Terr ☑
EX32. . . . . .155 A4
Chackrell La EX16. . . . .50 F2
Chaddiford La EX31 .154 D7
CHADDLEWOOD 251 B6
Chaddlewood Ave
PL4. . . . . .263 B3
Chaddlewood Cl
Plymouth PL7 . . . . .250 F5
Plymouth PL7 . . . . .251 A4
Chaddlewood Ho
PL7. . . . . .251 B5
Chaddlewood Prim Sch
PL7. . . . . .251 A5
Chad Rd PL9. . . . . .140 A8
Chaffcombe Cross
EX17. . . . . .78 F5
Chaffcombe La EX17 . .79 A6
Chaffinch Dr EX15 . . .163 B2
Chaffinch Rise EX5. . . .99 B6
CHAGFORD 111 A6
Chagford CE Prim Sch
TQ13. . . . . .111 A5
Chagford Cross TQ13 111 E5
Chagford Wlk PL6. . . .249 E8
Chains Rd EX16. . . . . . .50 D1
Chalcombe Rocks La
TA4. . . . . .34 E5
Chalfield Cl TQ2 . . . . .213 C3
Chalk Pit Rd TA20 . . . . .69 F7
Chalk St EX4. . . . . .174 D2
CHALLABOROUGH. . . .142 E3
Challabrook La TQ13 180 B6
CHALLACOMBE. 11 F3
Challacombe Cotts
PL20 . . . . .120 F6
Challacombe Cross
Chagford TQ13 . . . . . .110 F2
Challacombe EX31. . . . .11 F3
Chulmleigh EX18. . . . . .45 A2
Challacombe Hill EX34 . 8 A5
Challacombe Hill Rd
EX34. . . . . .7 F6
Challenger Cross
EX13. . . . . .87 E7
Challeycroft Rd TQ5. .230 A1
Challgood Cl ☑ PL9. .255 F5
Challgood Rise PL9 . .255 F5
Challices Cotts EX18 . .59 E4
Challock Cl PL6. . . . . . .245 D4
Challowell La
Braunton EX33 . . . . . .152 B8
Knowle EX33. . . . . .8 D1
Chaloner's Rd EX33 . .152 D6
CHAMBERCOMBE 150 D5
Chambercombe La
EX34. . . . . .150 E4
Chambercombe Manor★
EX34. . . . . .150 E5
Chambercombe Park Rd
EX34. . . . . .150 E5
Chambercombe Pk
EX34. . . . . .150 E5
Chambercombe Pk Terr
EX34. . . . . .150 E5
Chambercombe Rd
EX34. . . . . .150 D5
Chamberlain Ave
EX8. . . . . .202 E7
Chamberlain Rd
Exeter EX2 . . . . .177 B4
Exeter EX2 . . . . .261 B4
Chamberlayne Dr
PL7. . . . . .250 E6
Chambers Cl EX14 . . .188 A8
Chambers La EX1 . . . .179 B8
Champernhayes La
DT6. . . . . .104 F7
Champernowne PL21 137 B3
Champernowne Cres ☑
EX34. . . . . .150 D5
Champford La TA21. . .160 D5
Champford Mews ☑
TA21. . . . . .160 D5
Champion Cross TA4. . .35 E3
Champion Way EX16. . .64 E8
Chancel Cl EX4 . . . . . . .174 D1
Chancel La EX4 . . . . . .174 D1
Chancellor's Way
EX4. . . . . .174 A2
Chandlers Ct ☑ EX39. .15 B1
Chandlers Hts TQ8 . . .259 D5
Chandlers' La EX10 . . .188 B5
Chandlers Wlk EX2. . .261 A1
Channel Park Ave
PL3. . . . . .249 B5

Channel View
Ilfracombe EX34 150 D5
Woolacombe EX34 1 A2
Channel View Dr
TQ7 147 B6
Channel View La
EX7 204 C3
Channel View Terr
PL4 263 C4
Channer Pl EX39 156 C6
Channings Dr EX1 179 B8
Channon Rd PL12 242 C4
Channons Ct 8 EX14 166 B6
Chanter Ct EX2 178 A2
Chanter's Hill EX32 155 B5
Chanters Rd EX39 157 A3
Chantry Ave EX39 157 A3
Chantry Cl TQ14 210 D7
Chantry Ct PL7 250 B5
Chantry Hill TQ7 145 D4
Chantry Mdw EX2 181 B8
Chantry Orch EX24 103 A5
Chantry The EX20 170 C5
Chapel Cl
Crediton EX17 79 C1
Gunnislake PL18 125 B5
Halberton EX16 65 A8
5 Horrabridge PL20 126 F4
Petrockstow EX20 56 F4
Chapel Cnr EX22 70 F5
Chapel Cotts PL7 132 F4
Chapel Cross
Dunkeswell EX14 67 C2
Iddesleigh EX19 57 E3
Petrockstow EX20 56 F8
Puddington EX16 62 B5
Thorverton EX5 81 D5
Thurlestone TQ7 143 A2
Chapel Ct
Chudleigh TQ12 123 F6
Exeter EX2 177 A4
Stoke Gabriel TQ9 227 F8
Swimbridge EX32 28 E8
Torquay TQ1 219 F7
Chapel Down La
PL21 137 F3
Chapel Down Lane End
PL21 137 E3
Chapeldown Rd
PL11 247 A2
Chapel Downs Dr
EX17 165 A6
Chapel Downs Rd
EX17 165 A6
Chapel Fields 6
TQ10 134 F3
Chapel Hill
5 Budleigh Salterton
EX9 198 A1
Cheriton Fitzpaine EX17 62 F1
Clyst St George EX3 183 C6
15 Exmouth EX8 202 A6
Longdown EX6 98 E2
5 Newton Abbot
TQ12 207 B3
Uffculme EX15 65 A6
Uffculme EX15 66 A7
Whiddon Down EX20 95 E3
Chapel Hill Cross
EX17 62 F1
Chapel Ho 4 EX39 156 F7
Chapel Knap EX13,
EX24 102 F7
Chapel La
Chilsworthy EX22 53 E1
Colaton Raleigh EX9 186 C4
11 Coldeast TQ12 122 F1
Coldeast TQ13 180 D1
Combe Martin EX34 3 A3
Dartmouth TQ6 233 F3
Folly Gate EX20 93 F8
4 Horrabridge PL20 126 F4
2 Horrabridge PL20 126 F5
Loddiswell TQ7 143 E7
Lutton PL21 133 B2
Malborough TQ7 147 E6
Mary Tavy PL19 117 E6
Ottery St Mary EX11 169 E4
Patsford EX31 9 B2
Stoke Fleming TQ6 146 B7
Totnes TQ9 223 D5
Withypool TA24 21 C6
Yealmpton PL8 257 F4
Chapel Mdw PL20 126 C3
Chapel Park Cl EX39 157 C2
Chapel Pk EX17 96 A8
Chapel Rd
Brampford Speke EX5 81 E1
Bratton Clovelly EX20 92 A2
Exeter EX2 177 B1
Lympstone EX8 195 D5
Newton Abbot TQ12 207 D3
Parkham EX39 39 E8
Saltash PL12 242 B3
Sidmouth EX10 188 B3
Yealmpton PL8 136 A2
Chapel Row TQ7 142 C6
Chapelry The 5
TQ13 123 C4
Chapel St
Axmouth EX12 192 D7
4 Bere Alston PL20 125 E1
18 Bideford EX39 157 A2
Blackawton TQ9 139 E1
Braunton EX33 152 D5
Buckfastleigh TQ11 236 B5
Budleigh Salterton
EX9 199 G2

Chapel St *continued*
Dolton EX19 57 F7
Dulverton TA22 33 D6
Ermington PL21 136 F4
Exeter EX4 261 B3
1 Exmouth EX8 202 A6
Georgeham EX33 8 A2
Gunnislake PL18 125 D6
Holsworthy EX22 164 C3
Honiton EX14 166 C6
Lifton PL16 105 E4
Morchard Bishop EX17 61 A2
Plymouth PL4 263 A3
Plymouth, Mount Wise
PL1 247 E2
Sidbury EX10 101 B2
Sidmouth EX10 188 B3
Tavistock PL19 171 B5
19 Teignmouth TQ14 210 B4
Tiverton EX16 64 C7
Tiverton EX16 161 D4
Woolfardisworthy EX39 38 F7
Chapel The 7 TQ9 223 D5
CHAPELTON 27 F5
Chapelton Cross EX37 27 F5
Chapelton Sta EX37 28 A4
Chapeltown Cross
EX5 63 C1
Chapel Way
Axminster EX13 167 E7
Plymouth PL3 249 A6
Chapman Ct PL12 242 B3
Chapmans Gn EX22 54 C4
Chapmans Ope PL1 247 D2
Chapple Cl EX6 201 B8
Chapplecroft Rd EX13 87 E5
Chapple Cross
Bovey Tracey TQ13 180 B5
Chagford TQ13 110 D8
Dolton EX19 57 E6
Chapple Cross Cross
TQ13 110 D7
Chapple Hill EX16 62 C5
Chapple La EX20 76 E4
Chapple Rd
Bovey Tracey TQ13 180 A6
Witheridge EX16 46 E1
Charberry Rise DT6 104 F4
Chard Ave 4 EX5 99 E8
Chard Barton PL5 244 B3
CHARD JUNCTION 88 E7
Chard Rd
Axminster EX13 88 B4
Axminster EX13 167 E6
Exeter EX1 178 A6
Plymouth PL5 243 D2
Chard St
Axminster EX13 167 D6
Chardstock EX13 88 B7
CHARDSTOCK 88 B7
Chard Stock Cl EX1 178 D6
Chardstone Gr EX13 88 B7
Charfield Dr
Plymouth PL6 245 A1
Plymouth PL6 249 A8
Charford Cross TQ10 135 B1
Chariot Dr TQ12 207 F6
Chariot Way EX20 170 D7
Charlacott Cross
EX31 27 B6
Charlbury Dr 7 PL3 249 D1
Charlemont Rd TQ14 210 B8
CHARLES 18 E3
Charles Ave EX39 157 A2
CHARLES BOTTOM 18 E2
Charles Cross
East Buckland EX32 18 E3
Plymouth PL4 263 A3
Charles Ct EX8 195 E5
Charles Dart Cres
EX32 155 A6
Charles Darwin Rd
PL1 247 F1
Charles Hankin Cl
PL21 237 E4
Charles Hudson La 2
EX31 155 A7
Charles Rd
Honiton EX14 166 C6
Kingskerswell TQ12 213 A2
Charles St
14 Barnstaple EX32 154 F6
Dartmouth TQ6 233 F3
3 Exmouth EX8 202 A7
Plymouth PL4 263 A3
Charles Terr PL3 249 A6
Charlestown Rd TQ3 225 D7
Charleton CE Prim Sch
TQ7 144 C1
Charleton Court Barns
TQ7 144 C1
Charleton Way TQ7 144 C1
Charlotte Cl TQ2 219 F8
Charlotte Ct TQ1 214 B1
Charlotte Mews 1
EX2 261 B2
Charlottes Oak TQ12 123 E1
Charlotte St
Crediton EX17 165 D5
Plymouth PL2 247 E4
Charlton Cres PL6 245 A2
Charlton Ho EX7 204 F6
Charlton Rd PL6 245 A3
Charlton Terr PL21 237 D5
Charlwood Ct TQ1 220 C8
CHARMOUTH 104 F4
Charmouth Bypass
EX13 104 F5

Charmouth Cl
Lyme Regis DT7 260 E4
Torquay TQ1 220 D6
Charmouth Ho DT7 260 C3
Charmouth Rd
Lyme Regis DT7 260 E4
Raymond's Hill EX13 104 C7
Charneymore Cross
EX18 44 E1
Charnhill Cl PL9 256 A6
Charnhill Way PL9 256 A6
Charnley Ave EX4 176 E5
Charter Cl EX16 161 B4
Charter Rd EX13 167 E7
CHARTON 104 A1
Charton Cross DT7 104 A2
Chartwell Cl TQ3 225 E7
Chartwell Dr TQ12 207 A4
Charwell Mdw EX5 82 F6
Chase The
Exeter EX3 182 D6
Honiton EX14 166 D7
Ivybridge PL21 237 D4
CHASTY 164 C2
Chasty La EX22 164 C3
Chatham Cl EX8 202 D8
Chatsworth Gdns
PL5 243 F3
Chatsworth Rd TQ1 220 B6
Chatto Rd TQ1 220 A7
Chatto Way TQ1 220 A7
Chatwell La PL21 137 B3
Chaucer Ave EX2 177 F3
Chaucer Grove EX4 177 F8
Chaucer Rd PL19 171 D5
Chaucer Rise 4 EX8 196 C3
Chaucer Way PL5 244 C1
Chaves Cl EX16 161 F3
CHAWLEIGH 60 B7
Chawleigh Cl PL18 125 C5
Chawleigh Hill EX18 59 F8
Chawleigh Week Cross
EX18 59 E8
Chawleigh Week La
EX18 59 D8
Chawleigh Week Mill
Cross EX18 59 D8
Cheavestone Lea
TQ9 139 E1
Checkridge La EX13 88 D2
Chedworth St PL4 263 A3
Cheeke St EX1 261 C3
Cheese La EX10 187 F4
Cheevor Pl TQ12 208 A3
Cheffers Mws EX3 182 D7
CHEGLINCH 8 F6
Cheglinch Cnr EX34 8 F5
Cheglinch La EX34 8 F6
CHELDON 60 D8
Cheldon Barton Moor La
EX18 60 D8
Cheldon Cross
Chawleigh EX18 60 D8
Chulmleigh EX18 45 D2
CHELFHAM 17 D6
Chelfham Mill Sch
EX32 17 C6
Chelmer Cl PL7 251 A5
Chelmsford Pl PL5 244 C4
Chelmsford Rd EX4 176 E6
Chelsea Pl 8 TQ14 210 B5
Chelsea Trad Ctr
EX2 178 E5
Chelson Gdns PL6 245 E3
Chelson La EX10 101 E1
CHELSTON
Torquay 219 E4
Wellington 52 D8
Chelston Bsn Pk TA21 52 D8
CHELSTON
HEATHFIELD 52 E7
Chelston Rd
Newton Abbot TQ12 207 B4
Torquay TQ2 219 E3
Chelston Terr TA21 52 D8
Cheltenham Cl EX4 176 E7
Cheltenham Pl PL4 263 B4
Chelwood Gr PL7 250 F5
Chene Ct 6 PL21 137 B2
Cheney's La EX14 166 E8
CHENSON 60 A4
Chepstow Ave PL6 245 C8
Chepstow Cl EX2 182 B8
Chequers Haigh PL8 140 F6
Chequer Tree Ct
PL18 125 C5
Chercombe Bridge Rd
Newton Abbot TQ12 206 C3
Ogwell TQ12 211 B8
Chercombe Cl TQ12 206 E4
Chercombe Valley Rd
TQ12 206 E4
CHERISTOW 22 D4
Cheriswood Ave EX8 196 D1
Cheriswood Cl EX8 196 D1
CHERITON 5 D3
CHERITON BISHOP 97 A4
Cheriton Bishop Com
Prim Sch EX6 97 B4
Cheriton Cl PL5 244 A3
CHERITON CROSS 97 B3
Cheriton Cross
Cadbury EX5 81 C8
Chilton EX17 80 D7
CHERITON
FITZPAINE 62 E1
Cheriton Fitzpaine Prim
Sch EX17 62 F1

Cheriton Hill EX35 5 D3
Cheriton Mill Cross
EX17 62 E2
Cheriton Rd EX35 151 D1
Cherry Arbour EX32 155 C3
CHERRYBRIDGE 5 A4
Cherrybridge Cross
EX35 151 A2
Cherry Brook Dr TQ4 229 B8
Cherry Brook Sq TQ4 229 B8
Cherry Brook Wlk
TQ4 226 B1
Cherry Cl
Cheriton Fitzpaine
EX17 62 F1
Exmouth EX8 196 C3
5 Honiton EX14 85 C2
Tiverton EX16 161 D5
Willand EX15 162 D4
Cherry Cross TQ9 223 C4
Cherry Ct PL19 116 E3
Cherry Dr EX12 192 A5
Cherryford La EX31 4 C4
Cherry Gdns
Crediton EX17 165 C5
Exeter EX2 178 A4
Paignton TQ3 226 A7
Cherry Gr EX32 155 C2
Cherry Mdw EX17 62 F1
Cherry Park Cl TQ2 219 D2
Cherry Pk
Appledore EX39 14 F1
Plymouth PL7 251 A3
Cherry Tree Cl
Exeter EX4 173 A2
Rockbeare EX5 99 B6
Cherry Tree Dr
Brixton PL8 257 A5
3 Landkey EX32 17 B2
Cherry Tree Gdns
EX16 161 E5
Cherry Tree La PL7 251 A4
Cherry Tree Rd EX13 167 E6
Cherrywood Cl TQ12 206 E4
Cheshire Dr PL6 244 D6
Cheshire Rd EX8 196 E2
Chesil Ct DT7 260 C3
Chesnut Cl PL12 242 D4
Chester Cl EX4 176 E7
Chester Ct EX8 201 F7
Chesterfield Rd PL3 249 B4
Chestermoor Cross
EX20 92 D5
Chester Pl 4 PL4 248 E4
Chester Terr 17 EX32 155 A4
Chesterton Cl PL5 244 C3
Chestnut Ave
Cullompton EX15 163 C2
Dartmouth TQ6 233 E4
Exeter EX2 178 A3
Plymouth PL9 255 C5
Torquay TQ2 219 F4
Chestnut Cl
22 Bere Alston PL20 125 E1
Braunton EX33 152 E6
Cheriton Bishop EX6 97 B4
Crediton EX17 165 D6
Exmouth EX8 196 C3
Lamerton PL19 116 E4
Seaton EX12 192 A7
Tavistock PL19 171 D2
Torpoint PL11 246 F3
Wellington TA21 160 E5
Wembury PL9 255 A1
Chestnut Cres
7 Chudleigh TQ13 123 F6
Stoke Canon EX5 173 F8
Chestnut Ct EX2 181 B8
Chestnut Dr
Bideford EX39 25 D4
Brixham TQ5 230 A2
Kingsteignton TQ12 207 F6
Newton Abbot TQ12 208 A1
Willand EX15 162 C4
Chestnut Gr TQ6 233 C4
Chestnut Mews EX14 84 E2
Chestnut Pk TQ7 149 D7
Chestnut Rd
Plymouth PL3 248 D7
Tiverton EX16 161 F5
Chestnuts The EX5 99 D2
Chestnut Terr PL19 116 E3
Chestnut View EX13 87 D6
Chestnut Way
Honiton EX14 166 A4
Newton Poppleford
EX10 186 F8
Chestnut Wlk EX7 204 C5
Chestnut Wy 11 TQ7 143 E7
Cheston Cross TQ10 134 E1
CHESTWOOD 155 B1
Chestwood Ave EX31 154 C3
Chestwood Cl EX31 154 D4
Chestwood Villas
EX32 16 E1
CHETTISCOMBE 161 F8
CHEVITHORNE 49 D2
Cheyne Beach 2
EX34 150 C6
Cheynegate La EX4 174 C3
Cheyne Rise EX4 174 D2
Cheyney Cross EX36 30 B2
Cheyney La EX36 30 B2
Chibbet Hill TA24 21 B8
Chibbet Post TA24 21 C8
Chichacott Cross
EX20 170 F7
Chichacott Rd EX20 170 D7

Chichester Cl
Barnstaple EX32 155 B2
Exmouth EX8 202 C8
Ilfracombe EX34 150 A4
11 Instow EX39 15 B1
Teignmouth TQ14 210 A8
Chichester Cres
Barnstaple EX32 155 B2
Saltash PL12 242 E1
Chichester Ct
Barnstaple EX32 155 C5
Horrabridge PL20 126 F4
Outer Hope TQ7 147 B7
Shirwell EX31 17 B8
Chichester Ho
Barnstaple EX31 155 B8
Exeter EX2 178 B5
Plymouth PL1 262 B2
Chichester Mews
EX1 261 B3
Chichester Pk EX34 8 A6
Chichester Pl 7 EX16 64 D7
Chichester Rd EX32 155 B2
Chichester Way
East Budleigh EX9 198 B6
Newton Abbot TQ12 207 F3
Westward Ho! EX39 156 C6
Chicory Cl TQ12 206 D5
Chideock Ct DT7 260 C3
Chieftain Wy EX2 177 A4
Chilbridge La EX31 17 B8
Chilcombe Cross
EX24 102 B7
Chilcombe La EX24 102 A6
Chilcote Cl TQ1 220 C8
Chilcott Cl 5 EX16 64 D7
Chilcott Cross TA22 33 A7
Chilcott La TA22 33 A7
Childrey Gdns PL6 245 C1
Childrey Wlk PL6 245 C1
CHILLA 73 E5
Chilla Chapel EX21 73 E4
Chilla Rd EX21 73 E3
CHILLATON 116 D8
Chillaton Cross TQ7 138 A1
Chillaton Ct PL16 106 E1
CHILLINGTON 145 A2
Chillmark Cl PL3 249 D1
Chill Park Brake EX1 175 D1
Chill Pits La EX13 88 B8
Chilpark EX31 153 D5
CHILSON 88 C6
CHILSON COMMON 88 D7
CHILSWORTHY
Gunnislake 125 B7
Holsworthy 53 E1
Chiltern Cl TQ2 219 D3
Chiltern Cross EX16 34 B2
CHILTON 80 E7
Chilton Ave TQ14 210 C6
Chilton Cl PL6 249 B7
Chilton Gate EX16 81 D8
Chilton La EX17 80 E7
Chilverton Cross
EX17 59 F1
Chilverton Hill Gate
EX17 59 F1
Chilverton La EX17 59 F1
Chineway Gdns EX11 169 F3
Chineway Head EX11 101 B6
Chineway Hill EX11 101 A6
Chineway Rd
Ottery St Mary EX11 100 F6
Ottery St Mary EX11 101 A6
Chingswell St 2
EX39 157 A2
Chinkwell Rise TQ2 219 B8
Chinon Ct EX16 64 D8
Chinon Pl EX16 161 A6
Chinston Cl EX14 85 B4
Chipmunk Wlk EX32 155 B6
Chipple Pk PL21 133 B2
CHIPSTABLE 35 E6
Chircombe La EX39 157 A4
Chiseldon Farm TQ5 230 B2
Chiseldon Hill TQ5 230 C2
Chiseldon Ho EX4 173 A1
Chitterley Bsns Ctr
EX5 82 A7
Chittleburn Bsns Pk
PL8 256 F6
Chittleburn Cross
PL8 256 E5
Chittleburn Hill PL8 256 E5
CHITTLEHAMHOLT 44 B8
CHITTLEHAMPTON 28 F4
Chittlehampton CE Prim
Sch EX37 28 F4
CHIVELSTONE 149 A6
Chivelstone Cross
TQ7 149 A5
CHIVENOR 15 E5
Chivenor Airfield
EX31 152 F1
Chivenor Ave PL5 243 D4
Chivenor Cross EX31 15 E5
Chiverstone La EX6 194 C4
Chiverstone Rd EX6 194 C4
Chockenhole La EX9 199 A8
Chockland Rd 12
TQ12 123 E1
Cholhouse La EX20 77 C7
Chollacott Cl PL19 171 C4
Chollacott La PL19 171 D3
Chollaton Cross EX22 39 E1
Cholwell Cross TQ9 222 F4
Chope Rd EX39 156 F6
Chopes Cl EX39 26 A4

Chough Cl
Launceston PL15 105 A2
Marhamchurch EX23 70 A8
Christ Cross EX5 82 C8
Christcross La EX5 82 D7
Christian Mill Bsns Pk
PL6 244 F4
Christina Par TQ9 223 F5
Christina Pk TQ9 223 E5
Christone Cross TQ9 138 D7
CHRISTOW 113 A3
Christow Com Prim Sch
EX6 113 B4
Christow Rd EX2 177 B2
Chrystel Cl EX10 100 D2
Chubb Dr PL3 248 B4
Chubb Rd EX39 26 A4
Chubby Croft Cl EX39 22 E3
Chubs Cross EX20 77 F5
Chubworthy Cross
TA4 35 D5
CHUDLEIGH 123 F6
Chudleigh Ave EX39 157 B1
Chudleigh CE Com Prim
Sch TQ13 123 E6
CHUDLEIGH
KNIGHTON 123 C4
Chudleigh Knighton CE
Prim Sch TQ13 123 C4
Chudleigh Rd
2 Bideford EX39 157 B1
Exeter EX2 181 B7
Kingsteignton TQ12 207 D8
Kingsteignton TQ13 123 E1
Plymouth PL4 249 A4
Chudleigh Terr 6
EX39 157 B1
Chudley Cl EX8 196 D1
Chuggaton Cross
EX37 28 C5
Chuley Cross TQ13 130 F3
Chuley Hill TQ13 130 F4
Chuley Rd TQ13 130 F4
CHULMLEIGH 44 F1
Chulmleigh Community
College EX18 44 E1
Chulmleigh Hill 10
EX18 44 E1
Chulmleigh Prim Sch
EX18 44 E1
Chulmleigh Rd
Morchard Bishop
EX17 61 A2
Winkleigh EX19 58 F3
Church Ave
Lamerton PL19 116 F3
Okehampton EX20 170 A5
Church Cl
Ashprington TQ9 139 F8
Aylesbeare EX5 99 D2
Bratton Fleming EX31 18 A8
Broadclyst EX5 175 C7
15 Chulmleigh EX18 44 E1
Dartmouth TQ6 233 F3
Dolton EX19 57 F6
Goodleigh EX32 17 B5
Kingsbridge TQ7 258 D5
Lapford EX17 60 D3
Plymouth PL7 250 B7
Puddington EX16 62 B5
Totnes TQ9 223 C5
Yealmpton PL8 257 F4
Church Cliff DT7 260 E3
Church Cross
Buckfastleigh TQ11 236 B6
Cheriton Fitzpaine EX17 62 E1
Exeter EX4 174 D3
Filleigh EX32 29 C6
Sandford EX17 80 A5
Church Cross Rd
TQ11 236 B6
Church Ct
Harberton TQ9 222 D2
Kingsteignton TQ12 207 E6
14 Newton Abbot
TQ12 207 B3
Plymouth PL6 245 A7
Church Dr TA21 52 F7
Church End Rd TQ12 212 F4
Church Farm TQ7 143 A1
Churchfield Rd 26
EX39 15 A1
Churchfields TA21 160 D7
Church Fields TA21 160 E6
Churchfields Dr
TQ13 180 D7
Churchfields Gdns
TQ6 233 D3
Churchfields W TQ6 233 D3
Church Flats EX6 201 B8
Churchford Rd EX33 8 D1
Church Gate EX36 30 E1
Church Gr EX32 155 B3
CHURCH GREEN 101 F7
Church Hill
Awliscombe EX14 85 B4
Beer EX12 191 D5
Blackawton TQ9 139 E1
Brendon EX35 5 F4
Buckfastleigh TQ11 236 C6
Calstock PL18 125 D3
Exeter EX4 174 E2
Fremington EX31 153 E5
Holbeton PL8 136 D1
Honiton EX14 166 D5

Church Hill continued
Ilfracombe EX34 . . . . . . **150** A5
Kingswear TQ6 . . . . **234** A2
Lynton EX35 . . . . **151** C5
Marldon TQ3 . . . . **218** D4
Milton Combe PL20 . . . **126** C1
Musbury EX13 . . . . **103** D5
Otterton EX9 . . . . **198** D7
Plymouth PL6 . . . . **245** B1
Tavistock PL19 . . . . **171** E2
Tedburn St Mary EX6 . . **97** F5
Winkleigh EX19 . . . . **58** F3
Church Hill Cl TQ9 . . . **139** E2
Church Hill Cross
EX20 . . . . **94** E7
Church Hill E 6 TQ5 . **230** C5
Church Hill La EX33 . . . **8** D1
Church Hill Rd PL9 . . **255** A6
Church Hill W 5
TQ5 . . . . **230** C5
Church Ho
Exeter EX2 . . . . **177** A4
Saltash PL12 . . . . **243** A2
Church House Cl 8
TQ13 . . . . **123** C4
CHURCHILL
Axminster **87** F4
Barnstaple **10** B3
Churchill EX34 . . . . **8** F4
Churchill Ave EX7 . . **204** D5
Churchill Cl
Barnstaple EX32 . . . . . **155** B6
Kenton EX6 . . . . **194** D3
Churchill Cotts PL21 **137** D6
Churchill Cres EX36 . **158** C3
Churchill Ct
7 Brixham TQ5 . . . . . . **230** C4
Lympstone EX8 . . . . . . **195** E6
Churchill Dr
Crediton EX17 . . . . **165** B6
Teignmouth TQ14 . . . . **210** C6
Churchill Gdns EX17 . **78** C7
Churchill Hill EX31 . . . **10** C4
Churchill La
Axminster EX13 . . . . . . **88** A5
Calverleigh EX16 . . . . . **48** C3
Chipstable TA4 . . . . . . **35** C5
Churchill Rd
Bideford EX39 . . . . **26** A4
Exeter EX2 . . . . **176** F4
Exmouth EX8 . . . . **196** D2
Tavistock PL19 . . . . **171** D2
Tiverton EX16 . . . . **161** A4
Churchill Rise EX13 . **167** E7
Churchills 11 EX15 . . . **67** B8
Churchills Nature
 Reserve ★ TQ12 . . . . **207** A5
Churchills Rise 16
EX15 . . . . **67** B8
Churchills The TQ12 **207** A4
Churchill Way
Appledore EX39 . . . . . . **14** F1
Northam EX39 . . . . . . **156** F6
Northam EX39 . . . . . . **157** A7
Plymouth PL3 . . . . **248** E6
Churchill Wlk PL12 . . **242** D1
CHURCHINFORD **68** D7
Church La
Alfington EX11 . . . . **84** F1
Aveton Gifford TQ7 . . . **143** C6
10 Barnstaple EX31 . . **154** F5
Bideford EX39 . . . . **25** E2
4 Bittaford PL21 . . . . **137** C8
Bridford EX6 . . . . **112** F5
Broadclyst EX5 . . . . . . **175** C7
Calstock PL18 . . . . **125** D3
Cargreen PL12 . . . . . . **238** F1
Cargreen PL12 . . . . . . **239** A1
Cheriton Bishop EX6 . . **97** B4
Christow EX6 . . . . **113** B3
Clyst St Mary EX5 . . . . **179** B2
Crediton EX17 . . . . **165** D5
Dulverton TA22 . . . . . . **33** D6
East Budleigh EX9 . . . . **198** B6
Exeter EX2 . . . . **177** A4
Exeter, Heavitree EX2 . **177** F5
Exeter, Pinhoe EX4 . . . **174** D2
Feniton EX14 . . . . **84** E2
Frithelstock Stone EX38 **40** F5
Great Torrington EX38 . **159** C5
Hatherleigh EX20 . . . . **75** C7
Holsworthy EX22 . . . . **164** C4
Kingsbridge TQ7 . . . . **258** F2
Langtree EX38 . . . . **40** F2
Membury EX13 . . . . . . **87** D5
Modbury PL21 . . . . . . **137** B2
Newton St Cyres EX5 . . **82** F8
North Tamerton EX22 . **89** D8
Parracombe EX31 . . . . **4** D1
St John PL11 . . . . **252** B8
Salcombe TQ8 . . . . . . **259** E5
Sheldon EX14 . . . . **66** F3
Shobrooke EX17 . . . . . **80** E4
Slapton TQ7 . . . . **145** D3
Stokeinteignhead
 TQ12 . . . . **209** B2
Swimbridge EX32 . . . . **28** E8
Tavistock PL19 . . . . **171** C5
Torquay TQ2 . . . . **219** F5
Trusham TQ13 . . . . **113** D1
Whitestone EX4 . . . . . . **98** E4
Winkleigh EX19 . . . . . . **58** F3
Yealmpton PL8 . . . . . . **257** F4
Church Lake 8 EX32 . . **17** B2
Churchlands EX17 . . . . **78** C4

Churchlands Cl PL6 . **245** E7
Churchlands Rd PL6 . **245** E8
Church Lane Cross
EX17 . . . . **59** F2
Church Lane Head
TQ13 . . . . **121** B2
Church Lea PL19 . . . . **171** E2
Church Mdw
High Bickington EX37 . . **43** B7
Ivybridge PL21 . . . . . . **237** A4
Landkey EX32 . . . . **17** B2
Langtree EX38 . . . . **40** F2
Church Mdws
Bratton Clovelly EX20 . . **92** A2
Okehampton EX20 . . . **170** A5
Church Mead EX14 . . . **85** B1
Church Mews TQ12 . . **207** E6
Church Park Cl TQ9 . **138** C7
Church Park Ct PL6 . **245** E8
Church Park Rd
1 Newton Ferrers
 PL8 . . . . **141** A7
Plymouth PL6 . . . . **245** E8
Yealmpton PL8 . . . . . . **136** A2
Church Parks EX17 . . . **80** A5
Church Path
Ashburton TQ13 . . . . . **130** F4
Barnstaple EX31 . . . . . **154** F7
Exeter EX1 . . . . **178** A5
Halberton EX16 . . . . . . **65** A7
Ipplepen TQ12 . . . . . . **211** C2
Okehampton EX20 . . . **170** A5
6 Paignton TQ3 . . . . **226** B6
Shute EX13 . . . . **102** F8
Churchpath La EX31 . . **10** D3
Church Path Rd EX2 . **176** F3
Church Pk
Bideford EX39 . . . . **25** A3
Cornwood PL21 . . . . . **133** C2
Horrabridge PL20 . . . . **126** F4
Kingston TQ7 . . . . **142** C6
Kingswear TQ6 . . . . . . **234** B3
2 Newton Ferrers
 PL8 . . . . **141** A7
Paignton TQ3 . . . . **225** D4
Church Pool EX34 . . . . **8** F5
Church Quillet TQ9 . **139** E1
Church Rd
Bishopsteignton
 TQ14 . . . . **209** A7
Brixham TQ5 . . . . **229** E5
Churchinford TA3 . . . . **68** C8
Churchstanton IA3 . . . **68** B8
Cockwood EX6 . . . . . . **201** A6
Colaton Raleigh EX10 . **186** E3
Dartmouth TQ6 . . . . . **233** E3
East Ogwell TQ12 . . . . **206** D1
Ermington PL21 . . . . . **136** F4
Exeter, Alphington EX2 **177** B1
Exeter, St Thomas EX2 . **177** A4
Exmouth EX8 . . . . **202** A7
Georgeham EX33 . . . . . **8** A2
Hennock TQ13 . . . . . . **123** B7
Highampton EX21 . . . . **74** C7
Ideford TQ13 . . . . **124** B4
Ilfracombe EX34 . . . . . **150** A5
Kenton EX6 . . . . **194** F5
Luton TQ13 . . . . **124** C4
Lympstone EX8 . . . . . . **195** E5
Newton Abbot TQ12 . . **207** C2
Plymouth, Plympton
 PL7 . . . . **250** F4
Plymouth, Plymstock
 PL9 . . . . **255** F7
Saltash PL12 . . . . **242** D2
Silverton EX5 . . . . **82** B5
Stoke Fleming TQ6 . . . **146** B7
Torquay, Barton TQ2 . . **214** A3
Torquay, St Marychurch
 TQ1 . . . . **220** B8
Wembury PL9 . . . . **140** D8
Whimple EX5 . . . . **99** E7
Church Row La PL5 . . **244** C4
Church St Mews 4
TQ3 . . . . **226** B6
Church Side EX5 . . . . **179** D7
Church St
Axminster EX13 . . . . . **167** D5
Axmouth EX12 . . . . . . **192** D7
Bradninch EX5 . . . . **83** A7
Braunton EX33 . . . . . . **152** D7
4 Brixham TQ5 . . . . . **230** C4
Buckfastleigh TQ11 . . **236** B5
Calstock PL18 . . . . **125** D3
Chulmleigh EX18 . . . . . **58** E8
Colyton EX24 . . . . **103** A5
Combe Martin EX34 . . . **3** A3
Crediton EX17 . . . . . . **165** D5
Cullompton EX15 . . . . **163** C3
Dawlish EX7 . . . . **204** C6
Dolton EX19 . . . . **57** F7
Exeter EX2 . . . . **177** F5
Exmouth EX8 . . . . **202** A6
Halwell TQ9 . . . . **139** B4
3 Honiton EX14 . . . . **166** C5
Ilfracombe EX34 . . . . . **150** B5
Kenton EX6 . . . . **194** D3
Kingsbridge TQ7 . . . . **258** D5
Kingsteignton TQ12 . . **207** E6
Lyme Regis DT7 . . . . . **260** E3
Modbury PL21 . . . . . . **137** B2
Morchard Bishop EX17 . **61** B2
Okehampton EX20 . . . **170** B5
Paignton TQ3 . . . . **226** B6
Plymouth PL3 . . . . **248** A4
Salcombe TQ8 . . . . . . **259** D5
Sandford EX17 . . . . **80** A5
Sidbury EX10 . . . . **101** C2

Church St continued
8 Sidford EX10 . . . . . **101** B1
Sidmouth EX10 . . . . . **188** B3
14 South Brent TQ10 . **134** F3
South Molton EX36 . . **158** C4
Starcross EX6 . . . . **201** B8
Tiverton EX16 . . . . **161** C4
Torquay TQ2 . . . . **219** F5
Uplyme DT7 . . . . **260** B5
Witheridge EX16 . . . . **60** B1
Churchstanton Prim Sch
TA3 . . . . **68** B8
Church Steps Cotts
EX5 . . . . **184** B3
Church Stile EX6 . . . . **182** B4
Church Stile EX5 . . . . **184** B3
CHURCHSTOW **143** E4
Churchstow Wlk
Plymouth PL6 . . . . **245** E1
Plymouth PL6 . . . . **249** E8
Church Terr
7 Bampton EX16 . . . . **34** B1
Exeter EX2 . . . . **177** F5
CHURCHTOWN
Bridgerule **71** A6
Parracombe **4** D2
Churchtown Cl PL21 . **133** C2
Churchtown Dr PL12 . **242** D1
Churchtown Vale
PL12 . . . . **242** D1
Church View
Bideford EX39 . . . . **26** A1
5 Chudleigh TQ13 . . **123** E6
Dawlish EX7 . . . . **204** C6
Kingsteignton TQ12 . . **207** E6
Ottery St Mary EX11 . . **169** D3
St Dominick PL12 . . . . **125** A2
Saltash PL12 . . . . **242** D2
Sutcombe EX22 . . . . . . **54** A6
Walkhampton PL20 . . . **127** B4
Church View Ho EX5 . **184** B3
Churchward Rd TQ3 . **226** B7
Churchwater La EX18 . **58** D8
Churchway TQ1 . . . . **220** C7
Church Way
Newton Abbot TQ12 . . **207** E1
Plymouth PL5 . . . . **247** E8
Yealmpton PL8 . . . . . . **257** F4
Church Ways EX20 . . . **95** B5
Church Wlk
Avonwick TQ10 . . . . . . **135** B1
17 Bideford EX39 . . . **157** A1
Stoke Gabriel TQ9 . . . **227** F7
Wembury PL9 . . . . **140** C8
Churchwood Ct TQ1 . **220** C5
Churchyard La EX17 . . **61** C7
CHURSCOMBE **218** E2
Churscombe Gn TQ3 **218** E2
Churscombe Pk TQ3 . **218** D2
Churscombe Rd TQ3 . **218** D2
Churston Broadway
TQ4 . . . . **229** B7
Churston Cl TQ5 . . . . **229** C5
Churston Cross
 Churston Ferrers
 TQ5 . . . . **229** E4
 West Putford EX22 . . . **39** B2
Churston Ct TQ7 . . . . **258** D4
CHURSTON
 FERRERS **229** E4
Churston Ferrers Gram
 Sch TQ5 . . . . **229** C5
Churston Rd TQ5 . . . . **229** E5
Churston Rise EX12 . . **191** F8
Churston Sta ★ TQ5 . . **229** C5
Churston Way TQ5 . . **230** B4
Chute SK1 . . . . **261** C4
Cider Press Rd PL15 . . **89** D2
Cider Way EX36 . . . . . **158** B4
Cinder Hill TA20 . . . . . **69** C5
Cinders La TQ6 . . . . . **146** B7
Cintra Terr EX39 . . . . **157** A4
Cistern St TQ9 . . . . . . **223** B5
Citadel Ope 12 PL1 . . **263** A2
Citadel Rd PL1 . . . . . . **262** B2
Citadel Road E PL1 . . **263** A2
Citadel Road W PL1 . **262** C2
City Arc EX4 . . . . **261** A2
City Bsns Pk PL3 . . . . **248** A4
City Coll Plymouth
 (Camels Head Tech Ctr)
 PL5 . . . . **247** E8
City Coll Plymouth (Deep
 Blue Sound) PL1 . . **263** A2
City Coll Plymouth
 (Goschen Ctr) PL2 . **247** E5
City Coll Plymouth (Kings
 Road Ctr) PL1 . . . . **248** A2
City Coll Plymouth
 (Learning Warehouse)
 PL1 . . . . **262** B2
City Coll Plymouth
 (Marine Skills Ctr)
 PL1 . . . . **247** F1
City Coll Plymouth
 (Prince's Trust Ctr)
 PL4 . . . . **263** A2
City Ind Est EX2 . . . . **261** B1
Claddon La TQ1, TQ2 . **214** A5
Clampet La 9 TQ14 . . **210** C4
Clampits Stile TQ11 . . **135** C6
Clampitt Cl TQ12 . . . . **211** D1
Clampitt Rd TQ12 . . . **211** D2
Clampitts EX15 . . . . . **163** B2
Clanage Cross TQ14 . **124** C1
Clanage St TQ14 . . . . **208** F3
Clannaborough Cross
EX17 . . . . **78** E5

CLAPHAM **114** B6
Claponmill Cross EX5 . **83** B2
Clappentail Ct DT7 . . **260** C4
Clappentail La DT7 . . **260** C5
Clappentail Pk DT7 . . **260** C3
Clapperbrook La EX2 **177** B1
Clapperbrook La E
EX2 . . . . **177** D2
Clapper Cross
Bondleigh EX20 . . . . . . **77** B8
Zeal Monachorum EX17 . **78** B5
Clapper La EX14 . . . . **166** C7
Clapps La EX11 . . . . . . **169** D3
Clapp's La
Beer EX12 . . . . **191** D5
Seaton EX12 . . . . **192** B5
CLAPWORTHY **29** D3
Clapworthy Cross
EX36 . . . . **29** D2
Clara Pl EX3 . . . . **182** E5
Claredale Rd EX8 . . . **202** B6
Clare Dr EX16 . . . . . . **161** F6
Clare Ind Est PL4 . . . **263** B2
Claremont Ave TQ12 . **213** A4
Claremont Field
EX11 . . . . **169** D3
Claremont Gr
Exeter EX2 . . . . **261** C1
Exmouth EX8 . . . . **202** B7
Claremont La EX8 . . . **202** C7
Claremont Pl EX20 . . . **75** C7
Claremont St PL1 . . . **262** C4
Clarence Cotts 5
EX34 . . . . **150** B6
Clarence Ct PL1 . . . . . **262** A3
Clarence Hill TQ6 . . . **233** F4
Clarence Ho TQ2 . . . . **219** E6
Clarence Pl
15 Barnstaple EX32 . . **155** B3
Exeter EX4 . . . . **261** C4
Plymouth, Morice Town
 PL2 . . . . **247** E4
Plymouth, Stonehouse
 PL1 . . . . **262** A3
Clarence Rd
Budleigh Salterton
 EX9 . . . . **198** A2
6 Exeter EX4 . . . . . . **177** A5
Exmouth EX8 . . . . **202** A7
Torpoint PL11 . . . . **247** B3
Clarence St TQ6 . . . . **233** F4
Clarendon TQ1 . . . . . . **220** C3
Clarendon Cl TQ1 . . . **219** F6
Clarendon Ct EX4 . . . **173** D1
Clarendon Gdns 3
EX31 . . . . **154** C1
Clarendon Ho 1 PL1 **247** E5
Clarendon La 11 PL3 . **247** F3
Clarendon Rd TQ12 . . **211** D2
Clare Pl PL4 . . . . **263** B2
Clare St PL21 . . . . **237** C4
Claridge The TQ3 . . . **226** C8
Clarke Cl EX15 . . . . **65** F7
Clarke Ctr The EX2 . . **177** C2
Clarke Mead EX2 . . . **178** C4
Clarks Barn Rd TQ7 . **143** E7
Clarks La EX20 . . . . . . **57** A6
Clatworthy La EX32 . . **29** E7
Claude Dix Cl 1
EX31 . . . . **155** A7
Claw Cross EX39 . . . . **38** F5
Clawford Cross EX22 . **72** D3
Clawford Vineyard &
 Fisheries ★ EX22 . . **72** D3
Claw Hill EX16 . . . . . . **62** F4
Claw Pk EX22 . . . . **72** B2
CLAWTON **72** B2
Clawton Prim Sch
EX22 . . . . **72** B1
Clayfield Villas 6
EX32 . . . . **155** B4
Clayford La TA22 . . . . **33** C5
Clayford Rd TA22 . . . . **33** C5
CLAYHANGER **35** C1
CLAYHIDON **52** E2
Clayhidon Crossway
EX15 . . . . **52** E2
Clay La
 Chudleigh Knighton
 TQ13 . . . . **123** C3
Colyton EX24 . . . . **102** F4
Colyton EX24 . . . . **103** A4
Copplestone EX17 . . . . **79** A6
Dartington TQ9 . . . . . **223** A8
Lympstone EX8 . . . . . . **195** E4
Teignmouth TQ14 . . . . **210** B5
Uffculme EX15 . . . . **66** A8
Clayland Cross TQ4 . **225** E4
Claylands Dr TQ4 . . . **225** E4
Claylands View EX14 . **166** B4
Claylands Way TQ3 . . **225** E4
Claymans Pathway
PL21 . . . . **237** A6
Claypark Hill EX16 . . . **47** D5
Clay Park Terr TQ9 . . **228** A7
Clay Pit Cl EX5 . . . . . **179** B3
CLAYPITS **34** C4
Claypits Covert Cross
EX31 . . . . **154** A2
Claypits Rd EX31 . . . . **154** A3
Claypits Way TQ13 . . **123** E2
Claytonia Cl PL6 . . . . **241** C1
Clayton Pl PL4 . . . . . . **249** B2
Clayton Rd
1 Plymouth PL4 . . . . **249** B2
CLEARBROOK **132** A8
Clearbrook Ave PL5 . **243** E1

Clear View PL12 . . . . **242** E3
Cleatlands Cl TQ4 . . . **225** E4
CLEAVE **10** C4
Cleaveanger La EX17 . **60** B1
Cleave Cl
Barnstaple EX31 . . . . . **154** D4
Folly Gate EX20 . . . . . . **75** F1
Tedburn St Mary EX6 . . **97** F4
Cleave Cross EX14 . . . **86** C3
Cleave Hill
Dolton EX19 . . . . **57** E6
Meshaw EX36 . . . . **46** A6
Cleave La
Bishop's Tawton EX32 . . **27** F7
Burrington EX37 . . . . . **44** A2
Chapelton EX32 . . . . . . **28** A7
Wilmington EX14 . . . . **86** C3
Cleave La End EX32 . . **28** A7
Cleaveland Rise
TQ12 . . . . **206** F3
Cleave Lane End EX32 **27** F7
Cleave Pk EX31 . . . . . **153** F5
Cleave Rd EX31 . . . . . **154** D4
Cleaves Cl EX5 . . . . . . **81** E5
Cleave The PL10 . . . . **253** B2
Cleavewood Dr EX39 **157** D1
Cleeve Dr PL21 . . . . . **237** B5
Cleeve Gdns PL21 . . . **248** A8
Cleeve The EX15 . . . . . **66** E8
Clegg Ave PL11 . . . . . **246** E3
Cleland Ct TQ14 . . . . **208** F8
Clematis Hill TQ7 . . . **142** E3
Clement Rd PL7 . . . . . **251** B5
Clement's La EX32 . . . **28** B8
Clennon Ave TQ4 . . . **226** B4
Clennon Ct
5 Brixham TQ5 . . . . . **230** C3
Torquay TQ2 . . . . **214** A2
Clennon Dr TQ4 . . . . **226** B4
Clennon Gdns TQ4 . . **226** B4
Clennon Hts TQ4 . . . . **226** B4
Clennon La TQ2 . . . . . **214** A2
Clennon Pk TQ4 . . . . **226** B4
Clennon Rise TQ4 . . . **226** B4
Clennon Summit
TQ4 . . . . **226** B4
Clennon Valley Ct
TQ4 . . . . **226** B4
Clennon View TQ3 . . . **226** B3
Clerk Cl FX8 . . . . **196** C2
Cleve Ct TQ1 . . . . **220** E5
Clevedon Cl EX4 . . . . **173** D1
Clevedon Ho EX10 . . . **188** C5
Clevedon Park Ave
PL2 . . . . **248** B6
Clevedon Pk EX39 . . . **157** C6
Clevedon Pk EX10 . . . **188** C5
Cleveland Ct
Exeter EX1 . . . . **261** C4
Paignton TQ4 . . . . **226** C5
Cleveland Dr TQ7 . . . **142** E3
Cleveland Gdns EX1 . **261** C4
Cleveland Pl
8 Dawlish EX7 . . . . . **204** C6
Exmouth EX8 . . . . **201** F6
Cleveland Rd
Paignton TQ4 . . . . **226** C5
Plymouth PL4 . . . . **263** C3
Torquay TQ2 . . . . **219** F6
Clevelands Pk EX39 . **157** C6
Cleveland St 7 EX4 . . **177** A5
Cleveland Terr EX39 . **156** C7
Cleverdon Cross EX22 . **53** F8
Cleverhayes La EX14 . . **86** B4
Cleve Terr TQ1 . . . . . . **220** E5
Cliff Bastin Cl EX4 . . **178** C4
Cliff Ct PL1 . . . . **262** B1
Cliffden Cl TQ14 . . . . **210** C5
Cliff La PL10 . . . . **252** A4
Cliff Mews TQ4 . . . . . **226** D5
CLIFFORD **38** C8
Clifford Ave TQ12 . . . **123** E1
Clifford Cl
13 Chudleigh TQ13 . . **123** E6
Exeter EX1 . . . . **178** B7
Kingsteignton TQ12 . . **207** E7
Plymouth PL5 . . . . **243** E2
Teignmouth TQ14 . . . . **210** A3
Clifford Cross EX6 . . . **112** C8
Clifford Dr TQ12 . . . . **180** F2
Clifford Gdns EX17 . . **165** D5
Clifford Mews TA21 . **160** E6
Clifford Rd EX4 . . . . . **177** E8
Clifford Rd Ind Est
EX4 . . . . **177** F8
Clifford St
Chudleigh TQ13 . . . . . **123** C4
14 Chudleigh TQ13 . . **123** E6
Kingsteignton TQ12 . . **207** E7
Clifford Terr TA21 . . . **160** E6
Cliff Park Ave TQ4 . . **226** C3
Cliff Park Rd TQ4 . . . **226** C4
Cliff Rd
Budleigh Salterton
 EX9 . . . . **199** G2
Paignton TQ4 . . . . **226** C4
Plymouth PL1 . . . . **262** B1
Salcombe TQ8 . . . . . . **259** C3
Sidmouth EX10 . . . . . . **188** C3
Teignmouth TQ14 . . . . **210** D2
Torquay TQ2 . . . . **219** F6
Wembury PL9 . . . . **140** D7
Cliffside EX34 . . . . **7** F6
Cliffside Rd TQ1 . . . . **220** C8

Cliff Terr EX9 . . . . **199** G2
Cliff View Terr PL18 . **125** D6
CLIFTON **10** C4
Clifton Ave PL7 . . . . . **250** C4
Clifton Bank 5 TQ3 . **226** A6
Clifton Cl
Paignton TQ3 . . . . **225** F6
Plymouth PL7 . . . . **250** C4
Clifton Cres TQ3 . . . . **226** A6
Clifton Ct
Croyde EX33 . . . . **7** E3
Exeter EX1 . . . . **177** E7
3 Ilfracombe EX34 . . **150** B5
Clifton Gdns TQ3 . . . **226** A6
Clifton Gr TQ3 . . . . . . **226** A6
Clifton Hill EX1 . . . . . **177** E7
Clifton Hill Sp Ctr
EX1 . . . . **177** E7
Clifton 17 TQ4 . . . . . . **210** C5
Clifton La EX31 . . . . . . **10** B4
Clifton Pl
Dawlish EX7 . . . . **204** C6
18 Ilfracombe EX34 . . **150** B5
Plymouth PL4 . . . . **263** A4
Salcombe TQ8 . . . . . . **259** E5
Clifton Rd
Exeter EX1 . . . . **261** C3
Paignton TQ3 . . . . **226** A6
Clifton Rise TQ3 . . . . **226** A6
Clifton St
Barnstaple EX31 . . . . . **154** F4
Bideford EX39 . . . . **157** B1
Exeter EX1 . . . . **177** E6
Plymouth PL4 . . . . **263** A4
Clifton Terr
Barnstaple EX31 . . . . . **154** F4
11 Northam EX39 . . . **157** A7
12 South Brent TQ10 . **134** F3
Torquay TQ2 . . . . **220** B4
Climsland Rd TQ4 . . . **226** A5
Clinket La EX33 . . . . . . **8** D1
Clinton Ave
Exeter EX4 . . . . **177** E8
Plymouth PL4 . . . . **249** A4
Clinton CE Prim Sch The
EX20 . . . . **57** A6
Clinton Cl EX9 . . . . . . **197** F2
Clinton Gdns EX20 . . . **57** A7
Clinton Rd EX3 ? **155** D3
Clinton Rise EX12 . . . **191** E6
Clinton Sq EX8 . . . . . **201** F6
Clinton Terr
11 Barnstaple EX32 . . **155** B3
Budleigh Salterton
 EX9 . . . . **198** A2
Great Torrington EX38 . **159** B5
Merton EX20 . . . . **57** A7
Millbrook PL10 . . . . . . **252** F6
Clipper Quay EX2 . . . **261** B1
Clipper Wharf EX8 . . **201** E6
Cliston Ave EX8 . . . . . **196** E2
Cliston Cross TQ9 . . . **139** C2
Cliston La EX20 . . . . . . **76** E4
Clittaford Rd PL6 . . . **244** F7
Clittaford Road Ind Est
PL5 . . . . **245** A7
Clittaford View PL6 . **244** E7
Cliveden Rd EX39 . . . . **26** A4
Cloake Pl PL12 . . . . . **239** A2
Cloakham Dr EX13 . . **167** E7
Clobells 3 TQ10 . . . . **134** F2
Cloepark La EX17 . . . . **60** B6
Cloford Cl PL3 . . . . . . **249** D1
Cloggshill Cross EX31 . **27** B1
Cloister Rd EX4 . . . . . **177** F7
Clonway 1 PL20 . . . . **126** F3
Clooneavin Path
EX35 . . . . **151** C5
Close The
Barnstaple EX32 . . . . . **155** C5
14 Bere Alston PL20 . . **125** E1
Brixham TQ5 . . . . **230** C6
Holcombe EX7 . . . . . . **210** F8
Paignton TQ4 . . . . **229** C8
Rewe EX5 . . . . **82** A2
Saltash PL12 . . . . **242** C3
Seaton EX12 . . . . **192** A5
Tiverton EX16 . . . . **161** E6
Closewood Gr EX36 . **158** B5
Cloud Berry Cotts
TQ3 . . . . **225** E3
Cloutman's La EX33 . . **7** E2
CLOVELLY **23** D3
Clovelly Apts 17
EX34 . . . . **150** B5
Clovelly Cl EX39 . . . . **156** E1
Clovelly Court Gdns ★
EX39 . . . . **23** D2
Clovelly Cross EX39 . . **23** D2
Clovelly Gardens N
EX39 . . . . **156** E1
Clovelly Gardens S 2
EX39 . . . . **156** F1
Clovelly Prim Sch
EX39 . . . . **23** D3
Clovelly Rd
Bideford EX39 . . . . **25** D4
Plymouth PL4 . . . . **263** C1
Clovelly Rise
Dawlish EX7 . . . . **204** D5
Paignton TQ3 . . . . **225** E6
Clovelly Road Ind Est
EX39 . . . . **25** D4
Clovelly View PL9 . . . **255** A7
Clover Ave EX4 . . . . . **176** E8
Clover Cl TQ3 . . . . . . **225** E2
Cloverdale Ct DT7 . . . **260** E3

Clover Dr
　Cullompton EX15 . . . . .163 B2
　Dawlish EX7 . . . . .204 E8
Clover Pk PL8. . . . . .257 A5
Clover Rise PL6. . . . . . . .245 E8
Clover Way EX32. . . . . . .155 E4
Clover Wlk PL12 . . . . . . .242 C3
Clover Wy TQ12. . . . . . .206 D5
Clowance Cl PL1. . . . . . .247 E1
Clowance La PL1. . . . . . .247 E1
Clowance St PL1. . . . . . .247 E1
Cluden Rd EX39. . . . . . .156 F6
Cludens Cl EX2 . . . . . . .181 B8
Clumpit La EX6 . . . . . . .194 A4
Clydesdale Cl EX5. . . . . .173 A1
Clydesdale Rd EX4 . . . . .173 A1
Clyde St PL2. . . . . .247 F5
Clyst Ave
　Brixham TQ5. . . . . . . .230 A2
　Clyst Honiton EX5. . . . .175 E2
Clyst Ct EX5 . . . . .179 F2
Clyst Halt Ave EX2 . . . . .178 E3
Clyst Hayes Gdns
　EX9. . . . . .197 E1
Clyst Heath EX2. . . . . . .178 D3
Clyst Heath Com Prim
　Sch EX2. . . . . .178 D3
CLYST HONITON 179 D8
CLYST HYDON 83 D4
Clyst Hydon Prim Sch
　EX15. . . . . .83 D4
Clyst Rd
　Exeter EX3 . . . . .178 F2
　Topsham EX3 . . . . . . .182 F7
CLYST ST GEORGE. 183 C6
CLYST ST
　LAWRENCE. 83 C3
CLYST ST MARY. 179 B3
Clyst St Mary Prim Sch
　EX5. . . . . .179 A2
Clyst Units EX2 . . . . . . .177 D1
Clyst Vale Com Coll
　EX5. . . . . .175 D5
Clyst Valley Rd EX5. . . . .179 B2
Clyst View EX1. . . . . . . .178 D7
Clyst William Cross
　EX15. . . . . .84 B1
Coach Cl EX39. . . . . . . .25 F4
Coach Ho La TQ2. . . . . .219 E4
Coach Ho The
　Grenofen PL19 . . . . . . .126 D6
　Paignton TQ3 . . . . . . .226 C7
Coach House Mews
　PL9. . . . . .256 B6
Coach House Mws **15**
　TQ13. . . . . .123 E6
Coach Pl TQ12 . . . . . . .207 C2
Coach Rd
　Newton Abbot TQ12 . . .207 B1
　Noss Mayo PL8 . . . . . .140 F6
　Silverton EX5 . . . . . . .82 B6
Coach Rd The DT7 . . . . .260 C8
Coaker Rd EX1. . . . . . . .174 F2
Coarsewell Cross
　PL21. . . . . .138 A5
Coastguard Cotts
　Challaborough TQ7. . . .142 D4
　Dawlish EX7. . . . . . . .204 F6
　Down Thomas PL9. . . . .254 F2
　Inner Hope TQ7. . . . . .147 B6
　Stoke EX39. . . . . .22 B3
　Torquay TQ1. . . . . . . .220 D2
Coastguard Hill EX9. . . . .199 H2
Coastguard Rd EX9 . . . . .198 B1
Coast Rd EX34 . . . . .2 E4
Coates Rd
　East-the-Water EX39 . . .26 B4
　Exeter EX2 . . . . .178 B5
COBB 260 D2
Cobbacombe Cross
　EX16. . . . . .49 D6
COBBATON 28 D5
Cobbaton Combat
　Collection (Mus)★
　EX37. . . . . .28 D5
Cobbett Rd PL5 . . . . . . .244 B2
Cobb La PL9 . . . . .255 F6
Cobblestone La PL1. . . . .248 A1
Cobb Rd DT7 . . . . .260 D2
Cobb Terr DT7. . . . . . . .260 D2
Cobb The★ DT7 . . . . . . .260 D1
Cob Castle TA21. . . . . . .52 D8
Cobden La EX5 . . . . . . .99 D7
Cobham Cl PL6 . . . . . . .245 C6
Coblands Cross EX5. . . . .82 A7
Cobley Ct EX1 . . . . .178 D8
Cobley La
　Bideford EX39. . . . . . .26 C6
　Lapford EX17 . . . . . . .60 E4
　West Worlington EX17 . .60 F6
Cob Mdw EX20. . . . . . . .75 C7
Cobourg St PL1. . . . . . .262 C3
COBURG. 123 E5
Coburg Cl TA21. . . . . . .52 F7
Coburg Cres **23** TQ13 123 E6
Coburg Pl
　Cullompton EX15 . . . . .163 C6
　Torquay TQ2 . . . . .220 B4
Coburg Rd EX10. . . . . . .188 A3
Coburg Terr
　8 Ilfracombe EX34 . . . .150 C6
　Sidmouth EX10 . . . . . .188 A3
Cockeram's Rd EX5. . . . .99 C8
Cockhaven Cl TQ14 . . . .208 F7
Cockhaven Mead
　TQ14. . . . . .208 F7
Cockhaven Rd TQ14. . . .208 F7

COCKINGFORD 121 B2
COCKINGTON 219 C4
Cockington Cl PL6 . . . . .245 E1
Cockington Com Prim
　Sch **8** TQ2. . . . . .219 F5
Cockington Ctry Pk★
　TQ2. . . . . .219 B4
Cockington La
　Paignton TQ3 . . . . . . .219 C1
　Torquay TQ2 . . . . .219 D4
Cockington Rd TQ3 . . . . .219 A3
Cockington Wlk PL6 . . . .245 E1
Cockland Hill TA21. . . . .19 D8
Cockland La EX16. . . . . .48 F3
Cockles La **2** EX17. . . . .165 D5
Cockles Rise EX17 . . . . .165 D5
Cockpit Hill EX15 . . . . . .163 C3
Cockrams Butt Cross
　EX37. . . . . .29 B1
Cockram's La EX37. . . . .43 F7
Cockrattle La EX17. . . . .61 B3
Cockspark La EX14. . . . .84 F8
Cocks Pk TQ7 . . . . .142 D7
Cocktree Throat EX20 95 C8
COCKWOOD 201 B5
Cockwood Prim Sch
　EX6. . . . . .201 B6
Codden Cross EX32. . . . .28 A8
Codden Hill Cross
　EX32. . . . . .27 E8
Coddiford Cross EX17. . . .62 E2
Coddiford Hill EX17 . . . . .62 E1
Coddiford La EX17 . . . . .62 F2
Codrington St EX1 . . . . .261 C3
Coffins La EX6 . . . . .181 F4
COFFINSWELL 213 A4
Coffinswell La TQ12. . . . .213 A4
Coffintree Cross EX17. . . .80 F6
Coffintree Hill EX17 . . . .80 F7
COFTON. 200 F5
Cofton Hill EX6 . . . . .201 A5
Cofton La
　Cockwood EX6 . . . . . . .200 F5
　Westwood EX6. . . . . . .201 A6
Cofton Rd EX2 . . . . .177 D1
Cohort Cl EX20. . . . . . . .170 D7
Coil Cross EX31 . . . . . . .10 B6
Coker Ave TQ2. . . . . . . .214 A4
Cokers Elm EX14. . . . . . .87 A7
Cokers Elm Cross
　EX14. . . . . .87 A7
Colands Ct EX2 . . . . . . .181 A8
Colaton La EX5 . . . . . . .81 E5
COLATON RALEIGH. 186 D3
Colaton Terr EX10 . . . . . .187 F4
Colborne Rd PL6. . . . . . .245 A2
Colcombe La
　Dalwood EX13 . . . . . . .86 F1
　Shute EX13. . . . . .102 F8
Colcombe Rd EX24. . . . .103 A5
COLDEAST. 180 D1
Cold East Cross
　TQ13. . . . . .121 C2
COLDHARBOUR 66 A7
Coldharbour
　Bideford EX39. . . . . . .157 A2
　3 Totnes TQ9 . . . . . .223 E5
　Uffculme EX15 . . . . . . .66 A7
Coldharbour Cross
　Chilsworthy EX22. . . . .53 E1
　Loddiswell PL21 . . . . . .138 B8
Coldharbour Mill (Mus)★
　EX15. . . . . .66 A7
Coldharbour Rd
　EX16. . . . . .161 A3
Coldrenick St PL5. . . . . .243 F1
COLDRIDGE 59 F2
Coldwell La EX12 . . . . . .192 D6
Coldwell Lane Terr
　EX12. . . . . .192 D7
Colebred Cl EX11 . . . . . .169 E4
COLEBROOK
　Cullompton 65 A1
　Plymouth. 250 E6
COLEBROOKE. 79 A3
Colebrooke La EX15. . . . .65 A1
Colebrook La PL7 . . . . . .250 E7
Colebrook Rd
　Plymouth, Plympton
　PL7. . . . . .250 E6
　Plymouth, St Budeaux
　PL5. . . . . .243 D1
COLEFORD 79 A3
Coleford Hill EX16 . . . . . .48 B6
Cole La
　Ivybridge PL21 . . . . . . .237 E6
　Ivybridge, Higher Keaton
　PL21. . . . . .237 C1
Coleman Ave TQ14. . . . .210 A5
Coleman Cl EX16. . . . . .64 D8
Coleman Dr PL9. . . . . . .255 F4
Colemans Cross
　PL15. . . . . .105 B5
Coleman's Cross
　EX24. . . . . .102 D6
Cole Moore Mdw
　PL19. . . . . .171 B6
Coleridge Ave PL6 . . . . .244 F2
Coleridge Barns TQ7 145 A2
Coleridge Cl EX8. . . . . . .196 C4
Coleridge Ct TQ2 . . . . . .219 E8
Coleridge La TQ7 . . . . . .145 A2
Coleridge Rd
　Exeter EX2 . . . . .176 F4
　Ottery St Mary EX11. . .169 D4
　10 Plymouth PL2. . . . .248 F4
　Plymouth PL4 . . . . . . .249 A4
　8 Tiverton EX16 . . . . .64 D7

Cole's Cnr EX18. . . . . . .59 C8
Coles Cotts PL9. . . . . . .255 C1
Cole's Cotts PL7 . . . . . . .250 E6
Coles Ct EX18. . . . . . . .58 E8
Cole's Ct TQ6 . . . . .233 F3
Coles Mead EX16 . . . . . .161 F4
Coles Mews EX2. . . . . . .177 A4
Coles Mill Cl EX22. . . . . .144 F5
Coles's La EX13 . . . . . . .104 B8
Colesworthy Cross
　TQ12. . . . . .180 B2
Coleton Fishacre★
　TQ6. . . . . .234 F2
Colhayne La
　Dalwood EX13 . . . . . . .86 F1
　Shute EX13 . . . . .102 F8
Colin Campbell Ct
　10 Plymouth PL1 . . . . .262 B3
　Plymouth PL3 . . . . . . .262 B3
Colin Rd TQ3 . . . . .226 C7
Collabear Cnr EX31. . . . .27 D8
Collabridge Hill
　Dunsford EX6 . . . . . . .97 D1
　Dunsford EX6 . . . . . . .112 E8
Collabridge La EX6. . . . . .112 E8
Collabridge Rd EX6. . . . .112 E8
Collacombe Cross
　PL19. . . . . .116 D4
Collacott Cl EX22 . . . . . .38 E1
Collacott Cross
　EX38. . . . . .40 F2
Collacotts La EX19 . . . . .59 B2
Collaford Cl PL7 . . . . . . .251 A4
Collaford Farm Bsns
　Units PL7. . . . . .136 A6
Collapark TQ9 . . . . .223 B6
Collard La PL7 . . . . .132 D4
Collaton Cross
　Halwell TQ9 . . . . .139 D4
　Malborough TQ7 . . . . .147 F6
　Yealmpton PL8 . . . . . . .141 B8
Collaton Ct TQ2. . . . . . . .219 C8
Collaton Ho **7** TQ1 . . . .220 D4
Collaton La PL19 . . . . . .117 F2
Collaton Mews TQ4 . . . .225 D4
Collaton Rd
　Malborough TQ7 . . . . .147 F6
　Torquay TQ2 . . . . .219 C8
COLLATON ST
　MARY 225 C4
Collaton St Mary CE Prim
　Sch TQ3. . . . . .225 C5
Collatons Wlk EX17. . . . .78 C4
Coll Ct EX15 . . . . .66 A7
College Cl TQ13 . . . . . . .180 E8
College Ave
　Exeter EX2 . . . . .261 C2
　Plymouth PL3 . . . . . . .248 E5
　Tavistock PL19 . . . . . . .117 C1
　Tavistock PL19 . . . . . . .171 D6
College Cl EX39. . . . . . .156 C6
College Ct
　Barnstaple EX31. . . . . .154 D3
　1 Torquay TQ1. . . . . .219 F6
College Dean Cl PL6 . .245 C5
College Gn
　Bideford EX39. . . . . . .156 F2
　Uffculme EX15 . . . . . . .66 A7
College La
　Clyst Hydon EX5, EX15 . .83 B5
　Ide EX2. . . . . .176 C2
　Plymouth PL4 . . . . . . .248 F4
College Park Pl PL3 . .248 E5
College Rd
　Cullompton EX15 . . . . .163 C4
　Exeter EX1 . . . . .261 C3
　Newton Abbot TQ12 . . .207 C2
　Plymouth PL2 . . . . . . .247 E5
　Shebbear EX21. . . . . . .55 F4
College Road Prim Sch
　PL2. . . . . .247 E5
College The
　Exeter EX2 . . . . .176 D2
　Ottery St Mary EX11. . .169 D4
College View
　Plymouth PL3 . . . . . . .248 E4
　Tiverton EX16. . . . . . . .161 C6
College Way
　Dartmouth TQ6. . . . . . .233 D4
　Exeter EX1 . . . . .178 E7
Colleton Cl EX8 . . . . . . .202 C8
Colleton Cres EX2. . . . . .261 B2
Colleton Ct **9** EX2 . . . . .261 B2
Colleton Gate EX18 . . . .44 C1
Colleton Gr EX2. . . . . . . .261 B1
Colleton Hill EX2. . . . . . .261 B1
Colleton Ho EX2 . . . . . . .261 B1
Colleton Mews EX2. . . . .261 B1
COLLETON MILLS 44 C2
Colleton Row EX2. . . . . .261 B1
Colleton Way EX8. . . . . .202 C8
Collett Way TQ12 . . . . . .207 E3
Colleybrook Cl **1**
　TQ12. . . . . .123 E1
Colley Cres TQ3. . . . . . .226 A6
Colley End Pk TQ3 . . . . .226 A6
Colley End Rd TQ3 . . . . .226 A6
Colley Farm La TQ3 . . . .69 B8
Colley La EX7, TQ13. . . .124 D5
Colley Lane Cross
　TQ13. . . . . .124 D4
Colley Park Rd EX33. . . .152 D5
Colliepriest View
　EX16. . . . . .161 B1
Colliers Cl **5** PL9 . . . . .140 D8

Collier's Mews **1**
　EX20. . . . . .170 B6
Collin Cl PL5. . . . . .243 D1
Collingsdown Cross
　EX39. . . . . .39 F4
Collingwood Ave
　PL4. . . . . .263 C2
Collingwood Cl
　Dartmouth TQ6. . . . . . .233 C3
　Torquay TQ1. . . . . . . .220 C2
Collingwood Rd
　Dartmouth TQ6. . . . . . .233 C3
　Paignton TQ4 . . . . . . .226 A5
　Plymouth PL1 . . . . . . .248 A3
Collingwood Villas **5**
　PL1. . . . . .248 A3
Collins Pk EX9 . . . . .198 B6
Collins Rd
　Exeter EX4 . . . . .173 E2
　Totnes TQ9 . . . . .223 B6
COLLIPRIEST. 161 C2
Collipriest Ho EX16 . . . . .161 C2
Collipriest La EX16. . . . . .161 C1
Collipriest Rd EX16. . . . .161 C2
COLLITON 84 C7
Colliton Cross EX14. . . . .84 C6
Colliver Cross EX9 . . . . .198 E5
Collyland La EX17. . . . . .62 C3
Colmer Cross PL21. . . . .138 A4
Colmer Ho PL21 . . . . . . .138 A4
Colne Gdns PL3. . . . . . .249 B5
Colombelles Cl EX31 .153 E5
Colscott Cross EX22. . . . .39 C1
Colston Cl PL6. . . . . . . .245 B6
Colston Cross EX13 . . . . .88 B4
Colston La EX16. . . . . . .47 E1
Colston Rd
　Buckfastleigh TQ11. . . .236 E3
　Rattery TQ9. . . . . .215 A3
Coltishall Cl PL5 . . . . . .243 F4
Coltness Rd PL9 . . . . . . .256 B5
Coltsfield Cl PL6 . . . . . .249 B8
COLUMBJOHN 82 C2
Columbjohn Cross
　EX5. . . . . .82 B2
Columbus Cl PL5. . . . . .243 C2
Colvin Cl EX8 . . . . .202 D7
Colway Cl DT7 . . . . .260 D5
Colway Cross TQ14. . . . .124 B3
Colway La
　Chudleigh TQ13. . . . . .123 F3
　Lyme Regis DT7 . . . . . .260 D4
Colway Rise DT7 . . . . . .260 D5
Colwill Rd PL6. . . . . . . .245 E3
Colwill Wlk
　Bideford EX39. . . . . . .156 D1
　Plymouth PL6 . . . . . . .245 F3
Colwyn Ct TQ1. . . . . . . .220 C5
Colwyn Rd PL11. . . . . . .247 A3
COLYFORD. 103 B3
Colyford Rd EX12 . . . . . .192 B7
Coly Rd
　Colyton EX24 . . . . . . .103 A4
　Honiton EX14 . . . . . . .166 C4
COLYTON. 103 A5
Colyton Bsns Pk
　EX24. . . . . .103 A5
Colyton Cross EX14. . . . .86 C2
Colyton Gram Sch
　EX24. . . . . .103 A3
Colyton Hill EX13,
　EX24. . . . . .103 B6
Colyton Prim Sch **26**
　EX24. . . . . .103 A4
Colyton Rd
　Colyton EX13, EX24. . . .103 A6
　Northleigh EX24. . . . . .102 C6
Colyton Sports Ctr
　EX24. . . . . .103 A3
Coly Vale EX24. . . . . . . .103 A4
Combas La EX33 . . . . . . .7 E2
COMBE
　Brixton 256 E5
　Buckfastleigh. 130 A2
Combe Beacon La
　TA20. . . . . .69 F2
Combe Cl EX13 . . . . . . .167 D5
Combe Cross
　Ashburton TQ13 . . . . . .131 C5
　Aveton Gifford PL21 . . .143 A8
　Ivybridge PL21. . . . . . .137 B6
　Kingsbridge TQ7 . . . . .258 D7
　Loddiswell TQ7 . . . . . .138 C3
　Shillingford EX16 . . . . .34 D4
　Strete TQ6. . . . . .145 E7
Combe Farm Barns
　TQ7. . . . . .143 A7
COMBE FISHACRE 217 E2
Combefishacre Cross
　TQ12. . . . . .217 D8
Combefishacre La TQ9,
　TQ12. . . . . .217 D6
Combe Hayes EX10. . . . .188 B8
Combehead Droveway
　EX13. . . . . .86 C3
Combehead La EX13 . . . .86 F3
Combe Hill EX15 . . . . . .52 C2
Combe Hill Cross
　TQ12. . . . . .123 F2
Combe Hill Dro TA20. . . .69 F5
COMBEINTEIGNHEAD
　. . . . . .208 E4
Combe La
　Dulverton TA22 . . . . . . .33 D6
　East Anstey TA22 . . . . .32 F6
　Galmpton TQ5. . . . . . .229 B3

Combe La continued
　Northleigh EX24. . . . . .102 B7
　North Tawton EX17 . . . .77 F1
　Spreyton EX17 . . . . . . .95 F8
　Torquay TQ2 . . . . .214 A1
　Whitestaunton TA20 . . .69 E5
Combeland La TA22 . . . .34 A5
COMBE MARTIN 3 B3
Combe Martin Mus★
　EX34. . . . . .2 F4
Combe Martin Prim Sch
　EX34. . . . . .2 F4
Combe Martin Wildlife &
　Dinosaur Pk★ EX34 . . .3 C2
Combe Moor La EX17 . .77 F1
COMBE PAFFORD 214 A4
Combe Pafford Sch
　TQ2. . . . . .214 B3
Combe Pk
　Ilfracombe EX34. . . . . .150 D5
　Torquay TQ3 . . . . .214 A1
COMBE RALEIGH 85 D5
Combe Rd
　Axmouth EX12, DT7 . . .193 B6
　Torquay TQ2 . . . . .214 B2
Comber's Cross EX31. . . .27 E8
COMBE ST NICHOLAS. . .69 F6
Combesdown Cross
　EX22. . . . . .72 C6
Combeshead Cross
　Cornwood PL21 . . . . . .133 F1
　Diptford TQ9 . . . . .138 C6
　Heasley Mill EX36. . . . .19 C2
Combeshead La
　Dunchideock EX2 . . . . .114 A7
　West Anstey EX36. . . . .32 A7
Combe Wood Rd TA20. . .69 F5
Combley Dr PL6 . . . . . . .245 D4
COMBPYNE 103 F3
Combpyne La DT7,
　EX13. . . . . .193 E8
Combpyne Rd EX13 . . . .103 D3
Combrew La EX31. . . . . .16 A3
Combsland Cross
　EX36. . . . . .31 B4
Combsland New Cross
　EX36. . . . . .31 B4
Comburg St EX8 . . . . . . .196 E3
Come Park La EX35 . . . .151 E2
Comer Cl EX1. . . . . .174 F3
Comer's Cross TA24. . . . .21 B6
Comer's Gate TA24. . . . .21 E6
Comers La EX34 . . . . . . .3 B3
Comfrey Ave TQ12 . . . . .206 B6
Comilla Cl EX38. . . . . . .196 C3
Commanders Cut
　TQ6. . . . . .233 E4
Commercial Ope PL4 263 B6
Commercial Pl PL4 . . . . .263 B1
Commercial Point EX34 1 F1
Commercial Rd
　Barnstaple EX31. . . . . .154 F5
　Calstock PL18. . . . . . .125 D3
　Crediton EX17. . . . . . .165 E5
　9 Dawlish EX7. . . . . .204 E6
　Exeter EX2 . . . . .261 A2
　Horrabridge PL20. . . . .126 F4
　Paignton TQ4 . . . . . . .226 B2
　Plymouth PL4 . . . . . . .263 B2
　Uffculme EX15 . . . . . . .66 A7
Commercial St
　Gunnislake PL18. . . . . .125 D6
　Plymouth PL4 . . . . . . .263 B2
Commin's Rd EX1 . . . . . .177 F7
Commodore Cl EX39 .156 E6
Common Head EX37 . . . .43 E2
Common Hill EX12 . . . . .191 D4
Common La
　Beer EX12. . . . . .191 D5
　Huish Champflower TA4 . .35 D7
　Kingskerswell TQ12 . . .212 E2
　Milton Combe PL6. . . . .241 B5
Commonmarsh La
　EX17. . . . . .165 E5
Common Moor La
　EX38. . . . . .56 A7
Common Moors La
　EX36. . . . . .158 A6
Commons Mews
　EX39. . . . . .156 E2
Commons Old Rd
　TQ14. . . . . .210 A6
Common The EX38. . . . .197 A4
Company Rd EX31. . . . . .153 E6
Compass Dr PL7 . . . . . .251 A7
Compass Quay EX2. . . . .261 B1
Compass South TQ1. . . .221 A3
COMPTON. 218 D6
Compton Ave PL3. . . . . .249 A5
Compton Castle★
　TQ3. . . . . .218 C8
Compton CE Prim Sch
　PL3. . . . . .249 A6
Compton Ho TQ1 . . . . . .220 C7
Compton Knoll Cl
　PL3. . . . . .249 A6
Compton Leigh PL3 . . . .249 A6
Compton Park Rd
　PL3. . . . . .248 F5
Comptonpool Cross
　TQ3. . . . . .218 C8

Compton Rd TQ7. . . . . .144 C1
Compton Vale PL3 . . . . .249 A5
Concorde Dr EX32. . . . . .155 C5
Concorde Rd EX8 . . . . . .196 F1
Condor Dr TQ2. . . . . . . .214 B2
Conduit Sq **11** TQ13 . . .123 E6
Coney Ave EX32. . . . . . .155 B3
Coney Ct EX2 . . . . .261 A1
Coneypark La EX34. . . . .3 A3
Congella Rd TQ2. . . . . . .220 C6
Congram's Cl **7**
　EX32. . . . . .155 B3
Congreve Gdns PL5 . . . .244 C1
Conifer Cl EX15. . . . . . .163 C5
Conifer Mews EX2 . . . . .178 D3
Conifers The
　Bovey Tracey TQ13 . . . .180 C4
　Torquay TQ2 . . . . .214 B3
Conigar Cl EX15. . . . . . .67 B8
Conigar La EX15 . . . . . .67 A7
Coniger Cross EX8 . . . . .196 B7
Coniston Cl TQ5 . . . . . . .230 A2
Coniston Gdns PL6. . . . .244 F4
Coniston Rd TQ12 . . . . . .211 F8
Conker Gdns **9** PL7. . . .251 B5
Connaught Ave PL4 . .248 F4
Connaught Cl EX10. . . . .188 A4
Connaught La **6** PL4 248 E4
Connaught Rd EX10. . . . .188 A4
Conniford La TQ12 . . . . .211 D1
Connybear Cross
　TQ12. . . . . .213 B8
Connybear La TQ12 . . . .213 C7
Conqueror Dr PL5. . . . . .244 E1
Conrad Ave EX4. . . . . . .178 B8
Conrad Rd PL5. . . . . . . .244 D1
Consols Cl PL21. . . . . . .237 E4
Consort Cl PL3. . . . . . . .248 E7
Consort Ho PL5. . . . . . .243 B2
Constable Cl PL6. . . . . .244 D3
Constance Pl PL1 . . . . . .262 A3
Constantine Cl EX12 . .191 F8
Constantine St PL4. . . . .263 A3
Constitution Hill
　EX32. . . . . .155 B4
Contour Hts TQ6. . . . . . .234 A3
Convent Cl
　Barnstaple EX32. . . . . .155 C2
　Saltash PL12. . . . . . . .242 F2
Convent Fields EX10 . . . .187 F4
Convent Lodge **3**
　TQ14. . . . . .210 B6
Convent Rd EX10. . . . . .187 F4
Conway Cres **2** TQ4 .226 A5
Conway Ct TQ1. . . . . . . .261 C2
Conway Gdns PL2. . . . . .248 B7
Conway Ho **4** TQ3 . . . .226 B5
Conway Rd TQ4. . . . . . .226 B5
Conybeare Cl EX4. . . . . .178 B7
Conybeare Dr EX39 . . . .156 E6
Conyngham Ct PL6. . . . .249 A8
Cooban Ct PL6. . . . . . . .249 A8
COOKBURY 73 A8
COOKBURY WICK. 72 E5
Cook Ct PL12 . . . . .242 B3
Cooke Dr TQ12 . . . . . . .211 C2
Cooks Cl
　12 Ashburton TQ13. . . .131 A5
　Kingsteignton TQ12 . . .207 F7
Cooks Cross EX36. . . . . .158 C3
Cooks Farm EX5 . . . . . .184 C6
Cooks La EX13 . . . . .104 B7
Cooksley Ct PL1. . . . . . .263 A1
Cooks Mead DT7. . . . . . .260 A6
Cookson's Rd EX6. . . . . .201 A8
Cookworthy Ct TQ7 . . . .258 C6
Cookworthy Forest Ctr★
　EX21. . . . . .73 A4
Cookworthy Mus of Rural
　Life★ TQ7 . . . . .258 C6
Cookworthy Rd
　Kingsbridge TQ7. . . . . .258 C6
　Plymouth PL2. . . . . . . .247 F6
COOMBE
　Tipton St John. 100 E2
　Tiverton 50 A4
Coombe Ave TQ14 . . . . .210 A5
Coombe Ball Hill
　East Worlington EX17. . .61 C8
　Witheridge EX16. . . . . .46 D1
Coombe Cl
　Bovey Tracey TQ13 . . . .180 E7
　Dartmouth TQ6. . . . . . .233 F4
　Goodleigh EX32 . . . . . .17 B5
　Honiton EX14 . . . . . . .166 C4
Coombe Cross
　Bovey Tracey TQ13 . . . .180 E7
　Christow EX6 . . . . .113 B2
　Goodleigh EX32 . . . . . .17 B4
　Great Torrington EX38 . .159 F8
Coombe Dean Sch
　PL9. . . . . .256 A6
Coombe Dean Sp Ctr
　PL9. . . . . .256 A6
Coombe Down La
　PL8. . . . . .140 F6
Coombe Dr PL12. . . . . . .239 A2
Coombefield La
　EX13. . . . . .167 D5
Coombehaven TQ8. . . . .259 D4
Coombe Hill EX16. . . . . .47 F1
Coombe House Cross
　TQ9. . . . . .224 F2
Coombe House La
　TQ9. . . . . .225 A2

Coombe La
Axminster EX13 . . . . . .167 D5
Bickleigh EX16 . . . . .63 C3
Bovey Tracey TQ13 . . .180 F8
Cadbury EX5. . . . . .81 C7
Cargreen PL12 . . . . . . .239 A2
Cheriton Fitzpaine EX16,
EX17. . . . . .63 B3
Chulmleigh EX18. . . . . .44 E4
Combe PL8 . . . . .256 E5
Harford EX6 . . . . .97 F7
Kingsbridge TQ7 . . . . .258 D8
Okehampton EX20 . . .170 E6
Plymouth PL5 . . . . . . .244 D7
Puddington EX16 . . . . . .62 B6
Silverton EX5 . . . . .82 B7
Silverton EX6 . . . . .82 B7
Teignmouth TQ14 . . . .210 A7
COOMBELAKE 169 B6
Coombe Mdw TQ12 . .180 E7
Coombe Mdws TQ7 . .134 F1
Coombe Orch EX12 . .192 E6
Coombe Park Cl
PL10 . . . . .253 A2
Coombepark La EX23 . 70 E7
Coombe Park La PL5 244 A3
Coombe Park Rd
TQ14. . . . . .210 A6
Coombe Pk
Kingsand PL10 . . . . . .253 A2
Saltash PL12 . . . . . . .242 F7
Coombe Pk La S
TQ12. . . . . .244 A3
Coombe Rd
Dartmouth TQ6 . . . . .233 F4
Paignton TQ3 . . . . . . .219 C1
Saltash PL12 . . . . . . .243 A2
Shaldon TQ14 . . . . . .209 C5
Coombesend Rd
TQ12. . . . . .207 F7
Coombesend Road E
TQ12. . . . . .208 A7
Coombeshead Acad
TQ12. . . . . .207 A4
Coombeshead Rd
TQ12. . . . . .206 F4
Coombe Shute TQ9 . .227 F7
Coombe St
Exeter EX1 . . . . .261 B2
Lyme Regis DT7 . . . . .260 E3
Coombes The [1]
EX31. . . . . .154 A2
Coombe Terr EX12 . .192 E6
Coombe The
Dartmouth TQ6 . . . . .233 F4
Galmpton TQ5 . . . . . .229 B5
Coombe Vale EX10 . .100 D2
Coombe Vale Rd
TQ14. . . . . .210 A5
Coombe Valley Nature
Reserve★ TQ14 . . .124 E1
Coombe View
Plymouth PL2 . . . . . .247 F7
Teignmouth TQ14 . . .124 E1
Coombe Way
Bishopsteignton
TQ14. . . . . .209 B8
Plymouth PL5 . . . . . .243 F1
Coopers Cross EX37. . 44 E6
Cooper's Cross
Chawleigh EX18 . . . . .60 C6
Lydford EX20 . . . . . . .107 A3
Coopers Dr EX31. . . .154 B2
Coopers Hill EX19 . . . .58 F3
Cooper St [11] EX39 . .157 A2
Coot Hide EX16 . . . . . .50 D1
Copland La TQ9. . . . .223 A6
Copland Mdws TQ9 .223 B6
Copleston Rd PL6. . . .244 E5
Copley Cl TQ3 . . . . . .225 F6
Copley Dr EX31 . . . . .154 D3
Coppard Mdws PL7 . .250 B6
Copper Beech Way
PL6. . . . . .245 C7
Copper Castle EX14 . .166 E6
Copper Cl EX39 . . . . . .38 F8
Copperfield TQ3 . . . .144 F1
Copperfield Cl EX8. . .196 E1
Copperfields PL20 . . .126 E5
Copper Pl PL1 . . . . . .262 A3
Coppers Pk PL5 . . . . .245 E7
Copperthorn Cross
TQ9. . . . . .222 D4
Copper Tree Cross
TQ9. . . . . .216 C5
Copperwood Cl
TQ13. . . . . .130 F4
Copp Hill La EX9 . . . .198 A2
Coppice Cl
Barnstaple EX32. . . . .155 E3
Fremington EX31 . . . .153 F6
Raymond's Hill EX13 . .104 B7
Coppice Gate EX32. . .155 C3
Coppice Gdns PL5 . . .244 E2
Coppice La EX17. . . . . .80 A7
Coppice The
Dawlish EX7 . . . . .204 D4
Ivybridge PL21 . . . . . .237 E4
Coppice Wood Dr
PL6. . . . . .245 C7
Coppledown Gdns
EX9. . . . . .197 F2
COPPLESTONE 79 B6
Copplestone Dr EX4. .173 A1
Copplestone La EX9. .186 C4

Copplestone Prim Sch
EX17. . . . . .79 B5
Copplestone Rd EX9 .198 A1
Copplestone Sta EX17 79 A6
Copp Path EX7. . . . . .204 C5
Copp's Cl EX39. . . . . .157 A3
Copse Cl PL7. . . . . . . .250 D4
Copse Hill La EX20 . . . .77 B7
Copse Rd PL7. . . . . . . .250 D4
Copse The
Barnstaple EX31. . . . .154 B3
Chillington TQ7 . . . . .145 A1
Exeter EX2 . . . . .182 C7
Exmouth EX8. . . . . . .196 C2
Newton Poppleford
EX10. . . . . .186 F8
Okehampton EX20 . . .170 D6
Totnes TQ9 . . . . .222 E6
Copsey La TQ12 . . . . .211 B6
Copstone EX39 . . . . . . .39 E7
Copstone Hill EX17. . . .61 D5
Copthorne Gdns PL9 .255 F5
Copydown La EX5. . . . .82 D6
Copythorne Cl TQ5. . .230 A4
Copythorne Pk TQ5 . .230 A4
Copythorne Rd TQ5 . .230 A4
Coral Ave EX39 . . . . .156 D7
Coram Ave DT7 . . . . .260 D2
Coram Ct DT7 . . . . . .260 D3
Coram Manor DT7 . . .260 D3
Corams La TA21 . . . . .160 B6
Cordery Rd EX2 . . . . .176 F3
Cordwents Vw EX16. . .65 A7
Corea Terr PL1 . . . . . .248 A2
Core Fields EX10 . . . .188 B8
Core Hill Rd EX10 . . . .100 F1
Coreway EX10 . . . . . .188 B8
Coreway Cl EX10 . . . .188 B8
CORFCOTT GREEN. . . .71 F2
Corfe Ave PL3 . . . . . . .248 F8
Corfe Cl PL21 . . . . . . .237 D4
Corfe Cres TQ2 . . . . . .213 F1
Corilhead Rd EX33 . . .152 B6
Coringdean Cl PL6. . .245 B6
Coriolis Way N EX1. . .178 D7
Cormelles Ct [13] EX34. . 3 A3
Cormorant Cl
Marhamchurch EX23 . . .70 A8
Seaton EX12. . . . . . . .192 B5
Torquay TQ2 . . . . . . .213 D3
Cornacre Cl TQ2 . . . . .219 C7
Cornacre Rd TQ2 . . . .219 C7
Cornborough Rd
EX39. . . . . .156 B6
Corn Cl EX5. . . . . .99 B6
Corndon Cross TQ13 .110 F4
Corner Brake PL6. . . .245 D7
Corner Cl TA21 . . . . . .160 D6
Corner Cotts EX16 . . . .65 A7
Corner La
Combe Martin EX34 . . . . 3 B3
Halberton EX16 . . . . . .65 A7
Cornermoor Cross
EX16. . . . . .47 C1
Cornerstone Ct [11] 247 B3
Cornfield Gdns PL7 . .251 B7
Cornfield Gn TQ2 . . . .214 B2
Cornfield Way EX20 . . .77 C4
Cornflower Cl
[4] Barnstaple EX31 . .154 B3
Willand EX15 . . . . . . .162 E5
Cornflower Cres
PL15 . . . . .105 A2
Cornflower Hill EX4 . .176 D8
Cornflower Way [1]
PL19 . . . . .171 A6
Cornflower Wy TQ12 .206 D5
Cornham Farm La
TA24. . . . . .12 E2
Cornhill
Hemyock EX15 . . . . . .67 B8
[5] Wellington TA21 . . .160 D6
Cornlands EX16. . . . . . .50 D1
Cornmarket St EX38 . .159 D5
Corn Mill Cl EX34 . . . .150 E6
Corn Mill Cres EX2. . .177 A1
Corn Park Rd TQ12 . . .212 A6
Corn Pk TQ10 . . . . . . .134 F2
Cornridge View EX20. . 93 C2
Corntown Cross
PL21. . . . . .133 C1
Cornwall Beach PL1. .247 D2
Cornwall Coll Saltash
PL12. . . . . .242 D2
Cornwall St
Bere Alston PL20 . . . .125 E1
[5] Exeter EX4. . . . . . .177 A5
Plymouth PL1 . . . . . .262 C3
Plymouth, Morice Town
PL1. . . . . .247 D2
CORNWOOD. 133 C2
Cornwood CE Prim Sch
PL21. . . . . .133 C2
Cornwood Rd
Ivybridge PL21 . . . . . .237 A5
Plymouth PL7 . . . . . .251 B4
CORNWORTHY. 227 B4
Cornworthy Cl PL2. . .248 A7
Cornworthy Cross
TQ9. . . . . .227 A4
Coronation Ave EX7. .204 D5
Coronation Cres EX15 66 A2
Coronation Pl
Plymouth PL5 . . . . . .247 E8
Shebbear EX21. . . . . . .55 E4
Coronation Rd
Bideford EX39. . . . . .156 F1

Coronation Rd continued
Exeter EX2. . . . . .178 A4
Kingsbridge TQ7 . . . .258 D5
Kingsteignton TQ12 . .207 E7
[1] Newton Abbot
TQ12. . . . . .207 B3
Salcombe TQ8. . . . . . .259 D5
[1] Teignmouth TQ14. .210 A3
Totnes TQ9 . . . . .223 D6
Coronation St EX32 . .154 F6
Coronation Terr
Abbotsham EX39 . . . .156 A2
[11] Ilfracombe EX34 . .150 C6
Starcross EX6 . . . . . .201 B8
Coronation Villas
EX18. . . . . .59 C4
Corondale Rd PL2. . . .248 B7
Coronet Cl EX2 . . . . .178 D3
Corporation Cres [14]
EX32. . . . . .155 B3
Corporation Rd PL2. .248 D7
Corporation St [12]
EX32. . . . . .155 B3
Corporation Terr [13]
EX32. . . . . .155 B3
Corry Ho TQ1 . . . . . . .220 E5
Corscombe La EX20 . . .94 E6
Corsham Cl PL6. . . . . .245 B6
Corsham Rd TQ4 . . . .226 A5
Corstone Cross EX19. .76 D7
Corvid Cl
Barnstaple EX31. . . . . .16 A3
[2] Roundswell EX31. .154 A1
Corvus Mws PL9 . . . .256 E8
Cory Ct TA21 . . . . . . .140 E8
Coryton Cl EX7. . . . . .204 E6
Coryton La EX13 . . . . .87 C1
Coscombe Circus [3]
PL3. . . . . .249 D1
Cosdon Pl PL6 . . . . . .244 F1
**Cosgates Feet or County
Gate** EX35 . . . . 6 D5
Cossick Cross TQ13 . .112 B5
Costly St PL21 . . . . . .237 D5
Cosway Rd EX16 . . . . .161 D5
Cotehele Ave
Plymouth, Keyham
PL2. . . . . .247 F5
Plymouth, Prince Rock
PL4. . . . . .263 C2
Cotehele Dr TQ3 . . . .225 D7
Cotehele House★
PL12. . . . . .125 C3
Cotehele Quay Mus★
PL12. . . . . .125 C3
Cotehele View PL18. .125 D3
Coteland La EX32 . . . . .18 F1
Coteland Lane End
EX32. . . . . .18 F1
Cotfield Cl EX14 . . . . .166 D7
Cotfield St EX2 . . . . . .177 C3
COTFORD. 101 C3
Cotford Cl EX10. . . . . .101 C3
Cotford Rd EX10 . . . . .101 C3
Cot Green Cross EX14 . 85 B5
Cothay La
Chittlehampton EX37 . .29 C1
Satterleigh EX37 . . . . .44 C8
Cothay Manor & Gdns★
TA21. . . . . .51 C8
Cot Hill PL7. . . . . .250 B5
Cot Hill Cl PL7. . . . . . .250 A6
Cot Hill Trad Est PL7. .250 B6
Cot La EX5. . . . . .82 B5
Cotlands EX10 . . . . . .187 F3
Cotleigh Cross EX14. . .86 C5
Cotleigh Crossing
EX14. . . . . .68 C1
Cotley La EX6. . . . . . .113 C8
Cot Manor [6] EX32. .155 B3
COTMATON 187 F4
Cotmaton Rd EX10 . . .187 F3
Cotmore Cl
Brixham TQ5 . . . . . . .230 A2
Chillington TQ7 . . . . .145 A1
Cotmore Way TQ7 . . .145 A1
Cotsford Cl EX5. . . . . .179 B2
Cotswold Cl TQ2 . . . . .219 D3
COTT. 222 F8
Cottage Cl EX33. . . . . . .8 D1
Cottage Cross
Ashburton TQ13 . . . . .131 B5
Cheriton Bishop EX6 . . .97 B4
Cottage Homes
EX36. . . . . .158 D4
Cottage La TA22 . . . . . .33 D6
Cottage Mews PL7. . .250 E4
Cottages The TQ7. . . .142 F2
Cott Cross
Ash Mill EX36 . . . . . . .31 C2
Chawleigh EX18 . . . . .59 E6
Dartington TQ9 . . . . .222 F8
Membury EX13 . . . . . .87 C7
Cotte Cl EX12 . . . . . . .190 B5
Cotterbury Gn TQ9 . .232 A2
Cotterell Rd EX5 . . . .175 E2
Cotters Cl EX15 . . . . . .66 A3
Cottey Brook EX16 . .161 B4
Cottey Cres EX4. . . . . .174 A2
COTTEYLANDS 161 A3
Cottey Mdw TQ12 . . .207 E6
Cott Hill EX11. . . . . . . .10 D1
Cottingham Cres
EX39. . . . . .156 F3
Cottington Ct EX10. . .188 A4

Cottington Mead
Sidmouth, Lower Woolbrook
EX10. . . . . .188 B6
Sidmouth, Weston Town
EX10. . . . . .188 A4
Cottisbourne TQ13. . .111 A6
Cott La
Croyde EX33. . . . . 7 E1
Petrockstow EX20 . . . . .56 F4
Totnes TQ9 . . . . .222 F8
Cottlass La PL21 . . . . .137 A2
Cottles La EX5 . . . . . .184 D4
Cottles View EX20. . . . .77 C4
Cotton Cl PL7 . . . . . . .250 F4
Cotton La
Cheriton Fitzpaine
EX17. . . . . .63 A3
Tiverton EX16. . . . . . .63 B5
Cotton Rd TQ6 . . . . . .233 B2
Cott Pk EX5. . . . . .184 C2
Cott Rd TQ9 . . . . .222 F8
Cotts PL20. . . . . .239 B7
Cottshayne La EX24 . .102 E5
COTTWOOD. 43 D1
Couches La EX5. . . . . .184 C2
Couchill Dr EX12. . . . .191 F8
Couchill La EX12. . . . .191 F8
Coulsdon Rd EX10 . . .188 B6
Coulson Cross EX20. . .76 F8
Coulsworthy Crook
EX34. . . . . 3 D2
Coulsworthy La EX34. . 3 E2
Council Chambers [2]
EX9. . . . . .198 A1
Council Hos
Brixton EX5. . . . . . . .257 B5
Clyst St Mary EX5 . . . .179 A3
Council Hos The EX5 .179 E7
Council Houses The
TQ7. . . . . .149 D7
Council La EX5. . . . . . .175 E4
Countessmead EX16 .161 F8
Countess Pl EX16 . . . .161 E5
COUNTESS WEAR 178 B1
Countess Wear Com Sch
EX2. . . . . .182 B8
Countess Wear Ho
EX2. . . . . .182 A8
Countess Wear Rd
EX2. . . . . .182 A8
Counties Cres EX6 . . .201 B7
COUNTISBURY. 5 E6
Countisbury Hill
EX35. . . . . .151 E5
Country Cousins
EX34. . . . . .150 B4
Country Ho [4] EX10 . .101 B1
County Cl PL7 . . . . . . .251 A5
Couper Mdws EX2 . . .178 D3
Coursebeer La EX20. . .95 E5
COURSHAY. 88 C3
Court Baron Cross
EX14. . . . . .84 E3
Court Barton TQ7 . . .147 D8
Court Barton Cl EX5. . .81 B4
Court Barton Cotts
Coffinswell TQ12. . . . .213 C6
Down Thomas PL9. . . .255 C1
Court Barton Hill
EX12. . . . . .191 C8
Court Barton La EX5 .172 A8
Court Barton Mews
PL19. . . . . .116 F4
Court Dr
Cullompton EX15 . . . .163 C5
Wellington TA21 . . . . .160 D5
Courtenay La EX14. . .166 A5
Courtenay Cl
[23] Colyton EX24 . . . .103 A4
Starcross EX6. . . . . . .195 A1
Courtenay Cotts EX16 . 48 F2
Courtenay Dr [24]
EX24. . . . . .103 A4
Courtenay Gdns
Exeter EX2 . . . . .181 A8
Newton Abbot TQ12 . .207 C2
Courtenay Manor
TQ1. . . . . .220 C4
Courtenay Park Rd
TQ12. . . . . .207 D3
Courtenay Pk TQ10. . .135 A3
Courtenay Pl TQ14 . . .210 C4
Courtenay Rd
Exeter EX2 . . . . .177 B3
Newton Abbot TQ12 . .207 C2
Okehampton EX20 . . .170 C4
Paignton TQ4 . . . . . .226 C2
Tavistock PL19 . . . . . .171 B6
Courtenay St
Newton Abbot TQ12 . .207 B3
Plymouth PL1 . . . . . .262 C2
Salcombe TQ8. . . . . . .259 D5
Courtenay Terr EX6 . .201 B8
Court Farm Barns
TQ12. . . . . .212 B6
Courtfield TQ9. . . . . . .223 F5
Courtfield Cl EX11. . . .168 D5
Court Field La TA20 . . .69 E5
Courtfield Rd PL3. . . . .248 F5
Court Fields Com Sch
TA21. . . . . .160 C5
Court Gate TQ12. . . . .211 C1
Court Gn TQ7 . . . . . . .258 E6
Court Grange TQ12 . . .212 B6
Courtis Gdns EX17 . . .165 D5
Court La
Morebath EX16. . . . . . .34 D4

Court La continued
Seaton EX12. . . . . . . .192 A6
Thurlestone TQ7 . . . . .143 A2
Courtlage Wlk TQ7. . .258 C6
Courtland Cres PL7 . .250 D7
Courtland Cross
TQ12. . . . . .211 A6
Courtland Rd
Paignton TQ3 . . . . . .226 B7
Torquay TQ2 . . . . . . .219 B5
Wellington TA21 . . . . .160 D6
Courtlands
Saltash PL12. . . . . . . .242 E1
Tiverton EX16. . . . . . .161 E7
Courtlands Cl PL19. . .171 B6
Courtlands Cross
EX8. . . . . .196 A3
Courtlands La EX8 . . .195 F3
Courtlands Rd
Newton Abbot TQ12 . .207 D2
Tavistock PL19 . . . . . .171 B6
Courtlands Sch PL6. . .244 F1
Court Moors La TA21. . .51 E5
Courtney Ho PL5. . . . .244 B4
Courtney Rd EX16. . . .161 E5
Court Orch EX5 . . . . . .81 A1
Court Pk TQ7 . . . . . . .143 A2
Court Pk Rd TQ7 . . . .143 A1
Court Rd
Abbotskerswell TQ12 . .212 B6
Newton Ferrers PL8. . .140 F7
Torquay TQ2 . . . . . . .219 C5
Court Royal EX5 . . . . .99 B6
Court St TQ13 . . . . . . .111 F4
Court Terr TA21 . . . . .160 C5
Court The
Dunsford EX6 . . . . . . .112 F4
Plymouth PL6 . . . . . .245 C7
Saltash PL12 . . . . . . .242 C2
Court View PL8 . . . . . .256 F4
Court Way EX16 . . . . . .50 D1
Court Wlk EX19 . . . . . .58 F3
Court Wood PL8 . . . . .140 E7
Courtyard Cotts
PL21. . . . . .136 C3
Cousens Cl EX7 . . . . . .204 F8
Cousin's Cross TQ7 . .149 A6
COVE. 49 B6
Cove Hill EX16 . . . . . . .49 C6
Cuve Mdw PL11. . . . . .247 A6
Coventry Cl EX14. . . . .84 D2
Coventry Farm Est
TQ2. . . . . .213 B2
Coventry Rd EX4 . . . .176 F4
Coverdale Pl PL5 . . . .244 C1
Coverdale Rd
Exeter EX2 . . . . .177 B3
Paignton TQ3 . . . . . .226 B6
Covert Cl EX13. . . . . . .167 E7
Coverts Cl [14] EX31 . .154 A2
Cow Down Rd TA20 . . .88 F8
Cowdray Cl PL12. . . . .242 E2
Cowdray Terr PL12. . .242 E1
Cowflop Cross EX18. . .43 A1
Cowick Ct EX2 . . . . . . .177 A2
Cowick Hill EX2 . . . . .176 F3
Cowick La
Exeter EX2 . . . . .176 F3
Exeter EX4 . . . . .176 F3
Cowick Rd EX2 . . . . . .177 A3
Cowick St EX4. . . . . . .177 A4
Cow La EX34 . . . . .150 B6
COWLEY. 172 E4
**Cowley Bridge Rd Bsns
Pk** EX4 . . . . .173 A1
Cowley Hill EX5. . . . . .172 F4
COWLEYMOOR 161 E5
Cowley Moor Rd
EX16. . . . . .161 E5
Cowley Pl EX5. . . . . . .172 E5
Cowley Rd PL5. . . . . . .244 D3
Cowley Wood Head
EX31. . . . . 4 A2
Cowley Wood Hill EX31. 4 A2
Cownhayne La EX24. .103 B4
Cowpark Terr [1]
EX39. . . . . .156 F7
Cowper Ave EX2 . . . .177 F3
Cowsen La
Sourton EX20 . . . . .92 F2
Sourton EX20 . . . . . . .93 A2
Cowslip Ave PL19 . . . .171 A5
Cowslip Cres TQ12 . . .206 D5
Cowslip Mdw EX7. . . .204 E8
Coxhill Cross EX11. . . .236 A3
Coxley La EX13, EX24. .102 F7
Coxmoor Cross EX17. . .78 A1
Coxmoor La EX17. . . . .78 A2
COXPARK. 125 A7
Cox Rd TA21 . . . . .160 C4
Cox's Cl PL6 . . . . .245 B1
COXSIDE. 263 B1
Coxs La EX33 . . . . 8 C3
Coxs Mdw EX22 . . . . . .89 F7
Cox Tor Cl [6] PL20 . .126 F3
Cox Tor Rd PL19 . . . . .171 E5
Coypool Rd PL7. . . . . .250 A6
Coysh Sq EX3 . . . . . . .182 E5
Crabadon Cross TQ9 .138 F5
Crabbers Cross TQ10 135 D4
Crabb La EX2 . . . . . . .177 A2
Crabbs Cl PL15. . . . . . .90 C1
Crabshell Quay TQ7 . .258 D4
CRABTREE. 249 E5
Crabtree Cl
Cranbrook EX5 . . . . . .99 A6
Plymouth PL3 . . . . . .249 E5
Crabtree Villas PL3 . .249 E5

Crackaway Cl EX34 . . . . 9 A4
Crackington Ave EX4 174 D1
Crackston Cl PL6 . . . .249 B7
CRADDOCK. 66 C7
Craddock Cl EX22. . . .164 C6
Cradlemans Cross
EX32. . . . . .155 E1
Craig Ct EX10 . . . . . . .188 C4
Craigie Dr PL1 . . . . . .262 A3
Craigmore Ave PL2 . .247 F5
Cramber Cl
Roborough PL6. . . . . .245 C8
[5] Tavistock PL19. . . .171 B4
Crammer Ash Cross
EX15. . . . . .84 C3
Crammers Cross
TQ13. . . . . .123 F7
Crampit La
Westleigh EX39 . . . . . .26 A7
Westleigh EX39 . . . . .157 C5
Cramp La EX36 . . . . . .31 E6
Cranapool Cross EX22 . 54 E3
Cranbourne Ave PL4 .263 C4
CRANBROOK EX5 . . . . .99 A6
**Cranbrook Education
Campus** EX5. . . . . . .99 B7
Cranbrook Rd EX2 . . .178 A5
Crandford Cl EX20 . . .107 F8
Crandons Cross EX14 . 87 B6
Cranesbill Way TQ12 .206 D5
Cranes La EX9 . . . . . .198 B6
Cranfield EX7 . . . . . . .250 C7
CRANFORD. 39 A8
Cranford EX10 . . . . . .188 B5
Cranford Ave EX8 . . . .202 D6
Cranford Cl EX8. . . . . .202 C6
Cranford Cross
Great Torrington EX38 . 42 C8
Woolfardisworthy EX39 . 39 A8
Cranford Ho EX8. . . . .202 D6
Cranford Rd TQ3 . . . .219 A1
Cranford View EX8. . .202 C6
Cranishaies La EX5. . . .83 B7
Cranleigh [4] EX32 . .154 F6
Cranleigh Terr [2] EX34. 3 A3
Cranley Gdns TQ13 . .111 A6
Cranmere Ct EX2 . . . .181 C8
Cranmere Rd
Okehampton EX20 . . . .170 E6
Plymouth PL3 . . . . . .249 A6
Cranmore View
EX16. . . . . .161 B1
Crannaford La EX5 . . . .99 B6
Crannafords Ind Pk
TQ13. . . . . .111 B7
Crantock Terr [7]
PL2. . . . . .248 A5
Craon Gdns EX20 . . . .170 D6
CRAPSTONE. 126 E2
Crapstone Rd PL19. . .126 E2
Crapstone Terr PL20 .126 E2
Crashaw Cl PL5 . . . . .244 D3
Craven Ave PL4 . . . . .263 C4
Crawford Gdns EX2 . .177 A3
Crawford Rd PL1 . . . .262 A4
CRAWLEY. 69 C3
Crawley Cutting TA20 .69 C3
CRC Units EX2 . . . . . .177 D1
Creacombe Barton Cross
EX16. . . . . .46 F6
Creacombe Cross
PL8. . . . . .141 E8
Creacombemoor Cross
EX16. . . . . .47 A6
**Creacombe Parsonage
Cross** EX16 . . . . .47 A6
Crealy Great Adventure
Pk★ EX5 . . . . .99 A1
Creamery Cl PL8. . . . .136 A2
Crease La
Millhill PL19 . . . . . . .116 F1
Tavistock PL19 . . . . . .117 A1
Tavistock PL19 . . . . . .171 A4
Creber Dr PL21 . . . . . .137 E8
Crebor Rd PL19 . . . . . .171 B7
CREDITON. 165 D4
Crediton Cross EX17. . .62 D3
Crediton Hospl EX17.165 A6
Crediton La EX6 . . . . . .97 C5
Crediton Lane End
EX6. . . . . .97 C4
Crediton Rd EX20. . . .170 C5
Crediton Sta EX17. . . .165 E4
Crediton Wlk PL6 . . . .249 E8
Creedy Bridge EX17. . .165 F7
Creedy Cross EX17. . . .62 A2
Creedy Rd
Crediton EX17. . . . . . .165 D5
Plymouth PL3 . . . . . .249 C5
Creedy View EX5. . . . . .80 F2
Creedy Vw EX17. . . . . .80 B5
Creek Cl TQ7 . . . . . . .144 E1
Creek Cross TQ13 . . . .131 B5
Creek End TQ7. . . . . .148 F7
Creek Rd
Camels Head PL2. . . . .247 E7
Dartmouth TQ6. . . . . .233 D4
Creely Cl EX2 . . . . . . .181 C8
Crelake Cl PL19 . . . . . .171 C4
Crelake Ind Est [1]
PL19. . . . . .171 B4
Crelake Pk PL19 . . . . .171 C4
CREMYLL. 253 E7
Cremyll Rd PL11 . . . . .247 B2
Cremyll St PL1. . . . . . .254 A8
Crescent Ave
Barnstaple EX31 . . . . .154 D3
Plymouth PL1. . . . . . .262 B2

Crescent Avenue Mews
PL1 . . . . 262 B2
Crescent Ct TQ6 . . . . 233 D4
Crescent Gdns PL21 . . 237 C6
Crescent Mansions Flats
EX2 . . . . 261 C2
Crescent Rd PL21 . . 237 C6
Crescent The
  Brixham TQ5 . . . . . 230 D3
  Brixton PL8 . . . . . 257 A5
  Crapstone PL20 . . . 126 E3
  Exmouth EX8 . . . . . 202 E8
  Gunnislake PL18 . . . 125 D6
  Kilmington EX13 . . . . 87 C1
  Langtree EX38 . . . . . 40 E2
  Lifton PL16 . . . . . . 105 E4
  Pathfinder Village EX6 . 98 B4
  Plymouth PL1 . . . . . 262 B2
Cresents Gdns PL21 . . 237 C6
Cressbrook Cl PL6 . . 245 F2
Cressbrook Dr PL6 . . 245 F2
Cressbrook Wlk PL6 . 245 F2
Cresswell Cl TQ12 . . 213 A5
Crestfield Rise PL21 . 237 A5
Crestfields TQ6 . . . 145 E5
Crest Hill TQ11 . . . . 236 B5
Cresthill Rd PL2 . . . 248 B7
Crestway TQ6 . . . . 145 E5
Crewkerne Rd EX13 . 104 C7
Crewkerne Turning
EX13 . . . . 88 C6
Creykes Ct PL1 . . . . 262 A3
Cricket Cl EX18 . . . . . 44 F1
Cricketers Gn TQ2 . . 219 E8
Cricketers The EX13 . 167 D7
Cricketfield Cl TQ13 . 123 F6
Cricket Field Ct EX9 . 198 A1
Cricket Field La EX9 . 198 A1
Cricketfield Rd TQ1,
TQ2 . . . . 219 F7
Cricket Field Rd [9]
TQ12 . . . . 207 C3
Cricket La TQ11 . . . . 236 A6
Cricket Pk EX23 . . . . 70 A6
Cricklepit Mill ★* EX2 . 261 A2
Cridlake EX13 . . . . . 167 E5
Crier St EX14 . . . . . 166 A6
CRIMP 37 D2
Crimps Cross TQ7 . . 258 F6
Crispin Rd TQ7 . . . 258 C5
Critchards EX5 . . . . 184 C2
Criterion Pl [16] EX8 . 202 A6
Crocadon Mdws TQ9 . 139 B4
Crockaton Cotts
TQ13 . . . . 130 F5
Crocken Tor Rd
EX20 . . . . 170 D5
CROCKERNWELL . . . 96 F3
Crockernwell Ct EX6 . 96 F3
Crocker's Row PL18 . 125 D6
Crockers Cl EX31 . . 154 A4
Crockwells Cl EX6 . . 182 B3
Crockwells Rd EX6 . . 182 B4
Croft Chase EX4 . . . 176 E4
Croft Cl TQ12 . . . . 206 D1
Croft Cotts TQ12 . . . 211 D2
Croft Ct TQ2 . . . . . 220 A5
Croft Hill TQ2 . . . . 220 A5
Croft Ho EX22 . . . . 164 C4
Croft La
  Brushford TA22 . . . . . 33 C4
  Charleton TQ7 . . . . 144 C1
  Skilgate TA4 . . . . . . 34 E6
  Spreyton EX17 . . . . . 96 A6
Croft Mdw TQ12 . . . 211 D2
Croft Orch TQ12 . . . 211 D2
Croft Pk TQ6 . . . . 245 C7
Croft Rd
  East Ogwell TQ12 . . 206 D1
  Holsworthy EX22 . . 164 C4
  Ipplepen TQ12 . . . . 211 D2
  Salcombe TQ8 . . . . 259 D5
  Torquay TQ2 . . . . 220 A5
Croft's Est EX17 . . . . 80 A5
Croftside [5] EX34 . . 150 B5
Crofts Lea EX34 . . . . . 2 E3
Crofts Lea Pk EX34 . 150 B5
Croftswood EX34 . . 150 D5
Croftswood Gdns
EX34 . . . . 150 D4
Croft The EX20 . . . . . 95 A4
Croft View Terr TQ8 . 259 E5
Crogg La DT7 . . . . 260 B5
Croker's Mdw TQ13 . 180 C8
Crokers Way TQ12 . . 211 D2
Cromartie Point Flats
TQ2 . . . . 219 E2
Cromartie Rd PL4 . . 249 B1
Cromer Cl PL6 . . . . 245 A7
Cromer Wlk PL6 . . . 245 A7
Cromlech Ho EX38 . . 159 B5
Cromwell Cl EX13 . . 159 F6
Cromwell Cotts TQ12 131 F7
Cromwell Ct EX1 . . . 178 A5
Cromwell Gate PL6 . 245 C7
Cromwell Pk
  Modbury PL21 . . . . 137 B3
  Tiverton EX16 . . . . . 64 D6
Cromwell Rd PL4 . . 263 C3
Cromwells Mdw
EX17 . . . . 165 E6
Cromwells Way
TQ13 . . . . 180 C8
Cromwell Terr [7]
EX2 . . . . 178 D5
Crook Copse [6] EX1 . 178 F8
Crookeder Cl PL9 . . 256 A5

Crooked Oaks EX36 . . 30 C1
Crooke La EX20 . . . . 77 E3
Crooklake Hill EX5 . . . 98 E8
Crookmans Cl EX32 . 155 A7
Crookmans Cnr EX32 155 C5
Croppins Cl TQ11 . . 236 C5
Croscombe La EX35 . . . 4 E4
CROSS 7 F2
Cross Cl EX31 . . . . 153 D5
Crosscut Way EX14 . 166 C5
Cross Farm [5] EX33 . 152 D6
Cross Farm Ct [6]
EX32 . . . . 16 E1
Cross Furzes TQ11 . . 129 F1
Crossgate EX18 . . . . 59 C7
Cross Gate EX32 . . . . 18 F6
Crossgates PL7 . . . . 132 C6
Cross Gn PL15 . . . . 105 E7
Crossgrange Trad Est
TQ12 . . . . 180 F3
Cross Hill
  Combeinteignhead
  TQ12 . . . . 208 D3
  Crediton EX17 . . . . . 79 E5
  East Buckland EX32 . . 18 D1
  East Village EX17 . . . 80 C8
  Plymouth PL2 . . . . 247 E4
Cross Hill Cross EX17 . 80 C8
Crosshill La EX6 . . . . 97 A5
Crossing Cross TQ9 . 222 F7
Crossingfields Dr
EX8 . . . . 196 A1
Crossings Cl PL19 . . 117 E6
Cross-in-Hand PL21 . 237 F5
Cross La
  Berrynarbor EX34 . . . . 2 E3
  Brendon EX35 . . . . . 6 A4
  East Portlemouth TQ8 . 259 F4
Crossland La EX14 . . 68 C2
CROSSLANDS 160 C8
Crosslands
  Barnstaple EX31 . . . 154 C4
  Thurlestone TQ7 . . . 143 A1
  Wellington TA21 . . . 160 B8
Cross Lane Cross
EX36 . . . . 19 D1
Cross Lanes
  Ashprington TQ9 . . . 139 F8
  Ashwater EX21 . . . . . 90 F6
  Launcells EX23 . . . . 70 D8
  South Pool TQ7 . . . 148 F6
Crossley Cl TQ12 . . 207 E7
Crossley Moor Rd
TQ12 . . . . 207 E8
Cross Mdw EX17 . . . 96 A7
Cross Mdws EX31 . . 154 A2
Crossmead EX35 . . . 151 B5
Crossmoor Cross
  Rackenford EX16 . . . 47 E1
  Templeton EX16 . . . . 47 E1
Cross Moor La EX36 . 31 E2
Crosspark Ave TQ2 . 219 C8
Cross Park Ave PL6 . 244 F1
Crosspark Cl EX31 . . 154 E7
Crosspark Cres EX31 . 17 A7
Crosspark Cross
  Bradworthy EX22 . . . 38 E1
  Holsworthy EX22 . . . 164 E5
Crosspark Hill EX16 . 48 C8
Cross Park Rd
  Plymouth PL6 . . . . 244 F1
  [3] Wembury PL9 . . 140 D8
CROSSPARKS 164 F5
Crossparks
  Dartmouth TQ6 . . . 233 D3
  Tiverton EX16 . . . . . 64 F6
Cross Parks
  Cullompton EX15 . . 163 A2
  High Bickington EX37 . 43 C7
Cross Park Way PL6 . 244 F1
Cross Pk
  Berrynarbor EX34 . . . . 2 E3
  Brixham TQ5 . . . . . 230 B3
  Brixton PL8 . . . . . 257 B5
  Buckland Monachorum
  PL20 . . . . 126 D3
  Combeinteignhead
  TQ12 . . . . 208 D4
  Ilfracombe EX34 . . . 150 B6
  South Zeal EX20 . . . . 95 A4
  Thurlestone TQ7 . . . 143 C3
  Totnes TQ9 . . . . . 223 E6
CROSS ROADS . . . 106 F5
Cross Side Hill EX36 . 31 F2
Cross St
  Barnstaple EX31 . . . 154 F5
  Combe Martin EX34 . . 2 F4
  Lynton EX35 . . . . . 151 B5
  Moretonhampstead
  TQ13 . . . . 111 F5
  Northam EX39 . . . . 157 A7
  Seaton EX12 . . . . . 192 A5
Cross Terr PL18 . . . 125 C5
Cross The
  Kilmington EX13 . . . . 87 D1
  St Dominick PL12 . . 125 A2
Crosstown EX23 . . . . 36 E2
Cross Tree EX9 . . . . 198 E7
Cross Tree Ctr [3]
EX33 . . . . 152 D6
Cross View
  Buckfastleigh TQ11 . 236 A2
  Exeter EX2 . . . . . 177 B1
Cross View Terr EX2 . 176 F2
Crosswater EX23 . . . 36 F1
Crossway
  Paignton TQ4 . . . . 226 C2

Crossway *continued*
  Plymouth PL7 . . . . 250 D7
Crossway Ave PL4 . . 249 B3
Crossway Cross EX20 . 94 E6
Crossway Hill EX17 . . 61 F2
Crossway Park Homes
TQ7 . . . . 258 A8
Crossways
  Cornwood PL21 . . . 133 C2
  Milton Damerel EX22 . 54 E5
  [9] Paignton TQ4 . . 226 B6
  Ringmore TQ7 . . . . 142 E4
  South Chard EX13 . . . 88 D7
  Tatworth TA20 . . . . . 88 D8
  [4] Wembury PL9 . . 140 D8
  Whitestone EX4 . . . . 98 E4
Crossways Ct EX34 . . . 7 F7
Crossways Sh Ctr
TQ3 . . . . 226 B6
Croucher Cl EX1 . . . 174 F2
Crowbeare Mdw
EX38 . . . . 159 E6
Crowborough La EX33 . 8 A2
Crowborough Rd EX33 . 8 A2
Crow Bridge EX15 . . 163 B3
Crowbridge Pk EX15 . 163 B2
CROWDEN 74 D2
Crowden Cres EX16 . 161 F3
Crowden Cross EX20 . 74 D2
Crowden Rd EX20 . . . 74 E2
Crowder Cross TQ10 . 135 A2
Crowder Mdw TQ10 . 135 A2
Crowder Pk TQ10 . . 135 A2
Crowder's Cross EX14 84 C3
Crowdhole Cross EX16 46 F4
Crowdhole Hill EX16 . . 46 F4
Crow Gn EX15 . . . . 163 B3
Crow La EX16 . . . . . 47 C3
Crown and Anchor Way
[5] TQ3 . . . . . . 226 B6
Crowndale Ave PL3 . 249 A6
Crowndale Rd PL19 . 126 A6
Crown Gdns PL6 . . . 245 A1
CROWNHILL 244 F2
Crown Hill
  Halberton EX16 . . . . 64 F7
  West Buckland TA21 . . 52 F7
Crownhill Cross
PL21 . . . . 137 B3
Crownhill Ct PL6 . . . 244 F2
Crown Hill Ct TQ2 . . 219 E6
Crownhill Fort ★* PL6 . 244 F3
Crownhill Fort Rd
PL6 . . . . 244 F3
Crownhill La EX5 . . . 81 C5
Crown Hill Pk TQ2 . . 219 E6
Crownhill Rd PL5 . . 244 C3
Crown Hill Rise TQ2 . 219 E6
Crown Hill Terr [9]
EX17 . . . . 165 C5
Crowley La
  Stoke Gabriel TQ3 . . 225 A1
  Stoke Gabriel TQ9 . . 227 F8
Crown Mews TA21 . . 52 F7
Crown Sq [6] TQ14 . 210 A3
Crown Way EX2 . . . 178 D3
Crow Pk PL3 . . . . . 248 F5
Crowther's Hill TQ6 . 233 F3
Crow View EX32 . . . 155 C5
CROYDE 7 E2
CROYDE BAY 7 D2
Croyden Cross EX22 . 55 A4
Croyde Rd EX33 . . . . 7 D1
Croyde Sands Bglws
EX33 . . . . 7 D2
Croydon Gdns PL5 . . 243 E4
Croylands Ct EX8 . . 202 C6
Croyle Cross EX15 . . . 66 A4
Crozier Rd [6] PL4 . . 248 F4
Cruel Cross TQ3 . . . 225 D8
Cruffen Cross EX33 . . 8 B1
Cruffen La EX33 . . . . 8 B1
Cruwys Morchard Hill
EX16 . . . . 63 A7
Cruwy's Morchard Mill La
EX16 . . . . 63 A7
Cruwys Morchar Hill
EX16 . . . . 62 F2
Crystal Cl TQ4 . . . . 226 C2
Cuckoo Down La
EX14 . . . . 166 E4
Cuckoo Hill EX17 . . . 61 C3
Cuckoo La DT7 . . . . 260 A4
Cuckoo's La EX32 . . . 28 B5
Cuddeford Cnr EX4 . . 98 C6
Cuddenhay La EX17 . . 46 A2
Cuddyford Cross
TQ13 . . . . 130 F5
Cudemoor Cross EX38 41 A1
Cudhill Rd TQ5 . . . 230 B4
CUDLIPPTOWN . . . 118 A6
Cudmore Pk EX16 . . . 64 D6
Cuffe Rd PL3 . . . . 248 C4
Culbin Gn PL6 . . . . 249 D7
Culdrose Cl PL5 . . . 243 E4
Cullaford Cross EX17 . 95 E8
CULLOMPTON 163 A3
Cullompton Com Coll
EX15 . . . . 163 C2
Cullompton Hill EX5 . 83 A7
Cullompton Rd
  Awliscombe EX14 . . . 85 C4
  Honiton EX14 . . . . 166 A4
Culmbridge La EX15 . 67 C7
Culmbridge Rd EX15 . 67 C8
Culm Cl
  Bideford EX39 . . . . 157 C2
  Exeter EX2 . . . . . 178 D4

Culm Cl *continued*
  Torquay TQ2 . . . . 219 B8
Culm Cross EX20 . . . 77 A4
CULM DAVY 52 A2
Culme Cl EX14 . . . . 67 C1
Culme Rd PL3 . . . . 249 A5
Culme Way EX14 . . . 67 C1
Culm Gr EX2 . . . . . 178 D4
Culm Haven EX15 . . 66 A7
Culm Lea EX15 . . . . 163 E3
CULMSTOCK 66 E8
Culmstock Prim Sch
EX15 . . . . 51 E1
Culmstock Rd EX15 . 67 B8
Culm Valley Sports Ctr
EX15 . . . . 163 C2
Culm Valley Way EX15. 65 F7
Culver Cl
  Bradninch EX5 . . . . 83 A6
  Plymouth PL6 . . . . 249 A8
  Tiverton EX16 . . . . 161 F3
Culver Ct PL12 . . . . 242 F2
Culverdale TQ9 . . . 223 E4
Culver Gdns EX10 . . 188 B4
CULVERHILL 116 C3
Culver Ho [12] TQ13 . 123 E6
Culver La
  [8] Chudleigh TQ13 . 123 F6
  Rattery TQ10 . . . . . 135 E3
Culverlake La EX13 . . 88 G3
Culverland Cl EX4 . . 177 D8
Culverland Rd EX4 . . 177 D8
Culver Park Cl TQ7 . 258 C3
Culver Rd PL12 . . . 242 F2
Culver Way PL6 . . . 249 A7
Culverwood Cl PL7 . 251 C6
Culvery Cl EX5 . . . . 184 C3
Culvery Cross EX17 . 165 C2
Culvery Gn TQ2 . . . 219 B8
Cumber Cl
  Brixham TQ5 . . . . 230 B5
  Malborough TQ7 . . 147 F6
Cumber Dr TQ5 . . . 230 B5
Cumberland Cl EX2 . 202 D8
Cumberland Dr EX2 . 178 D4
Cumberland Gn TQ5 . 230 B5
Cumberland Rd PL1 . 247 F1
Cumberland St PL1 . 247 E2
Cumberland Way
  Exeter EX1 . . . . . 178 E2
  Exeter EX4 . . . . . 178 B8
Cumbernauld TQ1 . . 220 D4
Cummings Cross
EX13 . . . . 180 C1
Cummings Ct TQ12 . 180 C1
Cummins Cnr EX6 . . 97 E5
Cummins La EX14 . . . 87 B6
Cundy Cl PL7 . . . . 250 A7
Cunliffe Ave PL9 . . 255 A6
Cunningham Ave
EX13 . . . . 167 F7
Cunningham Rd
  Exmouth EX8 . . . . 196 D2
  Plymouth PL5 . . . . 244 C8
Cunningham's La
EX10 . . . . 187 F3
Cunningham Way
PL12 . . . . 242 D3
Cuppiers Piece Cross
EX19 . . . . 43 A1
Curie Mews EX2 . . . 177 E4
Curium Ct [9] EX12 . 192 B4
Curledge St TQ4 . . 226 B5
Curledge Street Acad [4]
TQ4 . . . . 226 B5
Curlew Cl
  Okehampton EX20 . . 170 A6
  Torquay TQ2 . . . . 213 C3
Curlew Dr
  Kingsbridge TQ7 . . 258 F1
  Torquay TQ2 . . . . 213 C2
Curlew Mews PL3 . . 249 C4
Curlew Rd EX23 . . . 70 A8
Curlew Way
  Dawlish EX7 . . . . 200 F2
  Dawlish Warren EX7 . 201 A2
  Exeter EX4 . . . . . 173 C2
Currington Mdw
EX31 . . . . 154 A3
Curriton Hill EX17 . . 61 C5
Curriton La EX17 . . . 61 B6
Curscombe Cross
EX14 . . . . 84 F4
Curscombe La EX14 . 84 F4
Cursons Way PL21 . . 237 A5
Curtis Cross EX22 . . 54 B3
CURTISKNOWLE . . . 138 D4
Curtis Rd EX31 . . . 154 F8
Curtis St PL1 . . . . 247 E1
Curve Acre EX33 . . . 152 E5
Curwood Cres [2]
EX16 . . . . 161 C3
Cussacombe Cross
EX36 . . . . 20 D1
Cussacombe Gate
EX36 . . . . 20 E1
Custance Ho [8] EX14 166 C6
Custom House Hill [4]
TQ14 . . . . 210 B4
Custom House La
PL1 . . . . 262 B1
Custom La EX16 . . . . 64 B4
Cuthays La EX13 . . . 88 B1
Cuthbert Cl TQ1 . . . 214 A1
Cuthbert Mayne Sch
TQ1 . . . . 214 A1
Cutland Cross EX18 . . 44 D4
Cutliffe La EX39 . . . 22 D3

Cutterburrow La
EX33 . . . . 152 C5
Cutteridge La EX4 . . 176 A6
Cut Tongue La TA20 . . 69 F7
Cutwell Cross TQ10 . 134 E1
Cuxton Mdws PL20 . 126 C3
Cygnet Ct EX2 . . . . 261 C1
Cygnet Units EX2 . . 261 C1
Cygnus Mws PL9 . . 256 E8
Cypress Cl
  [12] Honiton EX14 . . 85 C2
  [6] Plymouth PL7 . . 251 C5
  Torquay TQ2 . . . . 220 A5
Cypress Dr EX4 . . . 176 F7
Cypress Gdns EX8 . . 202 B6
Cyprus Rd EX8 . . . 202 B6
Cyprus Terr EX32 . . 155 B3

Dark La *continued*
  Thorverton EX5 . . . . 81 E5
Darklake Cl PL6 . . . 245 E5
Darklake La PL6 . . . 245 D8
Darklake View PL6 . 245 E5
Dark Street La PL7 . 250 C4
Darky La
  Chulmleigh EX18 . . . 59 E8
  Kingsbridge TQ7 . . 258 C2
Darlick Cnr EX36 . . . 20 C4
Darlick Corner EX36 . 20 C4
Darnell Cl EX10 . . . 188 B6
Darracombe Cres
TQ12 . . . . 206 E5
DARRACOTT 8 B2
Darracott
  Great Torrington EX38 . 41 E7
  Great Torrington EX38 159 E7
  Huntshaw EX39 . . . . 26 F1
Darracott Cross EX38 . 41 E8
Darracott Hill EX39 . . 37 B4
Darran Cl TQ12 . . . 207 F7
Darran Rd TQ12 . . . 207 F7
Dart Ave TQ2 . . . . 219 C7
Dartbridge Cross
TQ11 . . . . 236 C6
Dartbridge Manor
TQ11 . . . . 236 C6
Dart Bridge Rd TQ11 236 C5
Dart Bsns Ctr TQ9 . . 215 F1
Dart Cl
  Braunton EX31 . . . . 15 E5
  Plymouth PL3 . . . . 249 D7
  St Giles on t H PL15 . . 90 C1
Dart Hill EX16 . . . . 46 D2
DARTINGTON 215 E1
Dartington CE Prim Sch
TQ9 . . . . 215 F1
*Dartington Cider Press Sh
Ctr* ★* TQ9 . . . . . 215 F1
Dartington Cl EX38 . 159 E6
*Dartington Crystal (Glass
Factory)* ★* EX38 . . 159 C5
Dartington Fields
EX38 . . . . 159 E6
Dartington Hall ★*
TQ9 . . . . 216 B2
Dartington La TQ9 . . 223 B7
Dartington Wlk
  Exminster EX6 . . . . 181 F5
  Plymouth PL6 . . . . 249 E8
DARTMEET 129 D8
Dartmeet ★* PL20 . . . 129 D8
Dartmeet Ave PL3 . 249 B6
Dartmoor Cotts PL7 . 132 D4
Dartmoor Ct TQ13 . . 180 C7
*Dartmoor Expedition Ctr,
Rowden* ★* TQ13 . . 120 C3
*Dartmoor Otters &
Buckfast Butterflies* ★*
TQ11 . . . . 236 D5
Dartmoor Prison Mus ★*
PL20 . . . . 119 A1
Dartmoor Rly ★* EX20 170 B3
Dartmoor View
  [2] Chulmleigh EX18 . 44 E1
  Okehampton EX20 . . 170 F5
  Plymouth PL4 . . . . 249 C3
  Saltash PL12 . . . . 242 D3
  Woolfardisworthy EX17 . 61 E4
*Dartmoor Visitor Ctr
(Princetown)* ★*
PL20 . . . . 128 A8
Dartmoor Zoological Pk ★*
PL7 . . . . 133 A1
DARTMOUTH 233 E3
Dartmouth Acad
TQ6 . . . . 233 D2
Dartmouth Castle ★*
TQ6 . . . . 234 B1
Dartmouth Hill TQ6 . 146 B7
**Dartmouth & Kingswear
Hospl** TQ6 . . . . 233 F3
Dartmouth La TQ5 . 229 C4
Dartmouth L Ctr TQ6 233 E3
Dartmouth Mus ★*
TQ6 . . . . 233 F3
Dartmouth Rd
  Brixham TQ5 . . . . 229 C2
  East Allington TQ9 . . 144 E7
  Paignton TQ4, TQ5 . 226 C3
  Stoke Fleming TQ6 . 146 B8
Dartmouth Steam Rly ★*
  Churston TQ5 . . . . 229 C5
  Kingswear TQ6 . . . 234 A4
  Paignton TQ4 . . . . 226 C2
Dartmouth Wlk PL6 . 249 E8
Darton Gr TQ9 . . . . 227 F7
Dart Pk EX36 . . . . 158 D4
Dartridge La EX18 . . 44 D1
Dartside TQ9 . . . . 223 B6
Dart View TQ6 . . . 228 C3
Dart View Rd TQ5 . . 229 B6
Dart Villas TQ9 . . . 223 C4
Darwin Cres
  Barton TQ2 . . . . . 213 F3
  Plymouth PL3 . . . . 249 D5
Darwin Ct [11] EX2 . 261 B2
Dashley Ct TQ9 . . . 131 D2
Dashpers TQ5 . . . . 230 B3
Daucus Cl PL19 . . . 171 C5
Daveycourt La EX20 . 95 F3

D

Dabby La EX6 . . . . . . 97 B4
Daccabridge Rd
TQ12 . . . . 212 F4
DACCOMBE 213 E5
Daccombe Cross
TQ12 . . . . 213 E5
Daccombe Hill TQ2,
TQ12 . . . . 213 E4
Daccombe Mill La
TQ12 . . . . 213 B4
DADBROOK 252 E4
Daddon Cl EX39 . . . . 25 C4
Daddon Hill EX39 . . 156 E6
Daddyhole Rd TQ1 . 220 D3
Daggeridge Plain
EX16 . . . . 63 B4
Daggers Copse TQ12 206 F3
Dagmar Rd EX8 . . . 202 A6
Dagmar St TQ14 . . . 210 A3
Dagra La TQ12, TQ14 . 209 B6
Daimonds La TQ14 . . 210 B5
DAINTON 212 A2
Dainton Elms Cross
TQ12 . . . . 211 F2
Dainton Mews TQ4 . 226 B5
Dairs Orch TA20 . . . 88 C8
Dairy Cl
  Exminster EX6 . . . . 182 B3
  Totnes TQ9 . . . . . 223 F5
Dairy Gr EX4 . . . . 174 E2
Dairy Hill TQ2 . . . . 219 C7
Dairy La PL21 . . . . 237 D5
Daison Cotts TQ1 . . 220 A7
Daison Ct TQ1 . . . . 220 B8
Daisy La TQ12 . . . . 206 C5
Daisy Links EX4 . . . 176 D8
Daisy Pk PL8 . . . . 257 A5
Dakota Way EX1 . . . 175 F1
Dalbury Cl TQ12 . . 207 C4
Dalditch La EX9 . . . 197 D3
Dale Ave PL6 . . . . 249 C7
Dale Gdns PL4 . . . . 248 D4
Dale Rd PL4 . . . . . 248 D4
Daleside Ct TQ1 . . . 220 E4
Daleside Rd EX4 . . . 173 E1
Daleswood Rd PL19 . 171 A4
Dalton Gdns PL5 . . 243 E3
Dalverton Ct TQ5 . . 230 C6
DALWOOD 87 B3
Dalwood La EX33 . . . 87 B3
Damerel Cl PL1 . . . 247 F2
Damson Cl EX15 . . . 162 D4
Damson Cres
  Wellington TA21 . . 160 E4
  Wellington TA21 . . 160 F7
Damson Row TA21 . 160 F7
Danby Heights Cl
TQ1 . . . . 220 E4
Danby Terr EX8 . . . 202 A7
Dandy La EX4 . . . . 174 D5
Dane Ct EX39 . . . . 157 A6
Daneheath Bsns Pk
TQ12 . . . . 180 F3
Danes Cl EX14 . . . . 68 C2
Danes Cross EX5 . . . 82 C2
Daneshay EX39 . . . 157 A7
Danes Hill EX4, EX5 . . 82 C2
Daneshill Cross EX13 . 87 B3
Danes Mead EX15 . . 163 C6
Danes' Rd EX4 . . . . 261 B4
Danesway EX4 . . . . 174 F2
Daniel's Grave EX16 . 62 D4
Daniel's La
  Broadhempston TQ9 . 131 E4
  West Charleton TQ7 . 144 C1
Danisco Pack Westward
  Burlescombe EX16 . . 51 C3
  Tiverton EX16 . . . . . 51 C3
Danum Dr PL7 . . . . 251 B3
Danvers Rd PL2 . . . 247 F2
Daphne Cl TQ1 . . . 220 D5
D'arcy Ct TQ12 . . . 207 C4
Dares Field EX13 . . . 87 C1
Dares Orch EX24 . . 103 A3
Darke La EX31 . . . . 153 B4
Darke La PL19 . . . . 117 B8
Darkey La
  Lifton PL16 . . . . . 105 E4
  Okehampton EX20 . . 170 A5
Dark La
  Ashbrittle TA21 . . . . 50 E8
  Barnstaple EX31 . . . 154 F7
  Budleigh Salterton EX9 197 F1
  Hockworthy EX16 . . . 50 B8
  Modbury PL21 . . . . 137 B3
  Northleigh EX20 . . . . 74 D2
  Sidmouth EX10 . . . 187 F6

Davey's Cross PL21 . . .137 B7
Daveys Elm Vw TQ4 . .226 B2
David Cl
  Braunton EX33 . . . . . .152 D5
  Plymouth PL7 . . . . .250 F6
David Rd TQ3 . . . . .226 A2
David's Cl EX10 . . . . .101 B2
David's Hill EX33 . . . . . . .8 A2
Davids La PL21 . . . . . .137 B7
David Southgate Ct
  PL1 . . . . .262 A2
Davies Ave TQ4 . . . . . .229 A8
Davies Cl EX5 . . . . .82 B6
Davis Ave TQ2 . . . . . . .219 D6
Davis Rd TQ6 . . . . .233 C3
Davy Cl PL11 . . . . .246 F3
Davy Rd PL5 . . . . .245 C4
Dawes Cl TQ12 . . . . . .211 F8
Dawes Ct TQ4 . . . . . . .226 B5
Dawes La
  Millbrook PL10 . . . . . .252 E5
  Plymouth PL9 . . . . . . .256 D7
DAWLISH 204 F6
Dawlish Bsns Pk EX7 200 F2
Dawlish Com Coll
  EX7 . . . . .204 F7
Dawlish Com Hospl
  EX7 . . . . .204 D6
Dawlish L Ctr EX7 . . .204 F8
Dawlish Mus ★ EX7 . .204 D6
Dawlish Park Terr
  EX8 . . . . .195 F4
Dawlish Rd
  Exeter EX2 . . . . .181 C8
  Exminster EX3 . . . . . .182 B3
  Teignmouth TQ14 . . . .210 C6
Dawlish Sta EX7 . . . . .204 E6
DAWLISH WARREN .201 A1
Dawlish Warren National
  Nature Reserve ★
  EX7 . . . . .201 D3
Dawlish Warren Rd
  EX6 . . . . .201 B4
Dawlish Warren Sta
  EX7 . . . . .201 B2
Dawlish Wlk PL6 . . . . .249 E8
Dawn Cl EX1 . . . . .178 A6
Daws Ct PL12 . . . . . . .243 A2
Daws Mdw TQ12 . . . . .207 E6
Dawson Cl PL5 . . . . . .243 E1
Daymond Dr TQ13 . . .180 F7
Daymond Rd PL5 . . . . .243 D2
Days-Pottles La EX6,
  EX2 . . . . .181 D4
Dayton Cl PL6 . . . . . . .244 E3
Deacon Cl EX2 . . . . . .181 B8
Deacon Dr PL12 . . . . .242 F1
Deacons Gn PL19 . . . .171 A3
Deadhorse La EX13 . . .103 C5
Dead La EX15 . . . . .65 F2
Deadman's Cross
  TQ6 . . . . .233 D2
Dead Road Cross
  EX15 . . . . .65 F2
Deaf Acad The EX8 . .202 B5
DEAN
  Combe Martin 3 E2
  Lynton 5 A5
  West Down 8 E5
Dean Clarke Gdns
  EX4 . . . . .261 B2
Dean Cross
  Combe Martin EX31 . . . .3 E1
  Gunn EX32 . . . . .17 E4
  Lynton EX35 . . . . .5 A5
  Plymouth PL9 . . . . . . .255 E7
  South Brent TQ10 . . . .135 C5
  West Down EX34 . . . . . .8 E5
Dean Cross Rd PL9 . . .255 E7
Deane Cl EX33 . . . . .8 D1
Deane La TQ12 . . . . . .209 D2
Deane Rd TQ12 . . . . . .209 B2
Deanes The EX16 . . . .161 B3
Deane Way TA20 . . . . . .88 D8
Dean Hill PL9 . . . . . . .255 E7
Dean Hill Rd EX15 . . .162 B3
Dean La
  Combe Martin EX31 . . . .3 E1
  Lynton EX34 . . . . .5 A5
  West Down EX34 . . . . . .8 F5
Dean Lane End
  TQ10 . . . . .135 D5
Dean Park Rd PL9 . . . .255 D7
DEAN PRIOR 135 C6
Dean Rd PL7 . . . . .250 D6
Deans Cl
  Bishopsteignton
  TQ14 . . . . .208 F8
  Northam EX39 . . . . . . .156 F7
Deans La EX16 . . . . .34 D7
Deans Mead EX10 . . . .188 A5
Deans Pk EX36 . . . . . .158 D5
Dean St
  Crediton EX17 . . . . . . .165 D5
  Exeter EX2 . . . . .261 B2
Dean Steep EX35 . . . . . .5 A4
Dean Wood La
  Dean EX31 . . . . .3 F2
  Dean EX31 . . . . .10 F8
Deave La
  Throwleigh EX20 . . . . . .95 C1
  Wonson EX20 . . . . .110 D8
De Bathe Cross EX20 . .77 C3
Debden Cl PL5 . . . . . . .243 D4
De Brionne Hts EX20 .170 C5

Deckport Cross
  Hatherleigh EX20 . . . . .75 D7
  Winkleigh EX19 . . . . . . .75 F8
De Courcy Rd TQ8 . . .259 B2
Decoy Com Prim Sch
  Newton Abbot TQ12 . .207 D1
  Newton Abbot TQ12 . .212 D8
Decoy Ctry Pk ★
  TQ12 . . . . .207 C1
Decoy Ind Est TQ12 . .212 D8
Decoy Rd TQ12 . . . . . .207 D1
Deeble Cl PL7 . . . . . . .250 F7
Deep Cut Cross EX14 . .67 C2
Deep Dene Cl TQ5 . . . .230 A3
Deepdene Pk EX2 . . . .177 E4
Deep La
  Bratton Fleming EX32 . . .17 F7
  Combe Martin EX34 . . .10 C7
  Crediton EX17 . . . . . . .165 C6
  High Bickington EX37 . . .43 D7
  Kentisbury EX31 . . . . . .3 C1
  Plymouth PL7 . . . . . . .251 C3
Deeplane Head EX22 164 C5
Deepway
  Branscombe EX12 . . . .190 D4
  Exeter EX2 . . . . .181 D4
  Exminster EX6 . . . . . . .182 A4
Deepways EX9 . . . . . . .197 F2
Deerhill La EX36 . . . . .158 C6
Deerhill Rd EX36 . . . . .158 B5
Deer La EX22 . . . . .89 D8
Deer Leap PL19 . . . . . .171 D4
Deer Park Ave TQ14 . .210 A6
Deer Park Cl
  Tavistock PL19 . . . . . .171 C5
  Teignmouth TQ14 . . . .210 A6
Deer Park Cres PL19 .171 C5
Deer Park Dr
  Plymouth PL3 . . . . . . .249 D7
  Teignmouth TQ14 . . . .210 A6
Deer Park Est TQ6 . . .146 B8
Deer Park La
  Daccombe TQ12 . . . . .213 E7
  Tavistock PL19 . . . . . .171 C5
Deer Park Rd
  Barnstaple EX32 . . . . .155 C2
  Newton Abbot TQ12 . .207 E8
  Stoke Fleming TQ6 . . .146 B8
  Tavistock PL19 . . . . . .171 C5
Deer Pk
  Chudleigh Knighton
  TQ12 . . . . .123 C6
  Ivybridge PL21 . . . . . .237 E5
  Saltash PL12 . . . . .242 F3
Deers Leap Cl TQ3 . . .219 B2
Deer Valley Rd EX22 . .164 C4
Deer Wood View 4
  EX32 . . . . .16 E1
De Ferrers Dr PL8 . . . .141 A7
Defoe Cl PL5 . . . . .244 C1
De Havilland Rd EX1 .175 F1
De la Hay Ave PL3 . . . .262 A4
Delamere Rd PL6 . . . . .249 D7
Delamore Cl PL21 . . . .237 A5
De La Rue Way EX4 . .174 D1
Delaware Com Prim Sch
  PL18 . . . . .125 C5
Delaware Cotts PL18 .125 C6
Delaware Ct PL18 . . . .125 C5
Delaware Gdns PL2 . .247 F7
Delaware Rd PL18 . . . .125 C6
Delderfield Gdns
  EX8 . . . . .202 C6
Delgany Dr PL6 . . . . . .245 A5
Delia Gdns EX5 . . . . . . .99 C5
Delius Cres PL2 . . . . . .178 C5
Dell Court TQ12 . . . . . .207 C3
Dellohay Pk PL12 . . . .242 D4
Dell The
  Plymouth PL7 . . . . . . .250 B6
  Tavistock PL19 . . . . . .171 B6
Delve's Grave Cross
  EX38 . . . . .41 F8
Demouville Gdns EX17 80 B5
Denarius Rd 8 EX1 . .178 E8
Denbow Cross PL5 . . . .99 A2
Den Brook Cl TQ1 . . . .220 D6
DENBURY 211 D3
Denbury Cross TQ12 .211 D3
Denbury Ct EX2 . . . . . .181 D8
Denbury Down Cross
  TQ12 . . . . .131 F3
Denbury Down La
  Denbury TQ12 . . . . . . .131 F3
  Denbury TQ12 . . . . . . .211 A7
Denbury Prim Sch
  TQ12 . . . . .211 A6
Denbury Rd TQ12 . . . .211 E6
Denby Ho TQ4 . . . . . . .226 C5
Den Cres TQ14 . . . . . . .210 C4
Dencroft La EX14 . . . . .87 A5
Dendy Rd TQ4 . . . . . . .226 B6
Dene Cl EX8 . . . . .196 D1
Deneridge Cross EX17. 60 F6
Deneridge Hill
  Lapford EX17 . . . . .60 F6
  Morchard Bishop EX17 . .61 A5
Dene's Cl 2 EX32 . . . .17 B2
Denes Rd EX32 . . . . . . .17 B2
Dengie Cl PL7 . . . . . . .251 B5
Denham Cl PL5 . . . . . .244 C2

Dening Ct EX8 . . . . . . .202 B8
Denise Cl EX2 . . . . . . .181 B8
Denmark Rd
  Exeter EX1, EX2 . . . . .261 C3
  Exmouth EX8 . . . . .202 D8
Denners Way EX15 . . . .66 A7
Dennesdene Cl EX8 . .196 B3
Dennington Cross
  EX32 . . . . .28 B1
Dennington Hill EX32 .28 D8
Dennington La
  Churchinford EX14 . . . .68 F6
  Dulverton TA22 . . . . . . .33 B4
Dennis Camp Rd PL6 245 A7
Dennis Cl PL5 . . . . . . .247 C7
Dennis Cross EX19 . . . .57 F7
Dennis's Down Cross
  EX6 . . . . .96 C5
Dennysmead Ct EX4. 173 A1
Den Prom TQ14 . . . . . .210 C4
Den Rd TQ14 . . . . .210 C4
Densdon Gate EX16 . . .46 E6
Densdon Rd EX36 . . . . .46 E6
Densham La EX17 . . . . .61 F4
Den The TQ14 . . . . .210 C4
Denver Cl EX3 . . . . . . .182 E6
Denver Rd EX3 . . . . . . .182 E6
Denys Rd
  Torquay TQ1 . . . . .220 C5
  Totnes TQ9 . . . . .223 C5
DEPTFORD 43 B5
Deptford Pl PL4 . . . . . .263 A4
Deptford Villas 2
  EX31 . . . . .154 C3
DERBY 155 B6
Derby Rd
  Barnstaple EX32 . . . . .155 B6
  Kingsbridge TQ7 . . . . .258 D4
  Plymouth PL5 . . . . . . .244 C4
Derick Rd EX16 . . . . . .161 B5
Derncleugh Gdns
  EX7 . . . . .210 F8
Derrell Rd TQ4 . . . . . . .226 A4
DERRIFORD 245 B4
Derriford Bsns Pk
  PL6 . . . . .245 A4
Derriford Health & L Ctr
  PL6 . . . . .245 B4
Derriford Hospl PL6 . .245 B4
Derriford Pk PL6 . . . . .245 A3
Derriford Rd PL6, ...245 A4
Derriford Villas 2
  EX22 . . . . .54 D6
Derriton Rd EX22 . . . . .71 E6
Derry Ave PL4 . . . . . . .262 C4
Derry's Cross PL1 . . . .262 B2
Derwent Ave PL3 . . . . .249 C5
Derwent Rd TQ1 . . . . . .220 B7
Derworthy Cross
  EX22 . . . . .54 D6
Derworthy La EX22 . . .54 D6
Desborough La PL4 . .263 C3
Desborough Rd PL4 . .263 C3
De Tracey Pk TQ13 . . .180 D7
Deveron Cl PL7 . . . . . .251 A5
Devon Bsns Pk EX15 .163 D4
Devon Cliffs Holiday Pk
  EX8 . . . . .203 B5
Devoncourt TQ5 . . . . . .230 E6
Devondale Ct EX7 . . . .201 B2
Devon East Bsns Ctr
  EX14 . . . . .85 C3
Devon Expressway
  Ashburton TQ13 . . . . .131 B6
  Buckfastleigh TQ11 . . .236 B4
  Lee Mill PL21 . . . . .136 C6
  Plymouth PL5 . . . . . . .243 C2
  Plymouth PL7 . . . . . . .250 C6
Devon Guild of Craftsmen
  The ★ TQ13 . . . . .180 D7
Devon Heath 2
  TQ13 . . . . .123 C4
Devon Ho TQ13 . . . . . .180 E8
Devon House Dr
  TQ13 . . . . .180 E8
Devonia Cl PL7 . . . . . .250 E7
Devon Oaks PL19 . . . .126 E5
Devon Pl 13 TQ9 . . . .223 D5
DEVONPORT 247 D4
Devonport High Sch for
  Boys PL1 . . . . .248 A2
Devonport High Sch for
  Girls PL2 . . . . .248 C6
Devonport Hill
  Kingsand PL10 . . . . . .253 A2
  Plymouth PL1 . . . . . . .247 F1
Devonport Leat PL6. .241 B5
Devonport Rd PL3 . . . .247 F3
Devonport Sta PL1. . .247 F3
Devon Railway Ctr ★
  EX16 . . . . .63 F2
Devon Rd
  Exeter EX4 . . . . .177 F8
  Salcombe TQ8 . . . . . . .259 D4
Devonshire Ct
  14 Honiton EX14 . . . . .85 C2
  Torpoint PL11 . . . . . . .247 B3
Devonshire Gdns
  EX20 . . . . .77 C4
Devonshire Ho
  Plymouth PL1 . . . . . . .262 B2
  2 Tavistock PL19 . . . .171 B5
  Torquay TQ1 . . . . .220 C8
Devonshire Pk EX39 . .157 A1
Devonshire Pl EX4 . . .177 D8
Devonshire Rd EX14. . .85 C2

Devonshire Rise
  EX16 . . . . .161 E3
Devonshire St PL4 . . . .263 A3
Devonshire Way 4
  EX14 . . . . .166 A4
Devon Sq
  Kingsbridge TQ7 . . . . .258 C5
  Newton Abbot TQ12 . .207 C3
Devons' Rd TQ1 . . . . . .220 C7
Devon Terr
  Plymouth PL3 . . . . . . .248 E5
  16 Totnes TQ9 . . . . . .223 D5
Devon Tors PL20 . . . . .127 A3
Devon Tors Rd 9
  PL20 . . . . .126 F3
Devon Units
  Exeter EX2 . . . . .177 C1
  Great Torrington EX38 .159 F6
Devon View EX7 . . . . . .201 B2
Dewberry Dr
  Barnstaple EX31 . . . . .154 B3
  Paignton TQ3 . . . . . . .225 E2
Deyman's Hill EX16 . . .161 D3
Dial Ho The EX9. . . . . .198 A1
Dial St EX19 . . . . .58 F3
Diamond Ave PL4 . . . .263 B4
Diamond La TQ10 . . . . .134 D5
Diamond Rd EX2 . . . . .261 A1
Diamond St EX2 . . . . .154 F5
Diana Cl PL16 . . . . . . .106 A8
Diane Cl
  Exmouth EX8. . . . . . . .196 D4
  5 Paignton TQ3 . . . . .225 F1
Dibbon's La EX34 . . . . . .1 D2
Dibble Dr EX2 . . . . . . .177 F3
Dickens Rd PL5 . . . . . .244 B1
Dickers Terr TQ12 . . . .207 E2
Dickiemoor La PL5. . . .244 C2
Dickna St PL15 . . . . . . .90 C1
Dick Pym Cl EX2 . . . . .178 C4
Dick's Hill EX36 . . . . . .46 E8
Dickshill La EX38 . . . .159 D5
DIDDYWELL 157 B8
Diddywell Cl EX39. . . .157 A8
Diddywell Rd
  Appledore EX39 . . . . . .14 F1
  10 Northam EX39 . . . .156 F7
  Northam EX39 . . . . . . .157 A8
  Northam EX39 . . . . . . .157 B8
DIDWORTHY 134 E5
Didworthy Bglws
  TQ10 . . . . .134 E5
Didworthy Pk TQ10 . .134 E5
Dieppe Cl PL1 . . . . . . .247 F2
DIGBY 178 D3
Digby Dr EX2 . . . . .178 D3
Digby Gr PL5 . . . . .243 F5
Digby Rd EX2 . . . . .178 C3
Digby & Sowton Sta
  EX2 . . . . .178 D4
Diggerland Devon ★
  EX15 . . . . .162 C2
Diggories La 5 EX14 166 B6
Dillons PL8 . . . . .141 A7
Dillybridge Hill EX6 . . .97 D4
Dinan Way EX8 . . . . . .196 E3
Dinan Way Trad Est
  EX8 . . . . .196 F1
Dince Hill Cl EX5. . . . . .99 E7
Dingle Cl PL17 . . . . . . .115 B1
Dingle Ct PL18 . . . . . . .125 C5
Dingle Rd
  Plymouth, North Prospect
  PL2. . . . . .248 A6
  Plymouth, Plympton
  PL7. . . . . .250 C6
Dingles Fairground
  Museum ★ PL16 . . . .106 A5
Dingwall Ave PL5 . . . .244 E3
Dinham Cres EX4 . . . .261 A3
Dinham Mews EX4 . . .261 A3
Dinham Rd EX4 . . . . . .261 A3
Dinneford St EX5 . . . . .81 E5
Dinnis Cl EX6 . . . . .97 F4
Dinsdale Rd PL4 . . . . . .263 C3
Dipford Gate EX16 . . . .48 C3
Dipford La EX16. . . . . . .48 C4
Dipper Dr PL19 . . . . . .171 D2
DIPPERTOWN 106 D3
DIPTFORD 138 C7
Diptford Ct TQ4 . . . . . .225 E3
Diptford Cross TQ9 . . .138 C7
Diptford Parochial CE
  Prim Sch TQ9 . . . . . . .138 C7
Dirty La PL12 . . . . .242 B5
Discover
  Wistlandpound ★ EX31
  . . . . .11 A5
Discovery Rd PL1 . . . .247 F1
Discovery Wharf 19
  PL4 . . . . .263 A2
Distine Cl PL3 . . . . . . .249 B7
Ditch End Cross EX32 .18 C7
Ditchett Cross EX16 . . .46 E6
Dittiscombe Cross
  TQ9. . . . . .145 A6
DITTISHAM 228 C3
Dittisham Ct TQ4 . . . .228 C3
Dittisham Wlk PL6 . . .249 E8
Ditton Ct PL6 . . . . .249 A8
Divett Dr 6 TQ12 . . . .122 F1
Dixon Cl TQ3 . . . . .218 E1
Dixon Rd EX5 . . . . .179 B3
Dixon Pl PL2 . . . . .247 F4
Dixon Terr PL8. . . . . . . .257 F3
Dix's Field EX1. . . . . . . .261 B3

Doatshayne Cl EX13. .103 D5
Doatshayne La
  Musbury EX13. . . . . . . .103 D6
  Musbury, Maidenhayne
  EX13. . . . . .103 D5
Dobbin Arch TQ12 . . .212 F4
Dobbsmoor Cross
  EX18. . . . . .44 F3
Dobles Cl EX22 . . . . . .164 C5
Dobles La EX22 . . . . . .164 C6
Dobles Lane Ind Est
  EX22 . . . . .164 C6
Dobles Terr EX22 . . . . .164 C5
Dobree Pk TA21 . . . . . .160 A4
DOCCOMBE 112 C5
Doccombe Cross
  TQ13. . . . . .112 B5
Dockeys La TQ7. . . . . . .145 D1
Dockray Cl PL6 . . . . . .245 D4
Dock Rd EX8. . . . . .201 F6
Dockworthy Cross
  EX18. . . . . .60 C8
Dockyard Sta PL2. . . .247 E4
Docton Mill Gdns ★
  EX39. . . . . .22 B1
Doctors Cnr EX16 . . . . .61 D7
Doctors Rd 3 TQ5 . . .230 C3
Doctors Wlk EX2. . . . . .176 E2
DODBROOKE 258 E5
Dodbrooke Ct TQ7 . . .258 D5
DODDISCOMBSLEIGH
  . . . . .113 C3
Doddiscombsleigh Prim
  Sch EX6. . . . . .113 D5
Doddridge Cl PL9 . . . .255 F4
DODSCOTT 42 C6
Dodscott Cross EX38. .42 B7
Doe Ct EX38 . . . . .159 F5
Dog Down Cross EX16 50 A8
Doggie La
  Higher Slade EX34 . . . . .8 E8
  Ilfracombe EX34. . . . . . .1 E2
DOG VILLAGE 99 E7
Doidges Farm Cl PL6 249 B8
Dokkum Rd EX17. . . . .165 A4
Dolbeare Rd 14 TQ13 131 A5
Dole Park Cross East
  EX37. . . . . .43 D5
Dolepark Cross West
  EX37. . . . . .43 C5
Dolepark La EX37 . . . . .43 D5
Dolphin Cl
  Lyme Regis DT7 . . . . . .260 E3
  Plymouth PL9 . . . . . . .255 F6
Dolphin Court Rd
  Paignton TQ3 . . . . . . .218 F1
  Plymouth PL9 . . . . . . .255 F6
Dolphin Cres TQ3 . . . .218 F1
Dolphin Ct
  Brixham TQ5 . . . . .230 C6
  Cullompton EX15 . . . .163 C3
  13 Honiton EX14. . . . .166 C6
  Northam EX39 . . . . . . .156 E7
  22 Teignmouth TQ14. .210 C4
  Torpoint PL11. . . . . . . .246 D3
Dolphin Ho 17 PL4 . . .263 A2
Dolphin Rd EX2 . . . . . .191 B5
Dolphin Sq
  Bovey Tracey TQ13 . . .180 C7
  Plymouth PL9 . . . . . . .255 F6
Dolphin St EX24. . . . . .103 A5
DOLTON 57 F7
Dolton CE Prim Sch
  EX19. . . . . .57 F7
Dolvin Rd PL19 . . . . . .171 C5
Domehayes EX20 . . . .170 B5
Dommett Cl EX13 . . . .167 E2
Donkey La
  Millbrook PL10 . . . . . .252 C4
  Ugborough PL21. . . . . .137 D6
Donkey Sanctuary The ★
  EX10. . . . . .189 B7
Donn Gdns EX39 . . . . .157 C2
Donnington Dr PL3 . . .249 C7
Doomsford La EX37 . . .44 B5
Doone Way EX34. . . . . .150 B4
Dorado St PL9 . . . . . . .256 E8
Dorchester Ave PL5. . .244 D4
Dorchester Gr TQ2. . . .213 F1
Dorchester Way EX8 .196 D4
Doreena Rd PL9 . . . . . .256 C7
Doriam Cl EX4 . . . . . . .173 C2
Dormy Ave PL3 . . . . . .248 F5
Dornafield Cl TQ12 . . .211 D2
Dornafield Cross
  Abbotskerswell TQ12 . .211 D5
  Ipplepen TQ12 . . . . . .211 D3
Dornafield Drive E
  TQ12 . . . . .211 E2
Dornafield Drive W
  TQ12 . . . . .211 D2
Dornafield La TQ12 . . .211 E4
Dornafield Rd TQ12 . .211 D3
Dornaford Cross
  EX20. . . . . .76 C2
Dorridge Gate EX37 . . .28 B2
Dorset Ave EX4 . . . . . .176 E4
Dorset Pk PL15 . . . . . . .89 D2
Dorsmouth Terr PL7 . .250 E8
Dosson Gr TQ1. . . . . . .219 E7
Dotheridge La EX39. . .25 A1
Dots Cl PL21. . . . . .90 E6
Dotton Cl EX10 . . . . . .186 E6
Dotton La EX10 . . . . . .186 E6
Doughy La TQ12 . . . . .211 A7

Douglas Ave
  Brixham TQ5 . . . . .230 E4
  Exmouth EX8. . . . . . . .202 C6
Douglas Dr PL9 . . . . . .256 A6
Douglas Ho 14 PL10 . .210 B5
Douglass Rd PL3. . . . . .249 C6
Douro Ct PL21 . . . . . . .237 D5
DOUSLAND 127 C3
Dousland Ho PL20 . . .127 B3
Dousland Rd PL20 . . . .127 B3
Dousland Terr PL20 . . .127 B3
Dove Cl
  Cullompton EX15 . . . .163 A2
  Honiton EX14 . . . . . . .166 B4
Dovedale Cl EX34 . . . .150 E5
Dovedale Rd PL2. . . . . .248 A7
Dove Gdns PL3 . . . . . .249 C6
Dove La
  Cranbrook EX5 . . . . . . .99 B6
  Sidmouth EX10 . . . . . .188 B3
Dover Rd PL6 . . . . .245 E3
Dover's Hill EX17 . . . . .80 E8
Dove Way EX2 . . . . . . .176 D3
Dowell St EX14 . . . . . .166 B6
Dower Ct TQ3 . . . . .226 C8
Dower Ho The TQ10 . .135 C4
Dower Rd TQ1 . . . . . . .220 A7
DOWLAND 57 F5
Downash La EX13 . . . . .88 E3
Downaway La TQ12 . .213 E5
Down Cl
  Newton Poppleford
  EX10. . . . . .186 D7
  Saltash PL12. . . . . .242 C2
Down Cross EX16 . . . . .47 A2
Down End EX17 . . . . . .165 F5
Downes Cl EX17 . . . . .165 E4
Downeshead La
  EX17. . . . . .165 E5
Downfield Dr PL7 . . . .250 F5
Downfield Way PL7 . .250 F5
Downfield Wlk PL7 . . .250 F5
Downgate Gdns PL2. .248 D8
Downhayes Rd PL5. . .244 C7
Downhayne Brake Rd
  EX24. . . . . .102 E6
Downhayne Hill EX17 .62 B1
Downhayne Rd EX24 .102 F6
Down Hill
  Morchard Bishop EX17 . .78 F8
  Rackenford EX16 . . . . . .47 A3
Down La
  Braunton EX33 . . . . . .152 E6
  Doddiscombsleigh EX6 113 D5
  Dunsford EX6. . . . . . . .112 D8
  East Buckland EX32 . . .18 C3
  Georgeham EX33 . . . . . .8 A4
  Georgeham, North Buckland
  EX33. . . . . .8 B3
  Kentisbury EX31. . . . . .10 F6
  Knowle EX33. . . . . .8 F2
  Molland EX36 . . . . .31 E7
  Rackenford EX16 . . . . . .47 A3
  Winkleigh EX19. . . . . . .58 D4
Downland Cross
  Clovelly EX39 . . . . .23 E1
  Clovelly EX39 . . . . .23 E2
Downlands Cross
  EX15. . . . . .66 E2
Downlands La TA3. . . . .52 F1
Downlea PL19 . . . . . . .171 B6
Downmoor Cross
  EX38. . . . . .55 B8
Down Park Dr PL19 . .171 D4
Down Rd
  Instow EX39 . . . . .15 B1
  Plymouth PL7 . . . . . . .251 C5
  Tavistock PL19 . . . . . .171 D4
DOWN ST MARY 78 E7
Downside Ave PL6 . . .249 C7
Downside Cl DT6 . . . .104 F4
Downs The TQ7 . . . . . .143 A2
DOWNSTOW 134 F5
Downstow Cross
  TQ10. . . . . .134 F5
Downs View EX22. . . . .54 D6
DOWN THOMAS 255 C1
Downton Cl PL1. . . . . .262 A4
Downton Cross TQ6. . .233 A4
Down View Rd TQ12 . .211 A6
Dowrich Cross EX17. . .80 A7
Dracaena Ave EX31. . .154 C4
Draco Dr PL2 . . . . .247 F6
Dragdown Hill EX17. . .95 F7
Dragon Hill EX38. . . . . .40 F2
Dragons Hill DT7. . . . .260 E5
Dragon's Mead EX13 167 C4
Dragon's Tail TQ5. . . .230 E4
Dragoon Cl TQ12 . . . .180 E3
Drake Ave
  5 Exeter EX2. . . . . . . .178 D5
  Ivybridge PL21 . . . . . .237 A5
  Teignmouth TQ14 . . . .210 A8
  Torquay TQ2 . . . . .219 C6
Drake Cir PL1, PL4. . . .263 A3
Drake Circus PL3 . . . . .262 C3
Drakecircus Sh Ctr
  PL1. . . . . .263 A3
Drake Cl EX39 . . . . . . .156 B6
Drake Ct
  Plymouth, Ernesettle
  PL5. . . . . .243 E4
  Plymouth, St Jude's
  PL4. . . . . .263 B3
Drake Dr TQ4 . . . . .226 B2

Drakefield Dr PL12. . . .243 A3
Drake Gdns PL19. . . . . .171 C4
Drake La TQ13. . . . . . . .180 E7
DRAKELAND
CORNER. 132 E1
Drake Mdws **5** TA3. . .68 D7
Drake Prim Sch PL2. . .247 E6
Drake Rd
Bovey Tracey TQ13. . . . .180 E4
Cullompton EX15. . . . . .163 C4
Newton Abbot TQ12. . . .207 F3
Salcombe TQ8. . . . . . . .259 C5
Tavistock PL19. . . . . . . .171 C6
Drake's Ave
Exmouth EX8. . . . . .202 A8
Sidmouth EX10. . . . . . .188 C8
Drake's CE Prim Sch
EX9. . . . . .198 B6
Drakes Cl PL6. . . . . . . .244 F4
Drakes Cres TA20. . . . . .88 D8
Drakes Ct TQ1. . . . . . . .220 B8
Drakes Farm EX2. . . . .176 E2
Drakes Gdns EX8. . . . . .202 D8
Drakes Mdw
Cheriton Fitzpaine
EX17. . . . . .62 F1
Yarcombe EX14. . . . . . .69 A3
Drakes Pk TA21. . . . . . .160 D7
Drake's Pk **3** PL20. . .125 E1
Drakes Pk N TA21. . . . .160 D7
Drakes Rd EX4. . . . . . . .177 A4
Drake's Rd TQ4. . . . . . .225 E4
Drakes Way DT7. . . . . .260 E3
Drake Villas
Tavistock PL19. . . . . . . .171 A4
Tavistock PL19. . . . . . . .171 B4
Drakewalls Gdns
PL18. . . . . .125 C5
Drakewalls Pl PL18. . . .125 C5
Drake Way PL9. . . . . . .255 E7
DRAKEWELLS. 125 C6
Drapers Cl EX34. . . . . . .3 B3
Draper Terr **3** PL19. . .171 B5
Drax Gdns PL6. . . . . . . .248 E8
Draycott Cl EX2. . . . . .178 A4
Dray Ct **21** EX8. . . . . .202 A6
Draydon La
Dulverton TA22. . . . . . .21 F2
Dulverton TA22. . . . . . .33 B8
Drayford Rd EX16. . . . . .46 E1
Drayton Rd PL5. . . . . . .244 C1
Drayway Cross EX16. . . .63 D1
Drayway La
Bickleigh EX16. . . . . . . .63 E1
Cadbury EX16. . . . . . . .81 E8
Drew's Cl EX6. . . . . . . .201 A8
Drews Field La TQ3. . . .218 D7
Drewsmead TQ13. . . . .122 C3
Drew St TQ5. . . . . .230 C3
DREWSTEIGNTON. 96 D2
Drewsteignton County
Prim Sch TQ13. . . . . . .96 D1
Drewston Cross
TQ13. . . . . .111 C6
Drewstone Cross
EX36. . . . . .30 E6
Dreys Ct EX1. . . . . . . .177 E6
Dreyton Cross TQ9. . . .139 F3
Drift La EX14. . . . . .66 F3
Drift Lane Cross EX14. . .66 F3
Drift The TA20. . . . . . . .88 E8
Drive The
Bishopsteignton
TQ14. . . . . .208 B4
Brixham TQ5. . . . . . . .230 C2
Dawlish EX7. . . . . .204 E6
East Budleigh EX9. . . . .198 D8
Exeter EX5. . . . . .99 B3
Hillfield TQ6. . . . . . . .232 C2
Holbeton PL8. . . . . . . .136 D1
Kingskerswell TQ12. . . .213 A4
Plymouth PL3. . . . . . . .248 E2
Droridge TQ9. . . . . . . .222 F8
Droridge La TQ9. . . . . .222 E8
Drovers Way
Ivybridge PL21. . . . . . .237 A6
Seaton EX12. . . . . .192 B8
Drove Way TA3. . . . . . .68 C8
Druid Cross TQ13. . . . .130 E5
Druid Rd TQ13. . . . . . .130 E6
Drum Bridge TQ12. . . .180 F1
Drummond Cl PL2. . . .247 F3
Drummond Pl PL1. . . .247 F3
Drummond Way
PL20. . . . . .239 E3
Drum Theatre PL1. . .262 C2
Drum Way TQ12. . . . . .180 F2
Drunken Bridge Hill
PL7. . . . . .250 D4
Drupe Farm Ct EX10. .186 D3
Drybridge Cross
TQ10. . . . . .135 C5
Dryburgh Cres PL2. . . .248 A8
Dryden Ave PL5. . . . . .244 C1
Dryden Cl EX8. . . . . . .196 C4
Dryden Cotts EX5. . . . .99 D2
Dryden Rd EX2. . . . . . .177 F4
Dryfield EX6. . . . . .182 B4
Dry La
Christow EX6. . . . . . . .113 B4
Okehampton EX20. . . . .93 D5
Drymump Hill EX36. . . .45 F7
Dry Wlk PL10. . . . . . . .253 E6
Dualstone Cross EX22. .71 C3
Dubbs Cross EX21. . . . .96 B3
Ducane Wlk PL6. . . . . .245 B1
Duchy Ave TQ3. . . . . . .219 B2
Duchy Coll PL17. . . . . .115 B1

Duchy Cotts PL17. . . . .115 B1
Duchy Ct EX8. . . . . . . .196 E1
Duchy Dr TQ3. . . . . . . .219 B2
Duchy Gdns TQ3. . . . . .219 A3
Duchy Pk TQ3. . . . . . . .219 A2
Duchy Rd EX14. . . . . . .166 A4
Duchy Sch The EX5. . . . .82 F6
Duckham La EX17. . . . . .60 C5
Duck La EX20. . . . . .76 C5
Duckpool Rd EX4. . . . .176 A4
Ducks Field EX36. . . . .158 E4
Ducksmoor Cross
EX16. . . . . .63 E8
Ducks Orchard Rd
EX6. . . . . .182 B3
Duckspond Cl TQ11. . .236 A4
Duckspond Rd TQ11. . .236 A4
Duckworth Rd EX2. . . .177 A4
Duckworth St **3** PL2. .248 A4
Ducky Row PL17. . . . . .125 E4
Dudley Gdns PL6. . . . . .249 B8
Dudley Rd PL7. . . . . . . .250 B5
Dudley Way PL39. . . . . .156 B6
Dudmoor La EX31. . . . . .10 E6
DUERDON. 38 E6
Duerdon Cross EX39. . . .38 E6
Duke of Cornwall Cl
EX8. . . . . .196 E1
Dukes Cl
Otterton EX9. . . . . . . .198 E7
Paignton TQ3. . . . . . . .225 E6
Dukes Cres EX8. . . . . .196 E1
Dukes Dr PL19. . . . . . .125 E4
Duke's Dr PL17. . . . . . .115 C4
Dukes Mead EX15. . . . .163 C2
Dukes Orch EX5. . . . . . .82 F6
Dukes Rd TQ9. . . . . . . .223 F5
Duke's Rd EX9. . . . . . . .197 F2
Dukes Ryde The **1**
PL9. . . . . .255 F7
Duke St
Cullompton EX15. . . . . .163 C2
Dartmouth TQ6. . . . . . .233 F3
Kingsbridge TQ7. . . . . .258 D5
Plymouth PL1. . . . . . . .247 E2
South Molton EX36. . . .158 C4
Tavistock PL19. . . . . . . .171 C6
Dukes Way EX13. . . . . .167 C4
Dukes Wlk **4** EX1. . . .178 D1
Dulcis Cross EX13. . . . . .87 C2
DULFORD. 84 B8
Dulford Bsns Pk EX15. . .66 A1
Dulford Cross EX15. . . . .66 B1
Dulings Mdw EX17. . . . .79 B5
Duloe Gdns PL2. . . . . . .248 C8
Dulverton La TA4. . . . . .35 D7
Dulverton Mid & Com Sch
TA22. . . . . .33 D6
Dumfries Ave PL5. . . . .244 D3
Dumpdon La EX14. . . . .85 F6
Dumpdon View EX14. . .86 A6
DUMPINGHILL. 55 F3
Duncan Ho TQ1. . . . . .220 C4
Duncannon La TQ9. . . .227 E7
Duncannon Mead
TQ9. . . . . .227 F7
Duncan St PL1. . . . . . . .247 E1
DUNCHIDEOCK. 114 A6
Duncombe Ave PL5. . . .244 A2
Duncombe Cross
TQ7. . . . . .144 C2
Duncombe St TQ7. . . . .258 D6
Dun Cross TQ9. . . . . . .222 C8
Dundas St **4** PL2. . . .248 A4
Dundonald St PL2. . . . .247 F4
Dundridge Ct TQ9. . . .222 B1
Dunes The **12** EX39. . .15 B1
Dune View
Braunton EX33. . . . . . .152 B7
Westward Ho! EX39. . . .156 D7
Dune View Rd EX33. . . .152 B6
Dunheved Rd PL12. . . .242 F2
DUNKESWELL. 67 C2
Dunkeswell Airfield
EX14. . . . . .67 B2
Dunkeswell Bsns Pk
EX14. . . . . .67 B2
Dunkeswell Cl PL2. . . .247 F8
Dunkeswell Meml Mus★
EX14. . . . . .67 B2
Dunkirk EX11. . . . . . . .169 C4
Dunley Cross TQ13. . . .123 B4
Dunley La TQ13. . . . . . .123 B5
Dunley Wlk PL6. . . . . . .245 C1
Dunlin Cl EX7. . . . . . . .200 F2
Dunlin Dr
Yelland EX31. . . . . .15 C3
Yelland EX31. . . . . . . .153 A5
Dunlins Wlk EX3. . . . . .182 E6
Dunmere Rd TQ1. . . . . .220 B6
Dunmore Ct TQ14. . . . .210 B2
Dunmore Dr TQ14. . . . .210 B2
Dunning Ct EX14. . . . . .166 A4
Dunning Gn **1** EX31. .154 C3
Dunning Rd TQ14. . . . .210 A7
Dunning Wlk TQ14. . . .210 A6
Dunn La EX39. . . . . .25 E2
Dunns Cl EX33. . . . . . .152 F4
Dunn's Hill TA21. . . . . .51 A6
Dunraven **20** EX32. . .155 A4
Dunraven Dr PL6. . . . . .245 A6
Dunrich Cl EX2. . . . . . .261 C2
Dunscombe La
Sidmouth EX10. . . . . . .189 B7
Trow EX10. . . . . .189 B7

Dunsdon Cross EX22. . . .53 C3
*Dunsdon Farm National
Nature Reserve★*
EX22. . . . . .53 B2
DUNSFORD. 112 F8
Dunsford Cl EX8. . . . . .202 D6
Dunsford Com Prim Sch
EX6. . . . . .112 F8
Dunsford Gdns EX4. . . .176 E3
Dunsford Hill EX5. . . . . .81 E3
Dunsford Rd EX2. . . . . .176 E3
Dunsford Way **1**
EX16. . . . . .161 C3
Dunsgreen La EX15. . . . .67 D8
Dunsland Cross EX22. . . .73 A6
Dunsley Hill EX16,
EX36. . . . . .32 D5
Dunster Cl PL7. . . . . . .251 C4
Dunsterville Rd PL21. . .237 E6
Dunster Wlk EX1. . . . . .181 F5
DUNSTONE
Chillington. 149 B7
Widecombe in the
Moor. 121 B2
Yealmpton. 136 B2
Dunstone Ave PL9. . . . .256 A7
Dunstone Cl
Paignton TQ3. . . . . . . .218 E1
Plymouth PL9. . . . . . . .255 F7
Dunstone Cross TQ7. . .149 C7
Dunstone Ct TQ3. . . . . .218 E1
Dunstone Dr PL9. . . . . .255 F7
Dunstone La PL9. . . . . .256 B7
Dunstone Park Rd
TQ3. . . . . .218 E1
Dunstone Prim Sch
PL9. . . . . .256 A8
Dunstone Rd
Plymouth, Plymstock
PL9. . . . . .255 F7
Plymouth, St Budeaux
PL5. . . . . .243 F3
Dunstone Rise PL9. . . .256 A7
Dunstone View PL9. . . .256 A7
DUNTERTON. 115 D6
Duntz Hill PL16. . . . . . .105 E4
Dunvegan Cl EX4. . . . . .177 A8
Dunwell Cross PL21. . . .137 D5
Dural Cross EX22. . . . . .38 B3
Durant House EX20. . . . .77 C4
Durban Rd PL3. . . . . . .248 D5
Durbin Cl EX14. . . . . . .166 D5
Durdon Cross EX20. . . . .75 A1
Dure La EX36. . . . . .30 E8
Durham Ave PL4. . . . . .263 C4
Durham Cl
Exeter EX1. . . . . .178 C7
Exmouth EX8. . . . . . . .196 D4
Paignton TQ3. . . . . . . .219 B1
Durham Way EX14. . . . .166 A4
Durleigh Rd TQ5. . . . . .230 B4
Durlestone Cross
TQ7. . . . . .149 B8
Durleymoor Cross
EX16. . . . . .50 F4
Durley Rd EX12. . . . . . .191 F7
Durnford St PL1. . . . . .248 A1
Durnford Street Ope
PL1. . . . . .248 A1
Durrant Cl
Northam EX39. . . . . . . .157 A5
Plymouth PL1. . . . . . . .247 E3
Durrant La
Northam EX39. . . . . . . .156 F5
Northam EX39. . . . . . . .157 A5
Durris Cl PL6. . . . . .245 D4
Durris Gdns PL6. . . . . .245 D4
Dursley Way EX39. . . . .156 E2
Durwent Cl PL9. . . . . . .255 A6
DURYARD. 173 A1
Duryard Halls of
Residence EX4. . . . . .173 A2
Duryardwood La EX5. . .172 E5
Dutchbarn La EX3. . . . .182 D7
DUTSON. 105 A4
Dux Cross EX22. . . . . . .71 B6
Duxford Cl PL5. . . . . . .243 E5
Dyehouse Cnr TA22. . . .34 A4
Dyehouse Cross TA22. . .33 F5
Dyehouse La TA22. . . . .34 A5
Dyers Cl
Braunton EX33. . . . . . .152 D6
West Buckland TA21. . . .52 F7
Dyers Ct EX2. . . . . .261 A2
Dyke Hill Terr TA20. . . . .88 D8
Dymock Way PL1. . . . . .237 A5
Dymond Ct (Kingdom Pl)
PL12. . . . . .242 F2
Dymond Rd EX39. . . . . .156 F1
Dynevor Cl PL3. . . . . . .248 F7

E

Eager Way EX6. . . . . . .181 F5
Eagle Cl
Kingsteignton TQ12. . . .123 E1
Plymouth PL7. . . . . . . .251 C4
Eagle Cotts EX4. . . . . . .177 A5
Eagle Cres TQ12. . . . . .207 A5
Eagle Ct TQ2. . . . . .219 E8
Eagle Ho EX4. . . . . .261 A2
Eagle Hurst Ct **5**
EX10. . . . . .188 A4
Eagle Hurst Lodge **4**
EX10. . . . . .188 A4
Eagle Pl TQ13. . . . . . . .111 F5
Eagle Rd PL7. . . . . .251 C4

Eaglescott Airfield
EX37. . . . . .43 C3
Eagles Nest EX2. . . . . .176 D4
Eagle Way EX2. . . . . . .178 F5
Eaglewood Cl TQ2. . . . .213 C2
Ealing Cl TQ5. . . . . . . .230 D3
Earl Richard's Road N
EX2. . . . . .177 E3
Earl Richard's Road S
EX2. . . . . .177 F2
Earl's Acre PL3. . . . . . .248 C4
Earls Ct TQ1. . . . . .219 F6
Earl's Dr PL10. . . . . . . .253 B3
Earl's Dr The
Cawsand PL10. . . . . . . .253 A1
Rame PL10. . . . . .140 I2
Earls Mill Rd PL7. . . . . .250 E6
Earls Wood Cl PL6. . . . .245 F3
Earlswood Dr TQ3. . . . .225 D7
Earls Wood Dr PL6. . . . .245 F3
EASTACOMBE. 27 C8
Eastacombe Cross
Barnstaple EX31. . . . . . .16 B1
Northlew EX20. . . . . . . .74 E2
Eastacombe La EX15. . . .15 E6
Eastacombe Rise
EX31. . . . . .15 E6
EASTACOTT. 28 E2
Eastacott Cross EX37. . .28 E2
Eastacott La EX34. . . . . .8 B6
EAST ALLINGTON. 144 E7
East Allington Prim Sch
TQ9. . . . . .144 D7
EAST ANSTEY. 32 E5
East Anstey Prim Sch
EX16. . . . . .32 E5
EAST ASH. 95 D2
East Ash Cross
Bradworthy EX22. . . . . .38 F3
Whiddon Down EX20. . . .95 D2
East Ave EX1. . . . . .177 E6
East Ball Hill EX39. . . . . .22 E3
Eastbourne Terr
EX39. . . . . .156 D7
Eastbrook Ho **7**
TQ14. . . . . .210 B6
EAST BUCKLAND. 18 D2
East Buckland Cross
EX32. . . . . .18 D2
EAST BUDLEIGH. 198 B6
East Budleigh Rd
Budleigh Salterton
EX9. . . . . .198 B3
East Budleigh EX9. . . . .198 C6
Eastbury Ave PL5. . . . .244 C2
EAST BUTTERLEIGH. . . .64 E3
East Butterleigh Cross
EX15. . . . . .64 E3
East Challacombe La
EX34. . . . . .3 B4
EAST CHARLETON. 144 D1
Eastchurch La EX6. . . . .96 D6
East Cl EX16. . . . . .46 E1
East Cliff DT7. . . . . . . .260 E3
East Cliff Cl EX7. . . . . .204 E7
East Cliff Gdns EX7. . . .204 E7
East Cliff Rd EX7. . . . . .204 E7
Eastcliff Wlk TQ14. . . . .210 D5
East Cliff Wlk TQ14. . . .210 D5
East Coombe Cross
EX17. . . . . .81 A6
Eastcoombe La EX17. . . .81 A6
Eastcote Cl PL6. . . . . . .245 B6
EASTCOTT. 37 D3
Eastcott Cross EX23. . . .37 D2
East Courts The **5**
PL1. . . . . .262 A3
*East Dartmoor Woods &
Heaths National Nature
Reserve★* TQ13. . . . .122 B5
East Devon Bsns Pk
EX14. . . . . .86 C3
EASTDON. 201 B4
Eastdown EX39. . . . . . .22 F3
EAST DOWN. 10 C4
Eastdown Cross
TQ9. . . . . .145 D8
East Down Cross
Combe Martin EX34. . . . .9 F6
Okehampton EX20. . . . .93 D8
East Dr EX8. . . . . .196 A1
Eastella Rd PL20. . . . . .127 A2
East End EX17. . . . . . . .62 D3
East End Terr **16**
TQ13. . . . . .131 A5
Easterbrook La EX6. . . .96 D8
Easter Close Cross
EX31. . . . . .3 D1
Easter Ct EX31. . . . . . .154 B2
Easterdown Cl PL9. . . .255 F7
Easterfield La TQ1. . . . .214 C2
Easter Ground La EX34. .8 F5
Easter Hill EX37. . . . . . .28 B2
Easter Hill La EX6. . . . .201 A4
Easter La
Berrynarbor EX34. . . . . .2 E3
Lower Tippacott EX35. . . .6 B4
Easter Lane Cross
TQ13. . . . . .121 B2
Easterley Terr EX31. . . .154 C3
Easterly Pk EX33. . . . . .152 F5
Eastern Ave
Barnstaple EX31. . . . . .155 C4
Exeter EX2. . . . . .182 C7
Eastern Backway
TQ7. . . . . .258 D5
Eastern Down La EX33. . .8 C3
Eastern Espl TQ4. . . . . .226 C6

Eastern Rd
Ashburton TQ13. . . . . .131 A5
Zeal Monachorum EX17. . .78 C7
Easterntown PL8. . . . . .136 D1
EASTERN TOWN. 188 B3
Eastern Wood Rd
PL7. . . . . .251 D4
Easter Rd EX36. . . . . . . .19 A2
Easter St EX32. . . . . . . .16 E1
East Farm TQ7. . . . . . . .144 D1
Eastfield EX11. . . . . . . .168 D4
Eastfield Ave PL9. . . . . .255 C6
Eastfield Cres PL3. . . . .249 A6
Eastfield Gdns EX11. . . .168 D4
Eastfield Orch
Uffculme EX15. . . . . . . .66 A8
West Hill EX11. . . . . . . .168 D4
East Grove Rd EX2. . . . .261 C2
Easthay La TA20. . . . . . .88 F4
East Hill EX33. . . . . . . .152 E6
East Horner La EX13. . . .87 B5
EAST ILKERTON. 5 B3
EASTINGTON. 60 E4
Eastington Cross EX17. .60 E4
Eastington Hill EX17. . . .60 E3
East John Wlk EX1. . . . .177 E6
EAST KNOWSTONE. . . .32 B2
Eastlake Ho **4** PL1. . .263 A2
Eastlake Ope PL1. . . . . .263 A3
Eastlake St PL4. . . . . . .262 C3
Eastlands EX15. . . . . . . .67 B8
EASTLEIGH. 26 C6
EAST LEIGH
Haberton. 222 B1
Zeal Monachorum. 77 F8
Eastleigh Cl EX13. . . . .103 D8
East Leigh Cross
Harberton TQ9. . . . . . .222 B1
Zeal Monachorum EX17. . .77 F8
East Lyn La EX35. . . . . .151 F2
East Mead EX15. . . . . . .67 B8
East Meadow EX31. . . . .27 B8
East Meadow Rd
EX33. . . . . .152 B7
East Mere Cross EX16. . .50 B2
EAST MIDDLETON. 4 B1
East Moore Cross
TQ9. . . . . .135 E1
East Nymph La EX17. . . .95 E6
EAST OGWELL. 206 E1
EASTON. 111 B7
Easton Cross
Hittisleigh EX6. . . . . . . .96 C5
West Alvington TQ7. . . .258 B3
Easton La EX1. . . . . .50 D1
Easton Moor Cross
EX31. . . . . .27 C1
Easton Rd EX6. . . . . . . .96 C4
East Pafford Ave
TQ2. . . . . .214 B3
East Park Ave PL4. . . . .262 C4
East Park Cl EX19. . . . . .58 F3
East Park Rd EX32. . . . .155 D4
East Pitton Barns
PL7. . . . . .136 A5
East Pk EX39. . . . . .38 F8
EAST
PORTLEMOUTH. 259 F4
EAST PRAWLE. 149 A3
East Pugsley Cross
EX37. . . . . .29 B2
EAST PUTFORD. 39 C3
East Ridge View
EX39. . . . . .157 B1
East Rowley La EX36. . . .45 D6
East Sherford Cross
PL8. . . . . .257 A8
East St
Ashburton TQ13. . . . . .130 F5
Bishop's Tawton EX32. . .16 E1
Black Torrington EX21. . .74 A8
Bovey Tracey TQ13. . . .180 D8
Braunton EX33. . . . . . .152 D6
Chittlehampton EX37. . . .28 F4
Chulmleigh EX18. . . . . .44 E1
Crediton EX17. . . . . . . .165 D5
Denbury TQ12. . . . . . . .211 A7
Great Torrington EX38. . .159 D5
Ipplepen TQ12. . . . . . .211 E2
Newton Abbot TQ12. . . .207 C3
North Molton EX36. . . . .19 E1
North Molton EX36. . . . .30 E8
Okehampton EX20. . . . .170 C5
Plymouth PL1. . . . . . . .262 A2
Sheepwash EX21. . . . . .56 C1
Sidmouth EX10. . . . . . .188 B3
South Molton EX36. . . . .158 D4
Torquay TQ2. . . . . .219 F6
Uffculme EX15. . . . . . . .66 A7
EAST STOWFORD. 28 F5
East Tapps La EX16. . . . .33 B2
East Terr
Budleigh Salterton
EX9. . . . . .199 H2
Exeter EX1. . . . . .178 A6
East View Terr EX39. . . .157 A1
EAST VILLAGE. 80 C8
East Village Cross
EX17. . . . . .80 C8

East Way PL21. . . . . . . .136 D6
Eastwell La TQ12. . . . . .217 C7
Eastwick Barton EX16. . .62 B8
East Wonford Hill
EX2. . . . . .178 B5
Eastwood EX35. . . . . . .151 B4
Eastwood Cres TQ12. . .206 E5
Eastwood La EX6. . . . . .96 C7
EAST WORLINGTON. . . .61 B8
East Worlington Cross
EX17. . . . . .61 B8
East Worlington Prim Sch
EX17. . . . . .61 B8
EAST YOULSTONE. 37 F2
East Youlstone Cross
EX23. . . . . .37 F2
Easy Bridge Cross
EX13. . . . . .102 F7
Easy La TQ13. . . . . .123 B7
Eaton Ct TQ14. . . . . . . .210 B7
Eaton Dr EX1. . . . . .261 C3
Eaton Hall Dr TQ6. . . . .233 E4
Eaton Ho EX1. . . . . .261 C3
Eaton Pl TQ4. . . . . .226 B5
Ebberley Lawn EX32. . .155 A5
Ebberly Arms EX38. . . . .42 F6
Ebberly Cross EX19. . . . .42 E5
Ebberly Ct **14** EX32. . .155 A5
EBBERLY HILL. 42 F6
Ebdon Ct EX10. . . . . . .101 B2
Ebdon Way TQ1. . . . . . .219 F6
Ebenezer Rd TQ3. . . . . .226 A5
EBFORD. 183 C4
Ebford La EX3. . . . . . . .183 C4
Ebrington Rd EX2. . . . .177 B3
Ebrington St
Kingsbridge TQ7. . . . . .258 D5
Plymouth PL4. . . . . . . .263 A3
Echo Cres PL5. . . . . . . .244 D2
Eco Way PL6. . . . . .245 C8
Eddy's La **10** EX32. . .155 B3
Eddystone Cl
Heybrook Bay PL9. . . . .140 A7
Plymouth PL3. . . . . . . .249 C6
Eddystone Rd
Down Thomas PL9. . . . .255 C1
Thurlestone TQ7. . . . . .258 B3
Eddystone Rise TQ7. . .147 D7
Eddystone Terr PL1. . . .262 B1
Eden Cl TQ5. . . . . .230 C3
Eden Gr TQ3. . . . . .225 F7
Eden Park Prim Sch
TQ5. . . . . .230 C3
Eden Pk TQ5. . . . . .230 C3
Edenside PL3. . . . . .248 F6
Edenvale Rd TQ3. . . . . .225 F8
Eden Valley Gdns
PL6. . . . . .245 D2
Eden Way EX10. . . . . . .186 A3
Edford St EX2. . . . . . . .177 C6
Edgar Terr PL4. . . . . . . .249 A4
Edgbaston Mead
EX2. . . . . .178 C4
Edgcumbe Ave PL1. . . .262 A3
Edgcumbe Cl PL18. . . .125 E1
Edgcumbe Cres PL10. .252 F6
Edgcumbe Ct **3** PL3. .248 A3
Edgcumbe Ho PL1. . . . .262 B2
Edgcumbe Park Rd
PL3. . . . . .248 D6
Edgcumbe Rd
St Dominick PL12. . . . .125 A2
Saltash PL12. . . . . .242 C5
Edgcumbe Terr
13 Bere Alston PL20. . .125 E1
Milton Abbot PL19. . . . .116 A6
Edgecombe Way
PL18. . . . . .125 B5
Edgecumbe Rd PL19. . .116 A6
Edgeland Cross
EX15. . . . . .217 D8
Edgelands La TQ12. . . .211 C1
Edgeley Rd TQ2. . . . . . .214 A2
Edgemill Wlk PL21. . . . .237 E4
Edgemount Ho **5**
TQ1. . . . . .220 B5
Edgerley Cross EX17. . . .60 C1
Edgerton Park Rd
EX4. . . . . .177 D8
Edgeworthy Hill EX16. . .62 C8
Edgiford Cross EX18. . . .45 B1
Edgiford La EX18. . . . . .45 A1
EDGINSWELL. 213 B5
Edginswell La TQ2,
TQ12. . . . . .213 A1
Edinburgh Cres EX8. . .195 E6
Edinburgh Dr EX4. . . . .176 E6
Edinburgh Rd TQ5. . . . .230 D3
Edinburgh St PL1. . . . . .247 C8
Edith Ave PL4. . . . . . . .263 C4
Edith St PL5. . . . . .243 D1
Edmonton Cl EX4. . . . .178 A8
Edmund St EX2, EX4. . .261 A2
Edmunds Way
1 Exeter EX1. . . . . . .178 D1
Exeter EX1. . . . . .182 D8
Edna Terr PL4. . . . . . . .263 C3
Edward Cl TQ7. . . . . . . .143 A1
Edward Dr EX11. . . . . . .169 B3
Edwards Cl PL7. . . . . . .251 B4
Edwards Cres PL12. . . .242 C2

Edwards Ct EX2......178 D4
Edwards Dr
　Plymouth PL7.......251 B5
　Westward Ho! EX39...156 E7
Edwards Rd PL15.....90 C1
Edwin Rd EX2........177 B3
Effingham Cres PL3..248 D7
EFFORD..............249 C5
Efford Barns EX17....81 B4
Efford Cres PL3......249 B6
Efford Fort PL3......249 E6
Efford La PL3........249 B5
Efford Marshes Nature
　Reserve★ PL3.......249 C6
Efford Pathway PL3..249 C6
Efford Rd PL3........249 B6
Efford Wlk PL3.......249 B6
Egerton Cres PL4.....263 C3
Egerton Pl PL4.......263 C3
Egerton Rd
　Plymouth PL4........263 C3
　Torquay TQ1.........220 C6
EGGBUCKLAND........249 A8
Eggbuckland Com Coll
　PL6................249 A8
Eggbuckland Rd
　Plymouth PL3.......249 A6
　Plymouth PL3.......249 C7
Eggbuckland Vale Prim
　Sch PL6............249 A8
Eggesford Cross EX17 60 A1
Eggesford Ctry Est
　EX18...............59 E6
Eggesford Fourways
　EX18...............59 E6
Eggesford Garden &
　Country Ctr★ EX18..59 E6
Eggesford Rd
　Winkleigh EX19......58 F3
　Winkleigh EX19......59 A2
Eggesford Sta EX18...59 E6
Egg Moor La EX13.....88 A7
Egham Ave EX2.......177 D3
Egremont Cross EX14..84 C6
Egremont Rd EX8.....202 A7
Egret Cl
　Dawlish EX7.........200 F2
　Millbrook PL10......253 A6
Egypt La EX2........44 E1
Fiffel Pl EX2 TQ9.....223 C5
Eight Acre Cl
　Paignton TQ3.......225 F1
　Plymouth PL7.......251 C5
Eight Acre Dr TQ3.....225 F1
Eight Acre La TA21...160 C5
Eight Trees TQ9......216 A5
Elaine Cl
　Exeter EX4..........174 A2
　Plymouth PL7.......250 B5
Elba Cl TQ4..........206 C5
Elberry Farm La TQ4..229 D7
Elberry La TQ5.......229 E5
Elbow La PL19.......171 C6
ELBURTON...........256 B6
Elburton Prim Sch
　PL9................256 C7
Elburton Rd PL9......256 B8
Elbury Cl EX4........175 E6
Eldad Hill PL1.......262 A3
Elderberry Way EX15 162 E5
Elder Cl PL7.........251 B5
Elder Gr EX17........165 E6
Eldertree Gdns EX4...177 A7
Eldridge Ho EX13.....167 F7
Eleanor Ho PL1.......262 A4
Electra Way PL9......256 E8
Elford Cres PL7......250 E7
Elford Dr PL9........255 C7
Elford Pk PL20.......127 A2
Elgar Cl
　Barnstaple EX32.....155 C5
　Exeter EX2..........178 C5
Elgin Cres PL5.......244 E3
Elim Cl EX10.........188 B5
Elim Ct PL3..........248 E5
Elim Terr PL3........248 E5
Elim Villas EX10.....188 B5
Eliot St PL1.........247 E8
Elizabethan EX39.....156 B7
Elizabethan Ct EX2..261 B2
Elizabethan Ho TQ9..223 D5
Elizabethan Wy TQ14 204 B1
Elizabeth Ave
　Brixham TQ5........230 A1
　Exeter EX4..........177 E8
Elizabeth Cl
　Barnstaple EX31.....154 D2
　Ivybridge PL21......237 F5
　Lyme Regis DT7.....260 E4
　Rockwell Green TA21 160 B4
　Whimple EX5........99 E8
Elizabeth Ct
　Plymouth PL1.......263 A2
　Torquay TQ2........219 F5
　Totnes TQ9.........223 F5
Elizabeth Dr EX31....154 D3
Elizabeth Gdns EX1..178 C7
Elizabeth House Mus &
　Arts Gall★ PL4......263 A2
Elizabeth Lea CT EX22 38 E1
Elizabeth Penton Way
　EX16................34 B1
Elizabeth Pl PL4.....263 A4

Elizabeth Rd
　Exmouth EX8........196 C2
　Seaton EX12........192 A7
Elizabeth Sq TQ12...207 F2
Elizabeth Way EX12..192 A6
Elkins Hill TQ5......230 D5
ELLACOMBE..........220 C6
Ellacombe Acad......220 B6
　TQ1................220 B6
Ellacombe Church Rd
　TQ1................220 B6
Ellacombe Rd TQ1....220 B6
Ellacott Rd EX2......181 C6
Ellards Cl EX2.......177 E3
Ellbridge La PL12....238 A3
Ellen Tinkham Sch
　EX1................178 E7
Ellen Tinkham Sch
　Further Ed Coll EX1 178 B7
Elleralie Ho PL14....210 B3
Ellerhayes EX5.......82 D4
Ellersdown La TA22...33 E4
Ellerslie Rd EX31....154 B4
Ellesmere TQ1.......220 C1
Ellesmere Rd TQ1....220 E5
Elley Cross EX17......79 B2
Ellimore Rd TQ13....122 C8
Elliot Cl
　Barnstaple EX32.....155 C4
　Ottery St Mary EX11.169 C3
Elliot Ho EX2........261 B2
Elliot Plain TQ11....236 C5
Elliots Hill TQ13.....130 C8
Elliot Sq PL11.......247 B3
Elliot St PL1........262 B1
Elliott Cl
　Exeter EX4..........173 E2
　Saltash PL12........242 D2
Elliott Ct TQ12......211 C2
Elliot Terr PL1.......262 C1
Elliot Terrace La PL1 262 C1
Elliott Gdns EX1.....174 F2
Elliott Gr TQ5.......230 B4
Elliott Rd PL4........249 B1
Elliotts Hill TQ13....258 A4
Elliott's Hill EX17....61 C3
Elliott Way EX2......178 D5
Ellis Dr TQ13........111 A6
Ellis Yard EX34......150 B5
Ellmead Cross EX20...93 F7
Ellwood Ct TQ1......220 B6
Ellwood Rd EX8......196 D2
Elm Bank TQ11......236 A4
Elmbank Gdns
　TQ4................226 A5
Elmbank Rd TQ4.....226 A5
Elmbridge Gdns EX4 177 A8
Elm Cl
　Broadclyst EX5......175 C6
　Stibb Cross EX38.....40 D2
　Tavistock PL19......171 C3
Elm Cotts
　Barnstaple EX31......16 A3
　Saltash PL12........242 C3
Elm Cres PL3, PL4....249 A4
Elm Croft PL2........248 B7
Elmcroft La TQ12....212 E6
Elm Ct EX6..........201 B8
Elmdale Rd EX4......157 A3
Elmdon Cl EX4.......173 D1
Elm Dr TQ12.........207 D1
Elm Farm La EX24....103 A3
Elmfield Cres EX8....196 B2
Elmfield Mdw EX20...74 E1
Elmfield Rd
　Barnstaple EX31......16 A3
　Seaton EX12........192 A7
Elmfield Terr EX39...157 A7
Elmfield Way TQ12...207 E6
Elm Gr
　Bideford EX39.......156 F2
　Exmouth EX8........201 F6
　Plymouth, Eggbuckland
　PL6................249 B8
　Plymouth, Plympton
　PL7................250 E5
　Teignmouth TQ14....210 B8
Elm Grove Ave EX3...182 F5
Elm Grove Cl EX2....204 E7
Elm Grove Dr EX2....204 E7
Elm Grove Gdns EX3 182 F5
Elm Grove Rd
　Dawlish EX7........204 E7
　Exeter EX4..........261 A4
　Topsham EX3........182 F5
Elmhirst Dr TQ9......223 E5
Elmhurst Ct TQ14....210 B5
Elm La EX8..........202 F7
Elmlea Ave EX31.....153 E5
El Monte Cl TQ14....210 B6
Elm Orch EX12.......192 D7
Elmoreswell Ave
　EX1................179 A8
Elmore Way
　Tiverton EX16........64 C8
　Tiverton EX16.......161 E5
Elm Pk
　Millbrook PL10......253 B6
　Paignton TQ3........225 F6
Elm Pk Way EX1......179 B8
Elm Rd
　Brixham TQ5........230 A2
　Exmouth EX8........202 C7
　Newton Abbot
　TQ12...............207 C3
　Plymouth, Glenholt
　PL6................245 D6

Elm Rd continued
　Plymouth, Mannamead
　PL3................248 F4
ELMSCOTT............37 B8
Elmscroft Terr.......157 A2
Elmside
　Budleigh Salterton
　EX9................198 A1
　Exeter EX4..........177 E7
　Willand EX15........65 D5
　Willand EX15........162 D3
Elmside Cl EX4.......177 E7
Elmsleigh EX32.......27 E8
Elmsleigh Pk TQ4....226 B5
Elmsleigh Rd TQ4....226 B5
Elms Mdw EX19.......58 F2
Elms Rd TA21.........160 F5
Elms The
　Colyford EX24.......103 A3
　Holsworthy EX22.....164 C4
　Plymouth PL3........248 A3
Elm Terr
　Honiton EX14........166 D6
　Plymouth PL3........248 F5
　Tiverton EX16.......161 B4
Elm Tree Cl
　Torquay TQ2........213 C2
　Yealmpton PL8......257 F4
Elm Tree Dr TQ9.....228 A8
Elm Tree Pk PL8......136 A2
Elm Units EX2........177 D1
Elm Villas EX24......103 A3
Elm Way EX10........101 A1
Elm Wlk TQ9.........223 F5
Elmwood Ave TQ12...206 E4
Elmwood Cl PL6......245 D5
Elmwood Cres EX7....204 E7
Elmwood Gdns EX24..103 A3
Elmwood Pk TQ7......143 E7
Elphinstone Rd PL2...248 C7
Elsdale Rd TQ4.......226 A4
Elsdon EX11..........168 E4
Elsdon La EX11.......168 E4
Elsdon's La DT6......104 D7
Elsie Pl EX1..........178 D6
Elspeth Sitters Ho
　PL4................263 A2
Elston Cross
　Churchstow TQ7......143 D4
　Copplestone EX17....79 C6
ELSTONE.............44 D3
Elstone Cross EX18...44 C3
Elston La EX17........79 B5
Elston Mdw EX17.....165 A5
Elton Cl EX16........161 B5
Elton Rd EX4.........177 E8
Elvestone EX9.........198 B1
Elvis Rd EX8.........202 D7
ELWELL..............18 C2
Elwell Cross EX32.....18 B2
Elwell Rd PL12.......243 A2
Elwick Gdns PL3.....249 B5
Elworthy Cross EX16..47 C2
Elworthy Dr EX17.....160 D4
Elworthy Hill EX16....47 D2
Elwyn Rd EX8........202 C6
Ely Cl
　Exeter EX4..........176 D6
　Feniton EX14........84 D2
Elysian Ct EX36......156 D5
Elysian Fields EX10...188 B5
Embankment La PL4..249 B2
Embankment Rd
　Kingsbridge TQ7.....258 D3
　Plymouth PL4.......249 B2
Embankment Road Lane
　N PL4................249 B2
Embankment The
　TQ14...............209 D5
Embercombe Cross
　EX32................18 F1
Ember Rd TQ8........259 C5
Embleford Cres
　TQ13...............111 F5
Embridge Cross TQ6 145 F7
Embridge Hill TQ6....146 A7
Embury Cl TQ12......213 A4
Emily Gdns PL4.......263 B4
Emma Gr PL19.......171 B7
Emmanuel Cl EX4.....177 A5
Emmanuel Rd
　EX4................177 A5
Emma Pl PL1.........248 A1
Emma Place Ope
　PL1................248 A1
Emmasfield EX8......202 D7
Emmetts Pk TQ13.....131 A5
EMPACOMBE.........253 D6
Emperor Way EX1.....178 E7
Empire Ct TQ1.......220 A7
Empire Rd TQ1.......220 A7
Empsons Cl EX7......204 C6
Empsons Hill EX7.....204 C6
Encombe St PL3......249 E1
Endeavour Ave PL4...182 C8
Endeavour Ct PL1.....263 A1
Endfield Cl EX1.......178 B6
Endsleigh Cres EX5..179 B7
Endsleigh Dr PL15,
　PL19...............115 D5
Endsleigh Gdns★
　PL19...............115 F5
Endsleigh Gdns
　PL4................263 A4

Endsleigh Park Rd
　PL3................248 D6
Endsleigh Pl EX23....70 A6
Endsleigh Pl PL4.....263 A4
Endsleigh Rd PL9.....255 C7
Endsleigh View PL21 237 A5
Energic Terr EX15....163 C4
Enfield Cl EX17.......165 A5
Enfield Cotts TQ1....220 D7
Enfield Rd TQ1.......220 C7
Engineers Way EX8...202 E7
England's Cl EX10....101 B1
Eningdale Rd PL19....171 A4
Ennaton Cross PL21..137 E7
Ennerdale Gdns PL6 244 E5
Ennerdale Way EX4...176 F6
Ennisfarne Rd EX39..156 B7
Ensign Ct EX39.......156 E7
Ensis Cross EX31......27 D5
Enterprise Ave EX16..64 E8
Enterprise Rd
　Roundswell EX31......16 B2
　Roundswell EX31.....154 B1
Entrance Cross EX37..44 B7
Epping Cres PL6......249 D7
Epworth Terr PL2.....247 F5
Erica Dr TQ2.........213 F3
Eric Rd
　Calstock PL18.......125 E5
　Plymouth PL4........263 C3
Erith Ave PL2........247 E2
Erle Gdns PL7.........250 F3
Erlstoke Cl PL6.......245 D1
Erme Bridge Wks
　PL21...............237 C4
Erme Ct PL21.........237 D5
Erme Dr PL21.........237 C5
Erme Gdns PL3.......249 C5
Erme Pk PL21.........136 F3
Erme Prim Sch The
　PL21...............237 D5
Erme Rd PL21........237 D5
Ermeside Cotts PL21 136 F4
Erme Terr PL21.......237 D5
ERMINGTON..........136 F4
Ermington Prim Sch
　PL21...............136 F4
Ermington Rd
　Ivybridge PL21......237 C3
　Ivybridge PL7.......136 F6
Ermington Terr PL4..240 F4
Ermington Workshops
　PL21...............137 A4
Ernborough Ct EX2..261 C2
ERNESETTLE.........243 E3
Ernesettle Com Sch
　PL5................243 F4
Ernesettle Cres PL5..243 E4
Ernesettle La PL5.....243 D4
Ernesettle Lane Ind Est
　PL5................243 E3
Ernesettle Rd PL5....243 E3
Ernsborough Gdns
　EX14...............166 B5
Erril Ret Pk PL7......250 C5
Escot★ EX11.........84 C1
Escot Cotts EX5......184 B2
Eskil Pl EX38.........159 C6
Esmonde Gdns PL5...247 B8
Esplanade
　Exmouth EX8........202 A5
　Seaton EX12........192 B4
　Teignmouth TQ14...210 C4
Esplanade Rd TQ4...226 C6
Esplanade The
　Dartmouth TQ6......233 F5
　Plymouth PL1........262 C1
　Sidmouth EX10......188 B3
　Woolacombe EX34....7 F7
Essa Rd PL12.........242 F2
Essex Cl EX4.........176 E4
Essex St PL1..........262 B4
Essington Cl EX8.....196 B3
Essington Ct EX20.....77 C4
Essington La EX20.....77 D4
Essington Rd EX20....77 C4
Esso Wharf Rd PL4...263 C1
Esthwaite La PL6......245 A4
ESTOVER.............245 E5
Estover Cl PL6.......245 F5
Estover Ind Est PL6..245 E4
Estover Rd PL6.......245 F4
Estuary Ave EX3......177 A5
Estuary Bsns Pk EX31 15 C3
Estuary Ct TQ14.....209 D7
Estuaryview TQ12....207 F8
Estuary View
　Budleigh Salterton
　EX9................198 B1
　Northam EX39.......157 A8
　Yelland EX31........15 C2
Estuary Vw EX8......196 A3
Estuary Wy PL5......247 C8
Esworthy Cross EX16. 32 F1
Ethelston's Cl DT7...260 A5
Ethelwynne Brown Cl
　EX39...............157 B2
Eton Ave PL1.........262 C4
Eton Cl EX39.........156 F3
Etonhurst Cl EX2.....178 D3
Eton Pl PL1..........262 C4
Eton St PL1..........262 C4
Eton Terr PL1........262 B3
Eton Wlk EX4........176 E4
Eugene Rd TQ3.......226 C8
Eureka Terr
　Bovey Tracey TQ13...180 D8

Eureka Terr continued
　Honiton EX14........166 C5
Europa Pk EX34......8 B6
Evans Ct PL1.........262 A3
Evans Field EX9......197 F2
Evans Pl PL2.........248 B5
Eveleigh Cl
　Brixham TQ5........230 C3
　West Clyst EX4......174 E3
Eveleighs Ct EX4.....261 B4
Evelyn Pl PL4........263 A4
Evelyn St PL5........243 D1
Evenden Ct PL11.....247 A3
Eventide Homes
　TQ5................230 C2
Everest Dr EX12.....192 A4
Everett Pl EX16......161 E6
Evergreen Cl EX8....196 D3
Evett Cl EX8.........202 E8
Evran Dr EX8.........196 E3
Ewings Sq EX2.......261 A2
Ewin's Ash EX14......85 C8
EWORTHY............91 E6
Eworthy Cross EX21..91 E6
EXBOURNE...........76 C4
Exbourne CE Prim Sch
　EX20...............76 C4
Exbourne Cross
　EX20...............76 C4
Excalibur Cl EX4.....174 A1
Excelsior Mews
　TQ1................220 B7
Exchange St PL4.....263 A2
EXEBRIDGE...........33 F3
Exebridge Ind Est
　TA22...............33 F3
Exe Bridge Retail Ctr
　EX4................261 A1
Exe Cl EX31..........15 E5
Execliff EX8..........202 A5
Exe Dene EX3.........182 E5
Exe Gdns PL3........249 C7
Exe Hill TQ2.........219 B8
Exe St
　Exeter EX4..........261 A3
　Topsham EX3.......182 F5
EXETER..............261 B4
Exeter Acad EX4.....173 D1
Exeter Airport Bsns Pk
　EX5................99 A4
Exeter Arena Athletics
　Stadium EX4........174 B1
Exeter Bsns Ctr EX2..177 C2
Exeter Bsns Pk EX1..178 E4
Exeter Cath (Church of
　St Peter)★ EX1......261 B3
Exeter Cathedral Sch
　Exeter EX2..........261 B2
　Exeter EX1..........261 A3
Exeter Central Sta
　EX4................261 A4
Exeter Cl
　Feniton EX14........84 D2
　Plymouth PL5.......243 D4
Exeter Coll EX4......261 A3
Exeter Coll Annexe
　EX4................261 A3
Exeter Coll Bishop
　Blackall Annexe
　EX4................261 B4
Exeter College
　Construction Training
　Centre (Falcon House)
　EX2................178 E4
Exeter Coll Maths &
　Science Ctr
　Exeter EX2..........177 B7
　Exeter EX4..........261 A4
Exeter Coll Tech Centre
　EX2................178 E4
Exeter Community Hospl
　(Whipton) EX1......178 C7
Exeter Cross
　Coldeast TQ12......123 A1
　Sidmouth EX10......188 B6
Exeter Foyer EX2.....261 A2
Exeter Gate EX36.....158 C3
Exeter Hill
　Cullompton EX15.....163 B2
　Kenton EX6.........194 D3
　Shobrooke EX17......80 F5
　Tiverton EX16.......161 E2
Exeter Hill Cross
　EX17................80 F4
Exeter Hospl, Nuffield
　Health (private)
　EX2................177 C4
Exeter International
　Airport EX5.........99 A4
Exeter Mathematics Sch
　EX1................261 B3
Exeter Racecourse★
　EX6................114 C2
Exeter Rd
　Braunton EX33......152 E4
　Chudleigh TQ13.....123 F7
　Crediton EX17......165 D4
　Cullompton EX15.....163 B2
　Dawlish EX7........200 D3
　Doccombe TQ13.....112 A5
　Exmouth EX8........196 A2
　Exmouth EX8........202 A7
　Honiton EX14.......166 A5
　Ivybridge PL21......237 C3
　Kennford EX6.......181 A2
　Kingsteignton TQ12..207 D8
　Moretonhampstead
　TQ13...............111 F4

　Newton Abbot TQ12..207 B5
Exeter Rd continued
　Newton Poppleford
　EX10...............186 C8
　Okehampton EX20...170 D5
　Ottery St Mary EX11..169 A3
　Rockwell Green TA21 160 B4
　Rockwell Green TA21..160 B5
　Silverton EX5.......82 B5
　South Brent TQ10...135 A3
　South Molton EX36...29 E3
　Teignmouth TQ14...210 B6
　Tiverton EX16........64 E4
　Topsham EX2, EX3...182 D6
　West Hill EX11......168 E7
　Whiddon Down EX20.. 95 F3
　Whimple EX5........168 B8
　Winkleigh EX19......58 F2
Exeter Road Bsns Pk
　TQ12...............123 E1
Exeter Road Com Prim
　Sch EX8............202 A7
Exeter Road Ind Est
　EX20...............170 C6
Exeter St David's Sta
　EX4................177 A7
Exeter Sch EX2.......177 E5
Exeter St
　North Tawton EX20....77 C4
　Plymouth, Barbican
　PL4................263 A3
　Plymouth, St Jude's
　PL4................263 B2
　Teignmouth TQ14...210 B5
Exeter's Underground
　Passage Mus★ EX4.261 B3
Exeter Trad Ctr EX2..181 E8
Exeter Tutorial Coll
　EX4................261 C2
Exe Units EX2........177 D1
Exe Vale Rd EX2......178 A1
Exe Vale Terr
　EX4................161 C3
Exe Valley Fishery★
　TA22...............33 F3
Exe Valley L Ctr
　EX16...............161 C5
Exe Valley Way EX5...81 F2
Exe Vicw Cotts EX4..176 F4
Exe View Rd EX8......196 C6
Exhibition Rd EX17...165 E6
Exhibition Way EX4..178 D8
EXMINSTER..........182 B4
Exminster Com Prim Sch
　EX6................182 A4
Exminster Hill
　Exminster EX6......182 B2
　Powderham EX6......194 B8
Exminster Marshes (RSPB
　Reserve)★ EX6......182 D3
Exmoor Cl EX16......161 E6
Exmoor Gdns TA22...33 D6
Exmoor La EX16......49 C1
Exmoor National Park
　Visitor Ctr★ EX35...151 C6
Exmoor View EX36...158 C5
Exmoor Way EX15....163 A3
Exmoor Zoo★ EX31...11 B3
EXMOUTH...........202 B7
Exmouth Archery Club
　EX8................197 B4
Exmouth Com Coll
　EX8................202 B8
Exmouth Ct
　Exmouth EX8........202 B6
　Plymouth PL1.......247 F5
Exmouth Hospl EX8...247 F5
Exmouth Model Rly★
Exmouth Mus★ EX8..202 A7
Exmouth Nature
　Reserve★ EX8......195 C2
Exmouth Rd
　Aylesbeare EX5......185 D8
　Budleigh Salterton
　EX9................197 E1
　Clyst St Mary EX5....179 A1
　Exton EX3..........183 C3
　Lympstone EX8......195 F5
　Lympstone EX8......195 F7
　Newton Poppleford
　EX10...............186 D5
　Plymouth PL1.......247 F5
Exmouth Sports Ctr
　EX8................201 F7
Exmouth Sta EX8.....201 F7
Exmouth Tennis & L Ctr
　EX8................202 B8
Exonia Pk EX2........176 D3
Explorer Ct PL2......248 B5
Explorer Wlk TQ2....213 F3
EXTON...............183 D2
Exton La EX3.........183 C2
Exton Rd EX2.........177 C3
Exton Sta EX3........183 C1
EXWICK..............176 E7
Exwick Ct EX4........176 F7
Exwick Heights Prim Sch
　EX4................176 E7
Exwick Hill EX4......176 F6
Exwick Ho EX4.......176 D7
Exwick La EX4........176 F7
Exwick Rd EX4........176 F7
Exwick Villas EX4....176 F7
Eyewell Gn EX12......192 A6
Eymore Dr EX11......168 C3
Eyrecourt Rd EX12...192 A4

Factory Cotts TQ9 . . . . **139** C7
Factory Cross TQ13 . . **110** F6
Factory La TA20 . . . . **88** D8
Factory Ope 🔳 EX39 . **15** A1
Factory Row
  South Molton EX36 . . . . . **158** E4
  Torquay TQ2 . . . . **220** A5
Fairacre Ave EX32 . . . . **155** C2
Fairby Cl EX16 . . . . . . **161** D6
Fairend La TA20 . . . . **69** D8
Fairfax Gdns EX2 . . . . **177** B2
Fairfax Pl TQ6 . . . . **233** F3
Fairfax Rd
  Cullompton EX15 . . . . . **163** C4
  Heathfield TQ12 . . . . . . **180** F3
Fairfax Terr 🔳 PL2 . **247** F4
Fairfax Way
  Great Torrington
   EX38 . . . . **159** F5
  Ottery St Mary EX11 . . **169** F5
Fairfield
  Bratton Fleming EX31 . . **18** A8
  Ilfracombe EX34 . . . . . **150** C5
  Plymouth PL7 . . . . **250** E7
  Sampford Peverell EX16 **50** D1
  South Brent TQ10 . . . . **135** A2
Fairfield Ave
  Exeter EX4 . . . . **178** C8
  Plymouth PL2 . . . . **248** C2
Fairfield Cl
  Axminster EX13 . . . . . **167** D5
  Bovey Tracey TQ13 . . . **180** C7
  Exmouth EX8 . . . . **202** B6
  Kingsbridge TQ7 . . . . . **258** D4
Fairfield Gdns EX14 . . **166** C5
Fairfield Gn TA3 . . . . . . **68** D7
Fairfield Pk DT7 . . . . . **260** E4
Fairfield Rd
  Crediton EX17 . . . . . . **165** C6
  Exeter EX2 . . . . **181** B8
  Exmouth EX8 . . . . **202** B5
  Kingskerswell TQ12 . . . **213** A3
  Torquay TQ2 . . . . **219** F8
Fairfield Terr
  Exeter EX2 . . . . **177** A4
  Newton Abbot TQ12 . . . **207** C3
Fairfield Way TQ7 . . . **145** A1
Fairholme Rd EX34 . . . . **7** F6
Fairies Hall TQ11 . . . . **236** C6
Fair Isle Cl TQ2 . . . . . **213** E2
Fairlands Ave EX10 . . . **188** B5
Fairlawns Pk TQ4 . . . . **226** B2
Fairlea TQ5 . . . . **230** C6
Fairlea Cl EX7 . . . . . . **200** F1
Fairlea Cres EX39 . . . . **156** F6
Fairlea Ct EX9 . . . . . . **197** E1
Fairlea Gdns EX39 . . . **156** E6
Fairlea Rd EX7 . . . . . . **200** F1
Fairleigh EX10 . . . . . . **186** B8
Fairlinch Cross EX33 **152** B8
Fairlynch Cl EX33 . . . . **152** B7
Fairlynch Gr EX33 . . . . **152** C7
Fairlynch La EX33 . . . **152** B7
Fairlynch Mus★ EX9 . **199** H2
Fairmead EX10 . . . . . . **187** F8
Fairmead Ct TQ2 . . . . **213** F2
Fairmead Mews
  PL12 . . . . **242** C3
Fairmead Rd PL12 . . . **242** C3
FAIRMILE **169** B7
Fair Oak Cl EX5 . . . . . . **99** A4
Fair Oak Ct EX5 . . . . . . **99** A4
Fair Oak Rd EX5 . . . . . . **99** A4
Fair Oaks TQ14 . . . . . **210** A6
Fairpark Cl EX2 . . . . . **261** C2
Fairpark Rd EX2 . . . . **261** B2
Fairplace Terr EX20 . . **170** B5
Fairseat Cl TQ9 . . . . . **223** D4
Fair View
  Barnstaple EX31 . . . . . **154** E6
  Bradworthy EX22 . . . . . **53** E8
  Colyford EX24 . . . . . . **103** A3
Fairview Ave
  Clyst St Mary EX5 . . . . **179** D2
  Plymouth PL3 . . . . **249** D5
Fair View La EX24 . . . **103** A3
Fairview Pk TQ13 . . . **180** C5
Fairview Rd TQ12 . . . . **211** A7
Fair View Rd
  Dartmouth TQ6 . . . . . . **233** E4
  Honiton EX14 . . . . . . **166** C5
Fairview Terr EX1 . . . **174** F1
Fairview Way PL3 . . . . **249** E5
Fairwater Cl TQ12 . . . **207** F7
Fairwaters TQ12 . . . . **207** E8
Fairway
  Appledore EX39 . . . . . . **14** F1
  Saltash PL12 . . . . **242** C2
  Tiverton EX16 . . . . **64** E8
Fairway Ave PL21 . . . **237** B5
Fairway Cl
  Braunton EX33 . . . . . . **152** B6
  Churston Ferrers TQ5 . . **229** D5
Fairway Gdns 🔳 PL7 . **136** A8
Fairways Cl EX37 . . . . . **43** B6
Fairways Dr EX37 . . . . . **43** B6
Fairways The EX39 . . **156** D7
Fairways View EX37 . . **43** C6
Fairway The
  Braunton EX33 . . . . . . **152** B6
  Exeter EX4 . . . . **173** E1
  Newton Ferrers PL8 . . . **140** F7
FAIRY CROSS **25** A3

Fairy La TQ11 . . . . **236** A4
Falcon Ct EX36 . . . . . . **158** C4
Falcon Pk TQ4 . . . . . . **224** F5
Falcon Rd
  Exeter EX2 . . . . **178** E4
  Mount Wise PL1 . . . . . **247** F1
Falcon Units TQ12 . . . **207** A3
Falcon Way 🔳 EX16 . **161** C6
FALKEDON **96** A6
Falkedon Cross EX17 . . **96** A6
Falkland Cl EX4 . . . . . **173** E2
Falkland Dr TQ2 . . . . . **207** F8
Falkland Rd TQ2 . . . . **219** F5
Falkland Way TQ14 . . **210** A6
Fallapit Turn TQ9 . . . **144** C8
Falloway Cl TQ2 . . . . **214** A2
Fallow Cl EX15 . . . . . **158** B5
Fallowfield Cl TQ12 . . **207** F3
Fallowfields TQ9 . . . . **223** A5
Fallow Fields EX32 . . **155** C2
Falmouth Cl TQ2 . . . . **219** B8
Fancy Cross PL21 . . . . **137** A2
Fanny's Cross EX36 . . . **46** E7
Fanny's La EX17 . . . . . . **80** B5
Fannys Lane Cross
  EX17 . . . . **80** B5
Fanshawe Way PL9 . . . **255** C6
Faraday Ho EX1 . . . . . **177** E6
Faraday Mill Bsns Pk
  PL4 . . . . **249** B1
Faraday Rd PL4 . . . . . **249** B1
Faringdon Rd PL4 . . . . **249** B1
Farleigh TQ12 . . . . . . **206** B5
Farleigh Back Rd
  EX16 . . . . **63** C2
Farleigh Cross TQ9 . . **139** A4
Farleigh Front Rd
  EX16 . . . . **63** C2
Farleigh Mdws EX16 . **161** A6
Farley Gr EX1 . . . . **174** F2
Farley Hill TQ13 . . . . **123** D8
Farley's Grave EX20 . . **77** E7
Farm Cl
  Exeter EX2 . . . . **178** C4
  Kingskerswell TQ12 . . . **212** F6
  Plymouth PL7 . . . . **250** C7
  Roundswell EX31 . . . . **154** A1
Farmer Frank's La
  EX19 . . . . **58** F2
Farm Hill EX4 . . . . . . **176** E8
Farmhouse Ave EX1 . . **178** F8
Farm House Rise
  EX6 . . . . **181** F4
Farm La
  Plymouth PL5 . . . . **244** B2
  Saltash PL12 . . . . **242** D1
Farm Mdw EX3 . . . . . **182** D8
Farm Rd
  Bideford EX39 . . . . **25** D4
  Rousdon DT7 . . . . **193** E6
Farm The EX5 . . . . **99** D8
Farm Way EX14 . . . . . . **84** D2
Farmyard La TQ3 . . . . **218** B6
Farnham Ho 🔳 DT7 . **260** D3
Farnham Terr 🔳
  TQ3 . . . . **226** B7
Farnley Cl PL6 . . . . . . **245** B6
Farpark Hill La
  Beara EX31 . . . . **9** A1
  Halsinger EX33 . . . . **8** F1
Farrant Ct EX10 . . . . . **188** A4
Farrant's Hill EX6 . . . **113** B8
Farriel La EX34 . . . . . . **8** F5
Farriers Cotts PL7 . . . **250** E7
Farriers The PL19 . . . **116** E4
FARRINGDON **99** B1
Farringdon Cross
  Chilton EX17 . . . . **80** E7
  Exeter EX5 . . . . **99** A1
Farringdon Ct EX5 . . . . **99** B2
Farringdon Hill EX17 . . **80** E7
Farringdon Ho EX5 . . . **99** B2
Farthing Cross
  EX32 . . . . **29** A7
Farthing Down TA21 . . **51** E7
Farthing La TQ3 . . . . . **218** C2
Farthing Lake Cross
  EX32 . . . . **29** A7
Farthingland Cross
  EX20 . . . . **76** B5
Farthings La EX10 . . . . **186** E7
Farthings Lodge Bsns Ctr
  EX15 . . . . **83** E6
Farthing's Pitts TA21 . **160** C4
Far View Rd EX20 . . . . **170** C5
FARWAY **102** A6
Farway CE Prim Sch
  EX24 . . . . **101** F7
Farway Common Rd EX14,
  EX24 . . . . **101** F7
Farwell Rd TQ9 . . . . . **223** B6
Farwood Cross EX24 . **102** C4
Fatacott Cross EX39 . . **23** F1
Fatherford Rd EX20 . . **170** D5
Faulkner Cl TQ6 . . . . **233** C3
Fawns Cl PL21 . . . . . . **136** F4
Fay Rd EX7 . . . . **204** E6
Fayre View PL12 . . . . . **242** B1
Fearnside Way PL12 . . **242** C3
Featherbed La
  Clayhanger EX16 . . . . . . **35** C1
  Exmouth EX8 . . . . **196** B2
  Monkton EX14 . . . . **86** D6
  Offwell EX14 . . . . **86** B2
Featherstone Rd EX8 **196** A4
Federation Rd PL3 . . . **249** C4
Fegen Rd PL5 . . . . **243** B1
Felixwell Ct EX4 . . . . **176** F5

Fell Cl PL8 . . . . **141** B8
Fellowes Ct 🔳 PL1 . . **262** A3
Fellowes Pl PL1 . . . . **248** A2
Feltrim Ave EX2 . . . . **261** C1
FENITON **84** E2
Feniton CE Prim Sch
  EX14 . . . . **84** E2
Feniton Gdns EX14 . . **84** D2
Feniton Sta EX14 . . . . **84** D2
Fenten Pk PL12 . . . . . **242** F3
Feoffe Cotts EX31 . . . **154** F7
Feoffees Cotts TQ7 . . **258** A4
Ferguson Cl PL1 . . . . **169** B3
Ferguson Rise
  West Clyst EX4 . . . . . . **174** F3
  West Clyst EX4 . . . . . . **175** A4
Fernbank Ave PL21 . . **237** A6
Fern Cl
  Brixham TQ5 . . . . **230** D4
  Okehampton EX20 . . . . **170** C6
  Plymouth PL7 . . . . **251** C5
Ferncombe Cl 🔳
  TQ12 . . . . **123** F1
Ferncombe Dr 🔳
  TQ12 . . . . **123** F1
Ferndale TQ6 . . . . **233** E8
Ferndale Ave PL2 . . . **247** E1
Ferndale Cl
  🔳 Honiton EX14 . . . . . . **85** C2
  Plymouth PL6 . . . . **245** D8
Ferndale Gdns EX2 . . **177** A4
Ferndale Mews TQ2 . **219** B7
Ferndale Rd
  Exeter EX2 . . . . **177** A4
  Plymouth PL2 . . . . **247** F7
  Teignmouth TQ14 . . . . **210** B6
  Torquay TQ2 . . . . **219** B7
Ferndown Cl EX39 . . . **156** E2
Ferndown Rd DT7 . . . **260** E3
Ferne Animal Sanctuary★
  TA20 . . . . **69** D2
Fernery The 🔳 EX34 . **150** D5
Fernham La EX32 . . . . . **18** D7
Fernhill DT7 . . . . **260** F7
Fernhill Cl PL21 . . . . **237** B5
Fernhill Cross TQ7 . . **143** E8
Fernhill Hts DT6 . . . . . **104** F4
Fernicombe Cl TQ3 . . **225** E7
Fernicombe Rd TQ3 . . **225** E7
Fernleigh Cl EX20 . . . . **77** C4
Fernleigh Rd PL3 . . . . **248** F5
Fern Mdw
  Okehampton EX20 . . . . **170** C6
  Tavistock PL19 . . . . . . **171** D6
Fernpark Cl
  Exeter EX2 . . . . **177** E2
  Exeter EX2 . . . . **177** E3
Fern Pk EX34 . . . . **150** B5
Fern Rd TQ12 . . . . . . **207** F1
Fern Way EX34 . . . . . . **150** B4
Fernworthy Cl
  Copplestone EX17 . . . . . **79** B5
  Torquay TQ2 . . . . **219** A7
Fernworthy Forest Trail★
  TQ13 . . . . **110** D2
Fernworthy Gdns
  EX17 . . . . **79** B5
Fernworthy Pk EX17 . . **79** B5
Ferrers Gn TQ5 . . . . . **229** E4
Ferrers Rd PL5 . . . . . **243** E1
Ferry La PL11 . . . . **246** D5
Ferryman's Reach
  TQ14 . . . . **210** B3
Ferrymans View TQ5 . **234** E8
Ferryman Way EX3 . . **182** D7
Ferry Rd
  Plymouth PL1 . . . . **247** E3
  Topsham EX3 . . . . **182** E5
  Topsham EX3 . . . . **182** F4
Ferry Slip TQ6 . . . . . . **233** F3
Ferry St PL11 . . . . **247** C3
Feversham Cl PL7 . . . **251** B6
Fiddlecott La EX17 . . . . **60** B6
Field Cl
  Braunton EX33 . . . . . . **152** C5
  Paignton TQ3 . . . . **219** B2
Field End
  Axminster EX13 . . . . . **167** E5
  Bideford EX39 . . . . **156** E2
Fieldings The EX37 . . . . **28** F4
Field La
  Ashford EX31 . . . . **16** B6
  Braunton EX33 . . . . . . **152** C5
Field Rd EX1 . . . . **175** B1
FILHAM **237** F4
Filham Ind Est PL21 . **237** D5
Filham Moor Cl PL21 **237** E4
Fillablack Way EX39 . **157** C2
Fillace La 🔳 PL20 . . . **126** F4
Fillace Pk PL20 . . . . . **126** F4
FILLEIGH **29** C7
Filleigh Com Prim Sch
  EX32 . . . . **29** C6
Filleigh Mill New Rd
  EX32 . . . . **29** D7
Filleigh Moor Cross
  EX17 . . . . **60** D5
Filleighmoor Gate
  EX21 . . . . **56** C3
Filmer Way EX2 . . . . . **177** B3
Fincer Dr PL21 . . . . . . **237** A6
Finch Cl
  Plymouth PL3 . . . . **249** D4
  Shillingford Abbot EX2 . **181** B7
Finches Cl PL9 . . . . . . **256** C7
Finch Foundary★
  EX20 . . . . **95** A5
Findon Gdns PL6 . . . . **245** D4

Finewell St PL1 . . . . . **262** C2
Fingle Bridge★ TQ13 . **111** E8
Fingle Cl EX4 . . . . **176** E8
Fingle Glen EX6 . . . . . . **98** B4
Finistere Ave EX7 . . . **204** E8
Finnigan Rd PL4 . . . . **249** B1
Finnimore Ind Est
  EX11 . . . . **169** C3
Finning Ave EX4 . . . . **174** D1
Fin St PL1 . . . . **262** B1
Firbank Rd EX7 . . . . . **200** F1
Fir Cl
  Honiton EX14 . . . . . . **166** B5
  Willand EX15 . . . . **162** D5
Firconia Terr EX21 . . . **73** B4
Fircroft Rd PL2 . . . . . **248** B7
Firebeacon Cross
  EX39 . . . . **37** C7
Fire Beacon Cross
  Bishop's Tawton EX31 . . **27** D7
  Chittlehampton EX37 . . **29** B2
Fire Beacon Hill Nature
  Reserve★ EX10 . . . . **100** F1
Firebeacon La
  Bolham EX16 . . . . **49** C3
  Chittlehampton EX37 . . **29** B2
Fire Beacon La EX10 . **100** E1
Fire Brigade Hos
  EX4 . . . . **261** A4
Firestone Cross EX20 . **95** C3
Fire Stone Cross EX20 **95** C4
Firestone La TQ12 . . . **212** A8
Fir La EX17 . . . . **62** F3
Firlands TQ14 . . . . . . **210** B7
Firlands Rd TQ2 . . . . **214** A2
Firleigh Rd 🔳 TQ12 . **123** E1
Firs Cross TQ9 . . . . . . **144** C7
Firs Gr EX32 . . . . **155** B5
Firs Pk EX2 . . . . **176** C3
First Ave
  Axminster EX13 . . . . . **167** F7
  Dawlish EX7 . . . . **204** D5
  Exeter, Countess Wear
   EX2 . . . . **182** D7
  Exeter, Heavitree EX1 . . **177** F6
  Plymouth, Billacombe
   PL9 . . . . **255** F8
  Plymouth, Stoke PL1 . . **248** A2
  Teignmouth TQ14 . . . . **210** A5
  Torquay TQ1 . . . . **220** A8
First Dr TQ14 . . . . **210** B5
First Field La EX33 . . **152** C5
Firs The
  🔳 Barnstaple EX32 . . . **155** B5
  Kennford EX6 . . . . **114** D4
  Wilmington EX14 . . . . . **86** D2
First Raleigh EX39 . . . **156** E3
Fir Terr EX36 . . . . **158** D4
Fir Tree Cl EX8 . . . . . . **196** E2
Firtree Rise PL21 . . . . **237** D5
Firway Cross EX16 . . . . **34** C3
Fir Wlk TQ2 . . . . **219** C8
Fisgard Way PL11 . . . . **246** D3
Fishacre Cl TQ3 . . . . . **225** E8
Fishacre Cross TQ9 . . **216** F6
Fishchowter's La
  TQ9 . . . . **223** C4
Fishcombe Rd TQ5 . . . **230** B6
Fisherman's Path
  TQ13 . . . . **111** B8
Fisher Rd
  Newton Abbot TQ12 . . . **207** B3
  Plymouth PL2 . . . . **248** A5
Fisher's Hill TA21 . . . . **51** D7
Fishers Mead TA22 . . . **33** D6
Fisher St TQ4 . . . . . . **226** B5
Fishers Way EX16 . . . . **65** A7
Fisherton Cross EX37 . **28** C2
Fishingclose Cross
  EX20 . . . . **76** F6
Fishleigh Cross EX20 . **75** C8
Fishleigh Rd EX31 . . . **154** B2
Fish Mkt PL4 . . . . **263** B2
Fish Quay PL4 . . . . . . **263** A2
Fistral Cl PL11 . . . . . **246** F4
Fitzford Cotts PL19 . . **171** B4
Fitzroy Rd
  Exeter EX1 . . . . **178** C5
  Plymouth PL1 . . . . **248** A3
Fitzroy Terr 🔳 PL1 . . **248** A3
Five Acres TQ13 . . . . . **180** C4
Five Acres La PL12 . . . **242** B5
Five Barrow La EX13 . **104** A4
Five Barrows Cross
  EX36 . . . . **19** D7
Five Bridges EX15 . . . **163** C6
Five Bridges Cross
  EX15 . . . . **67** C7
Five Cross TQ12 . . . . . **122** C1
Five Crosses
  Modbury PL21 . . . . **137** A2
  Rackenford EX16 . . . . . **47** C1
Five Crossway EX36 . . . **46** D8
Five Cross Way
  Brayford EX31 . . . . **18** F8
  Plymtree EX15 . . . . **83** E8
  West Buckland TA21 . . . **52** F6
Five Cross Ways TA22 . **32** F7
  South Molton EX36 . . . . **30** D4
Five Elms Cross EX5 . . **80** C1
Five Elms La EX5 . . . . . **80** E1
Five Hos TA21 . . . . . . **160** B8
Five Lane End EX38 . . **159** A1
Five Lanes
  Buckfastleigh TQ13 . . . **236** E5
  Dawlish EX7 . . . . **200** A3
  Hennock TQ13 . . . . . . **123** B7
  🔳 Kingsteignton TQ12 **123** E1
  Marldon TQ3 . . . . **218** E3

Five Lanes Cross EX22 **54** D8
Five Lanes Rd TQ3 . . . **218** D2
Five Mile Hill EX6 . . . . **98** C4
Five Mile Hill Cross
  EX6 . . . . **98** C4
Five Oaks TQ11 . . . . . **130** C2
Five Oaks Cross
  Brampford Speke EX5 . . **81** C1
  Burrington EX37 . . . . . . **43** D4
Five Turnings EX34 . . . . **3** A4
Five Wyches Cross
  TQ13 . . . . **180** B7
Flagstaff Rd TQ6 . . . . **233** F4
Flamborough Rd
  PL6 . . . . **245** A7
Flamborough Way
  PL6 . . . . **245** A6
Flamsteed Cres PL5 . . **243** E1
Flavel Pl TQ6 . . . . **233** F3
Flavel St TQ6 . . . . **233** F3
Flaxmeadow La EX13 **167** E6
Flayes Almshouses 🔳
  EX4 . . . . **178** C8
Flay Field EX1 . . . . . . **179** B8
Fleet Court EX12 . . . . **192** B5
Fleet St
  Plymouth PL2 . . . . **247** E6
  Torquay TQ1, TQ2 . . . . **220** B4
Fleet Walk Sh Ctr
  TQ2 . . . . **220** B4
Fleetwood Gdns PL6 . **245** A7
Fleming Ave EX10 . . . **188** C8
Fleming Way EX2 . . . . **177** E4
Flemons Ct 🔳 TQ4 . . **226** A5
Fletcher Cl TQ2 . . . . . **219** E7
Fletcher Cres PL5 . . . . **244** A5
Fletcher Ind Est EX39 **25** E4
Fletcher Way PL9 . . . . **256** A6
Flete ★ PL21 . . . . **136** E2
Flete Cl TQ12 . . . . **207** F2
Flete Ho PL21 . . . . . . **136** E2
Fletemoor Rd PL5 . . . **243** E1
Flete View Terr 🔳
  PL21 . . . . **137** C8
Fletewood Sch PL4 . . **262** C4
Flexapark EX34 . . . . **3** A3
Flexton The EX11 . . . **169** D4
Flightway EX14 . . . . . . **67** B3
Flightway Bsns Pk
  EX14 . . . . **67** B3
FLITTON BARTON . . . **19** B1
Floaters Rd TQ6 . . . . **233** F4
Flood's La EX15 . . . . . **163** B3
Flood St TQ9 . . . . **227** F8
Flora Cl EX8 . . . . **196** D1
Flora Cotts PL1 . . . . . **262** B2
Flora Ct PL1 . . . . **262** B3
Flora St PL1 . . . . **262** B2
Florence Cotts TQ7 . . **145** D1
Florence Pl
  Newton Abbot TQ12 . . **207** D1
  Plymouth PL4 . . . . **263** C3
Florence St PL5 . . . . . **243** D1
Florence Way EX1 . . . **178** D6
Florida Dr EX4 . . . . . . **173** D2
Florida Gdns PL3 . . . . **249** C6
Florida Rd TQ1 . . . . . **220** C6
Flower La EX5 . . . . . . **184** C3
Flowerpot La EX4 . . . **177** A5
Flowers Mdw 🔳
  TQ12 . . . . **122** F1
Flower St EX5 . . . . . . **184** C3
Flow La TQ14 . . . . . . **208** F7
Floyd Cl PL2 . . . . **247** F7
Floyers-Hay Ct EX2 . **261** A1
Floyte La EX6 . . . . **98** B5
Fluder Cres TQ12 . . . **213** B3
Fluder Hill TQ12 . . . . **213** B3
Fluder La TQ12 . . . . . **213** F5
Fluder Rise TQ12 . . . **213** B3
FLUXTON **100** C3
Foldhay Cross EX17 . . **78** A6
Foldhay Rd EX17 . . . . **78** A6
Foliot Ave PL2 . . . . . . **248** A6
Foliot Rd PL2 . . . . **248** A6
Follafield Pk TQ5 . . . . **230** B2
Follaton Bglws TQ9 . . **223** A5
Follaton Gate TQ9 . . . **222** E4
Follaton Mount TQ9 . . **223** A5
Follaton Rise TQ9 . . . **222** E5
Follett Cl TA21 . . . . . **160** D8
Follett Rd
  Tiverton EX16 . . . . **64** D7
  Topsham EX3 . . . . **182** E5
Folley La EX4 . . . . **98** D4
Folly Cross EX20 . . . . **134** C1
Folly Ct TQ13 . . . . **180** C4
Folly Farm Cl EX33 . . **152** C6
FOLLY GATE **93** E8
Folly Gate Cross EX20 **93** F8
Folly Goyle Cross
  EX19 . . . . **43** B3
Folly Hill TQ7 . . . . . . **142** E3
Folly La
  Buckland St Mary
   TA20 . . . . **69** D8
  South Molton EX36 . . . . **30** D4
Folly The PL9 . . . . **256** B7
Football La TQ12 . . . . **207** E8
Footland La
  Daccombe TQ12 . . . . . **213** F5
  Ipplepen TQ12 . . . . . . **217** F5
Footland Rd TQ4 . . . . **226** A5
Forbes Cl TQ12 . . . . . **180** F2
Forbes Cl EX15 . . . . . **163** B2
Forcefield Rd EX15 . . **163** B2
Forces Cross TQ9 . . . **139** E3

Forches Ave EX32 . . . **155** C4
Forches Cnr EX17 . . . **165** C6
Forches Cross
  Burrington EX37 . . . . . . **43** F4
  Crediton EX17 . . . . . . **165** C6
  Langtree EX38 . . . . **40** F1
  Newton Abbot TQ12 . . . **206** D7
  Newton Abbot TQ12 . . . **206** E7
Forches Cross Com Prim
  Sch EX32 . . . . **155** C4
Forches Cross Rd
  TQ12 . . . . **206** C7
Forches Green Flats 🔳
  EX32 . . . . **155** B4
Forches Head EX5 . . . **175** E4
Forches Hill TQ12 . . . **209** B2
Forches Row EX1 . . . **179** A8
FORD
  Bideford **25** B3
  Chillington **149** A7
  Holbeton **136** D1
  Holcombe Rogus **50** F5
  Plymouth **248** A5
Ford TQ6 . . . . **233** E3
FORDA **93** B1
Fordbarn Cross TQ9 . **222** E2
Fordbrook La PL9 . . . **256** C4
Ford Cl PL21 . . . . **237** A5
Ford Cres EX22 . . . . . . **53** E8
Ford Cross
  Ash Mill EX36 . . . . **31** D1
  Chawleigh EX18 . . . . . . **59** E7
  Chulmleigh EX18 . . . . . **44** D2
  Ford TQ7 . . . . **149** A7
  Hittisleigh EX6 . . . . **96** D4
  Kentisbury EX31 . . . . . **10** D5
  Molland EX36 . . . . **31** F7
  Monkton EX14 . . . . **86** A5
  Oakford EX16 . . . . **48** D5
  Shirwell EX31 . . . . **17** C8
  South Zeal EX20 . . . . . . **95** A4
  Staverton TQ9 . . . . . . **216** C5
  Tedburn St Mary EX17 . . **97** D8
Ford Down La EX36 . **158** A3
Forde Abbey & Gardens★
  TA20 . . . . **88** F8
Forde Cl
  Abbotskerswell
   TQ12 . . . . **212** A7
  Newton Abbot TQ12 . . . **207** D3
Forde Cross EX17 . . . . **80** F8
Forde Gdns TQ12 . . . . **207** D1
Forde La EX38 . . . . **26** E2
Fordens La EX7 . . . . . **204** C3
Forde Pk TQ12 . . . . . **207** D2
FORDER
  Cawsand **252** F1
  Saltash **242** C1
Forder Cross
  Bishopsteignton
   TQ14 . . . . **208** D7
  Blackawton TQ9 . . . . . **145** C8
  Chagford EX20 . . . . . . **110** D8
  Ugborough PL21 . . . . . **137** E7
Forde Rd TQ12 . . . . . . **207** D3
FORDER GREEN **131** C2
Forder Hill PL10 . . . . **252** F1
Forder Hts PL6 . . . . . **245** B1
Forder La
  Bishopsteignton
   TQ14 . . . . **208** E8
  Bovey Tracey TQ13 . . . **122** E7
  Cawsand PL10 . . . . . . **252** F1
  Dartington TQ9 . . . . . . **222** A3
  South Brent TQ10 . . . . **135** B4
  Ugborough PL21 . . . . . **137** D7
Forder Valley Nature
  Reserve★ PL6 . . . . . **249** D8
Forder Valley Rd
  PL6 . . . . **249** D8
Ford Farm Ct EX6 . . . **194** D3
Ford Hill
  Bow TQ7 . . . . **78** F4
  Cheriton Bishop EX6,
   EX17 . . . . **97** C6
  Hartland EX39 . . . . **22** B3
  Kentisbury EX31 . . . . . **10** D5
  Plymouth PL2 . . . . **248** A5
  Thorverton EX5 . . . . . . **81** E6
Fordishaies La EX5,
  EX15 . . . . **82** F8
Ford La
  Cheriton Fitzpaine
   EX16 . . . . **63** B6
  Clifton EX31 . . . . **10** B5
  Hittisleigh EX6 . . . . **96** D4
  South Molton EX36 . . . . **30** A6
  West Hill EX11 . . . . . . **168** D3
  Whitestone EX4 . . . . . . **98** E4
Fordland Bottom Rd EX2,
  EX6 . . . . **176** B2
FORDLANDS **156** F5
Fordlands Cres EX39 **156** F4
Fordlands Rd TQ13 . . **111** F5
Ford Mill Cross EX16 . **34** D1
Fordmill Cross EX16 . **48** C8
Ford Moor Cross
  EX18 . . . . **59** E7
Ford Orch EX16 . . . . . **50** D1
FORD PARK **248** D4
Ford Park La PL4 . . . **248** E4
Ford Park Rd PL4 . . . **248** D4

Ford Pk
6 Chudleigh Knighton
TQ13................**123** C4
Plymouth PL4........**248** E4
Ford Plain EX5.......**81** E5
Ford Prim Sch
Plymouth PL2........**247** F5
Plymouth PL2........**248** A5
Ford Rd
Abbotskerswell TQ12 .**212** B7
Bampton EX16 ....**34** C1
Tiverton EX16........**64** D7
Totnes TQ9 ....**223** B6
Wembury PL9 ....**140** D8
Yealmpton PL8 ......**136** A2
Ford Rise EX39.......**25** F4
Fords Rd EX2........**261** A1
Ford St
Moretonhampstead
TQ13..............**111** F5
Tavistock PL19 ......**171** B5
Wellington TA21 .....**160** F4
FORD STREET......**52** D5
FORDTON..........**165** E3
Fordton Cross EX17..**165** E2
Fordton Ind Est EX17 **165** E3
Fordton Plain EX17...**165** E3
Fordton Terr EX17....**165** D3
Ford Valley TQ6......**233** E3
Ford Way Arrow EX1 .**175** B1
Fordworth Cotts TQ7 **149** D5
Foredown La TQ12....**212** E4
Foredown Rd TQ12....**211** E2
Foreland Ho EX34....**150** A4
Foreland View EX34...**150** A4
Fore St Hill 11 EX18...**44** E1
Fore St
Aveton Gifford TQ7 ...**143** C6
9 Bampton EX16.......**34** B1
Beer EX12...........**191** D5
Bere Alston PL20 ....**125** E1
Bere Ferrers PL20 ...**239** F3
Bishopsteignton TQ14.**208** F8
Bovey Tracey TQ13 ...**180** D7
Bradninch EX5 ....**82** F6
Bridestowe EX20 .....**107** F8
Brixham TQ5 ....**230** C5
Buckfastleigh TQ11...**236** C5
Budleigh Salterton
EX9...............**199** G2
Calstock PL18........**125** D3
Cargreen PL12 ......**239** A2
Chudleigh TQ13......**123** E6
Cornwood PL21 ......**133** C2
Cullompton EX15 ....**163** C3
Culmstock EX15 .....**66** E8
Dartmouth TQ6......**234** A3
Dolton EX19 ....**57** F7
Dulverton TA22......**33** D6
Exbourne EX20 ......**76** C5
Exeter EX4 ....**261** A2
Exmouth EX8........**201** A6
Great Torrington EX38 .**159** D5
Gunnislake PL18 .....**125** D6
Gunnislake, Albaston
PL18..............**125** C5
Harberton TQ9 ......**222** D2
Hartland EX39 ....**22** E3
7 Hemyock EX15.......**67** B8
Holbeton PL8 ....**136** D1
Holbeton PL8 ....**142** A8
Holcombe Rogus TA21 .**50** F5
Holsworthy EX22......**164** C4
Ide EX2.............**176** E2
Ideford TQ13 ....**124** B4
Ilfracombe EX34......**150** C6
Ipplepen TQ12 ......**211** D2
Ivybridge PL21.......**237** D5
Kentisbeare EX15 ....**66** A3
Kenton EX6..........**194** D3
Kingsand PL10 ......**253** A2
Kingsbridge TQ7 .....**258** C6
Kingskerswell TQ12 ..**212** F4
Kingskerswell TQ12 ..**213** A4
Kingsteignton TQ12 ..**207** E7
Langtree EX38 ......**40** E2
Lifton PL16 ....**105** E4
Loddiswell TQ7 ......**143** E7
Luton TQ13 ....**124** C3
Millbrook PL10 ......**252** E5
Milton Abbot PL19 ...**116** A6
Morchard Bishop EX17 .**61** A2
Moretonhampstead
TQ13..............**111** F5
Northam EX39 ....**156** F6
North Molton EX36....**30** D8
North Tawton EX20 ...**77** B4
Okehampton EX20 ...**170** B5
Otterton EX9.........**198** E7
Plymouth, Devonport
PL1...............**247** F2
Plymouth, Plympton
PL7...............**250** D4
Plymouth, Tamerton Foliot
PL5...............**244** B6
Salcombe TQ8........**259** E4
Saltash PL12........**242** F2
Seaton EX12.........**192** B5
Shaldon TQ14 ....**210** A3
Shebbear EX22.......**55** D1
Sidbury EX10 ....**101** B2
Sidmouth EX10 ......**188** B3
Silverton EX5 ....**82** B5

Fore St continued
13 South Brent TQ10...**134** F3
South Tawton EX20 ...**95** B5
Tatworth TA20.......**88** D8
19 Teignmouth TQ14...**210** B5
8 Teignmouth TQ14...**210** C4
Tiverton EX16........**161** D4
Topsham EX3 ....**182** F5
Torpoint PL11 ....**247** B3
4 Torquay TQ2.......**220** B8
Torquay, Barton TQ2 .**214** A2
Uffculme EX15 ....**66** A7
Ugborough PL21.....**137** D6
Wellington TA21 .....**160** D6
Winkleigh EX19......**58** F3
Witheridge EX16.....**46** E1
Yealmpton PL8 ......**257** F4
Forest Ave PL2......**248** C7
Foresters Rd
Holsworthy EX22 .....**164** C5
Plymouth PL6 ....**255** D7
Forester's Terr TQ14 **210** B4
Forest Hill
Bideford EX39........**25** F4
Budleigh Salterton EX9 **198** B1
Forest Hos EX11 .....**73** B4
Forest Rd
Stover TQ13 ....**123** B1
Torquay TQ1.........**220** A7
Fore Street Ctr EX4 ..**261** A2
Fore Street Hill EX9 ..**199** H2
Fore Street Mews 15
EX4...............**261** A2
Forest Ridge Rd TQ3 .**218** F1
Forestry Hos PL20...**120** B4
Forest View PL6 .....**245** D7
Foretown EX15 ....**83** D3
Forge Cl EX9 ....**197** F2
Forge End EX19......**58** F2
Forge La
Butterleigh EX15 .....**64** D3
Saltash PL12........**242** C4
Forge Pl
Bovey Tracey TQ13 ...**180** C7
Uffculme EX15 ....**162** F7
Forge Rd EX15.......**162** F7
Forges Hill EX15 ....**64** F3
Forget Me Not La
PL6...............**245** F5
Forge Way EX15 .....**163** C3
Forgeway Cl TQ2.....**219** D4
Fork Cross TQ9 ......**222** A5
Forresters Bsns Pk
PL6...............**245** F5
Forresters Dr PL6....**245** D7
Forrest Units EX12 ...**177** D1
Forster Rd TQ8 ......**259** D5
Forsythia Dr PL12....**242** C3
Fort Austin Ave PL6 .**245** C1
FORTESCUE........**188** D7
Fortescue Bglws EX34. .**8** C6
Fortescue Cl EX33....**152** E5
FORTESCUE CROSS....**44** C4
Fortescue Cross EX5 ..**81** E2
Fortescue Pl PL3.....**249** A6
Fortescue Rd
Barnstaple EX32.....**155** B2
Exeter EX2 ....**177** B3
Ilfracombe EX34......**150** B6
Paignton TQ3 ....**219** C1
Salcombe TQ8.......**259** C4
Sidmouth EX10 ......**188** B3
Fortescue Terr PL19 ..**171** A6
Fortessque Ct PL19 ..**116** E3
Fortfield EX12 ....**192** B5
Fortfield Gdns EX10..**188** A3
Fortfield Terr EX10...**188** A3
Forth Gdns PL3 .....**249** D6
Fort Hill Dr EX32....**155** B5
Fortibus Rd EX3 .....**182** B7
Fortmead Cl EX32....**155** A5
Forton Rd EX8........**196** C1
Fort Picklecombe
PL10..............**253** F4
Fort Rd EX20.........**170** D6
Fort St EX32 ....**155** A5
Fort Terr
13 Barnstaple EX32 ...**155** A5
5 Bideford EX39......**157** B1
Plymouth PL6 ....**244** F3
Fort The PL10........**253** A1
Fortune Way TQ1 ....**220** B7
Forum La EX20.......**170** E2
Forward Gn EX5......**82** E7
Fosbrooke Ct 10 PL3 .**248** F6
Foseth Hill EX39 .....**156** C6
Foseth Terr EX39.....**156** C6
FOSS..............**253** A5
Fossa Ct EX20........**170** D6
Fosse Rd TQ7........**258** D6
Fosse Way EX13 .....**88** C7
Fosseway Cl EX13....**167** D5
Fosse Way Ct 2
EX12..............**192** B4
Foss Slip TQ6........**233** F3
Foss St TQ6.........**233** F3
Fosterlea EX15 ......**163** B3
Fosters Mdw PL18....**125** A6
Foulston Ave PL5.....**247** B8
Foundary Mews
PL19..............**171** D6
Foundry Ct 1 TQ13 .**123** E6
Foundry La PL8.......**140** F6
Foundry Mews PL19 ..**171** D6
Fountain Ct TQ13....**180** D7
Fountain Fields EX37 ..**43** B7
Fountain Hill EX9....**203** F8

Fountain Ho TQ1.....**220** C4
Fountains Cres PL2 ..**248** C8
Fouracre Cl EX4......**174** A1
Four Acres EX39.....**156** D2
Four Acres Cl EX14...**86** B2
Fouracre Way EX12...**207** F8
Four Cross
Axminster EX13 ......**167** B7
Ilsington TQ12 ......**122** C2
Kingston TQ7 ....**142** C7
Wilmington EX14 ....**86** C4
Four Cross Elms
EX24..............**103** A4
Fourcross Hill EX13 ..**167** B7
Four Cross Lanes
TQ9...............**228** A8
Four Cross Way EX12 ..**11** C1
Four Crossways EX18 ..**44** E1
Four Cross Ways
Cheriton Bishop EX6 ...**97** A4
North Tawton EX20 ...**77** D4
Willand EX15 ....**162** D5
Winkleigh EX19......**58** D2
Four Elms
Holcombe Rogus TA21 .**51** A6
Sidmouth EX10 ......**187** C8
Four Elms Hill EX10 ..**187** B8
Four Firs EX5........**185** A1
Four Lanes EX34.....**84** B8
Fourlanesend Com Prim
Sch PL10...........**252** F3
Four Mills La EX17 ...**165** D4
Four Oak EX32.......**17** B2
Four Oak Cross EX32..**17** B2
Four Oaks Cl 1 EX32..**17** B2
Four Oaks Rd EX6....**97** F4
Four Seasons Village
EX19..............**58** E3
Fourth Ave TQ14.....**210** A6
Fourview Cl TQ3 .....**219** C1
Four Ways Cotts EX18 .**59** E4
Four Ways Dr 3 EX18 ..**44** E1
Four White Gates Cross
EX37..............**29** B4
Fowelscombe Gate
PL21..............**137** F6
Fowey Ave TQ2......**219** B8
Fowey Cl EX1........**177** F7
Fowey Gdns PL3.....**249** D6
Fowey Rd EX31 ......**15** E5
Fowler Cl EX6........**102** A4
Fowley Cross EX20....**93** D5
Fowlmere Cl PL5.....**243** E6
Foxbeare Rd EX34....**150** E5
Fox Cl
Okehampton EX20 ....**170** D6
Rockwell Green TA21 ..**160** A6
Foxdown Hill
Wellington TA21 .....**52** B6
Wellington TA21 .....**160** C4
Foxdown Ho TA21....**160** C4
Foxdown Terr TA21...**160** D4
Foxes' Cross EX38....**26** E1
Foxes Lair EX20......**170** A6
Fox Field Cl PL3......**249** C5
Foxglove Chase
EX15..............**162** D5
Foxglove Cl
Barnstaple EX32.....**155** E4
Dunkeswell EX14 ....**67** C1
Launceston PL15 .....**105** A2
Newton Abbot TQ12 ..**206** C5
9 Tiverton EX16......**161** F6
Fox Glove End EX11...**169** D2
Foxglove La 2 PL19 ..**171** A6
Foxglove Rd EX12....**192** B7
Foxglove Rise EX4 ...**176** D8
Foxglove Way
Paignton TQ3 ....**225** E2
Saltash PL12........**242** B3
FOXHAYES.........**176** F7
Foxhayes Rd EX4.....**176** F6
Fox Hill EX39 ....**156** F6
Foxhill La TQ12 .....**211** A2
Foxhole Hill EX6 .....**113** B4
Foxhole La EX39 .....**156** F6
Foxhole Rd
Paignton TQ3 ....**225** F7
Torquay TQ2 ....**219** D5
Foxholes Hill EX8 ....**202** D4
Foxhollows TQ12 ....**208** A2
Fox & Hounds Cross
EX20..............**108** A5
Foxlands Wlk TQ1....**220** C8
Foxleigh Cres TQ12 ..**206** F3
Fox Rd EX4 ....**174** B2
Fox's Cnr EX10.......**187** F2
Fox's Cross EX17.....**63** B1
Foxtor Cl PL5 ....**244** B3
Fox Tor Cl TQ4.......**229** B7
Foxtor Rd EX4 ....**176** E8
Foxwell La TQ12 .....**207** A4
Foxwood Gdns
Plymouth, Plymstock
PL9...............**255** F5
Plymouth, Southway
PL6...............**244** E5
Foxworthy Rd TQ13 ..**111** F1
Foyle Cl PL7.........**251** B5
Frances Homes EX1 ..**261** C3
Francis Cl EX4 ....**176** F4
Francis Court Cotts
EX5...............**82** D2
Francis Cres 4 EX16 ..**64** D7
Francis Ct
3 Crediton EX17......**165** C5
Exeter EX2 ....**177** C5

Francis Dr EX39......**156** C6
Francis St PL1.......**262** A3
Francis Way EX24....**103** B3
Franeth Cl TQ12 .....**207** D8
Frankford La
Pathfinder Village EX6 .**82** A6
Tedburn St Mary EX6 ..**97** F5
Frankfort Gate 9
PL1...............**262** B3
Franklea Cl EX11.....**169** D3
Franklin St EX1......**261** B2
Franklyn Ave EX33 ...**152** E6
Franklyn Cl EX2......**176** F3
Franklyn Dr EX2......**176** F3
Franklyn Hospl EX2 ..**176** F3
Franklyns' PL6.......**245** A4
Franklyns Cl PL6.....**245** A4
Frankmarsh Pk EX32 **155** B6
Frankmarsh Rd EX32 **155** B6
Frankmills Hill TQ13 .**113** A1
Frank Webber Rd
TA21..............**160** A5
Fraser Dr TQ14......**210** A6
Fraser Pl PL5........**244** C7
Fraser Rd
Exmouth EX8........**196** D2
Plymouth PL5 ....**244** C7
Fraser Sq PL5........**244** C7
Frederick Street E
PL1...............**262** B3
Frederick Street W 6
PL1...............**262** B3
Frederick Terr 6
EX7...............**204** D6
Fredington Gr PL2....**248** B6
Free Cotts EX4.......**261** A3
Freedom Sq PL4......**263** B4
Freelands Cl EX8.....**202** D8
Freemans Wharf PL1 **254** A8
Freestone Rd TQ12...**207** D8
Fremantle Gdns 4
PL2...............**247** F4
Fremantle Pl PL2 ....**247** F4
FREMINGTON.......**153** E6
Fremington Com Prim
Sch EX31...........**153** D5
Fremington Nature
Reserve★ EX31......**153** E6
Fremington Quay
EX31..............**153** F7
Fremington Rd EX12 .**191** F7
French Cl EX5........**82** B6
French Furze Rd TQ9 **139** E2
French St 7 TQ14....**210** C4
Frenchstone Cross
EX36..............**30** B2
Frensham Ave PL6...**245** C7
Frensham Gdns PL6..**245** C7
Freshford Cl PL6.....**245** C1
Freshford Wlk PL6....**245** C1
Freshwater Dr TQ4...**229** B8
Frewin Gdns PL6.....**245** B6
Frewins EX9.........**197** F2
FRIARS' GREEN.....**261** A2
Friar's Hele Cross
EX20..............**57** B2
Friars Lodge EX2.....**261** B2
Friars Wlk PL19 .....**171** E2
Friars' Wlk EX2......**261** B2
Friary Pk PL4........**263** B3
Friary St PL4........**263** B3
Friendship Ct PL19...**117** E6
Friernhay Ct EX4.....**261** A2
Friernhay St EX4.....**261** A2
Frith Rd PL12 ....**242** D3
FRITTISCOMBE.....**145** B2
Fritz's Grave TQ11 ...**236** A7
Frobisher App PL5...**244** D2
Frobisher Cl TQ14....**210** A8
Frobisher Dr PL12....**242** D2
Frobisher Gn TQ2....**219** C6
Frobisher La TQ8 ....**259** C5
Frobisher Rd
Exmouth EX8........**196** C2
Newton Abbot TQ12 ..**207** F4
Frobisher Way
Paignton TQ4 ....**226** B2
Tavistock PL19 ......**171** B5
Torpoint PL11 ....**246** D3
Frogbury Cross EX17. .**59** F1
Froggy Mill Cross EX6 **97** C5
Frog La
Braunton EX33 ......**152** D7
Clyst St Mary EX5 ....**179** A3
Holcombe Rogus TA21 .**50** F5
South Molton EX36 ...**158** B5
FROGMORE.........**144** E1
Frogmore Ave PL6....**249** B7
Frogmore Cross EX5 ..**82** F3
Frogmore Ct PL6.....**249** B7
Frogmore Farm TQ9 .**139** F7
Frogmore Rd EX9 ....**198** C6
Frogmore Terr TQ7 ..**258** C4
Frogs La TA21 ....**52** F7
Frog St
Bampton EX16.......**34** B1
Exeter EX1, EX2 .....**261** A2
Woolacombe EX34 ...**7** F6
Frogstreet Hill EX33...**8** A2
Frogwell Cross TA4 ...**34** D6
Frogwell La TA22 ....**34** B6
Frome Cl PL7........**251** A4
Frontfield Cres PL6 ..**244** E5

FROST..............**61** A1
Frost Cross
Bovey Tracey TQ13 ...**123** B6
Morchard Bishop EX17..**61** B1
Frost's Cnr EX19 .....**42** D1
Froude Ave TQ2......**214** B3
Froude Rd TQ8 ......**259** B2
Fry's La 5 EX10......**101** B1
Fry St EX22 ....**164** C4
Fuge Cross TQ6......**145** E6
Fuidge Cross EX17....**96** A5
Fuidge La EX17 ......**96** A5
Fulda Cres EX17 .....**165** D4
Fulford Cl
Bideford EX39........**157** D1
Tedburn St Mary EX6 ..**97** F4
Fulford Dr EX15......**163** B2
Fulford Gdns EX20 ...**77** C4
Fulford Rd
Cheriton Bishop EX6 ...**97** D1
Dunsford EX6........**112** F8
Exeter EX1 ....**177** F7
Fulford Way EX5.....**184** C2
Fullaford Cross
TQ11..............**236** B4
Fullaford Hill EX31....**18** E8
Fullaford Pk TQ11....**236** A4
Fullaford Pool Cross
TQ11..............**236** A4
Fullers Ct 12 EX2.....**261** A2
Fullers Pl TQ12 .....**123** E5
Fullerton Rd PL2.....**248** A5
Fullingcott Cross
EX39..............**153** A2
Fulton Cl TQ12 ......**211** D2
Fulton Ho 2 EX12....**192** A5
Furland Cl PL9.......**255** C5
Furleigh Cross EX13...**87** D6
FURLEY............**87** D7
Furley Cross EX13....**87** D6
Furlong Cl TQ11 .....**236** B7
Furlong Cotts EX16 ...**51** A4
Furneaux Ave PL2....**248** B5
Furneaux Rd PL2.....**248** B6
Furness Cl TQ4 ......**226** A2
Furrough Cross TQ1 .**220** C8
Furrough Ct TQ1 ....**220** C8
Fursdon Cl PL9 ......**256** C6
Fursdon Cross
East Allington TQ7....**144** E4
Hittisleigh EX6 ......**96** C5
Fursdon House★
EX5...............**81** E7
Fursdon La EX6, EX17 .**96** B5
Furse Pk PL5 ....**247** C2
Fursham Cross EX6...**96** B4
Furzeacre Cl PL7.....**251** A7
Furzebeam Row
EX38..............**159** B5
Furzebeam Terr 14
EX39..............**157** B1
Furzebrake Cl TQ2...**213** C2
Furzebrook EX11.....**169** E4
Furze Cap 3 TQ12 ...**123** E1
Furze Cross
Bridgerule EX22......**71** A5
Chittlehampton EX37 ..**29** A5
Cornworthy TQ9......**227** A2
Kingsbridge TQ7 .....**144** D3
Furze Ct EX4.........**176** E3
Furzedown Cross
TQ12..............**213** A5
Furzedown Rd
TQ12..............**213** A5
Furze Gdns
Shop EX23 ....**37** A1
Totnes TQ9 ....**223** F5
Furzegood TQ3......**218** D3
Furzeham Ct TQ5....**230** B5
Furzeham Pk TQ5....**230** B5
Furzeham Prim Sch
TQ5...............**230** C5
Furzehatt Ave PL9....**256** A6
Furzehatt Park Rd
PL9...............**256** A6
Furzehatt Rd PL9.....**255** F6
Furzehatt Rise PL9...**256** A6
Furzehatt Way PL9...**256** A6
Furzehill Cl EX10.....**101** B2
Furzehill Cross TQ9 ..**227** B3
Furzehill Rd
Heybrook Bay PL9.....**140** A7
Plymouth PL4 ....**248** F4
Torquay TQ1 ....**220** A6
Furze Hill Rd EX34 ...**150** B4
Furze La 2 TQ5......**230** D5
Furzeland Hill EX17...**79** C6
Furzeleigh Cross
TQ13..............**122** F6
Furzeleigh La
TQ13..............**180** D8
Furzendown Rd
TQ7...............**147** F6
Furzepark Cross
Bittaford PL21.......**137** C7
Dolton EX19 ....**58** A5
Furzepark La
Hartland EX39 ......**22** E3
Kentisbury EX31......**10** E6
Zeal Monachorum EX17 .**78** C6
Furze Park Rd EX31 ..**18** A8
Furze Pk EX34.......**2** F3
Furze Pk La EX31.....**9** B2
Furze Rd
Totnes TQ9 ....**223** F5
Woodbury EX5 ....**184** C3
FYLDON............**19** D4
Fyldon Hill EX36 .....**19** D5

Gabber La PL9.......**140** B8
Gable Pk TQ1........**220** C6
Gables Lea EX15 ....**162** C4
Gables Rd EX15 .....**162** C4
Gables The
Combe Martin EX34 ...**2** F4
Exmouth EX8.........**202** D6
Rousdon DT7 ....**193** F7
Teignmouth TQ14.....**210** A5
Wellington TA21 .....**160** C6
Willand EX15 ....**162** C4
Gabriel Ct
11 Exeter EX2.........**261** A2
Stoke Gabriel TQ9 ...**227** F7
Gabriels Wharf EX2 ..**177** C3
Gabwell Hill TQ1,
TQ12..............**214** C7
Gabwell La TQ12.....**214** C7
Gaddacombe Cross
EX20..............**91** D1
Gainsborough Cl
TQ1...............**220** B4
Gainsborough Dr
EX39..............**156** B6
Gainsborough Ho
Exeter EX1 ....**177** E6
Tavistock PL19 ......**171** B6
Gains Cross EX22.....**53** C3
Gala Cross PL8.......**257** F1
Galahad Cl EX4.......**174** A1
Galbraith Rd EX20....**170** F6
Gale Rd TQ13 ....**131** B5
Gales Crest 3 TQ13 .**123** C4
Gales Hill 18 TQ13 ...**209** F6
Gale Wy EX16.......**161** B5
Galileo Cl PL7 ....**250** E6
Gallacher Way PL12..**242** B3
Galleon Way EX39...**156** E7
Gallery Cl 4 EX14....**166** B6
Galloping La EX39....**39** B8
Gallops The PL12 ....**242** D4
Galloway Dr TQ4.....**124** E1
Gallows Cross TQ12 .**207** C8
Gallows Gate TQ3....**218** F6
Gallows Park Cross
TQ13..............**131** B5
GALMPTON
Malborough..........**147** C7
Paignton.............**229** B5
Galmpton CE Prim Sch
TQ5...............**229** B5
Galmpton Cross TQ7 **147** D7
Galmpton Ct TQ5 ....**229** B5
Galmpton Farm Cl
TQ5...............**229** B5
Galmpton Glade TQ5 **229** B5
Galmpton Rise EX4 ..**173** E1
**GALMPTON
WARBOROUGH**.....**229** B5
Galpin St PL21.......**137** C2
Galsworthy Cl PL5 ...**244** C2
Galsworthy Sq EX4 ..**178** C8
Galva Rd
Hemerdon PL7.......**251** C8
Sparkwell PL7.......**132** E1
Gamberlake EX13.....**167** C4
Gamberlake Cross
EX13..............**167** C4
Gamblyn Cross TA4 ...**34** F5
Gamlin Cl TA21......**160** D8
GAMMATON........**26** C4
GAMMATON MOOR..**26** D3
Gammaton Moor Cross
EX39..............**26** D3
Gammaton Rd EX39....**26** B4
Gammons Hill EX13 ..**87** D1
Gammon Walk 23
EX31..............**154** F5
Ganders Pk TQ2 .....**213** A2
Gandy St EX4 ....**261** A3
Ganges Rd PL2.......**248** A5
Ganna Park Rd PL3...**248** D6
Gappah Cross TQ12 ..**123** E4
Gappah La TQ13 .....**123** E4
Gara Cl PL9..........**256** D6
Gara Lodge TQ12 ....**212** F4
Gard Cl TQ2 ....**214** A3
Garden Cl
Braunton EX33 ......**152** B6
Exeter EX2 ....**178** C4
Holbeton PL8 ....**142** A8
Plymouth PL7 ....**251** D5
Rattery TQ10........**135** D4
Garden Cotts TQ7....**258** C5
Garden Ct EX9 ......**198** A1
Gardeners La PL8.....**257** E4
Garden Gn EX32 ....**155** C2
Garden House The★
PL20..............**126** D3
Gardenia Dr
Bolham EX16........**49** C3
Tiverton EX16........**161** E7
Garden La PL19 .....**171** B5
Garden Mill Ind Est
TQ7...............**258** D4
Garden Park Cl PL9 ..**256** C7
Garden Pk TQ10 .....**135** D4
Garden Rd TQ1 ......**220** B6
Garden Spot La TQ13 **123** F6
Garden St PL2 ....**247** C4
Gardens The
6 Chudleigh TQ13....**123** E6
Dulverton TA22......**33** D7
Holemoor EX22......**73** B7

Gardens The *continued*
Rousdon DT7 . . . . .193 E5
1 Wellington TA21 . .160 D5
Garden Terr
Cullompton EX15 . . . .163 C4
Wellington EX21 . . . . .160 B7
Garden Village PL9 . .255 F8
Gardiner Cl EX5 . . . . . . .82 A1
Gards La PL5 . . . . .243 E2
Gareth Cres EX4 . . . . .173 F2
Garfield Pl 12 TQ9 . . .223 C5
Garfield Rd TQ4 . . . . . .226 C6
Garfield Terr
PL3 . . . . .248 A3
Garland Cl EX4 . . . . . . .176 E8
Garland Cross EX37 . . .45 B5
GARLANDHAYES 52 F2
Garlandhayes La EX15 .52 E2
Garland Meadow
EX1 . . . . .179 B8
Garlic Rea TQ5 . . . . . . .230 D5
Garliford La EX36 . . . . . .30 F4
Garners Cl TQ12 . . . . . .206 D1
Garners La TQ12 . . . . . .206 D1
Garratt Cl EX8 . . . . . . .196 C3
Garratt Rd EX5 . . . . . . .179 B3
Garrett Cl EX12 . . . . . .192 B6
Garrett St PL11 . . . . . . .253 A1
Garrick Cl PL5 . . . . .244 C2
Garrison Cl PL1 . . . . . . .247 E1
Garrow Cl 1 TQ5 . . . . .230 C3
Garston Ave TQ12 . . . . .207 B4
Garston Cl PL9 . . . . .256 A8
Garth Rd TQ2 . . . . .214 A2
Gascon Cl TQ12 . . . . . .211 F8
Gascoyne Ct PL4 . . . . . .263 A3
Gascoyne Pl PL4 . . . . . .263 A3
Gashay La EX13 . . . . .88 H3
Gashouse La PL4 . . . . . .263 B2
Gasking St PL4 . . . . . . .263 A2
Gas La EX38 . . . . .159 D5
Gatcombe Ash EX12 . .102 E2
Gatcombe La
Beer EX12 . . . . .191 C8
Seaton EX12 . . . . .102 F6
Gatcombe Mws 2
EX31 . . . . .154 C1
Gate Cl EX13 . . . . .88 E3
Gate Cross EX24 . . . . . .102 F6
Gatedown La
Salcombe Regis
EX10 . . . . .101 E1
Sidmouth EX10 . . . . . . .189 D8
Gate Field Rd EX39 . . .156 C2
Gatehouse ACE Academy
EX7 . . . . .204 E8
Gatehouse Cl
Cullompton EX15 . . . .163 B3
Dawlish EX7 . . . . .204 E7
Gatehouse Hill EX7 . .204 E7
Gatehouse La 2
PL7 . . . . .250 D5
Gatehouse Rise EX7 . .204 E7
Gate Reach EX2 . . . . . .177 E2
Gater La EX1 . . . . .261 B2
Gatesfield DT7 . . . . . . .260 C2
Gate Tree Cl TQ12 . . . .207 F7
GATHERLEY 105 D1
Gattery La TQ5 . . . . . . .229 F1
Gavel The EX36 . . . . . . .158 D4
Gaverick Ct TQ12 . . . . .123 B1
Gawton Way PL19 . . . .171 E7
Gay Cl TA21 . . . . .160 E6
Gaydon St EX32 . . . . . .155 A5
Gays Cross EX17 . . . . . .79 C7
Gays La EX17 . . . . .79 C7
Gay St TA21 . . . . .160 E6
Gaze Hill TQ12 . . . . . . .206 F5
Gdn Ct PL12 . . . . .242 D1
Gdynia Way
Plymouth PL3 . . . . .249 B2
Plymouth PL4 . . . . .263 C2
Geasons La PL7 . . . . . . .250 E5
Gees La PL21 . . . . .137 C2
Gemini Rd PL9 . . . . . . .256 E7
Generals Cl EX6 . . . . . .201 A7
Generals La EX6 . . . . . .201 B7
Genesis La 3 EX34 . . . . .3 A3
Geneva Cl EX2 . . . . .177 E4
Geneva Ct
Bideford EX39 . . . . .156 F1
Exeter EX2 . . . . .177 E4
Geneva Pl EX39 . . . . . . .156 F1
Gennys Cl PL18 . . . . . . .125 B6
Gentian Cl TQ12 . . . . . .218 D2
George Ave PL7 . . . . . . .250 F6
George Cross PL7 . . . . .250 F5
George Downing Ho
PL6 . . . . .245 A1
GEORGEHAM 8 B2
**Georgeham CE Prim(VC)
Sch** EX33 . . . . .8 A2
Georgeham Cross
EX33 . . . . .152 D7
Georgeham Rd
Croyde EX33 . . . . .7 F2
Woolacombe EX34 . . . . . .8 B5
George Hill EX17 . . . . .165 B6
Georgehill Cross
EX17 . . . . .165 A6
George La
Kilmington EX13 . . . . . .87 C1
Plymouth PL7 . . . . .250 F5
GEORGE NYMPTON 30 A1
George Nympton Cross
George Nympton EX36 . .30 A2
George Nympton EX37 . .29 F1

George Nympton Rd
EX36 . . . . .158 C2
George Pl PL1 . . . . .262 A2
George Rd TQ3 . . . . . . .219 B1
Georges Cl EX1 . . . . . . .178 B6
George Shopping Mews
EX36 . . . . .158 C4
George Sq PL1 . . . . . . .247 F1
George's Sq DT7 . . . . . .260 E3
George St
Axminster EX13 . . . . . .167 D6
12 Barnstaple EX32 . . .154 F6
Exeter EX1 . . . . .261 A2
1 Exmouth EX8 . . . . . .202 A7
Honiton EX14 . . . . .166 C6
Newton Abbot TQ12 . . .207 B3
Okehampton EX20 . . . .170 B5
Plymouth PL1 . . . . .247 F1
11 Teignmouth TQ14 . .210 C4
Wellington TA21 . . . . . .160 D6
George Teign Rd
EX6 . . . . .113 D2
Georgia Cres PL3 . . . . .249 C6
Georgian Ct TQ1 . . . . . .220 E6
Georgian Ho The
EX6 . . . . .201 B8
Gerald Dinnis Units
EX2 . . . . .177 D1
Geraldine Terr PL12 . .242 C1
Gerbera Ho EX4 . . . . . .176 E8
Gerbera Way EX15 . . . .163 D3
Gerbestone La TA21 . . .52 E6
GERMANSWEEK 91 D5
Gerrydown Rd EX19 . . .58 D3
Gerston Cross TQ9 . . . .223 A3
Gerston La TQ7 . . . . . . .258 C1
Gerston Pl 8 TQ3 . . . . .226 B6
Gerston Rd TQ4 . . . . . .226 B6
Gervase Ave EX2 . . . . . .261 A1
Gerway Cl EX11 . . . . . . .169 D2
Gerway La EX11 . . . . . . .169 E2
Gestridge Cross
TQ12 . . . . .207 D7
Gestridge Rd TQ12 . . .207 D7
Giant's Grave TQ9 . . . . .69 D7
Giant's Grave Rd TA20 .69 D7
Gibb Hill PL21 . . . . .133 B2
Gibbon La PL4 . . . . .263 A3
Gibbon St PL4 . . . . .263 A3
Gibbs Plantation
EX31 . . . . .153 C5
Giblands Cross EX20 . .170 D5
Giblands Pk EX20 . . . . .170 D5
Gibraltar Rd EX8 . . . . .195 E6
Gibson Cl EX8 . . . . .196 E1
Gibson Ct TQ4 . . . . .226 A1
Gibson Dr TQ4 . . . . .226 A1
Gibson Gdns TQ4 . . . . .226 A1
Gibson Rd TQ4 . . . . . . .226 A1
Gidcott Cross EX22 . . . .55 A4
GIDLEIGH 110 D7
Gidley Arms Cross
EX36 . . . . .46 A5
Gidley Cross EX36 . . . . .46 A5
Gidleys Mdw TQ9 . . . . .222 F8
Gidley's Meadow Ind Est
EX6 . . . . .113 B4
Gidley's Turn EX6 . . . . .113 C4
Gifford Cl EX39 . . . . .22 E3
Gifford Pl PL3 . . . . .248 D4
Gifford Terrace Rd
PL3 . . . . .248 E5
Gilbert Ave
Exeter EX2 . . . . .178 C4
Teignmouth TQ14 . . . . .210 A7
Gilbert Cl TQ2 . . . . .219 D6
Gilbert Ct PL7 . . . . .251 B6
Gilbert Gr 6 EX34 . . . .150 C6
Gilbert La PL2 . . . . .248 C5
Gilbert Rd TQ12 . . . . . .207 E3
Gilbert Way TQ4 . . . . . .226 A3
Gilbrook Cl EX5 . . . . . . .184 B2
Gilchrist Way EX10 . . .188 C5
Gillard Rd
Brixham TQ5 . . . . .230 F4
Brixham TQ5 . . . . .231 A5
Gillards Cl TA21 . . . . . .160 B4
Gillards Mead TA3 . . . . .68 D7
Gillard Way PL21 . . . . .136 D6
Gilley Cl TQ13 . . . . .180 F7
Gill Pk PL3 . . . . .249 B5
Gillscott Cross EX17 . . .60 B1
Gill's Cross TQ9 . . . . . .222 D2
Gill's Nursery 13 TQ9 .223 C5
Gilly's Wlk PL18 . . . . . .125 C5
Gilpin Cl EX7 . . . . .204 F8
GILSCOTT 24 E2
Gilston Rd PL12 . . . . . .242 D4
Gilwell Ave PL9 . . . . . . .256 B7
Gilwell Pl PL4 . . . . .263 A3
Gilwell St PL4 . . . . .263 A3
Gimbletts Ct 14 EX22 .164 C4
Gingaford Cross
TQ10 . . . . .135 A5
Gipsies Cnr EX17 . . . . . .79 F6
Gipsies La EX17 . . . . . . .79 F6
Gipsy Cnr
Bovey Tracey TQ13 . . . .122 D5
Budlake EX5 . . . . .82 E1
Whiddon EX5 . . . . .9 C1
Gipsy Cross EX14 . . . . . .67 A5
Gipsy Dro TA20 . . . . .69 F4
Gipsy Hill La EX1 . . . . .178 F8
Gipsy Hill Mews EX1 . .178 F7
Gipsy La
Bideford EX39 . . . . .25 B4
Bittadon EX31 . . . . .9 F3
Buckfastleigh TQ11 . . . .236 A4

Gipsy La *continued*
Exeter EX1 . . . . .178 F8
Exmouth EX8 . . . . .200 B8
Ilfracombe EX34 . . . . . .150 D5
Ivybridge PL21 . . . . . . .136 D7
Muddiford EX31 . . . . .9 F2
Sampford Arundel TA21 .51 D5
Girt La EX34 . . . . .3 B4
Gissage Hill EX17 . . . . .78 B/
Gissage View 7
EX14 . . . . .166 B6
Gissons EX6 . . . . .182 B4
Gissons La EX6 . . . . . . .114 D4
GITTISHAM 85 B1
Gittisham Cl EX1 . . . . .178 D6
Gittisham Farm Cross
EX14 . . . . .85 A1
Gittshayne Cross
EX24 . . . . .102 F5
Glade Cl PL6 . . . . .245 A4
Glades The EX16 . . . . . .161 E3
Glade The PL20 . . . . . . .126 E2
Glade Wlk EX5 . . . . .179 E2
Gladstone Pl 11
TQ12 . . . . .207 C3
Gladstone Rd EX1 . . . . .177 E6
Gladstone Terr
8 Teignmouth TQ14 . .210 C5
Wellington TA21 . . . . . .160 E6
Glanville Ave 1
PL19 . . . . .171 B5
Glanville Rd
Offwell EX14 . . . . .102 A8
Tavistock PL19 . . . . . . .171 B6
Glanvilles Mill PL21 . .237 D5
Glanvilles Rd PL21 . . . .237 D5
Glanville St PL1, PL4 . .262 C3
Glanville Terr PL21 . . .242 F3
Glanvill's Cl EX6 . . . . . . .98 C4
Glanvill Way EX14 . . . .166 B4
Glascott Cl EX20 . . . . . .75 B6
Glasshouse La EX2 . . . .182 B7
Glastonbury Cl
Exeter EX4 . . . . .174 A2
3 Plymouth PL2 . . . . .248 A7
Glave Saunders Ave
EX2 . . . . .178 C4
Glazebrook Ct TQ10 . .134 E2
Glazegate Cross TQ3 .224 F7
Glazegate La TQ3, TQ4,
TQ9 . . . . .224 E6
Glazon Way EX39 . . . . .157 A8
Gleaner Cl TQ12 . . . . . .244 D1
Glebe Ave PL12 . . . . . . .242 F3
Glebe Cl
Exmouth EX8 . . . . .202 F7
Hatherleigh EX20 . . . . . .75 C7
Lympstone EX8 . . . . . . .195 E6
Newton Abbot TQ12 . . .206 F3
Otterton EX9 . . . . .198 E7
Upton Pyne EX5 . . . . . .172 F7
Glebe Cotts EX5 . . . . . . .99 B1
Glebe Cl EX39 . . . . .156 F6
Glebefield EX33 . . . . .8 A2
Glebe Field TQ7 . . . . . .143 A2
Glebefields EX39 . . . . . .156 F6
Glebe Hos EX39 . . . . . . .156 A1
Glebe Houses
Abbotsham EX39 . . . . . .25 C5
Abbotsham EX39 . . . . . .156 A1
Glebeland
Churchstow TQ7 . . . . . .143 E4
Down St Mary EX17 . . . .78 E7
Glebe Land TQ7 . . . . . .143 C6
Glebeland Ct TQ2 . . . . .219 A8
Glebelands
Buckfastleigh TQ11 . . . .236 A6
Cheriton Bishop EX6 . . . .97 B4
12 Chudleigh TQ13 . . .123 F6
Exminster EX6 . . . . .182 A4
Holsworthy EX22 . . . . . .164 B4
Holsworthy TA20 . . . . . . .71 F6
Lympstone EX8 . . . . . . .195 E6
Newton Poppleford
EX10 . . . . .186 F8
Puddington EX16 . . . . . .62 B5
Sidmouth EX10 . . . . . . .188 A4
Uplyme DT7 . . . . .260 B5
Wrafton EX33 . . . . .152 E4
Glebelands Rd EX16 . . . .64 D7
Glebelands The TQ13 .111 F4
Glebeland Villas EX36 . .31 A2
Glebeland Way TQ2 . . .219 B8
Glebe Mdw EX22 . . . . . .164 B4
Glebe The
Bratton Fleming EX31 . . .18 B8
Ipplepen TQ12 . . . . . . .211 C2
Poughill EX17 . . . . .62 D3
Thorverton EX5 . . . . .81 E4
Glenarm Terr 6 TQ9 .223 C6
Glenavon Rd PL3 . . . . .248 E5
Glenburn Cl PL3 . . . . . .248 E7
Glenburnie Ho EX39 . .157 A3
Glenburnie Rd EX39 . .157 A3
Glencarnock Cl TQ1 . .219 E7
Glen Cl
Clyst St Mary EX5 . . . . .179 E2
Sidmouth EX10 . . . . . . .188 A3
Glencoe EX2 . . . . .177 E5
Glendale Rd EX20 . . . . .170 A6
Glendale Terr EX39 . . .157 A3
Glendaragh Rd 12
EX34 . . . . .210 C5
Glendenning Acad
TQ12 . . . . .207 F3
Glendon Cross EX20 . .170 F4
Glendorgal Pk PL18 . . .125 C5
Glendower Rd PL3 . . . .248 D5

Gleneagle Ave 4
PL3 . . . . .248 F6
Gleneagle Rd PL3 . . . . .248 F6
Gleneagle Villas 5
PL3 . . . . .248 F6
Glen Farm Cres
EX14 . . . . .166 D5
Glenfield Cl PL6 . . . . . . .245 D6
Glenfield Rd
Bideford EX39 . . . . .157 A4
Plymouth PL6 . . . . .245 C6
Glenfield Way PL6 . . . .245 E6
Glengarth Cl EX39 . . . .157 A5
Glen Gdns EX39 . . . . . . .156 F4
Glenholme DT7 . . . . . . .260 D2
GLENHOLT 245 D6
Glenholt Cl PL6 . . . . . . .245 D6
Glenholt Rd PL6 . . . . . .245 D6
Glenhurst Rd 5 PL3 . .248 E6
Glen Isla EX10 . . . . .188 B3
Glen Lyn 21 EX32 . . . .155 A4
Glen Lyn Gorge ★
EX35 . . . . .151 C5
Glen Lyn Pk TQ13 . . . .180 D5
Glenmore Ave PL2 . . . .247 F5
Glenmore Rd
Brixham TQ5 . . . . .230 C4
Exeter EX2 . . . . .178 A5
Glennaven Cl PL7 . . . . .251 C6
Glenorchy Ct 5 EX8 . .202 A7
Glen Park Ave PL4 . . . .262 C4
Glen Park Prim Sch 6
PL7 . . . . .251 B5
Glen Rd
Paignton TQ3 . . . . .226 B7
Plymouth, Mannamead
PL3 . . . . .248 F5
Plymouth, Plympton
PL7 . . . . .250 F6
Sidmouth EX10 . . . . . . .188 A3
Glenside Cl 5 TQ14 . .210 B6
Glenside Ct TQ1 . . . . . .220 E5
Glenside Rise PL7 . . . .250 E6
Glen The
Beer EX12 . . . . .191 E6
3 Newton Abbot
TQ12 . . . . .207 F2
Okehampton EX20 . . . .170 B4
Uplyme DT7 . . . . .260 B5
Glenthorne Cl TQ1 . . . .220 D4
Glenthorne Rd EX4 . . .173 A1
Glentor Rd PL3 . . . . . . .248 E7
Glentorr Rd EX39 . . . . .157 A3
Glenview EX14 . . . . . . .166 D5
Glenwater Cl EX12 . . . .192 D6
Glen Wlk EX4 . . . . .173 D2
Glenwood Dr EX31 . . . .154 A1
Glenwood Rd PL3 . . . . .248 E6
Glenwood Rise
EX2 . . . . .261 C1
Globe Ct EX15 . . . . .163 C3
Globefield EX3 . . . . . . .182 F5
Globe Hill EX5 . . . . .184 B3
Globe La EX3 . . . . .182 F4
Globe Ley EX3 . . . . .182 F5
Gloster Rd EX32 . . . . . .155 A4
Gloucester Cl
Honiton EX14 . . . . .166 A5
Torquay TQ2 . . . . .213 F1
Gloucester Cres
EX14 . . . . .166 A5
Gloucester Ct PL1 . . . . .262 C4
Gloucester Pl PL1 . . . . .262 C4
Gloucester Rd
Exeter EX4 . . . . .176 E7
Exmouth EX8 . . . . .196 E3
Newton Abbot TQ12 . . .207 C3
9 Teignmouth TQ14 . .210 B5
Glove Ct EX38 . . . . .159 C5
Glovers Cl 11 EX22 . . .164 C4
Gloyn Pk EX22 . . . . .53 E1
Glynsmead TA20 . . . . . .88 C8
Gnaton Cotts PL8 . . . . .141 C8
*Gnome Reserve & Wild
Flower Gdn* ★ EX22 . . .39 B2
Goad Ave
Plymouth PL4 . . . . .263 C2
Torpoint PL11 . . . . .246 E3
Goad Cl PL11 . . . . .246 F3
Goaman Pk EX39 . . . . . .22 E3
Goaman Rd EX39 . . . . . .26 A4
Go Ape! (Haldon) ★
EX6 . . . . .114 A3
Goats Hill Rd EX39 . . . .157 A6
Goblin Hill EX17 . . . . . . .79 C4
Goblin La EX15 . . . . . . .163 C4
Godborough View
EX39 . . . . .156 D2
Godding Gdns PL6 . . . .244 E6
Godford Cross EX14 . . . .85 B5
Godfrey Ave TQ3 . . . . . .219 B2
Godfrey Cl EX11 . . . . . . .169 C3
Godfreys Gdns EX17 . . .78 C4
Godhams La TA4 . . . . . . .35 A7
Godolphin Cl EX5 . . . . . .81 A1
Godolphin Ho PL19 . . .171 C5
Godwell La
Ivybridge PL21 . . . . . . .237 D3
Ivybridge PL21 . . . . . . .237 F5
Ivybridge PL7 . . . . .136 F6
Gogwell La
Cove EX16 . . . . .49 B5
Tiverton EX16 . . . . .161 F1
Goldburn Cross EX20 . .76 B1
Golden Bay Ct EX39 . . .158 C5
Golden Cl TQ5 . . . . .230 B2
*Golden Hind (Mus Ship)
The* ★ TQ5 . . . . .230 D5

Golden Inn Cross
EX21 . . . . .74 C7
Golden Joy EX7 . . . . . . .165 D6
Golden Cl EX14 . . . . .66 F2
Golden Lane Cross
EX14 . . . . .66 F2
Golden Lion St TQ13 . .130 F4
Golden Park Ave
TQ2 . . . . .213 F4
Golden Pk Ave TQ3 . . .214 A4
Golden Square EX14 . . .86 E6
Golden Terr 20 EX7 . .204 D6
Goldfinch Cl
Kingsteignton TQ12 . . .207 C8
Launceston PL15 . . . . .105 A2
Goldfinch Gdns PL19 .171 D2
Goldfinch Gr
Cullompton EX15 . . . .163 C4
Saltash PL12 . . . . .242 D4
Golds Cross EX6 . . . . . . .97 E4
Goldscross Hill EX6 . . .97 D4
Golds La EX6 . . . . .97 E5
Goldsmith Gdns PL5 . .244 D3
Goldsmiths La EX13 . . .88 E4
Goldsmith St
Exeter EX1 . . . . .261 A3
Exeter, Heavitree EX1 . .177 F6
Goldsmoor Cross
EX16 . . . . .50 E3
Gold St
Ottery St Mary EX11 . . .169 D4
Tiverton EX16 . . . . .161 D4
GOLDWORTHY 24 F1
Golf Links Rd
South Brent TQ10 . . . . .134 D1
Westward Ho! EX39 . . . .156 D7
Yelverton PL19 . . . . . . .126 F1
Golland La EX37 . . . . . . .44 B2
Gollands TQ5 . . . . .230 B5
Gollands Cl TQ5 . . . . . .230 A5
Gollands La
Copplestone EX17 . . . . .79 B8
Morchard Bishop EX17 . .61 B1
Golvers Hill Cl TQ12 . .207 B8
Golvers Hill Rd TQ12 .207 C8
Goodacre Cross PL16 . .91 B1
Goodeve Cl PL9 . . . . . . .255 E6
Goodgates Cl EX33 . . . .152 C6
Goodgates Cres
EX33 . . . . .152 B6
Goodgates Gr EX33 . . .152 C6
Goodgates Pk EX33 . . .152 C6
Goodgates Rd EX33 . . .152 B6
Goodiford Cross EX15 . .63 F3
Gooding Rise EX16 . . . .161 B4
GOODLEIGH 17 C5
Goodleigh CE Prim Sch
EX32 . . . . .17 B5
Goodleigh Cross
EX32 . . . . .155 F7
Goodleigh La EX19 . . . .58 E3
Goodleigh Rd
6 Barnstaple EX32 . . .155 B5
Barnstaple EX32 . . . . . .155 D5
Goodleigh View 4
EX32 . . . . .155 C5
GOODRINGTON 226 B2
Goodrington Rd
Paignton TQ3 . . . . .225 F1
Paignton TQ4 . . . . .226 B1
Goodrington Sands Halt ★
TQ4 . . . . .226 C4
Goodshelter Cross
TQ8 . . . . .148 E5
Good Shepherd Dr 5
EX2 . . . . .261 B2
GOODSTONE 131 C6
Goodstone Cross
TQ12 . . . . .131 C6
Goodstone Way TQ4 . .225 F3
Goodwells Head EX32 .18 C3
Goodwin Ave PL6 . . . . .245 A6
Goodwin Cres PL2 . . . .248 A6
Goodwood Park Rd
EX39 . . . . .157 A5
Gooseberry La PL1 . . . .262 B2
Gooseford Cross EX20 .95 D2
Gooseford La PL11 . . . .252 C6
Goose Gn EX38 . . . . . . .159 E5
GOOSEHAM 37 B3
GOOSEMOOR 186 B7
Goose Moor La EX6 . . .114 B4
GOOSEWELL 2 D4
Goosewell Hill
Plymouth PL6 . . . . .245 C1
Plymouth PL6 . . . . .249 C8
Goosewell Park Rd
PL9 . . . . .255 F6
Goosewell Prim Sch
PL9 . . . . .255 F6
Goosewell Rd PL9 . . . . .255 F5
Goosewell Terr PL9 . . .255 F6
Gora La EX34 . . . . .8 A6
Gorbut Gdns PL19 . . . .171 D4
Gordon Ct
6 Plymouth PL1 . . . . .262 A3
Saltash PL12 . . . . .242 D2
Gordon Rd
Exeter EX1 . . . . .177 E7
Topsham EX3 . . . . .182 E6
Gordon's Pl EX1 . . . . . .177 F5
Gordon Terr
Beer EX12 . . . . .191 D5
Plymouth PL4 . . . . .248 E4
Gore La
Exmouth EX8 . . . . .202 E4
Kilmington EX13 . . . . . .103 C5

Gore La *continued*
Uplyme DT7 . . . . .260 A4
Gorfin Cl EX8 . . . . .202 E8
Gorhuish Cross EX20 . .75 C1
Gorlegg TA21 . . . . .51 E5
Gornhay Cross EX16 . . .64 D8
Gornhay Orch EX16 . . . .64 D8
Gorrans Down EX39 . . .22 F1
Gorse Ho EX4 . . . . .176 E8
Gorse La EX4 . . . . .196 D4
Gorse Way
Ivybridge PL21 . . . . . . .237 E4
Sidmouth EX10 . . . . . . .187 F4
Gorsey Cl PL5 . . . . .244 A3
Gorvin Cross EX39 . . . . .38 B6
Gorway TQ12 . . . . .210 C6
Gorwell Rd EX32 . . . . . .155 C5
Gorwood Rd EX39 . . . . .40 B7
Gorwyn La EX6 . . . . .97 C4
Gosceline Wlk EX14 . .166 C4
GOSFORD 169 D7
Gosford Cl EX11 . . . . . .169 C7
Gosford Rd EX11 . . . . . .169 D7
Goshawk Units EX2 . . .178 F6
Goshen Rd TQ2 . . . . . . .219 E4
Goshen St PL5 . . . . .247 E5
Goslings The TQ7 . . . . .145 A1
Gosling Wlk EX12 . . . . .192 A8
Goss Mdw EX17 . . . . . . .78 C4
Gostwick Cl EX20 . . . . . .77 C4
Goswela Cl PL9 . . . . . . .255 F5
Goswela Gdns PL9 . . . .255 F5
Gothic Rd TQ12 . . . . . . .207 B2
Gould Cl EX32 . . . . .155 B4
Gould Pl TQ12 . . . . .207 F4
Gould Rd
Barnstaple EX32 . . . . . .155 C4
Exeter EX1 . . . . .178 E8
Salcombe TQ8 . . . . .259 D5
Gourders La TQ12 . . . .212 F2
Goutsford Gate PL21 . .136 F2
Govers Mdw EX24 . . . .103 A4
GOVETON 144 C5
Govetts EX5 . . . . .184 C3
Gower Ridge Rd
PL9 . . . . .255 D6
Gowman's Terr EX20 . .77 B4
Goyleacre La EX13 . . . . .87 D6
Goyle Acre La EX13 . . . .87 D4
Grace Gdns TQ14 . . . . .209 E8
Grace Parade EX2 . . . .177 B2
Grace Road Central
EX2 . . . . .177 C2
Grace Road S EX2 . . . .177 D1
Grace Road W EX2 . . . .177 B2
Graddon Cross
Black Torrington EX21 . .73 F6
Okehampton EX20 . . . . .93 E4
Grafton Ct TQ1 . . . . . . .220 B4
Grafton Hts 8 TQ1 . . .220 C5
Grafton Pl 12 TQ12 . .207 B3
Grafton Rd
Exeter EX4 . . . . .173 B1
Plymouth PL4 . . . . .248 E4
Torquay TQ1 . . . . .220 B4
Grafton Terr TQ1 . . . . .220 B4
Graham Cl EX16 . . . . . .161 D5
Graham Rd TQ3 . . . . . . .219 A1
Graham Way EX39 . . . .156 C6
Grainger Cl EX2 . . . . . .178 C5
Grainge Rd PL6 . . . . . . .245 A1
Grambrel Rise 4
EX1 . . . . .178 F8
Gramercy Fields TQ5 .230 B2
Grammar La EX10 . . . .189 D7
Grampian Cl TQ4 . . . . .225 D4
Granary La EX9 . . . . . . .198 C1
Granby Ct PL1 . . . . .247 E2
Granby Gn PL1 . . . . . . .247 E2
Granby Pl PL1 . . . . .247 E2
Granby St PL1 . . . . .247 E2
Granby Way PL1 . . . . . .247 E2
Grand Hotel Rd PL1 . . .262 B1
Grandison Ave TQ14 . .209 A8
Grandison Ct EX2 . . . . .178 A2
Grandisson Dr EX11 . .169 E3
Grandisson St TQ12 . .123 D6
Grand Par PL1 . . . . .262 B1
**Grand View Rd
(Cliff Rd)** TQ7 . . . . . . .147 B7
*Grand Western Canal Ctry
Pk Nature Reserve* ★
EX16 . . . . .64 F7
**Grand Western Canal
(Ctry Pk Nature
Reserve)** ★ EX16 . . . . .50 F2
Grange Ave
Barnstaple EX31 . . . . . .154 C2
Exmouth EX8 . . . . .202 B8
Paignton TQ4 . . . . .226 D2
Grange Bglws EX39 . . .157 B1
Grange Cl
Bratton Fleming EX32 . . .18 A8
Exmouth EX8 . . . . .202 B8
Ipplepen TQ12 . . . . . . .211 C3
Lympstone EX8 . . . . . . .195 F5
Newton Abbot TQ12 . . .207 D1
Wellington TA21 . . . . . . .52 C7
Wellington TA21 . . . . . .160 E5
Grange Cotts EX5 . . . . . .99 C6
Grange Cross EX14 . . . .84 D7
Grange Ct
4 Barnstaple EX32 . . .155 A6
Teignmouth TQ14 . . . . .210 A5
Grange Dr TQ14 . . . . . .210 B6

Grange Heights Cl
TQ4.................226 A1
Grange Hill EX32......18 B8
Grange Hill Ind Est
EX31.................18 B8
Grange Hts TQ4......226 A2
Grange La EX31......57 A7
GRANGE PK.........208 D8
Grange Pk TQ12......212 A6
Grange Rd
Abbotskerswell TQ12 .212 B6
Bideford EX39........157 B1
Buckfast TQ11.......236 B7
Paignton TQ4.......226 B2
Plymouth PL7.......251 A4
Torquay TQ2........220 C5
Yelverton PL20......126 F3
Grange The
Braunton EX33.......152 E5
Dousland PL20.......127 B3
Grange View TQ4.....226 A2
Grant Ct EX39........156 D1
Grantham Cl PL7.....250 B4
Grantland Hill EX16,
EX17...............63 A4
Grantlands EX15......66 A7
Grantley Gdns PL3 ...249 A5
Grant's Hill EX16, TA22. 33 F2
Granville Ave EX32....154 F6
Granville Pl EX15.....162 C5
Granville Rd EX34....150 B6
Grapple Cl EX31......153 E6
Gras Lawn EX2.......177 E4
Grasmere Cl
Plymouth PL6.......244 E5
Torquay TQ2........214 B2
Grasmere Ct EX4.....176 F5
Grassendale Ave PL2 247 F7
Grass La PL2.........248 C6
Grasslands Dr EX1....178 F8
Grassmere Way
PL12................242 D4
Grasspark Hill EX32...18 E3
Grass Rd TQ13.......131 A3
Grassy La PL8........136 C4
Grattan La EX31.......16 B6
Grattans Way EX17....78 C4
GRATTON............54 F5
Gratton Cl TQ6.......146 B8
Gratton Cross
Shebbear EX22.......55 A5
Yelverton PL20......127 A2
Gratton Ct EX31......154 C2
Gratton Dr TQ7.......145 A1
Gratton La
Bittadon EX31........9 C5
Chulmleigh EX18......59 D3
Combe Martin EX31....3 F2
Lower Tippacott EX35...6 A4
Parracombe EX31......4 C2
Yelverton PL20......127 A2
Gratton Pk **10** EX5...99 A6
Gratton Pl PL6.......245 A1
Grattons La TQ9......216 E2
Gratton Way EX31....154 C2
Gravel La EX12.......192 B7
Gravel Pit Cross EX36.20 A6
Gravel Wlk EX15.....163 C3
Gravesend Gdns
PL11................247 B3
Gravesend Wlk PL5 ..243 D4
Graybridge Rd PL20..126 F4
Gray Cres PL5........247 C8
Graynfylde Dr EX39..157 B2
Grays Cotts TQ1......220 D7
Grays Ct TQ13........112 B3
Gray's Hill EX15.......52 D1
Gray's La EX15.......52 D1
Grays Mdw TQ13.....111 F5
Great Ambrook Ave
TQ12................217 A7
Great Berry Rd PL6...244 F1
Great Bridge TQ13....130 F5
Great Burrow Rise
EX39................156 F8
Great Churchway
PL9................256 A7
Great Cl EX15.........51 E1
Great Fellingfield
PL19................117 E6
Great Field Gdns
EX33................152 C5
Great Field La EX37...45 A6
Greatfield Rd PL3....249 B7
Great Furlong TQ14..208 E8
Great Gate Flats 13
TQ5................230 C4
GREAT HAYNE......63 A2
Great Headland Cres
TQ3................219 D1
Great Headland Rd
TQ3................219 C1
Great Hele La EX36...158 D2
Great Hill **3** TQ13...123 E6
Great Hill Cross TQ1 .213 F5
Great Hill Rd TQ2....213 F5
Great Hill View EX4 ..173 E2
Great La TQ7........147 E6
Greatlands Cres PL2 .248 A6
Greatlands Pl **5** PL2.248 A5
Great Lightleigh La
EX18................44 F5
Great Links Tor Rd
EX20................170 E5

Great Longlands Dr
PL12................242 B5
Great Mdw TA22......33 D6
Great Mead EX6......112 F7
Great Meadow **3** EX5 99 A6
Great Mis Tor Cl 5
PL20................126 F3
Greatoak Cross TQ12 212 C5
Great Oak Cross EX5..81 D2
Great Oak Gdns PL16 105 F4
Great Oak Mdw EX22 164 C5
Great Orchard Cl
PL9................255 C6
Great Park Cl
Bishopsteignton
TQ14..............208 F7
Greatpark La TQ3....225 D6
Great Parks Rd TQ3 .225 D6
Great Pitford La EX18.58 D6
Great Pk TQ7.......147 E6
Great Rea Rd TQ5....230 D5
Great Ringaton La
EX36................32 B6
Great Tor Cl TQ3....218 F1
**GREAT
TORRINGTON**......159 D6
**Great Torrington
Bluecoat CE Prim Sch**
EX38................159 E5
**Great Torrington Com
Sch & Sports Coll**
EX38................159 E5
Great Tree Cl TQ4....225 F1
Great Tree Pk TQ13...96 A1
Great Tree Pl TQ4....228 F8
Great Tree View TQ4 228 F8
Great Tree Vw TQ4...225 F1
Greatweek Cross
TQ13................111 B6
GREAT WEEKE.....111 B6
Great Western Cl
TQ4................226 C4
Great Western Ind Est
EX32................155 B3
Great Western Rd
12 Paignton TQ4....226 B6
Plymouth PL1.......262 B1
Great Western Way
EX16................161 D3
Great Woodford Dr
PL7................250 B6
Grebe Cl PL7.........250 F5
Grebe Row EX7......200 E2
Grebe Way TQ2.....207 C8
Grecian Way EX2....178 C4
Greebys The TQ3....226 A6
Greenacre
Braunton EX33.......152 C6
Cranbrook EX5........99 C6
Green Acre EX16......65 B7
Greenacre Cl
Bradworthy EX22......53 E8
Northam EX39.......157 A7
North Tawton EX20....77 C4
Greenacres
Exeter EX4.........173 A3
Plymouth PL9.......255 F8
Torquay TQ1.......220 D5
Greenacres Cl EX14...84 D1
Greenaway EX17......61 A2
Greenaway Ho EX22.164 C3
Greenaway La TQ12 .213 B6
Greenaway Rd TQ12 207 A4
Greenaway Villas 4
TQ12................207 B4
Greenawell Cl TQ13 .111 D2
Greenbank EX38......159 F6
Green Bank EX10.....186 E8
Greenbank Ave
Kingsteignton TQ12 .207 D8
Plymouth PL4.......263 B3
Greenbank Cl EX38...159 F6
Greenbank Cottages
PL4................263 B4
Greenbank Rd
Barnstaple EX32.....155 C4
Brixham TQ5........230 B4
Plymouth PL4.......263 B4
Greenbanks TQ7.....145 C3
Green Banks Cl TQ7 .145 C3
Greenbank Terr
Plymouth PL4.......263 B4
Yelverton PL20......127 A3
Green Cl
Cornworthy TQ9.....227 B4
Exmouth EX8........202 C8
Kingsbridge TQ7.....258 D6
Greenclose Ct 3
EX24................103 A4
Green Close La EX31..10 B5
Greendale Bsns Pk
EX5................174 A5
Greendale Cross EX5 183 F7
Greendale La
Exeter EX5.........99 A1
Woodbury Salterton
EX5..............184 A8
Greendale Rd PL2....248 A7
Greendown Cross
EX20................74 C2
Green End La EX15....83 F5
Greenfield Cl EX39...156 E2
Greenfield Dr
Ivybridge PL21......237 D4
7 South Brent TQ10..134 F2

Greenfield Rd
Paignton TQ3.......219 A1
Saltash PL12........242 D7
Greenfield Terr TA20..88 D8
Greenfinch Cres
PL12................242 E4
Greenford Villas EX2 261 A1
Green Gables EX10...188 A4
GREEN GATE........50 B2
Green Gate EX16.....50 B2
Green Gdns EX39....156 E6
GREENHAM..........51 B7
Greenhaven EX9....197 F2
Greenhayes
Charmouth DT6......104 F4
Dartington TQ9......222 E8
Greenhays Foot EX13 .88 B6
Greenhead EX10......101 B2
Green Hedges EX19...58 E8
GREENHILL.........207 E5
Greenhill
East Allington TQ9...144 D7
Kingsteignton TQ12 .207 E6
Green Hill
Lamerton PL19......116 E3
Poughill EX16, EX17...62 D3
Sampford Courtenay
EX20..............76 F3
Tavistock PL19......171 D5
Greenhill Ave
Exmouth EX8........202 C7
Lympstone EX8......195 E5
Greenhill Cl PL9.....255 F5
Greenhill Cross
East Knowstone EX36..32 B2
Knowle EX33.........8 E1
Poughill EX17........62 D3
Sampford Chapple EX27 77 A3
Greenhill Gdns TQ12 .212 F4
Greenhill Ind Units
TQ12................207 E6
Greenhill La TQ12...211 B6
Greenhill Rd
Kingskerswell TQ12 .212 F4
Kingsteignton TQ12 .207 E6
Plymouth PL9.......256 A5
Greenhill Terr TQ12 .207 E6
Greenhill Way TQ12 .207 E6
Greenhouse Gdns
EX15................163 D3
Greenings Rd EX39...40 C7
Green Knap La TA20...69 F2
Green La
23 Appledore EX39....15 A1
Axmouth EX12......193 C8
Axmouth EX12, DT7 ..193 B8
1 Barnstaple EX31...154 F5
Beaford EX19.........42 D1
Bittaford TQ10......137 E8
Blackawton TQ9.....139 B1
Braunton EX33.......15 D7
Braunton EX33.......152 E6
Buckfastleigh TQ11..236 F4
Chard Junction TA20...88 D7
Chardstock EX13......88 B7
Cheriton Bishop EX6...97 F8
Churchstanton EX15...68 B8
Churston Ferrers TQ5 .229 E5
Colyford EX24.......103 A3
East Allington TQ9...144 D8
Exeter EX4.........176 E5
Exton EX3..........183 B2
Feniton EX14........84 E2
Hatherleigh EX20.....75 D7
Ilsington TQ13......122 C4
Kemacott EX31.......4 C4
Kingsand PL10......253 A2
Merton EX20.........57 A7
Molland EX36........31 B8
North Molton EX36...19 F1
Rackenford EX16.....47 C5
Raymond's Hill EX13..104 C7
Rewe EX5...........82 A2
Rousdon DT7.......193 F8
Sampford Arundel TA21 51 F4
Sidbury EX10.......101 D2
Southleigh EX24.....102 D3
Spreyton EX17.......96 A7
Swimbridge EX32.....28 B8
Tavistock PL19......171 E5
Totnes TQ9.........223 A4
Venn Ottery EX10....100 B2
West Sandford EX17...79 F6
Whitstone EX23......70 E1
Yelverton PL20......126 F1
Greenlake Cross EX39 22 D1
Greenland PL10......252 F5
Greenland Head Cross
Churchstow TQ7.....143 E6
Pennymoor EX16.....62 E6
Greenlands Ave TQ3 219 D1
Greenlands Est PL19 171 D5
Greenlane Cross EX36 31 C8
Green Lane End
Blackawton TQ9.....139 B1
Buckfastleigh TQ11..236 E4
Green Lanes Sh Ctr
EX31................154 F5
Greenlees Dr PL7.....251 B3
Greenmeadow Dr
EX31................155 A7
Green Mews EX9.....198 A1
Green Mount EX10...188 C6
Greenover Cl TQ5....230 B3
Greenover Rd TQ5...230 B3
Greenpark Ave EX1...178 D7

Green Park Ave PL4 .248 D4
Greenpark Rd EX8...196 D2
Green Park Rd
Paignton TQ3.......218 F1
Plymouth PL9.......255 E5
Green Park Wlk TQ3 .218 F1
Green Pk PL10.......253 A2
Green Park Way TQ7 145 A1
Greenslade Cross
EX20................77 A3
Greenslade Rd
Blackawton TQ9.....139 E1
Totnes TQ9.........145 B8
Witheridge EX16......46 E1
Greenslinch La EX5...82 D6
Greensway Rd PL19 .171 A4
Greenswood Cl 9
TQ5................230 C3
Greenswood La TQ6 .232 B1
Greenswood Rd 4
TQ5................230 C3
Green The
Ashburton TQ13.....130 F4
Bridgerule EX22......70 F5
Brushford TA22.......33 E4
Denbury TQ12.......211 A6
Down St Mary EX17...78 E7
East Ogwell TQ12....206 E1
Exeter EX1.........178 D1
Exeter EX3.........182 D8
Exmouth EX8........202 F8
6 Horrabridge PL20 ..126 F5
Ide EX2.............176 D1
Kingsand PL10......253 A2
Meavy PL20.........127 C2
Milton Combe PL20..240 F8
Otterton EX9........198 E7
Plymouth, Ernesettle
PL5..............243 E3
Plymouth, Hooe PL9 .255 B6
Saltash PL12........242 C3
Teignmouth TQ14...210 A8
Whimple EX5........99 E8
Green Tree La EX5...175 D6
Greenville Way EX15.163 C4
Greenway
Crediton EX17.......80 A3
Crediton EX17.......165 B5
Plymouth PL9.......256 A5
Greenway Ave PL7...250 B6
Greenway Cl
3 Horrabridge PL20 .126 F5
Ivybridge PL21......237 D5
Torquay TQ2........214 A1
Greenway Dr EX39...156 E8
Greenway Gdns
Budleigh Salterton
EX9..............198 A2
Tiverton EX16.......161 C4
Torquay TQ2........214 A2
Greenway La
Ashcombe EX7.......124 F5
Awliscombe EX14.....85 B5
Beacon EX14........85 D8
Budleigh Salterton
EX9..............198 A2
Sidmouth EX10......187 E8
Torquay TQ1.......220 B8
Greenway Pk TQ5....229 B4
Greenway Rd
Galmpton TQ5......229 B4
Paignton TQ5.......228 E3
Rockwell Green TA21 .160 A5
Torquay, Chelston TQ2 219 E4
Torquay, St Marychurch
TQ1...............220 B8
Greenways EX34.....150 A5
Greenwich Pl PL12...242 F3
Greenwood Cl
Aveton Gifford TQ7...143 C6
Ivybridge PL21......237 D5
Greenwood Ct EX39..156 D1
Greenwood Dr EX2...178 D5
Greenwood Park Cl
PL7................251 B6
Greenwood Park Rd
PL7................251 B6
Greenwoods The EX39 22 E3
Gregory Cl
Bow EX17...........78 C4
Tiverton EX16.......161 F4
Gregorys Cres TA21 .160 D7
Gregory's Ct TQ13...110 F6
Gregory's Wlk PL5 ...105 A2
Gregory Terr EX39....22 E3
Grenadier Rd EX1....178 E7
Grenadine Cl TQ2....213 E3
Grendon Almshouses
EX1................177 E6
Grendon Bldgs **2**
EX1................261 A2
Grendon Ct TQ4.....210 A5
Grendon La EX16......46 E4
Grendon Rd EX1.....177 E6
Grenfell Ave PL12....242 D3
Grenfell Gdns PL12...242 D3
Grenofen Cross PL19 126 D6
GRENOFEN.........126 D6
Grenofen Cl PL19.....126 D6
Grenville Ave
Exeter EX4.........178 D8
Paignton TQ4.......225 E4

Grenville Ave continued
Torquay TQ2........219 D6
Grenville Cl
Dartmouth TQ6......233 D3
Newton Abbot TQ12 .207 E3
South Molton EX36..158 C4
Stokenham TQ7......145 B2
Grenville Ct PL7.....251 C6
Grenville Dr PL19....171 B3
Grenville Estate Cres
Bideford EX39........25 E4
Bideford EX39.......156 E1
Grenville Est The
EX39................25 E4
Grenville Ho EX31...155 A8
Grenville Pk PL20....127 A2
Grenville Rd
Exmouth EX8........196 C2
Plymouth PL4.......263 C3
Salcombe TQ8......259 D4
Grenville Road Lane S
PL4................249 B2
Grenville St **16** EX39..157 A2
Grenville Terr
4 Bideford EX39.....157 B1
Northam EX39......157 A7
Grenville Way TQ4...226 B3
Gresham Cl PL5......244 C7
Greycoat La TQ12...206 F7
Greyfriars Rd EX4....177 F8
Greyhill Cross TQ7...138 A1
Greysand Cres 31
EX39................15 A1
Greysholt Cross EX32 .28 B8
Greystoke Ave PL6 ..249 D7
Greystone Cross EX6...96 C3
Greystone Wlk EX15. 163 A3
Gribble Cl EX32......155 C4
Gribbleford Cross
EX20................75 A4
Gribble La EX5........99 D6
Gribblemead EX24...103 A4
Grieg Dr EX32........155 C5
Griffin Way PL9......256 C6
Griggs Cl
Northam EX39.......157 A6
Plymouth PL7.......251 B4
Griggs Gdn EX31....153 D5
Grigg's La EX10......188 D3
Grimspound Cl PL6 .249 E8
Grimstone Terr PL20 126 E2
Grinacombe Cross
PL16................91 B2
GRINACOMBE MOOR .91 B2
Grinacombe Moor cross
PL16................91 B2
Grindhill Cross EX20 .92 D5
Grindle Way EX5.....179 B2
Grizedale Rd PL6.....249 D7
Gronau Cl EX14.....166 C4
Grooms Orch TA21...160 C5
Gropers La
Ipplepen TQ3, TQ12 .218 C8
North Whilborough
TQ12..............212 B1
Gropy La
Ash Mill EX36........31 D1
South Molton EX36...46 D8
Grosvenor Ave TQ2 .213 C1
Grosvenor Cl TQ2....213 C1
Grosvenor Cotts 1
PL4................248 F4
Grosvenor Ct
3 Barnstaple EX32...155 A5
Ivybridge PL21......237 C5
Grosvenor Pl EX1....261 C4
Grosvenor Rd
Paignton TQ4.......226 B5
Plymouth PL6.......244 F4
Grosvenor St 2
EX32................155 A5
Grosvenor Terr
4 Barnstaple EX32...155 A5
Paignton TQ4.......226 B5
4 Teignmouth TQ14..210 B6
Groundhead Rd EX14.. 86 F6
Grove Ave **12** TQ14...210 B5
Grove Cl
Plymouth TQ12.....244 D6
3 Totnes TQ9.......223 C5
Grove Cres **6** TQ14 .210 B5
Grove Cross EX22.....39 D3
Grove Ct
Dawlish EX7.........204 F6
Teignmouth TQ14...210 C6
Grove Hill
12 Colyton EX24......103 A4
Topsham EX3.......182 F5
Grove Ho EX3........182 F5
Grove La
Copplestone EX17....79 B7
West Anstey EX36....32 D6
Grove Mdw EX20.....94 F5
Grove Mews **16** TQ9 .223 C5
Grove Pk
Tavistock PL19......171 D5
Torpoint PL11......246 E3
Grove Sch The 19
TQ9................223 C5
Groves The PL21.....237 C6
Grove Terr **11** TQ14..210 B5
Grove The
5 Bittaford PL21.....137 C8
Blackawton TQ9.....139 E1
Exeter EX4.........174 E2
Paignton TQ4.......225 E4

Grove The continued
Plymouth, Plymstock
PL9................255 D8
Plymouth, Stoke PL3..248 A4
Sidmouth EX10......188 B4
Totnes TQ9.........223 C5
Woolacombe EX34....7 F6
Guardian Rd EX1....178 E6
Gubbin's La EX33....152 C5
Guelder Way TQ12...244 C6
Guernsey Ave EX4...174 E2
Guernsey Cnr EX24..102 F4
Guestland Rd TQ1...220 C7
Guildford Cl
Exeter EX4.........176 E6
Plymouth PL5.......244 E3
Guildford St PL4.....263 A3
Guildhall Sh Ctr EX4 261 A3
Guildhall Sq PL1.....262 C2
Guinea St EX1........261 A2
Guinevere Way EX4 .174 A1
Guinness La EX4.....176 E6
Gulland Cross TQ12 .212 B4
Gullet Cross TQ7.....148 F6
Gulliford Cl EX8......195 F6
Gulliford Cotts EX8 .195 F6
Gulliver La EX20......77 D7
Gullyhole Hill EX36...31 F7
Gully La EX14........86 C5
Gully Shoot EX24....103 A3
Gulway Mead TA20...88 D8
GULWORTHY.........125 E8
Gulworthy Cotts
PL19................125 E7
Gulworthy Cross
PL19................125 E7
Gulworthy Prim Sch
PL19................125 E7
Gun La
Heasley Mill EX36....19 D4
North Heasley EX36...19 D4
Plymouth PL5.......247 E2
GUNN................17 F4
Gunn Cross EX32......17 F3
GUNNISLAKE........125 D6
Gunnislake Prim Sch
PL18................125 C6
**Gunnislake Rural
Workshops** PL18....125 C6
Gunnislake Sta PL18 125 C6
Gunsdown Villas
EX36................158 C5
Gunstone Cross EX17 .79 E1
Gunstone Mill Cross
EX17................79 E1
Gunswell La EX36...158 B5
Gurnard Wlk PL3....249 C6
Gurney Cl PL11......246 F3
Gurneys The TQ3....226 A5
GUSCOTT............26 E2
Guscott La EX38......26 E2
Gussiford La EX8.....202 B6
Guy Miles Way PL5...244 B3
Guys Rd EX4........176 F6
Gwel Avon Bsns Pk
PL12................242 D2
Gwithian Cl PL11....246 F4
Gwyn Rd PL4.......263 C4
Gwythers EX36......158 D4
Gypsy La
Simonsbath TA24......13 E1
Simonsbath TA24......20 E8

H

Hacche La
South Molton EX36....30 B8
South Molton EX36...158 C6
South Molton EX36...158 C8
Haccombe Cl EX4....176 E6
Haccombe Cross
TQ12................213 C4
Haccombe Path
TQ12................208 A2
Haccombe View
TQ12................207 F6
Hacker Cl EX10......186 F7
Hackney La
Kingsteignton TQ12 .207 F6
Newton Abbot TQ12 208 B4
**Hackney Marshes Nature
Reserve** TQ12......207 E6
Hackpen Cross Way
EX15................66 C6
Hackworthy Cnr EX4.98 F5
Hackworthy Cross
EX6................97 F6
Hackworthy Cross La
EX6................97 F6
Hackworthy La
Nadderwater EX4.....98 F5
Tedburn St Mary EX6..97 D4
HADDACOTT.........26 E3
Haddacott Cross EX38. 26 F3
Haddo Dr EX2.......178 D4
Haddington Rd PL2 .247 F4
Haddon Cnr EX13....103 C8
Haddon Ct **2** TQ3...226 B5
Haddon Hill TA4......34 D7
Haddon La TA4........34 F7
Haddon Rd EX13....103 B8
Hadfield Ct **4** TQ13 .123 C4
Hadrian Cl EX4......176 E6
Hadrians Way EX8...196 C1
HALBERTON..........65 B8
Halberton Prim Sch
EX16................65 A7

Halcyon Ct PL2 248 A6
Halcyon Rd
Newton Abbot TQ12 207 B3
Plymouth PL2 248 A6
Haldene Terr 6
EX32 154 F6
Haldon Ave TQ14 210 C6
Haldon Belvedere★
EX6 113 F5
Haldon Cl
2 Newton Abbot
TQ12 207 F2
Topsham EX3 182 E6
Torquay TQ1 220 D4
Haldon Ct EX8 196 B2
Haldon Dr EX6 114 A4
Haldon La TQ13 124 B4
Haldon Lodge EX6 114 B5
Haldon Pl PL5 244 A3
Haldon Plain EX6 114 B3
Haldon Rd
Exeter EX4 177 A6
Torquay TQ1 220 D4
Haldon Ridge EX6 114 C2
Haldon Rise 1 TQ12 207 F2
Haldon Terr 14 EX7 204 D6
Haldon View TQ13 123 F6
Haldon View Terr
EX2 177 F5
Haldron's Almshouses
EX16 161 C4
Halecombe Rd PL3 249 D1
Hale La
Honiton EX14 85 F3
Honiton EX14 166 E6
Haley Barton 4 PL2 248 A5
Haley Cl EX8 196 C2
Half Farthing La EX20 77 C7
Halfmoon Ct TQ11 236 A3
Half Moon The EX13 87 E8
HALF MOON
VILLAGE 172 C7
HALFORD 122 F1
Halford Cross TQ12 122 E1
Halfpenny Cross EX16 49 B7
Halfpenny Ct PL1 248 A2
Halfsbury Cross EX37 43 E4
Halfway House Flats
TQ5 230 F6
Halfyard Ct TA21 160 F4
Hallamore La PL21 133 B2
Hall Cross PL21 133 E2
Hallerton Cl PL6 245 E2
Hallett Cl PL12 242 B3
Hallett Ct DT7 260 D4
Halletts Way EX13 167 E6
Halley Gdns PL5 243 E1
Hall Hill EX35 6 B5
Hall La
Holcombe EX7 210 E8
Morchard Bishop EX17 60 F2
HALLSANDS 149 E5
HALLSANNERY 25 F3
Halls Cross EX31 10 E4
Hall's La TQ12 212 F4
Hall's Mill La EX31 154 E8
HALLSPILL 26 B2
Hallswell Ct TQ4 226 B6
Halmpstone Cross
EX32 28 C7
Halsbury Rd EX16 161 F4
Halscombe La
Ide EX2 176 C1
Sidbury EX10 101 F8
Halsdon Ave EX8 196 A1
Halsdon Cross EX22 54 C1
Halsdon La EX8 196 A2
Halsdon Rd EX8 202 A7
Halsdon Terr EX38 159 C5
Halsdon Wildlife
Reserve★ EX19 57 D6
Halsegate Cross EX20 77 D3
Halse Hill EX9 197 F1
Halse La
North Tawton EX20 77 D4
West Worlington EX17 61 B6
Halses Cl EX4 176 D8
Halsewood Gate EX15 64 E2
Halsey Lake Cross
EX31 10 D1
HALSFORDWOOD 98 F4
Halsfordwood La
EX4 98 F4
Halshanger Cross
TQ13 130 F8
HALSINGER 8 E1
Halsteads Rd TQ2 214 A2
Halswell Cross EX36 29 D2
Halt The EX2 177 B1
HALWELL 139 B4
Halwell Bsns Pk TQ9 139 C3
Halwell Cross
Denbury TQ12 211 A5
Halwell TQ9 139 C4
Halwell Ho TQ7 148 E7
HALWILL 73 C2
Halwill Com Prim Sch
EX21 73 E2
HALWILL JUNCTION 73 E2
Halwill Mdw EX21 73 D3
Halyards EX3 182 E5
HAM
Axminster 86 F4
Plymouth 248 A8
Wellington 52 D8
Hambeer La
Exeter EX2 176 E3
Exeter EX4 176 F2
Hamberhayne Cross
EX24 102 D6
Hamble Cl PL3 249 D7
Hamblecombe La
TQ13 124 A4
Hambleton Ho 4
TQ14 210 C5
Hambleton Way TQ4 226 A2
Ham Butts TQ7 143 F7
Ham Cl PL2 248 B8
Ham Cross EX13 86 F4
Ham Dr PL2 248 B8
Hameldown Bsns Pk
EX20 170 E6
Hameldown Cl TQ2 219 B7
Hameldown Rd EX20 170 E5
Hameldown Way
TQ12 207 D4
Hamelin Way TQ2,
TQ3 219 A8
Ham Farm La TA20 69 F8
Ham Gn PL2 248 A7
Ham Green Ct PL2 248 A7
Ham Green La PL2 248 A7
Ham Hill
Ashreigney EX18 43 E1
Ashreigney EX18 58 E8
Street Ash TA20 69 F8
Tracebridge EX16 51 A8
Ham Ho PL2 248 A8
Hamilton Ave EX2 177 F2
Hamilton Cl
Bideford EX39 25 E4
14 Sidford EX10 101 B1
Hamilton Ct 4 EX8 202 B6
Hamilton Dr
Exeter EX2 178 D5
Newton Abbot TQ12 207 B5
Hamilton Gdns PL4 248 D4
Hamilton Gr EX6 201 B7
Hamilton La EX8 202 C7
Hamilton Rd
Exmouth EX8 202 D7
Topsham EX3 182 E6
Hamiltons The TQ14 210 A3
Ham La
Colyton EX24 103 A4
Combe St Nicholas TA20 69 D8
Dittisham TQ6 228 C3
Plymouth PL2 248 A8
Shaldon TQ14 209 D4
Sidmouth EX10 188 B3
South Molton EX36 158 E4
Hamley La TA20 69 E8
Hamlin Gdns EX1 178 A7
Hamlin Ho EX1 178 A7
Hamlin La EX1 178 A7
Hamlintoo La EX17 95 E7
Hamlyns La EX4 176 F8
Hamlyns Way TQ11 236 B5
Hammett Rd EX15 163 B3
Hammetts La
Barnstaple EX32 155 B1
Bishop's Tawton EX32 16 E1
Hammond Croft Way
EX2 181 B8
Hamoaze Ave PL5 247 D8
Hamoaze Pl PL1 247 D2
Hamoaze Rd PL11 247 B2
Hampden Pl EX2 261 A1
Ham Pl 10 EX16 161 C3
Hampshire Cl EX4 176 E4
Hampson Cross EX17 78 A4
Hampson La EX17 78 A4
Hampstead Farm La
Littlehempston TQ9 216 C1
Littlehempston TQ9 223 C8
HAMPTON 103 C7
Hampton Ave TQ1 220 C8
Hampton Bldgs EX4 261 C4
Hampton Ct EX13 103 C6
Hampton La
Torquay TQ1 220 C8
Whitford EX13 103 C6
Hampton Pk EX39 156 E4
Hampton Rd
Newton Abbot TQ12 207 C3
Whitford EX13 103 C7
Hampton St PL4 263 A3
Ham Rd
Dalwood EX13 87 A3
Wellington TA21 52 D8
Hamslade Cross EX16 48 D8
Hamslade Hill EX16 48 D8
Hams The EX2 176 D1
Hamstone Ct TQ8 259 D4
Hamway La TA20 69 F8
Hancock Cl PL6 244 D6
Hand and Pen La EX5 99 E6
HAND & PEN 99 E6
Hand & Pen Cotts EX5 99 E6
Handy Cross EX39 25 E4
Hangar La PL6 245 B5
Hanger La EX14 84 F8
Hanging La EX35 5 A3
Hangman Path EX34 2 F4
Hangman's Cross
PL21 138 A2
Hangman's Hill EX16 48 D7
Hangman's Hill Cross
EX16 48 E7
Hankford Cross EX22 39 E2
Hannaburrow La
Braunton EX33 14 F8
Saunton EX33 14 F8
HANNAFORD 28 C8
Hannaford Cross EX32 28 C8
Hannaford La EX32 28 D8
Hannaford Rd
Lifton PL16 105 E3
Noss Mayo PL8 140 F5
Hannahs at Ivybridge
PL21 237 B5
Hannaton Cross EX32 28 D8
Hanniford Gdns EX1 175 A3
Hann Rd EX16 64 F8
Hanover Cl
7 Brixham TQ5 230 C3
Exeter EX1 177 F6
Plymouth PL3 249 B5
Hanover Ct
Dulverton TA22 33 D7
Exeter EX2 181 C8
15 Plymouth PL1 263 A2
Hanover Gdns EX15 163 C5
Hanover Ho TQ1 220 D3
Hanover Rd
Exeter EX1 177 F6
Plymouth PL3 249 C4
Hansetown Rd TA4 34 F8
Hansford Cross
Ashreigney EX18 44 A1
Burrington EX37 44 B2
Hansford Ct EX14 166 C5
Hansford Way EX11 169 C3
Hanson Pk
Bideford EX39 156 F4
Bideford EX39 157 A4
Happaway Cl TQ2 214 A2
Happaway Rd
Torquay TQ2 213 F2
Torquay TQ2 214 A2
HARBERTON 222 D1
Harberton Cl TQ4 225 E3
HARBERTONFORD 139 C6
Harbertonford CE Prim
Sch TQ9 139 C7
Harbour Ave
Plymouth PL4 263 A2
Plymouth, Camels Head
PL5 247 E8
Harbour Ct
Exmouth EX8 201 F6
6 Seaton EX12 192 B4
Harbourne Ave TQ4 225 F3
HARBOURNEFORD 135 B5
Harbourneford Cross
TQ10 135 B4
Harbour Rd EX12 192 B4
Harbourside 3 EX34 150 C6
Harbour St PL11 247 B3
Harbour The
Lynmouth EX35 151 C6
Seaton EX12 192 C5
Harbour View
Plymouth PL9 255 A7
Saltash PL12 242 E2
Harbour View Cl 1
TQ5 230 C5
Harbour View Rd
PL5 247 E8
HARCOMBE
Chudleigh 124 A8
Sidford 101 D1
HARCOMBE
BOTTOM 104 D6
Harcombe Cross
Raymond's Hill EX13 104 C6
Sidbury EX10 101 C1
Harcombe Fields
EX10 188 D8
Harcombe La EX10 188 D8
Harcombe Lane E
EX10 188 E8
Harcombe Rd
Raymond's Hill DT7 104 D6
Uplyme DT7 260 D8
Hardaway Head 7
EX32 155 A5
Harden Ho TQ3 225 E7
Harding Cres EX16 161 E5
Harding Ct TQ11 236 B5
Hardings Cl PL12 242 E3
HARDISWORTHY 37 A7
Hardisworthy Cross
EX39 37 B7
Hardway Rd TA22 21 D2
Hardwick Farm PL7 250 C3
Hardy Cl
Exeter EX2 182 C8
Torquay TQ1 220 C2
Hardy Cres PL5 244 E1
Hardy Rd EX2 178 D5
Hardys Ct EX10 186 D4
Harebell Cl PL12 242 D4
Harebell Copse EX4 176 D8
Harebell Dr EX15 162 E5
Haredon Cross PL21 137 D6
Harefield Cl EX4 177 A8
Harefield Cotts EX8 195 D5
Harefield Dr
Lympstone EX8 195 F5
Stoke Fleming TQ6 146 B7
Harefield Rd EX8 195 F6
Harefoot Cross TQ13 121 D3
Hare La EX4 98 D4
Harepath Hill EX12 192 A8
Harepath Ind Est
EX12 192 A8
Harepath Rd EX12 192 A7
Harepathstead Rd EX5 83 B1
Harepie Cross EX31 27 D6
Hares Cl TQ13 111 A6
Haresdown Cross
EX36 47 C7
Hares Gn EX36 158 C4
Hares La TQ13 130 F4
Hareston Cl PL7 251 B3
Hareston Cross PL8 257 D8
Harestone Cross EX13 88 B7
Hare Tor Cl EX20 170 E5
HAREWOOD 125 E4
Harewood TQ11 236 B5
Harewood Cl PL7 250 E5
Harewood Cres PL5 244 B2
Harewood Rd PL18 125 D3
HARFORD
Cornwood 133 F2
Tedburn St Mary 97 F7
Harford Cross EX32 17 C2
Harford La EX6, EX17 97 F7
Harford Rd
Ivybridge PL21 237 D6
Landkey EX32 17 B2
Harford Way 14 EX32 17 B2
Hargood Terr 6 PL2 247 F4
Hargreaves Cl PL5 243 F2
Harker La EX6 114 B2
Harlech Cl PL3 249 A7
Harlequins Sh Ctr
EX4 261 A3
HARLESTON 145 A4
Harleston Cross TQ7 144 F4
Harley Ct PL21 237 D5
Harlington Ct TQ12 207 C4
Harlseywood EX39 156 E2
Harlyn Drive PL2 248 D8
Harman Wlk EX32 155 C5
Harnorlen Rd PL2 248 D7
Harold Cl EX11 169 B3
Haroldsleigh Ave
PL5 244 E2
Harper's Hill
Northlew EX20 74 E2
Totnes TQ9 223 A5
HARPFORD 100 C1
Harpins Ct TQ12 213 A6
Harpitt Cl EX15 162 C3
Harp La EX5 99 E2
Harp's Corner Cross
EX36 46 C6
Harpson Hill EX36 31 F1
Harpson La
Bishops Nympton
EX36 31 F1
South Molton EX36 46 F8
Harracott Cross EX31 27 E6
Harraton Cross PL21 137 D1
Harrier Pl TQ12 207 A5
Harriers Cl EX12 192 A6
Harrier Way EX2 178 E4
Harriet Gdns PL7 250 B6
Harringcourt Rd EX4 174 E2
Harrington Dr EX4 174 E2
Harrington Gdns EX4 174 E1
Harrington La EX4 174 D2
Harris Cl EX16 51 A4
Harris Cotts
Blackawton TQ9 139 E1
Ivybridge PL21 237 C5
Harris Cross EX39 38 D8
Harris Ct PL9 255 B6
Harrison St 7 PL2 247 F4
Harrisons Way EX5 173 F8
Harris Pl EX1 174 F3
Harris Way PL21 136 B6
HARROWBARROW 125 A4
Harrowbarrow Sch
PL17 125 A4
Harrowbeer La PL20 126 F3
Harrowby Cl EX16 161 F4
Harston Rd PL21 237 A5
HARTFORD 34 C8
Hartford Rd TA4 34 B8
HARTLAND 22 E3
Hartland Abbey & Gdns★
EX39 22 C3
Hartland Cl PL6 245 A7
Hartland Cross EX17 79 C4
Hartland Prim Sch
EX39 22 E3
Hartland Quay Mus★
EX39 22 A3
Hartland Tor Cl TQ5 230 A2
Hartland View Rd EX34 8 C6
HARTLEY 248 E7
Hartley Ave PL3 249 A6
Hartley Ct PL3 249 A6
Hartley Park Gdns
PL3 248 F6
Hartley Rd
Exmouth EX8 202 A6
Paignton TQ4 226 A5
Plymouth PL3 248 E6
Hartleys The EX8 202 A6
HARTLEY VALE 249 A8
Hart Manor EX33 152 E3
Hartnoll Cross EX16 64 E8
Harton Cross EX39 22 E3
Harton Way EX39 22 E3
Harton Way Ind Pk
EX39 22 E3
Hartopp Rd EX8 202 A8
Hartop Rd TQ1 214 B1
Harts Cl
1 Exeter EX1 178 E8
Teignmouth TQ14 210 A6
Harts La EX1 178 E8
Hart's La EX1 178 D8
Hart's Path TA4 35 E7
Hart St 9 EX39 157 A2
Hart Way
Oareford TA24 6 F3
Oareford TA24 13 F8
Hartwell Ave PL9 256 D7
Harvest Cl
Plymouth TQ12 244 C8
4 Roundswell EX31 154 A1
Harvest La
Bideford EX39 156 D2
Exeter EX3 182 D7
Harvey Ave PL4 249 B1
Harveys Cl
11 Chudleigh Knighton
TQ13 123 C4
Sampford Courtenay
EX20 76 F4
Harvey St PL11 247 B3
Harveys Walk TQ7 143 F7
Harveys Wk 13 TQ7 143 E7
Harwell Ct 8 PL1 262 B3
Harwell La TQ10 135 A3
Harwell St PL1 262 B3
Harwood Ave PL5 244 C7
Harwood Cl EX8 196 D1
Haskins Cross EX14 84 C5
Hask La EX6 96 D3
Haslam Ct TQ1 220 A7
Haslam Rd TQ1 220 A7
Hastings St PL1 262 B3
Hastings Terr PL1 262 B3
Haswell Cl PL6 249 A8
HATCH 143 E5
Hatcher Cl EX14 166 C3
Hatcher St 10 EX7 204 D6
Hatchland Rd
Poltimore EX4 174 F6
Poltimore EX4 175 A6
Hatchmoor Common La
EX38 159 F6
Hatchmoor Est EX38 159 E5
Hatchmoor Ind Est
EX20 75 B6
Hatchmoor Lane Ind Est
EX38 159 F6
Hatchmoor Rd EX38 159 F5
Hatfield TQ1 220 B6
Hatfield Rd TQ1 220 B6
Hatherdown Hill
TQ13 123 B6
HATHERLEIGH 75 C6
Hatherleigh Com Prim
Sch EX20 75 C7
Hatherleigh La TQ13 122 D7
Hatherleigh Rd
Exeter EX2 177 A2
Okehampton EX20 93 F7
Winkleigh EX19 58 E2
Hatherton La EX20 76 E2
Hat La PL10 252 F2
Hatris La EX32 18 D2
Hatshill Cl PL6 132 A2
Hatshill Farm Cl PL6 132 A5
Hatswell Rd EX2 181 E7
Hatway Hill EX10 101 C3
Hauley Rd TQ6 233 F3
Havelock Rd TQ1 214 B1
Havelock Terr
Lutton PL21 133 B2
Plymouth PL2 247 F3
Haven Banks EX2 261 B1
Haven Banks Ret Pk
EX1 261 A1
Haven Cl EX2 261 A1
Haven Ct 5 EX12 192 B4
Haven Rd EX2 261 A1
Haven The TQ14 208 F7
Havenview Rd EX12 192 A5
Have's Hill EX17 61 C8
Hawarden Cotts PL4 249 B1
Hawcombe La EX33 8 E1
Haweswater Cl PL6 244 E4
Hawk Ave TQ12 207 A5
HAWKCHURCH 88 E3
Hawkchurch CE Prim Sch
EX13 88 E3
Hawkchurch Cross
EX13 88 E2
Hawkchurch Rd EX13 88 E3
Hawkerland Rd EX10 186 C4
Hawkers Ave PL4 263 A2
Hawkers Dr EX23 37 A1
Hawkers La PL3 248 E5
Hawkesdown Cl
EX12 192 D7
Hawkinge Gdns PL5 243 E4
Hawkins Ave TQ2 219 C7
Hawkins Cl PL6 245 A5
Hawkins La EX11 168 E3
Hawkin's La TA4 35 E7
Hawkins Pl EX15 163 C4
Hawkins Rd
Exeter EX1 174 F3
Newton Abbot TQ12 207 E3
West Clyst EX4 175 A4
Hawkins Way EX17 165 E5
Hawkins Wlk EX20 170 D5
Hawkmoor Cl PL7 250 D5
Hawkmoor Cotts
TQ13 122 E7
Hawkmoor Hill EX13,
DT6 88 H2
Hawkmoor Pk TQ13 122 E7
HAWKRIDGE 21 D1
Hawkridge Cross
Hawkridge TA22 21 D1
Umberleigh EX37 28 C4
Hawkridge Loop Rd
TA22 21 D2
Hawkridge Rd EX31 15 E5
Hawksdown View
EX12 192 A7
Hawks Dr 8 EX16 161 E6
Hawks Pk PL12 242 C2
Hawks Way EX32 17 F4
Hawkwood Cl TQ12 206 D5
Hawkwell Cross EX16 32 F4
Hawkwell La
Brushford TA22 33 A4
East Anstey EX36 32 F4
Hawley Cl EX32 155 C5
Hawley Cross EX13 86 F3
Hawley Manor EX32 155 C5
Hawson Cross TQ11 130 B3
Hawthorn Ave
Ilfracombe EX34 150 D5
Torpoint PL11 246 F3
Hawthorn Cl
Cullompton EX15 163 B2
Honiton EX14 166 B5
Kingsbridge TQ7 258 C4
Plymouth, Hooe PL9 255 C5
Plymouth, Woolwell
PL6 245 D7
Hawthorn Dr
Sidmouth EX10 187 F8
Wembury PL9 140 D7
Hawthorne Cl
Newton Abbot TQ12 212 F8
West Hill EX11 168 D4
Hawthorne Rd
10 Tiverton EX16 161 F6
Wellington TA21 160 F5
Hawthorn Gr
Exmouth EX8 196 E1
Plymouth PL2 248 C7
Hawthorn Park Cl
TQ2 219 D3
Hawthorn Park Rd
PL9 140 D7
Hawthorn Pk
Bideford EX39 156 E1
Lydford EX20 107 F4
Hawthorn Rd
Barnstaple EX32 155 E4
Crediton EX17 165 C5
Exeter EX2 177 F3
Tavistock PL19 171 C2
Hawthorns PL12 242 D2
Hawthorn Way
Exeter EX2 181 A8
Ivybridge PL21 237 F5
Plymouth PL3 249 B7
Haxter Cl PL6 241 B1
Haxter Wood Chase
PL6 241 B2
Haxton Down La EX31 18 B8
Haxton La EX31 18 A8
Haycock La TQ5 230 E5
Haycroft Ho 3 EX39 157 A1
Haycroft Mws PL3 249 D1
Haycross Hill EX21 55 D4
Haydn Cl EX32 155 C5
Haydon Cross EX16 48 C4
Haydon Gr PL5 243 C1
Haydon Rd EX16 161 B5
Haydons Pk EX14 166 C5
Haye Barton DT7 260 C4
Haye Cl DT7 260 C4
Haye Gdns DT7 260 C4
Haye La
Colyford DT7, EX13 103 D3
Lyme Regis DT7 260 D4
Haye Rd PL7, PL9 250 C1
Haye Road S PL9 256 C7
Hayes Barton★ EX9 197 E7
Hayes Barton Ct EX4 177 A5
Hayes Cl
Budleigh Salterton
EX9 198 A2
Otterton EX9 198 E7
Totnes TQ9 223 E4
Hayes Copse EX32 17 B2
Hayes Cross EX21 55 E3
Hayes Ct
Lyme Regis DT7 260 D3
Paignton TQ4 225 F5
Hayes End EX11 168 C4
Hayes Gdns TQ4 226 A4
Hayes La
Ashreigney EX18 58 D8
East Budleigh EX9 198 A6
Otterton EX9 198 E7
Hayes Pl PL6 249 B8
Hayes Rd
Paignton TQ3, TQ4 226 A5
Plymouth PL9 255 C7
Hayes Sch TQ4 225 F5
Hayes Square 24 EX5 99 A6
Hayes The TQ5 229 E5
Hayeswood La EX9 198 A6
Hayfield Rd EX20 76 C5
Hay La TQ7 147 E6
Hayle Ave TQ4 229 B8
Hayley Pk TQ12 212 F3
Hayman's Cl EX15 163 B2
Haymans Gn EX15 163 B2
Haymans Orch EX5 184 C3
Hayne Barton Cotts
EX15 163 E6
Hayne Cl
Exeter EX4 178 A7
Tipton St John EX10 100 D2
Hayne Cross
Ashill EX15 66 F5
Bishops Nympton EX36 31 A4
Cheriton Fitzpaine EX17 63 A2

Hayne Cross *continued*
Lewtrenchard EX20 . . . 106 B5
Lustleigh TQ13 . . . . 121 F7
Morebath EX16 . . . . 34 B4
Plymtree EX15 . . . . 83 F6
Zeal Monachorum EX17 . 78 B6
Hayne Ct
Bolham EX16 . . . . 49 C1
Tiverton EX16 . . . . 161 E7
Hayne Hill EX10 . . . . . . 100 D2
Hayne Ho EX16 . . . . 49 B2
Hayne La
Bolham EX16 . . . . 49 B2
Butterleigh EX15 . . . . . . 64 C2
Honiton EX14 . . . . 85 C2
Silverton EX5 . . . . 82 C4
Wilmington EX14 . . . . . . 86 D3
Hayne Pk
Barnstaple EX32 . . . . . . 155 B4
Tipton St John EX10 . . . 100 D2
Haynes La EX6 . . . . 176 A2
Hayne Town Cross
EX37 . . . . 44 B8
Hayridge Mws EX14 . . . 84 E2
Hayrish Cross EX20 . . . 95 B7
Haystone Pl PL1 . . . . . 262 B4
Haytor Ave TQ4 . . . . . . 225 F3
Haytor Cl
Plymouth PL5 . . . . 244 B3
Teignmouth TQ14 . . . . . 209 D8
Haytor Ct TQ13 . . . . . . 122 A4
Haytor Dr
Exeter EX4 . . . . 176 E7
Ivybridge PL21 . . . . 237 D4
Newton Abbot TQ12 . . . 208 A3
Haytor Gr TQ12 . . . . . . 208 A3
Haytor Pk TQ12 . . . . . . 207 E7
Haytor Rd
Bovey Tracey TQ13 . . . . 122 C5
Torquay TQ1 . . . . 220 B7
Haytor Rocks* TQ13 . 121 F3
Haytor Terr 17 TQ12 . . 207 B3
Haytor Vale TQ13 . . . . 122 B4
Haytor View
Chudleigh Knighton
TQ12 . . . . 123 C5
Heathfield TQ12 . . . . . . 123 B3
Haytor View Com Prim
Sch TQ12 . . . . 207 F3
HAYTOWN 39 E1
Haytown Pottery*
EX22 . . . . 39 E1
Haywain Cl TQ2 . . . . . . 213 B1
Haywards Prim Sch 5
EX17 . . . . 165 D5
Hay Webb Cl EX1 . . . . . 174 F3
Hazel Ave
Braunton EX33 . . . . 15 D8
Braunton EX33 . . . . 152 E7
Hazel Cl
Kingsbridge TQ7 . . . . . . 258 C4
Newton Abbot TQ12 . . . 208 A1
Newton Poppleford
EX10 . . . . 186 F8
Plymouth PL6 . . . . 245 B6
Seaton EX12 . . . . 192 A7
Teignmouth TQ14 . . . . . 210 C8
Hazel-Crest TQ13 . . . . 123 B7
Hazeldene TQ8 . . . . . . 259 C3
Hazeldene Cl PL21 . . . 136 B6
Hazeldene Gdns
Exmouth EX8 . . . . 196 A1
Plymouth PL9 . . . . 256 C8
Hazeldown Rd TQ14 . . 210 B7
Hazeldown Sch TQ14 210 B8
Hazel Dr PL9 . . . . 256 C7
Hazel Gr
4 Barnstaple EX31 . . . 154 C2
Plymouth PL9 . . . . 256 C7
Rockbeare EX5 . . . . 99 C5
Yelverton PL20 . . . . 127 A3
Hazel La PL21 . . . . 237 F5
Hazelmead Rd EX5 . . . 179 E2
Hazel Mws EX36 . . . . . 158 D5
Hazel Rd
Exeter EX2 . . . . 177 F2
Tavistock PL19 . . . . 171 C2
Hazelwood 6 TQ1 . . . 220 D5
Hazelwood Cl EX14 . . 166 C4
Hazelwood Cres PL9 . 256 D7
Hazelwood Dr
Dawlish Warren EX7 . . . 201 A2
Plymouth PL6 . . . . 245 D8
Hazelwood Pk EX7 . . . 201 B2
Headborough Rd
TQ13 . . . . 130 F5
Headgate EX36 . . . . 20 B1
Head Hill EX18, EX37 . . . 44 C5
Headingley Cl EX2 . . . 178 C4
Headland Cl EX1 . . . . 178 C7
Headland Cres EX1 . . . 178 C7
Headland Cross EX17 . 96 A6
Headland Ct
8 Brixham TQ5 . . . . . . 230 D5
Woolacombe EX34 . . . . . . 7 F8
Headland Gr TQ3 . . . . 219 C1
Headland La EX17 . . . . . 96 A5
Headland Park Rd
TQ3 . . . . 219 C1
Headland Pk PL4 . . . . . 263 A4
Headland Rd TQ2 . . . . 219 E2
Headlands The TQ2 . . 219 E2
Headlands View Ave
EX34 . . . . 1 B1
Headless Cross TQ13 112 B6
HEADON 72 C5
Headon Cross EX22 . . . 72 C5
Headon Gdns EX2 . . . . 178 A1
Headson Cross EX20 . . 91 E1
Headstock Rd TA20 . . . 88 E7
Headway Cl TQ14 . . . . 209 D7
Headway Cross Rd
TQ14 . . . . 209 D8
Headway Rise TQ14 . . 209 D8
Head Weir Rd EX15 . . 163 C5
HEALE 4 A3
Heale Down La EX31 . . . 4 A3
Heal Park Cres EX31 . 153 D5
Heal's Field EX13 . . . . 167 F7
Healy Ct 9 PL2 . . . . . . 247 F4
Healy Pl PL2 . . . . 247 F4
Heanton Cl EX33 . . . . . 152 E6
Heanton Ct TQ1 . . . . . . 220 C4
Heanton Hill EX33 . . . . 152 F4
Heanton Hill La EX31 . . 15 E6
Heanton Lea EX31 . . . . . 15 E6
HEANTON
PUNCHARDON 15 E6
Heanton St EX33 . . . . . 152 D5
Heanton Terr PL10 . . . 252 E6
Heard Ave EX8 . . . . 202 E8
Heard Cl EX39 . . . . 22 E3
Hearl Rd PL12 . . . . 242 B3
Hearson Cross EX32 . . . 28 B8
Heasley Cross EX36 . . . 19 C3
Heasley La EX36 . . . . . . 19 D3
HEASLEY MILL 19 D3
Heasley Mill Cross
EX36 . . . . 19 D3
HEATH 175 D6
Heathayne Cross
EX24 . . . . 102 F5
Heathbrook Mews
EX4 . . . . 174 C2
Heath Cl
Heathfield TQ12 . . . . . . 123 B2
15 Honiton EX14 . . . . . . 85 C2
Heathcoat Prim Sch
EX16 . . . . 161 B3
Heathcoat Sq EX16 . . . 161 C4
Heathcoat Way EX16 . 161 F5
Heath Comm EX13 . . . . 87 E6
Heath Cross
Cheriton Fitzpaine
EX16 . . . . 63 A5
Spreyton EX17 . . . . 96 A8
Tedburn St Mary EX4 . . . 98 C5
Heath Ct
Brixham TQ5 . . . . 230 E6
1 Totnes TQ9 . . . . 223 C5
Heather Cl
Exeter EX1 . . . . 178 B6
9 Honiton EX14 . . . . 85 C2
Newton Abbot TQ12 . . . 206 F4
Okehampton EX20 . . . . 170 B5
Seaton EX12 . . . . 192 B7
Tavistock PL19 . . . . 171 D4
Teignmouth TQ14 . . . . . 210 B7
8 Tiverton EX16 . . . . . . 161 F6
Heatherdale EX8 . . . . . 202 C6
Heatherdene TQ13 . . . 180 C7
Heather Est TQ12 . . . . 180 F3
Heatherfield EX6 . . . . . 98 C4
Heather Grange
EX11 . . . . 168 D4
Heather Pk TQ10 . . . . . 135 A3
Heathers The
Okehampton EX20 . . . . 170 D6
Plymouth PL6 . . . . 245 D7
Heather Terr PL20 . . . 128 A8
Heatherton Park Ho
TA4 . . . . 52 E8
Heather Way TQ5 . . . . 230 A4
Heather Wlk PL21 . . . . 237 D4
HEATHFIELD 180 F2
Heathfield Cl TQ13 . . . 180 C5
Heathfield Cross
Axmouth DT7 . . . . 193 D8
Cornwood PL21 . . . . . . 133 B3
Heathfield TQ12 . . . . . . 123 B2
Modbury PL21 . . . . 137 E2
Poltimore EX4 . . . . 174 C7
Woodbury Salterton
EX5 . . . . 184 A7
Heathfield Ind Est
TQ12 . . . . 180 F3
Heathfieldlake Hill
Chudleigh TQ12 . . . . 123 F7
Chudleigh TQ13 . . . . 123 F7
Heathfield Mdw
TQ13 . . . . 180 D5
Heathfield Pk PL20 . . . 127 A3
Heathfield Rd
Bideford EX39 . . . . 157 C1
Cornwood PL21 . . . . . . 133 C2
Denbury TQ12 . . . . 211 A6
Plymouth PL4 . . . . 249 B3
Heathfield Terr
Bovey Tracey TQ13 . . . . 180 C6
Denbury TQ12 . . . . 211 A6
Heath Hill TQ12 . . . . . . 123 B2
Heath La
Cheriton Fitzpaine
EX16 . . . . 63 A6
Hollocombe EX19 . . . . . . 58 F5
Tedburn St Mary EX4,
EX6 . . . . 98 C4
Heathlands Ct TQ14 . . 210 A8
Heathlands Rise
TQ14 . . . . 210 A8
Heathland View EX38 . 40 D1
Heathpark Ind Est
EX14 . . . . 166 A5
Heathpark Way 13
EX14 . . . . 85 C2
Heath Pk
Brixham TQ5 . . . . 230 E5
Newton Abbot TQ12 . . . 208 A1
Heath Rd
Brixham TQ5 . . . . 230 E5
Dunsford EX6 . . . . 112 F7
Exeter EX2 . . . . 178 B5
Spreyton EX17 . . . . 95 F8
Heath Rise TQ5 . . . . . . 230 E5
HEATHSTOCK 87 A6
Heath Terr PL18 . . . . . 125 C5
Heatree Cl TQ14 . . . . . 210 B8
Heatree Cross TQ13 . . 121 D7
Heaviside Cl TQ2 . . . . . 214 B3
HEAVITREE 178 B6
Heavitree Gallows
EX1 . . . . 178 C5
Heavitree Pk EX1 . . . . 178 A5
Heavitree Rd
Exeter EX1 . . . . 177 E6
Kingsand PL10 . . . . 253 A2
Hebditch Cl TQ13 . . . . 180 E7
Heberton Cl EX5 . . . . . . 99 E8
Heckpen View EX15 . . . 66 D6
Hectors Cl EX19 . . . . . . 57 F7
Heddeswell Cross
TQ7 . . . . 143 E2
HEDDON 29 B7
Heddon Cross
Heddon EX32 . . . . 29 A7
Milton Damerel EX22 . . . 54 C5
Hederman Cl EX5 . . . . . 82 B5
Hedge Cross EX20 . . . 107 C4
Hedge Field Cl EX14 . . . 85 C2
Hedgend Rd EX14 . . . . . 86 B5
Hedgerow Cl
Crediton EX17 . . . . 165 E6
Plymouth PL6 . . . . 245 E8
Hedgerows The PL12 242 B3
Hedingham Cl PL7 . . . 251 C4
Hedingham Gdns
PL6 . . . . 245 B7
Heggadon Cl EX5 . . . . . 83 A7
Heiffers La EX16 . . . . . . 47 A5
Heights The PL19 . . . . 171 A6
Heirland Cross TQ7 . . 143 D3
HELE
Bradninch 82 F5
Ilfracombe 150 F6
Torquay 219 F8
Hele Almshouses
PL9 . . . . 140 E8
Hele Barton Cross
EX17 . . . . 61 D6
Helebridge Rd EX23 . . . 70 A6
Hele Cl
Barnstaple EX31 . . . . . . 154 A3
Bickleigh PL6 . . . . 132 A5
Torquay TQ2 . . . . 213 F1
Hele Corn Mill*
EX34 . . . . 150 E5
Hele Cross
Ashburton TQ13 . . . . . . 130 E5
Bradworthy EX22 . . . . . . 38 E4
Cornwood PL21 . . . . . . 133 D4
King's Nympton EX37 . . . 44 D7
St Giles on t H PL15 . . . . 90 B3
Torquay TQ2 . . . . 213 F1
Hele Gdns PL7 . . . . . . 251 A4
Hele Hill EX17 . . . . 61 C5
Hele La
Barnstaple EX31 . . . . . . 154 A3
Bickington EX31 . . . . . . 154 A3
Frithelstock Stone EX38 . 40 F5
Roborough PL6 . . . . 241 F2
Shaugh Prior PL6, PL7 . 132 A6
Hele Lane Hill EX17 . . . 61 D6
Hele Manor La EX16 . . . 33 E3
Helena Pl 7 EX8 . . . . . 202 A6
Helens Mead Cl TQ2 . 214 A4
Helens Mead Rd TQ2 214 A4
Hele Park TQ12 . . . . . . 206 C5
Hele Rd
Bradninch EX5 . . . . 82 F6
Exeter EX4 . . . . 261 A4
Kingsteignton TQ12 . . . 123 E1
Torquay TQ2 . . . . 213 F1
Torquay TQ2 . . . . 219 E8
Hele Rise EX31 . . . . . . 154 A3
Hele Sq EX5 . . . . 82 F5
Hele's Sch PL7 . . . . . . 250 C6
Hele's Terr PL4 . . . . . . 249 B2
Helford Dr TQ4 . . . . . . 229 B8
Helford Wlk TQ4 . . . . . 229 B8
Heligan Dr TQ3 . . . . . . 225 E8
Hellevoetsluis Way
TQ3 . . . . 218 F4
Hellier Cl EX14 . . . . . . 166 A4
Hellinghayes La EX16 . 46 C3
Hellings Gdns EX5 . . . 175 C7
Hellings Parks La
EX5 . . . . 175 E4
Helmdon Rise TQ2 . . . 219 B8
Helmers Way TQ7 . . . . 145 A1
Helston Cl TQ3 . . . . . . 225 F7
HELTOR 112 D6
Heltor Bsns Pk TQ12 . 180 F4
Hembury Cock Hill
TQ11 . . . . 236 A7
Hembury Cotts TQ9 . . 131 E1
Hembury Cross
Holbeton PL8 . . . . 141 F8
Stibb Cross EX38 . . . . . . 40 C4
Hembury Fort* EX14 . . 84 F6
Hembury Fort Cross
EX14 . . . . 84 E5
Hembury Pk TQ11 . . . . 236 B7
HEMERDON 251 D7
Hemerdon Hts PL7 . . . 251 A6
Hemerdon La PL7 . . . . 251 C8
Hemerdon Way PL7 . . 250 D6
Hems Brook Ct TQ2 . . 219 B8
HEMSFORD 216 F4
Hems La TQ9 . . . . 216 D7
Hemsworthy Gate
TQ13 . . . . 121 E3
HEMYOCK 67 C8
Hemyock Castle*
EX15 . . . . 67 B8
Hemyock Prim Sch
EX15 . . . . 67 B8
Hemyock Rd EX15 . . . . . 66 E8
Henacre Rd TQ7 . . . . . 258 D5
Henacroft Cross EX19 . 58 B3
Henbury Cl TQ1 . . . . . . 220 B6
Henceford Cross EX17 62 A6
Henderbarrow Cross
EX21 . . . . 73 E1
Henders Cnr 6 PL3 . . 248 F6
Henderson Pl PL2 . . . . 247 F6
Hendon Cross EX16 . . . 50 B8
Hendwell Cl PL6 . . . . . 244 E6
Heneaton Sq EX2 . . . . 182 B8
HENFORD 90 C5
Henlake Cl PL21 . . . . . 237 B6
Henley Cl EX13 . . . . 88 B7
Henley Dr PL5 . . . . 244 C7
Henley Ho TQ7 . . . . . . 143 A1
Henley Rd EX8 . . . . 202 C7
Hennapyn Rd TQ2 . . . . 219 E3
HENNOCK 123 B7
Hennock Com Prim Sch
TQ13 . . . . 123 B7
Hennock Ct EX2 . . . . . 181 D8
Hennock Rd TQ4 . . . . . 225 F2
Hennock Rd Central
EX2 . . . . 177 C1
Hennock Road E EX2 177 D1
Hennock Road N
EX2 . . . . 177 C2
Henrietta Pl 7 EX8 . . 202 A7
Henrietta Rd 8 EX8 . . 202 A7
Henry Avent Gdns
PL9 . . . . 256 C8
Henry Cl PL21 . . . . 136 B6
Henry Gdns EX11 . . . . 169 C3
Henry Lewis Cl 7 EX5 . 99 F8
Henry's Run 9 EX5 . . . 99 A6
Henry's Way DT7 . . . . . 260 E4
Hensbury La PL20 . . . . 239 F4
Hensford Mews EX7 . . 200 C3
Hensford Rd EX7 . . . . . 200 C2
Hensleigh Dr EX2 . . . . 177 E5
Hensleigh Rd EX16 . . . . 63 F7
Henson Ct EX20 . . . . 77 C4
Hensons Dr EX16 . . . . . . 51 A3
Hen St EX5 . . . . 83 A7
Henstill La EX17 . . . . . . 79 F7
HENSTRIDGE 3 A1
Henty Ave EX7 . . . . 204 F7
Henty Cl EX7 . . . . 204 F8
Heppenstall Rd EX32 155 B6
Heraldry Way EX2 . . . . 178 D4
Herbert Ho TA22 . . . . . . 33 D6
Herbert Pl PL2 . . . . 247 E4
Herbert Rd
Exeter EX1 . . . . 177 F7
Salcombe TQ8 . . . . 259 D4
Torquay TQ2 . . . . 219 D4
Herbert St PL2 . . . . 247 E4
Hercules Rd
Plymouth PL9 . . . . 256 D8
Sherford PL7 . . . . 250 F1
Herdicott Cross EX22 . . 71 F2
Hereford Cl EX8 . . . . . 196 D4
Hereford Rd
Exeter EX4 . . . . 176 D6
Plymouth PL5 . . . . 244 B5
Heritage Cl PL12 . . . . . 242 C3
Heritage Ct 15 EX14 . . 166 C6
Heritage Pk PL19 . . . . 171 D6
Heritage Rd EX1 . . . . . 178 D6
Heritage Way
Brixham TQ5 . . . . 230 E5
Sidford EX10 . . . . 188 B8
Hermes Ave EX16 . . . . 161 E3
Hermitage Ct 1 PL4 . . 248 E4
Hermitage Rd
Dartmouth TQ6 . . . . 233 D4
Ilfracombe EX34 . . . . . . 150 B6
Plymouth PL3 . . . . 248 E5
Hermitage The 1
EX34 . . . . 150 B5
Hermosa Gdns 5
TQ14 . . . . 210 B5
Hermosa Rd TQ14 . . . . 210 B5
Hernaford Cross TQ9 139 B6
Hernaford Rd TQ9 . . . 139 C6
Hern La PL8 . . . . 257 F4
Heron Cl PL10 . . . . 252 F6
Heron Cres EX12 . . . . . 192 C5
Heron Ct
Barnstaple EX32 . . . . . . 155 E4
Exmouth EX8 . . . . 202 C6
Heron Ind Units EX2 . 178 E5
Heron Rd
Drakewalls PL18 . . . . . . 125 C5
Exeter, Middle Moor
EX2 . . . . 176 D3
Exeter, Sowton EX2 . . . . 178 E5
Honiton EX14 . . . . 166 B4
Herons Brook EX20 . . 170 A6
Herons Reach
Charleton TQ7 . . . . 258 F2
Herons Reach *continued*
West Charleton TQ7 . . . 144 C1
Heron Way
Cullompton EX15 . . . . . 163 B2
Kingsteignton TQ12 . . . 207 C8
Torquay TQ2 . . . . 213 C3
Herschel Gdns PL5 . . . 243 E1
Herschell Rd EX4 . . . . 177 E8
Hertland Wlk PL2 . . . . 248 A7
Hescane Pk EX6 . . . . . . 97 B4
Hesketh Cres TQ1 . . . . 220 D3
Hesketh Mews TQ1 . . 220 D3
Hesketh Rd TQ1 . . . . . 220 D3
Hessary Dr PL6 . . . . . . 241 C1
Hessary Terr PL20 . . . . 128 A8
Hessary View
Princetown PL20 . . . . . . 120 B8
Saltash PL12 . . . . 242 E4
Tavistock PL19 . . . . 171 B6
Hestow Rd TQ12 . . . . . 123 F1
Hetling Cl PL1 . . . . 262 B3
Hewer's Row PL4 . . . . 263 A3
Hewetson Wy EX39 . . . 156 D1
Hewett Cl TQ12 . . . . . . 208 A3
Hewitt Cl PL12 . . . . 242 C1
Hexdown Barns TQ7 . 142 F3
Hexham Pl PL2 . . . . . . 248 A8
Hexton Hill Rd PL9 . . . 255 B6
Hexton Quay PL9 . . . . . 255 C6
HEXWORTHY 129 B7
Hexworthy Ave EX4 . . 176 E8
Heybrook Ave PL5 . . . . 243 D1
HEYBROOK BAY 140 B8
Heybrook Dr PL9 . . . . . 140 A7
Heydon's La EX10 . . . . 188 A4
Heyridge Mdw EX15 . . 163 B1
Heyswood Ave EX32 . . 155 C2
Heywood Cl
Hartland EX39 . . . . 22 E3
Torquay TQ2 . . . . 219 E7
Heywood Cross EX18 . . 59 D5
Heywood Dr EX6 . . . . . 201 A8
Heywood Est TQ12 . . . 207 D6
Heywood Rd EX39 . . . . 156 F5
Heywoods Cl 11
TQ14 . . . . 210 C5
Heywoods Rd TQ14 . . 210 C5
Hibernia Terr PL5 . . . . 247 E8
Hickory Cl EX14 . . . . . . 166 E5
Hickory Dr PL7 . . . . . . 251 B5
Hick's La PL4 . . . . 263 A2
Hide Market Rd
EX15 . . . . 162 C5
Hides Rd EX10 . . . . 188 C8
Hidewood La EX15 . . . . 52 F1
Hiern Dr EX32 . . . . 155 A2
Hierns La EX34 . . . . . . 150 C6
High Acre Dr PL21 . . . 237 A6
HIGHAMPTON 74 C7
Highampton Com Prim
Sch EX21 . . . . 74 C7
Highampton Cross
EX21 . . . . 74 C7
Highaton Head Cross
EX36 . . . . 32 C4
High Bank
Exeter EX4 . . . . 178 B8
West Hill EX10 . . . . 100 A4
West Hill EX11 . . . . 168 D3
Highbank Cl PL19 . . . . 171 A4
Highbarrow Cross
EX22 . . . . 54 A4
HIGH BICKINGTON 43 B7
High Bickington CE Prim
Sch EX37 . . . . 43 B7
High Bolham EX16 . . . . 33 C1
HIGH BRAY 18 F5
High Bray EX32 . . . . 18 F5
Highbridge Ct PL7 . . . . 250 E5
HIGH BULLEN 42 B7
High Bullen EX5 . . . . . . 82 B6
High Bullen Cross
EX36 . . . . 19 E1
High Bullen La EX35 . . . . 5 B3
Highbury Cres PL7 . . . 250 D7
Highbury Hill EX39 . . . 157 A8
Highbury Pk EX8 . . . . . 196 A1
Highbury Rd
Barnstaple EX32 . . . . . . 155 C3
Torquay TQ1 . . . . 220 B6
High Cl TQ13 . . . . 180 E7
Highclere Gdns PL6 . . 245 B8
Highcliff Ct EX7 . . . . . . 204 E6
Highcliffe Cl
Lympstone EX8 . . . . 195 D4
Seaton EX12 . . . . 191 F6
Highcliffe Cres EX12 . 191 F6
Highcliffe Ct EX8 . . . . 195 D4
Highcliffe Mews TQ4 226 C4
Highcliff Rd DT7 . . . . . 260 C3
Highclyffe Ct EX12 . . . 191 F6
Highcombe La PL9 . . . 255 C4
High Croft EX36 . . . . 19 C2
High Creek Cross
EX10 . . . . 188 F8
Highcroft EX4 . . . . 173 A1
Highcroft Ct EX4 . . . . . 173 A1
Highcroft Pk TQ12 . . . . 123 E7
High Cross
Bampton EX16 . . . . 34 A1
14 Combe Martin EX34 . . . 3 A3
High Cross Ho* TQ9 . 216 A1
Highcross Rd EX4 . . . . 177 C8
Highdown Cross
EX39 . . . . 23 A4
Higher Aboveway
EX6 . . . . 182 B3
Higher Aller La TQ13 . 122 E6
Higher Alston Farm
TQ5 . . . . 229 D3
Higher Anderton Rd
PL10 . . . . 252 F5
HIGHER ASHTON 113 D3
Higher Audley Ave
Torquay TQ2 . . . . 219 F8
Torquay TQ2 . . . . 220 A8
Higher Axmouth Cotts
EX12 . . . . 192 F6
Higher Barley Mount
EX4 . . . . 176 E5
HIGHER BATSON 259 C6
Higher Beara Cross
TQ11 . . . . 236 F4
Higher Bedlands EX9 197 F2
Higher Beetham TA20 69 D7
Higher Bibbery TQ13 180 E7
Higher Birch Dr 1
EX1 . . . . 178 E3
HIGHER BLAGDON . . . 225 A7
Higher Blagdon La
TQ3 . . . . 225 A7
Higher Borough TQ7 149 A4
Higher Brand La
EX14 . . . . 166 C4
Higher Brimley Rd
8 Teignmouth TQ14 . . . 209 F8
Teignmouth TQ14 . . . . . 210 C5
HIGHER BRIXHAM . . . 230 B3
Higher Broad Oak Rd
EX11 . . . . 168 D2
Higher Broad Pk
TQ6 . . . . 233 D3
Higher Brook Mdw 1
EX10 . . . . 101 B1
Higher Brook Pk
PL21 . . . . 237 A5
Higher Brownston Cross
PL21 . . . . 138 A4
Higher Buckeridge Rd
TQ14 . . . . 210 B7
Higher Budleigh Mdw
TQ12 . . . . 206 F3
Higher Bulkamore Cross
TQ10 . . . . 135 E5
Higher Bull Ring
EX15 . . . . 163 C3
Higher Bulworthy Cross
EX16 . . . . 47 E4
Higher Bulworthy La
EX16 . . . . 47 E4
HIGHER
BURROWTON 99 A8
Higher Buzzacott La
EX34 . . . . 3 B3
Higher Cadewell La
TQ2 . . . . 219 C8
Higher Cheglinch La
EX34 . . . . 8 F6
HIGHER CHERITON . . . 84 E3
Higher Church St 6
EX32 . . . . 155 A4
Higher Churchway
PL9 . . . . 256 A7
Higher Clevelands
Northam EX39 . . . . 156 F6
Northam EX39 . . . . 157 A6
HIGHER CLOVELLY . . . 23 D2
Higher Collaton Cross
TQ7 . . . . 147 F6
Higher Colleybrook
TQ13 . . . . 124 B4
Higher Combe La
TA24 . . . . 21 E8
Higher Combe Rd
TA22 . . . . 33 C8
Higher Commons
TQ3 . . . . 214 D8
HIGHER COMPTON . . 249 A6
Higher Compton Barton
TQ3 . . . . 218 E6
Higher Compton Rd
PL3 . . . . 248 F6
Higher Contour Rd
TQ6 . . . . 234 B3
Higher Coombe Dr
6 Teignmouth TQ14 . . . 209 E8
Teignmouth TQ14 . . . . . 210 A7
Higher Coombses
TA20 . . . . 88 D8
Higher Copythorne
TQ5 . . . . 230 A4
Higher Cotteylands
EX16 . . . . 161 B3
Higher Cross EX15 . . . . 51 C1
Higher Cross Rd
EX31 . . . . 154 B4
Higher Davis Cl EX32 . . 17 F6
HIGHER DEAN 135 C7
Higher Dean TQ11 . . . 135 C7
Higher Dean La EX34 . . . 3 B3
Higher Doats Hayne La
EX13 . . . . 103 D5
Higher Down EX6 . . . . 194 D3
Higher Down Pk EX14 . 85 C2
Higher Downs Rd
TQ1 . . . . 220 C8
Higher Dr EX7 . . . . 204 F8
Higher East St EX36 . . . 30 D8
Higher Edginswell La
TQ2 . . . . 219 B8
Higher Efford Rd
PL3 . . . . 249 B5
Higher Elmwood
EX31 . . . . 154 C3
Higher Elstone Cross
EX18 . . . . 44 D3

Higher Erith Rd TQ1. .220 D4
Higher Exeter Rd
 TQ14. . . . . .124 E2
Higher Exwick Hill
 EX4. . . . . .176 E7
Higher Ferry Slip 233 F4
Higher Forches Cross
 EX17. . . . . .60 D4
Higher Fortescue
 EX10. . . . . .188 D7
Higher French Pk
 TQ12. . . . . .206 F3
Higher Furlong Rd
 EX5. . . . . .99 C6
Higher Furzeham Rd
 TQ5. . . . . .230 C6
HIGHER GABWELL. . . .214 B7
Higher Gn TQ10. . . . . .135 A2
Higher Green Cross
 TQ7. . . . . .145 C4
Higher Greenhead
 EX10. . . . . .101 A2
Higher Greenway La
 Sidmouth EX10. . . . . .187 D8
 Sidmouth EX10. . . . . .187 E7
Higher Gunstone
 EX39. . . . . .158 E1
Higher Hayes La TQ5 229 F5
Higher Hendham Barns
 TQ7. . . . . .138 E1
Higher Hewish La EX31. 9 D4
Higher Hill View
 EX10. . . . . .188 A5
Higher Ho EX38. . . . . . .42 B5
Higher Holcombe Cl
 TQ14. . . . . .210 C7
Higher Holcombe Dr
 TQ14. . . . . .210 C8
Higher Holcombe Rd
 Holcombe EX7. . . . . .204 B3
 Teignmouth TQ14. . . .210 C8
Higher Hoopern La
 EX4. . . . . .173 C1
Higher Island TQ9. . . .139 E2
HIGHER KEATON. 237 D1
Higher Kelly PL18. . . . .125 D3
Higher King's Ave
 EX4. . . . . .177 D8
Higher Kingsdown Rd
 TQ14. . . . . .209 D7
Higher Kinsman's Dale
 TQ13. . . . . .111 F5
Higher La
 Axmouth EX12. . . . . .192 E7
 Axmouth EX12. . . . . .193 A6
 Plymouth PL1. . . . . . .262 C2
 Sampford Courtenay
 EX20. . . . . .76 D5
Higher Lane Cl EX12 .192 D7
Higher Ley EX17. . . . . . .60 B3
Higher Lincombe Rd
 TQ1. . . . . .220 E3
Higher Longford Cvn Site
 PL19. . . . . .117 F1
Higher Loughborough
 EX16. . . . . .161 B5
Higher Manor Rd
 TQ5. . . . . .230 C5
Higher Manor Terr **1**
 TQ3. . . . . .226 A5
Higher Marley Rd
 EX8. . . . . .196 D4
Higher Maudlin St **7**
 EX32. . . . . .155 A6
Higher Maunders Hill
 Otterton EX9. . . . . . .198 E5
 Otterton EX9. . . . . . .198 E7
Higher Mdw EX5. . . . . .99 A5
Higher Mdws
 Beer EX12. . . . . .191 D5
 High Bickington EX37 . .43 B7
Higher Mead EX15. . . . .67 B8
HIGHER
 METCOMBE. 168 D1
Higher Mill DT7. . . . . .260 D4
Higher Mill Flats
 DT7. . . . . .260 D4
Higher Millhayes EX15 52 B1
Higher Mill La
 Buckfast TQ11. . . . . .236 B7
 Cullompton EX15. . . .163 C3
Higher Mogworthy Cross
 EX16. . . . . .47 D4
Higher Moor TQ10 . . .135 B1
Highermoor Cross
 EX22. . . . . .53 B1
Higher Moor Sq **4**
 EX16. . . . . .161 F6
Higher Mowles PL3 .249 B6
HIGHER MUDDIFORD. . .9 D1
Higher Newclose La
 EX31. . . . . .16 B6
Higher Park Cl PL7. . .251 E3
Higher Park Rd EX33 152 E5
Higher Penn TQ5. . . . .230 D3
Higher Pk TQ7. . . . . . .149 A3
Higher Polsham Rd
 TQ3. . . . . .226 B7
Higher Port View
 PL12. . . . . .242 F2
HIGHER
 PRESTACOTT. 90 F7
Higher Preston Cross
 TQ12. . . . . .123 D1
Higher Queens Terr
 TQ1. . . . . .220 B5
Higher Rake La TQ7. .143 F6

Higher Raleigh Rd
 EX31. . . . . .155 A7
Higher Ramshill La
 TQ3. . . . . .225 C8
Higher Ranscombe Rd
 TQ5. . . . . .230 D4
Higher Rd
 Crediton EX17. . . . . .165 B6
 Fremington EX31. . . .153 E5
 Woodbury Salterton
 EX5. . . . . .184 B7
Higher Redgate
 EX16. . . . . .161 D5
Higher Ridgeway
 EX11. . . . . .169 E4
Higher Ringmore Rd
 TQ14. . . . . .209 D4
Higher Roborough **8**
 TQ13. . . . . .131 A5
Higher Rocombe
 TQ3. . . . . .214 B5
HIGHER ROSCOMBE
 BARTON. 214 A6
Higher Row PL10 . . . .253 A2
Higher Rydons TQ5 . .230 A4
Higher Sackery TQ12 208 D4
Higher Shapter Cl
 EX3. . . . . .182 F4
Higher Shapter St
 EX3. . . . . .182 F4
Higher Shippon EX6. . .97 B4
HIGHER SLADE. 1 E3
Higher Slade Rd
 EX34. . . . . .150 A2
Higher Spring Gdns
 EX11. . . . . .169 E3
Higher St
 Brixham TQ5. . . . . . .230 C5
 Cullompton EX15. . . .163 C4
 Dartmouth TQ6. . . . .233 F3
 Dittisham TQ6. . . . . .228 B2
 Hatherleigh EX20. . . . .75 C7
 Kingswear TQ6. . . . .234 A3
Higher Stert Terr
 PL4. . . . . .263 C3
Higher Stockley Mead
 EX20. . . . . .170 F6
Higher Summerlands
 EX1. . . . . .261 C3
HIGHER TALE. 84 A4
Higher Tamar Terr
 PL18. . . . . .125 D7
Higher Thorn Cl
 EX33. . . . . .152 D5
HIGHER TOWN. 236 A5
Higher Town
 Malborough TQ7. . . .147 E6
 Sampford Peverell EX16 50 C1
Higher Tuckers Pk
 EX22. . . . . .38 E1
Higher Union La TQ2 220 A5
Higher Union Rd
 TQ7. . . . . .258 C5
Higher Venn Cross
 EX32. . . . . .17 A1
Higher Warberry Rd
 TQ1. . . . . .220 D5
Higher Warborough Rd
 TQ5. . . . . .229 B6
HIGHER WARCOMBE. . .1 B2
Higher Warcombe Cross
 TQ7. . . . . .144 A5
Higher Warren Rd
 TQ7. . . . . .258 E3
HIGHER WAY EX10 . .187 A8
HIGHER WEAR. 178 A1
Higher Wear Rd EX2 .182 C7
Higher Weaver Cross
 EX15. . . . . .83 E7
Higher Weir TQ9. . . . .223 B7
Higher Wellbrook St
 EX16. . . . . .154 D3
Higher Well Rd TQ9 .228 A8
Higher Westlake Rd
 4 Barnstaple EX31. . .154 A2
 Barnstaple EX31. . . .154 B2
Higher Westonfields
 TQ9. . . . . .223 E5
Higher Wlk PL10. . . . .253 E5
Higher Woodfield Rd
 TQ1. . . . . .220 D7
Higher Woodford La
 PL7. . . . . .250 C7
Higher Woodway Cl
 TQ14. . . . . .210 C7
Higher Woodway Rd
 TQ14. . . . . .210 B8
HIGHER
 WOOLBROOK. 187 F7
Higher Woolbrook Pk
 EX10. . . . . .187 F7
HIGHER
 YALBERTON. 225 C3
Higher Yalberton Rd
 TQ4. . . . . .225 D3
Higher Yannon Dr
 TQ14. . . . . .210 A6
Highfield
 Honiton EX14. . . . . . .166 B5
 Lapford EX17. . . . . . . .60 D3
 Northam EX39. . . . . .156 F6
 Sidmouth EX10. . . . . .188 A5
 Topsham EX3. . . . . . .182 F7
Highfield Cl
 Barnstaple EX32. . . . .155 B4
 Brixham TQ5. . . . . . .230 A4
 High Bickington EX37 . .43 B7
 Plymouth PL3. . . . . . .249 C5

Highfield Cres TQ3. . .225 E6
Highfield Ct **3** EX8 . .202 B6
Highfield Dr
 Kingsbridge TQ7. . . . .258 D4
 2 Wembury PL9. . . . .140 D8
Highfield Gdns EX34. . . .3 A3
Highfield La EX8. . . . . .202 B6
Highfield Pk PL12. . . . .242 B3
Highfield Rd
 Dunkeswell EX14. . . . .67 C1
 Ilfracombe EX34. . . . .150 C5
Highfield Terr
 Beer EX12. . . . . .191 D5
 2 Bishop's Tawton
 EX32. . . . . .16 E1
 4 Bittaford PL21. . . .137 C7
 8 Ilfracombe EX34. . .150 C5
Highfield View TQ12 .244 E8
High Gate EX16. . . . . . .62 F6
Highglen Dr PL7. . . . . .251 B7
Highgow Cl EX31. . . . .154 A2
Highgrove EX31. . . . . .154 D1
Highgrove Pk TQ14 . .210 C7
High House Cl EX7. . . .204 E7
High House La
 Kingsbridge TQ7. . . . .144 B2
 Kingsbridge TQ7. . . . .258 D4
Highland Cl TQ2. . . . . .219 C6
Highland Pk EX15. . . . . .66 A7
Highland Rd TQ2. . . . .219 C5
Highlands
 Ottery St Mary EX11. .169 D3
 Wembury PL9. . . . . . .256 B3
 Yealmpton PL8. . . . . .257 F4
Highlands Pk **9**
 TQ13. . . . . .123 E6
Highland St PL21. . . . .237 D5
Highland Terr
 6 Tiverton EX16. . . . .161 D4
 Uffculme EX15. . . . . . .66 A7
Highland View EX20. .170 C3
High Mdw EX10. . . . . .188 B7
High Mdws EX4. . . . . .176 E5
High Park Cl EX39. . . . .25 D4
High Path TA21. . . . . .160 C7
High Rd PL9. . . . . .140 C8
Highridge Cross EX7. . .45 B7
High School for Girls
 PL4. . . . . .263 A4
High St
 Bampton EX16. . . . . . .34 B1
 Barnstaple EX31. . . . .154 F5
 Bideford EX39. . . . . . .157 A2
 Budleigh Salterton
 EX9. . . . . .199 G2
 Chagford TQ13. . . . . .111 A6
 Clovelly EX39. . . . . . . .23 D3
 Combe Martin EX34. . . .3 A3
 Crediton EX17. . . . . .165 C5
 Cullompton EX15. . . .163 C3
 Dawlish EX7. . . . . . . .204 E6
 Dulverton TA22. . . . . .33 D6
 East Budleigh EX9. . . .198 B6
 Exbourne EX20. . . . . . .76 C4
 Exeter EX4. . . . . .261 B3
 Exmouth EX8. . . . . . .202 A6
 Great Torrington EX38 .159 D5
 Halberton EX16. . . . . .65 A7
 Hatherleigh EX20. . . . .75 C7
 Hemyock EX15. . . . . . .67 B8
 High Bickington EX37. . .43 B7
 Honiton EX14. . . . . . .166 C6
 Ide EX2. . . . . .114 B8
 Ide EX2. . . . . .176 D1
 Ilfracombe EX34. . . . .150 B6
 Kentisbeare EX15. . . . .66 A3
 Kenton EX6. . . . . .194 D3
 Newton Poppleford
 EX10. . . . . .186 E8
 North Tawton EX20. . . .77 C4
 Okehampton EX20. . . .170 B5
 Plymouth, Stonehouse
 PL1. . . . . .248 A2
 Sidford EX10. . . . . . .188 B8
 Sidmouth EX10. . . . . .188 B4
 Silverton EX5. . . . . . . .82 B6
 Stoke Canon EX5. . . . .81 F1
 Stoke Canon EX5. . . .173 F8
 Swimbridge EX32. . . . .28 E8
 Topsham EX3. . . . . . .182 E6
 Totnes TQ9. . . . . . . .223 C5
 Uffculme EX15. . . . . . .66 A7
 Wellington TA21. . . . .160 E6
 Winkleigh EX19. . . . . .58 F3
Highstead Cross EX22 73 C8
Highstone Gr EX8 . . . .195 F5
High Street Prim Sch
 PL1. . . . . .248 A2
High Street & Waterloo
 Street Flats PL1. . . .248 A1
High Trees EX7. . . . . . .204 E7
High View
 Bideford EX39. . . . . . .156 E1
 Feniton EX14. . . . . . . .84 E2
 Sheepwash EX21. . . . . .56 C1
High View Gdns EX8. .202 B7
High View Prim Sch
 PL3. . . . . .249 D6
High View Sch PL3 . .249 C5
High View Terr EX39 .156 C6
High Wall EX31. . . . . .154 E4
High Way EX16. . . . . . .48 D8
Highwaymans Gr EX20 93 B1
HIGHWEEK. 206 F5
Highweek Com Prim Sch
 TQ12. . . . . .207 A3
Highweek Cross EX21 73 E8

Highweek Rd TQ12. . .207 A4
Highweek St TQ12 . . .207 B3
Highweek Village
 Newton Abbot TQ12. .206 F5
 Newton Abbot TQ12. .207 A5
Highweek Way TQ12 .207 B3
Highwell Rd EX12. . . .192 A5
Highwood Grange
 TQ12. . . . . .207 B2
Highworthy Cross
 EX21. . . . . .55 E3
Hilary Cl EX13. . . . . . .167 E6
Hilary Gdns EX13. . . .167 E6
Hill Barton Bsns Pk
 Clyst St Mary EX5. . . .179 F2
 Exeter EX5. . . . . .99 A1
Hill Barton Cl EX1. . . .178 C7
Hill Barton La EX1. . . .178 C7
Hill Barton Rd EX2. . .178 C7
Hillbrook Rd TQ9. . . . .223 E5
Hillbrook Rise **2**
 TQ9. . . . . .223 E5
Hill Budge Terr **8**
 EX17. . . . . .165 C5
Hill Cl
 Exeter EX4. . . . . .173 D1
 Plymouth PL7. . . . . . .250 D4
Hillcliffe Terr **30** EX39 15 A1
Hill Cres EX14. . . . . . .166 D6
Hillcrest
 Cullompton EX15. . . .163 C4
 Ilsington TQ13. . . . . .122 C3
 Oakford EX16. . . . . . . .48 D5
 Ottery St Mary EX11. .169 D3
Hill Crest
 Exminster EX6. . . . . .182 A4
 Kilmington EX13. . . . . .87 C1
 Plymouth PL3. . . . . . .248 E5
 South Tawton EX20. . . .95 B5
 Tiverton EX16. . . . . . .161 B6
Hillcrest Cl
 Plymouth PL7. . . . . . .251 A5
 9 Wembury PL9. . . .140 D8
Hillcrest Dr PL7. . . . . .251 A4
Hillcrest Gdns EX1. . .196 E1
Hillcrest Pk EX4. . . . . .173 C2
Hillcrest Rd
 Barnstaple EX32. . . . .155 B2
 Bideford EX39. . . . . . .26 A4
 Silverton EX5. . . . . . . .82 C6
Hillcroft Terr **5**
 EX39. . . . . .157 A2
Hill Cross
 Cobbaton EX32. . . . . . .28 B5
 Kingsbridge TQ7. . . . .144 B5
Hilldale Rd PL9. . . . . .255 E6
Hilldean Cl PL5. . . . . .244 C7
Hilldown TQ9. . . . . . .223 E5
Hilldown Cross EX17. . .78 D2
Hilldown La EX17. . . . .78 D3
Hilldown Rd EX17. . . . .78 C3
Hill Dr EX8. . . . . .196 B3
Hilldrop Terr TQ1. . . .220 B5
Hiller La EX20. . . . . . .208 B2
HILLERTON. 78 C1
Hillerton Cross EX17. . .78 B1
Hillesdon Rd TQ1. . . .220 B4
HILLFIELD. 232 C3
Hillfield
 South Zeal EX20. . . . . .95 A4
 Stoke Gabriel TQ9. . . .227 F7
Hill Garden Cl **10**
 EX39. . . . . .157 A2
Hill Gdns PL12. . . . . . .239 A2
HILLHEAD. 234 F8
Hillhead
 Colyton EX24. . . . . . .103 A4
 Halberton EX16. . . . . .65 A7
 Noss Mayo PL8. . . . . .140 F6
Hill Head EX37. . . . . . .28 F4
Hillhead Bglws **13**
 EX24. . . . . .103 A4
Hillhead Cross PL21. .137 D7
Hill Head Cross
 Chittlehampton EX37. . .28 F4
 King's Nympton EX37. . .44 C5
Hillhead Pk TQ5. . . . .234 E8
Hillhead Terr EX13. . .167 D5
Hillhouse EX14. . . . . . .69 A3
Hilliers EX19. . . . . .57 F7
Hillingdown Cross
 TQ7. . . . . .143 D1
Hillington EX34. . . . . .150 A4
Hill La
 Chipstable TA4. . . . . . .35 C6
 Exeter EX1. . . . . .178 B7
 Plymouth PL3. . . . . . .248 F7
 Waterrow TA4. . . . . . .35 E5
 Whitestone EX4. . . . . .98 E4
Hillmans Rd TQ12. . . .207 D2
HILLMOOR. 66 E8
Hillmoor Cross EX21. . .73 F7
Hillmorhayes EX6. . . . .96 D1
Hillpark EX39. . . . . . . .40 C7
Hill Park Cl TQ5. . . . . .230 E4
Hill Park Cres PL4. . . .263 A4
Hill Park Mews PL4. . .263 B4
Hill Park Rd
 Brixham TQ5. . . . . . .230 E4
 Newton Abbot TQ12. .206 F4
 Torquay TQ1. . . . . . . .220 A4
Hill Park Terr TQ4. . . .226 C5
Hill Path PL5. . . . . . . .243 F5
Hill Pk
 Ashprington TQ9. . . . .139 F8
 Kellaton TQ7. . . . . . .149 C6
Hill Rd
 Bondleigh EX20. . . . . .77 C7

Hill Rd *continued*
 Lyme Regis DT7. . . . .260 D3
 Newton Abbot TQ12. .207 B2
Hillrise TQ5. . . . . .229 B5
Hill Rise EX1. . . . . . . .178 C7
Hillrise (Patha) TQ5. .229 B5
Hill Rise Rd DT7. . . . .260 D3
Hillsborough
 2 Plymouth PL4. . . .248 F4
 Torquay TQ1. . . . . . . .220 B4
Hillsborough Ave
 EX4. . . . . .261 B4
Hillsborough Cross
 EX22. . . . . .71 C7
Hillsborough Nature
 Reserve ★ EX34. . . . .150 E6
Hillsborough Park Rd
 EX34. . . . . .150 E5
Hillsborough Rd
 Ilfracombe EX34. . . . . .2 A4
 Ilfracombe EX34. . . . .150 D5
Hillsborough Terr **15**
 EX34. . . . . .150 C6
Hillsborough Terr Mews
 16 EX34. . . . . .150 C6
Hillsdunne Rd PL3 . . .248 E6
HILLSIDE. 135 A3
Hillside
 Bittaford PL21. . . . . .137 C8
 Branscombe EX12. . . .190 B5
 14 Colyton EX24. . . . .103 A4
 George Nympton EX36. .30 A2
 Honiton EX14. . . . . . . .85 E5
 Newton Poppleford
 EX10. . . . . .186 D8
 Northleigh EX24. . . . .102 B6
 Payhembury EX14. . . . .84 C4
 Rawridge EX14. . . . . . .68 C1
 Sidbury EX10. . . . . . .101 B2
 South Brent TQ10. . . .135 A3
 Southleigh EX24. . . . .102 C4
 Talaton EX5. . . . . .84 B1
Hill Side PL7. . . . . . . .133 B2
Hillside Ave
 Exeter EX4. . . . . .261 B4
 Plymouth PL4. . . . . . .248 D4
 Saltash PL12. . . . . . . .242 F3
Hillside Cl
 Buckland Monachorum
 PL20. . . . . .126 C3
 South Brent TQ10. . . .135 A3
 Teignmouth TQ14. . . .124 E1
Hillside Cotts
 Abbotskerswell
 TQ12. . . . . .212 A6
 Noss Mayo PL8. . . . . .140 F6
Hillside Cres PL9. . . . .255 F8
Hillside Cross EX21. . . .72 F4
Hill Side Cross EX36. . .45 F5
Hillside Ct TQ11. . . . .236 C5
Hillside Dr
 Kingsbridge TQ7. . . . .258 D4
 Okehampton EX20. . . .170 E6
 Yealmpton PL8. . . . . .257 F3
Hillside Ind Units
 EX32. . . . . .155 F1
Hillside Pk TQ4. . . . . .224 F5
Hillside Rd
 Brixham TQ5. . . . . . .230 E4
 Ilfracombe EX34. . . . .150 E5
 Paignton TQ3. . . . . . .225 F7
 Saltash PL12. . . . . . . .242 F3
 Sidmouth EX10. . . . . .188 C4
Hillside Terr
 4 Bideford EX39. . . . .157 A2
 Kingswear TQ6. . . . . .234 A3
 2 Paignton TQ3. . . . .226 A6
Hillside Way PL8. . . . .136 A2
Hill's La EX14. . . . . . . .86 C5
Hill St PL4. . . . . .263 A3
Hills The EX10. . . . . . .188 B5
Hills View
 Barnstaple EX32. . . . .155 A5
 Braunton EX33. . . . . .152 D6
Hill The EX13. . . . . . . .87 C1
Hilltop TQ7. . . . . .142 F6
Hill Top EX31. . . . . . .153 E6
Hilltop Cotts
 Brixton PL8. . . . . . . .257 A5
 Combe PL8. . . . . .256 F5
Hilltop Cross EX11. . .153 E5
Hill Top Crest PL5. . . .243 E4
Hilltop Mdw TQ12. . .207 D2
Hill Top Rd EX39. . . . .156 E4
Hilltown Cross
 Chittlehampton EX37. . .29 B2
 Okehampton EX20. . . .93 E5
 Rackenford EX16. . . . .47 D2
 Warkleigh EX37. . . . . .31 C5
Hilltown La
 Chawleigh EX18. . . . . .59 F5
 Northlew EX20. . . . . . .74 E2
Hill View
 Buckland Monachorum
 PL20. . . . . .126 C3
 Ottery St Mary EX11. .169 D3
 Sidmouth EX10. . . . . .188 B5
Hill View Terr **4**
 TQ1. . . . . .220 B5
Hillway La EX1. . . . . .178 C7
Hillyfield Rd EX1. . . . .178 C7
Hilly Gardens Rd
 TQ1. . . . . .214 B1
Hilly Head TA21. . . . .160 B5

Hillymead EX12. . . . . .192 B6
Hilton Ave PL5. . . . . .244 D1
Hilton Cres TQ3. . . . . .219 C1
Hilton Dr TQ3. . . . . . .219 C1
Hilton Park Homes
 EX33. . . . . .152 C5
Hilton Rd
 Marhamchurch EX23. . .70 A6
 Monkleigh EX39. . . . . .40 F7
 Newton Abbot TQ12. .207 C5
Hil Top Rd **4** EX1. . . .178 E8
Hinam Cross TA22. . . .33 B7
Hindharton La EX39. . .22 E3
Hind St
 Bovey Tracey TQ13. . .180 D8
 Ottery St Mary EX11. .169 D3
Hingston Ct PL6. . . . .249 A8
Hingston Post TQ9. . .144 E8
Hingston Rd TQ1. . . . .220 C7
Hingston Rise TQ7. . .142 F5
Hinham La
 Dulverton TA22. . . . . .33 A8
 Dulverton TA22. . . . . .33 B7
Hinton Ct PL6. . . . . . .245 C1
Hirmandale Rd PL5. . .243 F3
HISCOTT. 27 C5
Hitchcocks Bsns Pk
 EX15. . . . . .162 F7
HITTISLEIGH. 96 D5
Hittisleigh Cross EX6. .96 D6
Hittisleigh Mill La EX6 96 D5
Hittsford La EX36. . . . .32 A1
Hobart St PL1. . . . . . .262 A2
Hobbacott La
 Marhamchurch EX23. . .70 A6
 Marhamchurch EX23. . .70 B7
Hobbacott Rise EX23. .70 A6
Hobbs Cl TA21. . . . . .160 A3
Hobbs Cres PL12. . . .242 C3
Hobb's Hill EX33. . . . . . .7 E2
Hobbs La EX32. . . . . . .18 E2
Hobbs Way EX17. . . . .78 B4
Hobby Dr The EX39. . .23 E3
Hobby House La EX36 30 C1
Hobbymoor Cross
 EX17. . . . . .60 A1
Hockey Fields TQ6 .146 A7
HOCKHOLLER. 52 E8
HOCKHOLLER GREEN. .52 E8
Hockings Gn EX1. . . .178 B6
Hockmoor Head
 TQ11. . . . . .130 C2
Hockmoor Hill TQ11. .130 C2
Hockmore Dr TQ12. . .207 F4
HOCKWORTHY. 50 D6
Hodder's La DT7. . . . .260 C8
Hodders Way EX38 . . .239 A2
Hodge Cl PL12. . . . . . .242 C2
Hodges Wlk EX38. . . .159 E5
Hodson Cl TQ3. . . . . .225 F7
Hoe App PL1. . . . . . . .262 C2
Hoe Ct PL1. . . . . .262 C2
Hoegate Cl PL1. . . . . .262 C2
Hoegate Pl PL1. . . . . .262 C2
Hoegate St PL1. . . . . .263 A2
Hoe Gdns PL1. . . . . . .262 C2
Hoe Rd PL1. . . . . .262 C2
Hoe St PL1. . . . . .262 C2
Hoe The PL1. . . . . . . .262 C1
Hofheim Dr EX16. . . .161 A6
Hogarth Cl PL9. . . . . .256 B6
Hogarth Ho **2** PL9. .191 B6
Hogarth Wlk PL9. . . .256 B6
HOGGS PARK. 54 A1
Hoile La TQ9. . . . . . . .224 E1
Hoker Rd EX2. . . . . . .178 A5
Holbeam Cl TQ12 . . .206 E4
Holbeam La
 Bickington TQ12. . . . .131 F6
 Newton Abbot TQ12. .206 E4
HOLBETON. 136 D1
Holbeton Sch PL8. . . .136 D1
Holborn Pl PL7. . . . . .250 E6
Holborn Rd TQ5. . . . .230 C6
Holborn St PL4. . . . . .263 B3
Holbrook Terr TQ7. . .145 B1
HOLCOMBE
 Lyme Regis. 104 B4
 Teignmouth. 204 D3
Holcombe Barton Cnr
 EX6. . . . . .98 D2
Holcombe Cross EX7 210 F8
Holcombe Down Cross
 TQ14. . . . . .124 F2
Holcombe Down Rd EX7,
 TQ14. . . . . .204 A4
Holcombe Dr
 Holcombe EX7. . . . . .210 F8
 Plymouth PL9. . . . . . .255 F5
Holcombe La
 Ottery St Mary EX11. .100 F7
 Uplyme DT7. . . . . . . .104 B4
Holcombe Rd EX7,
 TQ14. . . . . .210 E8
HOLCOMBE ROGUS. . .50 F5
Holcombe Village
 TQ14. . . . . .210 E8
Holcroft Cl PL12. . . . .242 D2
Holden Cross EX6. . . .113 E2
Holdridge La EX36. . . .30 D8
Holdstone Way EX34. . .3 B2
Holdsworth St PL4. . .262 B4
Hole Ball Cross EX21. .92 A8
Holebay Cl PL9. . . . . .256 A5
Holebrook Cross EX20 76 C4

Holebrook La EX20.....76 C5
Hole Cleave Rd EX33...8 A1
Hole Cross
  Halwill EX21.........73 F1
  Hittisleigh EX6......96 E4
  Yelverton PL20......239 E7
Hole Ct EX20.........75 C7
Hole Hill
  Branscombe EX12....190 C5
  Exbourne EX20......76 C4
  Witheridge EX16.....46 F2
Hole La
  Chulmleigh EX18......45 B3
  Combe Martin EX31...10 B6
  Croyde EX33..........7 F1
  North Tawton EX20...77 E6
HOLEMOOR..........73 B8
Holemoor Cross EX22.73 C8
Holemore Cross EX14.68 C5
Hole Rd PL20........239 F7
Hole's La
  Broadhempston TQ9...131 B3
  Staverton TQ9......216 B8
Holestone La EX9...187 A1
HOLEWATER.........19 A6
Holewater Cross EX32 19 A6
Holewater Hill EX32...19 A6
Holewell La EX6......96 E4
Hole Well La TA20....69 F8
HOLLACOMBE.........72 D6
Hollacombe Brake
  PL9...............256 C1
Hollacombe Cross
  Holsworthy EX22.....72 D6
  Yeoford EX17.........79 D3
HOLLACOMBE HILL...256 A2
Hollacombe La TQ3..219 D1
Hollam Cross TA22....33 E7
Hollam Dr TA22......33 D6
Hollam La TA22.......33 D7
Hollamoor View
  EX31..............154 B3
Hollam Way TQ12....207 F8
Holland Cl EX31.....154 A4
Holland Copse EX6...98 C4
Holland Dr
  West Clyst EX1.....175 A3
  West Clyst EX4.....174 F3
Holland Pk EX2.....178 D1
Holland Rd
  Exeter EX2.........176 F4
  Exmouth EX8.......196 C1
  Plymouth, Chaddlewood
    PL2..............251 D5
  Plymouth, Peverell PL3 248 E6
  Plymouth, Plymstock
    PL9..............255 C5
Holland's La TA4.....35 E8
Hollands Park Ave
  EX34..............154 B3
Hollands Rd 4 TQ14 .210 C4
Holland St 6 EX31...154 F5
Holland's Wash Dro
  TA20...............69 F5
Hollerday Dr EX35...151 B6
Holley Cl EX6.......182 A4
Holley Pk EX6.......170 D6
Holleys Cl TA20......88 D8
Hollicombe Cross
  PL21..............136 E3
Hollicombe Head
  TQ7...............149 D5
Hollow Hayes PL6...249 B8
Hollow Head Cross
  EX10..............100 F2
Hollow La EX1.......178 E4
Hollow Pits Ct EX2..181 B8
Hollows The
  Exmouth EX8........202 B7
  Plymouth PL9.......256 B8
Hollow Tree Cross
  EX18...............60 A7
Hollowtree Ct 5
  EX32..............155 B3
Hollowtree Rd EX32..155 B3
Holly Ball La
  Whimple EX10......100 A8
  Whimple EX5........99 F8
Hollyberry Rd PL7...136 B7
Holly Cl
  Broadclyst EX5......175 C7
  2 Chudleigh TQ13...123 F6
  Halwill Junction EX21..73 D3
  Honiton EX14........166 C4
  Tiverton EX16......161 E5
Hollycombe Cross
  EX20...............95 E4
Hollycombe La TQ9..216 E7
Hollycroft Rd PL3...249 A7

Holly Ct PL6.......249 E7
Hollyford La EX17....62 C2
Hollyhead Cross
  EX12..............191 C7
Hollyhead Rd EX12..191 B8
Holly Ho 2 EX34....150 B6
Hollyhock Cres TQ12 206 C4
Hollyhock Way PL6..245 A2
Hollymount Cl EX8..196 C3
Holly Park Cl PL5...244 A5
Holly Park Dr PL5...244 A5
Holly Rd
  Exeter EX2.........177 F3
  Tiverton EX16......161 E5
Holly Villas TQ9....139 F8
Hollywater Cl TQ9..139 F8
Holly Water Rd EX17 .62 E1
Holly Way EX15.....163 C5
Holly Wlk
  Cullompton EX16.....64 F2
  Exmouth EX8.......196 D3
Hollywood Terr 2
  PL1...............262 A3
HOLMACOTT.........26 E7
Holmacott Cross EX39.26 E7
Holman Cl EX7......204 F8
Holman Ct PL2......248 C8
Holman Hill TQ12...212 A2
Holmans Bldgs PL1..247 D2
Holmans Mdw PL15..105 B1
Holman Way
  Ivybridge PL21.....237 A6
  Topsham EX3.......182 F5
Holmbush Way PL8..257 A4
Holm Cross EX17.....59 F2
Holmdale EX10......188 B4
Holmead Cross EX16..48 B3
Holme Ct 3 TQ1....220 D4
Holmer Down PL6...245 D7
Holmes Ave PL3.....249 B5
Holmes Field EX20...95 A5
Holmes Rd TQ12.....180 F2
Holm Hill EX17.......59 E2
Holmleigh Rd TQ7...145 D1
Holmsleigh Cross
  EX14..............86 C5
HOLMSLEIGH GREEN .86 C5
Holmwood Ave PL9..255 E5
HOLNE.............130 A4
Holne Chase PL6....245 B7
Holne Cross TQ13...130 C5
Holne Ct EX4.......176 E8
Holne Moor Cl TQ3..225 E7
Holne Rd TQ11......236 B6
Holne Rise EX2......178 B4
Holne Turn
  Ashburton TQ13....130 E5
  Holne TQ13.........130 B5
Holset Cross TQ8...148 D5
Holsome La TQ9....138 D7
Holstock Cross EX20..74 D3
HOLSWORTHY........164 D5
**HOLSWORTHY
  BEACON**...........54 C3
Holsworthy CE Prim Sch
  EX22..............164 C5
Holsworthy Com Coll
  EX22..............164 C5
Holsworthy Hospl
  EX22..............164 D6
Holsworthy Ind Est
  EX22..............164 C7
Holsworthy L Ctr
  EX22..............164 C5
Holsworthy Mus★
Holsworthy Rd
  Hatherleigh EX20....75 B6
  Okehampton EX20...93 D5
Holt The
  19 Appledore EX39..15 A1
  Honiton EX14......166 E7
Holtwood Dr PL21...237 A5
Holtwood Rd PL6....245 D6
Holway TA20.........88 D8
Holwell Cl PL9......256 A5
Holwell La EX16......64 B5
Holwell Rd PL5.....230 B4
Holwill Dr EX38....159 D5
Holwill Tor Wlk TQ4..225 F3
HOLY CITY..........87 F7
Holy Cross RC Prim Sch
  PL4...............263 A4
Holyford La EX24...102 F3
**Holyford Woods Nature
  Reserve★** EX12....102 E3
Holy Moor Cross EX36 32 C1
Holy Moor La EX36...32 C1
Holyoake St TA21...160 C7
Holyrood Pl PL1....262 C2
Holyshute Cross
  EX14..............166 D6
Holyshute Gdns
  EX14..............166 D6
Holywell CE Prim Sch
  EX31...............27 D8
Holywell Cross EX36..19 F2
HOLYWELL LAKE......51 E7
Holywell Pk EX21....73 D3
Homebaye Ho 3
  EX12..............192 B4
Homebourne Ho
  TQ4...............226 C5
Home Cl
  Brixham TQ5.......230 C3
  Chillington TQ7....145 A1
  Cranbrook EX5......99 B6

Homeclose La EX13,
  TA20...............88 A8
Homeclyst Ho EX2...261 A1
Homecombe Ho TQ1 220 C8
Homecourt Ho EX4..261 A2
Homedown Cross
  EX37...............28 F4
Home Farm EX6.....114 E1
Home Farm Cl
  Croyde EX33.........7 E2
  Kingston TQ7.......142 C6
Home Farm Cross
  EX15...............65 F4
Home Farm Ct TQ12..209 B2
Home Farm N DT7...193 E6
Home Farm Rd
  Fremington EX31....153 D5
  Plymouth PL9.......255 E8
Home Farm S DT7...193 E6
Homefield
  Thurlestone TQ7....143 A1
  Wellington TA21....160 E4
Homefield Cl EX11...169 E3
Homefield Cotts TQ7 143 A1
Homefield Rd EX1...177 F6
Home Gate EX6.......98 A3
Home La EX34.........1 C3
Homelace Ho EX14...166 C4
Homelands Pl TQ7..258 C6
Homelands Prim Sch 1
  TQ1...............220 B8
Home Mdw TQ9.....223 C5
Homemeadows Ho
  EX10..............188 B5
Home Orch
  Sampford Peverell
    EX16...............50 D1
  Tiverton EX16.......50 D1
Homepalms Ho 3
  TQ1...............219 F6
Home Park Ave PL3..248 E6
**Home Park (Plymouth
  Argyle FC)** PL2...248 C5
Home Park Rd PL12..243 A3
Home Pk
  Ashburton TQ13....130 F5
  Plymouth PL2.......247 F4
Homer Cl EX31.....18 A8
Homer Cres EX33...152 B7
Homer Ct EX33.....152 B7
Homer Dr EX33.....152 B7
Homer La EX12......191 F8
Homer Park Lane S
  PL9...............255 C5
Homer Pk
  Plymouth PL9.......255 C5
  Saltash PL12.......242 D3
Homer Rd EX33.....152 B7
Homer Rise PL9.....256 B7
Homers Cl TQ12....207 D6
Homers Cres TQ12..207 D6
Homers La TQ12...207 D6
Homersleigh Rd EX14..86 A5
Homestead Rd TQ1..220 A8
Homestead Terr TQ1 220 A8
Home Sweet Home Terr
  PL4...............263 C2
Hometeign Ho TQ12 207 D4
Hometor Ho EX8....202 A8
Homeyards The
  TQ14..............210 A3
Homing Down Cross
  EX20...............75 A1
Honcray PL9........255 D8
Hone Cross EX16.....34 F5
Honest Heart Cross
  EX15...............66 A3
Honestone St EX39..157 A1
Honeybeetle Cross
  EX37...............29 A5
HONEYCHURCH.......76 E5
Honeychurch La EX6 76 E5
Honeychurch Moor Cross
  EX20...............76 F6
Honey Cl EX39......157 D2
Honeycroft Cross
  EX22...............54 A4
Honey Ditches Dr
  EX12..............191 B8
Honey Farm Cl 9
  EX36..............158 C5
Honeyford Cl PL6...245 A4
Honey La
  Daccombe TQ1,
    TQ12.............213 F5
  Exeter EX1.........174 F2
  Woodbury Salterton
    EX5..............184 D7
**Honeylands Childrens Ctr
  (Royal Devon & Exeter
  Hospl)** EX4.......178 B7
Honeylands Dr EX4..178 A7
Honeylands Way
  EX4..............178 A7
Honey Mdws EX22..164 C4
Honeymead TA24....13 D2
Honeymoor La EX16..48 E7
Honey Park Rd EX9..198 B2
Honey St EX39......157 A7
Honeysuckle Cl
  2 Barnstaple EX31..154 B3
  Paignton TQ3......225 E8
  Plymouth PL6.......245 E7
  Saltash PL12.......242 D4
  Tiverton EX16......161 F6
Honeysuckle Ct EX4..176 D8

Honeysuckle Dr
  Dawlish EX7.......204 D8
  Honiton EX14.......85 C2
  Tavistock PL19.....171 A6
Honeysuckle Gdns
  PL15..............105 A2
Honeywell TQ12....207 E6
Honeywell Cl EX32..155 B2
Honeywell La TQ13..122 C3
Honeywell Rd TQ12..207 E6
Honeywins Cross
  EX36...............19 C2
HONICKNOWLE......244 B4
Honicknowle PL5...244 B4
Honicknowle Gn PL5 244 B2
Honicknowle La PL5 .244 B1
Honicombe Cnr PL17 125 B5
Honicombe Pk PL17..125 B5
HONITON...........166 D4
Honiton Bottom Rd
  Honiton EX14.......166 C3
  Honiton EX14.......166 C3
Honiton Bsns Pk
  EX14..............166 B6
Honiton Cl PL5.....244 B3
Honiton Com Coll
  EX14..............166 C6
Honiton Cross EX36..29 F3
Honiton Hospl EX14..166 C5
Honiton La EX36.....29 E3
Honiton L Ctr EX14..166 C7
Honiton Prim Sch
  EX14..............166 C6
Honiton Rd
  Blackhorse EX5.....179 C7
  Cullompton EX15....163 E3
  Exeter EX1.........178 C5
  Honiton Sta EX14...166 C5
  Honiton Wlk PL5....244 B4
Honors Farm EX15...173 F8
Hooda Cl EX32.......17 E1
Hood Dr EX2.........182 C8
Hoodown La TQ6....234 B4
HOOE.............255 C5
Hooe Hill PL9......255 C5
Hooe La PL9........255 D3
Hooelake La PL10...253 C4
Hooe Manor PL9....255 C5
Hooe Prim Sch PL9..255 B5
Hooe Rd PL9........255 C5
HOOK..............88 B8
Hook Cross FX13....137 E7
Hook Dr EX2........178 D2
Hooker Cl EX9......197 F2
Hookhill La EX17.....62 A3
Hookhills Dr TQ4...226 C1
Hookhills Gdns TQ4 .229 B7
Hookhills Gr TQ4...226 C1
Hookhills Rd TQ4...226 B1
Hookmoor Cross
  PL21..............137 E7
Hooksbury Ave PL7 .251 B3
Hooks Cross TQ12...131 C7
Hookway EX17.......80 D1
Hookway Cross EX5..80 D1
Hookway Hill
  Lynton/Lynmouth EX35..6 F3
  Oareford TA24.......6 F3
Hookway La EX16....63 B5
Hookwell Down La
  EX36...............30 A8
HOO MEAVY........132 A8
Hoop Cross EX15.....83 B4
Hooper Cl EX20......75 B7
Hooperhayne Rd
  EX24..............102 E5
Hoopern Ave EX4...173 D1
Hoopern La EX4....177 C8
Hoopern St EX4.....261 B4
Hoopern Terr 4 EX7 204 D6
Hoopers Cl TQ9....223 F5
Hoopers Cross EX16..34 D3
Hoopers La PL18....125 C6
Hooper St PL11.....247 C3
Hoopers Way EX38..159 F5
Hooperton Cross EX6 96 E3
Hooper Turn EX6....96 E3
HOOPS.............24 D2
Hope By-Pass TQ7..147 B7
Hope Cl TQ9........223 F5
Hope Close PL7.....248 A7
Hope Rd EX2........178 A5
Hope Reach Ave TQ9 223 E4
Hope's Cl TQ14.....210 A6
Hopes Cove La TQ1..220 F5
Hope Wlk TQ9.......223 F5
Hopkins Ct 3 TQ12 207 C3
Hopkins La TQ12....207 C3
Hopperstyle EX31...154 B3
Hopton Cl PL6......248 F8
Hopton Dr EX38....159 F8
HOPWORTHY........71 C5
Horace Rd TQ2.....213 F2
Hore Down Gate EX34..9 B6
Hore's Cross PL21...137 D7
Horestone Cross EX16..47 F4
Hornapark Cl PL16..105 E3
Hornbeam Cl
  Honiton EX14......166 A4
  Tiverton EX16......161 F5
Hornbeam Gdns EX5..83 A7
Hornbeam Hollow 1
  EX31..............154 C2
Hornbeam Rd EX1...178 C6
Hornbrook Gdns PL6 244 D6
Hornby St 2 PL2....247 F4
Hornchurch La PL5..243 E4
Hornchurch Rd PL5..243 E5

Horn Cross
  Kentisbeare EX15....65 F2
  Plymouth PL9......255 E7
Horn Cross Rd PL9..255 F7
HORNDON...........118 A7
Horndon Field EX5..184 C2
Hornebrook Ave 9
  EX34..............150 B5
Horne Park Ave 14
  EX34..............150 B5
Horne Park Rd EX34 .150 B5
Horne Rd EX34......150 B5
Horner Tongue TQ9 138 F5
Horner Turn Cross
  TQ9...............139 A5
Horn Hill
  Dartmouth TQ6.....233 F3
  Poltimore EX4......174 E4
Horn La
  Brixton PL8........257 A5
  Plymouth PL9......255 F7
Horn Lane Flats 4
  PL9...............255 F7
Horn Rd EX15........65 E2
HORNS CROSS.......24 C2
Hornshayes Knap Cross
  EX14..............86 F7
Hornshayne Rd EX24 102 B5
Horns Pk TQ14.....208 E2
HORRABRIDGE......126 F5
**Horrabridge Com Prim
  Sch** PL20........126 F4
Horridge La EX18....59 A8
Horry Mill La
  Hollocombe EX18....58 F6
  Hollocombe EX18....59 A6
Horsdon Rd EX16...161 F4
Horsdon Terr EX16..161 F4
HORSEBRIDGE......116 A1
HORSEBROOK......135 B1
Horsecombe Cross
  TQ8...............259 B7
Horseguards EX4...261 B4
Horse Hill EX17......60 F7
Horsehill Cross EX17..60 F7
Horse Hill Cross EX22 .38 F1
Horse La TQ14......210 B3
Horsepond Mdw
  EX36..............158 C3
Horsepool St TQ5...230 B3
Horse Rd EX23.......36 F1
Horseshoe Bend TQ1 226 C2
Horseshoe Cl 19
  TQ13..............123 E6
Horseshoe Dr
  Newton Abbot TQ12..207 A5
  Plymouth PL7......250 D5
Horseway TA20.......69 E6
Horsewell Rd EX5...99 B6
Horsham La
  Plymouth, Honicknowle
    PL5..............244 C2
  Plymouth, Tamerton Foliot
    PL5..............244 C7
Horslears EX13.....167 C4
Horslett Hill EX22...89 E8
Horswell Cl PL7.....251 B5
Horton Cross EX22...38 C3
HORWOOD..........26 E6
Horwood Cross EX39 .26 D7
**Horwood & Newton
  Tracey Com Prim Sch**
  EX31..............27 A6
Horwood Sq 11 EX31 154 F5
Hosegood Way TQ12 207 D7
Hosford Cl PL9.....256 A4
Hoskings Ct TQ11...236 B5
Hospital Hill EX7....204 D6
Hospital La
  17 Ashburton TQ13..131 A5
  Exeter EX1.........178 C4
Hospital Rd PL4....263 B4
Hostel Hill TQ6.....233 E4
Hostle Park Gdns 12
  EX34..............150 C6
Hostle Park Rd EX34 150 C6
Hostle Pk EX34.....150 C6
Hotham Pl PL1......262 A4
Hothill La
  Ashprington TQ9....139 E4
  Cornworthy TQ9....227 A4
Hotspur Terr PL1....262 C4
HOUGHTON.........206 C6
Houghton Gr EX4...174 F4
Houghton La EX10..187 A5
Houldsworth Rd PL9 255 C7
Houndbeare La EX5..99 E4
Houndhead Cross
  TQ9...............216 D8
Houndiscombe Rd
  PL4...............248 E4
Hound Tor Cl TQ4...229 B7
Hounster Dr PL10...252 D4
Hounster Hill PL10..252 D4
Housman Cl PL5....244 D3
Hove Villas EX2....261 A1
Howard Ave EX32...155 B4
Howard Cl
  Exeter EX4.........176 F8
  Okehampton EX20..170 D6
  Plymouth PL5.......243 F2
  Saltash PL12.......242 D4
  Tavistock PL19.....171 A4
Howard Cross EX6...96 D7
Howard Ct TQ14....210 A7

Howard La
  Hittisleigh EX6......96 D7
  Marhamchurch EX23..70 B8
Howard Rd
  Plymouth PL9......255 E8
  Wellington TA21...160 D7
Howards Cl EX36...158 C2
Howards Way
  Ivybridge PL21.....237 A6
  Newton Abbot TQ12..207 F4
Howarth Cl EX10...188 A8
Howden Ind Est EX16 161 B3
Howden La EX16....161 B3
Howden Rd
  Tiverton EX16.......64 B7
  Tiverton EX16......161 C3
Howell Rd EX4......261 A4
Howeson Ct 10 PL1..262 A3
Howeson La PL6....245 A4
HOWLEY............69 C4
Howley Pk La EX32...18 D2
How St PL4.........263 A2
Howton La TQ12....206 B5
Howton Rd
  Newton Abbot TQ12..206 C6
  Newton Abbot TQ12..206 C7
Hoxton Rd TQ1.....220 B5
Hoyles Cl TA21.....160 E4
Hoyles Ct TQ3......225 F8
Hoyles Rd TA21....160 E4
Hoyle's Rd TQ3....225 F8
Hubbastone Rd EX39 157 C8
HUCCABY...........129 C7
Huccaby Cl TQ5....229 F2
HUCCOMBE.........149 C7
Huckham Barn Cross
  TQ7...............149 C7
Huckham La EX31....10 F3
Huckland Cross EX20..76 E4
HUDDISFORD........38 C6
Huddisford Cross
  EX39...............38 D7
Hudley Mill Hill EX32..18 D3
Hudson Cross EX22...53 B4
Hue La EX33.........47 E1
Hughball Cross EX19..76 A8
Hughes Ave EX32...155 B3
Hughes Gdns EX39..156 D2
Hugh Squier Ave
  EX36..............158 D5
HUISH............57 B6
HUISH
CHAMPFLOWER....35 B3
Huish Cleeve TA4...35 E7
Huish Cross TQ13..123 C6
Huishlane End EX6..97 F5
Hukeley Head Cross
  EX16...............34 D3
HULHAM...........196 B3
Hulham Rd
  Exmouth EX8.......196 B1
  Exmouth EX8.......196 B2
Hulham Vale EX8...196 C2
Hulk La EX5.........81 F4
HUMBER...........124 C2
Humber Cl PL3.....249 D6
Humber La TQ12,
  TQ14..............124 B1
Hume Ave EX35.....151 A5
Hummingbird Cl EX1 174 C1
Humphrey's Cross
  TQ13..............130 C4
Humphreys Rd TA21 160 E7
Humphries Pk EX8..196 D1
Humpy The EX7.....204 C7
Hungerford Rd PL2..248 B5
Hungry Fox Est EX5 175 E3
Huniver's La EX17...165 C4
Hunivers Pl EX17...165 C4
Hunsdon Ct TQ1....220 C4
Hunsdon Rd
  Ivybridge PL21.....237 A3
  Lee Mill PL21......136 D6
  Torquay TQ1.......220 C4
Hunstone Cross EX36..19 B2
Huntacott Way TQ2 219 B8
Hunter Cl PL6.......244 F2
Hunter La EX34......7 F6
Hunters Cl PL21....237 B5
Hunters Gate EX20..170 D6
Hunters Hill EX15....51 E1
Hunters Moon TQ9..222 F7
Hunters's Oak PL20..126 A2
Hunters Tor Dr TQ4 229 B7
Hunter's Way PL5....51 E1
Hunterswell Rd
  TQ2...............207 A3
Hunterswood EX38..159 F5
Hunthay Bsns Pk
  EX13..............167 A6
Hunthay La EX13...167 B6
Huntingdon Gdns
  PL5...............244 D4
Huntley Cl EX13....167 F7
Huntley La EX13.....88 B4
Huntley Pl PL3.....249 C6
Hunton Cl EX3......195 F5
Hunts Cross PL21...137 B1
HUNTSHAM..........50 A7
Huntsham Rd EX1...178 D7
HUNTSHAW.........26 D2
Huntshaw Cross EX31..27 B1
Huntshaw Moor Cross
  EX38...............26 F2
HUNTSHAW WATER..26 E2
Hurdwick Rd PL19..171 A5
Hurrabrook Cl PL6..245 E2

Hurrabrook Gdns PL6 ....245 E2
Hurrell Cl PL6 ....244 D6
Hurrell Ct
　Kingsbridge TQ7 ....258 C5
　Plymouth PL3 ....249 C5
Hurrell Rd TQ7 ....258 C5
Hursley Bsns Pk PL6 .241 D1
Hurst Ave EX2 ....178 B4
Hurst Cl PL9 ....255 F5
Hurstone Nature Reserve★ TA4 ....35 F3
Hurst's Almshouses EX2 ....261 C2
Husseys Cross EX14 ....86 F6
Hussey's La EX14 ....86 F6
Hutcherleigh Cross TQ9 ....139 B1
Hutcherleigh Turn TQ9 ....139 D1
Hutchings Cl PL6 ....244 D6
Hutchings Dr
　Clyst Honiton EX1 ....179 B8
　Clyst Honiton EX1 ....179 C8
Hutchings Mead EX1 178 F8
Hutchings Way TQ14 209 D8
Hutgate Rd EX14 ....86 A4
Hutton Rd TQ3 ....219 A1
Huxford La EX37 ....44 F7
HUXHAM 174 B8
Huxham Cl PL6 ....249 A6
Huxham's Cross TQ9 215 E3
Huxham's Cross Est TQ9 ....215 E3
HUXHILL 26 D2
Huxley Cl PL7 ....250 F7
Huxley Vale TQ12 ....212 F3
Huxnor Cross TQ12....212 F2
Huxnor Rd TQ12 ....212 F3
Huxtable Hill TQ2 ....219 E4
Huxtable La EX32 ....18 C2
Huxton Cross TQ7 ....143 D3
Huxton Fork TQ7....143 D3
Hyacinth Terr TA21 ....160 C5
Hyde Park Infs & Jun Sch
　[1] PL3 ....248 E5
Hyde Park Rd PL3 ....248 E5
Hyde Rd TQ4 ....226 B6
Hyfield Gdns TQ1 ....220 B4
Hyfield Pl [4] EX39....157 A1
Hylands Cl EX11 ....168 D3
Hylton Gdns EX4 ....176 F6
Hyne Town TQ6 ....145 E5
Hynetown Est TQ6 ....145 E5
Hynetown Rd TQ6 ....145 E5
Hyperion TQ2 ....219 E2

I

Ian Hay Cl EX39 ....157 C1
Ibex Ct EX39 ....15 A1
Ice House La EX10 ....187 F7
Icy Pk TQ7 ....143 C6
IDDESLEIGH 57 F3
Iddesleigh Cross EX19. 57 E3
Iddesleigh Rd EX4 ....177 E8
Iddesleigh Terr [10]
　EX7 ....204 E6
IDE 176 D1
IDEFORD 124 A4
Ide La EX2 ....177 A1
Ide Prim Sch EX2 ....176 E1
Idestone Brook Cross
　EX2 ....113 F7
Idestone Cross EX2 ..114 A7
Idestone La EX2 ....114 A8
Ide Village Rd EX2 ....176 E2
Idewell Rd TQ2 ....214 B2
Idston Cross TQ7....143 D7
Ikea Way EX1 ....178 D2
Ilbert Cotts PL7 ....250 E4
Ilbert Rd
　Kingsbridge TQ7 ....258 C5
　Thurlestone TQ7 ....143 A1
Ilbert St PL1 ....262 B4
Ilex Cl
　Exeter EX4 ....174 B2
　Shillingford St George EX2 ....114 C6
ILFRACOMBE 150 B6
Ilfracombe Acad EX34....150 C5
Ilfracombe Academy EX34 ....150 C5
Ilfracombe Aquarium★ EX34 ....150 D6
Ilfracombe CE Jun Sch EX34 ....150 C5
Ilfracombe & District Tyrrell Hosp EX34..150 B5
Ilfracombe Inf Sch [18] EX34 ....150 B5
Ilfracombe Mus★ EX34 ....150 B6
Ilfracombe Rd
　Braunton EX33 ....152 D7
　West Down EX34 ....8 F5
Ilfracombe Swimming Pool EX34 ....150 D5
Ilkerton Hill EX35 ....151 A4
Ilsham CE Prim Sch TQ1 ....220 F5
Ilsham Cl TQ1 ....220 F5
Ilsham Ho TQ1 ....220 F5
Ilsham Marine Dr TQ1....221 A4

Ilsham Mws TQ1 ....220 D5
Ilsham Rd TQ1 ....220 F5
ILSINGTON 122 C3
Ilsington CE Prim Sch TQ13 ....122 C3
Ilton Cross TQ7 ....259 A7
Ilton Way TQ7 ....258 D5
Immenstadt Dr TA21 .160 D4
Imperial Bldgs TQ12 .207 D8
Imperial Ct
　Lynton EX35 ....151 C5
　Torquay TQ1 ....220 C7
Imperial Mews [12] TQ12 ....207 C3
Imperial Rd EX8 ....201 F6
Imperial St EX4 ....176 F5
Impham Cl PL19 ....171 B7
Improvement Pl [5] TA21 ....160 D5
Ince Cl PL11 ....246 F4
Inchcoulter Rd EX8 ....202 C5
Inchkeith Rd PL6....244 F7
Incledon Hill EX33 ....8 A3
Indicombe La EX32....18 B2
Indio Rd TQ13 ....180 C6
Indus Pl PL9 ....256 E8
Inglebrook Hts EX39 .156 E7
Ingleside EX13 ....167 E6
Ingleside Ct EX9 ....198 A1
Ingrams Pl EX5 ....99 C6
Ingra Rd PL3 ....249 A6
Ingra Tor Cl [2] PL20..126 F3
Ingra Wlk PL6 ....245 B8
INLEIGH GREEN 58 C2
Innerbrook Rd TQ2....219 E5
INNER HOPE 147 C6
Inner Relief Rd [11] EX31 ....154 F6
Inner Ting Tong EX9 .197 C3
Inner Westland [2] EX5 ....99 A6
Innes Ho PL1 ....262 B3
Instaple Cross EX22...53 D6
INSTOW 15 B1
Instow Com Prim Sch EX39 ....15 C2
Instow Ho [4] EX39 ....15 B1
Instow Wlk PL5 ....244 A3
Inswell Ct PL19 ....171 A6
INSWORKE 252 F6
Insworke Cl PL10 ....253 A6
Insworke Cres PL10 ..252 F6
Insworke Pl PL10 ....253 A6
International Ho TQ12 ....180 F2
Inverdene PL3 ....248 D5
Inverteign Com Nursery & Prim Sch TQ14....209 D8
Inverteign Dr TQ14...210 A5
Inverteign Hts TQ14..209 D8
INWARDLEIGH 75 E2
Inwardleigh Cross EX20 ....75 D2
Iolanthe Dr EX4 ....174 A2
Iona Ave EX8 ....196 A2
IPPLEPEN 211 C2
Ipplepen Bsns Pk TQ12 ....217 D8
Ipplepen Cross TQ12.211 C6
Ipplepen Prim Sch TQ12 ....211 D1
Ipplepen Rd TQ3 ....218 C4
Ipswich Cl PL5 ....244 C4
Irene Way EX16 ....161 F6
Iris Ave
　Exeter EX2 ....177 B4
　Exeter EX2 ....261 A1
Irishcombe Gate EX4..46 B5
Irishcombe La EX36....46 C4
Iron Bridge EX4 ....261 A3
Iron Bridge Cross EX20 ....77 B3
Iron Letters Cross EX34. 2 B1
Iron Mine La PL20....127 B3
Iron Post TQ22 ....33 B5
Iron Shovel La EX36...31 A3
Irsha St EX39 ....15 A1
Irving Cl EX33 ....152 B6
Isaac Cl EX9 ....198 E7
Isaac Gr TQ2 ....213 F3
Isaacs Rd TQ2 ....214 A2
Isabella Rd EX16 ....161 D5
Isambard Brunel Way PL3 ....262 A2
Isambard Ct TQ2 ....214 B3
Isambard Kingdom Brunel Prim Sch TA21 ....160 E7
Isambard Par EX4....177 A7
ISCA Coll of Media Arts EX2 ....177 E2
Isca Ct EX2 ....177 D1
Isca Rd
　Exeter EX2 ....261 A1
　Exmouth EX8 ....202 C5
Isigny Rd TQ7 ....258 C5
Isis Cl EX14 ....166 E7
Island Lodge Camping & Cvn Site TQ7 ....144 B6
Island Quay TQ8 ....259 E5
Island St TQ8 ....259 E5
Island Terr TQ8 ....259 E5
Island View TQ7 ....143 A2
Isleworth Rd EX4 ....176 F5
Iter Cnr EX17 ....78 C4
Iter Cross EX17 ....78 C4

Iter Ct EX17 ....78 C4
Iter Pk EX17 ....78 C4
Itton Cross EX20 ....77 D2
Itton Moor La
　North Tawton EX17 ....77 F2
　Spreyton EX17 ....95 E8
　Spreyton EX20 ....77 F1
Itton Rd EX17 ....77 E2
Ivanhoe Rd PL5 ....243 D2
Ivatt Rd TQ6 ....233 C3
Iveagh Ct EX4 ....176 F8
IVYBRIDGE 237 C6
Ivybridge Com Coll PL21 ....237 D6
Ivybridge La PL20 ....120 B8
Ivybridge L Ctr PL21 .237 D4
Ivybridge Rd
　Ermington PL7 ....136 F4
　Tavistock PL19 ....171 C8
Ivybridge Sta PL21 ..237 F6
Ivy Cl
　Exeter EX2 ....178 A4
　Sidmouth EX10 ....188 B7
Ivycombe Hill
　South Allington TQ7 ..149 B5
　South Allington TQ7 ..149 A4
Ivy Cotts PL18 ....125 C6
Ivy Cross TA21 ....51 D7
Ivy Ct [28] EX39 ....15 A1
Ivydale EX8 ....196 D3
Ivydale Rd PL4 ....248 F4
Ivydene Rd EX21 ....237 C5
Ivy Dr TQ12 ....244 C6
Ivy Glen PL21 ....237 D6
Ivy Ho TA21 ....160 C6
Ivyhouse Cross PL16 ..91 A4
Ivy La
　Dartmouth TQ6 ....233 F3
　[15] Teignmouth TQ14...210 B4
Ivy Tree Hill TQ12 ....209 A2

J

Jack Backs Cross EX17 ....79 F7
Jack Bears Ho [10] TQ4 ....226 B6
Jackdaw Rd PL6 ....245 B2
Jackets La EX39 ....156 F7
Jacketts EX9 ....198 E7
Jacketts Cotts EX9 ...198 E7
Jackey's La EX17....78 C5
JACK-IN-THE- GREEN 99 B6
Jack Leslie Way PL2 .248 C6
Jackmans Cl TQ9 ....222 E6
Jackman's La TQ9 ....222 F4
Jackman's Mdw PL10 ....253 A3
Jackmans Meadow PL10 ....252 F3
Jackmoor Cross
　Brampford Speke EX5...81 C1
　Newton St Cyres EX5 ...81 B1
Jack Sadler Wy EX3 ..178 E1
Jacks Cl TQ9 ....223 F5
Jack's La
　St John PL11 ....252 B8
　Torquay TQ2 ....213 F3
Jackson Cl PL5 ....247 F8
Jackson Mdw EX8 ....195 E5
Jackson Pl PL2 ....247 F4
Jackson Way PL12 ...242 E3
Jacks Wy EX5 ....179 F2
Jacobs Field EX39 ....39 E8
Jacob's Pool EX20 ....170 B5
JACOBSTOWE 96 A4
Jacolind Wlk TQ5....230 D5
Jago Ave PL11 ....247 B3
James Ave TQ3 ....218 E1
James Cl PL9 ....256 B6
James Ct EX4 ....261 B2
James La EX14 ....69 C2
James Lane Cross EX13 ....69 C2
James Owen Ct EX4..261 C4
James Rd PL19 ....171 E2
James St
　Plymouth PL4 ....262 C4
　Plymouth, Mount Wise PL1 ....247 E1
James's Week EX18...59 E8
James's Week La EX18 ....59 E8
Jane Way's Grave EX17 ....61 B1
Jardine Pk EX2 ....177 C1
Jarmins Pit Cross EX15 ....66 A4
Jarvis Cl EX8 ....202 E7
Jasmine Cl EX16 ....161 F6
Jasmine Gdns
　Plymouth, Chaddlewood PL7 ....251 B5
　Plymouth, Glenholt PL6 ....245 E6
Jasmine Gr TQ3 ....225 E8
Jaspers Cotts TQ9 ...227 B4
Jawbone Hill TQ6....233 E2
Jays Cross PL15 ....105 B6
Jean Cres EX8 ....195 E5
Jedburgh Cres PL2...248 A8
Jeffery Cl
　Hartland EX39 ....22 E3
　Plymouth PL6 ....244 D6
Jefford Ho EX4 ....173 A1
Jeffries Rd TA21 ....160 F5

Jeffs Way EX13 ....167 E6
Jellicoe Rd
　Newton Abbot TQ12 ...207 F3
　Plymouth PL5 ....244 E1
Jellicoe Villas TQ9 ...223 B5
Jenker's Hill EX33 ....8 B2
Jenkins Cl PL9 ....256 A5
Jenner Rd EX16 ....161 B6
Jennifer Cl EX2 ....177 F3
Jennings Gdns EX1 ..179 B8
Jenns Cross EX22 ....53 D7
Jennycliff La PL9 ....255 A6
Jennys Combe Cl PL9 ....255 F4
Jenny's Portion EX5 ..82 A6
Jenwood Rd EX14 ....67 B1
Jephson Rd PL4 ....249 B3
Jericho DT7 ....260 D4
Jericho St EX5 ....81 E5
Jerrard Cl EX14 ....166 C5
Jerrard Cres EX14 ....166 C5
Jersey Rd EX4 ....174 E2
Jesmond Rd EX1 ....177 E7
Jessops PL7 ....250 D7
Jesu St EX11 ....169 D3
Jetstream Wy PL4 ....245 B5
Jetty Marsh Nature Reserve★ TQ12 ....207 C5
Jetty Marsh Rd TQ12 .207 B5
Jewell Cres EX32 ....155 C6
Jewell Meadow EX39...39 E8
JEWEL'S CROSS 70 E6
J.H.Taylor Dr EX39...157 A7
Jimmy's La EX18 ....45 F6
Jingles La EX32 ....155 A4
Jinkin Ave PL4 ....263 B4
Joan Spry Cl EX16....46 E1
Jobble's La EX24 ....102 E4
Jocelyn Mead EX17 ..165 B6
Jocelyn Rd EX9 ....198 A2
Jockey Hill EX17 ....165 C6
Jodel Cl PL6 ....245 B5
Joeys Field EX36 ....30 F3
John Acres La TQ12 ..123 D3
John Cole Cl TA21....160 D7
John Gay Cl EX32 ....155 C4
John Gay Rd EX32....155 C4
John Greenway Cl EX16 ....161 D3
John Grinter Way TA21 ....160 D4
John Hannam Ho EX1 ....261 C3
John Howe Cl EX38 ..159 D5
John La PL4 ....262 C4
John Levers Way EX4 ....176 F5
John Nash Dr EX7....204 C4
John Smale Rd EX31 .154 C4
Johnson Cl [2] PL20 ..125 E1
Johnson Pk PL18....125 D3
John Sparke Ho [16] PL1 ....263 A2
John St
　Plymouth PL1 ....247 E3
　Tiverton EX16 ....161 C4
John's Terr [7] EX16..161 B4
Johnstone Dr EX16 ...161 B5
Johnstone La EX36....30 D4
Jones's Hill EX33 ....7 E2
Jonida Cl TQ1 ....220 A7
JORDAN 121 A2
Jordan Cl EX32 ....155 C3
Jordan Cross TQ13 ...121 A2
Jordan Dr TQ14 ....209 D8
Jordan La PL20 ....126 F5
Jordan Mdw [15] TQ13 ....131 A5
Jordan Orch TQ11 ...236 A5
Jordans Brook TQ9 ..222 E6
Jordan St TQ11 ....236 A5
Joseph Locke Wy EX17 ....165 E4
Jose's Cross EX37....44 F8
Jose's La EX31 ....4 B5
Joslin Ct TQ12 ....207 D8
Joslin Rd EX14 ....166 B5
Joy St EX31 ....154 F5
Jubilee Cl
　Dartmouth TQ6 ....233 C3
　Exminster EX6 ....182 B4
　Great Torrington EX38 .159 E6
　Holcombe TQ14 ....204 B1
　[2] Ilfracombe EX34 ...150 B5
　Ivybridge PL21 ....237 F6
　Okehampton EX20 ....170 B5
　Saltash PL12 ....242 D2
Jubilee Cotts PL12 ...242 C1
Jubilee Ct
　Ashwater EX21 ....90 E6
　Exeter EX4 ....261 A3
　Torquay TQ1 ....220 B5
　[8] Wellington TA21...160 D5
Jubilee Dr
　Exmouth EX8 ....196 C3
　[8] Hemyock EX15....67 B8
Jubilee Gdns
　Cullompton EX15 ....163 C2
　North Molton EX36 ....30 D8
　Sidmouth EX10 ....188 C8
Jubilee Gr EX8 ....195 F5
Jubilee Lodge EX12 ..192 B5
Jubilee Pl EX3 ....249 C4
Jubilee Rd
　Appledore EX39 ....14 F1
　Bradninch EX5 ....82 F6
　Exeter EX1 ....177 E7
　Malborough TQ7 ....147 F6

Jubilee Rd continued
　Newton Abbot TQ12 ...207 B2
　Plymouth PL5 ....243 F3
　Totnes TQ9 ....223 E6
Jubilee Sq [21] EX39...157 A2
Jubilee St TQ7 ....143 C6
Jubilee Terr
　[1] Bittaford PL21 ....137 C7
　Copplestone EX17 ....79 B5
　Kingswear TQ6 ....234 B3
　Paignton TQ3 ....226 A6
　Plymouth PL4 ....249 B2
Julian Cotts PL21 ....136 D6
Julian Rd PL21 ....237 B5
Julian St PL4 ....263 C2
Julian Wlk PL6 ....245 E6
Jump Cl PL6 ....241 C1
Junction Gdns PL4....263 C3
Junction Rd EX17 ....78 C4
Juniper Cl
　Exeter EX4 ....174 B2
　[3] Honiton EX14....166 A4
　Paignton TQ3 ....225 D2
　[3] Tiverton EX16 ....161 F6
Juniper Ct EX31 ....154 C3
Juniper Dr
　Dawlish EX7 ....200 E1
　Dawlish EX7 ....204 E8
Junipers (Hosp) The EX2 ....177 F4
Juniper Way PL7....251 B5
Junket St EX37 ....43 B7
Jupes Cl EX6 ....182 B3
Juries La EX38 ....159 D6
Jurston Cross TQ13 ..110 F4
Jurston Ct TA21 ....160 F5
Jurston Fields TA21 ..160 F5
Jurston La TA21 ....160 E6
Jury Hill TA22 ....33 C6
Jury Pk EX36 ....158 B4
Jury Rd TA22 ....33 C6
Jurys Cnr TQ12 ....213 A4
Jurys Corner Cl TQ12 ....213 A4
Justment Cross EX17...77 F2
Jutland Way [5] EX1 ..178 D1

K

Kabale Cl EX16 ....161 A4
Kala Fair EX39 ....156 E7
Karen Cl EX39 ....157 D1
Katherines La EX11 ..169 E4
Kathleaven St PL5 ...243 D1
Kathleen Grange EX39 ....157 D1
Kay Cl
　Exmouth EX8 ....202 C8
　Plymouth PL7 ....250 F7
Keals Croft EX35 ....151 B5
Keaton Barns PL8....141 E6
Keaton La
　Ivybridge PL21 ....237 D1
　Ivybridge PL7 ....136 F4
Keaton Rd PL21 ....237 C4
Keats Cl
　Exmouth EX8 ....196 C4
　Teignmouth TQ14 ....124 E1
Keats Mill La TA20 ...69 C7
Keat St PL2 ....247 E4
Kedlestone Ave PL5..244 A3
Keep Cotts TQ4 ....224 B7
Keepers Cross EX16...49 A2
Keeper's Ct EX11 ....169 B7
Keephill Bglws EX22 .164 E1
Keep La TQ6 ....233 E4
Keep The PL12 ....242 C2
KELLACOTT 105 C5
Kelland Cl TQ3 ....226 A5
Kelland Cnr EX6 ....98 A1
Kelland Cross EX17 ...60 C2
Kelland Hill EX17 ....60 C2
Kellands La EX20....170 E6
Kellands Row TQ7 ...258 D5
KELLATON 149 B6
Kellaton Cross
　East Allington TQ9....144 E7
　Kellaton TQ7 ....149 C6
Kellett Cl [10] TQ13 ..131 A5
Kellock Dr TQ9 ....223 B5
KELLY 115 F8
Kelly Cl
　Plymouth PL5 ....247 C7
　Torquay TQ1 ....220 C2
Kelly Coll Preparatory Coll PL19 ....117 D3
Kelly Coll Prep Coll PL19 ....171 E8
Kelly Coll Prep Sch PL19 ....171 D7
Kelly Cross TQ13 ....122 D8
Kelly La EX16 ....62 E8
Kelvin Ave PL4 ....263 C4
Kelvin Ct
　Brixham TQ5 ....230 D5
　Torquay TQ1 ....214 C1
Kelway Rd TA21 ....160 E7
KEMACOTT 4 C4
Kemmings Cl TQ4....225 F1
Kempe Cl PL7 ....247 F6
Kempland La EX18 ...45 B2
Kempley Rd EX20 ...170 B5
Kemp's Field [25] EX5...99 A6
Kemp's La EX12 ....192 D7
Kemps Way TA22 ....33 D6

Kempton Terr PL11 ...247 B2
Kemyell Pl PL2 ....247 E4
Kenbury Cres EX6 ....201 B6
Kenbury Dr EX2 ....181 C8
Kendall Cl EX4 ....261 C4
Kendall Gr TQ13 ....180 F7
Kendall Ho PL4 ....166 C5
Kendal Pl PL5 ....244 E4
Kendlewood Cl TQ4 ..225 F3
Kenilworth TQ1 ....220 D3
Kenilworth Rd PL2 ...248 B7
Kenley Gdns PL5 ....243 F4
Kenmare Dr PL7 ....251 A5
Kenmay Mws EX3 ....182 D7
KENN 114 C4
Kennacott Cross EX22. 72 B1
Kennaway Rd EX11...169 F4
Kenn CE Prim Sch EX6 ....181 B1
Kenn Cl PL5 ....244 B3
Kennedy Way
　Dunkeswell EX14 ....67 C2
　Tiverton EX16 ....161 C5
Kennel Bridge Cross EX20 ....92 E8
Kennel Hill PL7 ....250 D4
Kennel Hill Cl PL7....250 C4
Kennel La
　Galmpton TQ5 ....229 B4
　Georgeham EX33 ....8 A2
　Ivybridge PL21 ....237 B5
Kennels Rd TQ5 ....229 C4
Kennels The PL21....237 B6
Kennerland Cross EX39 ....38 E8
KENNERLEIGH 61 F2
Kennerley Ave EX4 ...178 B8
Kennet Cl PL21 ....249 B6
Kenneth Ct TQ2 ....219 C8
KENNFORD 181 B2
Kennford Rd EX2....177 B3
Kennicott House TQ9 ....223 B6
Kenniford Cross EX5 183 D8
Kenn La
　Exeter EX6 ....181 F1
　Exminster EX6 ....182 A2
　Powderham EX6 ....194 B6
Kennydown La EX18...59 B7
Kensall Cross EX36....205 D1
Kensey Cl TQ1 ....220 E6
Kensey Valley Mdw PL15 ....105 A3
Kensham Ave EX5....83 A6
Kensham Cl EX5 ....82 F6
Kensington Cl [1] EX31 ....154 C1
Kensington Pl [8] PL4 .248 F4
Kensington Rd PL4...263 B4
Kenson Hill EX5 ....82 B5
Kent Cl EX2 ....178 A4
KENTISBEARE 66 A3
Kentisbeare CE Prim Sch EX15 ....66 A3
KENTISBURY 10 E6
KENTISBURY FORD ...10 E5
Kentisbury Prim Sch EX31 ....10 E6
Kentisknowle TQ1 ...220 E5
KENTON 194 E3
Kenton Brook Ct TQ2 ....219 B8
Kenton Hill EX6 ....194 E4
Kenton Mews EX6....194 D3
Kenton Pl EX2 ....177 C2
Kenton Prim Sch EX6 ....194 D3
Kenton Vineyard★ EX6 ....194 A2
Kent Rd
　Plymouth PL2 ....247 F5
　Tatworth TA20 ....88 D8
Kent's Bglws TA20 ...88 D8
Kents Cavern★ TQ1 ..220 E5
Kents Cavern Rd TQ1 ....220 D5
Kents Cl
　Tatworth TA20 ....88 C8
　Uffculme EX15 ....66 A7
Kent's Cotts TA20 ....88 D8
Kents La
　Tatworth TA20 ....88 D8
　Torquay TQ1 ....220 E5
Kent's Orch TA20 ....88 C8
Kents Rd TQ1 ....220 D5
Kenwith Dr TQ7 ....258 D5
Kenwith Rd EX39 ....156 F4
Kenwith Terr EX39 ...156 F3
Kenwith Valley Nature Reserve★ EX39 ....156 F3
Kenwin View EX39 ...156 D2
Kenwyn Rd TQ1 ....220 C6
Kenyon Ct EX3 ....182 F5
Kenyon St TA21 ....160 F5
Keppel Pl PL2 ....247 F4
Keppel St PL2 ....247 F4
Keppel Terr [8] PL2...247 F4
KERNBOROUGH 149 B8
Kernou Rd TQ4 ....226 C6
Kernow Cl PL11 ....246 E3
Kernow Ct PL11 ....246 E3
Kernow Gate PL5 ....243 C2
Kernstone Cross EX39. 22 B2
Kerria Cl TQ3 ....225 E8
Kerries Ct TQ10 ....135 A2

Kerries La TQ10 . . . . . .135 A2
Kerries Rd TQ10 . . . . . .135 A2
Ker St Ope PL1 . . . . . . .247 E2
KERSBROOK 198 B3
Kersbrook Gdns DT7 .260 D3
Kersbrook La EX9 . .198 A3
KERSCOTT 28 F8
Kerscott EX32 . . . . 28 F8
Kerscott Hill EX32 . . . . 28 F8
Kerse Cross
 Thurlestone TQ7 . . . . . .143 B2
 Thurlestone, South Milton
 TQ7 . . . . .143 C2
Kerse La TQ7 . . . . .143 B2
Kerslake's Ct 🔟
 EX14 . . . . .166 C6
Ker St PL1 . . . . .247 E1
KERSWELL 66 C1
Kerswell Cl PL21 . . . . .237 C4
Kerswell Cross TQ13 .124 A7
Kerswell La
 Kingskerswell TQ12 . . .213 A5
 Molland EX36 . . . . 31 C8
Kerswill Cross TQ9. . .135 C1
Kerswill Rd EX4 . . . . .176 F4
Kestell Rd EX10 . . . . . .188 C4
Kestor Cl
 Okehampton EX20 . . . .170 D5
 🔟 Plymouth PL2. . . . .248 A2
Kestor Dr
 Exeter EX4 . . . . .176 E8
 Paignton TQ3 . . . . . . .219 A2
Kestral Bsns Pk EX2. .178 F5
Kestral Units PL5 . . . .244 A1
Kestrel Cl
 Kingsteignton TQ12 . . .207 C8
 Okehampton EX20 . . . .170 B6
 Plymouth PL6 . . . . . . .245 D8
 🔟 Tiverton EX16 . . . . .161 E6
Kestrel Ct TQ1 . . . . . .220 C8
Kestrel Pk PL19 . . . . . .171 D2
Kestrel Way
 Barnstaple EX32. . . . . .155 E5
 Dawlish EX7 . . . . .200 F2
 Exeter EX2 . . . . .178 E5
Keswick Cres PL6 . . . .245 D2
Keverel Rd EX8 . . . . . .196 A1
Kew Ct EX2 . . . . .178 C3
Keyberry Cl TQ12 . . . .207 D1
Keyberry Mill TQ12. .207 D1
Keyberry Pk TQ12 . . . .207 D1
Keyberry Rd TQ12. . . .207 D1
Keyes Cl PL1. . . . . .247 F2
KEYHAM. 247 E5
Keyham Barton RC Prim
 Sch PL2 . . . . .247 E6
Keyham Ct PL2 . . . . . .247 E4
Keyham Rd PL2 . . . . . .247 E4
Keyham St PL5 . . . . . .247 E6
Keyham Sta PL2 . . . . .247 E6
Keymelford Cross
 EX17 . . . . 79 C2
Keysfield Rd TQ4 . . . .226 C5
Khartoum Pl TQ7 . . . .258 C5
Khyber Cl PL1 . . . . . . .247 A3
Kiddicott EX17 . . . . . .165 E5
Kidland La
 Bishops Nympton
 EX36 . . . . 31 E1
 South Molton EX36 . . . . 46 E8
Kidwelly Cl PL7 . . . . . .251 C4
Kiel Pl PL3 . . . . .249 D5
Kieran Ct 🔳 TQ1 . . . .220 A6
Kigbeare Cross EX20 . . 93 B5
Kilbarran Rise EX4 . . .177 A8
Kildere TQ7 . . . . .258 C4
Kilgannon Gdns EX1 .174 F3
Killatree Cross EX22 . . 71 E7
Killerton Cl 🔳 TQ3 . . .226 B7
Killerton House★ EX5 . 82 D3
Killerton La PL9 . . . . . .249 D1
Killerton Wlk EX6 . . . .181 F5
KILLINGTON 4 C3
Killington Cross EX31 . . 4 D2
Kilmar St PL9 . . . . .249 D1
KILMINGTON 103 D8
Kilmington Prim Sch
 EX13 . . . . .103 D8
Kilmorie TQ1 . . . . .220 F3
Kilmorie Cl TQ1 . . . . . .220 F3
Kiln Cl
 Bovey Tracey TQ13 . . . .180 C5
 Cawsand PL10 . . . . . . .253 A1
 Millbrook PL10 . . . . . .252 F6
 Plymouth PL5 . . . . . . .247 C8
Kiln Close La 🔳 EX39. . 15 B1
Kiln Cross TQ13 . . . . . .218 D3
Kilnford Rd TQ12 . . . . .207 F7
Kiln Ho TQ7 . . . . .258 C4
Kiln La
 🔳 Barnstaple EX32 . . .155 A4
 Branscombe EX12 . . . . .190 B4
 Combe Martin EX34 . . . . 3 B2
 Stokenham TQ7. . . . . . .145 B1
Kiln Orch TQ12. . . . . . .206 F3
Kiln Path TQ5. . . . . . . .230 C4
Kiln Rd
 Bovey Tracey TQ13 . . . .180 C5
 Galmpton TQ5. . . . . . . .229 A5
 Marldon TQ3 . . . . .218 C3
Kilnwood Pk EX31. . . .154 A4
Kilworthy TQ1 . . . . . . .220 B8
Kilworthy Hill PL19. . .171 C6
Kilworthy Pk PL19 . . . .171 C6

Kilworthy Rd PL19 . . . .171 C6
Kimber Cross EX20. . . . 74 E2
Kimberlands EX20. . . . 74 E2
Kimberley Ct PL21 . . .237 D5
Kimberley Pk EX39. . . .157 A7
Kimberley Rd EX2. . . .261 B2
Kimberley Terr EX39 .157 A8
Kimberley Villas
 PL21 . . . . .237 C4
Kimberly Dr PL6 . . . . .245 B1
Kimbland Cross EX32 .18 C5
Kincraig EX8 . . . . .202 C6
Kinevor Cl EX34. . . . . . . 7 F8
King Alfred Cres
 EX39. . . . . .157 A6
King Alfred Way
 EX10. . . . . .186 E8
King Arthur's Rd EX4 .174 A1
King Ave EX2 . . . . .182 C8
King Charles I Bsns Pk
 TQ12. . . . . .180 E4
King Charles Way
 EX10. . . . . .188 B8
Kingdom Ave EX36. . . .158 B5
Kingdom Fields EX31. .18 B8
Kingdom Mews EX4. .177 A7
Kingdom's Cnr EX16 . . 63 C4
Kingdom St PL3. . . . . .262 B1
Kingdon Ent Pk EX39. . 25 D4
Kingdons Ct EX36. . . .158 D5
Kingdon Wy EX22 . . . .164 C6
King Edward Rd
 Axminster EX13 . . . . . .167 C5
 Saltash PL12. . . . . .242 F2
King Edward St
 🔳 Barnstaple EX32 . . .154 F6
 Exeter EX4 . . . . .173 A1
King Edward Studios
 EX4. . . . . .173 A1
King Edward VI Coll
 Lower Sch TQ9 . . . . . . .223 B7
King Edward VI Com Coll
 (Kennicott Sixth Form)
 TQ9. . . . . .223 B6
Kingfisher Ave EX2. .176 D4
Kingfisher Cl
 Newton St Cyres EX17 . . 81 A1
 Plymouth PL6 . . . . . . .245 E6
 Tavistock PL19 . . . . . . .171 D2
 Torquay TQ2 . . . . .213 D2
Kingfisher Ct EX4 . . . .174 D1
Kingfisher Dr
 Barnstaple EX32. . . . . .155 E4
 Exeter EX4 . . . . .173 D2
 Okehampton/North Tawton
 EX20. . . . . .170 A6
Kingfisher Gdns
 EX15 . . . . .163 B2
Kingfisher Gn EX2 . . .176 D3
Kingfisher Way
 Exeter EX2 . . . . 58 F3
 Kingsteignton TQ12 . . .207 C8
 Plymouth PL9 . . . . . . .255 C7
KINGFORD 43 E6
King Henry's Rd EX2 .177 E3
King James Way PL7 .250 E8
King Pl EX15 . . . . .162 F7
Kingsacre EX33 . . . . .152 C6
Kingsacre Prim Sch
 EX33 . . . . .152 C6
King St Bsns Pk 🔳
 EX1 . . . . .261 A2
Kingsale Rd TQ8 . . . . .259 C4
KINGSAND 253 A2
King's Ash Cross TQ3 .225 E6
King's Ash Prim Sch
 TQ3. . . . . .225 E7
King's Ash Rd TQ3 . . .225 E6
Kings Ave
 Ottery St Mary EX11. . .169 F4
 Paignton TQ3 . . . . . . .226 C7
KINGSBRIDGE. 258 E5
Kingsbridge TQ1. . . . .220 B8
Kingsbridge Com Coll
 TQ7. . . . . .258 C4
Kingsbridge Com Prim
 Sch TQ7 . . . . .258 C6
Kingsbridgefork Cross
 TQ9. . . . . .144 C5
Kingsbridge La TQ13 .130 F4
Kingsbridge Rd TQ10 .137 B8
Kings Cl PL6 . . . . .245 E6
King's Cl EX2 . . . . .155 C2
Kings Cl Field TQ9 . . .131 E1
King's Cnr TA22. . . . . . 33 D6
Kings Coombe Dr 🔳
 TQ12. . . . . .123 F1
KINGSCOTT. 42 B5
Kingscott Hill EX38. . . 42 B4
Kings Cotts
 🔳 Newton Abbot
 TQ12. . . . . .207 C3
 Salcombe TQ8. . . . . . . .259 E5
King's Cres EX16. . . . .161 E4
King's Cross TQ13. . . .122 E6
Kings Ct
 🔳 Tiverton EX16. . . . . .166 C6
 Kingsbridge TQ7. . . . . .258 D3
 Kingsteignton TQ12 . . .207 B8
 Plymouth PL1 . . . . .248 A3
 🔳 Seaton EX12 . . . . . .192 B4
Kingsdale 🔟 TQ1 . . . .220 D4
KINGSDON. 103 B5
Kingsdon Hill EX24. . .103 B5
Kingsdown Cl
 Dawlish EX7 . . . . .204 E7
 Teignmouth TQ14 . . . . .209 D7

Kingsdown Cres
 EX7 . . . . .204 E7
Kingsdown Rd TQ14. .209 D7
Kings Dr TQ9 . . . . .228 A8
King's Dr The TQ2. . . .219 F4
Kings Farm La EX19 . . 58 F3
Kingsgate EX4 . . . . . . .177 D8
Kingsgate Bsns Ctr 🔟
 EX14. . . . . .166 A4
Kingsgate Cl TQ2 . . . .214 B4
King's Gdns EX14 . . . .166 C6
Kingsholme EX24 . . . .103 B3
Kingshurst Dr TQ3 . . .226 B8
KINGSKERSWELL. 213 B4
Kingskerswell CE Prim
 Sch TQ12. . . . . .213 A5
Kingskerswell Cross
 TQ2. . . . . .213 C3
Kingskerswell Rd
 Newton Abbot TQ12 . . .212 D7
 Torquay TQ2 . . . . .213 B3
Kings La EX10 . . . . . . .188 B3
King's La
 Bishop's Tawton EX32. . . 27 F7
 Lynton EX31 . . . . 4 B5
Kingslade La EX10 . . .187 B2
Kingslake Ct EX8. . . . .202 A8
Kingslake Rise EX8. . .202 A8
Kingsland Ct TQ4 . . . .225 E4
Kingsland Dr TQ4 . . . .225 E4
Kingsland Gardens Cl
 PL3 . . . . .248 E6
Kingsleigh Manor 🔳
 TQ1. . . . . .220 C5
Kingsley Ave
 🔟 Appledore EX39. . . . 15 A1
 🔳 Barnstaple EX32 . . .154 F6
 Exeter EX4 . . . . .178 B8
 Ilfracombe EX34. . . . . .150 B3
 Torpoint PL11 . . . . .247 B2
 Torquay TQ2 . . . . .213 F3
Kingsley Cl PL21 . . . . .136 D6
Kingsley Ct EX39. . . . .156 C6
Kingsley Ho EX31 . . . .155 A8
Kingsley Pk EX39 . . . .156 E7
Kingsley Rd
 Bideford EX39. . . . . . . .157 A3
 Kingsbridge TQ7 . . . . .258 C4
 Plymouth PL4 . . . . . . .248 E4
 Westward Ho! EX39 . . .156 C6
Kingsley Sch EX39 . . .156 E2
Kingsley St EX39. . . . .157 A2
Kingsley Terr
 🔟 Bideford EX39. . . . .157 A1
 🔳 Combe Martin EX34. . 3 A3
Kings Mdw TQ12. . . . .212 F4
Kingsmead Dr EX38 . .159 E6
Kingsmead Ho TQ3 . .226 C7
Kings Meadow Dr
 EX19. . . . . 58 F3
King's Mews EX14 . . . .166 C5
Kingsmill Ind Est
 EX15. . . . . .163 E5
Kingsmill Rd PL12. . . .242 C5
King's Mill Rd EX15 . .163 E5
Kingsmoor Cross
 EX26 . . . . 73 E7
KING'S NYMPTON 44 E6
King's Nympton County
 Prim Sch EX37. . . . . . . 44 E6
King's Nympton Sta
 EX37. . . . . 44 C3
Kings Orch TQ9 . . . . . .223 E5
Kings Pk EX18 . . . . 44 E1
King's Quay TQ6 . . . . .233 F4
King's Quay Ho TQ6. .233 F4
Kings Rd
 Barnstaple EX32. . . . . .155 B6
 Paignton TQ3 . . . . . . .226 C7
 Plymouth, Devonport
 PL1. . . . . .247 F2
 Plymouth, West Park
 PL5. . . . . .243 F3
King's Rd
 Dunchideock EX6 . . . . .113 F5
 Dunchideock EX6 . . . . .114 A5
 Exeter EX4 . . . . .177 E8
 Honiton EX14 . . . . .166 D6
 Plymouth PL1 . . . . . . .248 A2
Kings Rydon Cl
 Stoke Gabriel TQ9 . . . . .227 F8
 Stoke Gabriel TQ9. . . . .228 A8
Kings Sch PL3. . . . . . . .226 B6
King's Sch The EX11. .169 B3
King St
 🔟 Bideford EX39 . . . . .157 A2
 Brixham TQ5. . . . . .230 D5
 Colyton EX24 . . . . .103 A5
 Combe Martin EX34 . . . . 3 A3
 🔳 Dawlish EX7 . . . . . . .204 D6
 Exeter EX1, EX4 . . . . . .261 A2
 🔳 Honiton EX14 . . . . .166 C5
 Gunnislake PL18. . . . . .125 D6
 Honiton EX14 . . . . 85 E3
 Honiton EX14 . . . . .166 C6
 Millbrook PL10 . . . . . .252 E5
 Newton Abbot TQ12 . . .207 C3
 Plymouth PL1 . . . . . . .262 B3
 Silverton EX5 . . . . 82 B6
 South Molton EX36 . . . .158 C4
 Tavistock PL19 . . . . . . .171 B6
 Tiverton EX16 . . . . .161 C3
 Torpoint PL11 . . . . . . .247 C3
KING'S TAMERTON . . .243 F2
King's Tamerton Rd
 PL5. . . . . .243 F2
KINGSTEIGNTON. 207 C6

Kingsteignton Rd
 Chudleigh Knighton
 TQ12. . . . . .123 D4
 Newton Abbot TQ12 . . .207 C4
Kingsteignton Sch
 TQ12. . . . . .207 C8
King Stephen Cl EX4 .261 B4
King's Terr EX14 . . . . .166 C6
KINGSTON
 Bigbury. 142 C6
 Colaton Raleigh 186 A4
 Stoke Climsland 115 C1
Kingston Ave 🔳 EX34 . . 3 A3
Kingston Cl
 Kingskerswell TQ12 . . .213 A5
 Plymouth PL7 . . . . . . .251 A5
Kingston Dr PL7 . . . . .251 B5
Kingston Gate Cross
 TQ9. . . . . .216 A6
Kingston La TQ6 . . . . .233 E3
Kingston Rd
 Exmouth EX8. . . . . . . .202 C7
 Stoke Climsland PL17. .115 C1
Kingston Workshops
 TQ9. . . . . .216 A7
Kings Tor PL20. . . . . . .127 B4
Kingswater Ct TQ5. . .230 C5
Kingsway
 Exeter EX2 . . . . .177 C5
 Kingsand PL10 . . . . . . .253 B2
 Langage PL7 . . . . .251 E5
 Lyme Regis DT7 . . . . . .260 E4
 South Molton EX36 . . . .158 C3
 Teignmouth TQ14 . . . . .209 D7
Kings Way TQ6 . . . . . .106 C5
Kingsway Ave TQ4 . . .226 A1
Kingsway Cl
 Kingsbridge TQ7 . . . . .258 C4
 Paignton TQ4 . . . . . . .226 A1
Kingsway Ct TQ4. . . . .226 A1
Kingsway Dr TQ4 . . . .226 A1
Kingsway Gdns PL6. .244 F3
Kingsway Pk TQ7 . . . .258 C4
KINGSWEAR 234 B2
Kingswear Cres PL6. .245 B1
Kingswear Prim Sch
 TQ6. . . . . .234 B3
Kingswear Rd
 Brixham TQ5 . . . . .230 A1
 Brixham TQ5 . . . . .234 E8
Kingswear Sta★ TQ6 .234 A3
Kingswood Cl EX4 . . .176 F8
Kingswood Ct TQ4 . . .226 C5
Kingswood Ct TQ10 . .134 F2
Kingswood Mdw
 EX22 . . . . .164 D5
Kingswood Park Ave
 PL3 . . . . .248 D6
Kingswood Rd PL18 . .125 D6
King William Ho EX4 .261 B4
King William St EX4 . .261 B4
Kinlacey Ct TQ1. . . . . .220 C4
Kinnard Cres PL6 . . . .244 F7
Kinnerton Ct EX4 . . . .176 E8
Kinnerton Way EX4 . .176 E8
Kinross Ave PL4 . . . . .249 A4
Kinsale Rd PL5. . . . . . .243 F3
Kinscome Ct TQ1 . . . .236 C5
Kinsford Gate Cross
 EX16. . . . . 48 D5
KITBRIDGE. 88 A6
Kitchadon Gate EX18. . 59 D4
Kitchadon Rd EX18. . . 59 D3
Kitcott Cross EX36. . . . 45 F6
Kitcott Hill EX36. . . . . . 45 F6
Kit Hill Cres PL5 . . . . .247 C8
Kitley View PL8 . . . . . .257 B5
Kitley Way PL5 . . . . . .243 D1
Kits Cl 🔳 TQ13. . . . . .123 F6
Kitter Dr PL9 . . . . .256 A5
Kitterford Cross
 PL21 . . . . .137 F7

Kittersley Dr 🔟 TQ12 .122 F1
Kittiwake Dr TQ2 . . . .213 C2
Kitts TA21 . . . . .160 D4
Kitts Cross EX10 . . . . .187 A7
Kitts La EX10 . . . . .187 B6
Kitt's La EX5 . . . . 81 F2
Kitwell St EX15 . . . . . . 66 A7
Kivell Cl EX22. . . . . . . .164 B6
Klondyke Rd EX20. . . .170 C3
Knackershole La EX17. 61 B2
Knacker's Hole La
 TA3. . . . . 68 D6
Knap Cross PL21. . . . .136 C4
KNAP DOWN 3 B4
Knap Down La EX34. . . 3 B4
Knapp Copse Nature
 Reserve★ EX11. . . . . .101 D6
Knapp Hill EX10. . . . . .188 A5
Knapp Park Rd TQ4 . .226 C2
Knapps Cl PL9 . . . . . . .256 C6
Knapp's La EX10 . . . . .100 D1
Knaves Ash Cross
 TQ9. . . . . .217 A5
Kneela Hill EX21 . . . . . 74 A8
Kneele Gdns PL3. . . . .248 E8
Kneller Cl EX14 . . . . . .150 C4
Knick Knack La TQ5 . .230 C3
Knightacott Cross
 EX31 . . . . 11 C2
Knighthayes Wlk EX6 .181 F5
Knightley Rd EX2 . . . .177 E3
KNIGHTON. 140 D8
Knighton Cross TQ12 .131 F8
Knighton Hill Bsns Ctr
 PL9 . . . . .140 D8
Knighton Rd
 Plymouth PL4 . . . . . . .263 C3
 Wembury PL9 . . . . . . .140 D8
Knighton Terr 🔳
 PL20 . . . . .126 F5
Knights Cres EX2 . . . .178 D3
Knights Field Rise
 EX39 . . . . .157 A8
Knightstone La
 Ottery St Mary EX11 . . .169 F3
 Ottery St Mary, Wiggaton
 EX11. . . . . .169 F1
Knightstone Rd EX11 .169 F1
Knightswood EX15. . .163 C2
Knill Cross PL10 . . . . .252 E5
Knill Cross Cotts
 PL10. . . . . .252 E5
Knobcrook St EX38. . . 56 C6
Knockworthy Cross
 EX38. . . . . 26 F1
Knoll Knap EX13 . . . . .103 E4
Knoll The PL7. . . . . . . .250 B6
KNOTTY CORNER. 25 B4
Knowland Cl PL1. . . . .247 F3
KNOWLE
 Braunton 8 D1
 Budleigh Salterton 197 E2
 Copplestone 79 C4
Knowle Ave PL2 . . . . .247 E6
Knowle Bsns Units
 EX2. . . . . .181 D8
Knowle Cl
 Ashburton TQ13 . . . . . .130 C4
 Cullompton EX15 . . . . .163 A3
 Honiton EX14 . . . . .166 C6
 Landkey EX32. . . . . 17 B2
Knowle Cnr EX9 . . . . .197 D1
Knowle Cross
 Copplestone EX17 . . . . . 79 C4
 Hennock TQ13. . . . . . . .123 C8
 Whimple EX5 . . . . 99 E8
Knowle Cross La EX5. . 99 E8
Knowle Ct TQ8 . . . . . .259 D5
Knowle Dr
 Exeter EX4 . . . . .176 F4
 Sidmouth EX10 . . . . . .188 A4
Knowle Fork TQ7 . . . .148 F4
Knowle Gdns
 Combe Martin EX34 . . . . 3 A3
 Kingsbridge TQ7 . . . . .258 C6
 Sidmouth EX10 . . . . . .187 F4
Knowle Grange 🔳
 EX10. . . . . .188 A4
Knowle Hill EX9. . . . . .197 C2
Knowle House Cl
 TQ7. . . . . .258 D6
Knowle Ind Est EX33 . . 8 D1
Knowle La
 Butterleigh EX15 . . . . . . 64 F1
 Copplestone EX17 . . . . . 79 C4
 Drewsteignton EX6. . . . . 96 D1
Knowle Mews EX9 . . .197 E2
Knowle Prim Sch
 PL5. . . . . .244 A4
Knowle Rd
 Knowle EX9. . . . . .197 C1
 Lustleigh TQ13 . . . . . . .122 C8
 Lustleigh TQ13 . . . . . . .122 D7
 Salcombe TQ8. . . . . . . .259 D5
Knowles Cross TQ13 .130 E4
Knowles Dr 🔳 EX24 . .103 A4
KNOWLES HILL 207 B4
Knowles Hill Rd
 TQ12. . . . . .207 B6
Knowle Terr PL20. . . .127 B4

Knowle The TQ12 . . . .207 F6
Knowle View EX20 . . .170 D6
Knowle Village EX9 . .197 E2
KNOWSTONE 32 A2
Knowstone Cross
 EX16. . . . . 47 D6
Knowstone Moor Cross
 EX36. . . . . 47 B8
Kola Dr EX4 . . . . .174 D1
Kyl Cober Parc PL17. .115 C1
Kynance Cl PL11 . . . . .246 F4
Kynock Ind Est EX39 . . 25 F4

L

Labatt Cl PL6 . . . . .245 D3
Labbett's Cross EX18. . 60 C6
Labdon La EX18. . . . . . 59 C7
Laburnham Gr TQ9. .223 A9
Laburnum PL19 . . . . . .171 C6
Laburnum Cl
 Exmouth EX8. . . . . . . .196 D3
 🔳 Honiton EX14. . . . . . 85 C2
Laburnum Cotts 🔳
 TA21 . . . . .160 D5
Laburnum Ct TQ12 . . .212 B6
Laburnum Dr
 Barnstaple EX32. . . . . .155 E3
 🔳 Wembury PL9 . . . . .140 D8
Laburnum Rd
 Exeter EX2 . . . . .177 F3
 Newton Abbot TQ12 . . .207 E1
 Wellington TA21 . . . . . .160 E5
Laburnum Row 🔳
 TQ2. . . . . .219 F6
Laburnum St TQ2 . . . .219 F5
Laburnum Terr TQ12 .212 B7
Laburnum Villas
 PL19 . . . . .117 E6
Laburnum Way
 East Allington TQ9. . . . .144 E7
 Okehampton EX20 . . . .170 C5
Lace Cres EX16 . . . . . .161 B6
Lace Wlk EX14 . . . . . .166 C6
Lacey Ho 🔳 TQ3 . . . .226 B6
Lackaborough Ct
 EX2. . . . . .181 A8
Lacy Rd TQ3 . . . . .219 A1
Ladford Mill Cross
 EX21. . . . . 55 C5
Lodics Mile EX31. . . . . 4 A4
Ladies' Mile EX32 . . . .155 A3
Ladram Rd EX9 . . . . . .199 A8
Ladybird La PL20. . . . .127 A3
Ladyfern Rd PL6 . . . . .241 C1
Lady Harriet Acland's Dr
 Bury TA22 . . . . 33 F5
 Bury TA22 . . . . 34 A6
Lady Harriet Acland's Dr
 TA22. . . . . 34 A8
Ladymead EX10. . . . . .187 F8
Lady Meadow Terr
 TQ13. . . . . .121 B2
Lady Modifords CE(VA)
 Prim Sch PL20. . . . . . .127 B4
Lady Park Rd TQ2 . . . .219 D3
Lady Seawards CE Prim
 Sch EX33. . . . . .183 C6
Ladysmith Ct PL4 . . . .263 C4
Ladysmith Inf Sch
 EX1. . . . . .177 F7
Ladysmith Jun Sch
 EX1. . . . . .177 F7
Ladysmith Rd
 Exeter EX1 . . . . .177 F7
 Plymouth PL4 . . . . . . .249 B3
Lady St TA22. . . . . 33 D7
Lady Victoria's Dr
 TA22. . . . . 33 E6
Ladywell EX31 . . . . . . .154 F7
Ladywell Mdws EX37. . 44 E1
Ladywell Path EX35. . .151 A5
Ladywell Pl PL4. . . . . .263 B3
Lafrowda Cott EX4 . . .177 C8
Lagge Hill Cross EX17. 80 F8
Lag Hill EX17 . . . . 62 F1
Lagoon View EX31. . . .153 A4
LAIRA 249 C4
Laira Ave PL3. . . . . . . .249 D4
Laira Bridge Rd PL4 . .249 B1
Laira Gdns PL3. . . . . . .249 C4
Laira Green Prim Sch
 PL3. . . . . .249 C4
Laira Park Cres PL4 . .249 B4
Laira Park Pl PL4 . . . . .249 B4
Laira Park Rd PL4 . . . .249 B4
Laira Pl PL4 . . . . .263 C2
Laira St PL4 . . . . .263 C3
Laity Wlk PL6. . . . . . . .244 C4
LAKE
 Barnstaple 154 E2
 Yelverton 127 B3
Lake Ave
 🔳 Teignmouth TQ14. . .209 E8
 Teignmouth TQ14. . . . .210 A7
Lake Cl EX14. . . . . .166 D5
Lake Cross TQ9 . . . . . .131 D2
Lake Ind Est EX21 . . . . 55 E4
Lake La
 Ashreigney EX18 . . . . . . 58 F7
 Dousland PL20. . . . . . . 127 B3
 Newton St Cyres EX5 . . . 80 F2
 Northlew EX20 . . . . 74 D2
 Stockleigh Pomeroy
 EX17. . . . . 81 A7
Lakeland TQ12. . . . . . .212 B6
Lakelands Cl EX16 . . . . 46 E1

Lakelands Dr EX4.....176 F6
Lake Mews PL10.....252 E5
Lakenham Cotts
　EX39.............156 E7
Lakenham Hill EX39..156 F7
Lake Rd PL9.........255 B6
Lakerise EX7.........201 A2
Lake Rural Workshops
　EX21.............55 E4
Lakes Cl EX5.........230 A5
Lakes Cross EX20.....57 A8
Lakes Ct EX10.......188 B3
Lakes Down EX5......172 F7
Lakeside
　Salcombe TQ8......259 D5
　Tavistock PL19.....171 B6
Lakeside Ave EX2....182 B8
Lakeside Cl TQ13....180 C4
Lakeside Dr PL5......243 E5
Lakeside Village
　TQ12.............123 C6
Lakes La EX4.........98 F4
Lakes Rd TQ5........230 A4
Lake St TQ6.........233 F3
Lakeview EX7........201 A2
Lake View EX17......165 E6
Lake View Cl PL5.....244 B6
Lakeview Dr PL5......244 B5
Lakewater Cross
　TQ9..............131 E1
Lalebrick Rd PL9.....255 B5
Lamacraft Cl EX7.....204 F8
Lamacraft Dr EX4....178 A7
Lama Cross EX18......59 C4
Lamaton Pk EX36....158 D3
Lambert Cl EX7......204 F8
Lambert Cross EX20...75 A3
Lambert La EX6......96 F3
Lambert Rd PL5......244 B6
Lambert's La TQ14...209 D4
Lambhay Hill PL1.....263 A1
Lambhay St PL1.......263 A1
Lamb Park Cl 10
　TQ12.............123 F1
Lambpark Ct TA3.....68 C6
Lamb Pk
　Chagford TQ13.....111 A6
　Drewsteignton EX6...96 D1
　Ilfracombe EX34....150 A4
Lambs Cl TQ7.........143 A2
Lambscombe Cross
　EX36.............31 A8
Lambscombe Hill
　EX36.............31 A8
Lamb The TQ9.......223 B5
Lamejohns Field
　EX17.............165 C6
Lamerhooe Cross
　PL19.............116 A1
Lamerhooe Dr PL19..116 A1
LAMERTON..........116 F3
Lamerton CE Prim Sch
　PL19.............116 E3
Lamerton Cl PL5.....244 B3
Lamerton Cross EX20..75 F2
Lammacott Cross
　EX17.............78 E5
Lammacott La EX17...78 E4
Lammas La TQ3......226 A8
Lamorna Pk PL11.....246 E4
Lampard Com Sch The
　EX32.............155 C3
Lamplighters 14
　EX14.............166 C6
Lamplough Rd EX8...196 A3
LANA
　Holsworthy........53 C2
　Tetcott...........89 F7
Lana Cotts EX22......89 F7
Lana Cross EX22......55 C1
Lanbridge Cross TQ9 222 F1
Lancaster Cl
　Cullompton EX15..163 C5
　Exeter EX2........178 B5
Lancaster Dr TQ4....226 B4
Lancaster Gdns PL5..244 D4
Lancaster Ho TQ4....226 C5
Lancelot Rd EX4......174 A2
Lancercombe EX10...100 D3
Lancercombe La
　EX10.............100 D3
Lancer Ct TA21......160 D6
Lanchitt Cross EX36...19 B2
Lancin La EX22.......69 E2
Lancock St TA21.....160 A5
Landacre La TA21.....21 A7
Landboat Cotts EX17..62 F1
Landboat View EX17...62 F1
Landcroft La
　Sheldon EX15......66 F4
　Sheldon EX15......67 A4
LANDCROSS.........26 A2
Lander Rd PL12......242 F3
Landhayes Rd EX4...176 F5
LANDKEY...........17 B2
LANDKEY NEWLAND..17 B1
Landkey Prim Sch 13
　EX32.............17 B2
Landkey Rd
　Barnstaple EX32....155 C2
　Barnstaple EX32....155 D2
　Barnstaple EX32....155 D4
Landland Hill EX17....61 A4
Landland La EX11....169 B7
Langlands Bsns Pk
　PL21.............237 B6
Langham Pl PL4.....263 C3
Langham Way PL21..237 C5
Langhill Rd PL3......248 D5
Langland Hill EX17....61 A4
Langland La EX11....169 B7
Langlands Bsns Pk
Langlands Cl TQ4....225 E4
Langlands Cross EX15 163 A3
Langlands Rd EX15...163 A3
LANGLEIGH.........150 A4
Langleigh La EX34...150 A4

Landrace Cl TQ12....211 F8
Landrake Cl PL5.....247 C8
Landscore EX17......165 B5
Landscore Cl
　Crediton EX17......165 B5
Landscore Prim Sch
　EX17.............165 A5
Landscore Rd
　3 Exeter EX4......177 A5
　Teignmouth TQ14..210 B5
LANDSCOVE........131 B1
Landscove CE Prim Sch
　TQ13.............131 B1
Landsend La EX17.....78 E3
Lands Pk PL9........255 F7
Lands Rd
　Brixham TQ5......230 F6
　Exeter EX4........174 D1
LANDULPH..........243 A7
Landulph Cross PL12 238 F1
Landulph Gdns PL5..247 C8
Landulph Sch PL12..238 F1
Landunvez Pl EX5....82 F6
Lane Cross EX22......53 F7
LANE END..........73 D3
Lane End Cl 1 EX33...15 B1
Lane End Pk EX14.....78 E3
Lane End Pool TQ9...227 B3
Lane Field Rd EX39...156 D2
Lanehead Ex2.......191 D5
Lane Head Cl EX33....7 E2
Lanehead Rd EX12...191 D5
Lane The
　Dittisham TQ6.....228 D2
　Lutton PL21.......133 B2
　Plymouth PL7......250 D6
LANGAFORD........73 B2
Langaford La EX21....73 B2
Langage Cross PL7...251 F6
Langage Ind Est PL7..251 D4
Langage Pk PL7.....251 C4
Langage Science Pk
　PL7..............251 D5
Langage South Rd
　PL7..............251 D4
Langaller Cl TQ13...180 B5
Langaller Hill TA22....33 D4
Langaller La
　Bovey Tracey TQ13..122 E3
　Bovey Tracey TQ13..180 B4
Langarra Pk EX15....162 B4
Langarron Pk EX32...155 B5
Langaton Gdns EX1..174 F1
Langaton La EX1.....175 A1
LANGBROOK........136 D3
Langbrook Cross
　PL21.............136 E3
Langdale Cl PL6.....245 D1
Langdale Gdns PL6..245 D1
Langdon Cross PL21 139 F7
Langdon Ct PL9.....256 B6
Langdon Down Way
　PL11.............246 E3
Langdon Fields TQ5..229 B6
Langdon Hospl EX7..200 E2
Langdon La
　Dawlish EX7......204 C8
　Galmpton TQ4, TQ5..229 B6
Langdon Rd
　Bradworthy EX22....38 E1
　Dawlish EX7......204 D8
　Paignton TQ3......219 C1
Langdons Way TA20...88 C8
Langdown Way EX5...179 B3
LANGDOWN..........95 D7
Langerwehe Way
　EX8..............201 F6
Langerwell Cl PL12..242 C3
Langerwell La PL12..242 C3
LANGFORD
　Brampford Speke...172 E8
　Plymtree..........83 C5
Langford Ave EX14..166 D6
Langford Cres TQ2...223 F3
Langford Cross EX17..78 C4
Langford Gate PL21..137 F8
Langford Gn EX15....83 D5
Langford Rd
　Honiton EX14......166 D7
　Langford EX5......172 E7
Lang Gdns PL18.....125 D3
Lang Gr
　Plymouth PL9......256 C7
　Tavistock PL19.....171 D5
Langham Cross EX19..57 D6
Langham La EX17....165 A4
Langham Levels
　PL21.............237 B6
Langham Pl PL4.....263 C3
Langham Way PL21..237 C5
Langhill Rd PL3......248 D5
Langland Hill EX17....61 A4
Langland La EX11....169 B7
Langlands Bsns Pk
Langleigh La EX34...150 A4

Langleigh Pk EX34...150 A4
Langleigh Rd EX34...150 A5
Langley Cl EX18......44 E1
Langley Ave TQ5....230 C4
Langley Cl
　Brixham TQ5......230 C4
　Plymouth PL6......245 A7
Langley Cres PL6....244 F7
Langley Gdns 6 EX18..44 E1
Langley La EX18......44 E1
Langman Ct 17 PL20..125 E1
Langmans Cross TQ7 143 A2
Langmead
　Westleigh EX39.....26 B7
　Westleigh EX39....157 E5
Langmead Cl PL6....249 C8
Langmead Dr EX39...157 E1
Langmead Rd PL6...249 C8
Langmoor Cl DT7....260 D3
Langmoor La EX13....88 D2
Langmore Cl PL6....249 A7
Langport La EX7.....200 D3
Langridge Cross EX37..27 F1
LANGRIDGEFORD....27 F1
Langridge Rd TQ3...225 E8
Langsfield EX33........7 D1
Langsford Rd PL19...117 C3
Langs Rd TQ3.......226 C8
Langston Cross
　Kingston TQ7......142 D7
　Whiddon Down EX20..95 D1
Langstone Cl
　Heathfield TQ12....180 F2
　Torquay TQ1......220 D6
Langstone Cross
　TQ13.............121 E8
Langstone Dr EX8...196 C1
Langstone Hill
　Lustleigh TQ13.....121 E8
　Moretonhampstead
　TQ13.............111 E1
Langstone Rd PL2...248 C7
Langstone Terr PL2..248 C7
Langton Rd 8 PL20...126 F3
LANGTREE..........40 F2
LANGTREE COMMON..41 A3
Langtree Com Prim Sch
　EX38.............40 F2
Langtreemoor La
　EX38.............40 E2
Lang Way TQ12.....211 E2
Langwells Ct TQ9...139 E1
Langworthys Barn
　TQ7..............143 E2
Lanherne EX7.......204 E6
Lanherne Fst Sch 26
　EX7..............204 D6
Lanhydrock Cl TQ3..225 D8
Lanhydrock Rd PL4..249 B2
Lannacombe Rd TQ7 149 C5
Lanscore La EX14....101 A8
Lansdowne EX2.....178 B4
Lansdowne La 2
　TQ2..............219 F5
Lansdowne Pk
　Budleigh Salterton
　EX9..............197 D1
　Plymouth PL6......244 F2
　1 Torquay TQ2....219 F5
Lansdowne Rd
　Bideford EX39.....156 F8
　Exeter EX2........261 B2
Lansdown Terr 2
　EX32.............155 A6
Lanteglos Cl 5 PL21 137 C7
LAPFORD...........60 C3
Lapford Com Prim Sch
　EX17.............60 D3
Lapford Cross EX17...60 C2
Lapford Sta EX17....60 D2
Laps Cottage TA20...69 C5
Lapthorn Cl PL9.....255 C7
Lapthorne Ind Est
　TQ12.............211 F3
Lapwing Cl
　Cullompton EX15...163 A3
　Dawlish EX7......200 F2
Lapwing Gr EX31.....15 C3
Larch Cl
　Exmouth EX8......196 D3
　Saltash PL12......242 C3
　Seaton EX12......192 A8
　Teignmouth TQ14..210 B6
Larch Dr PL6........245 E7
Larch Gr
　Plympton PL7......132 B1
　Sparkwell PL7.....132 C1
Larch Rd
　Dawlish EX7......204 E8
　Exeter EX2........176 F3
Larch Wlk TQ2......219 C8
Larcombe End TQ9...135 F1
LARKBEARE........100 B8
Larkbeare Ave EX5..100 B8
Larkbeare Cross EX5 100 B8
Larkbeare Rd EX2...261 B1
Lark Cl EX4..........173 D1
Larkey La EX16.......63 D4
Larkhall Rise PL3....249 A8
Larkham Cl PL7.....250 C6
Larkham La PL7.....250 C6
Lark Hill PL2.........248 A6

Larkin Cl TQ13......180 F7
Lark Rise
　5 Barnstaple EX31..154 A2
　Newton Poppleford
　EX10.............186 E8
Larks Cl TQ14.......209 D4
Larkshayes Cross
　EX13.............86 E3
Larkshayes Droveway
　EX13.............86 F3
Larkshayes Knap EX13 86 F3
Larksmead Cl TQ12..207 A1
Larksmead Way
　TQ12.............207 A1
Larkspur Ct TQ3....225 E2
Larkspur Dr TQ12...206 E5
Larkspur Gdns EX32..155 E4
Larks Rise EX15.....163 A2
Larkstone Cres 3
　EX34.............150 D5
Larkstone Gdns
　EX34.............150 D5
Larkstone La EX34...150 D6
Larkstone Terr EX34 150 D6
Larks Way EX34.......17 F4
Lashbrook EX5........84 B2
Lashingcott Cross
　EX31.............27 B3
Lashingcott Lane End
　EX31.............27 B2
Laskeys Heath 1
　TQ12.............122 F1
Laskeys La EX10....188 C4
Latches Wlk EX13...167 D6
Latchgate Cross EX36..31 F7
Latchgate Hill EX36...31 F7
Latch La EX38.......40 E2
Latchmount Gdns
　EX13.............167 D6
Latham Cl PL6......249 A7
Latham Ct EX39.....156 F2
Latimer Cl PL7......251 B5
Latimer Rd EX4.....178 A8
Latimer Wlk PL6....244 E2
Lauderdale 2 EX32..155 B4
Lauderdale Dr EX32..155 B4
Lauder La EX31.....154 C1
LAUNCESTON.......105 B2
Launceston Cl PL6...245 B7
Launceston Head EX5..83 C1
Launceston Rd
　Bridestowe EX20...107 E8
　Tavistock PL19.....171 A5
Laundry Cotts EX5....98 F8
Laura Ave TQ3......226 B8
Laura Gr TQ3.......226 A8
Laura Pl 3 TQ3......226 A6
Laurel Ave EX39....156 E1
Laurel Bank EX14....85 B4
Laurel Cl PL2........248 A7
Laurel Dene PL2.....248 A7
Laurel Dr PL6........245 E5
Laurel La TQ14......209 D5
Laurel Rd
　Exeter EX2........177 F3
　1 Honiton EX14....166 A4
　Plymouth PL2......248 A7
Laurel Rise EX8.....202 D8
Laurels The
　Barnstaple EX31....154 B2
　Dunkeswell EX14....67 C3
　Gunnislake PL18...125 B5
　Sidmouth EX10....188 A5
　Torquay TQ1......220 D8
Laurie Ave TQ14....206 F2
Lauriston Cl TQ2....220 A5
Lavender Cl TQ5....230 A4
Lavender Rd EX4....176 E8
Lavender Wy EX32...155 C4
Lavington Cl PL7....251 B5
Lavinia Dr PL7......250 C5
LAWHITTON........105 B1
Lawhitton Down
　PL15.............105 A1
Law Memorial Ho 5
　EX32.............16 E1
Lawn Cl
　2 Plymouth PL7....251 C5
　Torquay TQ2......213 F4
Lawn Dr
　Chudleigh TQ13....123 C6
　14 Chudleigh TQ13 123 F6
Lawn Gdns 16 TQ13 123 E6
Lawn Hill 3 EX7.....204 E6
Lawn Rd EX8........202 A7
Lawns End TQ14....208 E8
Lawns The
　Barnstaple EX32....155 D2
　Plymouth PL5......244 E1
　Torpoint PL11......247 A4
Lawn Terr 25 EX7...204 D6
Lawn The
　3 Budleigh Salterton
　EX9..............198 A1
　1 Wellington TA21..160 D6
Lawn Vista EX10....188 B5
Lawrence Ave EX4...177 A4
Lawrence Cl EX14....84 D7
Lawrence Pl TQ2....220 B4
Lawrence Rd PL9....255 A6
Lawrence Wlk EX6..181 F5
Lawson Gr PL9......255 C7
Law Wlk PL6........244 D6
Laxton Ave EX1......178 C6
Layne Cl EX6........113 B4
Layne Fields EX6....113 B4

Laywell Cl TQ5......230 B2
Laywell La TQ5......230 A3
Laywell Rd TQ5......230 A3
Lazenby Rd EX16....161 F3
Leach Ave TQ13....180 B6
Leaches La EX18.....60 B7
Leachway La EX2....113 F7
Leachway Lane Cross
　EX2..............113 F7
Lea Combe EX13....167 D5
Leadengate Cl EX33...7 E1
Leadengate Fields
　EX33.............7 D1
Leader Cl TQ5.......230 E5
Leader La
　Marldon TQ3......218 C1
　Marldon TQ3......218 D2
　Paignton TQ3......225 D8
Leaholes Ave EX20..170 C5
Lea La EX5..........198 F7
Lealands TQ13......180 C6
Lea Mount TQ14....209 A8
Lea Mount Cl EX7...204 D5
Lea Mount Dr EX7...204 D5
Lea Mount Rd EX7..204 D5
Leander Ct 18 TQ14 210 B4
Leander Way PL5....244 D2
Leanway EX12.......242 E2
Lea Rd
　Otterton EX9......198 E7
　Tiverton EX16.....161 F6
　Torquay TQ2......214 B3
Lear La EX13........167 C4
Lear Pk EX15........83 F5
Lears La TQ13.......123 F6
Leary Cross EX32....29 B8
Lease Cotts EX5......82 D4
Lease Hill EX5.......82 E4
Lea Side EX6........112 E8
Leas Rd EX9........198 A1
Leas The EX34......150 A3
Leat Cl
　Dousland PL20.....127 B3
　Kingsteignton TQ12 207 E2
Lea Terr EX39........15 A1
Leatfield Dr
　Plymouth PL6......244 F4
　Plymouth PL6......245 A4
Lea The TQ14.......209 C2
Leatherby Cl PL6....244 F7
Leather Tor Cl 4
　PL20.............126 F3
Leat Mdw
　3 Coldeast TQ12...122 F1
　Tiverton EX16.....161 B5
Leat Rd PL16........105 F3
Leat St
　Tiverton EX16.....161 B5
　Tiverton EX16.....161 C6
Leat View
　Ivybridge PL21.....237 D5
　Saltash PL12......242 B3
Leatway Gdns EX15 163 B3
Leat Wlk
　Plymouth PL3......248 E6
　Roborough PL6....241 D1
　Saltash PL12......242 D4
Lea Vale Rd TQ12...207 A3
Lea View EX15......162 D5
Leaway Cotts EX16..161 E4
Leaze Rd TQ12......207 D8
Lebanon Cl EX4.....173 E1
Leburnick Cross
　PL15.............115 B8
Ledgate La PL7......251 F8
Ledsgrove TQ12....211 E2
LEDSTONE.........144 B5
Ledstone Cross TQ7 144 B5
LEE..............1 C3
Lee Ave EX39........25 F1
Lee Ball Cross EX31..11 E3
Lee Ball Hill EX31....11 D3
Leechwell La TQ9...223 C5
Leechwell St TQ9...223 B5
Lee Cl EX14.........166 B6
Lee Cliff Pk EX7......201 B1
Lee Cross
　Broadhempston TQ9..131 E1
　Great Torrington EX37..42 F7
　North Molton EX36...30 B8
　Woolacombe EX34....1 C1
Lee Lane End TQ7...148 F8
Lee Mdw EX34......150 A3
LEE MILL...........136 C1
Lee Mill Hospl PL7..136 C2
Lee Mill Ind Est PL21 136 D1
LEE MOOR.........132 F5
Lee Moor La PL7....132 E4
Lee Pk TA21.........52 F7
Lee Pl EX34.........150 C6
Lee Rd EX35........151 B5

Lak-Lev 291

Leeside Ct 7 PL2...248 A4
Lees Mdw EX5.......84 A2
Lee Terr 2 TQ13....123 E6
Leeward Ct FX8.....201 E6
Leeward La TQ2.....213 E3
Leeze Pk EX20......170 B4
Leggetts La EX7.....193 C7
Legion Hall La PL18..125 C5
Legion La PL8.......257 A5
Legion Way EX7.....177 B2
Legis Wlk PL6.......245 B8
Leg O Mutton Corner
　PL19.............126 F2
Leicester Mead EX4..176 F2
LEIGHAM..........249 E8
Leigham Ct
　7 Dawlish EX7.....204 E6
　Plymouth PL1......262 B2
Leighammanor Dr
　PL6..............245 F1
Leigham Manor Dr
　PL6..............249 F8
Leigham Prim Sch
　PL6..............245 E1
Leigham St PL1.....262 B1
Leigham Terr PL7....258 C5
Leigham Terrace La
　PL1..............262 B2
Leigham Terrace Lane W
　PL1..............262 B2
Leighan Bsns Units
　EX2..............181 D8
Leigh Cl PL21.......137 C8
Leighcott Cross EX17..62 A2
Leighcott La EX17....62 A2
Leigh Cross
　Ashill EX15........66 F6
　Bittaford PL21......137 D8
　Bridford EX6......113 B6
　Chulmleigh EX18....59 C8
　Hennock TQ13....123 C7
　Kingsbridge TQ7...258 A8
　Modbury PL21.....137 F3
　South Brent TQ10..135 A4
　Zeal Monachorum EX17..77 F7
Leigh Ct PL6........249 A8
Leighdene Cl EX2....177 E4
Leigh Dene Cl EX2...177 E4
Leigh La
　Bittaford PL21......137 C8
　Chawleigh EX17....60 C6
　Combe Martin EX34...3 C2
　Moorhaven Village
　TQ10.............137 C8
　Roborough PL6....241 D2
Leighmoor Cross
　PL21.............137 F3
Leighon Rd TQ3.....226 C7
Leigh Rd
　Bideford EX39.....156 E1
　Chulmleigh EX18....44 D1
　Combe Martin EX34...3 B2
Leighton Rd PL3....248 F8
Leighton Terr EX4...261 B4
Leighty Water EX38...42 A6
Leigh Villas EX18....44 E1
Leland Gr PL21......237 D4
Le Locle Cl EX10....187 B8
Lembury Rd TQ9....225 A1
Le Marchant Cl EX14..67 E4
Le Molay-Littry Way
　TQ13.............180 E7
Lemon Cl 18 TQ12..207 C3
Lemonford La TQ12 131 D7
Lemonford Mills
　TQ12.............131 D6
Lemon Pl TQ12.....207 C3
Lemon Rd TQ12....207 C3
Lenards Rd EX39....156 F6
Lenda La TQ12......122 C2
Lendon Way EX19....58 F2
Lennard Rd 6 EX17..165 C5
Lennards Ct EX10...188 B3
Lennox Ave EX10....188 B4
Lentney Cl PL9......140 A8
Lenton La EX37.....44 C6
Lenwood Ctry Club
　EX39.............156 E5
Lenwood Pk EX39...156 E4
Lenwood Rd EX39...156 E5
Leo Ave PL9.........256 E8
Leofric Rd EX16.....161 D6
Leonard Moor Cross
　EX15.............65 F8
Leonards Cl TQ7....143 A1
Leonards Rd PL21...237 D5
Lerwell Beech Tree Cross
　EX37.............29 A5
Leslie Rd EX8.......202 A4
Lester Cl PL3.......249 B6
Lestock Cl EX4......202 F7
Lethaby Rd EX32....155 B6
Lethbridge Rd EX2..178 B4
Lethbridge's & Davey's
　Almshouses EX1...261 C4
Letheren 's La EX20...77 B5
Letherens Mdw EX20..77 B5
Lettaford Cross TQ13 111 B3
LEUSDON..........130 A8
Level The TQ6......228 C2
Lever Cl EX39.......156 F8
Leverlake La
　Chettiscombe EX16..49 C1
　Tiverton EX16.....161 F7

Lewdon Cross EX6 . . . . . . .97 A5
LEWDOWN. 106 E5
Lewesdon Ct **2** DT7. .260 D3
Lewes Gdns PL5 . . . . . . .244 C4
Lewhaven Cl EX20 . . . . .106 E5
Lewis Ave EX16 . . . . . . .161 E4
Lewis Cres EX2 . . . . .178 D3
Lewis Ct **4** EX34. . . . . .150 B5
Leworthy Cross
　Holsworthy EX22. . . . . . .71 A4
　Woolfardisworthy EX39. .39 B6
Leworthy Dr EX4. . . . . .174 E3
Leworthy Hill EX31. . . . .11 D1
Leworthy Post EX31. . . .11 C1
Lewsley Cross EX13. . . . .87 E4
Lewsley La EX13 . . . . . . .87 E4
Lewthorn Cross
　TQ13. . . . . .122 B3
LEWTRENCHARD. 106 F4
Lew Trenchard CE Prim
　Sch EX20. . . . . .106 F5
Lexhayne La EX13. . . . . .103 A7
Leyburn Gr TQ4. . . . . . .226 A4
Ley Cl TQ12. . . . . .180 B1
Ley Cres TQ12. . . . . .180 B1
Ley Cross
　Ashreigney EX18 . . . . . . .58 F8
　Aveton Gifford PL21. . . .143 A8
　Ermington PL21. . . . . . .136 D4
　Holsworthy Beacon
　　EX22. . . . . .54 F3
　North Molton EX36. . . . .30 F8
　Widecombe in the Moor
　　TQ13. . . . . .121 C6
Leyfield Wlk EX7. . . . . . .204 E7
Leyford Cl PL9. . . . . .140 D8
Leyford La PL9. . . . . .255 F3
Ley La
　Bere Ferrers PL20 . . . . .239 D6
　Kentisbury EX31. . . . . . . .10 D6
　Kingsteignton TQ12. . . .207 D8
Ley La Cross TQ12. . . . .207 D8
Leyland Cross EX22 . . . . .53 E8
Ley Meadow Dr EX31 154 A3
Leypark Ave PL21 . . . . .237 E4
Leypark Cl EX1. . . . . .178 C7
Leypark Cres EX1 . . . . . .178 C7
Leypark Ct PL6. . . . . .245 E2
Leypark Dr PL6 . . . . .245 E2
Leypark Rd EX1. . . . . . . .178 C7
Leypark Wlk PL6. . . . . . .245 E2
Ley's Cross EX17. . . . . . . .62 E2
Ley's La EX31. . . . . .4 C1
Leys Rd TQ2 . . . . .219 D5
Leyton Ct EX15. . . . . . . .163 C4
Leywood EX14. . . . . .86 D7
Libby Ct PL12. . . . . .242 C5
Liberator Way EX14. . . . .67 C1
Liberty Rd EX31. . . . . . . .154 E2
Liberty Way EX2 . . . . . . .178 E1
Libra Ave PL9. . . . . .256 E8
Libra Gdns EX34 . . . . .2 F4
Libra Sch The EX36. . . . . .19 E3
Lichfield Ave TQ12 . . . . .214 A1
Lichfield Cl TQ5. . . . . . . .230 A4
Lichfield Dr TQ5. . . . . . .230 A4
Lichfield Rd EX4 . . . . . . .176 D6
Lichgate Rd EX2. . . . . . .181 C8
Lidburn Hill EX6 . . . . .97 E5
LIDDATON. 106 F1
Liddle Way EX7. . . . . . . .251 B6
Lidford Tor Ave TQ4. . . .225 F3
Lidstone La TQ3 . . . . . . .225 C1
Lidyates La DT7, EX13 103 F3
Lifeboat La
　4 Shaldon TQ14. . . . . .209 F5
　Shaldon TQ14 . . . . .210 A4
Liffey Rise EX4. . . . . .176 E8
LIFTON. 105 E4
Lifton Com Prim Sch
　PL16. . . . . .105 E4
LIFTONDOWN. 105 C4
Liftondown Cross
　PL16. . . . . .105 C4
Lifton La EX19 . . . . .59 B3
Lighthouse Cross
　EX39. . . . . .23 B3
Light La TQ5. . . . . .229 B8
Lightleigh Cross EX18. 44 F5
Lilac Cl PL9. . . . . .255 C5
Lilac Haven EX14. . . . . . .166 C5
Lilac Rd
　Exeter EX2. . . . . .177 F3
　Tiverton EX16. . . . . .161 F5
Lilac Terr **2** EX16. . . .161 E4
Lilac Way **3** EX32. . . .155 C4
Lilford Gdns TQ12. . . . . .244 A2
Lilian Cl EX17. . . . . .78 B4
Lillage La EX9 . . . . .198 D2
Lillebonne Cl TA21. . . . .160 F6
Lillebonne Wy TA21. . . .160 D7
Lilley Wlk EX14. . . . . . . .166 D5
Lillicrap Ct EX20. . . . . . .170 B5
Lillybrook La EX24 . . . . . .98 A5
Lillycombe La TA3,
　EX15. . . . . .67 E8
Lilly La EX5. . . . . .172 A8
Lilybridge EX39. . . . . . . .157 A7
Lily Cl EX19. . . . . .157 A4
Lilylake Cross EX24 . . . .102 F7
Lily Mount EX4. . . . . .99 F8
Lilypond La EX5. . . . . .99 F8
Limberland Ave TQ9 .215 E1
Lime Ave TQ2. . . . . .219 F5

Limeburners Rd PL4 . .255 B6
Lime Cl
　Broadclyst EX5. . . . . . . .175 C6
　Tiverton EX16. . . . . .161 F5
Lime Cres EX15 . . . . . . .162 C4
Lime Gr
　Bideford EX39. . . . . .156 F2
　Bideford EX39. . . . . .157 A2
　Exminster EX6. . . . . . . .182 A5
　Exmouth EX8. . . . . .196 C3
　Kingsbridge TQ7. . . . . . .258 C5
Limegrove Rd EX4 . . . . .176 F5
Limehayes Rd EX20 . . . .170 C5
Limekiln La EX31. . . . . . .16 A6
Lime Kiln La
　Exeter EX2. . . . . .178 A1
　Uplyme DT7 . . . . .260 A6
　Uplyme DT7 . . . . .260 A7
Lime Kiln Rd EX16. . . . .161 F5
Limekilns Cl EX36. . . . . .158 B3
Lime Rd EX16. . . . . .161 F5
Limerick Pl PL4. . . . . . . .263 C3
Limers Cross
　Chittlehampton EX37 . . . .29 A4
　Wolverstone EX14 . . . . . . .85 C7
Limer's Hill EX38. . . . . . .159 B5
Limers La
　Merton EX20. . . . . .57 A7
　Northam EX39 . . . . .156 F5
　Northam EX39 . . . . .157 A5
　Wolverstone EX14 . . . . . . .85 C7
Limer's La EX36. . . . . . . .158 B2
Limer's Lane Cross
　EX36. . . . . .158 B2
Limes Cotts EX6 . . . . . . .182 A4
Limes La EX6 . . . . .182 B4
Limes La PL19. . . . . .171 A6
Lime St
　Moretonhampstead
　　TQ13. . . . . .111 F5
　Sheepwash EX21. . . . . . .56 C1
Limes The PL6. . . . . .244 F2
Limestone Dr EX4. . . . . .174 F2
Lime Tree Cl EX2. . . . . . .178 C3
Limetree Cross EX16 . .64 D6
Limetree Gr EX33. . . . . .152 C6
Lime Tree Mead **1**
　EX16. . . . . .64 D7
Limetree Rd PL3 . . . . . . .248 D7
Lime Tree Wlk TQ12. . . .207 E1
Lime Wy EX12 . . . . .192 A7
Lime Wy EX36 . . . . .158 C6
Linacre La TQ12. . . . . . . .213 C6
Linacre Rd TQ2 . . . . .213 F4
Lincoln Ave PL4. . . . . . . .263 C4
Lincoln Cl
　Exmouth EX8. . . . . .196 E4
　Feniton EX14. . . . . .84 D2
Lincoln Gn TQ2 . . . . .214 A1
Lincoln Rd EX4 . . . . .176 E6
LINCOMBE. 1 D3
Lincombe Cross
　Diptford TQ9. . . . . .138 D8
　Salcombe TQ8. . . . . .259 D7
Lincombe Dr TQ1 . . . . . .220 E3
Lincombe Hill Rd
　TQ1. . . . . .220 E4
Linda Cl EX1. . . . . .178 B5
Linden Cl
　Barnstaple EX31. . . . . . .154 C3
　Braunton EX33. . . . . . . .152 D6
　Exmouth EX8. . . . . .196 D2
　Great Torrington EX38 .159 C5
Linden Ct **2** TQ5. . . . .230 C5
Linden Gdns EX31. . . . . .154 C3
Linden Hill
　Rockwell Green
　　TA21. . . . . .160 A6
　Wellington TA21. . . . . . .160 A6
Linden Rd
　Cullompton EX15 . . . . . .163 C4
　Dawlish EX7. . . . . .204 D5
Linden Terr
　Newton Abbot TQ12. . . .207 A3
　Plymouth PL4 . . . . .263 C3
Lindfield Cl TQ2 . . . . . . .219 F8
Lindisfarne Way TQ2 213 E2
Lindridge Cl **5** TQ12.123 E1
Lindridge Hill
　Kingsteignton TQ12. . . .123 F1
　Kingsteignton TQ12. . . .124 A2
Lindridge La **6** TQ12 123 E1
Lindridge Pk TQ14. . . . . .124 B2
Lindridge Rd
　Ashwell TQ14 . . . . .124 B1
　Torquay TQ1. . . . . .220 C8
Lindsay Rd TQ3 . . . . . . .219 A2
Lindthorpe Way TQ5. . . .230 B4
Linett Cl TQ12. . . . . .207 C8
Linfield Gdns EX14 . . . . .176 F4
Linhay Bsns Pk TQ13. .131 A5
Linhay Cl
　Brixham TQ5. . . . . .234 F8
　Honiton EX14 . . . . .166 B3
　Millmoor EX15 . . . . .51 E1
Linhay Dr
　Fremington EX31. . . . . . .153 F6
　Kingsteignton TQ12. . . .207 F6
Linhay La PL9 . . . . .249 D1
Linhay Pk EX17. . . . . .80 A5
Linhay Rd EX5 . . . . .99 C6
Linhey Cl TQ7. . . . . .258 C5
Linkadells PL7. . . . . .250 D6
Linketty La E PL6 . . . . . .245 A1
Linketty Lane W PL6. . . .248 F8
Linkhay TA20 . . . . .88 D8

Linkhay Cl TA20. . . . . .88 D8
Link House Cl EX39. . . . .156 C7
Link Rd EX20 . . . . .170 C6
Links Cl
　Churston Ferrers
　　TQ5. . . . . .229 E6
　Exmouth EX8. . . . . .202 C8
Links Ct TQ7. . . . . .143 A1
Links Rd EX9 . . . . .203 E8
Links The
　Northam EX39 . . . . .156 E7
　Torquay TQ2. . . . . .214 C1
Linnet Cl EX4. . . . . .173 D2
Linnet Ct PL12. . . . . .242 C2
Linnet Dene EX15 . . . . . .163 A2
Torquay TQ2. . . . . .213 D1
Linscott Cres EX31. . . . .153 A4
Linseed Dr EX13 . . . . . . .167 E6
Linton Cl PL5 . . . . .244 C8
Linton La EX39. . . . . .37 B5
Linton Rd
　Exeter EX1. . . . . .178 D6
　Plymouth PL5 . . . . .244 C7
Linton Sq PL5. . . . . .244 C8
Lion Cl TQ2. . . . . .258 C5
Lion Ho EX8. . . . . .202 A5
Lion's Close Hill
　EX24. . . . . .103 A5
Lions Mill EX31. . . . . . . .154 E7
Lions Rest Eco Pk
　EX6. . . . . .182 D3
Lion's Rump EX32,
　EX36. . . . . .18 F1
Lippell Dr PL9 . . . . .255 E6
Lipscomb Ave EX8 . . . . .202 E7
LIPSON. 263 C4
Lipson Ave PL4. . . . . .263 C4
Lipson Cooperative Acad
　PL4. . . . . .249 C4
Lipson Ct PL4. . . . . .263 B3
Lipson Rd PL4 . . . . .263 B4
Lipson Sp Ctr PL4. . . . . .249 B4
Lipson Terr PL4. . . . . . . .263 C4
LIPSON VALE. 249 A4
Lipson Vale PL4 . . . . . . .249 A4
Lipson Vale Prim Sch
　PL7. . . . . .249 A4
Lipson Cres PL4. . . . . . . .263 C4
Lisa Cl EX2. . . . . .178 A4
Lisburne Cres **18**
　TQ1. . . . . .220 D4
Lisburne Pl **10** TQ1 . .220 D4
Lisburne Sq TQ1 . . . . . . .220 D4
Liscaw Terr PL11 . . . . . .247 B3
Liscombe Cl PL18 . . . . . .125 D7
Lisham's Drain EX24 .103 A5
Lishaperhill Cross
　EX22. . . . . .53 B2
Liskeard Rd PL12 . . . . . .242 B3
Lisson Gr PL4. . . . . .248 F4
Lister Cl
　Exeter EX2. . . . . .177 E4
　Plymouth PL7 . . . . .250 F6
Lister Way TQ9 . . . . .144 E7
Litchardon Cross EX31 26 F8
Litchaton Cres PL7. . . . .250 B7
Litchaton Cross
　East Buckland EX32 . . . . .18 F1
　North Molton EX36. . . . .30 A8
Litchaton Hill
　East Buckland EX36 . . . . .18 F1
　North Molton EX36. . . . .30 A8
Litchaton Way PL7. . . . .250 B7
Litchdon La EX32 . . . . . .154 F4
Litchdon St EX32. . . . . . .155 A4
Litchfield Cl PL7 . . . . . . .251 B6
Litelbury Rd EX16. . . . . . .64 D7
Littabourne EX31 . . . . . .154 F7
Little Ash Gdns PL5 . . . .243 B1
Little Ash Rd PL5 . . . . . . .243 B1
Little Barley EX4. . . . . . .176 F5
Little Barton **7**
　TQ12. . . . . .123 F1
Little Batten Rd TQ9. .223 D8
Little Bewden TQ13. . . .130 A4
Little Bickington
　Courtyard EX38. . . . . . . .43 C7
Little Bickington La
　EX38. . . . . .43 C7
Little Bicton Ct **18**
　EX8. . . . . .202 A6
Little Bicton Pl EX8 . . . .202 A6
Littleborough Cross
　EX17. . . . . .62 A5
Little Bossell La
　TQ11. . . . . .236 B4
Little Bray Cross EX32 18 C8
Littlebray La EX32. . . . . . .18 E6
Little Bridge Bsns Pk
　EX5. . . . . .179 D1
Little Bridge Cross
　EX22. . . . . .70 F5
Littlebridge Mdw
　EX22. . . . . .70 F5
Little Buddies Pre-school
　10 PL7. . . . . .251 B5
Little Butts PL9 . . . . .255 E6
Little Castle St EX4. . . . .261 B3
Little Chockenhole La
　EX9. . . . . .187 A1
Little Cl
　Kingsteignton TQ12. . . .207 E8
　Ottery St Mary EX11. . .169 D3
Little Court EX39. . . . . . . .26 A4
Little Cross TQ13. . . . . . .130 A4
Little Dock La PL5. . . . . .244 B2
Littledown Cl EX8. . . . . .202 F7
Littledown La EX10. . . . .186 D7

Little Down La
　East Budleigh EX9. . . . . .198 A5
　Roborough PL6. . . . . . . .241 E3
Little Down Orch
　EX10. . . . . .186 D7
Little Esworthy La
　EX16. . . . . .48 A1
Little Fancy Cl PL6 . . . .245 C7
Littlefield TQ14 . . . . .208 E8
Little Field
　Bideford EX39. . . . . .156 D2
　Cranbrook EX5 . . . . .99 C6
Littlefield Cl
　Barnstaple EX32. . . . . . .155 D4
　Torquay TQ2. . . . . .213 D1
Little Field Ct PL19 . . . .171 E5
Littlefields EX12 . . . . . . .192 A7
Littleford Cross EX22. . 53 E8
Little Gate TQ7. . . . . .143 F7
Littlegate Rd TQ3 . . . . . .226 B6
Little Gornhay La
　Chevithorne EX16. . . . . . .49 D1
　Tiverton EX15. . . . . .64 D8
Little Hayes **12** TQ12. 123 F1
Little Hayes La EX15. . . 58 D8
Little Heath Cross
　EX16. . . . . .63 A6
Little Helstonbench Cross
　TQ13. . . . . .123 B6
Little Hill
　Buckland St Mary
　　TA20. . . . . .69 D7
　Salcombe TQ8. . . . . .259 C5
Little Hill Cl TQ12 . . . . . .123 F1
Little John's Cross Hill
　EX2. . . . . .176 E3
Little John's Wlk
　TQ13. . . . . .122 F6
Littlejoy Rd TQ12. . . . . .206 C4
LITTLE KNOWLE. 197 F1
Little Knowle EX9. . . . . .197 F1
Little Knowle Ct EX9 .197 F1
Little La
　Beer EX12. . . . . .191 D4
　Bishop's Nympton EX36 . .30 F3
　Bishop's Nympton EX36 . .31 A3
　Kingsand PL10 . . . . .253 A2
　Staddiscombe PL9. . . . .255 D3
Little Liverton Bsns Pk
　TQ12. . . . . .122 F1
Little Marsh Rd EX20 .170 E6
Little Mdw
　Clyst Honiton EX1. . . . . .175 B1
　Exmouth EX8. . . . . .196 E3
　Pyworthy EX22. . . . . .71 D5
Little Mdws EX18 . . . . . . .59 C4
Little Mead EX5. . . . . .99 B6
Littlemead La EX8 . . . . . .196 B3
Little Meadow Way
　EX39. . . . . .156 E2
Littlemoor Cl EX31. . . . .153 A4
Little Normans EX15. . 83 F6
Little Park Rd TQ3 . . . . .226 A6
Little Point Cres
　PL10. . . . . .252 F5
Little Princes TQ1. . . . . .220 C3
Little Queen St EX4 . . . .261 B3
Little Rackenford La
　EX16. . . . . .47 E5
Little Rack St **4** EX1 .261 A2
Little Raddon Cross
　EX17. . . . . .80 F6
Little Roborough
　TQ13. . . . . .130 F5
LITTLE SILVER. 63 D4
Little Silver
　Exeter EX4 . . . . .261 A4
　Tiverton EX16. . . . . .161 D3
Little Silver La
　Exeter EX2. . . . . .181 D5
　Wellington TA21. . . . . . .160 D2
Little Toms EX15. . . . . . . .65 A2
Littleton Pl PL2. . . . . . . .247 F4
LITTLE TORRINGTON .41 D3
Little Torrington
　EX38. . . . . .159 B1
LITTLETOWN. 166 B4
Littletown Prim Sch
　EX14. . . . . .166 C4
Littletown Rd EX14. . . . .166 B4
Littletown Villas
　EX14. . . . . .166 C4
Littleway EX2. . . . . .176 F3
Little Week Cl EX7. . . . .200 F1
Little Week Gdns
　EX7. . . . . .200 F1

Little Week La EX7. . . .200 F1
Little Week Rd EX7. . . .200 F1
Little Wiveliscombe La
　TA4. . . . . .35 D6
Littlewood Cl PL7 . . . . . .251 A4
Little Wood Cl EX5 . . . . . .99 A5
Littleworth Cl EX1 . . . . .179 B8
Livarot Wlk EX36. . . . . . .158 B4
Livaton Cross EX20. . . . . .95 D4
LIVERMEAD. 219 E2
Livermead Hill TQ2 . . . .219 E2
Livermore Rd EX4. . . . . .166 C5
Liverpool Hill EX4. . . . . .176 E7
LIVERTON. 180 A1
Liverton Bsns Pk EX8 196 F1
Liverton Cl EX8 . . . . .202 E8
Liverton Ct TQ12 . . . . . .180 A1
Liverton Hill EX8. . . . . . .197 B1
Livery Dole Almshouses
　EX2. . . . . .177 E5
Living Coasts (Zoo) ★
　TQ1. . . . . .220 B3
Livingshayes Rd EX5. . 82 C6
Livingstone Ave PL8. .141 B8
Livingstone Rd TQ14 . . .210 C6
Livonia Rd EX10. . . . . . . .188 B6
Lixton Pk EX31. . . . . .137 F1
Lizard Cl PL6. . . . . .244 F7
Lizard Wlk PL6. . . . . .245 A7
Llantilio Dr PL2 . . . . .248 B8
Lloyd Ave TQ2 . . . . .219 D7
Lloyd Maunder Rd
　EX15. . . . . .162 C5
Lloyds Cres EX1. . . . . . . .178 C8
Lloyds Ct EX1 . . . . .178 C8
Loatmead Cross EX22 . .38 B3
LOBB. 152 A8
Lobbthorn Stile EX33. . . .8 B1
LOBHILLCROSS. 107 A5
Locarno Ave TQ3. . . . . . .219 D1
Locarno Rd EX4. . . . . . . .176 E4
Lock Cl EX10. . . . . .188 A8
Lockeridge Rd EX20 . . . .125 E1
Lockfield Ct EX2. . . . . . . .177 B1
Lockington Ave PL3. . . . .248 F7
Lock La EX31. . . . . .10 E4
Lock Lane Cross EX31 . 10 F3
Locks Cl
　Braunton EX33. . . . . . . .152 D5
　Torquay TQ1. . . . . .220 D7
Locksey's La EX12. . . . . .190 C5
Locksey's La EX12. . . . . .190 D8
Lock's Gate Cross
　TQ13. . . . . .129 F8
Locks Hill TQ1 . . . . .220 D7
Locks Wlk PL1. . . . . .247 E1
Lockyer Ave EX10. . . . . .188 C8
Lockyer Cres EX16. . . . .161 A6
Lockyer Ct PL1. . . . . .262 C2
Lockyer Mews PL9. . . . . .171 C6
Lockyer Rd PL3. . . . . . . .248 E5
Lockyers Quay PL4. . . . .263 B2
Lockyer St PL1. . . . . .262 C2
Lockyer Terr PL12. . . . . .243 A3
LODDISWELL. 143 F7
Loddiswell Butts TQ7 143 E8
Loddiswell Prim Sch
　TQ7. . . . . .143 F7
Lodgecastle Ham
　EX20. . . . . .170 A6
Lodge Cl PL6. . . . . .244 E3
Lodge Cnr EX31. . . . . .27 D8
Lodge Cross
　Chulmleigh EX18. . . . . . .45 A1
　Longdown EX6. . . . . .98 E1
Lodge Gdns PL6 . . . . . . .244 E3
Lodge Hill
　Exeter EX4. . . . . .177 A8
　Okehampton EX20 . . . . .170 B5
Lodge La
　Axminster EX13 . . . . .88 B2
　Bratton Fleming EX31. . . .18 E8
　Brixton PL8. . . . . .256 F5
　Shute EX13. . . . . .103 A8
　Tudhay EX13. . . . . .88 C3
Lodge Rd EX16. . . . . .161 E4
Lodge The
　Crediton EX17. . . . . .165 A6
　1 Ilfracombe EX34. .150 D5
Lodge Trad Est EX5. . . .175 E3
Lofoten Cl PL1. . . . . .247 E5
Loftus Gdns PL5 . . . . . . .243 C2
Logan Rd TQ3 . . . . .226 C7
Logan Way EX15 . . . . .67 B8
Lolesbury Cross PL8 .136 A1
Lollabury Rd PL12. . . . . .242 E3
Lombard CI EX39. . . . . . . .25 D4
London Cl **5** EX20 . . .170 C5
London Ct The PL21.237 D5
London Inn Sq EX1. . . . .261 B3
London Rd
　Whimple EX11. . . . . .168 A8
　Whimple EX5. . . . . .99 D6
Longacre PL7. . . . . .250 B7
Long Acre PL12 . . . . .242 B4
Long Acres EX2. . . . . . . .261 C2
Long Barton **5**
　TQ12. . . . . .123 F1
Long Barton Ave
　EX20. . . . . .170 C6
LONGBRIDGE. 249 F2
Longbridge Cl PL6. . . . . .249 F2

Long Bridge Cross
　EX13. . . . . .87 B8
Longbridge Meadow Trad
　Est EX15. . . . . .163 D4
Longbridge Rd
　Plymouth, Laira PL3 . . . .249 C4
　Plymouth, Longbridge
　　PL6. . . . . .249 F2
Longbridge Wharf **13**
　EX39. . . . . .157 A1
Longbrook TQ7. . . . . .145 A1
Longbrook Barton
　PL7. . . . . .250 D5
Longbrook Cl PL21. . . . .237 B5
Longbrook La EX4 . . . . . .195 F4
Longbrook Rd PL21 . . . .237 B5
Longbrook St
　Exeter EX4 . . . . .261 B4
　Plymouth PL7 . . . . .250 D5
Longbrook Terr EX4. . . .261 B4
LONGCAUSE. 223 A7
Longcause EX7 . . . . .250 F4
Longcause Com Specl
　Sch PL7. . . . . .250 F4
Longcause Cross
　TQ9. . . . . .223 A7
Longcombe Cross
　TQ9. . . . . .224 C5
Long Copp EX9 . . . . .198 A2
Longcroft Ave TQ5 . . . . .230 B3
Longcroft Dr TQ5. . . . . . .230 B3
Long Cross
　Dartmouth TQ6. . . . . . . .233 C3
　South Pool TQ7. . . . . . . .148 F3
Longcross Cotts
　PL19. . . . . .116 D6
Long Cswy EX8 . . . . .202 B6
Longdogs Cl EX11. . . . . .169 E3
Longdogs La EX11. . . . . .169 E3
LONGDOWN. 98 E2
Long Down Gdns
　PL6. . . . . .245 E3
Longdown Rd EX2,
　EX6. . . . . .176 B3
Long Drag EX15. . . . . .65 E3
Longdrag Hill EX15. . . . .161 A4
Long Entry DT7 . . . . .260 E3
Longfield
　11 Appledore EX39. .15 A1
　Lutton PL21. . . . . .133 B1
Longfield Ave TQ12 . . . .207 F8
Longfield Cl
　Braunton EX33. . . . . . . .152 C5
　Lutton PL21. . . . . .133 B2
Longfield Dr TQ8 . . . . . . .259 C5
Longfield Est EX6. . . . . . .201 A8
Longfield Pl PL4 . . . . . . .263 B4
Longfields TQ7. . . . . .258 A4
Longfield Terr **7**
　EX34. . . . . .150 C5
Longfield Villas PL9 . . . .255 D8
Longford Cross TQ12 207 E8
Longford Down Head
　PL21. . . . . .137 F6
Longford Field EX8 . . . . .195 A1
Longford La TQ12. . . . . . .207 E8
Longford Pk TQ12. . . . . .207 E8
Longforth Rd TA21. . . . . .160 D6
Long-Go La EX14. . . . . . . .84 E8
Long Hill EX12. . . . . .191 C4
Long Holcombe Cross
　EX36. . . . . .20 A6
Long La
　Appledore EX39 . . . . .14 F1
　Ashford EX31. . . . . .16 B6
　Blackmoor Gate EX31. . .11 A6
　Bradiford EX31. . . . . . . .154 A4
　Calverleigh EX16. . . . . . .48 D2
　Combe Martin EX31,
　　EX34. . . . . .3 D1
　Dawlish EX7. . . . . .200 B3
　Exmouth EX8. . . . . .202 C6
　Georgeham EX33 . . . . .8 B1
　Newton Abbot TQ12. . . .208 B1
　Northam EX39 . . . . .157 A8
　Shaldon TQ14. . . . . .209 C4
　Tiverton EX16. . . . . .161 A7
　Wolverstone EX14 . . . . . .85 B8
Longland Cl EX32 . . . . . . .17 B5
Longland Cross TQ9. . . .227 C3
Longland La EX33. . . . . . .8 A2
LONGLANDS. 242 A1
Longlands
　Dawlish EX7. . . . . .204 D6
　Plymouth PL9 . . . . .255 D8
Longlands Cross
　Ashwater EX21. . . . . .90 A1
　Corfcott Green EX22. . . . .71 F2
Longlands La PL12 . . . . .242 B1
Longlands Way EX14 . . 85 C2
Long Ley PL3 . . . . .249 B6
Long Mdw
　Plymouth PL7. . . . . .250 D7
　South Brent TQ10 . . . . .134 F2
Long Mdw Rd EX5. . . . . . .99 C6
Longmead
　Hemyock EX15 . . . . .67 B8
　Huish Champflower TA4 . .35 E8
　Lynton EX35 . . . . .151 A5
Longmead Cl TA21. . . . .160 B8
Longmead Cotts
　TA21. . . . . .160 B8
Longmead La EX20. . . . . .76 F4
Longmeadow
　Budlake EX5. . . . . .82 C1
　Tiverton EX16. . . . . .161 D5

Longmeadow Cl PL7 .250 E7
Long Meadow Dr
　EX32. . . . . .155 B6
Longmeadow Rd
　Lympstone EX8. . . . .195 F5
　Saltash PL12. . . . . . .242 E3
Longmeadows EX17. .165 D6
Longmead Rd TQ3 . .218 F1
Longmead Wlk TQ3 .218 F1
Long Moor
　Cullompton EX15. . . .163 F6
　Willand EX15. . . . . . .162 E1
Long Orch PL20. . . . .125 E1
Long Park Cl PL9. . . .255 F5
Long Park Dr PL6 . . .245 D7
Longpark Hill TQ1 . .214 C6
Long Park Rd PL12 . .242 D2
Long Pk
　Ashburton TQ13 . . . .131 A5
　Cranbrook EX5. . . . . .99 C6
　Modbury PL21. . . . . .137 B3
　Woodbury EX5 . . . . .184 C3
Longpot La EX31. . . . . .17 D8
Long Pot La EX31 . . . .10 D1
Long Ragg Ct EX13. .167 D5
Long Range Pk EX10 .100 A7
Long Rd
　Paignton TQ4 . . . . . .225 D1
　Saltash PL12. . . . . . .242 B4
Long Rowden PL3. . .248 E6
Long Rydon TQ9 . . . .227 F8
Long Rydon Lower
　TQ9. . . . . .228 A7
Longstem Dr TQ9 . . .215 E1
Longstone Ave PL6. .245 A6
Longstone Cross ■
　TQ13. . . . . .131 A5
Longstone Rd TQ4 . .225 E4
Long Terrace Cl ■
　PL7. . . . . .251 C5
Longthorn Rd TQ13 .124 B4
Longview Rd PL12 . .242 D3
Longview Terr PL3 . .249 B7
Long Walk Dr EX32. . .29 C6
Longwood Cl PL7 . . .251 C4
Longwood La TA21. . .51 C4
Longwool Mdw EX23. .70 A6
Longwool Run EX15. .163 A3
Long Wools TQ4 . . . .229 D7
Lonsdale Rd
　Exeter EX1. . . . . . . .178 B5
　Newton Abbot TQ12 .207 D2
Loo Cross TQ7. . . . . .144 F1
Looe Rd EX4. . . . . . .177 A7
Looe St PL4. . . . . . . .263 A2
Lookout Cotts EX31. . .16 B6
Loom End
　Tiverton EX16. . . . . . .64 A8
　Tiverton EX16. . . . . .161 B6
Looseall La TA22. . . . .33 D8
Loosebeare Cross
　EX17. . . . . .78 B8
Loosebeare La EX17. . .78 B8
Loosedon Cross EX19 . .58 B4
Looseland Cross EX16 .47 D1
Looseleigh Cl PL6. . .245 A4
Looseleigh La PL6. . .244 F5
Looseleigh Pk PL6. . .244 E5
Lopes Cres EX20. . . .170 C5
Lopes Dr PL6 . . . . . .241 C1
Lopes Rd
　Dousland PL20 . . . . .127 B3
　Plymouth PL2. . . . . .248 B6
Lopwell Cl PL6. . . . . .244 F5
Lopwell Dam Nature
　Reserve PL6. . . . . . .240 C7
Loram Way EX20 . . .155 A4
Lord Louis Cres PL9 .254 F6
Lord Mamhead Homes
　EX2. . . . . .177 E4
Lord Nelson Dr TQ6 .233 C3
Lords Mdw ■ EX16 . . .49 B8
Lords Meadow Ind Est
　EX17. . . . . .165 C5
Lords Meadow La ■
　EX16. . . . . .34 B1
Lords Meadow L Ctr
　EX17. . . . . .165 C5
Lords Pl TQ1. . . . . . .220 B6
Lords Way EX2. . . . .178 C4
Loretto Gdns EX13. .167 E5
Loretto Rd EX13 . . . .167 E5
Loring Rd TQ8 . . . . .259 D4
Lorrie Dr TQ14. . . . . .210 B6
Lorrimore Rd PL2. . .247 F5
Lotherton Cl PL7. . . .251 B3
Lotus Cotts TQ9. . . .227 F7
Loughboro Rd PL5 . .243 C1
Loughwood La EX13. . .87 B2
Louisa Gate TA22 . . . .33 F7
Louisa Pl EX8. . . . . .202 A5
Louisa Terr EX8. . . . .202 A5
Louise Terr
　Great Torrington EX38 . .41 D6
　Great Torrington EX38 .159 C5
Louis Way EX14. . . . . .67 C1
Loup Ct EX13 . . . . . .167 F5
Louvigny Cl EX14 . . . .84 E2
Louville Ct TQ4 . . . . .226 C2
Lovacott Cross EX31 .153 F2
Lovacott Gr EX31. . . . .26 F6
Lovacott School Cross
　EX31. . . . . .27 A6
LOVATON. 127 C1
Love La
　Ashburton TQ13 . . . .130 F4
　Bickington TQ12 . . . .131 D7

Love La continued
　Bideford EX39. . . . . .156 E1
　Colyton EX24 . . . . . .103 A4
　Marldon TQ3. . . . . . .218 D4
　Marldon TQ3. . . . . . .218 F4
　Saltash PL12. . . . . . .242 E2
Lovelace Cres EX8 . .202 D8
Lovelace Gdns EX1. .181 B8
Loveland Cross EX20. .74 C1
Love Lane Cl TQ3 . . .218 F1
Lovell Cl EX8 . . . . . . .196 C3
Lovell Rd PL3 . . . . . .248 F6
Loventor Cres TQ3 . .218 D2
Loventor La TQ3, TQ9 .217 F3
Loveridge Dr EX2 . . .181 C6
Loveridge La TA20 . . .88 D8
Lovering Cl EX8. . . . .196 C3
Loverings Ct ■ EX31 .154 F5
Lowena La
　West Hill EX10 . . . . .100 A5
　West Hill EX10 . . . . .168 D5
　West Hill EX11. . . . . .168 D5
Lower Albert St EX1. .261 C3
Lower Aller La TQ13. .122 E6
Lower Almshouses ■
　EX31. . . . . .154 F6
Lower Anderton Rd
　PL10. . . . . .252 F5
Lower Argyll Rd EX4 .173 A2
LOWER ASHTON. . . .113 C3
Lower Audley Rd
　TQ2. . . . . .219 F8
Lower Ave EX1. . . . . .177 F6
Lower Barton ■ EX5 . .99 A6
LOWER BATSON. . . .259 D6
Lower Biteford Cross
　EX39. . . . . .38 B6
LOWER BLAGDON. . .225 B6
Lower Blagdon Cross
　TQ3. . . . . .225 B6
Lower Blagdon La
　TQ3. . . . . .225 C6
Lower Brand La
　EX14. . . . . .166 C4
LOWER BRIMLEY . . .180 A5
Lower Brimley Cl ■
　TQ14. . . . . .210 C5
Lower Brimley Rd
　Teignmouth TQ14 . . .210 B6
　Teignmouth TQ14 . . .210 C5
Lower Broad Oak Rd
　EX11. . . . . .168 E4
Lower Broad Path
　TQ9. . . . . .228 A7
Lower Broad Pk
　Dartmouth TQ6 . . . . .233 D3
　West Down EX34 . . . . .8 F5
Lower Brookfield Cotts
　TQ13. . . . . .122 C8
Lower Brookfield Terr
　TQ13. . . . . .122 C8
Lower Brook Mdw ■
　EX10. . . . . .101 B1
Lower Brook Pk
　PL21. . . . . .237 A5
Lower Brook St ■
　TQ14. . . . . .210 C5
Lower Budleigh EX9 .198 B5
Lower Budleigh Mdw
　TQ12. . . . . .206 F3
Lower Bulkamore Cross
　TQ10. . . . . .135 C5
Lower Bull Ring
　EX15. . . . . .163 C3
Lower Bulworthy Gate
　EX16. . . . . .47 D4
Lower Bulworthy La
　EX16. . . . . .47 D4
Lower Burston EX17. . .78 B5
Lower Burwood Rd
　EX38. . . . . .159 E5
Lower Cannon Rd
　TQ12. . . . . .123 B2
LOWER CHERITON. . .84 E4
Lower Church St
　■ Barnstaple EX32 . .155 A4
　Colyton EX24 . . . . . .103 A4
Lower Cl EX16 . . . . . . .65 A7
Lower Claypark EX34. . .7 F7
Lower Cleave
　Braunton EX33 . . . . .152 C7
　Northam EX39. . . . . .157 B5
Lower Cloister Wlk
　EX6. . . . . .181 F5
Lower Cobbaton EX37 28 D5
Lower Collapark
　TQ9. . . . . .223 B6
Lower Collins Rd
　TQ9. . . . . .223 B6
LOWER COMPTON. . .249 A5
Lower Compton Rd
　PL3. . . . . .248 F5
Lower Congella Rd
　TQ1. . . . . .220 C6
Lower Contour Rd
　TQ6. . . . . .234 B3
Lower Cookworthy Cross
　PL16. . . . . .106 A4
Lower Coombe La
　EX16. . . . . .63 D4
Lower Coombe Rd
　TQ12. . . . . .207 F7
Lower Coombe St
　EX1. . . . . .261 A2
Lower Coombses
　TA20. . . . . .88 D8
Lower Coppice EX1 .175 A2

Lower Cotteylands
　EX16. . . . . .161 B3
Lower Court Rd PL8. .140 F7
Lower Crooked Mdw
　EX20. . . . . .170 C5
Lower Cross EX15. . . .51 C1
Lower Cross Rd EX31 154 B4
Lowerdale Turn TQ9 .144 B8
Lower Dawlish Water Rd
　EX7. . . . . .204 A7
LOWER DEAN. 236 A2
Lower Dean Cross EX31 3 F2
Lower Dean La EX31 . .3 B3
Lowerdown TQ13 . . . .122 D5
Lower Dr EX7. . . . . . .204 F8
Lower Duck St EX6. . .182 B3
Lower Dunscombe La
　TQ13. . . . . .124 A5
Lower Ellacombe Church
　Rd TQ1. . . . . .220 C6
Lower Erith Rd TQ1. .220 D4
Lower Fairview Rd
　TQ6. . . . . .233 E3
Lower Farm Rd PL7 . .251 A4
Lower Farthings
　EX10. . . . . .186 F8
Lower Fern Rd
　Newton Abbot TQ12 .212 F8
　Newton Abbot TQ12 .213 A8
Lower Forches Cross
　EX17. . . . . .60 D4
Lower Fore St
　■ Exmouth EX8 . . . .202 A6
　Saltash PL12. . . . . . .243 A2
Lower Fowden TQ4 . .229 D6
Lower Foxmoor Rd
　TA21. . . . . .160 B5
Lower French Pk
　TQ12. . . . . .206 F3
Lower Furlong Cl EX5 .99 C6
Lower Fyldon Cross
　EX36. . . . . .19 D4
LOWER GABWELL. . .214 B8
Lower Gaydon St ■
　EX32. . . . . .155 A5
Lower Green TQ10 . . .135 A2
Lower Green Cross
　TQ7. . . . . .145 C4
Lower Green Way
　EX14. . . . . .85 C2
Lower Greystone EX34 1 C3
Lower Griggs EX10. . .188 D7
Lower Gunstone
　EX39. . . . . .157 A2
Lower Harrington La
　EX4. . . . . .174 E1
Lower Haske Cross
　EX17. . . . . .165 F7
Lower Hill Barton Rd
　EX1. . . . . .178 C6
Lowerhill Head Rd
　EX5. . . . . .179 B2
LOWER HOLDITCH. . .88 D5
Lower Holditch La
　EX13. . . . . .88 D5
Lower Hollicombe Cotts
　TQ3. . . . . .219 D1
LOWER KEATON. . . .237 E1
Lower Kelly PL18 . . . .125 D3
Lower King's Ave
　EX4. . . . . .177 D8
Lower Kingsdown Rd
　TQ14. . . . . .209 D7
Lower Kinsman's Dale
　TQ13. . . . . .111 F5
Lower La
　Chulmleigh EX18. . . . .59 C8
　Dalwood EX13 . . . . . .87 B2
　Ebford EX3 . . . . .183 C4
　■ Plymouth PL1. . . . .263 A2
　Sampford Courtenay
　EX20. . . . . .76 D5
Lower Ladram La
　Otterton EX9. . . . . . .198 F7
　Otterton EX9. . . . . . .199 A7
Lower Lodfin EX16. . . .34 B2
Lower Loughborough
　EX16. . . . . .161 B5
LOWER LOVACOTT . . .27 A6
Lower Lowton La
　EX6. . . . . .112 E6
LOWER LOXHORE . . .10 D1
Lower Manor Rd
　TQ5. . . . . .230 C5
Lower Marlpits Hill
　EX14. . . . . .166 D4
Lower Mead EX13. . .167 E6
Lower Meadow Rise
　EX7. . . . . .204 C6
Lower Meddon St ■
　EX39. . . . . .157 A1
LOWER MILCOTT. . . .173 A4
Lower Millhayes EX15 67 C8
Lower Mill La EX15. .163 C3
Lower Moor EX32. . . .155 D4
Lower Moor Way
　EX15. . . . . .64 D8
LOWER NETHERON. .208 C4
Lower Northcote Rd
　EX14. . . . . .166 D4
Lower North St EX4 .261 A3
Lower Park EX37. . . . .28 D2
Lower Park Dr PL9 . .255 F4
Lower Park Rd EX33. .152 E5
Lower Penns Rd EX19 C1
Lower Pk ■ TQ3. . . . .226 A7
Lower Polsham Rd
　TQ3. . . . . .226 C7

Lower Port View
　PL12. . . . . .242 F2
Lower Preston TQ12 .123 D1
Lower Preston Cross
　TQ9. . . . . .138 E2
Lower Rackclose La
　EX1. . . . . .261 A2
Lower Raleigh Rd
　Barnstaple EX31. . . .155 A7
　Barnstaple EX32. . . .154 F6
Lower Ray EX5. . . . . . .99 B6
Lower Rd EX5. . . . . . .184 B7
Lower Rea Rd TQ5 . .230 D5
LOWER RIDGE. 86 F4
Lower Ridings PL7. . .251 B7
Lower Row PL10 . . . .253 A2
Lower St German's Rd
　EX4. . . . . .177 C8
Lower Saltram PL9. .255 C7
Lower Shapter St
　EX3. . . . . .182 F4
Lower Shirburn Rd
　TQ1. . . . . .220 A7
Lowerside PL2. . . . . .248 A8
LOWER SLADE. 150 B2
Lower Sladesmoor Cres
　PL15. . . . . .90 B1
Lower St
　Chagford TQ13 . . . . .111 A6
　Dartmouth TQ6. . . . .233 F3
　Dittisham TQ6. . . . . .228 B3
　Plymouth PL4 . . . . . .263 A3
　West Alvington TQ7. .258 A4
Lower Summerlands
　EX1. . . . . .261 C3
LOWER TALE. 84 A5
Lower Tamar Terr
　PL18. . . . . .125 D7
Lower Terr EX22 . . . . .38 E1
Lower Three Acres
　Cranbrook EX5. . . . . .99 C6
　Rockbeare EX5. . . . . .99 C6
Lower Thurlow Rd
　TQ1. . . . . .220 A6
Lower Tidderson Cross
　EX16. . . . . .47 E6
LOWER TIPPACOTT. . .6 A4
LOWER TOWN
　Ashburton. 130 A7
　Buckfastleigh 236 C5
　Halberton 65 A7
Lower Town
　Halberton EX16 . . . . .65 A7
　Malborough TQ7. . . .147 E6
　Sampford Peverell EX16 50 D1
　Stoke Climsland PL17 .115 C1
　Winkleigh EX19. . . . . .58 F2
　Woolfardisworthy EX39 .38 F7
Lowertown Cotts
　EX20. . . . . .107 A3
Lower Trindle Cl 24
　TQ12. . . . . .123 C6
Lower Union La TQ2. .220 B5
Lower Union Rd TQ7 .258 C5
LOWER WADSTRAY. .232 B2
Lower Warberry Rd
　Torquay TQ1 . . . . . . .220 B5
　Torquay TQ1 . . . . . . .220 C4
Lower Warcombe Cross
　TQ7. . . . . .144 A6
Lower Warren Rd
　TQ7. . . . . .258 D3
Lower Way EX10 . . . .187 A8
LOWER WEAR. 182 B7
Lower Wear Rd EX2 .182 B8
Lower Westaway Ct
　EX31. . . . . .27 A6
LOWER WESTFORD. .160 A6
Lower Westlake Rd
　EX31. . . . . .154 A2
Lower Wheathill
　EX10. . . . . .188 B8
Lower Winsham Rd
　EX33. . . . . .8 D1
Lower Woodfield Rd
　TQ1. . . . . .220 C4
Lower Woodhayes Ct
　EX5. . . . . .99 E7
LOWER
　WOOLBROOK. 188 A6
Lower Yalberton Rd
　TQ4. . . . . .225 C2
Lowery Cross PL20. .127 C4
Loweswater Ho EX4. .176 F6
Lowley Brook Ct TQ2 219 B8
Lowman Cross EX16. . .50 B2
Lowman Gn EX16 . . .161 D4
Lowman Units EX16. . .64 D8
Lowman Way EX15. . . .64 D8
Lowmoor Ind Est
　TA21. . . . . .160 B8
Lownard Cross TQ9 .222 E8
Low Rd PL9. . . . . . . .140 D8
Lowton Cross EX20. . .77 C7
Lowton La EX6. . . . . .112 E6
Lowtrow Cross TA4 . . .35 A8
LOXBEARE. 48 C3
Loxbury Rd TQ2. . . . .219 D4
Loxbury Rise TQ2. . . .219 D5
Loxdown Rd EX39. . . .41 A7
LOXHORE. 10 D1
LOXHORE COTT. 10 D1
Loxhore Cross EX31. . .17 D7
Lucas Ave EX4. . . . . .177 D8
Lucas La PL7. . . . . . .250 D6
Lucas Terr PL4. . . . . .249 B2
Lucas Wy EX15. . . . . .162 F7
Luccombe Oak EX5 . . .99 B6

Lucerne ■ TQ1. . . . .220 D4
Lucius St TQ2. . . . . . .219 F5
Luckhams La TQ7. . . .147 E6
Lucky La EX2. . . . . . .261 B2
Lucombe Ct EX4 . . . .261 C4
Lucombe Oaks EX5 . .179 B6
LUDBROOK. 137 C5
Ludbrook Gate PL21. .138 C5
Ludford Cl EX2. . . . . .178 A3
Ludlow Rd ■ PL3 . . . .248 E6
Ludwell Rise EX1 . . . .178 B4
LUFFINCOTT. 89 F5
Lugsmoor La EX10 . .189 E7
Lugworthy Cross EX21 91 B5
Lukes Cl TA21. . . . . . .160 D8
Lukesland Gardens ★
　PL21. . . . . .237 E8
Luke St EX16. . . . . . . .34 B1
Lulworth Cl TQ4 . . . .225 F2
Lulworth Dr PL6 . . . .245 B7
Lumley Cl EX6. . . . . .194 E3
Lummaton Cross
　TQ2. . . . . .214 A2
Lummaton Pl TQ2. . .214 B1
Lundy Cl
　Barnstaple EX32. . . .155 C5
　Plymouth PL6. . . . . .244 F7
Lundy View EX39. . . .156 E6
LUPPITT. 67 E1
Luppitt Rd EX14. . . . . .86 A5
Lurley Cross EX16. . . .48 E2
Luscombe Ave PL19 .171 B7
Luscombe Cl
　Ipplepen TQ12 . . . . .211 D1
　Ivybridge PL21. . . . .237 A4
　Paignton TQ3 . . . . . .225 E7
Luscombe Cres TQ3. .225 E6
Luscombe Cross
　TQ9. . . . . .139 D8
Luscombe Hill
　Dawlish EX7. . . . . . .204 A6
　Teignmouth EX7. . . .124 E3
Luscombe La TQ3. . . .225 D8
Luscombe Rd TQ3 . . .225 E6
Luscombe Terr 12
　EX7. . . . . .204 D6
LUSON. 136 C1
Luson Cross PL8. . . . .136 C1
LUSTLEIGH. 122 C8
Lustleigh Cl EX2 . . . .181 C8
Lusways Ct EX10 . . . .188 C4
Lutehouse La EX19. . .58 E3
LUTON
　Cornwood. 133 B2
　South Brent 134 F4
Lutyens Dr TQ3 . . . . .225 D7
Lutyens Fold PL19. . .116 A6
Luxmoore Way EX20 .170 D6
Luxmore Cl PL6. . . . .245 E1
LUXTON. 68 D6
Luxton Cl EX21. . . . . .73 C3
Luxton Ct EX15. . . . . .163 C3
Luxton La EX20 . . . . . .77 B8
Luxton Moor La EX20. .59 A1
Luxton Rd TQ12 . . . .211 F8
Luxtons Pk EX11. . . . .169 C3
Lych Cl PL9. . . . . . . .255 A6
Lychgate Pk EX17. . . .79 A5
Lydacott Cross EX31. .153 F3
LYDCOTT. 18 F7
Lydcot Wlk PL6. . . . .245 A1
Lyddicleave EX31. . . .154 A3
Lyddon Cl TA21. . . . .160 D4
LYDFORD. 107 F4
Lydford Castle & Saxon
　Town ★ EX20. . . . . .107 E3
Lydford Cl PL21. . . . .237 D4
Lydford Gorge ★
　EX20. . . . . .107 F4
Lydford Ho TQ12. . . .207 D4
Lydford Park Rd PL3 .248 D5
Lydford Prim Sch
　EX20. . . . . .107 F4
Lydgates Rd EX12. . .192 A6
Lyd Gdns PL19. . . . . .171 C5
Lydia Cl EX10 . . . . . .186 D8
Lydiate La EX35. . . . . . .5 A5
Lydia Way PL4 . . . . .263 B4
Lydon La TA4. . . . . . . .35 D5
Lydwell Par TQ1. . . . .220 E5
Lydwell Rd TQ1. . . . .220 D6
Lye La EX14. . . . . .87 A8
Lym Cl DT7. . . . . .260 E3
Lyme Bay Ct ■ DT7 .260 D3
Lyme Bay Rd TQ14 . .210 C7
Lymeborne Ave
　EX10. . . . . .188 B6
Lymeborne Ho
　EX10. . . . . .188 B6
Lymeborne La EX10 .188 B6
Lymeborne Pk EX10 .188 B6
Lyme Cl EX13. . . . . . .167 D5
Lyme Mews 10 EX12 .192 B4
Lyme Rd
　Axminster EX13 . . . .167 C5
　Uplyme DT7. . . . . . . .104 B5
LYME REGIS. 260 E2
Lyme Regis Ind Est
　DT7. . . . . .260 E3
Lyme Regis Mus ★
　DT7. . . . . .260 E3

Lyme St EX13. . . . . . .167 D4
Lyme View Cl TQ1. . .220 D7
Lyme View Rd TQ1 . .220 D7
Lymington Rd TQ1 . .220 A6
Lympne Ave PL5 . . . .243 F5
LYMPSTONE. 195 E5
Lympstone CE Prim Sch
　EX8. . . . . .195 E5
Lympstone Commando
　Sta EX8 . . . . .195 C8
Lympstone Ct EX34. .150 B6
Lympstone Village Sta
　EX8. . . . . .195 D5
Lynbridge Cl ■ PL19 171 B5
Lynbridge Hill EX35. .151 B3
Lynbridge Rd EX35. .151 C4
Lynbro Rd EX31. . . . .154 F7
Lynch Cl
　Axminster EX13 . . . .167 D7
　Thorverton EX5. . . . . .81 E5
Lynch Head EX10 . . .100 C1
Lynch Rd EX5. . . . . . . .81 D5
Lyncombe Cl EX4 . . .173 E1
Lyncombe Cres TQ1. .220 E3
Lyncombe La EX35 . . .12 D8
Lyncourt TQ1. . . . . . .220 D3
Lyn Cross EX35 . . . . .151 D2
Lyndale Rd TQ12 . . . .207 D8
Lyndhurst Ave TQ12 .213 A5
Lyndhurst Cl
　Kingskerswell TQ12 .213 A5
　Plymouth PL2 . . . . . .248 C6
Lyndhurst Rd
　Exeter EX2. . . . . . . .177 E5
　Exmouth EX8. . . . . .202 A8
　Plymouth PL2. . . . . .248 C6
Lyndon Ct PL12 . . . .242 D4
Lyndons The EX2 . . .177 E5
Lyndrick Rd PL3 . . . .248 E7
Lyndridge Ct ■
　EX20. . . . . .170 A5
LYNEHAM. 257 F7
Lyneham Cross TQ13 123 D6
Lyn & Exmoor Mus ★
　EX35. . . . . .151 C4
Lyn Gr TQ12 . . . . . . .212 F6
Lyngrove Ct TQ12 . . .212 F6
Lynhayes EX13. . . . . . .87 C1
Lynher Ct PL12. . . . . .242 F1
Lynher Dr PL12 . . . . .242 F1
Lynher St PL5. . . . . . .243 D2
Lyn Hill
　Lynton EX35. . . . . .5 C5
　West Lyn EX35. . . . . .151 C3
Lynhurst Ave EX31. . .154 C4
Lyn La EX35. . . . . . . .151 D3
LYNMOUTH. 151 F5
Lynmouth Ave TQ4 . .225 F2
Lynmouth Cl PL7. . . .250 C7
Lynmouth Hill EX35. .151 C5
Lynmouth St EX35. . .151 C6
Lynn Terr EX38 . . . . .159 C5
LYNTON. 151 F5
Lynton & Barnstaple Rly ★
　EX31. . . . . .4 D3
Lynton CE Prim Sch
　EX35. . . . . .151 C5
Lynton Cross EX34 . . . .9 B6
Lynton & Lynmouth Cliff
　Rlwy ★ EX35. . . . . .151 C6
Lynton Rd EX34 . . . . . .3 B3
Lynway EX35. . . . . . .151 C4
Lynway Ct TQ1. . . . . .220 B6
Lynwood TQ12 . . . . .206 F1
Lynwood Ave
　Exeter EX4 . . . . .177 A5
　Plymouth PL7 . . . . . .250 B6
Lynx La PL9. . . . . . . .256 E8
Lyra Vale PL9 . . . . . . .256 E8
Lysander La PL6 . . . .245 B5
Lyster Ct ■ PL1. . . . .262 A3
Lyte Hill La TQ2. . . . .213 F3
Lyte La TQ7. . . . . . . .144 C1
Lyte's Rd TQ5. . . . . . .230 D4
Lythe-Land Cross
　EX16. . . . . .63 A6
Lytton Ho TQ2 . . . . .220 A4

M

Mabel Pl TQ4. . . . . . .226 B5
Mabry Way EX12. . . .192 C5
Macadam Rd
　Plymouth PL4. . . . . .263 C1
　Plymouth PL9. . . . . .255 B8
Macandrew Wlk
　PL21. . . . . .237 E6
Macaulay Cres PL5. .244 C5
Macauley Cl EX14. . .166 E6
Macey St PL11. . . . . .247 C3
Macford Court EX13. .167 F8
Machine Cross TA22 . .33 F6
Mackenzie Pl PL5. . .243 C2
Mackenzie Way
　EX16. . . . . .161 F4
MACKHAM. 67 D4
Mackrell's Almshouses
　TQ12. . . . . .207 A2
Maclins Cl EX36. . . . .158 C4
Macwood Dr PL2 . . .192 A6
Madagascar Cl EX8 .202 E8
Maddacombe Cross
　TQ12. . . . . .212 C4

Maddacombe Rd
TQ12. . . . .**212** D4
Madden Rd PL1. . . . . .**247** F2
Maddick Rd EX1. . . . . .**174** F3
Maddock Cl PL7. . . . . .**251** A4
Maddock Dr PL7. . . . . .**251** B4
Maddocks Cross EX22 **38** D2
Madeira Ct EX8. . . . . . .**202** B5
Madeira Pl TQ2. . . . . . .**220** A5
Madeira Rd PL1. . . . . . .**263** A1
Madeira Villas
Exmouth EX8. . . . .**202** A7
1 Horrabridge PL20 . .**126** F5
Madeira Wlk EX9 . . . .**199** H2
MADFORD. **67** D6
Madford Cross EX15 . .**67** C6
Madge Ct **3** PL19. . . . .**171** B6
Madge La PL19 . . . . . .**171** B6
Madgeon La TA20. . . . .**69** B8
Madges Cross
Aylesbeare EX5. . . . .**99** E2
Rockbeare EX5. . . . .**99** E6
Madicks Orch TQ9 . . . .**227** F8
Madison Ave EX1. . . . .**178** A6
Madison Cl EX5. . . . . . .**173** F8
Madison Wharf EX8. . .**201** E6
Madrepore Rd TQ1. . . .**220** B4
Maer Bay Ct EX8 . . . . .**202** B5
Maer La EX8. . . . .**202** C5
Maer Nature Reserve
The ★ EX8 . . . .**202** B5
Maer Rd EX8. . . . .**202** C5
Maer Top Way EX31. . .**155** A7
Maer Vale EX8. . . . .**202** C6
Magdala Rd EX31 . . . .**154** C4
Magdalen Bridge Ct **3**
EX2. . . . .**261** B2
Magdalen Court Sch
EX2. . . . .**177** E5
Magdalene Cl TQ9 . . . .**223** C5
Magdalene Lawn **9**
EX32. . . . .**155** A6
Magdalene Rd TQ1. . . .**220** A6
Magdalene Way
EX36. . . . .**158** B4
Magdalen Gdns
Exeter EX2. . . . .**177** E5
Plymouth PL7. . . . .**250** F3
Magdalen Rd EX2. . . . .**177** E5
Magdalen St EX1, EX2 **261** B2
Magnolia Ave
Exeter EX2. . . . .**178** A3
Exmouth EX8. . . . .**202** E8
Magnolia Cl
Barnstaple EX32. . . . . .**155** E4
3 Plymouth PL7. . . . . .**251** B5
Magnolia Ct
Bolham EX16. . . . .**49** C1
5 Exmouth EX8. . . . .**202** B6
3 Plymouth PL9. . . . . .**255** F7
Tiverton EX16. . . . .**161** C7
Magnolia Ho **10** EX8. .**202** A6
Magnolia Way EX20. . .**170** C5
Magnolia Wlk **2**
EX8. . . . .**202** A6
Magnus Cl **1** TQ12. . . .**244** E6
Magpie Cres EX2. . . . . .**176** D4
Magpie Hill TQ13 . . . .**130** C4
Maida Vale Terr PL4 . .**248** F4
MAIDENCOMBE. **214** D6
Maidencombe Cross
TQ1. . . . .**214** C6
Maidencombe Ho
TQ1. . . . .**214** C4
MAIDENHAYNE. **103** D6
Maidenhayne La
EX13. . . . .**103** D6
Maidenhead Cross
EX16. . . . .**51** C2
Maiden St **17** EX31. . . .**154** F5
Maidenway La TQ3. . . .**225** F8
Maidenway Rd TQ3. . . .**225** F8
Maidenwell Rd PL7. . . .**250** C5
Maidstone Pl PL5. . . . .**243** E4
Main Ave TQ1. . . . .**220** A8
Maine Cl EX33. . . . .**156** D2
Maine Gdns PL2 . . . . . .**247** F7
Main Rd
Exeter EX4 . . . .**174** E2
Exminster EX3. . . . .**182** A4
Salcombe TQ8 . . . .**8** B4
Mains Down La EX33 . . . .**8** B4
Main St TQ9 . . . .**139** E1
MAINSTONE. **245** F2
Mainstone Ave PL4. . . .**263** C2
Maire Rd EX36 . . . .**46** E5
Maisy Mws EX3 . . . . . .**182** D8
Maitland Dr PL3 . . . . . .**248** F8
Major Cross EX16 . . . . .**64** A2
Majorfield Rd EX3 . . . .**182** F5
Major's Mdw EX20 . . . .**170** C5
Major Terr **3** EX12. . . .**192** A5
Maker La PL10 . . . .**253** B4
Maker Rd PL11. . . . . . .**247** A2
Maker View
Plymouth PL3 . . . .**248** B4
Plymouth PL5 . . . .**248** B4
Maker View Rd PL10 . .**253** A6
MALBOROUGH **147** E6
Malborough Gn TQ7 . .**147** E6
Malborough Pk TQ7. . .**147** E6
Malborough with South
Huish CE Prim Sch
TQ7. . . . .**147** E6
Malden Cl EX10. . . . . .**188** B7

Malden La EX10. . . . . .**188** B8
Malden Rd EX10 . . . . . .**188** C8
Malderek Ave TQ3 . . . .**219** C1
Mallands Mdw TQ12 .**212** A7
Mallard Cl
Plymouth PL7 . . . .**250** F5
Torquay TQ2 . . . .**213** D3
Mallard Rd EX2 . . . . . .**178** E5
Mallet Rd PL21. . . . . . .**237** A6
Malletts La EX32 . . . . .**155** A5
Mallingbrook Cross
EX18. . . . .**44** E1
Mallison Cl EX4. . . . . .**176** F8
Mallock Rd TQ2. . . . . .**219** E5
Mallocks Cl EX10 . . . .**100** D2
Mallow Ct
Dartmouth TQ6. . . . . . .**233** B2
Willand EX15 . . . .**162** D5
Mallow Pl TQ12 . . . . . .**206** C4
Malmesbury Cl PL2 . .**248** B8
MALMSMEAD. **6** C4
Malmsmead Bridge
EX35. . . . .**6** D4
Malory Cl PL5. . . . .**244** D2
Malson La EX16. . . . . . .**47** B4
Malston Cross TQ7 . . .**144** D4
Malt Field EX8 . . . .**195** F5
Malthouse The
Bridgend PL8 . . . .**141** A7
5 Totnes TQ9. . . . .**223** D5
Malting Ct **4** EX7 . . . .**204** E6
Maltings The
21 Appledore EX39. . . . .**15** A1
Black Torrington EX21. .**74** A8
Crediton EX17. . . . .**165** D5
Exeter EX2 . . . .**177** F5
South Allington TQ7 . . .**149** B5
Malt Mill TQ9 . . . .**223** B6
Malvern Gdns EX2 . . . .**178** A4
Malvernleigh TQ1. . . . .**220** B8
Malvern Rd EX10. . . . .**188** B6
Malvern Way EX39 . . .**156** D2
Mambury Cross EX22. . .**39** D3
Mamhead Bsns Units
EX2. . . . .**181** D8
Mamhead Rd
Exeter EX2 . . . .**178** C4
Kenton EX6. . . . .**194** C2
Kenton EX6. . . . .**200** B8
Mamhead Sensory Trail ★
EX6. . . . .**124** E7
Mamhead View EX8 .**201** E6
MANADON. **244** D1
Manadon Cl PL5 . . . . .**244** E1
Manadon Dr PL5. . . . .**244** E1
Manadon Football Ctr
PL2. . . . .**244** D2
Manadon Hill PL5,
PL6. . . . .**244** E8
Manadon Vale Prim Sch
1 Plymouth PL5. . . . .**248** E8
Plymouth TQ12. . . . . . .**244** E1
MANATON **121** F8
Manaton Cl EX2. . . . . .**181** C8
Manaton Ct EX2 . . . . .**181** C8
Manaton Tor Rd TQ3 .**218** F1
Manby Gdns PL5. . . . . .**243** F5
Manchester Rd EX8 . .**201** F6
Manchester St EX8. . . .**201** F6
Mandarin Way TQ12. . .**207** C8
Mandrake Cl EX2 . . . . .**177** B1
Mandrake Rd EX2. . . . .**177** A1
Manifold Gdns PL3. . . .**249** D5
Manitoba Gdns EX15 .**163** B3
Manley Cl **1** EX5. . . . . .**99** E8
Manley La EX16. . . . . . .**64** E7
Manley Mdw EX4 . . . .**174** F4
Manleys La EX4 . . . .**4** C4
Manna Ash Ct EX2 . . .**261** C1
Mannacott La EX31 . . . .**4** C4
Mannacott Lane Head
EX31. . . . .**4** C4
Manor Ave
Lyme Regis DT7 . . . . . .**260** D4
Paignton TQ3 . . . .**226** C8
Manor Bend TQ5. . . . . .**229** C5
MANOR BOURNE **140** A8
Manor Bourne Rd
Down Thomas PL9. . . . .**255** C1
Heybrook Bay PL9. . . . .**140** A8
Manor Cl
Abbotskerswell
TQ12. . . . .**212** A7
Awliscombe EX14. . . . . .**85** C3
Barnstaple EX31. . . . . .**154** C3
Dawlish EX7. . . . .**204** D6
Fremington EX31. . . . . .**153** E6
Ivybridge PL21. . . . . . .**237** C5
Kentisbeare EX15. . . . . .**66** A3
Kingskerswell TQ12. . . .**213** A3
1 Seaton EX12. . . . . . .**192** A5
Sidmouth EX10. . . . . . .**188** A5
Tavistock PL19. . . . . . .**171** A6
Uffculme EX15. . . . .**66** B8
Wrafton EX33. . . . .**152** E4
Manor Cotts
15 Newton Abbot
TQ12. . . . .**207** B3
Rackenford EX16. . . . . .**47** C6

Manor Court Barns
TQ7. . . . .**147** F8
Manor Cres
Honiton EX14. . . . .**166** C4
Paignton TQ3 . . . .**226** C8
Manor Ct
Barnstaple EX32. . . . . .**155** F1
5 Dawlish EX7. . . . . . .**204** D6
Galmpton TQ5. . . . .**229** A5
Kingskerswell TQ12 . . .**213** A3
Landkey EX32. . . . .**17** B2
Paignton TQ12 . . . .**226** C7
Seaton EX12. . . . .**192** A5
9 South Brent TQ10. . .**134** F3
Stoke Fleming TQ6 . . . .**146** B7
Torquay TQ2 . . . .**219** F6
Manor Dr
Chagford TQ13. . . . . . .**110** F6
Clyst St Mary EX5. . . . .**179** B1
Ivybridge PL21. . . . . . .**237** C5
Kingskerswell TQ12 . . .**213** A3
Manor Est
Horrabridge PL19. . . . .**126** E4
Horrabridge PL20. . . . .**126** E4
Manor Farm PL20. . . . .**127** B3
Manor Farm Cl TA20 . .**88** C8
Manor Farm Mews
EX5. . . . .**99** E4
Manor Gdn TQ1. . . . . .**220** E3
Manor Gdns
Abbotskerswell TQ12 . .**212** B6
Exbourne EX20. . . . .**76** C5
Halwill Junction EX21. . .**73** E2
Horrabridge PL20. . . . .**126** E4
Kingsbridge TQ7. . . . . .**258** D6
Kingskerswell TQ12 . . .**213** A3
Millbrook PL10 . . . .**252** F6
Paignton TQ3 . . . .**226** C8
Plymouth PL1 . . . .**262** B4
Seaton EX12. . . . .**192** B5
Manorglade Ct **1**
TQ1. . . . .**220** D5
Manor Gn EX14 . . . .**68** C2
Manor Ho
Lympstone EX8. . . . . . .**195** D5
Torquay TQ1. . . . .**220** E3
Manor Ho The TQ9 . . .**223** C6
Manor La PL3. . . . .**249** D5
Manor Mead TQ12 . . .**131** D7
Manor Mill Rd EX33 . . .**8** D1
Manor Park Cl PL7. . . .**250** F5
Manor Park Dr PL/. . .**251** A4
Manor Pavilion Theatre ★
EX10. . . . .**188** A3
Manor Pk
Ashwater EX21. . . . .**90** E6
Barnstaple EX31. . . . . .**154** C3
Bradworthy EX22 . . . . .**53** E8
Clyst St Mary EX5 . . . .**179** A3
Dousland PL20. . . . . . .**127** B3
Kingsbridge TQ7. . . . . .**258** D6
Saltash PL12. . . . .**242** D2
Woolfardisworthy EX39 .**38** F8
Manor Prim Sch
PL21. . . . .**237** C5
Manor Rd
Abbotskerswell TQ12 . .**212** B7
Bishopsteignton TQ14. .**208** F8
Chagford TQ13. . . . . . .**110** F6
Exeter EX4 . . . .**177** A5
Landkey EX32. . . . .**17** A2
Landkey EX32. . . . .**17** B2
Landkey EX32. . . . .**155** F1
Newton Abbot TQ12 . . .**206** F3
Newton Abbot TQ12 . . .**207** A3
Paignton TQ3 . . . .**226** C8
Plymouth PL9 . . . .**255** E8
Seaton EX12. . . . .**192** A5
Sidmouth EX10. . . . . . .**188** A3
Tavistock PL19. . . . . . .**171** B6
Torquay TQ1. . . . .**220** C8
Manor St
Dittisham TQ6. . . . .**228** D2
Plymouth PL1. . . . .**262** A3
Manor Terr
Brixham TQ5. . . . .**230** C5
Paignton TQ3 . . . .**226** C8
Manor Vale Rd TQ5 . . .**229** C5
Manor View TQ12. . . . .**207** A3
Manor Way
Ivybridge PL21. . . . . . .**237** C5
Tavistock PL19. . . . . . .**171** B6
Totnes TQ9. . . . .**223** C6
Manot Gdns **23** EX7 . .**204** E6
Mansands La TQ5 . . . .**235** B8
Mansbridge Rd TQ2 . .**219** D3
Manscombe Cl TQ2 . . .**219** D3
Manscombe Rd TQ2. . .**219** D3
Mansfield Rd EX4. . . . .**176** C7
Mansfield Terr EX9 . . .**198** B2
Mansion Ho EX1. . . . . .**181** F5
Mansion Ho The PL1 .**254** B8
Mansion House St
TQ6. . . . .**233** F3
Mansion Terr **6** EX34 . . .**3** A3
Mansion The PL21. . . .**137** C8
Manston Cl PL5. . . . . . .**243** E5
Manston Ct PL5. . . . . . .**243** E5
Manstone Ave EX10. . .**188** A7
Manstone Cl EX10. . . .**188** B7
Manstone La EX10. . . .**188** B7
Manstone Mead
EX10. . . . .**188** B8
Manstone Workshops **3**
EX10. . . . .**188** B7
Manston Rd EX1. . . . . .**177** E7
Manston Terr EX2. . . . .**177** E5
Manstree Cross EX2. . .**114** A6

Manstree Rd EX2 . . . . .**114** B6
Manstree Terr EX2. . . .**114** C6
Manteo Way EX39. . . . .**157** C2
Mantle Gdns PL5. . . . .**247** D8
Mantle St TA21. . . . . . .**160** C5
Maple Ave
Bovey Tracey TQ13. . . .**180** C4
Torpoint PL11. . . . .**247** A3
Maple Cl
Brixham TQ5. . . . .**230** A2
10 Chudleigh Knighton
TQ13. . . . .**123** C4
7 Honiton EX14. . . . . . .**85** C2
Kingsteignton TQ12 . . .**207** E6
Plymouth PL6. . . . .**245** E6
Seaton EX12. . . . .**192** A7
Tavistock PL19. . . . . . .**171** C3
Willand EX15. . . . .**162** C4
Maple Ct
Cheriton Bishop EX6. . . .**97** B3
Paignton TQ4 . . . .**226** B2
2 Plymouth PL6. . . . . .**255** F7
Mapledene Cl TQ9 . . . .**227** F8
Maple Dr EX8. . . . .**196** D3
Maple Gr
Barnstaple EX31. . . . . .**154** C3
Ivybridge PL21. . . . . . .**237** F5
Plymouth, Mutley PL4. .**248** D4
Plymouth, Plympton
PL7. . . . .**250** B5
Tiverton EX16. . . . .**161** D4
Maple Rd
Brixham TQ5. . . . .**230** A2
Broadclyst EX5. . . . . . .**175** D6
Exeter EX4 . . . .**177** A5
Teignmouth TQ14. . . . .**210** B3
Maples Ct **7** EX32. . . .**154** F6
Maple St **4** EX32. . . . .**155** C4
Mapleton Cl TQ12. . . . .**206** F4
Maple Way PL6. . . . . . .**245** C2
Maple Wlk TQ2 . . . . . .**219** C8
Mapstone Hill
Lustleigh TQ13 . . . . . .**112** B1
Lustleigh TQ13 . . . . . .**112** B1
Marazion Wy **2** PL2. .**248** D8
Marber Cross TQ7 . . . .**149** A8
Marcent Row TQ5. . . . .**230** D3
Marchant's Cross
PL20. . . . .**127** C1
Marchant's Way
PL20. . . . .**127** C2
March Ct EX20. . . . . . .**170** B5
Marchweeke La EX16 . .**61** D6
Marcombe Rd TQ2 . . . .**219** E5
Marcom Ct EX8 . . . . . .**196** D3
Marcus Rd
Dunkeswell EX14. . . . . .**67** B2
Exmouth EX8. . . . .**196** D1
Marder's Bequest
DT7. . . . .**260** E3
Mardle Way TQ11 . . . .**236** B5
Mardle Way Bsns Pk
TQ11. . . . .**236** B5
Mardon Cl PL6. . . . . . .**245** D4
Mardon Cross EX6 . . . .**112** C2
Mardon Hill EX4 . . . . .**173** B1
Mare Hill EX17. . . . .**61** C5
Mare La
Beer EX12. . . . .**191** B5
Middle Marwood EX31. . . .**9** B1
Marepark Cross TQ7 .**144** D3
Marepark Gate EX20 . .**77** C7
Marett Rd PL5 . . . .**243** F3
Margaret Cl
East Ogwell TQ12. . . . .**206** F1
Kingsteignton TQ12 . . .**207** E2
Margaret St **7** EX4 . . .**178** C8
Margaret Gdns
TQ12. . . . .**207** F2
Margaret Pk PL3. . . . . .**248** E8
Margaret Rd
East Ogwell TQ12. . . . .**206** F1
Exeter EX4 . . . .**173** E1
Kingsteignton TQ12 . . .**207** E2
Margaret St **4** EX8. . .**202** A6
Margrove Terr **10**
EX32. . . . .**154** F6
Marguerite Cl TQ2 . . .**206** F4
Marguerite Rd EX16. . .**161** F6
Marguerite Way
TQ12. . . . .**213** A4
MARHAMCHURCH **70** A6
Marhamchurch CE Prim
Sch EX23. . . . .**70** A6
MARIANSLEIGH. **30** D1
Mariansleigh Cross
EX36. . . . .**30** E1
Marina Cl TQ5. . . . .**230** E5
Marina Ct
Brixham TQ5. . . . .**230** F6
Exmouth EX8. . . . .**202** B5
Paignton TQ4 . . . .**226** C5
23 Teignmouth TQ14. . .**210** C4
Marina Dr TQ5. . . . . . .**230** C5
Marina Rd
Brixham TQ5. . . . .**230** E4
Plymouth PL5 . . . .**243** F3
Marina Terr **7** PL4. . .**248** F4
Marina Way **6** EX12. . .**62** E4
Marine Acad Plymouth
PL5. . . . .**243** E1
Marine Aquarium ★
DT7. . . . .**260** D2
Marine Cres **6** EX12 .**192** A4
Marine Ct
Budleigh Salterton
EX9. . . . .**199** H2
Instow EX39. . . . .**15** B1
Torpoint PL11. . . . .**247** B2

Marine Dr
Bigbury-on-S TQ7 . . . .**142** E3
Heybrook Bay PL9. . . . .**140** A7
Paignton TQ3 . . . .**226** C7
Topsham EX3 . . . .**182** E7
Torpoint PL11. . . . .**247** B2
Woolacombe EX33, EX34 . **7** F5
Marine Gdns **9** EX23 .**191** D5
Marine Mount TQ1. . . .**221** A3
Marine Par
Appledore EX39. . . . . . .**15** A1
Budleigh Salterton
EX9. . . . .**199** H2
Dawlish EX7. . . . .**204** E5
Instow EX39. . . . .**15** B1
Lyme Regis DT7 . . . . . .**260** D2
Paignton TQ3 . . . .**226** D8
Teignmouth TQ14. . . . .**210** B3
Marine Pk
Ilfracombe EX34. . . . . .**150** B6
Seaton EX12. . . . .**192** A4
Marine Rd PL9. . . . . . .**255** D7
Mariners Cl EX33 . . . .**152** D5
Mariners Ct
7 Brixham TQ5. . . . . . .**230** D5
13 Dawlish EX7. . . . . . .**204** E6
Mariners Way TQ3 . . .**218** F1
Mariner's Way **33**
EX39. . . . .**15** A1
Marine Terr **17** TQ14 .**210** B4
Marine Theatre ★
DT7. . . . .**260** E3
Marine Way
Exmouth EX8. . . . .**201** F7
Exmouth EX8. . . . .**202** A8
Marino The EX10. . . . .**187** F3
Marions Way EX8 . . . .**196** D3
Marion View TQ1 . . . . .**220** C4
Maristow Ave
Exmouth EX8. . . . .**196** B2
Plymouth PL2 . . . .**247** F5
Maristow Cl PL6. . . . . .**244** F5
Maristow La PL12 . . . .**242** F3
Marist Way EX32. . . . .**155** C2
Maritime Sq PL1 . . . . .**247** F1
Marjon Hill PL6. . . . . . .**245** R4
Marjorie Ct PL12. . . . .**242** C4
Marjory Kelly Way
PL21. . . . .**237** D4
Marjory Wlk PL8. . . . .**257** E3
Markadon Cotts EX39 .**22** B4
Markers EX15. . . . .**66** A7
Marker's Cottage ★
EX5. . . . .**175** D7
Markers Pk EX14. . . . . .**84** C4
Markers Rd EX15. . . . . .**66** A7
Marker Way EX14. . . . .**166** C4
Market Ave PL1. . . . . .**262** B3
Market Cl
Ashburton TQ13 . . . . .**130** F4
4 Bampton EX16. . . . . .**34** B1
Brushford TA22. . . . . . .**33** E4
Buckfastleigh TQ11. . . .**236** B5
Plymouth PL1 . . . .**248** A1
Market Field EX38 . . . .**40** C2
Market Forum the (Sh
Ctr) TQ1. . . . .**220** B5
Market Mws EX3. . . . .**182** D7
Market Pl
Bideford EX39. . . . .**157** A2
Burlescombe EX16. . . . .**51** B4
Colyton EX24 . . . .**103** A5
Sidmouth EX10. . . . . . .**188** B3
Willand EX15. . . . .**162** C5
Market Rd
Plymouth PL7 . . . .**250** D5
Tavistock PL19. . . . . . .**171** C5
Market Sq
Axminster EX13. . . . . . .**167** D6
Dartmouth TQ6. . . . . . .**233** F3
3 Ilfracombe EX34. . . .**150** B6
Plymouth PL1. . . . .**262** C3
Market St
2 Appledore EX39. . . . .**15** A1
4 Barnstaple EX31. . . .**154** F5
8 Brixham TQ5. . . . . . .**230** C5
Buckfastleigh TQ11. . . .**236** B5
Crediton EX17. . . . .**165** C5
Dartmouth TQ6. . . . . . .**233** F3
Exeter EX1, EX4 . . . . . .**261** A2
Exmouth EX8. . . . .**202** A6
Hatherleigh EX20 . . . . .**75** C7
Ilfracombe EX34. . . . . .**150** B6
Kingsand PL10 . . . .**253** A1
Lynton EX35 . . . .**151** C5
Newton Abbot TQ12 . . .**207** B3
North Tawton EX20 . . . .**77** C4
Okehampton EX20 . . . .**170** B5
Plymouth PL1. . . . .**248** A1
Salcombe TQ8. . . . .**259** E5
South Molton EX36. . . .**158** C4
Tavistock PL19. . . . . . .**171** C5
Torquay TQ1. . . . .**220** B5
Yealmpton PL8. . . . . . .**257** F4
Market Terr EX16. . . . .**161** C4
Market Way
7 Chudleigh TQ13. . . .**123** E6
Plymouth PL1. . . . .**262** C4
Market Wlk **7** TQ12. .**207** B3
Market Wlk EX16. . . . .**161** C4
Markham Cross EX2. . .**114** B8
Markham La
Exeter EX2 . . . .**181** B7
Ide EX2. . . . .**114** C8

Mark's Cross EX6 . . . .**176** B2
Mark Twain Ho **1**
EX4. . . . .**178** C8
Marland Cross PL8. . . .**136** B1
Marland Prim EX39. . . .**156** B6
Marland Sch EX38 . . . . .**56** B8
Marland Terr EX39. . . .**156** F1
Marlborough Ave
TQ1. . . . .**220** D5
Marlborough Cl
Exmouth EX8. . . . .**196** E2
Ilfracombe EX34. . . . . .**150** B5
Musbury EX13. . . . .**103** D5
Saltash PL12. . . . .**242** F1
Marlborough Cross
EX5. . . . .**179** D6
Marlborough Ct
Bideford EX39. . . . .**157** A3
Exeter, Alphington EX2 .**181** C8
Exeter, Heavitree EX2. .**177** E5
Marlborough Dr **9**
EX2. . . . .**178** C5
Marlborough Pk **7**
EX34. . . . .**150** B5
Marlborough Pl
TQ12. . . . .**207** A4
Marlborough Prim Sch
PL1. . . . .**247** E2
Marlborough Rd
Exeter EX2 . . . .**261** C2
Ilfracombe EX34. . . . .**2** A3
Ilfracombe EX34. . . . . .**150** C5
Musbury EX13. . . . .**103** D5
Plymouth PL4. . . . .**263** A4
Marlborough Row
PL1. . . . .**247** E2
Marlborough St PL1. . .**247** E2
Marlborough Terr
TQ13. . . . .**180** C7
Marlborough Way
EX34. . . . .**150** C4
Marlcombe Cross
EX14. . . . .**85** A6
MARLDON **218** C3
Marldon Ave TQ3 . . . .**226** A6
Marldon CE Prim Sch
TQ3. . . . .**218** D3
Marldon Cl PL5 . . . . . .**244** F5
Marldon Cross TQ3 . .**218** D2
Marldon Cross Hill
TQ3. . . . .**218** D3
Marldon Gr TQ3. . . . . .**218** D3
Marldon La TQ3. . . . . .**218** B4
Marldon Rd
Dainton TQ12 . . . .**212** A1
Ipplepen TQ12 . . . .**211** F2
Paignton TQ3 . . . .**225** F8
Torquay TQ2 . . . .**219** B7
Marldon Way TQ3. . . .**218** E2
Marlen Ct EX39 . . . .**25** F4
Marles Cl EX14. . . . .**85** B4
Marles The EX8 . . . . . .**196** C2
Marley Cl EX16. . . . . . .**161** D6
Marley Dr EX8 . . . .**196** D5
Marley Head TQ10 . . . .**135** C3
Marley Rd EX8 . . . .**196** C3
Marlow Cres PL16. . . .**106** D1
Marlow Ct EX39. . . . . .**156** D7
Marlowe Cl TQ2. . . . . .**219** D7
Marlow Gdns PL9. . . . .**255** F5
Marlpit Cl EX12 . . . . . .**191** F7
Marlpit Cross EX14. . . .**87** A6
Marlpit La EX12. . . . . .**192** A5
Marlpits La EX14. . . . .**166** C5
Marl Pk
Harbertonford TQ9. . . .**139** C7
Holne TQ11. . . . .**130** A3
Marmora Terr EX12 . .**191** D5
Marnham Rd TQ1. . . . .**220** B7
Marpool Cres EX8. . . . .**202** C8
Marpool Hill EX8. . . . .**202** B7
Marpool Prim Sch
EX8. . . . .**202** C8
Marridge Cross PL21 .**137** F5
Marriott Way TQ13 . . .**180** B6
Marrowbone Slip
PL4. . . . .**263** B2
Marryat Gdns PL5. . . .**244** E1
MARSH. **69** B5
Marshall Cl
Tavistock PL19. . . . . . .**171** D4
Tiverton EX16. . . . .**161** F3
Marshall Dr PL21 . . . .**237** D4
Marshall Rd
Plymouth PL7 . . . .**250** A4
Tavistock PL19. . . . . . .**171** D2
Marshalls Field PL21 **237** E5
Marshalls Mead EX19 .**42** D1
Marsh Barton La
EX5. . . . .**172** D8
Marsh Barton Rd
EX2. . . . .**177** B3
Marsh Barton Trad Est
EX2. . . . .**177** C2
Marshbridge Cross
TA22. . . . .**33** C7
Marsh Cl PL6 . . . .**249** F6
Marshclose Hill TA22. .**21** D4
Marsh Cotts **14** EX39 . .**15** B1
Marsh Cross EX15. . . . .**83** E4
Marsh Dro EX2 . . . .**87** B2
Marsh End EX17 . . . . .**165** F5
MARSH GREEN **99** C5
Marsh Green La EX5. . . .**99** C5
Marsh Green Road E
EX2. . . . .**177** C2
Marsh Green Road N
EX2. . . . .**177** C2

Marsh Green Road W
EX2...................**177** C2
Marsh Hill
 Cheriton Fitzpaine
 EX16................**63** A4
 Dulverton TA22......**33** C8
 Lynton EX35........**151** C5
Mars Hill Way EX35 ..**151** C5
Marsh La
 Bow EX17............**78** B5
 Calstock PL18......**125** D3
 Cheriton Fitzpaine EX16 . .**63** A4
 Chudleigh TQ13.....**123** F8
 Chudleigh TQ13.....**124** A8
 Clyst St George EX3 .**183** B6
 Crediton EX17......**165** E5
 Instow EX39.........**15** B1
 Newton St Cyres EX5 . .**98** F8
 North Molton EX36 ....**30** E6
 Seaton EX12........**192** B7
 South Molton EX36...**158** F7
 Stockland EX14.......**87** A7
 West Charleton TQ7 ..**144** C1
Marsh La Cross TQ13 .**123** F8
Marsh Mill Ct EX5..**172** D7
MARSH MILLS........**249** F6
Marsh Mills PL6.....**249** F7
Marsh Mills Pk PL6..**249** F6
Marsh Mills Ret Pk
 PL6................**249** E7
Marsh Mills Sta★
 PL7................**250** A7
Marsh Path TQ13 ...**180** C7
Marsh Rd
 Crediton EX17......**165** E5
 Newton Abbot TQ12...**207** C3
 Seaton EX12........**192** B5
Marshrow La EX3 ...**182** C1
Marston Cl EX7......**204** F7
MARTINHOE...........**4** C5
Martinhoe Cross EX31 . .**4** E3
Martin La PL4.......**263** A2
Martin Rd EX32......**155** B5
Martins Bldgs 4
 TA21...............**160** D5
Martins Cl
 Great Torrington
 EX38...............**159** F5
 Okehampton/North Tawton
 EX20................**75** C7
 Wellington TA21....**160** D5
Martins Gate - City Coll
 PL4................**263** A2
Martins La EX16.....**161** D4
Martin's La EX1, EX4 . .**261** B3
Martins Rd EX8......**196** E2
Martin St PL1.......**262** B2
Martlesham Pl PL5...**243** F4
Marvell La PL4......**263** B3
Marven Ct DT7.......**260** B6
Marwell Cross TQ7...**142** E6
MARWOOD.............**16** C8
Marwood Cross EX5 ....**99** B3
Marwood Ct EX38.....**159** D5
Marwood Hill Gdns★
 EX31................**16** C8
Marwood La EX5......**99** C3
Marwood Pl EX14 ....**166** D6
Marwood's Cross EX31 . . .**9** D7
Marwood's Cross
 TQ10...............**134** D1
Mary Arches St EX4..**261** A3
Mary Cross PL21.....**237** C7
Mary Dean Ave PL5..**244** C7
Mary Dean Cl PL5....**244** C7
Mary Dean's CE Prim Sch
 PL5................**244** C7
Maryfield Ave EX4...**177** D8
Mary La 10 EX16......**34** B1
Maryland Gdns PL2..**247** F7
Mary Newman's Cottage★
 PL12................**243** A2
Marypole Rd EX4.....**173** F1
Marypole Wlk EX4....**173** F1
Mary Rose Ho
 9 Hemyock EX15.......**67** B8
 Torquay TQ2........**220** D7
Mary Seacole Rd
 PL1................**262** A3
Mary St TQ13........**180** D8
MARYSTOW............**106** D1
MARY TAVY............**117** E6
Mary Tavy & Brentor Com
 Prim Sch PL19......**117** E6
Marythorne Rd 15
 PL20...............**125** D2
Masefield Ave
 Barnstaple EX31......**154** F7
 5 Barnstaple EX32 ...**155** A7
Masefield Gdns PL5..**244** B1
Masefield Rd EX4....**178** C8
Masey Rd EX8........**202** D8
Mashford Ave PL4....**233** C4
Masons Row PL18.....**125** C6
Masons Yard PL8....**136** D1
Massey Rd EX16......**161** E6
Masterman Rd PL2...**247** F4
Masters Cl DT7......**260** A6
Masterson St EX2....**177** F3
Matford Ave EX2.....**177** E4
Matford Bsns Pk EX2 **181** C8
Matford La EX2......**261** C1
Matford Mews EX2...**181** D7
Matford Park Rd
 EX2................**181** D8
Matford Rd EX2......**177** E4

Matford Wy EX2......**181** D7
Mathew Ho 2 TQ1....**219** F6
Mathews Cl EX14.....**166** B4
Mathill Cl TQ5......**230** B3
Mathill Rd TQ5......**230** B3
Maton Cl PL21.......**237** D4
Matthews Cross EX15 . **66** B1
Matthew's Ct EX15...**163** C3
Matthews Pas TQ7....**258** C5
Mattiscombe Cross
 TQ7................**145** B1
Mattys Cross EX14....**68** A3
Maudlin Dr TQ14.....**210** B8
Maudlin Rd TQ9......**223** C5
Maudlins La PL19....**171** A5
Maudlins Pk PL19....**171** A5
Maunder's Hill EX9..**198** E7
MAUNDOWN............**35** F7
Maundown Rd TA4.....**35** F7
Maunsell Cl PL2.....**247** F7
Maurice Mws PL7.....**250** E4
Mavisdale PL2.......**247** F6
Mawes Ct PL18.......**125** A5
Maxstoke Ct 4 TQ1..**220** D5
Maxwell Rd PL4......**255** B8
Maybank Rd PL4......**263** C3
Maybrook Dr PL12....**242** D2
May Ct EX39.........**157** D1
Mayers Way PL9......**255** D6
Mayfair PL21........**237** A4
Mayfair Cres PL6....**245** B1
Mayfair Ho PL4......**263** A3
Mayfair Rd TQ12....**211** D2
Mayfield PL21.......**237** A4
Mayfield Cres TQ12 .**206** F3
Mayfield Dr EX8.....**202** D6
Mayfield Rd
 Exeter, Pinhoe EX4...**174** E1
 Exeter, Wonford EX2...**178** A5
 Mayfield Sch TQ2....**214** B3
Mayfield Sch Chestnut
 Centre TQ5........**230** A2
Mayfield Way 1 EX5 ..**99** A6
Mayfield Wy 11 EX5 ..**99** A6
Mayflower Ave
 Exeter EX4.........**173** D2
 Newton Abbot TQ12...**207** F2
Mayflower Cl
 18 Bere Alston PL20 ..**125** E1
 Chittlehampton EX37 ...**28** F4
 Dartmouth TQ6......**233** D4
 Dawlish EX7........**204** E6
 Plymouth PL9.......**255** F7
Mayflower Com Acad
 PL2................**248** A7
Mayflower Ct TQ6....**233** F4
Mayflower Dr
 6 Brixham TQ5......**230** C3
 Plymouth PL2.......**248** B5
Mayflower St PL1....**262** C3
Mayhew Gdns 3 PL7 .**250** E7
Maynarde Cl PL7.....**251** B5
Maynard Sch The
 EX1................**261** C3
Mayne Cl EX20........**75** B7
Mayor's Ave TQ6.....**233** F4
May St EX4..........**261** C4
May Terr
 Plymouth PL4.......**263** B3
 Sidmouth EX10......**188** B4
Maytree Cl EX21......**73** D3
Mazard Tree Hill
 Ash Mill EX36.......**31** C1
 South Molton EX36....**46** C8
Mazzard Cl 9 EX32...**17** B2
McCoys Arcade 18
 EX1................**261** A2
McDonald Ct 12 PL1..**262** A3
Mcilwraith Rd TQ8..**259** C5
Mckay Ave TQ1......**219** F6
MEAD.................**37** A4
Mead Cl
 Cullompton EX15....**163** B2
 Ivybridge PL21......**237** A6
 Paignton TQ3.......**226** C7
Mead Cnr EX39........**37** A4
Meadcombe Rd TQ7..**143** A1
Mead Cotts EX8......**202** F7
Meadcourt TQ3.......**226** C7
Mead Cross
 Ashburton TQ13.....**131** B6
 13 Rockbeare EX5.....**99** A6
Mead Dr TQ7........**143** A1
Meadfoot TQ7.......**143** A1
Meadfoot Cl TQ1.....**220** F4
Meadfoot Ct TQ1.....**220** F4
Meadfoot Grange
 TQ1................**220** C3
Meadfoot La TQ1.....**220** C3
Meadfoot Rd TQ1.....**220** C3
Meadfoot Sea Rd
 TQ1................**220** D3
Meadfoot Terr 2
 PL4................**248** F5
Meadhurst Ct EX10..**188** A3
Mead La
 Paignton TQ3.......**226** C7
 Thurlestone TQ7....**143** A1
Meadow Acre Rd
 EX14................**85** C2
Meadow Ave EX12...**192** A6
Meadow Bank EX13...**87** D1
Meadowbrook 19
 TQ9................**223** D5
Meadow Brook
 Barnstaple EX31....**154** B2

Meadow Brook continued
 Tavistock PL19......**171** A4
 18 Totnes TQ9.......**223** D5
Meadowbrook Cl
 EX4................**176** E8
Meadow Bsns Pk
 EX17...............**165** F5
Meadow Cl
 Bratton Fleming EX31 ..**18** A8
 Budleigh Salterton EX9 **197** F1
 Clyst St Mary EX5...**179** B3
 Harberton TQ9......**222** D2
 Ilfracombe EX34....**150** B4
 Kingskerswell TQ12..**212** F6
 Landkey EX32........**17** C1
 Lympstone EX8......**195** F5
 7 Newton Ferrers
 PL8................**141** A7
 Ottery St Mary EX11..**169** E4
 Plymouth PL7.......**251** D4
 Saltash PL12........**242** F3
 Totnes TQ9.........**223** F5
Meadow Cotts TQ6...**228** C2
Meadow Court Barns
 TQ7................**145** B1
Meadow Cres EX8.....**203** A6
Meadowcroft Dr
 TQ12...............**123** E1
Meadow Dr
 Brixton PL8........**257** A4
 Newton Poppleford
 EX10...............**186** F8
 Saltash PL12.......**242** D4
Meadowfield Pl PL7..**251** B3
Meadow Gdns EX17..**165** D5
Meadow Halt TQ12...**207** A1
Meadow La
 Croyde EX33..........**7** E2
 Cullompton EX15....**163** C2
 Instow EX39.........**15** B1
Meadowlands
 Newton St Cyres EX5 . .**98** F8
 Plymouth PL6.......**245** D7
Meadowlands L Pool 7
 PL19...............**171** B5
Meadow Lea EX5......**82** B6
Meadow Park Dr
 EX37................**43** F3
Meadow Pk
 Barnstaple EX31....**154** B2
 Bideford EX39.......**25** D4
 Brixham TQ5.......**230** B5
 Dawlish EX7........**204** C7
 Marldon TQ3.......**218** D3
 Molland EX36........**31** E7
 Plymouth PL9.......**255** C5
 Shebbear EX21.......**55** E4
 South Molton EX36..**158** C3
 Willand EX15.......**162** C4
Meadow Rd
 Barnstaple EX31....**154** E7
 Budleigh Salterton EX9 **197** F1
 Budleigh Salterton EX9 **203** F8
 Seaton EX12........**192** A5
 Torquay TQ2.......**219** E3
Meadow Rise
 Dawlish EX7........**204** C7
 Mile End TQ12......**206** D5
 Northam EX39......**157** A6
 Plymouth PL7.......**251** A4
 Spreyton EX17........**96** A7
 Teignmouth TQ14....**124** E1
 Torquay TQ1........**220** F5
Meadows Cres EX14..**166** C5
Meadows Edge EX6...**97** B4
Meadowside
 Ashford EX31........**16** B6
 Chillington TQ7....**145** A1
 Plymouth PL9.......**255** F7
 Rockwell Green TA21 .**160** B5
Meadow Side
 Burrow EX10........**186** E8
 Newton Abbot TQ12..**207** A3
Meadowside Rd EX17 .**80** B5
Meadowside SE EX8..**202** A7
Meadows The
 Beer EX12..........**191** D5
 East Portlemouth TQ8..**259** F4
 Kingsteignton TQ12..**207** F6
 Okehampton/North Tawton
 EX20................**74** E2
 St Dominick PL12...**125** A4
 Torpoint PL11......**246** E4
 Yeoford EX17........**96** A6
Meadowstone Cl EX38..**40** F5
Meadowsweet La
 3 Barnstaple EX31..**154** B3
 Paignton TQ4.......**225** E2
Meadowsweet Pk
 PL12...............**242** C2
Meadow Vale EX20....**57** A7
Meadow View
 2 Bampton EX16.....**34** B1
 Bishops Nympton EX36..**30** F2
 Bishopsteignton TQ14..**208** C7
 East Ogwell TQ12...**206** F2
 Hartland EX39.......**22** E3
 Holsworthy EX22....**164** C4
 Lympstone EX8.....**195** F5
 Rackenford EX16.....**47** B7
 Uffculme EX15.......**66** A7
Meadow View Cl
 Sidmouth EX10......**188** C5
 Woodbury EX5......**184** B2
Meadowview Rd EX8..**196** E2
Meadow View Rd
 PL7................**250** D5
Meadows Ct EX39.....**157** A3

Meadowville Rd
 EX39...............**157** A3
Meadow Way
 Colaton Raleigh
 EX10...............**186** D3
 Exeter EX2.........**177** F5
 Gunn EX32...........**17** F4
 Plymouth PL7.......**250** D7
Mead Park Cl EX31...**16** A3
Mead Pk EX31.........**16** A3
Mead Rd TQ2........**219** D2
Meads Cl EX15........**67** B1
Mead The
 Plymouth PL7.......**250** D7
 Silverton EX5.......**82** B5
Mead View Rd EX14..**166** C5
Meadville TQ1.......**220** D3
Meadway
 Newton Abbot TQ12..**212** D8
 Saltash PL12.......**242** E1
 Sidmouth EX10......**188** B6
Mead Way EX12......**192** A6
MEADWELL............**116** A8
Meadwood TQ1.......**220** D3
Mear Top EX31......**154** F7
Measbury Moor Cross
 EX18................**45** C5
Meatherel Cl PL21...**237** B4
MEAVY................**127** C2
Meavy Ave
 Plymouth PL5.......**244** E2
 Torquay TQ2.......**219** B7
Meavy Bourne PL20..**127** A2
Meavy CE Prim Sch
 PL20...............**127** C2
Meavy La PL20.......**127** A2
Meavy Villas PL20...**127** A2
Meavy Way
 Plymouth PL5.......**244** E2
 Tavistock PL19.....**171** D5
Medard Ho 17 EX32..**155** A5
MEDDON...............**37** F4
Meddon Cross
 Edistone EX39.......**37** F5
 Welcombe EX39......**37** F4
Meddon Green Nature
 Reserve★ EX39.......**37** F4
Meddon St
 5 Bideford EX39....**156** F1
 Bideford EX39......**157** A1
Mede The
 Exeter EX4.........**178** B8
 Topsham EX3.......**182** E5
Medland Cres PL6...**244** D6
Medland Cross EX6...**97** C6
Medland La EX6......**97** B6
Medley Ct EX4......**176** E8
Medway Pl PL3.......**249** D6
Medway Rd TQ2......**214** B2
Meerhay La DT6.....**104** F6
Meetford Cross EX6..**97** F7
MEETH.................**37** C3
MEETHE................**29** D1
Meethe Gate Cross
 EX36................**29** D2
Meethe Hill EX36....**29** D1
Meeting La EX8......**195** E6
Meeting St
 Appledore EX39......**15** A1
 Exmouth EX8.......**202** A7
Melbourne Cotts PL1 **262** B3
Melbourne Ct
 10 Exeter EX2......**261** B2
 Torquay TQ1........**220** A6
Melbourne Gn 2
 PL1................**262** B3
Melbourne Pl
 Exeter EX2.........**261** B2
 Plymouth PL1.......**262** B4
Melbourne St
 Exeter EX2.........**261** B2
 Plymouth PL1.......**262** B3
 Tiverton EX16......**161** B4
Melbury Rd EX39.....**39** E8
Melcot Cl TQ12......**207** E7
MELDON...............**93** E3
Meldon La EX20.......**93** E3
Meldon Quarry Sta★
 EX20................**93** E3
Meldon Rd TQ13.....**111** A6
Meldrum Cl EX7......**204** E6
Melhuish Cl EX16....**46** E1
Mellons Cl TQ12.....**206** D4
Mellons Wlk TQ12...**206** D4
Mellowmead TQ13...**121** F7
Mellows Mdw TQ12..**206** F3
Melrose Ave
 Exeter EX1.........**178** D6
 Plymouth PL2.......**248** C8
Melrose Cl EX16.....**161** D4
Melville La TQ1.....**220** B4
Melville Pl 1 PL2...**248** A5
Melville Rd PL2.....**248** A5
Melville St TQ1.....**220** B4
Melville Terrace La
 PL2................**248** A5
MEMBLAND............**141** B7
Membland Ct PL8....**141** C6
MEMBURY..............**87** D6
Membury Cl EX1.....**178** D6
Membury Prim Sch
 EX13................**87** D6
Membury Rd
 Axminster EX13......**87** E3
 Axminster EX13.....**163** B8
 Wambrook TA20......**69** D2
Memory Cross TQ13..**215** E8
Memory La PL9......**255** E7

Mena Park Cl
 Paignton TQ4.......**225** D1
 Plymouth PL9.......**256** B7
Mena Park Rd PL9...**256** B7
MENDENNICK..........**252** C7
Mendip Rd TQ2......**219** D3
Menors Pl EX22.....**164** C5
Merafield Cl PL7....**250** B5
Merafield Dr PL7....**250** C4
Merafield Farm Cotts
 PL7................**250** B4
Merafield Rd PL7....**250** B4
Merafield Rise PL7..**250** C6
Mercer Ct EX2......**178** A2
Mercers Dr EX16....**161** E6
Merchant Row EX3..**182** C7
Merchants Cnr EX17..**61** C1
Merchant's Gdn TQ7 **143** A1
Merchant's House
 (Mus)★ PL1.........**262** C2
Meredith Rd PL2....**248** C6
Mere La 15 TQ14....**210** C5
Meresyke EX8........**202** C6
Merewood Cl EX31...**16** C7
Meriden TQ14.......**210** C7
Meridian Ho PL4....**263** A3
Meridian Pl EX34...**150** B6
Merivale PL20......**126** F2
Merivale Cl TQ14....**210** C7
Merley Rd EX39.....**156** B7
Merlin Bsns Pk EX5 ..**99** A4
Merlin Cl PL6.......**245** E8
Merlin Cres EX4.....**174** A1
Merlin Way TQ2.....**213** D2
Mermaid Ct 6 EX1..**261** A2
Mermaid Yd EX1.....**261** A2
MERRIFIELD...........**70** F4
Merrifield Cross
 Bridgerule EX22.....**70** E4
 Slapton TQ7........**145** C6
Merrifield Rd TQ11..**130** C1
Merrion Ave EX8....**202** D6
Merritt Flats 5 TQ3 **226** A5
Merritt Rd TQ3.....**226** A5
MERRIVALE...........**118** C2
Merrivale Cl TQ2....**214** B4
Merrivale Rd
 Exeter EX4.........**176** A1
 Okehampton EX20...**170** E6
 Plymouth, Ham PL2..**248** B7
 Plymouth, Honicknowle
 PL5................**244** B3
Merrivale View Rd
 PL20...............**127** B3
Merrow Down Dr
 EX12...............**191** F8
Merrydale Cres EX31 . .**27** D6
Merryfield La EX6....**95** F2
Merryfield Rd EX39..**157** C1
Merryland Cl TQ3...**219** B2
Merryland Gdns TQ3 **219** B2
Merrylees Dr EX32..**155** C3
Merrymeet
 Tedburn St Mary EX17..**97** F8
 Whitestone EX4......**82** F4
 Whitestone EX4......**98** E4
Merryside Villas EX16 **61** E8
Merrythorn Rd EX31.**153** D5
Merryweather Way
 EX36...............**158** B4
Merrywood TQ12.....**206** F1
Mersey Cl PL3.......**249** D6
MERTON................**57** A7
MESHAW................**45** F6
Meshaw Cross Rds
 EX36................**46** A5
Meshaw Moor Cross
 EX36................**46** A5
Meshaw Rectory Cross
 EX36................**46** A5
METCOMBE...........**100** B2
Metcombe Cross EX31 . .**9** B2
Metcombe La EX31....**9** B2
Metcombe Rise EX11 **100** C2
Metcombe Vale
 EX11...............**100** C2
Meteor Wlk 2 EX32..**155** B5
METHERELL...........**125** A4
Metherell Ave TQ5..**230** D3
Metherell Avenue Ind Est
 TQ5...............**230** D3
Metherell Cross EX21 . .**91** F8
Metherell Rd EX39..**156** F1
Metley Cross TQ12..**131** E5
Mettaford Cross EX39 **22** F3
Metticombe La
 Barbrook EX35.......**5** C4
 Barbrook EX35.....**151** B1
Mews Ct EX7........**204** E6
Mews Gdns TQ6.....**233** F3
Mews The
 1 Bittaford PL21...**137** C8
 Dawlish EX7........**204** E6
 Exmouth EX8.......**196** F3
 Plymouth, Devonport
 PL1................**248** A3
 Plymouth, Stonehouse
 PL1................**262** A3
 7 Teignmouth TQ14..**210** B4

Mar–Mil 295

Michelcombe La
 TQ13...............**130** A4
Michigan Way
 Exeter EX4.........**173** C2
 Plymouth PL3.......**249** C6
Mid Churchway PL9..**256** A7
Mid Devon Bsns Pk
 EX15...............**162** D6
Middle Blagdon La
 TQ3................**225** B6
Middleborough La
 EX33..................**7** D3
Middle Budleigh Mdw
 TQ12...............**206** F3
Middle Combe Dr
 EX31...............**154** A3
Middlecombe La PL8 **140** F6
MIDDLECOTT..........**73** B8
Middlecott Cross
 Holemoor EX22......**73** B8
 Virginstow EX21.....**90** E4
Middlecott Hill EX32 **18** D3
Middlecott La EX17..**60** F2
Middle Down TQ9...**222** F5
Middle Down Cl PL9..**256** A5
Middlefield Cl PL12 **242** B2
MIDDLE GREEN........**160** D3
Middle Green TQ10..**135** A2
Middle Green Rd
 TA21...............**160** E3
Middle La EX33........**8** E1
Middle Leigh PL8....**140** F7
Middle Lincombe Rd
 TQ1................**220** D3
MIDDLE LUXTON........**68** C5
MIDDLE MARWOOD.......**9** B1
Middlemead Rd
 EX16...............**161** D5
Middle Mill La EX15 **163** C3
MIDDLEMOOR...........**171** F2
MIDDLE MOOR.........**178** D4
Middlemoor Cross
 EX37................**43** C3
Middlemoor Police
 Training Coll EX2 ..**178** D5
Middle Park Terr
 TQ7................**143** B1
Middle Ramshill La
 TQ3................**225** C7
Middle Rd PL9......**140** D8
MIDDLE ROCOMBE.....**213** F7
Middle St
 Brixham TQ5.......**230** C5
 East Budleigh EX9..**198** B6
 Teignmouth TQ14...**210** A3
Middleton Rd EX39..**156** F1
Middleton Wlk PL5..**243** D4
Middletown EX9....**198** B6
MIDDLE
 WADSTRAY..........**232** A3
Middle Warberry Rd
 TQ1................**220** D5
Middle Westerland Cross
 TQ3................**218** D1
Middlewood EX6.....**201** A5
MIDDLE
 WOOLBROOK........**188** A8
Midella Rd PL20.....**127** A2
Midvale Rd TQ4.....**226** B5
Midway
 Exmouth EX8.......**202** E8
 Kingskerswell TQ12..**212** F6
Midway Cl EX2......**177** A1
Midway Terr EX2....**177** A1
Miers Cl PL5........**247** C8
Miglo Ind Est TQ4..**225** E3
Mignonette Wlk
 EX39...............**157** A3
MILBER...............**207** F1
Milber La
 Coffinswell TQ12...**213** B6
 Newton Abbot TQ12..**208** A1
Milber Trad Est
 TQ12...............**208** A1
Milbury Cl EX6.....**182** B5
Milbury Farm Mdw
 EX6................**182** A5
Milbury La EX6.....**182** B4
Milch Pk PL12......**242** C2
Mildmay Ct EX4.....**176** F7
Mildmay St PL4.....**263** A4
Mildren Wy PL1.....**247** E2
MILE END............**206** E5
Mile End Rd TQ12...**206** E5
Mile Gdns EX4......**173** F2
Milehouse Rd PL2...**248** A5
Mile La EX1.........**174** A1
Miles Mitchell Ave
 PL6................**245** A1
Milestone Cotts EX6 **182** B3
Milestone Cross
 TQ13...............**123** F8
Milestone La TQ13..**123** F8
MILFORD..............**22** B1
Milford Ave EX10...**188** B4
Milford Cl TQ1......**210** A5
Milford Cotts EX6..**181** B4
Milford Cross EX39..**22** B1
Milford La PL5......**244** B5
Milford Rd EX10....**188** B4
Military Rd
 Millbrook PL10.....**252** C3
 Plymouth PL3......**249** C6
 Rame PL10.........**140** I2

Milizac Cl PL8 . . . . . .257 E4
Milkaway La EX33. . . . . . 7 E1
Milk Hill EX5. . . . . .81 D7
Milky Way Adventure
Pk ★ EX39 . . . . 23 E1
Milland Cross EX20 . . .75 B1
Millards Hill 10 EX39 . . 15 B1
Mill Ave EX17. . . . . .79 A6
Millbarn Cross EX16. . . 61 F8
MILLBAY 262 B2
Millbay Rd PL1. . . . . . .262 A2
Mill Bottom La
  Stokeinteignhead
  TQ12. . . . . .209 A3
  Stokeinteignhead
  TQ14. . . . . .209 A2
Mill Bridge PL1 . . . . . .262 A2
MILLBROOK
  Axminster. 167 E6
  North Molton 19 F1
  Torpoint 252 E5
Millbrook Bsns Ctr
  PL11. . . . . .252 C6
Millbrook CE(VA) Prim
  Sch PL10. . . . . .252 E5
Millbrook Cross
  EX13. . . . . .167 E6
Millbrook Dale EX13 . .167 E6
Millbrook La EX2 . . . . .177 F2
Millbrook Park Rd
  TQ2. . . . . .219 E5
Millbrook Rd 2 TQ3 . .226 B6
Mill Cl
  Lee Mill PL21 . . . . . . .136 D6
  Newton Abbot TQ12 . .206 F4
Millcombe Cnr TQ9 . . .139 E1
Millcombe La TQ9 . . . .224 C3
Mill Cotts
  Okehampton EX20 . . .170 B5
  Stoke Canon EX5. . . . .173 F7
Mill Cres TQ6 . . . . .233 D4
Millcroft EX11 . . . . . . .169 D3
Mill Cross
  Bickington TQ12 . . . . .131 F7
  Halwill EX21 . . . . .73 C1
  Harberton TQ9 . . . . . .222 C2
  Rattery TQ10. . . . . . . .135 D4
Milldale Cres EX14 . . .166 B5
Mill Dr EX2 . . . . .177 F1
Mill End 1 TQ12. . . . . .123 F1
Millenium St PL2 . . . .248 C8
Millen La TQ12. . . . . . .209 C2
Millennium Way
  Cullompton EX15 . . . .163 C5
  Westward Ho! EX39 . .156 E7
Miller Cl EX2 . . . . .178 C4
Miller Court Workshop
  Units PL1 . . . . .262 A2
Miller Cres EX32 . . . . .155 A5
Miller Ct PL1 . . . . .262 A2
Miller Gr EX4 . . . . .174 F4
Millers Brook EX33. . . . 7 E2
Millers La TQ9 . . . . . . .227 E7
Millers Way
  Honiton EX14 . . . . . . .166 B5
  Tedburn St Mary EX6 . .97 F4
Miller Way
  Exminster EX6 . . . . . .181 F5
  Plymouth PL6 . . . . . . .245 E3
Milletts Cl EX6. . . . . . .182 A4
Millfields Trust Bsns
  Units 11 PL1 . . . . . . .262 A3
Millford Rd EX10. . . . .188 B4
Mill Ford Sch PL5. . . .243 F4
Mill Gn DT7. . . . . .260 E3
Millgreen Ct DT7. . . . .260 E3
Millgreen La EX13. . . . . 87 D1
Millham La TA22 . . . . . .33 D6
MILLHAYES
  Hemyock. 52 C1
  Honiton. 86 F6
Millhayes Cross EX14 . 86 F6
Millhayes Rd EX14 . . . .86 F6
Mill Head EX34 . . . . . .150 C6
Millhead Rd
  Honiton EX14 . . . . .85 D3
  Honiton EX14 . . . . . . .166 B5
MILLHILL 116 F1
Mill Hill
  Barnstaple EX31. . . . . . 16 A3
  Fremington EX31 . . . .153 F5
  Stoke Gabriel TQ9. . . .227 F7
  Witheridge EX16. . . . . . 61 F7
Mill Hill Cotts PL19. . .116 F1
Mill Hill Ct TQ9 . . . . . .227 F7
Mill Hill La
  Millhill PL19 . . . . .116 F1
  Tavistock PL19 . . . . . .117 A1
  Tavistock PL19 . . . . . .171 A6
Millhouse Pk PL11 . . .247 A2
Millin Wy EX7. . . . . . . .201 A2
Mill La
  Alfington EX11 . . . . . . .84 F1
  Ashill EX15 . . . . .66 D6
  Aveton Gifford TQ7 . .143 C6
  Axminster EX13 . . . . . .88 F3
  Barnstaple EX31. . . . . .154 E6
  Barton Town EX31. . . . 11 E3
  Beaford EX20 . . . . .42 C1
  Berrynarbor EX34. . . . . 2 D4
  Bow EX17. . . . . .78 B4
  Branscombe EX12 . . .190 D4
  Brixham TQ5. . . . . . . .230 A1
  Burrington EX37. . . . . .44 B2

Mill La continued
  Charmouth DT6. . . . . .104 F6
  Cheriton Fitzpaine EX17 . 62 E2
  Clyst Honiton EX1. . . .175 C1
  East Buckland EX32 . . 18 E2
  East Ogwell TQ12 . . . .206 D1
  Exebridge EX16 . . . . . .33 F3
  Exeter, Higher Wear
  EX2. . . . . .177 F1
  Exton EX3 . . . . .183 D2
  Frithelstock Stone EX39 . 40 E6
  Galmpton TQ5. . . . . . .229 A4
  George Nympton EX36 . 30 A1
  Loddiswell TQ7 . . . . . .138 C7
  Lower Loxhore EX31. . . . 17 F8
  Lyme Regis DT7 . . . . .260 E3
  Meshaw EX36. . . . . . . .45 F7
  Millhayes EX14 . . . . . . .86 F6
  Newton Poppleford
  EX10. . . . . .186 F6
  North Tawton EX20 . . .77 B4
  North Whilborough
  TQ12. . . . . .212 D2
  Offwell EX14. . . . . .86 B1
  4 Paignton TQ3 . . . . .226 B7
  Sandford EX17 . . . . . . .80 B5
  Stockland EX13. . . . . . .87 B7
  Stoke Fleming TQ6 . . .146 A7
  Teignmouth TQ14 . . . .209 D7
  Torpoint PL11. . . . . . .247 A2
  Torquay TQ2 . . . . .219 F5
  Totnes TQ9 . . . . .223 D5
  Uplyme DT7 . . . . .260 C5
  Wambrook TA20 . . . . . .69 F2
  Whitestaunton TA20 . . 69 F2
  Woolacombe EX34 . . . . 7 F6
  Wootton Fitzpaine
  EX13. . . . . .104 F7
  Wrafton EX33 . . . . . . .152 F4
Mill Lane Cotts EX20 . . 77 B4
Mill Leat
  14 Hemyock EX15. . . . . 67 B8
  Totnes TQ9 . . . . .223 D6
Mill Leat Cotts EX14 . .78 B4
Mill-Leat Gdns EX32 . . 17 B2
Millmans Rd TQ3. . . . .218 D3
Mill Mdw
  Ashburton TQ13 . . . . .130 F5
  10 Combe Martin EX34. . 3 A3
  Harbertonford TQ9 . . .139 C7
  Ivybridge PL21. . . . . . .237 D5
MILLMOOR 51 E1
Millmoor EX15. . . . . . .166 E8
Millmoor Cross EX37. . 44 B2
Millmoor La EX10 . . . .186 F8
Millmoor Vale EX10 . .186 F8
Mill-on-the-Mole Mobile
  Home Pk EX36 . . . . . .18 E4
Mill Park Ind Est EX5 .184 E8
Mill Path TQ13 . . . . . . .130 F4
Mill Pk 2 TQ12. . . . . . .123 E1
Millpool Head PL10 . .252 E4
Millpool Rd PL10. . . . .253 A6
Millpool The TQ9 . . . .228 A7
Mill Rd
  Barnstaple EX31. . . . . .154 E5
  Beaford EX20 . . . . .57 C8
  Bradworthy EX22 . . . . .38 E1
  Exeter EX2 . . . . .177 F1
  Fremington EX31 . . . .153 E5
  High Bickington EX37 . . 43 B7
  Landkey EX32. . . . . 17 B1
  Lustleigh TQ13 . . . . . .122 C7
  Millbrook PL10 . . . . . .253 A5
  Okehampton EX20 . . .170 B4
  Totnes TQ9 . . . . .222 E8
Mill Rise EX14 . . . . .85 F8
Mill St Comm EX38. . .159 B4
Mills Dr TA21 . . . . .160 F7
Millsome La
  Bondleigh EX18. . . . . . .77 C8
  North Tawton EX18 . . . 59 D1
Mills Rd PL1 . . . . .247 F2
Mill St
  Bideford EX39. . . . . . .157 A2
  Chagford TQ13 . . . . . .110 F6
  Crediton EX17. . . . . . .165 D5
  Great Torrington EX38 .159 C4
  Honiton EX14 . . . . . . .166 B5
  Kingsbridge TQ7 . . . . .258 C5
  Ottery St Mary EX11 . .169 C3
  Plymouth PL1 . . . . . . .247 E2
  Sidmouth EX10 . . . . . .188 B4
  South Molton EX36 . . .158 D4
  Uffculme EX15 . . . . . . .66 B7
Mill Steep
  Bishopsteignton
  TQ14. . . . . .208 E8
  Twitchen EX36 . . . . . . .20 C1
Mill Stile EX33 . . . . . . .152 C5
Millstream EX2 . . . . . .177 F2
Mill Stream Ct EX11 . .169 D3
Mill Stream Gdns
  Halberton EX16 . . . . . .65 A7
  Wellington TA21 . . . . .160 B7
Millstream Mdw 4
  TQ13. . . . . .123 F6
Mills Way EX31 . . . . . .154 F6
Mill The EX2. . . . . .261 C1
MILLTOWN 9 D1
Milltown Hill EX36 . . . .45 F7
Milltown La EX10 . . . .188 C6
Mill View 13 TQ13 . . . .123 F6
Mill View Gdns PL10 .252 F5
Mill View Rd PL10. . . .252 F5
Mill Water Sch EX9 . .186 B2
Millway
  Bradninch EX5. . . . . . .82 F6

Millway continued
  18 Chudleigh TQ13 . . .123 E6
  Wambrook TA20 . . . . . .69 F2
Millway Gdns EX5. . . . .82 F6
Millway Pl PL9. . . . . . .255 D8
Millwey Ave EX13 . . . .167 F7
Millwey Ct EX13. . . . . .167 F7
MILLWEY RISE 167 F7
Millwey Rise Ind Est
  EX13. . . . . .167 F7
Millwood TQ13 . . . . . .180 C4
Millwood Bsns Pk
  TQ12. . . . . .207 E3
Millwood Dr PL6. . . . .245 E1
Millwood Terr EX37 . . .28 C2
Milne Pl PL1 . . . . .247 F3
Milsfords La EX5. . . . . .81 E5
MILTON ABBOT 116 B6
Milton Abbot Sch
  PL19. . . . . .116 B5
Milton Cl
  Brixham TQ5 . . . . .230 B2
  Exmouth EX8. . . . . . . .196 C4
  Plymouth PL5 . . . . . . .244 D2
MILTON COMBE 240 F8
Milton Cres
  Brixham TQ5. . . . . . . .230 B2
  Tavistock PL19 . . . . . .171 D5
Milton Ct
  2 Newton Abbot
  TQ12. . . . . .207 C2
  Plymouth, Cattedown
  PL4. . . . . .263 C2
  Plymouth, Prince Rock
  PL4. . . . . .249 B1
MILTON DAMEREL 54 D5
Milton Fields TQ5. . . .230 A2
MILTON GREEN 116 B5
MILTON HILL. 124 E5
Milton La TQ6 . . . . . . .233 C2
Milton Pk TQ5 . . . . . . .230 B2
Milton Pl EX39. . . . . . .156 F1
Milton Rd
  Exeter EX2 . . . . .177 F3
  Newton Abbot TQ12 . .207 B4
Milton St TQ5. . . . . . . .230 A2
Miltons Yard EX13 . . .167 D5
Milverton Rd TA21 . . .160 B8
Mimosa Cl 2 EX16. . . .161 F6
Mimosa Ct EX9 . . . . . .198 C1
Mimosa Wy TQ4 . . . . .225 F2
Minacre La TQ12 . . . . .212 E1
Mincent Cl TQ2 . . . . . .214 A3
Mincent Hill TQ2. . . . .214 A3
Minchin La EX5. . . . . . .99 D2
Minchin Orch EX5. . . . . 99 E2
Mincinglake Rd EX4. . .173 F1
Minden Rd 4 TQ14 . . .210 B5
Minehead La TA24 . . . . 33 F7
Miners Cl 11 TQ13. . . .131 A5
Minerva Bsns Pk
  TQ12. . . . . .207 E3
Minerva Cl PL7 . . . . . .251 A6
Minerva Way
  Newton Abbot TQ12 . .207 E3
  Okehampton EX20 . . .170 F7
Mines Rd EX39. . . . . . .157 C1
Miniature Pony Ctr The ★
  TQ13. . . . . .111 B3
Minifie Rd EX14. . . . . .166 B6
Minniemoor Cross
  EX31. . . . . 4 B1
Minniemoor La EX31. . . 4 C1
Minses Cl PL9 . . . . . . .256 C7
Minster Rd EX2 . . . . . .182 B5
Mint Park Rd EX33 . . .152 F7
Mint The EX4 . . . . .261 A3
Mirador Pl PL4. . . . . . .249 C3
Miranda Rd TQ3 . . . . .225 F8
Mire La
  Sidmouth EX10 . . . . . .189 B7
  Trow EX10. . . . . .189 B7
Mirey La EX5 . . . . .184 C3
Misdon Cotts EX20. . . .75 F1
Mission Ct EX1. . . . . . .261 A2
Misterton Cl PL9 . . . . .256 B8
Mistletoe View 15
  TQ12. . . . . .123 F6
Mitchell Cl PL9 . . . . . .255 D5
Mitchell Gdns 13
  EX13. . . . . .167 D5
Mitchell Ho EX4 . . . . .177 D8
Mitchell's Pool TA21 .160 E6
Mitchell St
  Wellington TA21 . . . . . .52 B8
  Wellington TA21 . . . . .160 C7
Mitre Cl
  Bishopsteignton
  TQ14. . . . . .208 E8
  Tavistock PL19 . . . . . .171 A3
Mitre Ct 14 EX1. . . . . .263 A2
Mitre La EX4. . . . . .261 A3
Mizzen Rd PL1 . . . . . . .247 F1
Moat Hill TQ9. . . . . . . .223 C4
Moat Pk PL6. . . . . .245 C1
Mockham Down Gate
  EX32. . . . . 18 C7
Mockham La EX32 . . . . 18 D6
MODBURY 137 C2
Modbury Cl PL21. . . . .244 B3
Modbury Cross PL21. .136 E2
Modbury Ct 5 PL21. . .137 B2
Modbury Prim Sch
  PL21. . . . . .137 B2
Model Terr 2 EX39 . . .157 A1
Modred Cl EX4. . . . . . .174 A1
Modyford Wlk PL20 . .126 C3
MOGWORTHY. 47 D4

Mogworthy La EX16. . . 47 D3
Mohun's Cl PL19. . . . .171 C4
Mohun's Pk PL19 . . . .171 C3
Mole Bridge La EX36 .158 E4
Mole Ridge Way
  EX36. . . . . .158 C5
Moles Cotts EX6 . . . . .182 A4
Moles Cross TQ3. . . . .218 E7
Moles La
  Kingskerswell TQ12 . .212 E1
  Paignton TQ3 . . . . . . .218 E8
Molesworth Rd
  Plymouth, Plympton
  PL7. . . . . .250 C6
  Plymouth, Stoke PL1,
  PL3. . . . . .248 A3
Molesworth Terr
  PL10. . . . . .252 F5
Molesworth Wy EX22 164 A4
Molford Ct EX36 . . . . .158 B3
MOLLAND 31 E7
Molland Cross
  Brayford EX36 . . . . 19 B4
  Chulmleigh EX18. . . . . .45 E3
Molland Hill EX32,
  EX36. . . . . 19 A5
Mollison Rd PL5 . . . . .243 E2
Moll Tall's Cross PL7 .136 A8
Molyneaux Pl 10 PL1 .247 F3
Molyneux Dr EX17 . . .165 E4
Monastery Rd TQ3 . . .226 A6
Mondeville Way
  Northam EX39 . . . . . . .156 F6
  8 Northam EX39 . . . . .156 F7
Money Acre Cross
  EX24. . . . . .101 E7
Money Acre Rd
  Church Green EX24. . .101 F7
  Farway EX24. . . . . .101 E7
Money Pit La EX13 . . . .69 D1
Monica Wlk PL4. . . . . .263 B4
Monitor Cl
  Exeter EX2 . . . . .261 A1
  South Molton EX36 . . .158 B5
MONKERTON 178 E8
Monkerton Com Prim Sch
  EX1. . . . . .178 E8
Monkerton Ct 2 EX1 .178 E8
Monkerton Dr EX1 . . .178 E8
Monkey La EX10 . . . . .186 E6
Monkey Puzzle Dr
  EX20. . . . . .170 C5
MONKLEIGH 40 F7
Monkleigh Mill La
  EX39. . . . . .40 D8
Monkleigh Prim Sch
  EX39. . . . . .40 F7
MONKOKEHAMPTON .76 B8
Monkokehampton Cross
  EX19. . . . . .76 A8
Monksbridge Rd TQ5 230 B3
Monks Cl
  Bideford EX39. . . . . 26 A4
  Crediton EX17. . . . . . .165 B6
Monks Hill PL15. . . . . .115 A4
Monksmead PL19 . . . .171 A4
Monks Orch TQ12. . . .212 A6
Monk's Rd EX4. . . . . . .177 F7
Monkstone Gdns
  EX13. . . . . .167 E5
Monkston Point TQ8 .259 D4
Monks Way TQ13 . . . .180 C6
Monkswell Rd EX4 . . .177 E8
MONKTON 86 A5
Monkton Rd
  Honiton EX14 . . . . . . .166 E7
  Monkton EX14 . . . . . . .86 A5
MONKTON WYLD. 104 D7
Monkton Wyld Camping
  Site DT6. . . . . .104 C7
Monkton Wyld Cross
  DT6. . . . . .104 C7
Monkton Wyld La
  DT6. . . . . .104 E7
Monmouth Ave EX3 . .182 F4
Monmouth Beach Chalets
  DT7. . . . . .260 C2
Monmouth Gdns PL5 244 C4
Monmouth Hill EX3 . .182 F4
Monmouth St
  Lyme Regis DT7 . . . . .260 E3
  Topsham EX3 . . . . . . .182 F4
Monmouth Way
  EX14. . . . . .166 D5
Monroe Gdns PL4. . . .262 B4
Monro Mead 7
  TQ12. . . . . .122 F1
Monshall EX19. . . . . . . 57 E3
Mons Terr 11 TQ10 . . .134 F3
Montacute Ave PL5 . .244 B2
Montagu Cl
  3 Exeter EX1. . . . . . . .178 D1
  Kingsbridge TQ7 . . . . .258 C6
Montague Gdns EX9 . .197 E1
Montague Pl EX39 . . .156 F1
Montague Rise EX4 . .261 B4
Montague Terr PL7 . . .132 F4
Montagu Rd TQ7. . . . .258 C5
Monterey TQ4 . . . . . . .226 C1
Monterey Cl TQ2 . . . . .219 E3
Monterey Gdns EX4 . .173 C1
Monterey Pk TQ12 . . .207 F1
Montery Pl 3 EX32 . . .155 B3
Montesson Cl TQ3 . . .225 D7
Montesson Rd TQ3 . . .225 D7
Montgomery Cl
  Ivybridge PL21. . . . . . .237 E5
  Saltash PL12. . . . . . . .242 D3

Montgomery Dr
  PL19. . . . . .171 A6
Montgomery Prim Sch
  Exeter EX4 . . . . .176 F5
  11 Exeter EX4 . . . . . . .177 A5
Montgomery Rd 6
  EX2. . . . . .178 D5
Mont Le Grand EX1 . .177 E6
Montpelier Ct
  Exeter EX4 . . . . .177 A7
  Paignton TQ3 . . . . . . .219 B1
Montpelier La 13
  EX34. . . . . .150 C6
Montpelier Prim Sch
  PL2. . . . . .248 B6
Montpelier Rd
  Ilfracombe EX34. . . . .150 C6
  Plymouth PL2 . . . . . . .248 C7
Montpellier Ct 1
  EX8. . . . . .202 B6
Montpellier Rd
  Exmouth EX8. . . . . . . .202 A6
  Torquay TQ1 . . . . .220 B4
Montrose Way TQ12. .244 B3
Montserrat Rise TQ2 .213 E3
Monument Cl TA21. . .160 E4
Monument Rd TA21. .160 E3
Monument St PL1. . . .247 E1
Monument View TA21 52 D8
Moonhayes Cross
  EX14. . . . . .68 C4
Moon Hill Cl EX2. . . . .181 C8
Moon La 4 PL21. . . . . .137 B2
Moonridge EX2 . . . . . .182 C7
Moon's Cross EX20. . . .95 B5
Moon St PL4. . . . . .263 A3
Moorashes 17 TQ9 . . .223 C5
Moor Cl TQ14. . . . . . . .210 C7
Moorcourt Cl EX10 . .187 F3
Moorcox Cross EX13 . .86 E2
Moor Cres PL20. . . . . .128 A8
Moorcroft Cl
  Okehampton EX20 . . .170 E5
  Plymouth PL9 . . . . . . .256 A7
Moorcroft Ct EX20 . . .170 E5
MOOR CROSS 133 C1
Moor Cross EX22. . . . . 71 C3
Moor Ct EX10 . . . . . . .187 F3
Moore Cl TQ12. . . . . . .212 F8
Moore Ct EX17. . . . . . .165 C5
Mooredge La EX5. . . . .82 E1
Mooremeadow EX1. . .179 B8
Moor Farm Cotts
  TQ8. . . . . .148 F4
Moorfield PL16 . . . . . .105 E4
Moorfield Ave 4
  PL6. . . . . .249 C7
Moorfield Cl EX8. . . . .202 C8
Moorfield Gdn TA24. . .21 C6
Moorfield Rd
  Exmouth EX8. . . . . . . .202 C8
  St Giles on t h PL15. . .90 C1
Moorfields
  6 Bittaford PL21. . . . .137 C8
  19 Colyton EX24 . . . . .103 A4
Moorfoot Cross
  TQ12. . . . . .131 C8
Moor Gate EX20 . . . . .170 C1
Moorhaven EX9. . . . . .197 F6
Moorhaven Cl TQ1 . . .219 E7
MOORHAVEN
  VILLAGE 137 C8
MOORHAYES 161 E6
Moorhayes TQ13. . . . .180 D7
Moorhayes Bglws
  EX16. . . . . .161 E5
Moorhayes Cross
  EX15. . . . . .67 B6
Moorhayes Ct EX5 . . . .84 A1
Moorhayne Cross
  EX15. . . . . .66 A2
Moorhen Cl TQ12 . . . .207 C7
Moorhouse La TA4. . . .35 A4
Moorings Reach TQ5 230 D5
Moorings The
  Braunton EX33 . . . . . .152 D6
  Exmouth EX8. . . . . . . .202 C5
  Exmouth, The Point
  EX8. . . . . .201 E6
  Kingsbridge TQ7 . . . . .258 D4
  Paignton TQ3 . . . . . . .226 C5
  Saltash PL12. . . . . . . .242 F1
Moor La
  Bittadon EX31. . . . . 9 C5
  Bovey Tracey TQ13 . . .180 C5
  Braunton EX33 . . . . . .152 A5
  Broadclyst EX5. . . . . . .175 C4
  Brushford TA22. . . . . . .33 F4
  Budlake EX5. . . . . .82 E1
  Budleigh Salterton EX9 197 F2
  Churchinford TA3 . . . . .68 D7
  Croyde EX33. . . . . 7 D2
  Exeter EX2 . . . . .178 F5
  Hatherleigh EX20 . . . . .75 D4
  Molland EX36. . . . . 31 E7
  Nethercott EX33. . . . . . 8 C2
  Plymouth PL5 . . . . . . .243 E1
  Poltimore EX4. . . . . . .174 F7
  Shobrooke EX17. . . . . .80 E4
  Staverton TQ9 . . . . . . .216 B5
  Torquay TQ2 . . . . .214 A3
  Venn Ottery EX11 . . . .100 C1
  Woodbury EX5. . . . . . .184 B5
  Yarnscombe EX31. . . . . 27 C2
  Zeal Monachorum EX17 . 78 B8
MOORLAKE 79 C2
Moorland Ave
  Denbury TQ12 . . . . . . .211 A2

Moorland Ave continued
  Plymouth PL7 . . . . . . .250 F6
Moorland Cl
  7 Bittaford PL21. . . . .137 C8
  Yelverton PL20. . . . . . .241 D8
Moorland Ct PL20. . . .126 F2
Moorland Dr PL7. . . . .250 E6
Moorland Gate
  Heathfield TQ12 . . . . .123 D8
  Roborough EX19. . . . . . 43 B3
Moorland Gdns PL7 . .250 F6
Moorland Pk TQ13 . . .180 D5
Moorland Rd PL7 . . . .250 E5
Moorland Rise EX36. .158 C4
Moorlands
  Chagford TQ13 . . . . . .110 F6
  Tiverton EX16. . . . . . .161 E6
  West Hill EX11 . . . . . .168 D5
Moorlands Cl TQ12 . .207 F2
Moorlands La PL12. . .242 C4
Moorlands Rd EX9 . . .197 E1
Moorlands Trad Est
  PL12. . . . . .242 C4
Moorland Terr EX38. .159 B5
Moorland View
  Buckfastleigh TQ11. . .236 A5
  Lapford EX17 . . . . .60 D3
  Newton Abbot TQ12 . .208 A2
  Plymouth, Derriford
  PL6. . . . . .245 A5
  Plymouth, Plymstock
  PL9. . . . . .256 B7
  Princetown PL20 . . . . .128 A8
  Saltash PL12. . . . . . . .242 F4
  South Molton EX36 . . . .46 D8
Moorland Way
  Exeter EX4 . . . . .176 F8
  Gunnislake PL18. . . . .125 C5
Moor Lane Cl TQ2. . . .214 A3
Moor Lane Cross N
  EX36. . . . . 31 E8
Moor Lea EX33. . . . . . .152 F5
Moormead EX9 . . . . . .197 F1
Moorpark
  Bittaford PL21. . . . . . .137 C8
  Exmouth EX8. . . . . . . .202 C6
Moor Park Cl EX33 . . . 7 D2
Moor Park Rd TQ12 . .212 F6
Moor Pk
  Chagford TQ13 . . . . . .111 A6
  Honiton EX14 . . . . . . .166 B3
  Kingskerswell TQ12 . .212 F6
Moor Rd
  Ipplepen TQ12 . . . . . .211 E3
  Staverton TQ9. . . . . . .216 B5
Moorsend TQ12. . . . . .206 E4
Moor's End TQ12. . . . .207 D8
Moorshead Cross
  Buckfastleigh TQ11. . .135 B6
  Yealmpton PL21 . . . . .136 D2
Moorside
  Malborough TQ7. . . . .147 E6
  Mary Tavy PL19. . . . . .117 E6
Moors Pk TQ14 . . . . . .208 F7
Moorstone Leat TQ4 .226 C1
MOORTOWN
  Great Torrington. 41 F7
  Tavistock 127 A8
  Tetcott 89 F7
Moortown EX18. . . . . . .59 F8
Moortown Cross
  Chulmleigh EX18. . . . . .59 F8
  Rackenford EX36 . . . . .47 B8
Moorview
  Broadhempston
  TQ13. . . . . .131 E1
  Marldon TQ3. . . . . . . .218 D2
  Payhembury EX14. . . . .84 D3
Moor View
  Bovey Tracey TQ13 . .180 C5
  Chudleigh TQ13. . . . . .123 E6
  Hatherleigh EX20 . . . . .75 B6
  Mary Tavy PL19. . . . . .117 E6
  Northlew EX20 . . . . . . .74 E2
  North Tawton EX20 . . .77 C4
  Pennymoor EX16 . . . . .62 E6
  Plymouth PL9 . . . . . . .255 D7
  Plymouth, Keyham
  PL2. . . . . .247 F5
  Plymouth, Laira PL3 . .249 C4
  Torpoint PL11. . . . . . .247 B3
Moorview Cl EX4. . . . .173 D1
Moor View Cl EX10. . .187 F7
Moorview Cres TQ3 . .218 D2
Moorview Ct PL6. . . . .245 F5
Moor View Dr TQ14 . .210 A6
Moorview End TQ3. . .218 D2
Moor View Terr
  9 Bittaford PL21. . . . .137 C8
  Plymouth PL4 . . . . . . .248 E4
  Yelverton PL20. . . . . . .127 A2
Moorview Way EX34 . . . 2 F4
Moothill Cross TQ9 . .216 A6
MORCHARD BISHOP . .61 D2
Morchard Bishop CE Prim
  Sch EX17. . . . . .61 D2
MORCHARD ROAD. . . .78 F7
Morchard Road Sta
  EX17. . . . . .78 F8
MOREBATH 34 B3
Morecombe Cross
  EX21. . . . . .73 A4
MORELEIGH. 139 A3
Moreton Ave
  Bideford EX39. . . . . . .156 E1
  Plymouth PL6 . . . . . . .244 F1
Moreton Dr EX39. . . . .156 E2

MORETONHAMPSTEAD 111 E4
Moretonhampstead Hospl TQ13 111 F5
Moretonhampstead Motor Museum★ TQ13 111 E4
Moretonhampstead Prim Sch TQ13 111 F5
Moretonhampstead Rd
Bovey Tracey TQ13 122 F6
Lustleigh TQ13 112 C1
Lustleigh TQ13 122 D8
Moreton Park Rd EX39 156 E1
Moreton Terr EX6 112 F5
Morgan Ave TQ2 220 A5
Morgan Ct EX8 202 A6
Morganhayes Cross EX24 102 D4
Morgans Quay TQ14 210 B3
Morgan Sweet EX5 99 B6
Morice Sq PL1 247 E2
Morice St PL1 247 E2
Morice Terr EX22 54 A6
MORICE TOWN 247 D3
Morice Town Prim Sch PL2 247 E4
Morin Rd TQ3 226 C8
Morlaix Cl EX7 204 E8
Morlaix Dr PL6 245 B4
Morleigh Cross TQ9 139 A3
Morleigh Gn TQ9 139 A3
Morleigh Green Cross TQ9 139 A4
Morleigh Rd TQ9 139 C6
MORLEY 206 B3
Morley Cl PL7 250 A5
Morley Ct PL1 262 B3
Morley Dr PL20 126 D2
Morley Rd EX4 177 E8
Morley View Rd PL7 250 C6
Mornacott Cross EX36 31 A4
Mornacott Rd EX36 31 A4
Morningside
Dawlish EX7 204 C4
Torquay TQ1 220 E5
Mornington Pk TA21 160 E5
Morrell's Cross EX16 34 B4
Morrell's La EX16 50 B6
Morris Cl EX20 75 B7
Morrish Pk PL9 255 F6
Morshead Rd PL6 244 F2
Mortain Rd PL12 242 D4
MORTEHOE 7 F8
Mortehoe Her Ctr★ EX34 7 F8
Mortehoe Station Rd EX34 1 B1
Mortimer Ave TQ3 226 B8
Mortimer Ct EX2 178 A2
Mortimer Ho EX1 177 E6
Mortimers Cross EX15 66 B4
Mortimore Cl PL12 242 D2
Morton Cres EX8 201 F6
Morton Crescent Mews EX8 201 F6
Morton Dr EX38 159 D5
Morton Rd EX8 201 F6
Morton Way EX13 167 D4
Morven Dr EX8 196 A2
Morwell Gdns PL2 248 A6
MORWELLHAM 125 E4
Morwellham Cl PL5 247 C8
Morwellham Quay★ PL19 125 E4
Morwenna Park Rd EX39 156 F7
Morwenna Rd EX23 37 A1
Morwenna Terr 2 EX39 156 F7
MORWENSTOW 36 E2
Moses Cl PL6 244 E7
Moses Ct PL6 244 E7
Mosshayne La EX1, EX5 179 B2
Mossop Cl EX11 169 D3
Mostyn Ave PL4 249 A4
Motehole Rd TQ12 211 D2
Mote Pk PL12 242 C3
MOTHECOMBE 142 A6
Mothecombe Wlk PL6 245 E1
Motherhill Ct TQ8 259 C5
Motton Rd EX16 161 B6
Mott's Cross EX15 84 A7
Motts La EX15 84 A7
Moult Hill TQ8 259 B2
Moulton Cl PL7 251 B5
Moulton Wlk PL7 251 B4
Moult Rd TQ8 259 B2
Mounson Hill EX6 97 C5
Mountain Cl EX8 202 F8
Mountain Hill EX8 197 A1
Mountbatten Cl
Exmouth EX8 196 D2
Plymouth PL9 255 D6
Mount Batten Ctr★ PL9 254 F7
Mountbatten Dr EX1 178 C1
Mountbatten Rd EX16 161 C5
Mountbatten Way PL9 255 E6
Mount Batton Dr EX2 182 C8
Mount Boone TQ6 233 F4
Mount Boone Hill TQ6 233 F4
Mount Boone La TQ6 233 F4
Mount Boone Way TQ6 233 E4
Mount Cl EX14 166 B5
Mount Dinham
Exeter EX4 177 A6
Exeter EX4 261 A3
Mount Dinham Ct EX4 261 A4
Mount Edgcumbe Ho & Country Pk★ PL10 253 E6
Mounter's Hill TA20 69 E2
Mount Ford PL19 171 A5
Mountford Dr
Bovey Tracey TQ13 123 A5
Bovey Tracey TQ13 180 F7
MOUNT GOULD 249 B3
Mount Gould Ave PL4 249 B2
Mount Gould Cres PL4 249 B3
Mount Gould Hospl PL4 249 B3
Mount Gould Rd PL4 249 B3
Mount Gould Way PL4 249 B3
Mount Hermon Rd TQ1 220 B6
Mounthill Cotts TQ12 122 F1
Mounthill Cross EX24 103 B5
Mounthill La EX13 103 E5
Mount House Sch PL19 171 E7
Mounticombe Cross EX18 45 C1
Mounticombe La EX18 45 C1
MOUNT LANE 90 B6
MOUNT PLEASANT 86 B3
Mount Pleasant
Bideford, East-t-W EX39 157 C3
Bideford, Littleham EX39 25 D2
3 Bishop's Tawton EX32 16 E1
10 Crediton EX17 165 C5
Millbrook PL10 252 E5
Moretonhampstead TQ13 111 F4
Plymouth PL5 244 B2
Mount Pleasant Ave EX8 196 B3
Mount Pleasant Cl
Kingsbridge TQ7 258 D6
Kingskerswell TQ12 213 A3
Mount Pleasant Ct EX8 196 B2
Mount Pleasant La 7 TQ14 210 A3
Mount Pleasant Mews TQ5 230 C4
Mount Pleasant Rd
Brixham TQ5 230 C4
Dawlish Warren EX7 201 B1
Exeter EX4 177 E8
Kingskerswell TQ12 213 A3
Newton Abbot TQ12 207 C2
2 Torquay TQ1 220 B6
MOUNT RADFORD 261 C2
Mount Radford Cres EX2 261 C2
Mount Radford Sq EX2 261 C2
Mount Raleigh Ave EX39 156 F4
Mount Raleigh Dr EX39 156 E3
Mount Rd TQ5 230 D5
Mount Ridley Rd TQ6 234 C3
Mount Rise EX6 114 E4
Mount Sandford Gn EX32 155 D2
Mount Sandford Rd
Barnstaple EX32 155 D1
Landkey EX32 155 E2
Mount St
Plymouth, Mount Wise PL1 247 E1
Plymouth, Mutley PL4 263 A4
MOUNTS THE 144 C7
Mount Stone Rd PL1 254 A8
Mount Street Prim Sch PL4 263 A4
Mount Stuart Hospl (Private) TQ1 219 F7
Mount Tamar Cl PL5 243 E2
Mount Tamar Sch PL5 243 E2
Mount Tavy Rd PL19 171 E6
Mount The
32 Appledore EX39 15 A1
Brixham TQ5 230 C6
Teignmouth TQ14 210 B6
Torquay TQ2 213 F4
Totnes TQ9 223 C4
Mount View
18 Colyton EX24 103 A4
Feniton EX14 84 E2
2 Ilfracombe EX34 150 D5
Mount View Cotts EX32 155 F2
Mount View Home Pk EX32 155 E2
Mount View Terr 2 TQ9 223 C5
Mount Wear Sq EX2 182 C8
MOUNT WISE 247 F1
Mount Wise Com Prim Sch PL1 247 E1
Mount Wise Cres PL5 247 F1
Mount Wise Ct PL1 247 F1
Mourne Villas PL9 255 F8
Mousebeare La EX16 48 E2
Mouseberry Cross EX17 46 A4
Mouseberry La TQ13 124 B4
Mousehole Cross EX14 84 D5
Mouse Hole La EX14 84 C4
MOUTH MILL 23 B5
Mowbars Hayes EX13 87 A3
Mowbray Ave EX4 261 B4
Mowbray Ct EX2 178 A5
Mowhay Mdw PL11 252 B8
Mowhay Rd PL5 244 A2
Mowhay The 15 EX22 164 C4
Mowlish La EX6 200 B7
Mowstead Pk EX33 152 B7
Mowstead Rd EX33 152 B7
Moxeys Cl EX17 62 E1
Moyses La EX20 170 B4
Moyses Mdw EX20 170 A4
Mrs Ethelston's CE Prim Sch DT7 260 A5
Mucky Duck EX20 107 E2
Mucky La EX19 57 D6
Mudbank La
Exmouth EX8 202 A8
Lympstone EX8 195 F1
MUDDIFORD 9 E1
Muddix Mews EX39 156 F6
MUDDLEBRIDGE 16 A3
Muddlebridge Cl EX31 16 A3
Muddle Brook EX31 16 A3
Muddy La
East Buckland EX32 18 E2
Ottery St Mary EX11 101 B7
Popham EX36 19 A3
Mudford Gate EX16 62 E7
Mudgate Cross EX36 20 D3
Mudge La TQ12 217 E6
Mudge's La EX17 78 D3
Mudges Terr PL18 125 D6
Mudge Way PL7 250 E5
Mudhouse Cross EX19 58 B7
Mudstone La TQ5 230 E3
Mulberry Cl
Exeter EX1 178 B6
Paignton TQ3 225 E6
Plymouth PL6 245 E7
Willand EX15 162 D4
Mulberry Gr PL19 171 C2
Mulberry Rd PL12 242 E1
Mulberry Rise EX12 192 A8
Mulberry St 3 TQ14 210 B4
Mulberry Way EX31 154 B2
Mulgrave St PL1 262 C2
Mullacott Cross EX34 1 E1
Mullacott Cross Ind Est EX34 1 F1
Mullet Ave PL3 249 C4
Mullet Cl PL3 249 C4
Mullet Rd PL3 249 C4
Mulligan Dr EX2 178 D2
Mullion Cl PL11 246 F4
Munro Ave PL8 141 B8
Munro Ho EX31 155 B8
Muralto Ho PL19 171 A4
MURCHINGTON 110 E7
Murchington Cross TQ13 110 E7
Murch Rise EX1 179 B8
Murdock Rd PL11 246 F3
Murhill La PL9 249 D1
Murley Cl EX17 165 A6
Murley Cres TQ14 208 E8
Murley Grange TQ14 208 E8
Murrayfield Cl PL2 248 C7
MUSBURY 103 D5
Musbury Castle★ EX13 103 E5
Musbury Prim Sch EX13 103 D5
Musbury Rd EX13 167 C4
MUSEHILL 106 F6
Museum Ct TQ7 258 C6
Museum Rd TQ1 220 C4
Musgrave Ho EX4 261 B3
Musgrave Row EX4 261 B3
Musgraves TA22 33 E6
Mushroom Rd EX5 99 A1
Musket Rd TQ12 180 F2
Mus of Barnstaple & North Devon★ EX32 154 F4
Mus of Dartmoor Life★ EX20 170 B5
MUTLEY 248 E4
Mutley Ct PL4 263 A4
Mutley Plain PL4 248 E4
Mutley Plain La PL4 248 E4
Mutley Rd PL3 248 E5
Muttersmoor Rd EX10 187 E5
MUTTERTON 83 D8
Mutton La
Exeter EX2 181 C8
Torrington EX38 159 C3
Muxbeare La
Willand EX15 65 E7
Willand EX15 162 D7
Muxey La
Great Torrington EX38 41 D5
Great Torrington EX38 159 D3
Muxworthy La EX32 19 A8
Mylor Cl PL2 248 D8
Myra Ct 27 EX39 15 A1
Myrtleberry La EX35 151 F3
Myrtlebury Way EX1 178 D6
Myrtle Cl
Exeter EX2 177 B1
Yelverton PL20 127 B3
Myrtle Farm View EX33 7 E2
Myrtle Gdns EX39 157 A2
Myrtle Gr
Bideford EX39 156 F2
Bideford EX39 157 A2
Myrtle Hill TQ14 210 C5
Myrtle La TA21 51 E7
Myrtle Rd EX4 176 E4
Myrtle Row
25 Exmouth EX8 202 A6
4 Torquay TQ1 220 B5
Myrtles Ct PL12 242 D4
Myrtle St 17 EX39 15 A1
Myrtleville Cres PL2 248 A6

N

Nadder Bottom EX4 176 B8
Nadder La
Nadderwater EX4 176 B8
South Molton EX36 158 B4
Nadder Mdw EX36 158 B4
Nadder Park Rd EX4 176 D5
NADDERWATER 176 B7
Nadrid Cross EX36 30 A8
Nadrid East Cross EX36 30 A8
Nags Head Rd EX14 85 B2
Naida Vale TQ6 233 F5
Naish's La EX13 87 B3
Nancarrows PL12 242 C2
Napier St PL1 247 F3
Napier Terr
Exeter EX4 261 A3
Plymouth PL4 248 E4
Nap La EX18 44 C1
Naps La EX10 186 C5
Nap View EX14 85 B4
NARFORD'S 69 F1
Narfords La TA20 69 F1
Narracott La
Hollocombe EX18 58 E7
South Molton EX36 158 A2
Narratons Rd EX20 93 E6
Narrow La
Botusfleming PL12 242 C7
Knowle EX17 79 C4
Tiverton EX16 161 C2
Narrowmoor Cross TQ7 144 D4
Narthmoor Hill TA22 33 B7
Naseby Dr TQ12 180 F2
Nash Cl
Exmouth EX8 202 E7
Plymouth PL7 251 A5
Nash Dr TA21 160 F6
Nash Gdns EX7 204 D4
Nash La DT6 88 H2
Nasmith Cl EX8 196 D1
NATCOTT 22 F2
Natcott La EX39 22 F2
National Marine Aquarium★ PL4 263 A2
Nats La
Cornwood PL21 133 D1
Sparkwell PL21 136 C8
Natsley La EX32 18 F8
Natson La EX6 97 C6
Natson Mill La EX17 78 B4
Nattadon Rd TQ13 111 A6
Natty Cross EX38 43 A5
Nautilus EX39 156 C7
Neadon La EX6 112 F5
Neal Cl PL7 251 B4
Neath Rd PL4 263 C4
Needlewood Cl EX11 168 C3
Needs Dr EX39 156 E1
Neet Way EX22 164 C6
Neilgate Cnr TQ13 131 A3
Nellies Wood View TQ9 223 B7
Nelson Ave PL1 247 F3
Nelson Cl
Staverton TQ9 216 A5
Teignmouth TQ14 210 A6
Topsham EX3 182 E5
Torquay TQ1 220 D2
Nelson Dr
Exmouth EX8 202 E8
Westward Ho! EX39 156 C7
Nelson Gdns 5 PL1 247 F3
Nelson Mews EX39 156 C7
Nelson Pl TQ12 207 B5
Nelson Rd
Brixham TQ5 230 C5
Dartmouth TQ6 233 C3
Exeter EX4 177 A5
Westward Ho! EX39 156 C7
Nelson St PL4 263 A4
Nelson Terr
Plymouth PL6 245 E6
Westward Ho! EX39 156 C7
Nelson Way 1 EX2 178 D5
NEOPARDY 79 D1
Neopardy Cross EX17 79 D1
Nepean St 1 PL2 247 F5
Neptune Ct 3 EX1 261 A2
Neptune Pk PL9 255 B8
Ness Dr TQ14 210 B2
Ness View Rd TQ14 210 C8
Neswick St PL1 262 B3
Neswick Street Ope PL1 262 A3
NETHERCOTT 8 C2
Nethercott Cross
Ashwater EX21 90 C7
Oakford EX16 48 C8
Nethercott Hill EX16 48 C7
Nethercott La
Oakford EX16 48 C7
Spreyton EX17, EX20 95 F6
Nethercott Rd EX33 8 C2
NETHEREXE 81 F2
Netherham Cross EX33 8 A2
Netherhams Hill EX33 8 A2
Netherleigh Rd TQ1 220 B7
Nether Mdw TQ3 218 D3
NETHERTON 208 C3
Netherton Cross EX34 3 A4
Netherton Est PL20 126 D3
Netherton Hill EX6 96 D1
Netherton La EX34 3 A4
Netley Rd TQ12 207 B4
NETTACOTT 81 C2
Nettacott Cross EX5 81 B2
Nettle Cl TQ12 206 C5
Nettleford Hill EX16 46 F5
Nettlehayes PL9 256 D7
Netton Cl PL9 256 B6
Nevada Cl PL3 249 D6
Nevada Ct 10 EX12 192 A5
Neville Rd
Newton Abbot TQ12 207 A4
Okehampton EX20 170 C5
Newacott Cross EX22 70 E5
New Barn Cross EX5 172 A7
New Barn Hill PL7 250 F3
New Barnstaple Rd EX34 150 E3
Newberry Cl EX34 2 E4
Newberry Cotts EX33 8 A2
Newberry Hill EX34 2 F4
Newberry La EX34 2 F4
Newberry Rd
Combe Martin EX34 2 F4
Georgeham EX33 8 A2
Newberry's Patch TA3 68 D7
Newbery Cl
Axminster EX13 167 E6
Colyton EX24 103 A4
Newbery Comm Ctr EX5 99 A4
Newberys EX13 87 A3
New Bldgs
3 Bampton EX16 34 C1
8 Barnstaple EX32 155 A6
Chittlehampton EX37 28 F3
Doddiscombsleigh EX6 113 D5
3 Exeter EX4 177 D8
Fremington EX31 153 E5
Thurlestone TQ7 143 C2
Newbridge Cl EX39 157 B4
Newbridge Cross
Bishop's Tawton EX32 27 F7
Cowley EX5 172 D6
New Bridge Cross EX31 27 E7
Newbridge Cswy EX31, EX32 27 E7
Newbridge Hill
Cowley EX5 172 E6
Gunnislake PL18 125 D6
Holne TQ13 130 A6
Witheridge EX16 46 D1
New Bridge St EX4 261 A2
NEWBUILDINGS 79 D6
Newbuildings Cross EX17 79 D6
Newbuilding's Hill EX17 63 A3
Newbury Cl PL5 244 B4
Newbury Dr TQ13 180 E7
Newcastle Gdns PL5 244 B5
Newcombe Cl EX20 170 D5
Newcombes 5 EX17 165 C5
Newcombe St EX1 178 A6
Newcombe Street Gdns EX1 178 A6
Newcombe Terr EX1 177 F6
Newcomen Rd TQ6 233 F3
Newcot Cross EX15 67 D5
NEWCOTT 68 F3
New Cotts EX8 202 F7
Newcourt Dr EX2 178 D1
Newcourt Rd
Silverton EX5 82 B5
Topsham EX3 182 E7
Newcourt Sta EX1 178 E1
Newcourt Wy EX2 178 D2
New Cross
Avonwick TQ10 135 C2
Kingsteignton TQ12 123 E1
Newcross Pk 10 TQ12 123 E1
New Cut
Beer EX12 191 D5
Crediton EX17 165 B5
New England Hill PL7 136 B5
New England Rd PL7 136 B5
New Esplanade Ct TQ4 226 C6
New Est EX5 81 A2
New Exeter St TQ13 123 E6
Newfoundland Cl EX4 173 E2
Newfoundland Rd TQ14 209 D6
Newfoundland Way 13 TQ12 207 B3
Newgate Cross TA22 33 D7
New George St PL1 262 C3
New Green St PL21 237 E4
Newground La
Parracombe EX31 4 D2
Parracombe EX31 11 D8
NEWHAVEN 24 F1
Newhay Cl EX7 204 C6
Newhay Cross TQ12 211 C1
Newhayes TQ12 211 C1
Newhayes Cl EX2 177 A2
Newhouse Hill
Bickington TQ12 131 E7
Witheridge EX16 46 E2
Newhouse La
Chipstable TA4 35 E6
Hittisleigh EX6 96 D5
New House Plain TA4 35 F7
New Houses TQ7 149 A5
New Inn Cross 5 EX5 99 E8
New Inn Ct
Cullompton EX15 163 C3
6 Holsworthy EX22 164 C4
New La
Bampton EX16 33 F2
Braunton EX33 15 D8
Broadhempston TQ9 131 E1
Knowle EX33 8 D1
Ottery St Mary EX11 169 E4
Staverton TQ9 215 F5
Tatworth TA20 88 C8
Newland EX32 17 C1
Newland Cotts EX32 17 C1
Newland Cross
King's Nympton EX37 44 C8
North Tawton EX20 77 B3
Rackenford EX16 47 B2
Newland La TA24 13 F1
Newland Pk Rd EX32 17 B1
Newlands
Dawlish EX7 204 E7
Honiton EX14 166 C6
Newlands Ave EX8 202 D8
Newlands Cl
Exeter EX2 177 A2
Landkey EX32 17 C2
Sidmouth EX10 188 B8
Newlands Cross PL21 237 D3
Newlands Dr TQ13 180 C4
Newlands Pk
Aylesbeare EX5 99 E1
Seaton EX12 192 A6
Newlands Rd EX10 188 B8
Newlane End TQ9 215 F5
New London PL20 128 B8
Newman Cres TQ9 222 F8
Newman Ct EX4 176 E5
Newman Rd
Exeter EX4 176 F5
Plymouth PL5 243 E2
Saltash PL12 242 F3
New Market Rd
Holsworthy EX22 164 D7
Holsworthy TA20 72 A8
New Mdw PL21 237 B6
New Mill La EX35 5 A4
New Mills Ind Est PL21 137 B2
Newnham Cross EX37 44 B4
Newnham Ind Est PL7 250 F6
Newnham La EX18, EX37 44 C4
Newnham Rd PL7 250 F7
Newnham Way PL7 250 F6
New North Rd
Exeter EX4 261 A4
Exmouth EX8 202 A7
New Orchard 9 TQ10 134 F2
New Park TQ13 180 C4
New Park Cl TQ5 230 D4
New Park Cres TQ12 207 D8
New Park Rd
Kingsteignton TQ12 207 D8
Lee Mill PL7, PL21 136 B6
Paignton TQ3 225 F7
Plymouth PL7 251 A4
New Passage Hill PL1 247 E3
New Path EX17 97 C7
New Pk
Bridford EX6 112 F5
East Anstey EX16 32 E4
Horrabridge PL20 126 F4
NEWPORT 155 B3
Newport Com Sch Prim Acad EX32 155 B3
Newport Rd
Barnstaple EX32 155 A3
Exeter EX2 182 C7
Newport St
Dartmouth TQ6 233 F3
Millbrook PL10 252 E5

Newport St *continued*
Plymouth PL1 . . . .**248** A1
Tiverton EX16 . . . .**161** D4
Newport Terr
Barnstaple EX32 . . . . . .**155** A3
7 Bideford EX39 . . . . .**157** B1
New Quay La TQ5 . . . .**230** D5
New Quay St
Appledore EX39 . . . .**15** A1
Teignmouth TQ14 . . . . .**210** B4
New Rd
Allercombe EX5 . . . . . .**168** B5
Barnstaple EX32 . . . . . .**155** A4
Beer EX12 . . . .**191** D6
Bere Alston PL20 . . . . .**125** E2
Bickleigh PL6, PL7 . . . .**132** A5
Bideford EX39 . . . .**157** A1
Bishop's Tawton EX32 . . .**16** E1
Brixham TQ5 . . . .**230** B4
Buckfastleigh TQ11 . . . .**236** B5
Cawsand PL10 . . . .**253** A1
Chard Junction TA20 . . . .**88** F8
Clyst St Lawrence EX5 . . .**83** B3
Great Torrington EX38 .**159** D4
Instow EX39 . . . .**15** C1
Kingsand PL10 . . . .**253** B2
Lifton PL16 . . . .**105** F4
Loddiswell TQ7 . . . .**143** F7
Lutton PL21 . . . .**133** B2
Merton EX20 . . . .**57** A6
Modbury PL21 . . . .**137** B2
Morchard Bishop EX17 . . .**61** B2
Oare EX35 . . . .**6** D4
Okehampton EX20 . . . . . .**93** F5
Okehampton EX20 . . . . .**170** A3
Roborough PL6 . . . .**241** D2
Saltash PL12 . . . .**242** E3
South Molton EX36 . . . .**158** D4
Starcross EX6 . . . .**201** A8
Stoke Fleming TQ6 . . . .**146** B7
Stoke Gabriel TQ9 . . . . .**227** F7
Teignmouth TQ14 . . . . .**210** C7
Totnes TQ9 . . . .**223** D6
Upottery EX14 . . . .**68** B1
Waterrow TA21 . . . .**35** F4
Wilmington EX14 . . . .**86** D2
Yealmpton PL8 . . . .**136** A2
New Road Cl PL10 . . . .**253** A2
New Road Cross
Milton Damerel EX22 . . . .**54** D3
Okehampton EX20 . . . . . .**93** F5
South Molton EX36 . . . . .**46** D6
Wilmington EX14 . . . .**86** D1
New Road Est EX14 . . . .**93** F8
New Road Gate EX35 . . . .**6** D5
New Row 8 EX39 . . . . .**157** A4
New Sch Exeter The
EX6 . . . .**182** A5
New Sidmouth Rd
EX24 . . . .**102** F4
New St
6 Appledore EX39 . . . . .**15** A1
13 Bideford EX39 . . . . .**157** A2
Chagford TQ13 . . . .**111** A6
14 Chulmleigh EX18 . . .**44** E1
Cullompton EX15 . . . . . .**163** B3
Exmouth EX8 . . . .**202** A7
Great Torrington
EX38 . . . .**159** C5
Honiton EX14 . . . .**166** C6
Millbrook PL10 . . . .**252** E5
Moretonhampstead
TQ13 . . . .**111** F5
Ottery St Mary EX11 . . .**169** E4
Paignton TQ3 . . . .**226** B6
Plymouth PL1 . . . .**263** A2
Sidmouth EX10 . . . .**188** B3
NEWTAKE **208** A1
Newtake Rd PL19 . . . . .**171** E2
Newtake Rise TQ12 . . .**207** F2
Newte's Hill EX16 . . . . .**64** D5
Newton Abbot **207** A4
Newton Abbot Coll
Newton Abbot TQ12 . . .**207** A4
Newton Abbot TQ12 . . .**207** B3
Newton Abbot Com Hosp
TQ12 . . . .**207** B5
Newton Abbot Hospl
TQ12 . . . .**207** C3
Newton Abbot L Ctr
TQ12 . . . .**207** A4
*Newton Abbot
Racecourse*★ TQ12 .**207** D5
Newton Abbot Sta
TQ12 . . . .**207** D3
*Newton Abbot Town &
GWR Mus*★ TQ12 . .**207** C3
Newton Ave PL5 . . . . .**243** E2
Newton Cl 3 PL8 . . . .**141** A7
Newton Cross
Blackawton TQ9 . . . . . .**145** B3
Denbury TQ12 . . . .**211** B6
Hartland EX39 . . . .**22** C2
Zeal Monachorum EX17 . .**77** F7
Newton Ct
14 Bampton EX16 . . . . .**34** B1
Newton Ferrers PL8 . . . .**140** F7
Newton Down PL16 . . .**106** B4
NEWTON FERRERS **140** F7
Newton Ferrers CE Prim
Sch PL8 . . . .**141** A7
Newton Gdns PL5 . . . .**243** F2
Newton Hall TQ12 . . . .**207** C2

Newton Hill
Daccombe TQ12 . . . . . .**213** F6
Newton Ferrers PL8 . . . .**140** F7
Newton Ho EX5 . . . .**80** F1
Newton La EX17 . . . .**77** F7
**NEWTON
POPPLEFORD** **186** E7
Newton Poppleford Prim
Sch EX10 . . . .**186** F8
Newton Rd
Bideford EX39 . . . .**157** A3
Bishopsteignton TQ14 . .**208** D7
Bovey Tracey TQ13 . . . .**180** C6
Heathfield TQ12 . . . .**123** A2
Heathfield TQ13 . . . .**180** E3
Kingskerswell TQ12 . . . .**212** F6
Kingskerswell TQ12 . . . .**213** A5
Kingsteignton TQ12 . . . .**207** D5
Littlehempston TQ9 . . . .**216** F1
Salcombe TQ8 . . . .**259** D4
Torquay TQ2 . . . .**213** B2
Torquay TQ2 . . . .**213** D1
Totnes TQ9 . . . .**223** D7
Newton Road Ret Pk
TQ12 . . . .**207** D6
NEWTON ST CYRES . . .**172** A8
Newton St Cyres Prim
Sch EX5 . . . .**172** A8
Newton St Cyres Sta
EX5 . . . .**81** A1
**NEWTON ST
PETROCK** **55** B7
Newton St Petrock Cross
EX38 . . . .**40** B1
Newton School EX38 . . .**55** C7
Newtons Orch EX13 . . . .**87** C1
Newton Sq 8 EX16 . . . . .**34** B1
Newton's Row PL7 . . . .**136** A4
NEWTON TRACEY **27** A5
NEWTOWN
Buckland St Mary **69** D7
Exeter **177** E6
South Molton **31** A4
Newtown
Cornwood PL21 . . . .**133** C2
Sidmouth EX10 . . . .**188** B4
NEW TOWN **188** B4
Newtown Cl EX1 . . . . . .**261** C3
Newtown Cross EX36 . . .**31** A4
Newtown La EX36 . . . . . .**31** A3
Newtown Prim Sch
EX1 . . . .**261** C3
Newtown Rd TA20 . . . . . .**69** D8
New Valley Rd EX4 . . . .**176** F7
New Village Cross
EX12 . . . .**59** F2
New Way EX5 . . . .**184** C6
New Way Est EX14 . . . . .**67** B2
New Wlk TQ9 . . . .**223** D5
New Wood Cl PL6 . . . . .**245** E8
New Zealand Ho PL3 . .**248** B4
Nexus Way EX20 . . . . .**170** C6
Nibbys Cross EX15 . . . . .**66** B5
Nicholas Cl TA22 . . . . . .**33** E4
Nicholas Mdw PL17 . . .**125** B4
Nicholas Rd EX1 . . . . . .**178** A6
Nicholas Way EX8 . . . .**202** E7
Nicholls Pl TQ13 . . . . . .**180** F7
Nichols Nymett Cross
EX20 . . . .**77** F4
Nichols Nymett La
EX20 . . . .**77** F5
Nichols Nymett Moors
Cross EX20 . . . .**77** F5
Nicholson Rd
Plymouth PL5 . . . .**244** E2
Torquay TQ2 . . . .**213** D1
Nichols Way 4 EX1 . . . .**177** E7
Nick Reed's La EX15 . . . .**52** D1
Nightcott La TA22 . . . . . .**33** C4
Nightingale Cl
Plymouth PL9 . . . .**256** C8
Torquay TQ2 . . . .**213** E2
Nightingale Hospital
Exeter EX1 . . . .**178** F6
Nightingale Lawns
EX15 . . . .**163** A2
Nightingale Wlk EX2 . .**176** D3
Nile Rd EX2 . . . .**182** C8
Nilgala Cl EX39 . . . .**156** E4
Nine Acre La EX17 . . . . .**190** C8
Nine Ash Cross EX16 . . .**49** D6
Nine Milestone Cross
PL21 . . . .**137** D7
Nine Oaks EX5 . . . .**99** C1
Nine Oaks Est PL20 . . .**127** C5
Nirvana PL21 . . . .**237** C5
Nirvana Cl PL21 . . . .**237** C5
Noctule Ave 3 TQ12 . .**207** A5
Noelle Dr TQ12 . . . .**207** A4
Noland Pk TQ10 . . . . . .**135** A2
Nomandsland Cross
EX16 . . . .**62** B8
No Mans Chaple EX5 . . .**81** D3
Nomansland EX17 . . . . .**80** D5
No Man's Land
Georgeham EX33 . . . .**8** B1
Whiddon EX31 . . . .**9** C1
Nook The PL19 . . . .**171** D6
No Place Hill EX16 . . . . .**131** E1
Norah Bellot Ct 2
EX31 . . . .**154** F5
Norbury Ct 3 PL1 . . . . .**262** A3
Norden La TQ7 . . . .**258** B5
Nordon Cross TQ12 . . .**131** F3
Norfolk Cl PL3 . . . .**249** C5
Norfolk Rd PL3 . . . .**249** C4
Norfolk Terr 25 EX32 . .**155** A4

Norleigh Cross EX20 . . .**75** C3
NORLEY **74** E3
Norley Rd EX33 . . . .**8** D1
Norman Cl
Axminster EX13 . . . .**167** D5
Exmouth EX8 . . . .**196** D2
Newton Abbot TQ12 . . .**206** E5
Norman Cres EX9 . . . . .**198** A2
Norman Ct EX2 . . . .**177** C1
Norman Dr EX15 . . . . . .**163** C5
Norman La EX15 . . . .**67** A6
Normandy Cl EX8 . . . . .**196** E1
Normandy Hill PL5 . . . .**243** B2
Normandy Ho 19
EX32 . . . .**155** A5
Normandy Rd EX1 . . . . .**177** F6
Normandy Way
Plymouth PL5 . . . .**243** C2
Salcombe TQ8 . . . .**259** E5
South Molton EX36 . . . .**158** B4
*Norman Lockyer
Observatory*★ EX10 **188** D5
Norman Mews EX2 . . . .**178** D4
Norman Pl EX2 . . . .**178** D4
Norman Rd TQ3 . . . . . .**226** C7
Normans Cleave
EX35 . . . .**151** B5
Norman Terr EX39 . . . .**157** A7
Norns La TQ6 . . . .**145** F6
Norris Dr TQ12 . . . .**244** E6
NORRIS GREEN **125** B4
Norse Pl EX1 . . . .**178** E8
Norsworthy's Grave
EX11 . . . .**97** E8
NORTHAM **157** A6
*Northam Burrows Cntry
Pk*★ EX39 . . . .**14** E1
Northam Ho EX39 . . . .**156** F8
Northampton Cl PL5 . .**244** B5
Northam Rd EX39 . . . .**156** F3
Northams Mdw EX20 .**170** A4
North Ave
Bideford EX39 . . . .**157** D1
Exeter EX1 . . . .**177** E6
Lyme Regis DT7 . . . .**260** D4
NORTHAY
Axminster **88** G3
Chard **88** F2
Northay Cross EX13 . . . .**88** H3
Northay La
Axminster EX13 . . . .**88** G3
Northay TA20 . . . .**69** G6
North Barton Cl EX32 . . .**18** B7
Northbeer Cross EX17 . .**96** A8
Northbeer La EX17 . . . . .**95** F8
North Beer La PL15 . . . . .**89** C3
North Boundary Rd
TQ5 . . . .**230** B5
NORTH BOVEY **111** E2
North Bovey Rd
TQ13 . . . .**111** E4
NORTH BRENTOR **117** C8
North Bridge Pl EX4 . .**261** A3
Northbrook Cl EX4 . . . .**174** A1
Northbrook La EX31 . . . .**10** F5
**Northbrook Swimming
Pool** EX4 . . . .**174** B1
NORTH BUCKLAND **8** C3
North Buckland Hill
EX33 . . . .**8** C3
North Castle Mews 8
TQ9 . . . .**223** C6
Northclose Rd EX18 . . . .**59** D2
North Combe Cross
EX16 . . . .**48** A3
Northcombe La TA22 . . .**33** E7
North Combe Rd
EX14 . . . .**86** C2
North Coombe La
EX16 . . . .**47** A3
Northcote Cross EX37 . .**43** E4
Northcote Hill EX14 . . .**166** F7
Northcote La
Honiton EX14 . . . .**166** B6
Pennymoor EX16 . . . . . .**62** F8
Northcote Rd EX14 . . . .**166** F7
NORTHCOTT **90** A3
Northcott Gdns EX39 .**157** A7
Northcott Terr 8
EX22 . . . .**164** C4
North Courts The 4
PL1 . . . .**262** A3
North Cross PL1 . . . . . .**262** C4
Northdene EX39 . . . . . .**156** E4
North Devon Cottage Rd
EX16 . . . .**161** B5
**North Devon District
Hospl** EX31 . . . .**155** A8
North Devon Farm Pk★
EX32 . . . .**17** D3
North Devon L Ctr
EX31 . . . .**154** F4
North Devon Link Rd
Ash Mill EX36 . . . .**31** D2
Bolham EX16 . . . .**49** C1
Filleigh EX32 . . . .**29** C8
Knowstone EX16 . . . .**46** F8
Loxbeare EX16 . . . .**48** F4
Rackenford EX36 . . . . . .**47** D7
Sampford Peverell EX16 .**50** C1
South Molton EX36 . . . . .**46** D1
South Molton EX36 . . . .**158** C8
Swimbridge EX32 . . . . . .**17** C2
Swimbridge EX32 . . . . . .**28** F8
Tiverton EX16 . . . .**49** E1
Tiverton EX16 . . . .**64** D8
Tiverton EX16 . . . .**161** E7
*North Devon Maritime
Mus*★ EX39 . . . .**15** A1

North Dimson Cotts
PL18 . . . .**125** C6
North Down Cres
PL2 . . . .**247** F6
North Down Cross
EX17 . . . .**79** B1
Northdown Dr EX39 . . .**156** F3
North Down Gdns
PL2 . . . .**247** F6
Northdown La EX36 . . . .**45** F6
Northdown Rd
Bideford EX39 . . . .**156** F2
Cadbury EX5 . . . .**81** F7
North Down Rd
Braunton EX33 . . . .**152** E6
Plymouth PL2 . . . .**248** B6
North East St EX39 . . .**157** A7
North Emb TQ6 . . . .**233** F4
NORTH END **51** E3
North End Cl TQ12 . . . .**211** C2
Northernhay 17
TQ12 . . . .**207** C3
Northernhay Gate 5
EX4 . . . .**261** A3
Northernhay Pl EX4 . . .**261** B3
Northernhay Sq EX4 . .**261** A3
Northernhay St EX4 . . .**261** A3
Northern La
Branscombe EX12 . . . . .**190** B5
Sidmouth EX10 . . . .**189** E8
Northesk St PL2 . . . . . .**248** A4
Northfield EX13 . . . . . .**103** D5
Northfield La EX31 . . . .**154** F7
Northfield Pk EX31 . . . .**154** F7
Northfield Rd
Bideford EX39 . . . .**157** C1
Georgeham EX33 . . . .**8** B2
Ilfracombe EX34 . . . . . .**150** B6
Okehampton EX20 . . . .**170** D5
Northfields Ind Est
TQ5 . . . .**230** B5
Northfields La
Brixham TQ5 . . . .**230** B4
Brixham TQ5 . . . .**230** B5
Northfield Terr 1
EX34 . . . .**150** B6
North Ford Rd TQ6 . . . .**233** F3
North Furzeham Rd
TQ5 . . . .**230** C6
North Garron 3
EX32 . . . .**155** B5
Northgate EX39 . . . .**22** D3
North Gate Ct EX4 . . . .**261** A3
Northgate La EX14 . . . . .**86** A3
North Gn 3 EX32 . . . . .**155** B4
North Grange EX2 . . . .**178** D3
Northground La
EX10 . . . .**101** D1
North Hayne Cross
EX36 . . . .**31** B4
NORTH HEASLEY **19** D4
North Heasley Cross
EX36 . . . .**19** C4
North Hill Cl TQ5 . . . . .**230** B5
North Hill La
Morchard Bishop EX17 . .**61** B3
Stockland EX14 . . . .**86** F8
North Hill Terr PL4 . . . .**263** A4
NORTH HUISH **138** B7
North Huish Cross
TQ10 . . . .**138** B8
North Jaycroft EX15 . .**162** D5
North La
Ashford EX31 . . . .**16** A6
Barnstaple, Bickington
EX31 . . . .**154** A4
Challacombe EX31,
TA24 . . . .**12** B4
Cheriton EX35 . . . .**5** D3
Cheriton EX35 . . . .**151** F7
Middle Marwood EX31 . . .**9** B3
Whiddon EX31 . . . .**9** D2
Northland Cnr EX31 . . . .**11** D2
Northland Cross EX36 . .**19** A1
North Lawn Ct EX1 . . . .**177** F6
Northleat Ave TQ3 . . . .**225** E5
NORTHLEIGH **102** B7
Northleigh Cross
Chelfham EX32 . . . .**17** C6
Northleigh EX24 . . . . . .**102** B7
Northleigh Hill EX32 . . .**17** C5
Northleigh Hill Rd
Honiton EX14 . . . .**166** B3
Offwell EX14 . . . .**86** A1
Northleigh Rd EX24 . . .**102** D6
NORTHLEW **74** E1
**Northlew & Ashbury
Parochial CE Prim Sch**
EX20 . . . .**74** E2
Northlew Rd EX20 . . . . .**93** D6
North Lodge Cl EX7 . . .**204** C5
NORTH MOLTON **30** D8
North Molton Cross
EX36 . . . .**30** D8
North Molton Sch
EX36 . . . .**30** D8
NORTHMOOR **38** C3
North Moor Cross
EX22 . . . .**38** C3
Northmoor Rd TA22 . . . .**33** D7
North Morte Rd EX34 . . .**7** F8
NORTHMOSTOWN **187** B7
Northmostown Ct
EX10 . . . .**187** A7
North Park Almshouses
EX2 . . . .**261** C2
North Park Cnr TQ9 . . .**139** C6

North Park Rd
Exeter EX4 . . . .**173** B1
Tedburn St Mary EX6 . . .**97** F4
North Park Villas
PL12 . . . .**242** C4
NORTH PROSPECT **248** A6
North Prospect Rd
PL2 . . . .**248** A5
North Quay PL4 . . . . . .**263** A2
North Radbarn **19** F5
NORTH RADWORTHY . . .**19** F5
North Rd
Barnstaple EX31 . . . . . .**155** A7
Bideford EX39 . . . .**157** A2
Bradworthy EX22 . . . .**38** E1
Hartland EX39 . . . .**22** D3
High Bickington EX37 . . .**43** B7
Holsworthy EX22 . . . . . .**164** D5
Lee Mill PL21 . . . .**136** C2
Lifton PL16 . . . .**105** F4
Okehampton EX20 . . . .**170** C7
Saltash PL12 . . . .**242** F3
Saltash PL5 . . . .**242** F3
South Molton EX36 . . . .**158** C5
Torpoint PL11 . . . .**247** B3
Yelverton PL20 . . . .**126** F3
Northridge Cross EX5 . .**98** E7
Northridge La EX5 . . . . .**98** E7
North Road E PL4 . . . . .**262** C4
North Road Ind Est
EX20 . . . .**170** C6
North Road W PL1 . . . .**262** B4
North Rocks Rd TQ4 . . .**229** C7
Northside TA21 . . . .**160** B5
North St
Ashburton TQ13 . . . . . .**130** F5
Axminster EX13 . . . .**167** D6
Braunton EX33 . . . .**152** D6
Chagford TQ13 . . . .**111** A6
Crediton EX17 . . . .**165** C5
Denbury TQ12 . . . .**211** A7
Dolton EX19 . . . .**57** F7
Exeter EX4 . . . .**261** A3
Exeter, Heavitree EX1 . .**177** F6
Exmouth EX8 . . . .**202** A7
Hartland EX39 . . . .**22** D3
Ipplepen TQ12 . . . .**211** D2
North Tawton EX20 . . . . .**77** C4
Okehampton EX20 . . . .**170** B5
Ottery St Mary EX11 . . .**169** C4
Topsham EX3 . . . .**182** F4
Wellington TA21 . . . . . .**160** D6
2 Totnes TQ9 . . . .**223** C6
Northumberland Pl
TQ14 . . . .**210** B4
Northumberland St
PL5 . . . .**247** E8
Northumberland Terr
PL1 . . . .**262** B1
North Upton Barns
TQ7 . . . .**143** B3
North View EX21 . . . . . .**55** E4
North View Ave EX39 . .**156** F3
North View Hill EX39 . .**156** F3
Northview Rd EX9 . . . . .**203** F8
North View Rd TQ5 . . . .**230** B5
North Villas 2 EX20 . . .**170** B6
Northville Pk TQ7 . . . . .**258** C6
Northville Rd TQ7 . . . . .**258** C6
North Walk Hill EX35 . .**151** C6
North Wlk
Barnstaple EX31 . . . . . .**154** F5
Lynton EX35 . . . .**151** B6
Northwood Cross
EX17 . . . .**61** B3
Northwood La
Buckfast TQ11 . . . .**236** C8
Buckland Brewer EX39 . .**40** C7
Morchard Bishop EX17 . .**61** A7
Northwoods PL5 . . . . . .**180** C4
North Wyke Cotts
EX20 . . . .**77** B1
NORTON
Dartmouth **233** A2
Hartland **22** E4
Norton Ave PL4 . . . . . .**263** C4
Norton Cross TQ6 . . . .**233** A3
Norton Pk TQ6 . . . .**233** A2
Norton Pl EX8 . . . .**202** E8
Nortons Cross EX5 . . . . .**81** A2
Norton View TQ6 . . . . .**233** C4
Nortonwood La EX17 . . .**81** A2
Norwich Ave PL5 . . . . .**244** B5
Norwich Rd EX4 . . . . . .**176** F5
Norwood Ave EX2 . . . .**261** C4
Norwood Ho EX4 . . . . .**261** B4
Norwood Rd EX16 . . . .**161** D6

NOSS MAYO **140** F6
Notley Gdns PL2 . . . . .**248** A8
Notte Dame Ho PL1 . . .**262** B3
Notre Dame RC Sch
PL6 . . . .**244** F5
Notte St PL1 . . . .**262** C2
Nottiston Cross EX31 . . .**16** A1
Nower Rd EX13 . . . .**87** C3
N St Mdw EX33 . . . .**152** D6
**Nuffield Health Exeter
Hospl (private)** EX2 .**177** E4
**Nuffield Health Plymouth
Hospl (private)** PL6 .**245** E4
Nurseries Cl
Exton EX3 . . . .**183** C1
Topsham EX3 . . . .**182** E6
Nursery Cl
Exmouth EX8 . . . .**202** C8
Paignton TQ3 . . . .**226** A5
Plymouth PL5 . . . .**244** B7
St Giles in the Wood
EX38 . . . .**42** B6
Nursery End EX31 . . . . .**154** F7
Nursery Gdns 7 EX1 . .**178** E8
Nursery Mews EX8 . . . .**202** C8
Nursery Rd TQ12 . . . . .**207** E7
Nursey Cl EX16 . . . .**49** B2
Nutaberry Hill EX39 . .**157** B1
Nutaberry Yd EX39 . . . .**157** B1
Nutbrook EX8 . . . .**196** B1
Nut Bush Cnr TQ2 . . . .**219** B7
Nut Bush La
Torquay TQ2 . . . .**219** B5
Torquay TQ2 . . . .**219** C6
Nutcombe Hill EX34 . . . .**3** C2
Nuthatch Cl
Drakewalls PL18 . . . . . .**125** C5
Torquay TQ2 . . . .**213** E2
Nuthatch Dr TQ2 . . . . .**213** E2
Nuttaberry EX39 . . . .**25** F4
Nuttaberry Bglws
EX39 . . . .**25** F4
Nut Tree Ct TQ5 . . . . . .**230** B2
Nut Tree Orch TQ5 . . . .**230** B2
Nutt's La
Combe Martin EX31 . . . . .**3** C2
Combe Martin EX34 . . . .**10** C8
Nutwell Rd EX8 . . . . . .**195** E7
Nymet Ave EX17 . . . . . .**78** C4
Nymet Bridge Cross
EX17 . . . .**60** B3
NYMET ROWLAND **60** B3
NYMET TRACEY **78** C3
Nymet Villas EX37 . . . . .**44** E6
Nymetwood Cross
EX6 . . . .**96** D8
Nymphayes La EX17 . . .**78** C8
Nynehead Rd TA21 . . . .**160** F8

O

Oakapple Cl PL7 . . . . . .**250** B7
Oak Apple Cl PL12 . . . .**242** D4
Oakbank TQ13 . . . .**180** C4
Oakbeer Orchard 4
EX5 . . . .**99** A6
Oak Cl
Bičkington EX31 . . . . . .**154** A3
Dulford EX15 . . . .**84** B8
Exeter EX4 . . . .**174** E1
Exminster EX6 . . . .**182** A4
Kingsteignton TQ12 . . .**207** F6
Ottery St Mary EX11 . . .**169** D3
Shillingford Abbot EX2 .**181** A6
Silverton EX5 . . . .**82** C6
Tiverton EX16 . . . .**161** D5
Oak Cottage Cross
EX22 . . . .**72** C2
Oak Cres EX15 . . . .**162** C4
Oakcroft Rd PL2 . . . . . .**248** B6
Oak Cross
Bondleigh EX18 . . . .**77** D8
Inwardleigh EX20 . . . . . .**75** C3
Oak Ct
Holsworthy EX22 . . . . .**164** C5
Lee Mill PL21 . . . .**136** D6
Oakdale Ave EX32 . . . . .**17** E1
Oakdene Ct EX6 . . . . . .**114** F1
Oakdene Rise PL9 . . . . .**255** F6
Oak Dr
Cullompton EX15 . . . . .**163** C5
Plymouth PL6 . . . .**244** B7
Oak End Ct TQ3 . . . . . .**218** D2
Oaken Ground TA21 . . .**160** B5
Oaken Hill
Great Torrington EX31 . .**42** E8
Yarnscombe EX31 . . . . . .**27** D1
Oakery Cres PL20 . . . . .**128** B8
Oakey Orch PL17 . . . . .**125** A4
Oakfield Cl PL7 . . . .**251** C6
Oakfield Pk TA21 . . . . .**160** E4
Oakfield Pl PL4 . . . .**249** B1
Oakfield Rd
Exeter EX4 . . . .**177** A5
Hatherleigh EX20 . . . . . .**75** C7
Plymouth PL7 . . . .**250** C6
Oakfields EX16 . . . .**161** D6
Oakfield St EX1 . . . .**177** F5
Oakfield Terr EX39 . . . .**157** A7
Oakfield Terrace Rd
PL4 . . . .**249** B1
OAKFORD **48** C3
Oakford TQ12 . . . .**207** D7
OAKFORDBRIDGE **48** D8
Oakford Cl EX36 . . . .**30** D8

Oakford Cross
Kingsteignton TQ12 207 D7
North Molton EX36 30 C8
Oakford Villas EX36 30 D8
Oak Gdns
Ivybridge PL21 237 E5
Uffculme EX15 65 F7
Oakham Rd PL5 244 B5
Oakhayes Rd EX5 184 B3
Oakhays EX36 158 D4
Oak Hill
Budleigh Salterton EX9 198 C6
Dawlish EX7 204 C5
East Budleigh EX9 198 B6
Oak Hill Cross Rd
Dawlish EX7 204 C4
Teignmouth TQ14 210 D8
Oak Hill Rd TQ1 219 F6
Oakhill Rise 3 EX31 154 C3
Oak La
East Anstey TA22 32 E6
Stockleigh Pomeroy EX17 81 A4
Whitstone EX22 70 E1
Oakland Ave EX31 154 D4
Oakland Dr EX7 204 D5
Oakland Park S EX31 154 B4
Oakland Pk EX31 154 D3
Oakland Rd TQ12 207 F2
Oaklands
Bideford EX39 25 D4
Petrockstow EX20 56 F4
Tavistock PL19 171 D2
Oaklands Cl
Buckfastleigh TQ11 236 A5
Plymouth PL6 245 C7
Seaton EX12 192 A8
Oaklands Ct EX31 154 D4
Oaklands Dr
Okehampton EX20 170 B6
Saltash PL12 242 C3
Oaklands Gdns EX31 154 D4
Oaklands Gn PL12 242 D3
Oaklands Pk
Buckfastleigh TQ11 236 A5
Okehampton EX20 170 A5
Oaklands Rd TQ11 236 A6
Oakland Wlk EX7 204 D5
Oak Lawn TQ12 207 C2
Oaklawn Ct TQ1 219 F7
Oaklawn Terr TQ1 219 F7
Oaklea
Honiton EX14 166 B6
Tiverton EX16 161 D6
Oaklea Cl TQ7 258 C4
Oaklea Cres EX31 153 D5
Oakleaf Cl EX21 73 E2
Oakleaf Way EX32 17 F4
Oaklea Pk TQ12 123 A1
Oakleigh EX15 66 F3
Oakleigh Rd
Barnstaple EX32 155 A4
Exmouth EX8 202 B7
Oakley Cl
Exeter EX1 174 E1
Teignmouth TQ14 210 B7
Oakley Wlk EX5 179 E3
Oak Mdw EX36 158 B4
Oak Park Ave TQ2 219 D8
Oak Park Cl TQ2 219 D8
Oakpark Cross PL21 137 E6
Oakpark La EX7 124 E6
Oak Park Rd TQ12 206 F4
Oak Park Villas EX7 204 E7
Oak Pl TQ12 207 D3
Oak Rd
Aylesbeare EX11 168 A2
Exeter EX4 176 F4
Okehampton EX20 170 C6
Tavistock PL19 171 C2
West Hill EX11 168 C2
Oakridge TQ1 220 C3
Oak Ridge
Exeter EX2 181 A8
Lifton PL16 105 E4
Oaks The
Bovey Tracey TQ13 180 E7
4 Hemyock EX15 67 B8
Mary Tavy PL19 117 E6
Newton Abbot TQ12 212 F8
Yeoford EX17 79 C1
Oaktree Cl
Broadclyst EX5 175 D6
Exmouth EX8 196 B3
Ivybridge PL21 237 A5
Oak Tree Cl EX14 68 C2
Oaktree Ct PL6 244 F1
Oak Tree Dr
Barnstaple EX32 155 E4
Newton Abbot TQ12 212 F8
Oaktree Fishery★ EX36 31 F4
Oak Tree Gdns
Ilfracombe EX34 150 B5
West Hill EX11 168 D4
Oak Tree Gr 8 TQ14 210 A3
Oak Tree La PL19 171 C3
Oak Tree Pk
Plymouth PL6 245 D6
Sticklepath EX20 95 A5
Oak Tree Pl EX2 181 C8
Oaktree Rd EX36 158 B4
Oak Tree Villas EX10 186 F8
Oak Units EX17 165 F5
Oak View
Honiton EX14 166 A3
Lyme Regis DT7 260 E5
Oak View *continued*
Totnes TQ9 222 F6
Oak View Cl TQ2 213 B1
Oakwell Cl EX38 159 E5
Oakwell La EX37 44 E8
Oakwood Cl
Barnstaple EX31 154 C2
Dartmouth TQ6 233 C3
Plymouth PL6 245 D7
Oakwood Ct EX36 158 D4
Oakwood Dr PL21 137 B3
Oakwood Pk TQ7 143 E7
Oakwood Prim Sch PL6 245 A6
Oakwood Rise EX8 196 E3
Oakwood Specialist Coll EX7 204 E7
Oakymead Pk TQ12 207 D6
OARE 6 E4
OAREFORD 6 F3
Oates Rd PL2 248 B5
Oathills Cres TQ3 225 F1
Oathills Ct 8 TQ3 225 F1
Oatlands Ave EX32 155 A1
Oatlands Dr TQ4 226 A4
Oberon Rd EX1 178 E7
Observer Cl EX36 158 B5
Occombe Cross TQ3 218 F3
Occombe Farm & Scadson Woods Nature Reserve★ TQ3 219 A3
Occombe Valley Rd TQ3 219 A2
Occombe Valley Woods Nature Reserve★ TQ3 218 F2
Ocean City Pl PL3 262 B3
Ocean Ct PL1 253 F8
Ocean Pk EX39 156 B7
Ocean St PL2 247 E6
Ocean View Cres TQ5 230 A1
Ocean View Dr TQ5 230 A1
Ochil Cl EX39 26 A4
Ockington Cl EX20 170 D5
Ockment Ct EX20 170 B5
Octagon St PL1 262 B3
Octagon The PL1 262 B2
Octans Way PL9 256 E8
Octon Gr TQ1 219 E7
Odam Cross EX36 45 E7
Odam La EX18 45 E6
Odam Moor Cross EX36 45 E5
Oddicombe Beach Hill TQ1 220 D8
Odette Ave TA21 160 A3
ODHAM 74 B5
Odhams Wharf EX3 183 B5
Odle Hill TQ12 212 A6
Odlehill Gr TQ12 212 A6
Odun Pl 34 EX39 15 A1
Odun Rd 22 EX39 15 A1
Odun Terr 36 EX39 15 A1
OFFWELL 86 B2
Offwell CE Prim Sch EX14 86 B2
Offwell Turn EX14 102 B8
Ogwell Cross TQ12 207 A1
Ogwell End Dr TQ12 206 F2
Ogwell Gn TQ12 206 E1
Ogwell Green TQ12 211 E8
Ogwell Mill Rd TQ12 206 E3
Ogwell Rd
East Ogwell TQ12 206 F1
Ogwell TQ12 211 E8
Oilmill Cross EX5 179 C2
Oilmill La
Clyst St George EX5 183 D8
Clyst St Mary EX5 179 C1
Oil Mill La EX6 184 A7
Okefield Ave EX17 165 C6
Okefield Rd
Crediton EX17 80 A3
Crediton EX17 165 C6
Okefield Ridge EX17 165 C6
OKEHAMPTON 170 A6
Okehampton Bsns Ctr EX20 170 F5
Okehampton Castle★ EX20 170 A3
Okehampton Cl PL7 251 B4
Okehampton Coll EX20 170 B4
Okehampton Com Hospl EX20 170 C6
Okehampton Pl 8 EX4 177 A5
Okehampton Prim Sch EX20 170 B5
Okehampton Rd EX4 177 A5
Okehampton St EX4 177 A5
Okehampton Sta EX20 170 C3
Okehampton Way PL21 237 D4
OKEMOOR PARK 170 E5
Oketor Cl EX20 170 D5
Oke Tor Cl TQ3 219 A2
Okewill Cross EX31 10 A2
Okewood Ct EX8 202 B5
Olands Rd TA21 160 D6
OLCHARD 123 F3
Olchard La TQ12, TQ13 124 A4
Old Abbey Ct EX2 177 E2
Oldaway La EX5 172 C7
Oldaway Tongue TQ7 143 E1
Old Bakery Cl EX4 176 F7
Old Bakery Cotts
Bickington EX31 154 A4
Yealmpton PL8 257 F4
Old Bakery The EX8 202 B8
Old Barn Cl
Stoke Canon EX5 173 F8
Winkleigh EX19 58 E2
Oldbarn Cross TQ12 212 A7
Oldbarn La EX16 33 E1
Old Barnstaple Rd
Bideford, East-t-W EX39 157 C2
Braunton EX31 15 F7
Ilfracombe EX34 150 D2
Old Beer Rd EX12 191 E6
Old Bell Hill EX16 47 D5
Oldberry La TA22 33 D6
Old Berrynarbor Rd EX34 150 F5
Old Bideford Cl EX31 154 B2
Old Bideford Rd EX31 154 C2
Old Blundell's★ EX16 161 D3
OLDBOROUGH 61 B1
Oldborough Cross EX17 61 B1
Oldborough La EX17 61 B1
Old Bridge Rd EX15 83 F6
Old Bridwell EX15 65 F7
Old Butterleigh Rd EX5 82 B6
Old Bystock Dr EX8 196 E3
Old Canal Cl EX23 70 A6
Old Chapel Gdns EX19 58 F3
Old Chapel Rd PL7 133 B2
Old Chapel Way PL10 252 F6
Old Chappel La PL7 132 F4
Old Chard Rd EX14 86 C6
Old Cider Press The 3 TQ4 226 B5
Old Cider Works La TQ12 212 A7
Old Cider Works The TQ12 212 A7
Old Coach Rd EX5 175 C6
Old Coal Yard The EX10 186 F8
Old Coastguard Cotts PL9 140 E7
Old Coastguard Sta EX12 192 D5
Old Coast Rd EX34 2 E4
Old Cooperage The EX2 177 F5
Old Court EX31 154 C4
Old Ct Mws 4 TA21 160 D6
Old Dairy The PL3 249 B6
Old Dawlish Rd EX6 181 C2
Old Ebford La EX3 183 C4
Olde Ct EX22 164 C3
Oldenburg Pk TQ3 226 C7
Old English Ind Est PL20 127 B3
Old Exeter Rd
Bishop's Tawton EX32 16 E1
Chudleigh TQ13 123 F8
Chudleigh TQ13, EX6 114 A2
Newton Abbot TQ12 207 B4
Tavistock PL19 171 D7
Old Exeter St TQ13 123 E6
Old Farm Bglws 2 EX10 188 B7
Old Farm Rd PL5 247 C8
Old Farm Way EX7 204 D4
Old Ferry Rd
Saltash PL12 242 F3
Saltash PL12 243 A3
Oldfields EX8 202 C6
Old Fire Sta The TQ13 110 F6
Old Fore St EX10 188 B3
Old Foundry The PL19 171 D6
Old Frogmore Rd TQ7 144 E1
Old Garden Pasture 22 EX5 99 A6
Old Gatehouse Rd EX7 204 E7
Old George St PL1 262 C2
Old Greystone Hill PL15, PL19 115 D6
Oldham Rd EX20 75 B7
Old Hayes 3 EX10 188 A4
Old Hazard Cotts TQ9 135 F2
Old Hill
Bickington TQ12 131 D7
Cullompton EX15 163 D2
Old Home Farm
Rousdon DT7 193 E6
Rousdon EX12 193 E6
Oldhouse La TQ7 142 E7
Old Ide Cl EX2 176 E2
Old Ide La EX2 176 E2
Old Inn Mews EX38 159 D5
Old Jaycroft
Willand EX15 162 D4
Willand EX15 162 E4
Old Laira Rd PL3 249 C4
Old Lake La EX35 5 A4
Oldlands Cl PL6 245 B6
Old Launceston Rd PL19 171 B6
Old Laundry The PL1 262 A3
Old Liverton Rd
Coldeast TQ12 122 F1
6 Coldeast TQ12 123 A1
Coldeast TQ12 180 D1
Old Lyme Hill DT6 104 F4
Old Lyme Rd DT6 104 F4
Old Main Rd TA20 69 C3
Old Manor Cl TQ13 130 E5
Old Manor Ct 21 EX7 204 D6
Old Manor Gdns EX24 103 B3
Old Market Cl EX2 177 B3
Old Market Dr EX39 38 F8
Old Market Field EX16 46 E1
Old Market Field Ind Est EX16 46 E1
Old Market Pl EX22 164 C3
Old Matford La EX6, EX2 181 E6
Old Mill Cl
Exeter EX2 261 C1
Tiverton EX16 161 C3
Old Mill Ct PL7 250 E5
Old Mill Ind Est EX5 173 E7
Old Mill La TQ6 233 C4
Old Mill Rd
Livermead TQ2 219 E2
Torquay TQ2 219 E4
Torquay TQ2 219 E5
Old Mill The
Culmstock EX15 66 E8
Harbertonford TQ9 139 B8
Old Mine La PL18 125 B6
Old Mkt The 15 EX15 67 B8
Old Newton Rd
Bovey Tracey TQ13 180 E4
Heathfield TQ12 123 A3
Kingskerswell TQ12 212 E5
Old Nursery Dr EX4 178 B8
Old Orchard TQ13 180 D7
Old Orchard Cl EX23 70 A6
Old Orchard The EX20 74 E2
Old Paignton Rd
Torquay TQ2 219 D2
Torquay TQ2 219 D3
Old Park Ave EX1 174 F3
Old Park Rd
Exeter EX4 261 B4
Plymouth PL3 248 D6
Old Pavilion Cl EX2 178 C4
Old Pinn La EX1 174 E1
Old Plymouth Rd
Kingsbridge TQ7 258 C6
Plymouth PL3 249 E5
Old Post Office Mews 19 EX39 157 A2
Old Printworks The TQ1 220 B4
Old Priory PL7 250 D5
Old Priory Jun Acad PL7 250 D5
Old Quarry Dr EX6 182 A5
Old Quarry Rd PL20 126 D3
Old Quay La 8 EX39 15 B1
Old Quay St TQ14 210 B4
Old Rd
Brixton PL8 257 A5
Galmpton TQ5 229 B5
Harbertonford TQ9 139 C7
Lutton PL21 133 B2
Okehampton EX20 170 A4
Stoke Fleming TQ6 146 B7
Tiverton EX16 161 E4
Old Rectory Cl EX39 15 C2
Old Rectory Cross TQ13 110 C7
Old Rectory Gdns
Morchard Bishop EX17 61 B2
Thurlestone TQ7 143 A2
Old Rectory La
Ashwater EX21 90 E6
Bratton Fleming EX31 18 A8
Oldridge Rd EX4 98 B6
Oldridge View EX6 97 F5
Old Rydon Cl EX2 178 E2
Old Rydon La EX2 178 D1
Old Rydon Ley EX2 178 D2
Old Saddlery The 18 EX14 166 C6
Old Sawmills Ind Est The EX10 186 C4
Old Sawmills The EX37 28 B1
Old School Cl EX16 161 B4
Old School Ct
6 Hemyock EX15 67 B8
6 Honiton EX14 166 C6
Topsham EX3 182 F5
Old School Ho The
Cawsand PL10 253 A1
North Tawton EX20 77 C4
Old School La EX31 153 E5
Old School Rd
Barnstaple EX32 155 C2
Plymouth PL5 247 C8
Old School The 5 EX16 161 D4
Old Show Field Way EX14 166 A6
Oldshute La TA22 33 C7
Old Sidmouth Rd EX24 103 A4
Old Smithy Cotts EX39 37 B4
Old Stables The
14 Bideford EX39 157 A1
Clyst St Mary EX5 179 A1
Old Station Rd
Barnstaple EX32 155 B4
Horrabridge PL20 126 F4
Old Station The PL20 126 E4
Old Station Yard 17 TQ10 134 F3
Old Sticklepath Hill EX31 154 E3
Old Stone Cl EX39 156 B6
Oldstone Cross TQ9 139 F2
Old's View EX4 177 A7
Old Tannery Bsns Pk The 4 PL4 263 A4
Old Tannery The EX32 28 D8
Old Taunton Rd
Dalwood EX13 86 F1
Dalwood EX13 87 A1
Old Teignmouth Rd EX7 204 D4
Old Tinhay PL16 105 F4
Old Tiverton Rd
Bampton EX16 34 C1
Bampton EX16 49 C8
Crediton EX17 165 E6
Exeter EX4 177 D8
Old Torquay Rd TQ3 226 C8
Old Torrington Rd EX31 154 D2
Old Torwood Rd TQ1 220 D4
Old Totnes Rd
Ashburton TQ13 130 F4
Buckfastleigh TQ11 236 C5
Cockington TQ2 219 C4
Newton Abbot TQ12 207 A1
Old Town EX39 157 A1
Old Town Hill TQ12, TQ13 122 C2
Old Town Park Nature Reserve★ EX20 170 A3
Old Town St
Dawlish EX7 204 D6
Plymouth PL1 262 C3
Old Tram Dr 1 EX31 154 A3
Old Turnpike Rd PL7 136 A6
Old Vicarage Cl EX2 176 D1
Old Vicarage Gdn DT7 260 D3
Old Vicarage Rd EX2 177 A4
Old Vicarage The
Sidmouth EX10 187 F3
Wellington TA21 160 E6
Old Walls Hill
Teignmouth TQ14 124 D1
Teignmouth TQ14 209 F8
Old Warleigh La PL5 244 B7
OLDWAY 226 A8
Oldway TQ13 123 E6
Old Way
Chipstable TA4 35 D6
Chudleigh TQ13 123 E6
Oldway Cl TQ12 123 E6
Oldway Ho TA21 160 F4
Oldway Mansion★ TQ3 226 B8
Oldway Pk TA21 160 F4
Oldway Prim Sch TQ3 226 B7
Oldway Rd
East Anstey TA22 32 F5
Paignton TQ3 226 B8
Wellington TA21 160 E4
OLDWAYS END 32 E3
Old Weighbridge The 19 EX8 202 A6
Old Wharf The PL9 255 C7
Old Widdicombe Rd TQ3 225 C7
Old Widdicome La TQ3 225 B8
Old Woodlands Rd PL5 244 D3
Old Woods Hill TQ2 219 E7
Old Woods Trad Est TQ2 219 E8
Old Workhouse Dr EX36 158 C5
Olga Terr EX8 195 F5
Olive Gdns EX7 201 B2
Olive Gr EX7 201 B2
Oliver Rd EX32 155 B5
Olivia Ct PL4 263 B4
Ollan Gwella PL18 125 A6
Olympian Wy EX15 163 A4
Olympic Wy PL6 245 C6
Olympus Bsns Pk TQ12 207 C4
Omaha Dr EX2 178 D1
Omaha Way EX31 153 E6
Omega Ctr The EX2 178 E5
One End St 4 EX39 15 A1
One Fir EX15 83 C4
OneSchool Plymouth Campus
Plymouth PL5 243 B1
Plymouth PL5 247 B8
Onslow Rd
Plymouth PL2 248 C7
Salcombe TQ8 259 D5
Ora Cl EX33 7 E2
Ora La EX33 7 E2
Orange Gr TQ2 214 A2
Orange Moor Cross EX18 44 F3
Orangery The EX6 181 F5
Ora Stone Pk EX33 7 E1
Orbec Ave TQ12 207 F7
Orchard Ave PL6 249 B7
Orchard Cl
Ashprington TQ9 139 F7
Barnstaple EX31 154 C3
Beesands TQ7 149 D7
Braunton EX33 152 C6
8 Brixham TQ5 230 C3
10 Chudleigh TQ13 123 F6
Coldridge EX18 59 C4
Colyford EX24 103 B3
9 Combe Martin EX34 3 A3
Dawlish EX7 204 D6
Denbury TQ12 211 A6
East Budleigh EX9 198 B6
East Ogwell TQ12 206 D1
Exeter EX1 174 F1
Exmouth EX8 196 B1
Exmouth, Littleham EX8 203 A6
Frogmore TQ7 144 E1
Galmpton TQ5 229 C5
Kingsteignton TQ12 207 F7
Kingsteignton, Sandygate TQ12 123 E2
Langford EX5 109 F7
Lympstone EX8 195 E5
Newton Poppleford EX10 186 D8
Okehampton EX20 170 B4
Ottery St Mary EX11 169 E3
3 Plymouth PL7 251 C5
Rockwell Green TA21 160 A5
St Giles on t H PL15 90 C1
Sandford EX17 80 A5
Shaldon TQ14 209 D5
Sidford EX10 188 C8
Sidmouth EX10 187 F3
Talaton EX5 84 A2
Tavistock PL19 126 A8
Uffculme EX15 66 A7
Upton Pyne EX5 173 A7
Whitford EX13 103 B6
Wilmington EX14 86 C2
Woodbury EX5 184 C3
Yealmpton PL8 257 F3
Orchard Cotts
Holbeton PL8 136 D1
Lamerton PL19 116 F3
Newton Tracey EX31 27 A6
Orchard Cres PL9 255 C7
Orchard Cross EX17 60 D3
Orchard Ct
1 Crediton EX17 165 C5
Exeter EX1 178 E6
Ivybridge PL21 237 B5
Lamerton PL19 116 E3
22 Newton Abbot TQ12 207 B3
Newton St Cyres EX5 81 A1
North Tawton EX20 77 C4
3 Whimple EX5 99 E8
Orchard Dr
Ipplepen TQ12 211 D2
Kingskerswell TQ12 212 F4
Otterton EX9 198 E7
Salcombe TQ8 259 C5
Orchard Farm EX14 85 A3
Orchard Gate EX19 57 F7
Orchard Gdns
Bideford EX39 157 A4
Broadclyst EX5 175 D6
15 Dawlish EX7 204 D6
Exeter EX4 176 F4
10 Teignmouth TQ14 210 C4
West Buckland TA21 52 F7
Orchard Gr
Brixham TQ5 230 C3
Croyde EX33 7 E1
Mile End TQ12 206 D4
ORCHARD HILL 157 A4
Orchard Hill
Bideford EX39 157 A4
Exeter EX2 176 F3
Talaton EX14 84 B2
Yealmpton PL8 136 B3
Orchard Ho
8 Chudleigh TQ13 123 E6
1 Teignmouth TQ14 210 C4
Torquay TQ1 220 C5
Orchard Ind Est's North & South TQ7 258 C5
Orchard La
Plymouth PL7 250 E6
Silverton EX5 82 B6
Starcross EX6 201 A4
Orchard Leigh EX16 161 C3
Orchard Manor Sch EX7 204 C5
Orchard Mdw TQ13 111 A6
Orchardon La EX33 8 B1
Orchard Pk
Dartington TQ9 222 F8
Dittisham TQ6 228 C3
Ivybridge PL21 237 C4
Orchard Pl 3 TQ1 220 A7
Orchard Rd
Ashburton TQ13 130 F4
Barnstaple EX32 155 B3
Brixton PL8 257 A5
Knowle EX33 8 D1
Plymouth PL2 248 B7
4 Torquay, Ellacombe TQ1 220 B6
Torquay, Hele TQ2 213 F1
Wrafton EX33 152 E3
Orchard Rise EX39 157 A4

Orchardside EX10 188 B7
Orchard Side EX10 101 C3
Orchards The
Galmpton TQ5 229 B5
Landkey EX32 17 B2
Lower Lovacott EX31 27 A6
Swimbridge EX32 28 E8
Orchard Terr
Abbotskerswell TQ12 212 B7
Barnstaple EX32 155 B2
3 Bovey Tracey TQ13 180 D8
Buckfastleigh TQ11 236 B5
Chagford TQ13 111 A6
Crediton EX17 165 B5
Kingskerswell TQ12 212 F5
Kingswear TQ6 234 B3
Totnes TQ9 223 C5
Tuckenhay TQ9 139 F6
Orchard The
Abbotskerswell TQ12 212 B6
Avonwick TQ10 135 B1
Barnstaple EX31 154 A3
Bishopsteignton TQ14 208 F8
Buckfastleigh TQ11 236 C5
Dunsford EX6 112 F7
Gunnislake PL18 125 D6
Holcombe EX7 210 E8
Holywell Lake TA21 51 E7
Honiton EX14 166 F8
Kilmington EX13 87 D1
Modbury PL21 137 C2
Seaton EX12 192 A5
Tipton St John EX10 100 D2
Totnes TQ9 223 C5
Whiddon Down EX20 95 C1
Yealmpton PL8 257 F3
Orchardton Terr 2
PL9 255 F5
Orchard Vale Com Sch
EX32 155 E4
Orchard View
Frogmore TQ7 144 E1
Halberton EX16 65 B7
Orchard Vw EX31 154 A3
Orchard Way
1 Bovey Tracey
TQ13 180 D8
Chillington TQ7 145 A1
Cullompton EX15 163 B2
Honiton EX14 166 D6
Kenton EX6 194 D3
Lapford EX17 60 D3
Stoke Gabriel TQ9 227 F8
Tiverton EX16 161 B3
Topsham EX3 182 E5
Uffculme EX15 66 A7
Willand EX15 162 D4
Orchard Waye TQ9 223 B5
Orchard Wy TQ2 213 B1
Orch Cres 5 EX1 178 E3
Orchid Ave
Ivybridge PL21 237 A6
Kingsteignton TQ12 207 E7
Orchid Cl
Barnstaple EX31 154 F8
7 Tiverton EX16 161 F6
Orchid Ho EX4 176 E8
Orchid Meadow
TQ13 124 A8
Orchid Vale 14 TQ12 123 F1
Orchid Wy TQ2 213 F2
Orch The EX14 84 E2
Orcombe Ct EX8 202 D8
Orcombe Gdns EX8 202 C5
Ordnance St PL1 247 E2
Ordulf Rd PL19 171 A5
Oregon Way PL3 249 D6
ORESTON 255 C7
Oreston Com Acad
PL9 255 C7
Orestone Cross TQ2 213 D3
Orestone Dr TQ1 214 C6
Orestone La TQ2,
TQ12 213 E3
Oreston Rd PL9 255 C8
Orient Rd TQ3 226 D8
Oriole Dr EX4 173 D1
Orion Dr PL9 256 F8
Orkney Cl TQ2 213 E2
Orkney Mews EX16 161 D6
Orleigh Ave TQ12 207 B5
Orleigh Cl EX39 40 C7
Orleigh Cross TQ12 207 B5
Orleigh Ct EX39 25 C1
Orleigh Mill Wlk EX39 25 D1
Orleigh Pk TQ12 207 B5
Orley Rd TQ12 211 B2
Ormonde Ct EX36 158 D4
Orpington Ct EX16 65 B7
Orstone Cross EX32 18 E3
Orway Ash Cross EX15 66 B2
Orway Cross EX15 66 C1
Orwell Garth EX4 178 C8
Osbern Rd TQ3 219 A2
Osborn Cl TQ12 211 D2
Osborne Cl EX39 156 D2
Osborne Ct PL1 262 C2
Osborne Gdns 4
EX31 154 C1
Osborne La EX39 156 D2
Osborne Pl PL1 262 C1
Osborne Rd
Ilfracombe EX34 150 A5
Plymouth PL3 248 A3
Osborne St TQ12 207 D3
Osborne Villas 2
PL3 248 A3
Osborne Dr TQ6 233 F5
Osborne Terr EX31 154 F4
Osmand Gdns PL7 250 D5
Osmond Lodge TQ4 226 C5
Osmond's La 12 TQ14 210 B4
Osney Ave TQ4 226 B4
Osney Cres TQ4 226 B4
Osney Gdns TQ4 226 B4
Osprey Ave
4 Newton Abbot
TQ12 207 A5
Seaton EX12 192 B5
Osprey Dr TQ2 213 D3
Osprey Gdns PL9 256 C7
Osprey Gr EX7 200 F2
Osprey Ho TQ1 220 D7
Osprey Rd EX2 178 F6
OSSABOROUGH 8 B6
Ossaborough La EX34 8 C6
Oswald Browning Way 4
EX31 155 A7
Otterbourne Ct EX9 198 B1
Otter Cl
Okehampton EX20 170 D6
Tipton St John EX10 100 D3
Torquay TQ2 219 C7
West Hill EX11 168 D4
Otter Ct
Bickington TQ12 131 F8
Budleigh Salterton
EX9 198 C1
Exeter EX2 181 C8
Otter Estuary Reserve★
EX9 198 D1
Otterhead Lake Nature
Reserve★ TA3 68 E8
Otter Rd TQ2 219 C7
Otter Reach EX10 186 F8
Otters The EX16 49 B2
OTTERTON 198 F7
Otterton CE Prim Sch
EX9 198 E7
Otterton Mews EX13 167 F7
Otterton Mill★ EX9 198 D7
Otter Vale Cl EX14 68 C1
Ottervale Rd EX9 198 C1
Otter Valley Pk EX14 166 F8
Otter Way EX32 155 D4
OTTERY 116 E2
Ottery Cotts PL19 116 E2
Ottery La EX10 101 A1
Ottery Moor La
Honiton EX14 85 D3
Honiton EX14 166 A6
Ottery Park Ind Est
PL19 116 E2
OTTERY ST MARY 169 E3
Ottery St Mary Hospl
EX11 169 C3
Ottery St Mary L Ctr
EX11 169 B3
Ottery St Mary Prim Sch
EX11 169 E3
Ottery St EX9 198 F8
Our Lady & St Patrick's
RC Prim Sch TQ14 210 A6
Our Lady's RC Prim Sch
EX32 155 B5
Outcrop Rd PL9 255 B7
Outer Down PL19 116 E3
OUTER HOPE 147 C7
Outer Ting Tong EX9 197 B3
Outland Rd PL2 248 C7
Overbeck's Mus & Gdn★
TQ8 259 B1
Overbrook EX7 204 D6
Overcliff Ct EX7 204 E7
Overclose TQ3 225 F8
Overcott La EX36 46 D8
Overdale Cl TQ2 213 F4
Overdale Rd PL2 248 A7
Overgang TQ5 230 D5
Overgang Rd TQ5 230 C6
Overland Ct EX4 174 E2
Overlangs TQ7 142 C6
Overseas Est TQ6 146 B6
Overton Cl DT7 260 E5
Overton Gdns 3 PL3 248 F5
Owen Dr PL7 250 C7
Owen St TA21 160 C6
Owlaborough La
EX36 32 B2
Owlacombe Cross
TQ12 131 A7
Oxenham Cross EX20 95 C5
Oxenham Gn TQ2 219 D6
Oxenpark Gate EX6 112 F5
Oxenpark La
Ilfracombe, Goosewell
EX34 2 C3
Ilfracombe, Two Pots
EX34 2 C2
Morchard Bishop EX17 61 C1
Stockleigh Pomeroy
EX17 80 F7
Oxford Ave PL3 248 E5
Oxford Cl EX8 196 E4
Oxford Cross EX33 8 A3
Oxford Ct TQ2 213 F1
Oxford Gdns PL3 248 E5
Oxford Gr EX34 150 B6
Oxford La TQ5 230 A4
Oxford Pk EX34 150 B5
Oxford Pl PL1 262 C3
Oxford Rd EX4 261 C4
Oxford St
Dartmouth TQ6 233 F3
Exeter EX2 177 A4
Plymouth PL1 262 B3
Oxford Terr
Crediton EX17 165 D5
4 Plymouth PL1 262 B3
Sandford EX17 80 A5
Oxham Cross EX36 45 D8
Oxham La EC36 45 D7
Ox Hill La EX24 102 F4
Oxlea Cl TQ1 220 E4
Oxlea Rd TQ1 220 E4
Oxman's Cotts EX39 157 E6
Oxmead EX5 99 D3
Oxmon's La EX39 157 A7
Oxton Ho EX6 114 E1
Oyster Bend TQ4 226 C2
Oystercatcher Ct 9
TQ14 210 A3
Oyster Cl TQ4 226 C2
Ozone Terr DT7 260 D2

P

Paccombe Pool La
EX10 189 C7
Pacehayne La
Dalwood EX13 87 A1
Shute EX13 103 A8
Packer Rd EX16 161 A6
Packhall La TQ5 230 A2
Packhorse Cl EX10 188 D8
Packington St PL2 248 A4
Packs Cl TQ9 139 C7
Packsheep Down
EX6 112 F3
Padacre Rd TQ2 214 A4
Paddock Cl
Plymouth PL9 255 E5
Saltash PL12 242 D4
Seaton EX12 191 F7
Paddock Dr PL21 237 D4
Paddocks The
Abbotskerswell TQ12 212 B7
Dolton EX19 57 F7
Honiton EX14 166 A2
Membury EX13 87 D6
Totnes TQ9 223 D6
Wellington TA21 160 E5
Whimple EX5 99 F7
Paddock The
Brixham TQ5 230 B4
Dawlish EX7 204 E7
Dulverton TA22 33 D6
Hemerdon PL7 251 C7
Torquay TQ1 214 B1
Paddons Coombe 9
TQ12 123 F1
Paddons La TQ14 210 A7
Paddons Row PL19 171 C6
Pafford Ave TQ2 214 B2
Pafford Cl TQ2 214 A2
Page Ho TQ4 226 C6
Page's Cross EX16 62 F7
Paige Adams' Rd
TQ9 223 B6
Paiges Farm PL9 255 C1
Paiges La 7 EX31 154 F5
PAIGNTON 226 D6
Paignton Com Coll
Paignton TQ4 225 D4
15 Paignton TQ4 226 B6
Paignton Com & Sports
Coll TQ3 225 E5
Paignton Health &
Wellbeing Centre 16
TQ3 226 B6
Paignton Hospl TQ3 226 B6
Paignton Rd TQ9 228 A8
Paignton Sta TQ4 226 B6
Paignton Zoological &
Botanical Gdns★
TQ4 225 F4
Pail Pk EX33 8 D1
Painsford Cross TQ9 139 D7
Painter's Cross EX13 102 F7
Painters Ct EX2 261 A1
Painton Water EX39 37 D8
Paisey La EX17 78 C5
Paizen La
Beer EX12 190 F6
Beer EX12 191 B6
Palace Ave TQ3 226 B6
Palace Cotts 10 EX8 202 A7
Palace Ct 23 PL1 263 A2
Palace Gate EX1 261 B2
Palace Gdns 22 TQ13 123 E6
Palace La PL21 137 B7
Palace Mdw TQ13 123 E6
Palace Pl TQ3 226 B6
Palace St PL1 263 A2
Palatine Cl TQ1 220 B5
Pale Gate Cl EX14 166 D7
Palegate Cross TQ7 258 A8
Palermo 12 TQ1 220 D4
Palermo Rd TQ1 220 C7
Palfrey's La EX16 49 C5
Palk Cl TQ14 209 D5
Palk St TQ2 220 B4
Palm Cl EX8 196 D3
Palm Cross 1 PL21 137 B2
Palm Ct
Dawlish Warren EX7 201 A2
Dawlish Warren EX7 201 B2
Palmer Cl EX4 175 A4
Palmer Ct EX9 198 A1
Palmers Cl EX33 152 D5
Palmers Ct EX38 159 E5
Palmer's La EX5 99 E5
Palmers Mead TA21 160 D8
Palmerston Dr EX4 176 E7
Palmerston Park Wood
Nature Reserve
EX16 161 B2
Palmerston Pk EX16 161 B2
Palmerston St PL1 262 A4
Palm Ho EX4 176 E8
Palm Rd TQ2 220 A5
Palm Rise TQ2 213 A3
Palms The 2 TQ1 220 D4
Palm Tree View TQ3 226 B1
Palstone La TQ10 135 A2
Pamela Rd EX1 177 F7
Pancheon Cl 10 EX31 154 A2
PANCRASWEEK 71 B8
Pandora Gr PL9 256 E8
Pankhurst Cl EX8 202 E7
Panney The EX4 178 A7
Pannier Mkt
Great Torrington
EX38 159 D5
Tavistock PL19 171 C5
Pannier Mws 16
EX39 157 A1
Panorama TQ2 219 E2
Panson Cross PL15 90 B3
Papaver Cl EX31 153 E6
Papermakers La
PL21 237 E6
Parade
Chudleigh TQ13 123 E6
Exmouth EX8 202 A7
Plymouth PL1 263 A2
Parade Bsns Pk 4
PL19 171 B4
Parade Ope PL1 263 A2
Parade Rd PL5 244 A3
Parade The
Chardstock EX13 88 A7
Millbrook PL10 252 E5
Milton Abbot PL19 116 A6
Paradise Glen TQ14 210 B6
Paradise Lawn EX36 158 D4
Paradise Pk EX22 70 E1
Paradise Pl
1 Brixham TQ5 230 D5
Plymouth PL1 248 A2
Paradise Rd
Plymouth PL1 248 A2
Teignmouth TQ14 210 C6
Paradise Wlk TQ4 226 C4
Paragon EX34 150 B6
Paramore Way EX36 158 C4
Parchment Pl PL21 237 D6
Par Dr EX16 64 E8
Parehayne La EX24 102 E7
Parely Hill TQ13 110 F6
Paris Rd TQ3 226 C8
Paris St EX1 261 B3
Park an Garrek PL12 239 A1
Park Ave
Barnstaple EX31 154 C4
Bideford EX39 157 A3
Brixham TQ5 230 B3
Plymouth, Devonport
PL1 247 E3
Plymouth, Plymstock
PL9 255 D7
Westward Ho! EX39 156 C7
Parkbay Ave TQ4 225 E2
Park Bglws EX16 51 B3
Park Cl
Clyst Hydon EX15 83 D4
Fremington EX31 153 E5
Holsworthy EX22 164 C6
Ivybridge PL21 237 C5
Plymouth PL7 250 B7
Silverton EX5 82 C5
Tiverton EX16 161 D5
Woodbury EX5 184 C2
Park Com Sch The
EX32 155 A3
Park Cotts
Bigbury TQ7 142 F5
Ugborough PL21 137 D6
Park Cres
Combe Martin EX34 3 A3
Plymouth PL9 255 C7
Park Cross EX17 62 C3
Park Ct
Brixham TQ5 230 E5
Chillaton PL16 106 D1
Honiton EX14 85 C2
Ilfracombe EX34 150 B4
Park Dr EX8 202 E7
Parkelands TQ13 180 C7
Parker Cl
Plymouth PL7 250 B5
Wellington TA21 160 E6
Parker Rd
Bigbury-on-S TQ7 142 E3
Plymouth PL2 248 B6
Parkers Cl TQ9 223 D4
Parkers Cross La
EX1 174 F2
Parker's Gn PL18 125 C6
Parkers Hollow EX31 154 B3
Parker's Rd EX6 201 A8
Parkers Way TQ9 223 D4
Parkes Rd EX38 159 F5
Parkesway PL12 242 D2
Parkfield TQ7 143 A2
Parkfield Cl
Marldon TQ3 218 D3
Parkfield Cl *continued*
Totnes TQ9 223 F5
Parkfield Cross TQ13 131 A3
Parkfield Dr PL6 245 F1
Parkfield Rd
Topsham EX3 182 F5
Torquay TQ1 219 F7
Park Field Terr EX12 190 D4
Parkfield Way EX3 182 F5
Parkfield Wlk TQ7 143 A2
Park Five Bsns Ctr
EX2 178 E4
Park Gate EX37 28 D2
Park Gdns EX35 151 B5
Park Grove EX22 164 C6
Park Hall TQ1 220 B3
PARKHAM 39 E8
PARKHAM ASH 39 C7
Parkham Cross EX39 24 F1
Parkham Glade TQ5 230 C4
Parkham La TQ5 230 C4
Parkham Prim Sch
EX39 39 E8
Parkham Rd TQ5 230 C4
Parkham Terr 12
TQ5 230 C4
Parkham Twrs 6
TQ5 230 C4
Parkhayes EX5 184 C7
Park Hill
Dainton TQ12 212 A2
Ipplepen TQ12 211 F2
Teignmouth TQ14 210 B5
Tiverton EX16 161 C5
Parkhill Cotts PL21 136 F4
Parkhill Ho TQ12 211 B3
Parkhill Rd TQ1 220 C3
Park Hill Rd EX34 150 B5
Park Hills Ind Units
EX34 3 A3
Parkhouse La
Stoodleigh EX16 48 E4
Stoodleigh EX16 48 F4
Parkhouse Rd EX2 176 F3
Parkhurst Rd TQ1,
TQ2 219 F7
Park La
Barnstaple EX32 155 A3
8 Bere Alston PL20 125 E1
Bideford EX39 157 A3
Blackawton TQ9 139 E1
Budleigh Salterton EX9 197 F1
Chittlehampton EX37 43 F8
Combe Martin EX34 2 F3
Combe Martin EX34 3 A3
Combe St Nicholas TA20 69 F6
Crediton EX17 165 B4
Exeter EX4 174 E2
Exmouth EX8 202 A8
Filleigh EX32 29 D7
Iddesleigh EX19 57 F3
Madford EX14 67 C4
Morchard Bishop EX17 61 A2
Otterton EX9 198 E6
Pennymoor EX16 62 D6
Plymouth PL9 255 C7
Sparkwell PL7 132 C1
Stowford EX31 11 B3
Torquay TQ1 220 B3
Wellington TA21 160 C1
Whitford EX13 103 B6
Parkland Dr EX2 178 C3
Parklands
Barnstaple EX31 154 C3
12 Hemyock EX15 67 B8
Okehampton EX20 170 B3
9 Seaton EX12 192 A5
South Molton EX36 158 B3
Totnes TQ9 223 C6
Parklands Cl EX36 158 B3
Parklands Rd TA21 160 D7
Parklands Way TQ13 180 C4
Park Lane Cotts EX32 29 D7
Park Lodge EX9 197 F1
Park Meadow Cl EX17 60 D3
Park Mews TQ5 230 E5
Park Mill Cross EX17 59 F3
Park Mill La EX18 59 F8
Park Pl
Exeter, Heavitree
EX1 177 F6
Exeter, Mount Radford
EX2 261 C2
Winkleigh EX19 58 F3
Park Place La 12 PL3 248 A4
Park Rd
Beer EX12 191 C5
Crediton EX17 165 D4
Dartington TQ9 216 B2
Dawlish EX7 204 D6
Exeter EX1 177 E7
Exmouth EX8 202 A8
Hatherleigh EX20 75 C7
Kingskerswell TQ12 212 F5
Lapford EX17 60 D3
Lifton PL16 105 E3
Plymouth PL3 249 A6
St Dominick PL12 125 A2
Silverton EX5 82 C5
Tiverton EX16 161 D5
Torpoint PL11 247 B3
Torquay TQ1 214 B1
Park Rise
Dawlish EX7 204 D4
Salcombe TQ8 259 C4
Park Row EX20 170 B5
Park School TQ9 216 C3
Parks Dr PL9 256 A5
Parkside
Ivybridge PL21 237 E5
Plymouth PL2 247 F5
Salcombe TQ8 259 D5
Parkside Cres EX1 174 F3
Parkside Ct EX2 261 B2
Parkside Dr EX8 196 E3
Parkside Rd
Exeter EX1 174 F3
Paignton TQ4 226 C6
Parkside Villas TQ1 220 C7
Park St
Crediton EX17 165 D5
Ivybridge PL21 237 C4
Lynton EX35 151 B5
Plymouth PL3 248 A4
Tiverton EX16 161 D5
Willand EX15 65 D6
Willand EX15 162 C5
Parkstone La PL7 250 F6
Park Street Mews
PL21 237 C4
Park Street Ope PL3 248 A4
Parks Villas EX33 152 D5
Park Terr
23 Barnstaple EX32 155 A4
Ivybridge PL21 237 C4
Plymouth PL4 263 A3
Tiverton EX16 161 D5
Park The PL8 257 A5
Parkview EX17 80 A5
Park View
Axminster EX13 88 A3
Beaford EX19 42 D1
Kenton EX6 194 F3
Lifton PL16 105 E4
Newton Abbot TQ12 212 F8
Plymouth PL4 263 C3
Pyworthy EX22 71 D5
Shute EX13 103 A7
Park View Cl 21 EX34 3 A3
Park View Cotts EX38 42 B6
Park View Rd EX32 155 A6
Park View Terr
Kingston TQ7 142 C6
Okehampton EX20 170 C3
Westward Ho! EX39 156 C7
Park Villas EX32 27 E8
Parkway
Exeter EX2 176 F3
Ilfracombe EX34 150 B3
Park Way
Exmouth EX8 202 C8
Woodbury EX5 184 C2
Parkway Ct PL6 249 E7
Parkway Ind Est The
PL6 249 E7
Parkway Rd TQ13 123 E6
Parkway The PL3, PL5,
PL6 244 B1
Parkwood Cl PL6 241 B2
Parkwood Ct PL19 171 D6
Parkwood Rd PL19 171 D6
Park Wood Rise
PL16 105 E4
Parkyns Cross EX19 43 B4
Parliament Ct 9
EX34 150 C6
Parliament St EX17 165 C5
Parlour Mdw EX8 202 F7
Parlour Mead EX15 163 A3
Parminter Cl EX8 202 E7
PARNACOTT 71 D8
Parnell Cl PL6 249 A8
PARRACOMBE 4 C2
Parracombe CE Prim Sch
Parracombe EX31 4 C1
Parracombe EX31 11 D7
Parracombe La EX31 4 D2
Parracombe Lane Head
EX31 4 D2
Parr Cl EX1 261 C4
Parricks La EX13 88 D3
Parr La PL4 263 B2
Parrocks La TA20 88 C8
Parr's La TQ13 123 E6
Parr St
Exeter EX1 261 C4
Plymouth PL4 263 B2
Parrys Farm Cl EX8 196 C2
Parsonage Cross
Chulmleigh EX18 44 F2
Dartington TQ9 215 F2
Germansweek EX21 91 D5
Staverton TQ9 216 E3
West Putford EX22 39 B2
Woodbury EX5 184 C3
Parsonage Ct PL16 105 E4
Parsonage Hill EX36 31 A3
Parsonage La
Awliscombe EX14 85 C1
George Nympton EX36 29 F2
Hittisleigh EX6 96 C6
Honiton EX14 166 D5
Kentisbury EX31 10 E5
Moreleigh TQ9 139 A3
Silverton EX5 82 B6
South Molton EX36 158 C5
Staverton TQ9 216 E4
Ugborough PL21 137 D6
Parsonage Lane Cross
EX32 18 B2
Parsonage Lane End
PL21 137 D6
Parsonage Rd PL8 141 A7
Parsonage St EX5 83 A7
Parsonage Way
Plymouth PL4 263 B2

Parsonage Way continued
Woodbury EX5 . . . .**184** C4
Parson CI EX8 . . . .**196** C2
Parsons CI
13 Holsworthy EX22 . .**164** C4
Newton Poppleford
EX1U. **186** D8
Plymouth PL9 . . . .**256** A4
Parson's CI EX15 . . . . . .**66** A3
Parsons CI PL10 . . . . . .**252** F6
Parsons Hill
Bridford TQ13 . . . .**112** C4
Heltor EX6 . . . .**112** D6
Parsons La
Branscombe EX12 . . . . .**190** E4
Rockbeare EX5 . . . .**99** B5
Parson St TQ14 . . . .**210** B5
Parthia PI EX8 . . . .**196** E1
Partridge Cross EX36 . . .**45** D7
Partridge Hill EX36 . . . . .**45** D7
Partridge La
Hittisleigh EX6 . . . .**96** C4
Tiverton EX16 . . . .**63** A8
Partridge Rd
Exmouth EX8 . . . .**196** C2
Plymouth PL6 . . . .**245** B2
Partways PL19 . . . .**116** E3
Pasley St PL2 . . . .**247** E4
Pasley Street E PL2 . . . .**247** F4
Passaford La
Colaton Raleigh
EX10 . . . .**187** A4
Hatherleigh EX20 . . . . . .**75** C6
Passage Rd PL8 . . . .**140** F6
Passmore Rd EX5 . . . .**82** B4
Pasture Cross TQ9 . . . . .**144** F8
Pastures The EX20 . . . . .**92** A2
PATCHACOTT **74** B1
Patchacott Cross
Bratton Clovelly EX21 . . . .**92** A8
Northlew EX21 . . . .**74** B1
Patchel Cross EX20 . . . . .**56** F3
Patches Rd EX16 . . . . . .**161** B4
PATCHOLE **10** D5
Paternoster La TQ12 . .**211** C2
Paternoster Row
8 Barnstaple EX31 . . .**154** F5
Ottery St Mary EX11 . . .**169** D4
Pathdown La EX33 . . . . . .**7** F2
Pathfield EX38 . . . .**159** F5
Pathfield CI
Barnstaple EX31 . . . . . .**154** A3
Totnes TQ9 . . . .**223** D5
Path Field CI EX32 . . . . .**18** B2
Pathfield Lawn EX31 .**154** E6
Pathfields
Croyde EX33 . . . .**7** E2
Totnes TQ9 . . . .**223** D5
Uffculme EX15 . . . .**66** A7
Pathfields Bsns Pk
EX36 . . . .**158** D6
Pathfield Sch
Barnstaple EX31 . . . . . .**154** A4
Barnstaple EX31 . . . . . .**154** F5
PATHFINDER
VILLAGE **98** C4
Path The 29 EX39 . . . . .**15** A1
Pathwhorlands EX10 .**188** A6
Patna PI PL1 . . . .**262** B4
Pato Point PL11 . . . .**247** A5
Patricia CI EX4 . . . .**173** C2
Patterson's Cross
EX11 . . . .**169** D8
Patteson CI EX11 . . . . . .**100** F8
Patteson Dr EX11 . . . . .**169** F4
Pattinson CI PL6 . . . . . .**245** E2
Pattinson Ct PL6 . . . . . .**245** E2
Pattinson Dr PL6 . . . . . .**245** F2
Paullet EX16 . . . .**50** C1
Paul St EX4 . . . .**261** A3
Pauntley Gdn EX10 . . . .**187** F3
Pavey Run EX11 . . . .**169** C3
Paviland Grange 6
PL1 . . . .**248** A3
Pavilion PI EX2 . . . .**261** B2
Pavilions CI TQ5 . . . . . .**230** B3
Pavilion Sh Ctr TQ2 . . .**220** B3
Pavilion View EX35 . . . . .**151** B5
Pavington Cross EX37 . .**43** E3
Pavor Rd TQ2 . . . .**214** B2
Pavo St PL9 . . . .**256** E8
Paws Rd EX37 . . . .**43** B7
Paxford House Sq
EX11 . . . .**169** D4
PAYHEMBURY **84** C4
Payhembury CE Prim Sch
EX14 . . . .**84** C4
Payne CI EX34 . . . .**178** B8
Payne's Cotts EX14 . . . . .**85** C3
Paynsford Mews
TQ12 . . . .**207** B4
Paynsford Rd 1
TQ12 . . . .**207** B4
Paynter Wlk 5 PL7 . .**251** B5
PAYTON **51** F7
Payton Rd
Holywell Lake TA21 . . . . .**51** F7
Rockwell Green TA21 . . .**160** A5
Peacegate Cross EX20 **76** E4
Peacehay La TA21 . . . . . .**51** E4
Peacock Ave PL11 . . . . .**247** A3
Peacock CI PL4 . . . .**263** C4
Peacock La PL4 . . . .**263** C4
Peacock PI EX16 . . . . . .**201** A8
Peacocks CI TA21 . . . . . .**52** F7

Peadhill La EX16 . . . . . .**49** D2
Peak Cnr EX16 . . . .**62** E7
Peak Cross TQ9 . . . . . .**222** F3
Peakfield Cross Ways
EX5 . . . .**82** E6
Peak Hill Llamas ★
EX10 . . . .**187** D2
Peak Hill Rd EX10 . . . . .**187** E3
Peak Tor Ave TQ1 . . . . .**220** C2
Pear Dr EX15 . . . .**162** D4
Peard Rd EX16 . . . .**64** D6
Peards Down CI
EX32 . . . .**155** D4
Pear La 8 PL7 . . . .**251** B5
Pearl Assurance Ho 2
TQ12 . . . .**207** C3
Pearmain CI EX15 . . . . .**162** D4
Pearn Cotts 2 PL3 . . . .**248** F6
Pearn Gdns PL3 . . . .**249** A7
Pearn Rd PL3 . . . .**249** A7
Pearn Ridge PL3 . . . . . .**249** A7
Pearse CI EX20 . . . .**75** B7
Pearson Ave 3 PL4 . .**248** F4
Pearson CI EX22 . . . . . .**164** C5
Pearson Rd PL4 . . . .**248** F4
Pear Tree CI
Kenton EX6 . . . .**194** E3
Westleigh EX16 . . . .**51** A4
Pear Tree Cotts PL8 . .**257** A5
Peartree Cross
Ashburton TQ13 . . . . . .**130** E4
Denbury TQ12 . . . .**211** A7
Pear Tree Way 5
EX32 . . . .**17** B2
Peasberry PI PL8 . . . . . .**257** F4
Peaseditch TQ5 . . . .**230** D3
Peasland Rd TQ2 . . . . . .**214** A4
Peaslands Rd
Sidmouth EX10 . . . .**188** A5
Sidmouth EX10 . . . .**188** B5
Peaspark Cross TQ7 . .**144** F3
Peazen Flats EX12 . . . .**191** C6
Pebblebed CI EX3 . . . . .**182** D7
Pebble CI EX39 . . . .**156** D7
Pebble Ct TQ4 . . . .**226** B8
Pebbleridge Rd EX39 **156** C8
Pebblestone PL12 . . . . .**192** A5

Penhill Chalets TQ6 . .**146** B7
Penhill Cross EX6 . . . .**113** F5
Penhill La
Brixham TQ5 . . . .**234** E8
Hillhead TQ5 . . . .**235** A7
Penhill View EX31 . . . . .**16** A3
Peninsula Medical Sch
Exeter EX2 . . . .**177** F5
Plymouth PL6 . . . .**245** D4
Peninsular Pk PL12 . .**242** C4
Penlee EX9 . . . .**199** G2
Penlee Cotts PL10 . . . .**140** L2
Penlee Gdns PL3 . . . . . .**248** A4
Penlee Pk PL11 . . . .**246** E4
Penlee PI 4 PL4 . . . . . .**248** F4
Penlee Rd PL3 . . . .**248** A4
Penlee Way PL3 . . . .**248** B4
Penleonard CI EX2 . . . .**177** E5
PENN **104** E6
Pennant Ho EX8 . . . . . .**201** E6
Pennant Way PL21 . . . .**136** D6
Pennball Cross TQ9 . . .**217** B3
Penn Court TQ5 . . . . . .**230** B3
Penn Cross DT6 . . . .**260** F7
Penn Ho TQ12 . . . .**207** E2
Pennine Dr TQ4 . . . .**225** D4
Pennington CI EX17 . . . .**79** A5
PENNINN **207** E1
Penn Inn CI TQ12 . . . . .**207** E2
Penn Kernow PL15 . . . .**105** A2
Penn La TQ5 . . . .**230** D3
Penn Mdws TQ5 . . . . . .**230** D3
Penn Meadows CI
TQ5 . . . .**230** D3
Pennsland La TQ13 . . . .**130** F7
Penns Way TQ1 . . . .**207** F6
PENNSYLVANIA **173** C1
Pennsylvania CI EX4 .**177** D8
Pennsylvania Cres
EX4 . . . .**177** C8
Pennsylvania Pk EX4 **173** D1
Pennsylvania Rd
Exeter EX4 . . . .**173** D1
Torquay TQ1 . . . .**220** B5
Penn Torr TQ8 . . . .**259** D4
Penn View TQ5 . . . .**230** D3
Pennyacre Rd TQ14 . . .**210** C6
Penny CI
Exminster EX6 . . . .**182** A4
Wellington TA21 . . . . . .**160** D7
Pennycombe La EX6 . .**114** E4
PENNYCOMEQUICK . .**262** B4
Pennycomequick Hill
PL4 . . . .**262** B4
PENNYCROSS **248** C8
Pennycross CI PL2 . . . .**248** B8
Pennycross Park Rd
PL2 . . . .**248** C7
Pennycross Prim Sch
PL2 . . . .**248** C8
Penny Hill EX33 . . . .**7** E2
PENNYMOOR **62** D6
Penny Plot DT7 . . . .**260** C4
Penny's Hill TQ1 . . . . . .**219** F7
Penny's La PL9 . . . .**256** D6
Penny's Terr EX13 . . . .**167** D5
Penny Thorn Cross
EX14 . . . .**85** E7
Pennywell CI TQ13 . . . .**131** B1
Pennywell Farm &
Wildlife Ctr ★ TQ11 .**135** E6
Penpethy CI TQ5 . . . . . .**230** B4
Penpethy Rd TQ5 . . . . .**230** B5
PENQUIT **237** F1
Penrith CI PL6 . . . .**245** D3
Penrith Gdns PL6 . . . . .**245** D3
Penrith Wlk PL6 . . . . . .**245** D3
Penrose Almshouses 4
EX32 . . . .**155** A4
Penrose St PL1 . . . .**262** B3
Penroses Terr 9
EX22 . . . .**164** C4
Penrose Terr 7 EX1 .**261** A2
Penrose Villas 5
PL4 . . . .**248** F4
Penryn PI 4 TQ14 . . . .**210** A3
Penry Rd EX3 . . . .**182** B7
Penscombe Cross
PL15 . . . .**115** A6
Penshill La EX36 . . . .**31** C2
Penshurst Rd TQ12 . . . .**207** B1
Pensilva Pk TQ5 . . . . . .**230** C2
Pens La EX15 . . . .**67** B7
Penson Cross EX20 . . . .**59** B1
Penson La EX20 . . . .**77** B8
PENSTONE **79** B3
Penstone Barns EX5 . . .**82** E4
Penswell Cross TQ10 **135** E4
Pentamar St PL2 . . . . . .**247** E4
Pentice La EX5 . . . .**3** A3
Pentillie CI 20 PL20 . .**125** E1
Pentillie Cres PL4 . . . . .**248** D4
Pentillie Rd
Bere Alston PL20 . . . . . .**125** E1
Plymouth PL4 . . . .**248** E4
Pentillie View 21
PL20 . . . .**125** E1
Pentire Rd PL11 . . . .**246** F3
Pentland CI PL6 . . . .**244** F7
Penton CI EX17 . . . .**165** D6
Penton La EX17 . . . .**165** D5
Penton Rise EX17 . . . . .**165** D6
Pentridge Ave TQ2 . . . .**219** C2
Pentyre Ct PL4 . . . .**263** C4
Pentyre Terr PL4 . . . . . .**263** C4
Penwill Way TQ4 . . . . . .**226** A4
PENHILL **16** A4

Peoples Park Rd
EX17 . . . .**165** C6
PEPPERCOMBE **24** E2
Pepperdon Common
TQ13 . . . .**112** B3
Pepperdon Hall La
TQ13 . . . .**112** B3
Pepper La
Kingswear TQ6 . . . .**234** E4
Plymouth PL9 . . . .**256** D7
Pepper's Cnr EX9 . . . . .**198** F7
Pepper St PL19 . . . .**171** C6
Peppery La TQ14 . . . . . .**209** D5
Pepys PI PL5 . . . .**244** E1
Perceval Rd EX4 . . . . . .**174** A2
Perches CI PL8 . . . .**141** B7
Percy Cross EX14 . . . . . .**67** B2
Percy Rd EX2 . . . .**177** B3
Percy St PL5 . . . .**243** D1
Percy Terr PL4 . . . .**249** A4
Peregrine CI TQ2 . . . . .**213** D3
Peregrine Rd PL6 . . . . .**245** B2
Perinville CI TQ1 . . . . . .**220** E6
Perinville Rd TQ1 . . . . .**220** D7
Periwinkle Dr
Barnstaple EX31 . . . . . .**154** B3
Plymouth PL7 . . . .**251** C5
Perkins Cross EX5 . . . . .**99** C1
PERKIN'S VILLAGE **99** C2
Perranporth CI PL5 . . .**243** E4
Perreyman Sq 7
EX16 . . . .**161** D4
Perriam's PI EX9 . . . . . .**199** G2
Perridge CI EX2 . . . .**176** E3
Perridge Cross EX6 . . . .**98** E1
Perridge La
Longdown EX6 . . . .**98** E1
Sidbury EX10 . . . .**101** F8
Perriman's Row EX8 .**202** A7
Perrin Way EX4 . . . .**174** D1
Perriton Cross EX5 . . . .**99** E8
Perros CI TQ14 . . . .**209** D8
Perry CI PL19 . . . .**171** B6
Perry Cross TQ12 . . . . .**206** D7
Perryfield PI
8 Plymouth PL3 . . . .**249** D1
Pomphlett PL9 . . . .**249** D1
Perry Hill EX17 . . . .**80** E8
Perry La
Doddiscombsleigh
EX6 . . . .**113** D5
Newton Abbot TQ12 . . .**206** D6
Perryman CI PL7 . . . . . .**250** E7
Perryman's Hill EX17 . .**79** F4
Perry New Rd TA22 . . . . .**33** F4
Perry Rd EX4 . . . .**177** B8
Perrys Gdns EX11 . . . . .**168** D4
Perry St TA20 . . . .**88** B8
PERRY STREET **88** E8
Perseus Cres PL9 . . . . .**256** E8
Perseverance Cotts 1
PL7 . . . .**250** E7
Perth CI EX4 . . . .**173** E2
Peryam Cres EX2 . . . . .**178** A4
Peryn Rd PL19 . . . .**171** A5
Peterborough Rd
EX4 . . . .**176** F7
Peterclose Rd EX16 . . .**161** F3
Peter Hopper's Hill
PL5 . . . .**240** C2
Peters CI TQ3 . . . .**225** F1
Peter's CI PL9 . . . .**256** C7
Peters Cres TQ3 . . . . . .**218** D3
Petersfield EX1 . . . .**174** F2
Peters Field PL8 . . . . . .**141** A7
Petersfield CI PL3 . . . . .**249** B6
PETER'S FINGER **105** B7
Peter's Gn EX17 . . . .**61** A1
PETERS MARLAND **56** C8
Peters Park CI PL5 . . . .**243** E1
Peter's Park La PL5 . . .**243** E1
Peter St EX5 . . . .**82** F7
Peter's Well Hill EX17 .**61** E5
PETER TAVY **117** F4
Petertavy Cross PL19 **117** E3
Pethericks EX16 . . . .**65** A7
Pethick CI PL6 . . . .**244** D6
Pethill CI PL6 . . . .**245** F2
Pethybridge TQ13 . . . .**122** B8
Petitor Mews PL1 . . . . .**214** B1
Petitor Rd TQ1 . . . .**214** C1
Petit Well La TQ1 . . . . .**214** B1
Petrel CI TQ2 . . . .**213** C3
Petre Street EX13 . . . . .**167** E7
PETROC
Barnstaple EX31 . . . . . .**154** E3
Tiverton EX16 . . . .**161** C6
Petroc (Brannams)
EX31 . . . .**154** C2
Petroc Ct PL18 . . . .**125** A6
Petroc Dr TQ12 . . . .**207** C4
PETROCKSTOW **56** F4
Petticoat La EX13 . . . . .**167** A6
PETTON **35** A3
Petton Cross EX16 . . . . .**35** A3
PEVERELL **248** D6
Peverell Park Rd
PL3 . . . .**248** D6
Peverell Terr PL3 . . . . .**248** D5
Pcw Tor CI
Tavistock PL19 . . . .**171** B5
3 Yelverton PL20 . . . .**126** F3
Phear Ave EX8 . . . .**202** B7
Phelps Rd PL1 . . . .**247** E2
PHILHAM **22** D1
Philham Cross EX39 . . .**22** D1

Philham La EX39 . . . .**22** D1
Philham Water EX39 . .**22** D1
Philip Ave EX31 . . . .**154** D2
Philip CI PL9 . . . .**256** A6
Philip Gdns PL9 . . . . . .**255** F6
Philip Ho FX1 . . . .**178** E6
Philip Rd EX4 . . . .**177** F8
Philips CI 2 EX33 . . . . .**152** D5
Philipps Ave 2 EX8 . . .**196** B1
Phillips Ct EX13 . . . . . .**167** D5
Phillips Path 12 TQ7 . .**143** E7
Phillips Sq EX14 . . . . . .**166** B6
Philpott La PL19 . . . . . .**171** B2
Phobe CI PL18 . . . .**125** B5
Phoenix Bsns Pk PL6 **245** F4
Phoenix CI 9 PL20 . . . .**126** F4
Phoenix La EX16 . . . . . .**161** D3
Phoenix PI
Kingsbridge TQ7 . . . . . .**258** C5
West Alvington TQ7 . . . .**258** B4
Phoenix Rd EX13 . . . . . .**161** B3
Phoenix St PL1 . . . .**262** A2
Piazza Terracina EX2 **261** B1
Picket Head Hill
TQ14 . . . .**210** A2
Picklecombe Dr
TQ12 . . . .**244** E4
Pick Pie Dr PL6 . . . .**245** E8
Picton PI TA22 . . . .**33** D6
Pidgeley Rd EX7 . . . . . .**204** F8
Pidgeon's La EX13 . . . .**104** B7
Pidgley Rd EX7 . . . .**200** E1
Pidland La EX16 . . . .**47** F1
Pidsley Cres EX3 . . . . . .**182** D7
Pidsley Hill EX17 . . . . . .**79** F7
Pidsley La EX17 . . . .**79** F8
Piece Hill EX6 . . . .**97** E4
Piend La EX17 . . . .**62** B1
Pier Head EX8 . . . .**201** E6
Pier La PL10 . . . .**253** A1
Piermont PI EX7 . . . . . .**204** E6
Pier St PL1 . . . .**262** B1
Piggy La EX13 . . . .**167** D6
Pig La EX13 . . . .**167** D6
Pigs Leg Cross EX20 . .**108** A8
Pigspark Cross TQ13 **131** A5
Pike Rd PL3 . . . .**249** D5
Pikes Hill EX6 . . . .**97** E3
Pike's Mead EX20 . . . . .**170** B4
Pilchers Field PL20 . . .**126** E3
Pilcock La
Alswear EX36 . . . .**30** B1
Alswear EX37 . . . .**45** B8
Pilemoor La EX16 . . . . . .**48** E3
Pilemore Cross EX16 . .**48** E4
Piley La TA21 . . . .**51** D8
Pilgrim CI
Brixham TQ5 . . . .**230** E5
Plymouth PL2 . . . .**248** B6
Pilgrim Ct 11 PL20 . . .**125** E1
Pilgrim Dr PL20 . . . .**125** E1
Pilgrim Prim Sch
PL1 . . . .**262** B3
Pilland Way EX31 . . . . .**154** D6
Pillar Ave TQ5 . . . .**230** B5
Pillar Cres TQ5 . . . .**230** B5
Pillar Ct TQ5 . . . .**230** B5
Pillar Flats TQ5 . . . .**230** B5
Pillar Wlk PL6 . . . .**244** F7
Pillavins La EX36 . . . . . .**158** F6
Pill Gdns EX33 . . . .**152** D5
Pillhead **157** F2
Pill Ho EX32 . . . .**155** A2
Pill La
Barnstaple EX32 . . . . . .**155** A2
Saltash PL12 . . . .**242** E4
Pill Lawn EX32 . . . .**155** A2
Pillmere Dr PL12 . . . . . .**242** D4
Pillory Hill PL8 . . . .**140** F6
Pill Rd EX39 . . . .**157** A2
Pill View EX31 . . . .**153** E6
Pilmuir Ave TQ2 . . . . . .**219** E5
PILTON **154** E6
Pilton Bluecoat CE Acad
Jun Sch EX31 . . . .**154** E7
Pilton Com Coll EX31 **154** E7
Pilton Cswy EX32 . . . . .**154** F6
Pilton Inf Sch EX31 . . .**154** F6
Pilton La EX1 . . . .**178** D8
Pilton Lawn
Barnstaple EX31 . . . . . .**154** F6
7 Barnstaple EX32 . .**155** A7
Pilton Quay EX31 . . . . .**154** F6
Pilton Row EX1 . . . .**175** A3
Pilton St EX31 . . . .**154** F6
Pimlico TQ1 . . . .**220** B5
Pimm Rd TQ3 . . . .**225** E7
Pinaster CI EX14 . . . . . .**166** C5
Pinbridge Mews EX4 **174** D1
Pinbrook Ind Est
EX4 . . . .**174** D1
Pinbrook Mews EX4 . .**174** D1
Pinbrook Rd EX4 . . . . . .**174** D1
Pinbrook Units EX4 . . .**174** D1
Pinces Cotts EX7 . . . . . .**177** A3
Pinces Gdns EX2 . . . . . .**177** A3
Pinces Rd EX2 . . . .**177** A3
Pinch Hill EX23 . . . .**70** A7
Pincombe Cnr EX36 . . . .**31** B3
Pincombe Rd EX39 . . . . .**25** C4
Pinder Ct PL19 . . . .**171** B5
Pine Ave EX4 . . . .**176** F7
Pine CI
Brixham TQ5 . . . .**230** B2

Pine CI continued
Ilfracombe EX34 . . . . . .**150** E4
Teignmouth TQ14 . . . . .**210** D7
Tiverton EX16 . . . .**161** B4
Pine Ct TQ1 . . . .**220** D5
Pinefields CI EX11 . . . .**168** E3
Pine Gdns
Honiton EX14 . . . .**166** D6
Plymouth PL2 . . . .**248** E6
Pine Gr EX14 . . . .**166** D6
Pinehurst Way PL21 . . .**237** A6
Pine Park Rd EX14 . . . .**166** D5
Pine Ridge DT7 . . . .**260** E5
Pineridge CI EX4 . . . . . .**176** F4
Pines CI
Hartland EX39 . . . .**22** E3
Westward Ho! EX39 . . .**156** B6
Pines The
Exmouth EX8 . . . .**196** D3
Paignton TQ3 . . . .**225** F8
Pine Tree CI EX7 . . . . . .**201** B2
Pine View PL18 . . . .**125** D2
Pine View Ave TQ1 . . . .**220** C6
Pine View Cl
Exmouth EX8 . . . .**196** F2
Halwill Junction EX21 . . .**73** E3
Pine View Gdns TQ1 . .**220** C6
Pine View Rd TQ1 . . . . .**220** C6
Pine Wlk DT7 . . . .**260** D5
Pinewood CI
Dawlish EX7 . . . .**205** A8
Plymouth PL7 . . . .**250** F6
Pinewood Dr PL6 . . . . .**245** E7
Pinewood La EX4 . . . . . .**174** B2
Pinewood Rd TQ12 . . . .**207** B2
PINHAY **104** B2
Pinhay Hollow DT7 . . . .**104** B2
Pinhey's Cross TQ9 . . .**144** F5
PINHOE **174** F2
Pinhoe CE Prim Sch
EX4 . . . .**174** E1
Pinhoe Sta EX1 . . . .**174** E1
Pinhoe Trad Est EX4 . .**174** D1
Pinkhams Cotts PL12 **242** B6
Pinksmoor La TA21 . . . .**51** E2
Pinkworthy Cross
EX16 . . . .**48** C8
Pinkworthy Hill EX16 . .**48** B7
Pin La PL1 . . . .**263** A2
Pinnacle Quay PL1 . . . .**263** B2
Pinnacle The TQ12 . . . .**207** A1
Pinnbridge Ct 7
EX1 . . . .**178** E5
Pinncourt La EX1 . . . . .**174** F2
Pinnex Moor Rd
EX16 . . . .**161** E6
Pinn La
Exeter EX1 . . . .**178** F7
Exeter EX1 . . . .**178** F8
Otterton EX10 . . . .**187** B2
Pinn Lane Cnr EX10 . .**187** A4
Pinn Valley Rd EX1 . . . .**174** F1
Pinslow Cross PL15 . . .**105** B8
Pins Pk EX22 . . . .**164** C5
Pintail La EX3 . . . .**182** E6
Pintail Way PL6 . . . .**245** B2
Pinwill Cres PL21 . . . . .**137** A4
Pinwood La EX4 . . . .**174** B1
Pinwood Meadow Dr
EX4 . . . .**174** B2
Pioneer Cotts EX12 . . .**191** D5
Pioneer Terr TQ11 . . . .**236** A5
Pipehouse La TQ13 . . . .**123** C4
Pipers Cross TQ7 . . . . .**142** C7
Pipers PI EX14 . . . .**68** C2
Piper St PL6 . . . .**245** B5
Pipistrelle Rd TQ12 . . .**207** A5
Pipistrelle Way TQ12 **207** C8
Pippin CI EX11 . . . .**178** C6
Pippin La PL9 . . . .**256** E7
Pippin PI TQ7 . . . .**258** D7
Pippins EX12 . . . .**191** D5
Pippins Field EX15 . . . . .**66** A7
Pippins The PL21 . . . . .**237** A5
Piran CI PL18 . . . .**125** A6
Pirates Bay Adventure
Golf ★ TQ4 . . . .**226** C6
Pisces St PL9 . . . .**256** E8
Piscombe La EX9 . . . . .**198** F7
Pissleton La
Crediton EX17 . . . .**61** A1
Morchard Bishop EX17 . .**60** F1
Pitcairn Cres TQ2 . . . . .**213** E3
Pitchingstone Cross
TQ7 . . . .**147** C7
Pitcombe La TA4 . . . .**35** B5
Pitfield CI EX15 . . . .**162** D3
Pitham La EX11 . . . .**169** F7
Pit Hill EX34 . . . .**2** D4
Pitland Cnr PL19 . . . . . .**117** B4
Pitland La TQ12 . . . .**213** E6
Pitlands La EX15 . . . .**67** A8
Pitley Cross TQ13 . . . . .**131** A5
Pitley Rd TQ13 . . . .**131** B5
Pitley Rd TQ13 . . . .**131** B5
Pitman's La PL21 . . . . .**133** C2
Pitsham La TA4 . . . .**34** E6
Pits La PL10 . . . .**140** H2
Pitson La EX10 . . . .**187** A5
Pitt Ave 12 EX39 . . . . . .**15** A1

Pitt Cres TQ4 . . . . . .224 B7
Pitt Cross EX39 . . . . . .22 C4
Pitt Ct
  8 Appledore EX39. . . .15 A1
  Loddiswell TQ7 . . . . .143 F7
Pitt Hill
  Appledore EX39. . . . .157 B8
  Crediton EX17. . . . . . .79 F3
  Kenton EX6 . . . . .194 D3
  Shebbear EX21. . . . . . .55 D4
Pitt Hill Rd TQ12 . . . .206 F4
Pitt Ho TQ13. . . . . . .123 D5
Pitt La
  Bideford EX39. . . . . . .157 A2
  Bow EX17. . . . . .78 B5
  Butterleigh EX16 . . . . .64 C4
  Cadbury EX5. . . . . . . .81 C8
  Chevithorne EX16. . . . .49 D2
  Dawlish EX7. . . . . . . .204 B7
  Huish Champflower TA4 . .35 E8
  North Molton EX36 . . . .30 F8
  Thorverton EX5. . . . . . .81 F7
  Waterrow TA4. . . . . . . .35 F5
Pitton Cross EX6. . . . . .96 E5
Pitt Pk **12** EX5. . . . . . .99 A6
Pitts Cleave Ind Est
  PL19. . . . . .117 D3
Pitts Cnr EX16 . . . . . .63 D4
Pitts Ct EX2. . . . . . . .261 C1
Pixey Plain EX16 . . . . .31 B3
Pixie Dell EX33 . . . . . .152 B7
Pixie La EX33 . . . . . . .152 C6
Pixie Wlk EX11. . . . . .169 B3
Pixon La PL19. . . . . . .171 B4
Pixon Trad Ctr **2**
  PL19. . . . . .171 B4
Pixton Cross EX19. . . . .58 B2
Pixton Way TA22. . . . . .33 E6
Place Cross
  Ashburton TQ13 . . . . .131 A6
  Okehampton EX20 . . . . .93 E5
Place de Brest PL1. . . .262 C3
Place La TQ13 . . . . . . .131 A5
Plainfield La EX16. . . . .63 C7
PLAINMOOR 220 B7
Plainmoor Rd **3**
  TQ1. . . . . .220 B7
Plainmoor (Torquay
  United FC) TQ1 . . . . .220 B7
Plains The TQ9 . . . . . .223 D5
Plaistow Cl PL5. . . . . .243 E2
Plaistow Cres PL5. . . . .243 E2
Plaistow Hill Inf Sch
  PL5. . . . . .243 E2
Plantagenet Dr EX15 163 C6
Plantagenet Wlk
  EX2. . . . . .178 D4
Plantation Cl TQ12 . . .207 F1
Plantation Terr EX7 . .204 E6
Plantation Way
  Torquay TQ2 . . . . . . .213 C3
  Torquay TQ2 . . . . . . .213 C2
  Totnes TQ9. . . . . . . .222 F6
Plant World (Gdns)★
  TQ12. . . . . .213 C7
Plassey Cl EX4. . . . . . .173 D2
Plaston Gn EX6 . . . . . .112 D5
Platt Cl TQ8 . . . . .259 B4
Plat The TQ6. . . . . . . .145 E5
Platway La TQ14 . . . . .209 D5
Play Cross TQ13 . . . . .130 A4
Playmoor Cotts EX1. .174 E1
Playmoor Dr EX1. . . . .174 F1
PLEAMORE CROSS 160 A2
Pleasant Terr **1** TQ3 226 A6
Pleasure Hill Cl PL9. .255 D8
Plintona View PL7 . . . .250 E7
Ploudal Rd EX15. . . . .163 B2
Plougastel Dr PL12. . . .242 E3
Plough Gn PL12. . . . . .242 C3
Ploughman Way PL8 136 A2
Plover Cl EX3. . . . . . . .182 E6
Plover Rise PL21. . . . . .237 B5
Plumbpk Ave EX8. . . . .202 E7
Plume of Feathers Cl
  EX11. . . . . .169 E4
Plumer Rd PL6. . . . . . .244 F2
Plumper's Cross EX38 41 A7
Plumtree Dr EX2. . . . .178 B4
Plumtree La EX5. . . . . .99 E7
Plum Way EX15 . . . . . .162 D4
Plymbridge Gdns
  PL7. . . . . .250 E5
Plymbridge La PL6. . . .245 B4
Plymbridge Rd
  Plymouth, Eggbuckland
  PL6. . . . . .245 C1
  Plymouth, Estover PL6 .245 E5
  Plymouth, Mainstone
  PL6. . . . . .245 F2
  Plymouth, Plympton
  PL7. . . . . .250 C7
Plym Cl TQ2 . . . . .219 B7
Plym Cres PL19. . . . . .171 D5
PLYMOUTH 262 C1
Plymouth Arts Ctr★
  PL4. . . . . .263 A2
Plymouth Athenaeum &
  Theatre★ PL1 . . . . . .262 B2
Plymouth Business Sch
  PL4. . . . . .263 A3
Plymouth City Mus & Art
  Gal★ PL4. . . . . .263 A3
Plymouth Coll Inf Sch **4**
  PL3. . . . . .248 F5

Plymouth Coll of Art
  PL4. . . . . .263 A3
Plymouth Coll Prep Sch
  PL1. . . . . .262 A3
Plymouth Coll (Senior
  Sch) PL4. . . . . .248 E4
Plymouth Discovery Ctr★
  PL3. . . . . .249 F6
Plymouth Ent Pk
  PL5. . . . . .243 D5
Plymouth Gin Distillery★
  PL4. . . . . .263 A2
Plymouth Hill PL20. . . .128 A8
Plymouth Hospl, Nuffield
  Health (private)
  PL6. . . . . .245 B4
Plymouth Life Ctr
  PL2. . . . . .248 C5
Plymouth Lipson Vale
  Prim Sch PL4. . . . . . .249 A4
Plymouth Marjon Univ
  PL6. . . . . .245 C4
Plymouth Medical & Tech
  Pk PL6 . . . . .245 A3
Plymouth Pavilions
  PL1. . . . . .262 B2
Plymouth Rd
  Buckfastleigh TQ11. . . .236 B4
  Buckfastleigh, Lower Dean
  TQ11. . . . . .236 A3
  Chudleigh Knighton
  TQ12. . . . . .123 D4
  Kingsbridge TQ7 . . . . .258 C6
  Plymouth PL7 . . . . . . .250 B6
  South Brent TQ10 . . . .134 F2
  Tavistock PL19 . . . . . .171 B4
  Totnes TQ9 . . . . .223 B5
Plymouth Road Ind Est
  PL19. . . . . .171 C3
Plymouth Sch of Creative
  Arts PL1. . . . . .262 A2
Plymouth Science Pk
  PL6. . . . . .245 C4
Plymouth Ski &
  Snowboard Ctr★
  PL6. . . . . .249 E7
Plymouth Sta PL4. . . . .262 C4
Plymouth Trade Pk
  PL4. . . . . .263 C1
Plymouth Univ Marine Sta
  PL3. . . . . .263 A3
Plymouth Univ Marine
  Stn PL1. . . . . .263 B1
PLYMPTON 250 E4
Plympton Cross TQ7 . .147 F5
Plympton Hill PL7. . . . .250 F3
Plympton St Mary Inf &
  Old Priory Jun Acad
  PL7. . . . . .250 D5
PLYMPTON ST
  MAURICE 250 E4
Plympton St Maurice
  Prim Sch PL7. . . . . . .250 F3
Plym St PL4 . . . . .263 A3
PLYMSTOCK 255 E6
Plymstock Rd PL9. . . . .255 D7
Plymstock Sch PL9 . . . .255 F8
Plymstock Sp Ctr
  PL9. . . . . .255 E6
PLYMTREE. 83 E5
Plymtree CE Prim Sch
  EX15. . . . . .83 F5
Plymtree Dr PL7 . . . . .250 C7
Plym Valley Mdws
  PL6. . . . . .249 F8
Plym Valley Rly★
  PL7. . . . . .250 A7
Plymview Cl PL3. . . . . .249 D6
Poadmarsh Cross
  EX36. . . . . .31 D1
Poadmarsh Hill
  Ash Mill EX36 . . . . . . .31 D1
  Bishops Nympton EX36. . .30 F1
  Rose Ash EX16 . . . . . . .46 D8
Pocklington Rise
  PL7. . . . . .250 E5
Pocombe Hill EX2. . . . .176 B3
Pode Dr PL7. . . . . .251 B4
Pod La EX13 . . . . .87 F4
Poets Corner TQ12. . . .244 C1
Point In View Cotts
  EX8. . . . . .196 B3
Point Terr EX8. . . . . . .201 E6
POINT THE. 201 E7
Polehayes. 74 B1
Polehouse La EX2. . . . .176 E1
Pole Rue La TA20 . . . . .69 F6
Pole Rue La TA20 . . . . .69 F6
Poles Hill EX31. . . . . .154 E7
Poleshill La EX31. . . . .154 D7
Polhearne La TQ5. . . . .230 B3
Polhearne Way TQ5. . .230 B3
Pollard Cl
  Plymouth PL9 . . . . . . .255 B5
  Saltash PL12. . . . . . . .242 B2
Pollardscl EX4. . . . . . .174 D1
Pollard's La TA21. . . . . .52 F7
Pollards Pl EX39 . . . . . .157 C2
Pollards The EX32. . . . .155 C3
Pollards Way
  Saltash PL12. . . . . . . .242 E3
  Saltash PL12. . . . . . . .242 E4
Pollyblank Rd **2**
  TQ12. . . . . .207 B3
Pollybrook EX5. . . . . .184 C2
Polmer Mews EX9 . . . .199 G2
Polperro Pl **3** PL2. . . .248 D8
Polruan Terr PL1. . . . .262 A3

Polsham Pk TQ3 . . . . .226 B7
Polsloe Bridge Sta
  EX4. . . . . .178 A7
POLSLOE PARK 177 E7
POLSLOE PRIORY 177 F8
Polsloe Rd EX1. . . . . . .177 E6
Polson Hill EX17. . . . . .61 A2
POLTIMORE 174 F6
Poltimore Cl EX36. . . . .158 D4
Poltimore Cross EX4 .174 F6
Poltimore Ct EX4 . . . . .174 F7
Poltimore Dr **6** EX1 . .178 E8
Poltimore House★
  EX4. . . . . .174 F5
Poltimore Lawn
  EX32. . . . . .155 B6
Poltimore Rd
  Farway EX24. . . . . . . .101 F7
  Offwell EX14, EX24. . . .102 A8
  South Molton EX36 . . . .158 D4
Poltimore Sq EX4. . . . .175 A4
Poltimore Way EX4 . . .175 A4
Polwhele Rd **14** EX16. . .64 D7
Polywell EX39 . . . . .14 F1
Polzeath Gdns **1**
  PL2. . . . . .248 D8
Pomarine Cl EX23. . . . .70 A8
Pomeroy Ave TQ5. . . . .230 A5
Pomeroy Pl **8** TQ12. . .122 F1
Pomeroy Rd
  Newton Abbot TQ12 . . .207 B3
  Tiverton EX16. . . . . . . .64 E8
Pomeroy Villas TQ9 . .223 D6
POMPHLETT 255 E8
Pomphlett Cl PL9 . . . . .247 F3
Pomphlett Farm Ind Est
  PL9. . . . . .249 E1
Pomphlett Gdns PL9 .255 D8
Pomphlett Prim Sch
  PL9. . . . . .255 E8
Pomphlett Rd PL9. . . . .255 E8
Pondfield Rd PL12 . . . .242 B3
Pond Hill EX16. . . . . . .65 A7
Pond La TA21. . . . . .51 D3
Ponsford Cross EX15. . .65 A2
Ponsford La EX15. . . . . .65 A2
Ponsonby Rd
  Plymouth PL3 . . . . . . .248 B4
  Plymouth PL3 . . . . . . .262 A4
PONSWORTHY 130 A8
Pooks La TQ13 . . . . . .130 F5
Pool Anthony Dr EX16 .64 E8
Pool Cross EX20 . . . . .107 F8
POOLE. 160 F8
Poole Cross TQ12 . . . .211 A1
Poole Gate EX4 . . . . . .177 B8
Poole Hill TA22. . . . . . .33 B5
Poole Ind Est TA21. . . .160 F8
Poole La EX36 . . . . .8 B7
Poole Park Rd PL5 . . . .247 C8
Poole's Ct DT7. . . . . . .260 E3
Pooley Cross TQ7. . . . .143 E4
Pool Hill
  Ashbrittle TA21. . . . . . .35 E1
  Bridestowe EX20 . . . . .107 F8
Pool La
  Burrington EX37. . . . . .44 A4
  Chittlehampton EX37 . . .29 A1
  Woolacombe EX34 . . . . .1 B1
Poolmill Cross TQ13 . .112 E1
Pool Pk TQ10 . . . . . . .135 A3
Pools Weir TQ12 . . . . .214 B8
Popes Cl EX11 . . . . . . .165 C6
Popes La EX24. . . . . . .103 A3
Pope'S La EX20. . . . . . .59 B1
Pope's La
  Lapford EX17 . . . . .60 D3
  Rockwell Green TA21. . .160 B4
POPHAM 19 A3
Popham Cl EX16. . . . . .161 F4
Popham Cross EX36. . . .19 A3
Popham Flats TA21 . . .160 D6
Popham La EX36. . . . . .19 A3
Popham Rd TA21. . . . . .160 F7
Pop La EX13, TA20. . . . .88 B8
Poplar Cl
  Brixham TQ5. . . . . . . .229 F2
  Exeter EX2 . . . . .177 A3
  Exmouth EX8. . . . . . . .196 D3
  Newton Abbot TQ12 . . .213 A8
  Plymouth PL7 . . . . . . .251 B5
Poplar Dr TQ7 . . . . . . .258 C5
Poplar Mount EX13 . . .167 D6
Poplar Row EX9 . . . . . .199 H2
Poplars Dr TQ3 . . . . . .218 D2
Poplars The
  7 Chudleigh Knighton
  TQ13. . . . . .123 C4
  Exeter EX4 . . . . .174 C2
Poplars Wlk EX5. . . . . .179 E2
Poplar Terr
  High Bickington EX37. . .43 C7
  Ipplepen TQ12 . . . . . .211 D2
Poplar Tree Cnr
  EX12. . . . . .88 A3
Poplar Tree Dr EX12 .192 A7
Popplestone Pk PL8. . .256 F5
Poppy Cl
  Exeter EX4 . . . . .176 D8
  Mile End TQ12. . . . . . .206 D5
  Tavistock PL19 . . . . . .171 A5
Popular EX7. . . . . .201 A2
Porch EX13. . . . . .88 A3
Porch Cotts **18** EX10. .101 B1
Porcher Dr EX5. . . . . .179 B3
Pork Hill PL19 . . . . . . .117 F1
Porlock Way TQ4 . . . . .225 F2

Porsham Cl PL6. . . . . .241 B1
Porsham La PL5 . . . . . .244 E8
Porspoder Pl PL10. . . .253 A2
Portal Pl PL21. . . . . . .237 B5
Portbridge Cross
  TQ9. . . . . .215 F8
Portchester Hts EX4 .261 C4
Port Cross
  Bishops Nympton
  EX36. . . . . .31 B4
  Kentisbury EX31. . . . . .10 F5
Porteous Cl PL1 . . . . . .247 F3
Porter's La EX8 . . . . . .195 E8
Porter Way PL7 . . . . . .242 C3
Portford Cross EX31 . . .27 C3
Portford La TQ10 . . . . .135 A2
PORTGATE. 106 C4
Portgate Cross EX36 . . .30 B8
Port Hill EX31. . . . . . . .10 F5
PORTINGTON 116 C3
Port La
  Bishops Nympton
  EX36. . . . . .31 C4
  Bury TA22 . . . . .34 A5
  Chillington TQ7 . . . . . .145 A1
  Wotter PL7. . . . . .132 C4
Portland Ave
  Exmouth EX8. . . . . . . .202 B6
  Teignmouth TQ14 . . . . .210 C7
Portland Bldgs **6**
  EX32. . . . . .155 A6
Portland Ct
  19 Barnstaple EX32 . . .155 A4
  Lyme Regis DT7 . . . . . .260 C3
  9 Plymouth PL1 . . . . .247 F3
  Torquay TQ1 . . . . .220 D7
Portland La
  Kilmington EX13 . . . . .103 C8
  Kilmington EX24 . . . . .103 C8
  Meavy PL20 . . . . .127 D2
Portland Pk EX34 . . . . .150 C6
Portland Rd
  Plymouth PL1 . . . . . . .247 F3
  Torquay TQ1 . . . . .220 D7
Portland Sq PL4 . . . . . .262 C4
Portland Sq La N
  PL3. . . . . .262 C4
Portland Square Lane N
  PL4. . . . . .263 A4
Portland St
  Barnstaple EX32. . . . . .155 B3
  Exeter EX1. . . . . .177 E6
  Ilfracombe EX34. . . . . .150 C6
Portland Villas PL4. . . .262 C4
Portledge Pl EX39. . . . .25 A3
Portlemore Cl TQ7. . . .147 E6
Portlemore Gdns
  TQ7. . . . . .147 E6
Portmarsh La EX32. . . .155 A4
Port Mer Cl EX8. . . . . .196 E3
Port Rd EX6 . . . . .200 D4
Portsmouth Arms Cross
  EX18. . . . . .60 B7
Portsmouth Arms Sta
  EX37. . . . . .43 F6
Portugal Way EX20. . . .170 D5
Portway EX15. . . . . . . .66 C7
Portway Cl PL9 . . . . . .256 D7
Portway Gdns EX15 . . .162 C3
POSBURY. 97 F8
Possession Cross
  EX37. . . . . .28 E7
Post Box Cross
  Bondleigh EX20. . . . . . .76 F6
  Cheriton Fitzpaine EX17 .63 B3
POSTBRIDGE. 120 A6
Postbury Pl EX1. . . . . .178 D7
Post Cl TA21. . . . . . . .160 E4
Post Coach Wy **19**
  EX5. . . . . .99 A6
Post Cross EX15 . . . . . .65 F2
Post Cross Bsns Pk
  EX15. . . . . .65 F2
Post Hill EX16. . . . . . . .64 E8
Post La
  Cotleigh EX14 . . . . . . .86 C7
  Malmsmead EX35. . . . . .6 C4
  Skilgate TA4 . . . . .34 E7
Post Office La
  Cheriton Fitzpaine
  EX17. . . . . .62 F1
  Tatworth TA20. . . . . . .88 C8
  Westleigh EX16 . . . . . .51 A4
Potacre St EX38. . . . . .159 D5
Potems' Cross EX35. . . .27 F1
Potshop Cross EX17. . . .79 D2
Potters Cotts **18** EX11. .168 D5
Potter's Cross TA4. . . . .35 C7
Potters Hill TQ1. . . . . .220 B5
Potters La TA20 . . . . . .69 E6
Potters Stile EX14. . . . .67 B1
Potters Way PL7 . . . . .250 D5
Potterswell EX31. . . . .154 B3
Potters Yd TQ12 . . . . .180 B1
Pottery Cl
  Bovey Tracey TQ13 . . . .180 C5
  Honiton EX14 . . . . . . .166 D6
Pottery Ct TQ6. . . . . . .233 D4
Pottery Est PL10 . . . . .252 E6
Pottery La EX31. . . . . .153 A4
Pottery Mews TQ3 . . . .218 D3
Pottery Rd
  Bovey Tracey TQ13 . . . .180 C5
  Kingsteignton TQ12 . . .207 D6
  Plymouth PL7 . . . . . . .250 D6
Pottery Units TQ12. . . .207 D4
POTTINGTON 154 C6

Pottington Bsns Pk
  EX31. . . . . .154 C6
Pottington Dr EX31 . . .154 C6
Pottington Ind Est
  EX31. . . . . .154 C5
Pottington Rd EX31. . . .154 C6
Pottles Cl EX6 . . . . . . .182 B3
POUGHILL 62 D3
Poultney Cl PL7. . . . . .251 A5
Pouncel La **15** EX5 . . . .99 A6
Pouncers Cross EX18. . .60 E6
Pound Cl
  Burrington EX37. . . . . .43 F3
  Exmouth EX8. . . . . . . .196 C1
  Sidbury EX10 . . . . . . .101 B3
  Topsham EX3 . . . . . . .182 E6
Pound Cnr
  Clyst Honiton EX5 . . . .179 E7
  Whitestone EX4 . . . . . .98 C5
Pound Cross EX5 . . . . . .99 B5
Pound Down Cnr EX4 . .98 D5
Pound Field TQ9 . . . . .227 F6
Pound Gate EX6 . . . . .112 F5
Pound Hill
  Axmouth EX12 . . . . . .192 D7
  Holcombe Rogus TA21. . .51 A5
Poundhouse Cross
  TQ6. . . . . .146 B8
Pound La
  Bridford EX6. . . . . . . .113 A5
  Buckland St Mary TA20. . .69 D8
  Colaton Raleigh EX10 . .186 C5
  15 Combe Martin EX34. . .3 A3
  Exmouth EX8. . . . . . . .196 C1
  High Bickington EX37 . . .43 C8
  Kentisbury EX31. . . . . .10 F5
  Kingskerswell TQ12 . . .212 F4
  Nadderwater EX4. . . . . .98 F4
  Parracombe EX31. . . . . .4 C2
  Parracombe EX31. . . . . .11 C8
  Raymond's Hill DT6. . . .104 D8
  Shaldon TQ14. . . . . . .209 C5
  Stoke Climsland PL17. . .115 C1
  5 Teignmouth TQ14. . .210 C4
  Topsham EX3 . . . . . . .182 E6
  Uplyme DT7 . . . . .260 B5
  Upottery EX14 . . . . . . .68 C1
  Woodbury EX5 . . . . . . .184 C3
  Yarcombe EX14. . . . . . .69 B2
Pound La End EX37 . . . .28 C3
Pound Lane End EX37 .43 D8
Pound Lane Trad Est
  EX8. . . . . .196 C1
Pound Mdw
  Great Torrington EX38 . .42 B7
  Hatherleigh EX20 . . . . .75 C7
  Parkham EX39 . . . . . . .39 E8
Pound Pk EX20 . . . . . .170 D6
Pound Pl
  Bovey Tracey TQ13 . . . .180 D8
  19 Newton Abbot
  TQ12. . . . . .207 B3
Pound Rd
  Axminster EX13 . . . . . .88 F2
  Crapstone PL20 . . . . . .126 E3
  Lyme Regis DT7 . . . . . .260 D3
Poundsclose EX14 . . . . .33 E4
Pound's Cross PL6. . . . .240 E5
POUNDSGATE. 130 A7
Poundsgate Cl TQ5 . . .230 E4
Pounds Hill EX17. . . . .165 D6
Poundshill Cross
  EX17. . . . . .165 D6
Poundsland EX5 . . . . . .175 C6
Pounds Park Rd
  1 Bere Alston PL20. . .125 E1
  Plymouth PL3 . . . . . . .248 D7
Pounds Pk PL12. . . . . .242 F3
Pound Sq EX15 . . . . . .163 C2
Pound St
  Exmouth EX8. . . . . . . .202 A6
  Lyme Regis DT7 . . . . . .260 D3
  Moretonhampstead
  TQ13. . . . . .111 F4
  Plymouth PL1 . . . . . . .254 A8
Poundstone Ct TQ8 . . .259 D4
Pound Terr **3** TA21. . .160 D5
Pound Wall EX4. . . . . .175 C6
Poundwell Ho **8**
  PL21. . . . . .137 B2
Poundwell Mdws **7**
  PL21. . . . . .137 B2
Poundwell St **9**
  PL21. . . . . .137 B2
Powderham Castle★
  EX6. . . . . .194 D4
Powderham Cl
  Newton Abbot TQ12 . . .207 B2
  Topsham EX3 . . . . . . .182 E6
Powderham Cres
  EX4. . . . . .177 D8
Powderham Ct
  20 Newton Abbot
  TQ12. . . . . .207 B3
  21 Teignmouth TQ14. . .210 C4
Powderham Rd
  Exeter EX2 . . . . .177 A4
  Newton Abbot TQ12 . . .207 B2
  Plymouth PL3 . . . . . . .248 F7
  Torquay TQ2 . . . . .213 C5
Powderham Terr
  Newton Abbot TQ12 . . .207 B2
  3 Shaldon TQ14. . . . .209 D6
Powderham Wlk EX6 181 F1
Powell Cl EX12. . . . . . .192 A6
Powells Way EX14 . . . .67 C1

Powis Gdns PL5. . . . . .244 B2
Powisland Dr PL6. . . . .245 A5
Powlers Piece Pk
  EX22. . . . . .39 C5
Powlesland La EX17. . . .95 C6
Powlesland Rd EX4 . . .177 B1
Powys Ho EX10 . . . . . .188 A4
Poyers EX33 . . . . .152 E4
Pratt's La TQ7 . . . . . . .143 B7
Precinct The TQ7. . . . .258 D6
Premier Pl EX2 . . . . . .261 C2
Prescot Rd EX4 . . . . . .176 E5
PRESCOTT. 51 C1
Prescott Rd EX15 . . . . .51 D1
Prestbury Ct EX4. . . . .176 D8
Prestbury Pk **4** TQ2 .219 F5
PRESTON. 226 B8
Preston Barns TQ9. . . .222 D1
Prestonbury Cl PL6 . . .245 B7
Preston Cross
  Loddiswell TQ7 . . . . . .138 E3
  West Alvington TQ7. . . .143 E2
Preston Down Ave
  TQ3. . . . . .219 B2
Preston Down Rd
  TQ3. . . . . .219 C1
Preston Fork TQ9 . . . .138 E2
Preston Gate EX31 . . . .10 E6
Preston La EX17 . . . . . .80 D7
Preston Prim Sch
  TQ2. . . . . .219 D2
Preston St EX1. . . . . . .261 A2
Preston Terr EX34 . . . .150 E3
Pretoria Rd EX1. . . . . .177 F7
Pretoria Terr EX34 . . .150 E3
Pretty Oak Main TA20 .69 F6
Pretty Top
  Little Torrington EX20. . .41 F1
  Petrockstow EX20 . . . . .56 F8
Prices Ave TA21 . . . . .160 D7
Prickly Ball Farm &
  Hedgehog Hospl★
  TQ12. . . . . .211 F7
Priddis Cl EX8 . . . . . . .196 C3
Priddles La TQ20 . . . . .69 F8
Prideaux Cl PL12. . . . .242 C5
Prideaux Cres EX16. . . .161 D6
Prideaux Ct **22** PL1. . .263 A2
Prideaux La TQ6 . . . . .145 F6
Prideaux Mdw EX3R . .159 F5
Prideaux Rd PL21. . . . .237 D5
Pridham La PL1. . . . . .248 D7
Pridhams Way EX6. . . .182 A4
PRIESTACOTT. 55 C1
Priest Hill EX15. . . . . .66 A3
Priesthood Terr
  PL10. . . . . .252 E5
Priestley Ave
  Exeter EX4 . . . . .178 B8
  Plymouth PL5 . . . . . . .243 E2
Prigg Mdw TQ13 . . . . .130 F4
Primley Cross TQ3 . . . .225 E5
Primley Ct TQ3 . . . . . .225 E5
Primley Gdns EX10. . . .188 C7
Primley Mead EX10 . . .188 C7
Primley Paddock
  EX10. . . . . .188 B7
Primley Park E TQ3 . . .226 A5
Primley Pk TQ3 . . . . . .225 F5
Primley Rd EX10. . . . . .188 B7
Primrose Ave EX32. . . .155 E4
Primrose Cl
  Chillington TQ7 . . . . . .144 F1
  Ivybridge PL21. . . . . . .237 D5
  Kingsteignton TQ12 . . .207 E2
  6 Tiverton EX16. . . . .161 F6
  Torpoint PL11. . . . . . . .246 E4
Primrose Dr
  Mile End TQ12. . . . . . .206 D5
  Newton Abbot TQ12 . . .206 D5
Primrose Gdns PL19 . .171 E4
Primrose La
  Northam EX39. . . . . . .157 B8
  Wrangaton TQ10 . . . . .134 E1
Primrose Lawn EX4 . . .176 D8
Primrose Mdw PL21. . .237 A6
Primrose Pk EX16. . . . .49 C8
Primrose Way
  Crediton EX17. . . . . . .165 E6
  Kingskerswell TQ12 . . .212 F6
  Seaton EX12 . . . . .192 B7
Primrose Wlk PL12. . . .242 D4
Prince Charles Cl
  EX8. . . . . .196 E1
Prince Charles Ct
  TQ2. . . . . .214 A3
Prince Charles Rd
  EX4. . . . . .177 F8
Prince Charles Way
  EX12. . . . . .192 A8
Prince Maurice Ct
  PL4. . . . . .263 B3
Prince Maurice Rd
  Plymouth PL3 . . . . . . .263 B4
  Plymouth PL4 . . . . . . .248 F6
Prince of Wales Dr
  Dartmouth TQ6 . . . . . .233 F4
  Exmouth EX8. . . . . . . .196 E1
Prince of Wales Rd
  Crediton EX17. . . . . . .165 C6
  Exeter EX4 . . . . .177 B8
  Kingsbridge TQ7 . . . . .258 C5
PRINCE ROCK 249 B1
Prince Rock Prim Sch
  PL4. . . . . .249 B2
Prince Rupert Way
  TQ12. . . . . .123 B2
Princes Ct **6** TQ1. . . .220 B6

Princes Point TQ1 . . .220 C3
Princes Rd
　Plymouth PL6 . . . . . . .245 E6
　Torquay TQ1 . . . . .220 B5
Princes Road E TQ1 . .220 C5
Princes Road W TQ1 .220 B5
Princess Alexandra Ct **9**
　EX4 . . . . .177 A5
Princess Ave
　Ilfracombe EX34 . . . . .150 C5
　Plymouth, Plymstock
　　PL9 . . . . .255 E6
　Plymouth, West Park
　　PL5 . . . . .244 A3
Princess Cotts TQ12 . .213 C6
Princess Cres PL9 . . . .255 E6
Princess Elizabeth Terr
　EX20 . . . . .107 F8
Princesshay Sh Ctr
　EX1 . . . . .261 B3
Prince's Sq EX2 . . . . .177 A3
Princess Rd
　Kingskerswell TQ12 . .213 A4
　Kingsteignton TQ12 . .207 D8
　13 Kingsteignton TQ13 .123 E1
Princess St
　Barnstaple EX32 . . . . .155 A6
　Ottery St Mary EX11 . .169 D3
　Plymouth PL1 . . . . . . .262 C2
Princess Street Ope
　PL1 . . . . .262 C2
Princes St
　16 Dawlish EX7 . . . . .204 D6
　23 Exmouth EX8 . . . . .202 A6
　Paignton TQ3 . . . . . . .226 B6
　Plymouth PL1 . . . . . . .247 E2
　Torquay TQ1 . . . . .220 D7
Princess Theatre ★
　TQ2 . . . . .220 B3
Prince's Street E EX2 177 A4
Prince's Street N
　EX2 . . . . .177 A4
Prince's Street S EX2 177 A4
Prince's Street W
　EX2 . . . . .177 A4
Princess Way PL1 . . . .262 C2
Prince St TQ12 . . . . . .207 C3
PRINCETOWN 128 B8
Princetown Com Prim
　Sch PL20 . . . . .128 A8
Princetown Rd PL20 . .127 B3
Prince William Ct **1**
　TQ5 . . . . .230 C4
Prince William Quay
　TQ5 . . . . .230 C5
Prings Ct **13** TQ5 . . .230 C5
Priorton Hill EX17 . . . .80 B7
Priorton La EX17 . . . . .80 B7
Priory
　Bovey Tracey TQ13 . . .180 C8
　Wellington TA21 . . . . .160 E6
Priory Ave
　Kingskerswell TQ12 . .213 A5
　Totnes TQ9 . . . . .223 C6
Priory Cl
　Barnstaple EX31 . . . . .154 F7
　East Budleigh EX9 . . .198 B7
　Ivybridge PL21 . . . . . .237 B5
　Tavistock PL19 . . . . . .171 D3
Priory Ct
　3 Totnes TQ9 . . . . .223 C6
　Wellington TA21 . . . . .160 E7
Priory Dr
　Plymouth PL7 . . . . . . .250 D5
　Totnes TQ9 . . . . .223 C6
Priory Gdns
　Barnstaple EX31 . . . . .154 F7
　1 Dawlish EX7 . . . . .204 E6
　Tavistock PL19 . . . . . .171 D3
　Totnes TQ9 . . . . .223 C6
　Wellington TA21 . . . . .160 E6
Priory Gn EX4 . . . . . . .178 A7
Priory Hill
　2 Dawlish EX7 . . . . .204 E6
　Totnes TQ9 . . . . .223 C6
Priory La EX6 . . . . . . .113 B4
Priory Lawn Terr
　PL3 . . . . .249 A6
Priory Mill PL7 . . . . . .250 D5
Priory Park Rd **13**
　EX7 . . . . .204 D6
Priory RC Prim Sch **3**
　TQ1 . . . . .220 B8
Priory Rd
　Abbotskerswell
　　TQ12 . . . . .212 C7
　Barnstaple EX31 . . . . .154 F7
　Dawlish EX7 . . . . .204 E6
　Exeter EX4 . . . . .177 E8
　Plymouth PL3 . . . . . . .249 A6
　Tiverton EX16 . . . . . .161 F6
　Torquay TQ1 . . . . .220 B8
Priory Ridge PL7 . . . . .250 D5
Priory St TQ6 . . . . .234 D4
Priory Terr **7** TQ9 . . .223 C6
Priory The
　Abbotskerswell
　　TQ12 . . . . .212 C7
　3 Modbury PL21 . . .137 B2
Priory View
　Cornworthy TQ9 . . . . .227 B4
　Exeter EX1 . . . . .178 E4
Priory Wall Cross
　EX15 . . . . .66 B2
Prisam La EX20 . . . . . .75 E2
Prisam Lane Cross
　EX20 . . . . .75 F2
Priscott Way TQ12 . . .207 E6
Prispen Dr EX5 . . . . . .82 B6

Prispen Ho EX5 . . . . . .82 B6
Prispen View EX5 . . . .82 B6
PRISTACOTT 27 C5
PRIXFORD 16 C7
Prixford EX31 . . . . . . .16 C7
Promenade
　Ilfracombe EX34 . . . . .150 B6
　Kingsbridge TQ7 . . . . .258 D5
　Paignton TQ3 . . . . . . .226 D8
　Paignton, Goodrington
　　TQ4 . . . . .226 C4
　Teignmouth TQ14 . . . .210 C4
Prospect EX7 . . . . .204 E6
Prospect Cnr EX31 . . . .27 A7
Prospect Cotts EX35 . .151 B5
Prospect Cres EX15 . . .66 A7
Prospect Gdns **2**
　EX4 . . . . .177 E7
Prospect Hill
　Okehampton EX20 . . . .170 B4
　Slapton TQ7 . . . . .145 C4
Prospect La PL12 . . . .242 C3
Prospect Pk EX4 . . . . .177 D8
Prospect Pl
　Barnstaple EX32 . . . . .155 B3
　Exeter EX4 . . . . .177 A4
　Ottery St Mary EX11 . .169 D3
　Plymouth PL1 . . . . . . .262 B2
　5 Tiverton EX16 . . . .161 B4
Prospect Rd **3** TQ5 . .230 C5
Prospect Row PL1 . . . .247 E1
Prospect St PL4 . . . . . .263 A3
Prospect Terr
　Gunnislake PL18 . . . . .125 D6
　Gunnislake, St Ann's Chapel
　　PL18 . . . . .125 B5
　Newton Abbot TQ12 . . .207 C3
Prospect Way EX17 . . . .60 D3
Prospect Wlk PL12 . . .242 C3
Protector Rd TQ12 . . .244 D2
Prouse Ave TQ13 . . . . .111 A6
Prouse Cres PL12 . . . .248 C8
Prouse Rise PL12 . . . .242 E2
Providence Pl
　Calstock PL18 . . . . . . .125 D3
　Lyme Regis DT7 . . . . .260 D3
　Plymouth PL1 . . . . . . .248 A3
Providence Row **15**
　EX39 . . . . .157 A2
Providence St PL4 . . . .263 A4
Provident Cl TQ5 . . . . .230 E5
Prowse La
　East Village EX17 . . . .80 C8
　Lapford EX17 . . . . .60 D3
Prowses EX15 . . . . . . .67 B8
Prowse's La EX16 . . . . .63 E1
Prustacott Rd EX23 . . .70 E8
Pryn Ct PL1 . . . . .262 A3
Prynne Cl PL1 . . . . . . .262 A3
Puckridge Rd EX4 . . . .174 D2
PUDDAVEN 223 A8
Puddavine Terr TQ9 . .223 A8
PUDDINGTON 62 B5
PUDDINGTON
　BOTTOM 62 B4
Pudleylake Rd
　Axminster EX13 . . . . .167 B1
　Musbury EX13 . . . . . .103 E6
Puffin Cl TQ2 . . . . . . .213 C2
Puffin Ct EX39 . . . . . . .156 C6
Puffin Way EX2 . . . . . .176 D3
Pugsley Rd **9** EX16 . .64 D7
Pulchrass St **11** EX12 .155 A4
Pullen's Row EX16 . . . .46 E1
Pulleys Cl EX17 . . . . . .143 C6
Pulling Rd EX4 . . . . . .174 D2
Pullins Terr **10** TQ13 .123 E6
Pulpit Wlk EX2 . . . . . .181 C7
Pump Field Cl EX15 . . .67 C1
Pump La
　Abbotsham EX39 . . . . .156 A2
　Lympstone EX8 . . . . . .195 D4
Pump St
　4 Brixham TQ5 . . . . .230 D5
　Newton St Cyres EX5 . .172 A8
Punchards Down
　TQ9 . . . . .222 F6
Purbeck Ave TQ2 . . . . .219 D2
Purcell Ct EX2 . . . . . . .178 C5
Purcombe Cross
　TQ13 . . . . .131 D3
Purlbridge Cross
　EX24 . . . . .102 D6
Purzebrook Cl EX13 . .167 D5
Purzebrook Cotts
　EX13 . . . . .167 D5
PUSEHILL 156 B5
Pusehill Rd EX39 . . . . .156 B5
PUTSBOROUGH 7 F3
Putsborough Cl EX33 . . .8 A2
Putsborough Rd EX33 . . .7 F3
Putshole La EX38 . . . . .40 E1
Putson Cross EX16 . . . .64 E8
Putts Cnr EX10 . . . . . .101 C7
Pye Cnr
　Brampford Speke EX5 . .81 D1
　Cullompton EX15 . . . .163 C3
　Kennford EX6 . . . . . . .181 B2
Pye La TA20 . . . . .88 E8
Pykes Down PL21 . . . .237 F4
Pyles Thorne TA21 . . .160 F4
Pyles Thorne Cl
　TA21 . . . . .160 E5
Pyles Thorne Rd
　TA21 . . . . .160 E4
Pym St
　Plymouth PL1 . . . . . . .247 F3
　Plymouth PL5 . . . . . . .247 F4

Pym St continued
　Tavistock PL19 . . . . . .171 C6
Pyne Gdns EX5 . . . . . .173 A7
Pyne Meadow Cross
　EX18 . . . . .44 D3
Pynes Cl
　Cheriton Fitzpaine
　　EX17 . . . . .62 E1
　East Budleigh EX9 . . .198 B6
Pynes Hill EX2 . . . . . .178 C2
Pynes Hill Bsns Pk
　EX2 . . . . .178 C3
Pynes La EX39 . . . . . .156 E1
Pynes Wlk EX39 . . . . . .25 E4
Pynsent Ct **4** TQ13 . .123 E6
Pyramids Swimming & L
　Ctr The EX1 . . . . .261 C3
Pytte Gdns EX3 . . . . . .183 C7
Pytte Ho EX3 . . . . .183 C7
PYWORTHY 71 C5
Pyworthy CE Prim Sch
　EX22 . . . . .71 D5

Q

Quadrangle The EX4 .177 C8
Quadrant The EX2 . . .261 C2
Quagmire La EX22 . . .164 C7
Quaker Lane PL3 . . . .248 E5
Quantock Rd TA21 . . .160 D7
Quantocks EX33 . . . . .152 B6
Quantocks Rd TQ2 . . .219 C3
Quant Pk PL19 . . . . . .171 C6
Quarries La EX37 . . . . .43 C7
Quarries The EX4 . . . .176 D4
Quarry Cl
　Bideford EX39 . . . . . .156 C2
　Totnes TQ9 . . . . .222 F6
　Totnes TQ9 . . . . .223 A6
Quarry Cotts
　Beer EX12 . . . . .191 B5
　Plymouth PL1 . . . . . . .262 A3
　Plymouth, Honicknowle
　　PL5 . . . . .244 B2
Quarry Ct EX16 . . . . . .161 D4
Quarryfields EX20 . . . .170 C6
Quarry Foot Cross
　EX17 . . . . .79 C4
Quarry Gdns TQ3 . . . .226 A7
Quarry Hts EX4 . . . . . .174 C2
Quarry La
　Beer EX12 . . . . .191 B5
　Down St Mary EX17 . . .78 F6
　Exeter EX1 . . . . .178 E4
　Exeter EX2 . . . . .178 C4
　Gunnislake PL18 . . . . .125 C6
　Silverton EX5 . . . . .82 B5
　Thorverton EX5 . . . . . .81 D4
Quarryman Cl **4**
　EX16 . . . . .49 B8
Quarry Park Ave PL9 .255 D7
Quarry Park Rd
　Exeter EX2 . . . . .178 C4
　Plymouth, Peverell
　　PL3 . . . . .248 D5
　Plymouth, Plymstock
　　PL9 . . . . .255 D7
Quarry Rd EX37 . . . . . .43 B7
Quarry St PL11 . . . . . .247 C3
Quarry Wood Ct **6**
　TQ3 . . . . .225 F1
Quarterdeck The
　PL1 . . . . .254 A8
Quarter Mile La PL5 . . .99 D3
Quartley Hill EX16 . . . .34 E4
Quartz Row EX4 . . . . .174 C2
Quayfield Rd EX34 . . .150 C6
Quay Hill EX1, EX2 . . .261 A2
Quay House Visitor Ctr ★
　EX2 . . . . .261 B2
Quay La
　Instow EX39 . . . . .15 B1
　Lympstone EX8 . . . . . .195 D4
Quay Rd
　Newton Abbot TQ12 . . .207 D3
　Plymouth PL1 . . . . . . .263 A2
　Teignmouth TQ14 . . . .210 B4
Quayside **6** PL19 . . .171 B5
Quayside L Ctr TQ7 . .258 D4
Quay Terr TQ12 . . . . . .207 D3
Quay The
　Appledore EX39 . . . . . .15 A1
　Ashprington TQ9 . . . . .139 F7
　Bideford EX39 . . . . . .157 A2
　Brixham TQ5 . . . . . . .230 D5
　Dartmouth TQ6 . . . . . .233 F3
　Dittisham TQ6 . . . . . . .228 D2
　Exeter EX2 . . . . .261 B2
　Ilfracombe EX34 . . . . .150 C6
　Plymouth PL9 . . . . . . .255 C7
　Salcombe TQ8 . . . . . . .259 C6
Quay View EX31 . . . . . .153 E6
Quay View Sch PL18 . .125 D3
Queen Annes **14**
　EX39 . . . . .157 A2
Queen Annes Copse
　TQ12 . . . . .206 F1
Queen Anne's Ct **14**
　EX31 . . . . .154 F5
Queen Anne's Mews **13**
　EX31 . . . . .154 F5
Queen Anne's Quay
　PL4 . . . . .263 B2
QUEEN DART 47 C3
Queen Dart Cross
　EX16 . . . . .47 B4
Queen Dart Hill EX16 . .47 B3

Queen Elizabeth Ave
　TQ6 . . . . .233 E4
Queen Elizabeth Ct
　EX39 . . . . .156 C6
Queen Elizabeth Dr
　Crediton EX17 . . . . . .165 A6
　Paignton TQ3 . . . . . . .225 E6
Queen Elizabeth's Sch,
　Barnfield Campus
　EX17 . . . . .165 B5
Queen Elizabeth's Sch,
　Western Road Campus
　EX17 . . . . .165 B6
Queen La **8** EX7 . . . .204 D6
Queen's Ave EX34 . . .150 C5
Queens Cl
　Kingsteignton TQ12 . .207 F8
　Plymouth PL6 . . . . . . .245 E6
　Westward Ho! EX39 . . .156 C7
Queen's Cres
　Brixham TQ5 . . . . . . .230 D3
　Exeter EX4 . . . . .261 B4
Queens Ct **25** EX24 . .103 A4
Queen's Ct **12** EX24 . .202 A6
Queen's Dr EX8 . . . . . .202 C5
Queen's Dr The EX4 . .177 B8
Queen's Gate
　Plymouth, Lipson PL4 .263 B4
　Plymouth, Stoke PL3 . .262 A4
Queen's Gate Mews
　PL4 . . . . .263 B4
Queen's Gate Villas
　PL4 . . . . .263 B4
Queenshays EX20 . . . . .95 A5
Queen's Ho **6** EX32 . .155 A5
Queensland Dr EX4 . . .173 E2
Queen's Park Rd TQ4 .226 C6
Queens Pk EX17 . . . . . .80 D4
Queen's Pk EX22 . . . . .55 C1
Queen Sq EX15 . . . . . .163 C3
Queens Rd
　Exeter EX2 . . . . .261 A1
　Plymouth PL5 . . . . . . .243 F3
　Wellington TA21 . . . . .160 E4
Queen's Rd
　Brixham TQ5 . . . . . . .230 C6
　Budleigh Salterton EX9 197 F2
　Moretonhampstead
　　TQ13 . . . . .111 F5
　Paignton TQ4 . . . . . . .226 C6
　Plymouth PL4 . . . . . . .263 B4
Queen's Sq
　Broadclyst EX5 . . . . . .175 C7
　8 Colyton EX24 . . . .103 A4
Queen St
　Barnstaple EX31 . . . . .154 F5
　Barnstaple EX32 . . . . .155 A5
　Bideford EX39 . . . . . .157 A2
　Budleigh Salterton
　　EX9 . . . . .199 G2
　9 Colyton EX24 . . . .103 A4
　Dawlish EX7 . . . . .204 D6
　Exeter EX4 . . . . .261 A3
　11 Exmouth EX8 . . . .202 A6
　17 Honiton EX14 . . . .166 C6
　Lynton EX35 . . . . .151 C5
　Newton Abbot TQ12 . . .207 D3
　Northlew EX20 . . . . . . .74 E2
　Plymouth PL1 . . . . . . .247 D2
　Seaton EX12 . . . . .192 A5
　South Molton EX36 . . .158 C4
　13 Teignmouth TQ14 . .210 B4
　Tiverton EX16 . . . . . .161 C3
　Torquay TQ1 . . . . .220 B5
　Winkleigh EX19 . . . . . .58 F3
Queen's Terr
　Exeter EX4 . . . . .261 A4
　Great Torrington EX38 .159 B5
　Stoke Canon EX5 . . . . .81 F1
　4 Torquay TQ1 . . . . .223 C6
Queensway
　Newton Abbot TQ12 . . .207 E2
　Tiverton EX16 . . . . . .161 F5
　Torquay TQ2 . . . . .219 D6
Queensway Cl TQ2 . . .219 E7
Queensway Cres TQ2 219 E7
Queensway Ho TQ12 .207 E2
Queensway RC Prim Sch
　TQ2 . . . . .219 D7
Queens Wlk DT7 . . . . .260 E4
Quentin Ave TQ5 . . . .230 B2
Quern Rise EX1 . . . . . .175 B1
Questant La EX10 . . . .188 C6
Quicks Wlk EX38 . . . . .159 F5
Quilletts The TQ7 . . . .147 E6
Quince Cross
　South Molton EX36 . . . .46 B8
　Spreyton EX17 . . . . . . .96 C7
Quince Hill EX36 . . . . .31 A1
Quince Honey Farm ★
　EX36 . . . . .158 C5
Quinnel Ho **7** TQ14 .210 B5
Quinta Cl TQ1 . . . . . . .220 C6
Quinta Ct TQ1 . . . . . . .220 C7
Quinta Rd TQ1 . . . . . .220 D6
Quintet Cl EX1 . . . . . . .178 C5
Quirk Hill EX16 . . . . . .63 D7
QUODITCH 91 A8
Quoditch Cross EX21 . .73 B1
Quoitgate Cross EX22 .38 D3

R

Raceworld Karting ★
　EX5 . . . . .184 D8
Rackclose La EX4 . . . .261 A2
RACKENFORD 47 D5

Rackenford CE Prim Sch
　EX16 . . . . .47 D5
Rackenford Cross
　EX16 . . . . .47 D5
Rackenford Rd
　Tiverton EX16 . . . . . .161 A6
　Witheridge EX16 . . . . .46 E1
Rackfield
　Rockwell Green
　　TA21 . . . . .160 A5
　6 Tiverton EX16 . . . .161 C3
Rackfield Cotts EX4 . .176 F8
Rackfield Ct EX32 . . . .154 F6
Rackfield Dr EX15 . . . . .67 C8
Rackleigh La EX17 . . . .46 A2
Rackmead EX37 . . . . . .28 F4
Rack Park St EX38 . . . .159 C5
Rack Park Rd TQ7 . . . .258 D5
Rack St EX1 . . . . .261 A2
Radar Rd PL6 . . . . . . .245 B5
Radcliffe Ct TQ3 . . . . .226 C7
Raddenstile Ct EX8 . . .202 B6
Raddenstile La EX8 . . .202 B6
Raddick La PL20 . . . . .127 F5
Raddicombe Cl TQ5 . .234 F8
Raddicombe Dr TQ5 . .234 F8
Raddicombe Farm
　TQ5 . . . . .234 F8
Raddicombe La TQ5 . .234 F8
RADDINGTON 35 B4
RADDON 81 D4
Raddon Cross EX17 . . .81 A5
Raddon Down Cross
　EX17 . . . . .79 D4
Raddon Hill EX17 . . . . .81 A6
Raddon Top EX17 . . . . .81 A6
Radford Ave PL4 . . . . .249 B1
Radford Grange EX7 . .204 A7
Radford Ho **11** TQ4 . .226 B6
Radford La PL10 . . . . .252 D4
Radford Park Dr PL9 . .255 D6
Radford Park Rd PL9 .255 D6
Radford Rd
　Exeter EX2 . . . . .261 C2
　Plymouth PL1 . . . . . . .262 B1
Radfords Orch TQ9 . . .131 E1
Radfordsturf EX5 . . . . .99 C6
Radfords Turf
　Cranbrook EX5 . . . . . . .99 C5
　Rockbeare EX5 . . . . . . .99 C6
Radford Way EX20 . . .170 E6
Radiant Ho PL1 . . . . . .262 B2
Radish La EX12 . . . . . .102 A2
Radley Cross EX36 . . . .30 D2
Radnidge La EX16 . . . .32 D4
Radnor Hall PL4 . . . . .263 A3
Radnor Pl
　Exeter EX2 . . . . .261 C2
　Plymouth PL4 . . . . . . .263 A3
Radnor St PL4 . . . . . . .263 A3
Radnor Villa EX2 . . . . .261 C2
Radsbury La EX35 . . . . .5 B3
Radshall Pk EX39 . . . .156 F4
Radway EX10 . . . . .188 B4
Radway Ct TQ14 . . . . .209 A8
Radway Gdns TQ14 . .209 A8
Radway Hill TQ14 . . . .209 A8
Radway La EX7 . . . . . .187 A1
Radway St TQ14 . . . . .209 A8
Ragged Field La EX34 . .8 E5
Ragged La EX37 . . . . . .44 B1
Ragg La EX9 . . . . .199 G2
Rag La
　Aylesbeare EX5 . . . . . . .99 C5
　Colebrooke EX17 . . . . .79 A2
　Yarcombe EX14 . . . . . .69 A2
Raglan Ct PL1 . . . . . . .247 F2
Raglan Gdns PL1 . . . .247 F2
Raglan Rd PL1 . . . . . . .247 F2
Raglans EX2 . . . . .181 C8
Railway Cotts
　Plymouth PL9 . . . . . . .255 D7
　Tavistock PL19 . . . . . .171 B6
Railway Terr
　3 Bideford EX39 . . . .157 B1
　Broadclyst EX5 . . . . . .175 C3
Rainbow Ct TQ2 . . . . .219 E7
Rainbow La
　Biscombe TA3 . . . . . . .67 F8
　Biscombe TA3 . . . . . . .68 A7
Rainsbury Hill TA4 . . .34 F8
Raisey La TA20 . . . . . . .69 F7
Rake Cnr TQ7 . . . . . . .143 F6
Rakeham Cotts EX38 . .41 B6
Rakeham Hill EX38 . . . .41 B6
Rakelane Cross TQ7 . .143 F6
RALEIGH 155 A7
Raleigh Ave TQ2 . . . . .219 D6
Raleigh Cl
　Dartmouth TQ6 . . . . . .233 D3
　Sidmouth EX10 . . . . . .188 B7
　South Molton EX36 . . .158 C4
　Torquay TQ2 . . . . .219 D6
Raleigh Cotts **3**
　EX31 . . . . .155 A7
Raleigh Ct
　Budleigh Salterton
　　EX9 . . . . .198 B5
　Plymouth PL7 . . . . . . .251 B6
　Torquay TQ2 . . . . .219 D6
Raleigh Dr
　Cullompton EX15 . . . .163 C4

Raleigh Dr continued
　Paignton TQ4 . . . . . . .226 B2
RALEIGH HILL 156 E4
Raleigh Hill
　Bideford, Raleigh Hill
　　EX39 . . . . .156 E4
　Bideford, Silford EX39 .156 D5
Raleigh Ho
　Exeter EX2 . . . . .261 C2
　Ottery St Mary EX11 . .169 D3
　1 Sidmouth EX10 . . .188 B7
Raleigh Hts EX31 . . . .154 F7
Raleigh Lawn EX31 . . .154 F7
Raleigh Mdw EX31 . . .155 A7
Raleigh Mead EX36 . .158 C4
Raleigh Pk EX36 . . . . .158 C4
Raleigh Rd
　Budleigh Salterton
　　EX9 . . . . .198 B2
　Dartmouth TQ6 . . . . . .233 E4
　Exeter EX1 . . . . .261 C2
　Exmouth EX8 . . . . . . .202 A6
　Ivybridge PL21 . . . . . .237 A6
　Newton Abbot TQ12 . . .207 F3
　Ottery St Mary EX11 . .169 E4
　Salcombe TQ8 . . . . . . .259 D4
　Teignmouth TQ14 . . . .210 A8
Raleigh St PL1 . . . . . . .262 B3
Raleigh View EX39 . . .157 A3
Raleigh Works EX31 . .154 E4
Raligh Mead EX36 . . .158 C4
Ralph Cl EX33 . . . . . . .152 B6
Ralph Rd EX33 . . . . . . .152 B6
Ralph's Ct PL19 . . . . . .171 B5
Ramage Cl PL6 . . . . . .245 F3
RAME 140 H2
Ramehead Cotts
　PL10 . . . . .140 H1
Ramehead La PL10 . . .140 H2
Rame La
　Cawsand PL10 . . . . . . .252 F1
　Rame PL10 . . . . .140 H2
Ramillies Ave PL5 . . . .244 A4
Ramparts Wlk TQ9 . . .223 C5
Ramsden La EX14 . . . . .86 A3
Ramsey Gdns PL5 . . . .244 D1
Ramsey La
　Runnington TA21 . . . . .51 F8
　Sampford Courtenay
　　EX20 . . . . .76 F3
Ramshill Cross TQ3 . .225 E8
Ramshill Rd TQ3 . . . . .225 E8
Ramsley EX20 . . . . .95 B4
Ramsoms Ct EX31 . . . .154 F8
Rance Dr EX8 . . . . . . .196 E3
Randell's Green EX8 . .202 E6
Randolph Cl PL5 . . . . .244 E3
Randolph Ct TQ12 . . .207 A4
Randwick Park Rd
　PL9 . . . . .255 D7
Ranelagh Rd EX20 . . .170 A5
Rangers Cl TQ11 . . . . .236 B4
Ranjan Pl EX1 . . . . . . .174 F2
Ranscombe Cl TQ5 . . .230 E5
Ranscombe Ct **9**
　TQ5 . . . . .230 D5
Ranscombe Hill
　TQ12 . . . . .123 E8
Ranscombe Rd TQ5 . .230 D5
Ransum Way PL19 . . .171 B4
Raphael Cl PL9 . . . . . .256 B5
Raphael Dr PL9 . . . . . .256 B4
Rapscott Cross EX36 . .18 F1
Rapscott Hill EX36 . . . .18 F1
Rashleigh Ave
　Plymouth PL7 . . . . . . .250 F7
　Saltash PL12 . . . . .242 D1
Rashleigh La EX18 . . . .59 D7
Ratcliffe Sch EX7 . . . .204 C4
Rathlin TQ1 . . . . .220 C7
Rathmore Rd TQ2 . . . .219 F4
Ratsloe Cross EX4 . . . .174 D8
RATSLOE 174 D8
Ratsloe Cross EX4 . . . .174 D8
Rattenbury Cotts
　EX12 . . . . .191 C6
Rattenbury Cross
　EX19 . . . . .76 A8
RATTERY 135 D4
Rattle St TQ13 . . . . . .113 D1
Ravelin Gdns **5**
　EX32 . . . . .155 B5
Ravelin Manor Rd
　EX32 . . . . .155 B5
Raven Cl
　Drakewalls PL18 . . . . .125 C5
　Exeter EX4 . . . . .173 C1
Ravenglass Cl PL6 . . . .245 D2
Ravensbourne La
　TQ6 . . . . .146 B7
Ravensbury Dr TQ6 . .234 A2
Rawlin Cl PL6 . . . . . . .249 C8
Rawlyn Rd TQ2 . . . . . .219 E4
Rawnsley La EX34 . . . . .7 F6
RAWRIDGE 68 C1
Rawridge Rd TA3 . . . . .68 C2
Rayer Rd **13** EX16 . . .64 D7
RAYMOND'S HILL 104 C7
Raymond Way PL7 . . .250 D6
Rayners PL6 . . . . .181 A1
Raynham Rd
　Plymouth PL3 . . . . . . .248 B4
　Plymouth PL3 . . . . . . .262 A4
Rea Barn Cl TQ5 . . . . .230 D4
Rea Barn Rd TQ5 . . . . .230 D4

Read Cl EX8 . . . . .196 C1
Reading Wlk PL5 . . . .244 C4
Rea Dr TQ5 . . . . .230 D5
Recreation Rd PL2 . . .248 C7
Recreation Road Ind Est
  PL2 . . . . .248 C7
Recreation Way PL7. .132 F4
Rectory Cl
  Filleigh EX32. . . . . .29 B6
  9 Whimple EX5 . . . . . .99 E8
  Willand EX15 . . . . .162 D4
  Wrafton EX33 . . . . .152 F4
Rectory Close Cross
  EX33. . . . . .152 F3
Rectory Cross TQ10 . .138 A7
Rectory Dr EX2 . . . . . . .181 B8
Rectory Hill
  Berrynarbor EX34. . . . . . .2 D3
  Cheriton Fitzpaine EX17 . 62 E1
  Sampford Courtenay
  EX20 . . . . .76 E3
Rectory La
  Dittisham TQ6. . . . . .228 C2
  Meshaw EX16 . . . . .46 A6
  Parkham EX39 . . . . .39 E8
  Stoke Fleming TQ6 . . . .146 B7
  Yelland EX39. . . . . .15 C2
Rectory Pk EX39 . . . . . .156 F2
Rectory Rd
  Ashbrittle TA21 . . . . .50 F8
  Bridestowe EX20. . . . . . .107 F8
  Buckland St Mary TA20 . 69 D8
  Combe Martin EX34 . . . . .3 A3
  Combe Martin EX34 . . . . 10 A8
  Dolton EX19 . . . . .57 F7
  East Ogwell TQ12 . . . . .211 E8
  Morchard Bishop EX17 . .61 A2
  Plymouth PL1 . . . . .248 A2
Rectory Rise EX20. . . . .56 F4
Recycling Way PL7. . . .136 A6
RED BALL 51 C4
Red Brook Cl TQ4 . . . .226 C1
Redburn Cl TQ3. . . . . . .226 A7
Redburn Rd TQ3. . . . . . .226 A7
Redcliff Ct EX9 . . . . . . .199 G2
Redcliffe Rd EX1 . . . . . .214 C1
Redcliffes The EX20. . .106 E5
RED COW VILLAGE. . . .177 A8
Redcroft Heights
  TQ6. . . . . .146 B7
Red Cross
  Colyton EX24 . . . . .102 F6
  Raymond's Hill EX13. . .104 C7
  Silverton EX5. . . . . .82 C5
Red Cross Hill EX17 . . .165 E6
Reddacleave Kiln Cross
  TQ11. . . . . .135 A6
Reddaway Dr EX6. . . . .182 A4
Reddenhill Rd TQ1. . . .220 C7
Red Devon Ct **10**
  . . . . .137 B2
Reddicliff Cl PL9. . . . . .255 E6
Reddicliffe Mws
  EX20. . . . . .106 E5
Reddicliffes The
  EX20. . . . . .106 E5
Reddicliff Rd PL9. . . . . .255 D5
Reddington Rd PL3 . . .249 B7
Redford Cross TQ7. . . .258 A8
Redford Way TQ7 . . . . .258 C5
Red Gate
  King's Nympton EX37 . . .44 E8
  Winkleigh EX19. . . . . . . .58 D2
Redgate Cl TQ1 . . . . . . .220 D6
Redgate La EX16 . . . . . .50 C5
Redhill Cl PL5 . . . . .243 E4
Redhill Cotts EX11 . . . .169 F6
REDHILLS. 176 E5
Redhills
  Budleigh Salterton
  EX9. . . . . .199 G2
  Exeter EX4 . . . . .176 E6
Redhills Cl EX4 . . . . . . .176 E6
Redhills Com Prim Sch
  EX4. . . . . .176 F6
Red Ho The EX17. . . . . .165 B5
Red House Cl **9**
  TQ13. . . . . .123 C4
Red La
  Churchinford TA3. . . . . . .68 C7
  Hatherleigh EX20 . . . . . .75 C7
  Hemyock EX15. . . . . .52 E3
  Raymond's Hill EX13 . . .104 C6
Redlake TQ9. . . . . .222 F8
Redlake Cross TQ9. . . .222 F8
Redlake Trad Est
  PL21. . . . . .137 B7
Redland Cross EX18. . .58 F7
Redlands EX16 . . . . . . .161 F4
Redlands Cl EX4 . . . . . .178 A8
Redlands Ct TQ3 . . . . . .225 F7
Redlands Rd EX31. . . . .153 F5
Redlands The EX10. . . .188 A3
REDLANE. 68 C7
Redlane Cross D77. . . .104 C6
Redlap Cross TQ6 . . . .146 C8
Redlap La TQ6 . . . . .146 B7
Redlap Rd TQ6 . . . . .146 C8
Red Lion Hill PL8. . . . .257 B5
Red Lion La EX1, EX4. .261 C4
Red Lion Pl **7** TQ4 . . .204 D6
Red Lion Yard EX20 . . .170 B5
REDMONSFORD. 38 C2
Redmoor Cl PL19 . . . . .171 A7

Redoubt Hill TQ6 . . . . .234 B3
RED POST 70 E8
Redpost Cross
  North Tawton EX20 . . . . .76 F5
  Sampford Courtenay
  EX20. . . . . .76 E5
Red Post Cross
  Burrington EX37. . . . . . . .43 F4
  Totnes TQ9 . . . . .217 C4
Red Rock EX5. . . . . .81 E2
Red Rock Rd EX5. . . . . .81 D1
Redruth Cl PL5 . . . . . . .244 A5
Redside Terr EX5 . . . . .172 E5
Redstart Cl TQ12. . . . . .206 F1
Redvers EX17 . . . . .165 E4
Redvers Gr PL7 . . . . . . .250 E4
Redvers Ho **7** EX17 . .165 C5
Redvers Rd EX4. . . . . . .177 A5
Redvers Way **5**
  EX16. . . . . .161 E6
Redwalls Mdw TQ6. . .233 E4
Redwell La TQ3 . . . . . . .225 F8
Redwell Rd TQ3. . . . . . .225 F8
Redwing Dr PL6 . . . . . .245 D8
Redwood Cl
  Bovey Tracey TQ13 . . . .180 C4
  Exmouth EX8. . . . . .196 D3
  10 Hemyock EX15. . . .67 B8
  4 Honiton EX14 . . . . .85 C2
Redwood Dr
  Loddiswell TQ7 . . . . . . .143 E7
  Plymouth PL7. . . . . .251 B5
Redwood Rd EX10 . . . .188 C5
Redwoods TQ13 . . . . . .180 C5
Redworth Terr TQ9 . . .223 C6
Redyeates Cross EX17 63 A2
Reed Mdw EX20. . . . . . .75 C7
Reeds Barn EX13. . . . . .88 F1
Reed's Cross
  Ashill EX15. . . . . .66 C6
  Bittadon EX31. . . . . .9 E4
Reedsdown Cross
  EX17. . . . . .79 F6
Reeds Pl EX15 . . . . . . .163 C3
Reed Vale TQ12. . . . . . .210 A5
Reed Walk EX2 . . . . . . .182 C7
REEDY. 113 A8
Reedy Hill EX6. . . . . . . .112 F8
Reeveacre Cross
  TQ9. . . . . .216 D5
Reeves Cl **3** TQ9. . . . .223 D5
Reeves Rd The TQ2 . . .219 D5
Reeves Way TQ7 . . . . . .143 D4
Reflections Rd PL4. . . .155 B6
Reform St **3** EX31 . . .154 F6
Regal Ct
  Exeter EX1 . . . . .178 E2
  Saltash PL12. . . . . .242 F2
Regard Cl TQ5 . . . . .230 E5
Regency Cres EX8 . . . .202 C6
Regency Ct **8** EX34 . .150 B5
Regency Dr EX31 . . . . .178 D1
Regency Gate EX10 . . .188 C5
Regent Cl
  Barnstaple EX31. . . . . . .154 C2
  Fremington EX31 . . . . . .153 F5
  Torquay TQ2 . . . . .219 E8
Regent Ct PL4 . . . . .263 A3
Regent Pl EX34 . . . . . . .150 B6
Regents Cl TQ4 . . . . . . .226 C5
Regents Gate EX8. . . . .202 B6
Regents Gdns **6**
  TQ14. . . . . .210 C4
Regent's Pk EX1 . . . . . .177 E6
Regent Sq EX1. . . . . . . .177 F5
Regent St
  Dawlish EX7 . . . . .204 D6
  Exeter EX2 . . . . .177 A3
  Plymouth PL4 . . . . .263 A3
  18 Teignmouth TQ14. . .210 C4
Regis Ct EX10. . . . . .188 C4
Reigate Rd PL9 . . . . . . .255 E8
Reme Dr EX14 . . . . .85 C2
Rena Hobson Ct
  EX16. . . . . .161 F3
Renaissance Gdns
  PL2. . . . . .248 C7
Rendells Mdw TQ13 . .180 E7
Rendlesham Gdns
  PL6. . . . . .245 E3
Rendle St PL1 . . . . .262 B3
Rennes Dr EX4 . . . . . . .173 C1
Rennes Ho EX1 . . . . . . .178 B7
Renney Rd
  Down Thomas PL9. . . . .255 C1
  Heybrook Bay PL9. . . . .140 B8
Rennie Ave PL5 . . . . . . .243 C1
Rennie Rd **2** EX16 . . .64 D7
Renoir Cl PL9. . . . . .256 A6
Renown St PL2 . . . . . . .247 E6
Rensey La EX17 . . . . . . .60 C4
Renslade Ho EX4. . . . . .261 A2
Renton La TQ7. . . . . . . .142 E7
Research Way PL6. . . . .245 C4
Reservoir Cres PL9. . . .256 B7
Reservoir Cross PL16. 91 A4
Reservoir La **1** PL3 . .248 F6
Reservoir Rd
  Plymouth, Hartley
  PL3. . . . . .248 F6
  Plymouth, Plymstock
  PL9. . . . . .256 B7
Reservoir Way PL9. . . .256 B7
Resolution Ho PL4. . . .263 B3
Resolution Rd EX1 . . .178 D1
Rest Hill TQ12. . . . . . . .131 D7
Restland La EX20 . . . . .94 F7
Restormel Rd PL4. . . . .262 C4

Restormel Terr PL4 . . .262 C4
Retail Park Cl EX2. . . .177 B3
Retreat Cl TQ7 . . . . . . .258 C5
Retreat Dr The EX3. . .182 D6
Retreat Rd EX3 . . . . . . .182 E6
Retreat The
  Exmouth EX8. . . . . .202 D7
  Paignton TQ3 . . . . .226 C8
  Plymouth PL3 . . . . .249 B7
  Tiverton EX16 . . . . .161 D4
  Topsham EX3 . . . . .182 D6
Revell Park Rd PL7. . . .250 E6
Revel Rd PL3 . . . . .249 A6
Revelstoke Rd
  Noss Mayo PL8. . . . . . . .140 F6
  Noss Mayo PL8. . . . . . . .141 A6
Revill Ind Units EX5 . .99 A4
REW
  Ashburton. 130 F6
  Malborough 147 F5
Rew Cross
  Ashburton TQ13 . . . . . . .130 F5
  Newton St Cyres EX5 . . .81 A2
Rewdown Cross
  TQ13. . . . . .130 F6
REWE 82 A2
Rewe Barton EX5 . . . . .82 A2
Rewe Cross EX5 . . . . . . .82 A2
Rewe Ct EX5. . . . . .82 B3
Rewe La EX5. . . . . .99 D6
Rewes Cross EX5 . . . . .82 F2
Rewlea Cotts TQ13 . . .130 F5
Rewlea Cross TQ13 . . .130 F6
Rew Rd
  Ashburton TQ13 . . . . . . .130 F5
  2 Ashburton TQ13. . . .131 A5
Rew's Cl EX34 . . . . .2 F4
Rews Cross EX36. . . . . .19 C2
Rews Mdw EX1 . . . . . . .174 F1
Rews Park Dr EX1. . . . .174 F1
REXON. 106 B7
Rexona Cl EX2 . . . . .177 A2
Rexon Cross PL16. . . .106 B7
Reynell Ave TQ12 . . . . .207 F3
Reynell Rd
  East Ogwell TQ12 . . . . .211 F8
  Newton Abbot TQ12 . . .211 F8
Reynolds Cl EX4 . . . . . .174 D1
Reynolds Gr PL5 . . . . . .247 C8
Reynolds Rd PL7. . . . . .250 C6
REZARE. 115 C4
Rheola Gdns PL6. . . . . .245 D3
Rhine Villas TQ9 . . . . . .223 D5
Rhodanthe Rd TQ3 . . .219 B1
Rhode Island Dr EX1 . .178 E1
Rhode La DT7. . . . . .260 C6
Rhodes Cl PL7 . . . . .250 E7
Rhododendron Ave
  Barnstaple EX31. . . . . . .154 D3
  Dunkeswell EX14 . . . . . .67 B1
RHS Gardens Rosemoor★
  EX38. . . . . .159 D2
Rhude Cross EX22. . . . .53 D2
Rhydda Bank Cross
  EX31. . . . . .4 A5
Rhyll Gate Cross TA22 .32 E7
Ribble Gdns PL3 . . . . . .249 D7
Ribston Ave EX1. . . . . . .178 C6
Ribston Cl EX1. . . . . . . .178 C6
Rices Mews EX2 . . . . . .177 A4
Richard Cl
  Bideford EX39. . . . . .25 E4
  Okehampton/North Tawton
  EX20. . . . . .170 D5
  Ottery St Mary EX11 . . .169 B3
Richard Ford Ct EX2. .177 F5
Richards Cl
  Dawlish EX7 . . . . .204 D5
  Exmouth EX8. . . . . .196 D2
  Wellington TA21 . . . . . . .160 C8
Richardson Dr PL8. . . .141 B8
Richards Row PL3. . . . .248 F7
Richards Terr PL10. . . .252 E5
Richina Dr EX20. . . . . . .77 B4
Richmond Ave EX34. . .150 A5
Richmond Cl
  Sampford Peverell
  EX16. . . . . .50 D1
  Torquay TQ1 . . . . .221 A4
Richmond Ct
  14 Dawlish EX7 . . . . . .204 E6
  Exeter EX1 . . . . .261 A3
Richmond Gn EX39. . . .14 F1
Richmond Hill TQ12. . .213 A5
Richmond Pk EX39. . . .156 F7
Richmond Pl
  13 Dawlish EX7 . . . . . .204 E6
  Ivybridge PL21 . . . . .136 C7
  Shaldon TQ14 . . . . .209 D5
Richmond Rd
  Appledore EX39 . . . . . . .15 A1
  Exeter EX4 . . . . .261 A3
  Exmouth EX8. . . . . .202 D7
  Ilfracombe EX34. . . . . . .150 A4
  Plymouth PL6 . . . . .245 A2
Richmond St EX32 . . . .155 A5
Richmond Terr
  9 Appledore EX39. . . .15 A1
  Buckland Monachorum
  PL20. . . . . .126 C3
  Kingsbridge TQ7. . . . . . .258 D6
Richmond Villas
  EX34. . . . . .150 A5
Richmond Walk Ind Est
  PL1. . . . . .247 F1
Richmond Wlk
  10 Barnstaple EX32. . .155 A6
  Plymouth PL1 . . . . .247 F1

RICKARD'S DOWN. 156 A3
Rickards Gn EX39 . . . . .156 B2
Rickards Row EX39 . . .40 B7
Rickham Cross TQ8 . .148 D4
Riddell Ave EX32. . . . . .154 F6
Ride The
  Beaworthy EX21. . . . . . .55 F4
  Plymouth PL7, PL9 . . . .249 D2
Ridge Cross
  Chillington TQ7 . . . . . . .149 B8
  Plymouth PL9 . . . . .256 A3
  Wilmington EX14 . . . . . .86 E4
Ridge Gr PL15 . . . . .105 A3
Ridge Hill
  Berrynarbor EX34. . . . . . .2 E3
  Combe Martin EX34 . . . . .3 A2
  Dartmouth TQ6 . . . . .233 F4
Ridge Ho PL4 . . . . .249 A4
Ridge La
  Chudleigh TQ13. . . . . . .124 B7
  Cornworthy TQ9 . . . . . . .139 F4
  Paignton TQ3 . . . . .218 F8
  Tiverton EX16 . . . . .63 F8
  Wilmington EX14 . . . . . .86 C3
Ridge Lane Cross
  TQ9. . . . . .139 E4
Ridgeleigh Ct **11**
  EX14. . . . . .166 C6
Ridgemark Cl TQ5 . . . .230 E5
Ridge Park Ave PL4 . . .248 D4
Ridge Park Rd PL7 . . . .250 F5
Ridge Pk PL7 . . . . .250 E5
Ridge Rd
  Combeinteignhead
  TQ12. . . . . .208 D2
  Maidencombe TQ1,
  TQ12. . . . . .214 B7
  Modbury PL21. . . . . .137 B4
  Molland EX36 . . . . .20 F1
  Molland TA22 . . . . .21 A1
  Molland TA22 . . . . .32 C8
  Plymouth PL7 . . . . .250 E3
  Stokeinteignhead
  TQ12. . . . . .209 A1
  Ugborough PL21. . . . . . .137 D7
  West Anstey TA22. . . . . .32 D7
Ridges The TQ6. . . . . . .233 D1
Ridgeway
  Exeter EX4 . . . . .173 A3
  Honiton EX14 . . . . .166 B4
  Ottery St Mary EX11 . . .169 E4
  Plymouth, Plympton
  PL7. . . . . .250 D5
  Saltash PL12. . . . . .242 D1
  Sidbury EX10 . . . . .101 B2
  Wellington TA21 . . . . . . .160 B6
Ridge Way EX6 . . . . . . .194 E2
Ridgeway Ave EX39 . . .156 E7
Ridgeway Cl
  Newton Abbot TQ12 . . .207 F1
  Sidbury EX10 . . . . .101 B2
  Westward Ho! EX39 . . . .156 D7
Ridgeway Ct EX39. . . . .156 D7
Ridgeway Dr EX39 . . . .156 D7
Ridgeway Gdns EX11 169 E4
Ridgeway Gn EX37 . . . .43 B7
Ridgeway Hts **17**
  TQ1. . . . . .220 D4
Ridgeway La
  Awliscombe EX14. . . . . .85 A5
  Coffinswell TQ12. . . . . . .213 D6
Ridgeway Mead
  EX10. . . . . .187 F7
Ridgeway Rd
  Newton Abbot TQ12 . . .207 F1
  Torquay TQ1 . . . . .220 E4
Ridgeway Sch PL7 . . . .250 E5
Ridgeway's Cross
  EX17. . . . . .79 E6
Ridgeway Sp Ctr PL7 250 E5
Ridgewood Cross
  EX15. . . . . .67 D8
Ridgewood La EX15. . .67 D8
Ridgey Cross TQ13. . . .130 B4
Ridgway Cross EX36. . .20 E1
Ridgway Ct EX13. . . . . .167 D5
Ridgway La EX24. . . . . .102 F4
Riding Cross EX37 . . . .29 A4
Ridings The EX3. . . . . . .183 C4
Ridley Hill TQ6. . . . . . . .234 A3
Rifford Rd EX2 . . . . .178 B4
Riflemans Walk PL6. . .245 B7
Rifton La EX16 . . . . .48 B4
Riga Terr PL3. . . . . .249 C4
Rigdale Cl PL6. . . . . . . .249 A7
Riggles Cross EX14. . . .68 A3
Rillage La TQ2. . . . . . . .219 F6
Rill Cnr EX5 . . . . .99 D3
Rill La EX9. . . . . .199 H2
Ringdown La EX15 . . . .52 F2
Ring Hill EX20 . . . . .95 C5
Ringhill Cross EX20. . .95 D5
RINGMORE
  Bigbury-on-Sea. 142 E4
  Teignmouth. 209 D4
Ringmore Cl TQ14 . . . .209 D5
Ringmore Dr TQ7 . . . . .142 E3
Ringmore Rd
  Shaldon TQ14 . . . . .209 D5
  Teignmouth TQ14 . . . . . .210 A3
Ringmore Way PL5. . . .244 B5
Ringrona TQ8. . . . . .259 B2
Ringsash Cross TQ13 .130 B4
Ringslade Cl TQ12. . . .206 F5
Ringslade Rd TQ12. . . .206 F5
Ringswell Ave EX1 . . . .178 C6

Ringswell Cross TQ9 .216 E6
Ringswell Pk **11** EX2. .178 D5
Riphay Corner EX16. . .33 E3
Riphay Cross TA22 . . . .33 E3
Ripon Cl EX4. . . . . .176 E6
Rippon Cl
  Brixham TQ5 . . . . .229 F2
  17 Tiverton EX16 . . . . .64 D7
Riscombe Hill EX5 . . . .98 F8
Risdon Ave PL4 . . . . . . .249 B1
Risdon Dr PL21 . . . . . . .237 A5
Rising Sun EX13 . . . . . .87 A3
Ritson La TQ9. . . . . .139 D3
Rivenford La EX5, EX17 81 C3
Riverbank Cotts
  EX39. . . . . .157 B4
River Cl
  Newton Abbot TQ12 . . .207 F6
  Stoke Canon EX5. . . . . .173 F8
River Ct
  3 Okehampton
  EX20. . . . . .170 B6
  Saltash PL12. . . . . .242 D5
  Sidbury EX10 . . . . .101 B2
  Tavistock PL19 . . . . .171 D6
Riverdale
  Harbertonford TQ9 . . . .139 C7
  Seaton EX12. . . . . .192 B7
Riverdale Cl EX12 . . . .192 B7
Riverdale Orch EX12 .192 B7
Riverdale Ave EX34 .150 A6
RIVERSIDE
  Plymouth 243 A1
  Wellington 160 B6
Riverside Apartments
  EX36. . . . . .158 E4
Riverside Bsns Pk
  PL1. . . . . .247 E3
Riverside Cl
  Bideford EX39. . . . . .157 B4
  Honiton EX14 . . . . .166 B6
  1 Horrabridge PL20. . .126 F4
Riverside Com Prim Sch
  PL5. . . . . .247 B5
Riverside Cott PL12 . .242 C1
Riverside Cross EX17. .62 A3
Riverside Ct
  12 Barnstaple EX31 . .154 F5
  Bideford EX39. . . . . .157 B4
  Dartmouth TQ6. . . . . . . .233 F3
  Exeter EX2 . . . . .261 B2
  Newton Abbot TQ12 . . .207 D4
Riverside L Ctr EX4 . . .261 A1
Riverside Mdw EX3 . . .182 D7
Riverside Mews PL12 243 A3
Riverside Pl
  Plymouth PL1 . . . . .247 D2
  Plymouth PL5 . . . . .247 D2
Riverside Rd
  Barnstaple EX31. . . . . . .154 C6
  Dittisham TQ6. . . . . .228 C3
  Lynmouth EX35. . . . . . . .151 C6
  Sidmouth EX10 . . . . .188 B3
  Topsham EX3 . . . . .182 E6
Riverside Road E PL8 140 F6
Riverside Road W
  PL8. . . . . .140 F6
Riverside Terr TQ9 . . .223 D5
Riverside Valley Pk★
  EX2. . . . . .177 E2
Riverside View EX11 .169 D3
Riverside Way
  Newton Abbot TQ13 . . .130 F7
  Seaton EX12. . . . . .192 C5
Riverside Wlk
  Plymouth PL5 . . . . .244 B6
  Yealmpton PL8 . . . . .136 A2
Riverside Workshops
  EX12. . . . . .192 C5
Rivermeet EX39. . . . . . .15 A1
Rivers The PL12. . . . . . .242 C6
Rivers Wlk EX2 . . . . . . .182 C7
River Tamar Way
  EX22. . . . . .164 C6
Riverton Rd EX31 . . . . .154 D2
Rivervale Cl TQ14. . . . .110 F6
River Valley Rd **13**
  TQ13. . . . . .123 C4
River View
  Barnstaple EX32. . . . . . .155 C4
  Exebridge TA22. . . . . . . .33 F3
  Gunnislake PL18. . . . . . .125 B5

River View continued
  Plymouth PL4 . . . . .249 B1
  Saltash PL12. . . . . .242 F3
River View Cl
  12 Chudleigh Knighton
  TQ13. . . . . .123 C4
  20 Colyton EX24 . . . . .103 A4
River View Commercial
  Ctr EX31 . . . . .154 D6
Riverview Dr EX4 . . . . .176 F8
River View Dr **21**
  EX24. . . . . .103 A4
River View La PL4. . . . .249 B1
Riverview Pl TQ7. . . . . .258 C5
River View Terr EX6. . .182 B3
Riviera Int Con Ctr★
  . . . . .219 F4
Riviera Terr
  Dawlish EX7 . . . . .204 F7
  Exminster EX6 . . . . .182 B3
Riviera The
  Paignton TQ4 . . . . .226 B5
  Torquay TQ1 . . . . .220 B3
Riviera Way TQ2 . . . . . .213 D1
Rixafer Rd TQ13. . . . . . .124 B4
Rixdale Rd TQ13 . . . . . .124 C4
Rixey La EX17. . . . . .61 B2
Rixeypark Cnr TQ13 . .123 D3
RIXLADE. 25 B5
Roach Hill EX36. . . . . . .31 F7
Roachill Cross EX36. . .32 C1
Roach La EX5. . . . . .82 C6
Road Down Cross EX6. 96 F7
Road End Cross EX14. .87 A8
Roadford Lake Nature
  Reserve★ EX21. . . . . . . .91 D4
ROAD GREEN. 103 A5
Road Pk TQ13. . . . . .123 B7
Roadway Cnr EX34. . . .8 A5
Robartes Ct EX2 . . . . . .261 C2
Robers Rd TQ12. . . . . . .207 D8
Robert Adams Cl PL7 250 B5
Robert Davey Rd
  EX2. . . . . .178 D1
Roberts Ave PL11 . . . . .247 B3
Roberts Cl
  Cullompton EX15 . . . . . .163 B2
  Torquay TQ2 . . . . .214 B2
Roberts Field EX36. . . .30 D8
Roberts Rd
  Exeter EX2 . . . . .261 B2
  Plymouth PL5 . . . . .247 D8
Roberts Way TQ12 . . . .206 F4
Robert Way EX10 . . . . .186 F8
Robin Cl EX15. . . . . .163 B2
Robin Dr PL15 . . . . .105 A2
Robin La EX5 . . . . .99 B6
Robins Cross EX16 . . . .63 A6
Robins Field TQ7 . . . . .144 F1
Robins Hill EX39 . . . . . .156 E4
Robins Park Ind Est
  TQ7. . . . . .143 E8
Robins Way PL9 . . . . . .255 E8
Robin Wlk **9** EX16 . . .161 E6
ROBOROUGH
  Great Torrington. 42 F3
  Plymouth 241 D1
Roborough Ave PL6. . .245 B5
Roborough Cl PL6 . . . .245 B5
ROBOROUGH
  DOWN. 126 F3
Roborough Down La
  PL6. . . . . .241 F6
Roborough Gdns **3**
  TQ13. . . . . .131 A5
Roborough La
  Ashburton TQ13 . . . . . . .130 F5
  Plymouth PL5. . . . . .244 D8
Roborough Rd EX31. . .155 A4
Roborough Terr
  TQ13. . . . . .130 F5
Robyns Cl PL7 . . . . .251 B5
Roche Gdn EX2 . . . . . . .182 A8
Rochester Rd
  3 Plymouth PL4 . . . . . .248 C4
  6 Plymouth PL4. . . . . .263 A4
Rochford Cres
  Plymouth PL5 . . . . .243 F5
  Plymouth TQ12 . . . . .244 A5
ROCK. 87 D5
Rock Ave
  Barnstaple EX32. . . . . . .155 A3
  Lynton EX35. . . . . .151 B5
ROCKBEARE. 99 C6
Rockbeare CE Prim Sch
  EX5. . . . . .99 B5
Rockbeare Hill EX5 . . .168 A5
Rock Cl TQ4 . . . . .229 C2
Rockcliffe Ct **1**
  EX34. . . . . .150 C6
Rock Cotts TQ7 . . . . . . .142 C6
Rock Cross EX17. . . . . .97 B7
Rockdale Rd PL8. . . . . .136 A2
Rock End Ave TQ1 . . . .220 C2
Rockerhayne Cross
  EX24. . . . . .102 C3
Rockey La
  Newton Poppleford
  EX10. . . . . .187 A6
  Northlew EX20 . . . . .74 E2
Rockfield Ave PL6. . . . .244 F6
Rockfield Cl TQ14. . . . .210 D7
Rockfield Cotts TA21. .51 F7
Rockfield Ho EX4 . . . . .261 B4
Rockfield Rd EX34 . . . .7 F4
ROCKFORD continued
Rock Gdns
  Barnstaple EX32. . . . . . .155 A3

Rock Gdns *continued*
Plymouth PL9 249 D1
Rock Gdns The★ TQ13 123 F5
Rock Head EX37 28 C2
Rock Hill
Aveton Gifford TQ7 143 C6
Berrynarbor EX34 2 D3
Braunton EX33 152 D6
Chulmleigh EX18 59 E8
Georgeham EX33 8 A2
Plymouth PL5 244 C7
Umberleigh EX37 28 C2
West Down EX34 8 F4
Rock House La TQ1 214 C5
Rockingham Rd PL3 249 A5
Rock La
Cheriton Bishop EX17 97 B7
Chudleigh TQ13 123 F8
16 Combe Martin EX34 3 A3
Offwell EX14 86 C1
Rocklands TQ13 123 E5
Rockley La EX32 11 F1
Rock Lodge Pk EX35 151 B5
Rockmount Terr 6 EX39 157 A2
Rockpark Cross TQ13 131 A5
Rock Park Terr 24 EX32 155 A4
Rock Pk
4 Ashburton TQ13 131 A5
Dartmouth TQ6 233 D4
Rock Rd
Chudleigh TQ13 123 E5
Torquay TQ2 220 B4
Rockshead Hill EX32 18 F3
Rockside EX4 177 A6
Rocks The EX39 156 B6
Rockstone The EX7 205 A7
Rock Terr PL7 250 D4
Rock The EX31 154 F7
Rock View EX16 65 B7
Rock Villas PL16 105 F4
Rockville Pk PL9 255 E8
Rock Walk Hts TQ1 220 A4
Rockwell Gate TA21 160 B5
Rockwell Gn TA21 160 B5
ROCKWELL GREEN 160 B5
Rockwell Green CE Prim Sch TA21 160 B5
Rockwood Rd PL6 245 E8
Rocky Hill PL19 171 B5
Rocky La
Abbotsham EX39 156 A3
Arlington EX31 10 C3
Buckfastleigh TQ11 236 A3
Combe Martin EX34 3 A4
Lydcott EX32 18 F7
Modbury PL21 137 E2
4 Teignmouth TQ14 209 E8
Teignmouth TQ14 210 A6
Rocky Park Ave PL9 255 E8
Rocky Park Rd PL9 255 E8
Rocombe Cl TQ2 213 F4
Rocombe Cross
Daccombe TQ12 213 F6
Raymond's Hill EX13 104 C6
Rocombe Hill TQ12 213 F7
Rodda Cl PL18 125 D7
Roddick Way 8 PL7 251 C5
Rodgements Cross EX18 59 E8
Rodgemonts Cross EX18 59 F8
Rodgemont's La EX18 59 F8
Rodgers Ind Est TQ4 225 D3
Rodney Cl
Dartmouth TQ6 233 D3
Exmouth EX8 203 A7
Rodney St PL5 247 D8
Rods La PL19 117 E6
Rodsworthy La EX36 31 C1
Rodway Cross EX14 87 A6
Roe Cl EX36 158 B5
Roeselare Ave PL11 247 A3
Roeselare Cl PL11 247 A3
Rogada Ct TQ5 230 D3
Rogate Dr PL6 245 D4
Rogate Wlk PL6 245 D4
Rogers Cl EX16 161 E6
Rogers Cres EX39 157 D2
Rogers Dr PL12 242 D4
Roland Bailey Gdns PL19 171 A6
Rolle Barton EX9 198 D7
Rolle Cotts EX9 197 E2
Rolle Ct EX38 159 C5
Rolle Rd
Budleigh Salterton EX9 199 G2
Exmouth EX8 202 A6
Great Torrington EX38 159 A5
Rolle's Quay EX31 154 F5
Rolle St
Barnstaple EX31 154 F6
Exmouth EX8 202 A6
Rolles Terr EX39 40 C7
Rollestone Cres EX4 173 E2
Rolle The EX9 199 G2
Rolle Villas EX8 202 A6
Rollis Park Cl PL9 255 C8
Rollis Park Rd PL9 255 C8
Rollstone La EX17 81 C1
Rolston Cl PL6 244 D6
Romaleyn Gdns TQ4 226 B4
Roman Rd
Feniton EX5 84 C2
Roman Rd *continued*
Kilmington EX13 87 C1
Kingsteignton TQ13 123 E2
Lyme Regis DT7 260 D4
Plymouth PL5 243 E2
ROMANSLEIGH 45 C7
Romansleigh Cross EX36 45 C7
Romansleigh Ridge EX18 45 C5
Romans Way EX16 161 F6
Roman Way
Honiton EX14 166 E7
Plymouth PL5 243 E2
Seaton EX12 192 A6
Roman Wlk EX4 261 B3
Roman Wy 8 EX5 99 A6
Romilly Gdns PL7 250 B5
Romney Cl PL5 244 B1
Romsey Dr EX2 177 E5
Ronald Gdns EX3 182 D7
Ronald Terr PL2 247 F5
Ronchetti Wy EX2 177 F3
Roncombe Cnr EX24 101 E5
Roncombe Gate EX24 101 E5
Roncombe Hill EX10 101 E5
Ronsdale Cl PL9 255 D8
Rookabear Ave EX31 154 A1
Rookbear La EX31 9 E2
Rookery Cvn Pk EX20 77 F5
Rookery Hill EX16 48 C8
Rookery La DT7 260 C8
Rookery Terr TA21 160 C5
Rook La PL21 133 C3
Rooklands 18 TQ12 207 B3
Rooklands Ave TQ2 219 E6
Rook Lane End PL21 133 C3
Rooksbridge View 3 EX31 154 A1
Rooks Cl EX31 154 B3
Rooks Cross EX31 27 D3
Rooks Farm Rd EX31 153 A4
Rooks Nest EX31 153 E5
Rooks Way EX16 161 E6
Rookswood Ct 1 EX31 154 A1
Rookswood La EX5 99 C5
Rookwood Cl EX14 166 B5
Rookwood Ho EX14 166 B6
Room Hill Rd TA24 21 D7
Roope Cl PL5 247 C7
Rooty Cross EX31 27 A7
Roper Ave PL9 255 D8
Roperidge Cross PL21 137 F6
Ropers Ct EX9 198 E7
Roper's La EX9 198 E7
Ropery Rd EX34 150 C6
Ropewalk
Bideford EX39 157 A2
Kingsbridge TQ7 144 A2
Kingsbridge TQ7 258 C4
Ropewalk Hill TQ5 230 C5
Ropewalk Ho EX8 201 E6
Rope Wlk
2 Teignmouth TQ14 210 B5
Wellington TA21 160 C4
Rorkes Cl PL5 243 E2
Roscoff Cl EX38 159 E5
Roscoff Rd EX7 204 E8
Roscoff Rise PL6 245 B4
Rosea Bridge La EX34 3 A4
Rose Acre Terr TQ5 230 D4
Rose And Crown Hill EX17 80 A5
Rose Ave EX1 178 D6
Rosebank Cres EX4 173 E1
Rosebarn Ave EX4 173 D1
Rosebarn La EX4 173 E1
Rosebery Ave PL4 263 C4
Rosebery La PL4 263 C4
Rosebery Rd
Exeter EX4 177 E8
Exmouth EX8 202 A7
Plymouth PL4 263 C4
Rose Cl
Rockwell Green TA21 160 A3
Tiverton EX16 161 F6
Roseclave Cl PL7 251 C6
Rose Cotts
Beer EX12 191 D5
9 Bishop's Tawton EX32 16 E1
Frogmore TQ7 144 E3
Plymouth PL6 249 B8
Rosedale Ave PL2 248 D7
Rose Dene TQ2 213 F2
ROSEDOWN 22 F3
Rosedown Ave PL2 248 A7
Rose Duryard EX4 173 A1
Rose Gdns
Ipplepen TQ12 211 E2
Plymouth PL6 245 E6
Rose Hill
Kingskerswell TQ12 212 F4
Wembury PL9 140 D7
Rosehill Cl TQ1 220 C5
Rose Hill Cl TQ12 212 F4
Rosehill Gdns TQ12 212 F4
Rosehill Rd TQ1 220 C5
Rose Hill Terr PL17 125 D3
Roseship Cl PL6 245 E7
Rose Ho TQ1 220 D7
Rose La EX32 155 C3
Roseland Ave EX1 178 A6
Roseland Cres EX1 178 A6
Roseland Cross EX22 54 C8
Roseland Dr EX1 178 A5
Roselands EX10 188 A4
Roselands Cotts EX24 103 A5
Roselands Dr TQ4 225 F2
Roselands Prim Sch TQ4 225 F2
Roseland Sq TQ12 207 E7
Roselands Rd TQ4 226 B2
Roselyn Terr EX31 154 E6
Rosemary Ave TQ12 206 F4
Rosemary Cl PL7 132 D4
Rosemary Ct TQ3 226 C8
Rosemary Gdns TQ3 225 F8
Rosemary La
Colyton EX24 103 A5
Dulverton TA22 33 D6
Holne TQ11 130 A3
Musbury EX13 103 D5
ROSEMARY LANE 52 D1
Rosemarylane Cross EX15 52 D1
Rosemary St EX4 176 F5
Rosemont 9 TQ1 220 D4
Rosemont Ct EX2 177 B1
Rosemoor Rd EX38 159 E5
Rose Moor Rd EX38 159 E5
Rosemount
Bideford EX39 156 E4
Paignton TQ4 226 C5
Rosemount Cl EX14 166 B5
Rosemount Ct TQ8 259 D5
Rosemount La EX14 166 B5
Rosery Rd TQ2 219 E5
Rosevean Ct 8 PL3 248 F6
Rosevean Gdns PL3 248 F6
Rosevean Ho 7 PL3 248 F6
Roseveare Cl PL9 256 A8
Roseville St TQ6 233 F3
Rosewarne Ave TQ12 207 F2
Roseway EX8 202 F8
Rosewell Cl EX14 166 D7
Rosewood Cl PL9 255 F5
Rosewood Cres EX5 179 E2
Rosewood Gr EX31 154 C3
Rosewood Terr 5 EX4 177 D8
Roslyn Gdns EX39 156 B7
Rospeath Cres PL2 248 D8
Rossall Dr TQ3 226 A5
Ross Cl EX1 174 F1
Rosse Rd EX16 161 D6
Rosshayne La EX14 68 F2
Rosslyn Park Rd PL3 248 D5
Ross Pk TQ12 211 E3
Ross St PL2 247 E4
Rosyl Ave EX7 204 C3
Rothbury Cl PL6 245 E4
Rothbury Gdns PL6 245 D4
Rotherfold TQ9 223 B5
Rothesay Gdns PL5 244 D3
Rougemont
Shaldon TQ14 209 F4
Shaldon TQ14 210 B2
Rougemont Ave TQ2 213 D1
Rougemont Cl PL3 249 B7
Rougemont Ct EX6 181 F4
Rougemont Dr EX1 175 B1
Rougemont Terr EX13 167 D5
Roundball Cl EX14 166 C4
Roundball La EX14 166 B2
Round Berry Dr TQ8 259 C4
Round Cross TQ11 236 B6
Roundham Ave TQ4 226 D5
Roundham Cres TQ4 226 D5
Roundham Gdns TQ4 226 D4
Roundham Ho TQ4 226 C5
Roundhead Rd TQ12 180 F3
Roundhill EX16 161 B3
Roundhill Cl EX4 173 A3
Roundhill Rd TQ2 219 D2
Roundhouse La EX8 196 B2
Roundings The TQ5 229 B5
Roundmoors Cl TQ12 213 A3
Roundsleys La PL19 117 E6
ROUNDSWELL 154 B2
Roundswell Com Prim Acad 3 EX31 154 A3
Roundtable Meet EX4 174 B1
Roundway The TQ12 212 F6
ROUSDON 193 F7
Rousdown Rd TQ2 219 E4
Rowan Cl
East Ogwell TQ12 206 F1
Great Torrington EX38 159 F6
2 Honiton EX14 85 C2
Plymouth PL7 251 B5
Tavistock PL19 171 C3
Tiverton EX16 161 F5
Rowancroft (Exeter Univ) EX2 177 F6
Rowan Ct PL12 242 C2
Rowan Dr EX12 192 A8
Rowan Lea EX15 162 C3
Rowan Pk 2 EX31 154 C2
Rowan Rd TQ3 225 E3
Rowans The PL16 105 E4
Rowan Tree Rd TQ12 207 E1
Rowan Way
Brixham TQ5 229 F1
Brixham TQ5 230 A2
Exeter EX4 176 F7
Plymouth PL6 245 E7
Rowan Wood Rd PL19 117 D3
Rowbrook Cl TQ4 225 E3
Rowcliffe Cotts TA21 50 F8
Rowcroft Cl EX14 166 B5
Rowcroft Rd TQ3 226 C8
Rowden Cross
Salcombe TQ7 148 A8
Teignmouth TQ14 124 C1
Widecombe in the Moor TQ13 121 A3
Rowden Ct PL8 141 A6
Rowdens Ho The TQ14 210 D6
Rowdens Rd TQ2 219 F5
Rowden St PL3 248 E5
Rowdens The TQ14 210 C6
Rowdon Brook EX6 112 F5
Rowdown Cl PL7 251 D4
Rowe Cl
Bideford EX39 25 E4
Rockwell Green TA21 160 A4
Rowell Cross EX20 107 F4
Rowells Mead 4 TQ12 122 F1
Rowena EX39 156 C6
Rowes Orchard EX15 162 C3
Rowe St PL11 247 B3
Rowhorne Rd EX4 176 C8
Row La
Dulverton TA22 33 A8
Hawkridge TA22 21 E1
Hawkridge TA22 32 F8
Plymouth PL5 243 E2
Rowland Cl PL9 255 E5
Rowley Cross EX31 4 D1
Rowley Gate EX31 11 B6
Rowley Rd TQ1 214 C1
Rowlstone Cl EX8 196 C3
Rowse Gdns PL18 125 D3
Rowsell's La TQ9 223 D5
Rows La
Bampton EX16 34 A1
22 Combe Martin EX34 3 A3
Row The EX36 30 A2
Row Tor Cl EX20 170 D5
Rowtry Cross EX20 76 F5
Royal Albert Meml Mus & Art Gall★ EX4 261 A3
Royal Ave The EX8 201 F7
Royal Charter Pk 7 EX18 44 E1
Royal Citadel★ PL1 263 A1
Royal Cl EX2 181 B7
Royal Clarence Appts 4 EX12 192 B4
Royal Clarence Apts 4 EX34 150 B6
Royal Cres EX2 178 D3
Royal Ct
Princetown PL20 128 A8
Torquay TQ1 220 D7
Royal Devon & Exeter Hospl (Heavitree) EX1 177 E6
Royal Devon & Exeter Hospl (Wonford) EX2 177 F4
Royal Eye Infmy PL4 248 E4
Royal London Ct EX10 188 B3
Royal Navy Ave
Plymouth PL2 247 F6
Plymouth PL5 247 F6
Royal Oak Cl EX15 67 B2
Royal Oak Cotts EX20 107 F8
Royal Oak Cross EX14 86 E6
Royal Observer Wy EX12 192 B5
Royal Par PL1 262 C2
Royal Pines TQ1 220 E3
Royal Way EX6 201 B8
Royal William Rd PL1 254 A8
Royal William Yard PL1 254 A8
Royston Ct 4 EX1 178 C8
Royston Rd
Bideford EX39 156 F1
Churchinford TA3 68 D7
ROYSTON WATER 68 F8
Rozel TQ1 220 D3
Rubby Cross EX6 97 E5
Ruby Cl
Holsworthy TA20 72 A6
Holsworthy TA20 164 C3
Ruby Red Row EX3 182 D8
Ruckamore Rd TQ2 219 E5
Ruckham La EX16 62 F6
Rudds Bldgs 4 EX16 161 B4
Rudyard Way EX39 156 B6
Rudyerd Wlk PL3 249 D6
Rudy La TA22 33 E6
Rue de Courseulles sur Mer TQ6 233 F4
Rue St Pierre PL21 237 E5
Rufford Cl 1 PL2 248 A7
Rugby Rd EX4 177 A4
Ruggaton La EX34 2 D2
Rule Cross EX23 37 B2
Rull Cross EX16 48 C5
Rull Hill
Oakford EX16 48 C5
West Worlington EX17 61 B8
Rull La EX15 163 B6
Rumbelow Rd EX16 161 E6
RUMSAM 155 B1
Rumsam Cl EX32 155 B2
Rumsam Gdns EX32 155 C2
Rumsam Mdws EX32 155 B2
Rumsam Rd EX32 155 B2
Runaway La PL21 137 A2
Rundle Rd TQ12 207 C4
RUNDLESTONE 118 F2
Runnacleave Rd EX34 150 B6
RUNNINGTON 51 F8
Runnon Moor La EX20 75 B7
Runnymede Ct PL6 245 E2
Runway Rd PL6 245 B5
Rupert Price Way TQ12 123 B2
Rupertswood EX34 150 C6
Rus Cotts EX17 165 A5
Rushcott Cl EX31 153 A4
Rushcott Cross
Newton Tracey EX31 27 B7
Stonyland EX31 27 B8
RUSHFORD 116 E3
Rushforth Pl EX4 176 E8
Rushlade Cl TQ4 225 F2
Rush Meadow Rd EX5 99 B6
Rush Park Terr PL18 125 C7
Rush Way TQ9 223 F5
Ruskin Cres PL5 244 D2
Rusper Cl EX15 83 F6
Russel Cl EX32 17 C1
Russel La EX15 65 A1
Russell Ave PL3 248 F7
Russell Cl
East Budleigh EX9 198 B6
Gunnislake PL18 125 D7
Plymouth PL9 256 B7
Saltash PL12 242 C3
Russell Court Gdns PL19 171 B6
Russell Ct
Plymouth PL1 262 C2
Salcombe TQ8 259 E5
Saltash PL12 242 C3
Tavistock PL19 171 B6
Russell Dr EX9 198 B6
Russell Pl PL1 262 B4
Russell St
Exeter EX1 261 C3
Sidmouth EX10 188 B3
Tavistock PL19 171 C5
Russell Terr EX4 261 A4
Russell Way EX2 178 D2
Russell Wlk EX2 178 C3
Russet Ave EX1 178 C6
Russet Cl
Uffculme EX15 66 A7
Wellington TA21 160 E7
Russet Gdns TQ7 258 E7
Russets La TQ11 236 C5
Russet Way PL8 257 A5
Russet Wood PL5 243 F4
Russon's La EX37 44 B7
Ruston Hill EX17 61 A6
Rutger Pl PL1 262 A4
Rutherford St EX2 178 A4
Ruthven Cl PL6 248 F8
Rutland Rd PL4 248 F4
Rutlery Field EX4 174 F3
Rutt's Cross EX14 84 E2
Ruxhill La EX31 10 D5
Ryall's Cnr
Beaford EX20 42 A1
Merton EX20 57 A8
Ryall's Corner EX19 57 A8
Ryalls Ct EX12 192 A5
Rydal Cl PL6 245 D2
Rydal Mews EX4 176 F5
Ryde Cl TQ2 214 A2
Ryder Cl 16 EX16 64 D7
Ryder Rd PL2 247 F4
RYDON 207 E8
Rydon Acres
Kingsteignton TQ12 207 E8
Stoke Gabriel TQ9 227 F8
Rydon Ave TQ12 207 E8
Rydonball Cross TQ12 211 F7
Rydon Cross
Denbury TQ12 211 D6
Stoke Gabriel TQ9 227 F8
Rydon Est TQ12 207 E8
Rydon Ind Est TQ12 207 D6
Rydon La
Abbotskerswell TQ12 212 C6
Exeter EX2 178 C3
Exton EX3, EX5 183 E2
Holsworthy EX22 71 E7
Payhembury EX14 84 B4
Rydon Lane Ret Pk EX2 178 C3
Rydon Orch EX9 198 F8
Rydon Prim Sch TQ12 207 E8
Rydon Rd
Holsworthy EX22 164 B5
Kingsteignton TQ12 207 E8
Rydons TQ5 230 A4
Rye Hill PL12 242 C2
Rye La TQ7 144 B5
Ryeland Cl PL9 140 D8
Ryelands Farm Ind Est TA21 160 B3
Rye Park Cl EX19 42 D1
Rye Pk
Beaford EX19 42 D1
Monkton EX14 86 C5
Ryll Cl EX8 202 B7
Ryll Court Dr EX8 202 B7
Ryll Gr EX8 202 B7

S

Sabre Cl TQ12 180 E3
Sabre Wlk 1 EX32 155 B5
Sackery TQ12 208 D4
Sackville Cl PL9 255 F7
Sacred Heart RC Sch 7 TQ3 226 B7
Saddleback Cl TQ12 211 F8
Saddlers Cl EX6 96 F3
Saddlers Way
Okehampton EX20 170 D6
Plymouth TQ12 244 C8
Saddle The TQ4 226 C2
Sadler Cl EX8 202 E8
Sadler Gn TQ13 180 C6
Saffron Ct TQ7 258 D5
Saffron Pk TQ7 258 D5
Sage Gr EX16 161 F4
Sage Park Rd EX33 152 B7
Sages Lea EX5 184 C6
Sailmakers Ct EX8 201 E6
St Agnes La TQ2 219 E3
St Albans Cl EX4 176 E6
St Albans La TQ1 220 C7
St Albans Pk PL20 127 A2
St Albans Rd TQ1 220 C7
St Andrew St N EX16 161 C3
St Andrew St S EX16 161 C3
St Andrew's CE Prim Sch
Buckland Monachorum PL20 126 C3
Chardstock EX13 88 A7
Plymouth PL1 262 B2
St Andrews Cl
Ashburton TQ13 130 F4
12 Bere Alston PL20 125 E1
Cullompton EX15 163 C3
Saltash PL12 242 C2
Sutcombe EX22 54 A6
St Andrew's Cl
Calstock PL18 125 D3
Feniton EX14 84 D2
Kennford EX6 114 E4
Yarnscombe EX31 27 E2
St Andrew's Cross 1 PL1 263 A2
St Andrews Ct
3 Tiverton EX16 161 E6
Torquay TQ2 219 C8
St Andrews Dr EX13 167 F7
St Andrew's Est EX15 163 B4
St Andrews Ho EX8 201 F6
St Andrews Mdw DT7 260 D4
St Andrews Orch EX24 103 A5
St Andrew's Pl PL10 253 A1
St Andrews Prim Sch EX15 163 B3
St Andrews Rd
Cullompton EX15 163 C3
Fremington EX31 153 D6
Paignton TQ4 226 C5
Tavistock PL19 171 D2
St Andrew's Rd
Cowley EX4 172 F2
Exmouth EX8 201 F6
St Andrew's Sq EX24 103 A5
St Andrew's St PL10 253 A1
St Andrew St
Millbrook PL10 252 E5
Plymouth PL1 262 C2
ST ANDREW'S WOOD 84 A8
St Annes EX6 194 D3
St Annes Cl EX22 70 E1
St Annes Ct TQ12 207 B3
St Annes Pl EX5 82 B5
St Anne's Rd
Exeter EX1 177 E7
Plymouth PL6 245 D6
Saltash PL12 242 E3
Torquay TQ1 220 D7
St Annes Well Brewery EX4 261 A3
St Annes Well Mews EX4 261 A3
ST ANN'S CHAPEL
Gunnislake 125 B6
Kingston 142 F6
St Anthony's Cl EX11 169 E4
St Ash TA20 69 F7
St Aubyn Ave PL2 247 F5
St Aubyn Rd PL1 247 E3
St Aubyns Pk EX16 161 F3
St Aubyn St PL1 247 E2
St Aubyn's Villas EX16 161 F3
St Aubyn Terr PL7 132 F4
St Augustines Cl TQ2 214 A3
St Austin Cl PL21 237 B5
St Barnabas Com Hospl PL12 242 F2
St Barnabas Ct PL1 262 A4
St Barnabas Terr PL1 262 A4
St Bartholomews Rd TQ12 211 F8
St Bartholomew Way TQ12 206 D1

St Bernard's Cl
 Buckfast TQ11 . . . . 236 B7
 Exeter EX2 . . . . 261 C1
St Boniface Cl PL2 . . . 248 C7
St Boniface Dr PL2 . . . 248 C7
St Boniface Rd EX17 . . 165 A5
St Boniface's RC Coll
 PL5 . . . . 244 E1
ST BRANNOCKS 152 C7
St Brannock's Hill
 EX33 . . . . 152 D7
St Brannock's Park Rd
 EX34 . . . . 150 B4
St Brannock's Rd
 EX34 . . . . 150 B4
St Brannock's Well Cl
 EX33 . . . . 152 D7
St Briac Way EX8 . . . . 196 E3
St Bridget Ave PL6 . . . 244 F1
ST BUDEAUX 243 D2
St Budeaux Bypass
 Plymouth PL5 . . . . 243 F1
 Plymouth PL5 . . . . 247 E8
 Plymouth TQ12 . . . . . . 244 A1
St Budeaux Cl EX11 . . 169 E3
St Budeaux Ferry Rd Sta
 PL5 . . . . 247 D8
St Budeaux Foundation
 CE (Aided) Jun Sch
 PL5 . . . . 243 F2
St Budeaux Orch
 EX11 . . . . 169 E3
St Budeaux Victoria Rd
 Sta PL5 . . . . 243 D1
St Catherines CE Prim
 Sch TQ12 . . . . 180 F1
St Catherines Pk 6
 PL8 . . . . 141 A7
St Catherine's Rd
 TQ1 . . . . 220 B8
St Chad Cl PL5 . . . . . . 244 C4
St Christopher's Prep Sch
 TQ9 . . . . 216 C5
St Clares Cl EX12 . . . . 192 B5
St Clements Ct TQ6 . . 233 D4
St Columba Cl TQ12 . . 207 E8
St Columba Cl TQ12 . . 207 E8
St Cyres Rd EX14 . . . . 166 B6
St Davids 11 EX39 . . . 157 A1
ST DAVID'S 177 B8
St Davids Cl EX13 . . . . 167 F7
St David's Dr EX13 . . . 167 F7
St David's Hill EX4 . . . 177 A7
St David's Pl EX4 . . . . 177 A7
St David's Prim Sch
 EX4 . . . . 261 A3
St Davids Rd TQ14 . . . 210 C8
St David's Rd PL19 . . . 171 C5
St David's Terr EX4 . . 261 A3
ST DOMINICK 125 A3
St Dominick CE Prim Sch
 . . . . 125 A2
St Dominic Pk PL17 . . 125 A4
St Dominic's Cl TQ1 . . 220 B8
St Dunstan's Rd TQ8 . 259 C4
St Dunstan's Terr
 PL4 . . . . 263 C3
ST DYMPNA'S 192 A8
St Edmunds Rd TQ7 . . 258 C6
St Edmund's Rd TQ1 . . 220 B8
St Edmunds wlk TQ7 . 258 C6
St Edward Gdns PL6 . . 245 B1
St Edward's CE Prim Sch
 PL6 . . . . 245 C1
St Efride's Rd TQ2 . . . 219 F5
Ste Honorine Du Fay Cl
 EX32 . . . . 28 E8
St Elizabeth Cl PL7 . . . 250 F3
St Elmo 3 EX12 . . . . . 192 A4
St Elmo Ct TQ8 . . . . . . 259 C3
St Erth Rd PL2 . . . . . . 248 D7
St Eval Pl PL5 . . . . 243 E4
St Francis Ct PL5 . . . . 244 B3
St Gabriel's Ave PL3 . . 248 D5
St Georges Ave PL2 . . 248 C7
St George's Ave PL2 . . 248 C7
St George's CE Prim Sch
 PL1 . . . . 262 A1
St George's CE (VA) Jun
 Sch EX39 . . . . 156 F8
St Georges Cl 15
 PL21 . . . . 137 B2
St Georges Cres TQ1 . 220 C7
St Georges Ct 1 PL2 . 247 F4
St Georges Hill DT7 . . 260 C4
St Georges La EX7 . . . 204 C3
St Georges Rd PL12 . . 242 D3
St George's Rd
 Barnstaple EX32 . . . . . 155 A6
 Saltash PL12 . . . . 242 E3
 Torquay TQ1 . . . . 220 C7
St George's Terr
 1 Barnstaple EX32 . . . 155 A6
 Plymouth PL2 . . . . 247 F4
 Shillingford St George
 EX2 . . . . 114 C4
St George's View
 EX15 . . . . 163 B4
St George's Way
 EX16 . . . . 161 C3
ST GEORGE'S WELL . . 163 C5
St George's Well Ave
 EX15 . . . . 163 B4
St Germans Rd EX4 . . 173 C1
St German's Rd EX4 . . 177 C8

ST GILES IN THE
 WOOD 42 B6
ST GILES ON THE
 HEATH 90 B1
St Giles on the Heath
 Com Sch PL15 . . . . 90 C1
St Gregorys Ct EX12 . . 192 A6
St Helens EX39 . . . . . . 156 A2
St Helen's CE (VA) Prim
 Sch EX39 . . . . 156 A1
St Helen's Cl EX33 . . . . 7 E2
St Helen's Ct EX10 . . . 187 F3
St Helens Wlk PL5 . . . 244 C5
St Hilary Sch of English
 14 TQ4 . . . . 226 B6
St Hilary Terr PL4 . . . . 263 C3
SAINT HILL 66 D3
St Hill Cl EX2 . . . . 177 A2
St Ida's Cl EX2 . . . . . . 176 D1
St Ives Ct 5 TQ1 . . . . 220 A6
ST JAMES' 177 D8
St James CE Prim Sch
 EX20 . . . . 170 D6
St James Cl
 Exeter EX4 . . . . 261 C4
 Landkey EX32 . . . . 17 C1
 Parkham EX39 . . . . 39 E8
St James Ct
 Exeter EX4 . . . . 177 E8
 Plymouth PL1 . . . . 262 B2
 Torpoint PL11 . . . . 247 B3
St James' Ho 16
 TQ14 . . . . 210 B5
St James Mews
 Plymouth PL1 . . . . 262 B2
 18 Teignmouth TQ14 . 210 B5
St James' Park (Exeter
 City AFC) EX4 . . . . 261 C4
St James' Park Sta
 EX4 . . . . 261 C4
St James Pl TQ1 . . . . . 220 D7
St James' Place E
 PL1 . . . . 262 B2
St James' Place W
 PL1 . . . . 262 B2
St Jame's Prec 19
 TQ14 . . . . 210 B5
St James Rd
 Torpoint PL11 . . . . 247 B2
 Torquay TQ1 . . . . 220 A7
St James' Rd EX4 . . . . 261 C4
St James Sch EX4 . . . 174 B1
St James St EX20 . . . . 170 B5
St James Terr
 Exeter EX4 . . . . 261 C4
 Plymouth PL1 . . . . 262 B2
St James Way 4
 EX16 . . . . 161 C6
St Joesph's RC Prim Sch
 TQ12 . . . . 207 A4
ST JOHN 252 C8
St John Cl 8 TQ13 . . . 180 C7
St Johns PL19 . . . . 171 C5
St Johns Ave PL19 . . . 171 C5
St John's Bridge Rd
 PL4 . . . . 263 B2
St John's CE Prim Sch
 Totnes TQ9 . . . . 223 C5
 Wellington TA21 . . . . . 160 E6
 Wellington TA21 . . . . . 160 E7
ST JOHN'S CHAPEL . . . 27 B8
St Johns Cl
 16 Colyton EX24 . . . . 103 A4
 Plymouth PL6 . . . . 245 D4
 11 Tiverton EX16 . . . . 161 E6
 Wellington TA21 . . . . . 160 E6
St John's Cl
 Bishopsteignton
 TQ14 . . . . 208 F7
 Bovey Tracey TQ13 . . . 180 C6
 Honiton EX14 . . . . 166 C6
 Ivybridge PL21 . . . . . . 237 B5
 Millbrook PL10 . . . . . . 252 E5
 Skilgate TA4 . . . . 34 E6
St John's Cotts TQ13 . 180 C6
St Johns Ct
 Bradworthy EX22 . . . . . 53 E8
 Tavistock PL19 . . . . . . 171 C4
St John's Ct 3 TQ3 . . 226 B6
St John's Dr
 Bradworthy EX22 . . . . . 53 E8
 Plymouth PL9 . . . . 255 B6
St Johns Farm Mews
 EX8 . . . . 196 F3
St Johns La PL11 . . . . 252 B8
St John's La
 Barnstaple EX32 . . . . . 155 C3
 Bovey Tracey TQ13 . . . 180 C7
St John's Pl TQ1 . . . . . 220 B4
St John's RC Prim Sch
 EX16 . . . . 161 B4
St John's Rd
 Exeter EX1 . . . . 177 E7
 Exmouth EX8 . . . . 196 E2
 Horrabridge PL20 . . . . 126 F4
 Ivybridge PL21 . . . . . . 237 B5
 Millbrook PL10 . . . . . . 252 F5
 Plymouth PL4 . . . . 263 B2
 Plymouth, Turnchapel
 PL9 . . . . 255 A6
St John's Sch EX10 . . 187 F5
St Johns St TQ12 . . . . 207 D4
St John's St PL4 . . . . . 263 B2
St John's Terr TQ1 . . . 223 B6
St John's Villas EX2 . . 177 F5
St John the Baptist RC
 Prim Sch TQ6 . . . . 233 C2

St Joseph's Cl
 Plymouth PL6 . . . . 244 F1
 Rumsam EX32 . . . . 155 C2
St Joseph's RC Prim Sch
 Exmouth EX8 . . . . 202 B7
 Plymouth PL1 . . . . 247 E2
St Jude's Rd PL4 . . . . . 263 B2
ST JUDE'S 263 B3
St Jude's Rd PL4 . . . . . 263 B2
St Julians Cres PL10 . . 253 E7
St Katharine's Rd
 TQ2 . . . . 219 E6
St Katherine's Cl
 EX31 . . . . 153 A5
St Katherine's Mews 5
 TQ9 . . . . 223 C5
St Katherines Rd
 EX4 . . . . 178 A8
St Katherine's Way
 TQ9 . . . . 223 C5
St Keverne Pl PL2 . . . . 248 D8
St Keyes Cl 10 EX32 . . 17 B2
St Kitts Cl TQ2 . . . . . . 213 F2
St Lawrence Cl 12
 EX1 . . . . 178 D6
St Lawrence Cres
 EX1 . . . . 178 D6
St Lawrence Dr EX17 . 165 B5
St Lawrence La TQ13 . 130 F4
St Lawrence Mews
 PL4 . . . . 263 A4
St Lawrence Rd PL4 . . 263 A4
St Lawrence's Gn
 EX17 . . . . 165 B5
St Leonard's Ave EX2 . 261 B1
St Leonard's CE Prim Sch
 EX2 . . . . 261 C1
St Leonard's Cl 16
 TQ12 . . . . 207 B3
St Leonard's Pl EX2 . . 261 C2
St Leonards Rd EX14 . 166 A5
St Leonard's Rd
 Exeter EX2 . . . . 261 C2
 Newton Abbot TQ12 . . 207 B3
 Plymouth PL4 . . . . 263 C2
St Leo Pl PL2 . . . . 247 E4
St Levan Rd PL2 . . . . . 247 F5
 Plymouth PL2 . . . . 250 C6
 Teignmouth TQ14 . . . . 210 A7
ST LOVE'S 178 A3
St Loye's Ct EX2 . . . . . 178 A4
St Loyes Gdns EX2 . . . 178 A5
St Loyes Rd EX2 . . . . . 178 A5
St Loye's Terr EX2 . . . 178 A4
Saint Luke's Campus
 EX1 . . . . 177 E6
St Luke's Cl TQ12 . . . . 207 F1
St Lukes Dr TQ14 . . . . 210 A6
St Lukes Pk TQ1 . . . . . 220 A4
St Luke's Pk TQ2 . . . . 220 A4
St Luke's Rd
 Kingskerswell TQ12 . . . 212 E8
 Torquay TQ2 . . . . 220 A4
St Luke's Road N
 TQ2 . . . . 220 B4
St Luke's Road S
 TQ2 . . . . 220 A4
St Luke's Science &
 Sports Coll EX1 . . . . . 178 D8
St Malo Cl EX8 . . . . . . 196 E3
St Marco Gdns TQ7 . . 258 D6
St Margaret Clitherow RC
 Prim Sch TQ5 . . . . 230 B3
St Margaret's Acad 2
 TQ1 . . . . 220 B8
St Margaret's Ave
 TQ1 . . . . 220 B8
St Margaret's CE (Aided)
 Jun Sch EX39 . . . . 156 F7
St Margarets Cl EX15 . 67 B8
St Margarets Cl TQ1 . 220 B8
St Margarets Ct EX3 . 182 E5
St Margaret's Ct 7
 EX39 . . . . 156 F7
St Margarets Gdn 1
 EX31 . . . . 154 F6
St Margarets La
 TA20 . . . . 88 C8
St Margarets Rd PL7 . 250 B7
St Margaret's Rd
 TQ1 . . . . 220 B8
St Margaret's Sch
 EX2 . . . . 177 C5
St Margarets Terr
 EX3 . . . . 182 F5
St Margaret's View
 EX8 . . . . 203 A4
St Marks 20 EX7 . . . . 204 E6
St Marks Ave EX1 . . . . 177 F7
St Mark's CE Prim Sch
 EX23 . . . . 37 B2
St Marks Dr TQ1 . . . . . 220 D3
St Marks Rd PL6 . . . . . 245 D5
St Mark's Rd
 Honiton EX14 . . . . 166 A4
 Torquay TQ1 . . . . 220 D3
St Martin's Ave PL3 . . 248 C7
St Martin's CE Prim Sch
 Cranbrook EX5 . . . . . . 99 A6
 Whimple EX5 . . . . 99 A6
St Martins Cl EX10 . . 188 B6
St Martin's Cl EX17 . . 78 C4
St Martins Ct TQ2 . . . 213 F1
St Martin's La EX17 . . 165 B6
St Martin's Mews
 TQ1 . . . . 220 C8
St Martins Rd EX23 . . 70 A8
St Marwenne Cl EX17 . 78 A4
ST MARYCHURCH 214 C1
St Marychurch CE Prim
 Sch TQ1 . . . . 214 B1

St Marychurch Rd
 Newton Abbot TQ12 . . 207 F1
 Torquay TQ1 . . . . 214 C1
 Torquay, Plainmoor
 TQ1 . . . . 220 B6
St Mary Church Rd
 TQ2 . . . . 213 F5
St Maryhaye PL19 . . . 171 A5
St Mary Magdalen Cl
 PL1 . . . . 208 F7
St Mary's CE Prim Sch
 EX39 . . . . 157 A4
St Marys Cl
 Abbotskerswell
 TQ12 . . . . 212 A6
 17 Chudleigh TQ13 . . 123 E6
St Mary's Cl
 Axminster EX13 . . . . . 167 F5
 Brixham TQ5 . . . . 230 B2
 Great Torrington EX38 . 159 B4
St Mary's Cotts EX7 . . 200 F4
St Marys Cl PL7 . . . . . 250 D5
St Mary's Ct
 4 Newton Abbot
 TQ12 . . . . 207 B3
 Paignton TQ3 . . . . 226 A6
 Torquay TQ1 . . . . 214 B1
St Marys Dr EX38 . . . . 43 C7
St Mary's Dr TQ5 . . . . 230 D3
St Mary's Flats 6
 EX39 . . . . 157 A1
St Marys Hill TQ5 . . . . 230 D3
St Mary's Hill TQ5 . . . 230 D3
St Marys Pk EX11 . . . . 169 F3
St Mary's Pk TQ4 . . . . 225 C4
St Mary's Pl TQ12 . . . 211 D2
St Mary's RC Prim Sch
 Axminster EX13 . . . . . 167 C5
 Buckfast TQ11 . . . . . . 236 C7
St Mary's Rd
 Barnstaple EX32 . . . . . 155 A6
 Brixham TQ5 . . . . 230 D2
 Croyde EX33 . . . . 7 E2
 Newton Abbot TQ12 . . 207 B3
 Plymouth PL7 . . . . 250 C6
 Teignmouth TQ14 . . . . 210 A7
St Mary St PL1 . . . . . . 262 A2
St Mary Steps Terr 8
 EX1 . . . . 261 A2
St Marys View
 Silverton EX5 . . . . 82 B5
 West Hill EX11 . . . . . . 168 E5
St Matthew's CE Prim and
 Nursery Acad PL6 . . . 245 C3
St Matthews Cl EX1 . . 177 E6
St Matthew's Rd TQ2 . 219 D4
St Matthews Wlk
 EX1 . . . . 261 C3
St Matthias Church Rd
 TQ1 . . . . 220 E5
St Maurice Ct PL7 . . . 250 F4
St Maurice Mews
 PL7 . . . . 250 E4
St Maurice Rd PL7 . . . 250 F3
St Maurice View PL7 . 251 B4
St Mawes Dr TQ4 . . . . 229 B8
St Mawes Terr 8
 PL2 . . . . 247 F5
St Michael Ave PL2 . . 247 F5
ST MICHAELS 226 A5
St Michaels Cl TQ7 . . 260 E4
St Michael's TQ2 . . . . 219 E6
St Michael's Bsns Ctr
 DT7 . . . . 260 E2
St Michael's CE Prim Sch
 Exeter EX1 . . . . 177 F6
 Kingsteignton TQ12 . . 207 E7
St Michael's CE (VA) Prim
 Sch DT7 . . . . 260 E4
St Michaels Cl
 Lawhitton PL15 . . . . . . 105 B1
 Otterton EX9 . . . . 198 E7
St Michael's Cl
 Clyst Honiton EX5 . . . . 179 D8
 Exeter EX2 . . . . 177 B1
 Plymouth PL1 . . . . 247 E1
 Torquay TQ1 . . . . 219 E6
St Michael's Ct
 Paignton TQ4 . . . . 226 A4
 7 Plymouth PL1 . . . . . 247 E1
St Michael's Hill EX5 . 179 D8
St Michaels Ho 4
 DT7 . . . . 260 D3
St Michaels Rd
 Kingsteignton TQ12 . . 207 D6
 Teignmouth TQ14 . . . . 210 C7
St Michael's Rd
 Newton Abbot TQ12 . . 207 D1
 Paignton TQ4 . . . . 226 B5
 Torquay TQ1 . . . . 219 E7
St Michaels Terr 5
 TQ10 . . . . 134 F2
St Michael's Terr
 Plymouth PL4 . . . . 262 C4
 8 Plymouth, Devonport
 PL1 . . . . 247 F3
 2 Torquay TQ1 . . . . . 220 B5
St Michaels View
 EX21 . . . . 55 E4
St Michaels Wy 14
 EX5 . . . . 99 A6
St Modwen Rd PL6 . . . 249 F7
St Nazaire App PL1 . . 247 F2
St Nazaire Cl PL1 . . . . 247 F2
St Nicholas CE Prim Sch
 1 EX10 . . . . 188 A7

St Nicholas Cl 5
 EX1 . . . . 178 F8
St Nicholas Priory ★
 EX1 . . . . 261 A2
St Nicholas RC Prim Sch
 EX1 . . . . 178 C6
St Nicholas Rise EX14 . 85 D5
St Olave's Cl EX4 . . . . 261 A3
St Olaves Mews EX4 . 261 A3
St Oswins TQ1 . . . . . . 220 B8
St Pancras Ave PL2 . . 248 D8
St Patrick's Cl TQ14 . . 210 A6
St Pauls Cl
 Bovey Tracey TQ13 . . . 180 D7
 Exeter EX2 . . . . 177 F3
 Plymouth PL3 . . . . 249 C5
St Paul's Cres TQ1 . . . 220 B7
St Paul's Ct 16 TQ12 . 207 C3
St Pauls Dr EX22 . . . . 164 B5
St Paul's Rd
 Honiton EX14 . . . . 166 A5
 15 Newton Abbot
 TQ12 . . . . 207 C3
 Paignton TQ3 . . . . 219 D1
 Torquay TQ1 . . . . 220 B7
St Paul's Roman Catholic
 Primary Sch PL5 . . . . 243 D1
St Paul's Sq EX16 . . . 161 C3
St Paul St
 Plymouth PL1 . . . . 254 A8
 Tiverton EX16 . . . . 161 C4
St Peter Cl PL7 . . . . . . 250 F4
St Peters EX22 . . . . . . 38 E1
St Peter's CE (Aided)
 Prim Sch EX9 . . . . 197 F2
St Peter's CE (Aided) Sch
 EX1 . . . . 178 D5
 EX2 . . . . 178 C5
St Peter's CE Sch
 EX2 . . . . 178 C5
St Peter's CE (VA) Jun
 Sch PL19 . . . . 171 D5
St Peter's CE (VA) Prim
 Sch PL1 . . . . 262 B3
St Peters Cl
 Shirwell EX31 . . . . 17 B8
 Torquay TQ2 . . . . 219 D6
 West Buckland EX32 . . 18 B2
St Peter's Cl TQ13 . . . 180 E8
St Peters Ct
 Plymouth PL1 . . . . 262 A3
 Sidmouth EX10 . . . . . . 188 B3
St Peter's Hill 5
 TQ5 . . . . 230 D5
St Peters Mount EX4 . 176 D7
St Peter's Quay TQ9 . 223 D4
St Peter's RC Prim Sch
 PL5 . . . . 244 B5
St Peters Rd
 Fremington EX31 . . . . 153 D5
 Holsworthy EX22 . . . . 164 B5
 Plymouth PL5 . . . . 244 C2
St Peter's Rd EX14 . . . 166 A5
St Peter's School
 EX8 . . . . 196 A6
St Peter St EX16 . . . . 161 C4
St Peters Terr 2
 EX34 . . . . 150 C5
St Peter's Terr 9
 EX31 . . . . 154 F5
St Peters Way PL21 . . 237 E3
St Peters Well La
 EX22 . . . . 53 E8
St Petrock's Cl EX2 . . 261 C2
St Phillips Ct EX4 . . . . 176 F4
St Ronans 2 TQ1 . . . . 220 C5
St Rumon's CE Inf Sch
 PL19 . . . . 171 C6
St Saviours Ho 20
 EX8 . . . . 202 A6
St Saviours Rd EX11 . 169 D3
St Saviour's Way
 EX17 . . . . 165 B5
St Scholastica's Abbey
 TQ14 . . . . 210 D7
St Sevan Way EX4 . . . 196 E3
St Sidwell's Ave EX4 . 261 C4
St Sidwell's CE Prim Sch
 EX4 . . . . 261 C4
St Sidwell's St EX4 . . 261 B4
St Simon's La PL4 . . . 249 B3
St Stephen Rd PL7 . . . 250 F3
ST STEPHENS 242 D2
St Stephens Com Prim
 Sch PL12 . . . . 242 E2
St Stephen's Hill
 PL12 . . . . 242 C1
St Stephen's Pl PL7 . . 250 E5
St Stephen's Rd PL12 . 242 E2
St Stephen St PL1 . . . 247 F1
St Swithin's St EX17 . 80 A5
St Teresa Ho PL4 . . . . 263 A3
St Teresa's Ct EX39 . . 156 F7
St Teresa's Ct 9
 EX39 . . . . 156 F7
St Therese's Ct PL1 . . 247 F2
ST THOMAS 177 A3
St Thomas Cl
 Bovey Tracey TQ13 . . . 180 E2
 Plymouth PL7 . . . . 250 D3
St Thomas Ct
 Exeter EX4 . . . . 177 A4
 2 Tiverton EX16 . . . . 161 E6
St Thomas Prim Sch
 EX4 . . . . 177 A4
St Thomas Sh Ctr
 EX4 . . . . 177 A4
St Thomas Ho EX4 . . . 177 A4
St Vincent Ho TQ1 . . . 220 C3

St Vincents Cl TQ1 . . 219 F6
St Vincent's Rd TQ1 . 219 F7
St Vincent St PL2 . . . 247 F4
St Werburgh Cl PL9 . . 140 D7
St Wilfrid's Sch EX4 . 261 A3
Salamanca St PL11 . . 247 B3
SALCOMBE 259 E4
Salcombe CE Prim Sch
 TQ8 . . . . 259 C5
Salcombe Cl EX10 . . . 188 C4
Salcombe Hill Cl
 EX10 . . . . 188 B4
Salcombe Hill Rd
 EX10 . . . . 188 C4
Salcombe Hts Cl
 TQ8 . . . . 259 C5
Salcombe Lawn
 EX10 . . . . 188 B4
Salcombe Maritime &
 Local History Mus ★
 TQ8 . . . . 259 E5
Salcombe Rd
 Malborough TQ7,
 TQ8 . . . . 147 F6
 Plymouth PL4 . . . . 263 C4
 Sidmouth EX10 . . . . . . 188 B4
SALCOMBE REGIS . . . 188 F6
Salcombe The TQ8 . . . 259 E4
Salcombe to Kingsbridge
 Nature Reserve ★
 TQ7 . . . . 148 C7
Salem Almshouses 7
 EX32 . . . . 155 A4
Salem Pl EX4 . . . . 261 C4
Salem St 8 EX32 . . . . 155 A4
Salisbury Ave
 Feniton EX14 . . . . 84 D2
 Torquay TQ2 . . . . 213 F1
Salisbury Cl EX14 . . . 84 D2
Salisbury Ope PL3 . . . 248 B5
Salisbury Rd
 Exeter EX4 . . . . 177 E8
 Exmouth EX8 . . . . 202 A7
 Newton Abbot TQ12 . . 207 D4
 Plymouth PL4 . . . . 263 C4
Salisbury Road Prim Sch
 PL4 . . . . 263 C3
Salisbury Terr
 Kilmington EX13 . . . . . 87 C1
 9 Teignmouth TQ14 . 210 C5
Sallicombe Rd EX24 . 101 F3
SALMONHUTCH 165 B2
Salmonhutch Cotts
 EX17 . . . . 165 B3
Salmon Leap Cl
 TQ11 . . . . 236 C5
Salmonpool La EX2 . . 177 E3
Salmons Leap TQ9 . . 223 B7
Salston Barton EX11 . 169 C2
Salston Ride
 Ottery St Mary EX10 . . 100 C5
 Ottery St Mary EX11 . . 169 D2
SALTASH 242 B1
Saltash Bsns Pk
 PL12 . . . . 242 C4
Saltash Com Sch
 PL12 . . . . 242 E1
Saltash Her Mus ★
 PL12 . . . . 243 A2
Saltash Ind Est PL12 . 242 C4
Saltash L Ctr PL12 . . 242 E2
Saltash Parkway Ind Est
 PL12 . . . . 242 B4
Saltash Rd
 Plymouth PL3 . . . . 262 C4
 Plymouth, Keyham PL2 247 E6
Saltash Sta PL12 . . . . 243 A2
Saltburn Rd PL5 . . . . 243 C1
Salterns Mdws EX9 . . 198 A2
Saltern Rd TQ4 . . . . . 226 C1
Salterns Terr EX39 . . 157 B2
Salter's Bldgs 4
 EX16 . . . . 161 C4
Salter's Cross EX10 . . 187 D6
Salters Ct EX2 . . . . . . 178 A4
Salter's La EX24 . . . . 103 A4
Salters Mdw EX10 . . . 188 B5
Salter's Rd EX2 . . . . . 178 A4
Salterton Ct EX8 . . . . 202 F8
Salterton Rd
 Budleigh Salterton EX8,
 EX9 . . . . 197 B1
 Exmouth EX8 . . . . 202 A7
Salterton Workshops 1
 EX9 . . . . 198 A1
Salting Hill EX9 . . . . . 199 I2
Saltings The
 Seaton EX12 . . . . 192 B7
 Shaldon TQ14 . . . . . . 209 D5
Saltmer Cl EX34 . . . . 150 A2
Salt Mill PL12 . . . . . . 242 F4
Saltmill Cl PL12 . . . . 242 F4
Saltram House ★ PL7 250 A4
Saltram Terr
 Lee Moor PL7 . . . . 132 F4
 Plymouth PL7 . . . . 250 E5
SALTRENS 25 F1
Saltrens EX39 . . . . 40 F8
Saltways La EX10 . . . 100 F1
Salt Wood La EX34 . . . 2 F3
Salty La TQ14 . . . . . . 209 D5
Salutary Mount EX1 . 177 F5
Salway Cl EX15 . . . . . 163 B3
Salway Gdns EX13 . . 167 F5
Samara Bsns Pk
 TQ12 . . . . 180 F3
SAMPFORD
 ARUNDEL 51 E5

Sampford Arundel Prim
  Sch TA21 . . . . 51 E5
SAMPFORD
  CHAPPLE 76 E3
SAMPFORD
  COURTENAY 76 F4
Sampford Courtenay Sta
  EX20. . . . . 77 A2
Sampford Cross EX20 . 76 F3
Sampford Gdns PL20 127 A5
SAMPFORD MOOR . . . 51 E5
SAMPFORD
  PEVERELL 50 E1
Sampford Peverell CE
  Prim Sch EX16. . . . . . 50 C1
SAMPFORD SPINEY . 127 B7
Sampford Terr **7**
  PL20. . . . . 126 F5
Sampson Cross EX37. . 44 E8
Sampson's Hill EX2 . 114 C6
Sampsons La EX1 . . . 177 E7
Sampsons Plantation
  EX31. . . . . 153 C5
Sams Cl EX39. . . . . . . 25 C4
Samuel Bassett Ave
  PL6. . . . . 245 B7
Sanctuary Cl
  Bishop's Tawton EX32. . . 16 E1
  9 Keyham PL2. . . . . 247 F5
Sanctuary La
  Hatherleigh EX20 . . . . . 75 C7
  Woodbury Salterton
  EX5. . . . . 185 B7
  Woodbury Salterton
  EX6. . . . . 184 F8
Sanctuary Rd EX22. . 164 C4
Sandaway La EX34 . . . . 2 F4
Sandclose La EX36. . . 31 D7
Sand Down La EX5. . 172 A8
Sanderling Cl **16**
  EX32. . . . . 155 A4
Sanders Cl EX5 . . . . 175 D6
Sanders Cross EX22. . 54 C8
Sanders La **8** EX2. . . . 16 E1
Sanders' La EX22 . . . 164 C5
Sanders Lea EX17. . . . 62 F1
Sanders Plantation
  TA4. . . . . 35 C7
Sanderspool Cross
  TQ10. . . . . 135 A2
Sanders Rd
  Bow EX17. . . . . 78 C4
  Brixham TQ5. . . . . . . 230 A5
  Exeter EX4 . . . . 174 E1
Sanders Way EX15 . . . 66 C6
SANDFORD 80 A5
Sandford Ash La EX17 79 A7
Sandford Cl EX32 . . . 155 D1
Sandford Cross EX20. . 77 E4
Sandford La EX20. . . . 77 F3
Sandford Orleigh
  TQ12. . . . . 207 E6
Sandford Rd PL9. . . . 255 F8
Sandfords EX6. . . . . . 181 B1
Sandford Sch EX17. . . 80 A5
Sandfords Gdns
  EX38. . . . . 159 B4
Sandford View TQ12 207 B4
Sandford Wlk EX1 . . . 261 C3
Sandgate La EX11. . . 100 D4
Sand Grove EX2. . . . . 178 D2
Sandheap Cross TQ7 143 C2
Sand Hill PL18 . . . . . 125 D6
Sandhill Cross TQ13. . 111 E5
Sand Hill Pk PL18 . . . 125 C6
Sandhills TQ8 . . . . . . 259 C3
Sandhills Rd TQ8 . . . 259 C3
Sandhole Cross EX39. . 37 A8
Sandick Cross EX32. . . 17 F2
Sand La
  Calstock PL18. . . . . . . 125 D3
  Littlehempston TQ9. . . . 223 F8
  Totnes TQ9 . . . . 224 A8
Sandoe Way EX4. . . . 174 E3
Sandon Wlk PL6 . . . . 245 A1
Sandown Rd TQ4 . . . 225 F2
Sandpark La EX11. . . . 10 D5
Sandpark Rd EX18 . . 159 D2
Sandpath Rd TQ12 . . 207 E6
Sandpiper Ct
  Exeter EX4 . . . . 174 D1
  Woolacombe EX34 . . . . 8 A6
Sandpiper Dr EX3. . . 183 C2
Sandpiper Gn EX2 . . 176 D3
Sandpiper Rd
  Marhamchurch EX23 . . . 70 A8
  Plymouth PL6. . . . . . . 245 B2
Sandpiper Way TQ2. 213 C2
Sandpit Hill EX24 . . . 101 E6
Sand Pit Hill La EX24 . 102 F4
Sandquay Rd TQ6 . . 233 F5
Sandquay Way TQ6 . 233 F5
Sandringham Dr TQ3 219 B2
Sandringham Gdn
  EX31. . . . . 154 C1
Sandringham Gdns
  TQ3. . . . . 219 C1
Sandringham Rd
  TQ12. . . . . 207 E3
Sands Ct
  Paignton TQ4 . . . . . . 226 B5
  Seaton EX12. . . . . . . 191 F7
Sands Gate Cross
  TQ13. . . . . 95 F1
Sands Rd
  Paignton TQ4 . . . . . . 226 C5

Sands Rd continued
  Slapton TQ7 . . . . 145 D3
Sands Sch TQ13. . . . 130 F4
Sandstone Cl **6** EX1. 178 E3
Sanduck Cross TQ13 .112 A2
Sandy Cross EX9. . . . 198 A8
SANDYGATE 123 E1
Sandygate TQ13 . . . . 123 E1
SANDY GATE. 178 F3
Sandygate Bsns Pk
  TQ12. . . . . 123 E1
Sandygate Mill TQ12 123 E1
Sandy La
  Brampford Speke EX5. . 81 E1
  Braunton EX33 . . . . . . 15 A6
  Broadclyst EX5. . . . . . 175 D5
  Chittlehampton EX37 . . 29 A5
  Croyde EX33. . . . . 7 E2
  Dawlish EX7. . . . . 204 F7
  Huxham EX4. . . . . 174 D8
  Ivybridge PL21. . . . . . 237 D5
  Kingsbridge TQ7,TQ9 . 144 B5
  Staverton TQ9. . . . . . . 216 A6
  Woolacombe EX34 . . . . 1 A1
Sandy Lane Cross
  EX21. . . . . 72 E1
Sandy Lane Ct EX34 . . 7 F6
Sandy Lane End TQ9 144 B6
Sandymere Rd EX39. 156 F7
Sandymoor Cross
  EX21. . . . . 72 E1
SANDY PARK. 111 B8
Sandypark La EX32. . . 18 E3
Sandy Rd PL7. . . . . . 251 C4
Sandy's La EX14 . . . . 68 C2
Sandy View **4** EX1. . 178 E3
Sandy Way
  Croyde EX33. . . . . 7 E1
  Michelcombe TQ11. . . 129 F3
Sandyway Cross EX36 . 20 D4
Sandyways Cross
  TQ13. . . . . 111 C7
Sanford Mws TA21. . 160 F5
Sanford Pl EX2 . . . . . 177 A4
Sanford Rd TQ2. . . . . 219 E5
Sanford Rise TA21 . . 160 F5
Sango Ct PL10 . . . . . 252 F6
Sango Rd PL11. . . . . 247 A2
Sannerville Way EX6 182 B5
San Remo Terr EX7 . 204 F7
San Sebastian Sq
  PL1. . . . . 262 C2
Sanson Cl EX5 . . . . . 173 F8
Sarah Cl PL20. . . . . . 125 E1
Sargent Cl EX1. . . . . 178 C6
Sargents Mdw EX23. . 37 A1
Sarlsdown Rd EX8 . . 202 D7
Sarum Cl PL3 . . . . . . 248 F7
SATTERLEIGH 29 C1
Satterleigh Cross
  EX37. . . . . 29 C1
Saturday's La TQ12. . 212 F1
Saundercroft Rd EX5. . 99 B7
Saunders Way
  Cullompton EX15 . . . . 163 E4
  West Charleton TQ7 . . 144 C1
Saunton Beach Villas
  EX33. . . . . 14 E8
Saunton Cl EX33 . . . 152 C6
Saunton Rd EX33. . . 152 B6
Savage Rd PL5. . . . . 247 D7
Savery Cl PL21. . . . . 237 E6
Savery Terr PL4. . . . . 249 A4
Savile Rd EX4. . . . . . 176 F5
Savoy Hill EX4 . . . . . 174 A2
Savoy St EX3 . . . . . . 182 D7
Sawmill La EX9 . . . . 197 F7
Sawmills Way **3**
  EX14. . . . . 166 C5
Sawpit La TQ9 . . . . . 222 F7
Sawrey St PL1 . . . . . 262 A2
Sawyer Dr TQ14 . . . . 124 E1
Sawyers Cl TQ13 . . . 111 F4
SAWYER'S HILL 52 E7
Sawyers Mill EX16 . . . 34 E2
Saxe St **20** TQ14. . . . 210 B5
Saxon Ave EX4. . . . . 174 F2
Saxon Cl EX17 . . . . . 165 D4
Saxon Hts **2** TQ5 . . 230 C4
Saxon Mdw TQ3 . . . 225 C5
Saxon Rd
  Exeter EX1 . . . . 177 F6
  Tavistock PL19 . . . . . 171 A6
Saxons Croft EX32 . . 155 C3
Saxon Way EX15 . . . 163 C6
Saxon Wy TQ12 . . . . 207 F7
Scabbacombe La
  TQ6. . . . . 235 A6
Scadsbury La EX20. . . 75 A4
Scalders La PL21. . . . 137 C2
Scalwell La EX12 . . . 192 A7
Scalwell Mead EX12. 192 A7
Scalwell Pk EX12 . . . 192 A7
Scannell Cl PL12. . . . 242 C1
Scarborough Pl TQ2 . 219 F5
Scarborough Rd
  Torquay TQ1 . . . . 220 A5
  Torquay TQ2 . . . . 219 F5
Scarhill Cross EX20 . . 95 D4
Scarsdale EX8. . . . . . 202 C5
Scattor View EX6 . . . 112 F5
Scholars Wlk TQ7. . . 258 D6
School Cl
  Bampton EX16 . . . . . . 34 B1
  Chulmleigh EX18. . . . . 60 A7
  Fremington EX31. . . . . 153 E5
  Plymouth PL7 . . . . . . 250 D7

School Cl continued
  Shobrooke EX17. . . . . . 80 E4
  Tavistock PL19 . . . . . 171 D5
School Cotts TQ12 . . 207 A8
School Ct TQ6 . . . . . 233 D3
School Dr PL6 . . . . . 245 D7
Schoolhayes EX20 . . 106 F5
School Hill
  Cockwood EX6 . . . . . . 201 B6
  7 Dawlish EX7. . . . . 204 D6
  Lympstone EX8. . . . . . 195 F5
  Stoke Gabriel TQ9 . . . 227 F7
  Whimple EX5 . . . . 99 E8
School House La EX13 . 88 F5
School La
  8 Bishop's Tawton
  EX32. . . . . 16 E1
  Blackawton TQ9 . . . . 139 E1
  Broadclyst EX5. . . . . . 175 C7
  Chilsworthy EX22. . . . . 53 E1
  5 Colyton EX24. . . . 103 A4
  Cornwood PL21. . . . . 133 C2
  Exeter EX2 . . . . 178 A1
  Exmouth EX8. . . . . . . 196 C1
  Great Torrington EX38 . 159 C6
  Hartland EX39 . . . . 22 E3
  Heathfield TQ13 . . . . 180 F3
  Honiton EX14 . . . . . . 166 C6
  Newton Poppleford
  EX10. . . . . 186 F8
  Plymouth PL7. . . . . . . 250 E4
  Rousdon DT7 . . . . 193 F7
  Stover TQ12 . . . . 123 B3
  Taleford EX10. . . . . . . 100 D8
  Taleford EX11. . . . . . . 169 C7
  Tatworth TA20. . . . . . . 88 C8
  Tedburn St Mary EX6 . . 97 F4
  3 Teignmouth TQ14 . 210 A3
  Thorverton EX5. . . . . . 81 E4
  West Hill EX11. . . . . . 168 E5
School Rd
  Brixham TQ5. . . . . . . 230 C5
  Ermington PL21 . . . . 136 F4
  Exeter EX2 . . . . 177 A4
  Kingskerswell TQ12 . . 212 F4
  Lydford EX20 . . . . 107 F4
  Newton Abbot TQ12 . . 207 C3
  Silverton EX5 . . . . 82 B5
  Stoke Fleming TQ6 . . 146 A7
  Stokeinteignhead
  TQ14. . . . . 209 B1
  Tavistock PL19 . . . . . 171 D2
  Teigngrace TQ12 . . . . 206 F8
School St **9** EX5. . . . 101 B1
School Way EX20 . . . 170 B5
Schooners Ct EX8. . . 201 E6
Schumacher Coll
  TQ9. . . . . 215 F2
Scobhill Rd EX35. . . . . 5 E3
Scoldens Cl **14** PL21. 137 B2
Sconner Rd PL11. . . . 247 A3
Scoresby Cl TQ2 . . . 214 B3
Score View EX34 . . . 150 C3
Scorpio Mws PL9 . . . 256 E8
SCORRITON. 130 A3
Scotchmead EX5. . . . . 99 D3
Scott Ave
  18 Appledore EX39. . . 15 A1
  Exeter EX2 . . . . 177 F3
  Plymouth PL5 . . . . . . 247 C8
Scott Bsns Pk PL2. . 248 A6
SCOTT CL TQ12 . . . . 207 C3
Scott Dr EX8. . . . . . . 196 B2
Scottleigh TQ2 . . . . . 219 F3
Scott Rd PL2. . . . . . . 248 A6
Scotts **1** EX16. . . . . 49 B8
Scott's Cl TQ7 . . . . . 143 E4
Scott's Hill TA4 . . . . . 35 E8
Scott's La
  Raymond's Hill EX13. . 104 C7
  Wellington TA21 . . . . 160 E6
Scouse Cross EX13. . . 88 E2
Scouse La EX13 . . . . . 88 E2
Scrapton La TA20 . . . 69 F5
Scratchface La
  Bideford EX39. . . . . . . 25 D4
  Bideford, Littleham
  EX39. . . . . 25 F2
  Buckland Brewer EX39 . 40 B6
  Stockleigh Pomeroy
  EX17. . . . . 81 B6
Scratch Face La EX2 .176 C2
Scratton Path TQ12 . 211 F8
Screechers Hill TQ13 130 F5
Sculptor Way PL9. . . 256 E8
Scurfield Cl EX33 . . . 152 D7
Seabee Wlk EX1 . . . . 178 E1
Sea Birds Pk EX33. . . . 7 E1
Seabourne Ct TQ4 . . 226 C4
Seabrook Ave EX2 . . 182 C7
Seabrook Mews EX2 . 182 C7
Seachange EX9. . . . . 198 B3
Seacliff TQ2 . . . . 220 B4
Seacroft Rd PL5 . . . . 243 C2
Seafield Ave EX6. . . . 196 A2
Seafield La EX10. . . . 188 A3
Seafield Rd
  Seaton EX12. . . . . . . 192 A5
  Sidmouth EX10. . . . . . 188 A4
Seafields TQ4 . . . . . . 226 C2
Seaforth Lodge EX12 191 F6
Sea Haven EX12. . . . 192 B4
Sea Hill
  Beer EX12. . . . . 191 B5
  Seaton EX12. . . . . . . 192 A4
Sea King Cl EX31. . . . 16 A3
Seaking Rd EX31. . . . 153 E6
Sea Lawn Terr EX7 . . 204 F7

Seale Cl TQ6. . . . . . . 233 D4
Seale Hayne TQ12. . . 206 B6
Sealey Ct EX19. . . . . . 42 F4
Seapoint **16** TQ14 . . 210 B4
Sea Point TQ4 . . . . . 226 D5
Searle St EX17. . . . . 165 C5
Searle Terr EX39. . . . 157 A7
Seashore Ctr ★ TQ4. 226 C4
Seaside Hill EX34 . . . . 2 F4
Seasons The **5** EX4. 178 C8
SEATON 192 B5
Seaton Cl TQ1. . . . . . 220 D7
Seaton Down Cl
  EX12. . . . . 191 E8
Seaton Down Hill
  EX12. . . . . 191 E8
Seaton Down Rd
  EX12. . . . . 192 A5
Seaton Hospl EX12. . 192 A6
Seaton La **4** EX12. . 248 A4
Seaton Orch PL7. . . . 136 A8
Seaton Pl PL2. . . . . . 247 F5
Seaton Prim Sch
  EX12. . . . . 192 A6
Seaton Rd
  Colyford EX24. . . . . . 103 A3
  Farway EX10, EX24. . . 101 E5
  Musbury EX13. . . . . . 103 D5
  Seaton EX24 . . . . . . 192 B8
Seaton Tramway ★
  EX12. . . . . 192 C7
Seaton Way PL20 . . . 126 B8
Sea Trout Mews TQ9 216 A5
Seaview TQ7 . . . . . . 149 A3
Sea View
  Gunnislake PL18. . . . . 125 B5
  Ilfracombe EX34. . . . . 150 D4
Sea View Ave PL4 . . . 263 C4
Seaview Cres TQ3. . . 225 C1
Sea View Dr **7** PL9 . 140 D8
Sea View Gdns TQ7 . 147 B7
Seaview Rd DT7 . . . . 104 B4
Sea View Rd
  Northam EX39. . . . . . 156 F7
  Thurlestone TQ7 . . . . 143 A2
Sea View Terr
  Beer EX12. . . . . 191 D5
  Brixham TQ5. . . . . . . 230 C6
  Plymouth PL4 . . . . . . 263 B4
  Sidmouth EX10. . . . . . 188 A5
  Thurlestone TQ7 . . . . 143 A2
Seaward Cl EX12. . . . 190 E4
Seaway Cl TQ2. . . . . 219 E3
Seaway Cres TQ3 . . . 226 D8
Seaway Ct TQ5. . . . . 230 B4
Seaway Gdns TQ3 . . 226 D8
Seaway La
  Tipton St John EX10. . 100 D2
  Torquay TQ2 . . . . 219 E3
Seaway Rd TQ3 . . . . 226 D8
Seckerleigh Cross
  EX16. . . . . 64 C5
Seckington Cross
  EX19. . . . . 58 E4
Secmaton Gdns EX7. 200 E1
Secmaton La EX7. . . 200 E1
Secmaton Rise
  Dawlish EX7. . . . . 200 E1
  Dawlish EX7. . . . . 204 F8
Second Ave
  Axminster EX13 . . . . 167 F7
  Dawlish EX7. . . . . 204 C5
  Exeter, Countess Wear
  EX2. . . . . 182 D7
  Exeter, Heavitree EX1. . 177 F6
  Plymouth, Billacombe
  PL9. . . . . 250 A1
  Plymouth, Devonport
  PL1. . . . . 248 A2
  Plymouth, Weston Mill
  PL2. . . . . 247 E7
  Teignmouth TQ14 . . . 210 A5
Second Dr TQ14 . . . . 210 B5
Second Field La
  EX33. . . . . 152 C6
SECTOR. 88 B1
Sector Hill EX13 . . . . . 88 B1
Sector La EX13. . . . . 167 F5
Sedemuda Cl EX10 . . 188 A8
Sedemuda Rd EX10 . 187 F8
Sedge Cl PL21. . . . . 174 F1
Sedgeclaire Cl EX1. . 174 F1
Sedgewell Cross EX21. 55 F4
Sedley Way PL5. . . . . 244 D3
Sefton Ave PL4 . . . . . 249 B3
Sefton Cl PL4. . . . . . 263 C4
Sefton Ct
  22 Dawlish EX7. . . . 204 E6
  Torquay TQ1. . . . . . . 220 D7
Segrave Rd PL2. . . . . 248 B6
Selcombe Cross TQ9 108 A4
Seldon Cres EX1 . . . 174 F3
Seldons Cl PL21. . . . 137 D6
Selkirk Cl PL21. . . . . 137 B2
Selkirk Ho **5** PL9 . . 255 F7
Selkirk Pl PL5 . . . . . 244 D2
Sellbed Cross TA24 . . 21 A8
Sellbed Rd TA22 . . . . 21 A8
Sellers Cl EX24 . . . . 103 B3
Seller's Grave EX24 . 103 A4
Seller's Wood Hill
  EX12. . . . . 190 E6

Sellick Ave TQ5 . . . . 230 D3
Selsden Cl PL9. . . . . 256 C6
Senate Ct EX8 . . . . . 196 E1
Senate Way EX8 . . . . 196 E1
Sendall's Way PL6 . . 244 F4
Sennen Cl PL11. . . . . 246 F4
Sennen Pl PL2. . . . . . 247 E5
Sentry Cnr EX39 . . . . 157 C1
Sentry Cross EX31 . . . 18 A8
Sentry La
  Bishop's Tawton EX32. . 16 E1
  Bishop's Tawton EX32. . 16 E1
  Huntsham EX16 . . . . . 49 E6
Sentrys Orch EX6 . . . 182 B3
Sercombes Gdns
  EX6. . . . . 201 B8
Serge Ct EX2 . . . . . . 261 A2
Serpell Cl PL6 . . . . . 244 E6
Serpens Vale PL9 . . . 256 E7
Serstone Cross EX17 . 78 C5
Sessland La
  North Tawton EX17 . . . 77 E1
  Spreyton EX17 . . . . . . 95 D8
Sestertius Rd EX1. . . 178 E8
Sett Cl TQ13 . . . . . . 180 D7
Seven Acre Cross
  EX36. . . . . 31 E6
Seven Acre La
  Braunton EX33 . . . . . 152 E5
  Bridford EX6. . . . . . . 112 F5
Seven Acres EX5. . . . . 99 A5
Seven Acres Pk EX33 152 E5
Seven Ash Cross EX34 . 3 C1
Seven Brethren Bank
  EX31. . . . . 154 F3
Seven Brethren Ind Est
  EX31. . . . . 154 F3
Seven Crosses EX16. . 63 F6
Seven Crosses Rd
  EX16. . . . . 161 A3
Seven Hills Ho TQ2. . 220 A5
Seven Stars La PL5. . 244 C6
Seven Stones Cross
  TQ7. . . . . 142 E8
Seventh St **15** EX32. 154 F6
Seven Trees Ct PL4 . 263 B4
Severn Pl PL3. . . . . . 249 C5
Severn Rd TQ2. . . . . 219 B7
Sewell Cl PL3. . . . . . 248 F5
Sexton's Cross EX6 . 113 E6
Seymore Cl EX8. . . . 196 B2
Seymour Ave PL4 . . . 263 B4
Seymour Bglws EX34. . 1 A1
Seymour Ct
  Exmouth EX8. . . . . . . 196 B2
  9 Totnes TQ9 . . . . . 223 D5
Seymour Dr
  Dartmouth TQ6 . . . . . 233 C3
  Plymouth PL3 . . . . . . 248 F5
  Torquay TQ2 . . . . 214 B4
Seymour Mews PL4 . 263 B4
Seymour Pk PL3 . . . . 249 A5
Seymour Pl
  Plymouth PL1. . . . . . . 262 A4
  Totnes TQ9 . . . . 223 D5
Seymour Rd
  Exmouth EX8. . . . . . . 196 B2
  Newton Abbot TQ12 . . 207 C4
  Plymouth, Mannamead
  PL3. . . . . 248 F5
  Plymouth, Plympton
  PL7. . . . . 250 C6
Seymour St
  Plymouth PL4 . . . . . . 263 A3
  Wellington TA21 . . . . 160 C6
Seymour Terr EX16 . . 161 C4
Seymour Villas EX34 . . 1 A1
Shackel Cross TA3 . . . 67 E8
Shackhayes EX34 . . . . 3 A4
Shackleton Cl PL5 . . 244 E1
Shackleton Ct PL5 . . 244 E1
Shackleton Wlk
  TQ14. . . . . 210 A8
Shadrack Cross TQ9 217 B3
Shadrick Way EX32 . 164 C6
SHADYCOMBE 259 D5
Shadycombe Ct TQ8 259 D5
Shadycombe Rd TQ8 259 D5
Shady La TQ6 . . . . . 146 B7
Shady Nook Pk TQ12 207 E6
Shaftesbury Cl **21**
  EX7. . . . . 204 D6
Shaftesbury Cotts
  PL4. . . . . 263 A4
Shaftesbury Ct **3**
  PL4. . . . . 263 A4
Shaftesbury Rd
  Exeter EX2 . . . . 177 A4
  6 Ilfracombe EX34 . 150 C5
Shaftesbury Theatre ★
  EX7. . . . . 204 D6
Shaftsborough La EX34. 1 C1
Shaftsbury Pl **9** TQ9 223 C5
Shaggs Flood La TA20. 69 E2
Shakespeare Cl
  Tiverton EX16 . . . . . . 161 D6
  Torquay TQ2 . . . . 219 D6
Shakespeare Prim Sch
  PL5. . . . . 244 B2
Shakespeare Rd
  Exeter EX2 . . . . 177 A3
  Plymouth PL5 . . . . . . 244 C2
Shakespeare Way
  EX8. . . . . 196 C4
SHALDON. 210 A8
Shaldon Bridge
  TQ14. . . . . 210 A4
Shaldon Cres PL5. . . 244 B3

Shaldon Prim Sch
  TQ14. . . . . 210 A3
Shaldon Rd
  Combeinteignhead
  TQ12. . . . . 208 F5
  Newton Abbot TQ12 . . 207 F2
Shaldon Wildlife Trust ★
  TQ14. . . . . 210 B2
Shale Row
  Blackhorse EX1. . . . . . 179 A8
  Clyst Honiton EX1. . . . 175 B1
Shales Rd EX4 . . . . . 174 C1
Shalford Terr EX13. . 103 B6
Shallowford Cl PL9. . 249 C8
Shallowford Rd PL6. . 249 C8
Shambles Dr EX17 . . . 79 A6
Shamble Way EX35. . 151 E2
Shameface La TQ12. . 123 B7
Shamel's End EX16. . . 64 E7
Shamrock Cl EX39 . . 156 E7
Shamrock St PL6 . . . 245 B2
Shamwickshire Cl
  EX39. . . . . 157 C1
Shand Pk
  Axminster EX13 . . . . 167 C5
  Axminster EX13 . . . . 167 D5
Shapcott La EX36 . . . 32 C2
Shapcott Wood Hill
  EX36. . . . . 31 F2
Shapland Pl EX16 . . . 161 C2
Shapleys Gdns PL9. . 256 C5
Shapley Tor Cl TQ5. . 230 A2
Shapley Way TQ12 . . 180 C5
Shapter Ct EX8 . . . . 202 F7
Shapters Rd PL4 . . . 263 C2
Shapters Way
  Plymouth PL4 . . . . . . 255 B8
  Plymouth PL9 . . . . . . 255 B8
Shaptor Cross TQ13 . 122 F8
Shaptor View TQ13. . 180 B5
Shareford Way EX5 . . 99 B6
Sharkham Ct TQ5. . . 230 D3
Sharkham Point National
  Nature Reserve ★
  TQ5. . . . . 230 F2
Sharland La EX17 . . . 78 F8
Sharland's La EX33. . 152 C6
Sharlands Rd EX23. . . 70 A6
Sharlands View EX1. . 175 B1
Sharon Way PL6 . . . . 245 A5
Sharper La TQ14 . . . 209 C5
Sharpham Dr TQ9. . . 223 D4
Sharpham Vineyard &
  Cheese Dairy ★ TQ9 227 B8
Sharp Hill EX20 . . . . 170 B4
Sharpitor Cl PL3. . . . 218 F1
Sharpitor Gdns **5**
  PL2. . . . . 248 A7
Sharpitor Row PL20. . 127 B4
Sharp Rock EX34. . . . . 7 F7
Sharps Cl TQ12 . . . . 123 B2
Sharps Crest TQ12 . . 123 B2
Sharps Ct
  Exmouth EX8. . . . . . . 201 E6
  Exmouth EX8. . . . . . . 201 F6
Sharrose Rd PL9 . . . 255 B5
SHAUGH PRIOR 132 C6
Shaugh Prior Prim Sch
  PL7. . . . . 132 C6
Shaw Way PL9 . . . . . 255 A7
Sheafhayne Cross
  EX14. . . . . 69 E4
Shearford Cl EX32 . . 155 A8
Shearman Ct **10** EX2. 154 F6
Shearwater Dr TQ2 . 213 D3
Shearwater Way
  EX12. . . . . 192 B5
Shearwood Cl PL7. . . 250 C6
SHEBBEAR. 55 D4
Shebbear Coll EX21. . 55 E4
Shebbear Com Sch
  EX21. . . . . 55 E4
Shebbear Cross EX38 . 41 A2
Shedden Hill Rd TQ2 220 A4
Sheepspine La EX13. . 88 F5
SHEEPSTOR 132 F6
Sheepstor Rd PL6. . . 245 D1
SHEEPWASH 56 C1
Sheepwash Cross
  EX36. . . . . 31 C6
Sheepwash Hill EX36. . 31 C6
Sheirs Orch EX9 . . . . 197 F8
SHELDON. 66 F3
Sheldon Cross EX14. . 66 F2
Sheldon La EX6. . . . . 113 B5
Sheldon's La TA22 . . . 33 A7
Shelduck Way EX7 . . 200 E2
Shell Cl PL6 . . . . 245 E1
Shell Cove EX7 . . . . . 204 D4
Shelley Ave
  Tavistock PL19 . . . . . 171 D5
  Torquay TQ1 . . . . 220 B8
Shelley Cl EX2 . . . . . 177 A2
Shelley Ct EX8 . . . . . 201 E6
Shelley Way PL5 . . . . 243 D1
Shell La EX16. . . . . . . 47 F1
Shells La EX24 . . . . . 103 A3
Shell's La TA20 . . . . . 69 D3
Shelly Ct EX20 . . . . . 95 B4
Shelly Rd
  Exmouth EX8. . . . . . . 201 E6
  South Zeal EX20 . . . . 95 B4
Shelly Reach
  Exmouth EX8. . . . . . . 201 E6
  Exmouth EX8. . . . . . . 201 F6

Shelston Tor Dr TQ4 225 F3
Shelton Pl EX1 177 F6
Shepherd Cl TQ3 225 E5
Shepherd's Hl EX2 178 A1
Shepherds La
Colaton Raleigh EX10 186 E4
Plymouth PL4 263 B2
Teignmouth TQ14 124 E1
Teignmouth TQ14 209 D8
Shepherd's La EX15 52 F1
Shepherds Mdw
Abbotsham EX39 156 A2
Beaford EX19 42 D1
Shepleigh Ct TQ9 145 B8
Sheppard Rd EX4 173 D2
Sheppard's Knap EX13 87 A2
Sheppard's Row EX8 202 A7
Sheppaton La EX18, EX19, EX37 43 B2
SHERBERTON 129 A8
Sherborne Cl PL9 256 C6
Sherborne La DT7 260 E3
Sherborne Rd TQ12 207 B3
Sherbrook Cl EX9 203 F8
Sherbrook Hill EX9 203 F8
Shercroft Cl EX5 175 E2
Sherdon Bridge EX36 20 D5
SHERFORD 144 F3
Sherford Cres
Plymouth, Elburton PL9 256 C7
Plymouth, West Park PL5 244 A3
Sherford Cross TQ7 145 A3
Sherford Down Cross TQ7 144 D3
Sherford Down Rd TQ7 144 E3
Sherford Rd PL9 256 D7
Sherford Vale Sch PL9 256 E8
Sherford Wlk PL9 256 E7
Sheridan Rd
Exeter EX4 178 C8
Plymouth PL5 244 C1
Sherman Ho EX11 169 E3
Sherracombe Cross EX36 19 C6
Sherracombe La EX36 19 C6
Sherratt's Oak EX31 155 B7
Sherrell Pk PL20 125 E1
Sherril Cl PL9 255 F4
Sherwell Arcade 9 PL3 263 A4
Sherwell Cl
Dawlish Warren EX7 201 A2
Staverton TQ9 216 A5
Sherwell Ct TQ11 236 B5
Sherwell Hill TQ2 219 E5
Sherwell La
Plymouth PL4 263 A4
Torquay TQ2 219 E5
Sherwell Park Rd TQ2 219 E5
Sherwell Rise S TQ2 219 D5
Sherwell Valley Prim Sch TQ2 219 C7
Sherwell Valley Rd TQ2 219 D6
Sherwill Cl PL21 237 A6
Sherwill La TQ9 216 A5
Sherwood DT7 260 C4
Sherwood Cl EX2 177 F5
Sherwood Cross EX14 84 D2
Sherwood Dr EX8 196 E3
Sherwood Gn EX38 42 E7
Shetland Cl TQ2 213 E2
Shewte Cross TQ13 122 D5
Shields The EX34 150 C4
Shieling Rd EX31 16 A3
Shillands
Tiverton EX16 161 B4
Tiverton EX16 161 B5
Shillingate Cl EX7 204 C4
SHILLINGFORD 34 E2
SHILLINGFORD ABBOT 181 A6
Shillingford La EX6 181 A3
Shillingford Rd
Alphington EX2 181 B8
Exeter EX2 181 A7
SHILLINGFORD ST GEORGE 114 C7
Shilstone Cross EX32 28 C5
Shilstone La TQ13 113 C1
Shilston Gate PL21 137 D4
Shindle Pk TQ7 144 F1
Shinners Cotts TQ6 228 C2
SHIPHAY 219 C7
Shiphay Ave TQ2 219 D7
Shiphay La TQ2 219 D7
Shiphay Learning Acad TQ2 219 C8
Shiphay Manor Dr TQ2 219 D7
Shiphay Park Rd TQ2 219 D8
Ship La EX5 179 D8
Shipley Cl TQ10 135 A3
Shipley Rd EX14 166 E6
Shipley Wlk PL6 245 A1
Shipney La TQ13 124 A7
Shippens Mead EX8 202 E7
Shirburn Rd
Plymouth PL6 249 B8
Torquay TQ1 220 A7
Shire Cl
Honiton EX14 166 A5
Paignton TQ4 229 B8
Shire Ct EX22 70 E1
Shire End DT7 260 D2
Shire La DT7 260 B3
Shirley Cl EX8 196 D4
Shirley Cnr EX17 79 B5
Shirley Ct 8 TQ1 220 D4
Shirley Gdns PL5 244 C1
Shirley Towers TQ1 220 C3
Shirmart Pk EX33 8 E1
SHIRWELL 17 B8
Shirwell Com Prim Sch EX31 17 B8
Shirwell Cross
Barnstaple EX31 16 E6
Shirwell EX31 17 B8
Shirwell Rd EX31 17 A7
Shoalgate Cross EX20 94 F8
Shobbrook Hill TQ12 206 E4
SHOBROOKE 80 E4
Shobrooke Cross EX17 80 D4
Shobrook La EX17 78 F7
Shoemaker's La PL12 242 E2
Shooting La EX18 60 B7
Shooting Marsh Stile EX2 261 A1
Shoot La EX32 17 D6
Shoots Barn Cross EX14 84 D3
Shoot's La EX14 67 A3
SHOP
Kilkhampton 37 A1
Milton Damerel 54 F6
Shop Cotts PL7 132 F4
SHORE BOTTOM 86 F6
Shore Head EX14 86 F5
Shoreland Cross EX18 44 F5
Shorelands Rd EX31 154 D3
Shorelands Way EX31 154 D3
Shoreland Way EX39 156 E7
Shorelark Way EX23 70 A8
Shoresgate Cross EX19 76 F8
Shoreside TQ14 210 A3
Shorland Cl EX7 204 F8
Shorneywell TQ7 145 A1
SHORTACOMBE 108 A5
Shortacombe Cnr EX31 10 A5
Shortacombe Dr EX33 152 B7
Shorta Cross TQ7 143 C7
Short Cl EX39 156 D2
Short Cotts PL11 247 A3
Short Cross TQ9 139 B3
Shorter Cross TQ9 135 D2
Short Furlong EX12 191 D5
Short La
Combe Martin EX34 2 F1
Halwell TQ9 139 B3
Shaldon TQ14 209 C4
Shortlands
Pyworthy EX22 71 D5
Yettington EX9 197 F8
Shortlands La EX15 163 B3
Shortlands Rd EX15 163 B3
Shortlands Way PL21 237 E4
SHORT MOOR 86 E7
Shortmoor Cross EX14 86 E6
SHORTON 219 A1
Shorton Rd TQ3 226 A8
Shorton Valley Rd TQ3 219 A1
Short Park Rd PL3 248 D5
Shortridge Cl
Honiton EX14 166 C4
Witheridge EX16 46 E1
Shortridge Mead 1 EX16 161 B4
Shorts Way TQ9 222 E6
Shortwood Cl EX9 197 F2
Shortwood Cres PL9 256 A7
Shortwood La EX9 197 D5
Shovelpiece La EX32 19 A7
Shrewsbury Ave
Torquay TQ2 213 F1
Torquay TQ2 214 A1
Shrewsbury Rd PL5 244 C4
Shrinkhill La EX16 161 D3
Shrubbery Cl EX32 155 C3
Shrubbery La EX14 86 E6
Shrubbery The
Axminster EX13 167 D5
Exbourne EX20 76 C5
SHUTE
Kilmington 103 A8
Newton St Cyres 81 A3
Shute TQ7 147 E6
Shute Barton* EX13 103 B8
Shute Com Prim Sch EX13 103 B8
Shute Cross
Newton St Cyres EX17 81 B2
South Brent TQ10 134 E1
Shute Ct TQ14 209 A8
Shute Hill
Bishopsteignton TQ14 209 A8
Malborough TQ7 147 E6
Teignmouth TQ14 210 C5
Shute Hill Cres 10 TQ14 210 C5
Shute Ho EX13 103 B7
Shute La
Cheston TQ10 134 E1
Combe Martin EX34 3 A4
Denbury TQ12 211 A6
Huish Champflower TA4 35 C8
Moretonhampstead TQ13 111 F5
Winkleigh EX19 58 F2
Shuteleigh TA21 160 E5
Shute Meadow St 2 EX8 202 A7
Shute Park Rd PL9 255 F6
Shute Pk TQ7 147 E6
Shute Rd
Kilmington EX13 87 C1
Shute EX13 103 A7
Totnes TQ9 223 D5
Shute Row TA21 160 E5
Shutes Mead EX11 169 E4
Shute Wood EX18 58 F6
Shutscombe Hill EX32 18 E5
Shuttern Cl EX5 172 A8
Shutterton Ind Est EX7 200 F1
Shutterton La EX7 201 A3
Shutter Water Rd
Westwood EX15 83 C1
Whimple EX5 99 C8
Sicklemans Cl TQ7 144 C1
SID 188 C5
Sidborough Hill EX17 61 B1
SIDBURY 101 B2
Sidbury CE Prim Sch EX10 101 C2
Sidbury Cl EX1 178 D7
Sidcliffe EX10 188 C6
Siddalls Gdns EX16 161 E5
Siddals Gdns EX16 161 E4
Sideling Cl EX2 114 A6
Sideling Fields EX16 161 F2
Side Wood La EX36 32 A1
SIDFORD 101 B1
Sidford Cross 7 EX10 101 B1
Sidford Rd EX10 188 B7
Sidgard Rd EX10 188 C6
Sidholme Cotts EX10 188 B5
Siding Cross TQ10 137 E8
Siding Rd PL3 262 C4
Sidings The
Braunton EX33 152 D6
Churston Ferrers TQ5 229 D5
Halwill Junction EX21 73 E2
Kingsbridge TQ7 258 C5
Sid La EX10 188 C5
Sidlands EX10 188 A4
Sidleigh EX10 188 C5
Sidmount Gdns EX10 188 A5
Sidmouth CE Prim Sch
Sidmouth EX10 188 B4
Sidmouth EX10 188 B7
Sidmouth Coll EX10 188 C7
Sidmouth Cotts 9 PL4 248 F4
Sidmouth Hospital EX10 188 B4
Sidmouth Junc Cross EX14 84 D2
Sidmouth Mus* EX10 188 B3
Sidmouth Rd
Bradninch EX5 83 B5
Clyst St Mary EX1 178 F3
Clyst St Mary EX2, EX5 179 A3
Clyst St Mary EX5 179 E2
Colyton EX24 102 F5
Colyton EX24 103 A4
Exeter EX2 178 D5
Exeter EX5 99 A1
Hele EX5 82 F5
Honiton EX14 166 A3
Lyme Regis DT7 260 C3
Ottery St Mary EX11 169 E2
Sidmouth Sp Ctr EX10 188 C7
SIDMOUTH VICTORIA 188 C3
Sidney Ct 3 EX7 204 D6
Sid Park Rd EX10 188 B5
Sid Rd EX10 188 C5
Sid Vale Cl 10 EX10 101 B1
Sidvale Ct 12 EX10 101 B1
Sidvale Mews 16 EX10 101 B1
Sidwell Ho EX1 261 C3
Sidwell St EX4 261 C4
SIGFORD 131 B8
Sigford Cross TQ12 122 B2
Sigford Rd EX2 181 D8
Signal Ct EX33 152 D5
Signals The EX14 84 D2
Signal Terr EX31 154 F4
Sign of the Owl Cross TQ10 137 E8
Signpost La EX17 80 A7
Silbury Place EX17 165 C5
Silbury Terr EX17 165 C5
Silcombe Cross EX36 30 F3
Silcombe Hill EX36 30 E4
Silent Woman Pk PL19 117 F1
SILFORD 156 D4
Silford Cross EX39 156 D5
Silford Rd EX39 156 E5
Silk Dr EX14 166 B6
Silvan Dr EX33 152 E7
Silverberry Cl EX1 178 C7
Silver Birch Cl
Exeter EX2 178 A3
Plymouth PL6 245 C7
Silver Birch Ct 5 EX31 154 C2
Silver Birch Vw EX32 155 B6
Silver Bridge Cl TQ4 229 C8
Silverdale
Exmouth EX8 196 E3
Silverton EX5 82 B6
Silverdale Cl TA22 33 E4
Silver Head Hill TQ9 216 F1
Silverhill Bldgs TQ12 212 D8
Silverhills Rd TQ12 212 D8
Silveridge La TQ7 144 A8
Silver La
Exeter EX4 261 C4
Rockbeare EX5 99 C5
Silver Lea EX13 87 C1
Silver Pk EX15 66 A3
Silver St
3 Appledore EX39 15 A1
Axminster EX13 167 D5
11 Bampton EX16 34 B1
Barnstaple EX32 154 F5
8 Barnstaple EX32 155 A5
Bere Ferrers PL20 240 A3
Berrynarbor EX34 2 E3
Bideford EX39 157 A1
Braunton EX33 152 D7
Buckfastleigh TQ11 236 B5
Colyton EX24 103 A5
Culmstock EX15 66 D8
Honiton EX14 166 C6
Ipplepen TQ12 211 C1
Kentisbeare EX15 66 A3
Kilmington EX13 87 C1
Lydford EX20 107 F3
Lyme Regis DT7 260 D3
Ottery St Mary EX11 169 D4
Saltash PL12 243 A2
Thorverton EX5 81 E4
Tiverton EX16 161 D4
West Buckland TA21 52 F7
Willand EX15 162 D4
Silvers The EX3 178 F2
Silver Stream Way PL8 257 B5
SILVER STREET 52 F8
Silver Terr
Exeter EX4 261 A3
Millbrook PL10 253 A6
SILVERTON 82 B5
Silverton CE Prim Sch EX5 82 B6
Silverton Rd EX2 181 D8
Silverton Rise EX14 84 E2
Silverway EX17 80 E4
Silverwell Pk PL21 137 C2
Silverwood Ave TQ12 207 E1
Silverwood Hts EX31 155 B6
Silworthy Cross EX22 38 F2
Simcoe Pl EX15 67 B8
Simcoe Way EX14 67 B1
Simey Cl EX4 176 F7
Simmonds Pl EX15 163 E4
Simmons Cl EX20 170 C5
Simmons Pk EX20 170 B4
Simmons Way EX20 170 C5
Simms Hill TQ12, TQ13 122 C2
Simon Cl PL9 255 E6
Simon Ct 5 TQ1 220 B6
SIMONSBATH 13 B2
SIMONSBURROW 52 C3
Simons Cross EX13 87 E4
Sims Terr PL18 125 D6
Sinai Hill EX35 151 C5
Singer Cl TQ3 226 A5
Singmore Rd TQ3 218 E2
Sing's La EX33 152 D5
Sink Well La TQ13 113 D1
Sion Cl EX14 166 B6
Sir Alex Wlk EX3 182 E5
Sir George Cl DT7 260 E5
Sir John Hunt Com Sports Coll PL5 244 D4
Sir Leonard Rogers Cl PL2 248 F6
Sir Robert's Path EX31 4 D5
Siskin Chase EX15 163 A2
Sisna Pk Rd PL6 245 F5
SITCOTT 90 C2
Sithney St PL5 243 C1
Sivell Mews EX2 177 F5
Sivell Pl EX2 177 F5
Six Acre Cross EX35 5 A4
Six Acre La EX35 5 A5
Six Acres EX6 98 C4
Six Mile Hill
Dunsford EX6 113 A8
Tedburn St Mary EX6 97 F5
Tedburn St Mary EX6 98 A5
Six O Clock La PL7 250 E3
Skardale Gdns PL6 249 D8
Skardon Pl PL4 263 A4
Skelmersdale Cl TQ7 258 D5
Skern Cl EX39 156 F8
Skern Way EX39 156 F8
Skerries Rd PL6 244 F7
SKILGATE 34 E6
Skinnard La PL18 125 C5
Skinner Cl 2 EX16 161 B4
Skirhead La EX34 3 B3
Skitt La
Lydford EX20 107 F3
Skitt La *continued*
Lydford PL19 108 A3
Skye Cl TQ2 213 E2
Skylark Cl TQ12 207 C8
Skylark Rise
Plymouth PL6 245 E8
Tavistock PL19 171 D1
Skylark Spinney 3 EX31 154 A2
Skyways Bsns Pk EX5 99 A4
Slade EX39 156 E2
Slade Cl
Ottery St Mary EX11 169 F4
Plymouth PL9 256 A5
Slade Cross
Kingsbridge TQ7 144 B6
Lustleigh TQ13 122 D8
North Tawton EX20 77 D5
Slade La
Abbotskerswell TQ12 212 B5
Abbotskerswell TQ12 212 B6
Combe Martin EX31 3 E1
Galmpton TQ5 229 B5
Hawkridge TA22 21 D1
Morchard Bishop EX17 61 A1
Sidmouth EX10 189 C7
West Anstey EX36 32 B6
Slade Lane Cross EX34 3 E1
Slade Rd
Ilfracombe EX34 150 A3
Ottery St Mary EX11 169 F3
Slade Valley Rd EX34 150 A3
Sladnor Park Rd TQ1 214 C5
Sladnor Pk TQ1 214 C5
Slanns Mdw TQ12 207 D6
Slappers Hill TQ4, TQ5 234 E7
SLAPTON 145 C4
Slapton Ley National Nature Reserve* TQ7 145 D2
Slate La PL1 262 A2
Slatelands Cl PL7 251 B3
Slattenslade La EX31 4 D5
Sleap Hill EX9 198 C7
Sleepy Hollow EX2 182 C7
Sleepy La TQ3 219 A1
SLERRA 23 D3
Slerra EX39 23 D3
Sletchcott Cross EX37 44 E8
Slew Hill EX34 2 C2
Slewhill Cross EX20 95 B5
Slewton Cres EX5 99 E8
Slip Ct 12 EX31 154 A2
Slipperstone TQ9 139 A7
Slipperstone Cross TQ9 216 C7
Slipper Stone Dr PL21 237 A6
Slipperstone La TQ9 216 C7
Slipway Quay PL12 239 B2
Slittercombe La EX6 194 E3
Sloe Gdns
Clyst Honiton EX1 175 B1
Clyst Honiton EX1 179 B8
Sloe La 4 EX32 17 B2
SLONCOMBE 111 E5
Slough La
Bishops Nympton EX36 30 F3
Upottery EX14 68 C5
Sluggett Pl EX4 174 E3
Smallack Cl PL6 244 F2
Smallack Dr
Plymouth PL6 244 F2
Plymouth PL6 245 A2
Smallacombe Dross TQ10 135 D6
Smallacombe Hill EX16, EX36 32 D4
Smallacombe La EX36 31 F8
Smallacombe Rd EX16 161 B4
Smallacott Hill EX6 97 D3
Smallcombe Cross TQ3 225 E8
Smallcombe Rd TQ3 225 E8
Smalldon La TQ1, TQ2 214 B3
Small La
Broadclyst EX5 175 D7
Burlescombe EX16 51 B2
Rattery TQ10 135 D3
Smallpark La TQ13 131 E1
Smallridge Cl PL9 255 F5
Smallridge Rd EX13 87 F4
Smallwell La
Ashprington TQ9 139 E7
Marldon TQ3 218 C3
Smardon Ave TQ5 230 A5
Smardon Cl TQ5 230 A5
Smaridge Row TQ13 180 B6
SMEATHARPE 68 B5
Smeathy La EX15 52 F3
Smeaton Sq PL3 249 D6
Smeaton's Twr* PL1 262 C1
Smiter's Pit La EX13 87 A1
SMITHALEIGH 136 A6
Smithay Mdws EX6 113 B4
Smithfield Dr PL12 242 B3
Smith Field Rd EX2 181 A8
Smithfields TQ9 223 A6
Smith Hill TQ14 208 F8
SMITHINCOTT 66 A6
Smiths Ct EX2 261 A1
Smith's La
Calverleigh EX16 48 E4
Hollocombe EX18 58 E6
Smith St TQ6 233 F3
Smiths Way PL12 242 B3
Smithy Cl PL12 242 C4
Smithys Way EX16 50 D1
Smockpark La PL9 140 B8
Smokey Cross TQ13 122 B3
Smoky House La EX32 155 B8
Smugglers' La EX7 210 F8
Smythen Cross EX34 9 E6
Smythen St EX1, EX4 261 A2
Smythes Cross EX15 67 F7
Snell Dr PL12 242 B3
Snodbrook Cross EX10 101 C1
Snowberry Cl TQ1 219 F7
Snowdonia Cl TQ4 225 D4
Snowdrop Cl 2 EX14 166 A4
Snowdrop Cres PL15 105 A2
Snowdrop Mews EX4 176 D8
Snows EX17 80 B5
Snydles La EX37 44 B6
Soap St PL1 262 A2
SOAR 147 E4
Soby Mws TQ13 180 C5
Sog's La EX10 100 C2
Solar Cres
Exeter EX4 176 F4
Plymouth PL6 245 D8
SOLDON CROSS 53 E5
Solidus Rd 9 EX1 178 E8
Solland Cross EX20 76 D4
Solland La EX20 76 D4
Soloman Dr EX39 157 A1
Solsbro Rd TQ2 219 E4
Solways DT7 260 C5
Somer Fields DT7 260 B3
Somerlea EX15 162 D5
Somerset Ave EX4 176 E4
Somerset Cotts 10 PL3 248 A4
Somerset Ct
10 Brixham TQ5 230 C5
17 Totnes TQ9 223 D5
Somerset Pl
20 Barnstaple EX31 154 F5
Plymouth PL3 248 A4
11 Teignmouth TQ14 210 B4
Totnes TQ9 223 D5
Somerset Place La 11 PL3 248 A4
Somerslea EX21 73 E2
Somers Rd DT7 260 C3
Somerthing La EX33 7 E1
Somerville Cl
Exmouth EX8 196 D1
Willand EX15 162 C5
Somerville Cres EX2 182 C8
Somerville Pk EX15 162 C4
Somerville Rd EX15 162 C5
Sommers' Cres EX34 150 C6
Sonnet Cl TQ12 244 C1
Soper Rd TQ14 210 A7
Sopers Hill PL6 241 A2
Soper's Hill PL5 240 E1
Soper Wlk TQ14 210 A7
Sophia Way TQ12 207 A2
SORLEY 143 F5
Sorley Green Cross TQ7 143 F5
Sorley La TQ7 143 F5
Sorrell Ct TQ12 207 D7
Sorrel Pl TQ12 206 D5
Sorrento 10 TQ1 220 C5
Sortridge Cl PL19 171 B7
Sortridge Pk PL19 126 E5
SOURTON 93 B1
Sourton Sq 5 PL3 249 D1
SOUTH ALLINGTON 149 B5
South Ave
Bideford EX39 157 D1
Exeter EX1 177 E6
Lyme Regis DT7 260 D4
Southay Cross TA20 69 D4
Southay La TA20 69 C4
Southbank TQ12 207 C4
South Bank Dr EX39 156 F2
SOUTH BRENT 134 F3
South Brent Prim Sch TQ10 135 A3
South Brent Rd TQ7 143 E7
Southbrook Cl 2 TQ13 180 C8
Southbrook La
Bovey Tracey TQ13 180 B8
1 Bovey Tracey TQ13 180 C8
Otterton EX10 187 B1
Rockbeare EX5 99 C7
Southbrook Mdw
Cranbrook EX5 99 C6
Rockbeare EX5 99 C6
Southbrook Rd
Bovey Tracey TQ13 180 C8
Exeter EX2 178 A2
Southbrook Sch EX2 178 A2
South Burrow Rd 11 EX34 150 B5
SOUTH CHARD 88 C8
South Church La EX20 170 A4
Southcombe Cross
Hittisleigh EX6 96 F4
Widecombe in the Moor TQ13 121 B3
Southcombe Hill EX6 96 F4
Southcombe St TQ13 111 A6

SOUTH COMMON 88 A4
South Common La
EX13 . . . . 88 A5
Southcoombe Terr
EX12 . . . . 192 E7
Southcote La EX14 . . . . 86 C1
Southcote Orch TQ9 . . 223 E5
SOUTHCOTT 157 D4
Southcott Cross
Chawleigh EX18 . . . . . . 60 A6
Langtree EX38 . . . . 40 F3
Okehampton EX20 . . . . . 93 C5
Southcott Rd EX39 . . . 156 F4
South Courts The 8
PL1 . . . . 262 A3
South Dartmoor Com Coll
18 TQ13 . . . . 131 A5
South Dartmoor Com Coll
Sixth Form Ctr
TQ13 . . . . 131 A6
South Dean Cir EX31 . . 4 A5
South Dean La EX31 . . . 4 A5
South Devon Coll
TQ4 . . . . 225 E1
South Devon Coll Brunel
Ctr TQ12 . . . . 207 E3
South Devon Highway
TQ2 . . . . 213 B2
South Devon Rly ★
Buckfastleigh TQ11 . . 236 E4
Staverton TQ9 . . . . . . 215 D4
Totnes TQ9 . . . . 223 C8
South Devon Steiner Sch
TQ9 . . . . 215 C3
SOUTHDOWN 253 B6
SOUTH DOWN 68 C6
Southdown Ave TQ5 . 230 B2
Southdown Cl
Beer EX12 . . . . 191 D5
Brixham TQ5 . . . . 230 B2
Southdown Cotts
PL10 . . . . 253 B6
Southdown Cross
Brixham TQ5 . . . . 230 B1
Burlescombe EX16 . . . . 51 B2
South Molton EX36 . . . 46 A5
South Down Cross
EX19 . . . . 76 C7
South Down Farm
TQ7 . . . . 147 E5
Southdown Hill
Brixham TQ5 . . . . 230 B2
Copplestone EX17 . . . . 79 D7
Meshaw EX36 . . . . 45 F6
Southdown Ho 5
TQ13 . . . . 180 B8
Southdown La EX37 . . 43 D3
South Down La EX36 . . 31 E6
Southdown Quay
PL10 . . . . 253 B6
Southdown Rd
Beer EX12 . . . . 191 D5
Brixham TQ5 . . . . 230 B1
Millbrook PL10 . . . . . 253 A6
South Down Rd
PL2 . . . . 248 B6
South Downs Rd
EX7 . . . . 204 D4
Southdown Terr
PL10 . . . . 253 A6
South Dr EX38 . . . . . 159 B5
Southella Rd PL20 . . 127 A2
South Emb TQ6 . . . . 233 F3
South End Cl 7
EX33 . . . . 152 D5
SOUTHERLY 108 A7
Southern Cl
Plymouth PL2 . . . . . . 247 F7
Torquay TQ2 . . . . 214 A4
Southernhay
Newton Abbot TQ12 . 207 C2
Winkleigh EX19 . . . . . 58 F2
Southernhay E EX1 . . 261 B3
Southernhay Gdns
EX1 . . . . 261 B2
Southern Rd EX8 . . . . 202 A8
Southerns Cross
EX13 . . . . 103 D5
Southern Terr PL4 . . 248 F4
Southernway PL9 . . . 256 A8
Southern Wood EX8 . 196 E2
SOUTHERTON 100 B1
Southey Cres TQ12 . . 213 A3
Southey Dr TQ12 . . . 213 A3
Southey La
Kingskerswell TQ12 . . 213 A3
Sampford Courtenay
EX20 . . . . 76 F3
South Farm Rd EX9 . . 198 D5
Southfield
Saltash PL12 . . . . 242 C3
11 Torquay TQ1 . . . . 220 D4
West Alvington TQ7 . . 258 A4
Southfield Ave
Paignton TQ3 . . . . . . 225 F8
Paignton TQ3 . . . . . . 226 A8
Southfield Cl TQ3 . . . 226 A8
Southfield Dr EX17 . . 165 B6
Southfield Rd
Bideford EX39 . . . . . 157 C1
Paignton TQ3 . . . . . . 226 A7
Southfield Rise TQ3 . 226 A7
Southfields
Bridgerule EX22 . . . . . 70 F5
Totnes TQ9 . . . . 224 B6
Southfield Way
Tiverton EX16 . . . . . . 64 A7
Tiverton EX16 . . . . . 161 B4

Southford La
Staverton TQ9 . . . . . 215 F4
Staverton TQ9 . . . . . 216 A4
South Ford Rd TQ6 . . 233 F3
South Furzeham Rd
TQ5 . . . . 230 C5
Southgate EX2 . . . . . 261 B2
Southgate Ave PL9 . . 255 E4
Southgate Cl PL9 . . . 255 E4
Southgate Ct 7 EX2 . 261 B2
South Gn 5 EX32 . . . 155 B4
South Grange EX2 . . 178 D3
South Hams Bsns Pk
TQ7 . . . . 143 E4
South Hams Hospl
TQ7 . . . . 258 C6
South Hayes Copse
EX32 . . . . 17 B2
South Hayes Mdw
EX5 . . . . 99 A5
South Hayne Cross
EX36 . . . . 31 B4
South Hele Cross
EX16 . . . . 35 C1
South Hill
Plymouth, Hooe PL9 . . 255 C5
Plymouth, Stoke PL1 . 248 A3
South Hill Cotts EX22 . 38 C1
South Hill Rd TQ1 . . . 220 C4
SOUTH HOLE 37 A7
Southholme Terr
EX39 . . . . 157 B2
SOUTH HUISH 147 D7
SOUTH KNIGHTON . . 131 F7
South La
Braunton EX33 . . . . . . 15 E8
Challacombe EX31 . . . 11 F3
Hartland EX39 . . . . . . 22 E2
Lynton EX35 . . . . 5 F5
Southland Park Cres 8
PL9 . . . . 140 D8
Southland Park Rd
PL9 . . . . 140 D8
Southlands
8 Braunton EX33 . . . 152 D5
Exeter EX1 . . . . 177 E6
Exeter EX1 . . . . 177 E5
Wrafton EX33 . . . . . . 152 E4
Southlands Dr EX38 . . 40 F2
Southlands Rd TQ2 . . 220 A5
South Lawn
Exeter EX2 . . . . 261 C2
Sidmouth EX10 . . . . . 188 C8
South Lawn Terr EX1 . 177 F6
Southlea EX39 . . . . . 156 E6
South Lea EX33 . . . . 152 E5
South Lea Cl EX33 . . 152 E5
South Lee Cross EX36 . 30 B7
SOUTHLEIGH 102 C4
Southleigh Hill Cross
EX24 . . . . 102 B3
Southleigh Rd EX24 . 102 B3
South Ley Cross EX31 . 3 D1
Southley Rd EX36 . . 158 C4
Southmead Prim Sch
EX33 . . . . 152 E4
SOUTH MILTON 143 D1
South Milton St PL4 . 263 C2
SOUTH MOLTON 158 D3
South Molton Com Coll
EX36 . . . . 158 C5
South Molton Com Prim
Sch EX36 . . . . 158 C5
South Molton & District
Mus ★ EX36 . . . . . . 158 C4
South Molton Hospl
EX36 . . . . 158 C4
South Molton Rd
Bampton EX16 . . . . . . 33 F1
Bampton EX16 . . . . . . 34 B1
Chulmleigh EX37 . . . . 44 C3
Oakfordbridge EX16 . . 48 F8
South Molton St EX18 . 44 E1
South Molton United CE
Jun Sch EX36 . . . . . 158 C5
South Molton United CE
Prim Sch
South Molton EX36 . . . 30 A4
South Molton EX36 . . 158 B3
South Moor La EX17 . . 59 C1
Southmoor Rise
PL21 . . . . 137 E8
South Par EX9 . . . . . 199 H2
South Parks Rd TQ2 . 213 F2
SOUTH PILL 242 E3
South Pk
Barnstaple EX32 . . . . 155 B3
Braunton EX33 . . . . . 152 F5
Woolfardisworthy EX39 . 38 F7
SOUTH POOL 148 F7
Southport Ave EX4 . . 176 E5
South Quay TQ4 . . . . 226 C5
SOUTH RADWORTHY . 19 F3
South Rd
16 Appledore EX39 . . 15 A1
Newton Abbot TQ12 . 207 B2
South Sands TQ4 . . . 226 C2
Southside EX17 . . . . . 59 F2
Southside Ope 13
PL1 . . . . 263 A2
Southside St PL1 . . . 263 A2
South Sq 10 EX24 . . 103 A4
South St
Axminster EX13 . . . . 167 D5
Barnstaple EX32 . . . . 155 B3
Braunton EX33 . . . . . 152 D5
Colyton EX24 . . . . . . 103 A4
Denbury TQ12 . . . . . 211 A6

South St continued
Dolton EX19 . . . . 57 F7
Exeter EX1 . . . . 261 B2
Exmouth EX8 . . . . . . 202 A6
Great Torrington EX38 . 159 C5
Hatherleigh EX20 . . . . 75 C7
Holcombe Rogus TA21 . 50 F5
Sheepwash EX21 . . . . 56 C1
Sheepwash EX21 . . . . 74 C8
South Molton EX36 . . 158 C4
Torquay TQ2 . . . . . . 219 F6
Totnes TQ9 . . . . 223 C5
Wellington TA21 . . . . 160 E5
Winkleigh EX19 . . . . . 58 F3
Woolacombe EX34 . . . 7 F6
SOUTH TAWTON 95 B5
South Tawton Prim Sch
EX20 . . . . 95 B4
Southtown
Dartmouth TQ6 . . . . . 233 F2
Kenton EX6 . . . . 194 F3
Southview PL10 . . . . 253 A6
South View
Abbotskerswell TQ12 . 212 B6
Barnstaple EX31 . . . . 154 D7
Bideford EX39 . . . . . 156 F2
Bishop's Tawton EX32 . 16 E1
Bovey Tracey TQ13 . . 180 D7
Bratton Fleming EX31 . 18 A8
Braunton EX33 . . . . . 152 D4
5 Hemyock EX15 . . . 67 B8
10 Horrabridge PL20 . 126 F4
Ilfracombe EX34 . . . . 1 E3
Lydford EX20 . . . . . . 107 F4
Mary Tavy PL19 . . . . 117 E6
Plymouth, Crownhill
PL5 . . . . 244 E2
Plymouth, Elburton
PL9 . . . . 256 B6
Prixford EX31 . . . . . . 16 C7
Tiverton EX16 . . . . . 161 D4
Westleigh EX16 . . . . . 51 A3
South View Cl
Braunton EX33 . . . . . 152 D4
Plymouth PL7 . . . . . . 250 D7
Willand EX15 . . . . . . 162 D5
South View Est EX15 . 162 D5
South View Pasture
EX5 . . . . 99 A5
South View Pk PL7 . . 250 D5
Southview Rd TQ3 . . 226 A7
South View Rd EX15 . 162 D5
South View Terr
Exeter EX4 . . . . 177 D8
Exminster EX6 . . . . . 182 B4
Plymouth PL4 . . . . . . 263 C3
Sidmouth EX10 . . . . . 188 A5
SOUTHVILLE 258 E3
Southville Gdns TQ7 . 258 E3
SOUTHWAY 244 F6
Southway
Sidmouth EX10 . . . . . 188 C4
Tedburn St Mary EX6 . 97 F4
Southway Ave TQ2 . . 213 F1
Southway Dr PL6 . . . 244 E6
Southway La
Plymouth TQ12 . . . . . 244 C6
Plymouth, Southway
PL6 . . . . 245 B6
Plymouth, Tamerton Foliot
PL6 . . . . 244 C6
Southway Valley Nature
Reserve ★ PL6 . . . . . 244 F6
SOUTH WONFORD . . . 54 E3
Southwood Cross EX5 . 99 C4
Southwood Ct TQ1 . . 220 C5
Southwood Dr EX39 . 157 A3
Southwood Mdws
EX39 . . . . 40 C7
South Yeo Cross
Northlew EX20 . . . . . . 74 F2
Poughill EX17 . . . . . . 62 E3
South Yeo Hill EX17 . . 62 E3
SOUTH ZEAL 95 B3
Sovereign Cl EX8 . . . 196 E1
Sovereign Ct
Exeter EX1 . . . . 178 D3
Plymouth PL7 . . . . . . 250 C5
Sovereign Rd TQ12 . 206 B3
Sowden La
Barnstaple EX32 . . . . 155 B5
Lympstone EX8 . . . . . 195 E4
Sowden Pk EX32 . . . 155 B5
SOWTON 179 B6
Sowton Ind Est EX2 . 178 E5
Sowton La EX5 . . . . . 179 B6
Sowton Rd PL20 . . . 241 D8
SOWTONTOWN 117 F3
Space Pl EX2 . . . . . . 177 C1
Spa Ct TQ1 . . . . 220 C4
Spanishlake Cross
EX6 . . . . 113 C6
Spanish Lane End
TQ9 . . . . 224 D3
Sparhanger Cross EX35 . 5 B3
Sparhanger La EX35 . . 5 B3
Sparkatown La PL20 . 127 B3
Sparke Cl PL7 . . . . . 251 B4
Sparkhays Dr TQ9 . . 223 D4
Sparks Barn Rd TQ4 . 226 B4
SPARKWELL 251 F8
Sparkwell All Saints Prim
Sch PL7 . . . . 136 A8
Sparkwell La TQ9 . . . 215 F8
Sparrow Dr EX5 . . . . 99 B6
Sparrow La TA24 . . . 21 C7
Sparrow Pk TQ7 . . . 147 F6

Sparrow Rd TQ9 . . . 223 B5
Speakers Rd PL21 . . 237 E5
Speares The PL12 . . 242 B2
Spearfield Cl EX36 . . 158 D4
Spcars La TA21 . . . . 35 F4
Speckled Wood Ct 16
EX31 . . . . 154 A2
Speedwell Cl
Barnstaple EX32 . . . . 155 E3
Bideford EX39 . . . . . . 25 E4
Brixham TQ5 . . . . . . 230 C3
Millbrook PL10 . . . . . 252 F5
Newton Abbot TQ12 . 206 D3
Speedwell Cres PL6 . 249 B7
Speedwell Units TQ6 . 233 C3
Speedwell Wlk PL6 . 249 B7
Spekes Cross EX18 . . 59 C4
Spence Combe Cross
EX17 . . . . 79 D4
Spence Cross EX14 . . 84 D4
Spence La TQ7 . . . . 104 F7
Spencer Cl EX8 . . . . 196 E2
Spencer Ct EX11 . . . 169 D3
Spencer Dr EX14 . . . 161 F3
Spencer Gdns PL12 . 242 F1
Spencer Rd
Newton Abbot TQ12 . 207 C2
Paignton TQ3 . . . . . . 225 E7
Plymouth PL9 . . . . . . 255 E8
Spenser Ave EX2 . . . 177 F3
Speranza Gr 17 TQ14 . 210 B5
Spestos La EX17 . . . . 78 C1
Spicer Cl EX15 . . . . 163 B2
Spicer Rd EX1 . . . . . 261 C3
Spicers Rd TQ13, EX6 . 114 A1
Spider's La EX8 . . . . 196 C3
Spindlebury EX15 . . 163 A2
Spindle Cres 7 PL7 . 251 B5
Spindlewood Cl
EX14 . . . . 166 C3
Spinnaker Quay PL9 . 254 F2
Spinners La TQ9 . . . 222 E8
Spinners Sq TQ12 . . 123 E5
Spinney Cl
Exeter EX2 . . . . 178 C4
15 Roundswell EX31 . 154 A2
Spinney The
Ivybridge PL21 . . . . . 237 A5
Plymouth PL7 . . . . . . 251 A4
Uffculme EX15 . . . . . . 66 A8
Spinning Bath Gdns
EX17 . . . . 165 C4
Spinning La EX13 . . . 104 B8
Spire Ct PL5 . . . . . . 249 B5
Spire Hill Pk PL12 . . 242 C2
Spirelake EX36 . . . . . 30 F2
Spire Lake Cl EX36 . . 30 F3
Spirelake Cross EX17 . 79 C8
Spirelake Hill EX17 . . 79 C8
Spires Coll The TQ1 . 220 C7
Spire's Cross EX20 . . 77 A3
Spitfire Ave
Clyst Honiton EX1 . . . 175 F1
Clyst Honiton EX1 . . . 179 E8
Spithead TQ6 . . . . . 233 F3
Spitlar Cross EX20 . . 95 C6
Spittis Pk TQ6 . . . . . 234 B3
Spittle Cross EX18 . . 44 D4
Spittles La DT7 . . . . 260 E4
Spitup La EX10 . . . . 187 E7
Splashdown@quaywest ★
TQ4 . . . . 226 C3
Splatford Dr EX15 . . 163 C5
Splatts Cross EX19 . . 76 C7
Splitwell Cross EX17 . 62 B2
Sportsmans CI PL15 . 115 A4
Spotter Cl EX36 . . . 158 B5
Spreacombe Gdns
EX33 . . . . 8 C4
5 Exeter, Middle Moor
EX2 . . . . 178 D5
Fremington EX31 . . . 153 E5
Gunnislake PL18 . . . 125 D6
Gunnislake, St Ann's Chapel
PL18 . . . . 125 B5
Hartland EX39 . . . . . 22 D3
5 Holsworthy EX22 . 164 C4
Inner Hope TQ7 . . . . 147 B6
Kingswear TQ6 . . . . 234 A3
Lutton PL21 . . . . 133 B2
Merton EX19 . . . . 57 A7
Moretonhampstead
TQ13 . . . . 111 F5
6 Northam EX39 . . . 156 F7
North Molton EX36 . . 30 D8
North Tawton EX20 . . 77 C4
Petrockstow EX20 . . . 56 F4
Plymouth, Stonehouse
PL1 . . . . 248 A2
Rockbeare EX5 . . . . . 99 C5
Saltash PL12 . . . . . . 242 C3
Sandford EX17 . . . . . 80 A5
Sandford EX17 . . . . . 80 B5
8 Seaton EX12 . . . . 192 A5
Shebbear EX21 . . . . . 55 D4
Sheepwash EX21 . . . . 56 C1
South Molton EX36 . . 158 C4
Uffculme EX15 . . . . . . 66 A7
Ugborough PL21 . . . 137 D6
8 Whimple EX5 . . . . 99 E8
Witheridge EX16 . . . . 46 E1
Squires Cl EX32 . . . 155 B2
Squires Cotts 1
PL20 . . . . 128 B8
Squire's La EX12 . . . 55 C6
Squires' La EX21 . . . 55 D6
Squirrel Cl EX2 . . . . 164 C5
Squirrel Cl PL5 . . . . 244 E4

Springfield Rd continued
Honiton EX14 . . . . . 166 F5
Ilfracombe EX34 . . . 150 B6
Offwell EX14 . . . . . . 86 A3
Plymouth PL9 . . . . . 256 B6
1 South Brent TQ10 . 134 F3
Torquay TQ2 . . . . . . 220 D7
Wellington TA21 . . . 160 C7
Woolacombe EX34 . . 8 A6
Springfield Rise PL9 . 256 B7
Springfields EX24 . . 103 A3
Springfield Terr
1 Bideford EX39 . . . 157 B1
12 Combe Martin EX34 . 3 A3
3 Northam EX39 . . 156 F7
Tatworth TA20 . . . . . 88 D8
Westward Ho! EX39 . 156 C7
Spring Flower Ave 2
EX32 . . . . 155 C4
Spring Gdns EX11 . . 169 E3
Springhead Cross
EX12 . . . . 193 A6
Springhead La EX13 . 87 C1
Spring Head Rd DT7 . 260 B6
Springhill
Lyme Regis DT7 . . . . 260 D4
Plymouth PL2 . . . . . 248 C8
Spring Hill PL19 . . . 171 B5
Springhill Down Hill
EX16 . . . . 47 D4
Springhill Gdns DT7 . 260 D4
Springhill Gn PL2 . . 248 C8
Springhill Rd TQ9 . . 223 E5
Spring Mdw EX8 . . . 195 E5
Spring Pk PL6 . . . . . 245 E7
Spring Rd PL6 . . . . . 140 B8
Springwood Cl
Ivybridge PL21 . . . . 237 E5
Plymouth PL7 . . . . . 251 A3
Spruce Cl
Exeter EX4 . . . . 174 B2
Exmouth EX8 . . . . . . 196 D3
Spruce Gdns PL7 . . 251 B5
Spruce Pk EX17 . . . 165 C4
Spruce Way TQ3 . . . 225 E8
Spry La
Lifton PL16 . . . . 105 F4
Lifton PL16 . . . . 106 A4
Sprys Shop Cross
EX22 . . . . 72 D2
SPRYTOWN 106 B4
Sprytown Cross PL16 . 106 B4
Sprywood Cross EX21 . 56 A1
Spur Cross EX39 . . . 22 E2
Spurfield Cotts EX6 . 182 A4
Spurge Rd TQ12 . . . 206 C5
Spurway Gdns EX34 . 3 B3
Spurway Hill EX16 . . 48 A7
Spurway Hill Cross
EX16 . . . . 48 A8
Spurway Rd EX16 . . 161 F3
Square's Quay TQ7 . 258 C4
Square The
Ashreigney EX18 . . . 58 E8
Barnstaple EX32 . . . 154 F5
Beer EX12 . . . . 191 D5
16 Bere Alston PL20 . 125 E1
11 Bishop's Tawton
EX32 . . . . 16 E1
Bradworthy EX22 . . . 38 E1
Bradworthy EX22 . . . 53 E8
Braunton EX33 . . . . 152 D6
Bridestowe EX20 . . . 107 F8
Cawsand PL10 . . . . . 253 A1
Chagford TQ13 . . . . 111 A6
Chittlehampton EX37 . 28 F4
12 Chulmleigh EX18 . 44 E1
Ermington PL21 . . . . 136 F4
Exeter, Exwick EX4 . . 176 F8

Sou – Sta 309

Squirrel Ct TA21 . . . 160 D5
Stabb Cl TQ4 . . . . . 226 A1
Stabb Dr TQ4 . . . . . 226 A1
Stabdon La EX19, EX20 . 59 C1
Stable Cotts PL7 . . . 250 E5
Stable Ct TQ7 . . . . . 147 F6
Stable Ctyd DT7 . . . 193 E6
Stable La TQ1 . . . . . 214 B1
Stables The TQ9 . . . 223 D6
Stadbury Cross EX14 . 86 B5
Stadbury La EX14 . . 86 B5
Staddens Lea La TQ2 219 C6
STADDISCOMBE . . . 255 F3
Staddiscombe Pk
PL9 . . . . 255 F4
Staddiscombe Rd
PL9 . . . . 255 F4
Staddle Stone Rd
EX1 . . . . 178 F8
STADDON 72 C6
Staddon Cl
Braunton EX33 . . . . 152 C6
Exeter EX4 . . . . 178 F7
Plympton PL7 . . . . . 132 C2
Staddon Court Cotts
PL9 . . . . 140 B8
Staddon Cres PL9 . . 255 E6
Staddon Cross EX22 . 72 C6
Staddon Gate EX20 . 77 D5
Staddon Gdns TQ2 . 214 B2
Staddon Gn PL9 . . . 255 D6
Staddonhill Rd TA24 . 21 F8
Staddon La PL9 . . . 255 E6
Staddon Moor Cross
EX20 . . . . 77 D5
Staddon Park Rd
PL9 . . . . 255 F6
Staddon Rd
Appledore EX39 . . . . 15 A1
Holsworthy EX22 . . . 164 F3
Tedburn St Mary EX6 . 97 E2
Whimble EX22 . . . . . 164 F2
Staddons View TQ13 . 180 C8
Staddon Terrace La
PL1 . . . . 262 B4
Stadium Dr TQ12 . . 213 A2
Stadium Way EX10 . 261 C4
Stadway Mdw EX10 . 187 E5
Staffick EX6 . . . . . . 194 E3
Stafford Cross EX24 . 102 D2
Stafford Ct 1 TQ9 . . 223 E5
Stafford Hill EX14 . . 84 F8
Stafford La EX24 . . . 103 A3
Stafford Moor Fishery ★
EX19 . . . . 58 B6
Stafford Rd
Dolton EX19 . . . . 57 F7
Exeter EX4 . . . . 176 F5
Paignton TQ4 . . . . . 226 C5
Stafford Terr La 8
PL3 . . . . 263 A4
Stafford Way EX19 . . 57 F7
Stag Cnr EX15 . . . . 162 E1
Staggers La EX33 . . 152 E3
Stag La
Plymouth, Elburton
PL9 . . . . 256 B8
Plymouth, Plympton
PL9 . . . . 250 B1
Stag Mill Cross EX16 . 50 B3
Stag's Head EX32 . . 29 D6
Stags Wood Dr EX21 . 73 E2
Stakes Hill TQ7 . . . . 143 A5
Stakes Rd TQ7 . . . . 143 A6
Stallards EX33 . . . . 152 C7
Stamford Cl PL9 . . . 255 A6
Stamford Fort Cotts
PL9 . . . . 255 A6
Stamford La PL9 . . . 255 A6
Stamford Rd PL9 . . . 255 A6
Stammery Hill EX13 . 88 C1
Stamps Hill PL8 . . . 257 A6
Stamps The PL17 . . 125 A5
Stanborough Cross
PL9 . . . . 256 C7
Stanborough Ct TQ9 . 139 A3
Stanborough Rd PL9 . 256 B7
Stanbridge Pk EX39 . 156 D2
Stanbury Ave PL6 . . 244 F1
Stanbury Cl PL15 . . 90 C1
Stanbury Copse
EX34 . . . . 150 A4
Stanbury Cross
Holsworthy EX22 . . . 164 D6
Morwenstow EX23 . . . 36 F1
Stanbury Ct EX17 . . 165 C5
Stanbury Rd
Knowle EX33 . . . . 8 D1
Torquay TQ2 . . . . . . 219 C2
Stanbury Row EX2 . . 181 B6
Stanbury Orch EX6 . . 96 F3
Stancombe Cross
TQ7 . . . . 144 E4
Standard Ct PL19 . . 117 E6
Standarhay Cl PL9 . . 256 C7
Standarhay Villas
PL9 . . . . 256 C7
Standle TA21 . . . . . 160 C3
Stanford Rd EX2 . . . 178 C5
Stang La EX34 . . . . . 8 F5
Stangray Ave PL4 . . 248 C4
Stanhope Cl EX22 . . 164 C5
Stanhope Dr EX10 . . 188 B6

Stanhope Rd PL5 . . . . .243 C1
Stanhope Sq **7**
  EX22. . . . . .164 C4
Stanhope Terr EX39 . .157 A3
Staniforth Dr PL21. . .237 D4
Stanley Cotts EX24. . .103 A3
Stanley Ct
  Parkham EX39 . . . . . . .39 E8
  Torquay TQ1. . . . . . . .220 C8
Stanley Gdns TQ3. . . .226 A7
Stanley Mews EX9 . . .198 A1
Stanley Pl PL4 . . . . . . .249 B2
Stanley Rd TQ1. . . . . .220 C8
Stanley Sq EX3 . . . . . .182 F4
Stanley St **10** TQ14 . . .210 B4
Stanley Wlk EX8 . . . . .196 D4
Stanmore Rise EX7. . .204 C8
Stanmore Tor TQ3 . . .226 A5
Stannary Bridge Rd
  PL19. . . . . .171 D6
Stannary Cl PL21. . . . .237 E5
Stannary Ct EX20 . . . .170 D5
Stannary La PL7 . . . . .250 E5
Stannary Pl TQ13 . . . .111 A6
Stansfield Ave TQ3 . . .226 A6
Stantaway Pk TQ1 . . .219 F7
Stanton Ct TQ7 . . . . . .138 A1
Stantor La PL7. . . . . . .218 F5
Stant Way TA20 . . . . . .69 F6
Stantyway Cross EX9 .198 F6
Stantyway Ct EX9 . . . .198 F5
Stantyway Rd EX9. . . .198 F5
Stanwell Dr EX39 . . . .156 C6
Stanwell Hill
  Bideford EX39. . . . . . .25 C4
  Westward Ho! EX39 . .156 C6
Stanwey EX1 . . . . .178 A5
Staplake La EX6 . . . . .201 A7
Staplake Rd
  Starcross EX6. . . . . . .195 B1
  12 Starcross EX6. . . . .201 A8
Staplake Rd EX6. . . . .195 A1
Staplanke Rd EX6. . . .194 F1
Stapleback Cross
  EX19. . . . . .57 E5
Staple Back La EX19. . .57 E5
Staple Cl PL6 . . . . .241 C1
Staple Cross EX19. . . . .57 F5
Stapledon Cotts EX22 . .72 E7
Stapledon La TQ13 . . .130 F5
Stapleford Dr TQ14 . .210 B7
Stapleford Gdns PL5 .243 F5
Staplegate EX16 . . . . . .50 A3
Staplehill Rd
  Coldeast TQ12. . . . . . .122 F1
  Newton Abbot TQ12. .206 B8
Staple Orch TQ9 . . . . .222 F8
Staples Mdw TA20 . . . .88 D8
Staples Mews **4**
  EX8. . . . . .202 A7
Staples Terr DT7 . . . . .260 E4
Stapleton Cl TQ4. . . . .225 E3
Stapleton Way EX2. . .181 E7
STAPLEY 68 A8
Star Barton La EX5 . . .172 D4
Starcombe La EX10 . . .101 C4
STARCROSS 201 A8
Star Cross EX13. . . . . . .87 E6
Starcross Prim Sch
  EX6. . . . . .201 A8
Starcross Sta EX6. . . .201 B8
Starkey Cl PL6 **10** EX16 . . .64 D7
Starling Dr PL6 . . . . . .245 A2
Starlings Roost EX15 .163 A2
Starpitten Gr TQ2 . . . .214 B3
Starpitten Lane W
  TQ2. . . . . .214 A2
Star Pk PL18. . . . . . . .125 D6
Starre Cl EX12 . . . . . . .192 A7
START. 145 B4
Start Ave
  Chillington TQ7 . . . . .145 A1
  Teignmouth TQ14 . . .210 C7
Start Bay Pk TQ6 . . . .145 F6
Start Cross TQ12. . . . .211 B7
Starved Oak Cross
  EX5. . . . . .81 D1
Station App
  Crediton EX17. . . . . . .165 E3
  South Brent TQ10. . . .134 F3
Station App Rd TQ12 .123 B3
Station Cl
  Braunton EX33 . . . . . .152 D5
  12 Holsworthy EX22. .164 C4
Station Cotts
  Bittaford TQ10 . . . . . .137 E8
  Brandis Corner EX22 . .73 A5
Station Cross
  Bittaford TQ10 . . . . . .137 E8
  Crediton EX17. . . . . . .165 E4
Station Ct TQ13. . . . . .180 C7
Station Fields EX17 . . .73 E2
Station High Rd EX21. .73 E3
Station Hill
  Barnstaple EX32. . . . . .18 A4
  Bideford EX39. . . . . . .157 B1
  Bratton Fleming EX31. .11 A1
  Bratton Fleming EX31. .18 A8
  Brixham TQ5. . . . . . . .230 C5
  Chudleigh TQ13 . . . . .123 E5
  Great Torrington EX38 .159 A6
  Lynton EX35 . . . . .151 B4
  Swimbridge EX17. . . . .17 E1

Station La
  Calstock PL18. . . . . . .125 D3
  Paignton TQ4 . . . . . . .226 B5
Station Rd
  Bampton EX16 . . . . . . .34 B1
  Barnstaple EX31. . . . .154 F4
  Bere Alston PL20 . . . .125 E2
  Bere Ferrers PL20 . . .239 E3
  Bickleigh PL6 . . . . . . .132 A5
  Bovey Tracey TQ13 . .180 C7
  Bow EX17. . . . . .78 B3
  Bratton Fleming EX31. .18 A8
  Braunton EX33 . . . . . .152 D5
  Bridestowe EX20 . . . .107 F7
  Broadclyst EX5 . . . . . .175 E3
  Buckfastleigh TQ11. . .236 C5
  Budleigh Salterton
   EX9. . . . . .198 A1
  Burlescombe EX16 . . . .51 B3
  Chard Junction TA20. . .88 D8
  Chulmleigh EX18. . . . . .44 C3
  Colyton EX24 . . . . . . .103 A5
  Crediton EX17. . . . . . . .79 A6
  Cullompton EX15 . . . .163 C4
  17 Dawlish EX7. . . . . .204 E6
  Exeter EX4 . . . . .176 F8
  Exeter, Pinhoe EX1 . . .174 E1
  Exeter, St David's EX4. .177 A8
  Exminster EX6 . . . . . .182 D3
  Exton EX3. . . . . .183 C1
  Feniton EX14 . . . . .84 D2
  Gunnislake PL18. . . . .125 C6
  Halwill Junction EX21. .73 E2
  Hele EX5. . . . . .82 F5
  Hemyock EX15 . . . . . . .67 B8
  Holsworthy EX22 . . . .164 C4
  Horrabridge PL20 . . .126 F4
  Ide EX2. . . . . .176 D1
  Ilfracombe EX34. . . . .150 A4
  Ivybridge PL21. . . . . .237 D6
  Lifton PL16 . . . . .105 F4
  Loddiswell TQ7 . . . . . .143 F7
  Lydford EX20 . . . . . . .108 A6
  Mary Tavy PL19 . . . . .117 E6
  Meeth EX20 . . . . .57 C2
  Moretonhampstead
   TQ13. . . . . .111 F4
  Newton Abbot TQ12 .207 D3
  Newton Poppleford
   EX10. . . . . .186 F8
  Newton Poppleford
   EX10. . . . . .187 A8
  North Brentor PL19 . .117 C8
  Northlew EX20 . . . . . . .74 E1
  Okehampton EX20 . . .170 B4
  Plymouth, Elburton
   PL9. . . . . .256 C7
  Plymouth, Keyham PL2 247 E5
  Plymouth, Plympton
   PL7. . . . . .250 C5
  Plymouth, Tamerton Foliot
   PL5. . . . . .244 A6
  Princetown PL20 . . . .128 A8
  Saltash PL12. . . . . . . .243 A2
  Sidmouth EX10 . . . . . .188 A4
  8 South Brent TQ10. . .134 F3
  South Molton EX36. . .158 D5
  3 Teignmouth TQ14 . .210 C4
  Tiverton EX16. . . . . . .161 D4
  Topsham EX3. . . . . . . .182 F5
  Totnes TQ9 . . . . .223 C6
  Wellington TA21 . . . . .160 C7
  Whimple EX5. . . . . .99 E8
  Willand EX15 . . . . . . .162 C5
  Woolacombe EX34 . . . .8 A6
  Yelverton PL20 . . . . . .127 A2
  Yeoford EX17. . . . . . . .79 C1
Station Road Ind Est
  EX15. . . . . .67 B8
Station View TQ9. . . . .117 C8
Station Yard EX13. . . .167 C5
Station Yard Bsns Pk
  TQ14. . . . . .210 C3
Station Yard Ind Est
  TQ7. . . . . .258 C5
STAVERTON 216 B5
Staverton Cotts TQ13 130 F4
Staverton Sta★ TQ9 .215 E4
Stawley County Prim Sch
  TA21. . . . . .51 B8
Steamer Quay Rd
  TQ9. . . . . .223 D4
Steamer Quay Wharf **11**
  TQ9. . . . . .223 D4
Steartfield Rd TQ3,
  TQ4. . . . . .226 C7
Steddaford Ct EX20 . . .95 A5
Stedhams Cl TA21. . . .160 D7
Steed Cl TQ4 . . . . .229 A8
Steel Cl EX14 . . . . .166 D6
Steeperton Ct EX20 . .170 D5
Steep Head EX36. . . . . .19 B1
Steep Hill TQ1 . . . . . . .214 D6
Steep La
  Hartford TA22. . . . . . . .34 C8
  Landkey EX32. . . . . . . .17 D2
Steeple Cl PL9 . . . . . . .255 F4
Steeple Dr EX2 . . . . . .181 B8
Steeple Mdw EX37 . . . .44 E6
Steer Park Rd PL7. . . .251 C5
Steer Point Cotts
  PL8. . . . . .256 F2
Steer Point Rd
  Brixton PL8. . . . . .257 A4
  Combe PL8. . . . . .256 F3
Stefan Cl PL9 . . . . .255 B5

Stella Maris Ct EX39. .157 A2
Stella Rd TQ3. . . . . . . .219 A1
Stemson Ave EX4 . . . .174 D1
Stenlake Pl PL4. . . . . .249 B2
Stenlake Terr PL4. . . .249 B2
Stentaway Cl PL9 . . . .255 F8
Stentaway Dr PL9 . . . .256 A8
Stentaway La EX33 . . . .7 E2
Stentaway Rd PL9. . . .255 F8
Stentiford Hill TQ7. . .258 D7
Stentiford Hill Rd
  TQ1. . . . . .220 B5
Stentiford La TQ13 . . .122 D4
Stepcote Hill EX1. . . . .261 A2
Stephens Way EX1. . . .179 B8
Steppes Mdw TQ12. . .207 A2
Steppingstone Cross
  EX33. . . . . .8 D1
Stepps Cross EX12 . . .192 E7
Stepps Rd EX12, DT7. .193 B5
Steps Cl EX1. . . . . .174 F1
Steps Cross TQ2 . . . . .214 B3
Stepstone La EX33 . . . .8 D1
Sterlings Wy EX20 . . .170 D6
Steven's Cross EX10. . .188 D8
Steven's Cross Cl
  EX10. . . . . .188 B8
Stevens La EX10 . . . . .188 A7
STEVENSTONE 42 A6
Stevenstone Ct EX38 . .42 A6
Stevenstone Rd EX8. .202 D1
Stewart Cl EX8. . . . . . .196 E1
Stewart Ct EX13. . . . . .167 E7
Stewart Gdns EX7. . . .204 E7
Stewart Ho EX7. . . . . .204 E7
Stewarts Rd EX22. . . . .70 C1
STIBB CROSS 40 C1
Stibb La PL21. . . . . . . .136 D7
STICKLEPATH
  Barnstaple 154 E4
  Okehampton. 95 A5
Stickle Path EX16 . . . . .35 C1
Sticklepath Com Sch
  EX31. . . . . .154 C3
Sticklepath Ct EX31. . .154 E3
Sticklepath Hill EX31 154 E4
Sticklepath Terr
  EX31. . . . . .154 C3
Sticksend La TQ13 . . .124 A8
Stidson Cross TQ10 . .135 B3
Stidston La TQ10 . . . . .135 A3
Stile Ct EX15. . . . . .163 B2
Stile Orch TQ7 . . . . . . .143 F7
Stillman Ct **6** PL4 . . . .263 A2
Stillman St PL4 . . . . . .263 A2
Stiniel Cross TQ13 . . .111 A4
Stintway La EX10. . . . .187 E5
Stirling Ct PL5. . . . . . .243 C1
Stirling Rd PL5 . . . . . .243 C1
Stitchill Rd TQ1. . . . . .220 C4
Stitworthy Cross EX39 23 C1
Stoat Pk EX32. . . . . . . .155 D4
Stoats Cl EX36 . . . . . .158 C2
Stoats Mews EX20 . . . .77 C4
Stockadon Farm Barns
  PL12. . . . . .238 B4
Stockadon La EX6. . . . .63 A1
Stockbridge La **16**
  TQ10. . . . . .134 F3
Stocker Rd EX4 . . . . . .173 B1
Stockeydown La EX17. 79 E2
Stockham Hill TQ22 . . .33 E8
Stockham La TA20 . . . .88 C7
Stock Hill EX35 . . . . . .151 A1
Stock La EX12 . . . . . . .192 A5
STOCKLAND 87 A8
Stockland CE Prim Acad
  EX14. . . . . .87 A7
Stockland Cross EX15 66 A3
Stockland Head Cross
  EX15. . . . . .84 B7
Stockland Hill EX14 . . .86 E6
Stockland La EX15 . . . . .8 D2
Stockland Rd TA20 . . . .69 D2
Stockleigh Cross
  Cheriton Fitzpaine
   EX17. . . . . .62 C1
  Stockleigh Pomeroy
   EX17. . . . . .80 F6
STOCKLEIGH
  ENGLISH 62 D1
Stockleigh La EX21. . . .74 F7
STOCKLEIGH
  POMEROY 81 A6
STOCKLEY HAMLET . . .94 D6
Stockman La EX20 . . . .88 C7
Stockmeadow Gdns
  TQ14. . . . . .209 A7
Stock Pk EX20 . . . . . . .170 E6
Stock Rd EX35 . . . . .5 B3
Stockstyle La EX15 . . . .88 A8
Stockton Ave EX7 . . . .204 E6
Stockton Hill EX7 . . . .204 D6
Stockton La **8** EX7. . . .204 D6
Stockton Rd EX7. . . . .204 D6
STOCKWELL 82 D5
Stockwell Cross EX5 . .82 D5
Stoford Lane TA21 . . . .52 F7
STOFORD WATER 66 B3
Stoggy La
  Frogmore & Sherford
   TQ7. . . . . .144 C3
  Plymouth PL7. . . . . . .250 F6
  Plymouth PL7. . . . . . .251 A6
  Plymouth PL7. . . . . . .251 B7
STOKE
  Ashburton. 129 F5

STOKE continued
  Hartland. 22 B3
  Plymouth 248 A3
STOKE CANON 173 E8
Stoke Canon CE Prim Sch
  EX5. . . . . .173 E8
STOKE CLIMSLAND. . .115 C1
Stoke Climsland Sch
  PL17. . . . . .115 B1
Stoke Cross PL8 . . . . .141 B6
Stoke Damerel Bsns Ctr
  9 PL2. . . . . .248 A4
Stoke Damerel Com Coll
  PL3. . . . . .248 B4
Stoke Damerel Prim Sch
  PL1. . . . . .248 A3
STOKE FLEMING 146 B7
Stoke Fleming Com Prim
  Sch TQ6. . . . . .146 A7
STOKE GABRIEL 227 F7
Stoke Gabriel Prim Sch
  TQ9. . . . . .227 F7
Stoke Gabriel Rd
  TQ5. . . . . .229 A5
STOKE HILL 173 E1
Stoke Hill
  Exeter EX4 . . . . .173 E2
  Stoke Canon EX5. . . .173 F6
  Stoke Climsland PL17. .115 B1
  Stoke Gabriel TQ9. . . .227 F7
Stoke Hill Cres EX4 . .173 E1
Stoke Hill Inf Sch
  EX4. . . . . .173 E1
Stoke Hill Jun Sch
  EX4. . . . . .173 E1
Stoke Hill La PL20. . . .126 E2
Stoke House Gdns
  TQ6. . . . . .146 B7
STOKEINTEIGNHEAD
  . . . . .209 B1
Stokeinteignhead Sch
  TQ12. . . . . .209 B1
Stokelake TQ13 . . . . . .123 D5
Stoke Lyne EX8 . . . . . .196 C1
Stoke Meadow Cl
  EX4. . . . . .173 E2
Stoke Mill La EX32 . . . .17 F6
STOKENHAM 145 C1
Stokenham Area Prim
  Sch TQ7. . . . . .145 B1
Stokenham Cross
  TQ7. . . . . .145 B1
STOKE POST 174 A5
Stoke Rd
  Higher Gabwell TQ1,
   TQ12. . . . . .214 C7
  Noss Mayo PL8. . . . . .141 A6
  Paignton TQ3 . . . . . . .225 B1
  Paignton, Higher Yalberton
   TQ4. . . . . .225 C3
  Paignton, Waddeton
   TQ5. . . . . .228 F6
  Plymouth PL1 . . . . . . .262 A3
  Stoke Canon EX4, EX5..173 D5
  Stokeinteignhead
   . . . . .209 B1
STOKE RIVERS 17 F6
Stokesay Ave PL6 . . . .245 A5
Stokes Cl TQ13. . . . . . .180 F7
Stokes La
  Plymouth PL1 . . . . . . .263 A2
  Tiverton EX16. . . . . . .161 D4
Stokes Mead EX5 . . . .173 E2
Stoke Valley Rd EX4. .173 D2
Stokewood La EX22 . . .17 F6
Stokingway Cl PL9 . . .255 E5
Stoneacre Cl TQ5. . . . .230 C3
Stone Ash La EX17 . . . .61 C3
Stonebarrow La EX13 . 88 F2
Stone Barton EX5 . . . . .99 B6
Stonebarton Cl PL7 . .250 C6
Stonebarton Rd EX1. .179 A8
Stoneborough Cnr
  EX9. . . . . .198 B1
Stoneborough Ct
  EX9. . . . . .198 B1
Stoneborough La
  EX9. . . . . .198 B1
Stone Cl EX14. . . . . . . .166 B4
STONECOMBE 10 C6
Stonecombe Hill EX31 10 C6
Stone Cross
  Chagford TQ13 . . . . . . .96 A1
  Lifton PL16 . . . . .105 E5
  Meeth EX20 . . . . .57 C4
  Molland EX36 . . . . .31 F7
  North Tawton EX20. . . .77 E4
  West Buckland EX32. . .18 A4
  Widecombe in the Moor
   TQ13. . . . . .121 B1
Stone Ct TQ2 . . . . .213 D1
Stonehall Flats PL1 . .248 A1
Stonehanger TQ8 . . . .259 D4
Stonehanger Ct TQ8 .259 D4
Stonehedge Cl PL21. .237 D4
STONEHOUSE 248 A1
Stonehouse Bridge
  PL1. . . . . .248 A1
Stonehouse St PL1. . .262 A2
Stone La
  Bickleigh EX5 . . . . . . .82 A8
  Cadbury EX5. . . . . .81 F7
  Chulmleigh EX17. . . . . .60 A8
  Drewsteignton TQ13. . .96 A1
  Lympstone EX8. . . . . .195 E5
Stoneland Cl EX5 . . . . .99 B6
Stoneland Cross EX16. 47 F4

Stoneland La EX16 . . . .47 F5
Stonelands EX6. . . . . . .96 F3
Stonelands Bridge
  EX7. . . . . .204 C6
Stonelands Mews
  EX7. . . . . .204 C6
Stonelands Pk EX7. . .204 C6
Stonelands Terr EX7 .204 C6
Stone Lane Gdns★
  TQ13. . . . . .96 A1
Stone Lane Ret Pk
  EX2. . . . . .177 B3
Stoneleigh
  Sidmouth EX10 . . . . . .189 C7
  Wellington TA21 . . . . .160 B8
Stoneleigh Cl TQ12. . .206 F4
Stoneleigh Dr TQ2 . . .219 D3
Stoneleigh Gdns
  EX15. . . . . .163 B3
Stoneman's Hill
  TQ12. . . . . .212 B7
Stonemans La EX38 . .159 C5
Stonemoor Cross
  EX38. . . . . .56 B7
Stone Moor Cross
  EX18. . . . . .45 C1
Stonemoor La EX36. . . .31 F7
Stonepark TQ13 . . . . .130 F4
Stonepark Cres TQ13 130 F4
Stone Pk TQ4 . . . . .229 D6
Stoneridge La TA4 . . . .35 D5
Stones Cl
  8 Kingsteignton
   TQ12. . . . . .123 F1
  Modbury PL21. . . . . . .137 C2
Stones Gallop
  Cranbrook EX5. . . . . . .99 C6
  Rockbeare EX5. . . . . . .99 C6
Stone's Hill EX17. . . . . .80 A7
Stoneshill Cross EX17 80 A7
Stonewall La EX17 . . .165 C6
Stone Wlk EX1. . . . . . .174 F3
Stoneybrook Rise
  EX20. . . . . .75 C7
Stoneycliffe Pl PL20. .128 B8
STONEYCOMBE 212 D3
Stoneyford
  Cullompton 163 E4
  Newton Poppleford . .186 A6
Stoneyford Pk EX9 . . .198 B1
Stoneyhill TQ12. . . . . .212 B3
Stoneyhouse La EX14 .86 D1
Stoney La
  Axminster EX13 . . . . .167 E6
  Bradninch EX5 . . . . . . .82 F7
  Honiton EX14 . . . . . . .166 D2
Stoneylands EX5. . . . . .99 C5
Stoney Lane Cross
  EX16. . . . . .50 B3
Stoney Lane Hill EX16 .48 C2
Stoney Park La EX20 .170 A4
Stoneywell **3** EX39 . . .15 B1
Stoning Cross EX20 . . .75 C7
Stonley Ct **13** PL1 . . . .262 A3
Stonybridge Cross
  EX36. . . . . .30 B8
Stonybridge Hill EX36. .30 B8
Stony Cnr EX34 . . . . . . .3 D3
Stony Hill Cross EX36 .31 A3
Stony La
  Gunnislake PL18. . . . .125 D6
  Landkey EX32. . . . . . . .17 B1
  Lympstone EX8. . . . . .195 F8
  Parracombe EX31. . . . . .4 D1
  Swimbridge EX32 . . . . .28 B8
  Winsham EX33 . . . . .8 E2
  Woodbury Salterton
   EX5. . . . . .184 C6
STONYLAND 27 B8
Stony Lane End EX32. . .17 B1
Stonyville Pl **3** PL20 .128 B8
STOODLEIGH 48 E5
Stoodleigh Cross
  Calverleigh EX16 . . . . .48 B4
  West Buckland EX32. . .18 B2
Stoodleigh Moor Cross
  EX16. . . . . .48 D6
Stooke Bridge Rd
  EX15. . . . . .83 C1
Stooks Cl EX15 . . . . . . .81 E1
Stoop EX39 . . . . .23 D3
Stoop Cross TQ9 . . . . .131 E1
Stooper's Hill TA20 . . .69 F6
Stopford Pl PL1. . . . . .247 F3
STOPGATE 68 F4
Stopgate Cross
  Yarcombe EX14 . . . . . .68 F4
  Zeal Monachorum EX17 .78 C8
STORMSDOWN 131 B7
Stormsdown Cotts
  TQ12. . . . . .131 B7
Storridge La EX13. . . . .88 B6
Storrs Cl TQ13 . . . . . .180 C8
Stott Cl PL3. . . . . .249 D5
Stour Cl PL3. . . . . .249 D6
Stourscombe 105 A2
Stourscombe Wood
  PL15. . . . . .105 A2
Stout Cross TQ14. . . . .68 F5
Stovar Long La
  Beer EX12 . . . . .191 D6
  Beer EX2. . . . . .191 C6
Stover Ct EX4. . . . . . . .261 C4
Stover Ctry Pk★
  TQ12. . . . . .123 B2
Stover Sch TQ12 . . . . .123 B1
Stowbrook EX10 . . . . .187 F8

Stowe Gdns PL5 . . . . .244 B2
Stowe La EX20 . . . . . . .76 C4
Stowell La TA20. . . . . . .88 D8
Stowe The EX23 . . . . . .37 A1
STOWFORD
  Bradworthy. 53 B8
  Challacombe. 11 B4
  Chittlehampton. 28 E5
  Colaton Raleigh 186 A3
  Halwill Junction 91 D8
  Lewdown 106 D5
  Sidmouth 187 E8
Stowford Bsns Pk
  PL21. . . . . .237 D4
Stowford Cl PL20 . . . .127 B3
Stowford Cross
  Bradworthy EX22. . . . .53 C8
  Chittlehampton EX37. .29 A5
  Cobbaton EX37. . . . . . .28 E5
  Halwill EX21. . . . . .91 D8
  South Molton EX36. . . .19 B2
  Stowford EX31. . . . . . . .11 C3
  West Putford EX22. . . .39 C2
Stowford Gate EX10. .187 E8
Stowford Hill EX17. . . .61 A7
Stowford Hts EX12 . . .191 F8
Stowford Prim Sch
  PL21. . . . . .237 D5
Stowford Rise EX10 . .187 F8
Straightway Head
  EX5. . . . . .100 A7
Strand
  Exmouth EX8. . . . . . . .202 A6
  Shaldon TQ14 . . . . . . .210 A3
  Topsham EX3. . . . . . . .182 F4
  Torquay TQ1 . . . . .220 B4
Strand Cl EX31. . . . . . . .16 B6
Strand Ct
  1 Bideford EX39. . . . .157 A2
  Topsham EX3 . . . . . . .182 F4
Strand Hill EX7 . . . . . .204 E6
Strand La EX31 . . . . . . .16 B6
Strand St PL1. . . . . . . .254 A8
Strand The
  Barnstaple EX32. . . . .154 F5
  Bideford EX39. . . . . . .157 A2
  3 Brixham TQ5 . . . . . .230 D5
  Culmstock EX15 . . . . . .66 E8
  Dawlish EX7 . . . . .204 E6
  18 Ilfracombe EX34. . .150 C6
  Lympstone EX8. . . . . .195 D5
  Ringmore TQ14 . . . . . .209 C5
  Starcross EX6. . . . . . .201 B2
  Topsham EX3 . . . . . . .182 F4
Strand View EX3. . . . .182 F4
Strashleigh View
  PL21. . . . . .136 D6
Stratford Ave EX4. . . .178 C8
Strathculm Rd EX5. . .82 F5
Strathmore Ct EX39 . . .25 E4
Stratton Dr EX3 . . . . . .182 E6
Stratton Wlk PL2. . . . .248 D8
Strawberry Ave EX2. .181 C4
Strawberry Fields
  EX20. . . . . .77 C4
Strawberry Hill EX8 . .195 F4
Strawberry La
  5 Exeter EX3. . . . . . . .182 C8
  Holcombe EX7 . . . . . .204 C5
  Ottery St Mary EX10. .100 C5
  Ottery St Mary EX11. .169 C2
Strawberry Terr
  TQ12. . . . . .207 E8
Strawberry Valley
  Dartmouth TQ6. . . . . .233 A3
  Hillfield TQ6. . . . . .232 E1
Straypark Cnr EX35 . . .5 E4
Stray Pk PL8. . . . . .257 F4
Streamcombe La TA22 33 A3
Stream Ct EX2 . . . . . . .261 A1
Streamers Mdws
  EX14. . . . . .166 C5
Streams La EX31. . . . . . .9 B2
Streatham Dr EX4. . . .177 B8
Streatham Rise EX4. .177 A8
STREET 190 B4
STREET ASH 69 E8
Street Ash La TA20 . . .69 F8
Street The
  Kilmington EX13. . . . . .87 C1
  Musbury EX13. . . . . . .103 D5
STRETE 145 E5
Strete Ralegh EX5 . . .168 A2
Strode Rd
  Buckfastleigh TQ11. . .236 B4
  Plymouth PL7 . . . . . . .250 F6
Stroma Cl PL6. . . . . . . .244 F7
Strongs Hill Cross
  EX21. . . . . .73 F1
Stroud Park Rd PL2 . .248 C7
STROXWORTHY 39 A6
Stroxworthy Cross
  EX39. . . . . .38 F6
Stuart Cres EX15. . . . .163 C6
Stuart Ct EX7 . . . . .204 D4
Stuart Rd
  Exeter EX1 . . . . .177 D1
  Plymouth PL2 . . . . . . .248 C4
  Plymouth, Pennycomequick
   PL3. . . . . .262 A4
Stuart Road Prim Sch
  PL1. . . . . .262 A4
Stuart Way EX5. . . . . . .99 A1
Stubbing Cross EX24 102 C5
Stubbins Cross TQ12 .211 D7
Stubborn Cross EX16. .62 C7
Stuckeridge Cross
  EX16. . . . . .48 D8

Stucley Rd EX39 . . . . . . 156 E1
Studd Dr EX32 . . . . 29 C7
Studhayes Cross EX13 87 C1
Studhayes La EX13 . . . . 87 B2
Studhayes Rd EX13. . . . 87 B2
Studley Ho 4 EX14. . 166 C5
Studley Rd IQ1 . . . . . 220 A7
Stumpy Cross
  Shobrooke EX17 . . . . . . 80 F4
  Silverton EX5 . . . . 82 B4
Stumpypost Cross
  TQ7. . . . . 144 B6
Sturcombe Ave TQ4 . 225 F3
Sturdee Rd PL2 . . . . . . 248 A5
Sturges Rd EX8 . . . . . 202 D8
Sturt Cotts EX17 . . . . . 78 E7
Sturtlebury La TQ7. . 143 F5
Style Cl EX32 . . . . 155 B2
Subway App EX15 . . . 162 C4
Suddon's Cross EX24 102 B6
Suddon's La EX24 . . . 102 B6
Sugar Ho Hill EX3 . . 182 F8
Sugar Loaf Hill & Saltern
  Cove Nature Reserve *
  TQ4. . . . . 226 C1
Sugar Mill Bsns Pk
  PL9. . . . . 249 C1
Sullivan Rd EX2. . . . . 178 C5
Summer Cl
  Exeter EX4 . . . . 178 B8
  Exmouth EX8. . . . . . 202 E8
  13 Hemyock EX15. . . . 67 B8
Summercourt Way
  TQ5. . . . . 230 A2
Summerfield
  Sidmouth EX10 . . . . . 188 B8
  Woodbury EX5 . . . . . 184 C4
Summer Field EX19 . . 58 E4
Summerfield Ave
  TA21. . . . . 52 D8
Summerfield Ct
  Ivybridge PL21 . . . . . 237 A5
  Paignton TQ4 . . . . . . 226 C4
Summerfield Rd TQ2 219 E8
Summerfields PL12 . . 242 D1
Summerfield Way
  TA21. . . . . 52 D8
Summer Green PL19 . 116 E3
Summerhayes EX7. . . 204 D4
Summerhill Cl 18
  TQ12. . . . . 122 F1
Summerhill Cres 17
  TQ12. . . . . 122 F1
Summerhill Cross
  TQ13. . . . . 130 E4
Summerhill Ho DT7 . 260 E4
Summerhill Rd
  16 Coldeast TQ12. . . . 122 F1
  Lyme Regis DT7 . . . . 260 E4
Summer House Hill Path
  EX35. . . . . 151 D3
Summering Cl EX20 . 170 E6
Summering Wlk
  Okehampton EX20 . . 170 D6
  Okehampton EX20 . . 170 E6
Summer La
  Alfington EX11 . . . . . 100 F8
  Bovey Tracey TQ13 . . 123 C2
  Brixham TQ5. . . . . . . 230 B2
  Exeter EX4 . . . . 174 B1
  Exmouth EX8. . . . . . 196 B4
  Northlew EX20 . . . . . . 74 F2
Summerland EX14 . . 166 C5
Summerland Ave
  EX7. . . . . 204 D7
Summerland Cl EX7. 204 D6
Summerland Cotts
  Alfington EX11 . . . . . 100 F8
  5 Newton Abbot
  TQ12. . . . . 207 C3
Summerland Ct 6
  TQ12. . . . . 207 C3
Summerland Pl
  12 Barnstaple EX32 . . 155 A4
  10 South Molton EX36 . 158 C4
Summerlands TQ12 . . 123 A1
Summerlands Cl
  Brixham TQ5. . . . . . . 230 A2
  Plymouth PL7 . . . . . . 251 C5
Summerlands Ct
  Brixham TQ5. . . . . . . 230 A2
  15 Coldeast TQ12. . . . 122 F1
  Exeter EX1 . . . . 261 C3
Summerlands Gdns
  PL7. . . . . 251 C5
Summerland St
  Barnstaple EX32. . . . 155 A5
  Exeter EX1, EX4 . . . . 261 C3
Summerland Terr 1
  EX34. . . . . 3 A3
Summer Mdw
  Lympstone EX8. . . . . 195 E5
  Rockbeare EX5 . . . . . . 99 A6
Summermoor La EX37. 28 E6
Summersby Cl EX12. . 192 A6
Summers Cl PL6 . . . . 249 B7
Summers' La EX17 . . . 79 D1
Summers Moor Cross
  EX19. . . . . 58 F1
Summerville Cross
  EX39. . . . . 37 F6
Summerway EX1 . . . 178 C8
Summerwell La EX16. 62 D1
Summer Well La EX34. . 9 A5
Sumner Rd 7 PL21 . . 137 C2
Sunbury Hill TQ1. . . 220 A6
Sunbury Rd TQ4 . . . . 226 B5
Sunbury Terr 4 TQ1 . 220 A6

Suncrest Cl TQ2 . . . . 213 F3
Suncrest Pk TQ2 . . . . 213 F3
Sun Ct 9 TQ12. . . . . . 207 B3
Sunderland Cl PL9 . . 255 A6
Sunflower Rd EX32. . 155 A5
Sunhill Ave EX3. . . . . 182 E6
Sunhill La EX3 . . . . . 182 F6
Sunleigh TQ1 . . . . . . 219 E2
Sunningbrook Rd
  EX16. . . . . 161 E5
Sunningdale EX39 . . 157 A3
Sunningdale Rd
  PL12. . . . . 242 C2
Sunnybank
  Kenton EX6. . . . . 194 E3
  Newton Abbot TQ12. . 207 B5
Sunny Bank EX32 . . . 155 B4
Sunny Cl TQ12 . . . . . 207 F3
Sunny Ct 1 EX16 . . . . 161 E6
Sunnydale
  Beesands TQ7. . . . . . 149 E8
  8 Bittaford PL21. . . . 137 C8
Sunnydale Cl PL21 . . 237 A4
Sunny Dene EX5 . . . . 243 D1
Sunnyfield EX5 . . . . . 175 C7
Sunny Gdns TQ1 . . . 220 A6
Sunny Hill
  Ottery St Mary EX11 . 169 E4
  Torquay TQ1 . . . . 220 C5
Sunnyhill Mews TQ1 . 220 C5
Sunny Hollow TQ12 . 211 D8
Sunnylands Cross
  EX13. . . . . 87 A2
Sunnylands Way EX7 210 F8
Sunnymead EX17 . . . . 79 B5
Sunnymead Terr 8
  TQ9. . . . . 223 C5
Sunnymoor Cl EX1 . . 174 F2
Sunnyside
  Awliscombe EX14 . . . . 85 C4
  9 Bideford EX39. . . . 157 B1
  3 Braunton EX33 . . . 152 D5
  Burlescombe EX16 . . . 51 C2
  Combe Martin EX34 . . 3 A3
  Cullompton EX15 . . . 163 C2
  St Giles in t W EX38. . . 42 B5
  Thurlestone TQ7 . . . . 143 C1
  Woolfardisworthy EX39 38 F8
Sunnyside Cotts 18
  EX34. . . . . 3 A3
Sunnyside La EX31. . . . 4 D1
Sunnyside Rd
  Kingskerswell TQ12 . . 213 A4
  Plymouth PL4 . . . . . . 249 B2
  Woolacombe EX34 . . . . 7 F6
Sunnyside Terr EX35 151 B5
Sunny View EX19 . . . . 58 F3
Sun Ray EX34. . . . . 2 F4
Sunset Heights EX21 . 55 E4
Sunset Ho 1 EX12 . . 192 A4
Sunset Hts EX32 . . . . 155 A5
Sunshine Terr PL19 . 171 D6
Sun Valley Cl TQ5 . . . 230 C5
Sunway Cl PL19 . . . . 171 A6
Sunwell La PL11 . . . . 252 A8
Sunwine Pl EX4 . . . . . 202 B6
Surbiton Cres EX4 . . 176 F4
Sussex Cl
  Exeter EX4 . . . . 176 E4
  Torquay TQ2 . . . . 214 A3
Sussex Pl PL1 . . . . . . 262 C2
Sussex Rd PL2 . . . . . 247 F5
Sussex St PL1. . . . . . 262 C2
Sussex Terr 5 PL2. . . 247 F5
Sutcliffe Cl TQ9. . . . . 222 F7
SUTCOMBE 54 A6
Sutcombe Com Prim Sch
  EX22. . . . . 54 A6
SUTCOMBE MILL. . . . 54 A6
Suter Dr 10 EX16. . . . 161 E6
Sutherland Cl TQ12 . 212 F8
Sutherland Dr 7 PL3 263 A4
Sutherland Pl 7 PL3 263 A4
Sutherland Rd
  Plymouth PL4 . . . . . . 263 A4
  Torquay TQ1 . . . . 220 C5
SUTTON 143 D1
Sutton Cl
  Dawlish EX7 . . . . 204 D7
  Torquay TQ2 . . . . 213 F2
Sutton Cross
  Moretonhampstead
  TQ13. . . . . 111 E5
  Thurlestone TQ7 . . . . 143 D1
Sutton Ct PL1. . . . . . 247 F1
Sutton Mews 21 PL4. 263 A3
Sutton Pl PL4 . . . . . . 263 B2
Sutton Rd
  Exmouth EX8. . . . . . 202 E7
  Plymouth PL4 . . . . . . 263 B2
Suttons Cross EX14 . . 86 D1
Sutton Wharf PL4. . . 263 A2
Swaddicott Cross
  EX21. . . . . 56 C2
Swain Cl EX13 . . . . . 167 D4
Swaindale Rd 3 PL3 248 E6
Swains Cl EX31 . . . . . 4 C5
Swains Ct EX3 . . . . . 182 E5
Swains La TA21. . . . . 160 D4
Swale Cl EX9 . . . . . . 198 B1
Sylvan Cl
  Plymouth PL3 . . . . . . 249 B6
  Torquay TQ2 . . . . 214 A3
Swale Cl
  EX34. . . . . 121 D6
Swallow Cl EX32 . . . 155 E4
Swallow Ct EX4 . . . . 176 F8
Swallow Ct EX16 . . . . 50 F1

Swallow Ct EX12 . . . 192 C4
Swallow Dr EX2. . . . . 176 D3
Swallow Field EX31 . 154 A2
Swallowfield Rd EX2 178 B2
Swallowfield Rise
  TQ2. . . . . 213 C2
SWALLOWFIELDS . . . 223 C7
Swallowfields 9 . . . 223 B7
Swallows Acre EX7. . 204 D4
Swallows End PL19 . 171 C2
Swallowtree Cross
  EX6. . . . . 96 C7
Swallow Units EX2. . 177 D1
Swallow Way EX15 . . 163 B2
Swallow Wy EX15. . . 163 A3
Swanaford Rd EX6 . . 112 F7
Swan Ave 1 EX16. . . . 161 E6
Swanborough Rd
  TQ12. . . . . 208 A2
Swan Cl PL10 . . . . . . 253 A6
Swan Ct
  Dartmouth TQ6 . . . . 233 E3
  Exeter EX2 . . . . 261 B1
Swan Gdns PL7 . . . . 250 F5
Swan Hill Rd EX24. . 103 A3
Swan Maisonettes 10
  EX2. . . . . 177 A5
Swannaton La
  Crediton EX17. . . . . . 79 E8
  Morchard Bishop EX17 . 61 E1
Swannaton Rd TQ6 . 233 F1
Swannywell Hill EX17 . 78 F8
Swan Rd
  Seaton EX12. . . . . . . 192 B5
  Starcross EX6. . . . . . 201 A8
Swan St TQ1. . . . . . . 220 B4
Swanswood Gdns
  EX39. . . . . 156 D7
Swan Units EX2. . . . . 178 E5
Swan Yd
  Exeter EX4 . . . . 177 A5
  12 Honiton EX14. . . . 166 C6
Swaynes Mews TQ1 . 220 C6
Sweb Entrance 3
  TQ3. . . . . 214 B2
Swedwell La TQ2 . . . 214 A4
Swedwell Rd TQ2 . . . 214 A4
Sweetbriar Cl EX7 . . 204 C3
Sweetbriar La EX7 . . 204 C3
Sweetbriar La 1 . . . 178 B6
Sweet Coppin EX5 . . . 99 B6
Swiddacombe La
  EX36. . . . . 32 C7
Swift Gdns PL5 . . . . 244 C2
Swift Ind Est EX32 . . 207 D6
Swift Rd EX7. . . . . . . 200 F2
SWIMBRIDGE 17 D1
Swimbridge CE Prim Sch
  EX32. . . . . 17 D1
SWIMBRIDGE
  NEWLAND 17 C2
Swinburne Gdns PL5 244 C1
Swincombe Dr TQ3 . 225 F6
Swincombe La EX31. . 11 F4
Swingate Cross EX22. 90 B8
Swing Gate EX6. . . . . 194 A4
Swing Gate Cross
  EX37. . . . . 29 A2
Swiss Cl EX8. . . . . . . 196 B3
Sword Cl EX31 . . . . . 153 E6
Swordfish Ave EX1. . 179 E8
Sybil Mead EX1 . . . . 178 F8
SYCAMORE 87 F8
Sycamore Ave
  Dawlish Warren EX7. . 201 A2
  Plymouth PL4 . . . . . . 263 C4
  Tavistock PL19 . . . . . 171 C2
Sycamore Cl
  Broadclyst EX5. . . . . 175 D6
  Exeter EX1 . . . . 178 E5
  Exmouth EX8. . . . . . 196 E2
  Honiton EX14 . . . . . . 166 A4
  13 Instow EX39 . . . . . 15 B1
  Paignton TQ4 . . . . . . 229 D7
  Willand EX15 . . . . . . 162 C4
Sycamore Dr
  Plymouth PL6 . . . . . . 245 C7
  South Molton EX36 . . 158 D5
  Torpoint PL11 . . . . . . 247 A3
Sycamore Rd
  Saltash PL12. . . . . . . 242 B3
  Tiverton EX16 . . . . . . 161 E5
Sycamore Way
  Brixham TQ5. . . . . . . 230 A2
  6 Chudleigh TQ13 . . . 123 F6
  Plymouth PL6 . . . . . . 245 E6
Sydenham TQ1 . . . . 220 D4
Sydenham Cross
  PL19 . . . . 116 B2
SYDENHAM
  DAMEREL 116 B2
Sydenham Ho 3
  EX4. . . . . 177 E7
Sydenham La EX16. . . 47 E6
Sydney Cl PL7 . . . . . 250 E4
Sydney Rd
  Exeter EX2 . . . . 177 A4
  Torpoint PL11 . . . . . . 247 B3
Sydney St PL1 . . . . . 262 B4
Sylvan Ave EX4 . . . . 173 D1
Sylvan Cl EX8 . . . . . 196 A2
Sylvan Ct
  Exmouth EX8. . . . . . 196 A2
  Plymouth PL1 . . . . . . 248 A3
Sylvania Dr EX4 . . . . 173 E2
Sylvan Rd
  Exeter EX4 . . . . 173 D1
  Wellington TA21 . . . . 160 E5

Symons Cl TQ13 . . . 180 F7
Symons Rd PL12 . . . 242 F2
Synagogue Pl EX4 . . 261 A3
Syncock's Cross
  EX39. . . . . 157 F3

T

Tabernacle Ct 9
  EX1. . . . . 261 A2
Tackbear Rd EX22,
  EX23. . . . . 70 D4
Taddiford Rd EX4. . . 177 A7
Taddiport EX38 . . . . 159 B4
Taddyforde Court Mans
  EX4. . . . . 177 A8
Taddyforde Ct EX4 . . 177 A8
Taddyforde Est EX4 . 177 A8
Tadworthy Rd EX39 . 156 E7
Tail Cnr EX17 . . . . . . 79 D7
Tailyour Rd PL6. . . . 244 F2
Tala Hill PL15. . . . . . 89 D2
TALATON 84 A2
Talaton Rd
  Feniton EX14. . . . . . . 84 C2
  Whimple EX5 . . . . 99 E8
Talbot Gdns PL5 . . . 247 D7
Talbot Rd DT7 . . . . . 260 D5
Tale Common Head
  Cross EX14 . . . . 84 B4
TALEFORD 169 C6
Taleford Cl
  Ottery St Mary EX11 . 169 C7
  Taleford EX10 . . . . . . 100 D8
Taleford Villas EX11 . 169 C7
Talewater Cross EX5 . 84 C2
Tallow Wood Cl
  TQ3. . . . . 225 E6
Tamar Ave
  Plymouth PL2 . . . . . . 247 E5
  Tavistock PL19 . . . . . 171 D5
  Torquay TQ2 . . . . 219 B7
Tamar Bridge PL5. . . 243 A2
Tamar Bsns Units
  EX22. . . . . 164 C6
Tamar Cl PL20 . . . . . 125 E1
Tamar Cotts PL19 . . 116 A1
Tamar Ho PL1 . . . . . 247 E1
Tamarind EX15 . . . . . 162 C4
Tamarisk Cl EX4 . . . . 174 B2
Tamar Rd EX31 . . . . . 15 E5
Tamar's Dr EX15 . . . 162 C4
Tamarside Sp Complex
  PL5. . . . . 243 F2
Tamar St
  Plymouth PL1 . . . . . . 247 E3
  Plymouth PL1 . . . . . . 247 E3
  Saltash PL12. . . . . . . 243 A4
  Torpoint PL11 . . . . . . 247 C3
Tamar Terr
  Calstock PL17. . . . . . 125 D3
  Horsebridge PL19. . . 116 A1
  Saltash PL12. . . . . . . 243 A2
Tamar View
  Milton Abbot PL19 . . 116 A6
  St Dominick PL12 . . . 125 A2
Tamar View Ind Est
  PL12. . . . . 242 D1
Tamar Villas PL9. . . . 255 D7
Tamar Way
  Gunnislake PL18. . . . 125 D6
  Plymouth TQ12 . . . . . 244 A2
Tamar Wharf PL1 . . . 247 D3
Tamerton Ave PL5 . . 243 D1
Tamerton Cl PL5 . . . 244 A6
TAMERTON FOLIOT . 244 B7
Tamerton Foliot Rd
  PL6. . . . . 244 D5
Tamerton Hill EX22 . . 89 D8
Tamerton Rd PL6 . . . 241 B2
Tamworth Cl TQ12 . . 211 F8
Tangmere Ave PL5 . . 243 E5
Tan La EX2 . . . . 177 B3
Tanners Cl EX15 . . . 163 B2
Tanner's Hill TA4 . . . 35 E7
Tanners Mews EX15 . 162 E5
Tanners Rd
  Landkey EX32. . . . . . . 17 C2
  Paignton TQ4 . . . . . . 226 C4
Tannery Cl EX36 . . . 158 B4
Tannery Flats 4
  EX17. . . . . 165 C5
Tanpits Cross TQ7 . . 145 A1
Tanpits La TQ7. . . . . 145 A1
Tanpits Mdw TQ7 . . 145 A1
Tanworth Ho TQ7 . . 143 A1
Tanyard La TQ12 . . . 217 F6
Tanyards Ct 7 EX12. 192 A5
Tape La EX14 . . . . . . 85 B8
Tapeley Park & Gdns*
  EX39. . . . . 157 F7
Tapfield Cross TQ7. . 142 F4
Tapley Gdns TQ14. . . 209 A8
Tappers Cl EX3 . . . . 182 F5
Tappers Knapp DT7 . 260 B5
Tappers La 8 PL8. . . 257 E4
Tappers Mdw EX20. . 170 D5
Tapp's La PL8. . . . . . 257 B5
Taps Cl EX6. . . . . 182 B4
Tapson Dr PL9 . . . . . 255 A6
Tarbet Ave EX1 . . . . . 177 F7
Tarka Cl EX20. . . . . . 170 D6
Tarka La EX34 . . . . . . 8 C6
Tarka Meade EX17 . . 79 A6

Tarka Way
  5 Braunton EX33 . . . . 152 D4
  Crediton EX17 . . . . . 165 E4
Tarn Wearfield Flats
  EX10. . . . . 188 B3
Tarraway Rd TQ3 . . . 219 D1
Tarr Post TA22 . . . . . . 21 C1
Tarr's Ave TQ12 . . . . 207 E2
Tarrs End TQ12 . . . . 207 E2
Tarr's End TQ12 . . . . 207 E2
Tarr Steps * TA22 . . . 21 B3
Tarr Stps Woodland
  National Nature
  Reserve * TA22 . . . . . 21 D3
TATWORTH 88 C8
Tatworth Prim Sch
  TA20 . . . . 88 C8
Tatworth St TA20 . . . 88 C8
Taunton Ave PL5. . . . 244 B5
Taunton Cl EX2 . . . . 177 A3
Taunton Cross EX13. . 87 A1
Taunton Ct 2 TQ2 . . 223 D5
Taunton Pl PL5 . . . . 244 B5
Taunton Rd EX1. . . . 160 E2
Taurus St PL9. . . . . . 256 E7
Tavern Gdns EX1 . . . 26 B1
Tavern Mews EX38. . 159 D5
Tavis Rd TQ3 . . . . . . 225 F8
Taviscote Coll PL19 . 171 A3
Tavistock Com Prim Sch
  PL19. . . . . 171 A5
Tavistock Cross PL20 125 F2
TAVISTOCK
  GENERAL 171 E5
Tavistock Hospl PL19 171 B5
Tavistock Mus *
  PL19. . . . . 171 C5
Tavistock Pl
  Paignton TQ4 . . . . . . 229 B8
  Plymouth PL4 . . . . . . 263 A3
Tavistock Rd
  Exeter EX4 . . . . 177 A7
  Launceston PL15 . . . . 105 A2
  Okehampton EX20 . . . 93 E4
  Plymouth PL6 . . . . . . 245 B5
  Plymouth, Manadon
  PL5. . . . . 244 E1
  Princetown PL20 . . . . 128 A8
  Yelverton PL20 . . . . . 126 F3
Tavistockretail Pk
  PL19. . . . . 171 C3
Tavistock Viaduct Wlk
  Nature Reserve *
  PL19. . . . . 171 A5
Tavistow Ct 2 TQ3. . 225 E8
Tavy Ave TQ2 . . . . . . 219 B8
Tavy Pl PL4 . . . . 248 F4
Tavy Rd
  Saltash PL12. . . . . . . 243 A3
  Tavistock PL19 . . . . . 171 D5
Taw Bridge Cross
  EX20. . . . . 77 B4
Taw Cl PL3 . . . . 249 D6
Taw Cres EX31 . . . . . 15 E5
Tawcroft Way EX31 . 154 D2
Taw Ct 14 EX32 . . . . 155 A4
TAW GREEN 95 B7
Tawgreen Cross EX18 59 C1
Taw Green Cross
  EX20. . . . . 95 B7
Tawgreen La EX18 . . . 59 C1
Tawgreen Rd EX20. . . 59 C1
Taw Meadow Cres
  EX31. . . . . 153 F6
Taw Mill Bsns Pk
  EX32. . . . . 155 C4
Taw Mills La EX18. . . 59 C1
Tawmoor Cross EX20. 95 C7
Tawny Cl EX36 . . . . . 158 C5
Tawny Rd 2 TQ12 . . 207 A5
Taw Rd EX31. . . . . . . 15 E5
Taw Trade Pk EX31 . 154 E6
Taw Vale EX32 . . . . . 154 F4
Taw Vale Ave EX20 . . 77 B4
Taw Vale Cl EX20 . . . 77 B4
Taw View
  1 Bishop's Tawton
  EX32. . . . . 16 E1
  Fremington EX31 . . . . 153 F6
  Umberleigh EX37 . . . . 28 D3
Taw Wharf EX31 . . . . 154 E5
Tayberry Ave TQ3 . . . 225 D2
Tay Gdns PL3 . . . . . . 249 D7
Taylor Cl
  Dawlish EX7 . . . . 204 D5
  Ottery St Mary EX11. . 169 B4
  Saltash PL12. . . . . . . 242 C3
Taylor Cres
  Exmouth EX8. . . . . . 202 E7
  Westward Ho! EX39 . . 156 C6
Taylor Rd PL12. . . . . 242 C4
Taylor's Cross EX17. . 62 E3
Taylor's La EX37 . . . . 43 D6
Taylors Ct
  Bolham EX16. . . . . . . 49 C1
  Tiverton EX16 . . . . . . 161 C2
Taylors Field EX20 . . 77 B4
Taylor's Hill EX16, EX17 62 E4
Taylor's Newtake 2
  TQ12. . . . . 122 F1
Taylor Sq PL19 . . . . . 171 B6
TDC Units EX2 . . . . . 164 C6
Teachers Cl PL9 . . . . 255 F6
Teal Cl
  Kingsteignton TQ12 . . 207 C8
  Torquay TQ2 . . . . 213 C2

Teal Pl EX7 . . . . 200 F2
Teats Hill Flats PL4. . 263 B1
Teats Hill Rd PL4. . . 263 B1
Teazle Ct EX2. . . . . . 261 A2
Technical Coll TQ12. . 207 E7
Tedburn Rd EX4 . . . 176 B5
TEDBURN ST MARY. . 97 F5
Tedburn St Mary Sch
  EX6. . . . . 97 F5
Tedburrow La EX15 . . 67 A8
Tedders Cl 3 EX15. . . 67 B8
Tedstone Ho EX6 . . . 196 A6
Tedstone La EX8 . . . 196 A7
Ted's Way EX20 . . . . 170 B5
Teeds The EX5 . . . . . 184 B2
Tees Cl PL3. . . . . 249 C7
Teignbridge Bsns Ctr
  TQ12. . . . . 180 F3
Teign Cl TQ14. . . . . . 208 E8
TEIGNCOMBE 110 D6
Teigncombe Ct EX6 . 113 B4
Teign Ct
  Bishopsteignton
  TQ14. . . . . 208 F8
  Bishopsteignton TQ14. 209 A8
  Stokeinteignhead
  TQ12. . . . . 209 B1
Teign Fort Dr TQ12. . 207 F2
TEIGNGRACE 206 F8
Teignharvey Rd
  TQ12. . . . . 209 A3
Teignholt Cross EX6 . 96 D7
Teign La
  Chudleigh TQ13. . . . . 123 D7
  Trusham TQ13. . . . . . 113 D1
TEIGNMOUTH 210 D4
Teignmouth Com Sch
  Teignmouth TQ14 . . . 209 F8
  Teignmouth TQ14 . . . 210 B5
Teignmouth Hill EX7 204 E5
Teignmouth Hospl
  TQ14. . . . . 210 A5
Teignmouth Rd
  Bishopsteignton
  TQ14. . . . . 209 B7
  Holcombe EX7, TQ14. . 210 E7
  Kingsteignton TQ12,
  TQ14. . . . . 208 B6
  Maidencombe TQ1. . . 214 C6
  Shaldon TQ1, TQ14 . . 210 A1
  Torquay TQ1 . . . . 220 A8
Teignmouth & Shaldon
  Mus * TQ14. . . . . 210 C4
Teignmouth Sta
  TQ14. . . . . 210 C5
Teign Rd
  Newton Abbot TQ12 . . 207 D4
  Plymouth PL3 . . . . . . 249 B6
Teign Sch TQ12 . . . . 207 D8
Teign St TQ14. . . . . . 210 B4
Teign Terr EX6. . . . . . 113 B5
Teign View TQ13. . . . 123 C4
Teign View Pl 14
  TQ14. . . . . 210 B4
Teignview Rd TQ14 . 208 F8
Teign Village TQ13. . 123 B7
Tekoa Units EX2 . . . 177 C1
Telegraph Cross
  PL21. . . . . 136 D4
Telegraph Hill EX6 . . 114 D2
Telegraph La
  Allercombe EX5 . . . . . 99 B5
  Allercombe EX5, EX11 168 B6
Telegraph View
  TQ12. . . . . 180 B1
Telegraph Wharf
  PL1. . . . . 254 A8
Telford Cres PL5. . . . 243 F2
Telford Rd EX4 . . . . . 177 A7
Temeraire Rd PL5. . . 244 D2
Temperance Pl 6
  TQ5. . . . . 230 D5
Temperance St TQ2. 220 A5
Templar Way TQ12 . . 123 C1
Temple Cres EX16. . . 161 F4
Temple Gdns EX10 . . 188 B5
Temple Mews EX10 . 188 B5
Temple Rd EX2 . . . . 261 B2
Templer Pl TQ13 . . . 180 D5
Templer Rd TQ3 . . . 219 A3
Templer Rd TQ12 . . . 207 D4
Templers Rd TQ12 . . 207 D4
Templer's Way 11
  TQ12. . . . . 123 E1
Temple St EX10. . . . . 188 B5
TEMPLETON 48 A1
Templeton Cross
  EX16. . . . . 48 A1
Templeton La EX16 . . 47 F1
Templetown Ct EX3 . 201 F6
Temple Wlk 6 PL2. . 248 A7
Tenacott Hts EX39 . . 26 A4
Ten Acre Gate EX13 . 87 E7
Tenby Rd PL5. . . . . . 243 C1
Tencery Orch EX14. . . 67 C2
Teneriffe 1 TQ1. . . . 220 C5
Tennacott La EX39 . . 26 B4
Tennyson Ave EX2 . . 177 F3
Tennyson Cl TQ1. . . 220 A8
Tennyson Gdns PL5 . 244 B1
Tennyson Way EX16. 196 C4
Tern Gdns PL7 . . . . . 250 F5
Terrace The
  Braunton EX33 . . . . . 152 D6
  Harrowbarrow PL17. . 125 A5

Terrace The continued
Loddiswell TQ7 . . . . .143 E7
Torquay TQ1 . . . . .220 B4
Terra Nova Gn PL2 . . .248 B5
Terris Cross EX20 . . . . .76 A6
Terr The
Dawlish EX7 . . . . .124 F3
Dawlish EX7 . . . . .204 A5
TETCOTT 89 F7
Tewkesbury Cl PL2 . .248 A8
Tews La
Barnstaple, Bickington
EX31 . . . . .154 A3
Barnstaple, Roundswell
EX31 . . . . .154 A2
Tewsley Cl EX31 . . . . .154 A3
Thackeray Cl EX11 . . .169 E5
Thackeray Gdns PL5 .244 B1
Thackeray Rd EX4 . . . .178 C8
Thames Gdns PL3 . . . .249 D5
Thanckes Cl PL11 . . . .247 A3
Thanckes Dr PL11 . . . .247 A4
Thatcher Ave TQ1 . . . .221 A3
Thatcher Dr TQ14 . . . .210 C8
Thatcher Hts TQ1 . . . .220 F3
Thatcher's La EX5 . . . . .81 E6
Thatcher's Lane End
EX5 . . . . .81 E5
Thatches The PL21 . . . .137 E2
Theatre La EX16 . . . . . .154 F5
Theatre Ope PL1 . . . . .247 F1
Theatre Royal Plymouth★
PL1 . . . . .262 C2
Thelbridge Cross
EX17 . . . . .61 D6
Thelbridge Hill EX17 . .61 C7
Thelma Hulbert Gall★
EX14 . . . . .166 C7
Therlow Rd PL3 . . . . . .249 B6
Thetford Gdns PL6 . . .249 D8
Third Ave
Dawlish EX7 . . . . .204 D5
8 Exeter EX2 . . . . . . .178 D5
Exeter, Countess Wear
EX2 . . . . .182 C7
Exeter, Heavitree EX1 . .177 F6
Plymouth, Billacombe
PL9 . . . . .250 A1
Plymouth, Camels Head
PL2 . . . . .247 E7
Plymouth, Stoke PL1 . . .248 A2
Teignmouth TQ14 . . . . .210 A5
Torquay TQ1 . . . . .220 A8
Third Dr TQ14 . . . . . . .210 B5
Thirlmere Gdns PL6 . .244 F4
Thistle Cl
Mile End TQ12 . . . . . . .206 D5
Plymouth PL6 . . . . .245 E7
Thomas Bassett Dr
EX24 . . . . .103 A3
Thomas Cl EX8 . . . . . . .196 C4
Thomas Fox Rd TA21 .160 B8
Thomas La
Exeter EX4 . . . . .177 A8
Plymouth PL3 . . . . .263 B4
Thomas Newcomen Ct
TQ6 . . . . .233 C3
Thomas Pl TA21 . . . . . .160 D7
Thomas's Cross EX6 . .112 F8
Thompson Rd
Exeter EX1 . . . . .178 A7
Plymouth TQ12 . . . . . .244 B4
THORN 110 E5
Thornberry Ave EX1 . .178 B6
THORNBURY 55 A3
Thornbury Cross
Sampford Courtenay
EX20 . . . . .76 E4
Thornbury EX22 . . . . . . .55 A4
Thornbury Mill EX22 . .55 A4
Thornbury Park Ave
PL3 . . . . .248 D6
Thornbury Primary Sch
PL6 . . . . .245 D4
Thornbury Rd PL6 . . . .245 E4
Thorn Cl
Exeter EX1 . . . . .178 B6
Newton Abbot TQ12 . . .206 E4
Thorncliff Cl TQ1 . . . .220 E5
Thorn Cnr EX18 . . . . . . .77 E8
Thorn Cotts
Combeinteignhead
TQ12 . . . . .208 D3
Woodbury EX5 . . . . . . .184 C3
Thorn Cross
Bovey Tracey TQ13 . . . .180 C5
Chagford TQ13 . . . . . . .110 E5
Slapton TQ7 . . . . .145 C6
Thorndale Cts EX4 . . . .176 D8
THORNDON CROSS . . .93 A4
Thorndon Cross EX22 .71 E5
Thorne Cotts EX11 . . . .169 B3
Thorne Cross EX6 . . . . .96 E4
Thorne Cross Way
TA21 . . . . .50 D8
Thorne Farm Way
EX11 . . . . .169 E5
Thorne La
Bow EX17 . . . . .78 D3
Spreyton EX17 . . . . .96 D8
Thorne Manor & Remains
of Chapel★ EX22 . . . . .71 C8
THORNE MOOR 105 E8
Thorne Moor Cross
EX6 . . . . .96 E4

Thornemoor La EX17 . .78 D2
Thorne Park Rd TQ2 . .219 D5
Thorne Pk EX34 . . . . . . .8 F5
THORNE ST
MARGARET 51 D8
Thornes Cross EX16 . . . .64 E5
Thornes Mdw EX2 . . . .114 A6
Thornes Terr EX36 . . . .158 C4
Thorney Cross EX21 . . . .90 E7
Thornfield Cl
Exmouth EX8 . . . . .196 A2
Seaton EX12 . . . . .192 A7
Thorn Gr TQ6 . . . . .233 C2
THORNHAM 237 E1
Thornham Chapel Cross
EX17 . . . . .46 B1
Thornhedges Cross
EX17 . . . . .80 B5
Thornhedges La EX17 . .80 B5
Thorn Hill EX16 . . . . . . .63 B6
THORNHILLHEAD 40 B3
Thornhillhead EX39 . . .40 B3
Thornhill Rd PL3 . . . . .248 E6
Thornhill Way PL3 . . . .248 E6
Thorning St TQ8 . . . . . .259 E5
Thorn La
Membury EX13 . . . . . . .87 D7
Saltash PL12 . . . . .242 C3
Thornlea Ave EX31 . . . .153 D5
Thornlea (Univ of Exeter)
EX4 . . . . .261 A4
Thornley Dr TQ14 . . . . .210 A5
Thorn Moor Cross
PL15 . . . . .105 E7
Thorn Orch TQ12 . . . . .211 E2
Thornpark Cross EX32 .18 C6
Thornpark Rise EX1 . . .178 B6
Thorn Pk PL3 . . . . .248 F5
Thorns Cross TQ13 . . . .111 C4
Thornton Ave PL4 . . . .263 B4
Thornton Cl
Bideford EX39 . . . . . . .156 E2
Budleigh Salterton
EX9 . . . . .199 G2
Thornton Hill EX4 . . . .261 B4
Thorntree Bsns Units
EX8 . . . . .196 A1
Thorntree Cl TQ12 . . . .206 F4
Thornville Terr PL9 . . . .255 C7
Thorny Park La EX31 . .167 E6
Thornyville Cl PL9 . . . .255 C8
Thornyville Dr PL9 . . . .255 D8
Thornyville Villas
PL9 . . . . .255 C8
Thorpe Ave EX8 . . . . . .196 B3
THORVERTON 81 D5
Thorverton CE Prim Sch
EX5 . . . . .81 E4
Three Acre Cl EX31 . . .167 E6
Three Ash Cross EX14 .87 B5
Three Close La EX33 . . .8 E2
Three Cnrs TQ12 . . . . .207 F8
Three Corner Cross
EX36 . . . . .45 C5
Three Corner Field
EX5 . . . . .79 B4
Three Corner Pl EX2 . .181 C8
Three Corners Cross
EX14 . . . . .85 A6
Three Crossways
4 Chulmleigh EX18 . . .44 E1
Zeal Monachorum EX17 .78 A6
Three Cross Ways
EX19 . . . . .58 D2
Three Elms Cross
EX15 . . . . .83 D3
Three Firs EX15 . . . . . . .83 D4
Threefoot Stool EX6 . . .98 A3
Three Gate Cross
Cheriton Bishop EX17 . .97 B6
Yeoford EX17 . . . . .79 D2
Three Gates Cross
Dulverton TA22 . . . . . . .33 C6
Huntsham EX16 . . . . . . .49 E6
Yarnscombe EX31 . . . . .27 D1
Three Gates Hill EX16 .49 E6
Three Hammers Cross
EX17 . . . . .61 A6
THREE HORSE
SHOES 172 E5
Three Horse Shoes
EX5 . . . . .172 E5
Three Lane End EX22 . .38 E1
Three Limbed Oak
EX5 . . . . .81 D3
Three Mariners Cross
EX14 . . . . .86 C6
Three Sycamores Cross
EX24 . . . . .102 F6
Three Tree La TQ14 . . .124 C2
Three Ways EX31 . . . . .18 A8
Threshers EX17 . . . . . .165 A5
Threwstones Cl EX16 .161 E5
Thriverton Cross
EX22 . . . . .39 B1
Throgmorton Ho 1
TQ9 . . . . .223 D5
Throwcombe Cross
EX16 . . . . .48 A6
Throwcombe La
Oakford EX16 . . . . .48 A6
Rackenford EX36 . . . . . .47 F6
Thrushel TQ5 . . . . .230 A2
THRUSHELTON 106 E6
Thuborough Cross
EX22 . . . . .54 A4

Thurlescombe Cross
EX16 . . . . .64 E6
THURLESTONE 143 A2
Thurlestone, All Saints CE
Prim Sch TQ7 . . . . . . .143 A2
Thurlestone Beach Ho
TQ7 . . . . .143 A1
Thurlestone Gdns
TQ6 . . . . .233 E3
Thurlestone Rd 3
TQ12 . . . . .207 B4
Thurlestone Rock
TQ7 . . . . .147 B8
Thurlestone Wlk PL6 .249 D8
Thurlow Cl EX17 . . . . .165 A5
Thurlow Hill TQ1 . . . . .220 A6
Thurlow Pk TQ1 . . . . .220 A6
Thurlow Rd
Exeter EX4 . . . . .177 E7
Torquay TQ1 . . . . .220 A6
Thursby Wlk EX4 . . . . .174 D1
Tichfield Gdns TQ3 . . .225 F7
Tick La EX6 . . . . .113 E5
Ticklemore St TQ9 . . . .223 D5
Tidcombe Cl 11 EX16 . .64 D7
Tidcombe La EX16 . . . . .64 D7
Tidcombe Prim Sch
EX16 . . . . .64 D7
Tidcombe Wlk 18
EX16 . . . . .64 D7
Tidderson Cross EX16 .47 F4
Tidderson La EX16 . . . .47 E3
Tiddy Brook Rd
Tavistock PL19 . . . . . . .171 E2
Whitchurch PL19 . . . . . .171 E2
Tideford Cross TQ9 . . .227 A1
Tidlake La EX36 . . . . . . .45 C8
Tidwell Bsns Units
EX8 . . . . .196 F1
Tidwell Cl EX9 . . . . . . .198 A3
Tidwell La EX9 . . . . . . .198 B5
Tidwell Rd EX9 . . . . . . .198 A2
Tiger Moth Rd
Clyst Honiton EX1 . . . . .175 E1
Clyst Honiton EX5 . . . . .179 E8
Tigers Wy EX13 . . . . . .167 E5
TIGLEY 135 F3
Tigley Cross TQ9 . . . . .135 F3
Tilery EX14 . . . . .69 A3
Tillage Way EX5 . . . . . .179 B3
Tillard Cl PL7 . . . . .251 C5
Tillerton Steep EX6 . . . .97 C6
TILLWORTH 88 D3
Tilly Cl PL9 . . . . .255 F4
Timber Hill DT7 . . . . . .260 E5
Timbers Cl TQ11 . . . . . .236 A3
Timbers Rd TQ11 . . . . .236 A3
Timber Terr TQ12 . . . . .212 F4
Times Mews 15 TQ9 . .223 C5
Timewell Hill EX16 . . . .34 C4
Timridge La EX6 . . . . . .113 E6
Tincombe PL12 . . . . . . .242 C2
TINHAY 105 F4
Tinhay Cross PL16 . . . .105 F4
Tinhay Mill Ind Est
PL16 . . . . .105 F4
Tinker's Cross EX18 . . .59 A5
Tinkers Wood Ct 4
TQ5 . . . . .230 C4
Tinkley La TQ13 . . . . . .123 C8
Tin La PL4 . . . . .263 A2
Tinners La TQ13 . . . . . .111 A6
Tinpit Hill EX5 . . . . .98 F7
Tinside Lido PL1 . . . . . .262 C1
Tintagel Cl
Exeter EX4 . . . . .174 A2
Torquay TQ2 . . . . .219 F8
Tintagel Cres PL2 . . . . .248 C8
Tintern Ave PL4 . . . . . .263 C2
Tip Hill EX11 . . . . .169 D3
Tipleyhill Cross
TQ12 . . . . .122 D2
Tipleyhill La TQ12,
TQ13 . . . . .122 D3
Tippacott La EX35 . . . . . .6 A4
Tipple Cross PL15 . . . . .105 B6
Tipton Cross EX11 . . . .168 B2
TIPTON ST JOHN 100 D2
Tipton St John CE VA
Prim Sch EX10 . . . . . . .100 C3
Tipton Vale EX11 . . . . .100 C3
Titan Ave PL9 . . . . .256 E8
TITCHBERRY 22 C6
Titchen's La
Calverleigh EX16 . . . . . .48 B8
Tiverton EX16 . . . . .63 B8
Titching Park La EX34 . .9 B5
Titham Hill EX16 . . . . . .47 C6
Tithebarn Copse EX1 178 F8
Tithe Barn Cross
EX15 . . . . .51 D2
Tithebarn La
Blackhorse EX1 . . . . . . .179 A8
1 Exeter EX1 . . . . . . .178 F8
Tithebarn Way EX1 . . .179 B8
Tithe Hill TQ7 . . . . . . .143 E4
Tithe Rd PL7 . . . . .250 B7
TITSON 70 C4
Titterton Cross EX20 . .77 D7
TIVERTON 161 D3
Tiverton Bsns Pk
EX16 . . . . .64 D8
Tiverton Castle★
EX16 . . . . .161 C4
Tiverton Cl PL6 . . . . . .245 B8
Tiverton & District Hospl
EX16 . . . . .161 C5

Tiverton High Sch
EX16 . . . . .161 C5
Tiverton Mus of Mid
Devon Life★ EX16 . . . .161 C3
Tiverton Parkway Sta
EX16 . . . . .65 E8
Tiverton Rd
1 Bampton EX16 . . . . .34 C1
Bampton EX16 . . . . .49 B8
Cullompton EX15 . . . . .163 B3
Silverton EX5 . . . . .82 B6
Tiverton Way EX16 . . .161 F5
Toadpit La
West Hill EX11 . . . . . . .168 C5
West Hill EX11 . . . . . . .168 E6
Tobruk Rd PL12 . . . . . .242 E3
Toby Cross PL21 . . . . . .137 D6
Toby La EX5 . . . . .184 E5
Tod Moor Cross
PL21 . . . . .237 A1
Tokesen Dr EX4 . . . . . .174 C1
Tolchers TQ9 . . . . .222 F8
Tolcis Cross EX13 . . . . .87 D3
Tollards Rd EX2 . . . . . .178 B2
Tollbar Cl PL21 . . . . . .237 F5
Toll Bar Cross EX18 . . .44 E3
Tolleys EX17 . . . . .165 C5
Tollit Gdn 12 TQ9 . . . .223 D5
Tollox Pl PL3 . . . . .249 B4
Tolman Cres EX12 . . . .192 B6
Tombstone La
Calverleigh EX16 . . . . . .48 C1
Tiverton EX16 . . . . .63 D8
Tomhead Cross EX4 . . .98 B6
Tom Maddock Gdns
PL21 . . . . .237 E4
Tomouth Cres 14
EX39 . . . . .15 A1
Tomouth Rd EX39 . . . . .15 A1
Tomouth Sq 15 EX39 . .15 A1
Tomouth Terr 13 EX39 .15 A1
Tom Sanders Cl EX34 . .3 A3
Tomsclose La EX18 . . . .59 C2
Tom's Field EX33 . . . . . .7 E2
Tom's La EX39 . . . . .25 A3
TONE 160 A8
TONEDALE 160 B7
Tonedale Bsns Pk
TA21 . . . . .160 B7
Tonedale Ind Est
TA21 . . . . .160 B8
Tone Hill TA21 . . . . . . .160 B8
Tongue End Cross
EX20 . . . . .94 E5
Tongue Gate EX36 . . . . .45 E7
Tongue Gate Hill EX36 .45 E7
Tongue La PL21 . . . . . . .137 F2
Tongue Lake La EX7 . . .44 E5
Tonyfield Wood Cross
EX17 . . . . .60 B4
Top Cliff TQ14 . . . . . . .209 D5
Topcliff Rd TQ14 . . . . .209 D5
Top of the Town Ctyd
PL12 . . . . .242 F2
TOPSHAM 182 F5
Topsham Mus★ EX3 . .182 F4
Topsham Rd
Exeter EX2 . . . . .178 A1
Exeter EX3 . . . . .182 B8
Exeter EX3 . . . . .182 C7
Topsham Sch The
EX3 . . . . .182 E5
Topsham Sta EX3 . . . . .182 F5
TOR 133 D3
Torbay Bsns Pk TQ4 . .225 E1
Torbay Ct TQ5 . . . . . . .230 E5
Torbay Hospl TQ2 . . . .219 D8
Torbay Hospl Annexe
TQ2 . . . . .213 D1
Torbay L Ctr TQ4 . . . . .226 B3
Torbay Rd
Paignton TQ4 . . . . .226 C6
Torquay TQ2 . . . . .219 F3
Torquay TQ3 . . . . .226 C2
Torbay Trad Est TQ5 . . .230 C7
Torbridge Cl PL12 . . . .242 D2
Tor Bridge High (Sec)
PL6 . . . . .245 D2
Tor Bridge Prim Sch
PL6 . . . . .245 D2
Torbridge Rd
7 Horrabridge PL20 . .126 F4
Plymouth PL7 . . . . .250 E6
TORBRYAN 211 A2
Torbryan Cl PL6 . . . . . .249 E8
Torbryan Hill TQ12 . . .211 A3
Torches Cnr EX19 . . . . .42 D1
Tor Church Rd TQ2 . . .220 A5
Tor Cl
Exeter EX4 . . . . .174 A1
Paignton TQ4 . . . . .229 B7
Plymouth, Hartley PL3 . .248 E2
Tor Cres PL3 . . . . .248 E7
TORCROSS 145 D1
Tor Dale 3 TQ1 . . . . . .220 A6
Tor Down EX20 . . . . . . .94 D5
Tor Haven TQ2 . . . . . . .220 B4
Tor Hill Rd
Torquay TQ2 . . . . .219 F5
Torquay TQ2 . . . . .220 A5
Torland Rd PL3 . . . . . . .248 E7
Torlands Ct PL20 . . . . .126 E2

Tor Lane End TQ9 . . . .144 C7
Tor Mare Ct TQ2 . . . . .219 E4
Toronto Ho EX4 . . . . . .177 E8
Toronto Rd EX4 . . . . . .261 C4
Tor Park Rd
Paignton TQ4 . . . . .225 D3
Torquay TQ2 . . . . .219 F6
Torpeek Cross PL21 . . .137 C7
TORPOINT 247 C3
Torpoint Com Coll
PL11 . . . . .247 A4
Torpoint Inf Sch
PL11 . . . . .247 B3
TORQUAY 220 B2
Torquay Acad TQ2 . . . .219 F8
Torquay Boys' Grammar
Sch TQ2 . . . . .219 D7
Torquay Girls' Grammar
Sch TQ1 . . . . .219 D7
Torquay Rd
Kingskerswell TQ12 . . . .213 A3
Newton Abbot TQ12 . . .207 C3
Newton Abbot, Milber
TQ12 . . . . .212 E8
Paignton TQ3 . . . . .226 C8
Teignmouth TQ14 . . . . .210 A3
Torquay Sta TQ2 . . . . . .219 F4
Torquay TQ2 . . . . .219 C4
Torr Bridge Pk PL8 . . .136 A2
Tor Rd PL3 . . . . .248 E7
TORRE 219 F5
Torre Abbey★ TQ2 . . .219 F4
Torre CE Prim Sch 1
TQ1 . . . . .219 E7
Torre Cl PL21 . . . . .237 F5
Torre Sta TQ2 . . . . .219 F6
Torres Vedras Dr
TA21 . . . . .160 F7
Torr Farm Cotts PL8 . .136 A2
Torr Hill PL8 . . . . .257 F4
Torridge Ave TQ2 . . . .219 B7
Torridge Cl
12 Bideford EX39 . . . .157 B1
Plymouth PL7 . . . . .251 A6
Torridge Hill EX39 . . . .157 A1
Torridge Ho 15 EX39 . .157 B1
Torridge Mount
EX39 . . . . .157 B1
Torridge Pl 13 EX39 . . .157 B1
Torridge Pool EX39 . . .157 A7
Torridge Rd
Appledore EX39 . . . . . . .15 A1
Drounton CX31 . . . . . . .15 C5
Plymouth PL7 . . . . .250 F6
Torridge St EX39 . . . . .157 B1
Torridge View EX38 . . .159 B5
Torridge View Bglws
EX38 . . . . .159 B5
Torridge Way
Holsworthy EX22 . . . . . .164 C6
Plymouth PL3 . . . . .249 C5
Torrington Com Hospl
EX38 . . . . .159 D5
Torrington Cross
EX37 . . . . .29 C4
Torrington Heritage
Mus★ EX38 . . . . .159 C5
Torrington La EX39 . . . .157 B1
Torrington Pl EX6 . . . . .194 D3
Torrington Pool
EX38 . . . . .159 C5
Torrington Rd EX19 . . . .58 E3
Torrington St 10
EX39 . . . . .157 B1
Torr La
East Allington TQ9 . . . . .144 A7
Plymouth PL3 . . . . .248 E7
Yealmpton PL8 . . . . . . .136 A2
Tor Royal La PL20 . . . .128 B8
Torr Quarry Ind Est
TQ9 . . . . .144 B7
Torr Rd PL3 . . . . .248 E7
TORRS PARK 150 A5
Torrs Pk EX34 . . . . .150 A5
Torrs Walk EX34 . . . . . .150 A6
Torr View Ave PL3 . . . .248 D7
Tor Sands 1 TQ4 . . . . .226 B5
Tors Pk EX35 . . . . .151 D5
Tor Square Ho 6
TQ2 . . . . .219 F6
Tors Rd
Lynmouth EX35 . . . . . . .151 C5
Okehampton EX20 . . . .170 B3
Tors The TQ12 . . . . . . .212 F4
Tors View EX39 . . . . . . .156 B6
Tor Vale TQ1 . . . . .219 F6
Torver Cl PL6 . . . . .245 D2
Tor View
Buckfastleigh TQ11 . . . .236 A4
8 Horrabridge PL20 . .126 F4
Princetown PL20 . . . . . .119 A1
Tor View Ave TQ12 . . .207 F2
Torview Flats 6
TQ13 . . . . .180 D8
Tor View Gdns TQ3 . . .226 A6
Torville Pk EX39 . . . . . .156 D7
Torwood Cl TQ1 . . . . . .220 C4
Torwood Ct TQ1 . . . . . .220 D4
Torwood Gables TQ1 220 C3
Torwood Gardens Rd
TQ1 . . . . .220 C4
Torwood Ho 4 TQ1 . . .220 D4
Torwood Mount 6
TQ1 . . . . .220 D4
Torwood St TQ1 . . . . . .220 C4
Torwood Villas TQ1 . . .220 C4
Tory Brook Ave PL7 . . .250 E6
Tory Brook Ct PL7 . . . .250 E6

Tory Way PL7 . . . . .250 D6
TOSBERRY 37 E8
Tosberry Cross EX39 . .37 E8
Tothill Ave PL4 . . . . . . .263 B6
Tothill Ct 2 PL4 . . . . . .210 A3
Tothill Rd PL4 . . . . .263 B6
TOTNES 223 B6
Totnes Castle★ TQ9 . .223 B6
Totnes Cl PL7 . . . . .251 B6
Totnes Costume Mus★ 20
TQ9 . . . . .223 C5
Totnes Cross TQ9 . . . .139 C3
Totnes Down Hill
TQ9 . . . . .223 D3
Totnes Elizabethan Ho
Mus★ TQ9 . . . . .223 C5
Totnes Hospl TQ9 . . . .223 C6
Totnes Littlehempston
Sta★ TQ9 . . . . .223 C7
Totnes Pavilion TQ9 . .223 C6
Totnes Progressive Sch
TQ9 . . . . .223 B7
Totnes Rd
Buckfastleigh TQ11 . . . .236 D5
Ermington PL7 . . . . . . .136 F3
Ipplepen TQ12 . . . . . . .211 F5
Marldon TQ3 . . . . .218 C1
Paignton TQ3 . . . . .225 D5
Paignton TQ3, TQ4 . . . .225 F5
10 South Brent TQ10 . .134 F3
Strete TQ6 . . . . .145 F5
Torquay TQ2 . . . . .219 C4
Totnes Sta TQ9 . . . . . . .223 C6
Tottons Ct EX2 . . . . . . .181 A8
Touts Cl EX36 . . . . .158 D4
Tovey Cres PL5 . . . . . . .244 D2
Towell La EX19 . . . . . . .42 D2
Tower Cross EX14 . . . . .86 A3
Tower Ct
Dunchideock EX6 . . . . .114 A5
Saltash PL12 . . . . .242 C2
Towerfield EX3 . . . . . . .182 E7
Towerfield Dr PL6 . . . .245 C8
Tower Gdns EX17 . . . . .165 C6
Tower Hill
Buckland Brewer EX39 . .40 B7
Cheriton Fitzpaine EX17 .62 A1
Holcombe Rogus TA21 . .50 D5
Tower Hill Cross EX17 .62 E1
Towerhill La TQ13 . . . .124 B4
Tower Hill Rd PL15 . . . .90 D1
Tower La
9 Dittisford PL21 . . . .137 C0
Buckland St Mary TA20 .69 D8
Moorhaven Village
PL21 . . . . .137 C8
Tower Moor EX37 . . . . .28 F6
Tower Pk EX36 . . . . . . .158 C3
Tower Rd
Honiton EX14 . . . . .166 F4
Offwell EX14 . . . . .86 A3
Paignton TQ3 . . . . .226 B6
Towers Cl PL6 . . . . .245 C4
Tower St
5 Bideford EX39 . . . .157 A1
13 Exmouth EX8 . . . .202 A6
Northam EX39 . . . . .156 F7
Tower View
Broadclyst EX5 . . . . . . .175 C5
Saltash PL12 . . . . .242 D1
Tower Way EX14 . . . . . .67 B1
Tower Wlk EX2 . . . . . . .181 C8
Town Cl TQ6 . . . . .233 E3
Town Cross EX13 . . . . . .87 A3
Town End EX5 . . . . .175 D7
Town End Cross EX20 . .76 C5
Town Farm TQ9 . . . . . .222 D0
Town Farm Bldgs
EX14 . . . . .85 B4
Town Farm Cl
6 Honiton EX14 . . . . .166 B6
8 Horrabridge PL20 . .126 F4
Town Farm Cotts
TQ9 . . . . .139 E5
Town Farm Ct
Braunton EX33 . . . . . . .152 C6
Ideford TQ13 . . . . .124 B4
Shirwell EX31 . . . . .17 B8
Town Farm La TQ13 . . .124 B4
Townfield EX6 . . . . .182 A4
Townhall Pl 8 TQ13 . . .180 D8
Town Hall Pl 4
TQ13 . . . . .180 D8
Town Hill
Broadclyst EX5 . . . . . . .175 C5
Culmstock EX15 . . . . . . .66 E8
Ermington PL21 . . . . . . .136 F3
Staverton TQ9 . . . . .216 A5
West Anstey EX36 . . . . .32 C6
Town La
Barton Town EX31 . . . . .11 E3
Rackenford EX16 . . . . . .47 D4
Woodbury EX5 . . . . . . .184 C3
TOWNLAKE 116 A1
Townland Rise EX20 . . .56 F4
Townlands
Bradninch EX5 . . . . .82 F6
Willand EX15 . . . . .162 D3
Town Living Cross
EX36 . . . . .30 D2
Town Living Cross
EX20 . . . . .76 B5
Town Marsh TA22 . . . . .33 D7
Town Mdw
Bridestowe EX20 . . . . .107 F8
Ilsington TQ13 . . . . . . .122 C3
Little Torrington EX38 . .41 D3
Town Mdws EX39 . . . . .38 E8

Town Mill Gdns PL19 .171 C6
Town Mills EX7 . . . . .204 C6
Town Mill The★ .. D7..260 E1
Town Moor Cross
FX17 . . . . .46 B1
Town Moor Hill EX17. .46 B1
Town Pk
Crediton EX17. . . . . . .80 A3
Crediton EX17. . . . . .165 B5
Great Torrington EX38 .41 D6
Great Torrington EX38 .159 C5
Loddiswell TQ7. . . . . .143 E7
West Alvington TQ7. . .258 B4
Town Rd TQ7. . . . . . .148 F3
Townsend EX12. . . . . .191 C6
Townsend Ave EX12. .192 A6
Townsend Cl TQ7 . . . .258 A4
Townsend Cross
Malborough TQ7. . . . .147 E6
Winkleigh EX19. . . . . .58 E2
Town's End Cross
TQ7. . . . . .145 C3
Townsend Farm La
EX16. . . . . .34 E6
Townsend Hill
Ipplepen TQ12 . . . . . .211 C3
Winkleigh EX19. . . . . .58 E2
Townsend Rd
Seaton EX12. . . . . . .192 A5
West Alvington TQ7. . .258 A4
Townsend Terr TQ9 . .144 E7
Townshend Ave PL2. .247 E5
Town's La TQ7. . . . . .143 E7
TOWNSTAL 233 D3
Townstal Cres TQ6. . .233 D4
Townstal Hill TQ6. . . .233 E3
Townstal Ind Est
TQ6. . . . . .233 C3
Townstal Pathfields
TQ6. . . . . .233 D3
Townstal Rd TQ6. . . .233 D3
Town Tree Hill 🔟
EX7. . . . . .204 D6
TRACEBRIDGE 51 A8
Tracey Ct PL1. . . . . . .262 B3
Tracey Gn EX16 . . . . .46 E1
Tracey Rd EX14 . . . . .166 A7
Traceys Ave EX12. . . .191 F8
Tracey Vale TQ13 . . . .180 C6
Tracey View 2 EX14. .166 B6
Trackfordmoor Cross
TA22. . . . . .33 B3
Trafalgar Arc 20 EX34. 3 A3
Trafalgar Cl
Newton Abbot TQ12 . .207 B5
Plymouth PL5 . . . . . .247 D8
Trafalgar Ct
Topsham EX3 . . . . . .182 E5
Uffculme EX15 . . . . . .66 A7
Trafalgar Dr EX38. . . .159 C6
Trafalgar Gdns EX32. .155 A3
Trafalgar Lawn EX32. .155 A3
Trafalgar Pl
4 Bideford EX39 . . . .156 F1
Exeter EX4 . . . . .261 C4
3 Plymouth PL1. . . . .247 F3
Trafalgar Place La
PL1. . . . . .247 F3
Trafalgar Rd
Exeter EX3 . . . . .182 C8
Lympstone EX8. . . . . .195 E6
Trafalgar St PL4 . . . . .263 A3
Trafalgar Terr TQ5. . .230 C6
Trafalgar Way EX13 . .167 C5
Trafalgar Way The
EX13. . . . . .87 E1
Trafford Mews EX2 . .178 C4
Trago Mills Sh & L Pk
TQ12. . . . . .123 A1
Traine Brake PL9 . . . .256 C1
Traine Rd
Wembury PL9. . . . . . .140 D8
Wembury PL9. . . . . . .256 B1
Traine Terr PL21. . . . .137 C2
Traine Villas PL21. . . .137 C3
Tramway Rd PL6. . . . .245 E7
Tramways TQ1. . . . . .220 B7
Transit Way PL5 . . . . .244 C3
Travellers Rest Cross
EX37 . . . . .28 D6
Travershes Cl EX8. . . .196 B1
Traylane EX37. . . . . . .28 B1
Trayne Hts EX37. . . . .155 A8
Treable La EX6 . . . . . .96 B3
Treacle Hill TQ12 . . . .207 E7
Treago Gdns PL6. . . . .245 C8
Treasbeare La EX5. . . .99 A5
Trebblepark Rd TQ7. .258 C6
TREBURLEY. 115 A4
Treburley Cl PL15. . . .115 A4
Treburley Ind Est
PL15. . . . . .115 A4
Treby Rd PL7. . . . . . .250 F4
TRECOMBE. 115 D4
Trecott Cross EX20. . .76 F3
Tree Beech Rural Ent Pk
EX32. . . . . .17 F4
Tree Cl EX32. . . . . . . .17 F4
Treefield EX31. . . . . . .18 A8
Treefields TQ5. . . . . .230 B4
Treefield Wlk EX32. . .155 D4
Trees Ct EX32. . . . . . .182 F5
Treesdale Cl TQ3 . . . .225 F6
Tree Surfers★ PL19 .125 D7
Treetop Cl PL12. . . . . .242 D4
Trefusis Gdns PL3. . . .249 A4
Trefusis Pl EX8 . . . . . .202 A5

Trefusis Terr
Exmouth EX8. . . . . . .202 A5
Merton EX20. . . . . . . .57 A7
Millbrook PL10 . . . . . .252 E6
Trefusis Way FX9 . . . .198 R6
Tregenna Cl PL7 . . . . .251 C4
TREGONHAWKE. 252 B4
Tregoning Rd PL11. . .246 F2
TREHAN 242 A1
Trehill Cl 3 TQ12 . . . .244 E6
Trehill Ho EX6. . . . . . .114 D3
Trehill La PL10. . . . . .140 H2
Trehill Rd PL21. . . . . .237 E5
TREKENNER 115 A5
Trekenner Com Prim Sch
PL15. . . . . .115 A5
Trelawney Ave PL5. . .243 D1
Trelawney Cl PL11 . . .246 E3
Trelawney Ct EX39 . . .157 A7
Trelawney Pl PL5 . . . .243 D1
Trelawney Rd
Plymouth PL3 . . . . . .248 D5
Saltash PL12. . . . . . .242 E2
Trelawney Rise PL11. .246 E3
Trelawney Way PL11 .246 E3
Trelawny Rd
Plymouth PL7 . . . . . .250 D6
Tavistock PL19 . . . . . .171 C6
Treledan Way PL12 . .242 C5
Trelissick Cl TQ3. . . . .225 D7
Trelissick Rd TQ3. . . .225 D7
Trelivan Cl EX8 . . . . . .196 B3
Trelorrin Gdns PL3. . .248 E5
Treloweth Cl PL2 . . . .248 D8
Tremaine Cl EX14. . . .166 D6
Tremarran Cl PL11. . .246 E4
Trematon Ave TQ1. . .220 A5
Trematon Cl PL11. . . .246 E4
Trematon Dr PL21. . . .237 E5
Trematon Terr PL4. . .248 A2
Tremayne Rise PL19 .171 B5
Tremlett Gr
Dartington TQ9 . . . . .215 E1
Ipplepen TQ12 . . . . . .211 D2
Tremlett Meadow EX5. 99 B6
Tremletts Cl EX6. . . . .97 F5
Trenance Dr PL19. . . .116 C3
Trenavin Cl EX17. . . . .165 B6
Trenchfirs Cnr TQ9 . . .139 E2
Trenchford Resr
Woodland Wlk★
TQ13. . . . . .112 E1
Trendle Gdns PL19 . . .112 E1
Trendlewood Rd PL6 245 D7
Trenemans TQ7. . . . . .143 B1
Trengrouse Ave PL11 246 F3
Treniffle La PL15. . . . .105 D2
Treninnow & Wiggle
Chalets PL10 . . . . . .252 C2
Trennaway Cross EX6. 96 C1
Trenode Ave EX34 . . . .2 F4
Trentbridge Sq EX2 . .178 C4
Trent Cl
Bideford EX39. . . . . . .26 A4
Plymouth PL3 . . . . . .249 B6
Trentham Cl
Paignton TQ3 . . . . . .225 E8
Plymouth PL6 . . . . . .245 B6
TRENTISHOE. 4 A5
Trentishoe Hill EX31. .4 A5
Trentishoe La EX31 . . .4 A5
Trentworthy Cross
EX22. . . . . .38 B2
Tresco Gdns TQ12. . . .244 F7
Trescote Way EX20. . . .92 F1
Tresillian Cotts EX3 . .182 F3
Tresillian Gdns
Exeter EX4 . . . . .177 E8
Topsham EX3 . . . . . .182 F4
Tresillian St PL4. . . . . .263 C2
Tresluggan Rd PL5. . .243 D1
Treston Cl EX7. . . . . . .204 E7
Trethewey Gdns PL7 .132 D4
Tretower Cl PL6 . . . . . .244 F5
Trevanna Rd TQ7 . . . .258 C4
Trevannion Cl PL6 . . . .249 A8
Trevelyan Rd EX12 . . .192 C4
Trevendon PL17 . . . . .115 B1
Treveneague Gdns
PL2. . . . . .248 D8
Trevenn Dr TQ12. . . . .213 A3
Treveor Gdns PL21. . .137 B3
Treverbyn Cl PL7 . . . .250 D6
Treverbyn Rd PL7. . . .250 D6
Trevessa Cl PL7. . . . . .248 D8
Trevethan Pk PL20. . .239 F4
Trevithick Ave PL11. .246 F4
Trevithick Rd PL5. . . .243 E2
Trevol Pl PL11 . . . . . .246 E3
Trevol Rd PL11. . . . . .246 E3
Trevone Gdns PL2 . . .248 D8
Trevorder Cl PL11. . . .246 F5
Trevorder Rd PL11 . . .246 F5
Trevose Way PL3 . . . .249 C6
Trevoya Pk PL15. . . . . .89 D2
Trewithy Ct PL6. . . . . .244 F1
Trewithy Dr PL6 . . . . .244 F1
Trews Weir Ct EX2 . . .261 C1
Trews Weir Reach
EX2. . . . . .261 C1
TREWYN. 164 B5
Trewyn Pk EX22. . . . .164 B5
Trewyn Rd EX22 . . . . .164 B5
Triangle Pl 15 TQ14 . .210 C4
Triangle The
4 Sidmouth EX10 . . .188 A3

Triangle The continued
16 Teignmouth TQ14. . .210 C4
Tribune Dr TQ12 . . . . .207 F6
Trickey Cl EX16. . . . . .161 F5
Trick's Terr FX19 . . . . .42 D1
Tricorn Cl TQ2 . . . . . .213 C1
Tridley Foot Cross
EX17. . . . . .61 F4
Tridley Foot Hill EX17. 61 F3
Trigger's Hill EX19 . . .42 D3
Trill Cross EX13. . . . . .103 E6
Trill La
Axminster EX13 . . . . .167 C2
Musbury EX13. . . . . .103 E6
TRIMSTONE. 8 E6
Trimstone Cnr EX34. . .8 F5
Trimstone Cross EX34. .8 E6
Trimstone La
West Down EX34 . . . . .8 E5
Woolacombe EX34 . . . .8 D6
Trinfield Ave EX8 . . . .196 B1
TRINITY 82 F8
Trinity CE VA Prim Sch
EX2. . . . . .182 C8
Trinity Cl
15 Bere Alston PL20. . .125 E1
1 Teignmouth TQ14. . .210 B6
Wellington TA21 . . . . .160 C5
Trinity Cotts EX5 . . . . .82 F8
Trinity Cross EX5 . . . . .83 A8
Trinity Ct
Sidmouth EX10 . . . . . .188 B3
Westward Ho! EX39. . .156 E6
Trinity Gdns EX34. . . .150 A5
Trinity Hill TQ1 . . . . . .220 C3
Trinity Hill Nature
Reseve★ EX13. . . . . .104 A6
Trinity Hill Rd
Axminster EX13 . . . . .167 F1
Raymond's Hill EX13. .104 B7
Uplyme EX13. . . . . . .104 B5
Trinity Mews TQ14. . .210 B7
Trinity Pl 15 EX32 . . . .155 A4
Trinity Rd EX8 . . . . . .201 E6
Trinity Row TA21. . . . .160 C5
Trinity Sch TQ14 . . . .210 B7
Trinity Sq EX13 . . . . .167 C6
Trinity St
Barnstaple EX32. . . . .155 A4
Plymouth PL1 . . . . . .262 B1
Trinity Way PL19. . . . .171 A4
Trinnaman Cl PL21. . .237 D4
Trinnicks Orch PL21. .137 D6
Tristan Cl EX4 . . . . . . .174 A2
Tristford Cross TQ9. . .223 A4
Tristford Rd TQ9 . . . . .222 D2
Trittencott Cross
EX36. . . . . .46 A8
Triumphal Cres PL7. . .250 A6
Triumph Pl PL11 . . . . .204 B1
Troarn Way 21 TQ13. . .123 E6
Trobridge Cross
EX17. . . . . .165 D2
Trojan Ind Pk TQ4 . . . .225 E3
Trood La EX2 . . . . . . .181 D6
Trough La
Bovey Tracey TQ13 . . .123 A6
Hennock TQ13. . . . . .123 A6
Trouville 16 EX32. . . . .155 A5
TROW 189 A7
Trowbridge Cl PL5. . . .244 C4
Trowell La TA4. . . . . . .35 E4
Trow Hill
Sidmouth EX10 . . . . .188 D8
Trow EX10. . . . . .189 A8
Truckham La EX34 . . .3 D2
TRUE STREET 224 A6
Trumans Ct EX4. . . . . .177 E8
Trumlands Rd TQ1 . . .214 B1
Trumpers Cl PL21. . . .237 A6
Trumpeter Pl EX7. . . .200 E7
Trumps Cross EX16 . . .50 E3
Trumps Ct EX10. . . . .188 B3
Trumps Orch EX15 . . .163 A4
Truro Ave TQ2 . . . . . .214 A1
Truro Dr
Exeter EX4 . . . . .176 F7
Exmouth EX8. . . . . . .196 D4
Plymouth PL5. . . . . . .244 A5
TRUSHAM 113 D1
Trusham Cross TQ13 .113 D1
Trusham Hill
Trusham TQ12. . . . . .123 C8
Trusham TQ13. . . . . .113 D1
Trusham Rd EX2 . . . . .177 C2
Tub Cnr EX5 . . . . .99 C7
Tucana Wlk PL9 . . . . .256 E6
TUCKENHAY 139 F7
Tucker Ct PL5. . . . . . .247 F8
Tucker Ct EX14 . . . . . .166 C6
TUCKERMARSH 125 C2
Tuckers Brook 12
PL21. . . . . .137 C3
Tuckers Cl EX17. . . . .165 A5
Tucker's Hill PL21. . . .133 C1
Tucker's Hill Head
PL21. . . . . .133 C2
Tuckers Maltings★
TQ12. . . . . .207 D4
Tuckers Mdw EX17. . .165 A5
Tucker's Moor Cross
EX16. . . . . .32 F3
Tuckers Pk
Bradworthy EX22. . . . .38 E1
Buckland Brewer EX39. 40 B7
Tuckfield Cl EX2 . . . . .178 A4
Tucking Mill La EX36 158 E3
Tuckmill Cross EX14 . .84 C4

Tuckwell Gr EX1 . . . . .175 A2
TUDHAY 88 C3
Tudor Cl
Lifton PL16 . . . . .105 E4
11 Newton Abbot
TQ12. . . . . .207 B3
Northam EX39 . . . . . .156 F6
Paignton TQ4 . . . . . .226 A2
Plymouth PL9 . . . . . .255 E5
Tudor Ct
Exeter EX4 . . . . .261 A2
Saltash PL12. . . . . . .243 A2
Tudor Dr EX31. . . . . . .154 D2
Tudor Gr EX15 . . . . . .163 C5
Tudor Rd TQ12. . . . . .207 B3
Tudor St EX4 . . . . . . .261 A2
Tuffery Ct EX4 . . . . . .177 F8
Tugela Terr EX5 . . . . .179 A3
Tully Gdns EX10. . . . .188 B7
Tuly St EX31. . . . . . . .154 F5
Tumbles The EX20 . . .76 C5
Tumbling Field La
EX16. . . . . .161 D3
Tumbling Fields
EX16. . . . . .161 D3
Tumbling Weir Way
EX11. . . . . .169 C3
Tumbly Hill TQ7 . . . . .258 D4
Tunnaford Cross
TQ13. . . . . .110 E4
Tunnel La EX14 . . . . .166 F8
Tuns La EX5. . . . . . . .82 B5
Tunworth Ct 1 EX1. .261 A2
Tuplins TQ12. . . . . . .207 E8
Turbill Gdns 4 PL7 . . .251 B5
Turbury Cross EX14. . .85 A8
TURFMOOR 87 D4
Turkey La EX5. . . . . . .99 E5
Turk's Head La EX14 .166 A6
Turlake Ho EX5 . . . . .172 F5
Turlake Mews EX5 . . .172 F5
TURNCHAPEL 255 B7
Turner Ave EX8 . . . . .202 C7
Turner Cl
Clyst Honiton EX1. . . .179 B8
Newton Poppleford
EX10. . . . . .186 F7
Turner Rise EX16 . . . .161 B2
Turners Cres EX39 . . . .22 E3
Turner's La DT6. . . . . .88 H2
Turning Ways EX17 . . .61 A2
Turnlake Rd TQ13. . . .111 A6
Turnpike
Gunnislake/Calstock
PL18. . . . . .125 B5
Halberton EX16. . . . . .65 C8
Honiton EX14 . . . . . .166 D6
Sampford Peverell EX16 50 C1
Turnpike Cl
Clovelly EX39 . . . . . . .23 D3
Whiddon Down EX20. . .95 F3
Turnpike Cres PL21 . . .237 E4
Turnpike Cross EX34. . .8 C6
Turnpike Rd EX20. . . . .95 F3
Turnquay PL9. . . . . . .255 C7
Turnstone Ave EX12. .192 C5
Turnstone Cl EX7 . . . .201 A2
Turnstone La EX31. . . .15 C3
Turnstone Rd EX2. . . .177 F2
Turpins Plot EX20 . . . .170 D5
Turret Gr PL4. . . . . . . .248 F4
Tute's La EX34 . . . . . .3 B4
TUTWELL. 115 E2
Tuxton Cl PL7. . . . . . .251 C3
Tweed Cl EX14. . . . . .166 C4
Tweenaway PL21 . . . .237 E4
Tweenaway Ct TQ4. . .225 E4
TWEENAWAYS 225 E4
Tweenaways TQ11 . . .236 A4
Tweenaways Cross
TQ4. . . . . .225 E4
Tween Moor Cross
EX17. . . . . .60 F6
Tweenways TQ12. . . .207 D7
Twelve Acre Post
TA22. . . . . .33 A4
Twelve Milestone Hill
EX17. . . . . .79 D7
Twelve Oaks Cross
EX18. . . . . .58 E6
Twickenham Rd
TQ12. . . . . .208 A1
Twickenham St PL2. .248 C8
Twinaway La EX2 . . . .114 B8
Twindle Beer TQ13. . .123 E6
Twiscombe Cnr EX4. . .98 D5
Twiscombe La EX4. . . .98 C6
Twisted Oak EX6. . . . .97 D5
Twistgates La EX14 . . .68 D4
TWITCHEN. 20 D1
Twitchen Ball Cnr
EX36. . . . . .20 C3
Twitchen Cross
Great Torrington EX38. 26 F2
West Down EX34 . . . . .8 E6
Twitchen Gate EX31. .11 F3
Twitchen La
Arlington EX31. . . . . . .10 F4
Burrington EX37. . . . . .43 F3
Stowford EX31. . . . . . .11 A3
Two Acre Cl TQ3 . . . . .225 E6
Twoacre Ct EX2. . . . . .181 A8
TWO BRIDGES 119 C1
Two Bridges Rd
Princetown PL20 . . . .128 B8
Sidford EX10. . . . . . .101 B1
Two Crosses
Dunsford EX6. . . . . . .113 A8

Two Crosses continued
Yealmpton PL8 . . . . .136 A1
Two Gate Cross EX37. .44 A4
Two Gates Cross EX16. 47 E5
Two Hills Pk PL12 . . . .242 C2
Two Mile Oak Cross
TQ12. . . . . .211 F5
Two Moors Prim Sch
EX16. . . . . .161 C4
Two Moors Way
PL20. . . . . .128 D7
Two Post Cross
Pennymoor EX16 . . . . .62 E7
Taw Green EX17. . . . . .95 D7
Two Post La EX17 . . . .95 D7
TWO POTS 2 B1
Two Rivers Ind Est
EX31. . . . . .154 E6
Two Stone La EX16. . .114 C5
Two Trees Rd EX31. . .153 D5
Twyford Pl
Tiverton EX16 . . . . . .161 D4
Wellington TA21 . . . . .160 D5
Tyes Orch EX15 . . . . . .83 F5
Tylers Mdw EX38. . . .159 E5
Tylney Cl PL6 . . . . . . .245 B6
Tylor Pl TA21 . . . . . . .160 D5
Tyndale Cl PL5. . . . . .244 B1
Tyrrell Mead EX10 . . .188 B7
Tyrrell Rd EX31. . . . . .161 B4
TYTHECOTT. 40 B4
Tytheing Cl EX5. . . . . .172 A4
TYTHERLEIGH. 88 C6
Tything Wlk 4 PL3. . .248 E6

U

UFFCULME 66 A8
Uffculme Ct EX15 . . . .66 A7
Uffculme Prim Sch
EX15. . . . . .66 A7
Uffculme Rd
Culmstock EX15 . . . . .66 D8
Uffculme EX15 . . . . . .66 A7
Willand EX15 . . . . . . .162 E6
Uffculme Sch EX15. . .66 A7
UGBOROUGH 137 D6
Ugborough Prim Sch
PL21. . . . . .137 D6
Ugborough Rd PL21. .137 C7
Ugbrooke House & Pk★
TQ13. . . . . .123 F5
Uggaton Cross EX14 . .84 D5
ULLCOMBE 68 D4
Ullcombe La EX14. . . .68 C4
Ullswater Cres PL6. . .244 E4
Ullswater Ct EX34. . . . .2 F4
Umber Cl EX34. . . . . .176 F5
UMBERLEIGH 28 D2
Umberleigh Com Prim
Sch EX37 . . . . .28 D2
Umberleigh Sta EX37. 28 C2
Umberside 19 EX34 . .33 A3
UMBORNE 102 F8
Undercliff TQ6. . . . . .233 F4
Undercliff Rd PL9. . . .255 B7
Underdown
Clovelly EX39 . . . . . . .23 D3
Kennford EX6. . . . . . .114 A4
Underdown La EX20. . .76 D4
Underfleet EX12 . . . . .192 B4
Underfleet The EX12 .192 B5
Underhay PL8 . . . . . .257 E4
Underhay Cl EX17. . . .204 F8
Underheath 5 TQ1. . .220 D5
Underhill EX8. . . . . . .195 E5
Underhill Cl EX8 . . . . .195 E4
Underhill Cres EX8. . .195 E4
Underhill Pk EX16. . . .161 C5
Underhill Rd
Plymouth PL3 . . . . . .248 A4
Torquay TQ2 . . . . . . .219 E3
Underhill Terr EX3. . . .182 F5
Underhill Villas 1
PL3. . . . . .248 A3
Underidge Cl TQ3 . . . .225 E6
Underidge Dr TQ3 . . . .225 E6
Underidge Rd TQ3 . . .225 E6
Under La
Bovey Tracey TQ13 . . .180 A5
Holsworthy EX22 . . . .164 C3
Sidbury EX10 . . . . . .101 C1
Underlane
Boyton PL15 . . . . .89 D3
Marhamchurch EX23. .70 A6
Plymouth, Plympton
PL7. . . . . .250 C5
Plymouth, Plymstock
PL9. . . . . .255 E6
Underleat Cl 3 TQ13 123 F6
Underleys EX12. . . . . .191 C5
Under Minnow Rd
EX31. . . . . .154 E7
Under Rd
Bridgerule EX22 . . . . .70 F5
Gunnislake PL18. . . . .125 D5
Undertown PL21. . . . .137 D6
Under Way TQ12. . . . .213 A6
Underways PL20 . . . . .125 E1
UNDERWOOD 250 C5
Underwood Cl EX7. . .204 D4
Underwood Cotts
EX15. . . . . .83 C4
Underwood Rd PL7 . .250 D4
Unicorn Cl PL7. . . . . .250 B6
Unicorn St EX2 . . . . . .178 D4
Union Cl EX39 . . . . . .156 F1

Union Hill EX17 . . . . . .78 E7
Union La 5 TQ5 . . . . .230 C5
Union Mine Rd PL19. .117 D3
Union Pl PL1. . . . . . . .262 A2
Union Rd
Crediton EX17. . . . . .165 C5
Exeter EX4 . . . . .177 D8
Union Sq Sh Ctr TQ1 .220 B5
Union St
Dartmouth TQ6. . . . . .233 F3
Dulverton TA22. . . . . .33 D6
Exeter EX2 . . . . .177 A4
5 Exmouth EX8 . . . . .202 A6
Newton Abbot TQ12 . .207 C3
Plymouth PL1 . . . . . .262 A2
Salcombe TQ8. . . . . .259 E5
Torquay TQ1, TQ2. . . .220 A5
Union Terr
Barnstaple EX32. . . . .155 A4
Barnstaple, Bickington
EX31. . . . . .154 A4
Crediton EX17. . . . . .165 C5
Unity Cl PL6 . . . . .245 D5
Unity Park PL3. . . . . .249 C6
Univ of Exeter EX4 . . .177 B8
Univ of Exeter (St Luke's
Campus) EX1 . . . . . .261 C3
Univ of Exeter (Streatham
Campus) EX4 . . . . . .173 B1
Univ of Plymouth
Exeter EX17. . . . . . . .177 E2
Plymouth PL4 . . . . . .263 A3
UPCOTT
Dolton. 57 F4
Holsworthy. 72 E7
Upcott Ave EX31 . . . .154 C6
Upcott Cross
Cobbaton EX32. . . . . .28 C5
Halwill EX21. . . . . . . .91 D8
Holsworthy EX22 . . . . .72 D7
Iddesleigh EX19 . . . . .57 F4
St Giles on t H PL15. . .90 E1
Welcombe EX39 . . . . .37 C5
West Buckland EX32. . .18 C3
Upcott Gate EX18 . . . .59 B3
Upcott Hill
Barnstaple EX31. . . . .154 D8
Bideford EX39. . . . . . .25 F4
Okehampton EX20 . . .170 A6
Upcott La
Thorverton EX5. . . . . .81 E6
West Buckland EX32. .18 C3
Upcott Mead Rd
EX16. . . . . .161 B4
Upcott Valley EX20. . .170 A6
UP EXE 82 A5
Upexe La EX5 . . . . . . .82 B5
UPHAM. 63 A3
Upham Cross EX17. . . .63 A3
Upham La EX5 . . . . . . .99 C1
Uphay La EX13. . . . . .167 B8
Uphill Cl PL21. . . . . . .237 E5
Upland Chase EX14 . .166 B3
Upland Dr PL6. . . . . .245 A5
Upland Gdns PL9 . . . .140 D8
Uplands
Saltash PL12. . . . . . .242 E1
Tavistock PL19 . . . . . .171 A4
Uplands Dr EX4. . . . .174 A1
Uplands Rd TQ3. . . . .219 A2
Uplands Terr
Holsworthy EX22 . . . .164 C3
Holsworthy TA20. . . . .72 A6
UPLOWMAN 50 B2
Uplowman CE Prim Sch
EX16. . . . . .50 B2
Uplowman Rd
Chevithorne EX16. . . .49 F1
Tiverton EX16. . . . . . .64 E8
Uplowman Rd N EX16 .64 E8
UPLYME. 260 B5
Uplyme Rd DT7. . . . . .260 C4
Uplyme Road Ind Est
DT7. . . . . .260 C4
UPOTTERY 68 C2
Upottery Prim Sch
EX14. . . . . .68 C2
UPPACOTT 27 D7
Uppacott Cnr EX31. . .27 D8
Uppacott Cross
Meshaw EX36. . . . . . .45 F8
Moretonhampstead
TQ13. . . . . .111 D7
Uppaton La PL21. . . . .133 D1
Upper Barton 5 EX5. .99 A6
Upper Braddons Hill Rd
TQ1. . . . . .220 C4
Upper Church St 9
EX8. . . . . .202 A6
Upper Churston Rise
EX12. . . . . .191 E8
Upper Claypark EX34. .7 F7
Upper Cloister Wlk
EX6. . . . . .181 F5
Upper Cockington La
TQ2. . . . . .219 C7
Upper Cockington La
(Path) TQ2 . . . . . . .219 D3
Upper Crooked Mdw
EX20. . . . . .170 C5
Upper Headland Park Rd
TQ3. . . . . .219 C1
Upper Hermosa Rd 1
TQ14. . . . . .210 B5

Upper Highfield
EX10. . . . .**188** A5
Upper Knollys Terrace La
PL3. . . . .**248** C4
Upper Longlands
EX7. . . . .**204** D7
Upper Manor Rd TQ3 **226** B8
Upper Mead EX13. . . . . **167** F6
Upper Morin Rd TQ3 **226** C7
Upper Paul St EX4 . . . **261** A3
Upper Penns Rd TQ3 **219** C1
Upper Richardson
Blackhorse EX1. . . . . . .**179** A8
Exeter EX1. . . . .**178** F8
Upper Ridings PL7. . .**251** B7
Upper Seaway La
EX10. . . . .**100** E2
Upper Stoneborough La
EX9. . . . .**198** A1
Upperton La PL6. . . . .**241** F3
Upperton Rd
Cheriton Bishop EX6. . . .**97** D1
Dunsford EX6 . . . .**112** E8
Upper Torrs EX34 . . . . . .1 E4
Upper Westhill Rd
DT7. . . . .**260** C3
Upper West Terr
EX9. . . . .**198** A1
Upper Wood La TQ6. **234** B3
UPPINCOTT. **81** A5
Uppincott Hill EX5 . . **63** C1
Uppincott La
Bickleigh EX5 . . . .**63** C1
Cadbury EX5. . . . .**81** C8
Upright Villas [4]
EX33. . . . .**152** D5
UPTON
Payhembury. **84** D5
Skilgate **34** F8
Torquay **220** A6
Upton Cl PL3 . . . .**249** B7
Upton Cross
Payhembury EX14. . . . . .**84** D5
Thurlestone TQ7. . . . . .**143** D2
Upton Ct [2] TQ1 . . . .**220** A6
Upton Farm La TA4 . . . .**34** E8
UPTON HELLIONS . . **80** C6
Upton Hill TQ1. . . . . .**220** A6
Upton Hill Rd TQ5. . .**230** C2
Upton Manor Ct TQ5 **230** C2
Upton Manor Pk TQ5 **230** C2
Upton Manor Rd
TQ5. . . . .**230** C2
UPTON PYNE. **173** A8
Upton Pyne Cross
EX5. . . . .**172** E4
Upton Pyne Hill
Upton Pyne EX17 . . . . . .**81** D1
Upton Pyne EX5 . . . . . .**172** F6
Upton Rd
[11] Bideford EX39 . . . .**157** B1
Torquay TQ1. . . . .**219** F6
Upton St James CE Prim
Sch [5] TQ1 . . . .**220** A7
Ursa Gdns PL9 . . . . . .**256** E8
Usticke La EX34. . . . . . . .3 B3
UTC Plymouth PL5 . .**247** E3
UTON. **165** B1
Uton Steep Cross
EX17. . . . .**165** B1
Uxbridge Dr PL5 . . . .**243** E4

V

Vaagso Cl PL1 . . . .**247** E2
Vachell Cres EX2. . . . .**178** D5
Vale Cl
Barnstaple EX32. . . . . . .**155** A6
Galmpton TQ5. . . . .**229** B5
Vale Ct [17] EX10 . . . .**101** B1
VALE DOWN **108** A5
Vale Dr EX2. . . . .**177** E3
Vale La EX13. . . . .**167** D6
Valentine Manor
TQ11. . . . .**236** C5
Valentines TA22 . . . . . .**33** E6
Vale Rd
Exmouth EX8. . . . .**202** D7
Kingskerswell TQ12. . . .**213** A5
Newton Abbot TQ12 . . .**207** D1
Valerian Pl TQ12. . . . .**206** D5
Vales Rd EX9 . . . .**198** B1
Valiant Ave PL5. . . . . .**244** A4
Valiant Soldier Mus The ★
TQ11. . . . .**236** C5
Valletort Flats PL1. . .**248** A2
Valletort Ho PL1 . . . . .**262** C3
Valletort La PL1. . . . . .**248** A3
Valletort Pk TQ5 . . . . .**230** A4
Valletort Pl PL1. . . . . .**248** A3
Valletort Terr PL1. . . .**262** A4
Valley Cl
Barnstaple EX32. . . . . . .**155** B3
Teignmouth TQ14. . . . . .**124** E1
Valley Dr PL9 . . . .**140** D8
Valley La [7] EX34 . . . . .3 A3
Valley of Rocks The ★
EX35. . . . . .5 A6
Valley Park Cl EX4 . . .**173** D2
Valley Path TQ12. . . . .**206** E4
Valley Rd
Clyst St Mary EX5 . . . . .**179** E3
Exeter EX4 . . . .**176** F7

Valley Rd *continued*
Plymouth PL7 . . . .**250** B5
Saltash PL12. . . . .**242** E2
Valleyside TQ7. . . . . .**143** A2
Valley View
Axminster EX13 . . . .**167** E5
Bideford EX39. . . . .**156** D2
Chagford TQ13. . . . .**111** A6
Farway EX24. . . . .**101** F6
Landkey EX32. . . . .**17** C1
Millmoor EX15. . . . .**51** E1
Morebath EX16. . . . .**34** B3
Plymouth PL6. . . . .**245** D7
Seaton EX12. . . . .**192** A6
Shebbear EX21. . . . .**55** E4
Valley View Cl
Plymouth PL3 . . . .**249** B6
Seaton EX12. . . . .**192** B6
Torquay TQ1 . . . .**219** F7
Valley View Rd PL3. . .**249** B7
Valley Way EX8 . . . . . .**196** E3
Valley Wlk PL6. . . . . . .**245** E6
Van Buren Pl EX2 . . . .**178** D3
Vanehill Rd TQ1 . . . . .**220** C3
Vanguard Cl PL5. . . . .**244** D1
Van Post EX16 . . . .**49** D6
Vanpost Hill EX16 . . . . .**49** D5
Vansittart Dr EX8 . . . .**196** C3
Vansittart Rd TQ2 . . . .**219** F6
Vapron Rd PL3. . . . . . .**248** F6
Varco Sq EX2 . . . .**178** C4
Varian Ct [4] TQ9 . . . .**223** E5
Varley Cl EX16 . . . .**161** E6
Varve Cl [2] EX31. . . . .**154** A3
Vauban Pl PL2. . . . . . .**247** F4
Vaughan Cl PL2 . . . . . .**248** C7
Vaughan Par TQ2 . . . .**220** B4
Vaughan Rd
Exeter EX1. . . . .**178** B6
Torquay TQ2 . . . .**220** B4
Vaughan Rise EX1 . . . .**178** B6
Vauxhall Ct [9] PL4 . . .**263** A2
Vauxhall Quay PL4 . . .**263** A2
Vauxhall St PL4 . . . . . .**263** A2
Vauxhall Street Flats [18]
PL4 . . . .**263** A2
Vavasours Slip TQ6 . . .**233** F4
Veale Cl EX20 . . . .**75** B6
Vealenia Terr TQ13 . . .**130** F4
Veales Rd TQ7 . . . .**258** C4
Veasypark PL9. . . . . . .**140** D8
Veille La TQ12 . . . .**219** C8
Velator EX33 . . . .**152** C4
Velator Cl EX33 . . . . . .**152** D4
Velator Dr EX33. . . . . .**152** D4
Vellacott La EX34 . . . . .3 C3
Vellaford Cross EX20. .**75** E7
Velland Ave TQ2 . . . . .**213** F4
Vellator Way EX33 . . . .**152** D4
Yellow Moor La EX19. .**58** F1
VELLY. **23** B3
Velwell Rd EX4 . . . . . .**261** A4
Venborough Cl EX12 . .**191** F8
Venbridge Hill EX6. . . .**97** B4
Venford Cl TQ4 . . . . . .**229** B8
Venford Hill
East Anstey TA22 . . . . . .**32** E8
Hawkridge TA22 . . . .**21** D1
Venford Villas EX36. . .**30** D4
Venhay Cross EX36. . . .**46** D6
Venlake DT7 . . . .**260** A5
Venlake Cl DT7 . . . .**260** A5
Venlake End DT7. . . . .**260** A5
Venlake Mdw DT7. . . .**260** A5
Venlock Cl EX32 . . . . . .**155** D4
Venmore Orch EX5. . . .**184** B2
VENN. **143** D5
Venn Bridge TQ10. . . .**137** E8
Venn Cl
Instow EX39. . . . .**15** C2
[6] Plymouth PL3. . . . . .**248** E6
Stoke Fleming TQ6 . . . . .**146** B7
Venn Cots EX39 . . . .**15** C2
Venn Cres PL3 . . . .**248** E6
Venn Cross
Barnstaple EX32. . . . . . .**155** D1
Broadhempston TQ12. . .**131** D4
East Allington TQ9. . . . .**144** E5
Stoke Fleming TQ6 . . . . .**146** B8
Ugborough PL21. . . . . . .**137** E7
Waterrow TA4. . . . .**35** D3
West Putford EX22 . . . . .**39** D3
Venn Ct
Brixton PL8. . . . .**257** A4
Plymouth PL3. . . . .**248** E6
Venn Dr PL8. . . . .**257** A4
Venn Gdns PL3 . . . . . .**248** E7
Venn Gr PL3 . . . .**248** E6
VENNGREEN. **54** D6
Venn Hill
Copplestone EX17. . . . . .**79** B8
Milton Abbot PL19 . . . . .**116** A6
Venn La
Cheriton Fitzpaine
EX17. . . . .**63** A1
Dartmouth TQ6. . . . . . .**233** B1
Plymouth PL2, PL3. . . . .**248** D7
Stoke Fleming TQ6 . . . . .**146** A8
Venn Lane End EX32. . .**17** B1
Venn Orch EX12 . . . . .**207** D7
VENN OTTERY. **100** B2
Venn Ottery Rd EX10 .**186** E8

Venn Pk TQ6. . . . .**146** B8
Venn Rd
Barnstaple EX32. . . . . . .**155** C1
Landkey EX32. . . . .**28** A8
Venn Way
Plymouth PL3 . . . .**248** E7
Stoke Fleming TQ6 . . . . .**146** B7
Venny Bridge EX4. . . .**174** D1
VENNY TEDBURN. . . .**98** A8
VENTERDON. 7 F3
Ventiford Cotts TQ12 **123** C2
VENTION. 7 F3
Vention La EX33. . . . . . .7 E3
Vention Rd EX33. . . . . . .7 E3
VENTON
Drewsteignton **95** F1
Ivybridge **136** B7
Venton Cross
Highampton EX21. . . . . . .**74** E6
Tigley TQ9. . . . .**135** F3
Venton Ct TQ9 . . . .**144** F5
Venton Dr
Westward Ho! EX39 . . . . .**25** D8
Westward Ho! EX39 . . . .**156** D7
Venture Ct TQ12 . . . . .**207** A3
Verbena Terr TQ14. . . .**209** D5
Verden Cl PL3 . . . .**248** E5
Vermont Gdns PL2. . . .**247** F7
Verna Pl PL5. . . . .**243** D2
Verna Rd PL5. . . . .**243** E2
Verney St EX1 . . . .**261** C4
Vernhill Cross PL7 . . . .**132** E3
Vernon Cl TQ1 . . . .**220** C2
Vernon Cres EX2. . . . . .**182** C8
Vernon Ct TQ1. . . . . . .**220** A4
Vernon Rd EX8 . . . .**196** D2
Vernons La [23] EX39 . . .**15** A1
Verona Ct [3] EX32 . . .**155** A6
Verwill La EX34 . . . . . . .3 D3
Veryan Cl EX1 . . . .**200** E1
Vestry Dr EX2. . . . .**181** B8
Vetch Pl TQ12 . . . .**206** D5
Veysey Cl EX2. . . . .**177** E2
Viaduct View EX22 . . .**164** C4
Vial's Cnr EX16 . . . .**48** D5
VICARAGE. **190** F4
Vicarage Ball TQ9. . . .**222** C2
Vicarage Cl
Brixham TQ5. . . . .**230** C5
Hartland TQ9 . . . .**22** D3
Stoke Gabriel TQ9. . . . . .**227** F7
Vicarage Gdns
Dawlish EX7. . . . .**204** C6
Milton Abbot PL19 . . . . .**116** A6
Plymouth PL5. . . . .**243** B1
Vicarage Gr TQ9 . . . . .**227** F8
Vicarage Hill
Brixham TQ5. . . . .**230** C5
Cornwood PL21 . . . .**133** D3
Dartmouth TQ6. . . . . . .**233** D3
Dulverton TA22 . . . .**33** D4
Holbeton PL8 . . . .**136** D1
Kingsteignton TQ12 . . . .**207** F7
Marldon TQ3. . . . .**218** E3
Torquay TQ2 . . . .**219** D4
Vicarage La
Exeter EX4 . . . .**174** E2
Longdown EX6 . . . .**98** E1
South Tawton EX20. . . . .**95** B5
Strete TQ6. . . . .**145** F6
West Alvington TQ7. . . . .**258** A4
Vicarage Lawn EX32. . .**155** A5
Vicarage Rd
Abbotskerswell TQ12 . . .**212** B6
Blackawton TQ9 . . . .**139** E1
Brixham TQ5. . . . .**230** C2
Cockwood EX6 . . . .**201** B6
East Budleigh EX9. . . . . .**198** B6
Landkey EX32. . . . .**17** B2
Marldon TQ3. . . . .**218** E2
Okehampton EX20 . . . . .**170** A5
Plymouth PL5. . . . .**250** C6
Sidmouth EX10 . . . .**188** B4
South Brent TQ10 . . . . . .**134** F3
Stoke Gabriel TQ9. . . . . .**227** F8
Torpoint PL11. . . . .**247** B2
Torquay TQ2 . . . .**219** D4
Vicarage St
Barnstaple EX32. . . . . . .**154** F5
Colyton EX24 . . . .**103** A5
Vicary Cl TQ12. . . . . . .**207** A3
Vickers Ground EX39 **156** F8
Vickery Cl
Cullompton EX15 . . . . . .**163** B3
West Clyst EX4 . . . .**174** F3
Vicks Mdw EX20 . . . . . .**75** C7
Victor Cl EX1 . . . .**178** A5
Victoria Ave PL1 . . . . .**262** A4
Victoria Cl
[7] Barnstaple EX32 . . . .**155** B4
[5] Exeter EX1. . . . .**178** E8
Kenton EX6. . . . .**194** D3
Willand EX15 . . . .**162** D4
Victoria Cotts
[2] Holsworthy EX22. . . .**164** C4
Lee Mill PL21 . . . .**136** D6
North Tawton EX20 . . . . .**77** C4
Plymouth PL6 . . . .**249** B8
Victoria Cres EX17 . . . .**165** D6
Victoria Ct
Dartmouth TQ6. . . . . . .**233** D3
[4] Totnes TQ9. . . . .**223** C5
Victoria Gdns
[1] Bideford EX39 . . . . . .**157** A1
Exmouth EX8. . . . .**196** A3
Victoria Gr EX39 . . . . .**157** A1
Victoria Hill [1] EX22. .**164** C4
Victoria Hts TQ6. . . . .**233** D3

Victoria La PL12 . . . . .**242** F2
Victoria Lawn EX32 . . .**155** B4
Victoria Par TQ1 . . . . .**220** B3
Victoria Park Rd
Exeter EX2 . . . .**177** E5
Torquay TQ1 . . . .**220** B7
Victoria Pl
Axminster EX13 . . . .**167** D6
Brixham TQ5. . . . .**230** C6
Budleigh Salterton
EX9. . . . .**199** G2
Chardstock EX13 . . . .**88** A7
Dartmouth TQ6. . . . . . .**233** F3
Kingsbridge TQ7 . . . . . .**258** D5
Newton Abbot TQ12 . . .**207** C3
Plymouth PL1. . . . .**262** A2
Plymouth, Devonport
PL2. . . . .**247** F4
Salcombe TQ8. . . . .**259** E5
Victoria Rd
Barnstaple EX32. . . . . . .**155** A4
Black Torrington EX21. . .**74** A4
Brixham TQ5. . . . .**230** F6
Dartmouth TQ6. . . . . . .**233** E3
[1] Exeter EX4. . . . .**177** D8
Exmouth EX8. . . . .**201** F6
Hatherleigh EX20 . . . . . .**75** C7
Ilfracombe EX34. . . . . . .**150** B5
Plymouth PL5 . . . .**243** D2
Saltash PL12. . . . .**242** F2
Sidmouth EX10 . . . .**188** B4
Topsham EX3 . . . .**182** F5
Torquay TQ1 . . . .**220** B6
Victoria Road Prim Sch
[1] PL5 . . . .**243** D1
Victoria Sh Ctr TQ4. . .**226** C6
Victoria Sq
[3] Holsworthy EX22. . . .**164** C4
Paignton TQ4 . . . .**226** C6
Victoria St
Barnstaple EX32. . . . . . .**155** B4
Exeter EX4 . . . .**177** D8
Holsworthy EX22 . . . . . .**164** C4
Okehampton EX20 . . . . .**170** C5
Paignton TQ4 . . . .**226** B6
Torpoint PL11. . . . .**247** B3
Totnes TQ9 . . . .**223** C5
Wellington TA21 . . . . . .**160** D6
Victoria Terr
Barnstaple EX32. . . . . . .**155** A4
[15] Bideford EX39. . . . .**157** A1
[2] Bovey Tracey TQ13 . .**180** D4
Cullompton EX15 . . . . . .**163** C3
Honiton EX14 . . . .**166** B6
Kingsteignton TQ12 . . . .**207** F7
Ottery St Mary EX11 . . .**169** C3
Plymouth PL4 . . . .**262** A4
Tiverton EX16. . . . .**161** B4
Victoria Way EX8 . . . .**201** F6
Victor La EX1 . . . .**178** A5
Victor St EX1 . . . .**178** A5
Victory Cl TQ12 . . . . . .**207** B5
Victory Dr EX2. . . . . . .**182** C8
Victory Rd
Dartmouth TQ6. . . . . . .**233** D3
North Tamerton EX22 . . .**89** D8
Victory St PL2 . . . .**247** E6
Victory Way EX38 . . . .**159** C6
Vieux Cl EX9 . . . .**198** E7
View Rd DT7. . . . .**260** D3
Vigilance Ave TQ5 . . . .**230** E5
Vigo Bridge Rd TQ9 . .**171** C6
Vigo Mews PL19 . . . . .**171** C6
Viking Gr EX1. . . . .**178** E8
Villa Capri TQ1 . . . . . .**220** D2
Villa Cl EX32. . . . .**155** B2
Villa Cl EX8 . . . .**202** F7
Village Cl
Coldridge EX17. . . . .**59** F2
Loddiswell TQ7 . . . .**143** E7
Morchard Bishop EX17 . .**61** A2
Village Cross EX6. . . . .**201** B6
Village Cross Rd TQ7 **143** E7
Village Dr PL6 . . . .**241** C1
Village Farm Cl EX23 . .**70** A6
Village Hill
Upton TA4 . . . .**34** F7
Upton TA4 . . . .**35** A8
Village Hts PL7 . . . . . .**250** E6
Village La EX14 . . . .**86** B1
Village Rd
Christow EX6 . . . .**113** B3
Marldon TQ3. . . . .**218** D3
Woodbury Salterton
EX5. . . . .**184** C6
Village St [10] EX32. . . .**16** E1
Village The
Buckland Monachorum
PL20. . . . .**126** C3
Milton Abbot PL19 . . . . .**116** A6
North Bovey TQ13. . . . . .**111** D3
St Giles in the Wood
EX38. . . . .**42** B6
Village Way PL19 . . . . .**117** F4
Villa Pardiso [4] TQ1 . .**220** C5
Villa Rd EX38 . . . .**159** C5
Villas The TQ12 . . . . . .**123** E1
Villiers Ave TQ12. . . . .**207** F2
Villiers Cl PL9 . . . .**255** D7
Vincents Rd TQ7 . . . . .**258** D5
Vine Cl EX2 . . . .**261** C2
Vine Cres PL2. . . . .**248** B6
Vinegar Hill EX39 . . . .**157** D2
Vine Gdns PL2 . . . .**248** B6
Vine Passage EX14. . . .**166** C6
Vine Rd TQ2 . . . .**219** F6
Vinery La PL7, PL9. . . .**250** E1

Vinery The TQ1 . . . . . .**220** B4
Vine St EX19. . . . .**58** F2
Vineton Pl EX14. . . . . . .**84** E2
Vineyard TQ9. . . . .**223** A8
Vineyard Hill TQ9 . . . .**223** A8
Vineyard La
Axminster EX13 . . . .**87** F2
Axminster EX13 . . . .**167** B7
Vineyards The EX22 . . .**164** C5
Vineyard Terr TQ9 . . . .**144** D7
Vineycroft La EX10 . . .**188** F7
Viney Cross EX14 . . . . . .**86** B6
Viney La
Monkton EX14 . . . .**86** C7
Upottery EX14 . . . .**68** C1
Viney Lane Cross
EX14. . . . .**86** B5
Vinivers Cross TQ8 . . .**148** F4
Vinnicombes Rd EX5 **173** F8
Vinstone Way PL5. . . . .**243** D1
Violet Dr
Dartmouth TQ6. . . . . . .**233** B2
Newton Abbot TQ12 . . .**206** C5
Plymouth PL6 . . . .**245** E8
Violet La PL19 . . . .**171** E6
Virginia Cl EX31. . . . . .**157** A1
Virginia Gdns PL2. . . .**247** F7
Virginia Lodge [14]
TQ1. . . . .**220** D4
VIRGINSTOW. **90** D3
Vision Hill Rd EX9. . . .**198** B2
Visitors Hill EX16 . . . . .**63** D4
Vittery Cl TQ5. . . . .**230** B5
Vivid App PL5. . . . .**247** D2
Vix Ct TQ5 . . . .**230** B5
Vixen Tor Cl
Okehampton EX20 . . . . .**170** E5
Yelverton PL20 . . . .**126** F3
Vixen Way PL5. . . . . . .**247** F7
Vognacott Cross EX22. **53** F3
Volans La PL9 . . . .**256** E8
Voley Cl EX1 . . . .**178** D7
Voley La EX31. . . . . .4 A3
Voscombe Cross EX31. **26** F7
Voulsdon Cross EX20. . .**92** A4
VOXMOOR. **160** F1
Voysey Hill EX17 . . . . . .**62** F1
Vranch House Sch
EX4. . . . .**178** B7
Vuefield Hill EX2. . . . .**176** E3
Vulscombe Cross
EX16. . . . .**63** A6
Vulscombe La EX16 . . . .**63** B6
Vyvyan Ct EX1 . . . .**178** A5

W

WADBROOK **88** C4
Wadbrook Cross EX13 **88** C4
Waddens Cross EX24 **102** D4
Wadderly Hill EX17. . . .**79** F7
WADDETON. **228** F6
Waddeton Cl TQ4 . . . .**225** F1
Waddeton Dr TQ3. . . .**225** F1
Waddeton Ind Est
TQ4. . . . .**225** F1
Waddeton Rd
Paignton TQ4 . . . .**225** F1
Stoke Gabriel TQ5. . . . . .**228** D6
Waddeton TQ3 . . . .**228** E7
WADDICOMBE **32** E6
Waddington Cross
EX36. . . . .**31** A3
Waddington La EX18 . . .**45** A5
Waddles Down Cross
EX4. . . . .**98** E5
WADDON. **124** A6
Waddon Cl PL7 . . . . . .**250** E7
Waddon La TQ13. . . . . .**124** A6
Waddons Cross TQ9. . .**216** C6
Wade Cl EX8. . . . .**202** E8
Wadham Cross
Knowstone EX36. . . . . . .**32** A2
West Anstey EX36. . . . . .**32** A2
Wadham Hill EX36. . . . .**32** A2
Wadham Ho EX4 . . . . .**173** A1
Wadham Terr [6] PL2 .**248** A5
Wadlands Mdw EX20 **170** D5
Wadley Hill DT7. . . . . .**260** A5
Waggoners Way EX4 **177** A8
Waggon Hill PL7. . . . . .**251** A4
WAGGS PLOT. **88** B4
Waggs Plot EX13. . . . . .**88** B4
Wagtail Ave PL8 . . . . . .**256** F8
Waie Cotts EX17 . . . . . .**78** C6
Waie Cross EX17 . . . . . .**78** B6
Wain La TQ12 . . . .**207** A4
Wain Pk PL7. . . . .**250** F6
Wakefield Ave PL5 . . . .**243** E1
Wakefields Yard [7]
TQ13. . . . .**180** C7
Wakeham Cl EX33. . . . .**152** E4
Wakehams Cl PL21. . . .**137** C2
Wake St PL4. . . . .**262** B4
Walcot Cl PL6. . . . .**245** E3
Walcott Way EX14. . . . .**67** C1
Walden Rd EX14 . . . . . .**67** C1
Waldland Gdns [4]
TQ12. . . . .**244** E6
Waldon Cl PL7. . . . .**251** B6
Waldon Ct TQ2 . . . .**220** B4
Waldon Ho TQ2 . . . . . .**220** B4
Waldon Point TQ2 . . . .**220** B4
Waldons Cross EX19 . . .**57** F2
Waldon Way EX22. . . . .**164** C6
Waldron's Cross TA21. .**35** E1
Walkers Gate TA21. . . .**160** D5

Walker Terr PL1 . . . . .**262** B1
Walkham Bsns Pk
PL5. . . . .**244** B1
Walkham Cl PL19 . . . . .**171** D5
Walkham Mdws PL20 **126** F4
WALKHAMPTON. **127** A4
Walkhampton Rd
PL20. . . . .**126** F4
Walkham Rise TQ2. . . .**219** B8
Walkham Terr [5]
PL20. . . . .**126** F5
Walk La EX36 . . . .**30** F6
Wallace Ave
Dawlish EX7. . . . .**204** E7
Exeter EX4 . . . .**178** B8
Torquay TQ2 . . . .**219** C8
Wallace La
Lynton EX35. . . . . .5 A3
West Alvington TQ7. . . . .**143** F1
Wallace Rd PL7. . . . . . .**251** A4
Wallaford Rd TQ11. . . .**135** C8
Walland Cross EX32. . . .**18** E3
Walland Dr EX39 . . . . . .**24** B1
Wallaton Cross TQ9. . .**145** A7
Walled Gdn The EX2 .**182** C7
Wallens La
Lutworthy EX16 . . . .**46** A3
Meshaw EX17. . . . .**45** F3
Wallfield Rd TQ13. . . . .**180** B5
Wallingford Rd TQ7 . .**258** D6
Wallis Gr TQ14. . . . . . .**209** A8
Wallon Cross TQ13. . . .**110** F7
Wallpark Cl PL7. . . . . . .**250** F7
Wall Park Cl TQ5 . . . . .**230** E5
Wall Park Rd TQ5 . . . .**230** E5
Wall Pk TQ9 . . . .**222** F6
Walls Cl EX8 . . . .**196** C5
Walls Hill Rd TQ1 . . . .**220** D7
Wall St PL1. . . . .**247** E2
Walnut Cl
[9] Chudleigh TQ13 . . . .**123** F6
Exminster EX6 . . . .**182** A4
Plymouth PL7 . . . .**251** B5
Totnes TQ9 . . . .**223** B6
Walnut Ct
Brixham TQ5. . . . .**230** D4
Torquay TQ2 . . . .**219** E4
Walnut Dr
Crediton EX17. . . . .**165** D6
Plymouth PL7 . . . .**251** C5
Tiverton EX16. . . . .**161** F5
Walnut Gdns PL7 . . . . .**251** C5
Walnut Gr EX8 . . . .**202** C7
Walnut La TQ2 . . . .**219** E4
Walnut Rd
Exeter EX2 . . . .**177** F2
Honiton EX14 . . . .**166** A4
Torquay TQ2 . . . .**219** E4
Walnut Way EX32 . . . .**155** D4
Walpole Cl EX4 . . . . . .**174** C1
Walreddon Cl PL19. . . .**171** B4
Walronds The EX16 . . .**161** C2
Walscott Hill
Newtown EX32 . . . .**18** F3
Popham EX36. . . . .**19** A3
Walshams EX14. . . . . . .**87** A1
Walsingham Ct PL7 . . .**251** B6
Walsingham Pl EX2 . . .**178** D4
Walsingham Rd EX2. . .**178** D4
Walson Cross EX17. . . . .**78** D3
Walson La EX19. . . . . . .**76** E7
Walson Rd EX17 . . . . . .**78** D3
Waltacre PL8 . . . .**257** F3
Walters Field EX31. . . .**154** A2
Walters Orch EX15 . . . .**163** C3
Walters Rd PL5 . . . .**243** C2
Walter Way EX31. . . . . .**153** E6
Waltham Pl PL2 . . . . . .**248** A8
Waltham Rd TQ12. . . . .**207** A3
Waltham Way PL21 . . . .**237** F4
Walton Cres PL5 . . . . . .**244** C1
Walton Rd EX2. . . . .**178** C5
Walton Way EX32 . . . .**155** C5
WAMBROOK. **69** F3
Wambrook EX20 . . . . . .**69** D2
Wandle Pl PL3 . . . .**249** D5
Wanstead Gr PL5 . . . . .**244** A2
Wantage Gdns PL1. . . .**262** A3
Warberry Ce Acad
TQ1. . . . .**220** C5
Warberry Rd W TQ1. . .**220** B5
Warberry Vale [3]
TQ1. . . . .**220** B6
Warboro Terr EX6 . . . .**201** B8
Warborough Hill EX6 **194** E3
Warborough Rd TQ5 **229** C6
Warbrightsleigh Hill
EX16. . . . .**48** B7
Warbro Ct [1] TQ1. . . .**220** B7
Warbro Rd TQ1 . . . . . .**220** C7
Warburton Gdns PL5 **243** C1
Warcombe La EX34 . . . .1 B2
Wardens Cl EX37. . . . . .**43** B7
Ward La EX19. . . . .**59** A2
Wardleworth Ct
TA21. . . . .**160** C7
Wardleworth Way
TA21. . . . .**160** C7
Wardlow Cl PL6. . . . . . .**248** F8
Wardlow Gdns PL6. . . .**248** F8
Ward Pl PL3 . . . .**249** B5
Wardrew Rd EX4 . . . . .**176** F5
Wards Cross EX5. . . . . .**99** C8

Ware Cl TQ12 . . . .**207** F7
Ware Cliff Chalets
  DT7 . . . .**260** D2
Warecroft Rd TQ12 . .**207** F7
Ware Cross
  Kingsteignton TQ12 . .**207** F7
  Ugborough PL21 . . . . .**137** D6
Warecross Gdns
  TQ12 . . . .**207** F7
Warefield Rd TQ3 . . . .**226** C7
Wareham Cross EX13 . .**88** E1
Wareham Rd EX13 . . . . .**88** E1
Ware Hill PL21 . . . .**137** D6
Ware La DT7 . . . .**260** B2
Warelwast Cl **1** PL7 .**250** D5
Waresfoot Dr EX17 . . .**165** B6
Warfelton Cres PL12 .**242** E2
Warfelton Gdns PL12 .**242** E2
Warfelton Terr PL12 . .**242** E2
Warfield Villas EX34 .**150** C5
WARFLEET **234** A1
Warfleet Creek Rd
  TQ6 . . . .**234** A1
Warfleet Rd TQ6 . . . . .**234** A2
Waring Bowen Ct
  EX2 . . . .**177** E1
Waring Rd PL6 . . . .**244** D7
Warkidons Way EX5 . .**185** A5
WARKLEIGH **29** A2
Warkleigh Cross EX37 . .**29** E1
Warland TQ9 . . . .**223** C5
Warleigh Ave PL2 . . . . .**247** E5
WARLEIGH BARTON . . .**243** F8
Warleigh Cres PL6 . . . .**244** F5
Warleigh La PL2 . . . . . .**247** E5
Warleigh Rd **2** PL4 . . .**248** E4
Warm Hill TQ13 . . . . . .**123** B7
Warmwell Rd PL5 . . . . .**243** E4
Warneford Gdns EX8 .**196** E2
Warne La PL19 . . . .**171** C6
Warnicombe La EX16 . .**64** D6
Warran La PL19 . . . . . .**171** C3
Warraton Cl PL12 . . . .**242** D3
Warraton La PL12 . . . .**242** D3
Warraton Gn PL12 . . . .**242** D3
Warraton Rd PL12 . . . .**242** D3
Warren Cl
  Great Torrington
    EX38 . . . .**159** C5
  Payhembury EX14 . . . . .**84** C4
  Wembury PL9 . . . .**140** D7
  West Hill EX11 . . . . . .**168** D4
Warren Cross EX16 . .**161** B7
Warren Dr EX9 . . . . . .**198** B2
Warren Hill TQ2 . . . . .**220** B4
Warren La
  Bickleigh PL5 . . . .**243** F8
  Chudleigh TQ13 . . . . .**124** A7
  Dartington TQ9 . . . . . .**216** B3
  Exeter EX4 . . . .**261** B4
  Farway EX24 . . . .**102** D7
  Great Torrington EX38 . .**41** C6
  Great Torrington EX38 .**159** C5
  Lee Mill PL21 . . . .**136** D6
  Plymouth PL5 . . . .**244** A8
  Wembury PL9 . . . .**140** E7
Warren Pk
  Plymouth PL5 . . . .**245** D7
  West Hill EX11 . . . . . .**168** D4
Warren Rd
  Bigbury-on-S TQ7 . . . .**142** E2
  Cockwood EX6 . . . . . .**201** B5
  Dawlish EX7 . . . .**205** A8
  Dawlish Warren EX7 . .**201** B2
  Kingsbridge TQ7 . . . . .**258** E3
  Mary Tavy PL19 . . . . . .**117** E6
  Simonsbath TA24 . . . . .**13** D3
  Thurlestone TQ7 . . . . .**143** A1
  Torquay TQ2 . . . .**220** B4
Warrens Mead EX10 .**188** D8
Warren St
  Plymouth PL2 . . . .**247** E4
  Rockwell Green TA21 .**160** A4
Warren The TQ12 . . . .**206** F3
Warren View EX39 . . .**156** E2
Warspite Gdns PL5 . .**244** D2
Warton Cl PL5 . . . .**244** D3
Warwick Ave
  Exeter EX1 . . . .**178** C5
  Plymouth PL5 . . . .**244** D3
Warwick Cl
  Feniton EX14 . . . .**84** E2
  Torquay TQ1 . . . .**220** E7
Warwick Orchard Cl
  PL5 . . . .**244** B3
Warwick Rd EX1 . . . . .**178** C6
Warwick Terr **8**
  EX32 . . . .**154** F6
Warwick Way EX4 . . . .**178** C8
Wasdale Cl PL6 . . . . . .**245** D2
Wasdale Gdns PL6 . . .**245** D2
WASH **215** B7
Washabrook La TQ7 .**258** E6
Washabrook Way
  TQ7 . . . .**258** E5
WASHBOURNE **139** D5
Washbourne Cl
  Brixham TQ5 . . . .**230** E5
  Plymouth PL1 . . . .**247** E3
Washbourne Cross
  TQ9 . . . .**139** D6
Washbrook View
  EX11 . . . .**169** E4
Wash Cross TQ11 . . . .**215** B8
WASHFIELD **48** F2
Washfield La
  Calverleigh EX16 . . . . .**48** F2
  Tiverton EX16 . . . .**49** A1

Washfield La *continued*
  Tiverton EX16 . . . .**64** A8
  Tiverton EX16 . . . .**223** D8
WASHFORD PYNE **61** F6
Washford Pyne Cross
  EX17 . . . .**61** E4
Washington Cl TQ3 . .**219** B1
Washington Ho **5**
  FX12 . . . .**192** A4
Wastor Cross PL21 . .**142** D7
Wastor Pk TQ7 . . . . . .**142** D7
WATCHCOMBE **102** F8
Watching Place Cross
  TQ13 . . . .**111** B3
Watch The TQ7 . . . . .**143** A2
WATCOMBE **214** B2
Watcombe Beach Rd
  TQ3 . . . .**214** C3
Watcombe Heights Rd
  TQ1 . . . .**214** C4
Watcombe Prim Sch
  TQ2 . . . .**214** B3
WATER **121** F7
Waterbeer St EX4 . . .**261** A3
Water Bridge Cross
  EX17 . . . .**78** F6
Watercolour Wy PL4 .**255** B6
Water Cotts TQ13 . . .**121** F7
Waterdale Pk TQ12 . .**213** A4
Waterford Cross TQ9 **131** E1
Waterford La EX13 . .**103** C5
Water Gate EX2 . . . . .**261** B2
Watergate Cotts PL9 .**140** D8
Watergate Cross
  EX20 . . . .**107** E6
Waterhaynes La TA20 . **68** F8
WATERHEAD **143** B6
Waterhead Cl TQ6 . . .**234** B4
Waterhead Terr TQ6 .**234** B4
Waterhouse Cross
  EX17 . . . .**62** E1
Waterhouse Hill EX20 . **74** F1
Waterhouse La EX13,
  EX14 . . . .**87** C6
Watering Ct EX9 . . . .**198** E7
Watering La EX9 . . . .**198** F8
Watering Pk La EX17 . .**60** A7
Water La
  Barnstaple EX32 . . . . .**155** B3
  Bow EX17 . . . .**78** C4
  Combe Martin EX34 . . . .**3** A3
  Cornworthy TQ9 . . . . .**227** A3
  Dartington TQ9 . . . . . .**215** B2
  Exeter EX2 . . . .**177** C3
  Kingskerswell TQ12 . .**213** A4
  Sidmouth EX10 . . . . . .**188** B5
  Tiverton EX16 . . . .**161** D4
  Torquay TQ2 . . . .**219** C8
Waterlake La EX31 . . . .**16** A7
Waterlake Rd TA20 . . . .**88** C8
Water Lane Cl **2**
  EX32 . . . .**155** B3
Water Lane Cotts **4**
  EX32 . . . .**155** B3
Water Lane End TQ9 .**215** B3
Waterlears Cross
  TQ7 . . . .**147** D8
Waterleat Ave
  Honiton EX14 . . . .**166** D5
  Paignton TQ3 . . . .**225** E6
Waterleat Cl TQ3 . . . .**225** F5
Waterleat Ct TQ3 . . . .**225** F5
Waterleat Rd TQ3 . . . .**225** F5
Waterleat Way TQ13 .**130** F6
Waterloo Cl PL1 . . . . .**248** A2
Waterloo Cotts EX15 .**163** C2
Waterloo Cross
  EX15 . . . .**65** F8
Waterloo Ct PL1 . . . .**248** A2
Waterloo Gdns EX38 .**159** F6
Waterloo Hill EX16 . . .**47** B6
Waterloo Path EX34 .**150** D6
Waterloo Rd
  Exeter EX2 . . . .**177** A3
  Holsworthy EX22 . . . .**164** D5
  Kingsbridge TQ7 . . . . .**258** D6
  Torquay TQ1 . . . .**220** B6
  Wellington TA21 . . . . .**160** C6
Waterloo St
  Plymouth PL4 . . . .**263** A4
  Plymouth, Stoke PL1. .**248** A3
  14 Teignmouth TQ14 .**210** C4
Waterloo Terr **1**
  EX39 . . . .**156** F1
Waterloo Yard Flats
  PL1 . . . .**248** A1
Watermark Way
  PL21 . . . .**237** D6
Water Mdw EX15 . . . .**163** C2
Watermead TA20 . . . . .**88** D8
Watermill St **5** TQ5 .**230** C4
Watermore Ct **1**
  EX4 . . . .**177** E7
Waterside
  Exeter EX2 . . . .**261** A1
  Kingsbridge TQ7 . . . . .**258** D4
  Newton Abbot TQ13 . .**180** D7
  Uplyme DT7 . . . .**260** B5

Waterside Ho
  Ivybridge PL21 . . . . . .**237** C4
  8 Totnes TQ9 . . . . . .**223** D5
Waterside La EX39 . . .**157** E6
Waterside Mews PL1 .**247** D3
Waterside Rd TQ4 . . .**226** C1
Waterside Vw TQ4 . . .**226** C1
Waterslade Dr PL21 . .**237** F4
Waterslade La EX5 . . .**179** E8
Waterslade Way
  Clyst Honiton EX5 . . .**175** E1
  Clyst Honiton EX5 . . .**179** E8
Waterstream Sq **5**
  TQ13 . . . .**123** F6
Water Terr **11** EX34. . . .**3** A3
Water Turn TQ13 . . . .**130** E5
Waterwell La TQ12 . .**213** C8
Waterworks La TQ14 **209** D4
Watery La
  Axminster EX13 . . . . . .**88** A3
  Beara EX31 . . . .**9** A1
  Braunton EX33 . . . . . .**152** F5
  Budlake EX5 . . . .**82** E3
  Colyton EX13, EX24 . .**103** A6
  Combe Martin EX34 . . . .**3** A3
  Croyde EX33 . . . .**7** E2
  Great Torrington EX38 .**159** B4
  Hawkridge TA22 . . . . . .**21** E3
  Milton Combe PL6 . . . .**240** D6
  Parracombe EX31 . . . . .**11** D6
  Stoke Canon EX5 . . . . .**81** F3
  Tiverton EX16 . . . .**161** E5
  Whiddon EX31 . . . .**9** C1
  Woodbury EX5 . . . . . .**184** B4
Watkins Way
  Bideford EX39 . . . . . .**157** C2
  Paignton TQ3 . . . .**225** D7
Watson Gdns PL4 . . . .**263** B3
Watson Pl
  Exeter EX2 . . . .**177** E4
  Plymouth PL4 . . . .**263** B2
Watts Park Rd PL2 . . .**248** C4
Watts Rd PL19 . . . . . .**171** B5
Watts' Rd PL4 . . . .**263** C3
Waveney Gdns PL5 . .**244** C3
Waverley Ave EX4. . . .**261** B4
Waverley Rd
  Exmouth EX8 . . . .**202** A8
  Kingsbridge TQ7 . . . . .**258** C4
  Newton Abbot TQ12 . .**207** B4
  Plymouth PL5 . . . .**243** D2
Waverley Terr EX35 . .**151** B5
Wavish Pk PL11 . . . . .**246** E3
Waybrook Cotts EX2 .**181** C8
Waybrook Cres EX2 . .**181** C8
Waybrook La EX2 . . . .**181** B6
Way Cnr EX16 . . . .**63** A5
Waycott Wlk PL6 . . . .**244** D6
Way Cross EX20 . . . . .**107** D8
Way Down Cross
  TQ13 . . . .**110** F8
Waye Cross TQ13 . . . .**110** F5
Wayfaring EX32 . . . . .**155** D3
Way La EX6 . . . .**98** B5
Wayland Ave EX2 . . . .**261** C1
Waylands Cnr EX16 . .**161** D7
Waylands Rd
  Bolham EX16 . . . .**49** C1
  Tiverton EX16 . . . .**161** D6
Wayside
  Brixham TQ5 . . . .**230** A4
  Ivybridge PL21 . . . . . .**237** C4
Wayside Cl TQ5 . . . . .**230** A4
Wayside Cres EX1. . . .**178** B7
Way's La EX15 . . . .**163** C2
WAYTOWN **24** D1
Waytown Cross TQ9 . .**131** D2
WAY VILLAGE **63** A5
Wear Barton Rd EX2 .**182** B7
Wear Cl EX2 . . . .**182** C7
WEARDE **242** F2
Wearde Rd PL12 . . . . .**242** E1
WEARE GIFFARD **26** B1
Weatherdon Dr
  PL21 . . . .**237** F5
Weatherill Rd EX4 . . .**166** C4
Weaver Cross EX15 . . .**83** E6
Weaver Ct TQ2. . . . . .**219** B8
Weaver La EX15. . . . . .**83** E7
Weavers Ct EX2. . . . . .**261** A2
Weavers Rd TQ12 . . .**123** C5
Weaver's Reach
  TA21 . . . .**160** B7
Weavers Way
  Dartington TQ9 . . . . . .**222** E8
  Kingskerswell TQ12 . .**213** A4
Weavers Wlk EX15 . . .**163** B2
Webber Cl TQ12 . . . . .**211** F8
Webber La EX17 . . . . . .**78** F3
Webbers CE Prim Sch
  TA21 . . . .**50** F5
Webbers Cl
  Wellington TA21 . . . . .**160** E4
  Whimple EX5 . . . .**99** E8
Webbers Mdw EX5. . .**184** D3
Webbers Way
  Dartington TQ9 . . . . . .**215** E1
  Dartington TQ9 . . . . . .**222** F8
  Tiverton EX16 . . . .**161** E6
  Willand EX15 . . . .**162** D4
Webbers Yard Est
  TQ9 . . . .**222** E8
Webberton Cross
  EX2 . . . .**113** F6
Webbery Cross EX39 . .**26** D4

Webbery Moor Cross
  EX36 . . . .**31** A3
Webble Green Cross
  EX13 . . . .**87** C8
Wcbbs Orch EX20 . . . .**77** C4
Webland La TQ10 . . . .**135** C3
Webley Rd EX2 . . . . . .**176** F3
Webster Cl TQ12 . . . .**207** C3
Weddicott Cross
  TQ13 . . . .**111** A4
Wedding Well La EX33 . **8** F1
Well Mead EX13 . . . . .**87** C1
Welcombe EX39 . . . . . .**37** B5
Wedgwood Ct **9**
  TQ14 . . . .**210** B4
Wedlake Mews **22**
  EX7 . . . .**204** D6
Wedlake Way EX31 . . .**154** A2
Weech Cl EX7 . . . .**204** C6
Weeches The EX16 . . . .**48** F2
Weech Rd EX7 . . . . . .**204** C6
WEEK
  Barnstaple **27** E6
  North Tawton **77** B4
  Totnes **215** D1
Weekaborough Dr
  TQ3 . . . .**218** D2
Weekaborough Oak Cross
  TQ12 . . . .**217** E4
Week Cross
  Bishop's Tawton EX31 . .**27** F6
  Bradninch EX5 . . . .**82** F7
  Burrington EX37 . . . . . .**43** C5
  Chulmleigh EX18 . . . . . .**45** D3
  Moretonhampstead
    TQ13 . . . .**111** C4
  Puddington EX16 . . . . .**62** D6
  South Zeal EX20 . . . . . .**95** B3
  Zeal Monachorum EX17 .**78** C7
Weeke Cross PL21 . . .**137** D4
Weeke Hill TQ6 . . . . .**146** C8
Weekes Mdw TA21. . . .**51** E6
Week La
  Dawlish Warren EX7. .**201** A1
  High Bickington EX37 . .**43** D5
Week Lane End EX31 . .**27** F5
Week Park Cross
  EX37 . . . .**43** C5
Weeksland Rd TQ2. . .**219** C6
Weeks Row PL18. . . . .**125** D6
Weekstone Cross
  EX22 . . . .**71** B8
Weir Cl PL6 . . . .**245** F2
Weirfield Ho EX2 . . . .**261** B1
Weirfield Rd EX2. . . . .**261** B1
Weirfields TQ9 . . . . . .**223** C6
Weirford La EX20 . . . . .**76** F4
Weir Gdns PL6 . . . . . .**245** F2
Weir Head Cotts TA22 .**33** B7
Weirside Pl EX2. . . . . .**261** B1
Weirside Way EX32 . .**155** B6
Welbeck Ave PL4 . . . .**262** C4
Welch Cl EX13 . . . . . .**167** D5
Welch's La EX31 . . . . .**15** C2
WELCOMBE **37** A5
Welcombe Cross EX39 .**37** B4
Welcome St EX2 . . . . .**261** A1
Weld Park Ave **4**
  EX34 . . . .**150** D5
Welland Gdns PL3 . . .**249** C5
Wellands Cl EX15 . . . . .**66** B7
Wellands Cross EX13. .**87** D4
Wellbrook Gn EX16 . .**161** B4
Wellbrook St EX16 . . .**161** C4
Wellbrook Terr
  10 Bideford EX39 . . .**157** A1
  8 Tiverton EX16 . . . .**161** B4
Wellclose Rd EX33 . . .**152** D5
Well Cross PL21 . . . . .**137** E6
Welle House Gdns
  TQ7 . . . .**258** D6
Weller Rd EX13 . . . . . .**167** D4
Wellesley Park Prim Sch
  TA21 . . . .**160** E4
Wellesley Pk TA21 . . .**160** D4
Wellesley Rd TQ12 . .**220** B6
Wellesley Way TA3. . . .**68** D7
Wellfield Cl PL7. . . . . .**251** C5
Wellfield Hill EX13,
  DT6. . . . .**88** H2
Well Gdns PL1 . . . . . .**262** B3
Wellhay Cl PL9. . . . . .**256** C6
Well Hill TQ7 . . . .**147** E6
Well Hill Cl TQ7 . . . . .**147** E6
Wellings Cl TA20. . . . . .**88** C8
WELLINGTON **160** D7
Wellington Cl **2**
  EX2 . . . .**178** D5
Wellington Com Hospl
  TA21 . . . .**160** B6
Wellington Hill TA21 .**160** F2
Wellington Jun Sch
  TA21 . . . .**160** E6
Wellington Mus *
  TA21 . . . .**160** D6
Wellington Pl **1** TQ1 **220** B6
Wellington Rd
  Exeter EX2 . . . .**177** A3
  Torquay TQ1 . . . .**220** B6
Wellington Relief Rd
  Wellington TA21 . . . . .**160** C3
  Wellington TA21 . . . . .**160** F4
Wellington Sch TA21 .**160** E5
Wellington Sports Ctr
  TA21 . . . .**160** C6
Wellington Sq **15**
  TQ10. . . . .**134** F3

Wellington St
  Plymouth PL4 . . . .**263** A4
  Plymouth, Stoke PL1. .**248** A3
  13 Teignmouth TQ14 .**210** C4
  Torpoint PL11 . . . . . .**247** B3
Wellington Way EX5 .**179** E8
WELLISFORD **51** D8
Well La
  Bradworthy EX22 . . . . .**38** E1
  Hartland EX39 . . . .**22** D3
  Welcombe EX39 . . . . . .**37** B5
Well Mead EX13 . . . . .**87** C1
Well Oak Pk EX2 . . . .**177** F3
Wellpark Cl EX4 . . . . .**176** F6
Well Park Flats EX38 .**159** D5
Well Park Pl TQ6. . . . .**146** A7
Well Park Rd PL18. . . .**125** C5
Well Park Rd
  Great Torrington
    EX38. . . . .**159** D5
  Torpoint PL11 . . . . . .**247** B3
Wellparks Hill EX17 . .**165** F4
Well Pk EX22 . . . .**164** C5
Wells Ave EX14 . . . . . .**84** E2
Wells Cl EX8 . . . .**196** E4
Wells Cl PL10 . . . .**252** E4
Well Spring Cl EX39 . . .**22** E3
Wellspring Pl PL9. . . .**256** D8
Wellsprings La EX20 . .**76** F3
Well St
  Exeter EX4 . . . .**261** C4
  Great Torrington EX38 . .**41** E7
  Great Torrington EX38 .**159** D5
  Loddiswell TQ7 . . . . .**143** F7
  Paignton TQ3 . . . .**226** B6
  Starcross EX6. . . . . . .**201** B8
Wells Terr EX17 . . . . . .**62** E1
Well Stones Cl PL21. .**237** E4
WELLSWOOD **220** D5
Wellswood Ave TQ1. .**220** E5
Wellswood Gdns
  TQ1 . . . .**220** D5
Wellswood Manor **3**
  TQ1 . . . .**220** D5
Wellswood Path TQ1 .**220** D5
Wellswood Pk TQ1. . .**220** D5
Well The TA21 . . . . . .**160** B5
Welman Rd PL10. . . . .**252** F6
Welsbere La EX17. . . . .**62** C3
WELSFORD **37** F8
Welsford Ave PL2 . . .**247** F5
Welstor Cross TQ13 . .**130** E7
Welsury Rd TQ2. . . . . .**213** C2
WEMBURY **256** B1
Wembury Dr TQ2 . . . .**214** B2
Wembury Marine Ctr *
  PL9 . . . .**140** C7
Wembury Mdw **1**
  PL9 . . . .**140** D8
Wembury Park Rd
  PL3 . . . .**248** D6
Wembury Prim Sch
  PL9 . . . .**140** D8
Wembury Rd
  Plymouth PL9 . . . .**256** A4
  Wembury PL9 . . . .**140** E8
WEMBWORTHY **59** C4
Wembworthy Down La
  EX18 . . . .**59** C6
Wembworthy Learning
  Ctr EX18 . . . .**59** C6
Wendover Way EX2 . .**178** B2
Wenlock Gdns PL2 . .**248** B8
Wensum Cl PL7. . . . . .**251** A4
Wentwood Gdns PL6 **245** E3
Wentwood Pl PL6. . . .**245** E3
Wentworth Gdns
  Crediton EX17. . . . . . .**165** E4
  Exeter EX4 . . . .**176** E4
Wentworth Pl PL4 . . .**249** B2
Wentworth Rd TQ12. .**180** F5
Wentworth Way
  PL12 . . . .**242** C2
Werstan Rd EX1 . . . . .**175** C4
Wesley Ave PL3. . . . . .**248** E5
Wesley Cl
  Exeter EX2 . . . .**177** A3
  3 Tiverton EX16 . . . . .**64** D7
  Torquay TQ2 . . . .**214** A4
Wesley Ct PL11 . . . . .**247** C3
Wesley La PL12 . . . . .**242** F2
Wesley Mews TQ2 . . .**214** A2
Wesley Pl
  Harberton TQ9 . . . . . .**222** D2
  Plymouth, Mutley PL3. .**248** E5
  1 Plymouth, Stoke
    PL2. . . . .**248** A4
Wesley Rd
  Holsworthy EX22 . . . .**164** B5
  Saltash PL12. . . . .**242** F2
Wesley Terr
  Hartland EX39 . . . .**22** D3
  Ipplepen TQ12 . . . . . .**211** D2
Wesley View TQ12 . . .**211** D2
Wesley Way EX2 . . . . .**181** B8
Wessex Cl EX3 . . . . . .**182** D6
Wessex Est EX4. . . . . .**177** A7
Wessex Ho **1** DT7 . .**260** D3
Wessex Way EX2. . . . .**233** C2
Wessiters EX12 . . . . .**192** A3
Westabrook Ave
  TQ13. . . . .**130** F5
Westabrook Cl TQ13 .**130** F5
Westabrook Dr TQ13 **130** F5
Westacombe EX31 . . . .**27** B8
WESTACOTT **155** F4

Westacott Cross
  Inwardleigh EX20 . . . . .**75** C3
  Meshaw EX36 . . . .**45** E8
  North Tawton EX20 . . . .**77** E5
Westacott La
  Coldridge EX17 . . . . . .**59** E2
  East Buckland EX32 . . . .**18** D2
  Mariansleigh EX36 . . . .**45** F8
  North Tawton EX20 . . . .**77** E5
Westacott Mdw EX32 **155** E3
Westacott Rd EX32. . .**155** E4
West Acres EX12. . . . .**191** F7
WEST ALVINGTON **258** B4
West Alvington Butts
  TQ7 . . . .**143** E2
West Alvington CE Prim
  Sch TQ7 . . . .**258** C5
West Alvington Hill
  TQ7 . . . .**258** C5
WEST ANSTEY **32** C6
West Anstey School Cross
  EX36 . . . .**32** C5
West Ave
  Barnstaple EX31 . . . . .**154** D3
  Exeter EX4 . . . .**177** C8
  4 Tavistock PL19 . . . .**171** B5
Westaway Hts EX31 . .**155** A8
Westaway La EX31 . . .**153** C5
Westaway Plain
  EX31 . . . .**155** A8
Westaway Rd **6**
  EX24 . . . .**103** A4
West Ball Hill EX39. . . .**22** D3
West Barton La EX20 . .**76** E4
West Beckon CI EX23. .**37** A1
Westbourne Gr EX34 **150** A5
Westbourne Rd
  Plymouth PL3 . . . .**248** B5
  Torquay TQ1 . . . .**220** A7
Westbourne Terr
  Budleigh Salterton
    EX9. . . . .**203** F8
  Saltash PL12. . . . .**242** F3
Westward Ho! EX39 . .**156** C7
Westbourne Villas
  EX34 . . . .**150** B6
Westbridge Cl EX20. .**170** B5
Westbridge Cotts
  PL19 . . . .**171** B4
Westbridge Ct EX2. . .**181** D8
Westbridge Ind Est **3**
  PL19 . . . .**171** B4
Westbrook Ave
  Teignmouth TQ14 . . . .**209** E7
  Teignmouth TQ14 . . . .**210** A5
Westbrook Cl EX4. . . .**178** B8
Westbrook Pl EX16. . .**161** C4
West Brushford La
  EX18 . . . .**59** C2
West Buckeridge
  TQ14. . . . .**210** B6
WEST BUCKLAND
  Barnstaple **18** B2
  Wellington **52** F7
West Buckland Cross
  EX32 . . . .**18** B2
West Buckland Prim Sch
  TA21 . . . .**52** F7
West Buckland Rd
  EX32 . . . .**52** D7
West Buckland Sch
  EX32 . . . .**18** C2
West Burridge Cross
  EX18 . . . .**60** E7
Westbury Cl PL5 . . . . .**244** B4
West Challacombe La
  EX34. . . . .**3** A4
WEST CHARLETON . . .**144** C1
West Charleton Ct
  TQ7. . . . .**144** C1
West Cl EX13 . . . .**167** C5
West Cliff EX7 . . . . . .**204** E6
West Cliff EX7 . . . . . .**204** D5
West Cliff Park Dr
  EX7. . . . .**204** D5
Westcliff Prim Acad
  EX7. . . . .**204** C5
Westcliff Rd DT6. . . . .**104** F4
West Cliff Rd EX7 . . . .**204** D6
West Cliff Terr **2**
  EX12 . . . .**192** A4
Westclyst EX1 . . . . . .**175** A3
Westclyst Com Prim Sch
  EX4. . . . .**174** F3
Westcombe EX2 . . . . .**181** B8
Westcombe Cres
  PL9 . . . .**255** D5
Westcombe La
  Bideford EX39 . . . . . .**156** F2
  Bideford EX39. . . . . . .**157** A2
Westcombes EX13 . . . .**88** B7
West Coombe La TA4 . .**35** D8
Westcots Dr EX19 . . . .**58** F2
WESTCOTT **83** C7
Westcott Cl PL6. . . . .**249** A8
Westcott Cross EX14. . .**66** F2
Westcott La
  Aylesbeare EX5. . . . . . .**99** D4
  Beara EX31. . . . .**9** A1
  Bridford EX6. . . . .**112** C6
  Witheridge EX16. . . . . .**61** E7
Westcott Rd **15** EX16 .**64** D7
West Cotts TA24 . . . . .**13** A2

Westcott Way EX14 . .**166** D6
Westcountry Cl PL2 . .**247** F7
Westcroft Ct **3** EX39 **156** F1
Westcroft Rd
  Holsworthy TA20. . . . . .**71** F6
  Holsworthy TA20. . . . .**164** B4
  Plymouth PL5 . . . .**243** D1
West Croft Rd EX22 . .**164** B4
West Croft Sch EX39 .**156** F1
West Cross EX33 . . . . .**152** D6
Westcroyde EX33 . . . . . . **7** D1
WEST CURRY **89** A4
West Devon Bsns Pk
  PL19. . . . .**171** B3
WEST DOWN. **8** F5
West Down EX16. . . . . .**65** A6
West Down County Prim
  Sch EX34. . . . . **8** F5
West Down Hill EX33,
  EX34. . . . . **8** F4
West Down La EX8 . . .**203** A6
West Down Rd PL2. . .**248** B6
West Down View
  EX8. . . . .**203** B6
West & East Putford Prim
  Sch EX22 . . . .**39** C2
West Efford La EX17. . .**81** A4
Westella Rd EX2 . . . . .**127** A2
West Emlett La EX17 . .**61** E3
West End Cross EX16. .**48** D5
West End La EX16 . . . .**48** D5
West End Rd
  Bradninch EX5 . . . .**82** F6
  Buckfastleigh TQ11. . .**236** B4
West End Terr
  Ashburton TQ13 . . . . .**130** F4
  Denbury TQ12. . . . . . .**211** A6
  South Molton EX36. . . .**158** C4
Westentown TQ7 . . . .**142** C6
Westeria Terr PL2 . . .**248** C7
WESTERLAND. **218** D1
Westerland TQ6 . . . . .**234** B3
Westerland Gn TQ3 . .**218** D1
Westerland La TQ3. . .**218** D2
Wester-Moor Cl **6**
  EX31. . . . .**154** A2
Wester-Moor Dr
  EX31. . . . .**154** A2
Wester-Moor Way
  EX31. . . . .**154** A2
Western App PL1 . . . .**262** B2
Western Ave
  Appledore EX39 . . . . . .**15** A1
  Exeter EX2 . . . .**182** D7
Western Bsns Pk
  TQ4. . . . .**225** F2
Western By-Pass
  TQ9. . . . .**223** B5
Western College Rd
  PL4. . . . .**248** F5
WESTERN COMMON. . .**19** D7
Western Cotts EX20 . .**107** E1
Western Ct EX10. . . . .**188** A3
Western Dr
  Newton Abbot TQ12 . . .**206** F4
  Plymouth PL3 . . . .**249** B4
  Starcross EX6. . . . . . .**201** B8
Western Field EX10 . .**188** A3
Western Gardens Rd
  EX34. . . . . **3** A3
Western Ho EX7 . . . . .**204** E7
Westernlea EX17. . . . .**165** A5
Western Piece La EX31. **9** D1
Western Pl **4** EX24 . .**103** A4
Western Rd
  Ashburton TQ13 . . . . .**130** F4
  Crediton EX17. . . . . . .**165** A6
  Exeter EX4 . . . .**177** A5
  Holsworthy EX22 . . . . .**164** C4
  Ivybridge PL21. . . . . . .**237** C4
  Newton Abbot TQ12 . . .**207** C3
  Torquay TQ1 . . . .**214** B1
  Zeal Monachorum EX17 . .**78** B6
Western Rise EX34. . . . .**8** A4
Western Side
  Clawton EX22 . . . .**89** E8
  Clawton TA20 . . . .**71** F1
Western Terr
  Barnstaple EX31. . . . .**154** E5
  Ilfracombe EX34. . . . . .**150** A4
  Totnes TQ9 . . . .**223** B6
WESTERN TOWN **188** A3
Western Units TQ13 . .**180** D5
Western Villas
  Crediton EX17. . . . . . .**165** B5
  Totnes TQ9 . . . .**223** B5
Western Way
  Exeter, Barnfield EX1,
  EX2. . . . .**261** C3
  Exeter, Friars' Green
  EX1. . . . .**261** A2
Western Way Ind Est
  EX15. . . . .**163** C4
Western Wood Way
  PL7. . . . .**251** D5
West Exe N EX16. . . . .**161** C4
West Exe S EX16. . . . .**161** C4
West Exe Tech Coll
  EX2. . . . .**177** A2
Westfield
  Bradninch EX5 . . . .**82** F6
  Plymouth PL7 . . . .**251** A6
Westfield Ave
  Barnstaple EX31. . . .**154** D4
  Plymouth PL9 . . . . . .**255** C6

Westfield Bsns Pk
  TQ3. . . . .**225** E1
Westfield Cl
  Brixham TQ5 . . . .**230** B3
  Budleigh Salterton
  EX9. . . . .**198** A1
Westfield Rd
  Budleigh Salterton
  EX9. . . . .**198** A1
  Tiverton EX16. . . . . . .**161** C3
West Field Rd EX6 . . .**182** B3
Westfield Terr **8**
  EX16. . . . .**161** C3
WESTFORD **51** F7
Westford Cl TA21 . . . .**160** A5
Westford Ct TA21 . . . .**160** A5
Westford Dr TA21 . . . .**160** A5
Westford Grange
  TA21. . . . .**160** A5
West Garth Ct EX4 . . .**172** F2
West Garth Rd EX4. . .**173** A3
Westgate EX17 . . . . . .**60** D3
West Golds Wy TQ12 .**207** B5
West Grove Rd EX2 . .**261** C2
Westhampnett Pl
  PL5. . . . .**243** F4
West Hartley TQ9 . . . .**139** E3
Westhay Cross EX13 . .**88** F3
Westhay Rd TA20 . . . .**69** C7
Westhays Cl PL9 . . . .**255** F1
Westhead Rd PL10 . . .**148** H2
WEST HILL **168** E4
West Hill
  Budleigh Salterton
  EX9. . . . .**203** F8
  Heybrook Bay PL9. . . .**140** A4
Westhill Ave TQ1 . . . .**220** B7
Westhill Avenue Cl
  TQ1. . . . .**220** B7
Westhill Cres TQ3. . . .**226** B7
West Hill Ct EX9 . . . . .**203** F8
West Hill Gdns EX9. . .**203** F8
West Hill La
  Braunton EX33 . . . . . .**152** C6
  Budleigh Salterton EX9 **197** F1
  Parracombe EX31. . . . . **4** B2
West Hill Prim Sch
  EX11. . . . .**168** D4
Westhill Rd
  Paignton TQ3 . . . .**226** A7
  Torquay TQ1 . . . .**220** B8
West Hill Rd
  Lyme Regis DT7 . . . . .**260** D3
  Ottery St Mary EX11. . .**169** B2
  Plymouth PL4 . . . .**248** F4
  West Hill EX10 . . . . . .**100** B5
  West Hill EX11 . . . . . .**168** D4
  West Hill EX11 . . . . . .**168** E5
Westhill Terr TQ12 . . .**213** A4
West Ho EX13. . . . . . .**167** D5
WEST HOE **262** B1
West Hoe Rd PL1. . . . .**262** B1
Westholme **6** TQ1. . .**220** C5
WEST ILKERTON **5** A3
West La
  Braunton EX33 . . . . . .**152** D6
  Challacombe EX31. . . . .**11** D4
  Dolton EX19 . . . .**57** E6
  Knowle EX33. . . . . **8** C2
  Lapford EX17 . . . .**60** C3
  Oakford EX16. . . . . . .**48** A7
  Paignton TQ3 . . . .**225** A6
  Templeton EX16 . . . . .**48** A1
WESTLAKE. **136** E4
Westlake Cl PL11 . . . .**246** F3
Westlake Rd PL9. . . . .**140** A8
Westlake Rise PL9 . . .**140** A8
Westland La EX16. . . . .**62** C6
Westlands
  Exmouth EX8. . . . . . .**202** C6
  Wrafton EX33. . . . . . .**152** E4
Westlands La TQ1. . . .**220** B7
Westleat Ave TQ3 . . . .**225** F6
WESTLEIGH
  Bideford **157** E6
  Wellington **51** A4
WEST LEIGH **77** E8
West Leigh Cross
  TQ9. . . . .**135** F1
Westleigh La EX34 . . . . **3** C2
Westleigh Wy PL9. . . .**249** D1
West Lodge DT7 . . . .**193** D5
West Lyn Rd EX35 . . .**151** C2
West Malling Ave
  PL5. . . . .**243** E5
West Manley La EX16. .**64** E7
Westmead Cl EX33. . .**152** C6
West Meadow Cl
  EX33. . . . .**152** B7
West Meadow Rd
  EX33. . . . .**152** A7
West Mill Cross
  TQ11. . . . .**236** B4
Westminster Cl
  Exmouth EX8. . . . . . .**196** D3
  Feniton EX14. . . . .**84** D2
Westminster Rd EX4 . .**176** E6
Westminster Villas
  EX34. . . . .**150** D5
West Molland La EX36 **31** D7
Westmoor Cl PL7 . . . .**251** C6
West Moor Cl EX39. . .**156** F8
Westmoor Pk PL9. . . .**171** C4
West Moor Way
  EX39. . . . .**156** F8
West Mount TQ12. . . .**207** D1
West of England Sch &
  Coll EX1. . . . .**178** B1

WEST OGWELL **206** A1
West Ogwell Cross
  TQ12. . . . .**211** C8
WESTON. **189** D6
Weston Cl
  Brixham TQ5 . . . .**230** C3
  Broadhembury EX14. . . .**84** D7
Weston Cross
  Awliscombe EX14 . . . . .**85** C3
  Sidmouth EX10. . . . . .**189** D8
Weston Ct TQ9. . . . . .**223** F5
Westonfields TQ9. . . .**223** E5
Weston La
  Awliscombe EX14 . . . . .**85** B4
  Totnes TQ9 . . . .**223** E4
WESTON MILL **247** E8
Weston Mill Com Prim
  Sch PL2. . . . .**247** E7
Weston Mill Dr PL5 . .**247** F8
Weston Mill Hill PL5 .**243** F1
Weston Mill La PL5. . .**244** A1
Weston Mill Rd PL5 . .**243** E1
Weston Park Rd PL3 .**248** D6
Weston Rd
  Totnes TQ9 . . . .**223** D5
  Wambrook TA20. . . . . .**69** F3
Weston Terr EX11. . . .**169** E4
WESTON TOWN **188** A3
Westover Cl
  Brixham TQ5 . . . .**230** D4
  Ivybridge PL21. . . . . .**237** B5
Westover Hill
  Charmouth DT6. . . . . .**104** F5
  Penn DT7 . . . .**260** F8
Westover Ind Est
  PL21. . . . .**237** C4
Westover La PL21. . . .**237** B4
Westown Rd EX2. . . . .**176** C1
West Pafford Ave
  TQ2. . . . .**214** B3
Westpark TA21 . . . . . .**51** D7
WEST PARK. **244** A3
Westpark EX36 . . . . . .**52** D7
West Park Dr PL7 . . . .**251** C5
West Park Hill PL7 . . .**251** B7
West Park Rd EX10. . .**188** A5
Westpark Villas **8**
  PL20. . . . .**126** F5
West Pk
  Braunton EX33 . . . . . .**152** C6
  Outer Hope TQ7 . . . . .**147** B7
  South Molton EX36. . . .**158** B4
  Stoke Fleming TQ6 . . .**146** B8
  Wellington TA21. . . . . .**160** D7
Westpoint (County
  Showground) EX5 . .**179** C3
West Pugsley Cross
  EX37. . . . .**29** A2
WEST PUTFORD. **39** C2
West Quay Rd PL20 . .**252** E5
West Rd
  Roborough PL6 . . . . . .**42** F4
  Sheepwash EX21 . . . . .**56** C1
  Woolacombe EX34 . . . . **7** F6
Westridge Cross EX16 **63** C4
West Rock Dr EX36. . . .**30** F2
WEST SANDFORD **79** E5
West Spurway La
  EX16. . . . .**48** A8
West St
  Ashburton TQ13 . . . . .**130** F4
  Axminster EX13 . . . . .**167** D5
  Bampton EX16 . . . .**34** B1
  Bishops Nympton EX36. .**30** F2
  Bishopsteignton TQ14. .**208** F8
  Denbury TQ12. . . . . . .**211** A6
  Exeter EX1, EX4 . . . . .**261** A2
  Hartland EX39 . . . .**22** D3
  Millbrook PL10 . . . . . .**252** E5
  Okehampton EX20 . . . .**170** B5
  South Molton EX36. . . .**158** C4
  Tavistock PL19 . . . . . .**171** B5
  Torpoint PL10 . . . .**252** E4
  Witheridge EX16. . . . . .**46** E1
West Terr
  Budleigh Salterton
  EX9. . . . .**198** A1
  Churston Ferrers TQ5. .**229** E4
  Exeter EX1 . . . .**177** F6
WEST TOWN
  Crediton **165** B5
  Newton St Cyres. **98** F8
  Woolfardisworthy. **38** E8
West Town Cross
  EX39. . . . .**38** E8
West Town Mdw
  TQ14. . . . .**208** E8
West Town Rd
  Newton St Cyres EX5 . . .**98** F8
  Newton St Cyres EX5 . .**109** A8
West Ugworthy Cross
  EX22. . . . .**53** E3
West Underleys
  EX12. . . . .**191** C5
West View
  Beer EX12. . . . .**191** D5
  Colyford EX24. . . . . . .**103** A3
  Holsworthy EX22 . . . . .**164** C5
  Tavistock PL19 . . . . . .**171** E2
Westview Cl EX5. . . . . .**99** E8
West View Cl TQ12 . .**206** F1
West View Rd
  EX32. . . . .**155** B4
West View Ct **1**
  EX32. . . . .**155** B4
5 Bere Alston PL20. . .**125** E1
  Marldon TQ3. . . . .**218** D2
  Okehampton EX20 . . . .**170** C5

West View Terr
  Exeter EX4 . . . .**261** A2
  3 Honiton EX14. . . . .**166** B6
  Lympstone EX8. . . . . .**195** F5
WESTON. **189** D6
Weston Cl
  Brixham TQ5 . . . .**230** C3
Westward Bsns Ctr
  EX17. . . . .**165** D5
Westward Ct TQ9. . . .**223** C5
Westward Dr EX8 . . . .**202** B7
WESTWARD HO!. **156** D8
Westward View
  TQ12. . . . .**208** A2
Westwater Hill EX6 . . .**97** E5
West Waters La EX31. . .**4** D5
Westway PL9 . . . .**255** B5
Westway Cross EX16. . .**61** F8
Whin Bank Rd PL5 . . .**244** E2
WHIPCOTT. **51** B5
Whippenscott Hill
  EX36. . . . .**46** B8
Whipple's Cross
  PL21. . . . .**136** E4
WHIPTON. **178** C8
Whipton Barton Ho
  EX1. . . . .**178** B7
Whipton Barton Inf Sch
  EX1. . . . .**178** B7
Whipton Barton Jun Sch
  EX1. . . . .**178** B7
Whipton Barton Rd
  EX1. . . . .**178** C7
Whipton La EX1. . . . . .**178** A6
Whipton Rd EX4 . . . . .**178** A8
Whipton Village Rd
  EX4. . . . .**178** B8
Whisselwell Cl TQ13 .**208** F6
Whistley Down PL20 .**126** E2
Whistley Hill TQ13 . . .**131** A4
Whistley Hill Cross
  TQ13. . . . .**131** A4
Whitaker Cl EX1 . . . . .**174** F3
Whitby Cres PL6 . . . .**245** A1
Whitby Rd PL6. . . . . .**245** A1
WHITCHURCH. **171** D3
Whitchurch Ave EX2 . .**178** B4
Whitchurch Com Prim
  Sch PL19. . . . .**171** D2
Whitchurch Rd
  Horrabridge PL20. . . . .**126** F5
  Tavistock PL19 . . . . . .**171** C3
Whitcott Hill EX36 . . . .**31** A8
Whiteabury Cross
  TQ13. . . . .**111** C7
Whitear Cl TQ14 . . . .**124** E1
Whitear's Way TQ12 .**207** E7
White Ash La TA20 . . .**69** D5
WHITE BALL **51** D6
Whiteball Rd EX16 . . .**51** E6
Whitebeam Cl
  Exeter EX4 . . . .**174** D7
  Paignton TQ3 . . . .**225** E7
Whitebeam Gr EX14. . .**67** B1
Whitebear Cross EX22. **54** F6
Whiteborough La
  Chudleigh TQ13. . . . . .**123** D8
  Trusham TQ13. . . . . . .**113** D1
Whitebridges EX14. . .**166** B4
Whitebrook Terr TA21. **50** F5
Whitechapel La EX36. .**30** F6
White Cl
  Paignton TQ3 . . . .**219** B2
  West Clyst EX4 . . . . . .**174** E3
Whitecleave Cross
  EX37. . . . .**43** F2
White Cliff **8** EX12. . .**192** B4
White Cross
  Aylesbeare EX5. . . . . . .**99** C1
  Cheriton Fitzpaine EX17 . .**62** F1
  Malborough TQ7 . . . . .**147** E6
  Ottery St Mary EX11. . .**100** F3
White Cross Ct PL4. . .**263** A3
Whitecross Gdns
  EX12. . . . .**192** B7
White Cross Hill EX17 . .**62** F1
White Cross Rd EX5. .**184** D6
White Ct **11** EX7. . . . .**204** E6
Whitedown Cross
  EX15. . . . .**67** E4
White Down Cross
  EX16. . . . .**64** E5
White Farm La
  West Hill EX10 . . . . . .**100** A4
  West Hill EX11 . . . . . .**168** D3
Whitefield EX14 . . . . . .**86** C3
Whitefield Cross
  EX36. . . . .**32** D3
Whitefield Hill EX31. . . . **9** E2
Whitefield La EX32. . . .**19** A6
Whitefield Terr PL4 . .**263** B4
White Friars La PL4 . .**263** B3
White Gate EX24 . . . .**102** E3
Whitegates EX34. . . . . . **2** F4
White Gates Cross
  TQ13. . . . .**110** F7
WHITEHALL. **52** A1
Whitehall Cl
  Morebath EX16. . . . . . .**34** B4
  South Molton EX36. . . .**158** C3
Whitehall Dr
  9 Bere Alston PL20. . .**125** E1
  Plymouth PL9 . . . .**256** B7
Whitehall La EX4 . . . .**182** F6
Whitehall Manor
  TQ7. . . . .**143** E4
White Hart La TA21 . .**160** D6
Whitehaven Way
  PL6. . . . .**245** A7

Whiddon Valley Ind Est
  EX32. . . . .**155** D3
Whidley La EX6. . . . . .**112** E8
Whilborough Rd
  TQ12. . . . .**212** E8
WHIMBLE. **164** E2
Whimble Hill EX22 . . .**164** D3
Whimbrel Ct EX3. . . . .**182** E6
Whimbrels Edge
  TQ7. . . . .**143** A1
Whimbrel Way PL9. . .**256** D8
WHIMPLE. **99** E7
Whimple Prim Sch
  EX5. . . . .**99** E8
Whimple St PL1. . . . . .**262** C2
Whimple Sta EX5 . . . . .**99** E8
Whin Bank Rd PL5 . . .**244** E2
WHIPCOTT. **51** B5
Westwood Ave PL6. . .**245** C6
Westwood Cl EX17. . .**165** A5
Westwood Cleave
  TQ12. . . . .**211** F8
Westwood Cotts EX6. .**98** E2
Westwood Hill EX6. . .**201** A5
Westwood La EX6. . . .**176** B4
Westwood Rd
  Crediton EX17. . . . . . .**165** A5
  East Ogwell TQ12 . . . .**212** A8
Westwoods EX6 . . . . . .**98** B4
Westwood Units EX6 .**177** D1
Westwood Way EX12 .**192** B7
WEST WORLINGTON . . .**61** A4
Westworthy Cross
  EX20. . . . .**77** E6
Westyard La EX18. . . . .**58** E8
West Yelland EX31. . . .**15** C2
West Yeo Cross EX16. .**46** C2
West Yeo Moor Hill
  EX16. . . . .**46** C3
WEST YOULSTONE **37** E2
Wethered Cl EX16. . . .**161** C3
Wet La
  Christow EX6 . . . .**113** B4
  17 Combe Martin EX34. . .**3** A3
WEYCROFT. **88** B2
Weycroft Ave EX13. . .**167** F7
Weycroft Cl EX13 . . . .**178** D6
Weymouth Pk TQ7 . . .**147** B7
Whalley La DT7 . . . . .**260** B4
Wharf Rd TQ12 . . . . .**207** D4
Wharf Road Ind Est
  TQ12. . . . .**207** D4
Wharf Theatre & Gall
  The* PL19 . . . .**171** B5
Whatley La PL19 . . . .**116** A7
Whatley Mws **4** PL3 .**249** D1
Wheadon Cross EX16. .**46** D4
Wheal Betsy* PL19. . .**117** E8
Wheal Maria PL19. . . .**116** C1
Wheal Maria Cotts
  PL19. . . . .**116** B1
Wheal Rd PL19. . . . . .**117** E6
Wheat Belt Rise **3**
  EX1. . . . .**178** F8
Wheatclose Cross
  EX36. . . . .**20** D2
Wheatcombe Ct TQ2 .**214** B3
Wheatfield Cl EX15. . .**163** B2
Wheatland Cross
  EX16. . . . .**48** D6
Wheatland La EX16 . . .**48** C6
Wheatlands Rd TQ4 . .**226** B4
Wheatley Cl EX4 . . . .**176** E5
Wheatley Ct **5** EX1 . .**261** A2
Wheatly Cotts EX17 . .**78** C4
Wheatly La EX31. . . . . .**4** B2
Wheat Pk TQ9 . . . . . .**138** D8
Wheatridge PL7 . . . . .**250** B7
Wheatridge La TQ2 . .**219** E2
Wheatsheaf **18** EX5 . . .**99** A6
Wheatsheaf Way
  EX2. . . . .**177** A1
Wheelbarrow La EX15 **67** C8
Wheel Cl **11** EX31 . . .**154** A2
Wheel Cross EX34. . . . .**2** F1
Wheeldon Off-road Bike
  Ctr* TQ9. . . . .**138** E5
Wheelers Cross EX22. .**39** E1
Wheelers Yard EX24 .**103** A5
Wheel La EX34. . . . . . . **2** F1
Wheelwright Ct PL20 **127** B4
Whelmstone Cross
  EX17. . . . .**78** E3
Whetcombe Cross
  PL21. . . . .**137** F6
Whey Cross EX37. . . . .**28** D3
Whidborne Ave TQ1. .**221** A4
Whidborne Cl TQ1. . .**220** F3
Whidborne Mews
  TQ14. . . . .**124** D1
WHIDDON. **155** D2
  Barnstaple **155** D2
  Marwood **9** D1
Whiddon Cross
  Abbotskerswell TQ12. .**212** B4
  Whiddon EX31 . . . . **9** D1
WHIDDON DOWN. **95** F3
Whiddon Down Rd
  TQ13. . . . .**111** C5
Whiddon Dr EX32. . . .**155** D3
Whiddon La
  Ide EX2. . . . .**114** A8
  Whiddon EX31 . . . . **9** D1
Whiddon Rd TQ12. . . .**212** B4

Whitehayes Cl
  Kilmington EX13. . . . . .**87** C1
  Wilmington EX14. . . . . .**86** D2
Whiteheads Cross
  TQ11. . . . .**135** C7
White Heather Terr
  TQ13. . . . .**180** D8
Whitehill Cl TQ12 . . . .**207** B5
Whitehill Cotts TQ12 .**206** F5
Whitehill Cross PL15 .**105** B6
White Hill Dro TQ4 . . .**69** F5
Whitehill Gdns PL7. . .**132** C4
Whitehill La TQ9, TQ9 **228** B8
Whitehill Rd TQ12. . . .**207** A5
Whitehorse La EX39. .**157** A8
Whitehouse Cl **2**
  EX39. . . . .**15** B1
Whitehouse Cross
  EX39. . . . .**156** B3
Whitehouse La EX18 . .**58** D5
White La PL1 . . . .**263** A2
White Ladies TQ6 . . . .**146** B7
White Lady Rd PL9 . .**255** D5
White Lady Waterfall*
  . . . .**107** A2
Whiteland Head EX20 .**57** B8
Whiteley Ave TQ9 . . .**222** F6
Whiteley Cross PL21 .**137** B5
White Lodge EX9 . . . .**198** B1
Whitemoor Cross
  PL8. . . . .**142** A8
Whitemoor Hill EX32. .**16** E1
Whitemoor La EX5,
  EX17. . . . .**81** C8
Whiteoxen Cross
  TQ10. . . . .**135** C4
White Pk TQ9 . . . . . .**139** A3
White Post EX36 . . . . .**20** F2
White Rock Cl TQ4 . . .**225** F1
White Rock Ct TQ4. . .**228** F8
White Rock Prim Sch
  TQ4. . . . .**229** A8
White Rock Rd
  Paignton TQ4 . . . .**225** F1
  Paignton TQ4 . . . .**229** A8
White Rock Wy TQ4 . .**225** F1
White Rock Wy TQ4 . .**225** F1
Whites Cotts EX20 . . . .**95** B4
Whiteside Cl EX2 . . . .**178** C4
Whites La EX31 . . . . .**154** F7
White's La
  Great Torrington
  EX38. . . . .**159** C5
  Stockland EX14. . . . . . .**86** F7
  Stockland EX14. . . . . . .**87** A7
White St EX3 . . . .**182** F4
WHITESTAUNTON. **69** D5
Whitestaunton Cross
  TA20. . . . .**69** E5
WHITESTONE **98** E4
Whitestone Cross
  TQ7. . . . .**145** C5
Whitestone Dr EX16. .**161** C6
Whitestone La EX33. . . .**8** D1
Whitestone Orch **2**
  TQ4. . . . .**226** B5
White Stones EX8. . . .**202** C6
Whitethorn Cl
  Honiton EX14 . . . .**166** C4
  Sidmouth EX10. . . . . .**187** F8
White Tor Cl EX20. . . .**170** E5
Whitewater Ct PL7. . .**250** E6
Whiteway Dr EX1 . . . .**178** B6
Whiteway La TQ1 . . . .**214** D8
Whiteway Rd TQ12. . .**207** D2
WHITFORD **103** B6
Whitford Rd EX13. . . .**103** C6
Witham Pk PL19 . . . .**171** C4
Whiting Cl EX39. . . . . .**25** F4
WHITLEIGH. **244** C5
Whitleigh Ave PL5. . .**244** C4
Whitleigh Com Prim Sch
  PL5. . . . .**244** D4
Whitleigh Cotts PL5. .**244** D4
Whitleigh Ct PL5. . . . .**244** D4
Whitleigh Gn PL5 . . . .**244** C4
Whitleigh Villas PL5. .**244** C4
Whitleigh Way PL5. . .**244** C4
Whitleigh Wood Nature
  Reserve* PL6. . . . . .**244** E4
Whitley Cross TQ7 . . .**143** C3
Whitley Rd
  Farway EX24. . . . .**101** F7
  Paignton TQ4 . . . .**226** A4
Whitley Rocks EX36 . .**31** C7
Whitlocks Mews
  TA20. . . . .**210** A6
Whitlow Copse EX2 . .**178** C4
Whitman Cl EX8 . . . . .**196** C4
Whitmore La PL21 . . .**137** C4
Whitmore Way EX14 .**166** A4
WHITNAGE **50** C2
Whitnage La EX16. . . .**50** C2
Whitnole Cross EX16. .**48** A5
Whitnole La
  Calverleigh EX16 . . . . .**48** A4
  Rackenford EX16 . . . . .**47** F4
Whitsam Cross PL20 .**125** D1
Whitson Cross PL5. . .**244** C3
Whitsoncross La
  PL5. . . . .**244** C2
WHITSTONE **70** E1
Whitstone Com Prim Sch
  EX22. . . . .**70** E1

Whitstone Head Sch
  EX22. . . . . .70 E1
Whitstone La
  Bovey Tracey TQ13 . . . .180 C8
  Meshaw EX36. . . . . .46 B5
Whitstone Rd TQ4 . . . . .226 B5
Whittingham Rd
  Ilfracombe EX34. . . . . . .150 C5
  Yealmpton PL8 . . . . . . .141 B8
Whittington St PL3. . . . .262 B4
Whitton Ct EX10 . . . . . . .187 F7
Whitton Way EX15 . . . .163 C4
Whitwell La EX24 . . . . . .103 A3
Whitycombe Way
  EX4. . . . . .176 D8
Whity Cross PL12 . . . . .242 A4
Whympston Cross
  PL21. . . . . .137 D1
Wicaford Cross EX36. . .31 A2
Wicaford La EX36. . . . . . .31 A2
Wick Cross EX14. . . . . . .85 F7
Wicket The EX7. . . . . . .178 C3
Wickham Cl
  Bideford EX39. . . . . . . .157 C1
  East-the-Water EX39 . . .26 A4
Wickington La EX20. . . . .95 B7
Widdicombe Cross
  Marldon TQ3. . . . . .218 F5
  Paignton TQ3 . . . . .218 E5
Widdicombe Dr
  PL21. . . . . .237 D4
WIDECOMBE IN THE
  MOOR. 121 B4
Widecombe in the Moor
  Prim Sch TQ13. . . . . .121 B3
Widecombe Way
  EX4. . . . . .173 E1
Widegate Nursery
  PL9. . . . . .256 D8
Widepost La EX13. . . . .167 C5
WIDEWELL. 245 B7
Widewell La PL6 . . . . . .245 C7
Widewell Prim Acad
  PL6. . . . . .245 B7
Widewell Rd PL6. . . . . .245 B7
Widey Court Prim Sch
  PL6. . . . . .244 F1
Widey Cross PL6. . . . . .244 F1
Widey Ct PL6 . . . . .244 F1
Widey Hill PL8 . . . . . . .141 A7
Widey La PL6 . . . . .244 F1
Widey View PL3. . . . . . .248 F6
Widgery Dr EX36. . . . . .158 C4
Widgery Rd EX4 . . . . . .178 A8
WIDWORTHY. 86 D2
Widworthy Ct EX14. . . . .86 C2
Wigeon Rd EX23. . . . . . .70 A8
Wigford Cross TQ7. . . .138 C1
Wigford La TQ7 . . . . . .138 D2
WIGGATON. 100 E4
Wiggaton Rd EX10 . . . .100 F4
Wigley Cross EX31. . . . .16 C8
Wilbarn Rd TQ3. . . . . . .226 C7
Wilburton Cross
  PL21. . . . . .136 C3
Wilburt Rd PL3 . . . . . . .249 D8
Wilbury Way EX7 . . . . .204 F7
Wilcocks Rd EX14. . . . .174 D1
Wilcombe Cross
  Brayford EX32. . . . . .18 E4
  Charles EX32. . . . . .18 E4
Wilcombe Prim Sch
  EX16. . . . . .161 F1
Wilcove Cl PL5 . . . . . . .247 A6
Wilcove Cl PL5. . . . . . .247 E8
Wilcove La
  Torpoint PL11. . . . . . . .246 E5
  Wilcove PL5 . . . . .247 A6
Wilderbrook Way EX34. . .1 F1
Wilderness La EX14. . . .84 D6
Wilderness Rd PL3. . . .248 E5
Wilder Pk EX34 . . . . . . .150 B5
Wilder Rd EX34 . . . . . . .150 B6
Wildersmouth Ct
  EX34. . . . . .150 B6
Wildmoor La TA21. . . . .52 F6
Wildner Top
  Barbrook EX35. . . . . .5 A4
  Lynton EX35. . . . . .4 F4
Wildwoods Cres
  TQ12. . . . . .207 F4
Wilford Rd EX2 . . . . . . .178 B5
Wilkey Cl EX32. . . . . . .155 C4
Wilkins Dr TQ12 . . . . . .225 E2
Wilkinson Rd PL5 . . . . .247 D8
Wilkke Rd TQ12 . . . . . .213 A5
WILLAND
  Taunton. 68 B8
  Tiverton 162 E4
Willand Ind Est EX15. .162 D5
WILLAND MOOR. 162 E5
Willand Moor Mews
  EX15. . . . . .162 E5
Willand Moor Rd
  EX15. . . . . .162 E5
Willand Old Village
  EX15. . . . . .162 C3
Willand Rd
  Braunton EX33. . . . . . .152 C6
  Cullompton EX15 . . . . .163 C4
  Willand EX15 . . . . .162 B6
  Willand Sch EX15 . . . . .162 D4
Willas Rd PL16. . . . . . .105 E4
Willcocks Cl 6 TA21 .160 D5
Willet St 3 EX39. . . . . .157 A2
Willey La EX20 . . . . .95 A6
Willeys Ave EX2. . . . . .261 A1
Willeys Ct EX2 . . . . . . .261 A1

Willhayes Cross EX6 .113 E6
Willhayes Hill EX6 . . . .113 E6
Willhayes Pk EX13 . . . .167 D6
Willhay La EX13. . . . . . .167 D7
Willhayne La EX24 . . . .102 F5
Willhays Cl 15 TQ12 . .123 F1
William Evans Cl
  PL6. . . . . .244 D5
William Prance Rd
  PL6. . . . . .245 A3
Williams Ave
  Exeter EX2 . . . . .177 B4
  Exeter EX2 . . . . .261 A1
  Plymouth PL4 . . . . .249 B1
Williams Cl
  Dawlish EX7 . . . . .204 C5
  Wrafton EX33. . . . . . . .152 E4
Williams Ct EX33. . . . .154 C4
Williams Ct TQ11 . . . . .236 B5
Williamson Cl EX33 . . . . .8 A2
Williamson Ho EX31. .155 A8
Williamson Way
  EX36. . . . . .158 C4
William St 3 EX16. . . . .161 D4
Willicombe Rd TQ3 . . .226 A5
Willie La EX17 . . . . .79 F7
WILLINGCOTT. 8 D6
Willingcott Cross EX34. . .8 C6
Willingcott Hill EX34. . . .8 D4
Willingcott Valley EX34. . .8 D5
Willing Cross TQ10. . . .135 F5
Willing Gate TQ10. . . . .135 F5
Willis Ct 1 TQ1. . . . . . .220 A7
Willis Dr EX4 . . . . .174 F4
Willis's Cross TQ12. . . .122 D2
Willmott Cl EX8. . . . . . .196 E1
Willoughby Cl EX8 . . . .196 C3
Willoughby Ho EX10 . .187 E2
Willoughby Rd TQ1 . . .220 C6
Willoughby Wy PL1 . . .262 B1
Willow Ave
  Exmouth EX8. . . . . .196 B3
  Torquay TQ2 . . . . .214 A3
Willoway Cl EX33 . . . .152 C6
Willoway Gr EX33 . . . .152 C6
Willoway La EX33 . . . .152 C7
Willowbank Prim Sch
  EX15. . . . . .163 B3
Willowbrook Ave 6
  EX4. . . . . .178 C8
Willowbrook Sch
  EX4. . . . . .174 B1
Willowby Gdns PL20 . .127 A2
Willowby Pk PL20. . . . .127 A2
Willow Cl
  Ilfracombe EX34. . . . . . .150 E4
  Newton Abbot TQ12 . . .213 A8
  Plymouth PL3 . . . . .249 E5
  Seaton EX12. . . . . .192 A8
  Stoke Canon EX5. . . . . .173 F8
Willow Cotts PL7. . . . . .250 D4
Willow Ct
  Exeter EX2 . . . . .178 A4
  Plymouth PL6 . . . . .249 E7
Willowdale Cl 1
  EX14. . . . . .166 B6
Willow Dr EX15 . . . . . . .65 F7
Willowfield
  Barton TQ2 . . . . .213 F2
  Braunton EX33. . . . . . .152 C7
Willow Gdns EX5. . . . .175 C6
Willow Gn PL12 . . . . . .242 D2
Willow Gr
  Bideford EX39. . . . . . . .25 D4
  Stibb Cross EX38 . . . . . .40 D2
Willow La
  Cornworthy TQ9. . . . . .227 B3
  Hemyock EX15 . . . . .52 F2
Willowpark La TQ12 . .213 C4
Willow Rd PL19 . . . . . .171 C3
Willow Rise EX17 . . . . .61 E8
Willows Cl TQ7 . . . . . . .144 E1
Willow St 2 TQ14. . . . .210 B4
Willows The
  Chilsworthy EX22. . . . . .53 E1
  Shillingford St George
  EX2. . . . . .114 C6
Willows The TQ12. . . . .213 D2
Willow Tree Cl EX20. . .170 C5
Willow Tree Rd EX33 . .155 B2
Willow View Pk EX5. . .100 A7
Willow Way
  Dawlish Warren EX7. . .201 A2
  Exeter EX4 . . . . .178 C8
Willow Wlk
  Crediton EX17. . . . . . . .165 E6
  2 Exeter EX4. . . . . . .177 D8
  Honiton EX14 . . . . .166 B4
  Plymouth PL6 . . . . .245 D5
Wills Ave TQ3. . . . . . . .219 C1
Wills Cl PL6 . . . . .244 E7
Willsdown Rd EX2 . . . .181 C8
Willshere Rd EX32 . . . .155 C4
Wills La EX1 . . . . .175 A2
Willsland Cl EX6 . . . . .194 D3
Wills Rd
  Bideford EX39. . . . . . . .156 D1
  Bovey Tracey TQ13 . . . .180 B6
  Totnes TQ9 . . . . .223 D6
Willsworthy Dr PL19 . .171 B7
WILMINGTON. 86 D3
Wilmington La EX13,
  EX14. . . . . .86 E2
WILMINSTONE. 117 D3
Wilminstone Ind Est
  PL19 . . . . .171 E7
Wilmot Gdns PL5 . . . . .244 D3

Wilncote Lodge 6
  TQ1. . . . . .220 A6
WILSHAM. 5 F5
Wilsham Cross EX35. . . .6 A5
Wilsham La EX35. . . . . . .5 F5
Wilson Cres PL2 . . . . . .248 B5
Wilson La
  Queen Dart EX16 . . . . . .47 B4
  Witheridge EX17. . . . . . .46 B1
Wilton Cl TQ12. . . . . . .212 B6
Wilton Rd
  Paignton TQ3 . . . . .219 B2
  Plymouth PL1 . . . . .248 A3
Wilton St PL1. . . . . . . .262 A4
Wilton Way
  Abbotskerswell TQ12 . .212 B6
  Exeter EX1 . . . . .178 D6
WILTOWN. 52 F3
Wiltown La EX15 . . . . . .52 F3
Wiltshier Cl EX5 . . . . . .175 C7
Wiltshire Cl
  Exeter EX4 . . . . .176 E4
  Plymouth PL4 . . . . .248 B5
Wilway La TQ21 . . . . . . .33 C6
Wimble Cross EX22 . . .164 D3
Winchester Ave
  Exeter EX4 . . . . .176 F7
  Torquay TQ2 . . . . .213 F1
Winchester Cl EX14 . . .84 D2
Winchester Dr EX8. . . .196 D4
Winchester Gdns
  PL5 . . . . .244 A5
Windabout Cross
  EX39. . . . . .39 B7
Windard Terr EX20. . . . .93 B1
Windbow La EX16. . . . . .48 D3
Windeatt Sq 4 TQ9 . . .223 D5
Winder Cres EX16. . . . .161 B6
Windermere Cl EX4 . . .176 F6
Windermere Cres
  PL6. . . . . .244 F4
Windermere Rd TQ1 . .220 C6
Windford Hill EX31. . . . .10 C4
Wind La EX32. . . . . .18 F7
Windmilland Cross
  EX21. . . . . .74 A6
Windmill Ave TQ3. . . . .219 A1
Windmill Cl TQ5 . . . . . .230 D4
Windmill Cross EX31. . .27 A3
Windmill Ct 9 TQ5. . . .230 C4
Windmill Gdns TQ3 . . .219 A1
Windmill Hill
  Brixham TQ5. . . . . .230 D4
  Saltash PL12. . . . . .242 E2
Windmill La
  Northam EX39. . . . . . . .26 A8
  Northam EX39 . . . . . . .157 B7
  North Whilborough
  TQ12. . . . . .212 D1
  Paignton TQ3 . . . . .218 F1
  West Hill EX10 . . . . . . .100 A5
  West Hill EX11 . . . . . . .168 D5
Windmill Rd
  Brixham TQ5. . . . . .230 D4
  Holsworthy EX22. . . . . .164 D4
  Paignton TQ3 . . . . .219 A1
Windout La EX6. . . . . . .97 E3
Windrush Rise EX11. . .169 D3
Windsbatch La 6
  PL3 . . . . .249 D1
Windsor Ave TQ12 . . . .207 F3
Windsor Cl
  Cullompton EX15 . . . . .163 C6
  Exeter EX4 . . . . .177 A7
  Ivybridge PL21. . . . . . .237 E4
  Newton Abbot TQ12 . . .207 C2
  Torquay TQ1. . . . . .220 B6
Windsor Ct
  Ilfracombe EX34. . . . . . .150 B5
  Kingsbridge TQ7 . . . . . .258 D5
Windsor Dr EX7 . . . . . .200 E2
Windsor Gdns EX31 . . .154 C1
Windsor Ho EX8 . . . . . .202 B7
Windsor La
  Saltash PL12. . . . . .242 E2
  Stokenham TQ7. . . . . . .145 B1
Windsor Mead EX10. . .101 A1
Windsor Pl PL1 . . . . . . .262 C2
Windsor Rd
  Barnstaple EX31. . . . . .154 E7
  Dartmouth TQ6. . . . . . .233 C3
  Kingsbridge TQ7 . . . . . .258 D5
  Northam EX39 . . . . . . .156 F7
  Plymouth PL3 . . . . .249 B7
  Torquay TQ2 . . . . .220 C6
Windsor Sq EX8. . . . . .202 A7
Windsor Terr DT7. . . . .260 D4
Windsor Villas PL1. . . .262 C2
Windthorn Cross
  TQ12. . . . . .218 A7
Windthorn La TQ3,
  TQ12. . . . . .218 B7
Windward La EX17 . . . .210 F8
Windward Rd TQ2 . . . .213 E3
Windway Hill TA4 . . . . .34 D6
Windwhistle Cross
  EX5. . . . . .81 C8
Wind Whistle Cross
  EX15. . . . . .66 C1
Windwhistle La EX16. . .49 B8
Windy Ash Cross EX32. .16 F1
Windy Ash Hill EX32. .155 C1
Windy Cnr TQ4 . . . . . . .229 B6
Windy Cross
  Ashford EX31. . . . . .154 D5
  8 Chulmleigh EX18 . . . .44 E1
Doddiscombsleigh EX6 .113 E7
  Great Torrington EX38 .159 C5

Windy Cross continued
  Holsworthy Beacon
  EX22. . . . . .54 F2
Windypost Cross
  FX35. . . . . .151 C2
Windys Way EX8 . . . . .202 D7
Wingate La EX20. . . . . . .75 C7
Wingfield TQ7 . . . . .143 A1
Wingfield Cl 8 EX16 .161 C3
Wingfield Mans PL3. . .248 A1
Wingfield Rd PL3 . . . . .262 A4
Wingfield Way PL3. . . .262 A4
Winham La EX15. . . . . . .83 B6
Winifred Baker Ct 5
  PL4. . . . . .263 A4
Winifred Cliff Ct 1
  EX16. . . . . .34 B1
Winifred Cliff Ct 7
  EX16. . . . . .196 C2
WINKLEIGH. 58 E2
Winkleigh Cl EX2 . . . . .177 A2
Winkleigh Com Prim Sch
  EX19. . . . . .58 F2
Winkleigh La EX6 . . . . .184 F8
Winkleigh Moor Cross
  EX19. . . . . .58 C7
Winneford La EX14. . . .85 C3
Winner Hill Rd TQ3. . . .226 A6
Winner St TQ3 . . . . . . .226 A6
Winnicott Cl PL6. . . . . .244 E7
Winnings Way TQ1 . . .220 D7
Winnow Cl PL9 . . . . . . .255 F4
Winsbeer La
  Rockwell Green
  TA21. . . . . .160 A6
  Runnington TA21. . . . . . .51 F8
Winsbury Ct PL6. . . . . .245 A1
Winscombe La EX6. . . . .96 D3
Winscott Cotts EX5 . . . .81 B1
Winscott Cross
  Holsworthy EX22. . . . . . .72 A4
  Newton St Cyres EX5. . .81 B1
WINSFORD. 156 C2
Winsford La EX21. . . . . .73 E3
Winsford Rd TQ2. . . . . .219 C3
Winsford Walled Gdn *
  EX21. . . . . .73 F4
WINSHAM. 8 E1
Winsham Cross EX33. . . .8 E1
Winsham Rd EX33. . . . . .8 D1
Winslade Cl TQ7 . . . . . .144 E1
Winslade Ct TQ7 . . . . . .144 E1
WINSLADE PARK. 179 B2
Winslade Park Ave
  EX5. . . . . .179 B2
Winslade Pk EX5. . . . . .179 B1
Winslade Rd EX10. . . . .188 B6
Winslake Mdw EX6. . . . .97 F4
Winsland Ave TQ9 . . . .222 E6
Winson Cross EX37 . . . .29 A4
Winsor Cross PL8. . . . .136 C4
Winsor Meadow
  EX36. . . . . .30 D8
Winstanley Wlk PL3. . .249 D6
Winstitchen Cross
  TA24. . . . . .13 C2
Winstitchen La TA24 . . .13 C2
WINSTON. 257 B4
Winston Ave PL4. . . . . .262 C4
Winston Cl TQ12 . . . . . .207 E7
Winston Ct TQ14 . . . . .210 C6
Winstone Ave TQ2 . . . .214 A1
Winstone Cotts PL8 . . .257 B4
Winstone La PL8. . . . . .257 B4
Winston Ho EX36 . . . . .158 C5
Winston Pk EX36. . . . . .158 C5
Winston Rd EX8. . . . . . .196 E2
Winsu Ave TQ3 . . . . . . .226 A8
WINSWELL. 56 D8
Winswell Water EX38 . .56 D7
Winswood EX17 . . . . . .165 D4
Winsworthy EX39 . . . . .23 D3
Winterbourne Rd
  TQ14. . . . . .210 C5
Winter Gdn TQ2 . . . . . .220 B4
Winterland La EX22. . . .164 D2
Winters Cross TA4 . . . . .35 C8
Wintershead Rd
  Simonsbath TA24. . . . . .19 F8
  Simonsbath TA24. . . . . .20 B7
Winters La EX11. . . . . .169 D3
Winter's La EX11. . . . . .169 D5
Winward Rise EX7 . . . .210 F8
Wiriga Way EX16. . . . . .46 E1
Wiscombe La TQ7. . . . .142 D6
Wishings Rd TQ5. . . . . .230 D3
Wish Meadow La
  EX5. . . . . .175 D3
Wisteria Cl EX19. . . . . . .57 F7
Wisteria Pl TQ7 . . . . . . .258 C5
Wistford Cross EX32 . . .18 C4
Wistman's Wood National
  Nature Reserve *
  PL20. . . . . .119 D4
Wiston Cross EX36. . . . .32 D2
Witch La EX14 . . . . .86 F8
Witcombe La EX6. . . . .194 D3
WITHACOTT. 40 D2
Witham Gdns PL3. . . . .249 C5
Witheby EX10. . . . . . . .187 F3
Withecombe Cross
  TQ13. . . . . .110 F8
Withen Cross EX5. . . . . .99 C1
Withen La EX5. . . . . .99 D2
Witherdon Cross
  EX21. . . . . .91 D5
WITHERIDGE. 46 F1
Witheridge CE Prim Sch
  EX16. . . . . .46 E1
Witheridge Cl EX22 . . . .38 E1

Witheridge Mill Cross
  EX16. . . . . .46 E2
Witheridge Moor Cross
  (East) EX16. . . . . .47 E1
Witheridge Moor Cross
  (West) EX16. . . . . .47 D1
Withey The EX5. . . . . . . .99 E8
Withies St PL3. . . . . . . .249 D1
WITHLEIGH. 63 D7
Withleigh Cross EX16 . .63 C8
Withleigh La EX16 . . . . .63 D7
WITHNOE. 252 A4
Withnoe La PL10. . . . . .252 B6
Withy Cl EX15. . . . . . . .161 F3
Withycombe Park Dr
  EX8. . . . . .196 C2
WITHYCOMBE
  RALEIGH. 196 C2
Withycombe Raleigh CE
  Prim Sch EX8. . . . . . .196 C1
Withycombe Rd EX8 .202 A8
Withycombe Village Rd
  EX8. . . . . .202 B8
Withy Cross EX38 . . . . . .42 E6
Withygate La EX32. . . . .19 A5
Withy La EX15 . . . . .52 B1
WITHYPOOL. 21 C6
Withypool Cross
  Hawkridge TA22. . . . . . .21 C2
  Twitchen EX36 . . . . .20 C8
Withywell La EX33. . . . . .7 E1
Withywine La TA22. . . . .34 C5
Witten Gdns EX39. . . . .157 A5
Wixenford Ct PL9 . . . . .255 F8
Wixon Cross EX18. . . . . .45 B3
Wixon La EX18. . . . . . . .45 B3
Woburn Cl TQ3 . . . . . . .225 D7
Woburn Terr PL9 . . . . .255 C7
WOLBOROUGH. 207 B1
Wolborough Church Path
  TQ12. . . . . .207 A2
Wolborough Cl TQ12 . .207 C2
Wolborough Gdns
  Brixham TQ5. . . . . .230 E6
  Newton Abbot TQ12 . . .207 C2
Wolborough St TQ12 . .207 B3
Wolbough CE (Aided)
  Prim Sch 18 TQ12 . . .207 C3
Wolford Cross EX14. . . .66 B4
WOLLATON. 257 B6
Wollaton Cross PL8 . .257 A6
Wollaton Gr PL5 . . . . . .243 F3
Wolrige Ave PL7 . . . . . .251 B5
Wolrige Way PL7 . . . . .251 A5
Wolsdon La
  Antony PL11. . . . . .246 A1
  St John PL11. . . . . .252 B8
Wolsdon Pl PL1. . . . . . .262 A3
Wolsdon St PL1. . . . . . .262 B3
Wolseley Bsns Pk 2
  PL2. . . . . .248 A5
Wolseley Cl PL2. . . . . .248 A5
Wolseley Rd
  Plymouth PL5 . . . . .247 E7
  Plymouth, Camels Head
  PL5. . . . . .247 F6
  Plymouth, St Budeaux
  PL5. . . . . .243 C1
Wolseley Road Flats
  PL2. . . . . .247 F6
Wolston Cl TQ5. . . . . . .230 B6
WOLVERSTONE. 85 A7
Wolverstone Cross
  EX14. . . . . .85 A8
Wolverstone Hill EX14 .85 A7
Wolverton Dr TQ12. . . .207 D7
Wolverwood Cl PL7. . . .251 C3
Wolverwood La PL7. . .251 B3
Wombwell Cres PL2. . .247 F2
Wonders Cnr EX38. . . . .40 D2
WONFORD. 178 A4
Wonford House Hospl
  EX2. . . . . .177 F4
Wonford Rd EX2 . . . . .261 C2
Wonford Sp Ctr EX1. .178 A3
Wonford St EX2. . . . . .178 A4
Wonnacott's Rd
  EX20. . . . . .170 C5
WONSON. 110 D8
Wonton Cross TQ9. . . .135 D2
WOODA. 157 C8
WOODACOTT. 54 E2
Woodacott Cross
  EX22. . . . . .54 E2
Wood Acre PL12 . . . . .242 B4
Woodacre Ct PL12 . . .242 B4
Woodah Rd EX4. . . . . . .176 F5
Wooda Rd EX39. . . . . . .157 C8
Woodberry Down Wy
  DT7. . . . . .104 B4
Woodbine Cotts PL7 .250 E4
Woodbine Pl 5
  EX12. . . . . .192 A5
Woodbine Terr EX4 . . .261 A4
Woodbridge La
  Bondleigh EX18. . . . . . . .77 D8
  Farway EX24. . . . . .102 B6
  North Tawton EX17. . . . .59 E1
Woodbrook Rd TQ9 . . .223 E5
Woodburn Cross EX16. .32 F2
Woodburn Hill EX16. . .32 E2
Woodburn Water Cross
  EX16. . . . . .32 F1
WOODBURY. 184 C3
Woodbury Bsns Pk
  EX5. . . . . .184 A1

Woodbury CE Prim Sch
  EX5. . . . . .184 C3
Woodbury Ct EX8 . . . .202 C6
Woodbury Gdns PL5 .244 A3
Woodbury La EX13. . . . .88 B7
Woodbury Pk EX13. . . .167 C4
Woodbury Rd EX3,
  EX5. . . . . .183 E5
Woodbury Rise TQ6. . .233 B2
WOODBURY
  SALTERTON. 184 C6
Woodbury Salterton CE
  Prim Sch EX5. . . . . . .184 C7
Woodbury View
  Broadclyst EX5. . . . . . .175 D6
  Exeter EX2 . . . . .177 A2
Woodbury Way EX13 .167 D4
Woodbury Wlk EX6 . . .181 F5
Woodchurch PL20 . . . .126 E3
Wood Cl
  Christow EX6. . . . . .113 B4
  Saltash PL12. . . . . .242 B3
Wood Cnr EX6. . . . . .97 C2
Woodcock Cl PL10 . . . .253 A6
Woodcock Way EX13. . .88 B7
Woodcote Ct EX5 . . . .184 C3
Wood Cotts TQ12 . . . . .180 C1
Woodcourt Rd TQ9. . . .139 C7
Woodcroft Cross
  EX19. . . . . .76 D7
Woodcroft La EX19. . . .76 D8
Woodcroft Mdws
  TA20. . . . . .69 B7
Wood Cross EX14. . . . . .86 C6
Woodend Rd
  Plymouth PL6 . . . . .245 D7
  Torquay TQ1. . . . . .220 D4
Wooder Wharf 12
  EX39. . . . . .157 A1
Woodfield Cl EX8 . . . .196 E2
Woodfield Cres
  PL21. . . . . .237 E4
Woodfield Ct TQ1. . . . .220 D3
Woodfield Prim Sch
  PL5. . . . . .244 C5
Woodfields EX12. . . . .192 A7
WOODFORD
  Blackawton. 139 D2
  Plymouth 250 C7
Woodford Ave PL7. . . .250 A7
Woodford Cl PL7. . . . . .250 A7
Woodford Cres PL7 . . .250 A6
Woodford Gdns
  EX32. . . . . .155 C2
Woodford Gn PL7. . . . .250 B6
Woodford Prim Sch
  PL7. . . . . .250 B6
Woodford Rd PL6. . . . .245 D6
WOODGATE. 51 E2
Woodhaye Cl 2
  TQ10. . . . . .134 F2
Woodhaye Gdns 5
  TQ10. . . . . .220 D4
Woodhayes Cl EX7. . . .204 F8
Woodhayes Dr EX15. . .67 C2
Woodhayes La
  Whimple EX5 . . . . .99 F7
  Whimple EX5 . . . . .100 A7
Woodhaye Terr 1
  TQ10. . . . . .134 F2
Woodhead Cross
  Branscombe EX12 . . . .190 E7
  Totnes TQ9 . . . . .217 E4
Woodhead La
  Cheriton Fitzpaine
  EX16. . . . . .63 A7
  Totnes TQ12 . . . . .217 E4
Woodhill View EX14. . .166 B4
Woodhouse Cl TQ7. . . .258 C4
Woodhouse Cross
  TQ13. . . . . .122 D3
Woodhouse Fields
  DT7. . . . . .104 B4
Woodhouse La
  Axminster EX13 . . . . . . .88 D1
  Uplyme DT7 . . . . .104 B4
Woodhouse Rd EX13. . .88 D1
Woodhuish La TQ5,
  TQ6. . . . . .235 B7
Wood La
  Abbotskerswell
  TQ12. . . . . .212 A5
  Ashreigney EX18 . . . . . .43 D1
  Broadhembury EX14. . . .84 E7
  Christow EX6. . . . . .113 B4
  Combe Martin EX34 . . . . .3 B2
  East Buckland EX32 . . . .18 F1
  Exmouth EX8. . . . . .196 D1
  Kingswear TQ6 . . . . . . .234 B3
  Monkton EX14 . . . . .86 C6
  Morchard Bishop EX17. .61 A2
  Slapton TQ7 . . . . .145 D4
  Stockleigh Pomeroy
  EX17. . . . . .81 B4
  West Alvington TQ7. . . .258 A4
  West Down EX34 . . . . . . .8 F4
WOODLAND
  Ashburton. 131 D3
  Ivybridge 237 A5
Woodland Ave
  Kingskerswell TQ12 . . .212 F5
  Plymouth PL9 . . . . .256 A8
  Teignmouth TQ14. . . . .210 D7
Woodland Bsns Pk
  TQ2. . . . . .219 E8

Woodland Cl
Barnstaple EX32....155 E4
Braunton EX33.......8 D1
Denbury TQ12......131 F3
Gunnislake PL18....125 C6
Ivybridge PL21.....237 B5
Staverton TQ9......216 A4
2 Tiverton EX16....49 B8
Torquay TQ2.......219 E8
Woodland Cotts
PL21............237 A5
Woodland Cross EX31. 27 B4
Woodland Ct
10 Barnstaple EX32...155 A4
Ivybridge PL21.....237 A5
Paignton TQ3......226 B7
Woodland Dr
Brixton PL8.......257 B5
Exeter EX1........178 E3
Plymouth PL7......250 B4
WOODLAND HEAD....97 C7
Woodlandhead Cross
EX17............97 B7
Woodland Hill
Cheriton Bishop EX17... 97 B8
Yeoford EX17......79 A1
Woodland La TQ9...227 D4
Woodland Mews
Broadclyst EX5....175 D6
1 Paignton TQ3....226 B7
Woodland Pk
Ivybridge PL21.....237 A5
Northam EX39......156 F5
Northam EX39......157 A5
Paignton TQ3......226 B7
Woodland Rd
Ashburton TQ13....130 F4
Broadclyst EX5....175 C6
Denbury TQ12......211 A6
Exeter EX1........178 D7
Harbertonford TQ9...139 C7
Ivybridge PL21.....237 B5
Lee Mill PL21......136 F7
Plymouth PL7......250 C6
Torquay TQ2.......219 E8
Woodlands
Budleigh Salterton
EX9............203 E3
Churchstow TQ7....143 E4
Combe Martin EX34...2 F4
Dousland PL20.....127 B3
Halwill EX21.......73 D3
Kingsteignton TQ12..123 E2
Newton St Cyres EX5.. 98 F8
Plymouth PL9......255 F6
Sidmouth EX10.....188 A4
Wellington TA21....160 F3
Whimple EX5.......99 F8
Woodlands Bsns Pk
EX16............51 C3
Woodlands Cl
Churchstow TQ7....143 E4
Offwell EX14.......86 B2
Teignmouth TQ14...210 C5
Woodlands Ct
Exmouth EX8......196 B3
Plymouth PL5......244 A3
Woodlands Dr EX8...196 B3
Woodlands End PL6..245 D5
Woodlands Gdns 5
TQ12............207 F2
Woodlands La PL6..245 F1
Woodlands L Pk ★
TQ9............139 F3
Woodlands Park Prim
Sch PL21.........237 A5
Woodlands Pk EX6...98 B4
Woodlands Rd TQ12..207 F2
Woodlands Special Sch
PL5............244 A4
Woodlands Way EX5.179 E3
Woodlands Wlk
TQ13............180 C4
Woodland Terr
Ivybridge PL21.....237 B4
Kingswear TQ6.....234 A3
Plymouth PL4......263 B4
Woodland Terr La
PL4............263 B4
Woodland View
EX22............164 C3
Woodland Way
Gunnislake PL18....125 D6
Torpoint PL11......246 F3
Woodland Wood Valley
Nature Reserve ★
PL5............244 A4
Woodlark La 2 EX31 154 A2
Wood Lea EX39.....39 E8
WOODLEIGH.......144 B7
Woodleigh Cl EX4...173 A3
Woodleigh Pk TQ14..210 B2

Woodleigh Rd TQ12..206 F3
Woodley Cross EX5...98 F8
Woodley La EX5.....98 E8
Woodleys Dr EX10...186 D8
Woodleys Mdw TQ2..219 D2
Woodman's Cnr
PL20............127 A3
Woodmans Cres 2
EX14............166 C5
Woodmans Orch EX5.. 84 A2
WOODMANTON.....196 C8
Woodmead Halls
DT7............260 D3
Woodmead Rd
Axminster EX13.....167 C5
Lyme Regis DT7.....260 D3
Woodmere Way
TQ12............207 C8
Woodpark Cross EX17 61 A8
Woodpark La
Molland EX36......31 E6
Paignton TQ3......210 C6
Wood Park La EX34...2 D3
Woodpecker Dr
TQ12............207 C8
Woodpecker Way
Cheriton Bishop EX6... 97 B4
Tavistock PL19.....171 D2
Wood Pk
Ivybridge PL21.....237 D6
Plymouth PL6......132 A2
Woodplace La
Cruwys Morchard
EX16............63 F3
Pennymoor EX16....62 F7
Woodridge Cross
EX19............57 D6
Wood Rock EX36....32 C5
Woodroffe Mdw DT7 260 C4
Woodroffe Sch The
DT7............260 C4
Woods Cross EX36...31 D6
Wood's Cross EX36...32 C5
Woods Field EX20...106 E5
Woodside
Crapstone PL20.....126 E2
Plymouth PL4......263 B4
Woodside Ave PL9...255 C6
Woodside Cl
Ivybridge PL21.....237 D4
Raymond's Hill EX13..104 C8
Woodside Ct
Lynton EX35.......151 D5
Plymouth PL7......250 E4
Woodside Dr TQ1...220 C4
Woodside La PL4....263 B4
Woodside Wlk EX14..166 D6
Woods Pasture 17
EX5............99 A6
Woods The TQ1.....220 E3
Woodstock Gdns
PL5............243 D1
Woodstock Rd EX2..178 A5
WOODTOWN
East-the-Water......26 D4
Fairy Cross........25 B2
Woodvale Ct 21
TQ12............207 B3
Wood View TQ12....207 A3
Woodview Pk PL9...256 A6
Woodview Rd TQ4...225 E1
Wood View Terr
PL21............136 F3
Woodville EX31.....154 C3
Woodville Ave PL20.128 A8
Woodville Cl EX31...154 C4
Woodville Cross EX23. 36 F1
Woodville Rd
Exeter EX2........177 B3
Exmouth EX8......202 A8
Morwenstow EX23...36 F1
Plymouth PL2......247 F7
Torquay TQ1......220 C6
Woodward Rd
Tiverton EX16......64 A6
Tiverton EX16......161 B2
Woodwater Acad
EX2............178 B4
Woodwater La EX2..178 B4
Woodway PL9......256 A7
Woodway Cl TQ14..210 C7
Woodway Dr TQ14..210 C6
Woodway Rd TQ14..210 C6
Woodway St TQ13..123 E6
WOODY BAY.......4 D6
Woody Bay Sta ★ EX31. 4 E3
Woody La
Lynton EX35.......5 C5
West Lyn EX35.....151 D3
WOOLACOMBE.....7 F7
Woolacombe Cross
PL20............125 F1
Woolacombe Ct EX34.. 8 A6
Woolacombe Rd
PL20............125 F1

Woolacombe Rise EX34 8 B6
Woolacombe Sch EX34. 8 A6
Woolacombe Station Rd
EX34............8 B6
Woolbarn Lawn
EX32............155 D4
Woolbrook Cl EX10..188 A6
Woolbrook Mdws
EX10............188 A7
Woolbrook Mead
EX10............187 F7
Woolbrook Pk EX10..188 A7
Woolbrook Rd EX10..188 A7
Woolbrook Rise
EX10............188 A7
Wool Cl EX15......163 A1
Woolcombe La
Ivybridge PL21.....237 D4
Ivybridge PL7......136 F6
Sidmouth EX10.....188 B5
Woolcott Way EX15.163 B2
WOOLFARDISWORTHY
............62 A3
Woolfardisworthy Cross
Clovelly EX39......23 D2
Woolfardisworthy EX17. 62 A3
WOOLFARDISWORTHY
OR WOOLSERY.....38 E7
WOOLHANGER.....4 F2
Woolhanger's La EX34. 2 E3
WOOLLATON.......56 B7
Woollcombe Ave PL7 250 F4
Woolleigh Cross EX19. 42 B3
WOOLLEY.........37 D3
Woolms Mdw PL21..237 A4
Woolpit La TA24....21 B7
Woolsery Ave EX4...178 B8
Woolsery Cl EX4....178 B8
Woolsery Gr EX4....178 B8
Woolsery Prim Sch
EX39............38 F7
Woolster Ct 7 PL4..263 A2
WOOLSTON.......147 F8
WOOLSTON GREEN.131 B1
Woolway Ave EX6...182 B4
WOOLWELL.......245 D7
Woolwell Cres PL6...245 C8
Woolwell Dr PL6....245 C7
Woolwell Rd PL6....245 D7
Wootton Cross EX13..88 F1
Worcester Cres
EX15............162 D4
Worden Cross
Milton Damerel EX22... 54 E6
Sutcombe EX22.....54 C8
Wordland Cross EX17. 80 F8
Wordsworth Ave
Barnstaple EX31....154 F7
6 Barnstaple EX32..155 A7
Wordsworth Cl
5 Exmouth EX8....196 C4
Torquay TQ2......219 E6
Wordsworth Cres
PL2............247 F7
Wordsworth Rd PL2..247 F7
Worham's La EX13...86 F2
Works The EX16....161 C4
World of Country Life ★
EX8............203 B6
WORLINGTON.....15 C1
Worlington Cross
EX39............15 C1
Worlington Hill EX39..15 C1
Wormsworthy Hill
EX16............48 D6
WORSTON........136 B3
Worthele Cl PL21...237 A4
Worthele Cross PL21 237 B1
Worth La
Hele EX5.........82 E5
Withypool TA22, TA24... 21 C4
Worth Rd EX34.....150 C5
Worthy La EX16.....47 C6
Wotten Way TQ9...216 D8
WOTTER.........132 D4
Wotton Cross TQ12..131 E4
Wotton La
Exmouth EX8......196 B5
Lympstone EX8.....195 F5
Wotton Pound EX8..196 A5
Wotton Way TQ9....131 E1
WRAFTON........152 E4
Wrafton Rd EX33...152 E4
Wragg Dr EX8......202 E7
WRANGATON.....137 D8
Wrangaton Bsns Pk
TQ10............137 D8
Wrangaton Rd
Bittaford PL21, TQ10..137 D8
Moorhaven Village
TQ10............137 D8
Wrangcombe La TA21 52 A4
Wrangcombe Rd
Wellington TA21....52 A4
Wrangway TA21....160 A1

WRANGWAY.......52 A4
Wrangway Rd EX15..52 A3
Wrangworthy Cross
EX39............39 E4
Wreford's Cl EX4...173 A3
Wreford's Dr EX4...173 A3
Wreford's La EX4...173 A3
Wreford's Link EX4..173 A3
Wren Cl
Honiton EX14......166 B4
Northam EX39.....157 A6
Wren Ct 10 TQ5....230 C4
Wren Gdns PL7.....250 C6
Wren Ret Pk TQ2...213 D2
Wrens Gate PL9.....255 E8
Wrentham Bsns Ctr
EX4............177 D8
Wrentham Est EX4..177 D8
Wrenwell Cross
TQ12............131 F3
Wressing View EX15..66 A3
Wrey Ave EX31.....154 D4
Wright Cl PL1.......247 E3
Wright Dr EX17.....79 A5
Wrights La PL8.....140 F7
Wright's La
Exmouth EX8......196 F6
Torquay TQ1......220 A7
Wrigwell Cross
TQ12............211 E1
Wrigwell La TQ12...217 F8
WRINKLEBERRY....23 D3
Wrinkleberry La EX39 23 D3
Wroxall Grange TQ1.220 C4
Wulphere Cl EX14...67 B1
Wyatts La PL19.....171 B6
Wychall Orch EX12..192 A6
Wychall Pk EX12....192 A7
Wych Ct EX13......88 E3
Wychwood Cl EX7..204 E7
Wycliffe Rd PL3....249 B4
Wye Gdns PL3.....249 D7
Wyke Cross EX17...80 F2
WYKE GREEN.....167 D1
Wykeham Dr 2 PL2..248 A7
Wyke Hill EX17.....80 F2
Wyke La EX15......167 D2
Wyke Moor Cross
EX20............95 C8
Wyke Rd EX13.....167 D3
Wykes Rd EX1......177 F7
Wylie Ho EX2......261 A1
Wynards EX2......261 B2
Wynards Cl EX9....198 B6
Wynards La 2 EX2..261 B2
Wynards Rd EX9....198 B6
Wyndham Ave EX1..177 F6
Wyndham La PL1...262 A3
Wyndham Mews 1
PL1............262 A3
Wyndham Pl PL1...262 A3
Wyndham Rd EX5...82 B6
Wyndham Sq PL1...262 A3
Wyndham Street E
PL1............262 B3
Wyndham Street W
PL1............262 B3
Wyndthorpe Gdns 17
EX34............150 C6
Wynford Rd EX4....173 F1
Wynstream Sch EX2.177 F3
Wyoming Cl PL3....249 C6
Wyre Cl TQ4.......226 A2
Wytch Gn EX13.....88 E3
Wythburn Gdns PL6..245 D3

Y
Yacht Haven Quay
PL4............255 C8
YALBERTON......225 C2
Yalberton Ind Est
TQ4............225 D3
Yalberton Ind
Management Units
TQ4............225 B3
Yalberton Rd TQ4...225 D3
Yalberton Tor Ind Est
TQ4............225 D3
Yalland Cross TQ10.134 F5
Yallop Way EX14...166 B4
Yanhey Hill EX16....32 E4
Yannon Dr TQ14....210 B5
Yannon La TQ12....212 E5
Yannons Ct TQ3....225 E2
Yannons Rd TQ4...225 E2
Yannons The TQ14..210 B6
Yannon Terr TQ14..210 B6
Yapham Cross EX39..23 A4
YARCOMBE.......69 A3
Yarda Wlk PL8.....257 A4
Yardbury Hill Rd
EX24............102 E7
Yard Cross EX14....86 B7

Yard Down Cross
EX36............19 C6
Yard Downs La EX5..82 C6
Yarde Cl EX10......188 B7
Yarde Cotts EX38...41 D1
Yarde Cross EX32...18 A4
Yarde Gate Cross
EX36............19 B5
Yarde Hill Orch EX10 188 B7
Yardelands EX10....188 B7
Yardelands Cl EX10..188 B7
Yarde Mead EX10...188 B7
Yarde's Grave Cross
TQ9............222 F7
Yard Hill TQ13.....111 D2
Yard La EX36......46 B8
Yardleigh Cross EX13. 88 D4
Yardley Gdns PL6..245 E3
Yards La
Brixham TQ5.......230 C1
Brixham TQ5.......230 C2
Yardwells Cross
EX36............19 B5
Yarlington Mill EX5..99 A6
Yarmleigh La EX17...79 E7
Yarnacott Cnr EX32..17 E1
Yarnapitts Cross
TQ13............110 E7
Yarner Wood Nature
Trail ★ TQ13......122 C5
YARNSCOMBE.....27 E2
Yarrow Mead PL9...256 D7
YAWL............104 B5
Yawl Cres DT7......104 B5
Yawl Cross DT7.....104 B6
Yawl Hill DT7......104 B5
Yawl Hill La DT7....104 B5
YEALMBRIDGE.....136 A2
Yealmbury Hill PL8..257 F4
Yealm Gr TQ2......219 C7
Yealm Pk PL8......257 E4
Yealmpstone Cl PL7.251 B4
Yealmpstone Dr PL7.251 B3
Yealmpstone Farm Prim
Sch PL7.........251 B3
YEALMPTON......257 E4
Yealmpton Prim Sch
PL8............257 E4
Yealm Rd PL8......140 F6
Yealm View Rd PL8.141 A6
Yearlstone Vineyard ★
EX16............63 F3
Yearnor Mill La TA24.. 6 F5
Yeats Cl PL5.......244 C2
Yeatt Cross TQ12...131 F3
Yellaford Way 1
EX31............154 B3
YELLAND........153 A4
Yelland Bglws TQ10..135 B5
Yelland Cross
Challacombe EX31...11 D4
Rattery TQ10......135 C5
Yelland EX31.......153 A5
Yelland Rd EX31....153 C5
Yellands Pk TQ7....142 C6
Yellaton La EX34....3 B1
Yellowmead Rd PL2.248 A7
Yellow Tor Ct PL12..242 C2
Yellow Tor La PL12..242 C2
Yellow Tor Rd PL12.242 B2
YELVERTON.......127 A3
Yelverton Bsns Pk
PL20............126 E2
Yelverton Cl PL5....243 E4
Yelverton Paperweight
Ctr ★ PL20.......126 F2
Yelverton Terr
Tavistock PL19.....171 D6
Yelverton PL20.....127 A2
Yendacott La EX17..81 B3
Yeo Bsns Pk EX5...179 E3
Yeo Cl PL3........249 B5
Yeo Cotts PL21.....133 D3
Yeo Cres EX17.....165 E4
Yeo Dr 20 EX39....15 A1
YEOFORD........79 C1
Yeoford Com Prim Sch
EX17............79 C1
Yeoford Mdws EX17..79 C1
Yeoford Sta EX17...79 C1
Yeoford Way EX2...181 D8
Yeo Gate EX36.....31 C4
Yeo Hill EX36......30 F1
Yeo La
Molland EX36......31 C5
North Tawton EX20... 77 B5
Yeoland Down
Crapstone PL20.....126 F1
Yelverton PL20.....241 E8
Yeoland La
Swimbridge EX32...17 F1
Yelverton PL20.....126 F1
Yeolands The TQ9..227 F8
Yeolland La PL21...237 D5
Yeolland Pk PL21...237 E5

Yeomadon Cross
EX22............71 D4
Yeomans Way PL7..251 A4
Yeo Mill Cross EX36..32 C5
Yeo Pk PL8........136 A3
Yeo Rd
Braunton EX31.....15 E5
Zeal Monachorum EX17. 78 D7
Yeotown Cross EX37.. 44 C8
Yeo Vale Cross EX17..60 C2
Yeo Vale Ho 5 EX32 154 F6
Yeo Vale Ind Est EX17.. 60 C2
Yeo Vale Rd EX32..154 F6
Yeo Valley Prim Sch
EX32............155 A6
Yeo View EX17.....79 C1
Yerris Rd EX15.....60 F8
Yetsonais Cross TQ9.144 D8
YETTINGTON......197 F8
Yettington Rd EX9..198 A7
Yew Cl
Brixham TQ5.......229 F2
Honiton EX14......166 A4
Yewdale Gdns PL6..245 D2
Yew Tree Cl
Exeter EX4........173 E1
Exmouth EX8......196 C3
Yew Tree Dr TQ12..207 E6
Yew Wood Cross
EX15............66 A4
Yolhey La TQ12....212 C5
Yonder Acre Way EX5. 99 B6
Yonder Cl EX11.....169 E3
Yonder Cnr EX11....169 E3
Yonder Hill Cotts
EX13............88 E7
Yonder Mdw TQ9...227 F8
Yonder Mount EX13.103 D5
Yonder St
Ottery St Mary EX11..169 E3
Plymouth PL9......255 B6
YONDERTOWN.....133 B1
Yon St TQ12.......212 F4
York Cl
Axminster EX13.....167 E6
Exmouth EX8......196 E2
Feniton EX14......84 D2
York Cres
Feniton EX14......84 D2
Torquay TQ1......220 C8
York Gdns TQ4.....226 B4
York Mews TQ4....226 B5
York Pl
Bideford EX39.....157 A3
Cullompton EX15...163 C5
Plymouth PL2......247 F4
York Rd
Exeter EX4........261 C4
Paignton TQ4.....226 B4
Plymouth PL5......247 E8
Seaton EX12......192 A5
Torpoint PL11......247 B3
Torquay TQ1......220 C8
York Rise EX39.....156 F2
York St
Plymouth PL1......247 E2
1 Sidmouth EX10..188 B4
York Terr
Exeter EX4........261 C4
7 Plymouth PL2...247 F5
Sidmouth EX10....188 B3
York Villas TQ1....220 C8
Youings Dr EX31...155 A7
Youlden La EX20...95 C7
Youldon Moor Cross
EX22............53 E4
Youldons Cl TQ9...139 C7
Youldon Way PL20.126 F4
Youlston Cl EX31....17 A7
Youltree Cross EX39.. 22 E4
Youngaton Rd EX39.156 F2
Younghayes Rd EX5.99 A6
Young's Park La TQ4 226 C4
Young's Park Rd TQ4 226 C4

Z
Zeal Cross EX6.....112 F8
Zealley Est TQ12...207 B4
ZEAL MONACHORUM 78 C7
Zeal Rd
Dunsford EX6.....112 F8
Tedburn St Mary EX6.. 97 F1
Zempson Cross TQ10 135 B5
Zephyr Cres EX32...155 B5
Zeth Hill La PL21...136 D8
Zion Pl
Dartmouth TQ6....233 F4
Ivybridge PL21.....237 C5
Zion Rd 3 TQ2....219 F5
Zion St PL1........262 C2